THE OXFORD HANDBOOK OF

DEWEY

THE OXFORD HANDBOOK OF

DEWEY

Edited by
STEVEN FESMIRE

OXFORD
UNIVERSITY PRESS

OXFORD
UNIVERSITY PRESS

Oxford University Press is a department of the University of Oxford. It furthers
the University's objective of excellence in research, scholarship, and education
by publishing worldwide. Oxford is a registered trade mark of Oxford University
Press in the UK and certain other countries.

Published in the United States of America by Oxford University Press
198 Madison Avenue, New York, NY 10016, United States of America.

Library of Congress Cataloging-in-Publication Data
Names: Fesmire, Steven, 1967– editor.
Title: The Oxford handbook of Dewey / edited by Steven Fesmire.
Description: New York : Oxford University Press, 2019. |
Includes bibliographical references and index.
Identifiers: LCCN 2019003452 (print) | LCCN 2019004110 (ebook) |
ISBN 9780190491208 (updf) | ISBN 9780190491215 (online content) |
ISBN 9780190491192 (cloth : alk. paper) | ISBN 9780197669259 (paperback)
Subjects: LCSH: Dewey, John, 1859–1952.
Classification: LCC B945.D44 (ebook) | LCC B945.D44 O94 2019 (print) |DDC 191—dc23
LC record available at https://lccn.loc.gov/2019003452

Paperback printed by Marquis Book Printing, Canada

The Oxford Handbook of Dewey is dedicated to the growing legacy of Jane Addams.

TABLE OF CONTENTS

I THE FUTURE OF PHILOSOPHICAL RESEARCH

II METAPHYSICS

III EPISTEMOLOGY, SCIENCE, LANGUAGE, AND MIND

IV ETHICS, LAW, AND THE STARTING POINT

V SOCIAL AND POLITICAL PHILOSOPHY, RACE, AND FEMINIST PHILOSOPHY

VI PHILOSOPHY OF EDUCATION

VII AESTHETICS

VIII INSTRUMENTAL LOGIC, PHILOSOPHY OF TECHNOLOGY, AND THE UNFINISHED PROJECT OF MODERNITY

IX DEWEY IN CROSS-CULTURAL DIALOGUE

Notes on Contributors

Thomas M. Alexander is professor of philosophy emeritus at Southern Illinois University, Carbondale. He is the author of *John Dewey's Theory of Art, Experience, and Nature: The Horizons of Feeling* (SUNY Press, 1987) and *The Human Eros: Eco-Ontology and the Aesthetics of Existence* (Fordham University Press, 2013). He is past president of The Society for the Advancement of American Philosophy. His research includes Dewey, Emerson, Santayana, Native American thought, classical philosophy, aesthetics, and metaphysics. He studied under the Dewey scholar James Gouinlock, to whom his essay is dedicated.

Roger T. Ames is Humanities Chair Professor of Philosophy at Peking University, and professor of philosophy emeritus at the University of Hawai'i. He has translated a number of the Chinese philosophical canons and has also authored several interpretative studies of Chinese philosophy and culture. He is the co-author with David L. Hall of *The Democracy of the Dead: Confucius, Dewey, and the Hope for Democracy in China* (Open Court, 1999). His most recent work centers on Confucian role ethics as a sui generis vision of the moral life and on writing articles promoting a conversation between American pragmatism and Confucianism.

Randall E. Auxier is professor of philosophy and communication studies at Southern Illinois University, Carbondale. He is the author of *Time, Will, and Purpose: Living Ideas from the Philosophy of Josiah Royce* (Open Court, 2013) and *Metaphysical Graffiti* (Open Court, 2017), and coauthor (with Gary Herstein) of *The Quantum of Explanation: Whitehead's Radical Empiricism* (Routledge, 2017). He was principal editor of eight volumes of the Library of Living Philosophers, three volumes of *Critical Responses to Josiah Royce*, and of the journal *The Personalist Forum* (1997–2005) and its successor *The Pluralist* (2006–2012).

F. Thomas Burke is professor of philosophy, University of South Carolina. He is the author of *What Pragmatism Was* (Indiana University Press, 2013) and *Dewey's New Logic* (University of Chicago Press, 1994) and coeditor of *Dewey's Logical Theory* (with M. Hester and R. Talisse; Vanderbilt University Press, 2002) and *George Herbert Mead in the Twenty-First Century* (with K. Skowronski; Lexington Books, 2013).

James Campbell is a distinguished university professor of philosophy at The University of Toledo, Ohio. He has served as president of the American Association of Philosophy Teachers, the Society for the Advancement of American Philosophy, and the William James Society. He was a Fulbright lecturer at the University of Innsbruck (1990–1991) and the University of Munich (2003–2004). He is the author of *The Community Reconstructs* (1992), *Understanding John Dewey* (1995), *Recovering Benjamin Franklin* (1999), *A*

Thoughtful Profession: The Early Years of the American Philosophical Association (2006), and *Experiencing William James* (2017).

Vincent Colapietro is liberal arts research professor emeritus at Pennsylvania State University. His principal area of historical research is American philosophy, broadly conceived, though pragmatism and Peirce in particular are at the heart of this research. His systematic interests focus on the intersection of such topics as reason, agency, subjectivity, and normativity.

Phillip Deen is senior lecturer of philosophy and humanities at the University of New Hampshire and the editor of John Dewey's *Unmodern Philosophy and Modern Philosophy*. His work on the history of American philosophy, the climate debate, civic education, and aesthetics has appeared in *The History of Political Thought*, *Metaphilosophy*, *Public Affairs Quarterly*, and *The Journal of Value Inquiry*, among others. He is currently writing a book on the ethics of humor.

Christine Doddington is university senior lecturer in education, Cambridge University and fellow emerita, Homerton College. She is coeditor of *Dewey and Education in the 21st Century: Fighting Back.* (Emerald Publishing, 2018) and has a chapter in *Philosophy as Interplay and Dialogue* (LIT Verlag, 2018). Recent publications include work in *The Routledge International Handbook of the Arts and Education* (2015) and *Wellbeing, Education and Contemporary Schooling* (2017), all with a research focus on arts education, aesthetics, and Dewey. She is an elected executive of the Philosophy of Education Society of Great Britain (PESGB) and a member of the International Editorial Board for *Education 3-13: International Journal of Primary, Elementary and Early Years Education*.

Andrea R. English is senior lecturer and chancellor's fellow in philosophy of education, University of Edinburgh, and senior fellow of the Higher Education Academy. She is the author of *Discontinuity in Learning: Dewey, Herbart, and Education as Transformation* (Cambridge University Press, 2013) and coeditor of *John Dewey's Democracy and Education: A Centennial Handbook* (Cambridge University Press, 2017), and her research on reflective teaching and transformative learning is published in a range of international journals and edited volumes. She is currently on the board of directors of the John Dewey Society, is an associate editor of *Dewey Studies*, and leads the Edinburgh Branch of The Philosophy of Education Society of Great Britain.

Steven Fesmire is professor of philosophy and chair of philosophy and religious studies at Radford University. He is the author of *Dewey* (Routledge Press, 2015), winner of a 2015 *Choice* "Outstanding Academic Title" award. He is also the author of *John Dewey and Moral Imagination: Pragmatism in Ethics* (Indiana University Press, 2003), winner of a 2005 *Choice* "Outstanding Academic Title" award. He was a 2009 Fulbright scholar at Kyoto University and Kobe University in Japan and a 2016 fellow at the Institute for Advanced Studies in the Humanities at the University of Edinburgh in Scotland.

Jim Garrison is a professor of philosophy of education at Virginia Tech and was chancellor's visiting professor at Uppsala University for 2014–2018. His work concentrates on philosophical pragmatism. Garrison is a past president of the John Dewey Society and the Philosophy of Education Society. Recent books include *Living and Learning*, coauthored with Buddhist philosopher and educator Daisaku Ikeda and Larry Hickman, director emeritus of the Center for Dewey Studies (Dialogue Path Press 2014), and *Democracy and Education Reconsidered: Dewey After One Hundred Years* (Routledge, 2016), coauthored with Stefan Neubert and Kersten Reich. His work is published in seven languages.

Peter Godfrey-Smith is professor of history and philosophy of science at the University of Sydney. He taught at Stanford, Harvard, the Australian National University, and the CUNY Graduate Center before moving to Sydney for his current position. His main interests are in the philosophy of biology and the philosophy of mind, and he also works on pragmatism. He has written five books, including *Darwinian Populations and Natural Selection* (2009), which won the 2010 Lakatos Award; *Theory and Reality* (2003); and *Other Minds: The Octopus, the Sea, and the Deep Origins of Consciousness* (2016).

Espen Hammer is professor of philosophy at Temple University, Philadelphia. He is the author of *Stanley Cavell: Skepticism, Subjectivity, and the Ordinary* (2002), *Adorno and the Political* (2006), *Philosophy and Temporality from Kant to Critical Theory* (2011), and *Adorno's Modernism: Art, Experience, and Catastrophe* (2015). He is the editor of *German Idealism: Contemporary Perspectives* (2006), *Theodor W. Adorno II: Critical Assessments of Leading Philosophers* (2015), and *Kafka's The Trial: Philosophical Perspectives* (2018). He is also a coeditor of *Stanley Cavell: Die Unheimlichkeit des Ungewöhnlichen* (2002), *Pragmatik und Kulturpolitik: Studien zur Kulturpolitik Richard Rortys* (2011), and the *Routledge Companion to the Frankfurt School* (2018).

Casey Haskins is associate professor of philosophy, Purchase College SUNY. He is coeditor of *Dewey Reconfigured: Essays on Deweyan Pragmatism* and is a contributor to the Oxford *Encyclopedia of Aesthetics*. He is currently writing a book on the history of the debate about autonomy in modern aesthetic theory.

Lisa Heldke is professor of philosophy, Gustavus Adolphus College, where she also teaches in the Gender, Women and Sexuality Studies Program. She is the author, co-author, or editor of a number of books in the philosophy of food, including *Exotic Appetites: Ruminations of a Food Adventurer* and *Philosophers at Table: On Food and Being Human*.

D. Micah Hester is chair of the Department of Medical Humanities & Bioethics and professor of medical humanities/pediatrics, University of Arkansas for Medical Sciences, and clinical ethicist, Arkansas Children's Hospital. He is author/editor of nine books, including *Community as Healing: Pragmatist Ethics in Medical Encounters* (2001), *Dewey's Logical Theory* (edited with F. T. Burke and Robert Talisse), *Dewey's Essays in Experimental Logic* (edited with Robert Talisse, 2007), and *End-of-Life Care and Pragmatic Decision Making* (2010), among others.

Larry A. Hickman is director emeritus, Center for Dewey Studies and professor emeritus, Department of Philosophy, Southern Illinois University-Carbondale. He is the author of *Modern Theories of Higher Level Predicates* (1980), *John Dewey's Pragmatic Technology* (1990), *Philosophical Tools for Technological Culture* (2001), *Pragmatism as Post-Postmodernism* (2007), and *Living as Learning: John Dewey in the 21st Century* (with Daisaku Ikeda and Jim Garrison, 2014). He is the editor or coeditor of more than a dozen volumes, including *Technology as a Human Affair* (1990), *Reading Dewey* (1998), *The Essential Dewey* (with Thomas Alexander, 1998), *The Correspondence of John Dewey* (1999, 2001, 2005, and 2008), *John Dewey: Between Pragmatism and Constructivism* (with Stefan Neubert and Kersten Reich, 2009), and *John Dewey's Educational Philosophy in International Perspective* (with Giuseppe Spadafora, 2009).

David L. Hildebrand is professor of philosophy at the University of Colorado, Denver. He is a past president of the Society for the Advancement of American Philosophy and the Southwest Philosophical Society. His work in American philosophy and pragmatism includes *Beyond Realism and Antirealism: John Dewey and the Neopragmatists* (Vanderbilt University Press, 2003); *Dewey: A Beginner's Guide* (Oxford: Oneworld Press, 2008); and a number of articles and reference articles including "John Dewey" (Stanford Encyclopedia of Philosophy) "Dewey" (*Cambridge Companion to Pragmatism*), "John Dewey" (*Routledge Companion to Pragmatism*), "Rorty and Dewey" (*A Companion to Rorty, Wiley*). Other research has included figures such as Hilary Putnam, Charles S. Peirce, A. N. Whitehead, and Kenneth Burke. His current research interests include neopragmatism, pragmatic objectivity, and the ways experience can shape (and be shaped by) practices in aesthetics, education, and technology.

Daniel R. Huebner is associate professor of sociology at the University of North Carolina, Greensboro. He is the author of Reintroducing George Herbert Mead (Routledge, 2022) and *Becoming Mead: The Social Process of Academic Knowledge* (University of Chicago Press, 2014). With Hans Joas he coedited *Mind, Self, and Society: The Definitive Edition* (2015) and *The Timeliness of George Herbert Mead* (2016), both published by the University of Chicago Press.

Mark Johnson is the Philip H. Knight Professor of Liberal Arts and Sciences in the Department of Philosophy at the University of Oregon. His research has focused on the philosophical implications of the role of human embodiment in meaning, conceptualization, reasoning, and values, especially from the perspective of the interaction of embodied cognitive science and pragmatist philosophy. He is coauthor, with George Lakoff, of *Metaphors We Live By* (1980) and *Philosophy in the Flesh* (1999), and author of *The Body in the Mind: The Bodily Basis of Meaning, Imagination, and Reason* (1987), *Moral Imagination: Implications of Cognitive Science for Ethics* (1993), *The Meaning of the Body: Aesthetics of Human Understanding* (2007), and *Morality for Humans: Ethical Understanding from the Perspective of Cognitive Science* (2014).

Philip Kitcher is the John Dewey Professor of Philosophy at Columbia University. He is the author of 17 books and more than 150 articles. Most relevant to this chapter is his *Preludes to Pragmatism* (Oxford University Press, 2012).

Joseph Margolis is Laura H. Carnell Professor of Philosophy at Temple University. A World War II veteran, he received his PhD from Columbia University in 1953. In addition to teaching philosophy continuously for seventy years, he has published about forty books and hundreds of articles, ranging over nearly all the main topics of philosophy, but especially the philosophy of art, pragmatism, the theory of human culture, and epistemology and metaphysics. *Toward a Metaphysics of Culture* (2016) is one of his most recent contributions to rounding out a comprehensive, fine-grained account of the development of pragmatism from the 1970s to current practice, within a global setting encompassing the whole of Western philosophy. The other is *Three Paradoxes of Personhood* (2017), the Venetian Lectures for 2016.

Noëlle McAfee is professor of philosophy and director of the Psychoanalytic Studies Program at Emory University. Her work is at the intersection of subjectivity and public life. She is editor of the *Kettering Review* and author of *Democracy and the Political Unconscious* (Columbia, 2008), *Julia Kristeva* (Routledge, 2003), *Habermas, Kristeva, and Citizenship* (Cornell, 2000), and a forthcoming volume with Columbia University Press on politics and the fear of breakdown. Her coedited volumes include a special issue of the philosophy journal *Hypatia* on feminist engagements in democratic theory and the volume *Democratizing Deliberation: A Political Theory Anthology* (Kettering, 2012). During the past decade she has worked on projects supported by the Kettering Foundation, the Ford Foundation, and the MacArthur Foundation. She is also a founding member and past codirector of the Public Philosophy Network.

Erin McKenna is professor of philosophy, University of Oregon. She is the coauthor, with Scott L. Pratt, of *American Philosophy: From Wounded Knee to the Present* (Bloomsbury, 2015), and the author of *Pets, People, and Pragmatism* (Fordham University Press, 2014) and *The Task of Utopia: A Pragmatist and Feminist Perspective* (Rowman & Littlefield, 2001). Her book *Livestock: Food, Fiber, and Friends* (University of Georgia Press, 2018) continues a pragmatist analysis of human relationships with other animal beings rooted in a Deweyan ethic. She is also the coeditor of *Animal Pragmatism: Rethinking Human-Nonhuman Relationships* (Indiana University Press, 2004) and *Philosophy and Jimmy Buffett* (Open Court, 2009). She has numerous articles and book chapters that cover a range of issues, from animal issues to the music of Neil Young to the work of William James.

Cheryl Misak is university professor and professor of philosophy at the University of Toronto. She is the author of numerous papers and five books: *Cambridge Pragmatism: From Peirce and James to Ramsey and Wittgenstein* (Oxford University Press, 2016), *The American Pragmatists* (Oxford University Press, 2013), *Truth, Politics, Morality: Pragmatism and Deliberation* (Routledge, 2000), *Verificationism: Its History and Prospects* (Routledge, 1995), and *Truth and the End of Inquiry: A Peircean Account of Truth* (Oxford University Press, 1991).

William T. Myers is professor of philosophy, Birmingham-Southern College, and adjunct associate professor at the University of Alabama-Birmingham School of Dentistry.

He has edited two volumes, *Philosophers of Process*, 2nd ed., with Douglas Browning (Fordham University Press, 1998), and *Thinking with Whitehead and the American Pragmatists: Experience and Reality*, with Brian G. Henning and Joseph D. John (Lexington Books, 2015). He has served as treasurer of the Society for the Advancement of American Philosophy since 2006.

Nel Noddings is Lee Jacks Professor of Education Emerita, Stanford University. She is a past president of the National Academy of Education, Philosophy of Education Society, and John Dewey Society. In addition to twenty-two books, she is the author of about three hundred articles and chapters on various topics ranging from the ethics of care to mathematical problem solving. Her latest book is *A Richer, Brighter Vision for American High Schools* (2015).

Gregory Fernando Pappas is a distinguished research fellow for the Latino Research Initiative at The University of Texas at Austin and professor of philosophy at Texas A & M University. He is the author of *John Dewey's Ethics: Democracy as Experience* and *Pragmatism in the Americas*. Dr. Pappas has been the recipient of a Ford Foundation Postdoctoral Fellowship, the William James and the Latin American Thought prizes from the American Philosophical Association, and the Mellow Prize from the Society for the Advancement of American Philosophy. He was a Fulbright scholar for the 2012–2013 academic year in Argentina and is currently president of the Society for the Advancement of American Philosophy.

Zachary Piso is an assistant professor of philosophy at University of Dayton. His work explores the social and ethical values at stake in environmental science, especially in interdisciplinary environmental research that draws on the social sciences in explanations of environmental change and resilience. Recently he is exploring ethical and epistemic questions arising in food systems research, including an ongoing study of ecological citizenship and environmental governance in Rust Belt urban agriculture. These public philosophical engagements emphasize stakeholder engagement and participatory methodologies that tie together interests in environmental philosophy, philosophy of science, and American pragmatism.

Scott L. Pratt is professor of philosophy at the University of Oregon. His research and teaching interests are in American philosophy, philosophy of education, and the history of logic. He is the author, coauthor or coeditor of seven books and many articles. His book, *Native Pragmatism: Rethinking the Roots of American Philosophy* (Indiana University Press, 2002) examines the influence of *Native American thought on European American philosophy*, particularly the origins of pragmatism. *Logic: Inquiry, Argument and Order* (Wiley-Blackwell, 2010) is the first introductory study of logic framed in terms of problems of knowledge that arise in the context of racial, cultural, and religious diversity. He is co-author, with Erin McKenna, of American Philosophy from Wounded Knee to the Present (Bloomsbury, 2015), a comprehensive history of philosophy in North America from 1890 to the present.

Naoko Saito is professor at the Graduate School of Education, University of Kyoto. Her area of research is American philosophy and pragmatism and its implications for education. For many years she has been working as a mediator in cross-cultural settings, especially between Japanese and Anglo-American cultures, and more recently European cultures. She was visiting fellow at the Institute of Education, London (October 2010–March 2011) and at Helsinki Collegium of Advanced Studies, University of Helsinki (September 2014–August 2015). Most recently she was engaged in an international research project called SPIRITS (Supporting Program for Interaction-based Initiative Team Studies), funded by Kyoto University. Her research theme is "Philosophy as Translation and Understanding Other Cultures: Interdisciplinary Research in Philosophy and Education for Bidirectional Internationalization." Her most recent publication is *Stanley Cavell and Philosophy as Translation*, coedited with Paul Standish (Rowman and Littlefield, 2017).

John R. Shook is also associate professor of philosophy at Bowie State and research ethics for the online Science and the Public EdM program for the University at Buffalo, New York. He is also a lecturer in philosophy at Bowie State University in Maryland. He is coeditor of the journal *Contemporary Pragmatism*. Among his recent books are *John Dewey's Philosophy of Spirit, with Dewey's 1897 Lectures on Hegel* (coauthored with James Good, 2010), *The Essential William James* (edited, 2011), *Neuroscience, Neurophilosophy, and Pragmatism: Brains at Work with the World* (coedited, 2014), *American Philosophy and the Brain: Pragmatist Neurophilosophy, Old and New* (coedited with Tibor Solymosi, 2014), *Dewey's Social Philosophy: Democracy as Education* (2014), and the *Oxford Handbook of Secularism* (coedited with Phil Zuckerman, 2017).

Maura Striano is professor of educational theory, social pedagogy, and history of education, University of Naples Federico II. She is cofounder and cochair of the Dewey Studies SIG within the Italian Society of Pedagogy (together with L. Bellatalla and G. Spadafora). She is founder and codirector (with R. Calcaterra and L. Hickman) of the international book series Dewey Studies, published by Fridericiana University Press. She served on the board of the John Dewey Society between 2011 and 2014. She has authored and edited a number of books, articles, and book chapters on Dewey and Dewey's legacy to educational research, among them *John Dewey in Italia: la ricezione/ripresa pedagogica* (with F. Cambi, 2010), *Il pensiero di John Dewey tra psicologia, filosofia e pedagogia, prospettive interdisciplinari* (with E. Frauenfelder and S. Oliverio, 2013); and *Per una teoria educativa dell'indagine, riflessioni pedagogiche sulla "Logica" di John Dewey* (2015).

John J. Stuhr is Arts and Sciences Distinguished Professor of Philosophy and American Studies at Emory University. Specializing in ethics, politics, contemporary cultural issues, and nineteenth- and twentieth-century American and European philosophy, he has published more than 150 journal articles and book chapters and is the author or editor of a dozen books, including most recently *Pragmatic Fashions: Pluralism, Democracy, Relativism and the Absurd* (Indiana University Press, 2016) and *Cosmopolitanism and Place* (coedited with Jessica Wahman and Jose Medina; Indiana University Press, 2017).

He is also the editor of the *Journal of Speculative Philosophy*, the founding director of the American Philosophies Forum, and the founding series editor of American Philosophy (Indiana University Press).

Shannon Sullivan is professor of philosophy and health psychology at the University of North Carolina at Charlotte (USA). She works in the intersections of American pragmatism/philosophy of the Americas, continental philosophy, feminist philosophy, and critical philosophy of race, especially critical whiteness studies. She is author or editor of ten books, including *Good White People: The Problem with Middle-Class White Anti-Racism* (2014), *The Physiology of Sexist and Racist Oppression (2015)*, *Feminist Interpretations of William James* (2015), and Thinking the US South: Contemporary Philosophy from Southern Perspectives (2021).

Sor-hoon Tan taught philosophy at the National University of Singapore from 2000 to 2018. Since July 2018 she has been professor of philosophy at the Singapore Management University. She authored *Confucian Democracy: A Deweyan Reconstruction* and edited *Bloomsbury Research Handbook of Chinese Philosophy Methodologies* and *Challenging Citizenship: Group Membership and Cultural Identity in a Global Age.* She is coeditor of *Feminist Encounters with Confucius, Filial Piety in Chinese Thought and History, The Moral Circle and the Self: Chinese and Western Perspectives*, and *Democracy as Culture: Deweyan Pragmatism in a Globalizing World.*

Paul B. Thompson is professor emeritus at Michigan State University, where he was the inaugural occupant of the W.K. Kellogg Chair in Agricultural, Food and Community Ethics from 2003 until 2022. *From Field to Fork: Food Ethics for Everyone* was the North American Society for Social Philosophy's Book of the Year for 2015. His book with *Patricia Norris, Sustainability: What Everyone Needs to Know*, was published by Oxford University Press in 2021.

Leonard J. Waks is distinguished professor of educational studies at Hangzhou Normal University and emeritus professor of educational leadership at Temple University. He received doctorates in philosophy (University of Wisconsin, Madison, 1968) and psycho-educational processes (Temple, 1984). He has taught philosophy at Purdue and Stanford and philosophy of education at Temple. In addition to co-editing with Andrea English John *Dewey's Democracy and Education: A Centennial Handbook* (Cambridge, 2017), his publications include *Education 2.0* (Paradigm, 2013) and *The Evolution and Evaluation of Massive Online Courses* (Palgrave, 2016), as well as more than one hundred journal articles and book chapters. He has been president of the John Dewey Society and a recipient of the John Dewey Society's Lifetime Outstanding Career Achievement Award.

Judy Whipps Judy Whipps is professor emerita of philosophy and integrative studies at Grand Valley State University. Her publications focus on pragmatism and the historical development of feminist pragmatism in the work of women philosopher-activists in the early twentieth century. She has published in journals such as *The*

Pluralist, Contemporary Pragmatism, Hypatia, Dewey Studies, the Journal of Speculative Philosophy, and the *National Women's Studies Journal*. She has contributed chapters on feminist pragmatism in a number of books. She is a former board member of the Society for the Advancement of American Philosophy. She is currently working on a book on the influence of feminist pragmatist political thought on U.S. politics in the 1920s and 1930s.

INTRODUCTION

STEVEN FESMIRE

JOHN Dewey (1859–1952) was the foremost figure and public intellectual in early to mid-twentieth-century American philosophy, working principally from the University of Chicago (1894–1904) and Columbia University (from 1905). He remains the most academically cited Anglophone philosopher of the past century, and he is among the most cited Americans of any century.[1]

Dewey's star as a cultural icon remained high for some years after his death. For example, he joins Jane Addams and W. E. B. Du Bois as the only twentieth-century philosophers to be honored with US postage stamps. Nevertheless, although Dewey has endured for well over a century as a towering figure among theorists housed in university schools of education, by the 1960s he and other American pragmatists such as Charles S. Peirce and William James were, with notable exceptions, dismissed among most professional Anglophone philosophers. What was of enduring worth in the classical pragmatists was presumed to have been incorporated into the purportedly more rigorous and exacting approach that had emigrated from Central Europe in the 1930s and 1940s. Anglophone philosophy concurrently grew isolated from contemporary conflicts, disparities, divisions, and drift, while philosophers who remained committed to dealing with urgent problems too often reached for intellectual tools that had not been critically reformed to meet the circumstances at hand.[2]

Generations of intellectuals have found an inspirational taproot in Dewey's notion that there is a public role for grown-ups who deliberately step back to critique the comfortable assumptions that color, shape, and prejudice our thinking. Dewey held that philosophy is impertinent when approached as a form of verbal conquest and scholasticism, restricted to supposedly timeless and placeless core problems manufactured by an esoteric class of symbolic technicians. Philosophic criticism advances when it deepens and perpetuates goods that are justified by open reflection, or when it helps us to mediate shared difficulties ([1925] 1929, LW 1:299–302; cf. 1916, MW 9:338). He famously summed up this spirit of public engagement in "The Need for a Recovery of Philosophy": "Philosophy recovers itself when it ceases to be a device for dealing with the problems of philosophers and becomes a method, cultivated by philosophers, for dealing with the problems" of humanity (1917, MW 10:46).

CONTENTS AND GOALS

The Oxford Handbook of Dewey reflects an exponential growth of interest in Dewey and American pragmatism across academic areas and philosophical traditions during the past three decades. As its chapters attest, the renascent interest in Dewey and pragmatism has produced a highly articulated framework for clarifying and extending contemporary philosophy's achievements while critiquing its deficiencies.[3] Some contributors to this volume would applaud Hilary Putnam's proposal of a third, Deweyan enlightenment, analogous to the Platonic and eighteenth-century ones (2004, 5–6ff.). Other contributors would deem such proposals overly idealistic, especially if decoupled from research to correct Dewey's own covert biases and limitations. If the volume nevertheless has a unifying theme, it is the conviction that a critical embrace of Dewey merits a central place in philosophical research, and that philosophy's recent past is not the best guide to its future.

The thirty-five chapters of the *Handbook* are written by leading scholars across topical areas. No comparable team has ever been assembled to engage with and critique Dewey's philosophy in a book of this scope. Scholarly emphases and trajectories of course differ from author to author—sometimes markedly so, as with Hammer's and Haskins's chapters on Dewey's aesthetics. In order to clarify and develop reflective tensions and differences, contributors have been asked to take and defend positions as they engage, inspire, and chart a course for emerging research "to determine the character of changes that are going on and to give them in the affairs that concern us most some measure of intelligent direction" (1930, LW 5:271).

The *Handbook* is written principally with an audience of researchers in mind: specialists, scholarly nonspecialists, graduate students, and undergraduates. It is distinct from a "companion" volume in that it is designed to help researchers access particular aspects of Dewey's thought and navigate the enormous and rapidly developing literature. Researchers seeking a companion to the *Handbook*, or readers relatively new to Dewey, may wish to consult a recent comprehensive introduction such as my *Dewey* (2015) in the Routledge Philosophers series, David L. Hildebrand's *Dewey: A Beginner's Guide* (2008), or Stéphane Madelrieux's *La philosophie de John Dewey* (2016).[4]

One measure of the success of any handbook is the extent to which it inspires and facilitates even better research. Accordingly, although each chapter includes some synthesis, exegesis, and summation by way of exploring the current scholarly landscape and orienting readers within contemporary discussions, the overall approach is not that of veterans describing the passing scene to novices. Contributors aim in each chapter to help other researchers *participate* in current scholarship in light of prospects in that area.

A rigid, formal structure designed a priori in the editor's armchair would be too taut to meet the *Handbook*'s goals, while an anarchic assemblage would be too slack and redundant to effectively analyze particular aspects of Dewey's philosophy. Accordingly, the final circumscription and honing of topical areas was determined through dialogue with and between contributors. Traditional philosophical signposts such as metaphysics, epistemology, ethics, and aesthetics are retained in chapter and section headings, leaving it to contributors to reveal and assess Dewey's radical reframing of a philosophical tradition from which he parted company in his search to promote a recovery of philosophical engagement with practical human questions of experience, knowing, moral life, and art.

Beginning with Philip Kitcher's framing chapter calling for a transformation of philosophical research, contributors interpret, appraise, and critique Dewey's philosophy under the following headings: Metaphysics; Epistemology, Science, Language, and Mind; Ethics, Law, and the Starting Point; Social and Political Philosophy, Race, and Feminist Philosophy; Philosophy of Education; Aesthetics; Instrumental Logic, Philosophy of Technology, and the Unfinished Project of Modernity; Dewey in Cross-Cultural Dialogue; The American Philosophical Tradition, the Social Sciences, and Religion; and Public Philosophy and Practical Ethics.

THE FUTURE OF PHILOSOPHICAL RESEARCH

Dewey frequently argued that much that is nominally called philosophy does not express the love of wisdom, if "by wisdom we mean not systematic and proved knowledge of fact and truth, but a conviction about moral values, a sense for the better kind of life to be led . . . . As a moral term it refers . . . not to accomplished reality but to a desired future which our desires, when translated into articulate conviction, may help bring into existence" (1919, MW 11:44). In a 1950 letter, he added that "wisdom is judgment about the uses to which knowledge should be put . . . . [P]ractical philosophy today is largely in academic doldrums—its 'professors' rarely make even an attempt to use it in its application to life's issues to say nothing of developing it so it can and will apply" (1950.04.10 [20434]: John Dewey to Earl C. Kelley).

In "Dewey's Conception of Philosophy," Philip Kitcher recommends to twenty-first-century philosophers the radical transformation that Dewey advocated a century ago in his watershed essay "The Need for a Recovery of Philosophy" (1917). Kitcher reconstructs, reconciles, and draws inspiration from Dewey's seemingly conflicting assertions about philosophy and its distinctive role in progressive social inquiry and practice. "Better it is for philosophy to err in active participation in the living struggles and issues of its own age and times," Dewey wrote, "than to maintain an immune monastic impeccability, without relevancy and bearing in the generating ideas of its contemporary present" (1908, MW 4:142; cf. Kitcher 2012).

METAPHYSICS

The more confidence we have that, from the widest angle, the world has one set of general characteristics rather than another, the more we try "to direct the conduct of life ... upon the basis of the character assigned to the world" ([1925] 1929, LW 1:309). Consequently, given the persistent tendency to damn as outcasts those who claim that existence has unauthorized traits, metaphysics was especially fertile ground for Dewey as a cultural critic.

Thomas M. Alexander, in "Dewey's Naturalistic Metaphysics," explores the development of Dewey's cultural naturalism, culminating in *Experience and Nature*'s "robust version of nonreductive naturalism that emphasized process and creative emergence." In contrast with British empiricism's conception of a receptive mind behind a veil of ideas, Dewey argued that our encounters with the world are creative. In Alexander's view, recognizing inquiry as one specialized kind of transaction rescues us from the intellectualist's fallacy, whereby philosophers have reduced all experience to knowing.

In "Dewey, Whitehead, and Process Metaphysics," William T. Myers explores divergent perceptions of Dewey's metaphysics among scholars and clarifies the traits of existence that Dewey took to be generic. Myers then offers an overview of Alfred North Whitehead's speculative process metaphysics and probes commonalities with Dewey on the mind/body problem and the starting point of inquiry.

EPISTEMOLOGY, SCIENCE, LANGUAGE, AND MIND

"I'm the one in the car with the map in his lap, ... often at the expense of seeing the actual landscape it depicts rolling past on the other side of the window," Mike Parker wrote in *Map Addict* (2009, 2). Like Parker, philosophers tend to be more map oriented than terrain oriented. There are consolations of such a retreat from the ambient buzz, but at our *philosophic* best we do not escape from existential peril into symbolic formulations and remain there. From Dewey's standpoint, the problem for philosophical method comes when we fail to review and revise the symbolic formulations (i.e., the maps) that guide us, reclining instead on familiar symbols cut loose from experimental feedback. Ultimately what mattered to Dewey was for philosophy to contribute to wiser practices, and he believed it could not do this unless it became more naturalistic and empirical so as to improve upon the stubbornly recurrent assumption, common to most historical idealisms and realisms, of an unaffected mind that mysteriously has no effects on the world it knows.

"Arguably, American pragmatism was the first self-consciously Darwinian movement in Western philosophy," Vincent Colapietro asserts in "Pragmatist Portraits of

Experimental Intelligence by Peirce, James, Dewey, and Others." Colapietro explores their reconception of human reason as active and not inherently limited, yet subject to distortions and failures.

David Hildebrand and Joseph Margolis criticize Robert Brandom and other linguistic pragmatists for supposing that it improves upon Dewey to perpetuate the idea that experience is essentially cognitive, a notion that stands on its head one of the very things Dewey was most concerned to reject. In a close and tightly argued reading of Brandom, Hildebrand explores the promises and limitations of linguistic neopragmatism in "Dewey, Rorty, and Brandom: The Challenges of Linguistic Neopragmatism." He concludes that Dewey's "melioristic, experiential starting point remains central and, indeed, indispensable to *any* pragmatism wishing to connect with everyday ethical, social, and political realities."

Leading up to a critical encounter with Brandom and the Pittsburgh School of pragmatism, Margolis in "Pragmatist Innovations, Actual and Proposed: Dewey, Peirce, and the Pittsburgh School" explores the classical pragmatists' "preference of flux over fixity, the deep informality of inquiry and judgment, Darwinian and post-Darwinian treatments of the continuum of the animal and the human, the treatment of the epistemological problem in terms inherently opposed to Kantian transcendentalism and Fregean rationalism, the abandonment of teleologism, essentialism, and fixities of any substantive or methodological kind."

Peter Godfrey-Smith's "Dewey and Anti-Representationalism" critiques Dewey's similarities to contemporary anti-representational positions in philosophy of mind and epistemology. A highlight of the chapter is an analysis of Dewey's discussion of cartographic maps in *Logic: The Theory of Inquiry*. Godfrey-Smith criticizes Dewey's use of false dichotomies, and he limits and qualifies Dewey's deflationary account of the link between accuracy and use. Nevertheless, Godfrey-Smith implies that maps are good models of at least some important sorts of symbol-mediated thinking and communication, so that an analysis of them helps to reveal projective, provisional, active, and constructive dimensions of specifiable sorts of inquiry.

ETHICS, LAW, AND THE STARTING POINT

Dewey argued that we can intelligently deal with problems and direct ourselves toward desirable goals, both individually and collectively, without transcendental standards that hide from inspection even as they pretend to guarantee the validity of judgments. The chief aim of ethical theory, in his view, is to systematically work through and generalize about situations in which the way forward is not well lit, when multiple paths beckon, and when incompatible goods and colliding duties "get in each other's way" (1932, LW 7:165).

Akin to Mill's notion in *On Liberty* of moral life as "experiments of living" (cf. Kitcher 2011), though unhampered by Mill's associationist psychology, Dewey approached our moral lives as cooperative, embodied, imaginative experiments in living. For Dewey, mind is constituted through social communication, so social pressures cannot simply be eliminated as extraneous undesirables. But neither—in contrast with Hegel's organicism—is mind "truly" to be identified with the larger social whole. Millian "negative freedom," taken on its own, does not shed light on how we can better learn to meet situations that destabilize, engage, and stimulate deliberate readjustment. In Dewey's moral psychology, in contrast, people reach out to grasp, assimilate, and transform subject matter that may nourish and consummate their life projects. He took steps toward a theory of ethical inquiry that emphasizes colloquy over detached soliloquy, a situational/systems outlook over hyperindividualism, creative flexibility over moral bookishness, and embodiment over emotionless separation from the intimacy of our own yearnings. A contemporary need, emphasized by Kitcher (2011) and Norton (2015), is for more cooperative diagnoses of problems and more collaborative deliberation. We are in need of more comprehensive conscientiousness in ethics, law, and politics.

Mark Johnson, in "Dewey's Radical Conception of Moral Cognition," explores implications of Dewey's naturalistic, social-psychological, reconstructive, fallibilist, and imaginative conception of moral cognition. Johnson argues that this conception squares well with recent work in moral psychology and cognitive neuroscience. We are adaptive biological organisms, and our embodied interactions are central to the emergence of any meaning, which recruits basic somato-sensory processes. Specifically, in Dewey's idiom, we get brought up short by troublesome circumstances (the problematic situation), we search for ways to deal with the need that has arisen, and our inquiry culminates (hopefully) in some relatively satisfactory way to reestablish relative equilibrium. This *need-search-consummation process* can be further clarified by scientific work on our embodied need for return to homeostatic equilibrium or to a dynamic trajectory or flow.

Cheryl Misak, in "Dewey on the Authority and Legitimacy of Law," grapples with "My Philosophy of Law," a neglected essay by Dewey on the nature, authority, and legitimacy of law. This essay deserves to be standard reading in philosophy of law or wherever legal theorists and ethicists are making sense of what it means to "get things right." Misak draws on Peirce, James, and Oliver Wendell Holmes Jr. to argue that Dewey offers "a truly promising account and justification of the law as a series of provisional punctuation points in a democratic process of inquiry."

In "Beyond Moral Fundamentalism: Dewey's Pragmatic Pluralism in Ethics and Politics," Steven Fesmire builds on Dewey's unpublished and published reflections on ethics to suggest that a vital role for contemporary theorizing is to lay bare and analyze the sorts of conflicts that constantly underlie moral and political action. Instead of reinforcing moral fundamentalism via an outdated quest for the central and basic source of normative justification, Fesmire argues that we should foster theories that, while accommodating monistic insights, better inform decision-making by opening communication across diverse elements of moral and political life, placing these elements in a wider context in which norms gain practical traction in nonideal conditions, and expanding prospects for social inquiry and convergence on policy and action.

Gregory F. Pappas, in "The Starting Point of Dewey's Ethics and Sociopolitical Philosophy," culminates the ethics section with a metaphilosophical bridge to politics. What should be philosophy's starting point? If we reply with some kind of empiricism, then what does it *mean* for philosophers to take experience seriously, and what are the implications for ethical and sociopolitical problems? According to Pappas, Dewey's proposal is more radical than his twenty-first-century allies who join him in advocating for "a shift from traditional approaches centered on ideal theories and abstractions toward a more nonideal contextualist, problem-centered, and inquiry-oriented approach." "For pragmatism," Pappas writes, "there are as many problems of injustice as there are problematic situations suffered in a particular way."

Social and Political Philosophy, Race, and Feminist Philosophy

When we open up decision-making to diverse voices and standpoints, it becomes more difficult to reject others' concerns out of hand. In this way, Dewey observed, democratic discourse can operate as a public check on exclusivity and knee-jerk partiality, though an imperfect and often inelegant one. Dewey's idea was that democratic communication maximizes the chance that we might find mutually workable paths forward that respect legitimate interests, evaluations, and evolving identities of different individuals, institutions, and groups. His approach is in some ways analogous to the more specific black feminist call for an intersectional imagination spotlighted by the Women's March on Washington in January 2017. Instead of developing a theory that determines in advance which valuational standpoints and idealizations are worth taking up, we improve our epistemic position by inhabiting the standpoint of intersecting loci and distancing ourselves from those who assume that only their values, concerns, and identities have overriding force. Dewey likewise eschewed overreliance on top-down, expert-driven decisions and championed participatory processes that engage communities in multifaceted social learning.

Dewey and Addams rejected the still-prevailing notion that there are only two alternatives to conservatism as an approach to social action: the tepid half-measures and sugar of the liberal reformist and the reactive wand-waving and vinegar of the revolutionary. If perceiving the need for radical changes makes one a radical, then as Dewey wrote in the middle of the Great Depression, "today any liberalism which is not also radicalism is irrelevant and doomed" (1935, LW 11:45). Yet Dewey's was a radicalism for those with the courage and patience to secure the "democratic means to achieve our democratic ends" (332). Or as Addams earlier made the point in her 1922 book *Peace and Bread in Time of War*: "Social advance depends as much upon the process through which it is secured as upon the result itself" (Addams 2002; quoted in 1945, LW 15:195).[5]

A distinctive feature of Dewey's and Addams's pragmatic progressivism was insistence on the inseparability of what we mean to do (ends-in-view, in Dewey's idiom), how we are going about it (means), and what we have actually done (ends). Moral and political intelligence necessitates a feedback loop in which we dramatically rehearse alternatives ex ante prior to acting on them irrevocably, then review and revise ex post in light of intended and unintended consequences.

Shannon Sullivan, in "Dewey and Du Bois on Race and Colonialism," converses with W. E. B. Du Bois to critique Dewey's views of colonialism and race during World War I. Sullivan charts a course for research to help correct the systemic injustices of white privilege concealed by our unacknowledged racist conceptual filters. By detecting the conceptual whiteness—"a white perspective that tends to ignore, overlook, and make invisible matters of race and racism"—in the 1910s writings of the great philosopher of the progressive era, Sullivan strives to disclose the indefensible not only in Dewey but also in the contemporary "souls of white folk." Sullivan's analyses may "help contemporary pragmatists avoid similar complicities in future work on Dewey."

Lisa Heldke, in "Dewey and Pragmatist Feminist Philosophy," explores Dewey's mixed record as a feminist theorist and appraises his influences in, and prospects for, feminist philosophy. After canvassing Dewey's influence on feminist work in epistemology, philosophy of education, and sociopolitical philosophy, Heldke argues that the conceptual resources of pragmatist feminist philosophy "could be put to further good use, particularly in feminist metaphysics, epistemology, and value theory."

In "Dewey's Pragmatic Politics: Power, Limits, and Realism About Democracy as a Way of Life," John J. Stuhr explores Dewey's central ontological, logical, and political commitments as a prelude to reassessing the ideal of democracy as a way of life. Stuhr proposes that a "pragmatism for realists" requires additions to and reconstructions of Dewey's account in light of three issues: "relations of power embedded in experimental inquiries; practical limits to the effectiveness of democratic means for democratic ends; and the gap between tribal political realities and Deweyan inclusive ideals."

In "Dewey, Addams, and Design Thinking: Pragmatist Feminist Innovation for Democratic Change," Judy D. Whipps concludes the section by examining philosophical and methodological resources in Dewey and Addams for strengthening the experimental and democratic approach of contemporary design thinking, "a method of problem-solving based in understanding the values and needs of people." Whipps draws from Addams and Dewey to contribute a pragmatist feminist perspective to experimental design thinking, including a focus on power and privilege in the design process.

PHILOSOPHY OF EDUCATION

Dewey's basic pedagogical idea was that children learn better when they organically assimilate knowledge in an active, personal, imaginative, and direct way. The increasingly dominant industrial model of content delivery and retrieval, in contrast, lacks any sense of students or teachers as live creatures actively exploring, navigating, reaching, and making. For Dewey, both students and their teachers are active and cooperative players in who they are becoming and in the world they are helping to make.

Nel Noddings explores curriculum, educational aims, and the vital contemporary import of interdisciplinary studies in "Dewey and the Quest for Certainty in Education." She draws from Dewey to argue that extremes of mere training, on the one hand, and elite intellectualism, on the other hand, do not lead to experimental knowledge that helps us live better.

In "Derridean Poststructuralism, Deweyan Pragmatism, and Education," Jim Garrison critically explores Derrida's philosophy of education in the historical context of Saussure, Husserl, and Heidegger. Garrison identifies areas of accord between Derrida and Dewey, including their mutual rejection of the metaphysics of presence and their openness to difference. He then discusses "Dewey's empirical pluralism and perspectivism" as "an alternative to Derrida's quasi-transcendental apriorism."

Maura Striano argues in "Dewey, the Ethics of Democracy, and the Challenge of Social Inclusion in Education" that Dewey's democratic approach to moral and sociopolitical inquiry anticipated many key issues within contemporary debates on human growth and development in the struggle for social justice and inclusion. "Dewey's approach," she urges, "suggests significant guidelines for contemporary democratic education in times of anxiety, disaffection, and distress."

Leonard J. Waks argues in "Dewey and Higher Education" that, although Dewey wrote "relatively little about higher education, he had a well-developed and largely unexplored conception of the university." Waks builds on Dewey's three-stage account of the logic of inquiry to explain Dewey's conception of higher education, especially with respect to teaching, service, and research. In addition to explaining Dewey's neglected critique of the university, Waks blazes a trail for contemporary educational researchers by extending that critique to twenty-first-century higher education.

Andrea English and Christine Doddington, in "Dewey, *Aesthetic* Experience, and Education for Humanity," explore implications of Dewey's conception of aesthetic experience for formal educational settings. With a special emphasis on the role of the teacher, they conclude that three of Dewey's insights have special import for educational policies that address contemporary educational crises: "the value of teachers, the role of art as an ethical-political force, and the special place of philosophy of education in the cultivation of our shared humanity."

AESTHETICS

Dewey strove to set forth the possibility and method by which techno-industrial civilization might be humanized. He intended this as an antidote to fatalistic acceptance that ordinary experience must be mostly characterized by subordination of present experiences to remote extrinsic goods. Without the methods of science, Dewey argued, we drift at the mercy of natural forces. But without lives rich in aesthetic consummations, he portended, we "might become a race of economic monsters, restlessly driving hard bargains with nature and with one another, bored with leisure or capable of putting it to use only in ostentatious display and extravagant dissipation" (1920, MW 12:152).

Dewey argued that artistic production and aesthetic experience reveal human experience in its full developmental potential. Experiences that are refined in the arts reveal the potential for the rest of our experiences to grow and be fulfilled. Such experiences serve as model, inspiration, and hope for establishing social and material conditions that improve the odds that our intellectual, moral, and everyday experiences may become as aesthetically complete as those peak experiences we justly celebrate in the fine arts. In *Art as Experience*, Dewey clarified his "instrumentalist" theory of inquiry in light of his lifelong emphasis on the felt significance of immediate experience: "I have from time to time set forth a conception of knowledge as being 'instrumental.' Strange meanings have been imputed by critics to this conception. Its actual content is simple: Knowledge is instrumental to the enrichment of immediate experience through the control over action that it exercises" (1934, LW 10:294).

Casey Haskins, in "Dewey's *Art as Experience* in the Landscape of Twenty-First-Century Aesthetics," explores *Art as Experience* as a vital resource for post-postmodern aesthetics, especially for "multidisciplinary discussions of 'everyday aesthetics,' the aesthetics of embodiment, and the dialogue between pragmatist and other traditions such as Adornean Critical Theory." Such aesthetic theorizing occurs, Haskins argues, "on a *landscape* of different possible linkages between belief and behavior," a Deweyan metaphor that invites dialogue about the nature of art and aesthetic theory.

Dewey took himself to be *respecting* art by revealing its naturalness; playing the cello was to him a *real* expression of nature, not virtually real. So he would likely, rightly or wrongly, interpret Adorno's critical theory of art as retreating from the real, and he would equally likely take issue with Adorno's concerns about the autonomy of art as a sanctuary. Indeed, his own use of the word *sanctuary* is consistently negative, as a hermetically sealed space violating the principle of continuity, such as when he criticized the idea of schools as "a fenced-off sanctuary" (1933, LW 8:58–59), or rejected the then-popular view of science as a sort of religious sanctuary "set apart; its findings were supposed to have a privileged relation to the real" (1929, LW 4:176).

But does Adorno's critical aesthetics notice something fundamental about aesthetic modernism that Dewey's cultural naturalism misses? Espen Hammer, in "Dewey, Adorno, and the Purpose of Art," explores this question and makes the case for Adorno's conception of modern art as "radically separated from the everyday and able to offer insight only in an indirect, self-negating manner."

Instrumental Logic, Philosophy of Technology, and the Unfinished Project of Modernity

Dewey remains a powerful ally today in the fight against deadening efficiency, narrow means-end calculation, "frantic exploitation" (1930, LW 5:268), and the industrialization of everything. He was a scalding critic of blind and ill-considered "technology as it operates under existing political-economic-cultural conditions" (1945, LW 15:190). A Dewey-inspired pragmatic approach rejects the persistent tendency to pit human intelligence in an antagonistic relation to nature, asks us to get clearer about our ends and values, and reflects on which technological innovations are functional or dysfunctional means to our most valuable ends. He argued that the operative method of intelligence is our best means to find out how far we can go in the direction of amelioration so that we are able to contribute to whatever progress is possible, but he held that there was nothing inevitable about progress toward greater and more widely shared human fulfillment, regardless of how rigorously experimental our method might be.

Larry A. Hickman, in "Dewey, Pragmatism, Technology," articulates Dewey's pragmatic philosophy of technology in contrast with positivism, Heidegger, Ellul, and critical theory. Hickman then situates Dewey's work within the context of contemporary work by Ihde, Latour, Verbeek, Feenberg, and Pickering. Dewey's account, Hickman argues, "is applicable beyond what are commonly regarded as the technosciences, even for example to logic and religion. It comprises a set of proposals for a continuing reconstruction of culture by means of systematic, regulated inquiry."

In "Dewey's Chicago-Functionalist Conception of Logic," F. Thomas Burke explores Dewey's view of logic "as a study of how abductive, deductive, and inductive forms of inference best work together in the course of inquiry." Burke spells out Dewey's functionalist approach in the context of mainstream contemporary logic, which has been deeply influenced by Russell's competing structuralist approach.

In the early 1940s Dewey worked intensively on a culminating book, which he envisioned as a historical critique of philosophy's lost opportunities. "The working motto of one and all" modern philosophies, he asserted, is to "get everything out into the open where it can be seen and examined" (2012, 169). This incomplete manuscript, or perhaps some less-fragmented revision of it, was lost in 1947. Phillip Deen recovered the infamous "lost" manuscript while combing the Dewey Papers at Southern Illinois University. Deen edited and published the book under Dewey's working title, *Unmodern Philosophy and Modern Philosophy* (2012). Dewey's "new" book radically reconstructs what Hammer, in a different context, calls "the framework of rationalized modernity" (chapter 22 this volume). In "Dewey, Habermas, and the Unfinished Project of Modernity in *Unmodern Philosophy and Modern Philosophy*," Deen explores the book's scholarly and contemporary relevance in relation to critical theory's account of scientific-technological reason.

DEWEY IN CROSS-CULTURAL DIALOGUE

The two and a half years Dewey spent in Japan and China (1919–1921) offered him an East-West comparative standpoint to examine Euro-American presuppositions. In subsequent work he took steps in the direction of a global philosophical outlook by promoting a fusion of aesthetic refinements with democratic experimentalism. Yet even a century on, we have barely begun to take in an emerging global philosophical culture that includes unfamiliar questions, angles, idioms, and emphases. In a sense, Dewey's pragmatism did not "grow up" in the United States; it originated there, and it is now growing up through cross-cultural dialogue.

Roger Ames, in "Dewey and Confucian Philosophy," argues that "American pragmatism might serve as a vocabulary to promote a positive dialogue" between the United States and China "at a moment in history when such a conversation is imperative." Ames compares "the central Confucian notion of relationally constituted persons (*ren* 仁)" with Dewey's conception of individuality. He also explores "the centrality of moral imagination in Confucian role ethics and in Deweyan ethics" and concludes that "these two traditions share the idea of a human-centered religiousness."

Naoko Saito, in "Two-Way Internationalization: Education, Translation, and Transformation in Dewey and Cavell," explores anxieties of inclusion, which are "experienced when we have to live with dissent and are exposed to discordant, disturbing voices." Building on Cavell's reflections on the experience of untranslatability, Saito argues that we must go beyond a politics of inclusion that merely recognizes and respects separate values without mutual destabilization and transformation. Dewey's own tendency to speak in a universal voice needs a corrective in this respect. Saito writes: "With the processes of self-criticism it so readily instills, translation is a metonym of such transformative experience." In light of this, "an alternative route to political education is explored, with the emphasis on two-way internationalization through the art of translation."

Is Confucian democracy an oxymoron? Could it work in China? Situating her inquiry within the setting of Dewey's historical visit, Sor-hoon Tan argues in "Experimental Democracy for China: Dewey's Method" that "Dewey's emphasis on experimentation in social reforms and his fallibilism regarding the political institutions of democracy open up new possibilities for China's democratization, and suggest where one might look to discover the indigenous conditions—the varied experiments being conducted in local governance and civil society—from which a Chinese democracy might be born."

THE AMERICAN PHILOSOPHICAL TRADITION, THE SOCIAL SCIENCES, AND RELIGION

James Campbell, in "John Dewey's Debt to William James," clarifies Jamesian themes that recur in Dewey's corpus, including "Dewey's melioristic, pragmatic account of social practice; his emphasis upon the importance of habits in organized human life; his presentation of the role of philosophy as a means of improving daily life; his recognition of the social nature of the self; and his call for a rejection of religious traditions and institutions in favor of an emphasis upon religious experience."

In "Mead, Dewey, and Their Influence in the Social Sciences," social scientist Daniel R. Huebner shares groundbreaking research on the relationship between Mead and Dewey and on their very considerable influence. Huebner documents Dewey's and Mead's work "to develop functional and later social psychology, social reform efforts, educational theory, the social history of thought, and other aspects of pragmatist philosophy." Dewey's influence also extended to "the sociologists and anthropologists at Columbia, institutional economists at Chicago and elsewhere, and later European social theorists."

In "Idealism and Religion in Dewey's Philosophy," Randall E. Auxier and John R. Shook explore the development of Dewey's shift from organicist idealism to his mature naturalistic view that "experience is ontologically continuous with nature." In conversation with James, Peirce, Royce, and Santayana, Auxier and Shook argue that *A Common Faith* "exemplifies this metaphysics as it explains the ethical growth of communities through religious experience."

Erin McKenna and Scott L. Pratt draw contemporary analogies to Dewey's controversial volume *German Philosophy and Politics* (1915) in "Philosophy and the Mirror of Culture: On the Future and Function of Dewey Scholarship." Dewey argued that Kant provided a "practical aid" to German absolutist politics, a commitment he reaffirmed in 1943. McKenna and Pratt argue that just as Kantian commitments mirrored and informed German culture, so the American linguistic turn in philosophy—exemplified for them by Robert Brandom's linguistic pragmatism—mirrors the rise of President Donald Trump's emotivist politics. McKenna and Pratt urge instead "a recovery of a Deweyan pluralist philosophy of resistance and freedom" that is democratic, fallibilistic, attuned to issues of power, and responsive to situated knowledge. They conclude by examining emerging trends in Dewey scholarship that offer a practical aid to democratic pluralism.

PUBLIC PHILOSOPHY AND
PRACTICAL ETHICS

Dewey argued in *Individualism, Old and New* (1930) that as industrial civilization developed, philosophers and other intellectuals were among the many individuals who lost any coherent social function. By facing problems and helping to guide inquiry into them, intellectuals could recover a public function. As seen for example in the work of environmental pragmatist Andrew Light (Light 2017), who serves as Assistant Secretary of Energy for International Affairs in the administration of President Biden, philosophers can help both experts and the public to engage problems in a way that aids deliberation and social learning so that change is directed more intelligently and less haphazardly than it otherwise might be.

Michael Sandel has observed that our philosophy of the public is implicated in all of our public philosophizing. It determines our aims and shapes our public discourse (Sandel 1998). In his philosophy of the public, Dewey held that the appropriate vocation of public intellectuals is *not* the construction of dogmas for "the people" to follow, as though foregone conclusions and an aura of absolute assuredness must replace experimental, fallibilistic, and participatory social inquiry in a pinch. In contrast with Walter Lippman, Reinhold Niebuhr (1932), and many twenty-first-century liberal intellectuals, Dewey did not think an enlighten-the-masses outlook revealed us at our philosophic or moral best (see 1927, LW 2; cf. Rogers 2008).[6]

Like Addams, Dewey warned against a double standard when it comes to justifications for inflaming people to value political ends irrespective of the results of the social means we use to achieve them (1939, LW 13:229). Such an approach undercuts democratic education, and it anti-pragmatically divorces means from ends. Dewey sounded a very different note than the so-called political realist who today offers the name Trump as incontrovertible proof that we can ultimately expect very little of the public. We have, Dewey held, long been running an educational experiment in low expectations, and the dismal results have been self-fulfilling (cf. Fesmire 2016). The answer to failures in democracy is to reorganize to expect *more* of public intelligence, not less (see 1927, LW 2; cf. 1935, LW 11:39). In Dewey's view, we must educate and communicate with the aim of creating a cultural context in which, in Eddie Glaude Jr.'s words, we "become the kind of people that a democracy requires."[7]

Noëlle McAfee leads off this section. In "Dewey and Public Philosophy," McAfee argues that Dewey would criticize the nondemocratic public philosophy latent in much recent public philosophizing. Such work "usurps the role of a public to identify problems and their sources and skips over any need for public deliberation on what should be done . . . . [P]ublic problems are best fathomed by the public itself, which may enlist experts or governments to fix the problems but alone is the best judge of what needs to be addressed and whether the remedy is successful."

In "Dewey and Environmental Philosophy," Paul B. Thompson and Zachary Piso explore environmental themes in Dewey's philosophy. Despite Dewey's conspicuous silence about environmental controversies that were central to contemporaries such as John Muir and Aldo Leopold, and in sharp opposition to cherry-picking misinterpretations of him as a scientistic technocrat, Thompson and Piso "conclude that an environmental philosophy oriented by Dewey's notion of organism-environment interaction provides promising approaches to interdisciplinarity, transdisciplinarity, and environmental justice."

In the volume's concluding chapter, "Dewey and Bioethics," D. Micah Hester draws from his background in medical humanities and clinical ethics—theorizing through practice, not merely deducing from prior principles—to appraise Dewey's "soft" particularism in moral philosophy in the context of contemporary conditions of wellness and affliction. In contrast with inhumane, atomistic, and merely mechanical approaches to healthcare, Hester builds on Dewey to defend a conception of healthcare as an art that uses science to heal living individuals.

At the close of *Unmodern Philosophy and Modern Philosophy*, Dewey made what he called a "cynical" suggestion that the "writing class" suffers from an inferiority complex. We place our own cognitive activities atop a value hierarchy while relegating practical activity to second-class status, as compensation for the fact that our wider social surroundings consistently place narrowly practical activity above knowing (Dewey 2012, 345). Philosophy should instead, he urged, speak to living.

Soon after his ninetieth birthday, Dewey was feted at his alma mater, the University of Vermont. Too tired to rise and speak to the crowd in Burlington, he simply said: "I'm thankful for the privilege of living on this good planet, Earth. But living on this Earth has become the supreme challenge to mankind's intelligence."[8] He urged philosophers to sympathetically meet problems with fresh hypotheses and to help interpret, evaluate, and redirect our confused cultures.

By what standard, then, would Dewey himself have appraised this handbook associated with his name? Whatever the quality of a philosophical work's schematic form or of its erudite chewing of a "historic cud" (1917, MW 10:47), or of its promise for manufacturing academic citations, by Dewey's standards it is *philosophically* valuable insofar as it interprets the contemporary scene and sheds light "upon what philosophy should now engage in" (1949, LW 16:361).

NOTES

1. According to Google Scholar. Of course, such comparisons break down when applied to figures who did their work prior to academic professionalization. Of such academic superlatives, Dewey had this to say in a letter to Scudder Klyce: "The thing I don't care about is ... your tendency to compare persons as to their greatness and goodness. It may be some defect in me but it does [not] interest me; it seems like a children's game. I confess I don't care how great or how good Christ or Buddha [were] anyway, especially as we don't know anything about them. And about our contemporaries of whom we know more, it seems

both hopeless and childish. That's the impression the Nobel prize makes on me; this sorting people out for prizes is of the mental age of twelve" (1915.07.05 [03542]: Dewey to Scudder Klyce).

2. Irwin Edman observed in the 1950s that postwar existentialists found Dewey "too hopeful," analytic philosophers found him "too large and vague," theologians and metaphysical idealists found him "too earthbound and secular," and doctrinaire conservatives did not "find in him fixed dogmas" (Edman 1955, 34). Dewey's heyday among professional philosophers was waning by the 1930s, and in that respect the rise of analytic philosophy completed a process that had begun earlier. See Campbell (2006). Also see the discussion of Campbell's 2006 book in *The Transactions of the Charles S. Peirce Society* 43, no. 2 (2007): 404–410.

3. Dewey wrote in a 1940 letter: "The word 'pragmatism' I have used very little, and then with reserves" (1940.09.06 [13667]: Dewey to Corliss Lamont). Dewey's pragmatism was, minimally, the critical attempt to replace received beliefs, distorting prejudices, and extant institutional structures with intelligent inquiry. Had Dewey ever formulated a maxim to clarify just what he thought made inquiry more intelligent—which for him was one with specifying what makes it experimental—it might spotlight his emphasis on the ends-means continuum: Always state ends in terms of the means we plan to use to achieve them. Then do our best to confer and pool experiences so that we track all of the rippling consequences of those means and not just the ones favored by our agenda. Review what we have actually done, and revise what we mean to do next accordingly. Alternatively, framed as a cautionary maxim: Beware anyone's ends which are asserted *ipse dixit* as finalities rather than "in terms of the social means" being proposed (Mead 1930, 104-5). Dewey held that the enriching and generative possibilities of human existence go unrealized except through action (Greek *pragma*), and he expanded and rigorously systematized Peirce's and James's pragmatism as a means for reconstructing philosophy and redirecting culture to meet life's evolving difficulties. In opposition to a popular sense of the word pragmatism, Dewey's writings ring with criticisms of shallow American practicality and acquisitiveness.

4. Readers seeking introductory works on Dewey may wish to consult (in alphabetical order) Boisvert (1998); Campbell (1995); Fesmire (2015); Hildebrand (2008); and Madelrieux (2016). For additional scholarly essays ranging over much of Dewey's philosophy, see Cochran (2010); Hickman (1998); and Shook and Kurtz (2011). For helpful online articles on Dewey's philosophy, consult the *Stanford Encyclopedia of Philosophy*. For general collections of Dewey's works beyond the critical edition, see Hickman and Alexander (1998); and McDermott (1981).

5. Dewey said that Addams and Hull House underscored for him the ever-growing happiness to be "found simply in this broadening of intellectual curiosity and sympathy in all the concerns of life" (1930, LW 5:422).

6. Journalist Walter Lippman, whose philosophy of the public Dewey famously critiqued in *The Public and Its Problems* (1927), wrote in *The Public Philosophy*: "It is a practical rule that the relation is very close between our capacity to act at all and our conviction that the action we are taking is right. This does not mean, of course, that the action is necessarily right. *What is necessary to continuous action is that it shall be believed to be right. Without that belief, most men will not have the energy and will to persevere in the action.* Political ideas acquire operative force in human affairs when, as we have seen, they acquire legitimacy, when they have the title of being right which binds men's consciousness. Then they possess, as Confucian doctrine has it, 'the mandate of heaven.'" (Lippman 1955, 135). In 1932, Reinhold

Niebuhr echoed Lippman in an implicit critique of Dewey that "[c]ontending factions in a social struggle require morale; and morale is created by the right dogmas, symbols and emotionally potent oversimplifications. These are at least as necessary as the scientific spirit of tentativity . . . . No class of industrial workers will ever win freedom from the dominant classes if they give themselves completely to the 'experimental techniques' of the modern educators" (Niebuhr 1932, xv).

7. Eddie Glaude Jr., public lecture, Green Mountain College, Poultney, Vermont, April 2017. See also Glaude (2007, 2016).

8. 1975.05.25? (22283): Herbert W. Schneider to American Humanist Association.

Works Cited

Citations of John Dewey's works are to the thirty-seven-volume critical edition published by Southern Illinois University Press under the editorship of Jo Ann Boydston. In-text citations give the original publication date and series abbreviation, followed by volume number and page number. For example, (1934, LW 10:12) is page 12 of *Art as Experience*, which was published as volume 10 of *The Later Works*.

Series abbreviations for *The Collected Works*:

EW *The Early Works* (1882–1898)

MW *The Middle Works* (1899–1924)

LW *The Later Works* (1925–1953)

Citations of Dewey's correspondence are to *The Correspondence of John Dewey*, 1871–2007, published by the InteLex Corporation under the editorship of Larry Hickman. Citations give the date, reference number for the letter, and author followed by recipient. For example: 1973.02.13 (22053): Herbert W. Schneider to H. S. Thayer.

Addams, Jane. 2002. *Peace and Bread in Time of War*. Urbana-Champaign: University of Illinois Press.

Boisvert, Raymond D. 1998. *John Dewey: Rethinking Our Time*. Albany: State University of New York Press.

Campbell, James. 1995. *Understanding John Dewey*. LaSalle, IL: Open Court.

Campbell, James. 2006. *A Thoughtful Profession: The Early Years of the American Philosophical Association*. Chicago: Open Court.

Cochran, Molly, ed. 2010. *The Cambridge Companion to Dewey*. Cambridge, UK: Cambridge University Press.

Dewey, John. 1908. "Does Reality Possess a Practical Character?" MW 4:125–142.

Dewey, John. 1915. *German Philosophy and Politics*. MW 8:135–204.

Dewey, John. 1916. *Democracy and Education*. MW 9.

Dewey, John. 1917. "The Need for a Recovery of Philosophy." MW:3–48.

Dewey, John. 1919. "Philosophy and Democracy." MW 11:41-53.

Dewey, John. 1920. *Reconstruction in Philosophy*. MW 12.

Dewey, John. (1925) 1929. *Experience and Nature*. LW 1.

Dewey, John. 1927. *The Public and Its Problems*. LW 2:235–372.

Dewey, John. 1929. *The Quest for Certainty*. LW 4.

Dewey, John. 1930. "What I Believe." LW 5:267–278.

Dewey, John. 1933. *How We Think*. LW 8:105-352.

Dewey, John. 1934. *Art as Experience*. LW 10.

Dewey, John. 1935. *Liberalism and Social Action*. LW 11:1-67.

Dewey, John. 1938. *Logic: The Theory of Inquiry*. LW 12.

Dewey, John. 1939. *Theory of Valuation*. LW 13:189-254.

Dewey, John. 1945. "The Revolt Against Science." LW 15:188–191.

Dewey, John. 1949. "Has Philosophy a Future?" LW 16:360–363.

Dewey, John. 2012. *Unmodern Philosophy and Modern Philosophy*. Edited by Philip Deen. Carbondale: Southern Illinois University Press.

Dewey, John, and James H. Tufts. 1932. *Ethics*. LW 7.

Edman, Irwin. 1955. *John Dewey*. New York: Bobbs-Merrill.

Fesmire, Steven. 2015. *Dewey*. Abingdon, UK, and New York: Routledge.

Fesmire, Steven. 2016. "Democracy and the Industrial Imagination in American Education." *Education & Culture* 32, no. 1: 53–62.

Glaude, Eddie, Jr. 2007. *In a Shade of Blue: Pragmatism and the Politics of Black America*. Chicago: University of Chicago Press.

Glaude, Eddie, Jr. 2016. *Democracy in Black: How Race Still Enslaves the American Soul*. New York: Crown.

Hickman, Larry A., ed. 1998. *Reading Dewey: Interpretations for a Postmodern Generation*. Bloomington: Indiana University Press.

Hickman, Larry A., and Thomas M. Alexander, eds. 1998. *The Essential Dewey*. 2 vols. Bloomington: Indiana University Press.

Hildebrand, David L. 2008. *Dewey: A Beginner's Guide*. Oxford: Oneworld Publications.

Kitcher, Philip. 2011. *The Ethical Project*. Cambridge, MA: Harvard University Press.

Kitcher, Philip. 2012. *Preludes to Pragmatism: Toward a Reconstruction of Philosophy*. Oxford: Oxford University Press.

Light, Andrew. 2017. "Climate Diplomacy." In *The Oxford Handbook of Environmental Ethics*, ed. Stephen M. Gardiner and Allen Thompson, 487-500. Oxford and London: Oxford University Press.

Lippman, Walter. 1955. *The Public Philosophy*. Boston: Little, Brown, & Co.

Madelrieux, Stéphane. 2016. *La philosophie de John Dewey*. Paris: Vrin.

McDermott, John J. 1981. *The Philosophy of John Dewey*. Chicago: University of Chicago Press.

Mead, George Herbert. 1930. "The Philosophies of Royce, James, and Dewey in Their American Setting." In *John Dewey*, 104-5. Cambridge, MA: Harvard University Press.

Niebuhr, Reinhold. 1932. *Moral Man and Immoral Society: A Study in Ethics and Politics*. New York: Scribners.

Norton, Bryan. 2015. *Sustainable Values, Sustainable Change: A Guide to Environmental Decision Making*. Chicago: University of Chicago Press.

Parker, Mike. 2009. *Map Addict*. London: Collins.

Putnam, Hilary. 2004. *Ethics Without Ontology*. Cambridge, MA: Harvard University Press.

Rogers, Melvin. 2008. *The Undiscovered Dewey*. New York: Columbia University Press.

Sandel, Michael. 1998. *Democracy's Discontent: America in Search of a Public Philosophy*. Cambridge, MA: Harvard University Press.

Shook, John R., and Paul Kurtz, eds. 2011. *Dewey's Enduring Impact*. Amherst, NY: Prometheus Books.

THE OXFORD HANDBOOK OF

DEWEY

I

THE FUTURE
OF PHILOSOPHICAL
RESEARCH

CHAPTER 1

DEWEY'S CONCEPTION OF PHILOSOPHY

PHILIP KITCHER

INTRODUCTION

DURING his long career, Dewey returned to the question of what philosophy is—or should be—on many occasions. His interest in the issue is easy to understand: he viewed himself as breaking with traditional ideas about the role and content of philosophy. The rupture, as he saw it, had begun in the work of his predecessors, particularly in the writings and lectures of William James (1910b, MW 6:92, 96–97; 1910c, MW 6:102). Yet, whether or not Dewey would have awarded himself the credit for any advance, it became far more evident and more systematic in his own writings.

The most prominent manifestations of his turn away from the philosophical tradition occur in his caustic critiques of large parts of metaphysics (1917, MW 10:46; 1920, MW 12:92–94) and epistemology (1917, MW 10:23; 1920, MW 12:149–151; 1929b; LW 4). As we shall see, Dewey envisaged replacing the misguided ventures of the past with valuable successors, forms of inquiry that help to advance the genuine task of philosophy. Richard Rorty (1982) laments this aspect of Dewey's program, regarding it as unfortunate backsliding. I argue to the contrary, that these hopes for renewal are not to be dismissed.

Rorty is, however, entirely correct in understanding just how radical a change in the character of philosophy Dewey envisaged. Reacting to the philosophical discussions of his own time, Dewey was convinced that philosophy had lost its way. If he had lived on into the early twenty-first century, I doubt that he would have found much to console him in the practices that dominate professional philosophical discussions in the English-speaking world. "High analytic philosophy" sees itself as addressing the enduring questions of "core philosophy"—metaphysics, epistemology, philosophy of language and mind—with increasing care and exactness. For Dewey, the idea of a timeless set of questions to be addressed by each new generation of philosophers was a harmful myth (1909, MW 4:14; 1928a, LW 3:131–132), and I suspect he would have viewed the mi-nute explorations celebrated by today's cognoscenti as "a kind of intellectual busy work carried on by socially absent-minded men" (1920, MW 12:164). He might have been encouraged, however, by the flourishing of philosophical inquiries outside "the core"—in studies of the arts and literature, of the methods of the sciences, of issues in normative ethics and large social questions, and especially in the attention now given to problems of race, class, and gender (Kitcher 2011).

Appreciating Dewey's profoundly original conception of what philosophy is and does is crucial for anyone who tries to read him. Those who take him to be addressing the questions contemporary philosophers typically view themselves as having inherited from the past are bound to find his writings disappointing. Indeed, his articles and books may come to appear so woolly and fuzzy, so directed toward irrelevant—nonphilosophical—issues that Dewey will appear as hardly a philosopher at all. Like the Cheshire Cat's smile, an impression of great earnestness may linger after the book has been closed, but there will be no consequences for doing "real philosophy."

My aim in this essay is to show why that—common—conclusion is thoroughly false.

A MISLEADING TITLE?

So what exactly is Dewey's conception of philosophy?

As already noted, Dewey discusses philosophy and its role in many different books and articles—in fact, from the very end of the nineteenth century through the 1940s. (I focus mainly on works from 1899 to 1939; there are other discussions in earlier and later writings.) We have characterizations aplenty. Unfortunately, they are different and seem, at least at first sight, incompatible with one another.

The diversity is already clear from the formulations provided in some of Dewey's most influential works. Here is the account offered by *Democracy and Education*:

> If we are willing to conceive education as the process of forming fundamental dispositions, intellectual and emotional, toward nature and fellow-men, philosophy may even be defined *as the general theory of education.*
>
> (1916, MW 10:338)

Four years later, Dewey says something apparently rather different.

> When it is acknowledged that under disguise of dealing with ultimate reality, philos-ophy has been occupied with the precious values embedded in social traditions, that it has sprung from a clash of social ends and from a conflict of inherited institutions with incompatible contemporary tendencies, it will be seen that the task of future philosophy is to clarify men's ideas as to the social and moral strifes of their own day.
>
> (1920, MW 12:94).

Five years later, in *Experience and Nature*, the characterization has changed again.

> The remarks are preparatory to presenting a conception of philosophy; namely that philosophy is inherently criticism, having its distinctive position among various modes of criticism in its generality; a criticism of criticisms, as it were.
>
> (1925a, LW 1:298).

Another four years pass, and we are offered a different image in *The Quest for Certainty*.

> Philosophy under such conditions finds itself in no opposition to science. It is a liaison officer between the conclusions of science and the modes of social and personal action through which attainable possibilities are projected and striven for.
>
> (1929b, LW 4:298).

Providing a theory of forming fundamental dispositions looks different from clarifying conflicts; clarification is a different activity from criticism; facilitating communication is something else again; and, in the last of these passages, the reference to "strifes" appears to have lapsed. So how do Dewey's various attempts reflect a single view?

Moreover, on other occasions, he identifies the goals of philosophy in yet other ways. Relatively early in his career, Dewey opposes any view of philosophy as "doctrine," preferring instead the idea of philosophy as "method" (1899, MW 1:129; 1904b, MW 3:76–77; 1909, MW 4:13). This formulation persists in works coeval with *Democracy and Education* (1917, MW 10:46) and even in the book that introduces the idea of philosopher as liaison officer (1929b, LW 4:200–202). Another early version of his vision of philosophy starts from identifying philosophy as a language, one "in which the deepest social problems of a given time and a given people are expressed in intellectual and impersonal symbols" (1904b, MW 3:73. See also 1920, MW 12:201). In other places, philosophy's task is taken to be one of providing intellectual order (1908b, MW 4:104–105; 1925b, LW 2:9; 1928a, LW 3:127–128) or serving as a source of goals or ends (1916, MW 9:339; 1929c, LW 5:30). There are also several works in which Dewey treats philosophy as a form of criticism but understands the specific nature of the criticism differently from the "criticism of criticisms" that figures in *Experience and Nature*. 1930, LW 5:141 takes the target to be the "familiar things" of everyday experience; 1929a, LW 5:164 sees criticism as directed against "beliefs that are so widely current socially as to be dominant factors in culture"; 1934b, LW 8:29 reiterates the idea, offering a "definition of philosophy as a critique of basic and widely shared beliefs."

In light of this diversity of formulations, my title may appear thoroughly mistaken. The singular should be replaced by the plural, and the topic should be Dewey's conceptions of philosophy. Yet careful attention to my references suggests a better reaction. Apparently rival accounts of philosophy appear in the same works, often in close proximity to one another. Indeed, discussions that foreground one idea often modulate into language that expresses others. The "criticism of criticisms" definition of *Experience and Nature* leads Dewey a few pages later to the figure of the "liaison officer," not quite in the form assumed in *The Quest for Certainty* (as a mediator between science and "social and personal action") but more generally as someone "making intelligible voices speaking provincial tongues" (1925a, LW 1:298, 306; 1929b, LW 4:298). In *Democracy and Education*, the "definition" in terms of forming "fundamental dispositions" (1916, MW 9:338) is juxtaposed with the view of philosophy as comprehensive (1916, MW 9:334, 336), in search of an "intellectual order" or Jamesian "world-formula" (James 1907, Lecture II); and the discussion quickly moves to identifying philosophy's "double task" of criticizing existing values and forming new ones (1916, MW 9:339). When *all* the passages I have cited are read carefully in their original contexts, it becomes evident that Dewey's approach—or approaches—to philosophy center(s) on a cluster of elements and that different elements in the cluster are emphasized on different occasions.

We can easily identify some of the elements. Philosophy starts from the existing constellation of ideas, including all parts of culture and lived experience. It is to proceed methodically, aiming at a synthesis relevant to the forms of existence present in a society at a time. Part of the method involves a critique of prevalent assumptions and entrenched values. Yet critique is combined with "appreciation" (1925a, LW 1:299–300), with the formation of new values. All this work leads to a theory, conceived as a set of tools, for instilling in people intellectual and emotional dispositions that will enable them to live better than they currently do.

Philosophy's great task is to help promote valuable human lives.

RENEWING THE TRADITION

Many philosophers have taken the central question of their subject to be one posed by Socrates: How to live? (see, for example, Williams 1985). Or perhaps it is not one question but two—How should I live? How should we live together? Dewey was one of those who identified philosophy's central focus in this way and who recognized both the individual and the community strands. As Sidney Hook points out in his introduction to *Experience and Nature*, "The distinctive function of philosophy for Dewey, to the extent that it can be marked off for emphasis but not separation from other disciplines, is the *normative consideration of human values*—or, most simply put, the quest for a good life in a good society" (1925a, LW 1:ix).

We can begin to appreciate the insights in Hook's phrasing by attending to other passages in which Dewey reflects on the nature and role of philosophy. In "Philosophy and Democracy," he suggests that

> we should return to the original and etymological sense of the word, and recognize that philosophy is a form of desire, of effort at action—a love, namely of wisdom; but with the thorough proviso, not attached to the Platonic use of the word, that wisdom, whatever it is, is not a mode of science or knowledge.
>
> (1919, MW 11:43)

Moreover, this conception of philosophy is retained throughout subsequent decades. In a very late essay, "Has Philosophy a Future?" Dewey reaffirms his vision of how the practice of philosophy should be modified:

> this turn-*about* is, after all, but a *re*-turn to the view of philosophy put forward of old by Socrates. It constitutes search for the wisdom that shall be a guide of life.
>
> (1949, LW 16:365)

That conception of wisdom pervades his writings, early and late. So

> wisdom is knowledge operating in the direction of powers to the better living of life.
>
> (1910a, MW 6:221)

> This aspect is expressed in the word "philosophy"—love of wisdom. Whenever philosophy has been taken seriously, it has always been assumed that it signified achieving a wisdom which would influence the conduct of life.
>
> (1916, MW 9:334)

> By wisdom we mean not systematic and proved knowledge of fact and truth, but a conviction about moral values, a sense for the better life to be led.
>
> (1919, MW 11:44)

> . . . wisdom, in its material and goal, was something more than science even though it was not possible without science. It was science enlisted in the service of conduct, first communal, or civic, and then personal. Most of the distinctive traits of philosophy throughout the ages are intimately connected with this fact.
>
> (1934b, LW 8:21–22)

The last passage is especially helpful for understanding Hook's interpolated remark about connections to other disciplines. The knowledge available at any given time is not yet wisdom—but it constitutes a resource for the methodical activity through which philosophy satisfies its desire for wisdom.

Philosophy is inevitably connected to and dependent on other modes of inquiry, and, as we shall see, not just to the natural sciences but to nascent investigations in the social and human sciences and ventures in the humanities and the arts. Philosophers join the practitioners of other disciplines in a common project, a project Dewey regards as the most important human enterprise. His accounts of that project often inspire his most passionate prose—as at the close of *A Common Faith*:

> We who now live are part of a humanity that extends into the remote past, a humanity that has interacted with nature. The things in civilization we most prize are not of ourselves. They exist by grace of the doings and sufferings of the continuous human community in which we are a link. Ours is the responsibility of conserving,

transmitting, rectifying and expanding the heritage of values we have received that those who come after us may receive it more solid and secure, more widely accessible and more generously shared than we have received it.

(1934a, LW 9:57–58)

Unlike many writers who use the first-person plural casually, Dewey is completely open about who "we" are—all human beings now alive. We are all heirs to the efforts of our predecessors and charged with the task of improving the quality of life for others now alive and for those who will succeed us.

In this great human project, philosophers have a distinctive role to play. They are not in the business of amassing new pieces of knowledge in the ways that chemists or anthropologists or historians of art might do. Their task is synthetic. Through reflection on the conditions of life as they find it and on the knowledge amassed by others, they attempt to show how the lives of individuals and the character of societies could be improved. How is that to be done? The answer is through all the various routes recorded in those apparently different definitions: through clarification of current moral and social conflicts, through critique of the most fundamental assumptions and institutions of the societies in which they live, through showing the practical import of the conclusions reached in other forms of inquiry, through constructing new kinds of intellectual order that make sense of the untidy diversity of human accomplishments, by pondering old values and constructing new ones, and by forging the methods through which all these activities can be carried out more effectively. The end result of philosophical practice is to be the translation of its deliverances into educational insights, so that contemporaries— even adult contemporaries—may re-form their fundamental dispositions for the better and so that the children of the future may have greater opportunities for living valuable lives.

That, in vague outline, is the guiding idea behind Dewey's conception of philosophy. It inspires his frequent castigations of the scholastic exercises of some of his contemporaries—and it is easy to imagine what he would say about much of the Anglophone philosophy of today. Reflecting on the flood of professional journal articles devoted to minute technical problems, apparently bereft of any connection to the enrichment of human lives, cut off from the questions pursued in other areas of inquiry, Dewey would have ample scope for complaining that the "philosophers" have simply deserted philosophy's central mission. They engage in displays of cleverness, showing their skill at games whose significance is never made clear.

The charge of irrelevance can of course be countered: today's "analytic philosophers" would contrast their own clarity and precision with Dewey's intolerable vagueness. Can that cloudiness be remedied? Can we sharpen his view of the valuable human life?

That view emerges most clearly in Dewey's writings on education, where he attends to the kinds of processes that must occur if people are to live well. Although it is very natural to confine these processes to a particular period—childhood, adolescence, and perhaps early adulthood—and to a particular location—the school and perhaps the university—Dewey insists that education is a lifelong matter: as he remarks early in

Democracy and Education, "all communication (and hence all genuine social life) is educative" (1916, MW 9:8). He is much concerned with the processes, both within formal education and in the exchanges of the broader society, that promote the growth of the individual. So, as a first formula, we might say that, for Dewey, the valuable life is one that exhibits continuous healthy growth.

But what exactly counts as growth? Dewey tells us in a section of *Democracy and Education* that offers a (surprising?) celebration of Plato's ideas about the aims of education. After admitting that much of what he has argued for "is borrowed from what Plato first consciously taught the world" (1916, MW 9:94), Dewey writes:

> We cannot better Plato's conviction that an individual is happy and society well organized when each individual engages in those activities for which he has a natural equipment, nor his conviction that it is the primary office of education to discover this equipment to its possessor and train him for its effective use.
>
> (1916, MW 9:96)

Education fulfills its proper function when people become acquainted with the possibilities for themselves, find their own paths, and are helped to acquire the abilities needed to travel happily and successfully along those paths.

When growth of this kind occurs, people are free in the deepest sense. As *Democracy and Education* goes on to explain, "the essence of the demand for freedom is the need of conditions that will enable an individual to make his special contributions to a group interest" (1916, MW 9:310). The same theme is reiterated in later discussions.

> In ultimate analysis, freedom is important because it is a condition both of realization of the potentialities of an individual and of social progress.
>
> (1937, LW 11:254)

> It is, then, a sound instinct which identifies freedom with power to frame purposes and to execute or carry into effect purposes so framed. Such freedom is in turn identical with self-control; for the formation of purposes and the organization of means to execute them are the work of intelligence.
>
> (1938a, LW 13:43)

Passages like these suggest that Dewey is not only building on Plato but also on John Stuart Mill. For part of his account of growth and the value of a life exhibiting growth seems to repudiate the idea that the decision about someone's "natural equipment" is externally imposed, in favor of the thought that the route to that decision is a form of self-discovery. People are not to be assigned their courses of life by outside authorities, however wise or discerning those experts may be (1916, MW 9:95). Rather they are helped to find and pursue their "own good" in their "own way."

Mill's *On Liberty* introduces the idea that the ability to discover and pursue one's own good is the "only freedom which deserves the name" (1859, chap. 1). That famous essay reworks the idea of the valuable life in terms of a notion of autonomy that Mill drew from Wilhelm von Humboldt: to live well is to find one's own life course—one's own "project" (Rawls 1971; Williams 1973)—and to carry it through successfully. If you are to discover the course that best suits you, your education must acquaint you with many possibilities—perhaps derived from what Mill calls "experiments of living." Thus Mill is led to a very ambitious program of education, one he outlines in the inaugural address he delivered as rector of the University of St. Andrews in 1867. That address draws on the account of the good life offered in *On Liberty* to advance a theory of what education in a democratic society should be—and, in doing so, it foreshadows some central themes of *Democracy and Education.*

Dewey does not spend much time either on Mill's ideas about education, nor on his conception of the good life. That is initially surprising, given Dewey's respectful attitude toward the man whom William James had seen as the intellectual godfather of pragmatism (James 1907, Dedication). Does it suggest that Dewey's views of the valuable life were at odds with Mill's emphasis on autonomy and that I have erred in linking them? I think not. It is highly probable that Dewey did not know the inaugural address, for, although it had been published shortly after its delivery, it is hardly one of Mill's more influential works. On the other hand, Dewey certainly knew *On Liberty.* Indeed, he drew on it, in framing "the problem of the public" (1927, LW 2, chap. 1).

And the character of that framing provides the clue to understanding how Dewey must have seen his ideas about the valuable life as fundamentally different from those advanced by Mill. *The Public and its Problems* begins by developing an analogue of Mill's harm principle, in the context of interactions among *groups* of people. Instead of thinking of societies as collections of individuals, each pursuing their own projects, Dewey regards them as composed of groups, formed to advance shared goals. Hence there are two faces of human freedom. The Millian "negative freedom" is needed for the groups to pursue their goals without colliding with one another. But prior to this there must also be a "positive freedom" to be able to engage with others, to formulate and to pursue joint efforts, directed toward common goals—goals that each of the group members freely and "intelligently" endorses. (The insufficiency of negative freedom is clearly stated at 1922, MW 14:210.)

From Dewey's perspective, Mill's accounts of social phenomena are pervaded by a fundamental error: the belief that individuals "have a full-blown psychological and moral nature . . . independently of their association with one another" (1935, LW 11:31), leading Mill to suppose that individuality needs "only the removal of certain legal restrictions to come into full play" (1935, LW 11:30. See also 1939, LW 13:138). Because he rejects Mill's form of individualism, he reinterprets Mill's requirement that the valuable life must be one in which the pattern (or project) is freely chosen. He takes over the Millian thought by linking it to a different notion of freedom, one in which the ability to enter into community with others is central.

We can begin to capture Dewey's idea by seeing him as adding a new requirement to Mill's emphasis on autonomous choice. Although Mill is skeptical about the value of an existence lived by a hermit upon a pillar, his account of freedom imposes no condition to exclude it. Autonomy is everything. Your own good might be a purely solitary occupation, lacking even the slightest interest to anyone else. For Dewey, by contrast, the path you choose and follow must be one in which you are constantly contributing to and receiving from the lives of others. The growth you enjoy is simultaneously part of a progressive modification of the society of which you are a part. The yoking of the realization of individual potential and social progress (1937, LW 11:254) is not accidental. The same conjunction occurs early in the section of *Democracy and Education* that celebrates—and corrects—Plato.

> No one could better express than did he the fact that a society is stably organized when each individual is doing that for which he has aptitude by nature in such a way as to be useful to others (or to contribute to the whole to which he belongs); and that it is the business of education to discover these aptitudes and progressively to train them for social use.
>
> (1916, MW 9:94)

But the link is not mere addition, as if Mill's idea of the autonomous choice of some path to pursue were now subject to the further condition that whatever is chosen must involve engaging in a community project. Autonomy is inevitably inflected—or, from Mill's perspective, compromised—by the social embedding through which an individual agent, capable of making choices, emerges.

> Through social intercourse, through sharing in the activities embodying beliefs, he gradually acquires a mind of his own. The conception of mind as a purely isolated possession of the self is at the very antipodes of the truth.
>
> (1916, MW 9:304)

Yet Dewey is adamant that the social intercourse must promote the individual's task of self-discovery. It must not overstep and become "an attempt to dictate to them what their good shall be" (1916, MW 9:128).

In sum: The function of philosophy is to play a distinctive role in generating social progress, where that progress is conceived in terms of the proliferation of more valuable lives. Lives gain value through their realization of the potentials of individuals, in ways that simultaneously contribute to the lives of others and to the advancement of the community.

The next step is to understand how Dewey conceives progress.

PROGRESS WITHOUT TELEOLOGY

Many philosophers and social theorists who deploy the concept of progress are utopians. They conceive of an ideal social state and understand progress in terms of the diminishing distance from it. Dewey, however, is no utopian. Once Darwin has displaced Hegel as his exemplary historicist, he thinks of progressive change in terms of adaptation to current difficulties rather than as movement toward some ideal goal. In an early discussion of ethics, he predicts that "as ethical writers become more habituated to evolutionary ideas, they will cease setting up ideals of a Utopian millennium, with only one end and law" (1904a, MW 3:57).

Teleological progress gives way in Dewey's writings to a notion of *pragmatic* progress. People and societies make progress by solving the problems that currently beset them. He illustrates the idea by explaining the character of progress in technology.

> The logic of the moral idea is like the logic of an invention, say the telephone. Certain positive elements or qualities are present; but there are also certain ends which, not being adequately served, are felt as needs.

> (1902a, MW 2:34).

It is not hard to articulate the view offered here and in many similar passages from Dewey's writings (1922, MW 14:194–199 provides the most extensive discussion). A concept of progress can be developed for many different kinds of systems—we can talk about the progress of smartphone technology or the progress of a young musician. When we do so we view later states of the system in relation to earlier states. If the later smartphone can do everything its predecessor could, while adding new functions or solving some of the glitches experienced earlier, we identify progressive change. If the musician is now more technically accomplished or more interpretively sensitive than she used to be, we rejoice in her progress. In neither instance does it make sense to talk of some goal toward which the system is tending. There is no Platonic Form of the smartphone, no ideal musician who performs every work to perfection. Moreover, with the concept of pragmatic progress, progress as problem-solving, in hand, it can be used to make sense of social change (Kitcher 2015, Kitcher 2017).

Dewey espouses *meliorism*. The human project he envisages, to which philosophy, along with many forms of substantive inquiry as well as the arts, contributes has no final goal. It is inevitably always a work in process. Our task is not to achieve perfection but to make things *better* than they currently are. If that task is to go forward, and to be based on something more than blind guesses, it needs diagnosticians, people who can identify the difficulties and handicaps and probe their sources. Hence it is easy to see why there might be an important place for critics, whose sharp vision enables them to see the places at which work needs to be done. At least one of the roles Dewey assigns to philosophy is not difficult to understand.

But what of the others? I start with the formulation from *Reconstruction in Philosophy*, in which Dewey assigns to philosophy the function of clarifying the "social and moral strifes" of the day. A helpful passage from an earlier essay takes up the charge that philosophy is unfruitful because it is the site of apparently endless controversies. Dewey thinks we sometimes do not need to resolve controversies but to understand their persistence in terms of the pulls of incompatible fundamental values (1919, MW 11:42–47). Or, as a later passage puts it, "In spite of conflicts philosophy serves the purpose of clarifying the source of opposition and the problems attendant on it; while with respect to some problems articulation and clarification are more significant than formal solution" (1934b, LW 8:27). Dewey does not tell us why that might be so, but, if we focus on "social and moral strifes," it is not hard to envisage the possibility. Two groups within a society clamor for moving in different directions. Initially each assumes that the way forward must follow one of the rival proposals. After the (philosophical) clarification, they see how the dispute turns on differences about how to rank competing values—and they turn their attention to seeing how to make institutional changes that will allow each to achieve enough of what it most deeply wants.

I alluded earlier to Dewey's historicism, and the importance of evolutionary ideas for his thinking (at least in the [long] period I am considering.) A particular aspect of his historicist perspective recognizes that the roles and institutions of societies are historical products, produced at moments of adaptation to the existing problems and being adjusted further as the problem environment changes. Attempts to address one problem not only give rise to new difficulties—smaller ones when the shift is progressive—but they can bring the inherited roles and institutions into new, and conflicting, relations with one another. The pressures induced by economic globalization are felt in many other spheres of life—in the character of education, to cite just one instance (Kitcher 2012, chap. 15). Dewey provides other examples:

> But when the scientific interest conflicts, say, with the religious, or the economic with the scientific or aesthetic, or when the conservative concern for order is at odds with the progressive interest in freedom, or when institutionalism clashes with individuality, there is a stimulus to discover some more comprehensive point of view from which the divergencies may be brought together, and consistency or continuity of experience recovered.
>
> (1916, MW 9:336)

The predicaments to which he alludes may call for the construction of an "intellectual order" or "comprehensive point of view," suited to the social and epistemic character of the age. Alternatively, they may demand the clarification of the "strifes" between incompatible proposals for remedying the situation. They may even demand a critique of particular institutions and roles, a return to understanding the historical circumstances under which they emerged and the problems they were introduced to address. Under this last aspect, Dewey's philosophical project finds unexpected kinship with other philosophical ventures—with Marx's attempts to probe the structural causes of social conditions, with the genealogical investigations of Nietzsche and Foucault, and with critical theory, especially as practiced by Jürgen Habermas, Axel Honneth, and Rahel Jaeggi.

The "general theory of education," dedicated to identifying changes in conditions that would promote more worthwhile lives—or, in the soaring words of *A Common Faith*, "conserving, transmitting, rectifying and expanding the heritage of values we have received"—thus stands at the center of a philosophical project that can be undertaken sometimes through criticism, sometimes through clarification, sometimes through evaluation, sometimes through the elaboration of new perspectives, sometimes by the proposal of new or modified aims and goals, as the situation demands. Dewey's apparent proliferation of rival roles for philosophy stems from a coherent underlying idea. That idea can be made fully explicit by combining his approach to the worthwhile life with his meliorism.

There is no ideal final state, no utopia in which all human beings live maximally worthwhile lives. That is not simply a practical matter, stemming from the impossibility of attaining any such state. Rather, the ideal itself is incoherent, tugged and torn in different directions by different values. Yet there are always social shortcomings, factors that detract from people's abilities to choose their own life path, factors that diminish their opportunities for community with others, factors that limit their attempts to pursue the projects they have chosen. It is useful to have a name for what these heterogeneous factors do: let's say that they *confine* human lives. Meliorists believe that confinement is an inevitable part of the human condition but that we can alleviate particular modes of confinement, indeed that we can do so to make the overall situation better—to make social progress.

Dewey's various definitions of philosophy point to the roles philosophers can play in helping to make social progress. The task of philosophy is to identify ways of *reducing confinement*.

PHILOSOPHY RECONNECTED

Rorty (1982) famously announced the end of philosophy—or at least of philosophy as traditionally practiced—and he claimed Dewey as an ally. To be sure, Dewey sometimes pointed in similar directions, as when, commenting on the irrelevance of the professional philosophy of a century ago, he remarked that "Direct preoccupation with contemporary difficulties is left to literature and politics" (1917, MW 10:4). Yet, within a paragraph or two, he made his aims evident: philosophy needs a transformation, not an obituary. So, while proposing an "emancipation of philosophy from too intimate and exclusive an attachment to traditional problems," he also denied that "we can turn abruptly away from all traditional issues" (1917, MW 10:4). Another question thus arises: How exactly does Dewey's—coherent—conception of philosophy relate to the tradition? Has he simply changed the subject, using a familiar name where he no longer has the right to do so?

If the tradition has *become* barren, scholastic, irrelevant, it was not ever thus. Dewey sympathizes with the history of philosophy, and his own writings display a clear interest in learning from that history. (A prime example is his wide-ranging and probing essay on Hobbes [1918, MW 11:18–40]. I conjecture that Dewey would find the

contemporary wealth of rich studies in the history of philosophy a positive development.) The problems bequeathed by the philosophical tradition once grew out of genuine difficulties in human life. They were originally questions generated by attempts
to discharge philosophy's proper function and to contribute to social progress. But
they have become fossils, objects of "intellectual busy work carried on by socially
absent-minded men" (1920, MW 12:164), toys in games or in contests for academic
prestige, because the social changes—some of them progressive—that have occurred
since they entered the philosophical agenda have divorced them from any current
concerns.

Dewey often sketches narrative explanations of the emergence of canonical
"core" philosophical questions. *Reconstruction in Philosophy*, perhaps his most passionate call for renewal of the subject, outlines a charitable tale about the origins
of abstract metaphysics. Socrates' probing of accepted values called for moving beyond accepting them "from custom and political authority" (1920, MW 12:89). Those
values were to be provided with rational justification or replaced if no such justification could be found.

> that which had rested upon custom was to be restored, resting no longer upon
> the habits of the past, but upon the very metaphysics of Being and the Universe.
> Metaphysics is a substitute for custom as the source and guarantor of higher moral
> and social values.
>
> (1920, MW 12:89).

It could not last, of course. Dewey has a further story to tell about how philosophy's
claims to discern "ultimate reality" were undermined in the seventeenth century by the
rise of modern science (initially in physics). But even in advance of hearing that story,
we can understand his charge that healthy philosophy can easily fall sick.

> there is danger that the philosophy that tries to escape the form of generation
> by taking refuge under the form of eternity will only come under the form of a
> by-gone generation. To try to escape from the snares and pitfalls of time by re-
> course to traditional problems and interests—rather than let the dead bury their
> own dead. Better it is for philosophy to err in active participation in the living
> struggles and issues of its own age and times than to maintain an immune mo-
> nastic impeccability, without relevancy and bearing in the generating ideas of its
> contemporary present.
>
> (1908a, MW 4:142)

Nevertheless, there are, as Dewey clearly recognizes, two different types of case: those in
which the old questions are simply abandoned (1909, MW 4:14) and those in which they
are reshaped to suit the needs of a later age.

Large parts of metaphysics have to go. For while it may once have been reasonable to
think of philosophical inquiry as able to disclose aspects of "ultimate reality" beyond

the reach of empirical investigation, the pretensions of philosophy in this regard have become absurd.

> It has no call to create a world of "reality" *de novo*, nor to delve into secrets of Being hidden from common sense and science. It has no stock of information or body of knowledge peculiarly its own; if it does not always become ridiculous when it sets up as a rival of science, it is also because a particular philosopher happens to be also, as a human being, a prophetic man of science. Its business is to accept and utilize for a purpose the best available knowledge of its own time and place. And this purpose is criticism of beliefs, institutions, customs, policies with respect to their bearing upon good.
>
> (1925a, LW 1:305)

Dewey's opposition to philosophy as aiming at a body of substantive knowledge, achieved through some special method of its own, is expressed throughout his career. It occurs in writings of the early twentieth century, where he disparages talk of philosophical intuitions—"The 'intuition' is declared to be a content of 'reason,' but reason is a mere label" (1902a, MW 2:27). Dewey's skepticism about appeals to intuition is foreshadowed in Peirce (1868a/1998a, 1868b/1998b). Yet there is a healthy substitute for the metaphysics of the past, one *Experience and Nature* endeavors to articulate. Through synthesis of the "best available knowledge" philosophy can arrive at a perspective—an "intellectual order"—from which its critical, clarificatory, value-forming tasks can better proceed.

> Philosophy, if it has a distinctive problem and purpose of its own, is not called upon to accept in a servile fashion the materials handed over by common sense and by natural science. If it have any claim to exist at all, it will have a distinct purpose of its own to serve, and will be free to reshape the materials it accepts in the interests of its own purpose.
>
> (1911, MW 6:51)

It *does* have a distinct purpose, and, consequently, a claim to exist. *Experience and Nature* is to supply the conceptual tools for fostering social progress, given the available knowledge and the sources of confinement as they occur in 1925, and it carries out its task by offering a comprehensive perspective, a "naturalistic metaphysics," informed by empirical investigations, and, in particular, the Darwinism of the day.

The same perspective—of problems originally introduced for understandable reasons, later becoming irrelevant fossils, and urgently needing replacement by more fruitful inquiries—is even clearer in the case of epistemology. Dewey recognizes that the question of how knowledge of an independent world is possible, the dominant problem of epistemology from the seventeenth century to his own time (and to ours?), had arisen from the "shock felt in the sixteenth century" (1928a, LW 3:121) as the adequacy of the Aristotelian synthesis began to be questioned. With scientific challenges to methods long deemed authoritative, "it was practically inevitable that modern thought should make the problem of knowledge its central problem" (1928a, LW 3:121). Yet as the new science generated success after success, the question of the possibility of knowledge should have been replaced: "The straightforward course would seem to have been an examination of the procedures by which knowledge is obtained in actual practice" (1928a, LW 3:122). Classical epistemology should have given way to what Dewey calls "experimental logic," or simply "logic," the general theory of inquiry—as it eventually did in the work of Peirce, on which Dewey hoped to build (most extensively in [1938b, LW 12]; for more recent developments, see Levi 1982, 1986).

The same diagnosis is formulated sharply in earlier writings. Those who feel that "current philosophy is entangled in epistemological questions that are artificial and that divert energy away from the logical and social fields in which the really vital opportunities for philosophy now lie" will welcome developments within psychology that help the "emancipation of philosophy" (1914, MW 7:55). Dewey's scathing references to "the industry of epistemology" contrast its futile controversies with the serious project of identifying "right ways of going about the business of inquiry" (1917, MW 10:23). As we might expect, *Reconstruction in Philosophy* offers an extended treatment of the theme. Dewey suggests that the "puzzles of epistemology" are "remote from the understanding of the everyday person and from the results and processes of science": a first task for reconstructing philosophy is to "emancipate philosophy" from these artificial questions (1920, MW 12:150). His envisaged renewal is by no means the end of philosophy.

> would not the elimination of these traditional problems permit philosophy to devote itself to a more fruitful and more needed task? Would it not encourage philosophy to face the great social and moral defects from which humanity suffers, to concentrate its attention upon clearing up the causes and exact nature of these evils and upon developing a better idea of social possibilities; ... ?
>
> (1920, MW 12:151)

As he admits, his proposal is vague—although we can easily use the ideas of earlier sections to articulate it further. Moreover, the specific directive to provide tools for identifying the causes of the confinement of human lives can be linked directly to Dewey's emphasis on the theory of inquiry. The sterile epistemology he denounced is prominent on the contemporary scene—in the innumerable attempts to analyze "*S* knows that *p*" and all the artificial questions spun off in "analytic epistemology." But it is counterbalanced by attempts to provide and critique methods for understanding complex causal situations. Outside the "core," the promise of fruitful epistemology is being realized (Spirtes, Glymour, and Scheines 2000; Cartwright 2007; Cartwright and Hardie 2012).

Philosophy does not end when we "get over" the venerable questions. It is renewed when philosophers emulate their predecessors by engaging in the kinds of processes through which those questions were originally generated—when they respond, reflectively, to the needs of their times.

PHILOSOPHY AT DIFFERENT LEVELS

Dewey's obvious respect for the sciences makes it easy to adopt an overly narrow form of the renewal he advocates. To be sure, he thinks philosophers ought to draw on the best available knowledge, and the natural sciences are prominent suppliers. If thought about social issues is not to be "speculative, romantic, Utopian or 'ideal,'" science must "give it body" (1904c, MW 3:207). Yet if the sciences should inform, they cannot substitute for philosophy. Dewey is unusually clear on the point.

> This reference to the sciences is not to be regarded, however, as implying an adoption of that conception of philosophy which identifies it exclusively with either an analysis or a synthesis of the results of the special sciences . . . . The only philosophy that can "criticize" the premises of the special sciences without running the danger of being itself a pseudo-science is that which takes into account the anthropological (in the broadest sense) basis of the sciences, just as the only one that can synthesize their conclusions, without running a like danger, is the one which steps outside these conditions to place them in the broader context of social life.
>
> (1928b, LW 3:46)

The close of *Experience and Nature* develops the theme at greater length, positioning "philosophic discourse" between science and literature (1925a, LW 1:304) and demanding that philosophy respond to "the entire human predicament" (1925a, LW 1:314).

This conception of philosophy leads Dewey to write books and articles of strikingly different kinds. As a first approximation, we can divide his works into three major types. Some focus on particular issues that arise for people in the societies he knows: these are the *problem-oriented* works. Others attempt to supply tools that can be put to work in addressing such particular issues: these are *methodological* works. Finally, there are some that reflect on philosophy itself, diagnosing the ills of current practice and advocating renewal: these are the *reformist* works.

If Dewey is dismissed as "hardly a philosopher," it is because so much of his attention seems to be devoted to problem-oriented writings. *Democracy and Education* appears to be focused on practical issues about how schools should be run, *The Public and its Problems* on the harmonious coordination of many overlapping groups in a complex society, *Art as Experience* on the detachment of aesthetic experience from daily life in the contemporary world, *A Common Faith* on how to preserve what might be valuable in religions after literal understandings of their doctrines become suspect, and *Liberalism and Social Action* on the disentangling of liberal ideals from the outdated economic institutions generated in the history of liberalism. Addressing such questions may be hailed as eminently worthy, but, for the devotees of "core philosophy" it is not "the real thing." The methodological writings—*Experience and Nature, Logic: The Theory of Inquiry, Theory of Valuation*, and large segments of *The Quest for Certainty*—look more promising at first glance. After a closer look, however, it becomes evident that Dewey is either providing odd and unclear answers to "the central questions" or simply pursuing "tangential" investigations. Finally, for those well satisfied with the state of professional philosophy, the reformist works—"The Need for a Recovery of Philosophy" and *Reconstruction in Philosophy*—are tiresome rants, bizarre attempts to change the subject or to put an end to it forever.

Seeing philosophy as an essential contributor to the project of reducing the confinement of human lives, Dewey recognized a need for works of all three types. The problem-oriented writings show the kinds of studies in which philosophy makes contact with that larger project. To undertake those studies, philosophers need tools, and those tools are forged in inquiries that renew the major subfields of the philosophical tradition. Liberating those inquiries from the outmoded questions and assumptions of the tradition requires awareness of the need for reform. So, throughout his career, Dewey moves among the three levels.

Proper practice of philosophy demands interaction: investigations at one level cannot be pursued in isolation from the other two. The tools supplied at the methodological level are tested by their performance in attending to specific problems. Success at problem-solving is appraised in light of overarching goals. The goals themselves cannot be adopted without reflection on the concrete possibilities for human lives. Hence my tripartite taxonomy is oversimple. Its shortcomings are exhibited in shifts of level within books and essays, even in works that are hybrids. *The Quest for Certainty* is part methodological, part reformist; *Human Nature and Conduct* contains problem-oriented and methodological discussions.

More common is the presence of themes from other levels in books or articles for which one level is dominant. *Democracy and Education* is, in large part, devoted to outlining a program for reforming schools so that they better serve the development of citizens within a democratic society. But, from early in his career, Dewey saw the connection between democracy and education as something far deeper than the addition of a new subject—"Civics"—to the curriculum (1902b, MW 2:82). So he offers us not only a new perspective on what it is to educate a child but a novel conception of democracy.

> A democracy is more than a form of government; it is primarily a mode of associated living, of conjoint, communicated experience.
>
> (1916, MW 9:93)

We move here from the practical to the methodological level. Later, in the chapter on philosophy of education, there is a further ascent: writing in reformist vein, Dewey gives us the definition of philosophy from which I began—the general theory of education.

Approaching Dewey without appreciating his conception of philosophy is, I believe, a recipe for misunderstanding him. Equipped with that appreciation, we can see why he poses the questions he does and how he shifts levels of inquiry in trying to answer them. And perhaps we can also recognize him as the most important philosopher of the twentieth century, a thinker whose works are models for how to practice philosophy in our—or any other—age.[1]

NOTE

1. My understanding of Dewey has been enriched by reading the writings of Richard Bernstein, Isaac Levi, Hilary Putnam, and Richard Rorty, as well as by discussions with all of these people. My greatest debt is to Sidney Morgenbesser, for illuminating conversations that first taught me how Dewey might profitably be read. But it should not be assumed that any of these eminent philosophers would agree with anything I have said here.
Many thanks to Steven Fesmire for some valuable suggestions about an earlier draft.

WORKS CITED

Citations of John Dewey's works are to the thirty-seven-volume critical edition published by Southern Illinois University Press under the editorship of Jo Ann Boydston. In-text citations give the original publication date and series abbreviation, followed by volume number and page number. For example: (1934, LW 10:12) is page 12 of *Art as Experience*, which is published as volume 10 of *The Later Works*.
Series abbreviations for *The Collected Works*
EW *The Early Works* (1882–98)
MW *The Middle Works* (1899–1924)
LW *The Later Works* (1925–53)
Cartwright, Nancy. 2007. *Hunting Causes and Using Them*. Cambridge UK: Cambridge University Press.
Cartwright, Nancy, and Jeremy Hardie. 2012. *Evidence-Based Policy: A Practical Guide to Doing It Better*. Oxford: Oxford: Oxford University Press.
Dewey, John. 1899. "'Consciousness' and Experience." MW 1:113–130.
Dewey, John. 1902a. "The Evolutionary Method as Applied to Morality." MW 2:3–38.
Dewey, John. 1902b. "The School as Social Centre." MW 2:80–93.
Dewey, John. 1904a. "Ethics." MW 4:40–58.
Dewey, John. 1904b. "Philosophy and American National Life." MW 3:73–78.
Dewey, John. 1904c. "The Philosophical Work of Herbert Spencer." MW 3:193–209.
Dewey, John. 1908a. "Does Reality Possess Practical Character?" MW 4:125–142.
Dewey, John. 1908b. "What Pragmatism means by Practical." MW 4:98–115.
Dewey, John. 1909. "The Influence of Darwinism on Philosophy." MW 4:3–14.
Dewey, John. 1910a. *How We Think*. MW 6:177–356.
Dewey, John. 1910b. "William James." MW 6:91–97.
Dewey, John. 1910c. "William James." MW 6:98–102.
Dewey, John. 1911. "The Problem of Truth." MW 6:12–68.
Dewey, John. 1914. "Psychological Doctrine and Philosophical Teaching." MW 7:47–55.
Dewey, John. 1916. *Democracy and Education*. MW 9.
Dewey, John. 1917. "The Need for a Recovery of Philosophy." MW 10:3–48.
Dewey, John. 1918. "The Motivation of Hobbes's Political Philosophy." MW 11:18–40.
Dewey, John. 1919. "Philosophy and Democracy." MW 11:41–53.
Dewey, John. 1920. *Reconstruction in Philosophy*. MW 12:80–201.
Dewey, John. 1922. *Human Nature and Conduct*. MW 14.
Dewey, John. 1925a. *Experience and Nature*. LW 1.
Dewey, John. 1925b. "The Development of American Pragmatism." LW 2:3–21.

Dewey, John. 1927. *The Public and its Problems*. LW 2:235–272.

Dewey, John. 1928a. "Philosophy." LW 3:115–132.

Dewey, John. 1928b. "The Inclusive Philosophic Idea." LW 3:41–54.

Dewey, John. 1929a. "Philosophy." LW 5:161–177.

Dewey, John. 1929b. *The Quest for Certainty*. LW 4.

Dewey, John. 1929c. *The Sources of a Science of Education*. LW 5:1–40.

Dewey, John. 1930. *Construction and Criticism*. LW 5:125–143.

Dewey, John. 1934a. *A Common Faith*. LW 9:1–58.

Dewey, John. 1934b. "Philosophy." LW 8:19–39.

Dewey, John. 1935. *Liberalism and Social Action*. LW 11:1–65.

Dewey, John. 1937. "Freedom." LW 11:247–255.

Dewey, John. 1938a. *Experience and Education*. LW 13:1–62.

Dewey, John. 1938b. *Logic: The Theory of Inquiry*. LW 12.

Dewey, John. 1939. *Freedom and Culture*. LW 13:63–188.

Dewey, John. 1949. "Has Philosophy a Future?" LW 16:358–382.

James, William. 1907. *Pragmatism*.

Kitcher, Philip. 2011. "Philosophy Inside Out." *Metaphilosophy*, vol. 42, 248–260.

Kitcher, Philip. 2012. *Preludes to Pragmatism*. New York: Oxford University Press.

Kitcher, Philip. 2015. "On Progress." In *Performance and Progress*. Edited by Subramanian Rangan, 115–133. Oxford: Oxford University Press.

Kitcher, Philip. 2017. "Social Progress." *Social Philosophy and Policy*, 34 (2), 46–65..

Levi, Isaac. 1982. *The Enterprise of Knowledge*. Cambridge MA: MIT Press.

Levi, Isaac. 1986. *Hard Choices*. Cambridge UK: Cambridge University Press.

Mill, John Stuart. 1859. *On Liberty*. New York: Holt.

Mill, John Stuart. 1867/1972. "Inaugural Address Delivered to the University of St. Andrews." In *Collected Works of John Stuart Mill*, Vol. XXI. Toronto: University of Toronto Press.

Peirce, Charles Sanders. 1868a/1998a. "Questions Concerning Certain Faculties Claimed for Man." In *The Essential Peirce*, Vol. 1. Edited by Nathan Houser and Christian Kloesel, 11–27. Bloomington: Indiana University Press.

Peirce, Charles Sanders. 1868b/1998b. "Some Consequences of Four Incapacities." In *The Essential Peirce*, Vol. 1. Edited by Nathan Houser and Christian Kloesel, 28–55. Bloomington: Indiana University Press.

Rawls, John. 1971. *A Theory of Justice*. Cambridge MA: Harvard University Press.

Rorty, Richard. 1982. *Consequences of Pragmatism*. Minneapolis: University of Minnesota Press.

Spirtes, Peter, Clark Glymour, and Richard Scheines. 2000. *Causation, Prediction and Search*. Cambridge MA: MIT Press.

Williams, Bernard. 1973. "A Critique of Utilitarianism." In *Utilitarianism: For and Against*. Edited by J. J. C. Smart and Bernard Williams, 77–150. Cambridge, UK: Cambridge University Press.

Williams, Bernard. 1985. *Ethics and the Limits of Philosophy*. Cambridge, MA: Harvard University Press.

II

METAPHYSICS

....

CHAPTER 2

DEWEY'S NATURALISTIC METAPHYSICS

....

THOMAS M. ALEXANDER

INTRODUCTION

....

THE subject of Dewey's treatment of nature in its most general features, his "naturalistic metaphysics," is a crucial but much misunderstood and maligned part of his philosophy. For many philosophers at the beginning of the twentieth century, the term "metaphysics" evoked either the intellectual edifices that had reigned prior to Kant—the Aristotelian-scholastic and rationalist systems—or the post-Kantian systems of absolute idealism. The former were thought to have tottered and crashed with the rise of Descartes and Locke, and the latter, the systems of absolute idealism, had become wearisome and remote to the younger generations of philosophers, from Bertrand Russell to Ludwig Wittgenstein and the positivists, who embraced mathematical logic and a minimalistic empiricism. For these thinkers the very word "metaphysics" stank to the heavens as illogical and unempirical—as a disreputable attempt to impose a "spiritual" meaning on a materialistic world or to supersede science when in fact science had superseded it. Classical American philosophy came of age in the last third of the nineteenth century with Charles S. Peirce's series of strange, brilliant essays espousing an evolutionary cosmology, a universe of creative growth, and William James's transformative *The Principles of Psychology* (1890), followed by books and essays whose pages still live and breathe, heralding pragmatism, radical empiricism, and a pluralistic universe. But it was manifestly clear: both Peirce and James were empiricists who sought to transform, not eradicate, metaphysics. Thus to the younger generation they seemed quaint, not fully purged of the past. There were those few to whom they did not seem so—to Alfred North Whitehead, Henri Bergson, and John Dewey, the last two both born the year Darwin's *The Origin of Species* appeared, 1859.

This background is important because many readers come to Dewey's work with these inherited prejudices: the suspicion of metaphysics as a subject, the fierce belief that "science" (by which is meant the most reductive sciences) has the last word, the vision of philosophy as an assistant to the scientific project, notably in the area of "epistemology." Dewey rejected all of these claims, though ironically he is often misunderstood as having endorsed them. He thought the expression "empirical metaphysics" was not only possible but salutary; he did not believe science was the final word on everything; he rejected the idea that philosophy ultimately was epistemology or that every instance of experience was also an instance of knowing. Though science plays a central role in Dewey's philosophy, it is primarily as an *example* of how ordinary experience can be fruitfully controlled and refined so that knowledge, provisional and fallible, may result. But this general method of inquiry is no substitute for the many other forms of experience that had nothing to do with the question of knowledge. Wherever knowledge became an issue, this same "pattern of inquiry" could—and should—be applied to avoid uncritical experience, dogmatism, or any other false method that ultimately was not tested by its results.

This study accordingly first takes up the development of Dewey's metaphysics from his absolute idealism to the emergence of his mature theory of experience and nature. Next it undertakes a close examination of Dewey's fullest statement of his metaphysical position in *Experience and Nature*, focusing in particular upon the "generic traits of existence."

The Development
of Dewey's Metaphysics

Dewey's metaphysics is fraught with critical problems, many stemming from the fact that Dewey's long career began with his advocacy of a form of absolute idealism. In graduate school he fell under the influence of the dynamic George Sylvester Morris (1840–1889) who, in turn, was deeply influenced by the British philosopher Thomas Hill Green (1836–1882). Green had introduced absolute idealism to England through his lengthy introduction to the works of David Hume. This essay was an exhaustive critique of Hume's reduction of the mind to atomic impressions and their mechanical laws of association. Not only did Green, like his German predecessors, claim for the mind a synthesizing, creative activity, but he saw in the individual's own mind a testament of universal consciousness that ultimately upheld ideals of community, religion, truth, and self-knowledge. Insofar as he had dedicated himself to liberal causes, Green's thought was a philosophy of social transformation and liberation, themes that would attract young John Dewey and become hallmarks of his own career. As Dewey became established at the University of Chicago beginning in 1893, he began "drifting" (as he puts it) away from idealism so that by the time of his move to Columbia University in 1905 he had broken with it altogether.[1] This leads not only to the historical question of Dewey's development but has caused many philosophers like Richard Rorty to dismiss aspects of

Dewey's mature philosophy (especially his metaphysics) as unresolved hangovers from his earlier idealist period.[2] In providing a sketch of the main themes of Dewey's naturalistic metaphysics, it is necessary to discuss first this period of philosophical development that may be called "Dewey's absolute idealism."

Absolute Idealism

Aside from two youthful essays, Dewey's earliest philosophy shows an exuberant embrace of absolute idealism. Many scholars loosely call this "Dewey's Hegelianism," but that is misleading. Dewey never incorporated Hegel's dialectical logic as the dynamism of his own thought. Insofar as the dialectic is the engine of Hegel's philosophy, to call Dewey an "Hegelian" is like describing someone as a "Thomist, but without God."[3] Dewey read the whole literature of British idealism then flourishing: the work of John and Edward Caird, F. H. Bradley, Bernard Bosanquet, and, of course, Thomas Hill Green (see 1930a, LW 5:152). Dewey read German, but there are no references in the *Psychology*, his major idealist work, to Fichte, Schelling, or Hegel. This is not because they were unread but because Dewey's idealism had set out on a nondialectical path in which psychology replaced the dialectic. While Morris was undoubtedly one of the greatest personal influences on Dewey, there was another teacher at Johns Hopkins who left his imprint: G. Stanley Hall. Hall had studied psychology under William James at Harvard and gone on to explore that nascent science in Germany in the work being done by Wundt and Helmholtz. And Dewey was drawn to psychology.[4]

The two themes, idealism and psychology, fused for Dewey—if absolute idealism studies the self, and the self as self-consciousness is the ultimate reality, and psychology is the science of consciousness, then psychology (not dialectic) becomes the method of philosophy. Dewey's first book, *Psychology*, though nominally a textbook, was in fact an introduction to the science of the self as ultimate reality. The "fact of consciousness" is "the fundamental characteristic of self"; that is, unlike a stick or stone, consciousness exists "*for itself*," that is, "*for* some consciousness" (1887, EW 2:7–8). Insofar as consciousness is presupposed in any endeavor, it cannot be defined. It is presupposed even by the unconscious. Psychology can only study the forms of consciousness as they arise. Consciousness as a "fact of the self" indicates that "the self is *individual*" though its content may be universal (1887, EW 2:8). Psychology studies the "reproduction" of universal content in an individual self through knowledge, will, and feeling, and it does so through introspection. What we would call "empirical psychology" is, for Dewey, at best an "indirect method," though a useful one. One can also study the creations of "Mind" or "Spirit" in the forms of culture. Here, perhaps, Dewey sounds a genuine Hegelian note.

Dewey's *Psychology* appeared in 1887. By 1905 he had rejected every one of these claims. This period, which Dewey vaguely describes as a "period of drifting," has yet to be carefully studied. But certain shifts can be detected. The most significant of these, as Dewey himself attests, was the impact of William James's *The Principles of Psychology* (1890). Not only did this masterpiece with its command of empirical detail combined with fresh philosophical thought throw Dewey's strange work into the void, but it presented a critique of any form of rationalism, including absolute idealism. The premise of idealism stemming from Kant was that the only answer to the sort of mechanical, fragmented, and passive view of mind represented by Hume and others was to point to the need for some innate "synthesizing" agency. This was the essential activity of mind or "Reason." Kant's aim had been to reconcile the objectivity demanded by science with the freedom demanded by ethics, but he did so by making science strictly limited to the phenomenal world as shaped by the active laws of the understanding—a heavy price to pay for the freedom of will demanded by ethics. As James said later, what was needed was not to go through Kant but "round him." (James 1977, 361–362). James did this by rejecting the problem of "how is experienced synthesized?" by denying, on empirical grounds, that experience was in need of "synthesis"; it comes to us as a living moving whole—in need of analysis, not synthesis. Concepts were abstractions made from this whole for the sake of negotiating our way through it. Relations were not imposed by lofty Reason but were intimately felt in the web of change. There are feelings of "if," "and," and "but," James insisted in the *Principles*—a theme he would later develop as his "radical empiricism" (James 1890: 245–246).

From the beginning, Dewey had sought to preserve the richness of experience from the desiccated, fragmented version of it offered by the British empiricists.[5] Hence the appeal of the Absolute as an ultimate synthesizing condition. James had upended that with his challenge that this was a solution to a nonexistent problem. Dewey was so impressed by James's *Principles* he wrote to James in the spring of 1891 that he was "going through" it with a group of students and found it a "stimulus to mental freedom."[6] The change in Dewey's thought can be seen in two essays of 1892 and 1893, both directed against Green: "Green's Theory of the Moral Motive" (1892, EW 3:155–173) and "Self-Realization as the Moral Ideal" (1893, EW 4:42–53). The only alternative to an ethics of hedonism (i.e., utilitarianism) or a "theological ethics" (presumably Kantian deontological ethics) is an ethics of self-realization. But how is this to be conceived? Green sees our aim to be this "Absolute Self" that is the actualization of all our possibilities. But, if this Self is already actual, why must there be this process of *our* experiences trying to replicate *that* in some way? Furthermore, how does this infinitely actualized Self help *me*, here and now, decide what actions are best in this finite world? The self must be conceived to be "a working, practical self, carrying within the rhythm of its own process both 'realized' and 'ideal' self" (1893, EW 4:53). Dewey does add that this view he criticizes is "falsely named Neo-Hegelian, being in truth Neo-Fichtean," indicating that he hoped Hegel's concept of Spirit as thoroughly mediated and concrete, truly "in and for itself," was thereby unlike the abstract idealisms of Fichte or Schelling.[7] In 1894, Dewey briefly referred to his position as "experimental idealism" (1894, EW 4:264), but appeals to any "Absolute Self" cease in his writing.

That same year, Dewey was appointed to set up the department of philosophy at the newly established University of Chicago. Not only was he head of a department of philosophy, he was also chair of psychology and pedagogy, a position he held until his resignation in 1904 (over a dispute concerning his wife's appointment as principle of the experimental schools).[8] These are the years of Dewey's focus on educational psychology, though the culminating statement of this aspect of Dewey's thought comes some years later with *Democracy and Education* (1916). This decade is marked by two developments. The first is Dewey's critical reconstruction of James's psychology in two important articles: "The Theory of Emotion" (1894) and the seminal "The Reflex Arc Concept in Psychology" (1896). The second lies in Dewey working out his basic ideas of inquiry in the four chapters he contributed to *Studies in Logical Theory* (1903) and which were included over a dozen years later in *Essays in Experimental Logic* (1916), Dewey's most extended discussion of his "instrumentalism" until *Logic: The Theory of Inquiry* in 1938.[9] The first pair of articles are gentle corrections of James to remove lingering dualisms so as to extend and improve Jamesian functional psychology. It is the second article, "The Reflex Arc Concept in Psychology," that is truly revolutionary. There Dewey articulates clearly the idea of organism and environment as a field or interwoven process of acting and undergoing, evincing a genuinely ecological understanding of action. The organism is implicated in its environment and its environment in it. Moreover the organism is a constant exploratory activity and not, as the mechanistic materialisms inherited from the seventeenth century imagined, passive matter waiting to be acted upon. This interactive field or process view of the living being would remain at the center of Dewey's subsequent thought, including his articulation of an ecological metaphysics.

The four essays initially written for *Studies in Logical Theory* mark a revolution in the approach to the question of knowledge. Again, here Dewey undertakes a fundamental critique of the assumptions of philosophical tradition, here that all experience is some form of "knowing." Knowing is the *outcome* of inquiry, and inquiry arises in the *context* of life activity through the disruption of habit, the thwarting of action. The goal is the reconstitution (or "reconstruction," as Dewey said) of habit. This is *never* a return to the previous state but involves an element of *growth or learning*. This marks a complete abandonment of the "transcendental" point of view in which reason was the constitutive ground of the possibility of experience. Here thought, reason as inquiry, arises out of nonreflective material. "The antecedents of thought are our universe of life and love; of appreciation and struggle" (1903, MW 2:298). When thought has done its job, it passes back into the "rhythm of direct practice" (1903, MW 2:299). Thinking is limited to its own context. "What we have to reckon with is not, How can I think *überhaupt*? but, How shall I think right *here and now*?" (10-3, MW 2:300). Questions dealing with "the relation of rational thought as such to reality as such"—the very source of idealist metaphysics—gives rise to the endless debates of epistemology: "logic is supposed to grow out of the epistemological inquiry and to lead up to its solution"; that is, "it is epistemology" (1903, MW 2:302–303). Over against this type of logic, Dewey contrasts his "instrumental type" whose "fundamental assumption is continuity" or "the natural history of thinking as a life-process having its own generating antecedents and stimuli, its own states and career, and its own specific object or limit" (1903, MW 2:304, 306, 309). For Dewey, this was carrying forward the agenda of James's *Principles*: to apply evolutionary method to consciousness and reflective thinking, "a logic of experience" (1903, MW 2:314).

Toward a Naturalistic Metaphysics

Having resigned his position at the University of Chicago, Dewey accepted an offer from Columbia University to begin teaching in the spring of 1905. He would remain there for the rest of his career. Whereas the department Dewey left was Dewey's creation, a veritable "school," as James called it, Columbia presented Dewey with established colleagues holding a variety of very different outlooks. One of these was the Aristotelian F. J. E. Woodbridge, who had a particular influence on Dewey in the area of metaphysics.[10] Perhaps instead of an absolute, a priori metaphysics of the idealist type, one could develop an empirical metaphysics, descriptive and detached from all questions of causality, first cause or otherwise. Such was Woodbridge's naturalistic reading of Aristotle. Also, Woodbridge (with James McKeen Cattell) had founded *The Journal of Philosophy* the year before Dewey's arrival.[11] It would carry in its pages many of the debates at the forefront of philosophy, not just including those of the new realists but the final flowering of James's thought in articles that boldly outlined his philosophy of radical empiricism.[12] These essays were also influential on Dewey, touching as they did the very heart of what had appealed to Dewey in *The Principles of Psychology*: the view that experience contained its relations within it, as felt and qualitatively embodied.[13]

It was in *The Journal of Philosophy* just after Dewey's move to Columbia that he published one of his most significant and bewildering essays, "The Postulate of Immediate Empiricism." It was a short, jaunty essay that advanced the metaphysical implications of Dewey's views of experience. In the name of experience Dewey had given up the Absolute and any transcendental philosophy. In doing so, he had placed reason as a mediating process of inquiry within what he now called "situations." Drawing inspiration from James's recent articles, Dewey now proclaimed himself an advocate of this "vital but still unformed movement" known as "radical empiricism, pragmatism, humanism, functionalism" or, now (Dewey proposes), "*immediate empiricism*" (1905, MW 3:158). "Immediate empiricism postulates that things—anything, everything, in the ordinary or non-technical use of the term 'thing'—are what they are experienced as" (1905, MW 3:158). Dewey uses a horse as an example: to a zoologist the horse "is" its taxonomic description; to a prospective rider, professional or amateur, it "is" a candidate for a ride, fast or slow; to a paleontologist, it "is" the outcome of evolution from the tiny Eohippus, and so on. One of these is not more—or less—"real" than the others. There is no "horse-in-itself" that makes these others "phenomena." What we have are "different reals of experience" (1905, MW 3:159).

Dewey seems to be flirting (or worse) with utter relativism (though he is not). The reason why is perhaps even more startling: The postulate that things are what they are experienced as is misunderstood if taken to mean things ultimately or truly are as they are *known* for some conscious knower. "This is the root paralogism of all idealisms," says Dewey (1903, MW 3:159). Knowing is just another type of experience and exerts no priority over all the other types. "To assume, because from *the standpoint of the knowledge experience* things *are* what they are known to be, therefore, metaphysically, absolutely without qualification, everything in its reality (as distinct from its 'appearance,' or phenomenal occurrence) is what a knower would find it to be, is, from the immediatist's standpoint, if not the root of all philosophic evil, at least one of its main roots" (1905, MW 3:160).[14] Thus it is wrong to say "reality" is what it is to some imagined "all-knower" or even to a finite and limited knower. What Dewey has done here, albeit none too clearly, is to deny one of the basic assumptions in the history of western philosophy going back to Parmenides, the claim that reality is identical with the object of knowledge: "Knowing and being are the same."[15] In modern philosophy, this has become the assumption that any given experience is also an instance of knowing—*to be* in pain is also *to know* one is in pain. Dewey has restricted "knowing" to the *process of inquiry* mediating between a prereflective situation and its outcome after it has been reflectively reorganized, whereupon it returns to the rhythm of life. Dewey therefore does not see an equivalence between "the knowledge experience" and "reality." The latter is inclusive of other sorts of experience. Moreover, Dewey has grasped that our ontologies and epistemologies have everywhere presupposed the omnipresent, silent, spectral knower.

Between 1905 and 1916 Dewey's thought explored this new position, itself the outcome of his growing criticisms of idealism and his concern for experience to be the basis of its own development.[16] Dewey's theory of inquiry, his "instrumentalism," is a key part of this new position, but it is only a part, for the very reasons just given: even if knowing is taken as pragmatic inquiry, it is not the whole picture. Two further insights were crucial in developing Dewey's mature metaphysics and the general theory of experience within which it was articulated. These are (a) the reality of the possible and (b) the idea of metaphysics as an empirical, descriptive enterprise instead of a search for ultimate causes. The first of these claims comes out clearly in an essay of 1908, "Does Reality Possess Practical Character?" Dewey sees the traditional Western elevation of the actual and eternal over the transitory and becoming as grounded in a denigration of praxis, of embodied, productive action. But, by the Postulate of Immediate Empiricism, "reality" (existence or nature) is revealed just as much in practical action as in contemplation. Insofar as practical conduct has been ignored or devalued compared with theoretical insight, it has not been given serious ontological status either. Indeed, knowing is part of the practical world of action; it seeks to make a difference in conduct. What follows if that is changed? What had been classified as "subjective" features, "such things as lack and need, conflict and clash, desire and effort, loss and satisfaction," are now to be "referred to reality" (1908, MW 4:125). As Dewey would put it later, it is the *situation* that is doubtful or consummatory, not some subjective mental "idea." Doubt is in the situation before it can be assigned either to an object or a subject. To give ontological weight to the practical is to reinstate the qualitative back into nature. If one believes that reality "is neatly and finally tied up in a packet without loose ends, unfinished issues or new departures" this makes no sense: the real is complete and our experience is a more or less successful copy of it. But if one believes "that the world itself is in transformation," then the issue is how to direct its processes intelligently (1908, MW 4:127). Put another way, if the individual is a living organism in an environment, then it is the interactive *situation* that is the locus of any quality or mood before it is assigned to the subject or the object. A further consequence follows: insofar as conduct, praxis, is an engagement with possibilities and not just actualities, the possible is just as much a dimension of existence as the actual. This means that the constituents of nature are temporal events with histories, not ultimate changeless self-identities.

The next stage in Dewey's development can be placed a few years later with the 1915 essay "The Subject-Matter of Metaphysical Inquiry." This, too, shows the influence of Woodbridge's naturalized, empirical Aristotelianism. Dewey rejects the idea of metaphysics as dealing with ultimate or nonnatural causes. But there is another sense in which metaphysics can be undertaken with regard "to certain irreducible traits found in any and every subject of scientific inquiry" (1915, MW 8:4).[17] It deals with "Aristotle's consideration of existence as existence" (1915, MW 8:6). Thus, for example, metaphysics would not claim to search for "the cause of life," an inquiry that might lead one to propose materialism, vitalism, or panpsychism as possible answers. Instead, metaphysics empirically notes that nature is such that life appears, here and there; that is, it notes that the universe is such that it can lead to the emergence of life. In short, while life is based on lifeless matter, it displays new orders of interaction, new consequences. Emergence of new types of order, then, is one of the things nature does. Thus "metaphysics would raise the question the sort of world which *has* such an evolution, not the question of the sort of world which causes it" (1915, MW 8:4). This is a question of "ultimate traits" that are "irreducible," such as "diverse existences, interaction, change" (1915, MW 8:6). Dewey believes that this is a salutary practice to counter the tendencies in metaphysics to seek "ultimate causes" and those in the sciences tending toward reductionism. To assume that nature is one unified actuality is another gratuitous claim that is belied by ordinary and scientific experience. As experienced, the world involves change, instability, and risk. Dewey cautiously argues that this allows for a limited reintroduction of the idea of "potentiality" into nature. He is clear to distinguish this from the Aristotelian idea of a pregiven end, a *telos* internal to the organism that determines its development. Dewey's teleology is ecologically situated as a play of possibilities *between* the organism and its environment.[18]

The year after "The Subject-Matter of Metaphysical Inquiry" appeared, the University of Chicago Press asked Dewey to reprint his four essays from *Studies in Logical Theory*, with supporting essays published in the subsequent years. The result, *Essays in Experimental Logic* (1916), was a powerful statement of Dewey's instrumental understanding of logic to which Dewey wrote an extended introduction. This introductory essay presents one of the most lucid discussions of what Dewey had been struggling to articulate for the previous dozen years, laying out the theory of experience that would guide his thought thereafter. After restating the intermediary nature of knowing over against the "primary character of non-reflectional experience," making the "intellectual element ... set in a context which is non-cognitive," he describes this noncognitive situation whose features, however diverse, "are saturated with a pervasive quality" (1916, MW 10:322). Here Dewey uses the Latin term *res* for "situation," connoting as it does "an affair, an occupation, a 'cause'; something which is similar to having the grippe, or conducting a political campaign, or getting rid of an overstock of canned tomatoes, or going to school, or paying attention to a young woman:—in short, just what is meant in non-philosophic discourse by 'an experience'" (1916, MW 10:322).[19]

A situation, or *res*, also has structure, "focus and context, brilliancy and obscurity, conspicuousness or apparency, and concealment and reserve, with constant movement of redistribution" (1916, MW 10:323). "'Consciousness,'" Dewey adds, "in other words, is only a very small and shifting portion of experience," although it is pervaded by the features of the situation or environment. "Experience" for Dewey now clearly stands for this inclusive, interactive, transforming process that is largely subconscious. Dewey was aware that "experience" as a philosophical term carries the weight of British empiricism associating it with conscious mental perceptions, impressions, and "ideas," and his insistence on using the term with a very different meaning would cause problems for readers and critics thereafter. Not only was "experience" for Dewey not necessarily conscious; it was not "mental": it was engagement with the world. "Experience" in Dewey's thought can be said to be what human beings make out of existence; it is *how* we exist in nature. In a set of notes for a course, *Syllabus: Types of Philosophic Thought* (1922–23), Dewey says, "The word 'experience' is here taken non-technically. Its nearest equivalents are such words as 'life,' 'history,' 'culture' (in its anthropological use. It does not mean processes and modes of experiencing apart from *what* is experienced and the way it is experienced, a totality which is broken up and referred to only in ready-made distinctions or by such words as 'world,' 'things,' 'objects' on the one hand, and 'mind,' 'subject,' 'person,' and 'consciousness' on the other" (1922, MW 13:351).

Experience, then, is a process within existence; it is the human transaction with nature. Because it is that part mediated by tools and symbols, the histories and possibilities of existence thereby *enter into the present directly and operatively*. This is a new type or, in Dewey's terms, "plateau" of existence. And it is to this localized field of history and possibility that Dewey gives the technical term "situation." A situation includes ~~involves~~ human involvement insofar as human beings have learned to respond to present events in terms of their possibilities and their histories, thereby making these features part of the *meaning* of the present as a field of activity. In that sense, they become part of the environment. Certain possibilities may be said to be in nature in an abstract way without their directly entering into the immediate present. Iron as an element may exist, but without the knowledge to smelt it the ore remains a rusty-colored rock. So iron forged after smelting at 2800° F is a possibility of nature in this abstract sense. But when the that possibility is known and the means of heating a furnace to reach 2800° F can be mastered, then smelting and forging iron is present operatively *in* the situation as part of the meaning of the situation.

Dewey insists that there are a plurality of situations; he is adamant that they do not add up to "one big situation." Those who wish to turn Dewey into an idealist make the mistake of thinking he is committed to there being ultimately "one big situation."[20] As Dewey says, "while there is no isolated occurrence in nature, yet interaction and connection are not wholesale and homogeneous. Interacting events have tighter and looser ties, which qualify them with certain beginnings and endings, and which mark them off from other fields of interaction" (1925, LW 1:207–208). Breaks, ruptures, and gaps are as real as connections. Also, situations are diverse by their various qualitative characters; each has its unique pervasive quality. This does not mean situations are well defined; situations are not "objects" or "things" in a discrete way. They are the indefinite settings within which objects of clearly discriminated focus exist—indeed, situations are what make "objects" denotatively possible: without situations, no discriminated objects or "things." In this sense situations can be called ontological environments.

As Dewey states in the "Introduction" to *Essays in Experimental Logic*, his general theory of experience was only dimly expressed and gradually worked out in the period leading up to the book, that is, from 1903 to 1916. The "Introduction" is where Dewey achieves for the first time an adequate expression of this idea. The opportunity to set forth his general views on experience and nature at length was provided in 1923 when Dewey was invited to give the first of the Carus Lectures. These lectures were subsequently worked up into his magnum opus, *Experience and Nature*, a synoptic view of his general position, which he then called his "humanistic naturalism" and later would term his "cultural naturalism." It is to this exposition we now turn.

The Metaphysics of Cultural Naturalism in *Experience and Nature*

Experience

Experience and Nature appeared in 1925; it was reissued in 1929 with a new first chapter written in response to the storm of confusion surrounding Dewey's new meaning of "experience" and its relation to "nature" or "existence." While the second version may have cleared up some confusions, it sowed others. If the first version had bravely said experience included death and insanity, the second, by trying to show how science itself is a form of experience, tended to give readers the idea that for Dewey science was the highest form of experience and the last word on nature, that is, "scientism," a view he set out to reject.[21] As discussed, Dewey had rejected several central assumptions in Western philosophy, and so his use of terms (like "experience") with meanings embedded in those traditions was risky. This strategy was, however, the sole alternative to coining a new, esoteric terminology in the manner of Whitehead or Heidegger. The danger facing the reader is that the habits of old meanings distort the understanding of Dewey's texts, at times causing almost an inversion of what Dewey explicitly said. In spite of Dewey's own extended warnings and the corrective labor of scholars, these problems continue to shackle readers new to Dewey. It is best when reading Dewey to place any seemingly familiar key term—experience, nature, mind, object, subject, and so on—in mental scare quotes followed by warning daggers: "experience"†, "nature"†, "mind"†, "object"†, "subject"†, and so on.

What is "experience" and what is "nature"? And how are they "related"? Dewey's aim is (a) to reject the primary characterization of "experience" as "mental" or even as "subjectivity," (b) to reject "nature" as primarily the object of scientific cognition, and (c) to reject the idea of them as somehow two separate things that then somehow are "related" by "interaction." The first point carries with it the rejection of experience as any sort of "phenomenal veil" separating human beings from nature. In his preface to the revised edition, Dewey says, "experience when intelligently used" becomes "a means of disclosing the realities of nature." It is *of* nature. Moreover, "It finds that nature and experience are not enemies or alien. Experience is not a veil that shuts man off from nature; it is a means of penetrating continually further into the heart of nature. ... a growing progressive self-disclosure of nature itself" (1925, LW 1:5). In the original 1925 version, Dewey says that his approach must be from "what is closest at hand, instead of from the refined products of science"—that is the lifeworld or what he terms "gross" or "macroscopic" experience, a "beginning back of any science." Scientific experience is then seen to be a developed phase of experience—but so are "magic, myth, politics, painting, poetry, and penitentiaries." "The domination of men by reveries and desire is as pertinent for the philosophic theory of nature as is mathematical physics." "Hence it is," Dewey adds, "that experience is something quite other than 'consciousness'" (1925, LW 1:369). For all that we prize clarity, "under other circumstances twilight, the vague, dark and mysterious flourish" and the subconscious "makes up a vastly greater part of experience than does the conscious field to which thinkers have so devoted themselves" (1925, LW 1:369–370; see 27–28). Experience is "something at least as wide and deep and full as all history on this earth" (1925, LW 1:370). "History" here includes all "natural history" in addition to human history. Experience "denotes just this wide universe" (1925, LW 1:371).

Experience is, for philosophy, not a subject matter but "method," and the method is that "denotation comes first and last" (1925, LW 1:371). Dewey does not mean "denotation"—"denotation"†—in the sense of designation of some ultimate particular. It is rather the denotation of the context or situation within which any such particular designations may occur.[22] To repeat: inquiry arises from embodied ongoing activity and takes its meaning from there. The objects and functions that so arise constitute what Dewey calls secondary experience. Dewey wishes to avoid the typical mistake of the "intellectualist fallacy" of taking the refined objects as the pre-existing constituents of primary experience whose "true being" is "revealed" by inquiry.[23] A refined metal is not the pre-existent reality of the ore but that ore modified and changed by human action. In a sense, then, the refined metal "denotes" the ore. It also denotes, in Dewey's usage, the functions to which it may be employed when shaped as tools. That is, it refers back to the world "of action and suffering" (1925, LW 1:374). The primary world is one of "being and having things in ways other than knowing them," which are "preconditions of reflection and knowledge" (1925, LW 1:377). Even in the process of inquiry, knowing is something *had* before it is *known* (1925, LW 1:379, 386). So "denotation comes first and last." Dewey insists: "We must conceive the world in terms which make it possible for devotion, piety, beauty, and mystery to be as real as anything else" (1925, LW 1:377). "Thus the value of the notion of experience for philosophical reflection is that it denotes both the field, the sun and the clouds and rain, seeds, and harvest, and the man who labors, who plans, invents, uses, suffers, and enjoys. Experience denotes what is experienced, the world of events and persons; and it denotes that world caught up into experiencing, the career and destiny of mankind" (1925, LW 1:384; see 18). To repeat: "experience" refers to the ways in which human beings *inhabit nature*; it is no more "mentalistic" than are farming or hunting. From flaked stone points to satellites and computers, from religions and their stories to political action, the spectrum of human existence is what Dewey means by "experience" instead of "mental states."[24] Above all, experience is not "a stuff or subject-matter" (1925, LW 1:386). As method, the term asks us to place all distinctions and concepts back into the lifeworld that gave them birth, to see the process whereby they arose and the ends they can serve. That is, instead of dichotomies and dualisms, Dewey asks us to think in terms of functions and processes.

Nature

What, then, is "nature" for Dewey? First of all "nature" is not an "it"; nature is not one thing, like Spinoza's substance or a class with only one member. But neither is it simply a collection of ultimate separate identities like atoms or monads. Dewey's alternative term for nature is "existence," a term that is used in nine of the ten chapter headings of *Experience and Nature*. But what is "existence"? Here we must be careful. One often encounters certain tough-minded naturalists claiming nature or existence is "all there is." This phrase is used as a spell to ward off the possibility of supernatural divinity beyond nature. But there are metaphysics, like Whitehead's, that make divinity part of nature or which, like Spinoza's or the Stoics', indiscriminately speak of "God or nature." Dewey has made the job of saying "what" nature is harder by urging that we not limit "it" to our conceptual or intellectual refinements. Nature as existence is prior to the essences we refine from it—but it includes them as well. Just as iron can come from ore, so refined conceptual meanings can come from existence. But they are not equivalent terms exactly. Nature is constituted by events or *res*, processes that change and interact. To repeat: Dewey is an irreducible pluralist. These pluralities of events come with fuzzy boundaries and creative potential; they merge and separate. As processes, they are temporal—indeed they are "histories" marked by realizations and failures. They have beginnings, middles, and ends. So nature—"existence"—is an "infinity term" of indefinite expanse that includes unmanifest potentialities and possibilities as well as present and past actualities. Existence cannot be just "all there *is*"—only actualities, only facts—since it includes "what is not" as well. "Nature" includes the "can be" as well as the "never was." Failures and tragedies are real in Dewey's universe.[25] In trying to think of nature or existence, as philosophy does, one tries to make it into some object of cognition, some essence. But existence or nature, precedes all cognition and all essentializing. Essences are the product of secondary experience, refinements that have selective emphasis and purposive focus. Thus Dewey agrees with James that truth is something that happens—it is a judgment in the process of inquiry— and so natural events prior to inquiry are *neither* true nor false. They are *existences* prior to those *meanings*. This does not mean that when they acquire meaning they are somehow destroyed or hidden. This would be to take the Kantian view that phenomena hide the world instead of revealing it. Nature has its know*able* side; but that does not mean it exists *only* as it is known. So nature does achieve realization in secondary experience—not just in science (as Dewey is often misread to say), but in all human activities that help show ways in which existence can *mean*. We must not forget the primary world of fraught ambiguity, the world as undergone, lived, or had that originates these meanings. If one must have a formula (though Dewey does not talk this way): Existence both precedes and includes essence.

The Generic Traits of Existence

Experience, that is, culture, includes the way nature opens itself to philosophical reflection. *Experience and Nature* presents Dewey's general theory of the ways in which human existence is embedded in nature. Instead of focusing on consciousness and "mental" events as epistemology has done, Dewey suggests an anthropologically informed approach: look at human life and its practices to see what it tells us about the world in which it occurs, that is, nature. *Experience and Nature* is Dewey's attempt to exhibit some of these features and their implications for philosophy. His account goes from the features of the stable and precarious to quality and relation, from symbolic interaction and community to individuality, from the preconscious "body-mind" to the field of conscious awareness (ranging from the unconscious to feeling to sense to signification), concluding with the topics of art, value, and the ideal of conduct guided by wisdom or intelligence. There is also a more specific project undertaken in the chapters of the book: the metaphysical project proper of describing the "generic traits of nature." As James Gouinlock observes, these two discussions, the broad issues of Dewey's philosophy of nature and the restricted one of describing the generic traits, are not easy to separate.[26] The problem is made more difficult insofar as Dewey did not attempt to give a list of what he considered the most important generic traits, though a fairly basic one can be constructed. Dewey's ultimate goal is that his "cultural naturalism" as a metaphysics should provide guidance to philosophy as "love of wisdom," that is, intelligent conduct. "If we follow classical terminology," he says, "philosophy is love of wisdom, while metaphysics is cognizance of the generic traits of existence" (LW 1:50). This claim is elaborated in the final chapter of the book:

> If philosophy be criticism, what is to be said of the relation of philosophy to metaphysics? For metaphysics, as a statement of the generic traits manifested by

existences of all kinds without regard for their differentiation into physical and mental, seems to have nothing to do with criticism and choice, with an effective love of wisdom. It begins and ends with analysis and definition. When it has revealed the traits and characters that are sure to turn up in every universe of discourse, its work is done. So the argument may run. But the very nature of the traits discovered in every theme of discourse, since they are irreducible traits of natural existence, forbids such a conclusion. Qualitative individuality and constant relations, contingency and need, movement and arrest are common traits of all existence. This fact is a source both of values and of their precariousness; both of immediate possession which is casual and of reflections which is a precondition of secure attainment and appropriation. Any theory that detects and defines these traits is therefore but a ground-map of the province of criticism, establishing baselines to be employed in more intricate triangulations.

(1925, LW 1:308–309)

If one were to force a little more systematic order onto Dewey's discussion of the generic traits, what might the list include? A list based on the chapters of *Experience and Nature* would include: situation, precarious/stable, qualitative immediacy, relational mediation, interaction or transaction (exemplified in communication), selectivity or individuality, continuity and emergence, field (fringe to focus, exemplified in consciousness), realization or the consummatory (exemplified in art), and value (intelligent conduct). As noted, many readers think that Dewey either lost the focus on what are truly generic traits of "existence as existence" to focus on such human things as communication and art. Others see in this a vindication of the charge that in the end Dewey was still an idealist of some strange sort. Another path is available: to say a trait is generic is to say it is found in *some form* everywhere one looks (if one looks carefully). The interaction between organisms is different from that between subatomic particles or between friends. They are all interactions, but they are of different sorts. To find a generic trait, then, does not mean reducing all instances to exactly the same features. Moreover, Dewey is an emergentist: new forms of existence arise from previous ones without necessarily being reducible to them. Organisms arise from chemical reactions but behave differently; humans, with symbolic communication, arise from earlier animals that do not exhibit this behavior. For Dewey, the more actualized or more complex tells us more about nature's possibilities than the simplest even though the complex may depend upon the previous, simpler stages. A poet may descend from the hooting Australopithecus as her ancestor, but the poet reveals nature in a fuller way and so tells us something more about nature. We may then distinguish between the generic traits as *inclusive*—as connecting all the diverse phenomena simpler and more complex that are encompassed by them—and certain *exemplary* instances in them that reveal their potential the most. Language is an instance of the *inclusive* generic trait of transaction or interaction, but it is *exemplary* in showing what interaction is in its fullest sense that we know.[27] With this in mind, let us discuss the salient generic traits of *Experience and Nature*, some of which will be discussed in their exemplary forms.

Situation

First of all, are *situations* generic traits? Human existence is characterized as being situated, so one might think so. But on the other hand the generic traits are traits *of* existence. For Dewey it is the *situation* that is precarious or stable. Situations are what ground meaning, so it might be better to think of the category of "situation" as what the generic traits are *of* rather than as a generic trait itself. There are alternate terms that Dewey uses for basic reality: "events," "histories," or "*res*." These terms indicate that situations are inherently *temporal*—that is, pervaded by the rhythmic *temporal quality* of *doing and undergoing* and *beginning and ending*. Even very stable situations have this rhythmic aspect, just as a slow harmonic movement in a piece of music is nevertheless marked by temporal development (1925, LW 1:92). So *situation* is a basic feature of any account of existence as experience (i.e., existence with human involvement), and by this is included the idea of it as an event pervaded by temporal quality as doing and undergoing and as development. But it is not an object as such; it is the context within which objects arise and are investigated.[28] What of nature or existence apart from human involvement? By Dewey's principle of continuity, there would be characteristics that prefigure situations, such as contexts, ecologies, or fields of energy. In this sense Dewey provides an ecological model for ontology.[29]

The Stable-Precarious

The first generic trait Dewey discusses is one of the most important: the generic trait of "the stable and the precarious."[30] Recall that being in a situation is the primary reality of human existence. Such situations are pervaded by general qualitative aspects that fall somewhere along the stable-precarious continuum. We can think of situations characterized by dominant stability, taking a Sunday stroll in a familiar neighborhood, for example. We can think of situations characterized by great instability, such as a battle with an unseen enemy in tall grass. And we can think of situations that change suddenly from stability to precariousness or which have a dominant quality of stability and an undercurrent of precariousness at variance with each other. The point is that by thinking of how stability and precariousness are reflected culturally, in tools, beliefs, practices, they are revealed to be pervasive features of existence. As one strolls along, the openness of streets and sidewalks indicates stability in society while a passing patrol car indicates that there is a need that also calls for a police force to protect the community. Soldiers in a firefight must use extreme caution, but they have disciplined responses, weapons, and reconnaissance tools to help stabilize the situation. Thus the stable-precarious is not simply to be read as some subjective feeling but as *a basic feature of situations* and so of nature. Philosophers may identify "real being" with the stable, as Plato did with his Forms or Democritus with his atoms, and relegate the unstable to a lower sort of existence, Plato's world of becoming or the atomists' derivative motion of the atomic bodies in the void. The aim of naturalistic metaphysics, as empirical method, is simply to acknowledge both aspects, stable *and* precarious, as features of situations, traits of existence, which are present wherever we turn, and the more we consider culture the more testimony to their existence it reveals.

Qualitative Immediacy

Situations have *qualitative immediacy*. Dewey discusses quality as a generic trait in Chapter 3 of *Experience and Nature* as well as in an important article of 1930, "Qualitative Thought." It was one of Dewey's major points to reintroduce quality back into nature after Galileo, Descartes, and Newton had excluded it. But he did not revert to Aristotelian realism—simply making qualities inhere in individual substances as predicates of a subject. For Aristotle, the proposition "The rose is red" reflects the ontological reality of a substance, the rose, exhibiting a predicate, redness. For Dewey, qualities are "in" the situation and do not necessarily have one specific location. If we are judging roses, we will refer the colors to the flowers. If we are studying the physiology of the optic system, we will refer color to the retina and optic nerve. And if we are photographers, we will see the color as a relational function of the source of light and its intensity and the distance and contour of the rose.

Quality also denotes the terminus or limit of a process, its brute here-and-now realization. As such, it denotes a radical, surd thatness, an ultimate finitude that, considered on its own, is unrelated, unique, ineffable and without name. It is an "end," not necessarily in the sense of the culmination of an event, a genuine fulfillment (such as Aristotle's *entelecheia*), but simply as its final determination, its "facticity." Philosophers, with their disciplinary disposition to regard existence as intelligible, resist this surd and try to focus on relations, concepts, classes, and so on.[31] "But in every event there is something obdurate, self-sufficient, wholly immediate, neither a relation nor an element in a relational whole, but terminal and exclusive," and, he adds "Immediacy of existence is ineffable" (1925, LW 1:74). Without this "phase of brute and unconditioned 'isness'" there would be no "footing" for relations and relational systems (1925, LW 1:75). It should be added, however, that this immediate, undergone phase of existence *may* be filled with consummatory or aesthetic meaning—meaning as had rather than instrumentally used. Then it becomes a funded outcome, a consummation. But this more developed aspect is rooted in the more primitive conditions Dewey points to: no quality, no consummation.

The last thing to note about the qualitative traits of situations is their transiency; they are as evanescent as they are irreducibly individual. Insofar as the qualitative may embody some "value"—something unreflectively welcomed or shunned long before it is the subject of critical judgment—its transitoriness begins to open up a directive for pursuit or avoidance, which is to say, it begins to open up the realm of possibility filled with anticipation and memory. A sudden good that is enjoyed may suddenly vanish, and, as infants, we weep or, if we are older, begin to look for it. Something painful or frightening goes away as quickly, but its shadow remains. Thus the hard shell of immediacy begins to crack and the dimension of relations and of the possible opens.

Relational Mediation

Dewey accordingly takes up in the fourth chapter this matter of relations and the mediated aspect of nature through an analysis of means, tools, and technology. (Note again how culture opens up a dimension of natural existence.) Existence is not just a matter of undergoing but of doing (technology being an exemplary instance of the generic traits of relation). In the desire to recover a lost good or to ensure that a present one does not go away, actions must be taken that impose an exploration of the features of situations in their capacities as means or relations. "By its nature technology is concerned with things and acts in their instrumentalities, not in their immediacies. Objects and events figure in work not as fulfillments, realizations, but in behalf of other things of which they are the means and predictive signs" (1925, LW 1:101). A tool literally refers to something beyond itself—the spear refers not only to the animal hunted but to the needs of the hunter. It is the world of need and labor that opens up nature in its interconnected relations and structures. The body itself in its organized habits or in the use of finger, hand, arm, foot, and pace began the process of turning existence into something known. Eventually, by focusing solely on knowing, the concept of nature became that of purely relational metaphysics illustrated in idea of nature as purely a set of mathematical transformations. The result was that quality was relegated to the world of subjective mind. The solution that Dewey proposes is to restore potentiality to natural events and to drop the view that reality is simply what is revealed through knowledge. One need not thereby conceive of potentiality as Aristotle did, a process aiming toward fixed ends. Potentialities are possibilities of relations in events; they are "in" the situation (1925, LW 1:109f).[32] Thus by insisting *both* upon the status of quality and relation in nature, Dewey proposes to resolve the "mind-matter" or "subject-object" dualism that as haunted modernity. Nature is a plurality of events that have a qualitative side and a relational side; the former is not concerned with knowing, while the latter is. To reiterate: nature is more than nature-as-known.

Another way of looking at the qualitative and relational traits of existence is in terms of the actual and the possible. Existence—nature—includes what is and was (the actual) as well as what is going to be (the potential) or what may be (the possible). Again, we are dealing here with a nuanced continuum insofar as "what there is" may reach beyond the present into the past, and what may be can extend from an immanent and highly likely future to a remote or merely logical possibility. As one goes from sheer undergoing, immediacy here and now, to regarding a situation in terms of what it will be or can be, one gains a sense of its possibilities as inherent or immanent in the present. Possibilities are rooted in what is; they are *of* it. The immediate situation thereby becomes a way of anticipating its closest possibilities. Its immanent possibilities form, as it were, a halo about its immediacy, and insofar as these are sensed and become operative they become meanings of the present. One may be trapped in a hole with a log. That log may be seen not just as a log but as a means for climbing out. In this way, when a possibility goes from being unrecognized to being recognized, it suddenly becomes part of the *meaning of the situation*; it becomes a perceived aspect of the situation at hand and something one can meaningfully use and respond to. In this way the situation is transformed. The operative environment expands.

Interaction/Transaction

The most powerful way the revelation of possibilities happens, according to Dewey, is through communication, the subject of the fifth chapter of *Experience and Nature*. At this point readers begin to wonder whether Dewey's project of describing generic traits of nature may have suddenly become the more limited project of describing nature solely in terms of human experience. But communication is an *exemplary instance* of the *inclusive* generic trait of *interaction*, or, in Dewey's words, "associated or conjoint behavior is a universal characteristic of all existences" (1928, LW 3:41).[33] Throughout nature there are many kinds of interaction (or "transaction" in Dewey's later terminology), but communication shows what it is at its fullest. We must recall that the sort of naturalism Dewey is developing is a nonreductive or "emergentist" naturalism. Here Dewey insists that he is making an empirical point: in nature we find all sorts of events, from the physical to the most culturally complex, and all these events are "natural." That nature can eventuate in poetry is as much as fact about the nature of nature as that iron can oxidize. Although modern philosophy has shown a preference for giving ontological priority to ultimate simples out of which complexities are generated and into which they can be reduced, Dewey questions this: "the more numerous and varied the forms of association into which anything enters, the better basis we have for describing an understanding it, for the more complex an association the more fully are potentialities released for observation" (1928, LW 3:42). As Dewey puts it in *Experience and Nature*: "For it is reasonable to believe that the most adequate definition of the most basic traits of natural existence can be had only when its properties are most fully displayed—a condition which is met in the degree of the scope and intimacy of interactions realized" (1925, LW 1:201). Thus although life, not to mention human life, is rare among natural events, nevertheless, as natural events, life in general and human life in particular show something of nature's potentialities. For Dewey, "the social, in its human sense, is the richest, fullest and most delicately subtle of any mode actually experienced" (1928, LW 3:44). This is a major point in grasping the focus of the later chapters of the book; it also lays to rest the charges that Dewey is being an "idealist" or even anthropocentric in his metaphysics. Nature is full of potentialities and existences *as* they are revealed these transactions.[34]

Dewey's discussion of communication also grows out of his earlier analysis of means, relations, and tools. The symbols and imaginative habits used in communication are tools and help reveal possibilities. But Dewey also describes language as "the tool of tools" (1925, LW 1:146–147). This is often misread as a "technological" or

·"instrumentalist" view of language, one that misses language as a form of poetic or emotional communion. This inverts the point Dewey is making, which is *precisely* to put the most emotional and expressive forms of human intimacy as the basis of technology. Language is the "tool" of tools because it is really the *condition* whereby other technologies even become possible; it is the means whereby the whole human world of sharing ideas, of imagination, cooperation, and shared experience—culture—comes into existence. Put another way: tools and technology are extensions of communication and language. The primary possibility that is revealed through communicative behavior is the ability to view oneself from the standpoint of another human being in order to try to interpret the meaning of one's *own* actions from *that* person's standpoint. Dewey uses the example of one individual asking another to bring him a flower. For this to work not only must the first individual try to see himself from the standpoint of the other so as to make the intention of one's actions convey what one wants, but the other person also must see herself from the other's standpoint to understand. Each sees the other in terms of social possibilities, not merely as a means toward an end, by means of empathetic moral imagination.[35]

Selectivity (Individuality)

For Dewey community and communication also require individuality, the subject of the sixth chapter. As communication is an intensified, and so exemplary, version of the generic trait of *interaction*, so individuality is a development of the generic trait of *selectivity*. All nature exhibits selectivity, but selectivity is most fully exemplified in the instance of "individual minds." "Mind" can be viewed as the impersonal inherited body of cultural habits, but individuality, the creative use of one's own experience, may also be developed. Dewey obscurely describes this contrast as the difference between "individuals with minds" and "individual minds" (1925, LW 1:169–170). His point, nevertheless, is clear: however much tradition may be venerated, each item of culture, each invention or action, originated with *some* unique individual. "Individuals with minds" refers to the inherited web of cultural habits; "individual minds" refers to the active use of individual preferences and habits. Some cultures may exist primarily as the passing on of inherited traditions in which deviance and innovation are discouraged. But other cultures may cultivate individualism to explore new possibilities, to take the future in an experimental way and regard the past with a reflectively critical attitude. The development of "individual minds" is something that really comes about with modernity, according to Dewey. In neither of these senses is "mind" to be understood as something "mental" or as "consciousness." Also, insofar as selectivity is a generic trait of all existences, so is the disposition toward individuality. In a late and highly important essay, "Time and Individuality," Dewey ascribes the nature of time itself to this individualizing tendency in all things. Time is a function of creative individuality in nature but is most fully exemplified in the biographies of human personalities (1940, LW 14:98–114).

Continuity (Emergence)

The seventh and eighth chapters of *Experience and Nature* are concerned with Dewey's response to the mind-body problem and the status of consciousness. These topics exhibit the generic trait of *emergence* or *continuity*. Recall Dewey's claim: even though "there is no isolated occurrence in nature, yet interaction and connection are not wholesale and homogeneous. Interacting events have tighter and looser ties." This is Dewey's pluralism. But he goes on to connect it with his emergentism: "Such relatively closed fields come into conjunction at times so as to interact with each other, and a crucial alteration is effected. A new larger field is formed in which new energies are released and to which new qualities appertain" (1925, LW 1:207–208). His emergentism is most fully on display in discussing the ways in which nature can pass from the physical level to the "psychophysical" or vital level and from thence to that of mind and consciousness, "that of association, communication, participation" (1925, LW 1:208). These are descriptive classifications, not "causes." As noted, though the physical may be a condition for the biological and the biological a condition of the cultural, being a condition is not the "cause" of the subsequent emergent level in the sense in which all features of the new level are found in and accounted for by the previous one. There is a level at which the writing or reading of a poem may be described by physics or biology, and one may insist that without physical and biological conditions there would be no poem. But to leave it at that is not to have an understanding of the poem. As an empiricist, then, Dewey insists that we take nature *as it is experienced*—as, for example, a place in which something like responding to poetry can happen—and not try to explain the phenomena away. Dewey's principle of continuity argues for such an emergent pluralism and rejects absolute ruptures, as is the case with dualisms and reductionisms. Continuity is a dynamic and elastic concept for Dewey. It is not to be thought of as a static continuum but as a process of growth in which there is not repetition so much as transformation.[36] "The distinction between physical, psycho-physical, and mental is thus one of levels of increasing complexity and intimacy of interaction among natural events" (1925, LW 1:200).[37]

Field

Against the background of this general view of emergence, Dewey develops his field theory of experience. Strictly speaking, this deals with the structure of situations, that is, transactions with humans as participants. But, as stated earlier, situations are anticipated throughout nature as fields of interactions by the principle of continuity. Situations, then, are exemplary of the contextual or "field" characteristics of all natural transactions. Consciousness is in the field of the body which is in the field of its environment. "The thing essential to bear in mind," Dewey admonishes, "is that living as an empirical affair is not something which goes on below the skin-surface of an organism: it is always an inclusive affair involving connection, interaction of what is within the organic body and what lies outside in space and time, and with higher organisms, far outside" (1925, LW 1:215). Dewey proposes the term "body-mind" as a way of designating what might be better termed an ecological theory of embodiment. The important thing is this: "To see the organism *in* nature, the nervous system *in* the organism, the brain *in* the nervous system, the cortex *in* the brain is the answer to the problems which haunt philosophy" (1925, LW 1:225).

Within the field of human experience we can distinguish three basic levels of increasing complexity of function, beginning with the wide expanse of tacit feeling, moving on to the qualitatively fused level of sense, and then to the gradually articulate and reflective use of symbols by the intensive, shifting center of consciousness. Feeling as such is merely "had," existing along the continuum from the preconscious or dimly aware to animal shock. But then there is the stage at which it begins to take on sense, something undergone but suffused with portent. Finally, with the use of symbols, a system of signs and consciously used meanings forms through social interaction. Mind "is an added property assumed by a feeling creature, when it reaches that organized interaction with other living creatures which is language, communication. Then the qualities of feeling become significant of objective differences in external things and of episodes past and to come. This state of things in which qualitatively different feelings are not just had but are significant of objective differences is mind. Feelings are no longer just felt. They have and make *sense*; record and prophesy" (1925, LW 1:198). As possibilities explicitly enter into the meaning of a present event, those possibilities can be responded to and used to transform the situation toward a desired end. In this way intelligence becomes manifest and the event becomes a genuine situation.

After presenting this description of the field of experience, from fringe to the focus of consciousness, Dewey addresses the nature of consciousness itself. He distinguishes consciousness as mere "had" or undergone feeling, an "anoetic occurrence," and consciousness as the perception of meanings and awareness of objects, attention "to the significance of events" (1925, LW 1:226). Dewey insists on this distinction. The former is an instance of what he has already said concerning immediate qualities; the latter implies the existence of communication. The subconscious also exhibits these features. The most conscious, reflective activities depend on a vast unconscious network of habits and their selective functions, that then forms the "fringe" or horizon of feeling (1925, LW 1:227).[38] Without this we would not experience the sense of immediate experience. Consciousness operates at the center of a field of experience—a situation—and allows us to respond to as yet unrealized possibilities; it expands the range of objects to which we respond just as eyes and ears expand our responses to the physical environment. Likewise there is a sharp distinction between mind and consciousness. "Mind denotes the whole system of meanings as they are embodied in the workings of organic life; consciousness is in a being with language denotes awareness or perception of meanings; it is the perception of actual events, whether past, contemporary or future, *in* their meanings, the having of actual ideas" (1925, LW 1:230). Mind extends far beyond any conscious act: "Mind is contextual and persistent; consciousness is focal and transitive" (1925, LW 1:230). Unlike many philosophers who dream of language fitting the "facts of existence," like a glove, Dewey recognizes that much remains unsaid and unsayable, full of nuance, poignancy, and vague implication. As transitive, consciousness is temporal, a summing up and carrying forward, a dramatic focus of a situation: "Every case of consciousness is dramatic; drama is an enhancement of the conditions of consciousness" (1925, LW 1:232).[39] More precisely, consciousness is "that phase of a system of meanings which at a given time is undergoing re-direction, transitive transformation" (1925, LW 1:233).

The Consummatory

Dewey's discussion of the possibility of funded and anticipatory consciousness prepares for his final two chapters which deal, respectively, with art as consummatory experience and value and the role of criticism in the conduct of life. Though some events may be simply endings and finalities, others, by utilizing possibilities, can be genuine fulfillments. Such experiences, when anticipated and cultivated, are art. "Art thus represents the culminating event of nature as well as the climax of experience" (1925, LW 1:8). Art and the aesthetic are exemplary of nature itself; they show what nature can do in its fullest sense. Not only does Dewey not make any initial distinction between fine and useful art, he treats science as a form of art. The only distinction that matters "is not between practice and theory, but between those modes of practice that are not intelligent, not inherently and enjoyable, and those which are full of enjoyed meanings. When this perception dawns, it will be a commonplace that art—the mode of activity that is charged with meanings of immediately enjoyed possession—is the complete culmination of nature, and that 'science' is properly a handmaiden that conducts natural events to this happy issue" (1925, LW 1:269). Art and consummatory experience are metaphysically significant for Dewey insofar as they realize potentialities of nature that other sorts of events do not; that is, they are exemplary of nature—manifestations of its genuine possibilities under certain circumstances.

Value (Intelligent Conduct)

Art and consummatory experience also show that human existence does not have to remain unfulfilled: by the use of critically appraised values, means can in some cases lead to the sense of immediate meaning. Art, in other words, can be applied to life. Dewey does not claim that all experiences may become aesthetically funded, but far more can be than we otherwise assume. The neglect of these possibilities lies largely in the separation of art from other activities.[40] This leads to Dewey's ultimate discussion of the role of intelligence in conduct. Critical reflection is the capacity to examine inherited or customary values in light of experience. In this process, those values may be deepened and expanded, or they may be seen to be far less worthwhile than thought—or possibly even something to be avoided. To undertake the journey of experience with criticism that can be applied to all facets of life is a liberating doctrine, allowing intelligence to operate in all areas. This is to make life itself a grand experiment in the search for meaning. This is where Dewey argues that we need metaphysics as the study of the generic traits of existence most of all. Our human tendency is to make practical distinctions, useful enough in some specific context, and then to erect them into absolute divisions for all time. By using the idea of generic traits, we can begin to detect common features and similarities in what might otherwise appear to be ultimate differences in kind. The generic traits identify those features that allow us to find continuities, not breaches, in nature. This is how metaphysics as a study of the generic traits of existence provides a "map" for criticism.[41] The role of metaphysics, then, is to keep the various specific modes of inquiry in communication and to fend off our valuation of only one subject over the others. It may be highly important to have a good understanding of the brain, especially when we are treating injuries or diseases that affect it. But it is gratuitous therefore to say that the human person "is" the brain or that "thoughts" are electrical impulses or that emotions like love are "nothing but" glandular secretions.

Conclusion

Dewey provided one of the richest forms of naturalism, and his metaphysics merits attention for that reason. Most of the varieties of naturalism both before his time and since have favored reductive views of nature and identified existence with the object of knowledge. Ancient atomism arrived at the ultimate objects of nature, atoms and the void, dialectically and maintained the theory dogmatically. Contemporary naturalisms tend to bow to whatever physics claims are the elements of matter or space-time and then proceed with assurance we actually know what nature is. Dewey's approach is to reject both identifying objects of knowledge with reality at large and to view nature as a web of creative processes such that, under the right conditions, life and consciousness can arise and manifest what nature can do under those circumstances. If a poet falls in love and writes poetry, then love and poetry are something that nature—in some instances—does.

Dewey was somewhat skeptical of overly systematic philosophies—he had, after all, produced such a system in his first book, his *Psychology* of 1887, which he eventually came to see as all wrong. Nevertheless, if Dewey's sort of naturalism is to be extended and critically examined, then a good deal of work remains to be done, especially in the area of further clarification of its main features. A critical and even somewhat systematic analysis of the generic traits would be especially salutary, the beginnings of which have been provided here.[42] The extension of Deweyan metaphysics into an ecological ontology or "eco-ontology" is another development.[43] There has already been fruitful dialogue between Deweyan metaphysicians and Process philosophers. The innovative work of Sandra B. Rosenthal extends the dialogue between Dewey and pragmatism in general not only to process philosophy but to Continental thought as well (Rosenthal

1986, 2011). There have also been other creative developments in American naturalism, such as the "ordinal naturalism" of Justus Buchler (Buchler 1990). The last fifty years has seen Dewey's philosophy pass from nearly total eclipse into lively reemergence and scholarly discussion. The publication of the critically acclaimed *Collected Works* and *Correspondence* have provided a large corpus of material worth serious attention. But it is at best a suggestive opening with plenty of original and creative work possible.

Notes

1. See Dewey (1930a).
2. See Rorty (1982), Bernstein (1961), Seigfried (2001), discussion in Alexander (1987), and responses by Myers (2004) and Myers and Pappas (2004).
3. In his autobiographical essay "From Absolutism to Experimentalism," Dewey says "acquaintance with Hegel has left a permanent deposit in my thinking" (1930a, LW 5:154). This seems to refer to Hegel's seeing philosophy as part of general cultural movements. This comment has led to extended debate on whether Dewey remained—and whether he ever was—"an Hegelian" in the sense of having a commitment to an Absolute. See next note.
4. See James Good (2005) for a defense of the mature Dewey as a "left-wing Hegelian." For criticism of this view see essays by Larry Hickman and Thomas Alexander *in Transactions of the Charles S Peirce Society*, vol. 44, no. 4 (2008) with response by Good. See also Dewey's 1897 lectures on Hegel, ed. Shook and Good (2010).This is a transcript of a class. The lectures give an exposition of Hegel's *Philosophy of Mind* (or "Spirit") without personal endorsement by Dewey and so this book's title is misleading: *Dewey's Philosophy of Spirit*. The introductory essays present a similarly distorted reading. For a careful reading of this period in Dewey's development see Rockefeller (1991).
5. See for example his 1884 essay "The New Psychology," in EW 1:48–60.
6. Dewey to James May 10, 1891. Quoted in Ralph Barton Perry, *The Thought and Character of William James*, Vol. 2 (New York: Little, Brown and Co., 1935), 517.
7. See Dewey's 1891 essay "The Present Position of Logical Theory" which defends Hegel as "the quintessence of the scientific spirit" (EW 3:138).
8. See discussion in Dykhuizen (1967: 110f).
9. The essays are: "The Relationship of Thought and Its Subject-Matter," "The Antecedents and Stimuli of Thinking," "Data and Meanings," and "The Objects of Thought" (1903, MW 2:298–367). As Dykhuizen points out, Dewey's essay "Some Stages of Logical Thought" of 1900 anticipates Dewey's rejection of transcendental for instrumental logic; it also was included in *Essays in Experimental Logic*. See Dykhuizen (1967: 82–83).
10. See Dewey, Jane (1939, 35–36).
11. Originally *The Journal of Philosophy, Psychology, and Scientific Methods*.
12. See especially, "Does Consciousness Exist?" and "A World of Pure Experience" (1904), "The Experience of Activity," "A Thing and Its Relations," 'and "The Place of Affectional Facts in a World of Pure Experience" (1905), all subsequently reprinted in James's posthumous work, *Essays in Radical Empiricism*. (James 1912.)
13. For a discussion of James's radical empiricism see John J. McDermott, "Introduction" in James (1977: xli f). For the impact of this aspect of James's thought on Dewey see xxxvii.

14. Hence this is not relativism, which asserts that all perceptions are equally cognitive and hence contradictory, as critiqued by Aristotle in *Metaphysics* IV.4.

15. Fragment DK B 3. My translation.

16. For a more detailed discussion of this period of Dewey's development, see Cherlin (2017). See also: "Beliefs and Existences" (MW 3:82–100), "Reality as Experience" (MW 3:101–106), and "Experience and Objective Idealism" (MW 3:128–129). Though Dewey still exhibits some deference to Hegel (MW 3:86), he stoutly declares for pragmatism and realism. The influence of Woodbridge is evident. Compare also Dewey's highly critical reviews of Royce's *The World and the Individual* (MW 1:241–256, MW 2:120–138) with his highly enthusiastic reviews of Santayana's naturalistic *The Life of Reason* (MW 3:319–322; MW 4:229–241).

17. There is some question as to whether Dewey means to limit these generic traits here to those only appearing within scientific inquiry. If so, he expands the scope to include all types of experience in *Experience and Nature*. But his discussion here is focused on the relation of metaphysics and science, so he may have intended the broader application. See Cherlin (2017: 68).

18. See Alexander (2014).

19. This anticipates Dewey's central insight of "having an experience" in *Art as Experience*.

20. A prime example is Bertrand Russell. See Dewey's response to Russell on this issue in 1939: LW 14:29–24. (This is Dewey's reply to the critics whose essays compose *The Philosophy of John Dewey*, ed. Paul A. Schilpp). Russell misses Dewey's rejection of the identity between reality and the object of knowledge, and so jumps to the unwarranted conclusion that the universe is the ultimate object of knowledge and so constitutes one ultimate situation, that is, the Absolute.

21. See Alexander, "Dewey's Denotative-Empirical Method: A Thread through the Labyrinth" in Alexander (2013, 54–71).

22. In the *Introduction* to *Essays in Experimental Logic*, Dewey distinguished between what he called "zero terms" and "infinity terms." A zero term would denote some discrete particular (Dewey uses "typewriter" as an example) while an infinity term would denote some "indefinite range of context," a "spatial and temporal environment" (1916, MW 10:324). "Experience" and "situation" are both "infinity terms."

23. See 1925, LW 1:375–376.

24. In this sense, "experience" for Dewey is close to the Greek *empeiria*, a skillful familiarity built up over repeated encounters. As Aristotle says, "For men, experience is born of memory" (*Metaphysics* I.1 950 b28).

25. John Greenleaf Whittier ends his poem "Maud Muller" with "For of all sad words of tongue or pen, the saddest are these: 'It might have been!'"

26. See Gouinlock (1972, 1).

27. This tension between the inclusively generic and the exemplary can be found in Aristotle's *Metaphysics* in which "first philosophy" is initially presented as the search for "being as being"—looking for what *all kinds* of beings share (the inclusive approach)—and looking for the *exemplary being* (his Unmoved Mover) that shows being in its fullest sense. See discussion by Boisvert (1992, 1998). Boisvert rejects the "both/and" approach followed here and says Dewey should have focused on exemplary instances.

28. See Dewey's discussion of situation in *Logic: The Theory of Inquiry* (1938, LW 12:72–77; 107–112). Note that not all situations are "problematic situations," but only those that provoke inquiry, the focus of *Logic: The Theory of Inquiry*.

29. See Alexander (2013) for a development of this idea.

30. The stable-and-precarious should be understood as *one* generic trait marking a relative distinction.

31. Unless they overemphasize it as the "absurd" in existentialism, for example, Sartre's "in it-self" or *en soi*.

32. See Alexander (2014).

33. "The Inclusive Philosophical Idea" (1927, LW 3:41–54) is a particularly important essay in understanding this part of Dewey's metaphysics. Dewey later came to prefer the term "transaction" to "interaction" to avoid the idea of two separate things existing on their own that subsequently "inter-act."

34. See George Santayana's highly critical essay attacking Dewey for his placing human interests in the foreground, "Dewey's Naturalistic Metaphysics" (Santayana 1928 in LW 3:367–384) and Dewey's feisty response, " 'Half-Hearted Naturalism' " (1928, LW 3:73–81).

35. See Fesmire (2003).

36. See discussion in Alexander (1987, 87f).

37. See Dewey's further development of the idea of continuity in *Logic: The Theory of Inquiry*, especially in Chapter 2. For example, "The idea of continuity is not self-explanatory. But its meaning excludes complete rupture on the one side and mere repetition of identities on the other; it precludes the reduction of the 'higher' to the 'lower' just as it precludes complete breaks and gaps. The growth and development of any living organism from seed to maturity illustrates the meaning of continuity" (1938, LW 12:30).

38. Dewey clarifies, "Indeed, the use of such words as context and background, fringe, etc. suggests something too external to meet the facts of the case. The larger system of meaning suffuses, interpenetrates, colors what is here and now uppermost; it gives them sense, feeling, as distinct from signification" (1925, LW 1:231).Dewey presents an extensive discussion of the role of this qualitative dimension even in logic in his important essay "Qualitative Thought" (1930b, LW 5:243–262).

39. See Fesmire (2003).

40. "The existence of activities that have no immediate enjoyed meaning is undeniable. They include much of our labors in home, factory, laboratory and study. By no stretch of language can they be termed either artistic or esthetic. Yet they exist, and are so coercive that they require some attentive recognition. So we optimistically call them 'useful' and let it go at that, thinking that by calling them useful we have somehow jus-tified and explained their occurrence. If we were to ask useful for what? We should be obliged to examine their actual consequences, and when we once honestly and fully faced these consequences we should probably find ground for calling such activi-ties detrimental rather than useful." The useful, Dewey goes on to say, must be traced back "the characteristic human need" which is for "possession and appreciation of the meaning of things," something "ignored in the traditional notion of the useful" (1925, LW 1:271–272).

41. For a discussion of the "map metaphor" see Boisvert (1998), Garrison (2005), Fesmire (2015), and Cherlin (2017).

42. See the chapter by William T. Myers in this volume and his distinction between the "plu-ralistic traits" and the "organic traits."

43. See Alexander (2013).

WORKS CITED

Citations of John Dewey's works are to the thirty-seven-volume critical edition published by Southern Illinois University Press under the editorship of Jo Ann Boydston. In-text citations give the original publication date, series abbreviation, followed by volume number and page number. For example: (1934, LW 10:12) is page 12 of *Art as Experience*, which is published as volume 10 of *The Later Works*.

Series abbreviations for *The Collected Works*

EW *The Early Works* (1882–98)

MW *The Middle Works* (1899–1924)

LW *The Later Works* (1925–53)

Alexander, Thomas M. 1987. *John Dewey's Theory of Art, Experience and Nature: The Horizons of Feeling*. Albany: State University of New York Press.

Alexander, Thomas M. 2013. *The Human Eros: Eco-ontology and the Aesthetics of Existence*. New York: Fordham University Press.

Alexander, Thomas M. 2014. "Potentiality and Naturalism: Dewey's Metaphysical Metamorphosis." In *Dewey and the Ancients*. Edited by Christopher C. Kirby, 19–46. London: Bloomsbury.

Bernstein, Richard. 1961. "John Dewey's Metaphysics of Experience." *The Journal of Philosophy*, vol. 63, 5–14.

Boisvert, Raymond. 1988. *Dewey's Metaphysics*. New York: Fordham University Press.

Boisvert, Raymond. 1992. "Metaphysics as the Search for Paradigmatic Instances." *The Transactions of the Charles S. Peirce Society*, vol. 28, no. 2, 189–202.

Boisvert, Raymond. 1998. "Dewey's Metaphysics: Ground-Map of the Prototypically Real." In *Reading Dewey*. Edited by Larry Hickman, 149–165. Indianapolis: Indiana University Press.

Buchler, Justus. 1990 (1966). *The Metaphysics of Natural Complexes*, 2nd expanded ed. Edited by Kathleen Wallace et al. Albany: State of New York Press.

Cherlin, Paul Benjamin. 2017. "John Dewey's Theoretical Framework from 1903–1916: Prefigurations of a Naturalistic Metaphysics." *The Pluralist*, vol. 12, no. 3, 57–77.

Dewey, Jane. 1939. "Biography of John Dewey." In *The Philosophy of John Dewey*. Edited by Paul A. Schilpp, 1–46. New York: Tudor.

Dewey, John. 1887. *Psychology*. Carbondale: Southern Illinois University Press. EW 2.

Dewey, John. 1892. "Green's Theory of the Moral Motive." EW 3:155–173,

Dewey, John. 1893. "Self-Realization as the Moral Ideal." EW 4:42–53,

Dewey, John. 1897. "The Reflex Arc Concept in Psychology." EW 5:96–110.

Dewey, John. 1901. Review of Josiah Royce, *The World and the Individual, First Series*. MW 1:241–256.

Dewey, John. 1902. Review of Josiah Royce, *The World and the Individual, Second Series*. MW 2:120–138.

Dewey, John. 1903. *Studies in Logical Theory*. ("The Relationship of Thought and Its Subject-Matter," "The Antecedent and Stimuli of Thinking," "Data and Meanings," "The Objects of Thought"). MW 2:293–378.

Dewey, John. 1905a. "The Postulate of Immediate Empiricism." MW 3:158–167.

Dewey, John. 1905b. Review of Santayana, *The Life of Reason* (vols. 1–2), MW 3:319–322.

Dewey, John. 1906. Review of George Santayana, *The Life of Reason* (vols. 1–5), MW 4:229–241.

Dewey, John. 1908. "Does Reality Possess a Practical Character?" MW 4:125–142.

Dewey, John. 1915. "The Subject-Matter of Metaphysical Inquiry." MW 8:3–13.

Dewey, John. 1916. "Introduction," *Essays in Experimental Logic*. MW 10:320–365.

Dewey, John. 1922. *Syllabus: Types of Philosophic Thought*. MW 13:349–396.

Dewey, John. 1925 (rev. 1929). *Experience and Nature*. LW 1.

Dewey, John. 1927. " 'Half-Hearted Naturalism' " LW 3:73–81.

Dewey, John. 1928. "The Inclusive Philosophical Idea." LW: 3:41–54.

Dewey, John. 1930a. "From Absolutism to Experimentalism." LW 5:247–260.

Dewey, John. 1930b. "Qualitative Thought." LW 5:243–262.

Dewey, John. 1938a. *Logic: The Theory of Inquiry*. LW 12.

Dewey, John. 1938b. "Experience, Knowledge, and Value: A Rejoinder." In *The Philosophy of John Dewey*. Edited by Paul A. Schilpp. LW 14:3–90.

Dewey, John. 1940. "Time and Individuality." LW 14:98–114.

Dykhuizen, George. 1967. *The Life and Mind of John Dewey*. Carbondale: Southern Illinois University Press.

Fesmire, Steven. 2003. *John Dewey and the Moral Imagination*. Indianapolis: Indiana University Press.

Fesmire, Steven. 2015. *Dewey*. London: Routledge.

Garrison, James. 2005. "Dewey on Metaphysics, Meaning Making, and Maps." *The Transactions of the Charles S. Peirce Society*, vol. 41, no. 4, 818–844.

Good, James A. 2005. *A Search for Unity in Diversity: The "Permanent Hegelian Deposit" in the Philosophy of John Dewey*. Lanham, MD: Lexington Books.

Gouinlock, James. 1972. *John Dewey's Philosophy of Value*. New York: Humanities Press.

James, William. 1890. *The Principles of Psychology* (2 vols.). New York: Henry Holt.

James, William. 1912. *Essays in Radical Empiricism*. New York: Longman Green.

James, William. 1977 (1896). "Philosophical Conceptions and Practical Results." In *The Writings of William James*. Edited by John J. McDermott, 345–361. Chicago: University of Chicago Press.

Lamont, Corliss. 1961. "New Light on Dewey's *Common Faith*. *The Journal of Philosophy*, vol. 58, no. 1, 26.

Myers, William T. 2004. "Pragmatist Metaphysics: A Defense." *The Transactions of the Charles S. Peirce Society*, vol. 40, no. 1, 41–52.

Myers, William T. and Pappas, Gregory. 2004. "Dewey's Metaphysics: A Response to Richard Gale." *The Transactions of the Charles S. Peirce Society*, vol. 41, no. 4, 679–700.

Rockefeller, Steven C. 1991. *John Dewey: Religious Faith and Democratic Humanism*. New York: Columbia University Press.

Rorty, Richard. 1982 (1975). "Dewey's Metaphysics." In *Consequences of Pragmatism*, , 72–89. Minneapolis: University of Minnesota Press.

Rosenthal, Sandra B. 1986. *Speculative Pragmatism*. Amherst: University of Massachusetts Press.

Rosenthal, Sandra B. 2011. "The Process of Pragmatism: Some Wide-ranging Implications. *The Pluralist*, vol. 6, no. 3, 5–18.

Santayana, George. 1984 (1928). "Dewey's Naturalistic Metaphysics." LW 3:367–384.

Schilpp, Paul Arthur. 1951 (1939). *The Philosophy of John Dewey*. New York: Tudor.

Shook, John R., and James A. Good. 2010. *John Dewey's Philosophy of Spirit*. New York: Fordham University Press.

Seigfried, Charlene Haddock. 2001. "Pragmatist Metaphysics? Why Terminology Matters." *The Transactions of the Charles S. Peirce Society*, vol. 37, no. 1, 13–21.

CHAPTER 3

DEWEY, WHITEHEAD, AND PROCESS METAPHYSICS

WILLIAM T. MYERS

INTRODUCTION

THE connection between process philosophy and pragmatism is significant. All of the classical American pragmatists are process philosophers, but not all process philosophers are pragmatists. Alfred North Whitehead and Charles Hartshorne are both noted process philosophers, and, while there are pragmatic elements in their respective philosophies, neither is properly called a pragmatist.[1] What connects Whitehead with the pragmatists is his process-oriented metaphysics. One common element to all process philosophies is that events are given ontological priority over objects. That is, in all process metaphysics, events are basic, while objects are characters of events. Thus there is an emphasis on relations and relativity. One significant difference between the pragmatists and Whitehead is in regard to system: Whitehead is nothing if not systematic, while the pragmatists are less so, by matters of degree. For example, *Experience and Nature*, Dewey's major work in metaphysics, is notoriously unsystematic. Unlike Whitehead's *Process and Reality*, *Experience and Nature* does not begin with a complete listing of his categories, or, as Dewey calls them, generic traits; rather, he uncovers them through a series of long dialectical arguments. This can make identification of exactly what Dewey takes to be generic difficult and sometimes even controversial. There are, however, a number of traits that stand out and are readily identifiable. Those will be delineated in a subsequent section.

Dewey's Metaphysics

Dewey's *Experience and Nature* from its very beginning has had a mixed reception. Its publication in 1925 came with much anticipation. In 1923, Dewey had delivered the first Carus Lectures, and this book grew out of that. Given the anticipation, the book was widely reviewed, getting some 35 reviews within the first three years of publication (1925, LW 1:403). While most of the reviews recognized the book as a major philosophical work, assessment of that work varied greatly. Many of the most critical reviews came from journals of religion (cf. Wieman, 1925), but even more sympathetic reviewers found the work problematic (cf. Perry, 1925). Perhaps even more interesting is the wide range of views on the quality of Dewey's writing, from Holmes's famous comment that the "book is incredibly ill written" (Howe 1942, 287) to Perry's observation that the book has "a certain eloquence and persuasiveness" (Perry 1925, 875).

The perception still holds today. In fact, there is a sense in which the book's reputation is in worse shape today than it was in the past. While there were critics in 1925 who disagreed with Dewey's position and those who thought poorly of his writing, today there are critics who are otherwise very sympathetic with Dewey who claim that the book was either misguided or that it does not do what it says it does, that is, metaphysics. Among contemporary interpreters, there are at least five sorts. I discuss them briefly in turn.

Those Who Think Dewey Does Not Do Metaphysics at All

Perhaps the most outspoken critic here is Charlene Haddock Seigfried. In her article, "Pragmatist Metaphysics? Why Terminology Matters," she writes:

> the pragmatists didn't just take an anti-positivistic turn; they didn't just reject the traditional subject areas of metaphysics. They grounded their analyses in the concrete conditions of everyday life. It is time to recognize that the formulation and analyses of these concrete conditions is a genuine alternative to metaphysics.
>
> (Seigfried 2001, 14)

Seigfried thus argues that the pragmatists were so tied to the concrete that metaphysics is precluded. Indeed, her feminist approach to pragmatism is one that distrusts the abstract as taking us away from concrete experience. Thus, whatever the pragmatists do, it certainly should not be called metaphysics.

Those Who Think Dewey Does Metaphysics
But Should Not

Here we find Richard Rorty, who divides Dewey into the "good" Dewey and the "bad" Dewey. Rorty finds Dewey most useful when he is "deconstructing" traditional philosophical problems. Naturally, Rorty is a fan of *The Quest for Certainty*. Dewey falls back into bad philosophical habits, though, when he tries to say something positive, as he does in *Experience and Nature*. It is interesting that, unlike Seigfried, Rorty recognizes that Dewey is at least attempting to do metaphysics; he just wishes that he had not done so (Rorty 1982, 72–89).

Those Who Think Dewey Does Metaphysics But Not
Very Well

This group actually has a long tradition, but one of the most recent vocal critics is Richard Gale. Gale clearly recognizes that Dewey is attempting to do metaphysics, but he claims that Dewey is deeply confused at every turn (Gale, 2002). Gale's approach to Dewey is largely analytic, reflecting Gale's own philosophical training. Reading Gale on Dewey is reminiscent of reading Bertrand Russell on Dewey. And for a Deweyan, it is at least as frustrating.

Those Who Think Dewey Does Metaphysics "Light" and
That Is Okay

Larry Hickman approaches Dewey largely from a technological and instrumentalist perspective (Hickman, 2009). For Hickman, Dewey's metaphysics is not as "transcendental" as traditional metaphysics—in my seminar on Dewey's metaphysics at the 2005 Summer Institute of American Philosophy, he called it "low-rise metaphysics."

Those Who Think Dewey Offers a Robust,
Process-Oriented Metaphysics

This is the position I defend in this chapter. Others who read Dewey this way include Thomas Alexander (Alexander, 1987), Raymond Boisvert (Boisvert, 1988), and Ralph Sleeper (Sleeper, 1986).

The Starting Point: The Postulate of Immediate Empiricism

In order to get a sense of Dewey's reconstruction of metaphysics, the best starting point is not *Experience and Nature* but his 1905 essay "The Postulate of Immediate Empiricism" (1905, MW 3:158–167). In this essay, Dewey describes his view of the relationship between experience, knowledge, and reality, calling his view "immediate empiricism." (He could have used James's term "radical empiricism.") The central thesis of the essay is "that things—anything, everything, in the ordinary or non-technical use of the term 'thing'—are what they are experienced as being. Hence, if one wishes to describe anything truly, his task is to tell what it is experienced as being" (1905, MW 3:158). Dewey goes on to use the example of describing a horse. The descriptions of a horse-trader, a jockey, a zoologist, and so on will of course vary, with both congruencies and divergences, but this is no reason to account any one description of the horse as being any more real than any other, or for reducing some accounts of the horse to being simply phenomenal. Each account of the horse, assuming the account is a description of what that horse is experienced as, is equally real.

But what about the contradictions among the accounts? These do not take away from the postulate. For Dewey, every experience is determinate—it is exactly what it is experienced as. It may be settled, confusing, frightening, illusory, and so on, but it is exactly what it is. Every experience is real—a confused experience is every bit as real as a knowing experience. Thus the distinction between a knowing experience and a confused experience is not one of Real versus Appearance but is simply a contrast between different reals of experience. Every experience is a concrete determinate experience, no more or less real than any other.

Notice that Dewey's thesis goes against the traditional philosophical notion of experience as being primarily cognitive. For Dewey, things are *not* what they are known to be but are exactly what they are experienced *as* being. That is, knowing is not the only mode of experience; it is but one type of experience. Dewey uses the example of a startling noise. "Empirically, that noise is fearsome; it really is, not merely phenomenally or subjectively so. That is what it is experienced as being" (1905, MW 3:160). If we investigate the noise, we discover, say, that the noise was caused by a loose shutter banging against the window. According to Dewey's thesis, the knowing experience, the experience that comes about as a result of inquiry, is no more real than the flustered experience, but they are not the same experience. That is, the thing experienced has changed; reality has changed. I may be embarrassed by my fright, but reality has been changed via the process of inquiry. It is, of course, correct to say that the latter experience is cognitively "truer" than the former, but it is no more or less real.

As Dewey points out in a note added to the end of the essay in response to reactions to the essay, commentators took much exception to the position he put forth. These exceptions, according to Dewey, are based largely on some fundamental misunderstandings of his position. One misunderstanding is that Dewey holds that human experience is somehow the "aboriginal stuff" out of which things evolve, thus making Dewey some kind of idealist. But, in the essay proper, Dewey says:

> So, when [the empiricist] talks of experience, he does not mean some grandiose, remote affair that is cast like a net around a succession of fleeting experiences; he does not mean an indefinite total, comprehensive experience which somehow engirdles an endless flux; he means that *things* are what they are experienced to be, and that every experience is *some* thing.
>
> (1905, MW 3:165)

This passage explicitly denies that experience is some kind of all-encompassing absolute. Again, in the added note at the end of the essay, Dewey says:

> [T]here is nothing in the text that denies the existence of things temporally prior to human experiencing of them. Indeed, I should think it fairly obvious that we experience things *as* temporally prior to our experiencing them.
>
> (1905, MW 3:167)

From "The Postulate of Immediate Empiricism," then, we can draw the negative conclusion that Dewey does *not* reduce everything to experience.

The foregoing still leaves open the positive question of what the relationship between experience and existence is for Dewey. One clear statement of Dewey's position is found in a later essay, "Experience and Existence: A Comment" (1949, LW 16:383–389), which was written in response to S. J. Kahn's essay "Experience and Existence in Dewey's Naturalistic Metaphysics" (Kahn, 1948, LW 16:456–462). At the end of his essay, Kahn asks, "Does [Dewey's] metaphysics include any existence *beyond* experience?" (Kahn, 1948, LW 16:462). Dewey answers this by saying that his "*philosophical* view, or theory, of experience does not include any existence which is beyond *the reach* of experience" (1949, LW 16:383). Notice the vast difference between these two phrases. According to Dewey, anything that exists does so within the reach of experience, at least in principle, and, even though an experiencing subject can and does change reality, reality is not ultimately dependent in any ontological way upon the subject for its existence.

Let's consider some of the implications of Dewey's radical empiricism. One of the first things that should be evident about Dewey's view is that it results in a denial of the spectator view of knowledge. Dewey has returned experience and knowing to its rightful place—right in the middle of things. Also, notice that there is an implicit process view of reality. If things are in fact *as* we experience them to be, then it must be that, ontologically speaking, things change. In "The Postulate of Immediate Empiricism" and in *Experience and Nature*, Dewey is actually talking about the nature of reality itself. The question is, though, can he do that? Obviously I think he can. In order to get at Dewey's reconstruction of the metaphysical enterprise, it will be useful to appeal to Arthur Murphy's characterization of Dewey's perspective (Murphy, 1927). Murphy describes

Dewey's metaphysics as "objective relativism." Stated most basically, Dewey is a process metaphysician who, in contrast with the tradition, inverts the traditional roles of objects and events. That is, events are basic and objects characterize them. In brief, objective relativism goes something like this. The world is made up of events. Every event emerges from a given context and is limited and conditioned by that context. This is the relative nature of events. But the properties of that event are real properties of that unique perspective. This is the objective nature of events. Finally, they are properties of the world as the world relates to that perspective. This is the interactive nature of events. Given this description, it becomes natural to say that our knowledge of the world is indeed relative. Yet, at the same time, it is still knowledge, that is, it is objective.[2]

Is Metaphysics Still Possible?

Does this perspectivalism leave room for metaphysical inquiry? In his 1915 essay "The Subject Matter of Metaphysical Inquiry" (1915, MW 8:3–13), Dewey argues that it does. The problem with traditional metaphysics has been its characterization of its subject matter. Traditional metaphysics has concerned itself with "ultimate origins" or "ultimate causes." Asking questions about such things, Dewey argues, is to ask meaningless questions. When we ask about causes, all we are really looking for are the antecedent circumstances that led up to the situation at hand. Once we establish these circumstances, we can ask the question once again, and, this time, we would look for the antecedent to the antecedent. Obviously there is a practical limit to how far we can go back with this line of inquiry. But the point is, questions about *ultimate* causes are meaningless. The only way it makes sense to speak of causes is in the scientific sense of antecedent circumstances. The primary cause of one situation is the antecedent situation that gave rise to it. And this account of cause and effect does not belong as much to the realm of metaphysics as it does to science. So the question still lurks, is there any place for metaphysics? Later in the same essay, Dewey says that this leads us to the question of "whether there are ultimate, that is, irreducible, traits of the very existences with which science is concerned" (1915, MW 8:6). Indeed, as Dewey points out, every scientific inquiry finds at least three such traits: pluralism, interaction, and change (1915, MW 8:6).

The problem with traditional metaphysics, then, is not its concern with ultimates but its concern with the wrong kind of ultimates. Instead of ultimate causes, origins, and realities, the proper subject matter of metaphysics is a plurality of ultimates all of which represent the ultimate, that is, irreducible, traits of existence. These generic traits are not anything mysterious, transcendental, or a priori; rather, just as in any investigative subject matter, they are discoverable through empirical inquiry.

A proper metaphysics, then, will consist of an inquiry into and an account of the generic traits of existence. Its function is to serve as a "ground-map for criticism" (cf. 1925, LW 1:308–309). In order to understand this, one must realize that, for Dewey, philosophy's job is primarily one of criticism. In his essay "Context and Thought," Dewey says:

> Philosophy is criticism; criticism of the influential beliefs that underlie culture; a criticism which traces the beliefs to their generating conditions as far as may be, which tracks them to their results, which considers the mutual compatibility of the elements of the total structure of beliefs. Such an examination terminates, whether so intended or not, in a projection of them into a new perspective which leads to new surveys of possibilities.
>
> (1931, LW 6:19)

So philosophy consists largely of criticism, and metaphysics is the categorical scheme that serves as the ground-map for this criticism. In the last chapter of *Experience and Nature*, Dewey says:

> When [metaphysical inquiry] has revealed the traits and characters that are sure to turn up in every universe of discourse, its work is done. So at least an argument may run. But the very nature of the traits discovered in every theme of discourse, since they are ineluctable traits of natural existence, forbids such a conclusion. Qualitative individuality and constant relations, contingency and need, movement and arrest are common traits of all existence. This fact is a source both of values and of their precariousness; both of immediate possession which is causal and of reflection which is a precondition of secure attainment and appropriation. Any theory that detects and defines these traits is but a ground-map for the province of criticism, establishing base lines to be employed in more intricate triangulations.
>
> (1925, LW1:308–309)

Dewey's use of the ground-map metaphor is revelatory of his view of the nature and purpose of metaphysics. It is clear that Dewey holds no finality on either his or any other metaphysical system. Given this, the purpose of a metaphysical system is to define basic traits of things in order that we may find our way more coherently while traversing a philosophical path. That is to say, the purpose of metaphysics is to aid in maintaining the coherence of the overall philosophical enterprise. Without the general metaphysical scheme, the philosopher is more liable to fall into incoherence. The ground-map, to follow the metaphor, keeps one on a coherent course.

THE GENERIC TRAITS

So what does this system look like? Perhaps the briefest way to describe it is with a list and summary of what I take to be Dewey's generic traits of existence.[3] But first a remark is in order. A century ago, in "The Need for a Recovery in Philosophy," Dewey said, "Dynamic connections are qualitatively diverse, just as are the centers of action. *In this sense*, pluralism, not monism, is an established empirical fact." And, "Empirically, then, active bonds of continuities of all kinds, together with static discontinuities, characterize existence" (1917, MW 10:11–12). Notice that here Dewey is describing the world as a place of "connected pluralism." Perhaps a more apt description of Dewey's position is that the world of events is one of "organic pluralism." The organic character of events points to the fact that events are dependent upon their context for their emergence. Every event comes from somewhere (i.e., a context structured by other events). The pluralistic character points to the fact that an event, once specified, is an individual. Dewey's organic pluralism consists in the interaction of these two characters. Now, given that categories are basic, Dewey's generic traits point to either an event's organicism or its pluralism.

The Pluralistic Traits

1. The Precarious—This points to the uncertain and the unpredictable character of the universe (1925, LW 1:42–68).
2. Immediacy—This points to the "present" of an event: it is exclusive, ineffable, self-sufficient. Events as immediate are not objects of inquiry, reflection, or experience (1925, LW 1:74–75).
3. Quality—Quality is immediate; it is had, not known. It is the basis of the unity of situations (1925, LW 1: 82, 94, 127–128, 11–112).
4. Temporal Quality—This points to duration; lived time, not to be confused with temporal ordering or measured time (1925, LW 1:92–93).
5. Novelty—This indicates the uniqueness of every event (1925, LW 1:97).
6. Selective interest—This is the basis of self-maintenance and the natural freedom of all things (1925, LW 1:186, 195).

The Organic Traits

1. The Stable—This allows for prediction and control; allows for science (1925, LW 1:42–68).
2. Sociality—This is a very general category. It indicates that all events occur in a context (1925, LW 1:63, 187–188).
3. Transitivity—This points to the giving over of one event to another; the continuity of process (1925, LW 1:85–86).
4. Transaction—This points to the interaction of events. It is the basis of Dewey's process metaphysics (1925, LW 1:138, 145, 207–208).
5. Potentiality—This points out that every event has infinite potentialities. An event's potentialities are revealed in transaction (1925, LW 1:27–28, 143, 241).

6. Tendency (Need)—This points to the tendency of every event to move toward completeness. Every event has a particular direction (1925, LW 1:58, 85–86, 279, 308).[4]

WHITEHEAD'S METAPHYSICS

In order to begin getting into the basics of Whitehead's metaphysics, one must start with his conception of speculative philosophy and his basic approach. In Part I, Chapter I of *Process and Reality*, Whitehead gives his classic account of speculative philosophy:

> Speculative philosophy is the endeavor to frame a coherent, logical, necessary system of general ideas in terms of which every element of our experience can be interpreted. By this notion of 'interpretation' I mean that everything of which we are conscious, as enjoyed, perceived, willed, or thought, shall have the character of a particular instance of the general scheme. Thus the philosophical scheme should be coherent, logical, and, in respect to its interpretation, applicable and adequate. Here 'applicable' means that some items of experience are thus interpretable, and 'adequate' means that there are no items incapable of such interpretation.
>
> (Whitehead 1929/1979, 3)

Whitehead's goal is grand in its scope. He wants a complete system that can account for everything and can do so in an adequate fashion. In order to construct this scheme, Whitehead uses the method of analogical generalization. That is, Whitehead's project begins with some aspect of ordinary experience and generalizes it to the greatest degree possible. Whitehead says:

> [the] construction [of such a system] must have its origin in the generalization of the particular factors discerned in particular topics of human interest; for example, in physics, or in physiology, or in psychology, or in aesthetics, or in ethical beliefs, or in sociology, or in languages conceived as storehouses of human experience. In this way, the prime requisite, that anyhow there shall be some important application, is secured. The success of the imaginative experiment is always to be tested by the applicability of its results beyond the restricted locus from which it originated.
>
> (Whitehead 1929/1979, 5)

Whitehead compares this process to the flight of an airplane. The airplane starts on the ground, in some aspect of concrete experience. It then lifts off into the air, into imaginative generalization. The airplane then returns to the ground, to check the results of the generalization to see if they aid in rational interpretation. To continue the metaphor, the more areas in which the airplane can land, the more adequate the generalization. Whitehead's goal is to use the method of analogical generalization in order to construct a system that can shed some interpretive light on every area of human experience.

In *Process and Reality,* Whitehead does not tell us which of the items in his suggested list of starting points he himself takes, if in fact he takes any of them. Rather, he simply proceeds to spell out the categories. Now, while Whitehead's defense and statement of speculative philosophy is classic, at least according to many, his litany of categories is notorious. Whitehead begins spelling out his scheme by listing one Category of the Ultimate, eight Categories of Existence, twenty-seven Categories of Explanation, and nine Categoreal Obligations. Fortunately, the purpose of this essay does not require a full account of all of these. Rather, I focus on The Category of the Ultimate and a few selections from the others.

THE CATEGORIES

Whitehead begins with what he calls "The Category of the Ultimate." The terms "creativity," "many," and "one," he says, "are presupposed in all of the more special categories" (Whitehead 1929/1979, 21). That is, there is nothing more basic than these notions. "Creativity" refers to the most fundamental character of all actuality. It is, Whitehead says, "the principle of *novelty*" (Whitehead 1929/1979, 21). By that he means that in every existence there is something that is not wholly derived from something else. Each actuality is in some sense novel and in some sense *causa sui.* The terms "many" and "one" express the working of creativity in the world.

> The ultimate metaphysical principle is the advance from disjunction to conjunction, creating a novel entity other than the entities given in disjunction. The novel entity is at once the togetherness of the 'many' which it finds, and also it is one among the disjunctive 'many' which it leaves; it is a novel entity, disjunctively among the many entities which it synthesizes. The many become one, and are increased by one. In their natures, entities are disjunctively 'many' in process of passage into conjunctive unity. This Category of the Ultimate replaces Aristotle's category of "primary substance."
>
> (Whitehead 1929/1979, 21)

Whitehead uses the term "concrescence" to describe this "production of novel togetherness."

> These ultimate notions of "production of novelty" and of "concrete togetherness" are inexplicable either in terms of higher universals or in terms of the components

participating in the concrescence. The analysis of the components abstracts from the concrescence.

(Whitehead 1929/1979, 21–22)

Whitehead calls these concrescing entities "actual entities," "actual occasions," or "occasions of experience," and they are the first of his Categories of Existence. They are "the final real things of which the world is made up" (PR 18); they are ontologically basic. Whitehead says, "The ontological principle declares that every decision is referable to one or more actual entities, because in separation from actual entities there is nothing, merely nonentity" (Whitehead 1929/1979, 43). Everything that is is explainable in terms of actual entities. They are the basis of all that is, and they are the basis of Whitehead's process metaphysics. Category of Explanation (CE) says "That the actual world is a process, and that the process is the becoming of actual entities" (Whitehead 1929/1979, 22).

To get a clear picture of actual entities, we need to look at six more CEs, somewhat rearranged to fit our purposes.

(iii) That in the becoming of an actual entity, the *potential* unity of many entities in disjunctive diversity—actual and non-actual—acquires the *real* unity of the one actual entity; so that the actual entity is the real concrescence of many potentials.

(v) That no two actual entities originate from an identical universe.

(xxii) That an actual entity by functioning in respect to itself plays diverse roles in self-formation without losing its self-identity. It is self-creative; and in its process of creation transforms its diversity of roles into one coherent role.

(xxiii) That this self-functioning is the real internal constitution of an actual entity. It is the "immediacy" of the actual entity. An actual entity is called the "subject" of its own immediacy.

(viii) That two descriptions are required for an actual entity: (a) one which is analytical of its potentiality for "objectification" in the becoming of other actual entities and (b) another which is analytical of the process which constitutes its own becoming.

(iv) That the potentiality for being an element in a real concrescence of many entities into one actuality is the one general metaphysical character attaching all entities, actual and non-actual . . . . [I]t belongs to the nature of a "being" that it is a potential for every "becoming." This is the "principle of relativity."

(Whitehead 1929/1979, 22–25)

Actual entities, then, are microcosmic pulses that are productive of novel togetherness. They are durational moments that in themselves do not change, but, rather, they *are* change. All actual occasions concresce to satisfaction and then perish in their subjective immediacy. During its duration, then, an actual entity is completely subjective (CE xxiii), and, when it perishes, it becomes an object with the potential of becoming objectified in a subsequent actual entity (CE viii). This objectification occurs by means of a "prehension" (a "Concrete Fact of Relatedness"), which is Whitehead's second Category of Existence. Regarding actual entities and prehensions, Whitehead says,

The analysis of an actual entity into "prehensions" is that mode of analysis which exhibits the most concrete elements in the nature of actual entities. This mode of analysis will be termed the "division" of the actual entity in question. Each actual entity is "divisible" in an indefinite number of ways, and each way of "division" yields its definite quota of prehensions. A prehension reproduces in itself the general characteristics of an actual entity: it is referent to an external world, and in this sense will be said to have a "vector character" . . . In fact, any characteristic of an actual entity is reproduced in a prehension. It might have been a complete actuality; but, by reason of a certain incomplete partiality, a prehension is only a subordinate element in an actual entity.

(Whitehead 1929/1979, 19)

A prehension, then, is the objectification of an aspect of one actual entity into a subsequent actual entity. It is, as was noted, a concrete fact of relatedness. A currently concrescing actual entity prehends its given past—that is, aspects of the past are objectified in the present. The entity then perishes and gives itself over as an object for subsequent occasions. Given that, CE xi describes what is involved in a prehension:

(xi) That every prehension consists of three factors: (a) the "subject" which is prehending, namely the actual entity in which that prehension is a concrete element; (b) the "datum" which is prehended; (c) the "subjective form" which is *how* that subject prehends that datum.

(Whitehead 1929/1979, 23)

The objectification of the given past in the concrescing occasion is called a physical prehension. Conceptual prehensions, on the other hand, are prehensions of eternal objects, which is Whitehead's fifth Category of Existence. Eternal objects are also called "Pure Potentials for the Specific Determination of Fact, or Forms of Definiteness" (Whitehead 1929/1979, 22). Regarding Eternal objects, CE vii says:

(vii) That an eternal object can be described only in terms of its potentiality for "ingression" into the becoming of actual entities; and that its analysis only discloses other eternal objects. It is a pure potential. The term "ingression" refers to the particular mode in which the potentiality of an eternal object is realized in a particular actual entity, contributing to the definiteness of that actual entity.

(Whitehead 1929/1979, 23)

Eternal objects, then, as pure potentials, have no say as to which actual entities they become ingredient in. They are merely possible forms of definiteness. And they are in stark contrast to actual entities in that eternal objects have no independent existence apart from their ingression in some actual entity. Included among the things that are eternal objects are colors, patterns and relations, grades of generic abstraction, and mathematical forms.

Up to this point, we have considered three of Whitehead's categories of existence, that is, actual entities, prehensions, and eternal objects. For the sake of this discussion, two more are needed, nexus and subjective form. In regard to the first, Whitehead says:

> Actual entities involve each other by reason of their prehensions of each other. There are thus real individual facts of togetherness of actual entities, which are real, individual, and particular, in the same sense in which actual entities and the prehensions are real, individual, and particular. Any such particular fact of togetherness among actual entities is called a nexus.
>
> (Whitehead 1929/1979, 20)

And CE xiv says:

> That a nexus is a set of actual entities in the unity of the relatedness constituted by their prehensions of each other, or—what is the same thing conversely expressed— constituted by their objectifications in each other.
>
> (Whitehead 1929/1979, 24)

A nexus, then, is a grouping of related actual entities that are connected by virtue of their prehensions of one another. Whitehead also calls these "Public Matters of Fact" (Whitehead 1929/1979, 22).

In contrast to the nexus as being a public matter of fact, a subjective form is a "Private Matter of Fact." Whitehead says that the subjective form "is *how* [the] subject prehends [the] datum" (Whitehead 1929/1979, 23). Some examples of subjective forms are "emotions, valuations, purposes, adversions, aversions, consciousness, etc." (Whitehead 1929/1979, 24). Notice that not all prehensions are conscious. In fact, most are not. Only a very few of the prehensions in the universe have the subjective form of consciousness.[5]

The Theory of Prehensions

Now that we have the basic terms and ideas spelled out, it is necessary to consider their interaction. Perhaps the best way to do this is to describe the becoming of an actual entity. As we already know, actual entities are made up of prehensions. They emerge from a given past, concresce into a novel event, and perish in a moment of satisfaction. All actual entities have both a physical and a mental pole. Each moment of experience begins with a simple, physical prehension of the immediate past. That is what is most prominent, and it constitutes the initial phase of an emerging actual occasion. In the second phase, the occasion will move to a conceptual prehension that originates from the mental pole. When I say "mental pole," this is not to say, again, that all occasions have consciousness. In his metaphysics, Whitehead distinguishes between subjectivity (exhibited in all occasions of experience—it is the immediacy of the present), mentality (a matter of degree, indicating the degree of complexity and capacity for novelty), and consciousness (only exhibited by very few, very complex occasions).

The actual occasion, then, begins with a simple physical prehension, then it moves to a conceptual prehension. We know that the simple prehension is of the immediate, physical past. The conceptual prehension is, again, of an "eternal object." Eternal objects are pure possibilities. They are similar to Plato's forms in that they are abstract, but they are different in that they are genuinely ingredient in actual entities, and they have no existence apart from their ingression in the actual occasion. Eternal objects are different kinds of things than actual occasions. One difference is that they do not emerge in the same way as actual occasions. They appear and disappear as needed, and yet wherever they appear they are always the same.

Because an actual occasion is only a "drop" of experience, we do not see individual ones. Rather, we perceive groups or nexus of actual occasions. A nexus is a set of actual occasions experienced as being fundamentally related to one another. Given certain other conditions, a nexus may constitute a "society" of occasions. In some societies, there is a directing nexus of very complex occasions which occur serially and exhibit consciousness. We would call it a psyche.

Each actual entity emerges from a particular context, with its unique particular past. No two actual occasions have identical pasts. This is indicative of the relative nature of Whitehead's system. This occasion begins to emerge and is the locus of the converging prehensions. As a new actual entity emerges, it has its own particular "subjective aim," which is the ideal for that occasion, given its limitations. The aim for an occasion serves to direct that occasion toward a particular satisfaction. Given that actual occasions are self-creative, this ideal may or may not be realized.

The key to what an actual occasion becomes lies in the interaction that takes place between the subject (emerging occasion) prehending and the data (past occasions/eternal objects) being prehended. How this interaction takes place is determined by the "subjective form," which is the particular mood or attitude by which the subject prehends a particular datum. While an occasion has only one subjective aim, it may involve a number of subjective forms.

So every act of prehension has its subjective form, but not every prehension contributes its particular datum to the concrescing actual occasion. That is, Whitehead distinguishes between positive and negative prehensions. A prehension whose datum is included as constitutive of an emerging occasion is a positive prehension, and one that is excluded is a negative prehension. This explains why a new actual occasion is constituted out of the past but is not just a mere repetition of it.

Once the actual occasion reaches its final satisfaction, it is not gone yet. Nothing is lost. Satisfied occasions have "objective immortality" in that they can serve as further data for future actual entities. The subjective immediacy of that moment is gone, that is, it can no longer experience, but it can serve as data for other actual entities.

It should be evident from this description that Whitehead is *not* a determinist. As an empiricist, he is convinced that the nature of our experience reflects the nature of reality. In which case, Whitehead postulates some measure of freedom, however primitive, in every actual entity at every level of the universe. But this is not unqualified freedom. Freedom for Whitehead always operates within a context of effective/relevant influences, so that the past is always influentially present in the present—it is felt "heavily," but its influence is persuasive and not coercive. Nevertheless, even in the simplest of entities, there is an element of self-creativity.

ON WHITEHEAD AND DEWEY

On the face of it, Dewey's and Whitehead's metaphysics look very different from each other. Whitehead is formal, systematic, and mathematical in his approach. Dewey, on the other hand, is rather notoriously unsystematic. However, their metaphysics share many important commonalities.[6] I mention two here: their starting point and their approach to the "mind/body" problem.

THE STARTING POINT

In a 1941 essay titled "The Philosophy of Whitehead" (1941, LW14:123–140), Dewey explores some of the similarities between his own philosophy and Whitehead's as the latter's is set out in *Adventures of Ideas*. The initial similarity Dewey considers is in regard to the starting point issue. In much of his philosophical writing, Dewey is critical of all philosophical methods that begin from any kind of axiomatic "first principles." The inadequacy of such a starting point for doing philosophy is that it fails to take into account the fact that we are all invariably and inevitably enmeshed in a particular context and background and that any first principles we formulate necessarily arise out of and/or because of this context and background.

As Dewey notes, few philosophers recognize this fact about our situation. Whitehead, Dewey notes, is one of the few who takes this into account. A passage from *Adventures of Ideas* quoted by Dewey is relevant here:

> The living organ of experience is the living body as a whole. Every instability of any part of it—be it chemical, physical, or molar—imposes an activity of readjustment throughout the whole organism. In the course of such physical activities human experience has its origin. The plausible interpretation of such experiences is that it is one of the natural activities involved in the functioning of such a high-grade organism. *The actualities of nature must be … explanatory of this fact ….*

Such experience seems to be more particularly related to the activities of the brain. But ... we cannot determine with which molecules the brain begins and the rest of the body ends. Further, we cannot tell with what molecules the body ends and the external world begins. The truth is that the brain is continuous with the body, and the body is continuous with the rest of the natural world. Human experience is an act of self-origination including the whole of nature, limited to the *perspective* of a focal region, located within the body, but not necessarily persisting in any fixed coordination with a definite part of the brain.

(1941, LW14:124, ellipses and emphases supplied by Dewey)

Notice that Whitehead's description puts us square in the middle of the world, so to speak. We are in fact part of and continuous with the world. A philosophy that does not take this into account will have no connection, or at best an accidental connection, to the world.

Traditional philosophy's failure to take background into account has arisen, perhaps, because of a narrow view of experience. As Dewey points out, Whitehead is critical of the view of experience that tends to limit experience to mere sensations. Whitehead's notion of perception in the mode of causal efficacy is an explicit repudiation of this view. In his rejection of the narrow view of experience, Whitehead writes:

We must appeal to evidence relating to every variety of occasion. Nothing can be omitted, experience drunk and experience sober, experience sleeping and experience waking, experience drowsy and experience wide-awake, experience self-conscious and experience self-forgetful, experience intellectual and experience physical, experience religious and experience sceptical, experience anxious and experience care-free, experience anticipatory and experience retrospective, experience happy and experience grieving, experience dominated by emotion and experience under self-restraint, experience in the light and experience in the dark, experience normal and experience abnormal.

(Whitehead, 1933, cited in 1941, LW14:126)

When it comes to doing metaphysics, then, since all of these things are part of our lives and thereby part of the world, they must be taken into account and adequately described. Indeed, Whitehead's list is reminiscent of Dewey's observation that a general account of the nature of things must not only account for our scientific knowledge of the world but also for "all the phenomena of magic, myth, politics, painting, and penitentiaries" (1925, LW1:27).

So Dewey's praise for Whitehead boils down to the fact that Whitehead recognizes that experience is much broader than has been traditionally conceived and that all of our experience makes up the background out of which our preconceptions arise. Regarding this fact, Dewey concludes: "For what I have called the background and point of departure seems to be the same for both of us, no matter what deviations may occur later" (1941, LW14:125). The starting point for each of them, then, is the here and now. This, of course, means that all of experience is philosophically relevant and must be taken account of.

The Mind/Body Problem

The final problem under consideration is the mind/body problem. To get a handle on this, let's consider what Dewey says first about matter. In *Experience and Nature*, Dewey says:

> The "matter" of materialists and the "spirit" of idealists is a creature similar to the Constitution of the United States in the minds of unimaginative persons. Obviously the real constitution is certain basic relationships among the activities of the citizens of the country; it is a property or phase of these processes, so connected with them as to influence their rate and direction of change. But by literalists it is often conceived of as something external to them; it itself fixed, a rigid framework to which *all* changes must accommodate themselves. Similarly what we call matter is that character of natural events which is so tied up with changes that are sufficiently rapid to be perceptible as to give the latter a characteristic rhythmic order, the causal sequence. It is no cause or source of events or processes; no absolute monarch; no principle of explanation; no substance behind or underlying changes—save in that sense of substance in which a man well fortified with this world's goods, and hence able to maintain himself through vicissitudes of surroundings, is a man of substance. The name designates a character in operation, not an entity.
>
> (1925, LW1:65)

Dewey conceives of matter as a "character of natural events." Where does this leave mind? Before getting to that question, some preliminary remarks are necessary. On the page immediately following the one just cited, Dewey notes that the only thing that stands in our way when it comes to conceiving of mind and matter as merely different characters of natural events is unfamiliarity. Given the tradition, "The idea that mind and matter are two sides or `aspects' of the same things, like the convex and the concave in a curve, is literally unthinkable" (1925, LW1:66). Going on in the next paragraph, Dewey says:

> A curve is an intelligible object and concave and convex are defined in terms of this object; they are indeed but names for properties involved in its meaning. We do not start with convexity and concavity as two independent things and then set up an unknown *tertium quid* to unite two disparate things. In spite of the literal absurdity of the comparison, it may be understood however in a way which conveys an inkling of the truth. That to which both mind and matter belong is the complex of events that constitute nature. This becomes a mysterious *tertium quid*, incapable of designation, only when mind and matter are taken to be static structures instead of functional characters.
>
> (1925, LW1:66)

So the initial description of mind is that, like matter, it is a character of natural events. That is not to say that there is no difference between matter and mind. In fact, Dewey draws a distinction between the physical, the psycho-physical, and the mental. The physical is descriptive of what we would normally call inanimate nature. The psycho-physical is descriptive, in general, of living things. The mental is mind. Dewey says:

> The distinction between physical, psycho-physical and mental is thus one of levels of increasing complexity and intimacy of interaction among natural events. The idea that matter, life and mind represent separate kinds of Being is a doctrine that springs, as so many philosophic errors have sprung, from a substantiation of eventual functions. The fallacy converts consequences of interactions of events into causes of the occurrence of these consequences—a reduplication which is significant as to the *importance* of these functions, but which hopelessly confuses understanding of them.
>
> (1925, LW1:200)

This quotation is consistent with and indicative of Dewey's notion of emergence. The more complex emerges from the less, yet, once emerged, the more complex is not reducible to the less.

In comparing Whitehead on the same problem, one striking similarity shows itself. Whitehead makes a distinction between subjectivity, mentality, and consciousness. Subjectivity is applicable to all events whatsoever as those events are concrescing. Mentality is indicative of an event's capacity for complexity, so it is a matter of degree. Consciousness is characteristic of very few events, and these are the most complex. While the parallels are not of course exact, a similar point is made. Both descriptions indicate that all events are natural events and their complexity is a matter of degree. The events that characterize mind or consciousness are not fundamentally different in kind, but they are different in their interaction and their complexity. So, for both Whitehead and Dewey, mind and body are simply different aspects of the same event.

CONCLUSION

Given the limited space of this chapter, the summaries of Dewey's and Whitehead's metaphysics are woefully inadequate, but hopefully they are suggestive of what they are all about. While the last section at least suggests some connections between Dewey's and Whitehead's metaphysics, it barely scratches the surface. This is at least partly due to the lack of systematic accounts of Dewey's metaphysics to date. Much has been written about Whitehead's metaphysics, but there are no similar systematic accounts of Dewey's metaphysics. It is an area that is in great need of further research.

NOTES

1. See Myers (2015) for my argument that Whitehead is not a pragmatist.
2. To fill this out with an example, let's consider an objective-relative interpretation of meaning. Meaning comes out of interaction, and interaction is the essence of an event. Dewey says, "Meanings are objective because they are modes of natural interaction; such an interaction … includes things and energies external to living creatures" (1925, LW1:149). So the basis of meaning is interaction and nothing is in and by itself a meaning. Meaning only and always occurs in a context and is the product of interaction. Given this, the same event may have many meanings in various relations. For example, a single event of rain may represent joy to the farmer, disaster to the baseball players, a job for the meteorologist, and so on. Such meanings are diverse and can be contradictory, yet each is objective and real, for each is a product of a natural interaction in various contexts. All relations are real, yet no relation can exhaust any given event's potentialities. Our perception of an event is never all there is to the story because we cannot see all of the infinite possibilities for the event. Yet each perspective of the same event is still a perception of *that* event—it is the same existential occurrence interacting with a variety of points of view. Dewey argues that to treat one particular meaning as what is really real and the others as being somehow artificial is to adopt a static view of things and to treat one potential relation as though it constituted the reality of the situation. Yet according to objective relativism, there is no "ultimate reality" of the situation. Every relation is a reality, and no one relation exhausts what a thing is.
3. The list of Dewey's generic traits is subject to some dispute. Some interpreters include others that I have not included, and some I have included are not in others. Sometimes the terminology varies also. My list comes from my own reading of Dewey's metaphysical works.
4. For a fuller discussion of the generic traits, see Myers (2008).
5. There are a number of interpreters who, because of Whitehead's generalization of the notion of experience, read him as being a panpsychist. This, I think, is a misunderstanding of what Whitehead means by experience. That he is not a panpsychist is supported in part, at least, by the fact that consciousness is a subjective form that is exhibited in very few of the occasions that make up the universe. Only those organisms that have a directing nexus (and not even the lower ones of those) have any actual occasions that exhibit the subjective form of consciousness, and, even then, it is only those occasions that make up the psyche.
6. For a more detailed analysis of their commonalities, see Myers (2015).

WORKS CITED

Citations of John Dewey's works are to the thirty-seven-volume critical edition published by Southern Illinois University Press under the editorship of Jo Ann Boydston. In-text citations give the original publication date, series abbreviation, followed by volume number and page number. For example: (1934, LW 10:12) is page 12 of *Art as Experience*, which is published as volume 10 of *The Later Works*.

Series abbreviations for *The Collected Works* are:

EW *The Early Works* (1882–1898)
MW *The Middle Works* (1899–1924)
LW *The Later Works* (1925–1953)

Alexander, Thomas M. 1987. *John Dewey's Theory of Art, Experience, and Nature: The Horizons of Feeling*. Albany: State University Press of New York.

Boisvert, Raymond D. 1988. *Dewey's Metaphysics*. New York: Fordham University Press.

Dewey, John. 1905. "The Postulate of Immediate Empiricism." MW 3:158–167.

Dewey, John. 1915. "The Subject Matter of Metaphysical Inquiry." MW 8:3–13.

Dewey, John. 1917. "The Need for a Recovery of Philosophy." MW 10:3–48.

Dewey, John. 1925/1929. *Experience and Nature*. LW 1.

Dewey, John. 1931. "Context and Thought." LW 6:3–21.

Dewey, John. 1941. "The Philosophy of Whitehead." LW 14:123–140.

Dewey, John. 1949. "Experience and Existence: A Comment." LW 16:383–389.

Gale, Richard. 2002. "The Metaphysics of John Dewey." *Transactions of the Charles S. Peirce Society*, vol. 38, no. 4, 477–519.

Hickman, Larry A. 2009. "Why American Philosophy? Why Now?" *European Journal of Pragmatism and American Philosophy*, vol. 1, no. 1, 41–44.

Howe, Mark DeWolfe. 1942. *Holmes-Pollock Letters: The Correspondence of Mr. Justice Holmes and Sir Frederick Pollock 1874-1932*. Cambridge, MA: Harvard University Press.

Kahn, Sholom J. 1948. "Experience and Existence in Dewey's Naturalistic Metaphysics." In LW 16:456–462.

Murphy, Arthur E. 1927. "Objective Relativism in Dewey and Whitehead." *Philosophical Review*, vol. 37, no. 2, 121–144.

Myers, William T. 2008. "John Dewey." In *Handbook of Whiteheadian Process Thought, Volume 2*. Edited by Will Desmond and Michel Weber. Frankfurt: Ontos Verlag.

Myers, William T. 2015. "Is Whitehead a Pragmatist? On the Pragmatic Elements in Whitehead's Metaphysics." In *Thinking with Whitehead and the American Pragmatists: Experience and Reality*. Edited by Brian G. Henning, Joseph D. John, and William T. Myers, 3–24. New York: Lexington Books.

Perry, Ralph B. 1925. "An Omnibus Philosophy." *The Saturday Review of Literature*, vol. 2, 874–875.

Rorty, Richard. 1982. *Consequences of Pragmatism*. Minneapolis: University of Minnesota Press.

Seigfried, Charlene Haddock. 2001. "Pragmatist Metaphysics? Why Terminology Matters." *Transactions of the Charles S. Peirce Society*, vol. 37, no. 1, 13–21.

Sleeper, Ralph. 1986. *The Necessity of Pragmatism: John Dewey's Conception of Philosophy*. Urbana and Chicago: University of Illinois Press.

Whitehead, Alfred North. 1929/1979. *Process and Reality*. Corrected edition, edited by David Ray Griffin and Donald Sherburne. New York: Free Press, 1979.

Whitehead, Alfred North. 1933/1967. *Adventures of Ideas*. New York: Free Press.

Wieman, Henry Nelson. 1925. "Religion in Dewey's 'Experience and Nature.'" *The Journal of Religion*, vol. 5, no. 5, 519–542.

III

EPISTEMOLOGY, SCIENCE, LANGUAGE, AND MIND

CHAPTER 4

PRAGMATIST PORTRAITS OF EXPERIMENTAL INTELLIGENCE BY PEIRCE, JAMES, DEWEY, AND OTHERS

VINCENT COLAPIETRO

INTRODUCTION: THE DARWINIAN TURN

PLATO described *logos* as the spark of divinity within humans. After the intellectual revolution wrought by Charles Darwin, however, a number of theorists conjectured[1] that human rationality is a singular instance of animal ingenuity.[2] It points to our kinship with other social animals rather than divine beings. The ingenuity of our species has been radically transformed by its use of symbols. The human mind is *symbolific*: it not only uses but makes symbols.[3] The importance of symbolization for the evolution of mind cannot be exaggerated. As Dewey notes, the "invention or discovery of symbols is doubtless by far the single greatest event in the history of man. Without them, no intellectual advance is possible; with them, there is no limit set to intellectual development except inherent stupidity" (1929, LW 4:121).

We find, among the first generation of thinkers to respond to the radical implications of Darwin's revolutionary theory, C. S. Peirce (1839–1914), William James (1942–1910), and eventually John Dewey (1859–1952).[4] As much as anything else, Dewey was awakened from his absolutistic slumber by James's *Principles of Psychology*, in particular, by the manner in which James reinterpreted mind, consciousness, and much else in light of biology.[5] This means nothing less than taking with the utmost seriousness "the fact that minds inhabit environments which act on them and on which they in turn react," that is, situating "mind in the midst of all its concrete relations" (1981 [1890], 19). In his notes for a course, James instructed himself: "Take evolution *au grand sérieux*" (1988, 367; also in Perry 1935, I, 444). But, in fact, he had been doing so for decades.

More than two decades before the publication of *Origin of Species*,[6] Darwin wrote, in one of his notebooks: "Experience shows the problem of mind cannot be solved by attacking the citadel itself.—The mind is a function of body" ("'N' Notebook"). It is not by the mind looking within itself but rather by situating itself in nature as an arena of action that the problem of mind but also that of intelligence can be fruitfully addressed. Introspection and intuition[7] are stumbling blocks to, rather than indispensable resources for, making sense of these topics.[8]

Classical American pragmatism is a sustained effort to respond to this Darwinian challenge. It is one of the first philosophical movements, if not *the* very first one, to define itself by the creative appropriation of an evolutionary perspective. Indeed, Peirce was convinced, "Now philosophy requires thorough-going evolutionism or none" (CP 6.14). Of his predecessor, Dewey would write in 1937: "Peirce lived when the idea of evolution was uppermost in the mind of his general. He applied it everywhere" (1937, LW 11:482–83). If anything, Dewey was an even more thoroughgoing evolutionist, certainly a far less hesitant Darwinian, than Peirce (Wiener 1965, 77).[9] In sum, the pragmatist movement marks a Darwinian turn in philosophical thought.

Toward a Pragmatist Reconstruction of Human Reason

One of the principal places in which this feature of pragmatism, in general, is most evident is how Peirce, James, Dewey, DuBois,[10] Mead, and other pragmatists reconstructed the conception of intelligence. To some extent, the focus shifts from reason to intelligence.[11] Even so, it is not a mistake to read this reconstruction as a significant contribution to the critical question of human rationality (Colapietro 1999). In various forms, the history of Western thought is a site in which critiques of human reason are proffered, hence one in which rival visions of rationality clash. Indeed, Hilary Putnam has gone so far as to claim, philosophy "is almost coextensive with [the] theory of rationality."[12] He however readily acknowledges, it is hardly easy to give "a sane and human description of the scope of reason."[13]

The pragmatist conceptions of experimental intelligence invite us to consider them in this connection. They are nothing less than attempts to provide just such a description. They are also nothing less than naturalistic critiques of experimental intelligence. While they are in important respects akin to views defended by such traditional figures as Aristotle, Kant, and Hegel, these critiques also mark a decisive break with the dominant traditions of Western philosophy (Colapietro 2013). It is impossible to understand the singular contribution of American pragmatism without appreciating their radically innovative theory of experimental intelligence.

In his first publication, James rescues Darwin from Spencer.[14] What is most relevant for our purpose are three points. First, there is his evolutionary portrait of the human animal: "there belongs to [the human] mind, from its birth upwards, a spontaneity, a vote. It is in the game, and not a mere looker-on [or spectator]; and its judgments of the *should-be*, its ideals, cannot be peeled off from the body of *cogitandum* as if they were excrescences."[15] The "knower is an actor," knowing one of the things humans *do*. The "knower is not a mirror floating with no foothold anywhere," but an implicated agent. Second, there is his instructive expression "intelligent intelligence." Human consciousness, as a biologically evolved function, "is not merely intelligent. It is *intelligent intelligence*."[16] We witness more than the pursuit of ends. "It seems to supply both the means and the standards by which they are measured. It not only *serves* a final purpose, but *brings* a final purpose—posits, declares it." In other words, such intelligence is not slavishly in the service of preordained ends, but irrepressibly engaged in the pursuit of novel purposes. Third, there is James' opposition to reductionism. Since an organism as complex as the human animal has evolved from much simpler ones, these simpler ones provide, Spencer argues, *the* means for understanding the more complex ones. But James asks, "if the polyp is to dictate our law of mind to us, where are we to stop?" The polyp "must be treated in the same way. Back of him lay the not-yet-polyp, back of all, the universal mother, fire-mist." To seek the reality of anything in ever more remote origins is, however, to reduce thinking to a nullity. The emergent features and functions of evolved species are continuous with, but not reducible to, the forms out from which they evolve. Human intelligence is hardly reducible to the functions of its far distant biological ancestors.

What Peirce calls "scientific intelligence" might also be designated "experimental intelligence" (and the pragmatists indeed tended to use *scientific* and *experimental* as synonyms). For our purpose, however, the *experimental* is better than the *scientific*, since it is less likely to encourage a *scientistic* interpretation of the pragmatist position. Part of what is at stake here is insisting upon a highly flexible meaning of this pivotal expression, rather than either a rigidly fixed or excessively narrow one. The form of intelligence in question might be as observable in the contexts of art, morals, and politics as in that of physics, chemistry, or astronomy. The point is not to reduce experimental intelligence to one of its most paradigmatic forms, that evident in the natural sciences. Rather it is to argue that something intimately akin to this form might operate, *mutatis mutandis*, in countless other spheres. The objective is to expand the scope of such intelligence so that it might transform the whole range of human practices. There can be no question that the operation of such intelligence in, say, the field of painting will be significantly different from this operation in the field of physics. But there is equally no question that, in some form, it is operative in all fields of our endeavors. Though the pragmatists, especially Peirce and Dewey, tended to stress the methodological character of experimental intelligence, it might at bottom be something different than a method. At any rate, I am more disposed to emphasize the pragmatic *temperament* or *sensibility*, admittedly vague but hardly vacuous words.[17]

In its most rudimentary sense, scientific or experimental intelligence is simply "an intelligence capable of learning by experience" (CP 2.227; cf. Peirce, x). The pragmatists see inquiry as the process by which we learn from experience and, in its more sophisticated forms, the process by which we deliberately (hence, self-consciously and self-critically) learn from experience. Whereas traditional logic took inference, principally deductive inference, as the focus of its concern, the pragmatists redefined logical theory. In their hands, it became nothing less than a theory of inquiry (what Peirce called "the quest of quests," an inquiry into the conditions of the success of inquiry). Such a theory is the work of a thoroughgoing experimentalist designed to facilitate experimental investigation. It is, in other words, an explicitly reflexive exercise of experimental intelligence— an experimentalist critique of experimental reason.

The seed from which it grows is the definition just quoted. The fruits to be gathered from the tree issuing from this seed include cooperative intelligence as one of the most pressing political ideals at the present time. Despite the tendency of so many scholars to overlook this contribution,[18] they also include a philosophical defense of religious faith, although one taking markedly different forms in Peirce, James, and Dewey. For this reason alone, we are compelled to see that the manner in which the pragmatists turned to experience was fundamentally different than the way in which either David Hume or the logical positivists conceived their appeal to experience (1917, MW 10:3–48; also Smith 1978, ch. 3; 1992, ch. 1). No animus against religion animated their appeal. To rule religion out of court on the basis of one's conception of experience was, in their judgment, to fall prey to apriorism; that is, it entailed practically betraying that to which one was nominally committed. Such a betrayal makes experience an instance of empiricide (Kaufmann 1958, section 15).[19] At the outset, however, it is to logic rather than ethics or politics, religion or aesthetics, that we must turn.

LOGIC REDEFINED AS THE THEORY OF INQUIRY

Dewey offers an astute assessment of Peirce's singular contribution to late modern thought. By implication, he connects this contribution to his own project: "the method urged by Peirce as a formulation of the method to arrive at scientific beliefs, has so far had little application in the thinking from which most beliefs in *social and moral* matters issue" (1935, LW 11:422). The application of this method to these matters is at the very center of Dewey's project.[20] Here is but one of numerous claims about the need to adopt an experimental stance toward human affairs: "The development of scientific inquiry is immature; it has not as yet got beyond the physical and physiological aspects of human concerns, interests and subjectmatters." As a result, this development has produced "partial and exaggerated effects. *The institutional conditions into which it enters and which determine its human consequences have not as yet been subjected to any serious, systematic inquiry worthy of being designated scientific*" (1920, MW 12: 267–68).

Peirce however was wary of subjecting human affairs to scientific "control." The differences between Peirce and Dewey on this point call for more careful scrutiny.

Ironically, Peirce felt the nature of experimental inquiry on the one side and that of human life on the other made such "control" impossible and, were it possible, ruinous, whereas Dewey held that such inquiry would never fulfill itself until it became an integral part of virtually every human institution, as human life would be a stymied affair until it assumed a self-consciously experimental character. But the ability to accomplish this assumes a grasp of this method. The difference between grasping the historical achievement of the experimental method and carrying through the implications of this achievement is considerable. Even so, Peirce's own achievement was singular. Indeed, Dewey is fulsome in his praise of Peirce: "To have grasped in its totality the significance of scientific experimental method and to have applied it to a restatement of traditional logic is, I am convinced, an achievement whose importance will stand out more and more as the years go by" (LW 11:422–23). In his judgment, then, Peirce grasped experimentalism in its totality and hence redefined logic as first and foremost the theory of inquiry (more precisely, the normative theory of objective inquiry). In other words, Peirce grasped the defining features of experimental intelligence and, as a result, was prompted to re-imagine the discipline of logic.

The implications of his sentimental conservatism (see, e.g., Peirce, CP 1.632f 661, 673) stand in marked contrast to the scope of Dewey's radical experimentalism (Colapietro 1999). Even so, Dewey was far from being uncritically generous when he asserted that Peirce grasped "in its totality the *significance* of scientific experimental method" (emphasis added). I am inclined to modify slightly this claim: Peirce was the first to have grasped the pragmatic significance of experimental intelligence in its essential character. This marks a break with formalist obsessions and an alliance with historical undertakings. The history of science becomes critical for understanding science, as does the history of logic become indispensable for comprehending logic.[21]

One of Peirce's historical observations calls for our careful attention.

> Upon the heels of that movement [the Reformation and the innovations in logic following its aftermath], came another, which has not yet expended itself, nor even quite completed its conquest of minds. It arose from the conviction that man had everything to learn from observation. The first great investigators in this line were Copernicus, Tycho Brahe, Kepler, Galileo, Harvey, and Gilbert. None of them seemed to have any interest at all in the general theory—and that for a simple reason; namely, they knew no way of inquiry but the way of experiment; and their lives were so many experiments in regard to the efficacy of the method of experimentation. (CP 4.31)

However it was with these inquirers, Peirce was more than anything else interested in devising *a theory of inquiry* grounded in the evolving practices of experimental inquirers (i.e., in the history of the success of science).

One of the ironies is that Peirce's misgivings regarding Dewey's early formulation of experimental logic tend to exaggerate the differences between Peirce's efforts and

Dewey's.[22] Peirce is partly responsible for this. He judged Dewey's essays in experimental logic to entail an abandonment of a normative theory (CP 8.239–44; Colapietro 2002). But he was almost certainly ungenerous in the manner he read Dewey's relatively early attempt to ground logical theory in a "natural history" of historical practices. After all, he himself explicitly announced his attempt to root his theory of logic in the history of the discipline. He brought profound, prodigious historical erudition to his efforts to redefine logic as a theory of inquiry (as a *normative* theory of objective inquiry).

CONJECTURAL REASON AND INERADICABLE FALLIBILITY

As we have already suggested, experimental reason eschews the methodological ideal of apodictic certainty and embraces the ineradicable fallibility of all of our epistemic claims. It might properly be designated *conjectural reason*, since the pragmatists recognize abduction (the logical operation[23] of framing testable hypotheses) as the heart of the matter. The business of rationality is bound up with hypotheses or conjectures. Deduction and induction are subordinate to abduction. Deduction serves to render our conjectures testable and induction actually to test them. We are bound to make mistakes. The trick is to make them *intelligently*.

No thread is indeed more important than Peirce's insistence upon fallibility. He writes: "[I]t is a truth well worthy of rumination that all the intellectual development of man rests upon the circumstance that all our action is subject to error. *Errare est humanum* is of all commonplaces the most familiar" (CP 6.86).

To repeat for emphasis, intellect or intelligence "consists of plasticity of habits." Intelligence is at bottom a more or less integrated network of habits, especially habits of a distinctive character (see, e.g., 1922, MW 14:47–48, 66–67, 91). To an extent far greater than we tend to realize "the working harmony" among these diverse dispositions is a precarious one (a point to which I will return eventually).

At the point where pragmatism most directly bears upon the problems of men and women,[24] the pragmatic import of Dewey's principally methodological reconstruction of creative intelligence is especially worth recalling in conclusion. In *Liberalism and Social Action*, he asserts: "It is no exaggeration to say that the measure of civilization is the degree in which the method of cooperative intelligence replaces the method of brute conflict" (1935, LW 11:57). At a very high level of generality, his conception of intelligence might be to some extent substantive, not merely methodological. For example, there is an explicit recognition of the constitutional needs of the human animal (see, e.g., Dewey's "Does Human Nature Change?" [1938]). But here one sees how Dewey's focus on the historical, cultural, and other contextual facets of these constitutional needs tends quickly to eclipse his recognition of these needs, arguably even the perception of these needs. In any case, he stresses the variable cultural and historical expressions of these constitutional needs far more than the unchanging character of human nature.

Needs and desires emerge in the course of history. Cultures are the sites of their fulfillment and frustration. This makes their formation, fulfillment, and frustration[25] a cultural affair in which inherited arrangements become focal objects of sustained critique. An ongoing, complex negotiation among cultural actors arises. For much of history, inherited arrangements have asserted their unquestionable status: its traditions are sacred. But a self-avowedly critical tradition has emerged in opposition to authoritarian ones, a critical tradition committed to subjecting traditional arrangements to even radical criticism. Ordinary people ought to take their lives to be singular experiments for which antecedently fixed patterns of human excellence are never anything more than suggestions. Just because human beings are social animals, however, the exercise of experimental intelligence in conducting these experiments in personal existence possesses a political dimension. It concerns regimes and relations of power.

EXPERIMENTAL INTELLIGENCE AND DEMOCRATIC CULTURES

At a very high level of generality, one might talk about *the* human form of life. But this form of life is by the very constitution of humans irreducibly and, in a sense, wildly diverse. It is less misleading to speak of human forms of life, in their utter heterogeneity and irrepressible profusion. The intra- and intercommunal conflicts generated by the very nature of these forms are at the center of the dramas of human history and the very stuff of our individual lives. Just as there is a dialectic between inter- and intrapersonal conflicts, so too there is one between inter- and intracommunal conflicts. The conflicts between groups tend to generate ones *within* those groups, just as the conflicts between, say, two individuals tend to unleash ones within each of the individuals.

An unblinking acknowledgment of human conflict is at the center of pragmatism (see, e.g., Dewey LW 5:279–88, cf. Appendix 5 to LW 5). One of the great ironies in intellectual history is that so many contributors to this field have seen the American pragmatists as naively optimistic children of the European Enlightenment. Hardly anything could be farther from the truth. They were neither naïve nor optimistic. Their fighting faith in creative intelligence was in their judgment nothing more than faith[26] (no dialectic of history secured the victory of such intelligence over its rivals), their hope in the project of replacing the method of brute conflict with the methods of cooperative intelligence (1935, LW 11:57) was either groundless or a hope in what all too easily could be made into its opposite (a fantastic hope in a statistical majority to produce wise decisions, or one in a militant reductionism bent on forcing human meaning into the Procrustean bed of brute facts, or an unwitting apology of American capitalism[27]).

To see the pragmatist faith in creative intelligence for what it was has turned out to be exceedingly difficult for the exponents no less than the critics of the pragmatist movement. Part of the problem has been that controversies regarding truth have tended to push to, if not beyond, the margins not only what was inaugural but also what continues to be central—the clarification of *meaning*, in particular, the clarification of meaning in terms of habits of feeling, imagining, and acting and, of greater import, in terms of the alteration of such habits. To put this in the technical terms of Peircean semeiotic, the "ultimate logical interpretant" of a sign is strictly speaking not a habit but a habit-change (see especially CP 5.476ff.). To put this in more Jamesian language, not only things but also meanings are *in the making* (James 1977, 77). Not meanings made, fixed once and for all by a reason presuming to stand above history, but meanings emerging from the flux of experience—and, thus, from the flux of history (see, e.g., 1925, LW 1:370). Moreover, they are used to plow back into experience for the purpose of ascertaining where we are, whence we came, and whither we are going. As much as whither we are directing ourselves, we must contend with whither we are driven by forces we hardly comprehend and, to a greater extent, barely control. Precisely because pragmatism is preoccupied with the outcomes of, and prospects for, our endeavors, it is painstakingly attentive to the past. Disciplined, probing recollection is vital for intelligence oriented to the exigencies of action. It is indeed constitutive of such intelligence.

As a logician devoted to reconstructing logic into a theory of inquiry, Peirce was a historian of science and, as a philosopher committed to the reconstruction of philosophy, Dewey was deeply engaged in the vital task of renarrating our intellectual history.[28] Recall Dewey's characterization of Peirce's achievement. His predecessor had "grasped in its totality the *significance* of scientific experimental method" (emphasis added). Peirce had, in Dewey's judgment, comprehended the meaning, the import, the function, and the implications of the instituted procedures by which experimental intelligence rendered itself an efficacious force in human history. One of his first steps in the direction of this accomplishment was, in "How to Make Our Ideas Clear" (1878), to have focused on the question of meaning and, in doing so, to have made the meaning of interrogation, the task of inquiry, integral to the meaning of meaning.[29] Meanings are not grasped intuitively, but *worked out* experimentally. In the context of inquiry, abstract definitions have indispensable but ultimately limited value. Their inherent limitations are to be overcome by pragmatic clarifications. The abstract is thereby to be rendered concrete, the verbal formula ultimately made to serve an experimental procedure yielding observable results.[30] So, in the context of inquiry, the clarification of meaning is formally tied to the procedures of the experimentalist.

But, as it turns out, the context of inquiry is not altogether a separable sphere of human activity. Indeed, *all* contexts (especially those of morals and politics) are in principle transformable into contexts of inquiry. Each one of them ought to be transformed into a sphere in which experimental intelligence is granted maximal authority. The seat of authority moves from inviolable traditions to continually self-corrective methods (1929, LW 4:40ff.; 1934, LW 9:22–27). The meaning of this entails instituting the inaugural procedure of the pragmatist movement. In other words, it demands deliberately cultivating the habits by which our words, assertions, and arguments are translated into the form most congenial to the distinctive work of the experimental inquirer.

We can all too readily take this to imply a narrow, superficial, scientistic approach to questions of meaning. It is only fair to acknowledge that Peirce at times encourages such a reading of pragmatism. But there is much in his writings and even more in those of James, Dewey, Mead, and other pragmatists to suggest that a more deep-cutting and far-reaching approach to meaning ought to be taken as the pragmatic import of experimental intelligence. Whatever else it means, such intelligence means the insistence on translating the significance of what we are saying into habits of various kinds, some being habits of overt doing. Whatever else such translation involves, it involves breaking out of the suffocating confines of a scientistic ideology and expanding the scope of intelligence. In terms of experimental intelligence, Duke Ellington composing on the piano, trying now this and now that, is at bottom akin to Gödel scribbling on a blackboard, following out now this sequence of steps and now that one. This is not quite right. At a high level of generality, the two are at bottom the same. There are of course specific ways in which experimental intelligence in the exacting context of musical composition differs from how such intelligence operates in the context of mathematics. These cannot be gainsaid. Even so, neither the intelligence of the composer nor the cast of that intelligence (the composer is clearly an instance of the experimentalist) can be denied.

Questions of meaning are logically prior to those of truth, even if the very meaning of some sentences demands the specification of the conditions in which they must or at least might be true. As a result, our attention ought to be directed in the first instance to questions of meaning, not least of all that of the meaning of meaning. Nowhere is the "bias" of pragmatism against reductionism more evident than in the refusal of the pragmatists to reduce the varieties of meaning to only one form. Richard Rorty was certainly not mistaken when he discerned an affinity between one of the later Wittgenstein's principal insights, the irreducible heterogeneity of language games, and one of the characteristic emphases of James and Dewey, fundamentally distinct modes of meaning-making.

Experimental intelligence is *personal* intelligence, also *cooperative* (and, hence, communal) intelligence, and finally *creative* intelligence. "Meaning is," as Jonathan Culler notes, "context-bound, but context is boundless" (Culler 2011, 68). For most of us, the diverse meanings with which experimental intelligence is preoccupied readily fall into such traditional categories as religious, scientific, moral, political, and aesthetic meanings, but just because they so easily sort themselves out in this fashion they pose fundamental questions rather than offer unproblematic demarcations. One of the most pressing tasks for experimental intelligence is to extricate itself from such traditional classifications and try, especially in the light of such fateful developments as high modernist art, psychoanalytic theory, and various emancipatory movements (Cavell 1990, 13), to reconstruct not only the meaning of these categories but also to suggest alternative frameworks to the inherited ones. This means nothing less than categoreal innovation. This might take an explicit, intricate form, as it does in the case of Peirce, or it might be done in a more implicit, less systematic manner, as it does in of James and Dewey. The pivotal terms in our intellectual disputes are "essentially contested concepts" (Gallie 1964) and, as such, they call for clarification, not least of all pragmatic clarification. This, too, indicates just how central the question of meaning is tied to the meaning of pragmatism.

As much as anything else, the meaning of pragmatism is bound up with the pragmatics of meaning. And this means the first step was not only a fateful one but also one that needs to be re-enacted, time and again. The painter or musician tries something new and is surprised, partly pleased and partly not, by the result. The result is then used to try something else and the result of this is very often the indefinite prolongation of an absorbing process in which experimental intelligence remakes both itself and what it is working on. Such intelligence and any practice in which it operates are after all inextricably intertwined. Such intelligence is always situated; that is, it is implicated in one or more practices. It is never a mere onlooker (James 1978 [1878], 21), but always a participant. In turn, human practices are always to some extent malleable affairs, not least of all ones modifiable by the immanent operation of experimental intelligence. They are indeed evolved and evolving traditions (typically intergenerational communities stretching across a significant stretch of human history—think here of the linguistic practices constituting a natural language).

Such languages are, in certain very important respects, the paradigm of what the pragmatists mean by a *practice* (cf. 1922, MW 14:57). It is instructive to recall here that in *Pragmatism* James explains his conception of truth by invoking analogies with law and language. Whatever its origin, language at present has evolved to the point where it has functionally transcended its historical origins. Unquestionably, the symbolific intelligence of *Homo sapiens* is not reducible to the signaling behavior of other species or even our rnearest ancestors (cf. 1925, LW 1:139–44). Such intelligence is principally not the instrument of antecedently fixed ends and desires, but rather the agency by which historically emergent goals and interests are rendered more secure, less fantastic, and less arbitrarily exclusive (1925, LW 1:191, 302, 305).[31] However innate or instinctual human intelligence might be in its origin (see, e.g., Peirce, CP 7.381), its forms and functions bear testimony to a cultural evolution stretching across largely unexplored millennia.

Human intelligence is an historically emergent function entangled in the exigencies of practice (though this might be the practice of the theoretical physicist or of the pure mathematician rather than the practice of an affectionate parent or that of the skilled artisan). As Dewey once remarked, the point is not to practilize intelligence but to intellectualize our practices (Eldridge 1998, 5). That is, it is to make our practices arenas in which the continuous growth of creative intelligence becomes one with participation in these practices. To some extent, this is what our practices have always been. But creative intelligence has tended to operate haltingly and even surreptitiously in many traditional religions and political communities. The history of politics no less than religion has been one in which the suppression or even vilifi-cation of such intelligence stands out. Those of other instituted practices, including schools, offer additional examples. Countless traditional authorities have judged ex-perimental intelligence to be an intolerable enemy of some shared practice. Many have libeled the pragmatists by charging especially James and Dewey with an oppor-tunistic and unprincipled stance toward the truth. The irony here is hard to miss: the absolutist critics of the classical pragmatists have been more often than not resolute champions of traditional institutions with a demonstrable record of trying to destroy experimental intelligence.

The absolutists have tried to eliminate the very possibility of error and imagined the failure to accomplish this would open the floodgates of skepticism. In a sense, the pragmatists have done the opposite: they have endeavored to expand the range of such possibilities and imagined their success in doing so would render the dread of skep-ticism beside the point. For absolutists, pragmatism is a variant of skepticism. What pragmatism is for the pragmatists themselves, however, is a resolute form of radical falli-bilism. "Our errors are surely," James insisted in "The Will to Believe," "not such awfully solemn things. In a world where we are so certain to incur them in spite of all our cau-tion, a certain lightness of heart seems healthier than this excessive nervousness on their behalf" (James 1979, 25).

THE PATHOLOGICAL FORMS
OF HUMAN INGENUITY

In its most basic sense, experimental intelligence is, as Peirce suggested, simply the ca-pacity to learn from experience. This practically means learning from our mistakes. "There is," as Archibald MacLeish wryly observed, "only one thing more painful than learning from experience and that is not learning from experience." As it turns out, however, both sides of his assertion require qualification. We can cultivate the capacity of learning from experience to the point where while not ceasing to be arduous and at times even frustrating the activity of learning from experience is sustaining and even ex-hilarating. In brief, learning from experience is not necessarily painful; it can be enjoy-able. Beyond this, nothing less than a life devoted to such learning is arguably the most noble form of human existence.

However painful are our failures not to learn from experience, we sometimes ap-pear to be pathologically addicted to the pain. Time and again, our desire to have been right wins out against our desire to be right (Quine and Ullian 1978). In any event, our capacity to learn from experience is very often severely limited by what William Blake called "mind-forged manacles." We have unwittingly shackled our own intelligence.

Herein lies one of the major lacunae of classical pragmatism. Any adequate account of experimental intelligence must include a deep-cutting understanding of human stupidity. It is not enough to celebrate our ability to learn from experience. It is also necessary to explore the reasons and causes why we so frequently fail to do so. Especially given the pragmatist portrait of human intelligence, what might be called the fragility of reason is a salient feature of any historical form of human rationality. In fairness, it must be noted that the pragmatists hardly ignored the obstructions to the operation of intelligence. In some contexts, Peirce stresses this in a manner reminiscent of Freud: "Men many times fancy they act from reason when, in point of fact, the reasons they attribute to themselves are nothing but excuses which unconscious instinct invents to satisfy the teasing 'whys' of the *ego*" (CP 1.631). Our propensity to self-delusion is so great as "to render philosophical rationalism a farce" CP 1.631).

The loftiest rationalists have been the most visceral racists. The tragic failure of intelligence to uproot itself from certain deeply visceral prejudices and to transplant itself in healthier soil is just that—a tragedy.[32] The pathologies of racism are only beginning to be confronted in a direct and painstaking manner, a manner characteristic of intelligence in Dewey's sense. The severe limits within which rational persuasion often operates are revealed by how otherwise intelligent individuals so quickly and adamantly enlist their intelligence in the service of their visceral prejudices. It is difficult to know how much of this is a failure of experience, in the sense of it being a function of very limited experience, and how much of it is an inability or unwillingness to attend to the disclosures of experience, however limited. Whatever is the case, humans time and again fail to learn from their experience.

According to Peirce, " 'rational' means essentially serf-criticizing, self-controlling, and self-controlled, and therefore open to incessant question," i.e., ceaseless self-interrogation (CP 7.77). So, too, intelligent intelligence is self-critical intelligence. While I have shifted the focus from reason (or rationality) to intelligence, and while I have stressed how Dewey especially set in sharp contrast his instrumentalist vision of intelligence to the traditional understanding of Reason (Logos, *intellectus, Vernunft*), even Dewey but especially Peirce did not jettison the terms *reason* or *rationality*. Their detailed depiction of intelligence was to a great extent a thoroughgoing reconstruction of reason.

The pragmatists were appreciative of the fragility of reason, the tenacious and resilient yet precarious and vulnerable constitution of our rationality. This becomes evident if we consider one of Dewey's most suggestive depictions of human rationality.

> Rationality ... is not a force to evoke against impulse and habit. It is the attainment of a working harmony among diverse desires. 'Reason' as a noun signifies the happy cooperation of a multitude of dispositions, such as sympathy, curiosity, exploration, experimentation, frankness, pursuit—to follow things through—circumspection, to look about at the context. ... Reason, the rational attitude, is the resulting disposition, not a ready-made antecedent which can be invoked at will and set into movement. (1922, MW 14:136)

If human rationality is essentially a working harmony among such diverse factors, it is easy to see how precarious it is. Possibilities of discord, disorder, and dysfunction *constitutionally* threaten rationality so conceived. This is true to such an extent that we might go so far as to define, in a pragmatic register, reason as a capacity constitutionally threatened by collapses into madness: to possess reason is to be susceptible to madness, but ordinarily susceptible not in a remote but in a more or less imminent way. The threat of such collapse is never far away.

The history of humanity is in no small measure that of the madness of reason. Less dramatically, it is the insufficiently intelligent or utterly misguided deployment of creative intelligence. As we have noted, James in his very first publication set intelligent intelligence in contrast to its opposite. His point was simple but profound: intelligence can be stupidly or unintelligently deployed, often to its own destruction and the destruction of the sphere in which it is exercised. Of course, the ideal is to use intelligence intelligently. The main conflict turns out to be not the conflict between intelligence and stupidity but that between a resolutely intelligent intelligence and an unintelligent intelligence. Tyrants and criminals can display a degree of intelligence beyond what is often observable in more benevolent or admirable figures. Their ingenuity is often remarkable. It perhaps should give us pause that *innocent* is often used as a polite synonym for *ignorant* (e.g., to say that someone is innocent of history or philosophy, as most Americans are, is to claim that that individual is ignorant of these fields). Rather than deny tyrants and criminals their due, we ought in some cases to grant their possession of intelligence but to press the point that their exercise of intelligence is at the expense of a world in which cooperative intelligence is an expansive force. The failure of cooperative intelligence is, at root, a failure of intelligence, not simply sociality. It is a self-stultification of intelligence.

THE EXPANSIVE SCOPE OF HUMAN INTELLIGENCE

As we have seen, intelligence basically means our capacity to learn from experience. Not infrequently, Dewey characterizes a failure to learn from experience as tragic. The exercise of this capacity is however not inherently limited (1929, LW 4:121), certainly not ineluctably tragic. The unrestricted exercise of this capacity drives toward a pragmatist critique of experimental intelligence, a critique in which our reliance on signs becomes a focus of concern. That is, it drives in the direction of logic reconstructed as a theory of inquiry and, in turn, this theory comes itself to be either identified with a general theory of signs or inclusive of such a general theory.

As important as the logical, semiotic, and methodological implications of the efforts of experimental intelligence to constitute itself as truly intelligent intelligence are, the moral, political, and arguably also religious implications are at least as important. In this regard, there is perhaps no assertion by any of the pragmatists more fitting to recall in our discussion than the one already quoted from Dewey's *Liberalism and Social Action*: "the measure of civilization is the degree in which the method of cooperative intelligence replaces the method of brute conflict" (LW 11, 57). But the brute conflicts of warring nations are ones in which we tragically witness both a phenomenal display of cooperative intelligence (e.g., think here of the Manhattan Project or, given its success, the ceaseless efforts on the part of the most powerful countries to build every more devastating weaponry, the life of Leonardo da Vinci illustrating this disheartening point) *and* the utter failure of a more inclusive cooperative intelligence. The brute conflicts are ones enlisting exemplary forms of experimental intelligence. But international cooperation is made impossible or, at best, largely ineffective in the face of the cooperative intelligence enlisted by individual nations and their strategic alliances (international associations falling far short of global cooperation).

One way of telling the story involves recalling a largely forgotten pragmatist and making him more central to the main narrative than most authors do. G. H. Mead's truly creative work on international cooperation seems a fitting way to move toward the conclusion of the present essay. If creative intelligence in its political deployment (hence, also in its moral one) stops short of global cooperation, it reveals itself to be an insufficiently intelligent intelligence. The inherent drive of scientific inquiry bursts the bounds of nationalism and all other forms of tribalism, however often historical actors betray this defining feature of the scientific community. The community of inquiry, as originally envisioned by Peirce and creatively appropriated by the other pragmatists, is in principle an infinite or unbounded one. In practice, such a community must continually contend and fight against countervailing forces, forces working against the limitless expansion of creative intelligence. It is hardly an accident that many of the most courageous political dissidents have been trained experimentalists who have devoted their lives to what is in a certain respect a paradoxical pursuit, the passionate yet dispassionate pursuit of novel truth by experimental methods.

The drive of capitalism no less than that of science pushes at least some of its participants beyond national and more broadly regional boundaries. In what on the surface appears to be a more problematic example, that of religions such as Islam, Christianity, Buddhism, and indeed virtually all of the other world religions likewise pushes beyond national and regional borders. There can be little doubt that there is an inherent drive in each one of these religious traditions to burst the bounds of their historical origin. This however engenders radical or intractable conflict and, in turn, such conflict can either engender violent confrontation or occasion the discovery of more humane forms of mutual recognition. Even if Mead's pragmatic defense of the need to adopt an international perspective is as politically compromised as Marilyn Fischer so learnedly argues (Fischer 2008), the moral imperative to *institute* a global orientation itself demands that this orientation be disentangled from the nationalistic biases with which it was so deeply entangled. The inherent scope of experimental intelligence must itself be experimentally determined. In principle, however, it is hardly an exaggeration, at least for a pragmatist, to insist this scope is boundless. The failures *in practice* to enlarge the scope of such intelligence need to be read as just that. This does not warrant despair; rather it sets an agenda for the reconstruction of our practices.

Long ago, certain imaginative individuals in widely scattered places, East and West, hit upon the moral importance of a deliberately cultivated *cosmopolitan* consciousness. In the work of Mead especially, the cosmopolitan ideal becomes a pivotal concern. It is perhaps too much to say that, for him, everything turns upon this ideal. It however would not be an exaggeration to say not only much does but also much of what is most important in his writings turns on this ideal.

Human history has been a tragicomedy in which the ability to institute effective methods of experimental inquiry has been conjoined to the devastating failures to expand the scope of creative intelligence. The resources provided by Peirce, James, Dewey, DuBois, Mead, and other pragmatists both to examine this history in a critical manner and, then, to learn from this tragicomedy in a creative way are indispensable.

The moral dimensions of experimental intelligence deserve painstaking attention. At bottom, the failure of such intelligence is, as Dewey so telling expressed it, a new failure of nerve (1925, LW 1:104; Hook, 1961). That is, it is an instance of cowardice. The link between intelligence and courage itself links the pragmatists to various figures in intellectual history. But there is more than courage to such intelligence. There is, to begin with, also, humility, forbearance, patience, industry, generosity, magnanimity, benevolence, and arguably also wonder, awe, reverence, and piety.

Despite their intense focus on the political dimensions of creative intelligence, neither Dewey nor Mead overlooked the intimately personal character of such intelligence. Indeed, experimental intelligence is ineluctably personal intelligence. Both these pragmatists are not only explicit but also emphatic about this. Pragmatically, this means that such intelligence must be personally cultivated if it is to be experimentally efficacious. For Dewey, "personal rationality or reflective intelligence" is nothing less than "the necessary organ of experimental initiative and creative invention in remarking custom" (1922, MW 14:56).

The emancipation of creative intelligence from historical and cultural limitations and disfigurements is of a piece with the struggle for human emancipation in its most urgent forms. This demands the reconstruction of our institutions, one undertaken and directed by experimental intelligence as a cooperative endeavor. Thus, "a sane and humane *description*" of the scope and function of human intelligence is insufficient; nothing less than *prescriptions* regarding the reformation of such intelligence will suffice. In this, the classical pragmatists reveal themselves to be the offspring of the European Enlightenment. They however are anything but naïve champions of a crudely empiricist reason or a fantastically rationalist capacity to jump outside of history. Their views regarding intelligence have been tempered and tutored by experience, their own personal experience but also the collective experience of countless generations (Peirce, CP 7.87).

CONCLUSION: EXPERIMENTAL INTELLIGENCE
AS CREATIVE AGENCY

The pragmatist portrait of the intelligent experimentalist is truly a new chapter in our intellectual history. It is a deliberate attempt to frame a modest yet bold vision of human reason in light of the Darwinian revolution. At the same time, it is an unblinkingly candid assessment of the failures of humans to learn from their experience. It is, in a qualified sense, a panacea. Whatever will prove to be effective in curing the ills afflicting us will do so in part by its strategic reliance on experimental intelligence. There might turn out to be ills for which there is no cure. But any one for which there is a cure, the cure will be discovered in the only way we have ever made any discovery, by painstaking observation, imaginative conjecture, opportune recollection, rigorous testing of rival hypotheses, and all of the other procedures by which such intelligence carries out its work.[33] The triad of recollection, observation, and forecast, in their complex interplay, is at the heart of human intelligence in the Deweyan sense.

The courage[34] to insist upon the propriety of exercising such intelligence in those contexts traditionally most hostile to this exercise is the virtue needed above all other virtues. The Enlightenment motto "Think for oneself" needs to be qualified: in the first instance, it might simply assume the form "Think" and very quickly thereafter "Do think for yourself but make a point of doing so with others." Thought only emerges when action is arrested, ordinarily by doubt.

The first task of intelligent intelligence then seems to be deliberate self-interruption, stopping ourselves from doing, saying, or even feeling what we habitually and hence effortlessly do, say, or feel. There are limits to the efficacy or practicality of self-interruption. But there are momentous disadvantages attached to the inability to stop oneself for the sake of creating opportunities to think over matters, even very familiar ones, anew. Dogmatism is defined by the presumption to know without the slightest doubt what others find perplexing. Experimentalism is, by contrast, marked by just this hesitancy: if informed, intelligent individuals argue the opposite of what one holds, one ought not to hold it tenaciously.[35] The doubts of competent or reasonable people ought to give us pause.

The scope of intelligence as envisioned by the pragmatists is staggeringly wide. It reaches from diplomatic efforts to institute international fora in which warring nations might replace the method of brute conflict with the method of cooperative intelligence (from such efforts) *to* the private resolve to stop oneself from doing—or saying or feeling—the done thing. It stretches from the global to the intimately personal. It assumes both the technical form of a renovated logic and the inherently informal modes of communicative habits constituting the innermost life of our communal associations. As Rorty suggests, these communicative habits are the Socratic virtues. The life of experimental intelligence depends upon the acquisition, exercise, and refinement of such virtues (Rorty 1982, 174). It possesses no magic except for the "miracle" of communication and this miracle occurs within the bounds of nature:

> Of all affairs, communication is the most wonderful. That things should be able to pass from the plane of external pushing and pulling to that of revealing themselves to man, and thereby to themselves; and that the fruit of communication should be participation, sharing, is a wonder by the side of which transubstantiation pales. (1925, LW 1:132)

The principal function of communication is however not to convey antecedently realized thoughts but to assist the emergence of efficaciously creative ones. The communicative facets of experimental intelligence indicate that art, rhetoric, linguistics, and much else must be taken into account to offer a comprehensive survey of experimental intelligence (see, e.g., Dewey's *The Public and Its Problems* no less than *Art as Experience*). Experimental intelligence is not experimental if it is not creative. In turn, creative intelligence is not creative if it is not effectively communicative.

Effective communication however turns out to be an instance of "poetic" utterance. That seemingly most prosaic of philosophical movements, American pragmatism, cannot be appreciated unless we discern the depth to which this orientation involves using ordinary language in ever new ways, always taking anything whatsoever as a medium for the realization of creative intelligence (Cf. Poirier). Already in the re-founding of pragmatism in 1898, James suggests: "Philosophers are after all like poets" (James 1975 [1898], 257).[36] For both are "pathfinders": What everyone can feel or know, "they sometimes find words for and express" (258).

Philosophers and poets can also help us to articulate what has not yet been felt or not yet discovered. In *Radical Hope*, Jonathan Lear defines the poet as "a creative maker of meaningful space" (Lear 2006, 51). Poetry concerns how we do things with words. But it also concerns how we transform and indeed create meanings, linguistic and otherwise. We might take Lear's definition of the poet to be a thoroughly pragmatist one. One might even say it is a pragmatic clarification of an implicit meaning of a highly elusive word. Shelley suggested that poets are the unacknowledged legislators of the world. Here it seems more apposite to suggest that pragmatists are among the unacknowledged poets in the world. In any event, their painstaking portrait of the intelligent experimentalist was in effect a self-portrait. Such an experimentalist could not fail being a poet in Lear's sense, "a creative maker of meaningful space," one who in making such space secures "the possibility for the creation of a new field of possibilities" (Lear 2006, 51). This means using language and other symbols to institute a meaningful space in which, say, international conflicts cease to be to such a large extent brute conflicts (1935, LW 11:57), or religious traditions open themselves to the world-shattering discoveries of scientific inquirers, or educational institutions to the contemporary expressions of newly emergent forms of social consciousness. Experimental intelligence is an instance of creative intelligence (1917, MW 10:44–48) and, as such, it is preoccupied with not only acting innovatively in established fields of human endeavor but also creatively instituting novel spaces.

NOTES

1. The fact that the pragmatists took themselves to be offering nothing more than a conjecture, however reasonable in the circumstances in which it was being elaborated and defended, is of the utmost significance. While Immanuel Kant denigrated hypotheses in philosophy as contraband, the pragmatists unqualifiedly accepted that, at bottom, even our most secure knowledge derives from conjectures. This implies that even our most secure knowledge is *not* absolutely secure or apodictically certain. As Peirce remarks, approximation has to be the fabric out of which our philosophy is woven (CP 1.404). This bears directly on our topic, since experimental intelligence can never be more than conjectural reason, that is, reason content with framing, elaborating, testing, revising, and rejecting conjectures. In other words, the pragmatist conjecture regarding human rationality marks a decisive break with the deductivist bias of the dominant traditions in Western thought. See Colapietro, "Conjectures Concerning an Uncertain Faculty Claimed for Humans," *Semiotica*, 153(1/4), 413–30.

2. See, for example, William James, *The Principles of Psychology* (Cambridge, MA: Harvard University Press, 1981); also A. N. Whitehead, *The Function of Reason* (Boston: Beacon Press, 1927). "There is," Whitehead contends, "Reason, asserting itself as above the world, and there is Reason as one of the many factors within the world. The Greeks have bequeathed to us two figures, whose real or mythical lives conform to these two notions—Plato and Ulysses. The one shares Reason with the Gods, the other shares it with foxes" (10). See Colapietro 1987.

3. See Terrence W. Deacon, *The Symbolic Species* (New York: W. W. Norton, 1997). Deacon makes use of Peirce in this informed, suggestive account of the human animal.

4. See Cynthia Eagle Russett, *Darwin in America: The Intellectual Response 1865–1912* (San Francisco: W. H. Freeman, 1976). Also see Colapietro 2003.

5. Though Dewey in "From Absolutism to Experimentalism" does not mention Darwin by name, there can be little doubt about the figure most responsible for "the immense progress made by biology since the time of Aristotle" (1930, LW 5:157). See especially Dewey's "The Influence of Darwinism on Philosophy" (1909, MW 4:3–14). In the autobiographical essay, Dewey stresses that there are two unreconciled strains in James's *Principles*, a subjectivist one and a biological, hence objective, strain. The former prolonged the dominant subjectivist tenor of prior psychological tradition, while the latter decisively broke with this modern tradition and inaugurated "a return to the earlier biological conception of the psyche," albeit "a return possessed of a new force and value due to the immense progress made by biology since the time of Aristotle." For Dewey, James's return to such a conception of the *psyche* or organism was the "one specifiable philosophic factor which entered my thinking so as to give it a new direction and quality." This was however a factor derived from Darwin by James and other thinkers from his generation.

6. The year 1859 was not only the year in which Darwin published his *Origin of Species* but also the one in which Peirce graduated from Harvard College as well as John Dewey, Henri Bergson, and Edmund Husserl were born. The coincidence of this publication with Dewey and indeed Bergson's births bears significance, even if it is coincidental.

7. While James argued for a place for introspection in his psychology, Peirce, Dewey, and Mead were much more circumspect in their evaluation of this "method." Of greater importance, Peirce's philosophy is virtually inaugurated by his critique of Cartesianism, at the center of which is his rejection of intuitionism. While qualitative immediacy is embraced

by the pragmatists, cognitive immediacy is rejected (though the case of James calls for qualification) (Bernstein, 1983, 2010). The emphasis decisively falls not on what occurs in consciousness, conceived apart from the body or the world in which the body is implicated, but on what agents do in the world (even more concretely, how organisms transact with their environments).

8. See Peirce's critique of intuitionism ("Certain Faculties Claimed for Man"), James's treatment of introspection in Chapter VII of *The Principles* ("The Methods and Snares of Psychology"), and Dewey's programmatic statement in "How Mind Is to Be Known" (1942, LW 15:27–33).

9. Philip P. Wiener, *Evolution and the Founders of Pragmatism*. Max H. Fisch, "Evolution in American Philosophy," reprinted as Chapter 3 of *Peirce, Semeiotic, and Pragmatism* (1986).

10. In *The American Evasion of Philosophy*, Cornel West has made a compelling case for counting W. E. B. DuBois as a pragmatist. More recently, Nancy Fraser has buttressed such an inclusion by an additional one ("Another Pragmatism").

11. In *The Quest for Certainty*, Dewey suggests, "the new scientific development [specifically, the transition from a view of nature derived from Newton to a vision derived from Heisenberg] effects an exchange of reason for intelligence. In saying this, 'reason' has the technical meaning given to it in classic philosophic tradition, the *nous* of the Greeks, the *intellectus* of the scholastics. In this meaning, it designates both an inherent immutable order of nature, superempirical in character, and the organ of mind by which this universal order is grasped. In both respects, reason is with respect to changing things the ultimate fixed standard" (LW 4, 169–70), indeed, the antecedently fixed standard. Reason in these overlapping traditional senses stands in marked contrast to *intelligence* in its historically emergent sense, the one it has acquired in conjunction with the actual procedures of experimental inquiry. In such procedures as these, intelligence "is associated with judgment; that is, with selection and arrangement of means to effect consequences and with choice of what we take as our ends" (170). This passage is remarkable for several important reasons, none more important than that it makes explicit the *semiotic* character of experimental intelligence: "Wherever intelligence operates, things are judged in their capacity of signs of other things. If scientific [or experimentally acquired] knowledge enables us to estimate more accurately the worth of things as signs, we can afford to exchange the loss of theoretical certitude for a gain in practical judgment" (Ibid.; see also "The Need for a Recovery of Philosophy"). We are led to an appreciation that intelligence in this sense has "a foothold and a function within nature which reason never possessed" (ibid.). So conceived, intelligence "is part and parcel of nature's own continuing interactions" (171). The intelligent activities of the human animal are, Dewey stresses, "not something brought to bear upon nature from without; it is nature realizing its own potentialities in behalf of a fuller and richer issue of events [including of course historical events in their uniquely human significance]. Intelligence within nature means liberation and expansion, as reason outside nature means fixation and restriction" (ibid.).

12. *Reason, Truth and History* (Cambridge: Cambridge University Press, 1981), 104–5.

13. Putnam, 103.

14. In "The Architecture of Theories," Peirce endeavors to do this principally in the context of cosmology, while James here does so primarily in reference to biology and, to an even greater degree, that of psychology. Both pragmatists however agree that Spencer's evolutionism is incompatible with his mechanism.

15. Dewey will pick up this emphasis and make it central to his project. Indeed, it would hard to exaggerate just how important his thoroughgoing rejection of the "spectator" theory of human knowledge is (Dewey 1917, MW 10:41; 1920, MW 12: 147).

16. "Remarks on Spencer's Definition of Mind" in *Essays in Philosophy* (Cambridge, MA: Harvard University Press, 1978), p. 67.

17. "'Tone,' to be sure, is," James readily admits, "a terribly vague word, but there is no other. . . . By their tone are all things human either lost or saved." Any word carrying the suggestion of militant reductivism or scientistic ideology cannot but fail to betray the tone with which the pragmatists spoke in favor of experimental intelligence.

18. John E. Smith was exemplary in bringing this important contribution into sharpest focus.

19. Walter Kaufmann, *Critique of Religion and Philosophy*, section 15.

20. One of the most important emphases, but also one of the least understood facets, of Dewey's project was his insistence that the methods of the natural sciences must be applied to the problems of human life. This is widely taken to be a reductivist or scientistic bias condemned to distorting what is singular about such life. It is moreover taken to be an uncritical celebration of "social engineering." To suggest that it is virtually the opposite of such engineering and such scientism indicates how profoundly Dewey has been misunderstood on this point. In his judgment, the experimental temperament (and it is as much if not more a temperament than it is a "method") could not but be radically modified when it is dealing with distinctively human affairs rather than narrowly natural phenomena. The main point concerns the rejection of apriorism and dogmatism, the exclusive reliance on the excessively thin conceptions of abstract reason and the purely formal proofs of deductive reason. Of course, experimental intelligence does not presume to dispense with abstraction or deduction; it simply subordinates these operations to those of framing, elaborating, testing, revising, and in countless cases rejecting hypotheses. The dogmatic impulse is diagnosed as an authoritarian one, while the experimental temperament is allied to a democratic orientation. In other words, Dewey conjoins the methodology of conjectural intelligence to a politics of democratic deliberation. This is at the heart of his insistence upon incorporating the attitudes, procedures, and habits of the experimentalist in the way humans in moral, political, and other contexts address problems. Another important respect in which Dewey's call to "apply" the methods of experimental inquiry to the conflicts of human life is that this call tends to be interpreted as transporting a fully determinate and indeed antecedently secured theory from a science such as physics or chemistry to these conflicts. This is however mistaken.

21. This is apparent in the readily available selections found in Philp P. Wiener's anthology subsumed under the heading of "Lessons from the History of Scientific Thought" (chapters 12–18). See also CP, 1: Chapters 1 ("Lessons from the History of Philosophy") and 2 ("Lessons from the History of Science").

22. Ralph W. Sleeper, *The Necessity of Pragmatism*, pp. 47–50; Larry Hickman (1986), "Why Peirce Didn't Like Dewey's Logic"; and my "Experimental Logic: Normative Theory of Natural History" (Colapietro 2002).

23. Whereas Karl Popper refuses to accord the operation of framing hypotheses the status of a logical operation (it being in his judgment merely a psychological process), Peirce insists upon according abduction this status. For him, there are three irreducible difference modes of inference: abduction, deduction, and induction. One can frame hypotheses more or less well, that is, more or less *intelligently*; and the character of our intelligence is

nowhere more evident than in this activity. This would seem to make the operation inherently normative. There is a *logic of abduction*, though it is marked different from either the logic of deduction or that of induction.

24. "Philosophy recovers itself," Dewey wrote in "The Need for a Recovery of Philosophy," "when it ceases to be a device for dealing with the problems of philosophers and becomes a method, cultivated by philosophers, for dealing with the problems of men" and women (1917, MW 10:46).

25. See, for example, Dewey's *Experience and Nature* (1925, LW 1:194–99).

26. Faith in intelligence is, for the pragmatists, truly a question of faith, but not blind or irrational faith. It is to some extent an historically grounded faith, even if human history offers countless examples of the tragic failures of human intelligence. In the face of such failures, Dewey is undeterred: "Faith in the power of intelligence to imagine a future which is the projection of the desirable in the present, and to invent the instrumentalities of its realization, is our salvation" (MW 10:48).

27. In response to criticisms along these lines pressed by Lewis Mumford, it is essential to consult such articles by Dewey as "The Pragmatic Acquiescence" (1922, LW 3:145–51) and "A Critique of American Civilization" (1928, LW 3:133–44).

28. This is strikingly apparent in Dewey's *Unmodern Philosophy and Modern Philosophy*, but no less so than in such works as *The Reconstruction of Philosophy* (MW 12) or *Experience and Nature* (LW 1).

29. It is noteworthy that, almost a decade before volume one of the *Collected Papers* appeared, Peirce became known to a wider readership because of an appendix in Ogden and Richards's *The Meaning of Meaning* (1923), also that he highly praised Victoria Lady Welby for simply posing the question of meaning in its full scope.

30. "The whole originality in pragmatism, the whole point in it, is," James insisted in *The Meaning of Truth*, "the concrete way of seeing. It begins with concreteness, and returns and ends with it" (1975, 281–82).

31. Philosophy, as an instance of intelligence, strives "to clarify, liberate and extend the goods which inhere in the naturally generated functions of experience" (Dewey 1925, LW 1:305). The work of clarifying, liberating, and extending as well as intensifying, deepening, and stabilizing values is, for Dewey at least, the most important work human intelligence sets for itself (and, in doing so, it proves itself to be what James identified as "intelligent intelligence," i.e., intelligently cultivated and directed intelligence).

32. See, e.g., W. E. B. DuBois, *Dusk of Dawn* (New York: Schocken Books, 1984); Cornel West, *Keeping Faith: Philosophy and Race in America* (New York: Routledge, 1993), Eddie S. Glaude, Jr., *Democracy in Black* (New York: Brown, 2016); Paul C. Taylor, *Race: A Philosophical Introduction* (Cambridge: Polity, 2008); and Shannon Sullivan, *Revealing Whiteness: The Unconscious Habits of Racial Privilege* (Bloomington: Indiana University Press, 2006). Each one of these theorists is rooted in the pragmatists' tradition.

33. "Memory of the past, observation of the present, foresight of the future are indispensable. But they are," Dewey insists, "indispensable to a present liberation, an enriching growth of action" (1922, MW 14:182; see also 195, 203, and 207).

34. Intelligence in Dewey's sense is impossible without courage. It is at once a moral and intellectual stance toward both the world and one's self. One of Dewey's most relentless critics nonetheless discerned just this aspect of Dewey's project. In "Action and Certainty'" reprinted as Appendix 2 in LW 5, W. E. Hocking astutely suggests: "The great public work

of the instrumental philosophy [i.e., of Dewey's pragmatism] has been to limber up the ways of knowing of this people, to reduce fixed dogmas to working-hypotheses fit for experience; to give the intellectually traditional, authority-seeking, hero-worshipping American *the courage of his own experience*" (Hocking, in Dewey LW 5:463; emphasis added).

35. "The man of science attaches," Peirce claims, "positive value to the opinion of every man competent as himself, so that he cannot but have a doubt of a conclusion which he would adopt were it not that a competent man opposes it; but on the other hand, he will regard a sufficient divergence from the convictions of the great body of scientific men as tending of itself to argue incompetence, and he will generally attach little weight to the opinions of men who have long been dead and were ignorant of much that has been since discovered which bears upon the question in hand" (CP 1.32).

36. Peirce goes so far as to claim, "Nothing is truer than true poetry" (CP 1.315).

WORKS CITED

Citations of John Dewey's works are to the thirty-seven-volume critical edition published by Southern Illinois University Press under the editorship of Jo Ann Boydston. In-text citations give the original publication date and series abbreviation, followed by volume number and page number. For example: (1934, LW 10:12) is page 12 of *Art as Experience*, which is published as volume 10 of *The Later Works*.

Series abbreviations for *The Collected Works*:

EW *The Early Works* (1882–98)

MW *The Middle Works* (1899–1924)

LW *The Later Works* (1925–53)

Citations to C. S. Peirce's *Collected Papers* are in accord with standard practice. For example, in (CP 6.14), CP refers to the *Collected Papers*, 6 to volume 6, and 14 to paragraph (not page) 14 of that volume.

Bernstein, Richard J. *Beyond Objectivism and Relativism: Science, Hermeneutics, and Praxis*. Philadelphia: University of Pennsylvania Press, 1983.

Bernstein, Richard J. *The Pragmatic Turn*. Cambridge: Polity Press, 2010.

Burke, F. Thomas, D. Micah Hester, and Robert B. Talisse (eds.). *Dewey's Logical Theory: New Studies and Interpretations*. Nashville, TN: Vanderbilt University Press, 2002.

Cavell, Stanley. *Conditions Handsome and Unhandsome: The Constitution of Emersonian Perfectionism*. Chicago: University of Chicago Press, 1990.

Colapietro, Vincent. "Toward a More Comprehensive Conception of Human Reason." *International Philosophical Quarterly*, 27 (1987), 281–298.

Colapietro, Vincent. "Peirce's Guess at the Riddle of Rationality: Deliberative Imagination as the Personal Locus of Human Practice." In *Classical American Pragmatism: Its Contemporary Vitality*, edited by Sandra B. Rosenthal, Carl R. Hausman, and Douglas R. Anderson. Urbana: University of Illinois Press, 1999, 15–30.

Colapietro, Vincent. "In the Wake of Darwin." In *In Dewey's Wake*, edited by William J. Gavin. Albany, NY: SUNY Press, 2003, 213–41.

Colapietro, Vincent. "Telling Tales Out of School: Pragmatic Reflections on Philosophical Storytelling." *JSP*, 27, 1 (2013), 1–32.

Colapietro, Vincent. "Experiemetal logic: Normative theory or natural history?" In *Dewey's Logical Theory: New Studies and Interpretations*, edited by F. Thomas Burke, D. Micah Hester, and Robert B. Talisse. Nashville: Vanderbilt University Press, 2002, 43–71.

Culler, Jonathan. *Literary Theory: A Very Short Introduction*. Oxford: Oxford University Press, 2011.

Dewey, John. 1909. "The Influence of Darwinism on Philosophy." MW 4:3–14.

DuBois, W. E. B. *Dusk of Dawn*. New York: Schocken Books, 1984.

Eldridge, Michael. *Transforming Experience: John Dewey's Cultural Instrumentalism*. Nashville, TN: Vanderbilt University Press, 1998.

Fisch, Max H. *Peirce, Semeiotic, and Pragmatism*. Bloomington: Indiana University Press, 1986.

Fischer, Marilyn. "Mead and the International Mind." *Transactions of the Charles S. Peirce Society*, 44, 3 (2008).

Fraser, Nancy. "Another Pragmatism: Alain Locke, Critical Race Theory, and the Politics of Culture." In *The Revival of Pragmatism: New Essays on Social Thought, Law and Culture*, edited by Morris Dickstein. Durham, NC: Duke University Press, 1999, 57–75.

Gallie, W. B. *Philosophy and the Historical Understanding*. New York: Schocken Books, 1964.

Hickman, Larry. "Why Peirce Didn't Like Dewey's Logic." *Southwest Philosophy Review*, 3 (1986), 178–189.

Hocking, William Ernest. "Action and Certainty." Appendix 2 of Dewey, LW 5.

Hook, Sidney. *The Quest for Being*. New York: Dell, 1961.

Glaude, Eddie S. Jr. *Democracy in Black*. New York: Brown, 2016.

James, William. *A Pluralistic Universe*. Cambridge, MA: Harvard University Press, 1977.

James, William. "Appendix 1 – 'Philosophical Conceptions and Practical Results.'" In *Pragmatism*. Cambridge, MA: Harvard University Press, 1978, 255–270.

James, William. *Manuscript Lectures*. Cambridge, MA: Harvard University Press, 1988.

James, William. "Remarks on Spencer's Definition of Mind as Correspondence." In *Essays in Philosophy*. Cambridge, MA: Harvard University Press, 1978, 7–22.

James, William. *The Letters of William James*. 2 vols. Edited by Henry James. Boston: The Atlantic Monthly Press, 1920.

James, William. *The Principles of Psychology*. Cambridge, MA: Harvard University Press, 1981.

James, William. *The Will to Believe and Other Essays*. Cambridge, MA: Harvard University Press, 1979.

Kaufmann, Walter. *Critique of Religion and Philosophy*. Princeton, NJ: Princeton University Press, 1958.

Lear, Jonathan. *Radical Hope: Ethics in the Face of Cultural Devastation*. Cambridge, MA: Harvard University Press, 2006.

Ogden, C. K., and I. A. Richards. *The Meaning of Meaning*. New York: Harcourt Brace Jovanovich, 1923.

Peirce, C. S. *The Collected Papers of Charles Sanders Peirce*. Vols. 1–6 edited by Charles Hartshorne and Paul Weiss, Vols. 7 and 8 edited by Arthur W. Burks. Cambridge, MA: Belknap Press of Harvard University Press, 1931–1958.

Perry, Ralph Barton. *The Thought and Character of William James*. 2 vols. Boston: Little, Brown, 1935.

Putnam, Hilary. *Reason, Truth, and History*. Cambridge: Cambridge University Press, 1981.

Quine, W. V., and J. S. Ullian. *The Web of Belief*. New York: McGraw-Hill, 1978.

Rorty, Richard. *Consequences of Pragmatism*. Minneapolis: University of Minnesota Press, 1982.

Sleeper, Ralph. *The Necessity of Pragmatism: John Dewey's Conception of Philosophy*. New Haven, CT: Yale University Press, 1986.

Smith, John E. *Purpose and Thought: The Meaning of Pragmatism*. New Haven, CT: Yale University Press, 1978.

Smith, John E. *America's Philosophical Vision*. Chicago: University of Chicago Press, 1992.

Sullivan, Shannon. *Revealing Whiteness: The Unconscious Habits of Racial Privilege*. Bloomington: Indiana University Press, 2006.

Taylor, Paul C. *Race: A Philosophical Introduction*. Cambridge: Polity, 2008.

Toulmin, Stephen. Introduction to Dewey 1929, LW 4 (*The Quest for Certainty*), vii–xxii.

West, Cornel. *Keeping Faith: Philosophy and Race in America*. New York: Routledge, 1993.

Whitehead, A. N. *The Function of Reason*. Boston: Beacon Press, 1929.

Wiener, Philip. *Evolution and the Founders of Pragmatism*. New York: Harper & Row, 1965.

CHAPTER 5

....

DEWEY, RORTY, AND BRANDOM

The Challenges of Linguistic Neopragmatism

....

DAVID L. HILDEBRAND

"*Temperaments, with their cravings and refusals do determine men in their philosophies, and always will. The details of systems may be reasoned out piecemeal ... [b]ut when the labor is accomplished, the mind always performs its big summarizing act, and the system forthwith stands over against one like a living thing, with that strange simple note of individuality which haunts our memory....*"

—William James, *Pragmatism* (2000, 21)

"*What is life but the angle of vision? A man is measured by the angle at which he looks at objects.*"

—R. W. Emerson, "Natural History of Intellect" (1903, 10)

INTRODUCTION

....

IMAGINE you are a person. You grow up among family and friends, live in a neighborhood, work various jobs, go to school, set up a household, and have children; you negotiate day-to-day problems as they arise, read the news, and become increasingly invested in problems happening in your town, country, and even across the world. You pay attention to the trees and creatures of the natural world; you find yourself curious about them, concerned about how their futures might unfold, likely in collision with human conduct. Such things matter because, like anyone else, you inhabit a personal and practical standpoint from which you feel, think, and act.

Now imagine you are also a philosopher. You became one because you cared and wondered about things in your personal and practical world. As a philosopher, though, you inherit many questions and answers originating in *others'* practical worlds. Intellectually, you begin to inhabit those earlier worlds, becoming enmeshed in their dialectic; eventually, you find yourself skeptical of others' *initial* questions—especially their assumptions. In other words, your engagement shifts toward the philosophic *systems* and *standpoints* which presume to answer not only the original (practical) questions but also the subsequent (dialectical) questions—regarding "grounds," "domain," and "plausibility," for example. Concomitantly, you notice emergent norms that make this a "credible" and "philosophical" enterprise—specifically, when answers provide a "system" that aims explicitly for consistency, comprehensiveness, and certainty.

This contrast, between philosophy's practical roots and its theoretical concoctions, provided the classical pragmatists (CPs) with what we may call their "metaphilosophical bedrock"—their *stance* or *starting point*.[1] This stance emerged from the lives of John Dewey and William James but arguably Charles Sanders Peirce as well. Motivated by the divide between their personal/practical standpoints and the theoretical ones expected by their professions,[2] they endeavored to bridge this gap not only by addressing philosophy to numerous nonphilosophical audiences but also by clearing away problematic, traditional dualisms. Their project was "American" in spirit insofar as the radical nature of their critiques (of largely European structures) intended to do something new and useful for *their* country. Their pragmatist philosophy would engage more directly, energetically, and practically with ideas germane to everyday life; it would amount to a return to philosophy's earliest wisdom traditions, a way to create more authentic selves and a more humane society, beyond the walls of academe.

Linguistic Neopragmatism

It has been more than sixty years since Dewey's last publication, and an enormous literature now interprets, comments upon, and develops the various dimensions of CP. Some mining these veins are called "pragmatists," while others add the prefix "analytic," "linguistic," "neo," or "new." Figures attracting (if not always embracing) these labels have included Richard Rorty, Hilary Putnam, Robert Brandom, Huw Price, Jeffrey Stout, Bjørn Ramberg, and Cheryl Misak.[3] While this chapter focuses on Rorty and Brandom, I label these figures "neopragmatists" because despite their differences they share (a) an intense concern with the nature (and relations between) language, truth, and logic (sometimes invoked by the aim of "getting things right"); (b) a disposition to either minimize or renounce CP notions of "experience"; and (c) a deep professional investment in debates *within* philosophy rather than with applications *outside* philosophy, for example, to issues and areas more practical or personal.

Parameters and Organization

Because this chapter's title is rather broad, let me define its parameters. How is Dewey "challenged" by neopragmatism? I take a "challenge" as potentially *obstructive* or *constructive*. *Obstructive* challenges frustrate readers' understandings of Dewey's specific projects (e.g., his "instrumentalism," his "naturalism," etc.) or his larger enterprise (his stance or starting point). *Constructive* challenges, in contrast, encourage readers to take Dewey further—correcting, improving, or extending his ideas by adding new ideas, tools, and venues of inquiry.

Second, more focus is placed upon Brandom than his teacher, Rorty. While "neopragmatism" used to connote Rorty and Putnam, Brandom has been consistently producing pragmatist-themed work for over twenty years, commenting at length on CP's history and advocating for new forms of pragmatism. With a large, creative, and growing influence, Brandom is undoubtedly the leading, living neopragmatist.

Third, despite a few critical comments regarding Rorty's and Brandom's interpretations of CP, my main objective is to illuminate how their readings challenge Dewey's vision and any future uses of it.

The takeaway, I hope, is a revealing and predictive contrast between Dewey and recent scholarship. By stating plainly the challenges of linguistic pragmatism, we may see what endures as fundamental to Dewey's enterprise. Not least, we illuminate ways Dewey's "temperament" or "angle of vision" differentiates him from newer pragmatists.

The chapter is organized as follows. The first section considers Rorty's neopragmatist challenges to Dewey; the second explicates Brandom's neopragmatism and considers its challenges. The third section summarizes the central Deweyan elements of meliorism and the practical starting point (stance), arguing that both are *only* possible in a pragmatism which retains the concept of "experience." The chapter concludes by inferring that, overall, the main challenge posed (to Dewey) is the creation of new strains of neopragmatism which lack the potency necessary to connect with everyday ethical, social, and political realities.

RORTY'S CHALLENGES TO DEWEY

For many years, Rorty posed Dewey's biggest challenge; his fame as an analytic philosopher vaulted his heterodox interpretations beyond many more seasoned and painstaking scholars. And while Rorty certainly elevated Dewey's stature—an unquestionably positive outcome, in my view—his dominance also filtered how many would approach Dewey and the CPs. But Rorty's interpretations have done more than merely provoke Americanists (like me) to "set the record straight." Along with Putnam's work, they have informed the agendas of contemporary philosophers wishing to develop "pragmatist" rubrics.[4] Prominent among these is Brandom. A doctoral student of Rorty's at Princeton, Brandom was deeply influenced by Rorty, calling him "the great neopragmatist of his generation." (Williams and Brandom 2013, 378) To appreciate present challenges, I begin with Rorty's neopragmatist interpretations of Dewey; these will provide a general basis for understanding newer pragmatisms, including Brandom's.

Good Dewey, Bad Dewey

One fundamental challenge Rorty posed concerned the unity of Dewey's philosophy. Dewey was nothing if not methodical, so while many can debate his contribution's significance, few dispute its coherence. Empirical, critical, and reconstructive, Dewey provided deep, detailed accounts ranging over natural, logical, psychological, educational, moral, political, and aesthetic domains. Rorty's Dewey, however, is a profoundly *self-divided*—and so, *divisible*—figure. There is a "good" and "bad" Dewey. Good Dewey is therapeutic, playful, imaginative, practical, and rhetorical; bad Dewey is constructive, serious, systematic, theoretical, and metaphysical. In Rorty's view, Dewey never reconciled these tensions:

> Throughout his life, [Dewey] wavered between a therapeutic stance toward philosophy and another, quite different, stance—one in which philosophy was to become "scientific" and "empirical" and do something serious, systematic, important, and constructive. ... Dewey never quite brought himself to [see] ... that philosophy's mission, like that of therapy, was to make itself obsolete.
>
> (Rorty 1982, 73, 82)

Rorty used these divisions as pivots for his "strong misreading" of Dewey (see Rorty 1982, 151). By excising retrograde elements (more on these in a moment), Rorty's improvised Dewey sported radical and *therapeutic* views which could artfully converse with Rorty's other heroes (Nietzsche, Wittgenstein, Quine, Sellars, Foucault, etc.).

Various reactions arose to Rorty's readings. Some took them not as *guides* but as constructive *uses* of Dewey for liberal ends (e.g., Voparil 2014); others saw Rorty *developing* a nascent *eliminativist* seed in Dewey, empowering Deweyans to "kick away the ladder," à la Wittgenstein (e.g., Conway 1999); still others denigrated them as cavalier and reckless readings in which "unwittingly but inexorably, Rorty threatens to undo Dewey's work, rather than carry it forward" (Gouinlock 1995, 87).

Experience

Rorty also, famously, challenged Dewey's central notion, experience. Toward the end of his life, Rorty said "I regard [Dewey's theory of experience] as the worst part of Dewey. I'd be glad if he had never written *Experience and Nature*" (Rorty 2006, 20) This is quite a statement. Experience developed Dewey's (and James's) thesis of mind-body continuity while maintaining the reality of both; experience meant an ongoing and co-constitutive mental-physical process, itself in transaction with larger contexts (natural, cultural, historical, and semiotic). Phenomenologically, much experience is "had" or "undergone," though (critically for survival—and philosophy) experience is also "known" or "reflective." Dewey endeavored to be empirical about experience, analyzing it both historically and phenomenologically. Besides offering analyses of experience's "generic traits," Dewey saw it as a way to return philosophy to everyday life—and wisdom. A philosophy of experience would renew cultural criticism and help breathe new life into education, aesthetics, morality, and religion.

Rorty would have none of this. He argued: Dewey's writings on experience were misdirected, vague, and superfluous to his critical and instrumentalist projects; his antidualism critiques were sufficient for cultural change, but his metaphysical descriptions of existence ("nature," "experience," etc.) were foolish lapses into an old philosophical hubris seeking *the thing itself*.[5] Dewey (and James) mistakenly believed that pragmatist epistemology needed to accommodate Darwinian biology by inventing some kind of vitalism—some "experience" to help mediate mind and world. But doing that made them miss the opportunity to eliminate metaphysics and simplify truth by tying truth to mere future *usefulness* rather than future *experience*. Their era, alas, lacked the (yet undeveloped) "linguistic turn," and they unwittingly toted metaphysical baggage of which philosophers now are free:

> I see it as the great virtue of Davidson's linguistification of Dewey's antirepresentationalism that it enables us to get rid of "experience" as the name of such an intermediary [between organism and environment]. It describes causal transactions between the environment and the linguistic behavior of speakers which are mediated only by, e.g., nerves and light waves.
>
> (Rorty 1995a, 219 n.10)

About this point, Rorty was fairly consistent: there are *causal* relations (sensory contacts with the world), and there are *rational* relations (among sentences), but there is nothing *intermediate* between them (including "experience"). As early as 1970, he denied "experience" was coherent, writing "The notion of a non-linguistic awareness is simply a version of the thing-in-itself—an unknowable whose only function is paradoxically enough, to be that which all knowledge is about." (Rorty 1970, 204) The common view "that awareness comes first and language must follow along and be adequate to the initial awareness" was "in fact, a remnant of what Sellars called the Myth of the Given" (Rorty 1970, 205).[6]

While Rorty was not discussing Dewey (or the pragmatists) in that piece, he might as well have been. His position is the same—all awareness is, as Sellars put it, a linguistic affair. As Steven Levine points out,

> Since Rorty follows Sellars in thinking that to possess a concept requires being able to use a word, for him conscious awareness is therefore bound up with the use of

language. This is the Sellarsian doctrine of psychological nominalism . . . [where] even the awareness of such sorts, resemblances, and facts as pertain to so-called immediate experience is presupposed by the process of acquiring the use of language.

(Levine 2010, 578)[7]

As we will see, Rorty celebrates his student's same move, writing, "Brandom can be read as carrying through on 'the linguistic turn' by restating pragmatism in a form that makes James's and Dewey's talk of experience entirely obsolete" (Rorty 1998, 122).

Language, then, cures the "experience" hangover and refashions pragmatism. Had Dewey taken the linguistic turn, he would made Rorty's move by resisting the urge to connect the causal-sensory with the rational-propositional.[8] And while Rorty *knows* that Deweyan experience is *not* the old-fashioned "given" (raw imprints on consciousness from cognitive content), it is nevertheless too close for comfort.[9] Had he foregone experience altogether, Dewey could have seen (with Wittgenstein and Sellars) that "there is no way to come between language and its object" and that philosophy "can only answer the question: can we perspicuously relate the various vocabularies we use to one another, and thereby dissolve the philosophical problems that seem to arise at the places where we switch over from one vocabulary to another?" (Rorty 1998, 127). Thus Dewey would have been tuned to the linguistic key of Rorty and Brandom, that is, to the notion that "philosophy can never be anything more than a discussion of the utility and compatibility of beliefs—and, more particularly, of the various vocabularies in which those beliefs are formulated" (Rorty 1998, 127).

As we will see, Brandom accepts Rorty's claim about Dewey (that "experience" is foundationalist backsliding), and about pragmatism (that its nobler aims are best extended by linguistic methods). Still, as other critics have pointed out, the challenge posed to Dewey by the loss of experience is enormous.[10]

Objectivity, Warrant, Truth, and Method

Rorty's efforts to repudiate realist (or objectivist) versions of truth found, however, a great ally in Dewey, who Rorty frequently enlisted to argue that "truth" deserves no theory and that "objectivity" is reducible to intersubjective agreement ("solidarity"). More important, for Rorty, was Dewey's "anti-authoritarianism," the view that ideas of absolute truth and reality had outlived their usefulness and were now "instruments of repression." (Rorty 1998, 77–78) Dewey's substitution of justification ("warrant") for truth suited Rorty.[11] So far, so good, from Dewey's perspective; indeed, Rortyan language of "solidarity" harbors new rhetorical possibilities for pragmatism.

Still another "bad" side to Dewey's view of warrant remained because, Rorty claimed, Dewey thought his method was *better* insofar as it was *more likely* to lead to truth.[12] This was bad faith, Rorty argued; Deweyan "warrant" (and its generators, "inquiry," "situation," and "scientific method") reeks of bankrupt metaphysics. Again, anything worth saving should instead be translated into a linguistic vocabulary.[13]

Rorty's criticisms complemented his attacks on experience; together they implied that *much* of central value to Dewey can simply be ignored. Rorty writes: Dewey's "whole idea of 'analysis of methods' is misconceived, and thus ... 'logic' ... as Dewey conceived of it, is a subject not worth developing" (Rorty 1985, 41). As with experience, questions regarding "methods" or "inquiry" or "situations" are better investigated via *linguistic practices*. We should *not* be asking (with Dewey and other epistemologists) "What method do scientists use?" Rather, Rorty says, we should realize that "Galileo was using some terminology which helped, and Aristotle wasn't. Galileo's terminology was the only secret he had—he didn't pick that terminology because it was 'clear' or 'natural,' or 'simple,' or in line with the categories of the pure understanding. He just lucked out" (Rorty 1982, 193). Dewey mistakenly sought a "method of critical intelligence"— none exists. Rather, "we muddle through as best we can" seeking to be "experimental, nondogmatic, inventive, and imaginative" without expecting (or trying for) certainty. *Pace* Dewey, it is fruitless to try teaching a "*methodical* way of being inventive and imaginative" because "method" promises more than Dewey "could offer—something positive, rather than the merely negative admonition not to get trapped in the past" (Rorty 1995a, 92).

BRANDOM'S NEOPRAGMATISM

Having examined Rorty's challenges to Dewey, I turn to Brandom. Brandom's stature in mainstream analytic philosophy is well established; with Putnam's recent (2016) death, he is the most productive and prominent neopragmatist alive. To sketch Brandom's challenges to Dewey, I start with the following preliminaries: (a) Brandom's angle of vision—his view of philosophy and his own role qua philosopher; (b) the gist of his relevant projects (inferentialist, pragmatist); and (c) the fit between Dewey, pragmatism and his own philosophy. These preliminaries permit an assessment, (d) regarding the challenges posed to Dewey.

Brandom and Philosophy

As William James reminds us, understanding a philosophy requires appreciating the individual who is also a philosopher; seeking out that "essential personal flavor in each one of them," James says, "is the finest fruit of our own accomplished philosophic education." For whatever universality their system promises, "what it is—and oh so flagrantly!—is the revelation of how intensely odd the personal flavor of some fellow creature is." (James 2000, 21) While I lack space to consider Brandom's biography, perhaps his take on philosophy's *general* mission can convey enough "personal flavor" to illuminate some affinities and differences from Dewey.

What is philosophy for Brandom? What needs to be understood? Above all else, understanding humans as *reasoners* is central:

> I am concerned to understand us as creatures defined by living in a normative space of reasons ... [and to explain] how we are linguistic creatures who use inference, argumentation, reasons. ... What's distinctive of human beings, which is radicalized, as I would see things, by the insight of analytic philosophers, is that language is the site of social normativity.
>
> (Williams and Brandom 2013, 374, 375, 380)

We possess, Brandom thinks, a special kind of self-consciousness, an

> awareness of ourselves as specifically *discursive* (that is, concept-mongering) creatures. [Philosophy's] task is understanding the conditions, nature, and consequences of conceptual norms and the activities—starting with the social practices of giving and asking for reasons—that they make possible and that make them possible.
>
> (Brandom 2009, 18)

Methodologically, philosophy's task is "an expressive and explicative one ... [to] make explicit how things are and what we are doing" (Brandom 2009, 18).

Unlike Rorty, who had a love-hate relationship with professional philosophy, Brandom is at peace: "For my own view, I think it's a good thing that philosophy became professionalized. It's done better what it does" (Williams and Brandom 2013, 395). Though Brandom is temperamentally inclined toward analysis and system-building, he is openminded about the various directions others' work might take. So, while "we are the kind of being whose self-conception is essential to our selves," he is open to the idea that "these different self-conceptions correspond to different aims for political activity. And they correspond to different conceptions of philosophy" (Brandom 2009, 18–19).

Inferentialism

Brandom is best known for his "inferentialism" or "inferentialist semantics." It aspires "to articulate something like a *logic* of the relations between meaning and use." (Brandom 2014, 65) Its motivating insight is that the traditional analyses of meaning are backwards; rather than understanding pragmatics as dependent on semantics, which in turn depends on syntax, Brandom argues that we can only provide an adequate account of semantics by first developing a normative pragmatics. As he puts it,

> [P]hilosophical reflection on us as rational creatures must deploy not only *logical*, but also *normative* concepts. The latter have the expressive job of making explicit what it is we are doing in engaging in discursive practices, applying concepts, and

exercising our sapient consciousness. For what we are doing is claiming authority
and undertaking responsibility, altering our commitments and entitlements in ways
that depend on what is a reason for what.

(Brandom 2009, 13)

The emphasis on practice is part of Brandom's pragmatism, of which more in a
moment; what is important, he explains, is that by rooting our understanding of
meaning and language in existing practices, inferentialism's value reaches *beyond*
those only interested in scientific discourse—toward fictional, religious, or political
discourse, too. "What philosophers need to do, and have been doing since Socrates,"
Brandom says, "is making explicit those inferences that are implicit in the concepts
that we use" (Williams and Brandom 2013, 385). By making concepts more explicit,
agents can become more self-conscious and critical of practices or norms that are
presently deficient.[14] Brandom's inferentialism, then, promises to be more *useful* than
the alternative (representational) semantics, because it is germane to wider arrays of
practical applications.[15]

Anglophone and Pragmatic Traditions: Reconciliation and Synthesis

However complicated Brandom's inferentialism—the logical, symbolic, and even dia-
grammatic details which make up its organizing principles—it is part of a larger historical story Brandom tells to explain why his neopragmatism should supersede earlier
systems. In this context much commentary on Dewey and pragmatism occurs; it pays to
glimpse its contours.

Brandom's strategy is to analyze historical tensions between Anglophone and
Pragmatist traditions, selecting what is compatible and valuable and then grafting
those with others drawn from German idealism. In his story, "pragmatism" means,
narrowly, CPs (e.g., Peirce, James, and Dewey), and more broadly "fundamental
pragmatism" (including late Wittgenstein, early Heidegger, Rorty, and Putnam).
While clearly frustrated over lingering antagonisms (especially from Anglophones),
he seeks common ground.[16] His "pragmatic semantic analysis" seeks to synthesize
traditions.

What do the traditions contribute? Analytic philosophy focused upon the semantic
relations between "vocabularies," seeking "whether and in what way one can make sense
of the meanings expressed by *one* kind of locution in terms of the meanings expressed
by *another* kind of locution" (Brandom 2014, 57). Most significant were "empiricist" and
"naturalist" vocabularies, whose analyses generally aimed to relate "base" with "target"
terms. An "empiricist" might appeal to *how the table appears* (a "base" vocabulary of
a phenomenalistic type) while trying to account for that appearance, that is, *what the
table actually is* (a "target" vocabulary constructed, with the help of logic, out of the base
vocabulary).[17]

Pragmatism (in Brandom's more catholic sense) contributes by challenging this analytic project in the mid-twentieth century, displacing "from the center of philosophical attention of the notion of <u>meaning</u> [semantics] in favor of that of <u>use</u> [pragmatics]" (Brandom 2014, 59; emphasis in original). Here, the Prime Mover for Brandom is Wittgenstein, whose influence informs both Sellars and Quine. Sellars, for example, criticized the empiricist program "on the basis of what one must *do* in order to *use* various vocabularies, and so to count as *saying* or *thinking* various things," and he argued (a point of signal importance to Brandom's later work) that "*none* of the various candidates for empiricist base vocabularies are practically *autonomous*, that is, could be deployed in a language game one played though one played no other." (Sellars quoted in Brandom 2014, 59) In other words, Sellars was arguing that the "proposed empiricist base vocabulary is not *pragmatically* autonomous, and hence not *semantically* autonomous. Observational vocabulary is not a vocabulary one could use though one used no other" (Brandom 2014, 96). Brandom attributes "an even broader pragmatist objection" to Quine, insofar as he attacked "the very notion of <u>meaning</u>" presupposed by both the empiricist and, indeed, the whole analytic semantic project. Quine's "methodological pragmatism" argues that "the whole point of a theory of meaning is to explain, codify, or illuminate features of the *use* of linguistic expressions" (Brandom 2014, 60).

But compared to the classical pragmatists, Brandom argues, Quine's attack upon the analytic project fell short. For while "Quine thought one could save at least the naturalist program by retreating semantically to the level of reference and truth-conditions," CPs such as James and Dewey already saw the new emphasis upon *use* could furnish "more sweeping sorts of semantic revisionism" (Brandom 2014, 60). Their revision was "more sweeping" in part because it shifted naturalistic *object* talk to talk about discursive *subjects*—on active *doings, abilities, practices*—all in ongoing dynamic and social environments; in other words, the CPs' "naturalism" encompassed far more than did traditional science and its objects.[18]

Still, Brandom sees *Wittgenstein* as more important qua pragmatist than the CPs because he went further in prioritizing *use* over *meaning*.[19] Moreover, Wittgenstein was also skeptical about whether it is even possible to isolate and privilege a *general kind of use*—such as "describing, stating facts, or representing states of affairs"—a move important to the analytic project (Brandom 2014, 61). Wittgenstein's doubt that such uses could be isolated put, he thought, the whole notion of meaning-as-isolable in jeopardy.[20]

Overall, these variegated pragmatist challenges to the analytic project highlight the *dynamism* of linguistic practice for Brandom, one evoking the rich embodied, historical, and contingent context of our discursive acts. But the lesson Brandom draws is not a stark either/or:

> I do not think we are obliged to choose between these approaches. They should be seen as complementing rather than competing with one another. Semantics and pragmatics, concern with meaning and concern with use, ought surely to be understood as aspects of one, more comprehensive, picture of the discursive.

> (Brandom 2014, 64)

Again, the crucial (Wittgensteinian) pragmatist insight is to look a vocabulary's *uses* to explain its meaning—"the practices by which that meaning is conferred or the abilities whose exercise constitutes deploying a vocabulary with that meaning" (Brandom 2014, 65). At the same time, the CPs can benefit from "the insight of analytic philosophers" by seeing "that language is the site of social normativity" and recognizing "just how transformative language is" (Williams and Brandom 2013, 380).

Hopefully, this cursory sketch of Brandom's synthesis of Anglophone and Pragmatist philosophies provides insight into how he would improve (constructively challenge) Dewey and CP: by amplifying the linguistic turn. Additionally, Brandom's project integrates the "rationalisms" of Kant and Hegel (post-processing by CP). The product, as we will see, is a new form of pragmatism ("linguistic pragmatism") combining the best of Anglophone, CP, and German idealist philosophies.

Toward a More Rationalist Pragmatism

The last section reviewed Brandom's synthesis of Anglophone and CP approaches to language noting that, for him, Wittgenstein's contribution qua pragmatist is the most important. But Brandom aims at more than a new philosophy of language; he is developing a new pragmatism, *tout court*, that promises to move beyond Dewey toward a "more specifically inferentialist pragmatism" informed by "a return to pragmatism's roots in German idealism" (Brandom 2014, 29). This rationalist (a.k.a. "linguistic") pragmatism would accomplish a kind of grand synthesis: "As Kant synthesized empiricism and rationalism, and the pragmatists synthesized naturalism and empiricism, I'm suggesting that a way forward from the pragmatists is to synthesize pragmatism and rationalism— in the form of the rationalist response to the demarcation question." (Brandom 2014, 29)[21] I will examine Brandom's neopragmatist invention in a moment; first, we need to quickly look at the Kantian and Hegelian contributions.

Kant and Hegel

Kant is a key ingredient for Brandom's pragmatist renovation, particularly how Kant demarcates the *discursive* in normative terms. For Kant, roughly, our judgments and intentional actions *commit* us to *doing* certain things, to being *responsible* in a certain way. We are *rationally* responsible insofar as we are able to justify our practical and theoretical commitments in ways that show (a) we understand what we are doing and (b) what the consequences might be. We must also be able to (c) critically revise commitments discovered as incompatible. This "normative turn" teaches the CPs the important lesson that human (sapient) discursive judgments and actions are categorically different from animals (sentient). Unlike animals, we can integrate our judgments into a whole, "a systematic, *rational* unity, dynamically created and sustained by drawing *inferential* consequences *from* and finding *reasons for* one's judgments, and rejecting commitments incompatible with those one has undertaken" (Brandom 2014, 7). Because reasoning also involves others, this is simultaneously a social responsibility.

Kant's second lesson for CP, Brandom says, was his "pragmatist methodology." Overturning the then-dominant order of explanation (concepts → judgments → syllogisms), Kant argues that "the minimal unit of *responsibility* is the judgment" and it is *that* unit that "one can invest one's authority in, commit oneself to" as part of a larger, rational whole (Brandom 2014, 8). Judgments are also, on Brandom's reading, "the minimal units of awareness and experience" (Brandom 2014, 8). Concepts should be understood analytically, in light of their eventual role in judgments.[22] The pragmatic basis for conceptual analysis should be clear, now; for if the interpretation of certain concepts relies on their function *for* judgments—and if judgments are interpretable insofar as they implicate what one must *do in the future* ("downstream" as Brandom likes to put it) then we can see that *what a concept is*, fundamentally, is *what it could do*, the "force" it has. For Brandom, that is a profoundly pragmatic insight.[23]

Hegel is Brandom's other central German idealist contributing to CP. Very briefly, in Brandom's narrative, Hegel begins naturalizing the normative linguistic commitments to which Kant drew attention. Hegel made clear that rational and linguistic norms are not only evident in our concrete sociocultural practices, they are also, in turn, *shaped by* those practices. "Normative statuses of responsibility and commitment," Brandom writes, "are *social* statuses: creatures of our practical attitudes of taking or treating each other *as* responsible and committed" (Brandom 2014, 29). This clearly designates immanent-practice as the source of our norms (rather than transcendent-reason) and puts to rest the supposition that norms are eternally fixed. Hegel set them into perpetual, creative evolution.

Empiricism and Experience

In Brandom's account, the CPs further transformed these idealists' advances (language's normative pragmatics and dialectical culture-churn) in ways that produced new and more complementary forms of naturalism and empiricism.[24] CPs such as Dewey took Kant's insight about concepts (as normative commitments) and Hegel's insight about sociality (as the immanent mode shaped by/shaping concepts) and adapted them to emerging statistical and Darwinian approaches in science. The result was new forms of explanation which looked predominantly toward a contingent and probable future rather than the necessary and exceptionless past. This organismic approach saw "habits" driving development, both for individuals ("learning") and species ("evolution"), with neither pledging more than probable regularities.[25]

The CPs recasting of nature and natural explanation was, of course, a recasting of empiricism. For Dewey and others, the experimental method was not restricted to lab samples and field expeditions—it applied to theorizing itself. It was "just the explicit, principled distillation of the selectional learning process that is the practical form common to intelligent creatures at all stages of development" (Brandom 2014, 11). Dewey's name for this process was, Brandom says, "experience," which transformed the "inner light" of a disembodied Cartesian consciousness to the "work" done (with effort and intention) by an agent attempting to adapt to challenges. As Brandom puts it,

Earlier empiricists had thought of experience as the occurrence of conscious episodes that provide the raw materials for learning, via processes such as association, comparison, and abstraction. For the pragmatists, experience is not an *input* to the learning process. It just *is* learning: the process of perception and performance, followed by perception and assessment of the results of the performance, and then further performance, exhibiting the iterative, adaptive, conditional-branching structure of a Test-Operate-Test-Exit loop.

(Brandom 2014, 12)

As Brandom construes it, what experience delivers is not "knowledge," exactly, but "understanding" which provides "a kind of adaptive attunement to the environment, the development of habits apt for successful coping with contingencies. It is knowing *how* rather than knowing *that*" (Brandom 2014, 12).

Experience and Fundamental Pragmatism

This take on experience is important for it helps us understand why Brandom believes, with Rorty, that "experience" can be *excised* from pragmatism entirely. While the CPs attempt to demystify (naturalize) experience—to "exhibit *discursive* intentionality as a kind of *practical* intentionality"—makes them "fundamental pragmatists" (Brandom's wider sense), ultimately they *can* leave experience behind (Brandom 2014, 15). For once it is understood that what is crucial is just our practices (especially our *discursive* acts and capabilities), then it becomes possible to make explicit what distinguishes sapients like us from sentients using a linguistic—but not an experiential—vocabulary.[26]

Brandom's explication of Deweyan experience does a couple of things. First, it celebrates the renovation of empiricism made possible (in part) by Dewey's deployment of experience as a "doing"—an *active* engagement with the environment using *predictive, adaptive,* and *selective* intentionality able to supersede the moderns' *passive* reception of ideas (or sense data). Second, it rereads Deweyan experience in a way that makes it integrable into his inferentialist project. To do this, Brandom pulls apart experience's "double-barreled" nature—as had/known (or undergoing/doing)—and makes it *rational*:

> The pragmatists' conception of *experience* is recognizably a naturalized version of the rational process of critically winnowing and actively extrapolating commitments, according to the material incompatibility and consequence relations they stand in to one another, that Kant describes as producing and exhibiting the distinctive synthetic unity of apperception.

(Brandom 2011, 8)

Deweyans must take note of the *challenge* issued here; viz., that experience has been cut in half. No longer an "undergoing" at all, Brandom's "experience," as Mark Johnson notes, is "primarily about rational inquiry and justification . . . that limits it to matters of belief, judgment, appraisal, and reason-giving (albeit, conceived as modes of action).

The experience that Brandom's pragmatist philosopher is interested in consists of experiences of assertion, reasoning, justification, and appraisal" (Johnson 2014, 17).

In a bit I will explore the upshot of this move; for now we should ask why Brandom treats experience this way. It seems, as mentioned a moment ago, that he aims to eliminate it by, as Rorty put it, making talk of it entirely obsolete. He *wants* to eliminate it because, as Levine rightly points out, he believes experience, even as modified by CP, (a) gives rise to the Myth of the Given and (b) is bound up with an inadequate ("instrumentalist") view of meaning and truth—one that focuses myopically on "desire" and the "downstream" (future consequences).[27] Let us consider these two concerns quickly.

Regarding (a), the Given is a danger because while experience qua undergone is not the (evil) conceptual given of modern epistemology, it still lies *somewhere* between "non-conceptual causal stimuli" and "conceptual responses" because it is not merely a cause of judgment but is yet able (Brandom thinks) to justify them.[28] This is something Brandom's system is designed to avoid.[29]

Regarding (b), Brandom faults the CPs for their narrow instrumentalism, a "school of thought centered on evaluating beliefs by their tendency to promote success at the satisfaction of wants" (Brandom 2002, 40). This also holds, Brandom believes, for the way CPs assess the "normative assessments of the truth of beliefs" (Brandom 2002, 51). This interpretation of CP and Dewey attracted *withering* criticism, but I have not yet discovered evidence Brandom modified these claims about Dewey.[30]

One final reason Brandom rejects the CP notion of experience—which may overlap with the reason given as (a)—regards experience as a "representation." Strategically, Brandom wishes to align Dewey (as a fundamental pragmatist) with his inferentialism; thus Brandom needs to reject any elements of Dewey construable as falling into *representationalist* bad faith—experience as "*die Sache Selbst*," in Rorty's poisonous phrase. So, by eliminating all experience, Brandom safeguards his linguistic pragmatism against one more Achilles' heel.[31]

Linguistic Pragmatism

Ultimately, Brandom is driving toward what he names a "rationalist" or "linguistic" pragmatism. Rooted in "fundamental pragmatism" (insisting that what we know or explain theoretically comes from more primary, practical uses and abilities), there are two principles that together create linguistic pragmatism. The first he names "methodological pragmatism"—it insists the motivation for associating meanings, extensions, and so on with linguistic expressions is to codify proper uses. The second principle is "semantic pragmatism," a "use-functionalism about meaning." It simply says that "in a natural language, all there is to effect the association of meanings, contents, extensions, rules, or other semantic interpretants with linguistic expressions is the way those expressions are *used* by the linguistic practitioners themselves" (Brandom 2014, 21).[32]

Linguistic pragmatism, then, is the view that "engaging in specifically *linguistic* practices is an essential necessary condition for having thoughts and beliefs in a full-blooded sense" (Brandom 2002, 47). This is also a "rationalist pragmatism" because it explains our linguistic practices (our discursive intentionality) in terms of our already implicit practical intentionality, "the kind that includes practices of making claims and giving and asking for reasons" (Brandom 2011, 31). But notice: the practices of claim/reason giving are no longer at base *conceptual*; following Sellars and Rorty, awareness—thinking—is a *linguistic* affair. Rationalist pragmatism *is* linguistic pragmatism because they partake of his more general "lingualism"—the "commitment to understanding conceptual capacities (discursiveness in general) in terms of *linguistic* capacities" (Brandom 2014, 19). Thus, Brandom says, "the philosophical way forward from the ideas of the American pragmatists must be a linguistic pragmatism, allied with the later Wittgenstein and the Heidegger of Division One of *Being and Time* (Brandom 2004b, 14).

BRANDOM'S CHALLENGES TO DEWEY

Finally, we can consider how Brandom's neopragmatism challenges Dewey, both constructively and obstructively. I focus on the most pivotal challenges; some others may be found in the notes.

Constructive Challenges

Brandom has paid sustained attention and respect to CP and Dewey; this overarching and positive aspect must be mentioned, first. He genuinely admires their progressive positions: their evolutionary naturalism, their conception of experience as *Erfahrung* (rather than *Erlebnis*), the priority they place upon semantics (over epistemology), rooted in the pragmatic-normative; their anti-intellectualism about knowledge (i.e., knowing *how* is equally important to knowing *that*) (Brandom 2004b, 14–15). So the first constructive challenge to Deweyans may simply be to appreciate the wide and deep sympathy expressed by this analytically trained philosopher.

A second constructive challenge is to appreciate Brandom's way of expanding pragmatism's "tent" via consonances identified in "non-canonical" figures such as Wittgenstein, Heidegger, and especially Sellars. These thinkers, as Richard Bernstein also points out, echo key pragmatic themes—such as repudiating the Given—shared by the CPs.[33] By illuminating connections between figures rooted in diverse traditions, Brandom provides Deweyans with powerful examples of alternate strategies toward common goals not always recognized *as* common.

Perhaps the most important constructive challenge lies in the detail and depth of Brandom's pragmatically oriented inferentialist semantics. It provides, as Levine notes, an impressive account of the top layer of our discursive activity; pragmatists would benefit by grappling with tools developed "to articulate, in a pragmatically satisfying way, this stratum of our intellectual lives" (Levine 2012, 138; see also Pihlström 2007, 276). And, as Pihlström suggests, Brandom's "distinctively pragmatist account of conceptuality and normativity" is useful for pragmatists who need "a conception of what normativity actually amounts to." Brandom can do this because he connects "pragmatism with the Kantian-Hegelian tradition" (Pihlström 2007, 279). This approach, Pihlström ventures, helps to both soften naturalism (render it less scientistic) and defend normativity against "non-pragmatists or reductive naturalists who want to explain [it] away" (Pihlström 2007, 280, 284).

Obstructive Challenges

Nevertheless, Brandom's work also presents various obstacles to fecund interpretations and uses of Dewey. One suspects that Brandom inherited some of Rorty's proclivities as a "strong misreader." If true, then, like Rorty, his use of Dewey is also a double-edged sword. I focus on several areas where caution is advised: experience, language, warrant, and instrumentalism.

Experience (and Language)

The preceding section reviewed Brandom's view of experience (à la CP and Dewey) and highlighted two key linguistic/rationalist positions he holds: first, that having thoughts and beliefs require specifically linguistic practices and, second, that claims of knowledge or meaning cannot repose (or even refer back to) experience that is non—or pre-linguistic. The dilemma Brandom forces, as Mark Johnson notes, is one where experience "is either already a linguistic construct, or else it has no standing in selecting out which concepts, truth claims, and modes of knowing are sanctioned by communities of inquirers" (Johnson 2014, 16). Insofar as Brandom talks about experience at all—and, then, mostly in a historical vein—it is as learning-feedback loops consisting in reasoning, justification, assertion, and so on. But experience in Dewey's more *primary* sense of "undergoing" is something Brandom can do without.[34]

One implication of Brandom's eliminativist view is that it obstructs some fruitful paths Dewey provided for relating thought and language. Johnson, building upon Dewey, argues we *can* think about the world *without* language for a couple of reasons. First, one need not accept Brandom's Sellarsian idea "that all thought is linguaform—linguistically expressible as a set of concepts, propositions, and their relations" (Johnson 2014, 19). Instead, Johnson provides an account where "meaning" can be "significant and normative" though *not* dependent on language.[35] There are, he argues, "meaning-making processes besides linguistic ones" and moreover "there is no language without our experience of language" (Johnson 2014, 19).[36] In other words, linguistic practices always "involve the whole relevant physically and culturally embodied situation or context in which you are operating" (Johnson 2014, 25). Once this is understood, Johnson notes, the "language" versus "experience" tension operative in some neopragmatists is dissolved.[37] Levine makes the complementary point that Brandom's approach attenuates the richer notion Dewey has of "practice," especially insofar as it is *embodied*.[38]

A second effect of Brandom's rejection of experience is that it obscures Dewey's capacious account of "language," which includes a range of experiential, meaning-making processes. As elaborated in Johnson's "embodied cognitive" approach, "linguistic meaning is rooted in a vast pre-conceptual and non pre-linguistic play of meaning structures" (Johnson 2014, 20). This helps explain how we have meaningful experiences that both generate inferences and open on to new ones, "not just on rare occasions (through, say, poetry and art), but much of the time in our lives when we grasp the meaning of what is happening in ways that do not rely on words" (Johnson 2014, 23).[39] This is a more expansive account of language—"language in its widest sense," as Dewey puts it—that can include sign relations between nearly anything standing for anything else. (See 1938, LW 12:27–28, 51–52.) In other words, some meanings are attributable to more than the fact we are individual perceivers or speakers; this is the sense in which *experience* connotes something communal—that is, *culture*.[40]

In short, there are many ways "experience" does more work and is more indispensable than Rorty or Brandom will admit. Where their account emphasizes how language makes sapients *dis*continuous from the rest of nature, CP strives instead for naturalistic continuities.[41] (I have indicated only a couple of interpretations of experience which facilitate such continuities. See, also, Pappas 2014, Margolis 2016.) Still, while I lack space to prove anything here, one whiffs in Brandom some lingering affection for *what might amount to* experience—for example, his notion of *thick*, "feedback-regulated practices"—and I half expect to see "experience" resurrected at some future point.[42] At various points, it seems that Brandom quietly lauds what other pragmatist scholars have championed—namely, how pragmatist accounts of inquiry-in-situations are not radically subjectivistic but simply flexible and nonabsolutistic forms of realism.

Instrumentalism: Belief and Desire

Brandom's account of CP and Deweyan instrumentalism is another obstructive challenge. As critiques have been mentioned, I will indicate how more accurate readings avoid the pitfalls Brandom thought, mistakenly, he had identified.

Brandom criticizes pragmatists for looking "only at the role of beliefs in justifying or producing actions" and ignoring "their role in justifying or producing further beliefs" (Brandom 2011, 30). Larry Hickman refutes this, pointing out that in *many* works Dewey argues that "beliefs are capable of producing not simply actions, which lack generality, but also new habits or beliefs" (Hickman 2013, 7; see also Hildebrand 2016, Dewey 1922, 1932, 1938, and works in education). Another problem supposedly infecting pragmatists' instrumentalism regards desire. Brandom reads Dewey, for example, as willing to replace "truth" with warrant, where warrant rests upon mere desire-satisfaction (Brandom 2011, 51). However as Hickman (and Putnam) point out, Dewey's rather more sophisticated account discriminated between *immediate* and *considered* desires, as well as between the *object* and *end* of desire. The end is not mere satisfaction, Hickman points out, but for the re-harmonization of a larger, fractured situation.[43] Understanding this nonsubjectivistic, experimentalist notion of "satisfaction" is a *basic* takeaway from Dewey's *Logic* (see 1938, LW 12: 21), and Hickman considers it possibly "the most astonishing of all Brandom's misreadings of classical pragmatism" (Hickman 2013, 12). Putnam comments that Brandom's misunderstanding (about the relation of belief-evaluation and desire) was "precisely the misunderstanding Dewey referred to when in a letter to James in 1903 he complained about the misunderstanding that pragmatism has no room for purely intellectual interests!" (Putnam 2002, 64).

Warrant

The errors Brandom makes about Deweyan belief and desire inform another error, on warrant. Brandom frames the issue thus: Just as pragmatists were too focused on desire (and the actions which would satisfy desire), they concoct a limited conception of "warrant" which is concerned only with "consequences" (what is "downstream") rather also factoring in earlier "circumstances" ("upstream") (Brandom 2004b, 12). But again, Dewey's supposed myopia is easily corrected by the texts. As Hickman points out, for Dewey "it is a mistake to attempt to determine meanings in the absence of context" (Hickman 2007, 110). And, specifically regarding warrant, Hickman notes that meaningful language has *logical* import *just because* it is determined by prior inquiries: "*As inquirential* it looks *upstream* to the results of logical work already done and thus to judgements that have been warranted as assertible" (Hickman 2007, 110; see also Dewey 1916, MW 10:354). Inquiry *in Dewey's own explication* looks both upstream (to previously established meanings which bear on present problems) and downstream (toward possible consequences). Brandom, thus, fails "to recognize the dynamism of Dewey's theory of inquiry" and so "seems to have misunderstood one of the key features of his version of pragmatism" (Hickman 2007, 113).[44]

CONCLUSION: WHAT IS AT STAKE
FOR DEWEYAN PRAGMATISM?

"Meaning is wider in scope as well as more precious in value than is truth, and philosophy is occupied with meaning rather than with truth."
— Dewey, "Philosophy and Civilization" (1927, LW 3:4)

Pragmatism is, and always will be, a big tent. Arising from multiple traditions (Kantian, Hegelian, utilitarian, German experimental psychology, and others), pragmatism spawned multiple shoots; its goals, methods, applications, and vocabularies will surely remain variegated for the foreseeable future. I have no objection to that. This chapter has tried only to specify the ways two recent neopragmatisms challenge what is central to John Dewey. To conclude, I briefly outline the major costs of overlooking the *obstructive* challenges posed by neopragmatism.

The Language Versus Experience Issue Is Really about Meliorism

As discussed, the neopragmatist dismissal of "experience" has generated a lot of debate, especially among Deweyans. While Bernstein clearly indicated that pragmatism cannot subsist *without* experience, he lamented that the competing orientations (linguistic versus experiential) had become a "reified dichotomy" and that taking sides had become a "cottage industry." He urged all pragmatists to forego such industry by appropriating what is best, thinking through differences creatively, and formulating a more robust pragmatism (Bernstein 2004, 77). To my mind, we push past the dichotomy by recognizing that the larger thing at stake is meliorism, a stance originary to CP and one which seeks to make philosophy less "monkish" and more oriented toward culture at large.[45] What I hope to briefly indicate in the remainder of this chapter is that *meliorism is so intertwined with experience that any pragmatism (linguistic or otherwise) which claims to be melioristic must have some commerce with experience.* In other words, the tension between language and experience can be resolved *if* linguistic pragmatism either disclaims meliorism for itself *or* finds some way to retract its disavowal of experience.

What is meliorism? At root, it simply means that the world can and should be made better by human effort. Meliorism stands against the certainty implied by both optimism and pessimism because certainty dampens or disables active efforts to make a practical difference. In other words, meliorism delegitimates theories which advocate or imply taking permanent moral holidays. Philosophical theories such as CP are guided by this stricture and insist that philosophy connect, sooner or later, with everyday life.[46]

If one agrees with this premise—that pragmatism must be melioristic—then a number of corollaries follow. Pragmatists must avoid methods and goals which isolate philosophy from making a difference in the world (e.g., skepticism, scholasticism, nonfallible system-building); philosophy must strive to connect theory with practice and be especially intentional about selecting those practices which protect or create value. Philosophy, in other words, must *care*.

For many pragmatists, care has required changing the foci of philosophy; for example, "epistemology" and "metaphysics" have long occupied a central place in traditional philosophy, but their connection to lived experience was, at best, remote. Pragmatists such as Dewey argued that these (and other areas) needed to be reconstructed. He shifted epistemology (concerned with abstract accounts of knowledge and truth) toward *learning* (specific patterns of habit and inquiry); concomitantly, he criticized the long speculative tradition in metaphysics-as-system-building (concerned with, e.g., time, substance, God) and argued for more empirical, concrete, and critical analyses of contemporary natural and cultural experiences. With such moves, Dewey nudged philosophy toward more direct and critical engagement with societal institutions (educative, scientific, governmental) empowered to make things better.

Experience and the Practical Starting Point

What lies behind such shifts is what I called in the introduction the "metaphilosophical bedrock" of CP—its stance. This is a caring stance, an insistence upon meliorism, which adopts for philosophy *itself* a practical starting point (PSP).[47] Dewey is most explicit about this, at one point calling it "intellectual piety." Such piety, Dewey says, requires a "respect for experience" that includes "an enforced attention to its joys and sorrows." Respect for others—each considered as a center of experience—is "a precondition of the direction of life and of tolerant and generous cooperation among men" (1925, LW1:393). This kind of experience, this PSP, is *integral* to any pragmatism I would call "fundamental." In contrast to Brandom's version, however, I insist that experience is indispensable not only because it is *learning* (a "Test-Operate-Test-Exit loop" in Brandom's reductive description) but because it is how persons *flourish* and even survive. As John McDermott notes,

> Experience … is potentially pedagogical, if we but pay attention. Everything we perceive teems with relational leads, many of them novel, and therefore often blocked from our experience by the narrowness and self-defining circular character of our inherited conceptual schema. *The human task is to let our experiences speak to us in all their manifold vagueness.* Naming, defining, cataloging, quantifying are activities of a last resort and have justification only for purposes of organization—necessary for enabling us to move on to still richer fields of experience—or of survival.
>
> (McDermott 2007, 147, emphasis mine)

The pedagogical lesson of experience—the intellectual piety or PSP—changes *how theory itself is understood and used.* Theory must be undertaken with a new mindfulness, one *as much* about openness toward novel encounters as about anticipation of arranged experiments. That openness requires that the system-building philosopher be courageous, not only to resist the siren-song of certainty and rational closure but to remain ready to *scrap* the system because it has become detached—*because it is profoundly unable to help in contexts which themselves are not philosophical.* To nevertheless persist in system-building which is extraneous to contemporary life is—and this is important—to indulge in the kind of idol worship against which pragmatism *initially* revolted. What is more, it leads to that philosopher's own personal impoverishment.[48]

Pragmatism, Ethics, and Activism

This way of seeing "experience"—not only as double-barreled (doing-and-undergoing) but also as how philosophy itself should be done—profoundly influences how to interpret Dewey and *what to do with* the philosophical equipment he left us. For example, Erin McKenna and Scott L. Pratt combine Dewey's philosophical goals (of dualism defiance and culture criticism) with an understanding of experience as pedagogical (in

McDermott's sense) to produce a Deweyan "philosophy of resistance"—to challenge dogma and systems of domination, to recognize the pluralism of experience, and to innovate alternative ways to think and live.[49]

Philosophy's mission, for Dewey, is, in its own way, Socratic: to help a culture engage in criticism. Sometimes criticism mitigates intergenerational tensions; sometimes it negotiates cultural differences threatening to fracture a nation—or cross an ocean. For McKenna and Pratt, Deweyan pragmatism is valuable when it reaches past the debates among old, dead, white guys—for example, the cast of Brandom's *Tales of the Mighty Dead*. Those figures *are* among our intellectual forebears, no question; some of their issues transcend time and place, and we grapple with them today. Still, McKenna and Pratt argue persuasively that the time has come to expand philosophy by appreciating, more sensitively, where we practically *start*. There is, they argue, a "tradition of resistance" rooted in an American history bound up with invasion, domination, and the struggle for liberation among a "plurality" of different cultures and traditions. Developing this tradition, philosophically, requires framing issues in new ways, linguistically; but more important, it requires actively *including* diverse voices with experiences and expressions that have been seriously heard or considered—for example, African Americans, Latino(a)s, women, Native Americans, and a variety of novely gendered identities. When, for example, McKenna and Pratt, investigate the Native American Kicking Bear, they take a philosophical approach that begins *not* from theoretical linguistics (as Brandom might) but from an episode in American history which played out clumsily and brutally due to the radically different conceptions of agency which separated the indigenous Sioux from westward-expansionist Americans. By first listening to Kicking Bear's concrete had (felt) experience, they are modeling what Dewey called "intellectual piety." The payoff is both a more nuanced historical understanding of a practical event and a new philosophical model (of agency), which is now instrumentally available for future use.[50]

This is but one illustration. Many other pragmatists are utilizing Dewey's pluralistic account of experience to make progress on educational, ethical, and political issues. It is a way of philosophizing that encourages and cultivates openness and respect toward others too often missing in more abstract and systemic approaches. Such openness directly fulfills a fundamental precept of pragmatism, meliorism, and this is why cutting experience out, as Bernstein says, makes pragmatism "gutless."

In a recent interview, Brandom is asked about a criticism Rorty made about his work; Rorty complained that Brandom's pragmatism lacked aspiration to a greater public calling—that it was too professionalized and was "only speaking to a few people inside philosophy" (Williams and Brandom 2013, 394). Brandom replied that Rorty was effectively correct—while he does care about what is going on in the world, he did not see his work as Rorty saw his own—as equipped to contribute to conversations which could affect events outside philosophical discourse. (Indeed, one is hard pressed to find much discussion of either ethics or education in Brandom's voluminous writings.) He expressed comfort with his role as professional philosopher and his aspiration to address issues of what he calls "high culture." At the same time, Brandom *also* stated he believed that "the ultimate endpoint of the philosophy of language should be a political theory" (Williams and Brandom 2013, 394). If he ever wants to fulfill that challenge, at least qua pragmatist in Dewey's tradition, he might reconsider his exclusion of experience and meliorism from his deeply impressive and intricate account of language. In the meantime, the challenge for Deweyans is to continue the dialogue with these neopragmatisms, always aiming to discover and build upon common ground.

NOTES

1. A foundational text regarding the notion of a "stance" in philosophy is Browning (1990). See also the entry by Gregory Pappas in this volume.

2. Dewey and James were beholden to at least two professions, philosophy and psychology; education constitutes, perhaps, a third for Dewey.

3. Because even CP has resisted a homogenized definition, I do not attempt to force one upon this motley crew. As I write, there is no entry for "neopragmatism" in the most recent *Encyclopedia of Philosophy* (2nd edition, 2006), *Stanford Encyclopedia of Philosophy* (online), or *Internet Encyclopedia of Philosophy* (online). For two recent encyclopedia entries see Pihlström (2013) and Hildebrand (2012). The so-called new or neo pragmatists have pushed back against what Maria Baghramian (2008) has called Rorty's "sociological account of truth," emphasizing ways which neopragmatism can, *pace* Rorty, admit more realist-leaning construals of "truth" and "objectivity." As Steven Levine encapsulates it, "While the new pragmatists agree with Rorty's 'humanist' and 'antiauthoritarian' notion that the norms that inform inquiry are *our* norms rather than the world's, they demur from his suggestion that this requires us to give up the notions of truth and objectivity. Implicit in human practices of dialogue and inquiry are norms of correctness, of getting things right, that go beyond what a community takes to be justified in the here and now. In being guided by such norms, we are not simply trying to convince a dialogical partner that our view of something is justified, as Rorty thinks, we are also trying to get our mutual beliefs of that something right" (Levine 2008: 167). See, also, Levine (2010) for related new pragmatist arguments (from Bjørn Ramberg, Jeffrey Stout, and Brandom) that such emphases are actually *consistent* with Rorty's *own* project; Baghramian (2008) is insightful regarding the Rorty-Putnam tension over cognitive and discursive norms and whether Brandom successfully adjudicates it.

4. For an in-depth look at Rorty's career-long entanglement with Dewey, see Hildebrand (In press); see also Voparil (2014). For a sustained examination of Rorty and Putnam, see Hildebrand (2003) and Pihlström (2004).

5. Rorty writes that Dewey "was never to escape the notion that what he himself said about experience described what experience itself looked like, whereas what others said of experience was a confusion between the data and the products of their analyses. . . . Other philosophers produced dualisms . . . because they 'erected the results of an analysis into real entities.' But a nondualistic account of experience, of the sort Dewey himself proposed, was to be a true return to *die Sache selbst*" (Rorty 1982, 79–80).

6. A somewhat fuller context helps makes Rorty's point clearer: "I think that the putative intuition that we will continue to have the same experiences no matter which words we use is in fact a remnant of what Sellars called the Myth of the Given—the view that

awareness comes first and language must follow along and be adequate to the initial awareness. . . . Indeed, the notion of a non-linguistic awareness is simply a version of the thing-in-itself—an unknowable whose only function is paradoxically enough, to be that which all knowledge is about. What does exist is the causal conditions of a non-inferential report being made. But there is no unique vocabulary for describing these causal conditions. There are as many vocabularies as there are ways of explaining human behavior" (Rorty 1970, 204–205). I am grateful to Levine for drawing my attention to this passage.

7. However, Levine points out, Rorty goes *beyond* Sellars in the following way: "Because of his reductive interpretation of what Sellars's psychological nominalism entails, Rorty takes it that the critique of the perceptual given results in . . . [a critique that] drains sense-impressions of the immediate qualitative and phenomenal aspects that were taken to be their hallmark by the classical tradition. . . . So when we respond to certain of our own inner causal states by deploying a concept . . . the character of our response is not de-termined *by the ontological nature of the states themselves* but by the vocabulary and the concepts that provide for the possibility of our giving a direct non-inferential report of these states" (Levine 2010, 579).

8. Levine: "[For Rorty] we know through higher-order philosophical reflection that there is causal constraint, but we can't, on pain of reinstating the myth of the given, answer the question of how this constraint rationally affects our view of the world. . . . Since we cannot explain how rational constraint from the world gets into the justificatory process in the space of reasons, and only items in this space can justify other items in this space, in thinking about knowledge we must ignore the 'vertical' relation of mind to world and focus exclusively on the result of 'horizontal' conversational or justificatory processes" (Levine 2010, 582).

9. Rorty's discomfort extends (beyond "experience") to Dewey's "pattern of inquiry," where an initial, *felt* phase leads to and "guides" inquiry (as the *pervasive quality* of the overall problematic situation). That, for neopragmatists like Rorty and Brandom, fails to respect the gap dividing (in Sellars' phrase), the "space of reasons" and the "space of causes."

10. A huge literature criticizes Rorty about Deweyan experience. One could do worse than start with Richard Bernstein who argues, *pace* Rorty, that Deweyan experience was *not* incoherent, was incorporative of Hegel and reflected a keen historical sense of how experience had changed over time (Bernstein 2010, 144, 145, 150). Joseph Margolis shows that Rorty's (and Brandom's) embrace of Frege and Sellars pushes both away from Dewey *and* Darwin insofar as both sought to depict an experiential *continuity* between humans and animals as concept-users. "Apart from some affinity for 'inferentialism' which they share with Brandom, Frege and Sellars also share an avoidance (at least implicit) of anything like a 'Darwinian' account of concepts with regard to the continuity between animal and human intelligence. Hence, if John Dewey (whom Rorty nominally favors) is the paradig-matic specimen of a philosophical pragmatist, then neither Frege nor Sellars (or indeed Donald Davidson or Rorty or Robert Brandom) can be proper pragmatists, since they all oppose as forcefully as possible any Darwinian account of concepts—essential to Dewey's conception of pragmatism. In this sense, reviewing Brandom's program, we may claim to be obliquely appraising the reasonableness of Rorty's transformation of classic pragma-tism" (Margolis 2002a, 118).

11. Here, Rorty links Dewey and Davidson: "Dewey (and, I have argued, Davidson) have suggested that there is little to be said about truth, and that philosophers should explicitly

and self-consciously confine themselves to justification, to what Dewey called 'warranted assertibility'" (Rorty 1999, 32).

12. About this, Rorty writes, "Philosophers have hoped to . . . [link] the temporal with the eternal, the transitory human subject with what is there anyway, whether there are humans around or not. That can be done if philosophy can show that the better justified a belief is, the more likely it is to be true. Failing that, it might try to show that a certain procedure for justifying belief is more likely to lead to truth than some other procedure. Dewey hoped to show that there was such a procedure; Davidson, and more pragmatists, seem to me right in suggesting that there is not" (Rorty 1999, 35).

13. E.g., Rorty thought Dewey's "indeterminate situation" was merely one where it "is not clear what language to use for describing what is going on" (Rorty 1985, 42–43) while Dewey's "inquiry" was us "fitting whatever comes down the pike into our previous experience and beliefs as best we can" (Rorty 1995b, 152).

14. "Having made that inference explicit," Brandom writes, "now you're in a position to be critical about it. Logic, and philosophical vocabulary more generally, is the organ of semantic self-consciousness. We can say and ask for reasons for or against something, to make explicit the inferential norms that are implicit in the concepts that we're reasoning with and that shape our thought" (Williams and Brandom 2013, 386).

15. Brandom writes, "There are many things we do with language, and on this inferentialist model, I give a set of formal tools for helping us to think about the different inferential roles that expressions can play. That's a vast, ambitious project, but perhaps you can see how it brings philosophy of language and formal semantics into contact with issues about language and human life that are of more traditional philosophical importance than the representational model lends itself" (Williams and Brandom 2013, 386).

16. Brandom writes, "There are good reasons on both sides for adopting somewhat adversarial stances, but I think that when we examine them more closely it becomes possible to see the outlines of a common project, in the service of which the two camps might find themselves joining forces" (Brandom 2014, 56). The problem, he notes, is that "the formal, mathematically inspired tradition of Frege, Russell, Carnap, and Tarski ... [and the] model-theoretic and possible worlds semantics" still oppose those "anthropological, natural-historical, [and] social-practical" approaches to inquiry which aim at both "demystifying our discursive doings ... and ... deflating philosophers' systematic and theoretical ambitions regarding them" (Brandom 2014, 64).

17. "The generic challenge," Brandom writes, "is to show how what is expressed by the use of such target vocabularies can be reconstructed from what is expressed by the base vocabulary, when it is elaborated by the use of logical vocabulary" (Brandom 2014, 58).

18. Brandom encapsulates the issue regarding naturalism as follows: "When we think today about naturalism, we tend to think of it first as a thesis about the *objects* represented by different potentially puzzling kinds of concepts: semantic, normative, probabilistic concepts, and so on. The question is how to see what those concepts represent as part of the natural world, as conceived by fundamental physics, or some special sciences, or even just by unproblematic empirical descriptive concepts. By contrast to this object naturalism, the American pragmatists were subject naturalists. Fundamental pragmatism counsels looking first to what discursive subjects are *doing*, to the abilities they exercise, the practices they engage in. If a naturalistic story can be told about *that*, it might well be that no questions remain that should trouble the naturalist" (Brandom 2014, 14–15).

19. Not only does Wittgenstein doubt the univocal use of singular terms (for picking out objects), and declarative sentences (for stating facts), he also "goes on to deny, in effect, that such uses even form a privileged center, on the basis of which one can understand more peripheral ones. ('Language,' he says, 'has no downtown')" (Brandom 2014, 60–61).

20. Brandom writes, "If we think of the uses as *very* different ... if we think of linguistic practice as a *motley*, of uses as not coming in a simple, or systematic, or even determinate variety, then the very idea that there is such a thing as *meanings* ... becomes contentious and in need of justification both in general and in each particular case" (Brandom 2014, 61). On Brandom's reading, Wittgenstein's "family resemblance" strategy suggested an alternative, *functional*, way to sort linguistic practices and vocabularies (e.g. "game," "description," "observation," etc.)—a more effective pragmatist approach amounting to "a straightforward denial of the possibility of semantic analysis in the classical sense" (Brandom 2014, 62).

21. "The demarcation question," Brandom writes "is definitional. How are *linguistic* practices and abilities ... to be distinguished from nonlinguistic ones? ... What sets them apart from prelinguistic or nondiscursive practices?" (Brandom 2014, 23, 25).

22. "So if one is to understand judging also as the application of concepts," Brandom writes, "the first question one must ask about the contents of those concepts [is] how the use of one or another concept affects those rational relations among the judgeable contents that result. This methodological inversion is Kant's commitment to the *explanatory primacy of the propositional*" (Brandom 2014, 8).

23. "The *functionalism* about conceptual contents that consists in understanding them as functions of judgment, which is the practical expression of methodological commitment to the explanatory primacy of the propositional, is motivated by an overarching methodological *pragmatism* according to which semantics must answer to pragmatics (in a broad sense)" (Brandom 2014, 9).

24. "The classical pragmatist versions of naturalism and empiricism," Brandom writes, " ... fit together much better than the versions that historically preceded and succeeded them. ... Both the world and our knowledge of it are construed on a single model: as mutable, contingent products of statistical selectional-adaptational processes that allow order to pop to the surface and float in a sea of random variability" (Brandom 2014, 13).

25. At both levels, Brandom notes, "selection" operates to serve adaptation, and all CPs shared the general view that, at any level, "There is no guarantee that any such accommodation will succeed permanently. As with habits learned by individuals, some of the law-like regularities may prove more robust and others more fragile" (Brandom 2014, 11).

26. In other words, Brandom thinks, it helps push CP further away from representationalism— since emphasizing the abilities and practices needed for believing and judging elevates our "implicit, know-how, skill, practical ability, practice side" over the older "explicit, conceptual, rule, principle, representation side" (Brandom 2014, 15).

27. Levine's (2012) essay gives a masterful summary and analysis of Brandom, along with defenses of Dewey.

28. Brandom's worry, as Levine points out, is that Deweyan "Experience is therefore something pre-judgmental, and therefore for Brandom pre-conceptual (insofar as concepts are essentially components of judgments), which, in having significance or sense, is nonetheless able to justify perceptual judgments rather than just cause them. On this conception then, experience has both causal and the conceptual properties that makes it fit to serve as an *interface* between mind and world. But in doing so it falls prey to the Myth of the Given" (Levine 2012, 134).

29. See Levine: "Brandom . . . avoids the Myth of the Given by *epistemically neutralizing* sense-impressions [making them merely causal rather than epistemically authoritative], by substituting for them pre-personal causal response dispositions that play no role in the space of reasons. As Brandom puts it, in placing 'the interface between non-conceptual causal stimuli and conceptual response at the point where environing stimuli cause perceptual *judgments*' his view avoids 'the Myth by seeing nothing non-judgmental that could serve to *justify* perceptual judgments, rather than just to *cause* them' " (Levine 2012, 134, quoting Brandom 2002a, 93–94).

30. See, for example, Putnam (2002), Sami Pihlström (2007), Richard Bernstein (2010), Larry Hickman (2013), and Levine (2012, especially 131–132). About Brandom's reading of Dewey and the CPs, Hickman calls it an " almost breathtaking misreading," Pihlström calls it "unfortunately naive," and Putnam calls it "a caricature." Putnam's criticisms were made contemporaneously in reply to Brandom's assertion. Putnam expressed remorse that "serious students of pragmatism have spent almost a century rebutting the sort of travesty of what the classical pragmatists thought that Brandom relies on, and it must not be allowed to go unrebutted now" (Putnam 2002, 59). While all three CPs (Peirce, James, and Dewey) believed that "all knowledge of fact presupposes value judgments" *none* believed anything like what Brandom suggests: that they "either (1) identified what is true with what promotes success in the satisfaction of wants; or (2) thought that we should forget about truth and just concentrate on finding what promotes success in the satisfaction of wants; or (3) thought that what promotes success in the satisfaction of wants is more important than what is true?" (Putnam 2002, 60).

31. Brandom writes, "Fundamental pragmatism is opposed to a *representationalist* order of explanation: one that begins with a notion of representational content, and appeals to that to make sense of what it is knowing and acting subjects do. That is not to say that pragmatists in this sense can have no truck at all with the concept of <u>representation</u>. It is to say at most that talk of representation should come at the end of the story, not the beginning" (Brandom 2014, 16). I am unsure whether Brandom's "representationalist" concern (with experience) overlaps with his Myth of the Given concern. This is due to the fact that while Dewey clearly immunizes his "experience" from the Given (which Brandom acknowledges), it remains unsafe for Brandom. Thus his objection to experience cannot *just* be its proximity to Givenness; it carries, too, an air of bad-representation.

32. Here are a couple of illustrations. For "methodological pragmatism," we might associate the use of "girl" with "female humans under eighteen years old" because in codifying certain *uses* as "proper" depends upon which ones we wish to reaffirm (e.g., avoid insults, indicate maturity, designate for benefits, etc.). For "semantic pragmatism," the idea is that our meanings (in a natural language) refer back to those practices or abilities we exercise that confer those meanings. If I say, for example, "Pass the salt," then we understand that meaning as governed or conferred by certain social and physical actions at a dining table.

33. As Bernstein notes, Peirce's 1868 rebuke of Cartesianism augurs Sellars' attack on the Myth of the Given and makes plausible Brandom's big tent approach. "Viewing Peirce's project and the pragmatic movement in this manner," Bernstein writes, "enables us to see the plausibility of Brandom speaking of Wittgensteinian and Heideggerian pragmatism. . . . Both of them are critical . . . to the critique of the Myth of the Given. They argue that subjectivism leads to unavoidable aporias" (Bernstein 2010, 18–19).

34. Brandom writes, "Indeed, though the word 'experience' is mentioned in the 750 pages of *Making It Explicit*, it is never used. I want to say, with Laplace, 'Je n'ai pas besoin de cette

hypothèse la.' The explanatory work done by what Sellars has taught us is the *theoretical* concept <u>experience</u> can be done without postulating a layer of potentially evidentially significant (hence conceptually articulated) states in between purely causally occasioned and physiologically specifiable responses to environing stimuli and full-blown perceptual judgments" (Brandom 2004a, 2).

35. Johnson writes, "Meaning in this sense reaches down deep into our ways of inhabiting and making sense of our world. It involves feelings, emotions, images, and qualities. When it gets expressed through language, it may achieve depth and scope of meaning that is not otherwise possible without language. But there is meaning there nonetheless, and sometimes it is a fullness of meaning that cannot be grasped by any linguistic structure" (Johnson 2014, 22).

36. See Dewey regarding situations where feelings "are no longer just felt. They have and they make *sense*; record and prophesy" (1925, LW1:198).

37. "One important consequence of this," Johnson writes, "is that you cannot use 'language' as a contrast term to 'experience,' in any way that pretends to deny experience a crucial role in our acts of thinking, meaning-making, communicating, problem-solving, and creativity" (Johnson 2014, 25).

38. In Brandom, Levine writes, "the practice that has priority over representation is the *discursive practice* of drawing inferences, and the norms of correctness implicit in this practice are norms that govern *conceptual activity* . . . But this makes it impossible for him to understand a richer sense of practice that is often at work in the classical pragmatists, namely, the *bodily* practices, habits, and skills through which subjects inhabit and cope with the environment, physical and social. For many pragmatists, the body is not a just an instrument that carries out orders that have their origin in the discursive realm, rather for them a subject's sensori-motor engagements with a physical and social environment already have *sense* before the operations of discursive reason get into the act. This type of bodily engagement is our basic way of 'being-in-the-world', and our representational dealings with things emerge from this background" (Levine 2012, 128).

39. Johnson argues "that the meaning of any thing, sign, action, or event is the experiences it in some way points to, enacts for us, or leads us to consider. . . . [T]here is meaning wherever and whenever some thing or event can stand as a sign of some experience. Natural languages are perhaps our most remarkable tools for establishing and stabilizing these sign relations, but they are not the sole means for shared meaning. Objects, qualities, and events can serve the signification function by employing various perceptual, motor, and affective processes, some of which are not language dependent" (Johnson 2014, 20, 21; see also Johnson 2007).

40. About "experience" being a term connoting "culture," Thomas Alexander notes, "One of the persistent causes of critical misinterpretation of Dewey is the understanding of his use of "experience" as if he were writing in the British empiricist tradition. . . . Dewey is quite explicit that he never held this view. . . . In other words, "experience" in Dewey's work is synonymous with "culture" as the term is used in anthropology: the structured practices and symbol systems by which human beings exist together as communities in the world and not as remote, individual mentalistic observers of sensations or holders of propositions" (Alexander 2014, 77).

41. Cf. Brandom: "What one misses most in the [classical] pragmatists—at any rate separates them from us—is that they do not share the distinctively twentieth-century philosophical

concern with *language*, and with the *dis*continuities with nature that it establishes and enforces" (Brandom 2011, 55).

42. See, for example, *Between Saying and Doing*, where Brandom describes how "thick" practices seem to be functioning as intermediaries between the categories "causal" and "reason-giving." He refers this idea back to the CPs for whom, he writes, "Feedback-governed practices are 'thick,' in the sense of essentially involving objects, events, and worldly states of affairs. Bits of the world are *incorporated* in such practices, in the exercise of such abilities. In this regard they contrast with words and sentences, considered merely as sign-designs or items in the natural world, which are 'thin' in that they can be specified independently of a specification of the objects or states of affairs they refer to or represent" (Brandom 2008, 178–79; virtually the same text appears in Brandom 2011, 17). A bit later he lauds Dewey for seeing that "the *thickness* of pragmatist semantics [was] one of its cardinal advantages over its more traditional thin rivals" and for recognizing his "functional system ... is *capacious enough* to include the environment being acted on and in as well as the organism transacting with it" (Brandom 2011, 18).

43. Hickman clarifies: "Desire is the result when some activity of the organism is blocked. But when blockage occurs, deliberation is called for. Objects are presented in imagination as solutions to the difficulty, and therefore as desired. But, Dewey reminds us, the end of desire is not to secure the object of desire. It is rather to reunite the disparate elements of the fractured situation and thereby to regain an ordered whole ... [to effect] a reconstruction of the total situation in such a way that the relative harmony and equilibrium of the [larger situation] is once again restored" (Hickman 2013, 9).

44. Levine concurs, noting that Brandom's criticism is a fault that *all* the CP's avoided "quite easily" (Levine 2012, 131).

45. As Thomas Alexander writes, "Thus, one of the major issues that divides 'us' (experiential pragmatists or cultural naturalists) from 'them' (linguistic pragmatists) is that 'they' think we are holding on to some archaic piece of epistemology when we have dropped epistemology altogether and the 'intellectualist' view of experience that comes with it and embraced instead an existentially embedded view of cultural existence that turns toward life, the lived body, culture and history. With this comes a different form of philosophical praxis than that esteemed by the Anglophone tradition. All debates will be pointless misunderstandings until this is recognized. By 'experience' we mean how people live in the world, how they inhabit nature together" (Alexander 2014, 79–80).

46. On Dewey and meliorism, see McDermott (1993) and (1998, 157).

47. On the starting point, see also Dewey (1925, LW1:366ff.), Browning (1998), Hildebrand (2003, 2011).

48. McDermott is incisive on this point: "To be open to the experience of another is of double salutary significance. Not only do we apprise, learn, and participate in diversity but, perhaps paradoxically, we come to appreciate the novelty, singularity, and preciousness of our own experience. To participate in the plurality of experiences is personally explosive for it trims our sails and curtails our arrogant provincialism while it widens our horizons and indirectly sanctions those experiences which are mundane to us, but exotic to others" (McDermott 2007, 163).

49. McKenna and Pratt write, "What then is a philosophy of resistance? First, it is one that challenges dogma and settled belief from a perspective that recognizes the pluralism of experience and the value of growth and change. It is resistance in an expected way because

it takes on systems of domination as a necessary step in a process of liberation. At the same time, American philosophies of resistance do not rest with criticism but actively work to establish alternative ways of thinking and living. It is a philosophy of the sort offered by Kicking Bear, for example, that begins outside the philosophical commitments of the dominant culture" (McKenna and Pratt 2015, 6).

50. Describing this new model, McKenna and Pratt write, "Pluralism of experience makes it clear that there are also different conceptions of agency (of who acts). . . . At the center of concern in all of these understandings of agency is the recognition that theories of who agents are intersect with the experience of agency to define individuals. The received account from Western philosophy recognizes human beings alone as agents, individual and autonomous. At the same time, indigenous philosophy recognizes human beings and other nonhuman beings as agents. Within the American tradition philosophers including Peirce, Royce, Addams and Deloria (among others) recognize both individuals and communities as agents. The centrality of agency has long been part of the American tradition of resistance. Agency is what was transformed in the mainstream in the wake of the Civil War and redefined—or reasserted practically—as part of the work of philosophers as well as activists. . . . The reemergence of indigenous sovereignty reasserted the agency of communities and their places and reframed the idea of recognition in the present world" (McKenna and Pratt 2015, 377).

WORKS CITED

Citations of John Dewey's works are to the thirty-seven-volume critical edition published by Southern Illinois University Press under the editorship of Jo Ann Boydston. In-text citations give the original publication date and series abbreviation, followed by volume number and page number. For example: (1934, LW 10:12) is page 12 of *Art as Experience*, which is published as volume 10 of *The Later Works*.

Series abbreviations for *The Collected Works*:

EW *The Early Works* (1882–98)

MW *The Middle Works* (1899–1924)

LW *The Later Works* (1925–53)

Alexander, Thomas M. 2014. "Linguistic Pragmatism and Cultural Naturalism: Noncognitive Experience, Culture, and the Human Eros." In *Special Issue: Language or Experience: Charting Pragmatism's Course for the 21st Century*. Edited by David L. Hildebrand. *European Journal of Pragmatism and American Philosophy*, vol. 6, no. 2, 64–90.

Baghramian, Maria. 2008. "Three Pragmatisms: Putnam, Rorty, and Brandom." *Poznan Studies in the Philosophy of the Sciences and the Humanities*, vol. 95, no. 1, 83–101.

Bernstein, Richard. 2010. *The Pragmatic Turn*. Cambridge: Polity.

Brandom, Robert B. 2002a. "Non-Inferential Knowledge, Perceptual Experience, and Secondary Qualities: Placing McDowell's Empiricism." In *Reading McDowell: On Mind and World*. Edited by Nicholas H. Smith, 92–105. London: Routledge.

Brandom, Robert B. 2002b. "Pragmatics and Pragmatisms." In *Pragmatism and Realism*. Edited by James Conant and Urszula M. Zeglen, 40–58. London: Routledge.

Brandom, Robert B. 2004a. "No Experience Necessary: Empiricism, Non-inferential Knowledge, and Secondary Qualities." Unpublished paper. http://www.pitt.edu/~brandom/mie/2421-w4.html

Brandom, Robert B. 2004b. "The Pragmatist Enlightenment (and Its Problematic Semantics)." *European Journal of Philosophy*, vol. 12, no. 1, 1–16. http://doi.wiley.com/10.1111/j.0966-8373.2004.00196.x

Brandom, Robert B. 2008. *Between Saying and Doing: Towards An Analytic Pragmatism.* Oxford: Oxford University Press.

Brandom, Robert B. 2009. *Reason in Philosophy.* Cambridge MA: Harvard University Press.

Brandom, Robert B. 2011. *Perspectives on Pragmatism: Classical, Recent, and Contemporary.* Cambridge, MA: Harvard University Press.

Brandom, Robert B. 2014. "Analytic Pragmatism, Expressivism, and Modality." Nordic Lectures in Pragmatism 3. Helsinki, Finland. 30 September–2 October 2014. Nordic Pragmatism Network. www.nordprag.org

Browning, Douglas. 1990. *Ontology and the Practical Arena.* University Park, PA: Penn State University Press.

Browning, Douglas. 1998. "Dewey and Ortega on the Starting Point." *Transactions of the Charles S. Peirce Society*, vol. 34, no. 1, 69–92.

Conway, Daniel W. 1999. "Of Depth and Loss: The Peritropaic Legacy of Dewey's Pragmatism." In *Dewey Reconfigured: Essays on Deweyan Pragmatism.* Edited by Casey Haskins and David Seiple, 221–246. Albany: SUNY Press.

Dewey, John. 1980 (1916). *Essays in Experimental Logic.* MW 10.

Dewey, John. 1981 (1925). *Experience and Nature.* LW 1.

Dewey, John. 1983 (1922). *Human Nature and Conduct.* MW 14.

Dewey, John. 1979 (1932). *Ethics.* MW 7.

Dewey, John. 1986 (1938). *Logic: The Theory of Inquiry.* LW 12.

Emerson, Ralph Waldo. 1903 (1893). "Natural History of Intellect and Other Papers." In *The Complete Works of Ralph Waldo Emerson: Natural History of Intellect, and Other Papers (vol. 12).* Boston, New York: Houghton, Mifflin, 1–110.

Gouinlock, James. 1995. "What Is the Legacy of Instrumentalism? Rorty's Interpretation of Dewey." In *Rorty and Pragmatism: The Philosopher Responds to His Critics.* Edited by Herman J. Saatkamp, 72–90. Nashville, TN: Vanderbilt University Press.

Hickman, Larry A. 2007. "Some Strange Things They Say about Pragmatism: Robert Brandom on the Pragmatists' " "Semantic 'Mistake.' " *Cognitio*, vol. 8, no. 1, 105–113.

Hickman, Larry A. 2013. "Robert Brandom's Three Strikes." Paper presented at Philosophical Revolutions: Pragmatism, Phenomenology and Analytic Philosophy 1895–1935, Conference. University College Dublin, Dublin, Ireland, June 21.

Hildebrand, David L. 2003. *Beyond Realism and Antirealism: John Dewey and the Neopragmatists.* Nashville, TN: Vanderbilt University Press.

Hildebrand, David L. 2011. "Could Experience Be More Than a Method? Dewey's Practical Starting Point." In *Pragmatist Epistemologies.* Edited by Roberto Frega, 41–60. Lanham, MD: Lexington.

Hildebrand, David L. 2012. "Neopragmatism." In *New Catholic Encyclopedia Supplement 2012–13: Ethics and Philosophy.* Edited by Robert L. Fastiggi, 1062–1065. Farmington Hills, MI: Gale/Cengage Learning.

Hildebrand, David L. 2016. "The Paramount Importance of Experience and Situations in Dewey's *Democracy and Education*." *Educational Theory*, vol. 66, nos. 1–2, 73–88.

Hildebrand, David L. In press. "Rorty and Dewey." In *The Wiley-Blackwell Companion to Rorty*. Edited by Alan Malachowski. Oxford: Wiley-Blackwell Press.

James, William. 2000 (1907). *Pragmatism and Other Writings*. (Giles B. Gunn, ed.). New York: Penguin Books.

Johnson, Mark. 2007. *The Meaning of the Body: Aesthetics of Human Understanding*. Chicago: University of Chicago Press.

Johnson, Mark. 2014. "Experiencing Language: What's Missing in Linguistic Pragmatism?" In *Special Issue: Language or Experience: Charting Pragmatism's Course for the 21st Century*. Edited by David L. Hildebrand. *European Journal of Pragmatism and American Philosophy*, vol. 6, no. 2, 14–27.

Levine, Steven. 2008. "Rorty, Davidson, and the New Pragmatists." *Philosophical Topics*, vol. 36, no. 1, 167–192.

Levine, Steven. 2010. "Rehabilitating Objectivity: Rorty, Brandom, and the New Pragmatism." *Canadian Journal of Philosophy*, vol. 40, no. 4, 1–29.

Levine, Steven. 2012. "Brandom's Pragmatism." *Transactions of the Charles S. Peirce Society*, vol. 48, no. 2, 125–140.

Margolis, Joseph. 2002a. "Dewey's and Rorty's Opposed Pragmatisms." *Transactions of the Charles S. Peirce Society*, vol. 38, no. 1, 117–135.

Margolis, Joseph. 2002b. *Reinventing Pragmatism: American Philosophy at the End of the Twentieth Century*. Ithaca, NY: Cornell University Press.

Margolis, Joseph. 2016. *Toward a Metaphysics of Culture*. London: Routledge.

McDermott, John J. 1993. "Why Bother: Is Life Worth Living? Experience as Pedagogical." In *Philosophy and the Reconstruction of Culture: Pragmatic Essays After Dewey*. Edited by John J. Stuhr, 273–284. Albany: State University of New York Press.

McDermott, John J., and Anderson, Douglas R. 2007. *The Drama of Possibility: Experience As Philosophy of Culture*. New York: Fordham University Press.

McKenna, Erin, and Pratt, Scott L. 2015. *American Philosophy: From Wounded Knee to the Present*. London: Bloomsbury.

Pappas, Gregory. 2014. "What Difference Can 'Experience' Make to Pragmatism?" In *Special Issue: Language or Experience: Charting Pragmatism's Course for the 21st Century*. Edited by David L. Hildebrand. *European Journal of Pragmatism and American Philosophy*, vol. 6, no. 2, 200–227.

Pihlström, Sami. 2004. "Putnam and Rorty on Their Pragmatist Heritage: Re-reading James and Dewey." In *Dewey, Pragmatism and Economic Methodology*. Edited by Elias Khalil, 39–61. London: Routledge.

Pihlström, Sami. 2007. "Brandom Sobre Pragmatismo." *Cognitio*, vol. 8, no. 2, 265–287.

Pihlström, Sami. 2013. "Neopragmatism." In *Encyclopedia of Sciences and Religions*. Edited by Anne Runehov and Luis Oviedo, 1455–1465. Dordrecht: Springer.

Putnam, Hilary. 2002. "Comment on Brandom." In *Pragmatism and Realism*. Edited by James Conant and Urszula M Zeglen, 59–65. London: Routledge.

Rorty, Richard. 1970. "In Defense of Eliminative Materialism." In *Mind, Language, and Metaphilosophy: Early Philosophical Papers*. Edited by Stephen Leach and James Tartaglia, 199–207. Cambridge: Cambridge University Press.

Rorty, Richard. 1982. *Consequences of Pragmatism*. Minneapolis: University of Minnesota Press.

Rorty, Richard. 1985. "Comments on Sleeper and Edel." *Transactions of the Charles S. Peirce Society*, vol. 21, no. 1, 39–48.

Rorty, Richard. 1995a. "Response to Gouinlock." In *Rorty and Pragmatism: The Philosopher Responds to His Critics*. Edited by Herman J. Saatkamp, 91–99. Nashville: Vanderbilt University Press.

Rorty, Richard. 1995b. "Response to Haack." In *Rorty and Pragmatism: The Philosopher Responds to His Critics*. Edited by Herman J. Saatkamp, 148–153. Nashville, TN: Vanderbilt University Press.

Rorty, Richard. 1998. *Truth and Progress: Vol. 3 of Philosophical Papers*. Cambridge: Cambridge University Press.

Rorty, Richard. 1999. *Philosophy and Social Hope*. London: Penguin.

Voparil, Chris. 2014. "Rorty and Dewey Revisited: Toward a Fruitful Conversation." *Transactions of the Charles S. Peirce Society*, vol. 50, no. 3, 373–404.

Williams, Jeffrey J., and Brandom, Robert B. 2013. "Inferential Man: An Interview with Robert Brandom." *Symplokē*, vol. 21, no. 1, 367–391.

CHAPTER 6

PRAGMATIST INNOVATIONS, ACTUAL AND PROPOSED

Dewey, Peirce, and the Pittsburgh School

JOSEPH MARGOLIS

INITIAL AFFINITIES AMONG THE CLASSICAL FIGURES

RATHER cleverly, John Dewey contrived his birth to coincide with the publication of Darwin's *Origin of Species*, in 1859. I view the feat as a stunning confirmation of the incorrigibly dialectical nature of philosophy, even if one treats the fact as fiction. But then, by the same liberty, Charles Peirce contrived *his* birth (in 1839) to conform with the possibility that he might then have been apprenticed to his celebrated father, Benjamin Peirce, for his first lessons in philosophy and science—with time enough to escape his father's philosophical limitations and to have anticipated the significance of pre-Darwinian evolutionary intuitions. In fact, in the very year of Dewey's birth, Peirce had already come to suspect (as a boy of 20)—though for somewhat less than adequate reasons—that Kant's transcendental assumption was both conceptually unnecessary and finally indefensible, a conviction Dewey was to share (by another route) with Peirce that would become firmer and more compelling in both their lifetimes. Peirce records his conviction in an unpublished paper (dated May 21, 1859), titled "That There is No Need of Transcendentalism."[1]

Peirce never abandoned his conviction. Indeed, it became increasingly settled and more compelling; so that, nearly 50 years later (c. 1905), when the first impressions of Peirce's pragmatism and his assessment of the relationship between Kant and pragmatism began to be published, Dewey, who was already well along in his career, was able to venture a first appraisal of affinities and differences between Peirce's pragmatism and his own intuitions (quite apart from James's uncertain renderings), which led, after another

30 or so years—well after Peirce's death (1914)—to Dewey's publication of *Logic: The Theory of Inquiry* (1938, LW 12), which follows (by about four to seven years) the posthumous publication (1931–1935) of the first six volumes of Peirce's *Collected Papers*. The latter event was Dewey's first sustained opportunity to read extensive parts of both Peirce's published and previously unpublished papers on pragmatism (chiefly collected in volume 5), that bring together a version of Peirce's "pragmatic maxim" (originally proposed and published in 1878 and in Baldwin's *Dictionary* in 1902) and Peirce's compelling verdict on Kant and Kant's relationship to pragmatism (unpublished until the appearance of the *Collected Papers* but bruited in some of Peirce's previously published pieces), pointedly brought to bear on Kant's treatment of the *Ding-an-sich* and realism.

It must be noted that Dewey's *Experience and Nature* (both the original 1925 and the revised 1929 edition) was published before Peirce's *Collected Papers* appeared in print; hence, although Dewey reviewed some versions of pragmatism (under various names) around 1925, his summary view at the time was essentially drawn from his own "instrumentalism": he did in fact tend, increasingly, to avoid the use of the epithet "pragmatism" (partly to escape suggestions of unsavory expediencies but also to emphasize his own distinctive "pragmatist" account of the enrichment of experienced life (as in *Art as Experience*), which remains a unique theme in Dewey's vision, quite distinct from Peirce's and James's alternatives, particularly with the appearance of, and after, *Experience and Nature*—very probably Dewey's most important publication. In that sense, the 1938 *Logic* cannot fail to be better informed about Peirce than *Experience and Nature*: of all Dewey's publications, *Logic* is undoubtedly the best placed to signal the distinct but limited convergence between Peirce and Dewey, however sparely acknowledged, from the vantage of an entirely different vocabulary and perspective.

In any event, Peirce made an extraordinary statement about Kant, which we must ponder if we are to assess pragmatism's—in particular, Dewey's—relationship with other movements that have engaged pragmatism one way or another in defining the state of play of contemporary philosophy, future as well as past and present well beyond, say, Quine's publication of *Word and Object* (1960):

> Kant (whom I more than admire) is nothing but a somewhat confused pragmatist. A real is anything that is not affected by men's cognitions *about it*, which is a verbal definition, not a doctrine. An external object is anything that is not affected by any cognitions, whether about it or not, of the man to whom it is external. Exaggerate this, in the usual philosopher fashion, and you have the conception of what is not affected by any cognitions at all. (5.525)

Peirce, James, and Dewey, I should say, tend to agree with the thrust both of Peirce's "pragmatic maxim" and his critique of Kant, though from different vantages with different weightings and different concerns. Peirce is more "Kantian" than Dewey in adhering to a substantive conception of "real things." In *Experience and Nature* and *Logic*, Dewey warns against the fixities of canonical realism, in both constructivist and fluxive terms; hence, he was still partly attentive to some version of idealism, though opposed (to be sure) to conceptual closure of any kind. Peirce also intends a form of evolutionary openness, which affects his fallibilism and which never quite shakes off its seeming Idealist and Kantian voice, as Josiah Royce charges (Peirce 8: Ch. 3). It's only toward his last years—when he begins to replace fallibilism with his "abductive turn"—that Peirce actually escapes Kant along lines congenial to Dewey's opposition to teleologies in nature and to any salient part of Kant's Critical program.[2] These distinctions may not be enough to qualify any sufficiently articulated pragmatism, though I doubt any reliable account of pragmatism's classical forms can be convincingly formulated without their being acknowledged. (I turn shortly to the bearing of these distinctions on selected "near"-pragmatist and "anti"-pragmatist positions in our time.)

I am already prepared to suggest that with the addition of some further themes—in particular, those regarding the import of Darwinian and post-Darwinian treatments of evolution, the continuum of the animal and the human, the relationship between experience and thinking, the critique of rationalism, the preference of a fluxive world over a world governed by telic or causal invariance, the import of the mastery of language, the meaning of naturalism and realism, the analysis of personhood and the distinction of the human mind, the idea of community and the relationship between individuals and societies, historied existence, and the constructed nature of norms and normativity—we should have collected a sufficient run of additional categories adequate for distinguishing the main features of nearly every historically important philosophical movement or career, pragmatist or other.

I am speaking chiefly of Dewey, of course, but I find it necessary to advance a pointed impression of Peirce's early conjectures and principal themes: not to provide a sustained comparison between the two but to suggest important convergences and differences between them—the principal systematizing talents of the classic pragmatists. In a way, James is the connective channel between the two of them: glossing Peirce in his (James's) uniquely consequential but somewhat unreliable and idiosyncratic way and qualifying Dewey's first (imperfect) impressions of Peirce's realist conceptions. I have in mind some oblique features of Peirce's formulation of his "pragmatic maxim," included in the 1903 "Lectures on Pragmatism," which James remembers as having been delivered at the Lowell Institute but which the editors of the *Collected Papers* report as having been given at Harvard, under the auspices of the Department of Philosophy. In the first of these lectures, Peirce himself cites the original formulation in "How to Make Our Ideas Clear" (published in 1878, which apparently appears, in identical form, in French, in *Revue philosophique*, also in 1878):

> Consider what effects [Peirce affirms], that might conceivably have practical bearings, we conceive the object of our conception to have. Then, our conception of these effects is the whole of our conception of the object. (5.402)

Peirce says, in "Pragmatic and Pragmatism" (from Baldwin's *Dictionary*), that he arrived at the maxim through his reading of Kant's first *Critique* (5.3). But it is really the

Descartes that Kant himself coopts (in fashioning his notion of apperceptive unity) that Peirce addresses, more than Kant, at least on this matter.[3]

What I especially wish to emphasize is the somewhat neglected fact that, increasingly (though by very different routes), Peirce, James, and Dewey clearly converge over time in the direction of opposing conceptual closure wherever Kant would insist on it (e.g., in reading the intended advice of the "pragmatic maxim"), in construing fallibilism in any teleologically explicit way (which, as far as I can see, Peirce always opposed in its literal form—*pace* Putnam), in outflanking the epistemological regress argument (chiefly in terms of the Darwinian continuum of the human and the animal), and in the need for (and possibility of) a determinate account of the sufficient, or necessary and sufficient, conditions of objective judgment (notably, in Peirce's replacement of infinitist fallibilism by the admission of abductive gaps—i.e., specifically epistemological gaps—in the most reliable achievements of the sciences).

I daresay Peirce took the initiative here in formulating the disjunction between the transcendental reading of Kant's first *Critique* and the thrust of pragmatism's replacement. But then Dewey arrived at much the same economy by a simpler and more direct route, by subtracting the Transcendental Idealist elements of his own early lessons and turning instead in the direction of a commonsense or Darwinian "empirical" schema rather than an "empiricist" atomism, which Peirce also opposes. It is in accord with these loosely shared themes (more nominalist in Dewey's account, more realist or Scotist in Peirce's) that I find a further, distinctly Peircean element (and rationale) in Dewey's notion of his "two" logics, which so many have found baffling in Dewey's philosophy— most tellingly, Bertrand Russell, but then, also, Peirce himself. I do not mince words about the matter: there is a distinctly lame quality in Dewey's handling of the completely figurative vocabulary of his "indeterminate" or "problematic situation"; but it could easily have been cast more explicitly (in my opinion) in terms of Peirce's simpler vocabulary (and conception). For the truth is, *Peirce* himself suggests a need for a larger "logic" of life (which Darwinism obliquely favors). A similar issue appears in Robert Brandom's (2008) "logic," insofar as Brandom is drawn to melding the contributions, allusively perhaps, of the Wittgenstein of the *Tractatus*, Kant, Sellars, Carnap, and Frege with those of Dewey, the Wittgenstein of the *Investigations* (not quite accurately), Rorty, and Hegel. But then, as I shall try to show, Brandom (possibly misled in some degree by Rorty) construes philosophical semantics as both autonomous and entitled to a certain primacy over epistemological inquiry. I consider that to harbor one of Brandom's fundamental (entirely unnecessary) mistakes—betrayed, in part, we may suppose, by Rorty's papers.[4]

In any event, these seemingly passing remarks begin to collect a sort of preliminary advice about how to approach a "late" reading of Dewey, aware of philosophical developments of both the first half of the 20th century (within Dewey's lifetime) and the work of the second half of the century continuing into the first decades of the new century, which bids fair to alter our characterization of what to understand, now, by "pragmatism" in general and the dialectical role of Dewey's entire *oeuvre* among a company of "near-" and "new-fangled" pragmatisms that Dewey could hardly have anticipated.

I think here, chiefly, of analytic figures including Quine, Davidson, Wittgenstein, Sellars, Rorty, McDowell, and Brandom—of course, a company that omits Heidegger and other figures associated with existentialism, hermeneutics, and phenomenology, a collection that deserves a separate hearing, as well as figures from the second surge of pragmatism dated roughly from the 1970s and 1980s, following the running debate nominally addressed to the definition of pragmatism, embedded in the exchange between Rorty and Putnam.[5]

Anti-Kantian and Antirationalist Tendencies

What I want to affirm first—a theme barely hinted at earlier, a theme especially congenial to pragmatism and philosophies akin to, or influenced by, classic pragmatism—is the daringly fluxive reading of the dialectical nature of philosophical work. What I mean specifically is that pragmatism characteristically advances in the direction of radicalizing the dialectical (or agonistic) confrontation of opposed approaches to the resolution of problems of the kinds tallied a moment ago. What I argue is that Peirce, James, and Dewey—each in his own way—tend increasingly, toward the end of their respective careers, to adopt a practice of philosophy that opposes the presumption of any unique or strongly convergent form of argumentative method, or fixed or foundational truths in accord with which we (somehow) are able to derive demonstrable, possibly even conclusively valid, solutions deemed to be addressed to the relatively well-defined problems of philosophical inquiry. The pragmatists believe there is and can be no determinate principle of conceptual or argumentative closure in philosophical confrontation: they proceed "dialectically," in the specific sense that questions of relevance, putative progress, practical confirmation, appraisals of competing approaches and claims are to be judged always and only "archivally" (oppositionally, perhaps) rather than "foundationally" (say, from primary or primal, self-evident, synthetic *a priori*, transcendental, or necessary truths). In short, pragmatism is unconditionally opposed to *rationalisms* of such sorts without opposing *rationality*: that is, some sort of conceptually ordered intelligence, whether discursive or not.

By "rationalism," then, I understand a doctrine (akin to Kant's purpose) that holds that reason is itself a cognitive faculty capable, within determinate boundaries, of discovering truths of the sorts (just noted) bearing on our possessing a true knowledge of the natural world, an understanding of how human beings ought to control and direct their lives and behavior, and an appropriate cognitively informed grasp of the right way to resolve such questions within human limitations. The pragmatists believe the world is best viewed as a flux rather than a closed or fixed plenum of any kind, that manifests (and requires) no more than legible regularities of provisional or contingent sorts to be humanly accessible: that is, apt for application to any given sector of the world, from the vantage of one program of inquiry or another, that belongs to our "archival" memory or may be generated inventively from the known exemplars of such programs. (Our "archive" obviously includes forms of rationalism as well as pragmatism and other philosophical ventures otherwise defined.)

Accordingly, the pragmatists construe Kant's Critical method as itself a "new" form of rationalism (more or less on Kant's own terms, though Kant rejects the idea)—on the grounds that Kant's transcendentalism does indeed claim to make a cognitively pertinent contribution to a viable realism, or is itself, (as Peirce affirms) "nothing but, a confused pragmatis[m]." Transcendentalists, the classic pragmatists argue, cannot distinguish, in principle, between transcendental and empirical truths. Would-be neo-Kantians, now, often grant themselves the right to speak of "natural" or "naturalistic" (or "weakly transcendental") necessities, not otherwise confirmed. The admission is effectively tendered by Sami Pihlström (2003) for instance, who wishes to "re-transcendentize" pragmatism (admitting the qualification just mentioned). So he must be counted a "progressive" (but, it seems, also, a stalemated) innovator. Whereas John McDowell (2009) effectively applies ("quietistically," we may say, in a sense apparently borrowed from Wittgenstein) Kant's own *a priori* truths, in reviving ("naturalistically") a very strong form of the concept of the "transcendental unity of apperception," though McDowell does not claim to be (and indeed is not) a pragmatist with regard to sensory perception, perceptual knowledge, or perceptual judgment. Purportedly, McDowell "naturalizes" the transcendental but does not explain the sense in which "discursive concepts" ("concepts" *tout court*, in McDowell's sense) necessarily accompany all instances of sensory perception. For instance, McDowell never directly examines the possibility, or the import of the possibility, of "perceptual [*non*linguistic] concepts" with regard to the intelligence of unlanguaged animals, the human infant that masters language, or even fully mature enlanguaged persons; and he does not indicate what should count as compelling evidence for his own position.[6] In this sense, he must be counted a "regressive" (and unconvincing) Kantian. I hasten to add that, on both analytic and broadly Darwinian grounds, it seems impossible to deny that if discursive concepts are learned in encultured ways they are bound to depend on accessing perceptual concepts. (I cannot find the issue developed in McDowell at all—it is Aristotle's thesis, of course.)

We must not lose sight of the point of these reflections. I have suggested that, from its beginnings, the classic phase of pragmatism (notably, Dewey's undertaking) has been mortally opposed to rationalism (as just characterized)—*a fortiori*, opposed to Kant's Critical transcendentalism; but then, opposed also to Cartesian rationalism, which Kant transforms along the lines of his doctrine of the "apperceptive unity" of perceptual knowledge, which McDowell thereupon invokes against the would-be inadmissible laxity of Sellars's reading of Kant's discursivity thesis; hence, then, also opposed (at least implicitly) to Fregean rationalism applied to the natural and practical world, which, on Brandom's reading of the fragmentary clues Brandom finds in Sellars's and Carnap's attraction to Frege, may nevertheless be capable of yielding a form of "analytic pragmatism" (Brandom's characterization of his own venture and of what is common to his inferentialism and Sellars's "pragmatics" of language).

This is a rather complicated affair. One strand of my reading of the classic pragmatists features the continually strengthened habit of Peirce, James, and Dewey to treat philosophical claims and disputes as "dialectical," meaning by that (as I have explained) that, throughout their careers, they tend, increasingly, to eliminate all reliance on "foundational" (and other fixed or privileged) cognitional sources in any and all inquiries. They tend, rather, to argue (as I have suggested) "archivally," that is, by engaging whatever belongs to the history of the questions they address and to what they can draw, inventively and agonistically, from any such sources, without pretending that they have discovered or could rightly claim to discover any uniquely right way of proceeding. They simply abandon cognitive privilege of any kind. Here, I find it helpful to cite Rorty and Brandom regarding the "pragmatism" each is committed to, which, then, bears (explicitly or allusively) on the cognate commitments of figures like Sellars, Carnap, and Quine—whose own views are said to exhibit clear affinities with the "pragmatisms" Rorty and Brandom specify. (Neither Quine nor Sellars, Brandom notes, characterizes himself as a pragmatist.) Rorty's succinct proposal is:

> The question is not whether human knowledge in fact has "foundations," but whether it makes sense to suggest that it does—whether the idea of epistemic or moral authority having a "ground" in nature is a coherent one. For the pragmatist in morals, the claim that the customs of a given society are "grounded in human nature" is not one which he knows how to argue about. He is a pragmatist because he cannot see what it would be like for a custom to be so grounded. For the Quine-Sellars approach to epistemology, to say that truth and knowledge can only be judged by the standards of the inquirers of our own day ... is merely to say that nothing counts as justification unless by reference to what we already accept, and that there is no way to get outside our beliefs and our language so as to find some test other than coherence. (1979, 178)[7]

But this is no more than Rorty's usual "overkill": he's right to remind us that we cannot escape the boundaries of (may I say?) the human *Lebensform*; although even that admission concedes that we are perfectly capable of improvising reasonable departures from the status quo—certainly to exceed considerations of mere "coherence," for instance by radical revision. Rorty's verdict is much too bleak—well-nigh irrelevant, too quick, if not deliberately equivocal. It's both true and false (in different senses) that, in morality as in science, "nothing counts as justification unless by reference to what we already accept." But what we thus "accept" is more than enough to escape Rorty's trap: the pragmatists are quite aware of the epistemological paradoxes and have never had any confidence in "foundational" solutions.

My own solution, which provides a way of improving on the options of the classic pragmatists, asks us to challenge the adequacy of the Darwinian account of evolution itself, applied to the unique transformation of the human primate into the human person—by way of the invention and mastery of language: a thoroughly cultural feat. (Here I go beyond the critique of Darwin mounted by Helmuth Plessner and the "philosophical anthropologists." No one among that company has been willing to admit, as a consequence of his own discoveries, that "persons" are, evolutionarily, artifactually altered hybrid creatures—actually thus yielded by their enlanguaged *Bildung*).[8] The fact that persons "always already" find themselves to be members of a society in which moral and cognitive questions may be legibly asked and successfully answered (also and instantly) solves Rorty's ersatz puzzle and shows us, at the same time, that we characteristically misunderstand the conditions under which answers may be rightly given.

Darwin failed to see that his evolutionary theory could not be convincingly applied to the whole of the human career—that is, that human evolution had to be a uniquely hybrid, largely artifactual affair—which outflanks Rorty's objection. The rejection of cognitive privilege (which Rorty shares with the pragmatists) does not lead inexorably to the impossibility of an objective morality or science: it merely obliges us to admit that reasonable questions and answers cannot fail to be constructed rather than straightforwardly discovered, cannot fail to be caught up in our archival and dialectical contests. The "archival" and "dialectical" space of cognitional questions simply displaces the "foundational" option—viably and compatibly—with the *kind* of views favored by the classic pragmatists: notably, Dewey's. Dewey's vision is more plausible and more responsive to human interests than is Rorty's. I express this fact by acknowledging that answers to our moral and cognitive questions cannot be more than "second-best," since pertinent such questions arise only among enlanguaged beings and among beings that lack an essential teleology. One form of pragmatism defeats another.[9]

I can perhaps improve my paraphrase of classic pragmatism a little by assigning a division of labor to the principal figures, with regard to the open schema of their primary concepts and vision: for instance, in opposing Kant's transcendentalism and in favoring an instrumentalist, "archival," even existentialist or hermeneutic treatment of pragmatist arguments. The stalemate of First Philosophy and "foundational" metaphysics and epistemology has never been more explicit. The pragmatists always treat cognitional questions as *arising* out of the human condition, viewed in Darwinian and/or existential terms; so that their epistemologies tend to morph into a kind of philosophical anthropology. In other words, the very idea of an autonomous epistemology is already conceptually ill-conceived. Peirce, as I have said, moves from his infinitist fallibilism (a laggard "Kantian" or "post-Kantian" maneuver, as Josiah Royce seems to have convinced Peirce was very likely true) to the primacy of abduction (which firms up the claim that epistemology can never be completed). Dewey moves from a blunderbuss conception of "experience" (in good part influenced by James) to an inadequately fashioned conception of the dawning functionality of an enlanguaged "culture" (incipient in both *Experience and Nature* and *Logic*), meant to accommodate the original animal powers of the human creature, that persist, authentically, within such cultures. I believe Dewey regarded both *Experience* (ultimately, *Culture*) *and Nature* and *Logic: The Theory of Inquiry* as falling far short of the philosophical *summa* he never quite attempted.[10]

James does not fit easily here, though *his* use of the epithet "experience" is not far removed from what Dewey had in mind by replacing "experience" with "culture." In any case, "experience" (for James) is, in *Essays in Radical Empiricism*, an omnibus term that has already lost nearly all semblance of conceptual constraint or special meaning. The term ("experience") had to be retired. James's account of religious "belief" and religious "truth" may, indeed, begin to approach the priorities Dewey recommends in *Unmodern Philosophy and Modern Philosophy*: I cannot parse the matter more closely. The best account of James's narrative that I have found appears in Philip Kitcher's *Preludes to Pragmatism*. The formula Kitcher ekes out, pursuing the dispute between James and W. K. Clifford, the principal site of James's best effort, pretty well comes to this:

> whether it is permissible to believe such claims on the basis of evidence that would not suffice for knowledge. Belief is permissible [the conjecture has it] provided that there is a way of embedding individuals' commitments to religion in a framework of social practices that will produce overall consequences at least as good as those of any alternative that forbids such commitments.
>
> (Kitcher 2012, 248)

Kitcher concludes that James fails to meet Clifford's test adequately. The fate of pragmatism rests, then, with related conceptions ("synechism" in Peirce's sense, "culture" or "experience" in Dewey's)—each admitting the need for two very different kinds of logic: one, that of pragmatism itself, existential (let us say), practical, inherently informal; the other, that of the technical instruments acquired by the sciences and allied inquiries. Both notions need to be "reconstructed" and made suitable for what Dewey came to call "cultural naturalism," meant to displace the canonical primacy of epistemology.

For the moment, we have gained some neglected ground—in the sense, primarily, of getting clear about what may be salvaged in pragmatism's interests: the pragmatic maxim, the Darwinian continuum, opposition to classic rationalism and epistemological privilege, the dialectical, archival orientation of philosophical dispute, the enlanguaged and encultured formation of persons, flux over invariance, the abandonment of natural teleologies among humans, the paradoxes of cognition and understanding, the logic of life or inquiry as distinct from mere formal logics, the instrumental warrant of beliefs as distinct from the narrow rigors of propositional truth, the human *Lebensform* (in a sense akin to Wittgenstein's usage), the idea of human community, specifically pragmatist treatments of concept, discursivity, normativity, realism, truth, belief, and judgment. All in all, this is a promising beginning and a displacement of epistemology's primacy in favor of a philosophical anthropology: the new emphasis defined as addressing the question of self-understanding: the very "meaning" of a human life.

I recommend a further, quite modest, but essential improvement. The pragmatist venture, I suggest, construes the "anthropological" question in terms of the human person's or human society's lacking any discernible *niche* or *telos* in the world, lacking any natural norms or assured holist channel of "true" knowledge or understanding of any kind; yet succeeding (by its own lights) in accord with its "second-best" constructions, in science, in morality, in every space of human interests. The single most absorbing discovery the human creature may rightly claim is just that it *is* indeed such a creature. The pragmatist corollary holds, then, that the perceived viability of its immensely diverse "form of life" provides, existentially (*not* epistemically, except derivatively) a ground for its "constructed," second-best conceptions of an objective order of nature and human nature.

On my reading, that is to concede that the natural languages we master (and that transform the human primate into persons capable of the range of mastery human societies actually exhibit) have themselves spontaneously produced stubborn "mongrel" sciences, epistemologies, metaphysics, and the like that, in spite of being demonstrably defective (according to our lights), remain remarkably hospitable in supporting our best conjectures about "the way the world is" and "how best to live"—which, in their own right, challenge the primacy of their own host's presumption. There's the startling lesson, for example, drawn, fairly enough, from contrasting Leibniz's monadology and Descartes's dualism of *res cogitans* and *res extensa*: Leibniz invents an ingenious but entirely contrived model of the world, which never becomes a spontaneous part of ordinary usage; whereas Descartes deliberately borrows from ordinary usage, entrenches (as the essential premise of his advanced metaphysics) the "mongrel" liberty of mind/body dualism (that we find too convenient to refuse), though all the while we agree with Descartes that our ("ordinary") dualism cannot be easily reconciled with the notion of an integral human being or whatever an improved science or philosophy may require as a correction of mongrel language itself. Similarly, the mongrel functionality of ordinary language permits us to shift at will, without the need for any explicit justification, from descriptive and explanatory efforts that are now causal, now rationalized, now motivational, despite the fact that such conceptual intermingling overrides their inherent incommensurabilities.[11] Evidently we require a heuristic-mongrel vocabulary to provide an air of "sharing a language" despite the conceptual uncertainties of whatever prevailing categories and theories we happen to favor. Pragmatism is committed to their quotidian, provisional adequacy and ineliminability.

ATTRACTION TO "TWO LOGICS"

I have now provided a rough sense of the convergent unity of the views of the classic pragmatists as they separately reach the end of their respective careers. Generally, they not only change their views over time, but they tend to improve and converge (from their separate vantages) with respect to the openness of concepts; the adequacy of an archival sense of progress; the rejection of transcendental apriorism (Kant) and all forms of cognitive privilege—in effect, all forms of classic rationalism (though not rationality); the continuum of the animal and the human, bearing on the analysis of human concepts; the relaxed treatment of realism, to accommodate the world of human reasons as well as physical nature; the rejection of dualism (especially between subjects and objects, in cognitive contexts); the distinction between (and need of) two logics—canonical formal logics that may be incorporated within the larger space of logics "of life" (or inquiry or practical commitment, or epistemology, for that matter) capable of bringing the norms of formal reasoning into accord with the norms of actual human life and interests; and the practical necessity of "mongrel" verbal liberties that ensure linguistic argumentative conveniences at the price of some inaccuracy and imprecision.

For my part, I have contributed very little: here at least, no more than the thesis (which I confess I take to be decisive for pragmatism and the rest of philosophy) of the hybrid artifactual nature of persons and the mongrel functionality of ordinary language. Viewed in Darwinian and post-Darwinian terms, I take the thesis to qualify both the artifactual nature of normativity (which penetrates the whole of human life) along "second-best" lines, and the ubiquity (or near-ubiquity) of discursive thinking and conception (which bears on the question of animal and human intelligence, the distinction between discursive and perceptual concepts, and the limitations of normative objectivity with respect to moral, political, economic, educational, religious, and other concerns of civilized cultures).[12]

I regard this as an instructive compendium. But now I must add a brief account of some further features of the work of the so-called Pittsburgh School—to include, very loosely, at least Rorty, Sellars, McDowell, and Brandom (and now, increasingly, a swelling population of allied figures who take up one or another of the questions favored by this small cohort). I add Wittgenstein, because Wittgenstein's views color important claims advanced by one or another Pittsburgher, and Frege, because Frege represents a particularly strong, pertinent form of rationalism that the Pittsburghers have been attracted to. Only Rorty and Brandom have explicitly claimed to be pragmatists themselves; although Sellars and Carnap have also been drawn to the possibility that a Fregean-"inspired" rationalism may be invoked to generate a form of "analytic pragmatism." (Indeed, Brandom offers an interesting interpretation of "Frege's fundamental *pragmatic* principle[:] in asserting a claim, one is [he says] committing oneself to its *truth*," to be explicated in terms of the inferentially implicated concepts tethered to such assertions [Brandom 2008, 11–13]).[13] The idea's a verbal stretch but a trim one.

Let me state at the outset (of this fresh conjecture) that I am persuaded that Frege's rationalism, as defined by his remarkable achievement in the *Begriffsschrift*, is not known to be straightforwardly applicable to *any* empirically defined inquiry (in the natural sciences or practical life). As far as I can see, Brandom admits the point and applies it to Kant's and Sellars's rationalist ventures:

> The key fact to appreciate, [Brandom says, regarding Frege's paradigm] is that outside of logic and mathematics (and possibly fundamental physics, though I doubt it), in ordinary language and the special sciences, material inference is massively *nonmonotonic*. That is, the fact that the inference from p to q is a materially good one in some situation does not mean that the inference from p and r to q must also be a good one, in the same situation. If I strike this dry, well-made match, it will light— but not if in addition all the oxygen is removed from the room, or a sufficiently strong magnetic field is applied, or ....
>
> (Brandom 2015, 192)[14]

That is to say, inferentialism is "true in general," but we have no adequate clue as to how to formulate the inferential *rules* that apply to particular assertions of ordinary language use. I conclude, provisionally, though firmly, that inferentialism must be at best a heuristic tool *and* that, if that is true, we must already possess a more informal way of understanding the meaning of what we say that cannot depend on the validity of the strong form of inferentialism itself (any form) said to yield explicit semantic rules for pragmatically qualified discourse. Furthermore, it looks as if, in admitting the verdict, Brandom subverts the primacy of inferentialism itself. I express this by insisting that semantics can never be separated from epistemology and that, therefore, inferentialism is inherently constrained by what Wittgenstein calls a *Lebensform* (or Husserl might have characterized as a *Lebenswelt*, if he were not himself a rationalist).

I think this means, quite simply, that the new rationalism ranging over Sellars, Brandom, Frege, and Kant cannot rightly challenge the commonsense pragmatism developed by Peirce and Dewey. If anything, it confirms, by its own limitations, that the *non*-inferential descriptive and explanatory powers of *any* valid form of inquiry relating to the experienced world cannot be seriously restricted, replaced, regulated, or defeated by Brandom's or Sellars's rationalist versions of "analytic pragmatism." Our noninferential sources of description and explanation must enjoy a measure of parity with inferentialism itself, partly at least because they implicate the question of the very *source* of discursive concepts. Recall, here, that it has been my contention that it is more than improbable that an infant's learning the *discursive* concepts of a natural language could be accounted for without admitting *perceptual* (and related sorts of) concepts—a doctrine that conflicts with the insistence (as with Brandom and McDowell) on restricting intelligent concept use entirely to the use of language. That cannot be squared with Darwinian evolution or studies of comparative intelligence—or the actual use of language.

But I have a stronger (if less ambitious) line of argument to offer. Frege's temptation to extend his *Begriffsschrift* lesson to the empirical domain is little more than a conjecture (which Brandom, as we have seen, effectively rejects).[15] About Kant's rationalism, Brandom says:

> Though he doesn't himself think of it this way, Frege is continuing and developing Kant's line of thought concerning the role that modality (including centrally the kind of necessity involved in causation) plays in distinguishing the expressive role of certain concepts that relate ground-level empirical descriptive concepts to one another from the expressive role of these descriptive concepts themselves.
>
> (Brandom 2015, 177–178)

But, of course, the thesis is valid only if Kant's transcendental structures in the first *Critique* are already able to *support* a Fregean-like account. But they cannot support such a claim if, say, arguments like Ernst Cassirer's, reviewing the history of the natural sciences, are at all reasonable in bringing Kant up to date on post-Newtonian physics. Because, what Cassirer's (1957) argument demonstrates is that, effectively, there cannot be "constitutive" or "regulative" principles of the kind Kant himself proposes for the rational ordering of scientific claims, that are constant or governed by higher-order constant principles, where such principles continually change (significantly) over the historical life of the sciences. Cassirer abandons constant "constitutive principles" for historical reasons; he appears to cleave, however, to "regulative principles." But precisely these, on my reading, cannot fail to be anything but vacuous if they cannot count on the constancy of constitutive principles. Kant himself seems uneasy about what can be said to be transcendentally necessary on these counts: little or nothing, I should say; and, if so, then, arguably, so too throughout the more detailed articulation of Kant's transcendental categories. If this line of reasoning is valid, then it is unlikely that Kant's transcendentalism can rise above the heuristic use I suggested earlier.

The gaps in the argument are adequately filled by Cassirer—and by Cassirer's reference to Kant's own texts (in the first *Critique*), that themselves allusively betray the stopgap nature of Kant's conjectures, where Kant appears to anticipate (abstractly) the possibilities of a physics that eclipses Newton's limitations. Cassirer's comments—which are explicitly addressed to Kant's summary remarks in the "Appendix to the Transcendental Dialectic" (A642/B670-A668-B696)—are clearly decisive, despite the fact that Cassirer himself clings loyally (as well as possible) to the transcendental invariance of "regulative" principles (where "constitutive" principles must be abandoned), though the former can have no determinate function where the latter no longer obtain:[16]

> The electron "as defined by modern physical theory," [Cassirer explains] does not precede the field but is first constituted by its relation to the field. Accordingly, even mechanics must depart from its strictly kinetic form. The development of quantum mechanics discloses a tendency toward increasing abstraction: in its most recent form it seems to renounce all "representation" of the processes within the atom, and all special images in general. But this must not be regarded as a purely negative achievement: it is rather the beginning, the first necessary step toward a new mode of formation and conceptual unity.
>
> Of course it is implicit in the character of this unity formation that the objectivity toward which it progresses and aims can never be conclusively determined. Whereas the "thing" of naïve intuition may appear as a fixed sum of definite properties, the physical object by its very nature can be conceived only in the form of an "idea of limit." For here it is not a matter of disclosing the ultimate, absolute elements of reality, in the contemplation of which thought may rest as it were, but of a never-ending process through which the relatively necessary takes the place of the relatively accidental and the relatively invariable that of the relatively variable. We can never claim that this process has attained to the ultimate invariants of experience . . . . Rather, the possibility must always be held open that a new synthesis will instate itself.
>
> (Cassirer 1957, 475–576)

I have cited the passage at some length, because, on its face, it provides the classic pragmatist with the strongest possible evidence that the Pittsburghers' drift toward Fregean rationalism can never adequately recover (beyond the heuristic) Brandom's monotonic vision of pragmatic contexts of discourse, or McDowell's necessities of discursivity, or the autonomy of Kantian or Fregean "transcendental" rationalism vis-à-vis any empirical or practical inquiry or commitment. I see no way in which strict rationalism can gain an advantage over the deliberate informalities of the last phases of classic pragmatism. Moreover, I take the argument to demonstrate the deep sense in which the Wittgenstein of the *Investigations* is indeed cousin to the pragmatists, though not a pragmatist himself—in his remarkable pronouncement (all too easily misunderstood):

> "So you are saying that human agreement decides what is true and what is false?"—It is what human beings *say* that is true or false, and they agree in the *language* they use. That is not agreement in opinions but in form of life.
>
> If language is to be a means of communication [he adds] there must be agreement not only in definitions but also (queer as this may sound) in judgments. This seems to abolish logic, but does not do so . . . [W]hat we call "measuring" is partly determined by a certain constancy in results of measurement.
>
> (Wittgenstein 1953, Pt. I, §§241–242)

What, obliquely, Wittgenstein is explaining here is that abandoning Fregean rationalism is tantamount to admitting the inseparability of discursivity and *Bildung* and that the rigors of anything akin to inferentialism are inescapably embedded in the contingencies of our form of life. The passage from Wittgenstein *does not* claim that there is any determinate, ineliminable empirical, or commonsense core of belief or knowledge on which true knowledge depends. Add that discovery, and the relative strengths of pragmatism, Kantianism, and the intended mediation (of the two) by inferentialism suddenly becomes crystal clear. The Pittsburgh maneuvers are instantly revealed to be regressive. That finding alone restores the agon between pragmatism and Kant's transcendentalism as the primary philosophical contest of our time, as it has been since the advent of pragmatism following the American Civil War.

THE "PRAGMATIC MAXIM" AND THE "INDETERMINATE SITUATION"

I must return, finally, to the most disputed and idiosyncratic of Dewey's themes: the analysis of the meaning of a "problematic situation" and its bearing on what I have loosely called the problem of the two "logics." We have already made considerable progress on the two-logics issue: I have already signaled that Peirce was himself clearly disposed to distinguish between various formal logics of restricted technical use and a larger "logic of inquiry" (cognitive, practically directed, normatively qualified), which the more technically specialized logics may be said to serve instrumentally. I cannot see how the 1903 Harvard Lectures—particularly Lectures I and V (bearing on the normative sciences and "three kinds of goodness") *and* their indicated involvement with the "pragmatic maxim"—can possibly fail to signal Peirce's undeveloped (but palpable) anticipation of a theme not too distant from Dewey's, though hardly formulated in terms congenial to Dewey's *Logic*. The fact is, Peirce begins the lectures with the sentence, "A certain maxim of Logic, which I have called *Pragmatism* has recommended itself to me for divers reasons and on sundry considerations." He claims to have taken it "as my guide in most of my thought" (5.14). In a way, I find the idea strengthened by Dewey's publication of "The Superstition of Necessity" (1893, EW 4:19–36), the year after Peirce published his essay, "The Doctrine of Necessity Examined," designed to lay a ground for the admission of "absolute chance," which is of course also congenial to the general thrust of Dewey's notion of an "indeterminate" or "problematic situation" in *Logic: The Theory of Inquiry*. Dewey is explicit about his having been prompted by Peirce's paper, though Dewey and Peirce proceed along very different lines.[17] In any case, the idea that pragmatism counts as a logical rule (for Peirce) is already a concession regarding the need for "two" logics, more or less in Dewey's sense.

My own suggestion proceeds along rather different lines, though it touches on the themes of the 1903 Harvard Lectures. Because the lectures are chiefly concerned with the "logic" of the essential "categories" of Firstness, Secondness, and Thirdness generated by the "normative sciences" and because Firstness is especially congenial to the basic argument of Dewey's 1938 *Logic*, notably adumbrated in his contributions to the earlier 1903 collection (involving other authors), published as *Studies in Logical Theory*, that were then included (with minor revisions) in Dewey's *Essays in Experimental Logic*[18] (1916). If one rereads Chapters 2 and 3 of *Experimental Logic* (already formulated in the 1903 *Studies* volume—hence, published close to the time of Peirce's delivery of the Harvard Lectures), one cannot fail to be struck by the fact that, in the two references to Peirce in the 1916 *Experimental Logic*, Dewey enthusiastically (as, earlier, James also) singles out the treatment of "pragmatism" as a logical rule involving the consequentialist theory of meaning. Thus, for instance, Dewey explicitly notes that Lotze's logic (which he is examining in the *Studies* volume) generates "the insoluble question of the reference of thought-activity to a wholly indeterminate unrationalized, independent, prior existence" and his failure (as well as the cognate failure of Kant's transcendental logic) "to view logical terms and distinctions with respect to their necessary function in the reintegration of experience." This is, of course, the puzzle Dewey means to resolve in his own *Logic*—now, as I am suggesting, by applying Peirce's theory of the essential categories of nature to his own account of an "indeterminate situation." (One can see, also, therefore, the relevance and distinction of Dewey's account of "necessity" pertinent to the *Logic*.)[19]

Dewey goes out of his way to oppose any suggestion that an "indeterminate" or "problematic situation" must be confined to (or at least implicates) conscious "subjective" states of some would-be agent: this must be a concession to James's use of "experience," which (on James's view) is perfectly compatible with "experience's" not being consciously "experienced" by anyone. Read here, approximatively: "the experienceable world . . . need not be experienced by anyone."[20] I am inclined to think Dewey may have espied an ordinary "mongrel" use of phrases having to do with the amorphous, rather uncertain, perhaps "uneasy" nature of some roughly identified "situation" that one might try to get clear about: e. g., "The entire situation bothered me. I couldn't put my finger on the problem." But then, it would have been better to draw on *such* verbal usages as actually appear in ordinary language. I think here, again, of Descartes's rather clever but ultimately unsuccessful maneuver regarding the mental and the physical. It is characteristically awkward to press a casual mongrel expression into a metaphysically specialized role (as in Dewey's explication of the "logic" of life or creaturely inquiry), unless (as with Descartes) the mongrel distinction is already nearly the whole of the would-be technical use intended. But then, Dewey himself seems to abandon the verbal decision he favors in *Logic*.

There is a final irony that I would like to note here but lack space enough to pursue: first, ordinary language already entrenches mongrel phrasings that are clearly useful (among apt speakers) in the press of spontaneous conversation, even though, if raised up to the level of a philosophical proposal, they tend to go wildly wrong; and, second, apt speakers are aware that they cannot normally defend, *as* philosophically valid, the apparent literal meaning of such phrasings. The explanation is plain enough: we cannot suppose that ordinary language has actually solved the complex conceptual puzzles that philosophers are (even now) unable to analyze satisfactorily (regarding the theory of mind, say). In that sense, our mongrel liberties are both benign and conditionally ineliminable. But if so, then, at one stroke, our reliance on ordinary usage obviates in good part Dewey's own complaint against the "mongrel" aspect of our discourse about "objective things": their seeming determinacy need not be fixed at all and, in any case, serves a use that probably cannot be bettered. Also, if that is true, then it is very likely true as well that the special forms of precision advocated by the Pittsburghers (partly at least against the classic pragmatists)—Sellars's disjunctive agon between the "manifest" and "scientific images," Brandom's primacy of inferentialism, McDowell's championing of the cognitional ubiquity of Kantian discursivity—are very likely distortions of one or another mongrel liberty read along rationalist lines. I mention these last complications in order to suggest how the argument might continue. I cannot address them further here. But mentioning them confirms, informally, the great distance between the undertaking of the classic pragmatists and the Kantianized or Fregeanized Pittsburgh rationalists, some of whom believe themselves to have demonstrated significant defects or limitations in the classic pragmatists' venture, due to their antirationalist tendencies. But the Pittsburghers are mistaken.

Notes

1. Remarked and discussed in Murphey (1993, 39–40). Murphey's account is one of the earliest overviews of Peirce's known output—originally published by Harvard University Press (1961), well before a reasonably accurate catalogue of Peirce's papers had been worked out. (The labor is still unfinished.) In a new preface, Murphey (1993) suggests possible revisions to his assessment; I suggest his advocacy of the decisive importance of abduction and the abandonment of Kantian formulations.

2. I am inclined to believe that Royce may well have "persuaded" Peirce to find a suitable replacement for the (Idealist) formulation of his "infinitist fallibilism." I find Peirce's final solution in his "abductive turn." See my *Toward a Metaphysics of Culture* (Margolis 2016, 130–136).

3. In *Collected Papers*, the editors add a long, extremely interesting, possibly only loosely linked note (5.402) seemingly written sometime between the 1903 "Lectures" and the 1878 publication of "How to Make Our Ideas Clear." The Kantian connection is caught up with Peirce's sense of the "architectonic" function of the maxim and his own theory of judgment and assertion. The essay itself, one of Peirce's best-known, which must be read together with "The Fixation of Belief" (1877), is actually focused on Descartes's treatment of "clear and distinct" ideas. Leibniz is mentioned but not (as far as I can see) Kant. What is especially intriguing is Peirce's development of the idea that pragmatism itself *is*, effectively, the pragmatic maxim—that is, a "rule," a "principle of logic," *not* "a skeptical and materialistic principle" but "only an application of the sole principle of logic which was recommended by Jesus: 'Ye may know them by their fruits', that is, a principle very intimately allied with the ideas of the gospel" (5.402n1). (Here, Peirce clearly anticipates Dewey on the nesting of the "two" logics needed—and in a deep way).

Peirce links his maxim to "the great principle of continuity" (Synechism) and to the collective "experience" of an actual society, not confined (nominalistically) to an "individual's" experiences (which James, of course, favors in his *Principles* and which Peirce explicitly opposes). Here, Peirce continues: "The great principle of logic is self-surrender [to the principle of continuity, in accord with which we] see how all is fluid and every point directly partakes the being of every other, [hence] it will appear that individualism and falsity are one and the same." This then also explains Peirce's notion of "collective" (or civilizational) solidarity, the idea that meanings issue in societally shared "habits of action"; accordingly, it also explains the constructivist nature of the meaning of our concepts.

In the same essay, Peirce links these features to what I have named his "infinitist fallibilism" regarding reality (and "settling opinion") and, even more profoundly, his commitment to Scotist or Scholastic realism, which marks one of the deepest divisions between Dewey and Peirce (5.405–407), apart from the explicit teleologism of the essay (made more acceptable as an article of "cheerful hope" rather than of what must be ontologically valid). Here, Peirce and Dewey seem to me to be as close to one another as they ever are—as pragmatists. In fact, if we add Peirce's strong disjunction (in the first of the 1903 Harvard lectures) between the analysis of "judgment" or "assertions" and the analysis of the "meaning" of "beliefs" or "propositions" (5.28–30), I think we may find that we have come very close indeed to an anticipation of the main lines of the metaphysical theme of Dewey's *Experience and Nature*, and possibly even to the distinction between canonical logics and Dewey's troublesome conception of the "logic" of practical life (in *Logic: The Theory of Inquiry* [Dewey 1938]). I find the suggestion entirely plausible. (There are important instructions in both the convergences and divergences involving Dewey and Peirce.)

I should add that there is an excellent account of Peirce's opposition to nominalism and his interpretation of Scotist realism in Murphey (1993, chap. 18: "Synechism"), which bears on the application of the idea of continuity and (on Peirce's view) community as well, that qualifies both his theory of science and his theory of normative conduct. In spite of this important divergence, then, I am persuaded, on pragmatist grounds strictly construed, that there remains a decisive convergence between Dewey and Peirce. ("Democracy," for instance, plays a double role in science and moral-political life, in Dewey's vision, that is, not unlike the role of Synechism in Peirce's.)

4. If we compare Richard Rorty's (1967/1992) introduction to the first edition of *The Linguistic Turn: Recent Essays in Philosophical Method* to the retrospective essay, "Twenty-five Years After," added to the 1992 edition of *The Linguistic Turn* (371–374), and then read Rorty's (1998) essay, "Dewey Between Hegel and Darwin," *the same year* as "Twenty-five Years After," we cannot fail to see that Rorty has reversed himself *utterly* and without any further option, except the rejection of epistemology itself. The irony is that Rorty's essay on Dewey might have alerted Brandom to the need for a *paired* logic resembling the thrust of the reflections of both Peirce and Dewey. In any case, the autonomy of semantics over epistemology is a hopeless maneuver, unless epistemology is already built into the "logic" and "semantics" that Brandom requires. See, particularly, Brandom (2008, chap. 4), which is reprinted (verbatim, to my eye), in Brandom (2015), also as chapter 4. The difficulties with Brandom's proposal lie largely with his adoption of the "Kantianized" or "Fregeanized" or combined reading Sellars favors regarding so-called "pure concepts" (in effect, modal concepts), picked up in chapter 5 in Brandom (2015, 174–175). I return to this issue shortly.

5. See my *Reinventing Pragmatism: American Philosophy at the End of the Twentieth Century* (Margolis 2000), especially "Prologue: Reconstruction in Pragmatism" (pp. 1–23). I regard this "Prologue" as a first pass at an essential part of the question I am addressing in the present essay.

6. See Sami Pihlström (2003), especially chapters 2 and 3 (e.g., pp. 108–110), and John McDowell (2009), especially Part I (the Woodbridge Lectures)—but see also, for a sense of needed concessions and the possible need for more, in "Avoiding the Myth of the Given," in the same volume, pages 256–272.

7. See further Rorty (1979, 179–182).

8. The details of my view of the matter may be found in my *Toward a Metaphysics of Culture* (Margolis 2016, chaps. 1–2).

9. I offer a full account of a "second-best" morality in my *Moral Philosophy After 9/11*, (Margolis 2001). Borrowing from Plato's *Statesman*, I argue that a pragmatist epistemology is a "second-best" epistemology.

10. See, however, John Dewey (2012), particularly Dean's helpful introduction. That book, of course, is simply Dewey's last book, promised but apparently lost in the 1940s, which treats "experience" as ranging over all human forms of functioning and "culture" as collecting (in a holist way, loosely derived from Hegel) an interpretive narrative that provides *not* an epistemology (which must be superseded) but the natural history (a *geistlich* history) of "knowing" viewed as part of the crowning activity of the human creature within its enabled world. Compare, here, Dewey (1938, chaps. 1–2), where the theme of the new book is clearly anticipated but only problematically advanced in terms of Dewey's puzzling heuristic category of an "indeterminate" or "problematic situation."

11. I have pursued the notion of the need for the "mongrel" functionality of ordinary language in *Three Paradoxes of Personhood* (Margolis 2017). One has only to think that the invention of a viable language cannot have been postponed until we had successfully solved our metaphysical and epistemological puzzles.

12. These last matters are discussed, most recently, in my *Toward a Metaphysics of Culture* (Margolis 2016); they are also largely neglected or misconstrued by figures like McDowell and Brandom.

13. Along these lines, Brandom finds that Frege, Kant, and Wittgenstein all favor "the priority of the propositional." Brandom (2008, 6) notes that he is speaking of "linguistic pragmatism," on the strength of the principle that "concept use is an essentially linguistic affair"—"taking it [it seems] that concept use is not intelligible in a context that does not include language use," which permits Brandom, rather easily, to include Davidson, Dummett, Quine, Sellars, the later Wittgenstein, James, and Dewey as "linguistic pragmatists" (of somewhat different sorts). I see little reason to oppose the extension. The question remains: What does the extension contribute to our conception of pragmatism, or how does it improve our sense of pragmatism's scope or powers?

14. Also see Frege's *Begriffsschrift*. An excellent account may be found in Macbeth (2005).

15. See Gottlob Frege, "*Begriffsschrift*, a Formal Language, Modeled upon that of Arithmetic, for Pure Thought," in van Heijenoort (1967/1970, 1–82).

16. Compare Kant, *Critique of Pure Reason*, A644/B672.

17. See John Dewey, "The Superstition of Necessity Examined" (EW 4:19–36).

18. The *Essays* do not appear in a single volume in Dewey's Collected Works. Rather, they are found in MW 1:151–174; MW 2:298–367; MW 4:78–97; MW 6:103–122; MW 8:14–97; MW 10:319–369.

19. Dewey (1915a, MW 8:95–96; 1915b, MW 10:366). Lotze's logical studies afford an important focus in Dewey's contributions from the *Studies* volume, which are essentially concerned with what was to become the theory of an "indeterminate situation"—made determinate by what I judge to be an adaptation of Peirce's theory of Firstness, which must be filled out by the operative function of Secondness and its mediation between Firstness and Thirdness, as explained in the Harvard Lectures. The references to Lotze appear in "The Antecedents and Stimuli of Thinking" (Dewey 1903, MW 2:134–136). There is also a short paper by Dewey, "Peirce's Theory of Quality" (Dewey 1935), that fits very nicely with my conjecture about Dewey's enthusiastic adoption of Peirce's discussion of discerning the "unity" of what is experienced relative to "indeterminate" situations (LW 11:86–94). I see this as part of a deliberate effort on Dewey's part to begin to limn the consequence of Peirce's, James's, and his own views as an up-to-date pragmatism. Compare, also, Dewey's *Logic: The Theory of Inquiry* (1938, LW 12), especially the opening chapters.

20. For a sense of James's metaphysics of "experience," see James (1992). This edition, edited by Ralph Barton Perry, omits essays IX–XII, in order to convey the critical sense of James's theory. I have been swayed by Perry's judgment.

WORKS CITED

Citations of John Dewey's works are to the thirty-seven-volume critical edition published by Southern Illinois University Press under the editorship of Jo Ann Boydston. In-text citations give the original publication date and series abbreviation, followed by volume number and page number. For example: (1934, LW 10:12) is page 12 of *Art as Experience*, which is published as volume 10 of *The Later Works*.

Series abbreviations for *The Collected Works*:

EW *The Early Works* (1882–1898)

MW *The Middle Works* (1899–1924)

LW *The Later Works* (1925–1953)

Citations of the critical edition of C. S. Peirce's work are to Collected Papers, "original publication year, CP n.m" where "n" is the volume number and "m" the paragraph number (e.g., CP 1.500 refers to volume 1, paragraph 500).

Brandom, Robert B. 2008. *Between Saying and Doing: Towards an Analytic Pragmatism* Oxford: Oxford University Press.

Brandom, Robert B. 2015. *From Empiricism to Expressivism: Brandom Reads Sellars.* Cambridge, MA: Harvard University Press.

Cassirer, Ernst. 1957. *The Philosophy of Symbolic Forms*, Vol. 3. Translated by Ralph Manheim. New Haven, CT: Yale University Press.

Dewey, John. 1893. "The Superstition of Necessity Examined." EW 4:19–36.

Dewey, John. 1915a. "The Existence of the World as a Logical Problem." MW 8:95–96.

Dewey, John. 1915b. "An Added Note to the Practical." MW 10:366.

Dewey, John. 1916. *Essays on Experimental Logic.* MW 1:151–174; MW 2:298–367; MW 4:78–97; MW 6:103–122; MW 8:14–97; MW 10:319–369.

Dewey, John. 1925/1929. *Experience and Nature.* LW 1.

Dewey, John. 1938. *Logic: The Theory of Inquiry.* LW 12.

Dewey, John. 2012. *Unmodern Philosophy and Modern Philosophy.* Edited by Phillip Dean. Carbondale: Southern Illinois University Press.

Heijenoort, Jean van (Ed.). 1967/1970. *Frege and Gödel: Two Fundamental Texts in Mathematical Logic.* Cambridge, MA: Harvard University Press.

James, William. 1909. *A Pluralistic Universe.* New York: Longmans Green, 1992.

Kitcher, Philip. 2012. *Preludes to Pragmatism: Toward a Reconstruction of Philosophy.* Oxford: Oxford University Press.

Macbeth, Danielle. 2005. *Frege's Logic.* Cambridge, MA: Harvard University Press.

Margolis, Joseph. 2000. *Reinventing Pragmatism: American Philosophy at the End of the Twentieth Century.* Ithaca, NY: Cornell University Press.

Margolis. Joseph. 2001. *Moral Philosophy After 9/11.* University Park: Pennsylvania State University Press.

Margolis, Joseph. 2016. *Toward a Metaphysics of Culture.* London: Routledge.

Margolis, Joseph. 2017. *Three Paradoxes of Personhood.* Milan: Mimesis International.

McDowell, John. 2009. *Having the World in View: Essays on Kant, Hegel, and Sellars.* Cambridge, MA: Harvard University Press.

Murphey, Murray G. 1993. *The Development of Peirce's Philosophy.* Indianapolis: Hackett.

Peirce, Charles Sanders. 1954–1960; 1962–1963. *Collected Papers.* Vols. 1–6 edited by Charles Hartshorne and Paul Weiss; vols. 7–8 edited by A. W. Burks. Cambridge, MA: Belknap Press of Harvard University Press.

Pihlström, Sami. 2003. *Naturalizing the Transcendental: A Pragmatic View.* Amherst, NY: Humanity Books.

Rorty, Richard. 1967/1992. *The Linguistic Turn: Recent Essays in Philosophical Method.* Chicago: University of Chicago Press.

Rorty, Richard. 1979. *Philosophy and the Mirror of Nature.* Princeton, NJ: Princeton University Press.

Rorty, Richard. (1998). *Dewey Between Hegel and Darwin* (Philosophical Papers, vol. 3). Cambridge, UK: Cambridge University Press.

Wittgenstein, Ludwig. 1953. *Philosophical Investigations.* Translated by G. E. M. Anscombe. New York: Macmillan.

CHAPTER 7

DEWEY AND ANTI-REPRESENTATIONALISM

PETER GODFREY-SMITH

INTRODUCTION

A comment in a letter by John Dewey to Charles Strong, quoted by Louis Menand in *The Metaphysical Club*, has become well known.[1] Dewey wrote in 1905 that "the chief service of pragmatism, as regards epistemology" will be "to give the *coup de grace* to *representationalism*" (Menand 2001, 361). The passage is quoted with approval by Huw Price (2009), drawing on Menand, and in Macarthur and Price (2007) it is used to support a statement of what pragmatism itself should be taken to *be*, a view in which opposition to representationalism is central: PRAGMATISM = LINGUISTIC PRIORITY without REPRESENTATIONALISM.[2] Whether or not they would agree with the " = ", quite a few others would agree that "representationalism" is a philosophical error, and Dewey helps us get past it—Rorty (1982) is a further example.

I set out instead from a viewpoint that sees representation as often overvalued and misunderstood, in philosophical contexts, but probably not as something to get *over*. Representationalist ideas are hard to deploy well but are not entirely on the wrong track. I am also an admirer of Dewey, and in general I think of Dewey's views as embodying much progress. But I am not sure this applies to Dewey's thinking about representation. Perhaps this is not a topic he handled as well as others? My aim in this chapter is to explore Dewey's place in these debates, both to work out what he thought and to see where his thinking leads—where it might have gone wrong, and where it might challenge my own cautious and qualified representationalism. The chapter focuses mostly (not entirely) on Dewey's later work, from the 1920s onwards.

REPRESENTATION
AND REPRESENTATIONALISM

Was Dewey an anti-representationalist, in the relevant sense? Was the "representationalism" of his letter to Strong the same sort of representationalism that Price, Rorty, and other philosophers now have in mind? If not quite the same (and surely it will not be), is it recognizably close?

The concept of representation is broad in ways that make this hard to answer. On one side, the idea of representation is used in a family of long-running but controversial projects that attempt to describe the goal of thought and the nature of meaning and truth, in terms of mirroring, copying, correspondence, and the like. But it is also possible to talk about representation in ways that seem harmless and unavoidable. Both in Dewey's day and now, "representation" can be used in a low-key manner to talk about all sorts of symbols and communicative devices, without commitment to any particular theory of how they work. Many objects of everyday public use, such as maps and blueprints, are representations. Almost everyone will accept that these things are real, even if they have an unusual story about how they work. Dewey himself made much of the importance of objects of this kind in social life.

> Where communication exists, things in acquiring meaning, thereby acquire representatives, surrogates, signs and implicates, which are infinitely more amenable to management, more permanent and more accommodating, than events in their first estate.
>
> (1925/1929, LW 1:132)

Evidently there are things normally called *representations*, and whatever it is they do, or are supposed to do, can naturally be called *representation*. To say this is not to offer much defense of representationalism as a philosophical doctrine. All representations represent (or are supposed to represent), but that is consistent with there being just about any degree of disunity in how they work and how they are used. Representations are all "stand-ins," perhaps, but there are so many ways of being such a thing. The idea of there being *any* definite role that representations have, any special representational relation of philosophical interest, might be wrong, for all that is on the table so far.

Alternatively, one might say that there *is* something distinctive that representations all do or try to do, but philosophers have offered such bad theories of this phenomenon that there is reason to talk quite differently about the whole business. Standard theories, based on representation as *reproduction of the form* of an object, or copying, might be seen as bad enough and central enough to the philosophical tradition to justify saying that one is an anti-representationalist even while offering a new theory of how these things, representations, work.

Yet another response is that what is wrong with "representationalist" ideas in philosophy is not the idea that representations exist and represent, or even the idea that "copying" is real in some cases; the problem is the fact that representation is given a role in entirely the wrong places. Everyday objects like street maps might be representations, but philosophers and psychologists tend to describe mental states, and other things that work nothing like public representational tools, in the same terms. A range of theories of perception, for example, hold that our contact with objects in the world is always mediated by more direct contact with representations of them.[3]

We might wonder where Dewey is in his much-quoted letter. Is he only rejecting some theories of perception? In fact, what Dewey says in the letter, and elsewhere, is quite close to anti-representationalism of a form recognizable now. The question is made complicated by some terminological issues; "representation" was not, in the period I am discussing, Dewey's usual way of marking out a target for criticism. But Dewey's treatment does show continuities with recent criticisms of representationalism. In the next section I work through some arguments from Dewey. Before then, I ask: what might be a reasonable statement of the ongoing controversy? What sorts of things might representations be, and what role might they be given, such that this *might* be a philosophical mistake, but might not be—so representation might instead be an important and poorly understood phenomenon that we could handle better in the future?

A person can have a representationalist view of thought, perception, language, scientific theories, or other things. I will talk of these as different "epistemic media." It is useful to also have a generic term for a sentence, thought, theory, or other entity within some particular epistemic medium, a term that does not prejudge the question of representationalism for that medium. I will use the term "epistemic device" for that role. Then:

> *Representationalism* about an epistemic medium is the claim that there is a relation
> *R* between epistemic devices in that medium and a subject-matter that these devices
> are used to deal with,
>
> (1) That is an achievable goal in the production of those epistemic devices, in a
>   given context of interpretation, and is hence a standard of assessment for the
>   devices themselves,
> (2) That involves
>   (2a) Veridicality, in the sense of satisfaction by the subject-matter of a condi-
>   tion specified by the epistemic device, and/or
>   (2b) Copying, picturing, or some other preservation of structure, between de-
>   vice and subject-matter,
> (3) And that has a causal relation to success (theoretical or practical) in the use
>   of these epistemic devices, where this link to success is part of why relation *R*
>   provides a goal and standard of assessment, as in (1).

If there is some relation *R* with that role, then representationalism is true for the medium in question. In this set-up, "representation" is a success-term; we try to represent what is going on, and we might succeed or fail. If we fail, we might *mis*represent, or perhaps not even manage that. There is such a thing as a *putative* representation, and only some of these succeed. One could also set things up so the target of analysis is the "putative" side. I do it in the way seen here because it leads to a simpler handling of the relation between conditions (1) and (3).

I will next say more about what is going on in clause (2). I think that in attempts to say what is distinctive about representation, when understood in more contentious forms, there have been two themes that can either be taken together as a package, or separated out. One is the idea of shared form—mirroring, mapping, and so on. The other is the idea that when there is representation, there is satisfaction of a condition specified by the representation—satisfaction of a truth-condition, or what I will call here, more generally, a veridicality-condition.[4] Perhaps the idea of representation does not involve picturing, mapping, or shared form in *any* sense at all; all that is required is (as Aristotle put it) saying of what is, that it is. Then the hard work is done, philosophically, in giving an account of what it is for something to *have* a veridicality condition.[5]

One possibility is that an explanation of what's going on in (2a) goes *via* (2b). By having a certain form (along with other features), a representation specifies a condition that the world is supposed to satisfy (Wittgenstein 1922). But one might also think this is a complete mistake, and there is a different route, for the epistemic devices in question, to the existence of a veridicality condition—a convention, for example.

If we shear (2a) away entirely from (2b), then condition (3) becomes harder to meet. It is harder for the relation in question to have a link to success of the required kind. Shared form between an epistemic device and some part of the world beyond it is a resource that can be exploited, when one has to deal with that part of the world and has that epistemic device available. Recent debates about truth have included a controversy over whether a view that features (2a) with none of (2b) preserves a suitably strong link between truth and success (Horwich 1998). I do not take sides on this matter, though I note that the road to (3) – a link to success of the right kind – is easier with (2b). I also accept, as implied in the previous summary, that one might have a view featuring (2b) without (2a). Those views are rare now, but perhaps some early modern theories of "ideas," such as Locke's view, would qualify.[6]

The word "copy" is often used to express what is problematic in this area—we will see this in the later discussion of Dewey. What is it for an epistemic device to copy something? There are two ways of unpacking the idea, ways that—again—may converge but may not. One way is with the idea of replication of form. Another is through the idea of satisfaction: a representation copies the world if it specifies a condition that is in fact satisfied. Again, one might approach the second sense of copying via the first: for some epistemic devices, having a particular form *is* (or is a part of) specifying how the world has to be for the device to be veridical. But this might not be how things are set up. Take a piece of simple declarative language: "the cat is on the mat." One might reasonably say that there is no need to put "shared form" onto the table here, no need for it to be anywhere in the story, no matter how attenuated. What matters is that through the conventions of the language, and the form of words used, a condition is specified. If the world is that way, then there is satisfaction of the veridicality condition. There is no picturing, but there is *telling it like it is*. In a sense, there is copying—not via similarity across representation and world but via specification of a condition, on the representation side, and satisfaction of that condition, on the world's side.

These uncertainties around the idea of "copying" are relevant because Dewey often chose "copy" as his target, as a term that picked out the bad options in this area. The term "correspondence," on the other hand, he often saw as salvageable. "Correspondence" is salvageable because of its helpful ordinary uses—two people might correspond by mail, each responding to the other.[7] "Copying" he saw as pointing more unambiguously in bad directions. Copying is the mere replication of form, passive and inert.

Once the two senses of "copy" are pulled apart, is Dewey only opposed to copying in a sense that includes replication of form? Might he be okay with the other sense (satisfaction of a veridicality condition), when it is made clear? No, I think. I am not sure about this, as the question is tied up with Dewey's views about meaning in *Logic* (1938) and related discussions of language, and I do not understand well enough how those views work. But Dewey is often clear enough in saying that representing things *as they are* is not the business of thought and knowledge. He does oppose such a view, at least sometimes. At other times he seems to say that it is good to represent *some* things or facts as they are but not the sorts of things supposed in traditional philosophy—I discuss all of this in the next section.

I realize that my (1)–(3) summary is complicated and set up differently from Dewey's discussions. But this whole area is so vexed that some imposition of order is needed, especially because representationalism about thought can be a very different beast from representationalism about language, and so on. Let us now sort through some strands in Dewey that bear on what he was against, why he was against it, and whether he was right to be.

STRANDS IN DEWEY'S TREATMENT

This section discusses three overlapping strands in Dewey's discussions of these issues. As noted, Dewey often does not treat "representation" as his target: he sees "copy" and to a lesser extent "correspondence" as guiltier parties. (In *The Quest for Certainty*, for example, the word "represent" is only used in the innocent senses introduced previously, and "representation" does not occur.) This makes it hard to work out whether and why he might be anti-representationalist in the sense of his contemporary allies. I note some the most important of these uncertainties as I go, but will not keep repeating this point every time the issue arises. The first two parts of this section concern broad features of Dewey's view that do bear on representationalism but in some ways are background to a more focused critique that is discussed in the third subsection.

Representation is a Solution to a Non-Problem Born of Dualism

For Dewey, a family of traditional epistemological concepts is motivated by attempts to solve a nonexistent problem, a spurious mystery that has resulted from a breach, gulf, or divide wrongly asserted between mind and nature. Once such a gap is in place, something special seems needed to bridge it. But establishing this divide is *such* an error, and so pervasive, that attempts to give accounts of mind-world relations in familiar philosophical terms are misconceived and tend to have a non-naturalistic character.

This is a central theme in *Experience and Nature* (1925/1929). Here is a passage from chapter 7, initially about life, but extended from there.

> [A]ll schemes of psycho-physical parallelism, traditional theories of truth as correspondence, etc., are really elaborations of the same sort of assumptions as those made by Spencer: assumptions which first make a division where none exists, and then resort to an artifice to restore the connection which has been wilfully destroyed.
>
> (1925/1929, LW 1:216)

Here he talks about correspondence, which I take to be a close cousin of representation in this context, and it shows Dewey's view of the false "breach" that has been established.[8] A better picture, for Dewey, will be one that does not require this kind of bridge between mind and world.

To this I reply: concepts like correspondence have indeed been used in misconceived projects, but that does not furnish much of an argument against them. The fact that a concept has been used in failed projects does not mean it cannot have a role in better ones. We have to see how the other projects turn out.

Representation Is Wrongly Seen as Ubiquitous

For Dewey, knowing is one mode of interaction with the world among others that are more basic: "things are objects to be treated, used, acted upon and with, enjoyed and endured, even more than things to be known" (1929 edition, LW 1:28).[9] This quote, along with others like it, is not about representation per se but about knowledge and "cognition." The error in this area he sometimes calls "intellectualism." But the point being made applies, especially to views that put weight on the idea of representation itself. In many traditional views, for example, all of our contact with objects is mediated by sensory representations of them. We are continually involved in tenuous and questionable inference from the representations to everyday objects. Dewey thinks that once nonepistemic interaction with objects is recognized in its own right, those views are shown to be misguided. We are not inferring when we eat food, put on clothes, and so on. We are interacting with objects in nonepistemic ways.

A link between my first and second strands is seen in the letter to Charles Strong with which I opened, in a passage leading up to his *coup de* grâce comment.

> I believe in the transcendent reference of knowledge, but it is a reference not beyond experience, but beyond the Experience qua knowing. Things are experienced by us practically & aesthetically as well as cognitively. Cognition, to my mind, is a harmonious adjusting of the non-cognitional (but nonetheless empirical) things to one another: it is this fact which gives the check on arbitrary subjectivism. Knowledge refers to or corresponds with non-cognitional things, but never copies nor means to copy.[10]

Dewey thinks that, once we have a better view of what the relations that figure in knowledge are *between* we will see that representation (copying) is not a good candidate for the crucial relation.

As the letter goes on, Dewey says he is okay with "correspondence" in an everyday sense.

> I correspond now with you. I have to adjust my ideas & my 'things'—paper, ink, envelope, address &c—|| to you—but no copying or resembling is required or involved.

For Dewey at this stage, knowledge is not a matter of relations that obtain solely between ideas or beliefs. What would now be called a "coherence" view of knowledge is denied. Knowledge involves reference to something outside cognition itself, but this need not be (and is not) reference to something outside of experience, because there is the nonepistemic side of experience. Once the right relata are in place in the epistemological picture, Dewey thinks there is no temptation to appeal to the idea of copying.

Here I have dipped back into an earlier stage in Dewey's work, 1905, rather than the naturalistic period that is the main topic of this chapter, and where I feel I understand him better. In any case, Dewey is right that traditional philosophy has been overly intellectualist in its treatment of experience. But misuse of the idea of representation in some traditional views of our dealings with the world does not yet tell strongly against the importance of representation in other philosophical projects.

Representation Is Part of a Bad View of the Function of Thought and Theory

Once we see cognition and knowledge as part of a larger pattern of involvement with the objects we encounter, our *goal* in the cognitive side of life becomes clear, and, for Dewey, it is not representation—not copying—but something else. *The Quest for Certainty* (1929) has a lot of material on this theme, though, as I noted earlier, the word "representation" does not appear—the target is copying, conformity, and so on. Here are three passages:

The business of thought is *not* to conform to or reproduce the characters already possessed by objects but to judge them as potentialities of what they become through an indicated operation.

(LW 4:110)

Knowledge which is merely a reduplication in ideas of what exists already in the world may afford us the satisfaction of a photograph, but that is all. To form ideas whose worth is to be judged by what exists independently of them is not a function that (even if the test could be applied, which seems impossible) goes on within nature or makes any difference there.

(LW 4:110)

Any instrument which is to operate effectively in existence must take account of what exists, from a fountain pen to a self-binding reaper, a locomotive or an airplane. But "taking account of," paying heed to, is something quite different from literal conformity to what is already in being. It is an adaptation of what previously existed to accomplishment of a purpose.

(LW 4:165)

There is a false dichotomy here, one that I think Dewey sometimes skirted and sometimes fell into. We can represent things as they are ("reproduce the characters already possessed") *in order to* change them: first one, then the other, with the first being a means to the second. An especially clear illustration is a military or agonistic one. Recall the saying: *know your enemy*. We want to first know them as they really are, but as a means to harming or destroying them.

The first quote falls into this. There can be immediate and more eventual "business." One kind of business can be instrumental to other kinds. In the second quote, "merely" provides a hedge, as it may mean: this is *all* that is done. But, if so, Dewey's example of a photograph is not very apt, as photographs can be instrumentally useful and often need to be accurate if they are to be useful (consider an aerial photo of enemy forces).

In the third quote, Dewey wants to contrast "taking account of" something with "conformity to what is already in being." "Taking account," he says, is a way of dealing with what previously exists, in order to accomplish a purpose. Yes, but "literal conformity" can be a good *route to* the adaptation or transformation of things to achieve such a purpose.

The possibility that Dewey seems to neglect is the possibility of an instrumental role for representation of a kind that involves copying or conformity. Maybe the "business" of some thought *is* to "conform to or reproduce the characters already possessed by objects" and *then* to make changes. It this possible? If not, why not? Might there be *some* of this? Dewey is rather wholesale in his rejections, especially in *The Quest for Certainty*.

Here is yet another example, in a 1915 letter discussed by Fesmire (2015, 106). Dewey says in the letter: "Philosophical errors come from taking propositional knowledge as referring to the world or 'corresponding' to it or 'representing' or 'presenting' it in some other way than as being direction for the performance of acts." That also seems an error. Surely we can represent now and direct change later.

This I think is the main problem with Dewey's claims in this area. One can also press further. It sometimes seems that Dewey himself cannot really avoid endorsing the view I just described, once he starts getting into details. In this passage in *The Quest for Certainty,* he is talking about experiment and science:

> Among these operations [of experimentation] should be included, of course, those which give a *permanent register of what is observed* and the instrumentalities of exact measurement by means of which changes are correlated with one another.
>
> (1929, LW 4:70, italics added)[11]

See also, from *Logic*:

> Just as a complex undertaking in any field demands prepared *materials* as well as pre-pared instrumentalities, so propositions which describe conjunctions of existential materials—ultimately reducible to space-time connections—are required in effec-tive inquiry.
>
> (1938, LW 12:139)

In both of these cases, Dewey might reply that this is not "representation" in a bad sense but only in a mild sense he generally endorses. Perhaps, but how can we tell? Why is this not a recognition of an important role for representation of things *as they are,* rather than "direction for the performance of acts"? (That phrase "direction for the per-formance of acts" is from the 1915 letter quoted earlier). It might be only very specific things, for Dewey, that we want to record and register (events observed, in the *Quest for Certainty* quote; conjunctions, in the quote from *Logic*), but this is still registration of what there is.[12]

Dewey does not seem to be keeping consistent track of what he wants to deny. There may, however, be a reason he cannot simply accept the view I outline here, the one in which copying has an instrumental role.[13] The following is a quote from *Human Nature and Conduct* (1922):

> Perception of things as they are is but a stage in the process of making them different. They have already begun to be different in being known, for by that fact they enter into a different context, a context of foresight and judgment of better and worse.
>
> (MW 14:206)

Applying this idea back to the *Quest for Certainty,* quote earlier, perhaps when we seek to record things, to make a "permanent register of what is observed," our making of that register already achieves some transformation of the things recorded. If so, this would block a view in which copying and conformity have an instrumental role. Even if we try to copy the way things are or were, when we do this, we transform them. If Dewey was genuinely and generally committed to something like this, it would be a significant move back toward idealism. Perhaps he did intend such a move, but, if so, one would then expect to find, in the later work, a clearer and more forthright statement of the argument. I have only found partial versions and hints, like the one cited here. Perhaps there is a detailed statement of an argument like this that I do not know of. I have never been sure what to make of that quote from *Human Nature and Conduct*.

I move on now to a close look at a particular discussion in Dewey's later work that bears on all these issues and does not fall into the false dichotomy that I have criticized in this section.

MAPS AND OPERATIONS

In the context of the critical line of argument I began earlier, ordinary cartographic maps are an important case. They are instruments for guiding behavior, *and* they are representations that can be assessed for accuracy—a truth-like property. They also lend themselves to analogies with belief and knowledge. Frank Ramsey said in 1929 that he saw beliefs as *maps by which we steer*, a comparison since echoed by Armstrong (1973) and others.

Dewey's *Logic* includes a discussion of maps that bears on these issues. Dewey writes there about maps because he wants to use them to help with a more difficult case, mathematical knowledge. But these pages include a fairly detailed grappling with the relation between accuracy and usefulness in maps.

Dewey first says that if we want to understand a map's relation to its territory, the right approach is with the idea of an *isomorphism*. We need to think not just about relations between map and terrain, but relations between different parts of the map and relations between different parts of the terrain:

> That the isomorphism in question is one of relations is evident in the fact that it does not exist between a point marked on the map and an element of the country mapped, town, river, mountain, but between the relations sustained by the former and the relations sustained by the latter. Relations of up-down in the map are isomorphic with relations of north-south in the country, and those of right-left with those of east-west of the country. Similarly, relations of distance and direction of the map are isomorphic with those of the country, not literal copies of actual existences.
>
> (1938, LW 12:397)

Something like this is probably the right approach, at this stage in the story. The view Dewey is sketching could be expressed more exactly by saying that a cartographic map is accurate when there is a *structure-preserving mapping*, in the mathematical sense, between elements of the map and elements of the terrain. I will make this more precise in a footnote (and will not use the words "mapping" or "map" in their mathematical senses in the rest of the main text of this chapter). Dewey's own examples are clear enough for us to move on to the next stage.[14] He says:

> [t]he isomorphic relation which subsists between the relations of the map and those of the country, or between *patterns* of relation, should be interpreted in a functional and operational sense.[2]

(1938, LW 12:398)

What does this mean? "Functional" opposed to what? The footnote he appends to that sentence does not help:

> [Footnote 2]. In other words, the issue concerns the *meaning* of isomorphic patterns, not their existence or importance.

He then makes clear what he means, and does so at some length.

> The relations of the map are similar (in the technical sense of that word) to those of the country because both are *instituted by one and the same set of operations*.
> [...]
> [This] is readily seen by noting the fact that both are products of execution of certain operations that may be summed up in the word *surveying*. The elements of the country are certainly existentially connected with one another. But as far as knowledge is concerned, as far as any propositions about these connections can be made, they are wholly indeterminate until the country is surveyed. When, and as far as, the country is surveyed, a map is brought into being. Then, of course, there is a common pattern of relations in the map and in the country as mapped. Any errors that result in the *map* from inadequacy in the operations of surveying will also be found in propositions about the relations of the *country*. The doctrine of structural (in the sense of nonoperational) similarity of the relations of the map and those of the country is the product of taking maps that have in fact been perfected through performance of regulated operations of surveying in isolation from the operations by which the map was constructed. It illustrates the fallacy that always occurs when propositions are interpreted without reference to the means by which they are grounded.
> Given the map as a pattern of relations, the "relation" of the ... pattern to that of the country mapped is functional. It is constituted through the intermediation of the *further* operations it directs—whose consequences, moreover, provide the means by which the validity of the map is tested. The map is instrumental to such operations as traveling, laying out routes for journeys, following movements of goods and persons.

(1938, LW 12:398–399)[15]

I am not sure how to read some of this. I think Dewey means that it is an *error* to say that there is an isomorphism between map and territory, with respect to the relations between elements present on each side, unless we think of the relations present in the territory as *dependent on acts of surveying*. In the last part of the passage Dewey adds another idea that I find more obscure. There is a relation between map and country, he says, with "relation" given scare-quotes, that is dependent on ("constituted through") a role for the "further" (additional or subsequent) operations that the map use involves.

Dewey may mean this: any relevant "similarity" between map and territory is dependent on the acts of surveying, and what makes the map a map *of* a particular place— this now being a reference-like feature of the map, as opposed to an accuracy-like feature—is the way it is used in subsequent operations such as traveling. Alternatively, he might mean that the accuracy of the map is also dependent on the map's subsequent use.

If he means the latter, it would have consequences for representationalism, as I described that project earlier. As I set it out, a central representationalist claim is that behavioral success can (often) be causally explained in terms of the use of accurate or veridical representations. If Dewey thinks, as he might, that the *fact that the map is accurate* is constitutively dependent on the fact that it was used in particular successful ways, by travelers and the like, then accuracy is not a cause of successful use in the way representationalism requires. I am not sure that Dewey means to say this; he might mean only that the accuracy-like features of the map are dependent on the upstream processes of surveying—certainly he does say that—and I am not sure what this claim would imply for representationalist explanations of success in term of accuracy. Then, at least, the features that make the map an accurate map of a given terrain would be in place prior to and independently of any episodes of successful use of the map by travelers. One reason I suspect that Dewey *does* mean his discussion to tell against representationalism of the sort I have in mind is something he says shortly after:

> When the directive function of the map is left out of consideration it must be said that no map is "true," not only because of the special "distortions" mentioned but because in any case a map represents a spherical upon a plane surface. On the functional interpretation, any map in any system is "true" (that is, valid) if its operational use produces the consequences that are intended to be served by the map.
>
> (1938, LW 12:399)

The "truth" (or, better, *accuracy*) of a map is constitutively dependent on the fact of its successful use. Accuracy is not a pre-existing feature (a relation to the terrain) that can give rise to successful use.

If this is what Dewey means, I think it is probably wrong about maps. In accurate cartographic maps, there is a relation between map and territory, which need not be isomorphism (not every bit of territory is mapped, etc.) but is something akin to it, that involves a preservation of structure across the two domains. As Dewey said, north-south as a relation between elements of the territory may correspond to up-down, and so on (see note 14). We have to know how to *read* the map for it to be useful. We have to know the interpretation rule to be applied, the one that gets us from elements of the map to elements of a territory (and also tells us which elements of the map are to be interpreted at all). We also need to know which bits of territory to use the map as a guide to. (This might be folded into the first reading rule, though it need not be.)

But once the navigation task has been identified, some fairly generic reading-rules can be applied to a great range of maps, and those maps will help us get around, in a nonaccidental way, only if there is a relationship between map and territory of the right sort, a relation that exists prior to any navigational use of this particular map.

I am not sure how much of this Dewey was meaning to deny. This passage from the long quote above seems important: "The elements of the country are ... existentially connected with one another. But as far as knowledge is concerned, as far as any propositions about these connections can be made, they are *wholly indeterminate* until the country is surveyed" (emphasis added). I take this to say that, independently of acts of surveying, there *are no* determinate relations between elements of the terrain of a sort that are relevant to "knowledge." I think this means that the fact that we can know what a piece of countryside is like by looking at a map is itself dependent on acts of surveying. In response, it's true that maps do not spring into existence without surveying or something similar (passive map-making by high-tech means, such as Google Earth, might press on this a little). But the fact that we can learn about a piece of countryside by looking at a map, and by making use of an isomorphism (or similar relation) between the two, does not depend on *there having been* a surveyor. Dewey seems to say that without a surveyor, there is an indeterminacy in the relations between aspects of the landscape. I think that is also wrong. He seems to think, wrongly, that a particular set of actions brings into being *both* the relations in the map and the relations in the terrain: "The relations of the map are similar ... to those of the country because both are *instituted by one and the same set of operations*." This means that the map would not have the relations it has between its parts were it not for surveying—a point that seems okay, give or take the passive cases—and, in addition, the country would not have the relations it has between *its* parts were it not for surveying. There I say no.

An idea Dewey may be heading toward can be better captured by talking about *selectivity*. Among all the relations between parts of the country, only some are mapped. (i.e., only some are mapped *at all*; not just: only some are mapped in a particular way. See note 14.) As I said, I am not sure what Dewey means to say at some points through here. What might be helpful is to next outline more explicitly what I think Dewey *should* have said about maps.

What he might have said instead is something like this: there are rules of map-making and rules of map-reading, in the service of navigation. The rules are different but complementary. The first set of rules is linked to surveying and related methods. These rules or procedures give rise to objects of a certain kind, objects which are *made to be read*. For any map-making rule there is a map-reading rule that is complementary to it (or a range of such rules). Map-making and map-reading rules come in complementary, interlocking pairs. Here is an example of such a pair:

Map-Makers: if Stowe is north of Waitsfield, put the "Stowe" mark higher on the
   page than the "Waitsfield" mark.
Map-Readers: if the "Stowe" mark is higher on the page than the "Waitsfield" mark,
   infer that Stowe is north of Waitsfield.

That is an easy case, one that uses Dewey's own example (north-south and above-below). Of course, this rule is not usually restricted to Stowe and Waitsfield; it is applied to all places in the territory—all of Vermont, as it might be. Many other pairs of rules are possible. *North-of* might map to *left-of*, or something weirder, by means of an unusual projection. The map-making rule can be very odd indeed, and all will go well as long as the map-reading rule takes it into account. In a context in which complementary rules of map-making and map-reading are in place, maps will be produced that have particular kinds of structure-preserving relationships to the territories being mapped, and map-users will be able to exploit those relations in projects of navigation. Maps will then be produced with relations to their terrain that fit the schema introduced earlier for representationalism about an epistemic medium. Specifically, when co-adapted rules of making and interpretation are in place, we have:

A relation R between maps and territories,

(M1) That is an achievable goal in the production of maps, in a given context of interpretation, and a standard of assessment for maps themselves,

(M2) That involves

(M2a) Veridicality, in the sense of satisfaction by the territory of a condition specified by the map, and

(M2b) Preservation of structure between map and territory,

(M3) And that has a causal relation to success (theoretical or practical) in the use of maps, where this link to success is part of why relation R provides a goal and standard of assessment, as in (M1).

I do not know whether Dewey's talk of "operations" is compatible with this. It would be fine with me if his treatment was a gesture in the right direction, even if wrong in many details or incomplete. I think, though, that Dewey was instead trying to *head off* a view like the one here—a view that may not have existed in worked-out form in the 1930s but whose outlines he saw and that he wanted to deny. This I infer from his saying things against "The doctrine of structural (in the sense of nonoperational) similarity of the relations of the map and those of the country." He wanted to steer us *away* from anything like that.[16]

I am still not sure that Dewey was wrong, or entirely wrong, to do this. I finish this section by taking my positive discussion of maps a little further, putting some additional pressure on the representationalist view of maps and related devices in a way Dewey might have endorsed.

In my general representationalist schema early in this chapter, and also in the version just applied to maps, I set things up so that R, the representation relation, is put in place (or not) by a producer and is either present or absent in the epistemic device itself. But there are two sides to sign use: production and interpretation. Perhaps most obviously in linguistic cases, producing a representation with particular properties requires a language community of the right sort to be in place. A producer per se cannot determine such things. In my schema, I accommodated this by talking about R as an achievable goal of device producers "in a given context of interpretation." But it might be objected that this underestimates the importance of interpretation rules. One argument along these lines is as follows.

In the representationalist schema I gave earlier, R is a property of epistemic devices themselves and a standard of assessment for them (this map is accurate; that one is not). But *any* object of sufficient complexity can be used as a map of any given piece of terrain, if the right interpretation rule is applied to it. Imagine a large abstract pointillist painting, with no two dots of exactly the same color. Such an image can be used as a map of Vermont, or of any other part of the United States, down to a certain level of grain. We first pair up points on the painting with points on the terrain—we do so arbitrarily, without any preservation of neighbor relations in the territory. Then the relations between the unique colors of dots on the painting can be used to recapture spatial relations on the terrain, when interpreted with a suitable rule. *If* the color of this point on the painting is C_1 and the color of this (perhaps distant) one is C_2, *then* Stowe is 19 miles north-north-east of Waitsfield. After the painting has been used as a map of Vermont, it could then be used to navigate Nevada, with the aid of a different rule. A map we call "accurate" could be replaced with a great many other objects, and we could do as well, if we had the right interpretation rule in place. So the idea that the *map* gets credit for accuracy, where that is a success-linked property, and the idea that the producer puts that feature in place now both seem wrong. A better view of the situation seems to be one in which *map plus rule* get the credit. In its shifting credit away from a pre-existing relation of similarity between map and terrain, and toward the rule of interpretation, this might be seen as a Deweyan objection.

I think there may well be some truth in this line of criticism, though I do not think it is yet a major threat to representationalism. In reply, we can note first that in any case of successful navigation through use of a map, there will be a complete story that includes (among other things), (a) the production of the map, (b) the intrinsic properties of the map (its array of marks), and (c) the interpretation rule applied by the navigator. Once the map and interpretation rule are in place, successful navigation can result, regardless of where the map came from; the producer plays no role once the map exists. Further, we can concede that if the navigator was given any of a large range of other ordinary objects instead of the map, together with a suitable interpretation rule, he or she could do just as well. It is not the map *as opposed to other objects* (including other maps) that suffices to get the navigator home. The proximate cause of success is map plus interpretation rule. We could pick many other objects (with enough complexity) instead, and in each case there will be some rule that allows us to navigate the terrain with it.

However, "there will be some rule . . . " is a very weak claim. Most such rules—rules that turn ordinary objects into useable maps of a given terrain—are very complicated and could only be used (if they can be *used* in a practical way at all) with very few maps, and can only be used in restricted ways. We see this in the example with the abstract painting mentioned earlier. The rule I gave for inferring the relations between Stowe and Waitsfield is a tiny fragment of what would be needed to get very far through

Vermont—we would need a long list of these conditionals, a list that could also only be used with this particular painting. We could use these rules to extract particular bits of information about distances and directions but could not use the painting to visually determine short-cuts and the like. In effect, a list of conditionals of this kind can turn a painting into a "lookup table" from which information can be extracted, and a cartographic map is more than that. Ordinary cartographic maps are worth making and paying money for because they enable people to navigate using rules that are simple, applicable to many maps, easily specified in advance, and allow more than the piecemeal extraction of facts. If we are restricted to rules of that kind, only a specific kind of producer can generate a map with the right intrinsic properties to enable successful navigation. This producer must make use of a survey, or something similar.

This puts the producer, and co-adapted rules of map-making and interpretation, back into the picture. And once we confine ourselves to practically useable interpretation rules that are not tailored, like an elaborate piece of encryption, to one specific case, there is much more constraint on which objects might be used as a map of a particular territory. Unusual projections are still possible, and the world really is, in a sense, full of very unobvious maps—things would be navigationally useful if we knew how to use them. But the notion of *accuracy* as a property of some ordinary cartographic maps, and a property that has links to successful navigation, has not yet collapsed.

Still, once we walk through all the steps in a full account of successful navigation of this kind, noting the roles of producer, map, and interpreter, there is uncertainty in my mind about whether some everyday habits of description of these practices, and representationalist philosophical commentaries, tend to misallocate credit in ways that are relevant here.[17]

In the last couple of sections I described what look to me like errors in some of Dewey's treatments of these topics. These errors undermine some of his arguments against representationalist positions. But as the just-previous discussion indicates, I do not think this debate is over. Dewey's falling into false dichotomies was a mistake, but there are many gaps in the story I have sketched, and the history of this area is one in which the nature and role of representation continually appears more straightforward that it really is. This has been a problem both for advocates of representationalism and critics such as Dewey.

Looking Ahead

Dewey came across a philosophical landscape littered with unsuccessful representationalist views, sometimes facile in their treatment of what representation involves, and often seeing it in the most unlikely places.[18] Part of his response was to treat representation-like things in a functionalist way, attending to their context of use. This is tied to his insistence that much of our interaction with objects is not epistemic at all. Dewey went too far, I think, in his rejections of representationalist views, especially in his rejection of the idea that part of what we want to do, even in practical and transformative projects, is understand and represent things as they are, perhaps as a preliminary to changing them.

Dewey's emphasis on sign use, on "operations," was certainly a good move. More recent views in this area are based explicitly around the pairs of behaviors on each "side" of a sign or representation—behaviors of production and display on one side and behaviors of interpretation and application on the other. In frameworks of this kind, the status of features like content, veridicality, and correspondence—considered as features of the mediating devices themselves—raises unresolved questions. Formal notions of similarity seem applicable to some cases, including maps and possibly some internal states of organisms (Shea 2014), but plenty of cases are not like this, and I allowed that a genuine representationalism could avoid the notion of preservation of structure completely. Such a road makes it harder to hang onto the link between accuracy and success that is especially useful in making a representationalist view into something substantive, making veridicality more than just an honorific label.

A point that Rorty made here is useful:

> The great fallacy of the tradition, the pragmatists tell us, is to think that the metaphors of vision, correspondence, mapping, picturing and representation which apply to small routine assertions will apply to large and debatable ones. (1980, 724).

I disagree with some of this passage but agree with its main point. I think it is not really true that the pragmatists, especially Dewey, tended to concede that "metaphors of vision," and so on, do apply to the small, routine cases.[19] Further, a representationalist treatment need not suppose that these concepts always do apply. Rorty seems to think that making sense of picturing is *the* road to representationalism, and he thinks that this does work for mundane cases. ("When we rap out routine undeliberated reports like 'This is water,' 'That's red,' 'That's ugly,' 'That's immoral,' our short categorical sentences can easily be thought of as pictures, or as symbols which fit together to make a map.")[20] Instead, there may be ways for signs to acquire veridicality conditions that do not involve picturing. But Rorty is right that even *if* some simple cases, some epistemic media, can be handled in representationalist terms, that does not amount to a wholesale vindication of representationalism, one that helps us make sense of large-scale scientific, political, or philosophical theories and debates.

I think there is no way round the fact that Dewey mishandled some of these questions, especially in his introduction of false dichotomies. The literature contains both excesses of representationalism, seeing representation as philosophical panacea, and excesses in denials. The landscape here is only slowly coming into view. A future account of these matters might be one that recognizes many different kinds of *involvement* of epistemic devices with the parts of the world they are directed on, where some of this involvement has a representational character. This character may be found to various degrees: a nontrivial notion of mapping or structure-preservation may be more or less salient; veridicality may play more or less of the role representationalism envisages. Illusions of explanation may come from describing cases with only a tenuously representational character as if they were more paradigmatically representational. And as Rorty presses, it may be that the most important areas are those where a representationalist view is most difficult to sustain.

NOTES

1. Many thanks to Steven Fesmire, Jessie McCormack, and Jane Sheldon for help with this chapter.
2. In work written after these papers, Price (2013) moved more toward rehabilitation of representation, as opposed to rejection of it. The "one cheer" for representationalism in Price's 2009 paper is now at least one and a half.
3. Note that some versions of "representative realism" may not see the representatives as representations (Lyons 2017).
4. In this discussion I set aside imperative contents (commands, etc.) and assume that satisfaction involves an indicative "direction of fit."
5. I do not know if he was the first, but Ramsey (1927) was early in seeing that things could be set up this way—a way in which the philosophical work goes not so much into *truth* but into the *having of truth-conditions*. Once we have explained that, explaining truth is easy.
6. I am not sure how some representational views of perception relate to the schema here, as it is not always clear that the sensory states are "produced" in the relevant way (see also note 3). For Locke, see Uzgalis (2017). Beliefs, in contrast, do fit the schema.
7. Many years later: "my own view takes correspondence in the operational sense it bears in all cases except the unique epistemological case of an alleged relation between a "subject" and an "object"; the meaning, namely, of *answering*, as a key answers to conditions imposed by a lock, or as two correspondents "answer" each other; or, in general, as a reply is an adequate answer to a question or a criticism-; as, in short, a solution answers the requirements of a *problem*" (1941, LW 14:179). See also LW 1:216. William James (1904) expressed similar attitudes—"correspondence" might be useable in a general account; copying is more problematic, though it may be present in a few cases.
8. "Representation" itself does not appear often in *Experience and Nature*. It is used once to refer to a view Dewey wants to reject (1925, LW 1:119–120) and once to talk about coins—"as money they are substitutes, representations, and surrogates, which embody relationships" (1925/1929, LW 1:137).
9. See also the 1925 edition of *Experience and Nature*: "*being* and *having* things in ways other than knowing them, in ways never identical with knowing them, exist, and are preconditions of reflection and knowledge" (LW 1:377).
10. The letter is 1905.004.28 (12501): John Dewey to Charles Augustus Strong. In the original Dewey struck-through some added letters in the word "non-cognitional," as follows: "non-cognitiveional."
11. Thanks to Lauren Alpert for bringing this quote and its importance to my attention.
12. Another example is seen in Dewey's account of what language does for us, and how this takes us beyond what other animals can do: "Organic biological activities end in overt actions, whose consequences are irretrievable. When an activity and its consequences can be rehearsed by representation in symbolic terms, there is no such final commitment. If the representation of the final consequence is of unwelcome quality, overt activity may be

foregone, or the way of acting be replanned in such a way as to avoid the undesired outcome" (1938, LW 12:57).

13. This issue is discussed in detail in Godfrey-Smith (2016).

14. A structure-preserving mapping, in this sense, is a function (an input-output rule) between a domain (a set of elements of a cartographic map, for example) and a codomain (elements of a territory) such that for each element of the domain the mapping assigns one element of the codomain, and vice versa, and for each relation r between elements in the domain, the mapping assigns a relation r^* between elements in the codomain, such that two elements of the domain are related by r if and only if their corresponding elements in the codomain are related by r^*. That is, if the mapping assigns x_1 to y_1 and x_2 to y_2 and assigns relation r_1 to r^*_1, then $r_1(x_1, x_2)$ if and only if $r^*_1(y_1, y_2)$. This is roughly what a lot of philosophical discussions mean by "isomorphism." The requirement that an ismorphism exist may be strong or weak, as a consequence of what is required for relations themselves to exist. A problem with this concept, applied to cartographic maps, is that it does not naturally accommodate the fact that any cartographic map is selective and partial; many elements in the territory and many relations between them will not be represented in any useable cartographic map. In response, one might see the map as isomorphic to some sort of abstraction from the territory, but it probably makes more sense instead to use a "morphism" concept that allows the structure on one side to be richer than the structure on the other (monomorphism?—this takes the discussion into more serious mathematics) and also to allow some role for approximation. Many cartographic maps also use representational tools that are not naturally understood in terms of discrete elements figuring in a structure-preserving mapping, such as continuous gradations of color shading. Representational devices that do not involve structure-preservation can also be freely added to maps—arbitrary icons, labels, and the like—along with the more pictorial elements. See Camp (in press) for discussion of the distinctive representational strategies seen in cartographic maps.

15. The second ellipsis here is a repeated "the" in the original.

16. I'd be interested to learn who he was thinking of when Dewey talked of this alternative, the "doctrine" of structural similarity between the relations in the map and in the country.

17. My approach in this section has been influenced by the recent development of "sender-receiver" models of sign use. These originate in Lewis (1969) and were revived and updated especially by Skyrms (2010). See also Millikan (1984), Shea (2014), and Godfrey-Smith (2017). My discussion of what Dewey should have said about maps draws specifically on Blackburn (2013), who discusses mapping in connection with arguments against representationalism in recent pragmatism. I (Godfrey-Smith 1996) and Kitcher (2002) also put pressure on pragmatism's anti-correspondence tendencies using cartographic maps, but neither of those discussions made use of a good account of how maps work, one based on sender-receiver or maker-reader complementarity. And none of us picked up Dewey's 1938 discussion, with its mix of good and less good moves; for this I am indebted to Fesmire (2015). Fesmire's book includes a detailed discussion of Dewey's account of maps, and he also applies the concept of mapping as a broader metaphilosophical tool.

18. Hylton (1990) includes a discussion of the ontologies of early analytic philosophers, and others around that time, that furnishes good examples, though some of the views are so strange that it is hard to work out how they related to the idea of representation: "Moore's metaphysics has a number of consequences which may, at first sight, strike the reader as

counter-intuitive. Perhaps the most extreme of these is his claim that ordinary things, which exist in space and time, are to be identified with propositions" (Hylton 1990, 138).

19. James perhaps conceded something a bit like this, in his discussion of our idea of a clock in Chapter 6 of *Pragmatism* (1907). Dewey, as discussed earlier, argued that notions of mapping do apply to some important cases (mathematics) but only after critical reinterpretation.

20. A bit more of the Rorty passage: "Given a language and a view of what the world is like, one can, to be sure, pair off bits of the language with bits of what one takes the world to be in such a way that the sentences one believes true have internal structures isomorphic to relations between things in the world. When we rap out routine undeliberated reports like 'This is water,' 'That's red,' 'That's ugly,' 'That's immoral,' our short categorical sentences can easily be thought of as pictures, or as symbols which fit together to make a map" (Rorty 1980, 721–722).

Works Cited

Citations of John Dewey's works are to the thirty-seven-volume critical edition published by Southern Illinois University Press under the editorship of Jo Ann Boydston. In-text citations give the original publication date, series abbreviation, followed by volume number and page number. For example: (1934, LW 10:12) is page 12 of *Art as Experience*, which is published as volume 10 of *The Later Works*.

Series abbreviations for *The Collected Works*

EW *The Early Works* (1882–98)

MW *The Middle Works* (1899–1924)

LW *The Later Works* (1925–53)

Citations of Dewey's correspondence are to *The Correspondence of John Dewey*, 1871–2007, published by the InteLex Corporation under the editorship of Larry Hickman. Citations give the date, reference number for the letter, and author followed by recipient. For example: 1973.02.13 (22053): Herbert W. Schneider to H. S. Thayer.

Armstrong, David M. 1973. *Belief, Truth, and Knowledge*. Cambridge: Cambridge University Press.

Blackburn, Simon. 2013. "Pragmatism: All or Some?" In *Expressivism, Pragmatism and Representationalism*, edited by Huw Price, Simon Blackburn, Robert Brandom, Paul Horwich, and Michael Williams. Cambridge: Cambridge University Press.

Camp, Elisabeth. (in press). "Why Maps Are Not Propositional." In *Non-Propositional Intentionality*, edited by A. Grzankowski and M. Montague. Oxford: Oxford University Press.

Dewey, John. 1922. *Human Nature and Conduct*. MW 14.

Dewey, John. 1925/1929. *Experience and Nature*. LW 1.

Dewey, John. 1929. *Quest for Certainty*. LW 4.

Dewey, John. 1938. *Logic: The Theory of Inquiry*. LW 12.

Dewey, John. 1941. "Propositions, Warranted Assertibility, and Truth." LW 14.

Fesmire, Steven. 2015. *Dewey* (The Routledge Philosophers). London: Routledge.

Godfrey-Smith, Peter. 1996. *Complexity and the Function of Mind in Nature*. Cambridge: Cambridge University Press.

Godfrey-Smith, Peter. 2016. "Dewey and the Question of Realism." *Noûs*, vol. 50, 73–89. doi: 10.1111/nous.12059.

Godfrey-Smith, Peter. 2017. "Senders, Receivers, and Symbolic Artifacts." *Biological Theory*, vol. 12, 275–286. doi 10.1007/s13752-017-0276-4.

Horwich, Paul. 1998. *Truth*, 2nd ed. Oxford: Blackwell.

Hylton, Peter. 1990. *Russell, Idealism, and the Emergence of Analytic Philosophy*. Oxford: Oxford University Press.

James, William. 1904. "Humanism and Truth." *Mind*, vol. 13, no. 52, 457–475.

James, William. 1975 (1907). *Pragmatism: A New Name for Some Old Ways of Thinking*. Cambridge, MA: Harvard University Press.

Kitcher, Philip. 2002. "On the Explanatory Role of Correspondence Truth." *Philosophy and Phenomenological Research*, vol. 64, no. 2, 346–364. doi 10.1111/j.1933-1592.2002.tb00005.x

Lewis, David. 1969. *Convention: A Philosophical Study*. Cambridge, MA: Harvard University Press.

Lyons, Jack. 2017. "Epistemological Problems of Perception." In *The Stanford Encyclopedia of Philosophy* (Spring 2017 Edition), edited by Edward Zalta. https://plato.stanford.edu/archives/spr2017/entries/perception-episprob/

Macarthur, David and Price, Huw. 2007. "Pragmatism, Quasi-Realism, and the Global Challenge." In *New Pragmatists*, edited by Cheryl Misak, 91–121. Oxford: Oxford University Press.

Menand, Louis. 2001. *The Metaphysical Club: A Story of Ideas in America*. New York: Farrar, Strauss and Giroux.

Millikan, Ruth Garrett. 1984. *Language, Thought, and Other Biological Categories*. Cambridge, MA: MIT Press.

Price, Huw. 2009. "One Cheer for Representationalism." In *The Philosophy of Richard Rorty*, edited by Randall E. Auxier and Lewis E. Hahn, 269–289. La Salle IL: Open Court.

Price, Huw. 2013. "Two expressivist programmes, two bifurcations." In *Expressivism, Pragmatism and Representationalism*, edited by Huw Price, Simon Blackburn, Robert Brandom, Paul Horwich, and Michael Williams, 67–84. Cambridge: Cambridge University Press.

Ramsey, Frank. 1927. "Facts and Propositions." In *F.P. Ramsey: Philosophical Papers*, edited by David H. Mellor, 34–51. Cambridge: Cambridge University Press.

Ramsey, Frank. 1929. "General Propositions and Causality." In *F.P. Ramsey: Philosophical Papers*, edited by David H. Mellor, 145–163. Cambridge: Cambridge University Press.

Rorty, Richard. 1980. "Pragmatism, Relativism, and Irrationalism." *Proceedings and Addresses of the American Philosophical Association*, vol. 53, no. 6, 719–738. doi: 10.2307/3131427

Rorty, Richard. 1982. *Consequences of Pragmatism*. Minneapolis: University of Minnesota Press.

Shea, Nicholas. 2014. "Exploitable Isomorphism and Structural Representation." *Proceedings of the Aristotelian Society*, vol. 114, 123–144. doi: 10.1111/j.1467-9264.2014.00367.x

Skyrms, Brian. 2010. *Signals: Evolution, Learning, and Information*. Oxford: Oxford University Press.

Uzgalis, William. 2017. "John Locke." In *The Stanford Encyclopedia of Philosophy* (Fall 2017 Edition), edited by Edward Zalta. https://plato.stanford.edu/archives/fall2017/entries/locke/

Wittgenstein, Ludwig. 1922. *Tractatus Logico-Philosophicus*. C. K. Ogden, trans. London: Routledge & Kegan Paul.

IV

ETHICS, LAW, AND THE STARTING POINT

CHAPTER 8

DEWEY'S RADICAL CONCEPTION OF MORAL COGNITION

MARK JOHNSON

IT is unfortunate that John Dewey's writings on morality and moral deliberation have not had much of an impact on twentieth- and twenty-first-century moral theory. The main reason Dewey's views have not caught on is that they necessitate a nearly total reconstruction of moral philosophy, and most philosophers are not ready for such a radical change. Dewey's ideas require a substantial reworking of our received notions about mind, thought, values, self, will, character, freedom, deliberation, principles, good, duty, and virtue. The inertia of traditional moral philosophy, as well as that of our commonsense notions about morality, resists the call for an overhaul of our most dearly held assumptions about moral experience and judgment.

There are parts of Dewey's view that have antecedents in earlier philosophical perspectives. For example, in the foreword to the Modern Language edition of *Human Nature and Conduct,* Dewey says, "Were it not for one consideration, the volume might be said to be an essay in continuing the tradition of David Hume." But Dewey is not just channeling Hume (1739, 1751). He is also challenging a number of deeply held cultural views about who we are, how we think, and how we ought to behave. Dewey's arguments cut so deeply against the grain of our Enlightenment notions about morality that it is no wonder that few philosophers have felt any resonance with his radical perspective.

Only in the past few years has there been a glimmer of renascent interest in Dewey's conception of morality. This is, I suspect, partly because parts of his view can now be validated by experimental cognitive science research on moral cognition. Recent developments in moral psychology are undermining some of our taken for granted notions about moral cognition and have opened the door for a reconsideration of Dewey's important contribution to a psychologically valid account of mind, self, habit, moral appraisal, and deliberation. Once we go through that door, there is no turning back, and the consequences for our new understanding of morality are many and profound.

In a nutshell, Dewey's view is naturalistic, social-psychological, reconstructive, fallibilist, and focused on imagination. It is *naturalistic* insofar as it treats moral agents as embodied social animals operating in the natural world, without possessing anything like an eternal soul, transcendent ego, pure reason, or other disembodied mental faculty. All our values, as well as our capacity to reason about them, have to arise naturally from our biological and social nature. Dewey's view is *social-psychological* because it sees morality as arising from our social embeddedness and interactions with others within communities of interdependent persons. It is *reconstructive* in that it regards moral appraisal and deliberation as part of an ongoing process of attempting to transform our developing experience for the better. It is *fallibilist* in recognizing that there is no all-encompassing or transcendent standpoint from which to make allegedly absolute moral judgments, so we have to understand moral deliberation as a self-critical process of continual re-evaluation in light of newly emerging problems, conditions, and opportunities for action. Finally, Dewey sees moral deliberation neither as rule following nor as mere emotional response but rather as *imaginative* exploration of how we might reduce conflict, harmonize competing ends, and deepen and enrich meaning within situations rife with conflict and tension.

Dewey's naturalistic approach requires us to begin our account of moral cognition with a description of the emergence of moral agency from the embodied and socially embedded activities of a biological/social organism as it engages its environment. What is needed is a nondualistic account of how increasing complexity of organism-environment interactions generates emerging functional organization, ranging from our automatic monitoring of our body states all the way up to our most reflective moral inquiries. We need to start, therefore, at a very basic biological level and work our way up to full-blown moral agency and cognition.

A NATURALISTIC PERSPECTIVE
ON ORGANISM-ENVIRONMENT INTERACTION

Dewey's most radical departure from traditional moral philosophies is his dismissal, on scientific and philosophical grounds, of any notion of a supernatural or transcendent basis for moral personhood and moral cognition. Dewey founds his account on the idea that we are embodied animals operating within natural environments, where nature includes not only the physical but also the social and cultural aspects of our being. This assumption runs directly counter to traditional theological and rationalist theories, in which moral agency is supposedly grounded in a soul, pure ego or other transcendent form of selfhood. I cannot provide the details of his many arguments for embodied agency in key books within his vast corpus of writings, but the view, in brief, runs as follows.

The first principle and grounding assumption for Dewey's naturalistic account of human being is that all experience, perception, thought, action, and communication is rooted in an embodied organism in ongoing interaction with its multidimensional physical, interpersonal, and cultural environments. In the chapter titled "The Live Creature" in *Art as Experience* (1934), Dewey explains:

> The first great consideration is that life goes on in an environment; not merely *in* it but because of it, through interaction with it. No creature lives merely under its skin; its subcutaneous organs are means of connection with what lies beyond its bodily frame, and to which, in order to live, it must adjust itself, by accommodation and defense but also by conquest. At every moment, the living creature is exposed to dangers from its surroundings, and at every moment, it must draw upon something in its surroundings to satisfy its needs. The career and destiny of a living being are bound up with its interchanges with its environment, not externally but in the most intimate way.
>
> (Dewey 1934, LW 10:13)

The first business of any living animal must be to secure the conditions for its continued existence. As neuroscientist Antonio Damasio explains, the fundamental value for any organism is the sustaining of the conditions of life, and this requires constant maintenance of a dynamic homeostasis within the semipermeable boundary of the organism: "Life requires that the body maintain a collection of parameter *ranges* at all costs of literally dozens of components in its dynamic interior" (Damasio 2010, 42). For example, an animal will need to maintain minimal levels of oxygen, proteins, and sugars, in the requisite proportions, if it is to continue living.

Changes in an organism's environment require the organism to monitor the effects of those changes on its body-state and then to make whatever changes are necessary to sustain or recover the homeostasis required for ongoing functioning. The result, for live animals, is a recurring need-demand-satisfaction process:

> By need is meant a condition of tensional distribution of energies such that the body is in a condition of uneasy or unstable equilibrium. By demand and effort is meant the fact that this state is manifested in movements which modify environing bodies in ways which react upon the body, so that its characteristic pattern of active equilibrium is restored. By satisfaction is meant this recovery of equilibrium pattern, consequent upon the changes of environment due to interactions with the active demands of the organism.
>
> (Dewey 1925/1929, LW 1:194)

Dewey's use of "need-demand-satisfaction" terminology can be a bit misleading in two respects. First, as Steven Fesmire has observed (in conversation), "search" might be a better term than "demand" for that part of the life process in which the organism seeks a resolution of the indeterminacy of a given situation, insofar as the organism is actively exploring its environment in search of a way to return to a relative internal equilibrium. Indeed, in his *Logic* (1938), Dewey describes the tripartite process in just that way:

> [L]iving may be regarded as a continual rhythm of disequilibrations and recoveries of equilibrium. . . . . The state of disturbed equilibration constitutes *need*. The movement toward its restoration is search and exploration. The recovery is fulfillment or satisfaction. (1938, LW 12:34)

The second caution is not to read "satisfaction" in an overly subjective and individualistic way, as if it consisted always in a feeling of fulfillment or satisfaction within an organism. Rather, this term is meant to include objective conditions and to involve the coordinated interplay of organism and environment when it achieves a certain stability and balance. Consciousness of fulfillment is not a necessary requirement for the recovery of equilibrium.

The process of achieving or recovering this balanced dynamic equilibrium state within certain required parameters is known in biology as *homeostasis*. Damasio concludes, just as Dewey did, that this need for homeostasis constitutes the ultimate source of values for any organism, from single-celled creatures all the way up to humans in complex patterns of social transaction with others: "For whole organisms, then, the primitive of value is *the physiological state of living tissue within a survivable, homeostatic range*," such that "objects and processes we confront in our daily lives acquire their assigned value by reference to this primitive of naturally selected organism value" (Damasio 2010, 49).

The term "homeostasis" can be somewhat problematic in the context of the dynamic process Dewey and Damasio are describing—a process in which an organism makes appropriate changes in itself, its environment, or both, in order to re-establish fluid action. The word "stasis" too readily conveys the idea of a fixed and finished state, whereas the opposite is often the case. Much of the time, animals do not return to a pregiven "steady state." Instead, the organism manages to establish a *new* dynamic equilibrium. In what follows, I will, on occasion, continue to use the term "homeostasis," but I am inclined to replace it with something like "dynamic equilibrium."

It cannot be emphasized strongly enough that the very possibility of morality, as well as the structure of moral cognition, is grounded in the pattern of development by which living beings sustain organic equilibrium as they engage their world. As we will see, the processes of moral problem-solving are modeled on, and are exaptations of, the biological processes of life maintenance, in which the organism falls in and out of harmony with its surroundings and must make adjustments to these changed conditions in order to restore relative equilibrium. Consequently, Dewey's naturalism requires that the "higher" social interactions of people that we call "moral" transactions are grounded in, and are continuous with, our bodily enactments of the need-search-satisfaction pattern.[1] That is what Damasio means (though without knowledge of Dewey) when he says that organic homesostasis is the primordial value upon which all "higher" values rest. Therefore, what we regard as moral cognition or moral thinking is isomorphic with, because it is rooted in, the very embodied processes of need-demand (search)-satisfaction by which living creatures occasionally fall out of harmony with their sur-roundings and then attempt to re-establish the requisite dynamic equilibrium they need to survive and flourish.

This point about the parallels between organic life processes and moral cognition is of crucial importance, insofar as it defines and makes possible a naturalistic account of morality. The only way to avoid bringing in allegedly external or transcendent causes or values is to see morality as an emergent level of functioning that arises from and recruits the basic life processes of the organism. From a naturalistic perspective, there must be a continuity between biological functions and cognitive operations. Dewey's version of this claim is his all-important *Postulate of Continuity*:

> (I)n order to account for the distinctive, and unique, characters of logical subject-matter we shall not suddenly evoke a new power or faculty like Reason or Pure Intuition. Positively and concretely, it means that a reasonable account shall be given of the ways in which it is possible for the traits that differentiate deliberate inquiry to develop out of biological activities not marked by those traits. (1938, LW 12:31)

In other words, the challenge for someone like Dewey, who has rejected the scientifi-cally and philosophically discredited notions of pure, transcendent, or absolute entities, causes, agents, or values, is to articulate an emergentist account of how higher functional wholes can arise naturally from lower processes of biological activity. We need to ex-plain how the very same patterns of need-search-satisfaction in biological functioning are operative in higher-level understanding and reasoning.

HABITS IN MORAL APPRAISAL

To say that we are creatures of habit is no overstatement. If anything, it is an un-derstatement. The story of morality is a story of habits and their reconstruction. Habits are experientially reinforced patterns of organism-environment interac-tion, realized neurally by vast arrays of neuronal connections. Consider the regular patterns of perception, action, and feeling that emerge over time as a human being lives in its environments. Under "normal" conditions of body-brain development, and assuming appropriate time sequencing in which various neural structures come on line, a human body grows certain specific types of perceptual systems that con-strain what it can perceive and how it makes sense of what it perceives. Likewise, it grows functional neuronal clusters that make possible certain specific kinds of body movement and object manipulations. It generates and tunes up its emotional response systems. Eventually, if all goes well, it wires up massive patterns of neuronal connectivity that underlie habits of language and abstract reasoning. At any given point in a creature's development, the current combinations of these habits of perception, feeling, movement, valuing, and thought constrain how we habitually experience our surroundings and what we regard as possible ways of thinking, feeling, and acting. Our physical-social-cultural environment thus provides what psychologist J. J. Gibson called "affordances" for possible ways of engaging our surroundings as we live and act in the world. The numerous habits we have developed will shape how we perceive the possibilities for action afforded us by a specific morally charged situation.

The neural/bodily systems responsible for our perception, action, and feelings typically involve dense arrays of interconnected neurons that form functional clusters whose connections are strengthened whenever we enact roughly the same experiential (sensory, motor, affective) patterns. For example, we develop and strengthen our tendency to see objects in certain ways, just as we develop and strengthen habits for handling those objects or using them to perform various tasks. These recurring activation patterns that emerge from regularities in our experience and action become the basis of habits of perception, feeling, action, valuing, and thought. Without such habits we would become completely unable to function fluidly in our day-to-day lives.

A fundamental aspect of Dewey's account of habits is his insistence that they are not merely structures internal to the organism but always incorporate within them aspects of our environment. As he says, there is no habit of breathing without the air we breathe, no habit of walking without the land we walk on and the legs we walk with. So, habits are neither exclusively inner nor outer but both at once, insofar as they reach out into the world beyond our skins. They constitute our means of being relatively "at home" in our world. In comparing habits to functions, Dewey emphasizes that they are "functions of the surroundings as truly as of a person. They are things done *by* the environment by means of organic structures or acquired dispositions" (1922, MW 14:15). What this entails, at the level of moral actions, is that our moral habits cannot be identified independent of the environments necessary for their operation.

One profound implication of Dewey's account of habits is that what we think of as the "self" that defines an individual person is not any sort of pure or transcendent disembodied ego, will, or rationality. Rather, the self is a complex blending of various habits of perceiving, feeling, valuing, moving, speaking, understanding, and reasoning. Dewey concludes that "a predisposition formed by a number of specific acts is an immensely more intimate and fundamental part of ourselves than are vague, general, conscious choices. All habits are demands for certain kinds of activity; *and they constitute the self. In any intelligible sense of the word will, they are will*" (1922, MW 14:21 [italics added]). Habits thus define the self, will, and character, which Dewey describes as "interpenetration of habits" (29).

NONCONSCIOUS DIMENSIONS
OF MORAL APPRAISAL

Another important implication of our habitual nature is that the vast majority of what we think of as our moral appraisal and choice goes on beneath the level of our conscious awareness, since what we care about, how we read situations, and how we are disposed to respond to certain situations is worked out mostly unreflectively through our habitual responses. Sad to say, but most of the time, we run on autopilot, and there is very little, if any, reflective thought involved. We just do what we are habitually prone to do. In this respect, Dewey anticipated by some eighty years certain parts of what has come to be known in our current moral psychology as the *dual-process (or dual-track) model* of moral appraisal. There is now a growing body of experimental evidence that the vast majority of our moral cognition goes on intuitively, beneath the level of conscious reflection and control, so that critical reflective reasoning plays only a very minor, almost negligible, role in shaping how we behave. Marc Hauser (2006) concisely summarizes the dual-process model of the intuitive versus the rational tracks:

> [I]ntuition and conscious reasoning have different design specs. Intuitions are fast, automatic, involuntary, require little attention, appear early in development, are delivered in the absence of principled reasons, and often appear immune to counter-reasoning. Principled reasoning is slow, deliberate, thoughtful, requires considerable attention, appears late in development, justifiable, and open to carefully defended and principles counterclaims.
>
> (Hauser 2006, 89)

The dual-track model of moral cognition is understandably upsetting to most people, insofar as it suggests that we are not the rational moral animals we may have thought we were. It appears that conscious rational reflection actually plays a very small role in our moral cognition. There is growing experimental evidence from moral psychology, developmental psychology, and neuroscience suggesting that people mostly make unreflective intuitive judgments about what's right or wrong based on their unconscious habits of appraisal and response. Then, only after the fact, do they proceed to gin up allegedly rational justifications for what they have already judged, via intuitive processes, to be the proper moral response (Hauser 2006; Haidt 2012).

Jonathan Haidt (2012) has appropriately named this the "elephant/rider" model, in which the elephant (our nonconscious, intuitive, habit-driven appraisal system) makes quick and unreflective judgments leading to action, and then the rider (our conscious, rational processes) makes up a good story about how he or she was actually planning and controlling the elephant's appraisals and movements. The fact is that the elephant pretty much goes where it will, and the rider gets carried along, all the while pretending that he or she is in rational control. Most of our moral cognition is actually the result of habits that we are seldom even aware of, and over which we have little, or sometimes no, control. At the intuitive level, it is our habits that define and direct our action in the world, and Dewey would probably agree that much of our purportedly conscious "rational" thought is somewhat impotent when it comes to guiding actions. It is in this respect that Dewey saw himself as furthering a basically Humean moral sentiment view.

Moral Deliberation as Imaginative Dramatic Rehearsal

Although Dewey's account of the key role of habits in our moral cognition appears to anticipate by eighty years the dual-process model's emphasis on intuitive, nonreflective dimensions of moral judgment, Dewey would *not* regard the dual-process account as a fully adequate explanation of human moral deliberation. He would see Haidt's conception of rationality as impoverished and overly narrow relative to the actual operations of human rational thought. He would argue that Haidt starts out with a false dichotomy between intuition and reason, reduces reasoning to justification of intuited values, and then more or less denies any serious role for intelligence in moral appraisal.

In contrast, Dewey proposed a much richer conception of rationality that includes a role for feelings and imagination. I (Johnson 2014) have argued that Dewey recognized, in addition to the intuitive track and the rational justification track, a third track of moral cognition, which he called deliberation. Deliberation is a process of imaginative "dramatic rehearsal" of possible ways experience might play out under the influence of this or that value, disposition, or choice. Dewey saw this imaginative process as a key part of human intelligence, and so he included it in his broad notion of reasonableness.

As I mentioned earlier, Dewey saw moral cognition as rooted in, and formed out of, our primitive biological processes of approach, avoidance, incorporation, expulsion, and so forth. Recall his argument that the transaction of an organism with its environment involves falling in and out of fluid engagement with one's surroundings, according to the need-demand (search)-satisfaction structure of animal experience. Dewey's whole notion of inquiry is predicated on precisely this pattern of organism-in-environment couplings and adjustments, as follows: Most of the time, we operate on autopilot, as our engrained habits carry us through the day, more or less enabling us to negotiate our engagement with our surroundings and other people. We maintain a relative homeostasis and fluid action in the world. Dewey describes this part of the experiential process as follows:

> The results of prior experience, including previous conscious thinking, get taken up into direct habits, and express themselves in direct appraisals of value. Most of our judgments are intuitive, but this fact is not a proof of the existence of a separate

faculty of moral insight, but is the result of past experience funded into direct outlook upon the scene of life. .... There is a permanent limit to the value of even the
best of the intuitive appraisals of which we have been speaking. These are dependable in the degree in which conditions and objects of esteem are fairly uniform and
recurrent.

(Dewey and Tufts 1932, LW 7:266–267)

These habitual modes and tendencies of appraisal operate well most of the time, until we
run into new situations that go beyond those conditions in which our habits of valuing
and judging were originally established. In such cases, our normal activity and engrained
habits tend to become frustrated and are felt to be inadequate to the task of managing
the complexities of our present situation, which now reveals an indeterminacy—a problematic character—about how to go forward. This is the "need" phase of the process that
leads us to inquire into what is going on and whether any changes are necessary to keep
things balanced and functioning.

Once we sense that something is wrong, we then have to figure out *what the problem
is*. This is the start of the "search" phase of the need-search-satisfaction structure of inquiry. The course of our moral inquiry begins with the fundamental question of how we
identify the problem we are facing. This is a matter of paramount importance, because
the direction of our deliberative reflection is a response to *this* particular situation (as
presently circumscribed and understood), and not some other context. The more partial and narrow our grasp of our situation is, the less likely we are to consider all of the
relevant dimensions that have given rise to the problem and that need to be harmonized
into a new direction of action.

The tradition-challenging aspect of this view is that, in formulating and addressing
a moral problem, there is no such thing as a distinctive moral faculty (e.g., conscience)
that generates a unique form of ethical reasoning in accordance with universal moral
principles or absolute values (Johnson 2014). Instead, moral inquiry is a process for
reconstructing experience to resolve the tensions and blockages that have arisen because of conflicting values, ends, practices, or ideals. As such, what we call moral inquiry is grounded in our biological problem-solving processes, but now developed
and transformed as an operation at the level of increased complexity, within human
communities, where moral appraisal is made possible by cultural systems of meaning,
thinking, and valuing.

Consequently, inquiry and problem solving are not rational or reflective procedures
or methods brought to experience from *outside* the processes of nature. Instead, moral
inquiry is a manifestation of the biological processes for the recovery of homeostasis
that underlie all life, but now operating at the higher level of our social transactions
within communities, and thus involving and being enriched by language, institutions,
and codes of behavior. Those organic processes *are* inquiry in its most fundamental
sense, and what we call "moral" inquiry—inquiry about matters of better and worse by
way of action—is just one (albeit more complex) manifestation of this type of embodied,
experiential problem-solving.

It need hardly be said that this orientation is fundamentally at odds with the Kantian rationalist point of view, which claims that a moral faculty of pure practical reason issues universally valid and binding imperatives. But it is also at odds with any view that reduces all moral appraisal to habitual, unreflective emotional response, as Haidt's model sometimes appears to do.[2] Dewey recognized that moral sentiment theory (e.g., Smith [1790] and Hume [1751]) is closer to what actually happens than is the rationalist program, but he found it necessary to supplement a sentiment based perspective with a more complex description of the imaginative dimensions of moral deliberation that are at once both reasonable and affectively charged with motivational power.

This constitutes the second part of the search phase of moral inquiry, namely, imaginative exploration of possible courses of action to see which best resolves the conflict of ends and values confronting us. This is a manifestation, at a higher (social and cultural) level of complexity, of the search (demand) phase by which organisms reconstructively engage their surroundings in an attempt to return to a state of relative dynamic equilibrium. Dewey's account of imaginative moral deliberation constitutes a third track, in addition to the intuitive and rational justification tracks of the dual-process model. This third track is basically part of Dewey's richer and more expansive notion of human intelligence and reasoning capacities. Dewey describes the reconstructive process as a form of "dramatic rehearsal" of possible courses of action, to determine which avenue offers the best chance for resolving the problem as it has been defined in the first phase of inquiry:

> Deliberation is a dramatic rehearsal (in imagination) of various competing possible lines of action. It starts from the blocking of efficient overt action, due to that conflict of prior habit and newly released impulse to which reference has been made. Then each habit, each impulse, involved in the temporary suspense of overt action takes its turn in being tried out. Deliberation is an experiment in finding out what the various lines of possible action are really like. It is an experiment in making various combinations of selected elements of habits and impulses, to see what the resultant action would be like if it were entered upon. But the trial is in imagination, not in overt fact.

> (Dewey 1922, MW 14:132–133)

Moral deliberation requires more than just imagining how one's situation would unfold under the influence of various values. More importantly, it requires an empathic grasp of what others are experiencing. Franz de Waal defines empathy as "the capacity to (a) be affected by and share the emotional state of another, (b) assess the reasons for the other's state, and (c) identify with the other, adopting his or her perspective. This definition extends beyond what exists in many animals, but the term 'empathy' ... applies even if only criterion (a) is met" (de Waal 2008). In order to understand whether, and how, a projected course of action might play out, and whether or not it would reconstruct our present situation for the better, we must have a basic understanding of the perspectives, needs, and feelings of those who are or might be affected by the anticipated action (Hoffman 2000).

The third ("satisfaction") phase of the deliberative process depends on how insightfully and sensitively we take the measure of our situation and discern a course of action, from among all of those surveyed as possible, so as to effectively harmonize competing and conflicting impulses and allow for the most comprehensive expression of the various impulses vying for attention in the situation. We are thus left with the key question of how we are to determine what constitutes better and worse moral deliberation.

REASONABLE MORAL DELIBERATION

So far in our account of the deliberative process, we have only reached the point where, if our understanding and capacity for imaginative exploration and empathy are sensitive and rich enough, we are able to imagine how various courses of action might be open to us, and what they mean to us. That, however, stops short of an ultimate judgment of what is the best course of action for the present situation. How is *that* decided? Dewey's answer is that, as we try out in imagination possible courses of action, we have to feel whether or not a particular projected course resolves the tension arising from competing or conflicting ends, values, and dispositions. We have to assess these outcomes not in some anticipated future but in the context of our present situation.

Neural imaging research on the human "mirror neuron" system suggests that parts of neuronal clusters that are activated when we execute certain bodily actions are also activated when we see others performing those specific actions. The same thing happens when we *imagine* ourselves or others performing such actions (Decety and Grezes 2006; Aziz-Zadeh et al. 2006). This mirror neuron system appears to make it possible for us to imaginatively explore various complex courses of action and to put ourselves in the place of others, so that we can appreciate, to a certain limited extent, their experience of a situation or event and feel how they might feel. Here is Dewey's description of that process:

> Deliberation is actually an imaginative rehearsal of various courses of conduct. We give way, *in our mind,* to some impulses; we try, *in our mind,* some plan. Following its career through various steps, we find ourselves in imagination in the presence of the consequences that would follow; and as we then like and approve, or dislike and disapprove, these consequences, we find the original impulse or plan good or bad. Deliberation is dramatic and active, not mathematical and impersonal; and hence it has the intuitive, the direct factor in it.
>
> (Dewey and Tufts 1932, LW7:275 [italics in original])

This account is bound to frustrate anyone who wants a definitive principle of moral evaluation. They will protest, "Are we left only with *feeling* whether a problematic situation is resolved or not? What kind of answer is that!" How could this not simply reduce to "If it feels right, do it?"

Dewey's answer is subtle, nuanced, and not likely to satisfy someone who believes that the dignity and importance of moral life requires clear and definitive principles and imperatives specifying how we ought to live. In brief, he builds his answer to emotivism and relativism around his notions of valuation and reasonableness.

The habits that drive our intuitive processes of moral appraisal are what Dewey called "direct *valuing*, in the sense of prizing and being absorbed in an object or person" (Dewey and Tufts 1932, 266). There is no sustained self-reflective or self-critical aspect to such valuings—we simply prize what it is our unreflective habit to prize. The possibility of a critical perspective arises only in "*valuation* as reflective judgment, based upon consideration of a comprehensive scheme" (266). Our moral deliberation has to go beyond merely imagining how various situations would unfold. It has to issue in some choice, through which experience is transformed as we move forward; that is, it drives toward the phase of satisfaction realized as a *choice* of a possible course of action.

What differentiates a reasonable from an unreasonable choice? It is tempting to believe, as most philosophers do, that rationality and reasonableness are defined *prior to* our deliberative acts. According to this view, certain acts are moral or immoral just insofar as they conform to pregiven criteria of reasonableness. Moral reasoning thus amounts to the bringing of specific cases under prior rationally derived moral principles to see whether the act is morally permissible or forbidden. This assumes that our moral universe is relatively static and completed, so that our moral categories are fixed, and right behavior is then defined through universal values and principles. Within this framework, moral reasoning requires understanding what the principles entail, and then seeing clearly that and how a particular case falls under a certain principle.

In sharp contrast, Dewey saw nature not as completed, with its moral categories fixed, but rather as always in process, evolving, and productive of newly emerging conditions. A "reasonable" choice is one that, as it is enacted through moral deliberation, transforms the situation for the better, that is, in a way that harmonizes competing values and ends, allowing for the expression of a greater range of impulses, both within ourselves and in relation to the desires and purposes of others. Dewey's seminal statement of this process of reasonable choice runs as follows:

> But reasonableness is in fact a quality of an effective relationship among desires rather than a thing opposed to desire. It signifies the order, perspective, proportion which is achieved, during deliberation, out of a diversity of earlier incompatible preferences. Choice is reasonable when it induces us to act reasonably; that is, with regard to the claims of each of the competing habits and impulses. This implies, of course, the presence of some comprehensive object, one which coordinates, organizes and functions each factor of the situation which gave rise to conflict, suspense and deliberation. (1922, MW 14:135)

The "comprehensive object" in this passage refers to the qualitatively unified situation in which one finds oneself and in which one has encountered some problematic indeterminacy about how to act. Within that situation "the objects experienced in following out a course of action attract, repel, satisfy, annoy, promote and retard" (134), and on that basis we eventually initiate some action.

Moral deliberation is about the resolution of a problematic *situation*, in all its complexity of persons, environmental conditions, desires, goals, feelings, and values. The challenge is to reconstruct the situation to establish a workable equilibrium. This culmination of fluid action is the *satisfaction* pole of the biological need-search (demand)-satisfaction structure present in all animals but now operating at the "higher" level of moral deliberation. In other words, moral deliberation is a higher level version of biological processes necessary for any animal to survive and flourish. Moral cognition is, in this way, rooted in organic bodily processes but not reducible to those processes.

It is crucial to note, however, that moral deliberation is typically or ideally not a solitary exercise of imagination. Morality is social, depending crucially on how others respond to what an individual says and does. What I can imagine in a given situation, and how I respond to what I imagine is possible, cannot be the whole story of reasonableness. For the question can always arise concerning whether what any individual can imagine adequately encompasses the full range of relevant and important factors in any given situation. What a particular individual sees as possible in a situation may be profoundly colored by childish, inaccurate, blind, or even psychotic impulses and habits. Human history is rife with horrific examples of how "problems" are solved by "solutions" such as murder, rape, genocide, enslavement, oppression, and exclusion. We need a way out of this form of moral relativism.

It is for this reason that Philip Kitcher (2011), in a Deweyan vein, insists that some sort of public dialogue is a crucial component of any moral deliberation that hopes to transcend, to the extent possible, the parochial perspectives and values of any particular person. What matters is not just what I or you might by ourselves be able to imagine as a possible resolution of an indeterminate, conflict-laden situation, since my vision and sensibilities may be so limited that I miss much of what is relevant in a morally-charged situation. What you and I need is others who point out to us what we cannot, or will not, see. Others lay claims on us to recognize them, to acknowledge their concerns as valid, to act in ways they approve of, and to respect them. Kitcher thus draws on Peter Singer's (1981) notion of "the expanding circle," which is the idea that in our moral deliberation we have to recognize the fullest range of beings who are affected by individual and group actions, practices, and institutions. Kitcher goes so far as to assert that we should seek dialogue based on "considerations and lines of reasoning that would be brought forward to achieve consensus were the entire human population to participate, *under conditions of mutual engagement*, in a conversation about the regulation of conduct" (Kitcher 2011, 340). Something like this might be the way that Dewey would interpret a Rawlsian conception of "reflective equilibrium" and "considered judgment" (Rawls 1972). In short, imaginative dramatic rehearsal should not be a solitary act of reflective soliloquy but rather a socially shaped process that seeks to reveal the full range of constructive possibilities present in a given situation. So there is a communal character to the imaginative process by which we *re*-view and *re*-vise a situation—a process in which we open ourselves to *new* ways of relating, interacting, and valuing that are fitted to the complexities of our newly emerging situation. This is the primary means available to us by which to expand our vision and discern the range of relevant considerations that should bear on our deliberations toward action.

The radical character of Dewey's conception of moral cognition is thus most evident in the way he rejects the traditional assumption that there must be correct values given in advance of any moral deliberation or judgment and capable of guiding our actions. He replaces this with an imaginative process of moral inquiry directed toward composing the situation in a way that enriches and deepens meaning, releases energies, and reduces conflict—not just for the individual moral agent but for the largest possible morally relevant community (which may include more-than-human nature).

It has been frequently noted that this makes moral deliberation more like the creation of an artwork than an exercise in rule following (Johnson 1993, 2014; Fesmire 2003; Shusterman 2000; Alexander 2013). Steven Fesmire (2003) has insightfully analogized the creative processes and dimensions of moral deliberation to the performance of a jazz ensemble or a musical quartet, in which each member of the group has to respond sensitively to the actions of others to craft a developing, consummatory musical experience. There are some standards and shared expectations for how a particular performance should proceed within a certain musical genre, including long traditions of jazz performances that recognize certain formal structures, ways of playing off of other members of the ensemble, and patterns of improvisation. This has to be realized relative to the particular history of the group one happens to be performing in. Each player has to sense where a musical development is moving and what is possible relative to its current manifestation. One needs to balance one's own skillful exuberance with a cultivated respect for others in the group who are jointly creating something. All of this happens over time, and it is made up (realized or enacted) in a temporal development whose end is, at any given point, still somewhat indeterminate and in the process of being explored. In Dewey's framework, then, reasonableness is understood as the artful re-making of experience, in the service of depth and richness of meaning, and the liberation of impulses in a manner that creates harmony and growth, rather than strife, domination, and alienation.

MORAL SELFHOOD

As we noted earlier, what we call "the self" is an intertwining or interpenetration of current habits of perception, acting, feeling, valuing, and thinking, but it is also a self-in-process as new habits develop and one's identity is revised. Selfhood is an ongoing process of developing reorganization, lasting from birth to death. There is stability only to the extent that our habits as presently constituted are relatively adjusted to experience as it comes to us. However, as new conditions arise that problematize our relation to our environment, we have opportunities to reconstruct aspects of our self as currently constituted toward a self structured by newly formed habits. Consequently, every instance of moral deliberation is a transition phase in our developing selfhood. Our present cluster of habits (i.e., our self as presently formed) constrains how we will construe a situation, while the degree of flexibility, which is proportional to the range of cultivated habits of thought and feeling, will shape what is possible for us in dealing with our moral difficulties. Dewey concludes that every such choice we make "sustains a double relation to the self. It reveals the existing self and it forms the future self. . . . Deliberation has an important function in this process, because each different possibility as it is presented to the imagination appeals to a different element in the constitution of the self, thus giving all sides of character a chance to play their part in the final choice. The resulting choice also shapes the self, making it, in some degree, a new self" (Dewey and Tufts 1932, LW 7:286–287).

We are thus brought to the ultimate question of what kind of self we should strive to cultivate if we hope to be a morally responsible person capable of intelligent valuation through deliberative processes. The answer to this is one of the most distinctive aspects of Dewey's moral philosophy. The "self" is always a self in the making. It is rooted in a temporally evolving process shaped by stabilized habits, but it is also changing as new habits are formed in response to changes in one's environment. There is no pregiven ideal form or fully realized self toward which a person could strive, as if his or her life consisted in a series of attempts to achieve what God, Reason, or some other transcendent source dictates as his or her moral essence and purpose.

In the absence of any such ultimate foundations of values, principles, or notions of selfhood, what, if any, type of character ought we to cultivate? Dewey's answer is that our best hope for intelligent moral deliberation rests on cultivating a self that conscientiously searches for growth in depth and richness of meaning:

> Except as the outcome of arrested development, there is no such thing as a fixed, ready-made, finished self. Every living self causes acts and is itself caused in return by what it does. All voluntary action is a remaking of self, since it creates new desires, instigates to new modes of endeavor, brings to light new conditions which institute new ends. Our personal identity is found in the thread of continuous development which binds together these changes. In the strictest sense, it is impossible for the self to stand still; it is becoming, and becoming for the better or the worse. It is in the *quality* of becoming that virtue resides. We set up this and that end to be reached, but *the* end is growth itself.
>
> (Dewey and Tufts 1932, LW 7:306)

Growth itself is *the* end, because it defines what it means to act for the better, once we realize that there are no ultimate final causes defining human purposes, no absolute values, and no unconditional moral laws. Growth means that, through inquiry, you become better able to appreciate the full range of impulses, habits, interests, and ends-in-view that are mixed up in your presently indeterminate experience. In other words, you develop an enriched, deepened, and expanded understanding of the meaning of your acts and selfhood. This is your best hope for discerning what the problem is and what projected courses of action have the best chance of reestablishing some measure of equilibrium among all of the competing values encountered.

This ongoing developmental process is not a simple linear unfolding of choices, one after the other, that progressively defines the self. For there are always multiple impulses, habits, and tracks of development in process at any given moment. The fact that we "choose" one track—select one course of action as "good in this situation"—does not do away with the other possible habits and impulses that remain part of our character, but perhaps in a diminished or sublimated way. Our selfhood is a many splendored creative process moved forward by a multitude of not always consistent impulses, desires, and habits.

To the question "What kind of person should I strive to be?" Dewey's answer is: *a sensitive, perceptive, empathetic, and conscientious person with some measure of flexibility and plasticity.* To the extent that Dewey has a virtue ethics, this is it. He prizes the virtues necessary for reflective, intelligent, imaginative problem-solving. Are we the slave of our previously established habits, or are we, as Dewey believes, capable of intelligently and expansively remaking experience in a way that fosters our growth and the growth and flourishing of others?

Dewey's most definitive statement of the nature of moral progress states that the present in which we dwell and must decide how to go forward, "is of *moral* moment because it marks a transition in the direction of breadth and clarity of action or in that of triviality and confusion. *Progress is present reconstruction adding fullness and distinctness of meaning, and retrogression is a present slipping away of significance, determinations, grasp*" (1922, MW 14:195 [italics added]).

Is Dewey's View of Moral Cognition Practical?

The human longing for absolutes, for certainty, and for fixed marks by which to navigate our way through troubled waters is deeply embedded in our common psyche. This longing is the basis of the rampant moral fundamentalism characteristic of all moral systems that assume that our ultimate values are given in advance of experience and that our moral obligation is to conform our behavior to those universal and absolute standards. Otherwise, the story goes, we are left with moral chaos. Within this kind of absolutist framework, Dewey's account of moral deliberation will seem impossibly relativist and lacking in the very moral guidance we so desperately need.

The general indifference and lack of interest among many contemporary moral philosophers and theologians for Dewey's moral theory most likely stems from their belief that he has nothing to offer by way of the kind of moral guidance they regard as the purpose and point of a moral philosophy. His moral pluralism, which recognizes multiple values, virtues, goods, and principles, strikes many people as undermining the very notion of ethics, which they think must have absolute foundations and produce universal and unconditionally binding moral principles. Add to that Dewey's fallibilism and his insistence that, absent absolutes, morality is an ongoing reconstructive project of continuous growth, and moral fundamentalists are sent scurrying away in horror.

The Deweyan response to these concerns is to observe that, once we develop an adequate social psychology, we come to realize that, in spite of our deepest longings for certainty, we humans never did have access to the kinds of absolute values and principles that many regard as definitive of our morality. Given what we are learning about human valuing, cognition, and action, we are led to conclude that we have mostly been demanding and looking for something that does not exist—an absolute moral foundation.

Moreover, in light of Dewey's account of moral inquiry as imaginative deliberation, moral fundamentalism (with its belief in absolute principles and values) turns out to be the *worst* possible strategy for dealing with morally problematic situations, since it peremptorily closes off the very kind of moral inquiry we most need. It sends us off in search of moral certainty, and in doing that it keeps us from the sensitive and appropriately critical perspective we need to bring to our lives (Johnson 2014).

Dewey therefore argues that we need to discard the traditional notion of conscience as a moral faculty that supposedly gives us access to pregiven and absolute moral values, principles, and motives for action. Conscience, Dewey claims, is just another term for the unreflective and unquestioned values and habits of moral appraisal that constitute intuitive valuing. He thus urges us to replace the mistaken idea of conscience with *conscientiousness*, which is the disposition to bring the appropriate level of critical reflection and imaginative deliberation to bear in cases of moral difficulty. Dewey explains, "The truly conscientious person not only uses a standard in judging, but is concerned to revise and improve this standard. ... Only by thoughtfulness does one become sensitive to the far-reaching implications of an act; apart from continual reflection we are at best sensitive only to the value of special and limited ends" (Dewey and Tufts 1932, LW 7:273).

The key to practical moral deliberation depends on realizing that humans are not what Dewey called "little gods"; that is, we are not possessed of any special insight, wisdom, or judgment stemming from some supernatural or transcendent source. Instead, we are humans—social animals, embedded in nature and society, drawing all our problem-solving resources from our modes of bodily engagement with our world. However modest our moral resources may be, they are what we have, and they have proved themselves invaluable in our attempts to make the world better. Dewey ends *Experience and Nature* with a beautiful statement of our human condition and the hope for intelligent moral inquiry:

> When a man finds he is not a little god in his active powers and accomplishments, . . .
> [w]hen he perceives clearly and adequately that he is within nature, a part of its
> interactions, he sees that the line to be drawn is not between action and thought, or
> action and appreciation, but between blind, slavish, meaningless action and action
> that is free, significant, directed and responsible.

> (Dewey 1925/1929 LW 7:324)

So, what is supposedly so radical about Dewey's moral philosophy? Well, for starters,
it calls into question and eventually undermines the very notion of morality as a
system of ultimate principles, laws, or imperatives binding on all rational creatures
and fixed for all time. It then proceeds to replace what I (Johnson 1993, 2014) have
called "the Moral Law Theory" with a view of moral reasoning as a form of situated
moral problem-solving. Dewey developed the Pragmatist notion of thinking and reasoning as forms of *doing,* that is, as ways of acting to change the world. Morality is thus
seen not as conforming one's choice and action to a pre-given moral framework but
instead as engaging in a deliberative process that reconfigures that world, making it
better. This imaginative process is part of our rational engagement with our world,
and, in exploring new possibilities for being and doing, it goes beyond our merely
intuitive processes of valuing. Consequently, Dewey identifies an imaginative rationality that transcends the confines of the dual-process model of moral appraisal. Moral
thinking is not about discovering, and then acting from, some pre-existent principle
or value; rather, it is about imaginatively, artfully, and intelligently transforming some
problematic experience in order to bring about growth of meaning and to reconstruct
experience (which involves oneself and others in ongoing interaction) for the better.

NOTES

1. One should not think of this developmental process as necessarily teleological, or purposive,
   as if the "lower" levels of organism-environment interaction are ultimately fully realized at the
   "higher" levels of conscious reasoning, decision-making, and acting. Dewey's account is evolutionary, but without any overarching purposes, goals, or goods toward which an organism's
   capacities might be directed. Instead, there is random variation and selection, in a loose sense,
   in which some structures emerge that may not be geared toward any obvious purpose or
   function. Dewey's view is rather that it is no miracle that we have the higher functions we do,
   since they have emerged from the same types of interactions, though perhaps resulting from
   higher complexity at some levels of organization, as our basic biological engagements with
   our environment. In this way, our embodiment grounds our capacity for conceptualization,
   reasoning, and action planning. I have articulated this *Embodied Cognition* perspective in *The
   Body in the Mind: The Bodily Basis of Meaning, Imagination, and Reason* (1987), *Philosophy
   in the Flesh: The Embodied Mind and its Challenge to Western Thought* (with George Lakoff,
   1999), and *The Meaning of the Body: Aesthetics of Human Understanding* (2007).
2. To be fair, Haidt recognizes at least a minimal role for rational reflection, though he consistently claims that the burden falls mostly on the intuitive processes (the "elephant"). In

summarizing his first principle of moral psychology—"Intuitions come first, strategic reasoning second"—Haidt says that Hume went too far in denying reason any significant role. Haidt recognizes two roles for strategic reasoning: "The elephant (automatic processes) is where most of the action is in moral psychology. Reasoning matters, of course, particularly between people, and particularly when reasons trigger new intuitions. Elephants rule, but they are neither dumb nor despotic. Intuitions can be shaped by reasoning, especially when reasons are embedded in a friendly conversation or an emotionally compelling novel, movie, or news story" (Haidt 2012, 71).

Works Cited

Citations of John Dewey's works are to the thirty-seven-volume critical edition published by Southern Illinois University Press under the editorship of Jo Ann Boydston. In-text citations give the original publication date and series abbreviation, followed by volume number and page number. For example: (1934, LW 10:12) is page 12 of *Art as Experience*, which is published as volume 10 of *The Later Works*.

Series abbreviations for *The Collected Works* are:

EW *The Early Works* (1882–1898)

MW *The Middle Works* (1899–1924)

LW *The Later Works* (1925–1953)

Alexander, Thomas. 2013. *The Human Eros: Eco-ontology and the Aesthetics of Existence*. New York: Fordham University Press.

Aziz-Zadeh, Lisa, S.M. Wilson, Giacomo Rizzolatti, and Marco Iacobini. 2006. "Congruent Embodied Representations for Visually Presented Actions and Linguistic Phrases Describing Actions." *Current Biology*, vol. 16, no 18, 1818–1823.

Damasio, Antonio. 2010. *Self Comes to Mind: Constructing the Conscious Brain*. New York: Pantheon.

De Waal, Frans. 2008. "Putting the Altruism Back in Altruism: The Evolution of Empathy." *Annual Review of Psychology*, vol. 59, 279–300.

Decety, Jean, and Julie Grezes. 2006. "The Power of Simulation: Imagining One's Own and Other's Behavior." *Brain Research*, vol. 1079, 4–14.

Dewey, John. 1922. *Human Nature and Conduct*. Vol. 14 of *The Middle Works, 1899–1924*. Edited by Jo Ann Boydston. Carbondale: Southern Illinois University Press, 1981.

Dewey, John. 1925. *Experience and Nature*. Vol. 1 *The Later Works, 1925–1953*. Edited by Jo Ann Boydston. Carbondale: Southern Illinois University Press, 1981.

Dewey, John. 1934. *Art as Experience*. Vol. 10 of *The Later Works, 1925–1953*. Edited by Jo Ann Boydston. Carbondale: Southern Illinois University Press, 1987.

Dewey, John. 1938. *Logic: The Theory of Inquiry*. Vol. 12 of *The Later Works, 1925–1953*. Edited by Jo Ann Boydston. Carbondale: Southern Illinois University Press, 1991.

Dewey, John, and James H. Tufts. 1932. *Ethics*. Vol. 7 of *The Later Works, 1925–1953*. Edited by Jo Ann Boydston. Carbondale: Southern Illinois University Press, 1989.

Fesmire, Steven. 2003. *John Dewey & Moral Imagination*. Bloomington: Indiana University Press.

Haidt, Jonathan. 2012. *The Righteous Mind: Why Good People Are Divided by Politics and Religion*. New York: Pantheon.

Hauser, Marc. 2006. *Moral Minds: How Nature Designed our Universal Sense of Right and Wrong*. New York: HarperCollins.

Hoffman, Robert. 2000. *Empathy and Moral Development: Implications for Caring and Justice*. Cambridge: Cambridge University Press.

Hume, David. 1751. *An Enquiry Concerning the Principles of Morals*. Edited by Tom Beauchamp. (The Clarendon Edition of the Works of David Hume). Oxford: Oxford University Press, 1998.

Hume, David. 1739–1740. *A Treatise of Human Nature*. Oxford: Clarendon Press, 2000.

Johnson, Mark. 1993. *Moral Imagination: Implications of Cognitive Science for Ethics*. Chicago: University of Chicago Press.

Johnson, Mark. 2014. *Morality for Humans: Ethical Understanding from the Perspective of Cognitive Science*. Chicago: University of Chicago Press.

Kitcher, Philip. 2011. *The Ethical Project*. Cambridge, MA: Harvard University Press.

Lakoff, George and Mark Johnson. 1999. *Philosophy in the Flesh: The Embodied Mind and Its Challenge to Western Thought*. New York: Basic Books.

Rawls, John. 1972. *A Theory of Justice*. Cambridge, MA: Harvard University Press.

Shusterman, Richard. 2000. *Pragmatist Aesthetics: Living Beauty, Rethnking Art*. Lanham, MD: Rowman & Littlefield.

Singer, Peter. 1981. *The Expanding Circle*. New York: Farrar, Straus, Giroux.

Smith, Adam. 1790. *The Theory of Moral Sentiments*. MetaLibri Digital Library.

CHAPTER 9

....

DEWEY ON THE AUTHORITY AND LEGITIMACY OF LAW

....

CHERYL MISAK

THE PRAGMATIST ACCOUNT OF TRUTH AND INQUIRY

....

PRAGMATIST accounts of truth and inquiry, including Dewey's, are entirely general. Every branch of knowledge is to be seen through the lens of human inquiry. In *Logic: The Theory of Inquiry*, Dewey sets out his conception of inquiry and its aim in a way that echoes Peirce, one of the two founders of the tradition:

> Doubt is uneasy; it is tension that finds expression and outlet in the processes of inquiry. Inquiry terminates in reaching that which is settled. This settled condition is a demarcating characteristic of genuine belief. In so far, belief is an appropriate name for the end of inquiry.
>
> (1938, LW 12:15)

Peirce had argued in the 1877 "The Fixation of Belief" that inquiry is the process by which some part of our settled body of belief, having been upset by a surprising experience, is replaced first by doubt and then by a newly settled, better belief. A belief that would be *really* settled, or indefeasible, or would stand up to all experience and reasons, would be true. Dewey, the first of the second generation of pragmatists, arrived at similar version of the pragmatist theory of truth, although he had some hesitation about using the label "true." Beliefs that are optimal, as far as the operative intelligence of inquiry goes, have the property of, if not truth, then warranted assertability.

While pragmatism is recognizably empiricist in its focus on inquiry, experience, and the operative consequences of belief, it diverges from the standard empiricist playbook in at least one significant way. While empiricists such as Hume and the logical positivists have also taken their principles to cover all of knowledge, they struggle with how to fit matters such as ethics and the law into their systems. Empiricists have usually wanted experience to be sensory, consequences to be invariable, and the conclusions of inquiry to be uncontestable. All these requirements seem out of place when it comes to normative questions about what we ought to do, morally or legally. Ethics and the law have seemed to empiricists to be *disputed* classes, not obviously a part of an experience-driven inquiry aimed at getting things right.

Peirce thought that the pragmatist conception of truth and inquiry held for all domains, including mathematics, ethics, and the law. In my own work, I have tried to show how we can excavate a promising position on what we ought to do from Peirce's work, even if he himself usually failed to see and articulate it. But Dewey, along with William James and Oliver Wendell Holmes, put ethics and the law front and centre.[1] Since pragmatism is the only brand of empiricism that promises, and delivers, an account of how moral inquiry is legitimate inquiry, this puts Dewey at the very heart of the pragmatist tradition.[2]

I have also argued that Dewey's attempt at providing a unified pragmatist account of knowledge and inquiry in the end does not quite manage to characterize inquiry in a way that is true to its practice. Dewey's twist on the Peircean account of inquiry is that he takes inquiry to be a matter of an organism trying to maintain stability or harmony in its environment.[3] The organism faces a problematic situation— instability or lack of equilibrium—and tries to resolve it so that it has "a decisive directive of future activities" (1938, LW 12:124). This is an idea that Peirce articulated in "The Fixation of Belief," and it is an idea that we find in all pragmatists. I have in the past suggested that Dewey's version of it is not, for want of a better word, "objective" enough. Especially in science, we are looking for a new belief that does not *merely* provide operative intelligence or a decisive directive. We are looking for a new belief that is responsive to the way things are or that gets the facts right. Peirce sorted the matter out in his own position by arguing in "The Fixation of Belief" that a belief resigns in the face of the acknowledgement that it was put in place by a method that did not take facts seriously. When an individual sees "that any belief of theirs is determined by any circumstance extraneous to the facts," he "will from that moment not merely admit in words that that belief is doubtful, but will experience a real doubt of it, so that it ceases to be a belief" (1877, W 3:253).

But as Peter Godfrey Smith (2013) and Steven Fesmire (2015, 53–59) have so helpfully argued, we can see Dewey also as requiring our beliefs to be connected to the facts. Fesmire directs our attention to Dewey's use of the metaphor of maps—an operational theory of representation—to unpack his pragmatist view of how we might get things right. A map is not a literal copy of the terrain. Rather, the isomorphic relationship between elements in the map and things in the landscape should be interpreted in a functional or operational sense. As Dewey puts it in *Logic: A Theory of Inquiry*:

> The elements of the country are certainly existentially connected with one another. But as far as knowledge is concerned, as far as any propositions about these connections can be made, they are wholly indeterminate until the country is surveyed.

> (1938, LW 12:397–401)

As when we move around using a map, when we have an experience we engage in "an affair of the intercourse of a living being with its physical and social environment" (1917, MW 10:6). That physical and social environment is, for Dewey, the factual. In what follows, I proceed with this reading of Dewey and show that this position works very nicely when we think through the difficult matter of how our moral and legal beliefs might aim at getting things right.

Indeed, Dewey's use of the idea of our "social environment" is an improvement on Peirce's stated view. One has to manually add, as I have done, social experience and social facts to Peirce's mix in order to get an appropriately general account of inquiry that upholds the commitment to not bifurcating fact and value. In this chapter, I explore Dewey's explicit and specific account of ethical and legal inquiry (as opposed to what I have done in the past: explore Peirce's implicit account of ethical inquiry). Along the way, I stop at William James's account of ethics and Oliver Wendell Holmes's account of law and build toward the conclusion that Dewey, utilizing some of the ideas of his pragmatist predecessors and adding his own important insights, gives us an answer to the hard and pressing question of what gives law its legitimacy or authority.

James on Ethical Inquiry

Pragmatists are committed to seeing ethics as a part of inquiry. One of the best arguments for this pragmatist, naturalist conception of morality comes from James's "The Moral Philosopher and the Moral Life."[4] It was published in 1891, in the first volume of *The International Journal of Ethics*, now known simply as *Ethics*. James argues that ethics and ethical theory cannot be made up in advance—they cannot be a priori. He asks us to imagine a rocky universe devoid of sentient beings. In that universe there would be no morality, for "good" is always "good for someone." He then asks us to imagine that there is only one person in the rocky universe and argues that we still do not have morality. We could not make sense of that person's beliefs about what is good as being true, for "Truth supposes a standard outside of the thinker to which he must conform" (1891, 335). There is no morality and no obligation in a solitude. There is only taste or preference. James asks us to add a second person to the universe and considers a number of possibilities:

1. Each continues to be concerned only with his or her own preferences. James believes that here too there would be no morality and no truth about what is good or bad, just or unjust. For there would be no unified, single point of view, and hence nothing anyone *ought* to do.
2. One of the entities is divine. James argues that even here, where there is a divine command, we want to know what the *ground* of the command or obligation is.
3. We understand morality in terms of our relationships with others. James argues that here and only here does morality enter the universe. For "we see not only that

without a claim actually made by some concrete person there can be no obligation, but that there is some obligation wherever there is a claim" (1891, 338).

The reason that the authority of morality does not reside in a divine commander is that obligation or duty starts with real people who make actual demands on us.[5] And this point holds not only for those who would ground authority in a Great Book or a Great Man but also in a Great Theory. *People* make demands on us, and morality starts with those demands. Pragmatism always directs us to experience and in ethics, it directs us to the experience of others.

In exploring possibility (1), James tells us that a tally of mere preferences is not enough to get morality going, that we need a "unified" view. That is not to say that there is an ideal system that might satisfy all demands. Such a system would require a "block universe," rejected by James. He thinks that there is "always a *pinch* between the ideal and the actual which can only be got through by leaving part of the ideal behind" (1891, 344). Whatever equilibrium we might find will be tinkered with or perhaps even overturned. All we can say is that "Ethical science is just like physical science, and instead of being deducible all at once from abstract principles, must simply bide its time, and be ready to revise its conclusions from day to day" (1891, 348–349). The pragmatist account of truth, when it comes to ethics, amounts to: "there can be no final truth in ethics any more than in physics, until the last man has had his experience and said his say." In the meantime, we need to go on what seems best to us here now, always taking in as much experience and fact as we can.

DEWEY: THE DEMOCRATIC METHOD

One of Dewey's signature contributions to pragmatism is to argue that a "real social organization and unity" requires the space in which we can "convince and be convinced by reason" (1916, MW 10:404). Inquiry is the experimental method put to service in solving practical problems. Inquiry or "deliberation" into moral matters is an instance of judging a problematic situation with the aim of resolving it—resolving it into one that is "morally satisfactory and right" (1938, LW 12:170). It is an application of "cooperative intelligence" and, as such, it requires democracy.

Dewey argued that a broadly democratic method is a precondition of every domain of inquiry, from physics to politics. For inquiry requires the unimpeded flow of information and the freedom to offer and to criticize hypotheses.[6] Democracy is the method that we must adopt if we are to get to warranted or true belief. These days this is called an "epistemic argument" for democracy. It follows straight on from the pragmatist account of truth. If a warranted or true belief is one that accounts for all the evidence, then if we are to aim at truth, everyone must, in principle, in some way or another, have a say.

This idea is a core tenet of pragmatism. We find it in James, Peirce, and Dewey. A warranted or true belief is one that would stand up to all our experience and argument. In any domain of inquiry, we have to take the perspectives and experiences of others seriously, given that we want to reach the right, or warranted, or true decision. Hence the "epistemic" nature of the pragmatist argument for "deliberative" democracy, on which legitimacy and authority flow from the fact that we employ a method that takes the experience of all into account and is thus more likely to give us warranted or true decisions.

While Peirce puts his account of truth and inquiry in terms of "indefeasibility" and Dewey criticizes the notion "that ideal goods should be shown to have, by means of knowledge of the most assured type, an indefeasible and inexpugnable position in the realm of the ultimately real" (1939, LW 4:27), they are not as far apart as they may seem. Dewey's words are from *The Quest for Certainty*, in which he is arguing that not even in principle or as a regulative ideal do we have a truth that escapes provisionality. But of course, Peirce was also what he called a "resolute fallibilist"—he was also against the quest for certainty. We cannot know when we have an indefeasible belief, and so all our beliefs are provisional.

PRAGMATISM AND THE AUTHORITY
OF THE LAW

While all pragmatists have the democratic method at the heart of their position, when it comes to the questions of legitimacy and authority of law, we must turn to Dewey and to Holmes for the best insights.

In *Logic: A Theory of Inquiry*, Dewey takes a legal trial to be a paradigmatic instance of a problematic situation that is resolved by inquiry. Its formal conceptions and definitions of, for instance, misdemeanor, crime, torts, and contracts arise out of "ordinary transactions"—they are not imposed "from on high or from any external or a priori source" (LW, 12:106; 1938). "But when they are formed, they are also formative; they regulate the proper conduct of the activities out of which they develop" (LW, 12:106; 1938). Dewey is gesturing here at one of the central questions in legal theory: What gives law the authority to regulate our conduct? Why should our behavior be constrained by the law, especially in those instances when we might not agree with it? He gives an excellent answer to this pressing question.

Dewey had direct engagement with legal theory and practice on two important occasions. The first occurred in 1922, when the young legal scholars at Columbia Law School convinced Dean Harlan Fiske Stone to invite Dewey to a "Special Conference on Jurisprudence." [7] His address was titled "Some Problems in the Logic and Ethics of Law," and a revised version was published as "Logical Method and Law" in the *Cornell Law*

Review. It is not surprising that in this address Dewey declined to put forward a grand theory of ethics and the law. It is not surprising that he talked, rather, about the logic of inquiry. He argued that inquiry or reasoning is always aimed at fixing a problem, and in a legal inquiry our aim, like our aim in other inquiries, is to reach decisions that subsequent experience will show to have been the best, under the circumstances. Thus begins Dewey's quest to say what it is that makes law binding on us. The results of legal inquiry are the best solution to our problem, and thus hold for the present, unless and until future experience and inquiry overturn them.

In 1941, Dewey was asked, with fifteen other American scholars, to set out his theory of law for a special volume titled *My Philosophy of Law: Credos of Sixteen American Scholars.* His article was naturally titled "My Philosophy of Law," and in it he takes the issue of the authority of law head on. He agrees with James on the need to avoid what James calls "intellectualist" theories. Such formalist theories hang on "scraps of paper" and "voices in the air,"[8] rather than attending to inquiry and experience. We must look to human experience or to a naturalized account of the authority or legitimacy of our laws and moral principles.

Dewey puts the problem as follows: What is the standard or criterion by which to evaluate laws? What *should* our regulations and practices be? Some traditions, he notes, make appeal to Reason, the Will of God, the Law of Nature found in medieval theory, Rousseau's General Will, or Kant's Practical Reason (1941, LW 14:120). That is, many have suggested that if we are to find a "sure ground for any genuinely philosophic valuation of law" we will find it in "a source higher and more fixed than that of experience" (1941, LW 14:116). We might add that some traditions have it that legal authority is vested in a different kind of Great Book: a constitution that can never be changed.

Dewey, of course, is set against these views. He is interested in "a program of action to be tested in action," not something that "can be judged ... on a purely intellectual basis" (1941, LW 14:117). Law is a "social phenomenon" and must be understood as thus. Like James, Dewey thinks that law and morality apply to human activities and forms of behavior, and their justification and authority must not try to transcend the human. Those theories of law that focus on agreement, contract, and consensus, Dewey suggests, are pointing to this social phenomenon, but they are overidealizing it.

So what is Dewey's conception of law as a program of action to be tested in action? He starts with the insight that law is a process, without a beginning and an end date, a process bound up with other human practices. We have to see law as it arises from social conditions and evaluate it in terms of what it does in and for society. One thing this picture entails is that the application of a law "is not something that happens *after* a rule or law or statute is laid down but is a necessary part of them" (1941, LW 14:117–118). A judge is not a spectator, nor is a judge a bastion of independent authority, nor is a judge the mere applicator of existing law. A judge has to use whatever exists—legal rules, policy, customary practice, efficiency—and shape the law for the future in the way that best solves the problem at hand. This is the core pragmatist thought about interpretation: we only know the meaning or the content of a law once we start to operate with it or interpret it. "A given legal arrangement *is* what it *does*" (1941, LW 14:118), and this action is a two-way phenomenon in that human beings react to applications of the law and change it in an ongoing process. Judges, that is, are not the only inquirers in legal inquiry. They can only respond to cases that are brought before them, and it is a citizen's right, duty, and responsibility to change law by bringing forward new claims. So judges, citizens, and law-makers all have a vital role to play in our ongoing legal inquiry.

Dewey offers us a pragmatist metaphor for how our customs and habits change via an inquiry that is sensitive to the way things are. It is a metaphor that perfectly aligns with the map metaphor discussed earlier—a metaphor of a changing landscape:

> The valley in its relation to the surrounding country, or as the "lie of the land," is the primary fact. The stream may be compared to the social process, and its various waves, wavelets, eddies, etc., to the special acts which make up social process. The banks are stable, enduring conditions, which limit and also direct the course taken by the stream, comparable to the customs. But the permanence and fixity of the banks, as compared with the elements of the passing stream, is relative, not absolute. Given the lie of the land, the stream is an energy . . . which forms and reforms its own banks.
>
> (1941, LW 14:118–119)

Anyone familiar with the later Wittgenstein will be astounded by this passage. For, despite his frequent attacks on pragmatism, Wittgenstein employs the very same metaphor, to the same purpose. He tells us that our beliefs are like the water flowing in a river, the banks being stable for the time being. But the riverbed can shift.[9] This is a deeply pragmatist point. If knowledge is to be possible at all, then at any given moment a large number of beliefs must be taken for granted, while each must remain in principle subject to revision, even those that seem immutable.

Dewey sees that his view might sound like Austin's idea that "sovereignty" is "something existing *within* social activities and relations, and not outside of them" (1941, LW 14:120). But Austin, Dewey thinks, wants to make law too rational and ignores the "comparatively unplanned results of customs interpreted in judicial decisions" (1941, LW 14:120). Dewey wants to focus on the experiential source of the law, not on the social institutions that might bring that experience under a rational structure.

One might ask at this juncture how Dewey is going to distinguish between odious social facts and good ones. What can we say to those who think that experience tells us, say, that we ought to make society substantively homogenous by eliminating those who do not fit in with our way of seeing things?[10] This is a question that worried Dewey the whole of his long career. In "My Philosophy of Law" he gives an answer. Social facts have consequences, "and the consideration of consequences may provide ground upon which it is decided whether they may be maintained intact or be changed" (1941, LW 14:121). There is nothing to go on but what we always go on: "intelligence, employing the best scientific methods and materials available, be used, to investigate in terms of the contexts of actual situations, the consequences of legal rules and of proposed legal decisions and acts of legislation" (1941, LW 14:122). In this way, we can improve our standards for judging and evaluating. There is nothing but human judgment, all the way down, as long as that judgment is responsive to the facts of human experience and need.

But another version of the worrying question is as follows. What is taken to be good here and now might well come apart from what is *really* good, and what is lawful might not only come apart from what is *really* just but also might come apart from what I sincerely think here and now is just. The question that Dewey, and any pragmatist, must answer is this: Why should I abide by a law that I disagree with? Here Dewey's important and fundamental point about democracy kicks in.

Dewey makes his argument succinctly in a paper titled "Creative Democracy: The Task Before Us." He argues that "Democracy is the faith that the process of experience is more important than any special result attained." Dewey's answer to our reformulated question is that the *process* drives the justification. Inquiry is controlled by what Peirce called a "hope" or a "regulative assumption of inquiry." Dewey's use of "faith" echoes Peirce. Inquiry requires faith in democracy: the faith of democracy in the role of consultation, of conference, of persuasion, of discussion, in formation of public opinion, which in the long run is self-corrective (1939, LW 14:227).

Dewey's answer to the question about the authority of the law is that authority resides in the fact that the conclusions of legal inquiry are put in place by the method that is best designed to get us the right answer. Whether or not we agree with the actual content of that answer, we are bound by the results of the method. The process of inquiry takes conflict and resolves it by way of adapting our practices and in coming, we have to assume, to a better answer.

It is important to see that, for Dewey, the requirements to keep inquiry open are deep and substantial. They involve, for instance, economic, education, and cultural commitments:

> Merely legal guarantees of the civil liberties of free belief, free expression, free assembly are of little avail if in daily life freedom of communication, the give and take of ideas, facts, experiences, is choked by mutual suspicion, by abuse, by fear and hatred. These things destroy the essential condition of the democratic way of living even more effectually than open coercion which—as the example of totalitarian states proves—is effective only when it succeeds in breeding hate, suspicion, intolerance in the minds of individual human beings.
>
> (1939, LW 14:228)

When we see fear, intolerance, and divide, we would do well to take that as a sign that our commitment to democratic structures is not as strong as it ought to be. This may well be Dewey's most enduring and important contribution—a point that we allow to fade into the background only at our peril.

DEWEY AND HOLMES

No one thought more about pragmatism and the law than Oliver Wendell Holmes Jr. Although he was wary of being lumped in with what he took to be the voluntarist "will to believe" strain in pragmatism, as exemplified by James, Holmes was indeed a pragmatist. He was a member of the Metaphysical Club, the reading group in which pragmatism was born in the 1860s. Those pragmatist ideas stayed with him for life, and are present in his classics *The Common Law* (Holmes 1882) and *The Path of Law* (Holmes 1952 [1897]).

Dewey, of course, was not a member of the Metaphysical Club. He was in the second wave of pragmatists, along with the likes of Jane Addams, George Herbert Mead, and George Santayana.[11] Peirce taught him for a year in the graduate program in Johns Hopkins, and in 1903 he reviewed Dewey's *Studies in Logical Theory* in the *Nation*, taking him to task in print and in private correspondence for his "genetical" approach. In Dewey's 1938 *Logic: A Theory of Inquiry*, we see Dewey shift to a full-out Peircean account of inquiry. Peirce clearly influenced him. Holmes did as well.

In 1928, Dewey published a paper in the *New Republic* titled "Justice Holmes and the Liberal Mind." He starts by quoting a 1919 passage by Holmes in his famous Abrams dissent, to which Dewey says he is indebted.[12] In that remarkable passage, Holmes makes three core pragmatist points. First, he says that "When men have realized that time has upset many fighting beliefs, they may come to believe ... that the ultimate good ... is better reached by free trade in ideas." This is one of Peirce's arguments in "The Fixation of Belief": once we see that others do not agree with our strongly held beliefs, we will adopt the method of science, or free trade in ideas, as our methodology. Second, Holmes says that "the best test of truth is the power of the thought to get itself accepted in the competition of the market." This is the pragmatist point, shared by Peirce, James, and Dewey, that warranted or true beliefs are those that survive the force of experience and argument. Third, Holmes says that men will see "that the truth is the only ground upon which their wishes safely can be carried out." This is Peirce's point in "Fixation" that the only action that will really be successful is that based on "circumstances not extraneous to the facts" (1877, W 3:253). Holmes, not referring to pragmatism or any of his fellow pragmatists (as was his habit), concludes with the strikingly pragmatist idea that the Constitution, like all of life, is an "experiment" (1929, LW 3:177).

It is not surprising that Dewey thinks these are "outstanding ideas." He rephrases them in his own words: "the conclusions of intelligence" are the "finally directive force in life"; "freedom of thought and expression" is "the condition needed in order to realize this power of direction by thought"; and life and thought have an "experimental character" (1929, LW 3:177). He then makes his argument about the pragmatist justification of the authority of the law.

It is similar to the argument we have seen him make about the justification of democracy. But in this paper it takes a new form. (It is also put in Holmes's voice, although it is clear that Dewey in is full agreement.) Holmes, Dewey asserts, does not have a substantive social philosophy. He does not have "a fixed social program" or "a social panacea to dole out"—"no code of fixed ends to be realized" (1929, LW 3:178). What he has is a *method*. Holmes sees "the processes and issues of law" in "an infinite perspective"—"that of a universe in which all action is so experimental that it must needs be directed by a thought which is free, growing, ever learning, never giving up the battle for truth, or coming to rest in alleged certainties, or reposing on a formula in a slumber that means death" (1929, LW 3:178). What a lovely expression of pragmatism. And notice that here, with respect to law, that most human of constructs, Dewey talks about truth, not warranted assertibility. That is, he was not always set against the idea that truth is that which we aim for, even if, as all pragmatists agree, our current beliefs are always fallible.

Dewey continues: "According to the framework of our social life, the community, the 'people,' is, through legislative action, the seat of social experiment stations." Dewey saw that judges can only respond to cases that are brought before them. This is how the law is appropriately revised and can become ever more responsive to human needs and experience. And this is what gives law its legitimacy or its call on us, even if we do not agree with what it issues. We are part of a process—a good process aimed at getting things right—in which law is forged.

Dewey notes that Justice Holmes argues that his fellow judges should have freedom and leeway to make their judgments, even if he himself would not vote for the measures they decree. Dewey thinks that judges, including Justice Holmes, are not God. Nor are legislators. Nor is some code, or formal logic, or set of complicated laws decisive for every legal problem. That formalism is merely "a mask for concealing unavowed economic beliefs concerning the causes and impact of social advantage which judges happen to hold" (1929, LW 3:181). Nor does the populist "voice of the people" carry infallible authority, nor "any idealization of popular judgment." What, then, is it that carries authority? Again, we see the deep pragmatist point do all the work: "experimentation is, in the long run, the only sure way to discover what is wisdom" (1929, LW 3:178). If our legal process is one of free, open, and democratic experimentation aimed at truth, we are justified—nay, required—to accept its outcomes.

As is so often the case, there is a meliorism, or an idea of ongoing potential for improvement, accompanying Dewey's position. Our laws are supposed to be getting better and better. But this meliorism holds, when it holds at all, only in very particular frameworks of social life. I have suggested that the pressure point on Dewey's position is that he owes us an account of those social frameworks and those legal systems in which the experimentation goes awry, in which the forces of intolerance or substantive homogeneity capture the mood of the people and the character of judges. Dewey meets the challenge as follows. He says that "within the limits set by the structures of social life (and *every* form of social life has a limiting structure), the organized community has a right to try experiments" (1929, LW 3:178). That right is grounded in the idea that only by significant experimentation will we get the truth, *as long as we pay attention to those prerequisites of inquiry and experimentation.* Those prerequisites are that our structures of education and economics must be such that people have the wherewithal to participate in democracy and to recognize their actual interests. There must be freedom of speech and thought so that we incorporate all the relevant ideas into our inquiries. Underrepresented views require special attention, again so that we integrate all the relevant points of view into our inquiries. And deep democratic and economic structures have to be such that, for instance, certain kinds of coercion and inequalities that would rob people of their abilities to challenge law or to press for its revision are eliminated.[13] Only if these conditions are in place is our faith in meliorism and improvement justified. We must ensure that we are getting as much of the evidence and perspective we can and reducing the number of blind spots we have and mistakes we make. If our aim in belief and assertion is to arrive at judgments that are responsive to all the relevant experiences, we need to include the experience of all, and include it in a robust way. Freedom must be effective, not merely legal and formal.

Dewey thus presents us, in concert with Holmes, with a compelling, human-centered, pragmatist account of how and why law is binding on us. We start with where we find ourselves, with a set of laws that embody all sorts of encrusted custom and accepted background belief. When conflicts arise, judges resolve them in an inquiry not unlike other kinds of inquiry. All inquiry is an experience-driven enterprise, with custom and background belief forming the banks of the riverbed, and with the force of new experience and challenges shifting those banks. The law is "a program of action to be tested in action" and these tests or evaluations will be complex matters, bringing into play all sorts of reasons, many of which anchor the traditional ethical theories. But there is no ultimate incorrigible value, such as freedom or equality. These and other values will be in the mix in democratic decision-making. If we put conditions of equality in place, if we set up inquiry so that its results should get better and better, then we have an allegiance to those results. Democratic decision-making has a normative call on us, for epistemic reasons.

Dewey's fundamental claim is that if we aim at getting the answer (or the set of acceptable answers) that best coheres with the experience and reasons of all, then we must take seriously the experience and reasons of all. Such "conscientiousness" leads us directly to deliberative democratic structures of decision-making and to the normative force of those structures. The legitimacy and authority of law lie in the structure of political and legal institutions: in whether or not they are engaged in *a culture of justification*.[14] If our institutions are democratic and offer reasons for the law's being such as it is, reasons that in principle speak to the subject, then that law is legitimate and authoritative for the subject. The claim is not that the subject has to endorse the content of the law, but he or she must understand how it makes a plausible claim to authority—the individual must be able in principle to understand that reasons stand behind the law, and that those reasons speak to him or her, whether or not they are actually convincing. Dewey, along with his fellow pragmatists, thus offers a justification of legal authority that does not start from a moral theory (about equality, rights, utility, need, and so on) but rather from thoughts about how reason-giving and the ongoing evaluation of belief are fundamental.

Another way of making Dewey's argument is as follows. It is sometimes thought that questions of justice, legitimacy, and authority on the one hand and morality on the other are fundamentally distinct in that justice is about not merely what is good for people to do but what they can be *made* to do. The idea is that a legitimate decision might not be a morally right decision. But the pragmatist, as is so often the case, sees an artificial barrier erected here. The pragmatist thinks that a good decision is the product of a democratic and open process. Could such a process give us the morally wrong answer? There is one obvious way in which it could. For Dewey and for all pragmatists, decisions are always provisional or in principle subject to revision, and a good process can give us a wrong answer in the sense that it will be revised or even overturned. But it is important to see that, for the pragmatist, there is nothing over and above well-conducted, conscientious inquiry that might provide us with more true or more moral answers. Truth and morality cannot be pulled apart from good belief evaluation and good decision-making.

Citizens can of course find themselves in the position where they think: I object to a law because it goes against my moral code. But a feature of authority is that the subject of authority does what he or she is told because the authority said so, not because the subject thinks the content of the command to be good. As Hobbes explained, that is the difference between command and advice. On Dewey's account of the authority of law, citizens who object to a law should nonetheless regard it as binding on them, because it was made by the best possible process, a process that is also moral. For instance, someone may disagree with laws that enshrine abortion rights but respect those laws nonetheless. If it is felt that the process or the result has been fatally flawed in some way, he or she might decide to engage in protest and even civil disobedience. But it is important to see that such measures are part of the very process that confers legitimacy on our laws and on our democracies. Even in the case of breaking the law through civil disobedience, citizens know where they stand—they understand that they are opening themselves up to sanctions. In a well-functioning democratic society, even civil disobedience has a part to play.

In political philosophy there is a distinction between authority in fact (de facto) and legitimate authority (de jure). The pragmatist account I have articulated here speaks to the latter—the conditions under which we should regard a de facto authority as legitimate. It explains the idea of authority—of when it is legitimate—and then *why* it is legitimate. It tells us that there is a fund of inherited social value that is unavoidable and is itself the product of experience. What the values are, how they should evolve, be revised, and replaced, and even how to understand them is open to experience. Hence, authoritative pronouncements are provisional punctuation points in a process of inquiry.

ACKNOWLEDGMENTS

I thank David Dyzenhaus and Steven Fesmire for extremely helpful comments on an earlier draft of this paper.

Notes

1. See Butler (2010), Hamner Hill (1997), Patterson (1950), and Schlegel (1995) for work on Dewey's legal theory and Howe (1957), Haack (2005), Kellogg (2007), and Misak (2017) for work on Holmes, pragmatism, and legal theory.
2. See Misak (2000) and (2013).
3. See the chapter by Johnson in this volume.
4. That is, it is one of the best accounts, if one ignores James's thoughts about supernatural religion, sticky-taped to the end of this naturalist paper.
5. See Fesmire, this volume, for the argument that, for Dewey, although the abstract concepts of good, duty and virtue start with demands, they do not reside exclusively in demands.
6. EW 3: 33; 1895, LW 11: 375; 1936.
7. See Schlegel (1995) for a full discussion.
8. 1941: 73–85.
9. 1969, OC: §§96–98. See Misak (2016) for an argument that Wittgenstein was in fact influenced by the pragmatists.
10. This is the view of Carl Schmitt, the Weimar legal theorist who jumped on the Nazi bandwagon. See Misak (2000) and (2013) for an extended discussion of the problem and its solution.
11. Santayana, like Holmes, was not keen on the label, but see Misak (2013) for the argument that both their positions were solidly within the pragmatist tradition.
12. Dewey, though, seems not to have bothered to read the whole dissent but pulls the quote from a secondary source.
13. I thank Bob Talisse for this point.
14. See Mureinik (1994) and Dyzenhaus (1998) for the use of the concept "culture of justification."

Works Cited

Citations of John Dewey's works are to the thirty-seven-volume critical edition published by Southern Illinois University Press under the editorship of Jo Ann Boydston. In-text citations give the original publication date and series abbreviation, followed by volume number and page number. For example: (1934, LW 10:12) is page 12 of *Art as Experience*, which is published as volume 10 of *The Later Works*.

Series abbreviations for *The Collected Works*:

EW The Early Works (1882–98)

MW The Middle Works (1899–1924)

LW The Later Works (1925–53)

Butler, Brian E. 2010. "Democracy and Law: Situating Law within John Dewey's Democratic Vision." *Etica & Politica/Ethics & Politics*, vol. XII, no. 1, 256–280.

Dyzenhaus, David. 1998. "Law as Justification: Etienne Mureinik's Conception of Legal Culture." *South African Journal on Human Rights*, vol. 14, no. 1, 11–37.

Fesmire, Steven. 2015. *Dewey*. London: Routledge.

Godfrey-Smith, Peter. 2013. "'Untimely Review' of John Dewey's Experience and Nature." *Topoi*, vol. 33, 285–291.

Haack, Susan. 2005. "On Legal Pragmatism: Where Does 'The Path of the Law' Lead Us?" *The American Journal of Jurisprudence*, vol. 50, 71–105.

Hamner Hill, H. 1997. "John Dewey's Legal Pragmatism." *Southwest Philosophy Review*, vol. 13, no. 1, 113–121.

Holmes, Oliver Wendell Jr. 1882. *The Common Law*. London: MacMillan.

Holmes, Oliver Wendell Jr. 1952 [1897]. "The Path of Law." In *Collected Legal Papers*. Edited by Oliver Wendell Holmes Jr., 167–202. New York: Harcourt, Brace, and Company.

Howe, Mark De Wolfe. 1957. *Justice Oliver Wendell Holmes: The Shaping Years*. Cambridge, MA: Belknap Press of Harvard University Press.

James, William. 1891. "The Moral Philosopher and the Moral Life." *International Journal of Ethics*, vol. 1, no. 3, 330–354.

Kellogg, Frederic R. 2007. *Oliver Wendell Holmes, Jr.: Legal Theory, and Judicial Restraint*. Cambridge, UK: Cambridge University Press.

Misak, Cheryl. 2000. *Truth, Politics, Morality: Pragmatism and Deliberation*. London: Routledge.

Misak, Cheryl. 2013. *The American Pragmatists*. Oxford: Oxford University Press.

Misak, Cheryl. 2016. *Cambridge Pragmatism: From Peirce and James to Ramsey and Wittgenstein*. Oxford: Oxford University Press.

Misak, Cheryl. 2017. "A Pragmatist Account of Legitimacy and Authority." In *Pragmatism and Justice*. Edited by Susan Dieleman. Oxford: Oxford University Press.

Mureinik, Etienne. 1994. "A Bridge to Where? Introducing the Interim Bill of Rights." *South African Journal of Human Rights*, vol. 10, no. 1, 31–48.

Patterson, Edwin W. 1950. "John Dewey and the Law: Theories of Legal Reasoning and Valuation." *American Bar Association Journal*, vol. 36, no. 8, 619–622, 699–701.

Peirce, Charles Sanders. 1982–. *The Writings of Charles S. Peirce: A Chronological Edition*. Edited by E. Moore. Bloomington: Indiana University Press. Cited as follows: "original publication year, Wn,m" where n is the volume and m the page number.

Schlegel, John Henry. 1995. *American Legal Realism and Empirical Social Science*. Chapel Hill: University of North Carolina Press.

Wittgenstein, Ludwig. 1969. *On Certainty*. Edited by G. E. M. Anscombe and G. H. von Wright. Translated by D. Paul and G. E. M. Anscombe. Oxford: Basil Blackwell. Cited as 1969: OC, section number.

CHAPTER 10

....

BEYOND MORAL FUNDAMENTALISM

Dewey's Pragmatic Pluralism in Ethics and Politics

....

STEVEN FESMIRE

EVEN as we confront increasingly complex problems that demand fine awareness, moral sensitivity, and rich responsibility (see Nussbaum 1990, 148–167), many have inherited a stark, one-way-street moral and political mentality: Those going the right way ("us") feel constantly endangered by others ("them") coming the wrong way, and each is convinced that the other has misread the signs. Such *moral fundamentalist* habits can cause people to oversimplify situations, neglect context, assume privileged access to the right way to proceed, ignore relevant possibilities for convergence, and shut off inquiry (Johnson 2014; Norton 2015). Moral fundamentalism, which logically requires the traditional monistic view that there is a single right or ideal way to formulate moral and political problems, also makes the worst of our native impulses toward social bonding and antagonism, driving the us–them wedge even deeper and depleting social capital (Putnam 2000) while making it harder for us to debate and achieve controverted social goals like justice, freedom, security, health, and sustainability (see Thompson 2010).[1] Meanwhile, exacerbating the one-way moral mentality, techno-industrial civilizations have arranged social networks and media communications into an infamous echo chamber that insulates "us" from having to learn anything new from "them" (Karsten and West 2016).

We must cultivate better cultural and cross-cultural conditions for dialogue, debate, and persuasion so that we can deal more intelligently and competently with complex and widely shared local, regional, national, and global problems (cf. 1927, LW 2:366). Over a century after Dewey's *Democracy and Education* (1916, MW 9), faith in the educative capacity of experience remains our best hope. Social inquiry and problem-solving are more honest, open, collaborative, rigorous, and productive when youths learn to be patient with the suspense of reflection, distrustful of tunnel vision, aware of the fallibility and incompleteness of any decision or policy, practiced in listening, and imaginative in pursuing creative leads.

Philosophical research can help to create a shared cultural context in which we culti-vate these conditions for sustained, communicative social inquiry. Drawing on unpub-lished and published sources from 1926 to 1932, this chapter builds on Dewey to argue that traditional ethical monism tends to stymie this creative possibility by legitimizing the "one way" feature of moral fundamentalism and that a deep pragmatic pluralism can accommodate valuable monistic insights without unduly exercising and reinforcing moral fundamentalist habits.[2]

Dewey's Pragmatic Pluralism in Ethical Theory

In ethics, pluralism implies affirmation of multiple values. Strong pluralists such as Williams (1985), Taylor (1982), Noddings (2013), and Appiah (2017) hold that ethical monism abridges moral life and edits out the diversity of situational tensions that mark real, unsettled circumstances.[3]

Values typically conflict and get in the way of each other, and, according to the strong pluralist, it would be an exceptionally easy case in which tensions could be resolved by appealing to a supreme value, principle, standard, law, concept, or ideal that devours whatever is of moral worth in the rest of our concerns. A strong pluralist position is well stated by Haidt and Bjorklund: "Monistic theories are likely to be wrong . . . . If there are many independent sources of moral value . . . , then moral theories that value only one source and set to zero all others are likely to produce psychologically unrealistic sys-tems" (2008, 215).[4]

Strong pluralists, especially in the pragmatist tradition, also tend to reject the quest for a self-sufficient "ideal theory," as Rawls (1971) called his idealized "original posi-tion" approach to a well-ordered society in which free, equal, and autonomous rational contractors fully comply with the requirements of justice.[5] This now-traditional ideal theory approach is exemplified by Rawls, Nozick (1974), and Dworkin (2000). Recent critics include, to various degrees, Mills (2005, 2017), Anderson (2009, 2013), Pappas (2008, 2020), Sen (2009), Valentini (2012), and Appiah (2017). Anderson, for example, has influentially argued that Rawls's approach to an ideal society blinds us to race-based and other social injustices to a degree that is "epistemologically disabling" (2013, 5).[6] These strong pluralists propose shifting to a nonideal starting point for sociopolit-ical inquiry. They do not, of course, object to idealizations in ethics, a subject recently canvassed in Appiah's As If: Idealization and Ideals (2017), but they do insist that values have to be appraised in light of the particular experiential contexts and purposes that generated them, and most advocate, in Pappas's words, a shift "toward a more nonideal, contextualist, problem-centered, and inquiry-oriented approach" (2020, 235). Pappas writes, "There are as many problems of injustice, as there are problematic situations suffered in a particular way." And even a plausible ideal theory, Appiah urges in his melioristic plea for nonideal (partial compliance) theories, "doesn't help much in the circumstances of an actual non-ideal world" (2017, 120; cf. 163).

Among pragmatists, such as Kitcher (2014), Johnson (2014), McKenna (2018), Pappas (2008), Thompson (2015), and myself (Fesmire 2003), pluralism is additionally an experimental *method* of moral and political inquiry. But pragmatism is not necessarily "a method of ethics" in the sense crystallized by Sidgwick: "a rational procedure for deciding what we ought to do" (Lazari-Radek and Singer 2014). Norton's "heuristic proceduralism" comes close (2005, 2015), but, like other pragmatists, he is critical of rational procedures that fail to fathom the extent to which we are all frogs in Zhuǎng Zǐ's well, inescapably limited and guided by our particular standpoints, contexts, and purposes. Moreover, like Kitcher and Johnson, Norton is focused on ethical inquiry as an experimental process rather than merely as incessant verbal argumentation. What Kitcher (2014) calls "the ethical project" is a process in which, as Johnson explains it, we actively try out "various modes of behavior (verbal and nonverbal), various institutional structures, and various life strategies." Verbal forms of argumentation remain important for philosophical ethics, but ethical theorists have neglected the way experiments in living *also* constitute "arguments" for and against various practices. Certain practices either address or fail to meet shared problems. Such "arguments," Johnson adds, are enactive, embodied, and embedded (Johnson 2014, 126), and they should be more central to the future of ethical theorizing.

Our actual experiments in living assuredly involve ideals and idealizations through which we appraise moral alternatives, as Appiah has argued (2017), but they must proceed without access to a noncontingent perspective or an ideal standpoint untainted by particular human drives, habits, and choices. Ethical inquiry is unending, and what we count as progressive or regressive is ultimately, in Kitcher's words, "something people work out with one another. There are no experts here" (2014, 286). Instead of another iteration of the old escape through faith or reason to an antecedently established "aperspectival position" (Johnson 2014, 120), the pragmatic pluralist embraces in her methodology the fact that when we ask different questions, we see different connections and possibilities. As is often observed, to ask the Kantian question (What is my duty?) or the utilitarian question (Which actions help us do the most good we can do?) is not to ask the Aristotelian question (Which character traits contribute to the *eudaemon* life?). To appropriate Heisenberg, what we observe is not the moral situation in itself, but the situation exposed to our method of questioning (see 1958, 32).

Nevertheless, as Kitcher and Johnson observe, rejection of aperspectival ethics "in no way keeps us from making reasonable claims about" the relative suitability of certain "values, principles, and practices" over others (Johnson 2014, 129; Kitcher 2014, 210). Given our actual contingent and nonideal starting point, pluralism is a strategy for more conscientious moral and political inquiry into what we should deem progressive and regressive, especially, I have argued, when our moral deliberations and choices are informed by broadly attentive, vital, and appreciative imaginative rehearsals and moral artistry (Fesmire 2003). If comparison to a world of agents fully compliant with the demands of justice makes us more sensitive to the particular pinch of an injustice and helps us singly or collectively hunt for ways to settle difficulties, creatively scope out alternatives, and picture ourselves taking part in them, then for the pragmatic pluralist it is a valuable heuristic. But it is the wrong starting point.

Dewey built on his more general theory of operative intelligence to chart a course making the best of our inescapable contingency and provincialism. He contended that no matter how carefully elaborated one's supreme moral principle (e.g., Gewirth 1978), it will rarely focus one's attention on all the relevant situational factors that one ought to note and deal with. He shared the spirit of James's pluralism: "The word 'and' trails after every sentence. Something always escapes. 'Ever not quite' has to be said of the best attempts made anywhere in the universe at attaining all-inclusiveness" (1977, 145).

The problem with ethical monism is not just that its usefulness to moral understanding is limited; indeed, the articulation of one-sided idealizations of incompatible theories may be a personal or collective help in specific contexts (see Appiah 2017). What is worse, from the standpoint of Deweyan moral epistemology, is that the traditional monistic quest for a single rational ruler to impose order on deliberation tends, as an unintended consequence, to enable the one-way feature of moral fundamentalism. More specifically, far from being an antidote to what J. Baird Callicott wittily dubs pluralism's "multiple personality disorder," monism tends to obstruct individual and communal inquiry into relevant situational features that "escape" our often-useful abstractions and idealizations. Of course monistic ethical theorists, in sharp contrast with prototypical fundamentalists, usually believe they have much to learn from those who disagree with them. But traditional monists hold that their moral house can, with some renovations and touch-ups here and there, fully accommodate whatever they need to learn. Using Dewey as a platform, I am arguing that it cannot. Even when we are aware, like Nozick, that we are "idealizing greatly" (1974, 151; cf. Appiah 2017, 119), we may be taken in by the putative value of our armchair theoretic clarities at the price of rendering actual moral and political problems more opaque.

Dewey asserted that "the growth of the experimental as distinct from the dogmatic habit of mind is due to increased ability to utilize variations for constructive ends instead of suppressing them" (1929, LW 1:7).[7] Accordingly, he saw variability in valuing and valuations as a useful starting point for further inquiry, rather than as a worrisome deviation to be squelched or intellectually standardized in the name of ethical truth. He held that there is no universal compass that allows us to rationally (or faithfully) navigate the social world, but through ongoing shared inquiry we can nevertheless steer reliably between the absolute and the arbitrary (cf. Elgin 1997).

As Dewey framed his pluralistic ethical theory, his central questions were: When we are morally conflicted, is this a superficial hesitancy that would invariably dissolve if only we could conduct our reasoning correctly, marshal the right data, or pray harder? Or is the experience of moral conflict often rooted in something deeper and intractable, a conflict *intrinsic* to the situation? Are a plurality of approaches to moral decision-making justified, or should we strive for a one-size-fits-all approach that organizes moral cognition under a single blanket category of good, right, or virtue? Do these blanket concepts spring from the same empirical source in our moral experience, or do they express distinctive roots of moral life? If leading moral concepts express independent forces with different roots, do these roots ultimately jibe well with each other (i.e., are they fully compatible)? Or do they get at cross purposes, often pulling us in different and seemingly legitimate directions, leaving us in a muddle about what to do? In sum, are there inherent conflicts as well as practical incommensurabilities between underlying primitive springs of moral action? If so, how can we practically manage and evaluate the normative claims made on us by these forces?

Dewey's partial and typically-for-him-programmatic answer to these questions pivoted on the thesis that there are "independent variables in moral action" (1930, LW 5:280), these several experiential factors are in tension with each other, and they are reducible neither to a single right or ideal starting point for moral inquiry nor to an ultimate foundation tethered to changeless universal truths. He did not simply assert the platitude that each vying monistic model has some truth to it; he developed and explored a hypothesis partially explaining how conflicting persistent values relate to one another and how they might be put into communication with each other without being hypostatized. Or alternatively, he suggested *how functionally isolated theories might be critically appraised within a wider normative context even as they sustain their distinctive selective emphases as idealized partial mappings or models of the terrain of moral action.* When divergent models of normative ideals are held to be true "independent of what they lead to when used as directive principles" (QC, LW 4:221), dogmatism results. But when normative models are understood as communicative and revisable experiments in living, as what Dewey in *The Quest for Certainty* called instrumentalities of direction, then he thinks they will mature through ongoing interactive engagement with the world and be truer to the mark.[8]

In the remainder of this chapter I explore Dewey's thesis, from its inception as a hypothesis in the 1920s to its elaboration in the early 1930s. Several standout features of Dewey's brand of strong axiological pluralism play a role in subsequent analysis: Dewey's theory rejects aperspectival positions and is marked by a naturalistic emphasis on the embodied context of moral action as a need-search recovery process (see Johnson 2020). He consequently emphasized conscientiousness, not native conscience, and he rejected the split between a moral realm sharply marked off from a nonmoral realm, observing that actions are so interconnected that any choice potentially has moral significance (1932, LW 7:170). He avoided extreme moral skepticism and extreme moral particularism (see Pappas 2008), and his outlook concurs with more recent strong pluralists that moral problems often admit of more than one approvable solution.

Moving to the four features central to what follows, (a) Dewey argued that moral uncertainty is often a sign of conscientiousness; (b) this uncertainty arises in part from conflicts between heterogeneous sources of moral action—irreducible basic factors in morals—to which reasonable moral agents ought to pay attention; (c) our choices and deeds are essential players in the moral situation, so what is good or bad, right or wrong, virtuous or vicious cannot be completely ascertained prior to acting and experimentally reviewing;[9] (d) although moral clarity and conviction are important (see Neiman 2008), moral fundamentalism robs them of their virtue and should be rejected in all forms, no matter how sophisticated, because there is no one right or ideal way to think *in advance* about moral or political problems and hence rarely a single "theoretically correct" diagnosis of any particular moral or political problem.

THREE INDEPENDENT FACTORS IN MORALS

On November 7, 1930, Dewey gave an address in English before the French Philosophical Society in Paris. As his French colleagues recognized in the ensuing discussion, he gave them "a première of his new ideas" (quoted in LW 5:503). The presentation was promptly published as "Trois facteurs indépendants en matière de morale."[10] In the 1960s, Jo Ann Boydston translated the French article back into English for *Educational Theory* as "Three Independent Factors in Morals," which eventually appeared in the critical edition (LW 5:279–288).

Soon after Boydston's translation appeared, an unpublished and undated typescript (mss102_53_3) was found in the Dewey archives at Southern Illinois University, titled in Dewey's hand "Conflict and Independent Variables in Morals" (Figure 10.1).[11]

The first five pages of the typescript were likely presented in 1926 or 1927 to a philosophy club at Columbia University (Dewey to Horace S. Fries [1933.12.26 (07682)]). Pages 6 to 12 closely track the French article, but there are several substantive revisions in Dewey's hand that do not appear in the critical edition. Pages 1 to 5 and page 13 remain unpublished. Dewey was likely reworking the typescript for an English publication. He instead incorporated the basic insights into the 1932 *Ethics* (LW 7), albeit in a less theoretical form that he judged to be better suited to the pedagogical and practical needs of undergraduate students (Dewey to Horace S. Fries [1933.12.26 (07682)]. In what follows, I incorporate material from the unpublished typescript whenever it offers a unique angle or metaphor that clarifies a point or adds something philosophically substantive.

In the 1930 presentation, Dewey hypothesized that each of the primary Western ethical systems (represented for him by Aristotle, Kant, and the British moralists) represents a basic, nonarbitrary force or factor of moral life: aspiration, obligation, and approbation, respectively (cf. Axtell and Olson 2009). Each factor is expressed in that system's leading fundamental concept: good, duty, and virtue, respectively. Each system seeks to bring divergent forces wholly within the logical scope of its own monistic category or principle. Other factors are subordinated and treated as derivative. For example, Kantians declare a trait to be virtuous because it maps to what is antecedently determined by autonomous reason to be right or obligatory. Yet, as examined here, Dewey contended that aspirations, obligations, and approbations are distinctive phenomena that cannot be blanketed by a single covering concept.

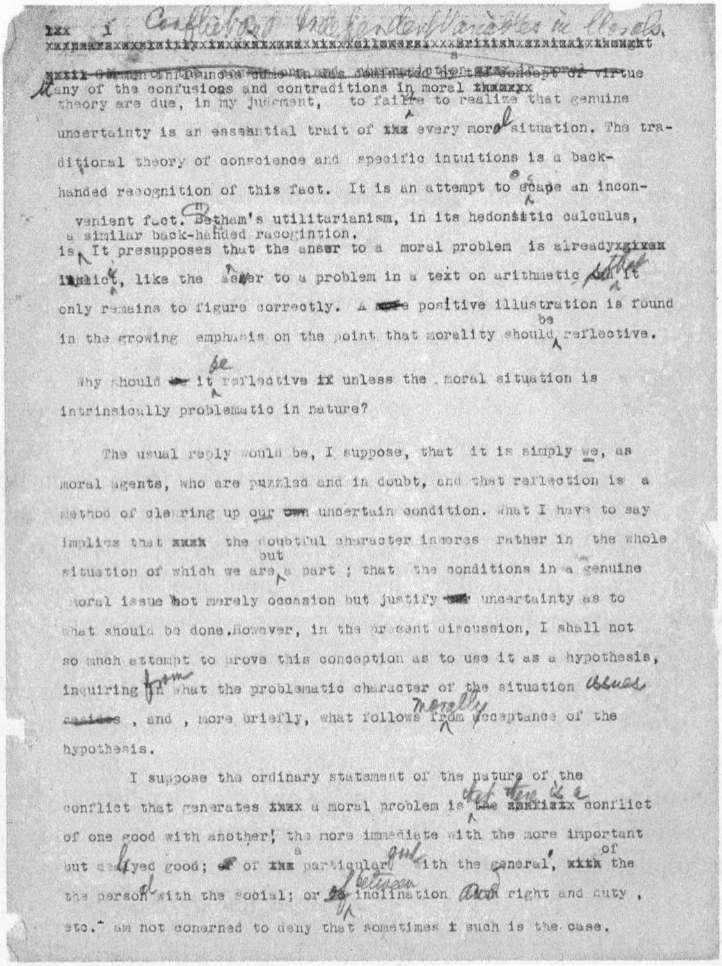

Many of the confusions and contradictions in moral theory are due, in my judgment, to failure to realize that genuine uncertainty is an essential trait of every moral situation. The traditional theory of conscience and specific intuitions is a backhanded recognition of this fact. It is an attempt to escape an inconvenient fact. Bentham's utilitarianism, in its hedonistic calculus, is a similar back-handed recognition. It presupposes that the answer to a moral problem is already given, like the answer to a problem in a text on arithmetic so it only remains to figure correctly. A positive illustration is found in the growing emphasis on the point that morality should be reflective.

Why should it reflective unless the moral situation is intrinsically problematic in nature?

The usual reply would be, I suppose, that it is simply we, as moral agents, who are puzzled and in doubt, and that reflection is a method of clearing up our own uncertain condition. What I have to say implies that the doubtful character inheres rather in the whole situation of which we are a part; that the conditions in a genuine moral issue not merely occasion but justify uncertainty as to what should be done. However, in the present discussion, I shall not so much attempt to prove this conception as to use it as a hypothesis, inquiring what the problematic character of the situation issues, and, more briefly, what follows merely from acceptance of the hypothesis.

I suppose the ordinary statement of the nature of the conflict that generates a moral problem is the conflict of one good with another, the more immediate with the more important but delayed good; of the particular with the general, the person with the social; or inclination between right and duty, etc. I am not concerned to deny that sometimes such is the case.

FIGURE 10.1 Used by permission of Special Collections, Morris Library, Southern Illinois University at Carbondale.

The subject matter of ethics is popularly taken to be about getting people to do the right thing when they are otherwise inclined. Accordingly, easy and uncomplicated cases such as "Should he embezzle the money?" are often spotlighted as prototypical, even though such cases are not usually occasions for much deliberation. Dewey recognized untangled cases in which habituated rule-following is best and excessive deliberation a waste of time, or worse, signifies a manically imbalanced character (1932, LW 7:170). Such trade-offs are unavoidable. Moreover, although Anscombe in her watershed "Modern Moral Philosophy" (1958) put it far more succinctly with her exceptionless prohibition against murdering the innocent, Dewey recognized that deliberation can at times lead us into temptation via ad hoc rationalizations (cf. Appiah 2017, 132). Additionally, recent moral psychology has revealed—with an experimental rigor that Dewey again left programmatic—the extent to which "moral reasoning" too often amounts to little more than a self-justifying ineffectual "rider" atop the headstrong "elephant" of habituated intuitions (Haidt 2012).

Any adequate defense of Dewey's general position requires some hedging of this sort, but his opening assertion in the 1930 presentation is uncomplicated: moral situations are not just *occasions* for uncertainty about what to do; problematic moral situations more typically *justify* our uncertainty. "Moral experience is a genuine experience" of real, systemic conflicts (in Koch 2010, 2.2270), so we generally *ought* to be reflective. And yet, Dewey argued, traditional moral theories have treated moral conflict as specious. Moral philosophers have acknowledged angst, but with their "Special Powers in their Special Armchairs" (Kitcher 2012, xix) they have for the most part postulated "one single principle as an explanation of moral life" (1930, LW 5:280), a correct standpoint from which we will in principle see that our initial hesitancy was based on momentary ignorance.

Because morally uncertain situations require us to reconcile conflicting factors, Dewey urged that "It is not without significance that uncertainty is felt most keenly by those who are called conscientious" (Dewey, undated ms, 13). Should a fifteen-year-old girl have an abortion? Should a soldier shoot upon command? Should a security analyst blow the whistle on government intrusions into privacy? Should John have had the affair with Anzia? To see these questions through the lens of only one factor—as at bottom a matter of rights not downstream consequences, of duty not virtue, of what is right not what is good, of what I should do and not who I should become—risks bringing deliberation to a premature close. When competing monistic concepts vie as bottom lines, this can of course elicit fruitful tension and dialogue. Pluralists, for their part, disagree with each other no less emphatically, but they are also committed in principle to nuanced perception and engaged problem-solving because they are keenly aware that their diagnoses have not precisely captured all that is morally or politically relevant.

Under the "one way" assumption legitimized by traditional ethical theorizing, conflict and diversity are merely apparent. A real situation may seem to be a quagmire, the supposition runs, but closer examination, or more data, or comparison to an ideally just world (see Rawls 1971) or egalitarian island world of rational albeit hapless contractors (see Dworkin 2000), will reveal that there had been a right or fair path through it all along. Uncertainty is seen mostly as a "hesitation about choice" between the moral and the immoral: we assume we must choose the good (vs. evil), will the obligatory (vs. giving way to appetite, inclination, and desire), or do the virtuous (vs. the vicious). "That is the necessary logical conclusion if moral action has only one source, if it ranges only within a single category" (1930, LW 5:280). "*We* may be in doubt as to what the good or the right or the virtuous is in a complicated situation," but under the restrictive one-way assumption "it is there and determination of it is at most a purely intellectual question, not a moral one. There is no conflict inhering in the situation" (Dewey, undated ms, 3).

Yet conflicts are rarely so superficial that a correct rational analysis could, even in principle, sweep the path clear toward what is "truly" good, right, just, or virtuous. In Latour's (1993) terms, "imbroglios" typify moral experience: moral predicaments are entanglements of often-incompatible forces. We are typically tugged in multiple ways, so one-way theorizing or decision-making at best leads to normative prescriptions that ignore factors relevant to our choices. This relative incommensurability of forces presents a practical problem, not primarily a theoretical one.[12]

Dewey acknowledged that "he exaggerated, for purposes of discussion, the differences among the three factors, that indeed moral theories do touch on these three factors more or less, but what he wanted to emphasize was the fact that each particular moral theory takes one of them as central and that is what becomes the important point, while the other factors are only secondary" (1930, LW 5:503). His point, then, was that there is a false hidden premise driving all projects that claim to give an account of metaethics and normative morality in terms of one supreme root. Each primary system misses, at least at the theoretical level, the inherent conflicts that constantly underlie moral and political action as irreducible forces, as when desired goods conflict with binding social demands. We should instead foster ethical and political theories that (a) lay bare and classify these practical conflicts within a wider "framework of moral conceptions" that puts basic roots in communication (1932, LW 7:309); (b) place these elements in a wider experimental context in which norms—for example, responsibility, self-respect, and authenticity, for Dworkin (2011)—gain practical traction in the entanglements of nonideal conditions; and (c) expand prospects for convergence on policy and action.[13]

Note, importantly, that Dewey nowhere *reduced* moral life to a triumvirate of root factors; he did not have a universal, cover-all ethical theory. He wanted to emphasize that, having long ago unseated the monarch of *custom*, Western moral philosophers continue to contest which monarch of *reason* shall rule from the old throne and issue truths about how we ought to live. What philosophers should do, in contrast, is to surrender the monarchical quest altogether so that we might "attend more fully to the concrete elements entering into the situations" in which we must act (1930, LW 5:288). In philosophy as in agriculture, we are in need of more polyculture, to borrow Vandana Shiva's image, not more monoculture.

Dewey's central question in the 1930 presentation was: Is there a single empirical source of moral action, or are there plural sources? His hypothesis was that moral problems require us to reconcile and coordinate "heterogeneous elements" (in Koch 2010, 2.2270) that include "at least three independent variables in moral action" (1930, LW 5:280) which "pull different ways" (Dewey, undated ms, 4). The variables are independent in the sense that one variable is neither logically derivable from another nor translatable without remainder into the terms of another. Hence the inadequacy, for Dewey, of any ethical theory analogous to a logical theory or mathematical theory that can solve any relevant problem with the right method or procedure.

Compare to Korsgaard, who says "Ethical truth is comparable to logical truth" (2014; cf. 1996). Dewey insisted in opposition that there is no logically right method in morals any more than there is a right map in cartography as some fixed and final charting of changeless territory, or a right climate model, isolated from an inclusive context, specified purposes, and objective results (see 1938, LW 12:138–139, 399). It is not possible to theoretically settle moral problems in advance of their occurrence because each variable in moral action "has a different origin and mode of operation," so "they can be at cross purposes and exercise divergent forces in the formation of judgment." "The essence of the moral situation is an internal and intrinsic conflict; the necessity for judgment and for choice comes from the fact that one has to manage forces with no common denominator" (1930, LW 5:280).

What ethical theory can do, despite (and at times perhaps even because of) its one-sided idealizations and emphases, is to help lay bare "the factors causing [problems] and thus make the choice more intelligent" (in Koch 2010, 2.2241–2.2245). In the contemporary ambit of Kitcher and Appiah, Dewey approached and evaluated ethical and political theories not on analogy to logical or mathematical problems but as experiments in "living together in ways in which the life of each of us is at once profitable in the deepest sense of the word, profitable to himself and helpful in the building up of the individuality of others" (1938, LW 13:303).

The 1930 presentation can be read as a blueprint to Dewey and Tufts' 1932 *Ethics*. Dewey approached his chapters (10–17) in the textbook with a conscious pedagogical goal: re-forge historical philosophic tools in light of contemporary needs so that students can use them to become more *comprehensively conscientious* in their deliberations and character development. Specifically, instead of egging on the outdated quest for a hierarchy that subdues variety among fundamental moral concepts, or merely venturing "an eclectic combination of the different theories" (1932, LW 7:180), Dewey's approach was to help students become more perceptive of moral complexity, study and assess their own circumstances in light of prior systems, and competently use diverse theories as deliberative tools in predicaments that require practical coordination among disparate elements.[14]

REIFICATION OF THREE INDEPENDENT
FACTORS INTO THREE FOUNDATION STONES

In a letter to Horace S. Fries [1933.12.26 (07682)] (Figure 10.2),

Dewey identified the key conceptual shift he made between his 1908 *Ethics* (MW 5)—and by implication earlier works such as *Outlines of a Critical Theory of Ethics* (1891, EW 2:238–388) and *The Study of Ethics: A Syllabus* (1894, EW 4:219–362)—and the 1932 *Ethics*. He had, he wrote, been committed in 1908 to a "socialized utilitarianism" that foreshortened moral action from the homogeneous perspective of the good. But he transitioned to a strong axiological pluralism that maintained the distinctness of variables in moral action, variables that are selectively emphasized—often to good effect—in leading abstract ethical concepts.

The new typology of "at least three" factors which are in some respects independent was the organizing principle of Dewey's spring 1926 course in "Ethical Theory" at Columbia University. Sidney Hook's lecture notes on that course contain clarificatory gems that emerge as Dewey surveys the history of ethical theory to lay bare "certain

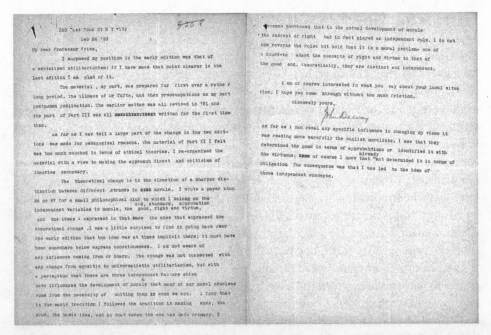

FIGURE 10.2 Used by permission of the Wisconsin Historical Society, Horace S. Fries papers, Mss 518, box 1, folder 6.

categories found to be involved in judgments which men actually pass in the course of moral conduct and which concepts have become the foundation stones of theories about ethics" (in Koch 2010, 2.2230).[15] Where helpful, I draw from Hook's notes in what follows.

To recap Dewey's hypothesis, moral situations are heterogeneous in their origins and operations. They elude full predictability and are not controllable by the impositions of any abstract monistic principle. Moral life has at least three distinct experiential roots that cannot be encompassed in one ideal way to proceed. Hence, most importantly, there is no foundation stone of ethics, whether procedurally constructed or "foundational" in the now old-fashioned sense. The unpublished typescript clarifies the hypothesis: "The three things I regard as variables are first the facts that give rise to the concept of the good and bad; secondly, those that give rise to the concept of right and wrong; thirdly, those that give rise to the conception of the virtuous and vicious . . . . What I am concerned to point out [is] that the concrete conflict is not just among these concepts, but in the elements of the actual moral situation that, when they are abstracted and generalized, give rise to these conceptions" (Dewey, undated ms, 2).[16] In this section, I clarify Dewey's hypothesis by interspersing the three factors and concomitant concepts, as emphasized in the 1930 presentation, with the parallel chapters in the 1932 *Ethics* (chs. 11–13). I hope at least to expose Dewey's own generalizations to scrutiny so that the promises and limitations of his approach can be critically evaluated.

First Factor: Good

The Good as a leading category in ethics arises from desires and aspirations. People have purposes they aim to realize; pervasive wants, drives, appetites, and needs that constantly demand satisfaction. Yet what *seems* good in the "short run" may not in fact *be* durably good. The isolated satisfaction we anticipate and crave may not be judged satisfactory when we take a wider view, so we need practice and wisdom to thought-fully discriminate between the real good and the mirage. Consequently, the teleological conception of a good that approvably speaks to human aspirations is "neither arbitrary nor artificial" (1932, LW 7:309). When we act hastily without reflective foresight, we just follow the strongest inclination and fulfill a desire without taking its measure. "But when one foresees the consequences which may result from the fulfillment of desire, the situation changes" (1930, LW 5:282). Foresight involves judgment and comparison as we envision consequences *ex ante* and track them *ex post*.

The capacity to imaginatively crystallize possibilities and transform them into di-rective hypotheses is explored in Dewey's theory of dramatic rehearsal in deliberation (e.g., 1922, MW 14, ch. 16; cf. Fesmire 2003, ch. 5). We rehearse in a developing social and historical context, and judgments can be "examined, corrected, made more exact by judgments carried over from other situations; the results of previous estimates and actions are available as working materials" (1930, LW 5:282). Consequently, we learn to organize and thoughtfully prioritize desires, and this led historically to candidates for the "chief good," the *summum bonum* (e.g., Aristotle 1999, Book I), such as hedon-istic pleasure, Epicurean wisdom, success (e.g., Plato 1992, Book I; Plato 1960), egoistic satisfaction, self-realization,[17] and asceticism. When this factor is uppermost, *reason* is conceived as "intelligent insight into complete and remote consequences of desire" (1932, LW 7:217). The contemplated action is right and virtuous because it is truly, far-sightedly good; it is wrong and vicious because it is short-sightedly bad.

As a contemporary example, in Singer's hedonistic utilitarian approach to "effec-tive altruism," reason calculates the objectively best quantifiable way to "maximize the amount of good you do over your lifetime" (Singer 2015, 65; cf. 198n10).[18] One need not be morally "on the clock" 24/7, but for Singer weighing your options to maximize the true, objective good that you do is what it *means* to be moral. For example, if you can work for Goldman Sachs and donate excess income to effective charities, you may do more life-saving good than if you espouse a deontological "do no harm" principle and refuse to participate in the capitalistic financial system due to its putative unfair-ness. The good you do *justifies* your participation, unless you could have aggregated more good in some other way. *If* struggling against structural inequalities adds up to the most good you can do, then it is justified, but fighting for justice is *not* good in it-self without regard for its utility. For Singer, answering a moral problem bears a strong analogy to answering a math problem. It requires us to calculate payoffs and pitfalls, debits and credits, and thereby determine the objective good (145). For instance, what priority should we give to expenditures on decreasing existential risk (from asteroids, etc.)? Singer (2015) quotes Bostrom, who deduces via utility calculations that it should be our highest global priority: "If benefiting humanity by increasing existential safety achieves expected good on a scale many orders of magnitude greater than that of alternative contributions, we would do well to focus on this most efficient philanthropy" (174).

Dewey responded to mathematizing approaches in the unpublished typescript: Appeals to "the dictates of conscience," intuition, a moral calculus, moral law, or divine command acknowledge moral puzzlement, but they mask existential uncertainty when they presuppose "that the answer to a moral problem is already licit, like the answer to a problem in a text on arithmetic that it only remains to figure correctly." Moral problems, Dewey held, typically bear little analogy to elementary arithmetic tasks in a schoolchild's textbook, or to being stumped by a hard puzzle. When puzzling over the square root of 81, there is a clear-cut way to formulate the problem and a right solution to calculate, so the only real problem is temporary ignorance of the answer. In moral life, however, "Genuine uncertainty is an essential trait of every moral situation" (Dewey, undated ms, 1).

Dewey is not simply commenting upon the uncertainty due to the *difficulty* of a puzzle, or to lack of *access* to relevant information to plug into our diagnostic machinery. He contended that a typical quandary about which choice to make among viable alternatives cannot *even in principle* be definitively formulated and finally answered by assembling data and then calculating profits and losses on an accounting spreadsheet, as neo-Benthamites persist in supposing. Dewey should have acknowledged that utilitarianism's economic-mathematical balancing model can function well as a heuristic for some purposes. What he rejected was the quest for a predetermined metric whereby we judiciously weigh matters so that the balance tips toward the good—many contemporary economists and policy analysts say "optimal"—outcome supported by a universal principle. Dewey acknowledged easy cases in which habituated rule-following may economize deliberation, but insofar as an approach fails to prioritize sensitivity to context, creative social inquiry, and experimental understanding of complex underlying structures, its actual result is too often reminiscent of an offhanded criticism that Dewey once made about "popcorn" solutions: put the right amount in the right mechanism and you get some "unnutritious readymade stuff" that will not sustain anyone for long (1951.02.14 [14090]: Dewey to Max C. Otto).

Second Factor: Duty

The way we express our cares, make sense of situations, and deal with problems is acquired through interaction with the physical, cultural, and interpersonal environments in which we are at home. Classic Greek theorists acquired through a sociocultural medium their intellectual habits of pulling toward the good, just as Roman and British theorists acquired habits of pulling respectively toward the right and virtuous.

Dewey argued that the intimacy of the Greek polis supported teleological intelligence and the idea that laws reflect our rational ability to patiently set and achieve purposeful goals together. Accordingly, theories of the good made sense to the ancient Greeks. The vast conglomeration of peoples in the Roman Empire, however, supported the development of centralized order and the imposition of demands. As a result, in the historical transition from Greek teleology to Roman law, as exemplified by the Stoics, compliance with authorized duty was placed at "the centre of moral theory" (1930, LW 5:284).

The resultant jural or deontological theories cover a fact in ordinary human behavior: We unavoidably make claims on each other through living together, such as the control of desire and appetite, companionship and competition, cooperation and subordination. Others' demands seem arbitrary unless they square with our own purposes, and our demands in turn seem arbitrary to others. We don't like to have our desires impeded and regulated, sorted into the forbidden and the permitted. So "there finally develops a certain set or system of demands, more or less reciprocal according to social conditions, which are . . . responded to without overt revolt." In this way, Dewey proposed, authorized rights and duties evolve, and continue to evolve, through demands and prohibitions on others' behavior. "From the standpoint of those whose claims are recognized, these demands are rights; from the standpoint of those undergoing them they are duties." This "constitutes the principle of authority, Jus, Recht, Droit, which is current" (284).

According to Dewey, duty as a leading concept arises, then, from authoritative control which imposes a ban on individual satisfactions and temptations. As such, the concepts of duty and the right are in many cases independent, in both existential origin and logical operation, from the concept of good. The good pivots on the element of aspiration; the right pivots on the element of exaction.

Because imperatives often inhibit the satisfaction of desires, the concept of duty is not, as Kant recognized, "reducible to the conception of the good as satisfaction, even reasonable satisfaction, of desire" (1932, LW 7:214). Nonetheless, as Kant also recognized, there is no moral quality in being bound by an authority we deem ultimately arbitrary. When my young son was grabbing and picking flowers in a public garden a few years ago, we told him "don't pick the flowers." He experienced this as an imposition in which a good was curtailed. If he begins to concur that it is reasonable for his liberty to be thus restrained, what began as enforced compliance may be converted into something with moral standing, something *right*. It would then operate as a *moral* demand that he acknowledges he should not refuse to meet.

Dewey here distinguishes the *origins* of each root factor from its eventual *operations*. That which *operates*, say, as a good may have had its origins in duty. A demand that comes to one as a duty operates via compliance, but one may eventually identify the injunction with an end one aspires to realize so that it operates as a good. If down the road my son desires to help that garden flourish, what began as an alien requirement that thwarted a desire to grab flowers, and may grow into something right to which he personally realizes the wisdom of submitting, may become a good. The same might eventually be said of his enforced duty to go to school. That is, cultivating the garden (or going to school) may enter his personal aspirations, despite its origins in obedience to communal regulations, "but when this happens, it loses its quality of being right and authoritative and becomes simply a good" (1930, LW 5:285).[19] Moreover, there are hybrid theories which happily defy tidy categorization. Rule utilitarianism, for example, operates in the main via compliance with universal rules, albeit rules theoretically justified solely by the welfare they are supposed to maximize: if you aspire to maximize the good, then conform to the rule.

In sum, "the Good is that which attracts; the Right is that which asserts that we *ought* to be drawn by some object whether we are naturally attracted to it or not" (1932, LW 7:217). When the latter factor is uppermost, *reason* (or, for some deontologists, a presumed innate faculty of conscience) is conceived as "a power which is opposed to desire and which imposes restrictions on its exercise through issuing commands" (217). It is good and virtuous to do it *because* it is right; it is bad and vicious because it is wrong. In consequence, to the degree that a deontologist is a monist, there are no morally relevant aspects of virtue or good that cannot be organized under the concept of duty, right, law, and obligation. To will what is right *because it is right*, and not because it is prudent, is consequently a common idea in moral judgments, and the category of lawful duty and compliance with constraints of the right is thus taken by many to be the foundation stone of ethics.

In the 1932 *Ethics*, Dewey applies these insights to Kantian deontology. According to Kantians, what is morally Good "is that which is Right, that which accords with law and the commands of duty" (214-216). Contemporary representatives include Rawls (1971), Donagan (1977), Gewirth (1978), Darwall (1983), and Korsgaard (1996). Central to his conception of justice as fairness, for example, Rawls distinctively holds with Kant that a deontological principle of right must take priority over consequentialist concepts of good (1971, 31; cf. Freeman 2007, 72). Rawls references *The Critique of Practical Reason*: "the concept of good and evil must not be determined before the moral law . . . , but only after it and by means of it" (Kant 2002, 37). One should, contra Singer, struggle against inequality or strive to change an unjust system *independent* of the net utility of what you've chosen. For Kantian deontologists, the good is a path to the right, and the right gets its governing authority by reasonably obliging—or in Korsgaard's idiom on the "source of normativity," moral obligations are assigned by autonomous consciousness (1996; cf. Schaubroeck 2010). Fully complying with your duty and thereby at least attitudinally intending to uphold the rights of others is what it *means* to be moral.

In Dewey's naturalistic and pragmatic view, how do social expectations take on justifiable moral authority? That is, how does Dewey reinterpret the locus and ground of rightfulness without falling back on God, the state, an inner law of pure practical reason, a law of nature, or idealized rational actors? The relationships that naturally bind us— say, as parents and children, friends, spouses or partners, and citizens—expose us to "the expectations of others and to the demands in which these expectations are made manifest." This is equally true of social demands within institutions and political alliances. Explicit and implicit claims and demands are "as natural as anything else in a world in which persons are not isolated from one another but live in constant association and interaction" (1932, LW 7:218). Although a child, friend, spouse, or citizen might be arbitrarily coerced into slavish conformity by despotic power, this is experienced as a brute imposition without moral standing. Expectations become *moral* claims because, even when inconvenient or exasperating, conscientious parents, friends, spouses, or citizens respond to relations of parenting, friendship, marriage, and citizenship as "expressions of the whole" to which they belong rather than as extrinsic impositions (218). "If we generalize such instances, we reach the conclusion that right, law, duty, arise from the relations which human beings intimately sustain to one another, and that their authoritative force springs from the very nature of the relation that binds people together" (219).

In his pragmatic-operational reconstruction of duty and the right, Dewey observed that in moral life we must meet the demands of the *situation*, which requires us to perceive and comprehensively respond to more than our own private satisfactions. The word duty is apt for those all-too-familiar occasions in which our own preferences or narrow desires run the other way, at cross-purposes from relational demands that should not be shirked merely because they may be irksome, discomforting, inconvenient, *or* perilous. Not only are Kantians right that we cannot rationally will a world of shoplifters or liars; they are also right to call for an inner sentinel alert to the exceptions we make of ourselves. Who better than Rawls, for example, for shining a light on the way we benefit from a practice while shirking to do our share in sustaining that practice for others? (cf. Appiah 2017, 203)[20] Kantians typically reject such aspectual pragmatizing as an abdication of morality; nevertheless, Dewey agrees with Kant that "to be truthful from duty is . . . quite different from being truthful from fear of disadvantageous consequences" (Kant 1993, 15). In sum, duty, right, and obligation are concepts that serve an experiential function as *one* constant and distinctive stream of morals. Kant's mistake was to hypostatize this factor and sharply separate moral conduct from our natural aspirations and practical purposes, inferring that "All so-called moral interest consists solely in respect for the law" (14n14).

Third Factor: Virtue

Dewey asserted in the 1930 presentation: "Empirically, there is a third independent variable in morals" centered on praise and blame, approval and disapproval, reward and punishment (LW 5:285). "Acts and dispositions generally approved form the original virtues; those condemned the original vices" (286). Approving and disapproving attitudes, in all of their popular variability and inconsistency within and across social groups, mark the virtuous as an independent primitive factor in morals. This factor differs fundamentally, at least in principle, from the deliberative pursuit of ends—which virtue theorists regard as too intellectualistic—or the demand for compliance—which virtue theorists regard as too legalistic. When teleological thinkers consider social approval, it is their *ends* to which they are devoting effort. Meanwhile, deontologists use praise and blame as sanctions for right and wrong (Dewey, undated ms, 10). "But as categories, as principles, the virtuous differs radically from the good and the right.

Goods, I repeat, have to do with deliberation upon desires and purposes; the right and obligatory with demands that are socially authorized and backed; virtues with widespread approbation" (1930, LW 5:286). Virtue ethicists extend this initial emphasis on acts that are praiseworthy or blameworthy to a search for consistency and coherence about which durable traits of character ought to be approved or censured. So they need some non-arbitrary standard of approbation to critique the "original" or spontaneous virtues and discover more appropriate and defensible ones. Typically they turn, like Anscombe, to some eudaemonistic conception of living well together.

In the Fries letter (Figure 10.2), Dewey credited his unconventional meta-ethical typology—which upends simple categorization of Aristotle as a virtue ethicist, or Mill as an aggregator of good consequences—to careful re-reading of eighteenth and nineteenth century British moral philosophers such as Hume, Smith, Bentham, Mill, and Sidgwick. This re-reading unfolds in Hook's 1926 course notes (in Koch 2010), and it led Dewey to a Jekyll-and-Hyde recasting of utilitarianism: the Benthamite strain has persisted as a teleological orientation mired in "an untenable hedonism," whereas Mill more securely received and renewed the torch of moral sentiment theory (e.g., Hume, Smith) by shifting the focus away from what we should *do* in pursuit of pleasures (e.g., Should I retaliate for what he did?) and toward cultivation of character (e.g., Should I *be* someone disposed to follow anger's directives?). "Although Mill never quite acknowledges it in words, a surrender of the hedonistic element in utilitarianism" enabled him to develop, or mostly develop, a robust welfarist standard implicit in our approbations that favors "worthy dispositions from which issue noble enjoyments" (1932, LW 7:245).

For both Hume and Smith, sympathetic sentiments were the singular source of morality. Hume wrote in the *Treatise* (regarding moral judgment) that "Sympathy is the chief source of moral distinctions" (1978, 618).[21] Sympathy necessarily brings approval, while antipathy brings disapproval. That is, we approve because we sympathize, and whatever calls out this sentiment we call good. Still, it's not *just* that we have antipathy toward Iago's treachery; for both Hume and Smith, our moral sentiments are subject to correctives and regulation by rational considerations. Dewey observed of moral sentiment theory: "In individuals, the exercise of sympathy in accordance with reason—i.e., from the standpoint of an impartial spectator, in Smith's conception—is the norm of virtuous action" (1935, LW 11:11).[22] The job of reason, for Smith, is to inform and secure the correctives of an impartial standard of approbation so that it plays a formative role in critically reflective ends. *Reason* seeks "a *standard* upon the basis of which approbation and disapprobation, esteem and disesteem, *should* be awarded" (1932, LW 7:255).[23]

Published discussions of Dewey's pluralism, including my own, have hitherto discussed utilitarianism of all stripes under the category of the good. But this is a half-truth, as becomes clear when carefully considering Smith's approach to the problem of nonarbitrary standards that do not simply kowtow to customary ridicule and esteem. This problem is uppermost in sentiment theory, Dewey argues, "even when the writer seems to be discussing some other question" (1930, LW 5:286). Again, within sentiment theory what is good or dutiful is derived from what our sentiments approve and disapprove. We spontaneously sympathize with and favor benevolent actions that serve others, while ill will arouses antipathy. For Hume and Smith, ethical theory gives its seal of rational approval to the implicit standard in such judgments: "the Good must be defined in terms of impulses that further general welfare since they are the ones naturally approved" (Dewey, undated ms, 10). In this way, according to Dewey, Hume and Smith accounted for both aspiration (the good) and compliance (duty) in terms of what they took to be *the more fundamental fact* of approval and disapproval (virtue). Nineteenth-century British utilitarianism inherited this legacy, as is especially evident in Mill's focus on social sympathy, but in Dewey's view it illogically tried to combine "Dr. Jekyll" with "Mr. Hyde": (a) the pursuit of general welfare as the legitimate standard implicit in social approval (or reproach) of dispositions and practices with (b) the hedonistic notion that individual pleasure is the *summum bonum*.

In sum, Dewey holds that for monistic theories rooted in the third factor, a practice or disposition such as generosity, courage, honesty, industriousness, curiosity, or compassion may be judged good and dutiful because our moral sentiments approve (and ought legitimately to approve) it as virtuous; a predisposition such as miserliness or retaliatory payback is bad and wrong because it is vicious (and rationally merits disapproval). To the degree that virtue theorists are monists—and Hume was a pluralist of sorts, at least with respect to fundamental conflicts among moral ends (see Gill 2011)—they infer that all morally relevant aspects of good or duty can be systematically organized under the concept of virtuous character traits, that is, traits we should approve because they are contributory to a rationally defensible conception of living and being well. Monistic virtue theorists hold that cultivating stable behavioral traits that are as virtuous as possible is what it ultimately *means* to be moral. Or, to update Dewey's analysis, the virtue theorist must at least fictionalize (see Alfano 2013) reliably stable traits of character—the sort of traits that situational psychologists are now claiming we are incapable of exhibiting in the requisite trans-contextual way (e.g., Appiah 2008, ch. 2).

CONCLUSION: BEYOND MORAL FUNDAMENTALISM

Dewey concluded "Three Independent Factors in Morals" with a call for imagination to be more perceptive and responsive to the situations in which we must act. Moral problems are entanglements, so theories will be ill-suited to practical conditions whenever "zeal for a unitary view" oversimplifies and standardizes moral life (1930, LW 5:288). Striving for systematic coherence can be a philosophic virtue. The problem is that traditional monists oversimplify moral experience by abstracting some factor as central and uppermost, hypostatizing it, then treating this factor as the self-sufficient starting point for moral inquiry and the foundational bedrock for all moral justification. The popular habit of singling out one trump value among a wide range of relevant values tracks the same pattern and perpetuates the same problems.[24]

To summarize Dewey's proposal, traditional concepts of good, duty, and virtue arise as distinct categories that express different experiential origins, and none operates as the bottom line that can accommodate all that is of moral worth in the rest. Hence, no single factor of moral life is the central and basic source of all moral justification. When our moral deliberations (our reflective excursions into what is possible) begin with the troubled situation—with a practical predicament rather than a theoretical starting point (Pappas 2020)—we discover that diverse factors are already in tension with each other.[25] Our foremost practical need is for fine-tuned habits that enable us to continuously co-ordinate and comprehensively integrate these tensions. Theories and practices that place primitive experiential factors in interplay and open a communicative field between them can better inform our moral deliberations. Dewey sought to analyze leading categories through which ethical theories have concentrated attention on these vital factors, in order to put them in communication for the sake of more intelligent choices.

The primitive strands discussed herein are conceptually distinct and have inde-pendent sources, Dewey argued, but in actual experiences they are intertwined and "cut across one another." Needs arise in which we must search for a way to reconcile them to each other by weaving them into a tapestry of action that more or less satisfactorily expresses the original tensions that set the problem at hand (Fesmire 2003, ch. 7).

In addition to such practical needs, there is a need for theoretical projects reconciling diverse factors. Such projects could change the terms of debate within and between eth-ical traditions. Dewey approached historical ethical theories, traditional codes of con-duct, and legal history as data for inquiry, not as finalities to be accepted or rejected wholesale (1932, LW 7:179; cf. Koch 2010). Future research in ethics could follow him in rejecting zero-sum theorizing. This would open a door for research recasting ethical theories as compensatory emphases, in dynamic tension with other emphases.[26] Classic moral philosophies were forged in part as idealized tools to interpret and deal with so-cial situations. Their enduring practical value for personal and social inquiry can be liberated—and Dewey's concern was to liberate, not to endorse or dismiss— by reforging traditional tools so that pretty good theoretical work stops getting in the way of better.

Dewey signaled a future for philosophical research in which we advance the growth of ethical traditions by rejecting both the quest for, and the tone of, finality in favor of experimentally developing robust communicative projects with distinctive dominant emphases, angles, and inferences. For example, Kant's corpus as a whole was more em-pirically informed and humane than is revealed in standard readings (Louden 2002), and a modified, non-absolutistic, broadly Kantian pluralism in ethics, fronting rough conformity to duty, has been plausibly defended as more than an oxymoron (Hill 2000).[27] As Neiman (2008) observes, we do not have to flee to an otherworldly metric or fancied preestablished harmony to see that "sometimes morality and self-interest part company" (20). The monistic Kantian inference that morality is thus *nothing but* auton-omous willing in accord with universal law, or that conformity with duty is what mo-rality essentially *is* (unlimited by the purpose at hand and wholly apart from whatever damage we imprudently though dutifully do), flows not from logic but from a hidden premise of theoretical correctness. That premise persists wherever anticonsequentialism is declared the victor in a theoretic prizefight, or wherever consequentialists overlook the practical bearings of attitudes and predispositions, of will. We enable this premise, or give it a "pass," at the *cost* of finding practical footholds to secure dignity and respect.

Should we abandon the quest for theoretical correctness in ethics, and, if so, what then? If being theoretically correct implies a completely enlightened ideal standpoint secured prior to confronting difficulties in particular contexts, a standpoint from which our general habits of moral thinking will be completely adequate to meeting every situation, then it is increasingly essential that we should abandon the quest for it. If, on the other hand, one understands "correctness" in an operative sense, as in "The map to the pub was correct," then it is a sensible ideal to strive for theories that help us to better navigate messy terrain (Fesmire 2015, 53–59).

The monistic quest for theoretical correctness can obstruct communication, constrict imagination, and underwrite bad choices. Getting beyond it would place ethical theorizing on a stronger footing, especially for dealing with those intractable and ubiquitous "wicked problems" in which problem formulation is itself among the key problems (because in these cases even the most sincere and informed participants formulate problems and interpret facts differently). When we see a moral or political problem only as given, not taken, the chief problem is presumed to be that others do not get the problem (see Norton 2015).[28] Or the main problem is presumed to be the general failure of the public, or of other nations, to adopt our brilliant solutions. Never mind the unnoticed parts of the mess occluded by our well-defended general principles, which are often assumed to be value-neutral and free of interest-driven rationalizations and inherited biases. If we think our diagnosis of the problem is incorrigible and has precisely captured all that is morally or politically relevant, then we will *predefine* what is relevant, and we will covertly prejudge alternative formulations.

What happens, then, to opportunities for learning our way together across a spectrum of values? In public disputes, from the local to the international, vying camps enlist enthusiasm through an evaluative conquest, restricting sympathies to a singular channel. They typically demand this to the logical exclusion of democratic attempts to secure shared toeholds to achieve social goals. In this way, moral fundamentalism, logically propped up by monism's assumption of theoretical correctness, offers a deep channel for our partialities and dearest inclinations, but it risks antagonism toward excluded standpoints, closure to being surprised by the complexity of many situations and systems, neglect of the context in which decisions are made, and a related general indifference to public processes and integrative values. This is a recipe for failed communication and bad decisions.

Moral fundamentalist habits, and the monistic one-way assumption that exercises and reinforces them, are obstacles to cultivating habits of moral and political inquiry that are better fitted to contemporary predicaments. We cannot create static utopias, but we would be better off if we would experiment with how far we can go in creating a shared cultural context for inquiry that checks both our inveterate moral fundamentalism and the reactionary nihilism that is fundamentalism's mirror image. An actual result of opposing "their" moral fundamentalism with our own is to perpetuate the root problem. To ameliorate the morasses we face, we need a more genuinely radical approach: we need confidence and resistance without puritanical zealotry, courage in mediating troubled situations without expectation of absolute certainty, frank speech without fatalistic resignation or paralyzing guilt, and moral clarity without incorrigibility and oversimplification.[29]

NOTES

1. For example, Paul Thompson (2015) observes of the food movement that "Advocates of both biotechnology *and* organic systems too often compare the most advanced and optimistic interpretation of their favored approach to the least successful applications of the alternative" (252). The result has been dichotomized either/or thinking, which comes attended by tendencies to oversimplification, ignoring context, and quests for purity (cf. Boisvert and Heldke 2016).

2. Monistic ethical theorists join pluralists in rejecting the arrogance that characterizes popular moral fundamentalist habits. Nevertheless, moral fundamentalism cannot logically stand without its monistic premise. I argue that we are better off without this premise. It is both empirically unwarranted and morally troubling, and there is little to be said in favor of it that cannot be accommodated by pragmatic pluralism.

3. It would be fruitful, though beyond the scope of this chapter, to compare and contrast Dewey's form of pluralism with other contemporaneous styles, such as W. D. Ross's (1930) intuitionist pluralism in *The Right and The Good*.

4. Haidt (2016) hypothesizes five moral foundations that operate as underlying universal intuitions: Care/harm, fairness/cheating, loyalty/betrayal, authority/subversion, sanctity/degradation. Dewey cautioned against innatist/universal instinct theories, and Haidt's theory could be strengthened by restatement in terms other than innate and universal modular foundations. For development of this line of criticism, see Johnson (2014).

5. Rawls proposed a division of labor between ideal and nonideal theories. The former's job is to determine "what a perfectly just society would be like" (1971, 8–9), whereas nonideal theories are tasked with discerning principles to deal with nonideal conditions in which people do not comply with the principles of justice, as with war or racial oppression, or in which conditions make perfect justice unrealizable. We need to start by constructing an ideal theory, Rawls thought, if we are to construct a moral compass for dealing with nonideal conditions. Anderson, Mills, Appiah, Pappas, and others are arguing that he was mistaken.

6. See Sullivan (2018) and Glaude (2007) to consider whether Dewey historically fared any better.

7. The idea that we should bring experimental method to bear on value inquiry traces most notably back to Hume's *Treatise*, the full title of which was *A Treatise of Human Nature: being an Attempt to introduce the experimental Method into Moral Subjects*.

8. Cf. Kitcher (2014) as well as Mill's (1986) *On Liberty* on "experiments of living" (65).

9. This is perhaps the most distinctively "pragmatist" feature of Dewey's ethical theory. Cf. Alexander 2013.

10. Originally published as "Trois facteurs indépendants en matière de morale," trans. Charles Cestre, in *Bulletin de la SFP* 30 (October–December 1930), 118–127.

11. A copy of the typescript was available to Abraham Edel and Elizabeth Flowers, who introduced the 1985 critical edition of the 1932 *Ethics*. This typescript was subsequently misplaced until 2016, when it was retrieved in a careful search by staff at Morris Library, Special Collections, Southern Illinois University at Carbondale.

12. I am indebted to Richard Bernstein for this insight (personal communication).

13. Rawls (1993) *hoped* to do this with his politics of "overlapping consensus," regardless of how one appraises his conception of "public reason" as a viable means to this end.

14. In his theory of moral judgment and knowledge (1932, LW 7, ch. 14), beyond my scope in this chapter, Dewey argued that the "comprehensive object" of moral choice is the option one foresees *ex ante* as most reliably expressing the situation's conflicting factors and recovering its dynamic equilibrium. Importantly, in Dewey's experimental view we must act and also see. *Re*-vision, review *ex post* is equally essential.

15. In these lectures, Dewey struggled with whether right and duty are fundamentally different concepts. For example, he explored Sidgwick's notion in *Methods of Ethics* that the right is the "Rational Good," which Sidgwick contrasted with a merely *natural* good (cf. Lazari-Radek and Singer 2014).

16. Dewey's typos silently corrected throughout.

17. Some commentators misrepresent Dewey's *mature* ethics as an ethics of self-realization. Not only would this be a monistic reduction, but he argues in the 1932 *Ethics* in a Kantian vein that self-realization as an ideal may deaden people to the experiences of others so that we value them like pleasantries.

18. Singer's (2015) *The Most Good You Can Do* is among the most engaging and teachable books available in contemporary practical ethics.

19. Along these lines, yet outside my scope in this chapter, Edel (2001) argues that Dewey respects the independence of each factor while making the content of each "responsible to the idea of the good" (11).

20. For Dewey the general social demand to do our fair share is justified in practice, not by compliance with the first principles of idealized contractors.

21. In *The Theory of Moral Sentiments*, Smith (1790) followed Hume in tracing the source of morals to the principle of sympathy: "By the imagination we place ourselves in his situation" (I.I.2).

22. Often neglected by scholars drawn to Smith's (1790) influential treatment of sympathetic imagination, Smith discusses the "impartial spectator" in terms of prescriptions and approvals of the authoritative "judge within the breast" (VI.iii.17–19). He writes: "When we first come into the world, from the natural desire to please, we accustom ourselves to every person we converse with . . . . [Yet] the fairest and most equitable conduct must frequently obstruct the interests or thwart the inclinations of particular persons, who will seldom . . . see that this conduct . . . is perfectly suitable to our situation. In order to defend ourselves from such partial judgments, we . . . conceive ourselves as acting in the presence of . . . . an impartial spectator who considers our conduct with the same indifference with which we regard that of other people" (Smith 1790, III.ii.36; cf. Frierson 2006, 148–149).

23. As deontologists fully appreciate, one's own hankerings may run counter to the "comprehensive object" of moral choice. But akin to Foot, and taking a cue from Hume and Smith,

Dewey was skeptical of the Kantian contention that our moral mettle is truly revealed only when we are motivated to pursue the comprehensive object by the force of reason independent of desire (Foot 1978, 161; cf. Trianosky 1990). Deweyan moral artistry (Fesmire 2003) does not rely on dispassionate pure reason (Kant), comparison to a world of agents fully compliant with the demands of justice (Rawls), detached moral bookishness (utilitarianism), or separation from the intimacy of our own yearnings (all of the above). Even in situations in which the comprehensive object has its origins in social demands, it is a matter of moral significance for Dewey that it be *desired* as (a hypothetical) good, not just coolly and disinterestedly assented to as dutiful.

24. For example, in environmental policymaking economic criteria are typically presumed to have supremacy over other key values (aesthetic, spiritual, recreational, ecological, etc.). See Norton (2005, 2015).

25. He states this most clearly in the unpublished typescript: "The three concepts in question represent forces that have different roots, not a common and single one. Because these forces pull different ways there is a genuine conflict—and a problematic quality pervades the whole situation" (Dewey, undated ms, 3).

26. For example, with notable exceptions such as McKenna and Light's (2004) *Animal Pragmatism* and the work of Paul Thompson (e.g., 2010, 2015), scholars working in the American pragmatist grain have taken a back seat to utilitarian and Kantian philosophers in responding to the far-reaching impact of human practices on other species and rising concern about animal use and treatment. Due to this neglect, the debate has been more anemic than it might have been. Abandoning the quest for a fully enlightened ideal standpoint may help us to secure a more comprehensive Rawlsian reflective equilibrium in animal ethics and in other areas of practical ethics.

27. To my knowledge Kantian pluralism has yet to be substantively defended in the "strong" sense of pluralism advocated herein.

28. It is a truism that people happily weigh in on matters concerning which they are incompetent, but no problem is so bad that we cannot make it worse through our way of dealing with it.

29. Research on this chapter was supported in part by a 2016 fellowship at the University of Edinburgh, Institute for Advanced Studies in the Humanities. In addition to helpful dialogue on this project with many peers at professional conferences, as well as with colleagues and students at Middlebury College and Green Mountain College, I am grateful to Erin McKenna and Anthony Weston for critical feedback on an earlier draft.

REFERENCES

Citations of John Dewey's works are to the thirty-seven-volume critical edition published by Southern Illinois University Press under the editorship of Jo Ann Boydston. In-text citations give the original publication date and series abbreviation, followed by volume number and page number. For example: (1934, LW 10:12) is page 12 of *Art as Experience*, which is published as volume 10 of *The Later Works*.

Series abbreviations for *The Collected Works*:

EW *The Early Works* (1882–98)

MW *The Middle Works* (1899–1924)

LW The Later Works (1925–53)

Citations of Dewey's correspondence are to *The Correspondence of John Dewey*, 1871–2007, published by the InteLex Corporation under the editorship of Larry Hickman. Citations give the date, reference number for the letter, and author followed by recipient. For example: Herbert W. Schneider to H. S. Thayer [1973.02.13 (22053)].

Alexander, Thomas. 2013. *The Human Eros*. New York: Fordham University Press.

Alfano, Mark. 2013. *Character as Moral Fiction*. New York: Cambridge University Press.

Anderson, Elizabeth. 2009. "Toward a Non-Ideal, Relational Methodology for Political Philosophy: Comments on Schwartzman's *Challenging Liberalism*." *Hypatia*, vol. 24, no. 4, 130–145.

Anderson, Elizabeth. 2013. *The Imperative of Integration*. Princeton, NJ: Princeton University Press.

Anscombe, G. E. M. 1958. "Modern Moral Philosophy." *Philosophy*, vol. 33, no. 124, 10.

Appiah, Kwame Anthony. 2008. *Experiments in Ethics*. Cambridge, MA: Harvard University Press.

Appiah, Kwame Anthony. 2017. *As If: Idealization and Ideals*. Cambridge, MA: Harvard University Press.

Aristotle. 1999. *Nicomachean Ethics*. Trans. Terence Irwin. Indianapolis, IN: Hackett.

Axtell, Guy and Philip Olson. 2009. "Three Independent Factors in Epistemology." *Contemporary Pragmatism* 6, no. 2:89–109.

Boisvert, Raymond D., and Lisa Heldke. 2016. *Philosophers at Table: On Food and Being Human*. London: Reaktion Books.

Darwall, Stephen L. 1983. *Impartial Reason*. Ithaca, NY: Cornell University Press.

Dewey, John. Undated manuscript (mss102_53_3). "*Conflict and Independent Variables in Morals*." Morris Library, Special Collections, Southern Illinois University at Carbondale.

Dewey, John, and James H. Tufts. 1908. *Ethics. MW* 5.

Dewey, John. 1916. *Democracy and Education. MW* 9.

Dewey, John. 1922. *Human Nature and Conduct. MW* 14.

Dewey, John. 1925/1929. *Experience and Nature. LW* 1.

Dewey, John. 1927. *The Public and Its Problems. LW* 2.

Dewey, John. 1929. *The Quest for Certainty. LW* 4.

Dewey, John. 1930. "Three Independent Factors in Morals." *LW* 5:279–288.

Dewey, John, and James H. Tufts. 1932. *Ethics*. Second edition. *LW* 7.

Dewey, John. 1938. *Logic: The Theory of Inquiry. LW* 12.

Dewey, John. 1938. "Democracy and Education in the World of Today." *LW* 13:294–303.

Donagan, Alan. 1977. *The Theory of Morality*. Chicago: University of Chicago Press.

Dworkin, Ronald. 2000. *Sovereign Virtue: The Theory and Practice of Equality*. Cambridge, MA: Harvard University Press.

Dworkin, Ronald. 2011. *Justice for Hedgehogs*. Cambridge, MA: Harvard University Press.

Edel, Abraham. 2001. *Ethical Theory and Social Change: The Evolution of John Dewey's Ethics, 1908–1932*. Piscataway, NJ: Transaction.

Elgin, Catherine Z. 1997. *Between the Absolute and the Arbitrary*. Oxford: Oxford University Press.

Fesmire, Steven. 2003. *John Dewey and Moral Imagination: Pragmatism in Ethics*. Bloomington: Indiana University Press.

Fesmire, Steven. 2015. *Dewey*. London and New York: Routledge.

Freeman, Samuel. 2007. *Justice and the Social Contract: Essays in Rawlsian Political Philosophy*. Oxford: Oxford University Press.

Frierson, Patrick. 2006. "Applying Adam Smith: A Step Towards Smithian Environmental Virtue Ethics." In Leonidas Montes and Eric Schliesser (eds.), *New Voices on Adam Smith*. London and New York: Routledge.

Gewirth, Alan. 1978. *Reason and Morality*. Chicago: University of Chicago Press.

Gill, Michael B. 2011. "Humean Moral Pluralism." *History of Philosophy Quarterly*, vol. 28, no. 1, 45–64.

Glaude, Eddie S. Jr. 2007. *In a Shade of Blue: Pragmatism and the Politics of Black America*. Chicago: University of Chicago Press.

Haidt, Jonathan. 2012. *The Righteous Mind: Why Good People Are Divided by Politics and Religion*. New York: Pantheon.

Haidt, Jonathan, and Fredrik Bjorklund. 2008. "Social Intuitionists Answer Six Questions About Moral Psychology." In Walter Sinnott-Armstrong (ed.), *Moral Psychology, Vol. 2, The Cognitive Science of Morality: Intuition and Diversity*. Cambridge, MA: MIT Press, 181–218.

Haidt, Jonathan. 2016. http://moralfoundations.org/; accessed July 13, 2018.

Heisenberg, Werner. 1958. *Physics and Philosophy: The Revolution in Modern Science*. New York: HarperCollins.

Hill, Thomas E. 2000. *Respect, Pluralism, and Justice: Kantian Perspectives*. Oxford: Oxford University Press.

Hume, David. 1978. *A Treatise of Human Nature*. Ed. L. A. Selby-Bigge. Oxford: Clarendon Press.

James, William. 1977. *A Pluralistic Universe*. Cambridge, MA: Harvard University Press.

Johnson, Mark. 2014. *Morality for Humans: Ethical Understanding from the Perspective of Cognitive Science*. Chicago: University of Chicago Press.

Johnson, Mark. 2020. "Dewey's Radical Conception of Moral Cognition." In Steven Fesmire (ed.), *The Oxford Handbook of Dewey*. Oxford and New York: Oxford University Press.

Kant, Immanuel. 1993. *Grounding for the Metaphysics of Morals*. Trans. James W. Ellington. Indianapolis, IN: Hackett.

Kant, Immanuel. 2002. *Critique of Practical Reason*. Trans. Werner Pluhar. Indianapolis, IN: Hackett.

Karsten, Jack, and Darrell M. West. 2016. "Inside the Social Media Echo Chamber." *Brookings*, December 9. https://www.brookings.edu/blog/techtank/2016/12/09/inside-the-social-media-echo-chamber/; accessed July 13, 2018.

Kitcher, Philip. 2012. *Preludes to Pragmatism: Toward a Reconstruction of Philosophy*. Oxford: Oxford University Press.

Kitcher, Philip. 2014. *The Ethical Project*. Cambridge, MA: Harvard University Press.

Koch, Donald (ed.). 2010. *The Class Lectures of John Dewey. Volume 2. Ethical Theory (1926) Class Lecture Notes by Sidney Hook*. Charlottesville, VA: InteLex Corp., 2.2230–2.2284.

Korsgaard, Christine M. 1996. *The Sources of Normativity*. Cambridge, UK: Cambridge University Press.

Korsgaard, Christine M. 2014. University of Groningen Interview on Ethics and Morality. https://www.youtube.com/watch?v=jzBLPDt-Blo; accessed July 13, 2018.

Latour, Bruno. 1993. *We Have Never Been Modern*. Trans. Catherine Porter. Cambridge, MA: Harvard University Press.

Lazari-Radek, Katarzyna de, and Peter Singer. 2014. *The Point of View of the Universe: Sidgwick and Contemporary Ethics*. Oxford: Oxford University Press.

Louden, Robert B. 2002. *Kant's Impure Ethics: From Rational Beings to Human Beings*. Oxford: Oxford University Press.

McKenna, Erin. 2018. *Livestock: Food, Fiber, and Friends*. Athens: University of Georgia Press.

McKenna, Erin, and Andrew Light (eds.). 2004. *Animal Pragmatism*. Bloomington: Indiana University Press.

Mill, John Stuart. 1986. *On Liberty*. Amherst, NY: Prometheus Books.

Mills, Charles W. 2005. "'Ideal Theory' as Ideology." *Hypatia*, vol. 20, no. 3, 165–184.

Mills, Charles W. 2017. *Black Rights/White Wrongs: The Critique of Racial Liberalism*. Oxford and New York: Oxford University Press.

Neiman, Susan. 2008. *Moral Clarity: A Guide For Grown-Up Idealists*. Princeton, NJ: Princeton University Press.

Noddings, Nel. 2013. *Caring: A Relational Approach to Ethics and Moral Education*. 2nd ed. Berkeley: University of California Press.

Norton, Bryan. 2005. *Sustainability: A Philosophy of Adaptive Ecosystem Management*. Chicago: University of Chicago Press.

Norton, Bryan. 2015. *Sustainable Values, Sustainable Change: A Guide to Environmental Decision Making*. Chicago: University of Chicago Press.

Nozick, Robert. 1974. *Anarchy, State, and Utopia*. New York: Basic Books, 1974.

Nussbaum, Martha C. 1990. *Love's Knowledge: Essays on Philosophy and Literature*. Oxford: Oxford University Press.

Pappas, Gregory. 2008. *John Dewey's Ethics: Democracy as Experience*. Bloomington: Indiana University Press.

Pappas, Gregory. 2020. "The Starting Point of Dewey's Ethics and Sociopolitical Philosophy." In Steven Fesmire (ed.), *The Oxford Handbook of Dewey*. Oxford and New York: Oxford University Press.

Plato. 1960. *Gorgias*. Trans. Walter Hamilton. New York: Penguin.

Plato. 1992. *Republic*. Trans. G. M. A. Grube and C. D. C. Reeve. Indianapolis, IN: Hackett.

Putnam, Robert. 2000. *Bowling Alone: The Collapse and Revival of American Community*. New York: Simon & Schuster.

Rawls, John. 1971. *A Theory of Justice*. Cambridge, MA: Harvard University Press.

Rawls, John. 1993. *Political Liberalism*. New York: Columbia University Press.

Schaubroeck, Katrien. 2010. Interview with Christine Korsgaard. *The Leuven Philosophy Newsletter*, vol. 17, 51–56. www.people.fas.harvard.edu/~korsgaar/Schaubroeck.Korsgaard.pdf; accessed July 13, 2018.

Ross, W. D. 1930. *The Right and The Good*. Oxford: Oxford University Press.

Sen, Amartya. 2009. *The Idea of Justice*. Cambridge, MA: Harvard University Press.

Singer, Peter. 2015. *The Most Good You Can Do*. New Haven: Yale University Press.

Sullivan, Shannon. 2018. "Dewey and Du Bois on Race and Colonialism." In Steven Fesmire (ed.), *The Oxford Handbook of Dewey*. Oxford and New York: Oxford University Press.

Taylor, Charles. 1982. "The Diversity of Goods." In Amartya Sen and Bernard Williams (eds.), *Utilitarianism and Beyond*. Cambridge: Cambridge University Press, 129–135.

Thompson, Paul. 2010. *The Agrarian Vision: Sustainability and Environmental Ethics*. Lexington: University Press of Kentucky.

Thompson, Paul. 2015. *From Field to Fork: Food Ethics for Everyone*. Oxford: Oxford University Press.

Valentini, Laura. 2012. "Ideal vs. Non-ideal Theory: A Conceptual Map." *Philosophy Compass*, vol. 7/9, 654–664.

Williams, Bernard. 1985. *Ethics and the Limits of Philosophy*. Cambridge, MA: Harvard University Press.

CHAPTER 11

THE STARTING POINT OF DEWEY'S ETHICS AND SOCIOPOLITICAL PHILOSOPHY

GREGORY FERNANDO PAPPAS

In order to appreciate the radical and promising character of Dewey's ethics and sociopolitical theory, we must understand how his approach in these areas of philosophy was a consequence of what he thought should be the starting point of philosophy, that is, his metaphilosophy. Dewey prescribed that philosophers should make an effort to be "empirical" and to take "experience" seriously, but these claims are subject to misunderstandings. In the first section of this chapter I first clarify what they mean. In the second section I consider the difference that Dewey's form of empirical philosophy makes in ethics, and in a third section the difference it makes in approaching sociopolitical problems. Dewey proposes a much more radical approach than similar contemporary approaches that are interested in a shift from traditional approaches centered on ideal theories and abstractions toward a more nonideal contextualist, problem-centered, and inquiry-oriented approach.

METAPHILOSOPHY: EXPERIENCE AS METHOD

It is commonly claimed that Dewey, like other theorists in the twentieth century, sought an empirical grounding for ethics and sociopolitical theory. This is true, but it is not illuminating unless Dewey's own brand of empiricism and his views about experience as method are made clear. Dewey's criticism of these two areas of philosophy presupposed a methodology, and it was informed by the systematic mistakes that he detected in other areas of philosophy.

We must first ask what one could mean by the claim that a philosophy is "empirical." A survey of the literature on this issue suggests the following possible tenets:

1. It adopts the subject matter, concepts, results, and judgments of the natural sciences;
2. it has as its starting point social psychology and evolutionary naturalism (i.e., based on scientific truths or standpoint);
3. it is like science in certain methodological respects (i.e., modeled on science);
4. it is informed by the natural sciences; and
5. it relies on experience as method. It takes lived experience as its starting point.

Many of the misdirected criticisms of Dewey's philosophy have assumed that he held tenet 1. Dewey's defenders rightly point out that this is a caricature of his view.[1] Dewey cannot be identified with a "naturalistic" reduction of moral or political judgments to scientific statements.[2] Tenet 2 is a more recent common interpretation.[3] Dewey had a tendency to describe everyday experience by using biological and psychological terms. This did the job of getting away from the modern view of the self as a subject or spectator of an antecedent reality, but it could mislead readers to think that Dewey is just a philosophy that adopts a scientific outlook on things or that starts with some theoretical truths given by the sciences. The pragmatists were influenced by Darwin and evolutionary naturalism. They saw these and other developments in the sciences (at the turn of the century) as providing an indirect validation of their philosophical views. However, this is different from claiming that pragmatism, in particular its view of lived experience, is based on or presupposes the truth of Darwinism or any evolutionary-type theory.

Instead of the narrow view assumed by tenets 1 and 2, tenets 3 and 4 better convey the sense in which for Dewey any area of philosophy can be empirical. Tenet 4 postulates how philosophy can be constantly nurtured and informed by the results of scientific inquiries. In this conception the philosopher is a more interdisciplinary creature than he or she typically is. Compared to tenet 4, tenet 3 seems to be making a stronger claim about the relation between science and philosophy. An empirical philosophy is one that adopts the general method of inquiry of the sciences. For example, Dewey did not see why the conclusions of moral philosophy could not have the same hypothetical character as those of the sciences.[4] However, these tenets are not sufficient to fully understand the radical nature of Dewey's reconstruction in philosophy. Dewey had a well-developed view of what it means for any area of philosophy to be empirical. It is to this view of an empirical philosophy that tenet 5 appeals. Dewey's view, although compatible with tenet 3, is not reducible to it. Dewey had some very substantive things to say about what it means for an area of philosophy to be empirical that were independent of how he conceived the relation between philosophy and science.[5]

A genuine empiricism in philosophy entails that no matter how abstract and remote our philosophical speculations might turn out to be, we need to start from and return to everyday situational lived experience.[6] Hence for Dewey experience is a "*starting point and terminal point*, as setting problems and as testing proposed solutions" (1925/1929,

redescription of moral experience. He believed that traditional ethics had become bankrupt because it begins with an isolated subject or self that has a purely cognitive apprehension of moral truths. However, this abstraction ignores the social (transactional) and affective (qualitative) character of moral experience. Dewey's ethics thus points to dimensions of moral life that still tend to be overlooked and undervalued in much of modern ethical thought. He rejects their intellectualist, passive, and possessive views of our moral life in favor of a conception of morality as a social, creative, imaginative-emotional, hypothetical, and experimental effort to ameliorate situations and bring new goods into existence.

Dewey characterized the generic elements and phases of our moral life as a process. There are three predominant stages in Dewey's model of moral inquiry. First, the agent finds herself in a morally problematic situation. Second, the agent engages in a process of moral deliberation. Finally, she arrives at a judgment that results in a choice. It is in light of this process that Dewey provided novel and provocative reconstructions of the traditional notions of character, moral deliberation, value judgments, principles, and moral problems. In contrast with the usual rationalistic-sterile account of moral deliberation, for example, Dewey describes moral deliberation as an experimental, emotional, and imaginative process. Moral deliberation results in a moral judgment—a decision to act in one way or another. However, judgments are not static; they continue throughout the entire deliberative process and are transformed as deliberation proceeds. Within this process Dewey distinguishes between the direct judgments of value ("valuing") and the reflective judgments ("valuations").

In Dewey's empirical ethics the self is not a substance but an organization of habits that is relatively stable and enduring. The self changes, therefore, as habits are modified. Because we are selves in the process of continuous formation, what we do at any point in time is not a creation *ex nihilo*. Instead, what we do depends on the history of the self. In deciding what to do we rely on the habitual tendencies, projections, and desires that constituted our character as it was formed, at least in part, from previous experience. Although having a good character does not guarantee that we will always do the right thing, it does increase our chances of doing so. The good habits we bring to a situation are among the means by which we are enabled to discover and do what is right. It is only by doing what we ought to do, however, that we can improve our habits. This is how being good and doing good are mutually dependent within any moral life that is both growing and educative.

In Dewey's ethics the moral self is an integral part of the process of reconstructing morally problematic situations. The self therefore affects and is affected by what goes on while transactions take place in a particular situation. This establishes a very important, organic relation between the quality of what we do and the quality of the character we bring to a situationThe self is composed of habits that some extent determine the quality of what we do and the experiences we have; but what we do in a situation sometimes has a significant effect on the habits and the character that makes up the self. Hence, a growing educative moral life requires both improvements of the habits that will determine the quality of present experience and of the present experiences that will determine the quality of our habits.

To take situations as the starting point of ethical theory does not entail a narrow or scaled-down view of moral experience. On the contrary, Dewey thought that much of the reductionism and oversimplification of the subject matter of contemporary moral theory had been caused by the failure to consider the complexity and richness of our moral experiences as they are had in unique situations. In "Three Independent Factors of Morals"[8] Dewey argued that the history of moral philosophy is characterized by one-sidedness because philosophers have abstracted one factor or feature of situations that are experienced as morally problematic and then made that factor supreme or exclusive. Hence moral theories have been classified according to whether they take good (teleological-consequentionalist), virtue (virtue ethics), or duty (deontological theories) as their central category or source of moral justification. As Dewey points out, however, good, virtue, and duty are all irreducible features found intertwined in moral situations. Dewey's pluralistic ethics is a promising alternative to the narrow, reductionistic views that have dominated the history of moral philosophy.

Dewey did not have a theory about *the* "good life." This notion is in fact antithetical to the pluralistic and contextualist thrust of his moral philosophy. Nevertheless, his ethics is unintelligible apart from some normative commitments and hypotheses about the conditions and instrumentalities for a better moral life that are central to his moral vision. Most traditional ethical theories treat situations as mere means to something else, for example the good life, the maximization of future pleasure, or the acquisition of a virtuous character. For Dewey, however, there is no ultimate and overarching end that defines and makes meaningful all moral activity. Each concrete, morally problematic situation presents a unique moral task with its own immanent end and meaning, even if its resolution happens to produce wonderful instrumentalities for further experiences. The moral tasks of responding to irreducible moral demands, judging, and deciding what I ought to do are always related to the unique context of a situation. What is sought in moral inquiry is therefore the very action among its alternatives that is called for by the situation, that is, the very action that better answers the particular experienced problem in the light of the context as it presents itself. To find this out requires an intelligent, open, sensitive, and full consideration of the situation in its uniqueness.

EMPIRICISM
IN SOCIOPOLITICAL PHILOSOPHY

Dewey's sociopolitical philosophy is based on a methodological criticism of this area of philosophy that simultaneously offers an alternative approach to the subject matter.

Starting with lived experience means that we cannot start with the dualisms that have plagued sociopolitical philosophy, nor with abstract and theoretical starting points. For instance, Dewey was critical of the dualistic starting points (e.g., individual/society, ideal/material, theory/practice) that have led to extreme positions and reductionisms in sociopolitical theory. In his work he tried to uncover how the dualistic starting points found elsewhere in traditional philosophy have made their way into sociopolitical theory. There is the dualism between theory/practice that we already addressed and ideal/actual but also between the individual (as a mind-subject) and institutions-social relationships, and how modern philosophy has oscillated between forms of individualism and collectivism.

For Dewey a theory of justice is as much a dangerous mistake in philosophy as is a theory of truth, and for the same reasons. They are both part of a philosophical quest that usually ends up committing the "philosophical fallacy"[9] and showing the ineptness of philosophy in helping to ameliorate concrete problems. Pragmatism is committed to basing philosophy in lived experience; in social philosophy this means a shift from the theoretical construction of a substantive normative conception of justice to a more contextualist, problem-centered, empirical, and inquiry-oriented approach. A pragmatist's approach must be distinguished from, and is critical of, approaches to justice that

1. start with a theory or theoretical abstraction about what justice is;
2. start with the assumption of a noncontextual ahistorical universal point of view (the "Archimedean standpoint"[10]); and
3. start with or presuppose a political ideology or even a political agenda.

    However, there are other contemporary approaches that reject these same views. In contrast to these views, it has been said that the proper approach should be nonideal, historical, contextual, and empirical. Philosophers such as Amartya Sen and Charles W. Mills have argued that ideal-type approaches are useless and ideological and may even function as blinders to actual injustices or mask existing oppressions. Instead, nonideal theorists insist that political philosophy should be empirical and realistic and should start with the actual circumstances in which we find ourselves. The diversity of views within nonideal theory includes the approaches to philosophy of Marxists, feminists, critical theorists, critical race theorists, and Latin American liberation philosophers. Many of these views seem to be in agreement that a proper approach to injustices (e.g., racism or inequality) should start with either or both:

4. a theory of historical evil: a theoretical-historical account of injustices in the world or of a particular problem of injustice at a particular time in the history of a particular country, nation, or civilization (e.g., the history of white supremacy or of colonization of the Americas); or
5. an empirical diagnosis provided by the social sciences via studies and analysis of the causes of the concrete problems of injustice. For example, philosophy should

begin with a sociological structural account of the systematic disadvantages imposed on people because of their race, class, or gender in our society.

Recently philosophers like Elizabeth Anderson have placed Dewey's pragmatism in the nonideal camp of the contemporary ideal versus nonideal debate (Anderson 2010).[11] She identifies the pragmatists' approach with (5) when she asserts that "philosophy must start from a diagnosis of injustices in our actual world, rather than from a picture of an ideal world" (Anderson 2010, 3). I argue that neither (4) nor (5) captures what pragmatism believes to be the proper philosophical-empirical approach to the problems of injustice. It is easy to see why (4) and (5) could be considered "empirical" starting points compared to the imaginary and theoretical abstractions of ideal theory. Since pragmatism is committed to empiricism, it is very sympathetic to the type of views presented in (4) and (5), and in fact it welcomes both historical accounts and scientific results as part of its resources. However, what distinguishes pragmatism from these other nonideal approaches is a more radical empiricism and contextualism that is not captured by these tenets.

What does beginning and returning to lived experience mean in the case of philosophical inquiry about justice? Instead of universal principles or imaginary contracts, philosophy must start and end with the "concrete problems of justice." On its face, what nonideal theorist would disagree with this statement? However, for pragmatism it means that an empirical philosophical approach to justice, no matter how theoretical, abstract, universal, or general in scope, must take as its ultimate focus and point of reference injustices as events suffered by concrete people at a particular time and in a situation. We need to start by pointing out and describing these problematic experiences. This is a different methodological prescription than starting with a theoretical account of these experiences (i.e., 4) or with a theoretical diagnosis of its causes (i.e., 5). These seem to be theoretical starting points.

Radical Contextualism and Pluralism

The sort of empiricism advocated by pragmatism entails a contextualism and pluralism that is radical. The contextualism is radical in the sense that for pragmatists the alternative to the universal aspirations of modern philosophy is not starting philosophical inquiry in the context of history, culture, practice, language, a socioeconomic system, or a plurality of socially constructed standpoints; these are usually nothing but theoretical abstractions or aspects we can discriminate in a present situation. A pragmatist perspective treats philosophical discourse as arising out of the lived experiences of culturally and historically situated people. However, these lived experiences are situations.[12] Like other nonideal theorists pramatists emphasize practice and history over some abstract theoretical starting point, but for pragmatists, "everyday praxis" is something that occurs in the context of a present situation and not in the context of history (as a historical totality) in which situations are events.

For pragmatism the problematic situations that occasion theories about injustice are problems of injustice, but this is too general a designation. Ultimately, it must mean an injustice suffered by someone in some relationship somewhere in a situation (primary situations of injustice). Of course, the situation of the theoretician or philosopher inquiring about an injustice may be somewhat removed from these primary situations and instead be more directly troubled by the incongruity between these injustice situations and existing social policies that are supposed to prevent such injustices from happening. As Dewey describes this situation, "when our laws, customs, and institutions no longer serve the purpose for which they were originally evolved, we are forced to ask, 'What's the trouble?' or 'Why aren't they working?'" (Dewey 1973, 47). This is a problematic situation, but it is related to the primary situations of injustice in the same way that a theoretician in medical research or a doctor is related to people suffering from an illness. If a medication that is supposed to work does not, then this provokes inquiry about why it does not work, but research must begin with and return to the situations of ill patients.

We could offer a general description of the primary situations of injustice, but Dewey refuses to provide some theoretical or universal criterion of them. Instead, he describes how these problems usually emerge in the historical context of a relationship between individuals or groups. Where inequities between groups or individuals are accepted as normal, the status quo is accepted by all and there is no problem of injustice that provokes communal inquiry or any action. However, if conditions change and lead to a disruption in smooth everyday relationships, there is an awareness that something is not right about the present treatment or recognition of some group or individual in particular contexts.

These vague generalities may be useful in designating the subject matter under investigation, but pragmatism stresses the importance of not underestimating the particularism of the problems that provoke inquiry. Social philosophy has witnessed how empirical approaches must be sensitive to the pluralism and particularism of our social experience; this makes it less prone to start with generalizations about entire groups and the masquerade of universality that has been used to conceal differences and injustices. For example, the history of feminism has witnessed how even its early criticism of the universalistic starting point in philosophy assumed the universality of some particular group experience (white women) at the expense of differences among women. Not acknowledging or concealing differences can have detrimental consequences for those groups ignored. Pragmatism is sensitive to this. In fact, the pluralism (hence recognition of difference) that it starts with is more radical than the idea of injustices particular to certain historical groups or people, civilizations, or cultures. As I have mentioned and continue to stress, for pragmatism there are as many problems of injustice as there are problematic situations suffered in a particular way. Dewey cannot be more clear on how strong his particularistic commitment is when he writes: "We need to develop the ability (and the disposition) to look for particular kinds of solutions by particular methods for particular problems which arise on particular occasions. In other words, we must deal with concrete problems by concrete methods when these problems present themselves in our experience" (Dewey 1973, 53).

Pragmatism and Systematic-Structural Injustices

The radical contextualism and pluralism of pragmatism is, however, compatible with the acknowledgment of the persistence of the same evil structures across situations. There are both unique and stable elements in situations. Dewey recognized the importance of habits, customs, and institutions in the latter category and in social life. These are stable and systematic structures across situations that regulate conduct; they can be both a means to freedom as well an obstacle to it. While they provide much-needed stability in a precarious world, we must be alert to their power to perpetuate evil. Their causal efficacy is in being taken for granted. If never subjected to criticism and inquiry, they will continue to cause injustice in situations. We therefore need an intelligent assessment of these stable structures. However, criticism and eradication of systematic or stable evil is not an end in itself but a means to ameliorate particular and present injustices.

In the matter of injustice, pragmatism navigates in between or avoids two extreme views. One is the view that treats each case of injustice as nothing more than an instance of a systematic and across-situations cause (e.g., white supremacy). This can lead to blindness to the uniqueness and complexity of the particular case and oversimplification as to the remedy. On the other hand, the pragmatists' view should not be confused with an atomistic form of particularism about injustices that may be even more blind and counterproductive. I have in mind those that refuse to inquire into the connections and continuities between situations of injustice because they are conceived as separate and self-contained contexts. Perhaps an example would help.

The atomistic particularist would consider a particular problematic case of seeming excessive force by the police toward a black person in the United States as an isolated incident. While this may seem to have the virtue of addressing the uniqueness of the details of a situation, the separation that is made from any precedent (similar situations) and society at large is as much a questionable abstraction as it is simply lumping all cases under one name or the effects of one historical cause (e.g., white supremacy). The atomistic particularist overlooks the idea that continuity, precedent, and cumulation (funded experience) are aspects of present situations. The alternative to the doctor who considers an ill patient as nothing more than an instance of a great historical and systematic disease that affects an entire population is not the doctor who pays attention to the individual-unique patient (illness) while ignoring the obvious connections with similar patients. One consequence of atomistic particularism is that no action is taken to ameliorate habits and institutional structures that are likely to recur in future similar situations of injustice. For instance, the unjust treatment of blacks by police in the United States will likely continue until it is recognized that there is a pattern of habits, via individuals or institutions, that needs to be questioned and stopped.

The particularism and contextualism of pragmatism is not incompatible with adopting, for the purposes of inquiry, a sociological and historical standpoint where we can make references to injustices shared by groups, nor is it incompatible with inquiry about injustices that are universal and general in scope. For example, there is a legitimate functional role in inquiry to speak of the problem of "white supremacy" at a global level. However, the pragmatists' approach is sensitive to historical particularity without succumbing to the grand causal narratives of some contemporary nonideal theories. For instance, Charles W. Mills claims that the starting point and alternative to the abstractions of ideal theory that masked injustices is to diagnose and rectify a history of an illness—the legacy of white supremacy in our actual society. The critical task of revealing this illness is achieved by adopting a historical perspective in which the injustices of today are part of a larger historical narrative about the development of modern societies that goes back to how Europeans have progressively dehumanized or subordinated others. Similary, radical feminists as well as third-world scholars, in reaction to the hegemonic Eurocentric paradigms that disguise injustices under the assumption of a universal or objective point of view, have stressed how our knowledge is always situated. This may seem congenial with pragmatism except the locus of the knower and of injustices is often described as power structures located in "global hierarchies" and a "world system," and not situations.[13]

Pragmatism only questions that we live in History or a "World-system" (as a totality or abstract context) but not that we are in history (lower case): in a present situation continuous with others where the past weighs heavily in our memories, bodies, habits, structures, and communities. It also does not deny the importance of power structures and seeing the connections between injustices through time, but there is a difference between (a) inquiring into present situations of injustice in order to detect, diagnose, and cure an injustice (a social pathology) across history and (b) inquiring into the history of a systematic injustice in order to facilitate inquiry into the present unique, context-bound injustice. To capture the legacy of the past on present injustices we must study history but also seek present evidence of the weight of the past on the present injustice.

If injustice is an illness, then the pragmatists' approach takes as its main focus diagnosing and treating the particular present illness, that is, the particular situation-bound injustice and not a global "social pathology" or some single transhistorical source of injustice. The diagnosis of a particular injustice is not always dependent on adopting a broader critical standpoint of society in its entirety, but even when it is we must be careful to not forget that such standpoints are useful only for understanding the present evil. The concepts and categories "white supremacy" and "colonialism" can be great tools that can be of planetary significance. One could even argue that they pick out much larger areas of people's lives and injustices than the categories of class and gender, but in spite of their reach and explanatory theoretical value they are nothing more than tools to make reference to and ameliorate particular injustices in a situation.

No doubt many but not all problems of injustice are a consequence of being a member of a group in history, but even in these cases we cannot a priori assume that injustices are homogeneously equal for all members of that group. Why is this important? The possible pluralism and therefore complexity of a problem of injustice does not always stop at the level of being a member of a historical group or even a member of many groups, as insisted on by intersectional analysis. There may be circumstances unique to particular countries, towns, neighborhoods, institutions, and ultimately situations that we must be open to in a context-sensitive inquiry. If an empirical inquiry is committed to capturing and ameliorating all of the harms in situations of injustice in their raw pretheoretical complexity, then this requires that we try to begin with and return to the concrete, particular, and unique experiences of injustice.

Pragmatism therefore agrees with Sally Haslanger's concern about Charles Mills's view. She writes: "The goal is not just a theory that is historical (v. ahistorical), but is sensitive to historical particularity, i.e., that resists grand causal narratives purporting to give an account of how domination has come about and is perpetuated everywhere and at all times" (1). For "the forces that cause and sustain domination vary tremendously context by context, and there isn't necessarily a single causal explanation; a theoretical framework that is useful as a basis for political intervention must be highly sensitive to the details of the particular social context" (Haslanger 2000).[14]

Although each situation is unique, there are commonalities among the cases that permit inquiry about common causes. We can "formulate tentative general principles from investigation of similar individual cases, and then ... check the generalizations by applying them to still further cases" (Dewey 1973, 53). However, Dewey insists that the focus should be on the individual case and was critical of how so many sociopolitical theories are prone to starting and remaining at the level of "sweeping generalizations." He states that they "fail to focus on the concrete problems which arise in experience, allowing such problems to be buried under their sweeping generalizations" (Dewey 1973, 53).

The lesson pragmatism provides for nonideal theory today is that it must be careful to not reify any injustice as some single historical force for which particular injustice problems are its manifestation or evidence for its existence. Pragmatism welcomes the wisdom and resources of nonideal theories that are historically grounded on actual injustices, but it issues a warning about how they should be understood and implemented. It is, for example, sympathetic to the critical resources found in critical race theory, but with an important qualification. It understands Derrick Bell's valuable criticism as context specific to patterns in the practice of American law. Through his inquiry into particular cases and civil rights policies at a particular time and place, Bell learned and proposed certain general principles such as the one of "interest convergence," that is, "whites will promote racial advantages for blacks only when they also promote white self-interest" (Bell 1980, 523). However, for pragmatism these principles are nothing more than historically grounded tools to use in present problematic situations that call for our analysis, such as deliberation in establishing public policies or making sense of some concrete injustice. The principles are falsifiable and open to revision as we face situation-specific injustices. In testing their adequacy, we need to consider their function in making us see aspects of injustices we would not otherwise appreciate.

Pragmatism definitely presents a very demanding methodological prescription to nonideal theory. Since most inquiry is, by nature, general or at least relies on theoretical categories that are general and abstract, its imperative to be sensitive to context seems to be asking the impossible. However, the view is not all or nothing. From the more abstract and general to the more particular and concrete is a matter of degree, as is our sensitivity to context.

CONCLUSION

I have explored how Dewey's commitment to an empirical philosophical method is key to understanding his ethics and sociopolitical philosophy and how it is the basis of his critiques of tradition and reconstructing a radical contextualist and pluralistic approach in both ethics and political philosophy. Dewey's approach to moral and sociopolitical problems continues to be the source of important lessons for those theorists interested in a shift from traditional approaches centered on ideal theories and abstractions toward a more contextualist, problem-centered, empirical, and inquiry-oriented approach.

Dewey proposed a way to avoid some of the most common dead-end problems in ethics and sociopolitical philosophy while at the same time presenting an alternative view on how to proceed. Even though I considered separately each of these areas of philosophy, their common starting point of lived experience entails a continuity between the moral and the sociopolitical. If moral experience is social, there is no separation between the quality of our most direct and personal relationships/communications and political forces (institutions and groups). Dewey's view of democracy cannot be understood apart from ethics and his views on lived experience.

In both his ethics and his sociopolitical philosophy, there is an important function for ideals. For Dewey ideals are imaginative constructions and projections that have arisen from trying to safeguard or bring to fruition what is good in a precarious world. This view requires that any presentation of an ideal needs to make reference to the problems from which it emerges. Dewey can only make sense of theories of justice or about ideals of the good society as things that have historically emerged from some concrete problems of injustice or some social conflict. This is how the ideal of democracy emerged, and Dewey reconstructs his ideal of democracy from this same experiential-historical starting point and not from some a priori source or by adopting some theoretical "Archimedean standpoint" or "veil of ignorance." Democracy is an ideal way of life that fruitfully embraces these traits of every lived experience: contingency, uncertainty, risk, ambiguity, contextualism, openness, pluralism, process, and intersubjectivity. Contrary to Richard Rorty's resistance to the idea that we need metaphysics to support our democratic ideals and hopes, Dewey and recent scholarship have argued that the value of a pragmatist approach to sociopolitical philosophy has everything to do with its radical-empiricist metaphysics.[15]

NOTES

1. See Ralph W. Sleeper, "Dewey's Metaphysical Perspective: A Note on White, Geiger, and the Problem of Obligation," *The Journal of Philosophy* 57 (1960): 100–115; James Gouinlock, "Dewey's Theory of Moral Deliberation," *Ethics* 88 (1978): 218–228; Robert L. Holmes, "The Development of John Dewey's Ethical Thought," *Monist* 48 (1964): 392–406.

2. I suspect that many of the scientistic interpretations of Dewey on ethics originate from confusing Dewey's suggestions in his writings that we must apply the methods of science to the problems of morality with applying the methods of science to ethical theory. These are entirely different things, and Dewey did not hold the second.

3. See, for example, Hugh LaFollete's "Pragmatist Ethics" entry in *Blackwell Guide to Ethical Theory* (Oxford: Blackwell, 1999), 400–419; and Elizabeth Anderson's "Dewey's Moral Philosophy" entry in *Stanford Encyclopedia of Philosophy* (spring 2005 edition), Edward N. Zalta (ed.), http://plato.stanford.edu/entries/dewey-moral, 2005.

4. Recent scholarship on Dewey has insisted that to appreciate that this was Dewey's view we must first understand what Dewey meant by "science" or the "scientific method." Jennifer Welchman, for example, claims that if one carefully studies Dewey's conception of the nature of science one finds that he thought that "every scientist acts in accordance with procedural rules" (Welchman 1995, 143) that can be experimentally confirmed. This indicates at least one respect in which for Dewey ethics can be like science. "Commitment to such rules, Dewey holds, is the essence of science. It is in this respect that he believes ethical theory ought to become scientific" (Welchman 1995, 143). If ethics is to advance it should "construct procedures for inquiries analogous to those used in the physical sciences." For James Campbell it was more the "scientific attitude" and the communal ("public") aspect of science that attracted Dewey to the notion of "ethics as a moral science" (Campbell 1995, 110).

5. From the point of view of the actual historical development of Dewey's philosophy there may be support for understanding his ethics through his views on science. This is what Jennifer Welchman has accomplished in *Dewey's Ethical Thought*. However, even if Dewey came to adopt an empirical view of ethics after or because he reexamined his own views about the nature of science, this does not mean that his views on science are the key to his ethics. My intention here is not to discredit but to supplement Welchman's work. We are in fact concerned about different things. She is concerned with Dewey's efforts to bring science and ethics closer together ("reconcile"), but this can be distinguished from his effort to show how to proceed in an empirical philosophical inquiry about morality. In this chapter I am concerned with the latter and not with the former.

6. For Dewey experience is a "*starting point* and *terminal point*, as setting problems and as testing proposed solutions" (1925/1929, LW 1:14, my emphasis).

7. For an explanation of all the different formulations of this fallacy see Gregory Pappas, *John Dewey's Ethics: Democracy as Experience* (Bloomington: Indiana University Press, 2008), 17–42.

8. Dewey's article "Three Independent Factors in Morals" (1930, LW 5:279–288) is a centerpiece of his moral thought. The tripartite description of our moral experience of this chapter explains why Dewey discussed good, duty, and virtue in separate chapters of his 1932 *Ethics*. Without this essay one misses important support for the situational and pluralistic thrust of his moral philosophy that is not evident in his discussions about value in

general. Dewey's faith in the instrumentalities of experience was tempered by the honest realization that the most intense moments of our moral life are tragic, in the sense that there is a irreducible and sometimes irresolvable conflict between positive moral demands or values. This is a different view and has different consequences than the general view of our moral life as merely a struggle between good and evil. Cf. Fesmire, this volume.

9. Dewey argues that the root of this fallacy is how philosophers neglect context. For Dewey's explanations of all the different formulations of this fallacy, see Gregory Fernando Pappas, *John Dewey's Ethics: Democracy as Experience* (Bloomington: Indiana University Press, 2008), pp. 17–42.

10. See http://en.wikipedia.org/wiki/Archimedean_point.

11. On the history of this debate, see Zofia Stemplowska and Adam Swift, "Ideal and Nonideal Theory," in *The Oxford Handbook of Political Philosophy*, ed. David Estlund (Oxford: Oxford University Press, 2012), pp. 379–392. I am hesitant to even use the parlance of ideal/nonideal because this seems to assume mutually exclusive categories when for the pragmatists there is no strict separation. It can be a functional distinction about theories that emphasize more or less abstractions/concrete conditions; ideals/realism (actual conditions), normative/empirical, conceptual/experimental, values/fact, theory/ practice. However, there is no doubt that pragmatism is more critical of the vices of ideal theoretical constructions that have no practical relevance and especially that do not start in the middle of things in problematic situations.

12. We must not neglect or forget the situational context of our lives and of our philosophical investigations. The ultimate context in which we philosophize is not history or culture but the unique situation in which we are, right here and now. It is in a situation that we find history, culture, nature, sticks and stones. While Dewey had a well-formulated naturalistic account of situations and the qualitative in terms of an evolutionary-biological theoretical framework, he never confused a theory of situations with the experience of situations. As Browning says: "The notion of a situation is introduced by Dewey in the *Logic* without appeal to any theory, logical or otherwise, which is already in place. It is a primitive notion" (Douglas Browning, "Designation, Characterization, and Theory in Dewey's Logic," in *Dewey's Logical Theory: New Studies and Interpretations*, eds. F. Thomas Burke, D. Micah Hester, and Robert B. Talisse (Nashville, TN: Vanderbilt UP, 2002), 174. In fact, Dewey writes: "I begin the discussion by introducing and explaining the denotative force of the word situation ... [W]hat is designated by the word 'situation' is not a single object or event or set of objects and events. For we never experience nor form judgments about objects and events in isolation, but only in connection with a contextual whole" (1938, LW 12:72). It is an experienced unifying quality that demarcates a particular situation, and each situation is unique. We can describe and have a theory about situations, but these forms of discourse point ("denotative") to something that is experienced. This sounded (and still sounds) mysterious or contradictory to philosophers who assume the ubiquity of knowledge or language (discourse) in life. Dewey's frustration with Russell on this issue is obvious in these passages: "Mr. Russell has not been able to follow the distinction I make between the immediately had material of non-cognitively experienced situations and the material of cognition--a distinction without which my view cannot be understood" (1939, LW 14:33). "Any one who refuses to go outside the universe of discourse—as Mr. Russell apparently does—has of course shut himself off

from understanding what a 'situation,' as directly experienced subject-matter, is" (31). "Mr. Russell is so wedded to the idea that there is no experienced material outside the field of discourse that any intimation that there is such material relegates it, ipso facto, to the status of the 'unknowable' " (33).

13. For an excellent article on this philosophical tradition, see "The Epistemic Decolonial Turn" by Ramon Grosfoguel in *Cultural Studies* 21 (2007): 211–223.

14. Haslanger also argues that large historical narratives about the domination of one group over another also need to be "vigilant in avoiding over-generalizations about the attitudes, experiences, or social position of members of the groups" as well as sensitive to the "overlapping nature of social groups" and the fact that "the meaning of group memberships can vary significantly with context." Moreover, we must be careful with our theoretical explanations of the causes of group domination since "it is the result of the complex interplay of multiple determinants [whose significance varies depending on context]." Haslanger issues these warnings as "desiderata" that arise out of "at least one strand of feminist/anti-racist theorizing," but they are also what follow from the Pragmatist's methodological commitments.

15. See Gregory Pappas, *John Dewey's Ethics: Democracy as Experience* (Bloomington: Indiana University Press, 2008); T. Throntveit, *William James's Ethical Republic: A Moral and Political Study* (New York: Palgrave Macmillan US, 2014); Nelson W. Keith, *Outline of a New Liberalism: Pragmatism and the Stigmatized Other* (Lanham, MD: Lexington Books, 2015); Alexander Livingston, *Damn Great Empires!: William James and the Politics of Pragmatism* (New York: Oxford University Press, 2016).

WORKS CITED

Citations of John Dewey's works are to the thirty-seven-volume critical edition published by Southern Illinois University Press under the editorship of Jo Ann Boydston. In-text citations give the original publication date and series abbreviation, followed by volume number and page number. For example: (1934, LW 10:12) is page 12 of *Art as Experience*, which is published as volume 10 of *The Later Works*.

Series abbreviations for *The Collected Works*:

EW *The Early Works* (1882–98)

MW *The Middle Works* (1899–1924)

LW *The Later Works* (1925–53)

Anderson, Elizabeth. 2010. *The Imperative of Integration*. Princeton, NJ: Princeton University Press.

Bell, Derrick A. Jr. 1980. "Brown v. Board of Education and The Interest Convergence Dilemma." *Harvard Law Review*, vol. 93, no. 3, 518–534.

Browning, Douglas. 2002. "Designation, Characterization, and Theory in Dewey's Logic." In *Dewey's Logical Theory: New Studies and Interpretations*. Edited by F. Thomas Burke, D. Micah Hester, and Robert B. Talisse, 160–179. Nashville, TN: Vanderbilt University Press.

Campbell, James. 1995. *Understanding John Dewey: Nature and Cooperative Intelligence*.Chica go: Open Court.

Dewey, John. 1925/1929. *Experience and Nature*. LW 1.

Dewey, John. 1930. "Three Independent Factors in Morals." LW 5:279–288.

Dewey, John, and James H. Tufts. 1932. *Ethics*. 2nd ed. LW 7.

Dewey, John. 1939. "Experience, Knowledge and Value: A Rejoinder." LW 14:3–90.

Dewey, John. 1973. *Lectures in China, 1919–1920*. Trans. and ed. Robert W. Clopton and Tsuin-Chen Ou. Honolulu: University Press of Hawaii.

Haslanger, Sally. 2000. "Comments on Charles Mills' 'Race and the Social Contract Tradition.'" Paper presented at the Central American Philosophical Association, April 22, 2000. http://www.mit.edu/shaslang/papers/MillsAPA2.html.

Welchman, Jennifer. 1995. *Dewey's Ethical Thought*. Ithaca, NY: Cornell University Press.

V

SOCIAL AND POLITICAL PHILOSOPHY, RACE, AND FEMINIST PHILOSOPHY

CHAPTER 12

....

DEWEY AND DU BOIS ON RACE AND COLONIALISM

....

SHANNON SULLIVAN

> "We need to recover something of the militant faith of our forefathers that
> America is a great idea, and add to it an ardent faith in our capacity to lead
> the world."
>
> —John Dewey, "America in the World" (1918b)

> "It is curious to see America, the United States, looking on herself first, as
> a sort of natural peacemaker, then as a moral protagonist in this terrible
> time. No nation is less fitted for this role."
>
> —W. E. B. Du Bois, "The Souls of White Folk" (1920b/1999b)

JOHN Dewey rarely discussed race in his scholarly publications and lectures. His 1922
essay on "Racial Prejudice and Friction" (Dewey 1922b, MW 13:242–254) and his
1932 "Address to the National Association for the Advancement of Colored People"
(Dewey 1932, LW 6:224–230) are two exceptions to the general rule of Dewey's professional silence on matters of race. Despite this fact, Dewey's pragmatist philosophy has
been a significant resource for contemporary scholars working critically on race and
racial justice. In response to Cornel West's (1993) charge that Dewey's philosophy lacks
an adequate sense of the tragic, for example, Eddie Glaude Jr. (2007) has argued that
Dewey's notion of contingency contains tragedy within it and is ripe for reconstruction in terms of race and racism. Glaude undertakes that Deweyan project, developing a
pragmatic approach to the evils of racism and white supremacy and to the tragic choices
the United States has made with regard to race. Shading Dewey's pragmatism with the
darker side of life—the blues—Glaude's "post-soul politics" turns away from abstract
or unified understandings of black identity, black history, and black agency and toward

a pragmatic African American politics that focuses on the actual practices and lived problems of black people.

Habit is another important Deweyan concept that has been developed by critical philosophers of race, especially for analyzing habits of whiteness.[1] Glaude (2016), Terrance MacMullan (2009), and Shannon Sullivan (2006) understand race in terms of racial habit: a predisposition to respond to and engage with the world in a particular way—and in the case of whiteness, in a way that tends to treat people of color as inferior to white people. Calling for a revolution of values to transform racial habits (Glaude 2016), new racial habits of ethnic remembrance and interracial compassion (MacMullan 2009), and strategies to thwart white people's habits of ontological expansiveness (Sullivan 2006), pragmatist scholars have demonstrated how Dewey's philosophy can be used to tackle problems of race.[2]

Dewey's pragmatism also can be problematic for a critical philosophy of race, however. In addition to West's concern that Dewey's alleged neglect of the tragic makes his pragmatism inadequate for grappling with racism, when Dewey does discuss explicitly discuss race, he tends to collapse it into either class concerns or equate it with a form of xenophobia that increased familiarity between people will easily dispel (Sullivan 2004).[3] Dewey's earlier work on education, including his laboratory schools for children, operates with a linear historicism and genetic psychology that privileges white people by explaining child development as the development from savagery to civilization (Fallace 2010). In the implicit logic of Dewey's pre-1916 educational philosophy, white children might be *like* so-called savages, but they are able to develop into civilized adults, unlike non-white people who are stuck in childlike savagery. Dewey's alignment of child development with the development of the (white) race resulted in both the treatment of African Americans and Native Americans as childlike races who were left behind in humanity's evolution toward Western civilization and, according to Fallace (2010, 101–112) the need to forcibly assimilate allegedly socially deficient immigrants such as the Polish, who were seen as resistant to but salvageable by America's educational system.[4]

Dewey's pragmatism thus is both promising and full of potential perils for contemporary philosophers of race. In this remainder of this essay, I take a fresh look at the value of Dewey's philosophy for a critical philosophy of race by examining his analyses of World War I (1914–1918), published primarily in 1918. After completing *Democracy and Education* in 1916, Dewey became a truly public philosopher beginning with his essays and articles analyzing the war. This moment in Dewey's career preceded a gradual, important shift to the cultural pluralism that characterizes his later work. That shift had not yet taken place in the late 1910s to the early 1920s, however, which is why I focus on this period of Dewey's work.

By examining Dewey's World War I essays, I seek to encourage future research on Dewey's pragmatism that corrects systemic injustice supported by unexamined conceptual filters. My argument is that Dewey's assessment of the war is saturated with white colonial privilege but that this privilege can be difficult to detect because it generally is hidden and unspoken in Dewey's work (and perhaps unrealized by Dewey himself). I do not make any claims about Dewey's conscious intentions when writing about the war. My interest here lies instead in what lessons we can learn by means of Dewey's philosophy about nonconscious forms of white domination. Dewey's essays on World War I are shaped by what Charles Mills (1998) has called conceptual whiteness: they are written from and reflect an unacknowledged white perspective that tends to ignore, overlook, and make invisible matters of race and racism, including many of the concerns, interests, and worldviews of people of color. To detect the conceptual whiteness of Dewey's work and the white privilege it supports, I read Dewey in conversation with W. E. B. Du Bois on the war. Dewey (1859–1952) and Du Bois (1868–1963) were contemporaries, both approximately at the midpoint of their long and productive careers at the time of World War I. Their radically different analyses of (a) the war's meaning, (b) the importance of the (white) working class for global stability, and (c) the solution for preventing future world wars help reveal Dewey's complicity with white colonialist domination. Juxtaposing Dewey and Du Bois' analyses hopefully also will help contemporary pragmatists avoid similar complicities in our own day.

THE MEANING OF WORLD WAR I

For Dewey, the meaning of World War I could be summarized as global interdependence. Technological and industrial changes especially in the late nineteenth century had radically shrunk the distance between nations that had once been far apart from each other. New developments in transportation and communication brought people closer together, but becoming closer also meant increased conflict and tension. Clashes between peoples thus are not necessarily surprising or alarming for Dewey. What they signal is a new world order trying to come into existence, with all the bumps and difficulties that birthing entails. Even in their most extreme form of global war, what can be seen is the future: "That nations from every continent on the globe are engaged in the war is the outer sign of the new world struggling to be delivered" (Dewey 1918b, MW 11:70).

The new world of the future is not necessarily an improvement upon the old, according to Dewey. It could be characterized by the same strife, hostilities, jealousies, and tensions that led to the Great War. This is likely, as Dewey (1918b, MW 11:70–71) claims, if the new world is guided by "the European idea," which has not managed to blend together different peoples and cultures so that they can peacefully and fruitfully coexist. This is what the United States uniquely was accomplishing. In 1918, as the war was nearing an end, Dewey celebrated what he saw as the exceptional position of the United States. The little former colony has grown up into "a continental state" and now has "an idea to contribute, an idea to be taken into account in the world reconstruction after the war," Dewey believed (1918b, MW 11:70, 71). The idea is federation, where the many are united but their unity does not eliminate the many. In particular, Dewey (1918b, MW 11:71) claims, the United States was successfully enacting this idea with respect to cultural differences by separating nationality from citizenship. Social, cultural, and linguistic differences were being completely divorced from political matters of state, making the United States "truly interracial and international in our own internal constitution" in ways that European nations are not (1918b, MW 11:71).

Dewey's description of American exceptionalism on this point is worth quoting at some length:

> One of the greatest problems which is troubling the Old World is that of the rights of nationalities which are included within larger political units—the Poles, the Irish, the Bohemians, the Jugo-Slavs, the Jews. Here too [as with federalism] the American contribution is radical. We have solved the problem by a complete separation of nationality from citizenship. Not only have we separated the church from the state, but we have separated language, cultural traditions, all that is called race, from the state—that is from problems of political organization and power. To us language, literature, creed, group ways, national culture, are social rather than political, human rather than national, interests. Let this idea fly abroad; it bears healing in its wings.
>
> (1918b, MW 11:71)

Dewey's confidence that the United States was successfully developing fair and inclusive political governance by relegating racial differences to the cultural sphere is remarkable. What is even more striking, however, is the complete omission of African Americans, Mexican Americans, and Indigenous people in Dewey's description of America's "interracial" mix. While many of the European peoples named by Dewey admittedly did not (yet) count as fully white in the United States in 1918, Dewey's interracial America tends to include European immigrants only. It excludes people native to the United States—not just Indigenous people but also the Mexicans who suddenly became Americans without moving an inch when Mexico ceded huge portions of its nation to the United States in 1848 at the end of the Mexican-American War. It also glaringly omits people who were forcibly brought to the United States from Africa as slaves. The unintended effect of Dewey's account of American exceptionalism is to suggest that immigrants to the United States from Europe can count as part of a successful interracial and international nation, but other peoples and nations cannot. What would it mean for *this* idea to fly across the Atlantic, we might ask. Would it also bear healing on its wings?

W. E. B. Du Bois resoundingly answered those questions in 1920 with a scathing analysis of "the souls of white folk" involved in World War I. While Du Bois's essay is not directed explicitly at Dewey, it does target anyone who thinks that the United States was in a position to make the world safe for democracy (as claimed then-President Woodrow Wilson, whose position on the war Dewey strongly supported). As Du Bois suggests in the previous epigraph, to send "the American idea" abroad to help Europe and the globe reconstruct itself after the war would be a disaster. This is because the American idea is not really any different than that of Europe. "America, Land of Democracy," as Du Bois (1920b/1999b, 29) argues, "stands today shoulder to shoulder with Europe in Europe's worst sin against civilization." That sin is the literal and metaphorical theft, enslavement, murder, and rape of people of color. The difference between the United States and

Europe is merely the location of these atrocities. Europe has colonies abroad in which it has pursued oppression and exploitation, while the United States primarily has done so at home. But their use and abuse of the darker world, as Du Bois calls it, for white benefit is equally problematic.

For Du Bois, World War I laid bare what people of color across the world had long known but that white people often liked to ignore or deny: that "whiteness is the ownership of the earth forever and ever, Amen!" (Du Bois 1920b/1999b, 18) World War I broke out because of fighting among white European nations about who would own which part of the earth and which nation would own the greatest share. Du Bois's claim is supported by prewar historical events such as the Partition of Africa (Keltie 1893), known more colorfully today as the Scramble for Africa (Pakenham 1991). In November 1884, Germany hosted an international conference in Berlin on Africa, which was attended by Russia and West European countries, namely France and Great Britain. German Chancellor Bismarck opened the conference by stating its aim: "to promote the civilization of the African natives by opening the interior of the [African] continent to commerce" (1991, 240). The years leading up to the conference included European excursions along the coasts of Africa, but in the 1870s most of Africa, including its vast interior, was "unexplored." By the end of the 19th century, in contrast, "Africa [had been] sliced up like a cake . . . . The Scramble gave Europe virtually the whole continent: including thirty new colonies and protectorates, 10 million square miles of new territory and 110 million dazed new subjects, acquired by one methods or another" (1991, 240). The Berlin conference marked the beginning of the full-scale scramble, forging agreement between rival European nations on the ground rules for dividing Africa. In this way, European powerhouses took steps to avoid war between themselves as they grabbed for the real and imagined riches of Africa, developed new markets in which to sell their own goods, protected maritime routes, and provided a place for emigrant sons (and perhaps daughters) to remain citizens of the nation when they stretched their wings and left the so-called motherland.

From one particular perspective, the Berlin conference could be considered successful: a major war did not break out between Europe nations for thirty full years after the scramble began. But break out it eventually did. "The passions generated by the Scramble had helped to poison the political climate in Europe" (Pakenham 1991, xxi), and that climate contributed to the tense environment leading up to World War I. There is another important sense in which the conference was "successful": the conference helped ensure European colonial conquest and imperial domination of much of Africa. During this period in history, managing tensions between European nations so as to avoid war cannot be separated from the tangle of race and colonialism as white European nations built empires in black Africa. When the 1914 assassination of Austrian Archduke Ferdinand triggered international alliances that escalated into a near-global war, what was at issue was not merely the national lines to be drawn between Austro-Hungary, Serbia, and Yugoslavia, for example, but also the larger question of which European nations would retain and/or strengthen their positions as imperial powerhouses.

Du Bois is on solid ground when he claims that competition for the best pieces of land and access to the native labor to exploit it, especially in Africa, was at the heart of the war and also when he links the issue of ownership of the world to whiteness. "Other causes have been glibly given and other contributing causes there doubtless were," Du Bois (1920b/1999b, 25) allows, "but they were subsidiary and subordinate to this vast quest of the dark world's wealth and toil." Du Bois could agree with Dewey that increased contact and thus friction between European nations played a role in starting the war, but he likely would find Dewey's focus on global interdependence misleadingly abstract and/or incomplete. What exactly were the concrete issues and problems at the heart of European friction, as Du Bois might pragmatically ask? The conceptual whiteness of Dewey's reflections on the war's meaning is evident in Dewey's evasion of this question, which demands the acknowledgement of racism and colonial oppression to answer it. Du Bois's response, in contrast, is clear and unequivocal: "Let me say this again and emphasize it and leave no room for mistaken meaning: The World War was primarily the jealous and avaricious struggle for the largest share in exploiting darker races" (Du Bois 1920b/1999b, 28).

THE IMPORTANCE OF THE (WHITE) WORKING CLASS FOR GLOBAL STABILITY

As Dewey considers both the possibilities and the need for social reorganization after the war's end, he focuses on the working class in Europe and the United States. "We need to ask ourselves what are the chief weaknesses in the existing order," Dewey (1918c, MW 11:74) urges, "which have been brought to light by the excessive stress and strain of war." The answer to this question, according to Dewey, is three-part: (a) unemployment and/or insecure employment for many in the working class, which is (b) accompanied by an unacceptably low, even "inhuman" standard of living and (c) caused by inefficiencies in the production and distribution of goods, which are still based on the old, noninterdependent models of social order (1918c, MW 11:75–78). These weaknesses were not created by the war, Dewey explains, but the war has helped bring them to light and made them a matter of public interest. In that way, the war has been "a tremendous education" (1918c, MW 11:74). Workers in all trades and occupations need more autonomy and more ability to control their industry, including the ability to secure steady employment and raise their standard of living (1918c, MW 11:84–85).

While the war did not begin because of dissatisfaction in the wage-earning classes, as Dewey acknowledges, the forces that the war has unleashed were having unexpected consequences. Namely, those forces were leading to the socialization of industry, and "is it not conceivable that some future historian may find this consequence outweighing any for which the war was originally fought?" (Dewey 1918f, MW 11:98) This is something worth fighting for, Dewey reassures his American readers in 1918. When intelligently organized via a federated body of nations, the socialization of industry on a global scale is what will produce "a world safe *for* democracy *and* a world *in* which democracy is safely anchored" (1918f, MW 11:105, emphasis in original). Ensuring democracy is "the ultimate sanction, for which [the United States is] fighting" in the war (1918f, MW 11:106). Since democracy is inextricably tied with wage-earning workers' economic stability, physical health, and satisfactory standard of living, to fight for democracy is to fight for social organization that respects working-class rights.

Du Bois also acknowledges the relevance of the working class to the war, but he tells a very different story about its role. Du Bois recognizes that working classes across the United States and Europe suffer from poor living conditions and exploitation by the wealthy owner class. "It is plain to modern white civilization that the subjection of the white working classes cannot much longer be maintained," Du Bois (1920b/1999b, 24–25) explains, due to their growing "education, political power, and increased knowledge of the technique and meaning of the industrial process." Dewey is right that something has got to give, as Du Bois might say, and it could very well be the case that the war has revealed and accelerated this process. But this is only half the story, Du Bois would add. The other and more important half is literally the other half of the world, which is not included in any of the working, middle, or wealthy classes. These are the darker people across the world, who have been barred from union membership and other protections and who are available "for exploitation on an immense scale for inordinate profit . . . . Here are no labor unions or votes or questioning onlookers or inconvenient conscience," only the "one test of success,—dividends!" (Du Bois 1920b/1999b, 25). Here if anywhere is a situation that cannot and should not be maintained. Not only the war itself but also what life will look like after the war will have a great deal to do with whether Africans, African Americans, and other people of color across the world continue to be exploited and oppressed.

The crucial issue for Du Bois, however, is not merely the exploitation of people of color by wealthy white nations, which Dewey omits or overlooks. It is also the growing complicity and participation of middle-class and even working-class white people in that very exploitation. If "the day of the very rich is drawing to a close" due to the changing situation of the white working classes, this is not because exploitation and subjection are ending (1920b/1999b, 25). It is because the white working classes, along with the white middle class, are being allowed into the exclusive club of those who may exploit people of color. The social reorganization bringing a more equitable distribution of power and control for which Dewey calls might be welcome by some, "but there is a loophole" (1920b/1999b, 25). As it was unfolding in the early twentieth century, the flattening out of differences between rich and poor white people meant an *increase* in the number of people who can benefit from the labor of darker peoples. This was becoming a privilege belonging "not simply to the very rich, but to the middle class and to the laborers" (1920b/1999b, 25).

Du Bois's criticism of the narrow scope of social and industrial reorganization shortly after the war is biting. Again acknowledging that "economic classes must give way" and that "the laborers' hire must increase, the employers' profit must be curbed," Du Bois (1920a/1999a, 58) continues sarcastically:

> But how far shall this change go? Must it apply to all human beings and to all work throughout the world? Certainly not. We seek to apply it slowly and with some reluctance to white men and more slowly and with greater reserve to white women, but black folk and brown and for the most part yellow folk we have widely determined shall not be among those whose needs must justly be heard and whose wants must be ministered to in the great organization of world industry.

World War I led the white world to slightly widen the circle of who counts, but white people continued to draw the circle and to leave people of color outside it. All the while, the white world lauded itself for pursuing universal values of equality, fairness, and democracy, making invisible both the circle itself and the rules that define it.

How to Avoid Future World Wars

Given Dewey's and Du Bois's different understandings of World War I, it will come as no surprise that they offer very different accounts of the national and international changes needed to avoid future global wars. Dewey thought that the war revealed the lack of an international political organization that could govern national relationships and disputes, thereby preventing war. Early in 1915, for example, in an essay on German philosophy and politics written in "the spectacle of the breakdown of the whole philosophy of Nationalism," Dewey (1915, MW 8:203) calls for "an international legislature." Such a legislature must be more than a bureaucratic device, however. To be effective, it must be part of a civilizing process, as Dewey calls it, one that would change isolationist habits by deepening and widening human intercourse and cooperation beyond national boundaries. As we saw earlier, Dewey firmly believes that the United States has these "interracial and international" habits as part of its "internal constitution" (1915, MW 8:203). The question in 1915 is whether the United States is willing to follow its constitution through to its conclusion and "make the accident of our internal composition into an idea, an idea upon which we may conduct our foreign as well as our domestic policy" (1915, MW 8:203). If it will do so, the United States could serve as a model for other nations and help guide the world toward a peace that is fruitful cooperation and not merely the absence of war.

Similarly, in 1916, before the United States had entered the war, Dewey urges European and other powerful nations to develop an international body in response to the rapidly changing global conditions of the times. Such a body would help civilize social relations among peoples much in the way that "the scientific conquest of nature" has helped secure the material side of civilization (Dewey 1916, MW 8:237). An international board whose interests in peace would "coincide with the interest of progress" would oversee commerce and tariffs between nations, and it would include a "board for colonies and one for the supervision of relations with those backward races which have not as yet been benevolently, or otherwise, assimilated by the economically advanced peoples" (1916, MW 8:243).

As the League of Nations was being championed by then-President Woodrow Wilson in 1918 and 1919, Dewey's dream of an international board seemed to be on the verge of coming true. Dewey cautioned that there were wrong ways to structure the League, however. If it were modeled on what he called "the old military-political system ... [based on] the ethics and politics of dignity, honor, aggression, and defense" (Dewey 1918d, MW 11:128), it would merely be concerned with adjudicating offenses between nation-states that refused to recognize their common interests. The superior version of the League, in contrast, would be one rooted in "newer ideas of association in common activities ... [focused on] the primacy of economic and industrial concerns" (1918d, MW 11:129). This would be, in other words, a version of the League modeled on the United States rather than the so-called Old World. "It is no accident," Dewey (1918d, MW 11:128) remarks in praise of the United States, "that the formulation of the new order came from this country, which by the fortune of history and geography escaped most completely from the ethics of maintaining a status of established dignity, and which has committed itself most completely to the ethics of industry and exchange." The contrast between the two models is a contrast between (European) feudalism and (American) democracy, and it is clear, Dewey argues (1918e, MW 11:131–134), that the world should choose the latter.

Dewey's dream was not to be. The League of Nations did not bring about the kind of reorganization for which he had hoped. "The League of Nations is not a League of Nations," Dewey (1918a, MW 11:79–80) charged in 1923, "but of governments, and of the governments whose policies played a part in bringing on the war and that have no wish to change their policies." Withdrawing his support for American membership in the League, Dewey lamented that nothing international had been created for the League to embody or to work with. It was merely a collection of bickering, self-interested nations—one that problematically excluded Russia and its interests, not to mention defeated Germany—identical to what Europe had been prior to the war. Why should the United States step back into that mess, as Dewey asks (1923, MW 15:81), especially now that it is wiser after the war? In the wake of the Treaty of Versailles, which Dewey and many others thought was a disaster, Dewey (1923, MW 15:81–82) bitingly remarked, "it is hard to find any evidence of readiness to cooperate in any definite and systematic way, much less to tie ourselves up with that League of governments which embodies all the forces that have brought the world to its present pass."

Dewey mentions European colonialism when discussing the League, but only in passing. He quickly—literally parenthetically—tucks the "adjustment of colonial problems" into what he sees as the larger "problem of the economic equality of nations" (1918a, MW 11:139). Without explicitly naming them as such, by "nations" Dewey means western, predominantly white European nations. Mere legal or formal equality between those nations will not be enough for a truly international board or league to succeed.

Smaller nations, such as Spain and Italy, have to be certain that they will not be squashed by larger, more powerful nations, such as Great Britain, France, and the United States. Speaking as Italy, for example, Dewey (1918a, MW 11:140) asks whether the League will "see to it that we get that relative share of the world's resources which an adequate development of our own powers requires?" Or is the League instead going to "enable the more powerful peoples to take advantage of our weaknesses?" Dewey insists that these questions of fairness and equity must be answered before smaller European nations will agree to join the League. The three or four most powerful nations in the world (France, Great Britain, the United States, and perhaps also Russia) must understand that it is in their enlightened self-interest—namely that of avoiding future global wars—to share access to the world's resources. Taking care of that problem will take care of any "colonial problems" since colonies are one of the world's resources that powerful nations would share or distribute in fair and equitable ways.

In contrast, European colonialism, American exceptionalism, and the racism infusing both are central to Du Bois's analysis of how to avoid future world wars. In some respects, Du Bois could agree with Dewey's statement that in postwar Europe "each nation felt its deep interests . . . in possession of land overseas, in the right to colonies" (Du Bois 1920b/1999b, 26). Like Dewey, Du Bois also recognizes the problem of "the rage for one's own nation to own the earth or, at least, a large enough portion of it to insure as big profits as the next nation" (1920b/1999b, 27). The solution to these problems according to Du Bois, however, is not to create a common interest in the fair distribution of colonies but to abolish the racist colonial system in which some nations and peoples own others. Addressing ownership, not organization, is the key task before the (white) world if it wants to avoid future wars, Du Bois would insist. The challenge before the world primarily is one of justice, not economics. Merely to reorganize relationships between European nations so that their ownership of other people does not lead to intra-European fighting is merely to rearrange the lounge chairs on the luxury deck of the Titanic.

Dewey's seemingly fair-minded concern about the economic equality of nations covers over a tremendous injustice. It effectively is a concern about which white nations and people will get to exploit darker people and nations. This concern conceals "the idea of white supremacy, [which] rests simply on the fact that white men are the creators of civilization . . . and are therefore civilization's guardians and defenders" (Baldwin 1955, 146). The inequity that Dewey thought that the League must avoid was an inequity among "civilized" European nations only. It did not include predominantly non-white people and nations, and it certainly did not include Africa and people of African descent. The questions of equity raised by Dewey did not apply outside the civilized circle of European and American whiteness. The darker people of the world, in Africa and elsewhere, did not count in the world's calculus of fairness.

As Du Bois recognized, this is because they do not count as full persons. Behind the political and economic issues of fair distribution and inclusion lies a crucial ontological question. While Du Bois (1920a/1999a, 58) notes the deplorable working conditions of laborers and coming changes in the industries in which they work, he also objects, "but this is not the need of the [coming] revolution nor indeed, perhaps, its real beginning. What we must decide sometime is who are to be considered 'men' [sic]." Black, brown, and yellow people are considered, whether explicitly or implicitly, merely subpersons in comparison to the full personhood that white people enjoy (Mills 1998). This difference in personhood is the "value gap" that fundamentally structures the United States and perhaps the world more broadly (Glaude 2016). The real revolution would be one that accords personhood to members of all racial groups. Until that revolution takes place, no genuine political, economic, or social reorganization can occur.

And that revolution is coming, Du Bois announces. In some of the most powerful sections of his analysis of the war, Du Bois warns that World War I was minor compared to the war to come if white people and nations continue to exploit people of color. "As wild and awful as this shameful war was," Du Bois portends, "*it is nothing to compare with that fight for freedom which black and brown and yellow men must and will make unless their oppression and humiliation and insult at the hands of the White World cease*" (1920b/1999b, 28, emphasis in original). If even more formidable world wars are to be avoided, the white world must change its ways. Europe and its partner in iniquity, the United States, must give up their consensual hallucination (William Gibson quoted in Mills 1998, 18) that they are upstanding, moral nations fit to govern inferior darker nations. This is a hallucination in real space, not cyberspace, with real consequences even though it is a fantasy. If the white world cannot do this, "if Europe hugs this delusion, then this is not the end of world war,—it is but the beginning!" (Du Bois 1920b/1999b, 28).

CONCLUSION: IN THE DAYS OF DAESH

Du Bois's foreboding prediction may yet be proved correct. Even if not, it now is clear that the aftermath of World War I is very much part of current global fighting ("terrorism") involving Europe and the United States. When Daesh (or ISIS) proclaimed itself to be a caliphate in 2014, for example, it released a propaganda video titled "The End of Sykes-Picot" (Tinsley 2015). Later in the year, when it moved into Syria from Iraq, Daesh tweeted the border crossing/conquest with the hashtag #SykesPicotOver. Both the video and the hashtag refer to the Sykes-Picot Agreement, which was a secret arrangement made between France and Great Britain during World War I (and exposed to the world in 1917) concerning the two countries' spheres of influence in and plan for divvying up the Middle East. In line with the agreement, after World War I France assumed rule of Syria, which Syrians vehemently opposed, along with Lebanon and portions of Turkey and Iraq (Pedersen 2015, 30). Promises made after the exposure of the Sykes-Picot Agreement to consult with Middle Eastern peoples and leaders about their postwar fate had been forgotten by European nations almost as quickly as they were made (Pedersen 2015, 2). While the issues involved in ISIS's establishment of a caliphate are extremely complex, part of the context for ISIS's actions was (is) the refusal of Europe and its allies to stop arrogantly ruling other parts of the world. Without condoning the violent acts committed by ISIS in Paris in 2015 and Nice in 2016, for example, we can say that it should not come as much of a surprise that ISIS targeted France in particular.

I am not arguing that Dewey could or should have known about the twenty-first-century emergence of ISIS. It is not anachronistic, however, to claim that Dewey could and should have seen World War I as a fight between white nations over which one could grab the most riches from the non-white part of the world. His contemporary Du Bois did, after all. Dewey's published writings on the war suffer greatly in comparison with those of Du Bois, revealing the conceptual whiteness and the lens of white American exceptionalism that shape this period of Dewey's work. While conceptual whiteness and American exceptionalism are not unique to Dewey's philosophy, and while talk of "civilized" people in contrast with "savages" was ubiquitous at the time—even Du Bois uses the terms on occasion[5]—Dewey failed to understand how an assumed white superiority was at the heart of international affairs in the early twentieth century. It is not an exaggeration to claim that Dewey's analyses of World War I "represent the gravest missteps in [his] career" (Dorzweiler 2016), and this is as much because of his silence on race and colonialism as it is because of his utopic, Wilsonian belief that World War I could be a war to end all global wars.

Dewey not only did not write explicitly about race very often, but some of his work that evades race is infused with an unspoken, "invisible" commitment to white privi- lege and white superiority. Dewey's approach to World War I is shaped by the same per- spective of white Western superiority found in his earlier educational work. As Fallace (2010, 168) observes, moreover, the shift in Dewey's thinking perhaps was never fully accomplished: "Dewey never explicitly denounced any of his earlier writings on educa- tion," and as late as 1934 Dewey wrote an introduction to a book on the Dewey school in which "he essentially defended the linear historicist curriculum he developed" earlier in Chicago. Nor did Dewey ever explicitly denounce, in his published work, his World War I writings.[6] This does not mean that Dewey's pragmatism cannot be a useful re- source for contemporary philosophers and scholars. We must read it, however, with a race-conscious eye for Dewey's complicity with the white colonialist domination of his time so that we do not replicate it in our own.

NOTES

1. On habit, see Dewey (1922a, MW 14).
2. For additional uses of Dewey's work to address race and/or racism, see also Pappas (2001) and the essays in part one of Lawson and Koch (2004).
3. The influence of Jane Addams on Dewey is evident here; on Addams and race, see Sullivan (2003). The remainder of this paragraph is adapted from Sullivan (2011).
4. In contrast, see Fesmire (2015, 22–23) for the argument that Dewey includes all immigrants when he opposes understanding assimilation as a "melting pot."
5. Thanks to Trevor Pearce for drawing this point to my attention.

6. Thanks to Steven Fesmire for this specific observation and, more generally, for helpful feedback on an earlier version of this essay.

Works Cited

Citations of John Dewey's works are to the thirty-seven-volume critical edition published by Southern Illinois University Press under the editorship of Jo Ann Boydston. In-text citations give the original publication date and series abbreviation, followed by volume number and page number. For example: (1934, LW 10:12) is page 12 of *Art as Experience*, which is published as volume 10 of *The Later Works*.

Series abbreviations for *The Collected Works*:

EW *The Early Works* (1882–1898)

MW *The Middle Works* (1899–1924)

LW *The Later Works* (1925–1953)

Baldwin, James. 1955. *Notes of a Native Son*. New York: Bantam Books.

Dewey, John. 1915. *German Philosophy and Politics*. MW 8:135–204.

Dewey, John. 1916. "Progress." MW 8:234–251.

Dewey, John. 1918a. "A League of Nations and Economic Freedom." MW 11:139–142.

Dewey, John. 1918b. "America in the World." MW 11:70–72.

Dewey, John. 1918c. "Internal Social Reorganization after the War." MW 11: 73–86.

Dewey, John. 1918d. "The Approach to a League of Nations." MW 11: 127–130.

Dewey, John. 1918e. "The League of Nations and the New Diplomacy." MW 11:131–134.

Dewey, John. 1918f. "What Are We Fighting For?" MW 11: 98–106.

Dewey, John. 1922a. *Human Nature and Conduct*. MW 14.

Dewey, John. 1922b. "Racial Prejudice and Friction." MW 13: 242–254.

Dewey, John. 1923. "Shall We Join the League?" MW 15:78–82.

Dewey, John. 1932. "Address to the National Association for the Advancement of Colored People." LW 6: 224–230.

Dorzweiler, Nick. 2016. "Democracy's Disappointments: Insights from Dewey and Foucault on World War I and the Iranian Revolution." *Constellations: An International Journal of Critical and Democratic Theory*. doi: 10.1111/1467-8675.12238.

Du Bois, W. E. B. 1920a/1999a. "Of Work and Wealth." In *Darkwater: Voices From Within the Veil*, 47–59 Mineola, NY: Dover.

Du Bois, W. E. B. 1920b/1999b. "The Souls of White Folk." In *Darkwater: Voices From Within the Veil*, 17–29. Mineola, NY: Dover Publications, Inc.

Fallace, Thomas D. 2010. *Dewey and the Dilemma of Race: An Intellectual History, 1895–1922*. New York: Teachers College Press.

Fesmire, Steven. 2015. *Dewey*. New York: Routledge.

Glaude, Jr., Eddie S. 2007. *In a Shade of Blue: Pragmatism and the Politics of Black America*. Chicago: University of Chicago Press.

Glaude, Eddie S. Jr. 2016. *Democracy in Black: How Race Still Enslaves the American Soul*. New York: Crown.

Keltie, John Scott. 1893. *The Partition of Africa*. London: E. Stanford.

Lawson, Bill E., and Donald F. Koch, eds. 2004. *Pragmatism and the Problem of Race*. Bloomington: Indiana University Press.

MacMullan, Terrance. 2009. *Habits of Whiteness: A Pragmatist Reconstruction.* Bloomington: Indiana University Press.

Mills, Charles. 1998. *Blackness Visible: Essays on Philosophy and Race.* Ithaca, NY: Cornell University Press.

Pakenham, Thomas. 1991. *The Scramble for Africa: 1876–1912.* New York: Random House.

Pappas, Gregory Fernando. 2001. "Dewey and Latina Lesbians on the Quest for Purity." *Journal of Speculative Philosophy,* vol. 15, no. 2, 152–161.

Pedersen, Susan. 2015. *The Guardians: The League of Nations and the Crisis of Empire.* New York: Oxford University Press.

Sullivan, Shannon. 2003. "Reciprocal Relations between Races: Jane Addams's Ambiguous Legacy." *Transactions of the C.S. Peirce Society,* vol. 39, no. 1, 43–60.

Sullivan, Shannon. 2004. "From the Foreign to the Familiar: Confronting Dewey Confronting Racial Prejudice." *The Journal of Speculative Philosophy,* vol. 18, no. 3, 193–202.

Sullivan, Shannon. 2006. *Revealing Whiteness: The Unconscious Habits of Racial Privilege.* Bloomington: Indiana University Press.

Sullivan, Shannon. 2011. "Review of *Dewey and the Dilemma of Race: An Intellectual History, 1895–1922,* by Thomas Fallace." *History of Education Quarterly,* vol. 51, no. 4, 558–561.

Tinsley, Meghan. 2015. "ISIS's Aversion to Sykes-Picot Tells Us Much About the Group's Future Plans." http://muftah.org/the-sykes-picot-agreement-isis/.

West, Cornel. 1993. "Pragmatism and the Sense of the Tragic." In *Keeping Faith: Philosophy and Race in America,* 107–118. New York: Routledge.

CHAPTER 13

....

DEWEY AND PRAGMATIST FEMINIST PHILOSOPHY

....

LISA HELDKE

How has the work of John Dewey been useful for feminist philosophers? And why should feminists find in Dewey a useful source of insight for future philosophical projects?

Several decades of feminist work on/with Dewey have already taken place, but such work does not necessarily put "paid" to the matter of its future usefulness—and the comparatively small impact of pragmatist feminist philosophy on feminist theory more generally (as, say, compared to feminist thought informed by continental philosophy) might count as evidence that pragmatism in general is *not* a particularly useful launching pad for feminism. Dewey, in particular, has been found lacking by feminist and other social theorists who have made a number of arguments about his positions on power, on race, and on women. Regarding power, some theorists argue that he does not have a critical analysis that recognizes it as something that can be used to oppress and manipulate (see, for instance, Hewitt 2007). Among the analyses of his philosophy with respect to questions of race and racism are these views: Dewey maintains a "relative silence about race in his published work" (Glaude 2007, 17); it is written from an unacknowledged white perspective that deploys conceptual whiteness (Sullivan this volume); and Dewey actually supported racist projects like segregated schools and Black assimilation (Curry 2011). Regarding women, theorists argue that despite clear admiration for women thinkers and women's rights, he did not outline a theory of women's liberation or acknowledge and explore its centrality to his own democratic project. (See Noddings 2012 and Seigfried 1996 for discussions of these positions.)

To some of these challenges, defenders have effectively responded. Hewitt (2007) and Hildreth (2009), for instance, have drawn out the conception of power they believe is implicitly present in Dewey.[1] And, despite Dewey's silence on race, Glaude argues that he offers unique resources that can be used to address problems of race and racism. Nevertheless, many challenges remain, as authors in this volume argue. Such charges must be taken seriously in any future feminist work that utilizes him. If Dewey's philosophy cannot effectively address the ways in which power and domination shape human interactions at individual and institutional levels, and if it cannot actively support thought that is robustly liberatory of women and of men of color, then it could well be concluded that his work is not of much use to transformative feminist philosophy.

This essay is written from an acknowledgement of these serious limitations but also from the conviction that his work has been an important source for pragmatist feminist philosophers. It is written from the belief that pragmatist feminism in general, and Deweyan feminism in particular, have yet to influence feminist philosophy to the degree warranted; that Dewey's experiential model of reality and of inquiry can be excellent resources with which to ground claims about the realness of oppression and concepts such as gender and race.

The chapter begins by sketching feminist influences *on* Dewey's writing from women who were his students, colleagues, and family. Next, it catalogues recent work in feminist philosophy that draws upon Dewey, identifying ideas that have proven most influential on feminists. I conclude with suggestions for future work in pragmatist feminism. Throughout, my aim is to provide evidence for my belief that not only does Dewey warrant the attention he has been given by feminists but also that the pragmatist feminism that has emerged in dialogue with him warrants greater influence than it has thus far had.

DEWEY AND HIS WOMEN CONTEMPORARIES

Dewey counts among those men philosophers who acknowledged the influence of women—including feminist women—on his thought. While those acknowledgements did not document the full extent to which he was shaped by the women around him, or provide many specific details about the particular ways his thought was influenced, they nevertheless served as useful clues from which subsequent scholars have traced the influences of those scholars, teachers, and activists on Dewey's thought. Charlene Haddock Seigfried's authoritative *Feminism and Pragmatism: Reweaving the Social Fabric* offers the most thorough and comprehensive research into those influences. Pragmatist feminist scholarship such as that of Seigfried, and of Judy Whipps and Marilyn Fisher, not only fills in more details about the emergence of Dewey's views and the women who influenced them but also independently recovers the work of these important women thinkers, making them accessible to subsequent philosophers and fleshing out the history of nineteenth- to twentieth-century thought.

Among the influences on Dewey, chief among them are his wife—born Alice Chipman—and Hull House founder Jane Addams. Alice Chipman Dewey is described by their daughter Jane (named for Addams) thus: "Awakened by her grandparents to a critical attitude toward social conditions and injustices, she was undoubtedly largely responsible for the early widening of Dewey's philosophic interests from the commentative and classical to the field of contemporary life. Above all, things which previously had been matters of theory acquired through his contact with her a vital and direct human significance" (Jane Dewey 1939, 21). An advocate of women's rights and a teacher who worked with the Lab School he founded at the University of Chicago, Alice inspired and shaped her husband's interest in education, a central focus of his work beginning in the mid-1890s (Whipps and Danielle 2016).

Alice Chipman Dewey directly, daily and intimately influenced Dewey's thought their entire life together; Jane Addams spent many fewer years in his direct company as friend and colleague, but her influence on him was also profound and lifelong. She was an important dialogue partner; one encyclopedist describes them as "intellectual soulmates," and Dewey dedicated *Liberalism and Social Action* to her. (Hamington 2014) He says she shaped his understanding of both democracy and education; as Jane Dewey notes, his "faith in democracy as a guiding force in education took on both a sharper and a deeper meaning because of Hull House and Jane Addams" (1939, 30). She influenced him even about the nature of philosophy itself, contributing to his transition away from Hegelian idealism. In a letter to Alice Dewey written in 1894 following an argument with Addams, he notes, "I have always been interpreting dialectic wrong end up, the unity as the reconciliation of opposites, instead of the opposites as the unity in its growth, and thus translated the physical tension into a moral thing" (as cited in Menand 2001, 313).

Beyond these two are Dewey's women students, who also sometimes became colleagues. That Dewey was influenced by women students is no small matter. As Judy Whipps notes, the era in which Dewey lived saw the first women going to college and university in the United States and entering academic life more generally. Dewey taught and was influenced by women students and teachers both in Chicago and in New York. Among them, three are most frequently mentioned and their influences on Dewey best documented.

Ella Flagg Young, his student at the University of Chicago and his colleague at the famed Lab School, is chief among these. Most often cited is her insistence that, as Ellen Lagemann put it, "respect for freedom means regard for the inquiring or reflective processes of individual [teachers]" (cited in Maher 2001, 18). Lageman is quoted as writing that Dewey acknowledged that Young, a mature woman with years of experience as a teacher before meeting him, had persuaded him to treat the (women) teachers at the Lab School as peers and colleagues and to offer them "freedom and intellectual cooperation" rather than "supervision and technical training" (as cited in Maher 2001, 18).

Columbia University student Elsie Ripley Clapp studied with Dewey and also served as his research and teaching assistant. Her feedback on his writings and course preparations shaped the writing of *Democracy and Education*, albeit in ways about which he is maddeningly unspecific. (See Seigfried 1996, 50ff for a discussion of the inadequate ways Dewey acknowledged what were obviously significant influences.) Lucy Sprague Mitchell, who knew Dewey in both Chicago and New York, became a student in his graduate classes at Columbia. An experienced educator and administrator, she founded programs that advanced the pragmatist model of education in which curriculum is shaped in response to the child.

Dewey was a thinker who explored ideas by inquiring *with* others. He chose the company of these brilliant, socially engaged women. Many of these women are credited with shaping lie at the heart of what is most "Deweyan" about Dewey, in terms of both subject matter (education and democracy) and philosophical approach (methods of inquiry as practiced, e.g., at Hull House and the Lab School).

These connections with women thinkers are more than just historically interesting. As I noted, Dewey can rightly be challenged for his failure to take up women's subordination as a serious philosophical topic. It is thus fair to ask for evidence of Dewey's feminist potential. Not so many decades ago, feminist philosophers struggled with the question of whether, in Audre Lorde's words, "the master's tools" could be used to "dismantle the master's house"—that is, whether the theories of an antifeminist or nonfeminist man could be used to do work that was genuinely liberatory for women. Feminists may no longer ask the question in that form, but it remains relevant to consider whether and how one can construct feminist thought that draws upon a thinker with no particular feminist agenda. As V. Denise James forthrightly observes, "Feminists do not need Dewey to help in their assertions of the validity and importance of their work" (2009, 94). Feminist thought can undergird itself. Nevertheless, while it is right to be disappointed that Dewey did not prioritize women's liberation, and while it is true that feminists do not "need" Dewey to create liberatory feminist philosophy, feminist philosophers are warranted in placing stock in Dewey. The influence these and other women had upon him counts in his favor; Dewey is worth contemporary feminists' attention in part just *because* feminists clearly influenced *him*. They stand as evidence that Dewey believed that women *could and should* influence him. It is not a patriarchy-smashing act, but it does render him a credible source for feminists.

TWENTIETH- AND TWENTY-FIRST-CENTURY FEMINIST DISCUSSIONS OF DEWEY

Feminist philosophers have primarily drawn from Dewey's work in the areas of philosophy of education, social and political philosophy, and epistemology. This section identifies some of the major threads of our work. I begin, however, with a discussion of his version of pragmatism, highlighting those features of his general approach to philosophy that have influenced feminists.

Dewey's Pragmatism. Dewey is committed to challenging dichotomous ways of thinking that undergird much Western philosophy. These dichotomies are linked, often in explicit and unsubtle ways, to oppressive gender, race, and class division. Women, and men of color, are associated with the bodily and practical, whereas men of privilege are associated with the mental and theoretical. Challenging these dichotomies is an important task for feminism, and Dewey offers valuable resources with which to do so, even though his own purposes for doing so do not address racism or sexism. *The Quest for Certainty* (1929), for instance, offers a powerful historical look at the emergence of dichotomous thinking in the West. Dewey's analysis of these hierarchical dichotomies—particularly those of theory/ practice, mind/body, human/nature, reason/emotion, and subject/object—makes clear the ways in which they are used to sort and grade both people and the work they do, though his analysis puts the matter only in terms of class hierarchies, not gender or race. For feminists, equally valuable as his critique of dichotomy are his efforts to get beyond dichotomies by getting "under" them. Excavating beneath dichotomies unearths shared assumptions that, once acknowledged, make it possible to dissolve or heal them. See the final section of this chapter, however, for a discussion of the limits of this strategy.

The frequency with which the word "experience" appears in the titles of Dewey's books points to another feature of his thought that has influenced feminist pragmatists. Experience, understood as the array of interactions and engagements we have with the world of which we are a part, is elemental. We begin *in* experience, and only on reflection and examination do we sort it into things like "objects." This feature of Dewey's thought is central to virtually all his work.

Inquiry always begins in, and returns to, a problem in one's experience. Inquiry is not different *from* experience; it is a different, less immediate, kind *of* experience. Thus does Dewey take philosophy down from its exalted perch and return it to the (everyday) world. Thus does it become a (particular) way of attempting to address the problems we encounter in our everyday world.

Dewey's word "interaction"—and his later "transaction"—encapsulate his notion that organisms and their environments constitute themselves and each other through dynamic exchanges. This understanding challenges subject/object dualism, by understanding subjects and objects not as having fixed, absolute boundaries but as porous entities that emerge in the context of particular transactions. See the later section on epistemology for further discussion of feminist uses of this concept.

For a Deweyan, a question that is always relevant is how does inquiry enable subsequent experience to be better—where "better" is understood to mean something we can articulate, disagree about, and develop experimentally? Denise James, for instance, finds in Dewey an important source of insight regarding "the task of theory." She suggests that he can help us think about how to do theory that initiates change. For a feminist philosopher, theory should do more than "uncover or state" the way things are. It should take seriously its origins in experience and also its obligation to improve subsequent experience. (James 2009, 92, 98) She quotes "The Need for a Recovery of Philosophy" (1917, MW 10:48), in which Dewey writes, "Faith in the power of intelligence to imagine a future which is the projection of the desirable in the present, and to invent the instrumentalities of its realization, is our salvation. And it is a faith which must be nurtured and made articulate: surely a sufficiently large task for our philosophy" (as cited in James 2009, 98).

This discussion has hinted at another feature of Dewey's pragmatism of central importance to feminists. For Dewey, inquiry of any sort, including scientific inquiry, is a value-laden activity taking place in a human world of human desires and interests. The rejection of a fact/value dichotomy has been virtually a defining principle for much feminist epistemology; Dewey's conception of inquiry, which leaves no room for the dichotomy, has informed the work of a number of writers, including Nelson (1990), Rooney (1993) and Heldke (1992).

Education. Dewey is heralded as a champion of progressive education and a founding influence on experiential education, two educational movements long in dialogue with feminist philosophy of education. (See, for instance, Warren and Rheingold 1993.) Feminists have drawn upon and extended features of Dewey's philosophy of education, most particularly its insistence upon the intertwining of knowing and doing ("head work" and "hand work") and the understanding of education as itself the practice of—not merely the preparation for—democracy. Some have also criticized his bringing gendered hand work into the classroom in ways that continue to marginalize it, and, more generally, his limited attention to the powerful roles gender plays in education.

Feminists have interrogated Dewey's reintegration of head work and hand work in progressive pedagogy from several vantage points, in an effort to ascertain whether that pedagogy can be considered—or can be made into—a genuinely feminist pedagogy. Is his scanty attention to both women and women's work more than an oversight; does it actually constitute a structural problem with his theory? Jane Roland Martin (1994) and Francis Maher both observe that, in Maher's words, "Formulations like Dewey's reflect an unstated assumption that inasmuch as education represents a developmental journey from the private to the public sphere as children grow, education itself is 'masculine'" (Maher 2001, 21) Similarly, I observe that the curriculum in a Deweyan school abandons domestic work when children progress beyond elementary school, as if such "women's work" is irrelevant to the work of an adult citizen of a democracy, as compared to, say, laboratory science. (Heldke 2002) Why does Dewey regard cooking and other homemaking tasks as forms of inquiry worth pursuing when the students are children but treat them only as sources of examples—not methods of intellectual engagement—when they are adults? Perhaps a more thorough-goingly Deweyan pedagogy would push harder against the dichotomy of public and private and would come to understand work in the home as a full part of the practice of democracy.[2]

Further to the matter of democracy and education, Elizabeth Minnich identifies in Dewey the inspiration and instigation for what she calls "aspirational democracy" These pragmatists call for "egalitarian, face-to-face, creative, engaged discussion among respectfully differing people that is throughout open-minded, exploratory, fallibilistic"

(Minnich 2002, 107). She sees Maxine Greene as "translating such a recentering of philosophy into a democratizing educational vision for today" (107), and quotes Greene as saying that, because "democracy . . . is a community always in the making," education is central to that making. It is in the "local spaces in which teaching is done" that "students will begin telling the stories of what they are seeking, what they know and might not yet know . . . . It is at moments like these that persons begin to recognize each other and, in the experience of recognition, feel the need to take responsibility for each other" (as cited in Minnich 2002, 107–108).

Ana M. Martínez Alemán draws upon Dewey's understanding of individuals as emerging through dialectical engagement with their worlds, and of democracy as emerging through, and depending upon, the presence of such individuals, to offer a vision of feminist classrooms as places that reject relativism. Borrowing a phrase from Lorraine Code, she argues that such classrooms demand participants to "move . . . from the realm of 'featureless abstraction' and the experience of psychic disequilibrium, to epistemologically significant agents in the classroom" (Martínez Alemán 2002, 126). Such classrooms "should be the passageways to self-realization in a 'democracy multicultural'" (128). Martínez Alemán picks up another theme common to much feminist use of Dewey; namely, the embracing of a view that rejects relativism while also eschewing absolutism. The particular way in which the pragmatist Dewey resists this dichotomy can be argued to be one of the most important contributions he can make to contemporary feminist philosophy; it is also a matter about which there is disagreement, as I discuss in a later section.

While Dewey continues to be an important influence on contemporary progressive education in general, and feminist progressive education in particular, his influence on these movements has not been as widespread among feminist philosophers as that exerted by Paolo Freire, author of *Pedagogy of the Oppressed*. Freire conceives of education as a means of radical social transformation. In contrast, Dewey understands education as one of the most powerful forms of democratic community building.

As Freire's title suggests, his work draws on a Marxist conception of oppression, as does much contemporary feminist work Perhaps then it is unsurprising that it has attracted more feminist philosophical attention than has Dewey's. To the degree that it is rooted in a belief that Freire is the more radical thinker than Dewey, this relative neglect is unwarranted. Dewey's radicalism can be found in his insistence that the *means* by which democratic communities can be built must be, themselves, democratic. Apropos this point Steven Fesmire, quoting Dewey (LW 11:332), writes that Dewey's radicalism calls upon "those with the courage and patience to secure the 'democratic means to achieve our democratic ends'" (Fesmire 2015, 164). Perhaps the radical title for Dewey's work would be *Democracy IS Pedagogy*.

Social and Political Philosophy. Given its centrality in his philosophy of education, it is no surprise that democracy lies at the center of Dewey's social and political philosophy and figures prominently in the thought of feminist theorists who employ him. Democracy is a term he associates with education, with the scientific method, and with growth, and associates tó such a degree that it seems democracy is synonymous with these other terms. Dewey's conception of democracy extends beyond traditional liberal conceptions to encompass collective inquiry aimed at addressing community problems and advancing the (collectively determined) common good. "The method of democracy—inasfar as it is that of organized intelligence—is to bring these conflicts out into the open where their special claims can be discussed and judged in the light of more inclusive interests than are represented by either of them separately" (1935 LW 11:56).

In *Deep Democracy,* Judith Green places Dewey's pragmatist conception of democracy in conversation with Habermas's critical theory, to explore the ways they "share the project of developing . . . a practical philosophy of democratic transformation in community life" (Green 1999, 15). She concludes that the two are "inadequate to generate [a] comprehensive philosophy of democratic transformation . . . unless they are reconstructed in conversation with other philosophical methodologies grounded in and motivated by a richer appreciation of diversity" (Green 1999, 48). Drawing feminism and cultural pluralism into the conversation, she develops a *"radical critical pragmatism"* that "draw[s] cross-culturally on all the great traditions of liberatory struggle" and that "express[es] a 'cultivated pluralism' learned through a critical multicultural education" (Green 1999, 49).

Denise James considers a critique of Dewey from Cornel West: that Dewey lacks a sense of the tragic, and thus is "too hopeful about the radical possibilities of social cooperation" (James 2009, 96). West, in essence, is suggesting that Dewey's philosophy does not take into account how bleak social reality is and thus has unrealistic expectations about the possibilities of democratic community building.

James replies that "West's prophetic pragmatism relies on not only a concept of evil but also a notion of utopia derived from Christianity that makes it a transcendent philosophy of the sort to which Deweyan pragmatism is necessarily opposed" (2009, 96). In other words, the demand that Dewey "name" evil, far from being an embrace of the real world and its horrors, ends up being a demand for a retreat to the abstract, "deexperientialized" philosophy Dewey rejects. While West seeks, in James's words, to "transcend the realities of experience," she quotes Dewey (1930, LW 5:267) asserting that " 'Faith in its newer sense signifies that experience itself is the sole ultimate authority' " (as cited in James 2009, 96). This conception of faith resonates with the theory of black feminists who "concentrate on the possibilities inherent in our current political situations, rather than the tragic elements of that experience" (James 2009, 96). Denise James connects Dewey's work to the "visionary pragmatism" of Stanley James and Abena Busia, as explored by Patricia Hill Collins (1998). Hill Collins writes that visionary pragmatism "points to a vision, [but] doesn't prescribe a fixed end point of some universal truth. One never arrives, but constantly strives. At the same time, by stressing the pragmatic, it reveals how current actions are part of some larger, more meaningful struggle" (as cited in James 2009, 97). Here, again, we encounter the pragmatist effort to reject both absolutism and relativism—or, as in this case, absolutism and absurdity.

While James distances Dewey from an abstract and transcendent utopianism, Erin McKenna's work *The Task of Utopia* begins with the contention that we need utopian thought to provide "visions to which we might aspire," so that we can better "understand ourselves both as we are and as we might be" (McKenna 2001, 1). That motivation leads her to develop a conception of utopia influenced by feminist utopian fiction and also (unexpectedly) Deweyan pragmatism. In contrast to both "end state" and "anarchist" conceptions of utopia, which promote dogmatism and passivity, her "process utopia" is characterized by the Deweyan belief that ends, as well as the means of achieving them, must be continually reconceived, reexamined, revalued—that the very picture of utopia must be continually reimagined. "On the process model it becomes critically important for us to critically examine the goals we choose to pursue, since what we choose to pursue now defines what we will be able to pursue in the future" (McKenna 2001, 167). Somewhat paradoxically, on this vision of utopia, the goal sought is not perfection; it recognizes, as the saying goes, that the perfect is the enemy of the good. Process utopia "seeks to create and sustain people willing to take on responsibility and participate in directing their present toward a better, more desirable future" (McKenna 2001, 167). Process utopia is radical in the way Dewey's pedagogy is radical.

Epistemology. Scholarship in feminist epistemology uses Dewey to challenge the sharp theory/practice dualism, which marginalizes the work of women and working-class men. Likewise, his description of the relationship between organism and environment as "interaction" provides a tool with which to challenge and reconceive the dualisms of self/world, subject/object, and organism/environment.[3]

Shannon Sullivan's *Living Across and Through Skins* explores Dewey's account of transaction. The title of the book is not meant metaphorically; Sullivan uses "across" and "through" to make the Deweyan acknowledgment that our skins do not hermetically seal us from each other or the world; bodies undergo "reconstitution through their constitutive relations with others" (Sullivan 2001, 13).

For Dewey, inquiry is simply one (albeit specialized) kind of transaction. Sullivan takes the notion of inquiry as a transactional relationship that changes both "inquirer" and "inquired" and builds a feminist pragmatist standpoint theory as well as a conception of objectivity.

As is evident in what I have said thus far, Deweyan pragmatism is valued by many pragmatist feminists for giving us ways to dismantle the dichotomy between absolutism and relativism; on this reading, Dewey rejects the insistence that *either* there are absolute truths *or* all truths are relative to a given context. Barbara Thayer-Bacon rejects this reading of Dewey as carving a third way; she instead grasps the nettle of relativism, arguing that Dewey is what she terms a "qualified relativist." She stresses the open-endedness and in-principle-unfinishedness of Dewey's understanding of inquiry, noting "For Dewey, inquiry is a *continuing* process . . . and settled beliefs are not necessarily settled for all time . . . . All settled beliefs are open to possibly becoming unsettled by further inquiry" (Thayer-Bacon 2003, 425). Such inquiry arrives not at absolute truth, but if all goes well, it may arrive at what Dewey called "warranted assertions" (Dewey 1938 LW 12:11).

She terms Dewey and the other classical pragmatists "qualified," as opposed to "vulgar" relativists. "Qualified relativists insist that all inquiry are [*sic*] affected by philosophical assumptions which are culturally bound, and that all inquirers are situated knowers who are culturally bound as well. However, we can compensate for our cultural embeddedness by opening our horizons and including others in our conversations" (Thayer-Bacon 2003, 417). She argues that these thinkers can be seen as the intellectual forebears of a range of contemporary feminist theorists, themselves qualified relativists, who:

> stress that the construction of knowledge is social, interactive, flexible, and on-going.... [F]eminists as qualified relativists argue along similar lines to Dewey's concept of a democratic community. They agree with Dewey that the more other voices are included and considered, the more each of us can trust that we have considered all available information and can hope to make a sound judgment.
>
> (Thayer-Bacon 2003, 434–435)

Whether this meliorism is best understood as "qualified relativism" or as a "third option" that is neither absolutist nor relativist is a question worth continued feminist consideration. (See also Heldke 1989.) While this way of putting the matter might mark it out as a pragmatist feminist question, it is of more general interest. Consider: How do we *justify* claims that systematic oppression is real and affects identifiable groups? Do those claims rest more securely on a qualified relativism, or on a reconfigured conception of objectivity? The question is far from idle, and is one on which Deweyan feminists can make helpful, relevant contributions.

Other Deweyan Resources for Feminist Philosophy.

This chapter began by claiming that Dewey's philosophy can contribute not only to pragmatist feminist philosophy but to feminist philosophy more generally. Feminist philosophy has drawn far more heavily from mainstream analytic and continental traditions than from pragmatism, despite what seem to be deep natural affinities between the underlying commitments and methods of the pragmatism and feminism. In concluding this section, I provide a list of the kinds of contributions a Deweyan feminist pragmatism can make to other feminist philosophical endeavors: (a) a conception of inquiry that never introduces (and thus does not need to heal) a fact/value dichotomy; (b) an understanding of humans as bodily and mindedness as a particular feature of bodily selves; (c) an embracing of chance, uncertainty, and change as genuine features of our world of experience that are not to be reasoned away; (d) a conception of reality grounded in the recognition that we and the world are constantly in the process of making ourselves up together; and (e) a commitment to the value and possibility of collective human inquiry, aimed at identifying and advancing toward shared notions of "the good."

FUTURE PROJECTS FOR DEWEYAN
FEMINIST PHILOSOPHY

Knowledge ... represents objects which have been settled, ordered, disposed of rationally. Thinking, on the other hand, is prospective in reference. It is occasioned by an unsettlement and it aims at overcoming a disturbance. Philosophy is thinking what the known demands of us—what responsive attitude it exacts. It is an idea of what is possible, not a record of accomplished fact. Hence it is hypothetical, like all thinking. It presents an assignment of something to be done—something to be tried. Its value lies not in furnishing solutions (which can be achieved only in action) but in defining difficulties and suggesting methods for dealing with them. Philosophy might almost be described as thinking which has become conscious of itself—which has generalized its place, function, and value in experience.

(Dewey 1919, MW 9:24)

Dewey's definition of philosophy here not only invites; it demands that we philosophize *about* his philosophy, that we address the "disturbances" and "unsettlements" that have arisen with respect to it. It is thus in the spirit of Dewey that feminists define the difficulties in his thought and suggest methods for dealing with them—methods that would enable that philosophy to be a more effective tool of human liberation.[4]

In the spirit of Dewey's vision of philosophy and of liberation, then, this last section attempts to deepen Dewey's value for feminism, by pointing to a current feminist discussion in which he should be included, and by suggesting a way to rethink his approach to dichotomies.

Dewey and Feminist Third Options.
Among the tasks that have occupied feminist philosophers, questions about the foundations for claims that women are oppressed and questions about the nature of fundamental categories like race and gender have loomed large. Against a backdrop of dualistic thinking, the choice of answers has sometimes been reduced to foundationalism and realism on the one hand, or relativism and antirealism on the other. To state these alternatives in their most naïve forms: Either there are "real women" (by virtue of their biological sex) who are "really oppressed" in ways that can be independently verified by "neutral" parties, or "woman" is a purely constructed category (call it "gender"), and oppression is a state of affairs entirely relative to a given cultural milieu. Even when stated in their most subtle and sophisticated forms, many feminist theorists regard these two options as neither exhaustive nor necessarily mutually exclusive. (Sex *or* gender only?) Many feminists have sought to develop a third option that is neither foundationalist nor relativist,

neither realist nor antirealist. The pursuit of this third option has led some feminist theorists to develop ontological positions that should have—but generally have not had—deep resonance with John Dewey.

Third options are difficult to establish and maintain, because it is difficult for those who view them from either of the two established positions to evaluate them on their own terms; to understand them as anything other than an unholy mashup between the existing apparently-polar opposites. The idea that the third is genuinely other—that it is generated out of genuinely different assumptions—is a difficult claim to advance. It is much easier for partisans of foundationalism or relativism to push third-option advocates over into the other camp (if they dislike its implications) or (if they *like* the third option) to draw it into their own camp and show how it can be redescribed on their terms. Placing feminist projects in conversation with Dewey might lead to new ways to think about how third options might be framed most effectively.

One important feminist exemplar will stand in to suggest the possibilities of such a project. Donna Haraway has been developing a way to talk about "what there is" that bears decided resemblance to Dewey's interactional, experiential model.[5] My account of Haraway here is indebted to Grebowicz and Merrick (2013), whose book situates Haraway's work within the debates I have just sketched.

Haraway well illustrates the perils faced by third options; her decades of efforts to develop such a position have met with frequent suggestions that she is actually a relativist or a thoroughgoing social constructivist (push-pull). At least one pragmatist feminist reads her *not* as a proponent of a third option but as a relativist. Mary Magada Ward suggests that what Haraway calls "pleasure in the confusion of boundaries" has the effect of pushing science into the category of myth and strikes her as irresponsible, perhaps even dangerous (as cited in Magada-Ward 2014, 474). Magada-Ward argues that the pragmatists, including Dewey, do not make such a move but remain advocates of a science that is committed to facts distinguishable clearly from fiction. Magada-Ward bluntly identifies the reason for her worry and for her insistence: "In a country in which intelligent design is still taught as respectable science at some public universities and national figures make claims about 'legitimate' rape, it is irresponsible to blur the boundaries between myth and science (or fact and fiction) in some all-encompassing notion of 'narrative' " (Magada-Ward 2014, 472).

The frequency of these kinds of challenges has led Haraway (2003) to assert her third-option status unambiguously: "I am neither a naturalist nor a social constructionist. Neither-nor. This is not social constructionism, and it is not technoscientific [n]or biological determinism. It is not nature. It is not culture. It is truly about a historical effort to get elsewhere" (as cited in Grebowicz and Merrick 2013, 34). "Elsewhere," understand, is something other than a scotch-taped-together nature-and-culture or a more fictional fact. To stress the "elsewhereness" of her position, she invents vocabularies that are just unfamiliar (or cumbersome) enough to interrupt one's normal way of approaching the world and, perhaps, create the possibility for another approach. Thus, for instance, her use of the phrase "being worldly," which does not automatically evoke either nature or culture. She acknowledges concepts that have served their purpose but have become stuck in either/or-ness. Sex and gender, for instance, are analytical tools that did a certain kind of good work to think into nature-culture at a certain time. The terms do not describe the way things (really, *really*) are. She states "Neither sex nor nature is the truth underlying gender and culture" (as cited in Grebowicz and Merrick 2013, 25).

Haraway's "worldly" third option bears important resemblance to Dewey's world of *experience*, a world that *is* all of the various things we encounter and experience it as being—fearsome, precarious, boring, stable, predictable, and so on. There is not some way the world is that underlies our experience of it and into which our experience can resolve itself when we come to realize how things really are. Rather, there are our experiences in and with our world. Those experiences change character as our situation in that world changes; they also change the dynamics of our relationships in the world. On a Deweyan view, we might say, for instance, that introducing a distinction between sex and gender does not reveal that sex was "there all along" but was obscured by our (enculturated) experiences. Rather, using the concepts of sex and gender to interact in our world enables us to engage with and in that world in a different set of ways, because those concepts *make* the world differently—and thereby make the *world* different.

For Dewey, that is, reality genuinely changes when we introduce new concepts—which might be thought of as creating new interactions or (as we more commonly think of them) as new pieces of knowledge. The world in which these relationships exist is a different world *because* it now contains these interactions. These interactions lead, in turn, to other ways of being and acting.

Some Dewey scholars are careful, at this juncture, to insist that Dewey is not claiming that reality is changing in the sense that "when we come to know stars light years away, a change has to take place, say in the nuclear reactions which feed the star," a notion one author calls "preposterous" (Tiles 1988, 25). Nature is different, on this reading, simply because the person observing the star is going to behave differently as a result of knowing this star. While such a reading is certainly cautious and responsible, and *may* represent the full extent of what Dewey was intimating, I want to push out its parameters, using Haraway to do so.

Haraway's exploration of natureculture recognizes that we are not the only ones organizing, ordering, and "making sense" of our world. As she puts it, "The actors are not all 'us'" (as cited in Grebowicz and Merrick 2013, 36). This is a world being "co-constructed" by all of the beings in it. In such a world, in which others are actors whose actions may have very different quality and form from ours (because their bodies are wildly different from ours, for starters), it is presumptuous to assume that we can summarize all the differences in reality that result from an interaction by framing them *purely* from the point of view of the human defined as the "knower." What if we read Dewey as *also* recognizing that the actors are not "all us," and thus that interactions might shape reality in ways irreducible what can be experienced and noted from the vantage point of a human knower?

Perhaps we cannot stretch far enough to imagine a distant star as such an actor. But it takes little effort so to understand other living beings with central nervous systems that live in our midst. For Haraway, this has meant, among other things, thinking hard about relationships with companion species such as dogs. Haraway argues that, when we realize there are other actors in the world, it becomes vital for us to figure out how to engage ethically with these others-as-actors. It will not do to speak for these others, nor will it do to assume that the modes of interaction that are most comfortable to humans (inquiry that produces knowledge) are the only relevant ones. "In order to co-construct nature, nonproductivist modes of relating between human and nonhuman that are expressed as articulations, relationality and respect are necessary" (Grebowicz and Merrick 2013, 37).

What does ethical relating "look like" between a human and her dog companion? What can we learn about such relating by putting Haraway in conversation with Dewey? What, if anything, does Dewey contribute to this discussion? How can Haraway help Dewey's account to become *more* Deweyan, by more robustly embracing the claim that reality is constituted (changed) by the relationships that happen *in* it, and by extending the scope of that claim beyond the changes to human actors?

Addressing Dualism Differently. Given the difficulties of getting beyond Western philosophical dualisms encountered by proponents of third options, I suggest we need additional methods of thinking about dichotomies, specifically, methods that actually live and work *with* them to arrive at third options. It behooves Deweyan feminists to consider the possibility that dichotomies ought not be busted or tunneled under or resolved or healed but rather *lived inside* and accepted as formative. That is, rather than trying to make these pervasive features of our world and our interactions in it "go away," we could choose rather to go inside them so as to acknowledge, and, perhaps, work with their power rather than continuing to attempt to neutralize it.

Earlier, I suggested that Dewey's standard method of addressing dichotomies—as represented by *The Quest for Certainty,* for example—was to conduct historical anthropology to explain how and why the dichotomy emerged and then to show how the seemingly intractable division could be eliminated. One technique Dewey frequently employs is to show that one side of the dualism is really a version or feature of the other side. Theory and practice, for instance, are two forms of practice, and mind is an emergent property of (some) bodies. In her quest for a third option, Haraway, similarly, acknowledges the long history of these dualisms in Western thought and similarly works to dissolve, heal, solve, or otherwise disappear them.

I have come to believe that part of the difficulty encountered by proponents of third options is (paradoxically?) their refusal to acknowledge the persistence, the durability, the attractiveness, and the usefulness *of* any given dichotomy and of dichotomous thinking more generally. Rather than fighting against their power, might there be merit in accepting their historic pervasiveness and living with them, not in a quietistic sense but in a transformative way?

The motivation for this suggestion comes from Michel Serres, whose work *The Parasite* undertakes the rather grandiose task of rethinking all dichotomies in Western philosophy, of reconceiving them as parasitic relationships in which each side of a dichotomy ekes out its identity, and really its existence, by chomping into the other side. Each side of the dualism is and has meaning because of its relation to the other. Drawing on a specifically French meaning of the term "parasite," as static or interference, Serres notes that, not only do the two sides of a dichotomy exist to eat into each other but also their parasitic relationship produces a third thing: noise, or residual stuff that does not fit into either side of the dualism. In other words, every dualism is always already not-just-two. This third body of stuff may be just chaotic noise from the vantage point of the dualism; experienced from another vantage point, it is information, a new direction.

How could this concept of the parasite resist dichotomy in a different way by *not* resisting it? Given the vitality, durability, and prevalence of dichotomous thinking in Western thought, perhaps we need to become, in a sense, more sympathetic to the selves that find themselves (ourselves) engaging in dichotomizing. Rather than showing the misguidedness of dichotomy and the resultant problems with it (a practice in which Dewey engages with skill), what might be achieved by experiencing and *noticing* the particular nature of its power? The suggestion is almost as much psychological as philosophical.[6]

Serres' parasite challenges the tendencies for dichotomies to oversimplify and decontextualize relationships. It also challenges the quest for pure concepts and the tendency toward "us/them" thinking. So far, this sounds like what Dewey and any self-respecting third option feminist would say. However, notably, Serres does *not* deny our *propensity* to dichotomize; indeed, he places this propensity at the heart of relationships. But he also reconceptualizes that propensity by observing that the two poles of the traditional dichotomy are in fact not the independent entities they are presented as being. Nor are they *inter*dependent in an always mutually supportive way. No; as the parasitic relationships that form much of the fabric of our natural world remind us, one member of the relationship is always needy, and needy *at a cost* to the other.[7] Nothing is really isolated.

This parasitic reformulation of dualism draws attention to the between-ness. For Serres, "The position of the parasite is to be between. That is why it must be said to be a being *or* a relation" (2007, 230)—a relationship that always already is "noisy." Perhaps a third option emerges from paying more attention to the "eating-in" relationships, which coexist uneasily with their ever-present noise, which threatens always to become the primary source of information.

The relevance to Dewey of this suggestion might come into focus if we recall the exchange between Dewey and Addams quoted earlier. Dewey later wrote to his wife, "I can [sense] that I have always been interpreting the Hegelian dialectic wrong end up—the unity as the reconciliation of opposites, instead of the opposites as the unity in its growth" (as cited in Menand 2001, 313). What can we learn—or, better, how can we grow—if we experience the growth Dewey describes here as a *parasitic* relation between opposites? This question has guided my recent research. In a set of unpublished papers, I explore the claim that, if we take parasitism to be metaphysically relevant and instructive, we will, in turn, be moved to reshape the dualism between self and other. The parasite calls us to refabricate models of personhood that rest on any tidy version of this division. This, in turn, requires us to reconstruct models of *healthy* personhood. Drawing on recent work to redefine the biological individual in ways that acknowledge the individual's dependence on its resident microbes, I argue that our conception of personhood—and of *healthy* personhood—must acknowledge and absorb the degree to which it's "chomping all the way down"—that is, the degree to which *my* personhood is a complex set of eating-in relationships, any of which can come in and out of balance at various points in the life cycle. I ask, "What if parasitism were the basal relationship, in terms of which we understand what it is to *be?*" (Heldke 2016). Rather than the thing to be explained *away,* what if it—this troublesome, sometimes life-threatening life form—were the thing *in terms of which* we explained? For me, the parasite is an ontological wakeup call to notice an elemental feature of our lived reality: the pervasiveness of eating and being-eaten-into relationships, and the instability, messiness, and unbracketable connectedness of those relationships. In the spirit of Dewey, who was brought to realize "opposites as the unity in [the dialectic's] growth," I suggest taking the parasite seriously.

CONCLUSION

As a remarkably prolific writer with diverse and evolving interests, Dewey published full-length philosophical works in virtually every major field of Western philosophy, from logic to aesthetics, epistemology to philosophy of religion. In this chapter I have sketched some of the main strands of pragmatist feminist research that have drawn insight from Dewey, including work in philosophy of education, social and political philosophy, and epistemology. Dewey was not a feminist theorist; he did not develop theories of women's subordination and liberation. He does, however, offer theoretical tools with which to advance feminist projects. In particular, his work is valuable for feminists seeking to ground theories of oppression and liberation in an ontological-epistemological third option that resists both relativism and foundationalism.

NOTES

1. For an effort to build a conception of power into Dewey's account, for the purpose of developing an "epistemology of the South" grounded in the question "How does this knowledge affect the condition of the oppressed?" see Nunes (2009). Nunes brings pragmatists such as Dewey and feminists such as Donna Haraway and Karen Barad in conversation with Boaventura de Sousa Santos to develop the latter's conception of an "epistemology of

the South," an ecology of knowledge that begins with "the world and experiences of the oppressed as a place of departure and arrival for another conception of what counts as knowledge" (Nunes 2009, par. 47).

2. At the same time, I use Jane Addams to caution against swinging the pendulum too far in the direction of a romanticized view of the role of the home as the most important tool for democracy, one that can be carried on in isolation from the public work of democracy (Heldke 2012).

3. Some pragmatist feminists have suggested that it is inappropriate to describe Dewey's theory of inquiry as an epistemology, because his understanding of the relationship between facts and values stands in such stark contrast to, for example, contemporary analytic epistemology that employing the term is more confusing than clarifying. (See, e.g., Seigfried 1996.)

4. In naming liberation as a goal of philosophy, I invoke a concept at the heart of feminist and other avowedly liberatory philosophies. But this term "liberate" also has a home in Dewey. In a paper on the value of a liberal arts college, Dewey suggests that we put at our disposal all forms of human inquiry (including the vocational) to "appraise the needs and issues of the world in which we live," an exercise that would be "liberating" "because it would do for the contemporary world what those [original 'liberal'] arts tried to do for the world in which they took form" (1944 LW 15:280).

5. Another feminist theorist who has undertaken a similar kind of work is Karen Barad, who uses the work of physicist Niels Bohr to develop a position she calls "agential realism." The book in which she develops the position is teasingly called *Meeting the Universe Halfway* (2007).

6. In a comment on an earlier draft of the essay, Steven Fesmire notes, "I'm reminded of the Buddhist approach: you embrace [i.e., understand and embrace contingency] in order to let go [i.e., let go of reactive habits, as they often give bad advice]."

7. An astonishing percentage of life forms have at least one stage of their lives that may be called parasitic. Furthermore, in response to those who would suggest that I mean something more benign or bucolic, like symbiosis, I would observe that the dividing line between relationships in which one party benefits at the expense of the other, and those in which neither party is harmed, is anything but clear and constant. Many so-called mutualistic relationships are not at all without cost to one or both organisms involved. Because I want to draw attention to the "at a cost" aspect of these relationships, I thus choose to use Serres's word "parasite."

WORKS CITED

Citations of John Dewey's works are to the thirty-seven-volume critical edition published by Southern Illinois University Press under the editorship of Jo Ann Boydston. In-text citations give the original publication date and series abbreviation, followed by volume number and page number. For example: (1934, LW 10:12) is page 12 of *Art as Experience*, which is published as volume 10 of *The Later Works*.

Series abbreviations for *The Collected Works*:

EW *The Early Works* (1882–98)

MW *The Middle Works* (1899–1924)

LW *The Later Works* (1925–53)

Barad, Karen. 2007. *Meeting the Universe Halfway: Quantum Physics and the Entanglement of Matter and Meaning*. Durham, NC: Duke University Press.

Curry, Tommy. 2011. "De-radicalization of Racism: How and Why Philosophy Under-Specializes the Development of (Critical) Race Theory." *Racism Review: Scholarship and Activism Toward Racial Justice*. http://www.racismreview.com/blog/2011/11/20/de-radicalization-of-racism-how-and-why-philosophy-under-specializes-the-development-of-critical-race-theory/

Dewey, Jane. 1939. "Biography of John Dewey." In *The Philosophy of John Dewey*. Edited by Paul Arthur Schilpp and Lewis Edwin Hahn, 1–46. Chicago: Open Court.

Dewey, John. 1919. *Democracy and Education*. MW 9.

Dewey, John. 1929. *The Quest for Certainty*. LW 4.

Dewey, John. 1935. *Liberalism and Social Action*. LW 11.

Dewey, John. 1938. *Logic: The Theory of Inquiry*. LW 12.

Dewey, John. 1944. "The Problem of the Liberal Arts College." LW 15: 276–280.

Fesmire, Steven. 2015. *Dewey*. New York: Routledge.

Glaude, Eddie. 2007. *In a Shade of Blue: Pragmatism and the Politics of Black America*. Chicago: University of Chicago Press.

Grebowicz, Margret, and Helen Merrick. 2013. *Beyond the Cyborg: Adventures with Donna Haraway*. New York: Columbia University Press.

Green, Judith. 1999. *Deep Democracy: Community, Diversity, and Transformation*. Lanham, MD: Rowman & Littlefield.

Hamington, Maurice. 2014. "Jane Addams." In *The Stanford Encyclopedia of Philosophy*. Edited by Edward N. Zalta. http://plato.stanford.edu/archives/fall2014/entries/addams-jane/

Haraway, Donna. 1991. "A Cyborg Manifesto: Science, Technology, and Socialist-Feminism in the Late Twentieth Century." In *Simians, Cyborgs and Women: The Reinvention of Nature*. Edited by Donna Haraway, 149–181. New York; Routledge.

Haraway, Donna. 2003. *The Companion Species Manifesto: Dogs, People, and Significant Otherness*. Chicago: Prickly Paradigm Press.

Heldke, Lisa. 1989. "Foundationalism and Relativism: The Issue for Feminism." *APA Newsletter on Feminism and Philosophy*, vol. 88, no. 2, 39–42.

Heldke, Lisa. 1992. "Foodmaking as a Thoughtful Practice." In *Cooking, Eating, Thinking: Transformative Philosophies of Food*. Edited by Deane Curtin and Lisa Heldke, 203–229. Bloomington: Indiana University Press.

Heldke, Lisa. 2002. "How Practical is John Dewey?" In *Feminist Interpretations of John Dewey*. Edited by Charlene Haddock Seigfried, 239–259. University Park: Penn State University Press.

Heldke, Lisa. 2012. "Community Gardeners or Radical Homemakers?" In *Contemporary Feminist Pragmatism*. Edited by Celia Bardwell-Jones and Maurice Hamington. New York: Routledge.

Heldke, Lisa. 2016. "It's Chomping All the Way Down: Guts, Dirt, and Fundamental(ish) Metaphysical Categories." Unpublished manuscript.

Hewitt, Randy. 2007. *Dewey and Power: Renewing the Democratic Faith*. Rotterdam: Sense Publishers.

Hildreth, R. W. 2009. "Reconstructing Dewey on Power." *Political Theory*, vol. 37, no. 6, 780–807.

James, V. Denise. 2009. "Theorizing Black Feminist Pragmatism: Forethoughts on the Practice and Purpose of Philosophy as Envisioned by Black Feminists and John Dewey." *Journal of Speculative Philosophy*, vol. 23, no. 2, 92–99.

Magada-Ward, Mary. 2014. "Why Pragmatists Should Not Be Cyborgs." *Journal of Speculative Philosophy*, vol. 28, no. 4, 472–488.

Maher, Frances. 2001. "John Dewey, Progressive Education, and Feminist Pedagogies: Issues in Gender and Authority." In *Feminist Engagements: Reading, Resisting, and Revisioning Male Theorists in Education and Cultural Studies*. Edited by Katherine Weiller, 13–32. New York: Routledge.

Martin, Jane Roland. 1994. *Changing the Educational Landscape: Philosophy, Women and Curriculum*. New York: Routledge.

Martínez Alemán, Ana M. 2002. "Identity, Feminist Teaching and John Dewey." In *Feminist interpretations of John Dewey*. Edited by C. H. Seigfried, 113–132. University Park: Pennsylvania State University Press.

Menand, Louis. 2001. *The Metaphysical Club*. New York: Farrar, Straus and Giroux.

McKenna, Erin. 2001. *The Task of Utopia*. Lanham, Md: Rowman and Littlefield.

Minnich, Elizabeth. 2002. "Philosophy, Education and Aspirational Democracy." In *Feminist Interpretations of John Dewey*. Edited by Charlene Haddock Seigfried, 95–110. University Park: Pennsylvania State University Press.

Nelson, Lynn Hankinson. 1990. *Who Knows: From Quine to a Feminist Empiricism*. Philadelphia: Temple University Press.

Noddings, Nel. 2012. *Philosophy of Education*. 2nd ed. Boulder, CO: Westview Press.

Nunes, Joao Arriscado. 2009. "Rescuing Epistemology." Translated by Karen Bennett. *RCCS Review*, vol. 1, no. 1. https://rccsar.revues.org/165

Rooney, Phyllis. 1993. "Feminist-Pragmatist Revisionings of Reason, Knowledge, and Philosophy." *Hypatia*, vol. 8, no. 2, 15–37.

Serres, Michel. 2007. *The Parasite*. Translated by Lawrence Schehr. Baltimore, MD: The Johns Hopkins University.

Seigfried, Charlene Haddock. 1996. *Pragmatism and Feminism: Reweaving the Social Fabric*. Chicago: University of Chicago Press.

Sullivan, Shannon. 2001. *Living Across and Through Skins*. Bloomington: Indiana University Press.

Thayer-Bacon, Barbara. 2003. "Pragmatism and Feminism as Qualified Relativism." *Studies in Philosophy and Education*, vol. 22, no. 6, 417–438.

Tiles, J. E. 1988. *Dewey*. New York: Routledge.

Warren, Karen, and Alison Rheingold. 1993. "Feminist Pedagogy and Experiential Education: A Critical Look." *Journal of Experiential Education*, vol. 16, 25–31.

Whipps, Judy, and Lake, Danielle. 2016. "Pragmatist Feminism." In *The Stanford Encyclopedia of Philosophy*. Edited by Edward N. Zalta. https://plato.stanford.edu/archives/win2016/entries/femapproach-pragmatism/

CHAPTER 14

....

DEWEY'S PRAGMATIC POLITICS

Power, Limits, and Realism About Democracy
as a Way of Life

....

JOHN J. STUHR

IMPERMANENT PRAGMATISM

....

MORE than a century ago, John Dewey wrote: "If changing conduct and expanding knowledge ever required a willingness to surrender not merely old solutions but old problems it is now" (1917, MW 10:4). For pragmatists like Dewey, time and change are real. Continents move, tectonic plates grind, and mountains rise up and are worn down. Species arise, evolve, migrate, and disappear. Languages and tools, dwellings and fashions, modes of transportation and forms of communication, and all the ways of making daily life are endlessly reconstructed, revised, revolutionized, replaced. Hatreds and loves, fears and hopes, indifferences and fascinations, and frustrations and satisfactions come and go—so too problems and solutions, even philosophical problems and philosophical solutions. And, of course, individual persons are born, live relatively shorter or longer lives, and die—passing in and out of existence, really passing away, not to return here and not to show up somehow the same someplace else. Things are contingent, unstable, temporal, and, thus, temporary. The only thing permanent, for pragmatists, is impermanence.

This means that temporality and change are not marks of mere appearance or only some foreground for an eternal background Being. They are not ephemeral instantiations or through-a-glass-darkly shadows of supposedly more real, fully real, transcendent Forms or some unseen, unexperienced in-itself world. They are not features of some dreamy or nightmarish prelude or journey to some supposed eternal salvation or unending damnation, some union or reunion with the really real. And they are not measures of the fixed limits or failings of human reason, knowledge, language, and imagination in the face of some earnestly posited and often ineffable Absolute.

Rather, for pragmatists, it is the notion of absolute, unchanging permanence that honest reflection on experience and nature shows to be an illusion. Of course, sometimes and for some persons and cultures, commitment to an eternal self-same is a comforting and genuinely consoling illusion—Dewey called it "the quest for certainty" and philosophy's "search for the immutable" (1929, LW 4:3–39). Beliefs in the eternal, the permanent, the unchanging, and the absolute proclaim in theory what has only been to a very small degree established in practice—namely, power and control sufficient to direct more and more regularly and successfully the flux of life in accordance with wills and desires (if frequently contested wills and desires).[1]

Dewey made this point over and over—perhaps an appropriate exercise for a philosopher who titled a 1930 autobiographical essay "From Absolutism to Experimentalism." The following are just three examples. First, in his "The Influence of Darwinism on Philosophy," Dewey listed three revisions made possible and demanded by a philosophy that takes seriously time and change and transfers "interest from the permanent to the changing" (1909, MW 4:7). He wrote that "in the first place, the new [Darwinian] logic outlaws, flanks, dismisses—what you will—one type of problem and substitutes for it another type. Philosophy foreswears inquiry after absolute origins and absolute finalities in order to explore specific values and the specific conditions that generate them" (1909, MW 4:10). In the second place, it looks "the facts of experience in the face" by turning away from any "wholesale transcendent remedy" for present evils and all cosmic guarantees of future fulfillment for goods now unrealized. Instead of all this futility, Dewey claimed that experience demonstrates "that knowable energies are daily generating about us precious values," and he concluded "to improve our education, to advance our politics, we must have recourse to specific conditions of generation" (1909, MW 4:12). Finally, Dewey concluded, a "genetic and experimental" philosophy of change and time, evolution and impermanence, finitude and particularity "introduces responsibility into the intellectual life: "[I]f insight into specific conditions of value and into specific consequences of ideas is possible, philosophy must in time become a method of locating and interpreting the more serious of the conflicts that occur in life, and a method of projecting ways for dealing with them: a method of moral and political diagnosis and prognosis. . . . In having modesty forced upon it, philosophy also acquires responsibility" (1909, MW 4:13).

As a second example, this same theme is everywhere evident in *Experience and Nature*. In fact, it can be found on almost every page of this book. Explaining why ancient Greek and modern European philosophers failed to take time and change centrally and seriously while also noting that post-Darwinian science presents "us with an immense amount of material foreign to, often inconsistent with, the most prized intellectual and moral heritage of the western world," Dewey observed:

> If classic philosophy says so much about unity and so little about unreconciled diversity, so much about the eternal and permanent, and so little about change (save

as something to be resolved into combinations of the permanent), so much about necessity and so little about contingency, so much about comprehending the universal and so little about the recalcitrant particular, it may well be because the ambiguous and ambivalence of reality are actually so pervasive. Since these things form the problem, the solution is more apparent (although not more actual), in the degree in which whatever of stability and assurance the world presents is fastened upon and asserted.

(1925, LW 5:46)

Some twenty pages later, Dewey again stressed that things are not permanent, stable, unchanging, or self-sufficient. Everything is in process and in relation, every "thing" is an event, and all events are irreducibly temporal. Dewey wrote:

Anything that can exist at any place and at any time occurs subject to tests imposed upon it by surroundings, which are only in part compatible and reinforcing. These surroundings test its strength and measure its endurance. As we can discourse of change only in terms of velocity and acceleration which involve relations to other things, so assertion of the permanent and enduring is comparative. The stablest thing we can speak of is not free from conditions set to it by other things. ... The fixed and unchanged being of the Democritean atom is now reported by inquirers to possess some of the traits of his non-being, and to embody a temporary equilibrium in the economy of nature's compromises and adjustments. A thing may endure *secula seculorum* and not be everlasting; it will crumble before the gnawing tooth of time, as it exceeds a certain measure. Every existence is an event.

(192, LW 1:63)

As a third and final example, consider the final section of Dewey's 1917 essay, "The Need for a Recovery in Philosophy" (reprinted in the 1945 *Creative Intelligence: Essays in the Pragmatic Attitude*). Dewey concluded that philosophy "must take, with good grace, its own medicine" and commit itself to a new task consistent with changing realities of experience: "Philosophy will have to surrender all pretension to be peculiarly concerned with ultimate reality, or with reality as a complete (i.e., completed) whole." He added: "Speaking summarily, I find that the retention by philosophy of the notion of a Reality feudally superior to the events of everyday occurrence is the chief source of the increasing isolation of philosophy from common sense and science ... philosophy in dealing with real difficulties finds itself hampered by reference to realities more real, more ultimate, than those which directly happen" (1917, MW 10:38–39)

A part of the point in these passages and throughout so much of Dewey's philosophy is that, because the world changes, ideas and habits formed under conditions no longer in existence must be remade and brought into line with current realities. This is especially important when the world not only changes but changes very rapidly. When change is rapid, ideas and habits must be reconstructed more fully and more frequently. Inquiries and problems, methods and explanations, and ideas and ideals must be grasped as temporal and anything but static or fixed. They arise and are deepened, expanded, maintained, revised, reframed, rejected, and abandoned. This holds for whole philosophies. It is why Dewey thought that it is not possible to hold Plato's view of human nature after Darwin, Aristotle's physics after Bohr and Einstein, John Locke's psychology after William James, or the flat earth cosmography displayed on the shield of Achilles after Galileo and Copernicus. And it is why we today should not expect that the philosophers we believe most illuminate yesterday and today can, will, or should recognize in full, much less resolve in full, tomorrow's problems.

Now I have stressed this Deweyan point because it is highly important that pragmatists keep it in mind not only when they consider philosophies and philosophers *prior to* pragmatism (or instrumentalism) and John Dewey; they must also keep it squarely in mind when they consider how the world, including our knowledge of the world, has changed in the many decades since Dewey passed away—how the world has changed *after* Dewey's pragmatism. If philosophers in general with good grace must take their own medicine, surely pragmatic philosophers must do so. This means that pragmatists must not take Dewey's philosophy as a compendium of eternal fixed truths, a philosophy independent from, and immune to, time. It means they must be alert to changes in the world, including our knowledge of it, that necessitate revision or reconstruction or even abandonment of some of Dewey's philosophy. And it means that they must consider seriously what, on one hand, has passed away and should be surrendered and what, on the other hand, still lives in Dewey's philosophy, its problems, and its solutions.

To do anything else is to miss much of the heart and spirit of Dewey's thought: the reality of impermanence and the practical importance of time and change. To fail to recognize that the world today is not Dewey's world is short-sighted and inattentive; to pretend that Dewey offered answers to problems that did not even arise in his lifetime is silly and anachronistic; to repeat in devotional tones Dewey's words as permanently established truths is tedious and nonpragmatic.

EXPERIMENTAL PRAGMATISM

As much as he held a view of reality as impermanent and changing, Dewey was committed to an experimentalist philosophy—a philosophy of, and by, experimental scientific *method*. In the opening pages of his *Logic: The Theory of Inquiry*, Dewey wrote

> The developing course of science thus presents us with an immanent criticism of methods previously tried. Earlier methods failed in some important respect. In consequence of this failure, they were modified so that more dependable results were secured. Earlier methods yielded conclusions that could not stand the strain put upon them by further investigation. It is not merely that *conclusions* were found to be inadequate or false but that they were found to be so because of methods employed. Other methods of inquiry were found to be such that persistence in them not only

produced conclusions that stood the strain of further inquiry but that tended to be self-rectifying. They were methods that improved with and by use.

(1938, LW 12:14)

Dewey's ontology of impermanence goes hand in hand with his experimentalist epistemology. Like Charles Peirce before him, Dewey believed that experience shows that experimental inquiry is the practically best method for responding to surprising facts, dealing with indeterminate situations, and arriving at warranted beliefs. Like William James also before him, Dewey was committed to a method of experiential, experimental inquiry rather than any imagined particular results in advance of the use of that method or any cherished views that fly in the face of the results of that method. Dewey offered no abstract, dialectical, or formal proof for this commitment. Rather, he thought its justification was a matter of practice: Experience bit by bit, time after time, case after case showed experimental method to be the most successful in practice. It is the most pragmatic or instrumental. Claiming that "we need to throw the emphasis on using the term "scientific" first upon methods, and then upon results through reference to methods," Dewey called this method "scientific" in the sense in which this term "means regular methods of controlling the formation of judgments" (1903, MW 3:3). He observed that in the actual "development of science, a tremendous change has come about":

> When the practice of knowledge ceased to be dialectical and became experimental, knowing became preoccupied with changes and the test of knowledge became the ability to bring about certain changes. Knowing, for experimental sciences, means a certain kind of intelligently conducted doing; it ceases to be contemplative and becomes in a true sense practical. Now this implies that philosophy, unless it is to undergo a complete break with the authorized spirit of science, must also alter its nature. It must assume a practical nature; it must become operative and experimental.
>
> (1923, MW 12:149)

For Dewey, this experimental method in a world of impermanence renders truth pragmatic. He put it this way:

> Just as to say an idea was true all the time is a way of saying *in retrospect* that it has come out in a certain fashion, so to say that an idea is 'eternally true' is to indicate *prospective* modes of application which are indefinitely anticipated. It's meaning, therefore, is strictly pragmatic. It does not indicate a property inherent in the idea as intellectualized existence, but denotes a property of use and employment. Always at hand when needed is a good enough eternal for reasonably minded persons.
>
> (1907, MW 4:71)[2]

Throughout his middle and later work, Dewey claimed that this experimental method had logic. Put differently, he claimed that logic, understood experimentally, simply is an account of the most practical, successful methods of inquiry. In his 1916 *Essays in Experimental Logic*, for example, Dewey asserted that logic is a "descriptive study," "an account of the processes and tools which have actually been found effective in inquiry, comprising in the term 'inquiry' both deliberate discovery and deliberate invention" (1916, MW 10:332).

He most fully developed this view of logic as an account of successful inquiry more than twenty years later. In *Logic: The Theory of Inquiry*, Dewey began by clarifying that his account of logic was "pragmatic" (despite the misunderstandings and "relatively futile controversy" surrounding this term). He observed: "In the proper interpretation of "pragmatic," namely the function of consequences as necessary tests of the validity of propositions, *provided* these consequences are operationally instituted and are such as to resolve the specific problem evoking the operations, the text that follows is thoroughly pragmatic" (1938, LW 12:4) He added:

> We know that some methods of inquiry are better than others in just the same way we know that some methods of surgery, farming, road-making, navigating or what-not are better than others. It does not follow in any of these cases that the "better" methods are ideally perfect, or that they are regulative or "normative" because of conformity to some absolute form. They are the methods which experience up to the present time shows to be the best methods available for achieving certain results, while abstraction of these methods does supply a (relative) norm or standard for further undertakings. ... Men think in ways they should not when they follow methods of inquiry that experience of past inquiries shows are not competent to reach the intended end of the inquiries in question.
>
> (1938, LW 12:108)

From this pragmatic, experimental perspective, Dewey defined inquiry as "*the controlled or directed transformation of an indeterminate situation into one that is so determinate in its constituent distinctions and relations as to convert the elements of the original situation into a unified whole*" (1938, LW 12:108). And he claimed that our many different inquiries in many different contexts have a common structure or pattern. This "pattern of inquiry" is thoroughly temporal and contains the following stages. First, there is a uniquely questionable, indeterminate situation—a state of affairs with outcomes that cannot be anticipated, consequences that cannot be foreseen, evoked responses that are at odds with one another, and significance that is unclear and confused. Dewey called this "the antecedent condition" of inquiry; its immediate concern is "what kind of response the organism shall make" (1938, LW 12:110–111). The second stage of inquiry is the "institution of a problem." Dewey observed: "The indeterminate situation becomes problematic in the very process of being subjected to inquiry. ... The first result of evocation of inquiry is that the situation is taken, adjudged, to be problematic. To see that a situation requires inquiry is the initial step of inquiry" (1938, LW 12:111). The third stage carries inquiry further: It is the "determination of a problem-solution." Here the determinate aspects of the indeterminate situation are noted—"no situation which is *completely* indeterminate can possibly be converted into a problem" (1938, LW 12:112)—and on this basis a possible resolution is suggested. This suggestion becomes an idea as its functional fitness is examined and assessed. This transformation of suggestions into ideas is the fourth stage of inquiry. Dewey called it "reasoning" and understood it to be the development of the meaning of an idea (within a system of meanings) that makes the idea "*relevant*" to the given problem by indicating "operations which can be performed to test its applicability" (1938, LW 12:115). Because reasoning renders operational the meaning of observed facts and the meaning of proposed ideas, it makes possible experimentation that resolves and unifies the original indeterminate situation or points to the need for further inquiry into other proposed ideas. Dewey called this the "operational character of facts-meanings" and he wrote that "ideas are operational in that they instigate and direct further operations of observation; they are proposals and plans for acting upon existing conditions to bring new facts to light and to organize all the selected facts into a coherent whole." As Dewey put it, facts "are not self-sufficient and complete in themselves." The facts that initiate and guide inquiry are "selected and described" "for a purpose, namely statement of the problem involved in such a way that its material both indicates a meaning relevant to resolution of the difficulty and serves to test its worth and validity." And, at the other end, the facts that result from experimental inquiry are, as Dewey put it, provisional or "trial facts." They may be observed, but they become facts only as their evidential function is confirmed in time by further experiment. Dewey concluded "the operative force of both ideas and facts is thus practically recognized in the degree in which they are connected with *experiment*" (1938, LW 12:116–117). The logical conditions or prerequisites of experimental inquiry, then, are (a) operationalized hypotheses concerning possible resolution of a formulated problem that (b) direct experimental observation and transformation of antecedent phenomena which (c) are continually assessed and revised on the basis of the consequences of this experimental action.

This is a crucial and far-reaching methodological point. In consequence, it means that every description or phenomenological account is the result of an act of selection, values, and purpose (whether conscious or not). It means that every fact is an operationally "taken" and not a mythical "given." And it means that traditional, now ever so tedious intramural debates between realists and anti-realists arise from presuppositions that should be rejected and a generalized problem that now should be surrendered. This is a point that Dewey stressed in his *Logic* in the context of social inquiry and social science: "Inquiry into social phenomena involves judgments of evaluation" and "even in physical inquiry, what the inquirer observes and the conceptions he entertains are controlled by an objective purpose—that of attaining a resolved situation" (1938, LW 12: 495–496). This is a methodological point Dewey stressed years earlier in "Experience and Philosophic Method," the opening chapter of *Experience and Nature*. Terming "selective emphasis" and its inclusions and exclusions "the heart-beat of mental life" and stating flatly that thinking independent of selective emphasis is impossible, Dewey wrote:

> But in philosophies, this limiting condition is often wholly ignored. It is not noted and remembered that the favored subject-matter is chosen for a purpose and that what is left out is just as real and important in its characteristic context. ... It is natural to men to take that which is of chief value to them at the time as *the* real. ... This

bias toward treating objects selected because of their value in some special context as the "real," in a superior and invidious sense, testifies to an empirical fact of importance. Philosophical simplifications are due to choice, and choice marks an interest *moral* in the broad sense of concern for what is good. ... Selective emphasis, choice, is inevitable whenever reflection occurs. This is not an evil. Deception comes only when the presence and operation of choice is concealed, disguised, denied. Empirical method finds and points to the operation of choice as it does to any other event. Thus it protects us from conversion of eventual functions into antecedent existence: a conversion that may be said to be *the* philosophic fallacy.

(1925, LW 1:31, 33, 34)

All philosophies are the result of selective emphases. Different philosophies are the result of different emphases. No philosophy, not even a philosophy that embraces experimental method, is independent of selective emphasis and choice, whether conscious or not. A philosophy that does embrace experimental method reflects a choice to attempt to formulate, investigate, and resolve problems in a particular way—a pragmatic way.

DEMOCRATIC PRAGMATISM

If Dewey's pragmatism reflects an interest moral in the broad sense of concern for what is good, that good is democracy. His commitment to experimental inquiry and his commitment to democratic culture mutually implicate one another. First, experimental inquiry and the open communication of its results require a democratic culture with democratic habits that provide persons with the freedom and conditions necessary for intelligent experimentation and the necessary protection from stifling and normalizing forces of custom, tradition and taboo, and from the many forms of authoritarian control practiced by self-interested political, economic, religious, and social elites on their own behalf. Second, commitment to democratic ways of life requires experimental method in order successfully and continually to fashion and reconstruct political institutions, practices, and policies in light of changing, impermanent cultural conditions. Experimental inquiry and democratic culture are two sides of the same coin. The "and" in Dewey's 1916 book title, *Democracy and Education*, expresses this point in the most succinct way possible. As Dewey explained in a few more words, "since democracy stands in principle for free interchange, for social continuity, it must develop a ... method by which one experience is made available in giving direction and meaning to another. The recent advances in physiology, biology, and the logic of the experimental sciences supply the specific intellectual instrumentalities demanded to work out and formulate such a theory" (1916, MW 9:355). More than twenty years later in "Democracy and Education in the World of Today," Dewey again stressed the link between democratic life and sound education. Democracy, he wrote, involves two ideas:

First, the opportunity, the right and the duty of every individual to form some conviction and to express some conviction regarding his own place in the social order,
and the relations of that social order to his own welfare; second, the fact that each individual counts as one and one only on an equality with others, so that the final social
will comes about as the cooperative expression of the ideas of many people.

(1938, LW 13:295–296)

Democracy, for Dewey, is first and foremost a way of life.[3] This idea—democracy as a
way of life—runs through almost all his political writings, including *Liberalism and
Social Action, Individualism: Old and New, Freedom and Culture*. It is given straightforward and often-quoted definition in *The Public and Its Problems*:

From the standpoint of the individual, it [the idea of democracy] consists in having
a responsible share according to capacity in forming and directing the activities of
the groups to which one belongs and in participating according to need in the values
which the groups sustain. From the standpoint of the groups, it demands liberation
of the potentialities of members of a group in harmony with the interests and goods
which are common. ... Regarded as an idea, democracy is not an alternative to other
principles of associated life. It is the idea of community life itself. ... Wherever there
is conjoint activity whose consequences are appreciated as good by all singular persons who take part in it, and where the realization of the good is such as to effect an
energetic desire and effort to sustain it in being just because it is a good shared by al,
there is in so far a community. The clear consciousness of a communal life, in all its
implications, constitutes the idea of democracy.

(1927, LW 2:327–328)

This democratic way of life—Dewey termed it "social democracy"--should not be confused with, or limited to, a democratic form of government—what Dewey called "political democracy as a system of government" (1927, LW 2:325). Regularly recurring
elections, wide suffrage, peaceful postelection transitions, majority rule, and minority
rights are, at best, the political phase of a democratic way of life. They are, Dewey wrote,
"means that have been found expedient for realizing democracy as the truly human way
of living" and they must not be considered or idolized as final ends in themselves (1937,
LW 11:218). Dewey claimed "there is no sanctity in universal suffrage, frequent elections,
majority rule, congressional and cabinet government" (1927, LW 2:326)—this claim a
suggestion that it is possible in the future that a democratic way of life may not be advanced by these practices and arrangements. Indeed, in light of changing, impermanent
cultural conditions, all "devices" of government must be understood as more or less
temporary; they must not be treated as dogmatic goods, goods independent of social
experimentation and new cultural conditions. Moreover, just as experimental methods
of inquiry must be transformed in light of the results of that inquiry, the very idea of a
democratic way of life also must be understood as temporary, incomplete, always in the
making, and never final or fixed. Dewey wrote the very idea of democracy must be "continually explored afresh" and "cannot stand still":

It has to be constantly discovered, and rediscovered, remade and reorganized; while the political and economic and social institutions in which it is embodied have to be remade and reorganized to meet the changes that are going on in the development of new needs on the part of human beings and new resources for satisfying those needs. ... It, too, if it is to live, must go forward to meet the changes that are here and that are coming. If it does not go forward, if it tries to stand still, it is already starting on the backward road that leads to its extinction.

(1937, LW 11:182)

The democratic task, in other words, is never nostalgic. It is never about making things "great again." It is always about making things greater anew. Democracy, Dewey observed, is always a shared creative task ahead (1939, LW 14:224–230).

This task, Dewey realized, is not easy because it requires faith, new kinds of inquiry and education, and the hard work of social change. In the first place, a democratic way of life requires, and includes, a democratic faith because there is no guarantee in advance of action on its behalf that it will be realized very fully—or realized at all. A democratic way of life does not have any God, chosen people, human nature, history, dialectic of history, or Enlightenment sure march of progress on its side. A democratic way of life includes no utopian promise and no cause for simple optimism. In the very same way, it provides no warrant for any general pessimism or dystopian vision. Neither present fulfillments nor present ills are fixed and necessarily permanent. In contrast, a democratic way of life includes a melioristic faith in the possibility of broader, deeper, and more meaningful democratic life. The warrant (or the lack of warrant) for this faith is a function of the consequences of actions, including ongoing reconstruction of the notion of a democratic way of life, to which this faith gives rise. It is a function of the consequences of experiment—a point at the heart of any genuinely pragmatic account of justification, knowledge, and truth. It is not a function of any philosophical foundation, communicative commitment, transcendental argument, quested-for certainty, or other clever or learned theoretical sleight of hand. In practice, faith in the real possibility of a more fully democratic way of life is one with faith in the possibilities of experimental method. Observing that "democracy is the faith that the process of experience is more important than any special result attainted, " Dewey concluded "since the process of experience is capable of being educative, faith in democracy is all one with faith in experience and education" (1939, LW 14:229). Creative democracy and creative intelligence are two sides of the same coin.

To be anything more than a mere wish or childlike fancy, this faith in the possible realization of democratic ends-in-view must include faith in the effectiveness of identified means to those ends. In the second place, this is an exceptionally strenuous, demanding faith because, as Dewey realized, a democratic way of life requires the development of new kinds of social inquiry and communication as well as a new kind of public education that effectively fosters democratic personal habits and outlooks. A democratic way of life requires that individuals participate intelligently in forming and directing the activities of groups in which their lives are bound up. But, contrary to classical liberal theory, this intelligence is not an automatic, original possession or "inherent endowment" (1935, LW 11:7) of each separate individual. It is not an antecedent of social life; it is a social product. It requires inquiry and it requires that the results of inquiry be communicated and understood. However, Dewey argued that views on social matters are not the result of experimental inquiry and that this needed social inquiry itself is in a "backward" state:

> The impact of cultural conditions upon social inquiry is obvious. Prejudices of race, nationality, class and sect play such an important role that their influence is seen by any observer of the field. . . . The evils in current social judgments of ends and policies arise, as has been said, from importations of judgments of value from outside of inquiry. The evils spring from the fact that the values employed are not determined in and by the process of inquiry: for it is assumed that certain ends have an inherent value so unquestionable that they regulate and validate the means employed, instead of ends being determined on the basis of existing conditions as obstacles-resources. . . . On the contrary, it means that ends in their capacity of values can be validly determined only on the basis of the tensions, obstructions, and positive potentialities that are found, by controlled observation, to exist in the actual situation.
>
> (1938, LW 12:482, 496–497)

Dewey argued that his backward state of experimental social inquiry is both paralleled and sustained by the absence of effective communication. He claimed that whatever limits publicity and communication "checks and distorts thinking on social affairs": "Without freedom of expression, not even methods of social inquiry can be developed" (1927, LW 2:339). In a moving passage, Dewey made clear that freedom of expression and effective communication are not ensured simply by institutions of democratic government—just as a democratic way of life more generally is not ensured simply by democratic government. Asserting that "a belief in intellectual freedom where it does not exist contributes only to complacency in virtual enslavement, to sloppiness, superficiality and recourse to sensations as a substitute for ideas: marked traits of our present estate with respect to social knowledge," Dewey continued:

> The belief that thought and its communication are now free simply because legal restrictions which once obtained have been done away with is absurd. Its currency perpetuates the infantile state of social knowledge . . . No man and no mind was ever emancipated merely by being left alone . . . the physical agencies of publicity which exist in such abundance are utilized in ways which constitute a large part of the present meaning of publicity: advertising, propaganda, invasion of private life, the "featuring" of passing incidence in a way that violates all the moving logic of continuity, and which leaves us with those isolated intrusions and shocks which are the essence of 'sensations'. . . . It is true that those who have the ability to manipulate social relations for their own advantage have to be reckoned with. They have an uncanny instinct for detecting whatever intellectual tendencies even remotely threaten

to encroach upon their control. . . . We seem to be approaching a state of government by hired promoters of opinion called publicity agents.

(1927, LW 2:340–341)

These extra-governmental limits and distortions of the inquiry and communication central to a democratic way of life also are both caused and produced by what Dewey termed the "hidden entrenchments" of emotional and intellectual habits of individuals. This point, put differently, is that societies that are not significantly democratic create and are sustained by individual habits that are not democratic—habits that await easy manipulation by powerful forces and their self-interests. At base, Dewey argued, these habits constitute a fear of the use of experimental method in human concerns and societal matters. Arguing that this fear is rationalized in all kinds of ways, Dewey concluded that these (frequently unconscious) fear-driven habits amount to a "social pathology" that "leads to withdrawal from reality and to unwillingness to think things through":

> [It] works powerfully against effective inquiry into social institutions and conditions. It manifests itself in a thousand ways: in querulousness, in impotent drifting, in uneasy snatching at distractions, in idealization of the long established, in a facile optimism assumed as a cloak, in riotous glorification of things 'as they are,' in intimidation of all dissenters—ways which depress and dissipate thought all the more effectually because they operate with subtle and unconscious pervasiveness. . . . But the evil does not stop there. The ultimate harm is that the understanding by man of his own affairs and his ability to direct them are sapped at their root.
>
> (1927, LW 2:341–342, 345).

And because Dewey believed that this point about inquiry applies equally to communication—because he believed that what has been said about the formation of ideas and judgments concerning the public apply as well to the distribution of the knowledge which makes it an effective possession of members of the public—he recognized that a democratic way of life demands both "the highest and most difficult kind of inquiry and a subtle, delicate, vivid and responsive art of communication" (1927, LW 2:349, 350).

This is not simply a matter of public institutions. It is a personal way of life—a matter of individual attitude, feeling, outlook, orientation, values, inquiries, beliefs, and action. Dewey observed that powerful enemies of democracy "can be successfully met only by the creation of personal attitudes in individual human beings" and not merely by "external means, whether military or civil." He continued:

> Democracy as a way of life controlled by a working faith in the possibilities of human nature . . . may be enacted in statutes, but it is only on paper unless it is put in force in the attitudes which human beings display to one another in all the incidents and

relations of daily life. . . . For what is the faith of democracy in the role of consultation, of conference, of persuasion, of discussion, in formation of public opinion, which in the long run is self-corrective, except faith in the capacity of the intelligence of the common man to respond with commonsense to the free play of facts and ideas which are secure by effective communication?

(1939, LW 14:226–227).

This faith, Dewey added in opposition to both right and left totalitarian regimes, is not utopian. That noted, Dewey recognized obstacles to the development of democratic personal habits. Chief among these obstacles, Dewey argued, is a kind of private capitalism buoyed by a long-outdated conception of rugged individualism which, in turn, "defines industry and commerce by ideas of private pecuniary profit." Dewey put it this way: "The virtues that are supposed to attend rugged individualism may be vocally proclaimed, but it takes no great insight to see that what is cherished is measured by its connection with those activities that make for success in business conducted for private gain" (1935, LW: 14:3).

Anti-democratic habits of individuals are the result of anti-democratic education. A democratic way of life requires a democratic conception of education—and institutions, practices, and policies that serve and advance this conception. Dewey stated this conception clearly, noting that in every social group there is some common interest and some interaction with other groups. "From these two traits," he argued, "we derive our standard": "How numerous and varied are the interests which are consciously shared? How full and free is the interplay with other forms of association" (1916, MW 9:89)? These criteria point to democracy:

> The first signifies not only more numerous and more varied points of shared common interest, but greater reliance upon the recognition of mutual interests as a factor of social control. The second means not only freer interactions between social groups (once isolated so far as intention could keep up a separation) but change in social habit—its continuous readjustment through meeting the new situations produced by varied intercourse. And these two traits are precisely what characterize the democratically constituted society.

(1916, MW 9:92)

Dewey concluded soberly this ideal of education, like the larger ideal of a democratic way of life, "may seem remote of execution, but the democratic ideal of education is a farcical yet tragic delusion except as the ideal more and more dominates our public system of education" (1916, MW 9:104).

Of course, if an ideal of democracy is to "dominate" public education and public life, this domination must be practical rather than only theoretical, must be enacted rather than merely conceptual. It requires social change—change in institutions, policies, practices, and associations. It requires a critical assessment of social groups in terms of democratic criteria. These are tough questions. What gap between rich and poor best advances a democratic way of life? What form of government most provides individuals with a responsible role in forming and directing the activities that impact their lives? What childcare, education, health, crime, and pension policies most fully address the needs and suffering of vulnerable members of a community? What social arrangements best ensure that each individual equally counts as one and only one? What societal changes would most fully eliminate the feelings, beliefs, and actions that undermine this equality—including (but not limited to) racism, sexism, classism, ageism, ableism, and discrimination based on sexual preference, ethnic background or family nationality, and religious belief? What is a genuinely democratic response to world climate change and to human transactions with the natural world? To what policy does a democratic way of life policy point concerning a nation's nuclear weapons or international proliferation of nuclear weapons?

As Dewey observed, effective answers to these questions in part depend on "a kind of knowledge and insight which does not yet exist." He added "In its absence, it would be the height of absurdity to try to tell what it would be like if it existed" (1927, LW 2:339) and, in a different context, cautioned "I do not see how it can be described until more progress has been made in its production" (1935, LW 14:3). The scope of cultural change required for a significantly more fully democratic way of life is immense. It is not difficult to grasp how the immense task of creative democracy can produce the "social pathology" of a "facile optimism" or an equally facile pessimism—a "riotous glorification" or a riotous denouncement of, or resignation to, things as they are.

PRAGMATISM FOR REALISTS

In this account, I have sought to sketch John Dewey's philosophy in three intimately interconnected but distinguishable movements of *impermanence, experimental inquiry,* and *democracy*: An *ontology* of time and change, impermanence and flux, finitude and relativity, and dynamism and process; a descriptive *method* or *logic* of experimental inquiry, scientific method, selective emphasis, and consequence-based assessment of operational hypotheses; and a democratic *politics* of individuals having opportunities to share equally in the direction of community decisions and activities that impact their lives, a politics of communities providing individuals resources needed for their fulfillment consonant with shared goods. It is by means of just this ontology, this logic, and this politics that Dewey sought to recover philosophy from old solutions and problems that, he thought, should be surrendered.

At the close of "The Need for a Recovery of Philosophy," Dewey claimed "we pride ourselves upon being realistic." He continued:

> We thus tend to combine a loose and ineffective optimism with assent to the doctrine of take who take can: a deification of power. All peoples at all times have been narrowly realistic in practice and have then employed idealization to cover

up in sentiment and theory their brutalities. But never, perhaps, has the tendency been so dangerous and so tempting as with ourselves. Faith in the power of intelligence to imagine a future which is the projection of the desirable in the present, and to invent the instrumentalities of its realization, is our salvation. And it is a faith which must be nurtured and made articulate: surely a sufficiently large task for our philosophy.

(1917, MW 10:48)

Today, more than a century after Dewey wrote these words, is this faith in intelligent experimental inquiry and democracy as a way of life in a world of impermanence a faith that should be embraced or surrendered? This is *the* pragmatic question *about* Dewey's pragmatism. And, if this faith is to be embraced, how does it avoid being just another idealization that covers up in theory myriad brutalities in practice? How is it possible without brutality to identify and project what is deemed desirable in the present? How is it possible without brutality to invent and deploy instrumentalities for the realization of these ideals? Is the notion of a temporal, experimental, democratic salvation realistically valuable without being narrowly realistic?

There are three points that press for consideration here—three large points at which Dewey's philosophy needs further articulation. The first point concerns experimental inquiry.[4] Now, Dewey correctly recognized that experimental inquiry is the source of the standard by which it is evaluated. The assessment of any method of inquiry is made on a basis furnished by that very same method of inquiry. Because experimental inquiry, in Dewey's account is an exercise of power—a "making of *some* change in environing conditions" (1938, LW 12:41), "a controlled or directed transformation of an indeterminate situation" (1938, LW 12:108), and a "control effected through acts" (1916, MW 10:338)—it is marked by selective interest, by some selective interest or other. It is surprising that Dewey never discussed the selective interests that guide his account of inquiry. Perhaps they are interests in a democratic way of life. I suspect this is the case, but, as Dewey says about all selective interest, it needs to be acknowledged rather than ignored or concealed—particularly because Dewey at times seems almost to suggest that his account of inquiry is not the product of any selective interest but instead is advanced "inclusively and exclusively upon the operations of inquiry itself" (1938, LW 12:527).

This point has far-reaching consequences in concrete cases. First, it means that different persons with different background beliefs, traditions, and selective emphases likely will experience multiple different indeterminate situations rather than the single one that Dewey identifies as the prerequisite or first stage in his pattern of inquiry. Second, it means that persons with different background selective interests likely will formulate problems in different ways rather than as a single, shared "determinate" problem, the next step in Dewey's pattern of inquiry. Whose interests are served by identifying an indeterminate situation in one way rather than another? Whose interests are served by formulating a problem in one way rather than another? What are the consequences of formulating, funding, or pursuing problems for experimental inquiry in the way some, rather than other, people do? When it is recognized that any particular actual inquiry has an irreducibly exclusionary dimension, how might democratic cultures nurture and recognize different, at times contested, experiences of indeterminate situations, problem formulations, and experimental transformations and the interests that sustain them? The group "interests and goods" that Dewey labeled "common" in the idea of democracy must be pluralistic rather than universal. As Reinhold Niebuhr observed: "By recognizing that men will remain selfish to the end we will be saved from the errors of both a liberalism which wants to achieve political ends by purely ethical means and a radicalism which hopes to achieve ethical ends by purely political means."[5]

The second point that merits additional thinking concerns the means to a democratic way of life. This is especially important in light of the massive gap or distance between the desired effects of democratic means and their actual outcome in social life. Dewey famously claimed that democratic ends require democratic means and observed: "If there is one conclusion to which human experience unmistakably points, it is that democratic ends require democratic methods for realization" (1939, LW 13:187). Understood in one context, this point is both very important and correct: Anti-democratic regimes cannot produce democratic ways of life. Dewey's 1939 warning rings true, perhaps even truer, in the present millennium:

> The progress of natural science has been even more rapid and extensive than could have been anticipated. But its technological application in mass production and distribution of goods has required concentration of capital; it has resulted in business corporations possessed of extensive legal rights and immunities; and, as is commonplace, has created a vast and intricate set of new problems. It has put at the disposal of dictators means of controlling opinion and sentiment of a potency which reduces to a mere shadow all previous agencies at the command of despotic rulers. For negative censorship it has substituted means of propaganda of ideas and alleged information on a scale that reaches every individual, reiterated day after day by every organ of publicity and communication, old and new. In consequence, for practically the first time in human history, totalitarian states exist claiming to rest upon the active consent of the governed.
>
> (1939, LW 13:156)

This point holds from Nazi propaganda and Maoist era "thought reform" to the Koch Industries political action committee and President Trump's web of "alternative facts" and "fake news."

Understood in another context, however, this point that democratic ends require democratic means is mistaken. Democratic means may be *necessary* for democratic ends, but frequently democratic means are not *sufficient* for democratic ends. Dewey recognized this fact when he supported US involvement in World War I. It was this recognition that led Randolph Bourne to declare that Dewey's philosophy had shown itself to be without any practical application, a fair-weather philosophy that is absolutely impotent in dealing with persons who do not already share its values, an illiberal and undemocratic mouthpiece of liberalism and democracy.[6] Sounding a different tone, some thirty years later, Dewey observed "our first defense is to realize that democracy can be served only by the slow day by day adoption and contagious diffusion in every phase of our common life of methods that are identical with the ends to be reached and that recourse to monistic, wholesale, absolutist procedures is a betrayal of human freedom, no matter in what guise it presents itself" (1939, LW 13:187). This is a pleasant thought, but there is little evidence that it is accurate. In the face of ethnic cleansing, genocide, terrorism, war, and the relentless authoritarian manipulation of feelings and beliefs, intelligence and experimental method alone have proven insufficient. No criticism of pragmatic theory can ring louder than evidence that the theory is not pragmatic in practice. Experimental inquiry is an instrument that, like all instruments, has finite and limited uses. In situations where it fails, it is imperative that genuinely democratic societies invent other effective means to preserve and advance their ideals. And it is imperative that they specify both the reach and the limits of those other means in specific contexts. The preferred ends do not justify any means; so too the preferred ends may not lead to preferred ends. It is easy to state this task and vexingly difficult to address it: How to create democratic personal habits and loyalties while effectively combatting war and terrorism and violence and abuse, anti-democratic institutions, concentrations of power and wealth, manipulative media, and manufactured helplessness? This is a task that Dewey did not much take up, much less complete, and it is an urgent research agenda item for any realistic pragmatism after Dewey.

Finally, the third point that presses for further articulation and action concerns the gap between Dewey's democratic ideals and the realities of social life. In the face of this gap—or multiple gaps—there are two possible general responses. One may affirm the ideals and claim that there is much work and change needed to bring realities closer to those ideals. This consistently was Dewey's strategy. When confronted with old notions of liberalism and individualism, anti-egalitarian forms of nationalism and imperialism, world wars, the limits of organized religion and museums and schools, tragedies and evils, powerful concentrations of economic capital, political power, and media might, Dewey explained how all these things needed to be reconstructed and transformed to bring them into line with his vision of a democratic way of life. The present unreality of democracy as a way of life was, for Dewey, a measure of work to be done and redone and a sign of the need to think long term. It was never a sign that ongoing great realization of the ideal itself simply is not realistically (as opposed to merely logically) possible. The ideal—democracy as a way of life—was a matter of faith.

A second, very different response also is possible. One may accept in largest contours present realities and claim that ideals that seem thoroughly out of touch with these realities are not realistic ideals but only folk theory, happy fictions, and beliefs that have taken on a supernatural quality. This is the strategy of self-branded realist critics of Dewey's political philosophy. When confronted by the fact that there is not and never has been a single nation (much less a single kingdom, empire, or dynasty) that very fully exhibits a democratic social life (as distinct, in Deweyan terms, from a democratic form of government), these critics conclude that it is Dewey's ideals that need to reconstructed and transformed in order to bring them into line with realities of social life. The present unreality of democracy as a way of life is, for them, a measure that their possibility is not supported by evidence produced by experimental inquiry. It was never a sign that the current social conditions are illusory. The way things are is a matter of warranted belief.

In *Democracy for Realists: Why Elections Do Not Produce Responsive Government*, Christopher H. Achen and Larry M. Bartels provide a representative and quantitatively-argued strong statement of this second response. In their concluding chapter, "Toward a Realist Theory of Democracy," they summarize what they call the "folk theory of democracy" and its commitment to the sovereignty of the people and the political judgment of the people as the basis for just government power. They write:

> Proponents of democracy have long thought that human dignity required self-government. People should choose their leaders at the polls and hold them accountable. Voters should be *represented*, not just governed ... good citizens would engage in thoughtful monitoring of their government. The abuses of kings, aristocrats, commissars, and dictators would be eliminated. Democratic norms would be enforced by the shared values of an enlightened populace. Mistakes would occur, of course, but they would be the people's own mistakes, and thus susceptible to quick recognition and reversal. ... Defenses of the conventional faith, conceding a few difficulties but affirming the fundamental verities, generally predominate in both popular and scholarly conversation. ... Those defenses, never very plausible to begin with, now are in tatters. ... However, many thinkers implicitly or explicitly continue to embrace the folk theory as a normative benchmark.[7]

The basis of this criticism—the reason why Achen and Bartels believe a Deweyan theory of democracy is "in tatters"—is that as a matter of fact people "are not much like the citizens imagined by the folk theory." They do not engage in experimental inquiry on political matters and they do not identify as members of a community of inquiry. Instead, they identify with "ethnic, racial, occupational, religious, or other sorts of groups" including a political party which they have been taught since childhood represents "people like us."[8] In short, they identify with their *tribe*. Tribalism is the driver of political life—tribalism and not commitment to experimental inquiry or the ideal of a democratic way of life. Tribalism is the social and political norm. To note that reason, even experimental inquiry, is not pure, is not to affirm irrationalism; it is to recognize that human reason, as part of human social life is tribal and perspectival—and so it is to hold no expectation that education will produce universal perspectives and wholly "freed intelligence."[9]

This point is echoed by many other theorists and empirical researchers. For example, observing that the tribes that best survived were those "most acutely aware of outsiders and potential foes" and noting that even though few actual tribes exist today nonetheless human beings now are genetically not much different from their ancestors,[10] Andrew Sullivan argues that successful modern democracies "co-opt" rather than abolish tribal bonds or feelings. "If I were to identify one profound flaw in the founding of America," he continued, "it would be its avoidance of our tribal nature":

What you end up with is zero-sum politics, which drags the country either toward alternating administrations bent primarily on undoing everything their predecessors accomplished, or the kind of gridlock that has dominated national politics for the past seven years—or both. Slowly our political culture becomes one in which the two parties see themselves not as participating in a process of moving the country forward, sometimes by tilting to the right and sometimes to the left, as circumstances permit, alternating in power, compromising when in opposition, moderating when in government—but one where the goal is always the obliteration of the other party by securing a permanent majority, in an unending process of construction and demolition.[11]

One of the large attractions of this tribalism, Sullivan concludes, is that you don't have to think very much—certainly you don't have to engage in shared experimental inquiry—because you always know "which side you're on": "You pick up signals from everyone around you, you slowly winnow your acquaintances to those who will reinforce your worldview, a tribal leader calls the shots, and everything slips into place. After a while, your immersion in tribal loyalty makes the activities of another tribe not just alien but close to incomprehensible."[12] In a similar vein, David Ropiek has observed that "tribalism is pervasive and it controls a lot of our behavior, readily overriding reason."[13] And Paul W. James has noted that globalization, itself pervasive, is not the opposite of pervasive tribalism or a sign that tribalism has been eradicated but, rather, exists concurrently with it.[14] As I have explained elsewhere, cosmopolitanism is a view from somewhere, the world view of a particular groups of people in particular times and places, the outlook and loyalty of a particular tribe.[15]

As Dewey's ontology of change illuminates, this does not mean that tribes or membership in a particular tribe is something permanent, fixed, or absolute. As Lawrence Rosen points out in "A Liberal Defense of Tribalism," empirical studies of actual tribes "show that even as they are defined by relatively narrow identities, they are also characterized by porous boundaries" and reciprocal influence with outside groups.[16] He adds pragmatically:

> Tribes are our common human heritage. But that doesn't mean they are some sort of primal, inescapable curse. Tribalism is a social resource that human beings ought to, and do, make use of depending on the circumstances we face.[17]

And, in language that recalls pragmatic claims that the solution to the shortcomings of inquiry and democracy are more inquiry and democracy (1927, LW 2:327), Rosen concludes with a "realistic assessment of tribalism": "Ultimately, there is nothing wrong with tribalism that can't be fixed by what is right with it."

Pragmatists must take this point, and the empirical evidence on which it is based, seriously. To do so—to make this an effective future research agenda for pragmatism--would be to return the focus of pragmatic politics to issues of education. Deweyan democracy awaits creation of a widespread kind of habit and practice that for the most part do not exist yet. This is a practical matter of social reconstruction of relationships, practices, and institutions, not mere theoretical articulation by scholars. The practical issue is this: Deweyan democrats must create a growing tribe of persons who from an early age self-identify, and identify each other, as members of a tribe of experimental inquirers committed to the value of fostering responsible and harmonious participants in the decisions and affairs that impact their lives and enable their growth. Political pragmatists are not a-tribal; they are members of a particular tribe.

The social enlargement of this tribe is a matter of education in its broadest, Deweyan sense—the formation of habits. As such it is not simply a matter of schooling but involves all the large institutions and practices that forge habits—including economies, governments, media, militaries, families, and much more. This education is not simply a matter of exposure to, or association with, other people, other tribes. As Amy Chua recently noted in *Political Tribes: Group Instinct and the Fate of Nations*, "exposure to people from different tribes is not sufficient"[18] because by itself it does not reconstruct habits, and it frequently can confirm existing biases and perspectives.

This pragmatic imperative to nourish, sustain, and greatly enlarge a tribe—plural tribes--committed to experimental inquiry and democracy as a way of life is no easy task in light of the fact that at present the myriad institutions, practices, and associations required are underfunded, technologically outmoded, often ineffective, and frequently embattled and actively opposed by powerful authoritarian forces. Surely it is a task that comes without any advance guarantee of success. However, any future pragmatism— which must be, among other things, a tribal pragmatism—that does not take up this task is neither realistic nor genuinely pragmatic.

Notes

1. For an account of this contrast between ancient Greek thought and Dewey's pragmatism in the context of the notion of force, see Stuhr (2016a).
2. See also the general introduction to Dewey's philosophy in Stuhr (2000).
3. I discuss Dewey's notion of democracy as a way of life and assess its strengths and challenges a century later in my "Democracy as a Way of Life, Democracy in the Face of Terrorism" in Stuhr (2003).
4. For an extended discussion of Dewey's theory of inquiry in this context, see "Power/ Inquiry" in Stuhr (2003).
5. Niebuhr (1933, 364).
6. See "Old Ideas Crumble: War and the Limits of Philosophy" in Stuhr (2016b) Also see "John Dewey's Philosophy" (1915), "The War and the Intellectuals" (1917), and "The Disillusionment" (1918) in Bourne (1977).
7. Achen and Bartels (2016, 297–298). This argument has important parallels with (and differences from) the claims advanced by Walter Lippmann in his 1925 *The Phantom Public*. Both argue that a Deweyan view of democratic politics is unrealistic. Lippmann argues that the notions of "the public" and "sovereign and omnicompetent citizens" are myths—phantoms that do not really exist. This argument leaves space for Dewey to re- spond that publics do exist but must be made self-aware and that democratic inquiry

and communication are needed to make possible democratic citizenship. Aachen and Bartels argue that, on the basis of a great deal of empirical evidence, individuals hold interests that they attribute to groups with which they deeply self-identify—groups that not only are not Deweyan democratic communities, whether self-conscious or not, but also sustain social conditions that work against the creation of such democratic communities. On this view, it is not simply that there is no democratic public at present; rather, it is that given the realities of tribal human nature, there can be no such democracy.

8. Ibid., pp. 291, 301. See also Hughey (1998) and Stuhr (2016b), "Democracy as Public Experiment: Beyond Mission Accomplished and Mission Impossible."
9. See Niebuhr (1943, 246; 1944, 16–18).
10. In this context, see Shermer (2012).
11. Sullivan (2017).
12. Ibid.
13. Ropeik (2016).
14. James (2006).
15. Stuhr (2017, 280–295).
16. Rosen (2018).
17. Ibid.
18. Chua (2018, 201).

WORKS CITED

Citations of John Dewey's works are to the thirty-seven-volume critical edition published by Southern Illinois University Press under the editorship of Jo Ann Boydston. In-text citations give the original publication date and series abbreviation, followed by volume number and page number. For example: (1934, LW 10:12) is page 12 of *Art as Experience*, which is published as volume 10 of *The Later Works*.

Series abbreviations for *The Collected Works*:

EW *The Early Works* (1882–98)

MW *The Middle Works* (1899–1924)

LW *The Later Works* (1925–53)

Achen, Christopher H., and Larry M. Bartels. *Democracy for Realists: Why Elections Do Not Produce Responsive Government*. Princeton, NJ: Princeton University Press, 2016.

Bourne, Randolph. *Randolph Bourne: The Radical Will: Selected Writings 1911–1918*. Edited by O. Hansen. Berkeley: University of California Press, 1977.

Chua, Any. *Political Tribes: Group Instinct and the Fate of Nations*. London: Penguin, 2018.

Hughey, Michael. W. *New Tribalisms*. London: Palgrave Macmillan, 1998.

James, Paul W. *Globalism, Nationalism, Tribalism: Bringing Theory Back In*. New York: SAGE, 2006.

Niebuhr, Reinhold. "Two Communications: Coe vs. Niebuhr." *The Christian Century*, March 15, 1933.

Niebuhr, Reinhold. *The Nature and Destiny of Man*, vol. 2. London: Nisbet and Co., 1943.

Niebuhr, Reinhold. *The Children of Light and the Children of Darkness: A Vindication of Democracy and a Critique of Its Traditional Defense*. New York: Scribner's, 1944.

Ropeik, David. "How Tribalism Overrules Reason, and Makes Risky Times More Risky." *Big Think Edge.* http://bigthink.com/risk-reason-and-reality/how-tribalism-overrules-reason-and-makes-risky-times-more-dangerous, 2016.

Rosen, Lawrence. "A Liberal Defense of Tribalism." *Foreign Policy Magazine*, January 16, 2018.

Shermer, Michael. "Evolution Explains Why Politics is so Tribal." *Scientific American*, June 1, 2012.

Stuhr, John J. *Pragmatism and Classical American Philosophy: Essential Readings and Interpretive Essays.* New York: Oxford University Press, 2000.

Stuhr, John J. *Pragmatism Postmodernism, and the Future of Philosophy.* New York: Routledge, 2003.

Stuhr, John J. "A permanência da mudança: Empédocles, Dewey e dois tipos de metafísicas pluralistas de força" (The Permanence of Change: Empedocles, Dewey, and Two Kinds of Pluralist Metaphysics of Force). *Cognitio: Revista de Filosofia*, vol. 17, no. 2, 2016a.

Stuhr, John J. *Pragmatic Fashions: Pluralism, Democracy, Relativism, and the Absurd.* Indianapolis: Indiana University Press, 2016b.

Stuhr, John J. "Somewhere, Dreaming of Cosmopolitanism." In *Cosmopolitanism and Place*, eds. Jessica Wahman, José M. Medina, and John J. Stuhr. Bloomington: Indiana University Press, 2017.

Sullivan, Andrew. "America Wasn't Built for Humans." *New York Magazine*, September 19, 2017.

....

CHAPTER 15

DEWEY, ADDAMS, AND DESIGN THINKING

Pragmatist Feminist Innovation for Democratic Change

....

JUDY D. WHIPPS

> The crisis that one hundred and fifty years ago called out social and political inventiveness is with us in a form which puts a heavier demand on human creativeness.... [T]he task can be accomplished only by inventive effort and creative activity. (1939, LW 14:225)

INTRODUCTION

....

THE ideal of a democratic society was an aspiration for both John Dewey and Jane Addams, a beacon that pulled them toward a future that has not yet been met in the twenty-first century. Their ideal of democracy is not exclusively or even fundamentally a system of governing; it is a way of being in community together. Democracy, as Dewey famously said, "is primarily a mode of associated living, of conjoint communicated experience" (1916a, MW 9:93). In reworking democracy though both philosophy and activism, Dewey and Addams developed powerful methods of democratic social change, methods that continue to be relevant today. This chapter examines various aspects of pragmatist social change methodology and its continuing relevance in contemporary social issues, linking it with other popular change methodologies. The methods of change developed by Dewey and Addams are central to the problem-solving pragmatist approach to philosophy and action. As Cornel West has said, "pragmatism is a philosophic orientation that highlights history, context and problem-solving" (2004, 225). In today's social, political, and professional environments, there are cultural and organizational imperatives around creating change. Employers and social change organizations are looking for people adept at creating change.[1] Dewey's and Addams' pragmatism can be brought into productive dialogue with the contemporary problem-solving methods of "human centered" design or design thinking. This is put forward in the spirit of a renewed recovery of the pragmatist method for innovation and change, reinvigorating the pragmatist approach to change and also enhancing the design thinking process.

Because of their mutual influence, Addams and Dewey are brought together here to examine pragmatist theory and practice of social change. For much of the twentieth century, Jane Addams' philosophic legacy lived in the shadow of Dewey, she as the activist who put Dewey's philosophies into practice. This diminished both Addams and Dewey—Addams was not seen as the philosopher that she was, and Dewey's activism was also sometimes seen as secondary or tangential to his own philosophy. Recent scholarship, starting with the work of Charlene Haddock Seigfried, has changed how we view this relationship. We now see Addams and Dewey as colleagues, whose joint work, both philosophical and activist, grew together in the social milieu of the Progressive Age. Examining both of them together in theory and practice allows for a more thorough look at their innovative methods of democratic change.

Dewey and Addams were both social activists, working locally, nationally, and internationally. Dewey's involvement in social causes began after his marriage to Alice Chipman, a Michigan woman who came from a family that had been deeply involved in issues of social justice.[2] Dewey's interest and involvement in social change continued to grow after he moved to Chicago to head the philosophy department at the University of Chicago. He began his career in Chicago with a visit to Hull House, the settlement Jane Addams founded. In his first year in Chicago, Dewey taught several classes at Hull House and in the late 1890s was elected to its board of directors. Later Addams guest-lectured in Dewey's classes, and Dewey named one of his daughters after Addams.

Addams was the founder, with Ellen Gates Starr, of Hull House, a settlement community that took on projects to change social, economic, and political conditions first in Chicago and then nationally. Addams committed her life to social activism, "refusing to be content," she said, "with a shadowy intellectual or aesthetic reflection" of a "really living world" (1910/1990, 39). As has been demonstrated in the past 30 years by many feminist pragmatist philosophers, Addams was also a philosopher, publishing 11 books and many essays and articles. As she developed her philosophies, she was always primarily concerned with putting ideas into action.

There is no indication that design thinking is historically connected to pragmatist or progressive change methods, but they both share an early interest in collaborative democracy. According to Stefanie Di Russo (2012) design thinking's origins can be traced to 1960s collaborative grassroots democratic methods. From there, she says it moved into "participatory design" methods in urban planning. Others trace the beginnings of the specific design thinking process to the art/design fields. The key innovation in moving from participatory design to what became "human-centered design" was to focus on the end-user at every stage of the process, developing innovations that meet the user's interests and needs, through continual dialogue/interaction. After the turn of the millennium, human-centered design as a method evolved into a particular approach known as "design thinking" (Di Russo 2012).[3] Today human-centered design and design thinking are often used interchangeably. It is a method increasingly used at all levels of education, in the non-profit world, and in social change/social entrepreneurship work.

Those trained in design thinking bring particular "mindsets" or philosophic attitudes/habits to the change processes that are also found in early pragmatist work. Most people in the design thinking field use a process that includes variations of some basic steps, including (a) empathy as a starting point, (b) a clear definition of the problem based on listening, (c) rapid ideation, (d) prototyping possible solutions, (d) testing the results of experimentation, and (e) continued revision. Rather than describing each of these steps in detail, which has been done elsewhere (Brown 2009, Hasso Plattner Institute of Design, n.d.), here we take a step back and look at the philosophic attitudes or "mindsets" of design thinking. We will see that pragmatist social change method shares many of these core elements. Pragmatists and contemporary design thinkers share a concern with process as well as result.

Even though it has early connections to community participation models, design thinking can be seen as problematic to many philosophers and academics today, often because it is closely associated with business and profit, as a method of product design. Even when moved to the realm of social innovation, the process itself is not always critically reflective about how the dynamics of power and privilege affects the processes of social innovation. A pragmatist and feminist approach brings a critical lens that can improve the process of innovation.

Bringing Dewey's and Addams' pragmatist philosophy and design thinking together demonstrates how the concept and practice of democracy is a site of innovation, since the practice of democracy is continuously in the process of reconstruction, even today. There are striking similarities between our twenty-first-century world and the American culture of the early twentieth century. The frustration with the status quo as exemplified in radical movements around the globe indicates a frustration with current levels of democracy similar the turn of the twentieth century. There is an increasing polarization between the rich and the poor, and an increasing wage gap between the CEO and the workers, discrimination against immigrants and minorities, a rising nationalism, and distrust of dialogue across the class and difference. A need for a flexible, collaborative method is needed to respond to these conditions as a way to engage in the reconstruction that Dewey called for. Can pragmatists, perhaps with some caution, utilize design thinking/human-centered design as a possible method of equitable pragmatist change?

DEMOCRACY AS ETHICAL PROCESS

The concept of "democracy" belongs to that small class of ideas that must be re-created in every generation and redefined by multiple thinkers depending on differing and local contexts. In "Philosophy and Democracy" Dewey asks "What is meant by democracy?" (1919, MW 11:49) Before answering he acknowledges that any definition of democracy must be arbitrary; democracy is an idea and an ideal, having never been perfected in actuality. In "The Ethics of Democracy," written while he was still at the University of Michigan, Dewey articulated a vision of democracy as the expression of a social organism. He said, "democracy approaches most nearly the ideal of all social organization; that in which the individual and society are organic to each other" (1888, EW 1:237). He disagrees with limiting the concept of democracy to vote-counting of distinct and isolated individuals but rather sees it as the expression of this social organism.

More than a political system "democracy" for Addams and Dewey refers to a way of method of living together in community, "a mode of associated living, of conjoint communicated experience" (1916a, MW 9:93). Viewed this way, democracy is seen as an aspiration not yet achieved, particularly in our contemporary divisive political and social environments. Dewey's vision of democracy changed over time. As his daughter Jane said in a biography that Dewey's collaborated on, once he moved to Columbia, his more "naïve" view of democracy came into conflict with the "irresponsible finance capitalism" he saw in New York (1939, 39). This is a good example of how one's understanding of democracy changes over time and experience. Democracy is a method, an active process, always becoming rather than a static reality. The ideal of democracy "is not a fact and never will be" (1927, LW 2:328). As an evolving way of living together not limited to political processes, democracy is "controlled by a working faith in the possibilities of human nature ... irrespective of race, color, sex, birth and family, of material and cultural wealth" (1939, LW 14:226). Addams once even referred to democracy as a "mystical" ideal, "continually demanding new formulation" (1909/1972, 146). And as an aspiration, it requires continuous effort; it "can have no end till experience itself comes to an end" since it is the work "of creation of a freer and more human experience in which all share and to which all contribute" (1939, LW 14:230).

Real democracy is also often radical, as Dewey said, it "requires great change in existing social institutions, economic, legal and cultural" (1937, LW 11:299), and it acts "to call into being things that have not existed in the past" (1939, LW 14:229–230). It attempts to correct maladjusted elements of society and as such requires and often responds to conflict. As Bernstein said about the evolution of Dewey's thinking about democracy, after the Pullman Strike in Chicago Dewey came to understand the importance of conflict and struggle. And as we have seen in any social movement, social change is most often the outcome of conflicting views. Conflict demonstrates the need for change and creates the conditions that call for adjustment, and hopefully that adjustment comes from democratic methods. Richard Bernstein points out that, for Dewey, "the key point is how one *responds* to conflict. And this requires imagination, intelligence, and a commitment to solve concrete problems" (Bernstein 2010, 84).[4] What Jane Addams understood so well was that conflict that leads to violence is never a democratic act. Violence is based in strength and dominance, acts of "power-over" others, the antithesis of the "power-with" democratic process. Instead, she says the change in society and institutions has to come from ethical, innovative participatory processes.

Responding to the need for a different democracy in the industrial age, Dewey points out "a democratic culture requires the courage of an inspired imagination" (1916b, MW 10:198). In 1939, facing the threat of Nazism, Dewey renewed his call for democracy to "re-create by deliberate and determined endeavor the kind of democracy" needed for that era. (1939, LW 14:225). Such work, he said, required inventiveness, courage, and philosophic reflection. And as Dewey notes, this interaction is not hierarchical interaction based on leadership by "geniuses or heroes or divine leaders" but rather "with associated individuals in which each by intercourse with others somehow make the life of each more distinctive" (1919, MW 11:53).

MELIORISM: BUILDING AN ATTITUDE OR A CULTURE OF CHANGE

According to the design firm IDEO, one of the leaders in the field of human-centered design, one of the mindsets of the design thinking process is an attitude that change is possible and that we, as individuals and communities, can be the agents of positive change.

> Embracing human-centered design means believing that all problems, even the seemingly intractable ones like poverty, gender equality, and clean water, are solvable. Moreover, it means believing that the people who face those problems every day are the ones who hold the key to their answer.
>
> (IDEO 2015, 9)

According to influential designers and Stanford d-school leaders Tom and David Kelley, the key to approaching design change is a sense of creative confidence, "believing in your ability to create change in the world around you" (2013, 2). In pragmatism, this attitude of change is often called "meliorism"—the belief that humans can effect change to make the world better. It is an essential element of the Addams' and Dewey's pragmatism, and it anchors their faith in the possibility of change and improvement. Meliorism, Dewey says, is not simply optimism, which may not see the problems that truly exist, but rather the "belief that the specific conditions which exist at one moment, be they comparatively bad or comparatively good, in any event may bettered" (1920, MW 12:181–182). Much has been made of Dewey's faith in the experimental methods of science, but his experimental approach went beyond science, to an overall attitude of innovation, with expectation of being able to create different social conditions. Dewey talks about the need to have "faith in the power of intelligence to imagine a future . . . and invent the instrumentalities of its realization" (1917, MW 10:48). He holds that faith in the process of democracy and "the possibilities of human nature" even into 1939 when confronting Nazi fascism (1939, LW 14:229).

One could say that anyone who takes on social action or engages in charity work is expressing meliorism, but the expectations of the pragmatists were different than what had gone before. Rather than only fixing existing problems, Addams and Dewey set out to understand and change the root causes of problems, to engage in reconstruction or "dovetailing" instead of the revolution or anarchy that was popular with some radicals in the early twentieth century. Significantly, as expressed by Dewey and Addams, early pragmatists saw this reconstructive work as the work of philosophy alongside of activism. Believing that they could significantly affect the intractable problems of society caused pragmatists to take an experimental approach to community life.

The fact that Addams and Starr would optimistically start their settlement household in an overcrowded, disease-ridden, foul-smelling neighborhood in hope of both understanding life and extending democratic practice illustrates their belief in the possibility of progress. As Addams said in 1907, she saw her work as part of "the beginning of a prolonged effort to incorporate a progressive developing life founded upon a response to the needs of all the people" (1907/2003, 92). Dewey too was being innovative in many ways at that time, such as creating, with Alice Chipman Dewey, the Dewey School, which "was genuinely experimental, with ideas tested, judged to be failures, and set aside even in the middle of the term" (Fesmire 2015, 20). In this work, the Deweys upended the traditional content lesson focus to place the emphasis on the child and his or her growth and learning. For Addams in particular, engaging in changing social conditions meant being open to changing oneself as well as the world. She is clear that she started Hull House for "subjective" reasons, for her own need for growth through engagement with others who had very different perspectives, resulting in mutually reciprocal transformation.

Addams described Hull House as "experimental effort to aid in the solution of the social and industrial problems." The story of Hull House is a story of social experiments of all kinds, with many successes but also with many failures. Yet, running through all of Addams' and her colleagues' work is the belief that through continued reflective experience they would learn what was needed to move forward. As David Hildebrand says, "meliorism is no sentimental faith, but a working hypothesis whose plausibility rests upon observation and experience" (2013, 59). It was this experimental and experiential approach that gave Addams and Dewey faith in new possibilities.

AN ETHIC OF EMPATHY

What distinguishes design thinking from earlier models of collaborative innovation is the focus throughout the process on the people affected by the problem in design language, sometimes called the "stakeholders." Earlier change methods may have researched the problem by talking to those involved, but a design thinker attempts to imagine him or herself in the place of the other, to understand as much as is possible the practical and emotional experience of those affected, and to return to engagement with those individuals throughout the problem-solving process. This is the process called "empathy." It requires deep listening and on-the-ground experience, working alongside others rather than working on behalf of others. It requires problem-solvers "to deeply understand the people they're looking to serve, to dream up scores of ideas, and to create innovative new solutions rooted in people's actual needs" (IDEO 2015, 9). For Addams and Dewey, this process that we now call empathy was the social ethic foundational to democracy.

It's important to distinguish the difference today between the processes of empathy and sympathy. Empathy is a newer term, arising in the early twentieth century. Dewey used the word "sympathy" rather than "empathy" in his writings, which was then the common term to encompass what we now may refer to separately as empathy and sympathy, although the term "empathy" would be a better way to describe both Dewey's and Addams' work. According to Simpson and Sacken, referencing Eisenberg and Strayer (1987), the English word "empathy" "arose in 1909 with unsettled and debatable meanings," which "may explain Dewey's almost exclusive use of sympathy for contemporary conceptions of both sympathy and empathy" (2014, 3). Even in Dewey's time, sympathy had problematic elements, especially when "sympathy" is experienced "as mere contagious feeling" (1908, MW 5:52). Feeling the emotions of sympathy does not change power structures. In contrast, empathy means coming alongside others and working to understand their lived experience as a basis of democratic change.

As an interpretative process of attempting to understand the lives and experiences of the other, empathy involves openness and humility and self-reflective practices. This is an approach that resonates throughout Dewey's work. Dewey said the emotion of sympathy was valuable morally, but for action, what was needed was "to put ourselves in the place of another, to see things from the standpoint of his [or her] aims and values, to humble our estimate of our own pretensions to the level they assume in the eyes of an impartial observer" (1932, LW 7:251). Empathy is "entering by imagination into the situations of others" (1908, MW 5:150), taking the point of view of the actual person experiencing the problem, "to assimilate, imaginatively, something of another's experience" (1916a, MW 9:8–9). This empathy work is part of the educational process, but it is also a part of community-based problem-solving work and is the basis of moral decision-making. As Dewey said at the end of *Democracy and Education*, "Interest in learning from all the contacts of life is the essential moral interest." (1916a, MW 9:370).

For Dewey, just listening or observing is not sufficient for moral ends; it is the action together, the communication and "joint participation" that leads to a democratic community (1920, MW 12:197). Empathy, understanding what people wanted and needed from the people themselves, is essential for democratic change. Rather than powerful people taking action based on what they think others need, Dewey said the starting place for democracy needs to be "asking other people what they would like, what they need, what their ideas are" (1938, LW 13: 295). Earlier, he connected this culture of empathic understanding to the work of social settlements like Hull House (1908, MW 5:150). Early in her career, Addams learned that careful listening was an integral part of her work. According to one visitor, Addams "was always in that listening attitude of mind of 'What is it?'" One resident commented that Addams worked "to understand and interpret (everyone) correctly and generously" (quoted in Knight 2005, 368).

Addams' first book *Democracy and Social Ethics* (1902) lays out the foundation for a newer approach to democracy, based on the ethics of empathy, claiming that empathy and acting with others is the basis of a twentieth-century democracy. Developing this empathy requires shared experiences—"mixing on the thronged and common road where all must turn out for one another"—but it also requires imagination, imagining oneself in the role of another. A lack of this ability to imagine oneself in the role of the other results in moral problems, "the insensibility and hardness of the world is due to the lack of imagination which prevents a realization of the experiences of other people" (1902/2002, 7–8).

Empathetic inquiry means starting with the lived experiences of the people involved. As Dewey wrote, experimental social inquiry should "grow out of the actual social tensions, needs, 'troubles'" of those involved, the "actual social situations which are themselves conflicting and confused" (1938, LW 12:492–493). At Hull House, the early residents did just that: they began by listening to the stories and experiences of their neighbors. These stories changed the residents' perspectives. Addams wrote to her step-brother George Haldeman in 1890 a year after Hull House opened that these stories were "the part of life ... which the residents care most for" (Knight 2005, 203). As a skilled writer and speaker, Addams listened carefully and engaged in shared experiences to develop empathy in her role as interpreter and storyteller. Yet she soon discovered the importance of asking an accompanying neighbor "to curb any hasty generalization" when she spoke to Chicago audience (1910/1990, 58). Addams' stories of the humanity and struggles of the immigrants in Chicago created a powerful impetus for social change. She carried that forward in her political work as well. In her discussion about the 1894 Pullman Railway strike, Addams reiterated the importance of really listening to workers. She critiqued the employer who "is good 'to' people rather than good 'with' them, when he allows himself to decide what is best for them instead of consulting them" (1902/2002, 70).

Marilyn Fischer points out how, in Addams' role as interpreter, she intentionally took differing perspectives and then worked to interpret the perspectives of one group to another (2011, 483). For example, in the Averbach situation, she alternated perspectives, first identifying the perspective of "the general public—primarily white, middle-class, and non-immigrant" (2011, 485) who had a general sense of fear and panic about anarchism, and then she shifted perspective to the fear of persecution experienced by the Russian Jewish immigrant population. In doing this, she worked to develop an interpretive empathy between the white and the Jewish populations, in an attempt to begin a starting place for understanding and dialogue in a fear-charged situation.

A Culture of Experimentation

The design thinking mindset creates and builds on a culture of innovation and experimentation. A continual process of iterative experimentation, testing and reforming and retesting all processes as well as products is basic to all design work. After careful listening and investigating the lived experiences of those involved, innovators approach problems asking "What if ... " or "How could we ... " in an attempt to imagine how the situation could be improved and to take action to improve it. In many ways this is a resurrection of the early-twentieth-century progressive pragmatist spirit with its trust in experience and in experimentation.

Continual experimental inquiry, building on an analysis of experience, is foundational to the aspirational democratic process posited by Addams and Dewey. As Dewey said, "Democracy is the faith that the process of experience is more important that any special result" (1939, LW 14:229). As such, democracy requires "a readiness to follow wherever experimental results lead" (Hickman 2008, 29). Dewey explicitly extends that experimental method to democracy in "Creative Democracy" saying that "the task of democracy is forever that of creation of a freer and more humane experience in which all share and to which all contribute" (1939, LW 14:232).

What distinguishes pragmatist inquiry from many other forms of philosophic inquiry in the emphasis on action in the world. Action is essential to the process of knowing. "The intellectual determinations can be tested and warranted only by *doing something* about the problematic existential situations out of which they arise" (1938, LW 12:492) Addams made a similar point early in her career: "action is the only medium man has for receiving and appropriating truth" (1910/1990, 73). And democratic inquiry requires experimental collaborative action with many others. For Addams, as well as for Dewey, Hull House was a site of action as well as reflective inquiry and analysis. As she said of the Hull House, it "is an experimental effort to aid in the solution of the social and industrial problems which are engendered by the modern conditions of life in a great city" (1910/ 1990, 75). Addams continued to experiment with social justice challenges throughout her life, working for industrial reform, women's rights, and international peace.

Dewey is most often known as a theoretical innovator, but he developed many of his ideas in collaboration with and action together with others. This is particularly true of his educational philosophies developed in dialogue with Addams, Ella Flagg Young,[5] and Elsie Ripley Clapp (Seigfried 1996). He also experimented with educational practice in the Lab School at the University of Chicago that he started with his wife Alice in 1896.

He directed the school, with Alice as principal, until he left Chicago for Columbia in 1904. Dewey attempted to devise an educational approach consistent with democracy, both to bring democracy into education and to educate future citizens to be prepared for a participatory democracy. Before starting the Lab School, he was active in the kindergarten movement; he participated in discussions about school reform in the Chicago Public Schools. Like Addams, Dewey had international stature and worked with officials and educators in many countries, most particularly in China.

Dewey's continuing commitment to participatory democracy can be illustrated by the long list of social reform movements that he was associated with. In 1920 he joined with Jane Addams, Clarence Darrow, and several others to form the American Civil Liberties Union. He was also involved in the forming of the National Association for the Advancement of Colored People. He was president of the People's Lobby from 1929 to 1936, an organization that worked for unemployment insurance and tax relief. He was one of the first presidents of the League for Independent Political Action, beginning in 1929, which called for a new political party that would include some of his ideals of democratic socialism. He continued to advocate for a third party for most of the rest of his life. He was also active with various organizations that worked for humanitarian causes, working with Hull House and the Henry Street Settlement in New York and conducting international work such as the Columbia Committee for relief for Russian children.

In the process of his work, Dewey also re-created philosophical political concepts basic to democracy, such as his reformulation of the "liberty" to embrace the ambiguity and processes of uncertainty and discovery. He defines "liberty as meaning a universe where there is real uncertainty and contingency . . . a world which in some respects is incomplete and in the making" (1919, MW 11:50). This acknowledgement of the incompleteness of our knowing and our actions is a hallmark of pragmatist thought.

A CULTURE OF DIVERSITY

The need for diverse perspectives in innovation problem solving is a basic principle in design thinking literature and practice. As Kelley and Kelley wrote: "The dynamic tension between different viewpoints is what makes diverse teams a fertile ground for creativity" (2013, 190). Sometimes design thinkers urge us to adopt a "traveler" perspective, to attempt to see the problem as someone from the outside would see it. Indeed, it is often that creative breakthroughs some from changing perspectives and hearing a new voice, whether that means listening to interdisciplinary views or shifting cultural perspectives.

It is clear that much of the energy of the Progressive Era came from those previously considered outsiders in the public realm, particularly women, immigrants, and people of color. In addition, journalists who took seriously and documented the living conditions of the poor, in their tenements and in their sweatshops, brought the lives of these previously marginalized peoples into the everyday lives of all Americans. Addams was inherently an outsider in the realm of politics and academia, as a woman disadvantaged in the male worlds of academia and business, as well as her perspective as an unmarried female facing family and social expectations. Although she only talks about this obliquely, often through the third person, surely this influenced her perspective on change. Even with that, there were many areas where Addams (and well as Dewey) needed to reach out to a new or larger perspective for change.

Dewey and Addams are both articulate about the need for diversity. From his time in Chicago with Addams, Dewey came to see democracy also as "a way of life that breaks down exclusionary social barriers and opens up diverse points of contact" (Fesmire 2015, 153). Addams' day-to-day community work made her more aware of the immediate need for diversity. She knew that for Hull House to be successful it must have "a deep and abiding sense of tolerance. It must be hospitable and ready to experiment" (1910/1990, 75). The communities that she worked in were always diverse in terms of class, race, and nationality, which led to many of the accomplishments of Hull House. As Marjorie Miller has pointed out, these diverse neighborhoods "gave Addams the base from which to develop the social intelligence which allowed her to recognize continually new problems—not just to generate new solutions" (2013, 243). Difference, whether it is in nationality, class, gender, or race, created the creative tension as well as a platform of creativity for change to occur and progress to be made. (Knight 2010, 107).

Addams' commitment to inclusive democratic life extended as well to the management of Hull House, where "policy decisions about residential life and joint projects were made by the residents as a collective body, not by Addams" (Knight 2005, 277). Although she was the founder, Addams did not attempt to dominate and was often voted down in residential decisions. She intentionally brought in residents from the neighborhoods to lead initiatives and worked closely with industrial workers, particularly women, to create programs. One such example is the creation of housing for women workers who were in vulnerable positions if they went on strike.

FALLIBILISM: TESTING AND FAILURE

The risk of failure is part of any experimental process, and failure is considered part of the learning process of design thinking. The prototype and testing phases of the design thinking process is meant to uncover early and obvious potential failures. In a prototype, innovators create a model of the proposed solution and test it with people who understand the issue to potentially find flaws in the process or product. Some design thinkers even evoke the mantra "fail fast, fail often" to embrace the process of trial and error. As business leader Rita McGrath said, "When you're tackling a fundamentally uncertain task, your initial assumptions are almost certain to be incorrect. Often the only way to arrive at better ones is to try things out" (2011). She continues by saying assumptions should be made explicit, so people are aware that the ideas/concepts are just that—provisional assumptions that can be disproved through experience. The bigger problem is when others start to act as if the assumptions are in fact real truth. Being open to learning from failure is one of the foundational traits of design thinking, "because we rarely get it right on our first try." (IDEO 2015, 21). While the process of prototyping and testing is not always easily applied to social change models, or to some philosophic thought, the basic openness to change and adaptation is clearly a pragmatist stance. A provisional approach to knowledge until confirmed by experience clearly resonates with pragmatist epistemology.

Fallibilism is a core part of pragmatist thought, the epistemological understanding that "truth" is never certain; theory and understanding are always being revised based upon the experiential and experimental outcomes of action. It acknowledges the limits of one's understanding. Rejecting certainty, holding open the possibility and need for adjustment, necessitates openness to change and re-creation. When ideas and possible solutions are put into practice, for pragmatists and designers, they must be open to change based on their workability. Dewey's embrace of the scientific method of experimentation and change throughout his work illustrates this openness. As Dewey said, concepts must be "subject to constant and well-equipped observation of the consequences they entail when acted upon, and subject to ready and flexible revision in the light of observed consequences" (1927, LW 2:362). Dewey's Lab School at the University of Chicago is an example of this, where the pedagogy was "was genuinely experimental, with ideas tested, judged to be failures, and set aside even in the middle of the term" (Fesmire 2015, 20).

Twenty Years at Hull House, Addams' most well-known book, is a record of the experiments—failures as well as successes—in the Hull House community. These experimental approaches taught the residents to "test the value of human knowledge by action" (Addams 1982, 186–187). The children's day care nursery was one of the early and successful experiments at Hull House, but it also led to one of its early failures in empathy. Working women could bring their small children there to be cared for during the day for a small fee. One mother abandoned her baby there, and, even though it was cared for at the nursery, the baby died after ten days. Addams and Hull House residents asked the county to take care of the burial since no family could be found. Upset neighbors confronted Addams, saying it was shameful and disrespectful to have a public/pauper's burial and eventually took up a collection for a private funeral. It was a blunder in their attempts to empathize with the community, and, as Addams said, their action "injured (Hull House) . . . deeply in the minds of some of its neighbors." She went on, "No one born and reared in that community could possibly have made a mistake like that" (1898, quoted in Knight 2005, 208).

Other failed experiments included the community kitchen, which prepared nutritious food for purchase by the neighbors who often worked long hours and did not have the time for cooking. While the kitchen distributed some of the food in the neighboring factories, the soups and stews were not popular with the local families. As one neighbor said, "she liked to eat 'what she'd ruther'" (1910/1990, 78.) Another venture, the Hull House Cooperative Coal Association, was hugely successful for the first three years but eventually failed because the kindness of the entrepreneurs running it, who gave away too much coal to stay profitable (1910/1990, 80). In all of the experiments that were tried and changed or abandoned, the residents of Hull House learned something and adapted, re-creating something new. As Addams said about one of the Hull House experiments, they learned "not to hold to preconceived ideas of what the neighborhood ought to have, but to keep ourselves in readiness to modify and adapt our undertakings" (1910/1990, 79).

Of course, there were many successful experiments at Hull House, more numerous that can be listed here, with its first public playgrounds for children, its innovations in support for labor, like the residential Jane Club for industrial working women, and the interactive Labor Museum, which became a model for Chicago's Museum of Science and Industry. Hull House, like the Lab School, continued long after Dewey's and Addams' lifetimes.

The adaption of processes and ideas, based on experience, is essential to pragmatist process and became a core part of Addams' philosophy. As she said, it "is so easy to commit irreparable blunders because we fail to correct our theories by our changing experience" (1907/2003, 92). Those failures fit within a framework toward progress and likely helped the Hull House residents develop resilience in the face of defeat, which served them well when they took on larger national and international work, like women's suffrage and peace activism.

The history of feminism is a great example of the trial-and-error approach to social change. The seventy-year battle for women's right to vote took many twists and turns as feminists tried various approaches to changing the public perception of women's roles. Although Addams did engage in direct political activism for women's suffrage later in her life, her earlier social reform work was intended partially as an example of the importance of having women in public leadership roles. As a storyteller, Addams effectively used the power of narrative to create an openness to change, using her public stage as an opportunity to highlight the conditions many women faced, an approach that had not been used extensively before Addams' time. Dewey was also involved with activist women's rights organizations. Along with writing on women's rights to education and political action, he gave several lectures in support of women's suffrage in the early part of the century. According to Dykhuizen's biography of Dewey, the press reported that at his 1912 lecture on suffrage "so many people came to hear him that many could not even get inside the doors" (1973, 150). Dykhuizen also reports that Dewey participated in occasional parades for women's suffrage rights, during one of which he is said to have carried a banner pushed into his hands that read "Men can vote! Why can't I?" (1973, 149–150) Women gained the right to vote it the United States in 1920, one of the huge successes of the progressive movement, but it has taken another century of trial and error, moving forward and falling back, to continuously work toward gender equality. More work is clearly still needed.

As feminists and pragmatists continue to work toward social change, models of design innovation can be useful contemporary methods of working with community-based change. Yet adopting this approach requires careful reflection and analysis as well, something that academics, particularly feminist pragmatists, can bring to the discussion.

FEMINIST PRAGMATIST CRITIQUES OF DESIGN METHODOLOGY: WHAT THE DESIGNERS CAN LEARN FROM THE PHILOSOPHERS

Design thinking demonstrates promise in solving complex social problems, and it can be a democratic methodology that communities can easily implement. Yet one needs to approach the process with some caution. The perspectives of philosophers and other academics bring a deeper context to some of its basic assumptions and can improve its inclusive processes. The work of Addams and Dewey demonstrates three areas of concern for design thinking. First is a concern about the validity and ethics of the empathic process, particularly in situations of power differences. Second, designers need to be more critically reflective about the diversity of those who are at the design table, as well as the perceived distinction between the active creative participants versus the potentially passive beneficiaries. And finally, philosophers can point to the need for critical reflective processes in the design method. As a problem-solving method, without intentional attention and reflection about power, the results of this method may end up primarily serving to reinforce the status quo. This reflection often requires a historical as well as a contextual understanding of the root causes of social issues.

The Ethics and Limits of Empathy

Innovators in all fields need to consider the limitations of empathy. Is it even possible to understand the lives of another? Our understandings, even when based on personal experience or deep listening, are always partial. For example, one could, with all good intent, go on a long fast in order to develop an empathic understanding of the lives of people who are starving. The experimenter may experience the physicality of lack of nutrition, but the experience would not be similar, since the experimenter knows that he or she could at any point decide to start eating.[6] Addams came to understand those limitations of empathy as she reflected on her privilege. She realized that even though she and other residents had the impulse to live with the poor that it was "mere pretense and travesty" as long as "the residents did not share the common lot of hard labor and scant fare" of those in their neighborhood (1910/1990, 142). Addams and most of the other residents continued to have choices that their neighbors did not.

Often, the process of design thinking does not intentionally account for disparities in power, such as in social position, race, and gender in the empathy process. In fact, these disparities can be accentuated if the design thinking process positions some as problem-solvers and others suffering from the problem as "benefactors." Power differentials affect communication and, as such, distort the empathy process. Understanding power requires reflection and analysis, personally and culturally to understand the multiple and deeper social inequalities that underlie the perspectives that people bring to the table. This is rarely discussed in the design literature.

Historically, philosophy has not been much better in terms of diversity. For much of its history, the field of philosophy has also not accounted for such disparities in power, instead aiming toward assumed universal truth. Pragmatism, with its focus on particulars and context, is one of the fields of philosophy that amends that search for universals. Danielle Lake points out that, for Dewey, all actions are individualized; little can be said about actions in general. She continues, "Abstracting, generalizing, and then universalizing our ideas for application in other complex circumstances is a dangerous, often high-stakes game" (Lake 2014, 68). Instead, pragmatists refocus on the discussion on what works in experience in a particular, which is always situated. Yet many pragmatist philosophers were not always cognizant of the underlying effects of privilege in their goals of democratic equality. When Dewey talked about equality in democracy, was he thinking about equality in terms of race or gender? When he talked about education, did he have in mind the vast racial inequalities of segregated education in the early twentieth century? Feminist philosophers, philosophers of race, and philosophers in non-Western cultures brought a new critical gaze to philosophy, demonstrating the range of voices that were missing in the philosophic dialogue. This reframing work of feminist pragmatists and pragmatist philosophers of race can be a model for design thinkers.

Awareness of these differentials in power need to be taught and practiced iteratively in the design process, so those entering into the empathy process are aware of the partiality of their understanding. Essential to that is an understanding of Addams' perspective of "working with" rather than "working for" others. Working with others for Addams and Dewey meant continual engagement, interaction, and dialogue. In addition, for design thinkers who come from the outside of the situated and historical context of the problem, the process may encourage "project-based" activism that leaves when the short-term "problem" is solved. That approach is too short term for real democratic change. Pragmatist democratic social change is continuously ongoing; change that is meaningful and lasting requires association and interaction with and among a pluralistic community.

Who Is at the Design Table?

Who are the ones doing the creative design work, and who are the "end-users" of the problem-solving process? As we saw already, advocates of design thinking point to the essential role of diversity in the design team as a sign that this process is necessarily inclusive of multiple identities. Most often, however, these references are to multiple disciplinary perspectives rather than cultural perspectives (See for example Maciver et al., 2016). A brief scan of the leaders of the creative/design thinking movement demonstrates the predominance of white male Americans, most of whom are highly trained professionals. Designers sometimes assume that the voices of those who may have previously been oppressed or marginalized have an equal standing in the innovation process. It is clear that simply saying the process is inclusive does not make it so, and many participants will attest to that. Privilege will determine who is invited to the table. As Dean Nieusma pointed out, even in participatory design methodologies, they are often "used to advance the goals of user-centered design without emphasizing the inclusion of marginalized perspectives in the design process." (2005, quoted in Oosterlaken 2009, 100). Unless planners of the design process have worked to become aware of implicit bias in their perceptions and in their organizations, some voices will be marginalized or discounted. But simply claiming there is equality is not enough for it to happen.

When working on a social change project, academics will often ask if marginalized communities are represented fairly. In the design thinking literature, even that coming out of universities, innovators rarely talk about how they handle the confidentially of participants in the design process. Academic researchers are generally aware of the need to obtain informed consent for any participants in a research project. But what about a community change project that is not intended for research but rather for community problem-solving? As my colleague Jody Vogelzang has asked: "Do the populations know what will be done with their thoughts, feelings, and values?"

Critical Reflection

Experience is a way of knowing in pragmatist thought, yet pragmatism also stresses careful reflection alongside that experience. Part of that reflection is an examination of oneself and one's position in relation to the question at hand. Along with intentionality toward listening this requires an awareness of one's own implicit biases as one works to understand the perspectives of another. We need more work on ourselves, understanding the multiple and deeper social inequalities that underlie the perspectives that people bring to the table. Addams was skilled in that reflective process, always questioning herself (Linn 2000, 373) and going back to write in order to process and re-examine what she experienced. She knew that experience, particularly experiences with diverse others, was essential for the empathy needed for democracy, but that experience also needed critical reflection.

The design thinking mindset of a "prejudice toward action" may often be at too superficial of a level to take time for that critical analysis and reflection. Yet action must be taken if change is to occur. It is here that philosophers and other academics could contribute an important added depth to the design thinking process. Philosophy is inherently a reflective process, and in the past decades philosophers have come to understand the need for critical analysis of self as well as theories. According to Marilyn Fisher, this is the role of reflective thought for which Addams was known, as an attempt to interpret oneself, each other, and society. She continues, "Essentially, thinking or reflection is a matter of delaying one's reaction to a situation to give oneself time to anticipate what others' responses to one's action or gesture will be, and then modifying one's action or gesture accordingly" (2011, 495). This reflective delay strengthens the design process, particularly in complex social situations, and can build rather than hinder creativity. In complex social issues, Dewey notes that reflection and creativity need to come together. " . . . When social change is great, and a great variety of conflicting aims are suggested, reflection cannot be limited to the selection of one end out of a number which are suggested by conditions. Thinking has to operate creatively to form new ends" (1932, LW 7:185). Design thinking could be useful as a way to bring philosophic work together with contemporary innovation, translating "philosophic reflection on the ultimate objectives" to "concrete design practice, including methods and tools" (Oososterlaken 2009, 101).

Conclusion

There is a critical need for a renewal of democracy worldwide today; we need our best innovative minds working on ways that we can come together for new solutions. Pragmatists and feminists, who begin with a belief in democratic social change and have a practice of reflective action, can increase their innovative capacities for change using the methods of design thinking. Design thinking could benefit from a feminist pragmatist approach that puts the emphasis on action alongside continuous cultural and self-examination. Pragmatists could gain from design thinking a "how to" collaborative approach for experimental change. As such, an intellectual and activist blending of pragmatism and design thinking can be a powerful social change tool for improving democracy.

NOTES

1. In the most recent Association of American Colleges and Universities survey of employers in 2015, 70 percent of employers rank problem-solving and 69 percent rank innovative skills as very important (Hart Research Associates 2015).
2. As his daughter said of Dewey, "things which had previously been matters of theory acquired through his contact with (Alice) a vital and direct human significance." This essay, written in collaboration between John Dewey and his daughters, also says that Alice Dewey was responsible for turning his attention to the "field of contemporary life" (Jane Dewey 1939, 21).

3. The early work of design theorist Nigel Cross as well as Richard Buchanan's 1992 "Wicked Problems in Design Thinking" were influential in the evolution of design thinking.

4. Citing Westbrook (1991), Bernstein claimed that Dewey's endorsement of conflict was one of the things that distinguished Dewey's philosophy from Addams' (2010, 84). The claim that Addams was opposed to conflict can only be true if by conflict Westbrook meant violence and war. However, in Dewey's discussion of the conflict that is part of democracy, there is no indication that he is referring to violence. To say that Addams was opposed to conflict is to not acknowledge her real work. Addams dealt with conflict and opposition continuously in her life work, as is true with any reformer who attempts to change unjust laws and social conditions. Of course, Addams firmly believed that nonviolence is always the best response to conflict, the basis of her peace work for which she received the Nobel Peace Prize.

5. Dewey believed that Ella Flagg Young exerted "the greatest influence" on his ideas on education. "She habitually and systematically thought out the implications of her actual experience" (Jane Dewey 1939, 29).

6. Sabrina Alkire uses this example in "Capability and Functionings: Definition and Justification" quoted in Oosterlaken (2009, 92).

Works Cited

Citations of John Dewey's works are to the thirty-seven-volume critical edition published by Southern Illinois University Press under the editorship of Jo Ann Boydston. In-text citations give the original publication date and series abbreviation, followed by volume number and page number. For example: (1934, LW 10:12) is page 12 of *Art as Experience*, which is published as volume 10 of *The Later Works*.

Series abbreviations for *The Collected Works:*

EW *The Early Works* (1882–1898)

MW *The Middle Works* (1899–1924)

LW *The Later Works* (1925–1953)

Addams, Jane. 1899/1982. A Function of the Social Settlement. In *The Social Thought of Jane Addams*. Edited by Christopher Lasch, 183–199. New York: Irvington.

Addams, Jane. 1902/2002. *Democracy and Social Ethics*. Urbana and Chicago: University of Illinois Press.

Addams, Jane. 1907/2003. *Newer Ideals of Peace*. In *Jane Addams's Writings on Peace Vol.1*. Edited by Marilyn Fischer and Judy Whipps, 1–176. Bristol, UK: Thoemmes Press.

Addams, Jane. 1909/1972. *The Spirit of Youth and the City Streets* (reissue ed.). University of Illinois Press.

Addams, Jane. 1910/1990. *Twenty Years at Hull House with Autobiographical Notes*. Urbana and Chicago: University of Illinois Press.

Bernstein, Richard J. 2010. *The Pragmatic Turn*. Cambridge, UK: Polity Press.

Brown, Tim. 2009. *Change by Design: How Design Thinking Transforms Organizations and Inspires Innovation*. New York: HarperCollins.

Buchanan, Richard. 1992. Wicked Problems in Design Thinking, *Design Issues*, vol. 8, no. 2 (Spring), 5–21.

Cross, Nigel. 2007. Forty years of design Research. *Design Studies*, vol. 28, no. 1, 1–4.

Dewey, Jane Mary, ed. 1939. "Biography of John Dewey." In *The Philosophy of John Dewey*. Edited by Paul Arthur Schilpp, 3–21. Evansville, IL: Northwestern University Press.

Dewey, John. 1888 "The Ethics of Democracy." EW 1.

Dewey, John. 1916a. *Democracy and Education*. MW 9.

Dewey, John---. 1916b. "American Education and Culture. MW 10.

Dewey, John. 1919. "Philosophy and Democracy." MW 11.

Dewey, John. 1920. *Reconstruction in Philosophy*. MW 12.

Dewey, John. 1927. *The Public and Its Problems. An Essay in Political Inquiry*. LW 2.

Dewey, John. 1937. "Democracy is Radical." LW 11.

Dewey, John. 1938. *The Logic of Inquiry*. LW 12.

Dewey, John. 1938. "Democracy and Education in the World of Today." LW 13.

Dewey, John. 1939. "Creative Democracy—The Task Before Us." LW 14.

Dewey, John, and James H. Tufts. 1908. *Ethics*. MW 5.

Dewey, John, and James H. Tufts. 1932. *Ethics* (rev. ed.). LW 7.

Di Russo, Stefanie. 2012. "A Brief History of Design Thinking: How Design Thinking Came to 'Be.'" Retrieved from https://ithinkidesign.wordpress.com/2012/06/08/a-brief-history-of-design-thinking-how-design-thinking-came-to-be/.

Dykhuizen, George, and Harold Taylor. 1973. *The Life and Mind of John Dewey*. Carbondale. Southern Illinois University Press.

Fesmire, Steven. 2015. *Dewey (The Routledge Philosophers)*. New York: Routledge Press.

Fischer, Marilyn. 2011. "Interpretation's Contrapuntal Pathways: Addams and the Averbuch Affair." *Transactions of the Charles S. Peirce Society*, vol. 47, no. 4, 482–506.

Hart Research Associates. 2015. "Falling Short? College Learning and Career Success." Retrieved from http://www.aacu.org/sites/default/files/files/LEAP/2015employerstudentsurvey.pdf.

Hasso Plattner Institute of Design. n.d. "An Introduction to Design Thinking Process Guide." Retrieved from https://dschool-old.stanford.edu/sandbox/groups/designresources/wiki/36873/attachments/74b3d/ModeGuideBOOTCAMP2010L.pdf?sessionID=573efa71aea50503341224491c862e32f5edc0a9.

Hildebrand, David. 2013. "Dewey's Pragmatism: Instrumentalism and Meliorism." In *The Cambridge Companion to Pragmatism*. Edited by Alan Malachowski, 55–80. Cambridge, UK: Cambridge University Press.

Hickman, Larry A. 2008. "The Genesis of Democratic Norms: Some Insights from Classical Pragmatism." In *Democracy as Culture: Deweyan Pragmatism in a Globalizing World*. Edited by Sor-hoon Tan and John Whalen-Bridge. Albany: State University of New York Press.

IDEO.org. 2015. *The Field Guide to Human-Centered Design*. Retrieved from http://www.designkit.org/resources/1.

Kelley, Tom, and David Kelley. (2013). *Creative Confidence: Unleashing the Creative Potential Within Us All*. New York: Crown Business.

Knight, Louise W. (2005) *Citizen: Jane Addams and the Struggle for Democracy*. Chicago: University of Chicago Press.

Knight, Louise W. 2010. *Jane Addams: Spirit in Action*. New York: W. W. Norton.

Lake, Danielle L. 2014. *Working With: Expanding and Integrating the Pragmatic Method for a Wicked World*. Retrieved from http://works.bepress.com/danielle_lake/7/.

Linn, James Weber. 1935/2000. *Jane Addams: A Biography*. Urbana and Chicago: University of Illinois Press.

Maciver, F., J. Malinsa, J. Kantorovitch, and A. Liapisc. 2016. "United We Stand: A Critique of the Design Thinking Approach in Interdisciplinary Innovation." Paper presented at DRS

2016, Design Research Society 50th Anniversary Conference. Brighton, UK, June 27–30. Retrieved from http://www.drs2016.org/037/.

McGrath, Rita. 2011, April. "Failing by Design." *Harvard Business Review*. Retrieved from https://hbr.org/2011/04/failing-by-design.

Miller, Marjorie C. 2013. "Pragmatism and Feminism." In *The Cambridge Companion to Pragmatism*. Edited by Alan Malachowski, 231–248. Cambridge, UK: Cambridge University Press.

Oosterlaken, Ilse. 2009. "Design for Development: A Capability Approach." *Design Issues*, vol. 25, no. 4, 91–102.

Seigfried, Charlene Haddock. 1996. *Pragmatism and Feminism: Reweaving the Social Fabric*. Chicago: University of Chicago Press.

Simpson, Douglas J., and D. Mike Sacken. 2014. "The Sympathetic-and-Empathetic Teacher: A Deweyan Analysis." *Journal of Philosophy & History of Education*, vol. 64, no. 1, 1–20.

West, Cornel. 2004. "Afterward: A Conversation between Cornel West and Bill E. Lawson." In *Pragmatism and the Problem of Race*. Edited by Bill E. Lawson and Donald F. Koch, 225–230. Bloomington: Indiana University Press.

Westbrook, Robert B. 1991. *John Dewey and American Democracy*. Ithaca and London: Cornell University Press.

VI

PHILOSOPHY OF EDUCATION

···

CHAPTER 16

DEWEY AND THE QUEST FOR CERTAINTY IN EDUCATION

···

NEL NODDINGS

ALMOST a century ago, John Dewey argued against the traditional philosophical search for certainty and the resulting separation of knowledge and action. Philosophy, like science, had been too long under the authority of religion and its claim to eternal verities. Instead of looking forever backward for certainties that justify our current actions, Dewey said, we should look forward, identify problems, reflect on our values and purposes, try out germinating hypotheses, and evaluate the results. Knowledge and action (or practice) are partners in the production of further knowledge. After a brief background discussion of Dewey's argument, I apply his advice to three major areas of current educational thought: curriculum, educational aims (or purposes), and disciplinary specialization.

SOME BACKGROUND

··

In *The Quest for Certainty*, Dewey (1929) discussed two ideas that he believed had long impeded science and were still holding back philosophy and moral theory:

> These two ideas ... are that knowledge is concerned with disclosure of the characteristics of antecedent existences and essences, and that the properties of value found therein provide the authoritative standards for the conduct of life.
>
> (1929, LW 4:58)

The two ideas referred to by Dewey were central in religious thought and helped to strengthen the authority of the Church. Even when science began to shake itself free of this authority, its influence continued:

But the supreme place of good as a defining property of the ultimately real remained the common premise of Jew, Catholic and Protestant. If not vouched for by revelation, it was warranted by the "natural light" of intellect. This phase of the religious tradition was so deeply ingrained in European culture that no philosopher except the thoroughgoing sceptics escaped its influence.

(1929, LW 4:43)

Dewey expressed concern over the insistence on starting a theoretical exploration by locating the "realities" established in antecedent Being. Practice, or action, was from this point of view a mere application of deeper, ultimate truths. Dewey argued for the recognition of a reciprocal relation between established knowledge and thoughtful practice—experimentation—that produces new knowledge:

When, on the other hand, it is seen that the object of *knowledge* is prospective and eventual, being the result of inferential or reflective operations which redispose what was antecedently existent, the subject-matters called respectively sensible and conceptual are seen to be complementary in effective direction of inquiry to an intelligible conclusion.

(1929, LW 4:144)

Dewey pointed out that, while the individual sciences have largely separated themselves from the authoritative grip of the past, there remains the need for integrated results:

The need, however, is practical and human, rather than intrinsic to science itself; the latter is content as long as it can move to new problems and discoveries. The need for direction of action in large social fields is the source of a genuine demand for unification of scientific conclusions.

(1929, LW 4:249)

Further,

The astronomer, biologist, chemist, may attain systematic wholes, at least for a time, within his own field. But when we come to the bearing of special conclusions upon the conduct of social life, we are, outside of technical fields, at a loss.

(1929, LW 4:249)

This integration and application is a job for philosophy, Dewey says, and he agreed that at least part of this job should be shared by education. Consider how well his advice to philosophy might be used in education:

It [philosophy] has to search out and disclose the obstructions; to criticize the habits of mind which stand in the way; to focus reflection upon needs congruous to present life; to interpret the conclusions of science with respect to their consequences for our beliefs about purposes and values in all phases of life.

(1929, LW 4:250)

How might this advice contribute to the analysis and direction of educational thought? Are we still largely held in the grip of traditional thinking?

CURRICULUM

Consider the basic, almost-standard high school curriculum: English, mathematics, science, history (or social studies), and a foreign language. We know that secondary education was designed to prepare males for public life, and in the next section of this chapter, we apply Dewey's thinking to an evaluation of educational aims and purposes. Here we discuss how firmly entrenched we are in the traditionally approved curriculum and the questions we might ask if we could shake free from it.

In the early twentieth century, American education made a novel, forward-looking move with the invention of the comprehensive high school. As the country made the transition from an agricultural to an industrial economy, it was widely recognized that more young people needed a high school education. There was, of course, considerable debate over the form that an expanded education should take (Kliebard 1995). Some insisted that the traditional, classical curriculum of the academies should be adopted in all secondary schools; others argued for a variety of programs to accommodate interests and talents that were not strongly academic. Fortunately, the latter won out, and the comprehensive high school was established, although the basic debate continues to this day. By mid-twentieth century, American high schools were graduating about 75 percent of their students, a figure close to today's graduation rate.

The most highly esteemed curriculum, however, continued to be the traditional academic program, and, despite the early world-leading graduation rate, many have considered the comprehensive high school to be a failure. David Angus and Jeffrey Mirel (1999), for example, argue that our high schools should "focus on their academic mission above all other considerations" (200). Why? The usual argument is offered— that the "best" curriculum traditionally offered to the most talented should be standard fare for all students. Even today, a time in which many courses are offered on a sliding scale of sorts—honors or advanced, standard, slow, remedial—it is still insisted that the "same" curriculum for all advances equality.

Vocational education, many of these critics say, should not be an option except for a few extracurricular courses or activities. Even Dewey worried that vocational "education" might deteriorate to mere vocational training and thus serve to maintain class biases: "Education would then become an instrument of perpetuating unchanged the existing industrial order of society, instead of operating as a means of its transformation" (1985/1916, 326).

During this long period of disagreement—still going on today—the questions suggested by Dewey's discussion have not been seriously addressed. Before we argue over curriculum, we should ask some fundamental questions. What problems are we trying to solve? If it is equality that we seek, does that imply sameness—the same curriculum for all students—or does it imply equal respect for the full range of human talents and interests? If the former, we seem to be working against our goal by using a system of tracking within each discipline. If the latter, then surely we should be organizing and supporting really fine programs in vocational education. As we work on this, we should heed Dewey's warning about the possible deterioration of vocational education into mere vocational training. How can we prevent this? I say more about this in the next section on aims and purposes.

Let's consider briefly what might be done if we continue on the present path—the same curriculum for all. What are the habits of mind that stand in the way? One such habit is clearly the devotion to the traditional structure of curriculum. In mathematics, is algebra really necessary for every student? In many states, barely 25 percent of high school students pass the PARC test in algebra. Is this because of poor teaching? Is it because of poor preparation in elementary school? Is it possible that many students simply dislike algebra and can see no real point in learning it? Or is it possible that most adults never use algebra and do not need it?

Andrew Hacker (2016) argues in favor of the last possibility. Most people never use any formal algebra. What they need is the mathematics of financial management and basic statistics. His argument is cogent. Yet even within a subject or discipline—never mind the whole curriculum—we encounter great difficulty in making any significant change. Suppose that it was suggested that just one year of mathematics devoted to personal finance and statistics be required for high school graduation? The usual academic sequence would still be available for those who choose it, but little or no algebra would be required for graduation. Think of the host of interesting questions that arise from this decision. Are there, for example, some elements of algebra that are really essential for intelligent adult life? What about variation, proportion, number systems, and probability? Why might these be important in everyday life?

Not only might the structure and content of each of the traditional disciplines be rethought. We might also consider changing the structure of the entire curriculum. Remember that it was designed by males for male participation in public life. How might the curriculum have been designed if there were equal concern for personal and home life (Kerber 1997; Noddings 2015)? Why do we teach almost nothing about parenting and homemaking when both are so important in adult life?

When it is decided that something is really important—moral life, for example—how does education acknowledge that importance? Again, we are trapped by the traditional structure. We might adopt a program of moral education for elementary school or middle school, but how in the world would we fit it into the high school curriculum? Add a course? In which year? Could it be required? Would it warrant college admission credit? Could it possibly "count" as much as biology or English literature? How would we decide whether it "works"? Add another test?

What stands in the way of considering such additions and changes? How should we identify "needs congruous to present life"? How should we interpret current conclusions that tell us many students are not acquiring competence in algebra? Should we reconsider, at least reflect upon, "our beliefs about purposes and values in all phases of life" as Dewey suggested?

AIMS AND PURPOSES

What might the high school curriculum look like if it had not been originally designed to prepare males for public life and occupations? Surely, if women had been involved, some attention would have been given to family life, homemaking, and parenting. Even when these matters appeared in the early colleges for women, however, they were not highly valued, and they were soon displaced in favor of the more prestigious subjects characteristic of the traditional male curriculum.

We should step back a bit and ask what we are trying to accomplish in education. What are our purposes? There are, of course, volumes on this question, and I do not intend to produce a comprehensive answer here. Rather, following Dewey, I simply want to draw attention to "our beliefs about purposes and values in all phases of life." Basically, through education, we hope to produce better people, people better equipped to meet challenges in every aspect of life: personal life, family life, vocational life, and civic life. As educators, we hope to contribute to the development of qualities that will help our students to cope well with these challenges. These qualities include at least moral, intellectual, empathic, and agreeable personality features. In addition, we must consider the skills required to cope adequately in all aspects of life. Conversations, explorations, and reflections on the characteristic aspects or categories of life and the qualities needed to thrive in each of them should be central, permanent facets of educational life.

Consider again the earlier discussion about vocational education and the fear expressed that it might collapse into mere vocational training. Some critics would eliminate all practical activities—even business and medicine from the college and college preparatory curricula (see Hutchins 1964). They hold fast to the idea that the main task of "real" education is to maintain and develop intellectual excellence. The logical conclusion for many of these critics is that college-oriented education should be reserved for those who display the requisite intellectual talent (see Murray 2008). This argument about the ultimate purpose of education is an old one that is unlikely to go away. Is it unfair? Does it work against our commitment to democracy and equality?

Concentrating on the education of the academically talented would certainly be unfair and against our devotion to equality. But suppose vocational programs were designed with as much care, expert attention, and financial investment as the excellent academic program? Suppose students could choose proudly among academic and vocational programs? An excellent vocational program would, like its academic counterparts, include attention to the full range of concerns for personal life, family life, vocational and civic life. And mechanical, hands-on work can be as challenging as the mental work offered in academic programs (Crawford 2009). A good mechanic can appreciate the beauty as well as the efficiency of a machine he has repaired. When, on the other hand, we insist on the same college preparatory program for all students in the name of equality, perhaps we convey an almost opposite message to the student who—if she had been given the choice—would have chosen a different program. Perhaps we, the academically talented, are unintentionally saying that everyone can (should?) be just like us. How does a mechanically talented student feel when he is told that he, too, can succeed at algebra and English literature but it may take a bit longer, require remedial work, separate him from his real interests, and force him to accept second- or third-place ratings? Is this equality?

As we consider designing new vocational programs for our secondary schools, we must keep Dewey's warning in mind. We should not want these programs to be "offered" as mindless alternatives to genuine education. But, then, neither should our universal academic programs be devoid of intellectual challenge and preparation for a full life. These, too, should be examined in the light of present purposes and values.

Perhaps more attention should be given to the idea of *choice*. Instead of assigning students to programs and courses according to our assessments of their abilities, perhaps we should allow them—with patient, adequate guidance—to choose their program. Not only might students proudly choose a vocational program; they might also choose what we now call an "honors" course in mathematics. With a sound understanding of how challenging the work will be and the sacrifice of free time demanded, an "average" student should be allowed to take the course if she wishes to do so. If she does not so choose, it will nevertheless be *her choice*. She will not find herself in an "average" course because she is not judged good enough by others for the more demanding course.

The role of choice should be discussed more often and more openly. Two centuries ago, the United States was properly labeled a *representative* democracy. It was the job of eligible voters (male landowners) to consider and elect the brightest among them to run the government. Today, we are moving closer to a *participatory* democracy—one in which all citizens are expected to participate in running the government. It is an exciting, but messy and complicated, process, and certainly the concept of choice is central in its operation. Citizens in a participatory democracy must learn to choose wisely and generously. In addition to assessing their own needs and possible contributions, they must consider the welfare of the whole community. To participate effectively, they must be generous listeners, adequate critical thinkers, and effective communicators.

Further, a participatory democracy puts great emphasis on the interaction of the groups that comprise its civil society. As Dewey points out, there are groups—such as criminal bands—that are held together by common goals and rules. These groups, however, do not qualify as *democratic* because they fail to interact cooperatively with other groups in the larger society. Dewey suggests a standard to apply to all groups in our society: "How numerous and varied are the interests which are consciously shared? How full and free is the interplay with other forms of association?" (1916, MW 9:89). As we consider our educational purposes in the context of our current problems in cross-class communication, it becomes vividly clear that something must be done to reduce the growing communication gap.

Today's communication gap has been increased by the movement toward gated communities, separate schools (or sharply separated programs within a school), separate shopping areas, even different doctors' offices and churches. Robert Putnam (2015) has described the differences dramatically in the account of how his hometown, Port Clinton, Ohio, has changed over the past fifty years. Moderately rich and moderately poor are no longer on a first-name basis; they rarely communicate with each other. His description of separate lives in a medium-size community is reminiscent in its tale of class differences of those recounted so vividly by George Orwell eighty years ago. Orwell reminded us then that it is extremely difficulty to overcome class differences: "To get rid of class-distinctions you have got to start by understanding how one class appears when seen through the eyes of another" (1937/1958, 131). This is advice that we should take seriously today. Before the 2016 US election season, few of us (the educated elite) were aware of the rising anger among the white working class.

Well-meaning "elites" often aggravate the communication gap. Elizabeth Anderson (2007) has described the attitude that is often conveyed by those who want to help people in need. Instead of working together with them to identify problems and explore solutions, they (the elites) diagnose and prescribe solutions. There is a failure of communication:

> Communicative competence is a shared good of the communicators. It is not a private possession that one party has and the other lacks. If A and B are not communicating effectively due to cultural differences, then both lack cultural capital with respect to each other . . . . When elites are overwhelmingly drawn from segregated advantaged groups, they share their deficits in cultural capital. (2007, 604)

In part, of course, it is these differences that education strives to overcome, but a structure of education that demeans or puts a label of "second-rate" on all but the most advanced intellectual programs may aggravate the very differences it is pledged to overcome.

The complications produced by class differences affect public/political life at every level. Well-meaning people ("liberators") at the international level often experience contradictory feelings about the oppressed people they are trying to help. They confess to feeling both sympathy and hostility. Michael Walzer, for example, comments:

> Sympathy, because the liberators don't just resent the foreign rulers—they really want to improve the lives of the men and women with whom they identify . . . . Hostility, because at the same time the liberators hate what they take to be the backwardness, ignorance, passivity, and submissiveness of those same people. (2015, 68)

All of this suggests that the difficulties of communicating across classes—either economic or educational—are real and important in our civic life. Where will we address them in our high schools? I have suggested installing a four-year seminar on social/moral/political issues, a seminar carefully composed of students from *all* of the programs (Noddings 2013; Noddings and Brooks 2016). If we are to produce better people—people better prepared to engage in a participatory democracy—we should start them in the process early and try to maintain the lines of communication into adult political life. This is one suggestion. Following Dewey, the crucial point is to recognize the problem and proceed with discussion, experimentation, analysis, careful (even temporary) implementation, and evaluation.

For illustrative purposes, let's consider another area that is badly neglected in our schools. Parenting is surely one of the most important responsibilities undertaken by most adults, and yet we teach almost nothing about it in our high schools. One reason for this has historical roots. Public secondary education was designed to prepare males for public life, and matters such as homemaking and childcare were considered to be women's work. Another, related reason is the closely held belief that public schools should not interfere with the private lives of citizens. A third reason—important today—is that poor parenting is often associated with poverty, and critics do not want to be accused of blaming the victim. Realistically, however, it must be noted that the poor are not immune to weaknesses and ignorance (Desmond 2016; Isenberg 2016; Vance 2016). As Walzer confessed, liberators and helpers often deplore the negative behaviors of those needing help. Further, weak or faulty parenting appears in all classes, but the wealthier can compensate with tutoring, private schools, travel, equipment, and high-powered summer camps. But what should schools do? I have suggested a four-year seminar on social issues. What else might schools do? Adding a course to an already full curriculum mired in traditional structure is not feasible. In the next section, however, I invite readers to think about possibilities in interdisciplinary arrangements.

Let's consider one more contemporary set of educational issues. How should we treat feeling or affect in our schools? This is an issue that gives rise to contradictions. Some of us believe that feelings are central to both life and education; we want to educate both heads and hearts. In acting on this belief, we urge teachers to encourage imagination, uncover fears, and work to resolve animosities. If we are working on a set of mathematical work problems, surely it is better to approach them with imagination and a sense of vital challenge than to tackle them with dull rules and dread. Volumes have been written about the importance of feeling in intellectual life. But a somewhat contradictory notion has arisen recently—that students must be protected from ideas that may induce bad feelings, and some teachers have accepted the responsibility to provide "trigger warnings" and other ways to shield students from ideas that may upset them. The downside of this response is that teachers may stick even more closely to the day's specified learning objective and produce one boring lesson after another.

On the positive side, it is useful to study and discuss how important feeling and imagination have been in scientific as well as artistic work. Alexander Von Humboldt, for example, approached the natural world with both scientific precision and artistic delight.

"Being with Goethe, Humboldt said, equipped him with 'new organs' through which to see the natural world" (Wulf 2015, 38). These new organs were clearly associated with sympathy, delight, surprise, and art.

Too often today, students treat their studies as merely a means to get good grades, a high GPA, and acceptance at the college they hope to attend. Once there, at the college level, studies are again considered a necessary form of drudgery. Imagination and intellectual excitement rarely color the required curriculum, and it should not be assumed that they are automatically satisfied by providing courses in art and literature. Dewey explained:

> It is, then, a serious mistake to regard appreciation as if it were confined to such things as literature and pictures and music. Its scope is as comprehensive as the work of education itself . . . . There are adequate grounds for asserting that the premium so often put in schools upon external "discipline", and upon marks and rewards, upon promotion and keeping back, are the obverse of the lack of attention given to life situations in which the meaning of facts, ideas, principles, and problems is vitally brought home.
>
> (1916, MW 9:244)

And a bit later,

> Only a personal response involving imagination can possibly procure realization even of pure "facts". The imagination is the medium to appreciation in every field. The engagement of the imagination is the only thing that makes any activity more than mechanical.
>
> (1916, MW 9:244)

Dewey is not talking about the play-acting or mind-wandering with which teachers often confuse the genuine use of imagination in education:

> The result is an unwholesome exaggeration of the fantastic and "unreal" phases of childish play and a deadly reduction of serious occupation to a routine efficiency prized simply for its external tangible results. Achievement comes to denote the sort of thing that a well-planned machine can do better than a human being can, and the main effect of education, the achieving of a life of rich significance, drops by the wayside.
>
> (1916, MW 9:245)

Does this sound familiar? It is just the sort of consequence that should worry us. When we closely examine our values and purposes in the present era of education, what should be questioned? What should we rethink and how? Does the current process of instructing, testing, recording, and repeating represent real education?

The contradictory part of the problem under consideration is one we hear today with some frequency—the need to protect students from language and expressed feelings that may hurt them. Surely, all thoughtful educators agree that potentially sensitive topics should be handled with care, care for the students directly affected and care for the welfare of the community and intellectual programs under discussion. But the need for sensitivity in discussing matters that arouse feeling should not cause teachers to avoid such matters entirely. The present climate pushes teachers more and more to "stick with the learning objective," avoid all distractions, and essentially take the heart out of teaching-learning. If Dewey is right about the central importance of imagination in learning, we simply must enrich our coursework if we are to justify our claims to educate.

DISCIPLINARY SPECIALIZATION

Whenever schools are asked to take on a new concept or area of attention, the response is either to claim that the matter under consideration is not a job for the school or, if it is acknowledged that it should be one for schools, the question arises where to put it. Does it belong in math? In English? In the arts? Or must we add a new course? This sort of response illustrates vividly how deeply we are stuck in the traditional mode of thinking that Dewey deplored.

If, instead, we started our conversation/debate with a description of the current problem, reflection on our current purposes and values, and an evaluation of what stands in the way of a solution, we might make some progress. We know, for example, that adding a course is rarely feasible. Our purpose is to produce better people—people better prepared to live competently and happily in all the categories of life mentioned earlier. If, for example, we are asked to do something that will make it more likely that our students will contribute to civic life, enjoy a rich personal life, and derive satisfaction from their vocations, what might we do? The temptation is to separate the three aspects of life (and all others) and ask where each "belongs" in the existing curriculum. This is almost certainly a mistake. We should ask instead how each discipline can contribute and how the disciplines might work together.

E. O. Wilson (2006) has argued for the "unity of knowledge" and focus on the connections of the individual disciplines to each other:

> As a consequence, what was once perceived as an epistemological divide between the great branches of learning is now emerging from the academic fog as something far different and much more interesting: a wide middle domain of mostly unexplored phenomena open to a cooperative approach from both sides of the former divide . . . . The middle domain is a region of exceptionally rapid intellectual advance. It, moreover, addresses issues in which students (and the rest of us) are most interested. (2006, 136)

In his focus on problem solving, Wilson adds:

> There is, in my opinion, an inevitability to the unity of knowledge. It reflects real life. The trajectory of world events suggests that educated people should be far better able than before to address the great issues courageously and analytically by undertaking a traverse of the disciplines. (2006, 137)

We have already mentioned Dewey's comments on the need to bring together the work of natural and social sciences. It seems, Dewey noted, that "we are at a loss" when it comes to using the conclusions of the disparate disciplines to guide social life. Dewey does not go as far as Wilson in claiming a unity of knowledge, but he does seek vital connections:

> The sheer increase of specialized knowledge will never work the miracle of producing an intellectual whole. Nevertheless, the need for integration of specialized results of science remains, and philosophy should contribute to the satisfaction of the need.
>
> (1929, LW 4:249)

Further,

> Were there any consensus as to the significance of what is known upon beliefs about things of ideal and general value, our life would be marked by integrity instead of by distraction and by conflict of competing aims and standards. Needs of practical action in large and liberal social fields would give unification to our special knowledge; and the latter would give solidity and confidence to the judgment of values that control conduct.
>
> (1929, LW 4:249)

Perhaps the closest we can come to the integrity offered by the variety and differences inherent in segmented knowledge is to make greater use of interdisciplinary approaches. Instead of confining appreciation to the arts, we should address it in all of the disciplines. The same is true of topics in religion, peace, morals, family life, and social policy. In all of the disciplines, we could make extensive use of biographies, stories, art, literature, humor, and games.

In mathematics, for example, we could share some biographical accounts of great mathematicians. I do not mean by this to ask each student to choose a mathematician and write a couple paragraphs citing his birthdate, birthplace, and major work for which he or she is best known. This sort of assignment would almost certainly suffer the same fate as the quadratic formula in the lives of most students; it would be soon and gladly forgotten. As Dewey reminded us, it is appreciation exercised through imagination that makes "information" come alive.

Math teachers might share with students Henri Poincare's description of creative work in mathematics. There is, he said, an initial period ("preparation") of mathematical labor distinguished mainly by hard work—even drudgery. This often ends—or passes—without a solution, and the math worker goes on to other daily events. But during these seemingly unproductive periods, unconscious mental activity continues; this is the period of "incubation." With good fortune, incubation is followed by "illumination" (the aha! experience), and all that remains is to write it all down. (See the accounts in E. T. Bell [1937/1965] and Newman [1956].) Teachers who share this dramatic account of mathematical experience with students should be prepared for daydreaming students to defend their behavior by saying, "I'm incubating, I'm incubating!"

Math teachers might also draw on the work of Douglas Hofstadter (1979) to discuss fascinating connections between math and art (Escher) and math and music (Bach). But they might also find his discussion of both "number numbness" and freedom of speech useful. On the former, he wonders how many of our citizens are able to read (put into words) the numbers 314,159,265,358, 979 and 271,828,182,845 (Hofstadter 1985, 130). In any class, we might check whether students can translate these numbers into words. In high school math classes, we might ask students whether they see anything more fascinating about these numbers. Suppose we put a decimal point after the 3 in the first number and after the 2 in the second. What do we see? Here is an opportunity to discuss the history of *pi* and *e*.

Discussion of number numbness gives us an opening to consider Hofstadter's handling—few pages before number numbness—of freedom of speech, a topic of great importance today. In the process of describing a moral tangle experienced by the American Civil Liberties Union, he expresses a worry that plagues us today:

> Patrick Henry spoke of "defending to the death your right to say it"—but does "it" include *anything*? Recipes for how to murder people? How to build atomic bombs? How to destroy the free press? Governments also face this sticky kind of issue. Can a government dedicated to liberty afford to let an organization dedicated to that government's downfall flourish? (1985, 109)

Hofstadter puts aside the question of whether some comments should be forbidden entirely (and we need to discuss this more fully today), but he addresses the important, more manageable question of where we should draw the line in separating science and pseudo-science. He tells us the story of how the *Skeptical Inquirer* magazine was founded to debunk fake science. Careful debunkers give a hearing to statements that are highly questionable, but they then go on to expose mistakes and untruths in these accounts. Can students name any sources today that take on this job?

Martin Gardner was one of the founders of *Skeptical Inquirer*, and many students today are still entranced by his puzzles. However, all students should have an opportunity to read his classic work, *The Annotated Alice* (1963). The logic puzzles are wonderful, and the misuse of mathematical data is hilarious. Indeed, Gardner's work on mathematics, magic, philosophy, religion, puzzles, logic, and pseudo-science stands as an exemplar of fascinating interdisciplinary work.

Mention of Gardner and his interdisciplinary interests gives us an opportunity to say a bit on religion in math class. Although he agreed with atheists about most of the formal beliefs of institutional religion, Gardner was not himself an atheist. Rejecting almost everything in formal religion, he believed in both God and immortality because, he said, "it consoles me" (1983, 208).

There are other interesting stories to be told about mathematicians and religion. G. H. Hardy, a pure mathematician, studied and taught at Cambridge and Oxford in the first half of the twentieth century. He was so averse to religion that he refused to attend the required services or even enter a house of worship. His mathematical genius was so appreciated, however, that the by-laws were amended to excuse him from chapel attendance.

Mention of Hardy and religion triggers two other matters of interest. Hardy, like so many great mathematicians, loved and treasured the *beauty* of mathematics. He disdained "useful" mathematics and even claimed, "I have never done anything 'useful'" (Hardy 1956, 2038). As it turns out, much of his work was in fact useful, but Hardy continued to insist that he did not intend that usefulness. The second matter of interest about Hardy has to do with friendship and generosity. While other British mathematicians ignored the self-taught Indian thinker Srinivasa Ramanujan, Hardy responded to his letters and papers with admiration and tangible help. And Ramanujan's expressed reactions seemed to increase Hardy's own interest and originality.

I hope readers will understand what I mean to illustrate. Imagination brings perception alive. Something interests us, and we begin to think, to seek connections. We review what we already know, what we are reading or hearing, and we try to make connections. We do not stick stubbornly to the day's learning objective in algebra. We draw on all of the disciplines to make connections. The connections enliven our thinking and encourage us to expand it. Imagine math connected to art, science, music, history, literature, religion, beauty, and ... fun! Not only does interdisciplinary work promise help with the identification and solution of social problems, it offers enrichment to the intellectual lives of communities and individuals.

CONCLUSION

The emphasis in this chapter has been on the advice Dewey gave to philosophy and education; it is worth repeating: "to search out and disclose the obstructions; to criticize the habits of mind which stand in the way; to focus reflection upon needs congruous to present life; to interpret the conclusions for our beliefs about purposes and values in all phases of life" (1929, LW 4:250).

His advice to start with an examination of current problems and current beliefs, values, and purposes is cogent. This does not mean that we should discard what has come down to us from the past. It means, rather, that the knowledge of the past should be reviewed in light of the present. Imagination, intelligently exercised, seeks to make the connections that may help to solve—or at least relieve—present problems.

On careful reflection, it seems unlikely that the structure of the high school curriculum will be changed. But, accepting the grip of that tradition on us, we might still expand the variety of programs offered and, in particular, renew our dedication to genuine vocational *education*. Moving in this direction requires a new analysis of what we mean by *equality* and a new emphasis on *choice*. To prepare students for effective life in a participatory democracy, we must provide them with the skills and commitment to communicate across class lines and to develop appreciation for the full range of human talents.

I have suggested that our major educational aim should be to produce better people, and this aim commits us to an ongoing conversation. What do we mean by "better people," and how does the curriculum we offer contribute to that aim?

Finally, in keeping with Dewey's analysis and that more recently offered by E. O. Wilson, I have suggested far greater emphasis on interdisciplinary studies. This emphasis not only invites new and exciting dialogues; it also holds the possibility for connecting specialized knowledge to our current social problems. As Dewey put it:

> To abandon the search for absolute and immutable reality and value may seem like a sacrifice. But this renunciation is the condition of entering a vocation of greater vitality. The search for values to be secured and shared by all, because buttressed in the foundation of social life, is a quest in which philosophy [and education] would have no rivals but coadjutors in men of good will.
>
> (1929, LW 4:248)

WORKS CITED

Citations of John Dewey's works are to the thirty-seven-volume critical edition published by Southern Illinois University Press under the editorship of Jo Ann Boydston. In-text citations give the original publication date and series abbreviation, followed by volume number and page number. For example: (1934, LW 10:12) is page 12 of *Art as Experience*, which is published as volume 10 of *The Later Works*.

Series abbreviations for *The Collected Works*:

EW *The Early Works* (1882–1898)

MW *The Middle Works* (1899–1924)

LW *The Later Works* (1925–1953)

Anderson, E. 2007. Fair opportunity in education: A democratic equality perspective. *Ethics*, vol. 117, no. 4, 595–622.

Angus, D. L., and Mirel, J. E. 1999. *The failed promise of the American high school.* New York: Teachers College Press.

Bell, E. T. 1937/1965. *Men of mathematics.* New York: Simon & Schuster.

Crawford, M. B. 2009. *Shop class as soulcraft.* New York: Penguin Press.

Desmond, M. 2016. *Evicted: Poverty and profit in the American city.* New York: Crown.

Dewey, J. 1916. *Democracy and education.* MW 9. Carbondale and Edwardsville: Southern Illinois Press.

Dewey, J. 1929. *The quest for certainty.* LW 4. Carbondale and Edwardsville: Southern Illinois Press.

Gardner, M. 1963. *The annotated Alice (Lewis Carroll).* New York: World Publishing.

Gardner, M. 1983. *The whys of a philosophical scrivener.* New York: Quill.

Hacker, A. 2016. *The math myth.* New York: New Press.

Hardy, G. H. 1956. A mathematician's apology. In *The world of mathematics.* Edited by James R. Newman, 2027–2038. New York: Simon & Schuster.

Hofstadter, D. R. 1979. *Godel, Escher, Bach: An eternal golden braid.* New York: Basic Books.

Hofstadter, D. R. 1985. *Metamagical themes: Questing for the essence of mind and pattern.* New York: Basic Books.

Hutchins, R. M. 1964. *The university of Utopia.* Chicago: University of Chicago Press.

Isenberg, N. 2016. *White trash: The 400-year untold history of class in America.* New York: Random House.

Kerber, L. 1997. *Toward an intellectual history of women.* Chapel Hill: University of North Carolina Press.

Kliebard, H. 1995. *The struggle for the American curriculum 1893–1958.* New York: Routledge.

Murray, C. 2008. *Real education.* New York: Random House.

Newman, James R., ed. 1956. *The World of Mathematics.* NY: Simon & Schuster.

Noddings, N. 2013. *Education and democracy in the 21st century.* New York: Teachers College Press.

Noddings, N. 2015. *A richer, brighter vision for American high schools.* Cambridge, UK: Cambridge University Press.

Noddings, N., and Brooks, L. 2016. *Teaching controversial issues: The case for critical thinking and moral commitment in the classroom.* New York: Teachers College Press.

Orwell, G. 1937/1958. *The road to Wigan pier.* San Diego: Harcourt.

Putnam, R. D. 2015. *Our kids: The American dream in crisis.* New York: Simon & Schuster.

Vance, J. D. 2016. *Hillbilly elegy: A memoir of a family and culture in crisis.* New York: Harper.

Walzer, M. 2015. *The paradox of liberation: Secular revolution and religious counterrevolution.* New Haven: Yale University Press.

Wilson, E. O. 2006. *The creation: An appeal to save life on earth.* New York: W. W. Norton.

Wulf, A. 2015. *The invention of nature: Alexander von Humboldt's new world.* New York: Alfred A. Knopf.

CHAPTER 17

DERRIDEAN POSTSTRUCTURALISM, DEWEYAN PRAGMATISM, AND EDUCATION

JIM GARRISON

INTRODUCTION

THERE has been little contact between Deweyan pragmatism and Derridean deconstruction. When deconstructionist philosophers of education turn to Dewey, they usually use him to expose the supposed limits of modernism and progressive education.[1] Here, the approach to Derrida comes from the side of pragmatism with decided Deweyan preferences. Limited space requires omitting several points of significant contact.[2] Thoughtful readers may readily fill in gaps.

DERRIDEAN DECONSTRUCTION, THE TRACE OF DIFFÉRANCE, AND ALTERITY

Derrida (1982) derives his notion of the deconstructive trace of *différance* from Ferdinand de Saussure's structuralist concept of "difference." He cites this critical passage from Saussure:

> [I]n language there are only differences. Even more important: a difference generally implies positive terms between which the difference is set up; but in language there are only differences without positive terms. Whether we take the signified or

the signifier, language has neither ideas nor sounds that existed before the linguistic system, but only conceptual and phonic differences that have issued from the system. The idea or phonic substance that a sign contains is of less importance than the other signs that surround it. (10–11)

Both ideational content and sound image depend on a web of differences without positive content. Derrida reminds us,

Now this principle of difference, as the condition for signification, affects the totality of the sign, that is the sign as both signified and signifier. The signified is the concept, the ideal meaning; and the signifier is what Saussure calls the "image," the "psychical imprint" of a material, physical--for example, acoustical—phenomenon. (10)

The ideal meaning in Saussure is something mental in a psychic sense as is the image corresponding to something in the world. It assumes a form versus content dualism.

For structuralist thinkers, any system of signs (e.g., a theory, a text, etc.) eventually terminates with the immediate intuitive presence of the "transcendental signified;" that is, some immediately present referent outside the semiotic system (Derrida, 1976, 158). Derrida (1973) first arrived at this insight analyzing Edmund Husserl:

Self-presence must be produced in the undivided unity of a temporal present so as to have nothing to reveal to itself by the agency of signs. Such a perception or intuition of self by self in presence would not only be the case where "signification" in general could not occur, but also would assure the general possibility of a primordial perception or intuition ... Later, whenever Husserl wants to stress the sense of primordial intuition, he will recall that it is the experience of the absence and uselessness of signs. (60)

In eidetic intuition, the mental empirical content of the noesis corresponds perfectly with the psychic form of thought or noema. Derrida rejects the entire western tradition of *nous* including Descartes' clear and distinct ideas and Heidegger's *aletheia*. Immediate noetic intuitions are instances of what Wilfrid Sellars (1997) calls "the myth of the given." It is not possible to complete "the quest for certainty" (1929, LW 4). There are no ultimate foundations (i.e., *arche*).

Surprisingly, Derrida retains a Husserlian stance toward the self and consciousness; he merely destabilizes the ability to secure the transcendental signified of self or object. Derrida (1976) adamantly insists "non-presentation or depresentation is as 'originary' as presentation" entails that *a thought of the trace can no more break with a transcendental phenomenology than be reduced to it"* (62).

Having critiqued Husserl and Heidegger, Derrida (1982) readily recognized that in Saussure's semiotics the play of semiotic differences never collapses into the immediate presence of a "transcendental" signified:

[T]he signified concept is never present in and of itself, in a sufficient presence that would refer only to itself. Essentially and lawfully, every concept is inscribed in a chain or in a system within which it refers to the other, to other concepts, by means of the systematic play of differences. Such a play, différance, is thus no longer simply a concept, but rather the possibility of conceptuality, of a conceptual process and system in general. (11)

Derrida (1976) introduces the neologism *différance* (with an "a") to depict a double meaning to the movement of difference. First, there is "difference": the signifier is different from the signified. Second, the meaning of the signifier is deferred to the signified (i.e., the deferred presence). The result is the "originary trace or arche-trace" of *différance* (61).

All there is of concepts (i.e., ideas, meaning) or psychic percepts (i.e., phenomenal content) is a trace of differences in which "the trace is not a presence [of the transcendental signified] but the simulacrum of a presence that dislocates itself, displaces itself, refers itself, it properly has no site—erasure belongs to its structure" (Derrida, 1982, 24). For Derrida, the trace is a track, path, or mark, of the originating *différance*. The originary trace (i.e., archi-trace) annuls the sign at the origin; it is, as Gayatri Spivak (1976) indicates, the "mark of the absence of a presence, an always already absent present" (xvii).

Derrida asserts that *différance* antecedes even the difference beyond the sensible and the intelligible:

It is not the question of a constituted difference here, but rather, before all determination of the content, of the pure movement which produces difference. *The (pure) trace is différance.* It does not depend on any sensible plenitude, audible or visible, phonic or graphic. It is, on the contrary, the condition of such a plenitude. Although *it does not* exist, although it is never a *being-present* outside of all plenitude, its possibility is by rights anterior to all that one calls sign (signified/signifier, content/expression, etc.), concept or operation, motor or sensory. This difference is therefore not more sensible than intelligible and it permits the articulation of signs among themselves within the same abstract order—a phonic or graphic text for example—or between two orders of expression. (62)

Furthermore, Derrida (1982) states, the trace "is no more an effect than it has a cause" (12). The arche-trace is the quasi-transcendental a priori condition of possibility of semiotics.

Unlike Kant's transcendental categories, différance is not any kind of form of human thought,

[W]e will designate as *différance* the movement according to which language, or any code, any system of referral in general is constituted "historically" as a weave of differences. "Is constituted," "is produced," "is created," "movement," "historically," etc., necessarily being understood beyond the metaphysical language in which they are retained, along with all their implications. (12)

Derrida employs words like "produced" or "movement" only for their strategic conven-
ience given our culturally entrenched use of language. Similarly, "*différance* is neither
simply active nor simply passive" (9). Production, movement, static, structural, active,
passive, or anything else eventually requires undertaking "their deconstruction at the
currently most decisive point" (9). *Différance* precedes Kant's transcendental categories
(quantity, quality, relation, and modality). However, like Kant's Free Will, God, and
Immortality, *différance* is thinkable but not knowable. Like all a priori principles, it is a
deliverance of pure thought devoid of content. His quasi-transcendentalism is aggressively anti-empirical. Derrida (1978b) states that "the true name of this renunciation of
the concept, of the a prioris and transcendental horizons of language, is *empiricism*. For
the latter has ever committed but one fault: the fault of presenting itself as philosophy"
(151; see also 139).

Derrida (1982) also argues that *différance* marks Heidegger's "ontico-ontological difference" (10). Between "Being" and instances of Being that present (disclose, unveil,
unconceal) themselves (i.e., *aletheia*); that is, "being." He asserts, "'Older' than Being
itself, such a différance has no name in our language" (26). Ever elusive, and allusive,
Derrida asserts that no name will suffice for the unnamable, "not even that of 'différance,'
which is not a name, which is not a pure nominal unity, and unceasingly dislocates itself
in a chain of differing and deferring substitutions" (10).

Restless, Derrida renders unsteady even the most stable terms in his or anyone else's
discourse:

> Now if we consider the chain in which *différance* lends itself to a certain number of
> nonsynonymous substitutions, according to the necessity of the context, why have
> recourse to the "reserve," to "archi-writing," to the "archi-trace," to "spacing," that is,
> to the "supplement," or to the *pharmakon*, and soon to the hymen, to the margin-
> mark-march, etc. (12)

These terms execute similar functions but are not identical. Derrida allows no word,
no concept, or even his own non-concepts to become a master term inhibiting semiotic movement. Derrida (1991) does not even think deconstruction "a good word" and
concludes, "It deconstructs itself" (275). Derrida depicts an aleatory world without
stable center or circumference.[3]

The illusion of the transcendental signified in Saussure arises out of his logocentric
metaphysics in conjunction with phonocentrism:

> The system of language associated with phonetic-alphabetic writing is that within
> which logocentric metaphysics, determining the sense of being as presence, has been
> produced. This logocentrism, this *epoch* of the full speech, has always placed in pa-
> renthesis, suspended, and suppressed for essential reasons, all free reflection on the
> origin and status of writing, all science of writing which was not technology and the
> *history of a technique,* itself leaning upon a mythology and a metaphor of a natural
> writing.
>
> (Derrida, 1976, 45)

Logocentrism implies the transcendental signified of a metaphysically immutable, indubitable, fixed, and final essence (object, self, etc.). Logocentrism is a quest for certainty.

Phonocentrism refers to the immediate self-presence of the knower's voice in speaking the words specifying the immediately present self-identical phenomena. Because of the immediate presence of the putatively "originary spoken language," Saussure privileges voice over the presumed absence of writing (29). Derrida rejects logocentrism, phonocentrism, and, as already shown, egocentrism.

Derrida ultimately retains Saussure's two-term theory of signs. As with Husserl, Derrida obligates to Saussure negatively and positively. Negatively, Saussure is guilty of logocentrism and phonocentrism arising from his commitment to the metaphysics of presence. Positively, Saussure's semiotics assumes the endless search for the transcendental signified that never arrives thereby providing the ground for the incessant deconstructive play of *différance*.

Derrida is a uniquely original post-Heideggerian neo-Kantian. The most significant aspect of that originality lies in his deconstruction of Western metaphysics. Derrida treats the pure trace as "something like an originary différance"; however, "one could no longer call it originary or final in the extent to which the values of origin, archi-, *telos, eskhaton*, etc. have always denoted presence—*ousia, parousia*" (9). Derrida (1978a) rejects all aspects of the metaphysics of immutable, indubitable presence:

> The entire history of the concept of structure . . . must be thought of as a series of substitutions of center for center, as a linked chain of determinations of the center . . . . It could be shown that all names related to fundamentals, to principles, or to the center have always designated an invariable presence—*eidos, arche, telos, energeia, ousia* (essence, existence, substance, subject. (279–280)

Eidos is something's characteristic properties, or essence. *Arche* indicates ultimate origin, foundation, or first principle. *Energeia* is the functioning of a capacity or potential to achieve its fulfillment and actualization. It conjoins with telos as completion, end, or purpose and *entelecheia*, the capacity or force to achieve its perfect self-actualization. For instance, a properly functioning acorn will become a giant oak. These various elements are interdependent and often collapse into each other. In the metaphysics of presence, Derrida (1973) writes: "The *eidos* is determined in depth by the *telos*" or more exactly the *entelecheia* (97). *Ousia* often converges with the *arche* as the ultimate underlying substance or *eidos*.

Derrida (1978a) does not attempt a Heideggerian destruction (*Destruktion*) of metaphysics:

> There is no sense in doing without the concepts of metaphysics in order to shake metaphysics. We have no language—no syntax and no lexicon—which is foreign to this history; we can pronounce not a single destructive proposition which has not already had to slip into the form, the logic, and the implicit postulations of precisely what it seeks to contest. (280)

As with Husserl's transcendentalism and Saussure's semiotics, Derrida leaves metaphysics in place as a platform from whence to launch endless deconstruction. Without the metaphysics of presence conjoined with its impossibility, deconstructive movement is unsustainable: "Metaphysically," writes Derrida (1978b), "the best liberation from violence is a certain putting into question, which makes the search for an *archia* tremble" (141). Derrida contends that in the pursuit of improved ethical-political relations, it always possible to conduct deconstructions thereby rendering metaphysical foundations precarious.

Derrida (1984) maintains, "Deconstruction always presupposes affirmation" (118). What Derrida most wishes to affirm is "an openness towards the other" (124). Deconstruction problematizes because it constantly points away from itself toward absence and Otherness. Derrida states deconstruction's affirmation thus:

> I mean that deconstruction is, in itself, a positive response to an alterity which necessarily calls, summons or motivates it . . . . The other precedes philosophy and necessarily invokes and provokes the subject before any genuine questioning can begin. It is in this rapport with the other that affirmation expresses itself. (118)

Deconstruction urges recognition and respect for what is different, dismissed, or unrecognized. This response to the Other, to those beings and situations different from the "norm," provides deconstruction with ethical-political efficacy.

There is an ethical-political concern regarding relentless deconstruction. There is no operative ethics without taking positions. Richard Bernstein (1992) wonders, "*how can we 'warrant'* . . . *the ethical-political 'positions' we do take*? This is *the* question that Derrida never satisfactorily answers . . . . What are we to do after we realize that all *archia* tremble?" (191). Derrida emphasizes deconstructing relatively stable contingent constructions. Meanwhile, Dewey emphasizes reconstructing relatively stable contingent constructions, a promising reply to Bernstein's query.

DERRIDEAN DECONSTRUCTION
AND EDUCATION

Derrida was a highly committed educator. Here the focus is on Derrida's (1983/2004b) Cornell inaugural lecture as professor-at-large along with Derrida's (1986/2004a) "The Antinomies of the Philosophical Discipline." He was a leader of the *Group de Recherches sur L'Enseignement Philosophique* formed in 1974 as a response to plans for reducing the teaching of philosophy in France. He was also prominent in establishing the *Collège International de Philosophie* in 1983, serving as its first director. Some of the remarks found in the report of a committee chaired by Derrida (1982/2004c) associated with the founding of the college prove especially pertinent. If readers substitute other educational institutions or "disciplines" *salva veritate* for what Derrida says about the "essence" of the university and philosophy here, they will *mutatis mutandis* readily approximate his philosophy of education.

It is useful to consider Derrida's philosophy of education in terms of his destabilization of Western metaphysics. His Cornell address Derrida (1983/2004b) focuses on the modern university's "reason to be":

> I will be talking about: reason [*logos*] and being [*ousia*], of course, and the essence [*eidos*] of the university in its relations to reason and being; but also the cause [*arche*], purpose [*telos*], necessity, justification, meaning and mission of the university; in a word, its *destination* [*entelecheia*]. (129)

He is challenging one of the principle dogmas of Western thought dating back to Parmenides's claim that To-Be and To-Think (and To-Know) are one and the same (see Kirk and Raven, 1957/1975, frag. 344). Parmenides's claim asserts being (*ousia*) in its essence (*eidos*) is immediately indubitable when thinking correctly (*logocentrism*).

Derrida (1983/2004b) is not only challenging the raison d'être of the university as "the institution of reason," but he is also challenging rationality as the developmental aim of education along with reason itself:

> But to answer *for* the principle of reason (and thus for the university) . . . is not simply to obey it or to respond *in the face of* this principle . . . . Are we obeying the principle of reason when we ask what grounds this principle that is itself a principle of grounding? (137)

Rejecting the Parmenidean principle requires rejecting the empire of rationality as the self-founding principle of any institutionalized educational structure.

Scholars must "interrogate the essence of reason . . . the *arche* in general . . . [and] attempt to draw out all the possible consequences in general of this questioning" (148). Derrida deconstructs not only pure rationality but also "End-oriented research," whether in "technology, economics, medicine, psycho-sociology, or military power" (141). He worries about the authoritarian use of rationality in all guises.

The dominance of the principle of reason accompanies "the interpretation of the essence of beings as *objects*, an object present as representation, an object placed and positioned *before* a subject" an "*ego* certain of itself" (139). Parmenides is the primary source for the quest for certainty. Disrupting the object destabilizes the subject matter of education while disrupting the subject destabilizes the version of humanism that assumes rationality is the essence of "Man" and, hence, the aim of education.[4]

Derrida turns to Kant who believed that unlike the "manual laborer" the "theoretical leader," as the one "having knowledge of causes and of principles" and "possessing reason or *logos*," is "in essence the teacher" (152). On the Kantian model, only beings possessed of pure reason are fully fit to teach. This enduring foundation of the university alienates it from the practical work it also conducts. The result is "an implacable political topology" wherein thinking "requires *both* the principle of reason *and* what is beyond the principle of reason, the *arche* and an-archy" (153).

While he deconstructs the role of rationalism as the *arche* and *ousia* of the university, he does not want to destroy either rationality or the university thereby yielding to irrationalism, obscurantism, and nihilism (see 138 and 147). Instead, he urges the necessity of "awakening" or "resituating" our sense of responsibility in the university (146). The hope is for "a new *affirmation*" (147).

Derrida (1986/2004a) identifies seven antinomies characteristic of the discipline of philosophy that readily extend to other disciplines. He acknowledges, "One could shorten or extend the list" (173). Here the list is shortened by eliminating his first, third and sixth antinomy.

Second:

> [W]e must protest the enclosure of philosophy ... [The] circumspection that would confine philosophy to a class or a curriculum, a type of object or logic, a fixed content or form .... [W]e should claim the proper and specific unity of the discipline .... How is one to reconcile this localizable identity and this ubiquity that exceeds all bounds? (170)

Fourth:

> [W]e consider it normal to demand institutions adequate to this impossible and necessary, useless and indispensable discipline .... Philosophy exceeds its institutions .... How is one to reconcile the respect and the transgression of the institutional limit? (170–171)

Fifth:

> [W]e require a ... the presence of a teacher .... But ... the teacher or master must be another, trained and then appointed by others, this heteronomic asymmetry ought not infringe on the necessary autonomy ... of the philosophical community .... How can that community bring about an agreement within itself between this heteronomy and this autonomy? (171)

Seventh:

> The teacher ... remains an other for the disciple. Guardian, guarantor, intercessor, predecessor, elder, he has to represent the speech, the thought or knowledge of the other: *heterodidactics* .... [O]n no account do we want to give up the autonomist and *autodidactic* tradition of philosophy .... What incredible topology do we require in order to reconcile the heterodidactic and the autodidactic? (172)

Derrida thinks these antinomies "sometimes configure aporias" (173).

His Cornell address refers to his report to the French government on the creation of an International College of Philosophy. He observes his report insists, "on stressing the dimension . . . . I am calling 'thinking'—a dimension that is not reducible to technique, nor to science, nor to philosophy" (148). In this college, "philosophy itself would be questioned" and it would be a place "open to types of research that are not perceived as legitimate today" (148). It would provide a place "to work on the value and meaning of the basic, the fundamental" in "opposition to end-orientation" in "all its domains" (148). These comments provide a good start regarding what Derrida expects from the college that he was so instrumental in creating.

The report of a committee Derrida (1982/2004c) chaired affirms, "if we propose the creation of a college *of philosophy*, it is not . . . to signal that this institution belongs integrally to what we might believe in advance as its *philosophical* destination or essence" (197). What he says next extends to every domain of inquiry: "In this regard, 'thinking' for the moment designates . . . an interest that is not philosophical first of all, completely and necessary" (197). In a typical statement of indissociability, "It is, *on the other hand*, to affirm philosophy and define what it can be and must do today in our society as regards new forms of knowledge in general" (197). Thinking, especially deconstructive often aprotic thinking that probes the nonlimitation and the limit of philosophy, constitutes the avant-garde work of the college. It emphasizes "interscience," "interferences," and "transferences" that establishes "zones of instability" beyond the "stable, accredited, habitable departments" in hopes of clearing "new paths" (206). The college operates beyond interdisciplinary among established disciplines; rather, the goal is to "bring forth new themes and new modes of research and teaching" (208). The report insists on opening possibilities for emergent *topoi*.

Dewey would have approved of Derrida's unconventional educational ideas as at least valuable experiments. After all, in "Education as Politics," Dewey declared schools should cultivate habits of suspended judgment, skepticism, inquiry, and "discussion rather than bias, inquiry rather than conventional idealizations" (1922, MW 13:334). He thought when this happened schools would become "dangerous outposts of a humane civilization" (1922, MW 13:334). He would join Derrida in calling for active student participation, creative questioning, and unconstrained thought. However, having made the *arche* of education tremble, it is fair to join Bernstein (1992) in wondering how Derrida or anyone else is to warrant the positions taken. Dewey's theory of inquiry would help.

DEWEYAN PRAGMATISM AND EDUCATION

Many of the divergences between Dewey and Derrida involve existential emphasis. In a chapter titled "Existence as Precarious and Stable," Dewey argues: "Man finds himself living in an aleatory world; his existence involves, to put it baldly, a gamble. The world is a scene of risk; it is uncertain, unstable, uncannily unstable" (1925, LW 1:43). In a risky world where destruction is a permanent possibility, Dewey understands the primary existential task as one of rendering the precarious relatively stable: "The striving to make stability of meaning prevail over the instability of events is the main task of intelligent human effort" (49). Dewey is primarily concerned with constructing and reconstructing contingent structures that may allow us to avoid destruction while enhancing the joy of existence. Derrida expends most of his effort deconstructing contingent constructions, opening them to alterity.

Human beings cannot survive without their constructions. Continuous deconstruction in an aleatory and uncannily unstable world where we may never be sure whether the Other will come to save or slay us invites destruction. Wisdom resides in deciding when and how to make the *arche* tremble without excessively risking destruction while responsibly warranting the relatively stable reconstructions undertaken. It is an endless task.

It is helpful to approach Dewey's philosophy of education through his rejection of the metaphysics of presence.[5] Dewey's owes much to Darwin:

> In laying hands upon the sacred ark of absolute permanency, in treating forms [*eidos*] that had been regarded as types of fixity and perfection as originating and passing away, the *Origin of Species* introduced a mode of thinking that in the end was bound to transform the logic of knowledge, and hence the treatment of morals, politics and religion.
>
> (1909, MW 4:3)

He might have added education.

A species is the ultimate ontological subject of evolutionary theory. Dewey does for essences what Darwin did for species: "The conception of εἶδος, species, a fixed form and final cause, was the central principle of knowledge as well as of nature. Upon it rested the logic of science" (6). Dewey, like Derrida, recognizes the determination of *eidos* by *telos* stating, "the classic notion of species carried with it the idea of purpose" (8). There is no ultimate cosmic beginning (*arche*) or ending (*entelecheia*): "Philosophy forswears inquiry after absolute origins and absolute finalities in order to explore specific values and the specific conditions that generate them" (10). Dewey rejects the metaphysics of substance (*ousia*). In his philosophy, existence or "nature is viewed as consisting of events rather than substances" (1925, LW 1:5–6). Hence, "A thing may endure *secula seculorum* and yet not be everlasting; it will crumble before the gnawing tooth of time, as it exceeds a certain measure. Every existence is an event" (63). Every "thing" eventually passes away in a Heraclitian universe, including the human species.

For educators, the rejection of metaphysics implies there is neither a fixed immutable human essence to actualize nor an absolute aim of education (e.g., a rational being). Dewey characterizes his philosophy as "naturalistic humanism" (1925, LW 1:10). In his essay "Does Human Nature Change?" Dewey answers emphatically, yes! (1938, LW 13:286). In an ever-evolving naturalism, "humanity" is an always already absent present:

> Since growth is the characteristic of life, education is all one with growing; it has no end beyond itself. The criterion of the value of school education is the extent in which it creates a desire for continued growth and supplies means for making the desire effective in fact. (1916, MW 9:58)

Lacking a transcendental signified the only aim of education is more education.

While Derrida retains metaphysics while constantly deconstructing it, Dewey dissolves most of Western metaphysics by transferring its various aspects (*arche, eidos*, etc.) to his logic where they serve as subfunctions of his theory of inquiry. He further affirms, "The formation of a self new in some respect or some degree is involved in every genuine act of inquiry" (1939, LW 14:70). This is part of what it means to be a participant in the events of existence and not a spectator.

To follow Dewey, one only needs to distinguish existence from the refined products of existence for human purposes (i.e., essences) while noting how language (i.e., meaning) connects them. Dewey states "there is a natural bridge that joins the gap between existence and essence; namely communication, language, discourse" (1925, LW 1:133). For Dewey to have a mind is to have meaning and meaning only emerges with language. Language acquisition is fundamentally *a three-term semiotic relation* between two conspecifics and a third thing; the relation can be reflexive and the third term another conspecific:

> Primarily meaning is intent and intent is not personal in a private and exclusive sense. *A* proposes the consummatory possession of the flower through the medium or means of *B*'s action; *B* proposes to cooperate—or act adversely—in the fulfillment of *A*'s proposal. Secondarily, meaning is the acquisition of significance by things in their status in making possible and fulfilling shared cooperation. In the first place, it is the *motion and sounds* of A which have meaning, or are signs. Similarly the movements of *B*, while they are immediate to him, are signs to *A* of *B*'s cooperation or refusal. But secondarily the *thing* pointed out by *A* to *B* gains meaning. It ceases to be just what it brutely is at the moment, and is responded to in its potentiality, as a means to remoter consequences. (142)

Note the movements (i.e., gestures) of A and B *become* meaningful signs; it is an emergent, naturalistic process.

Meaning is acquired by taking the attitude of *others* toward "things" in a three-term semiotic relation. Likewise, our sense of self arises from taking the attitude of the others toward our own actions. It is also crucial to recognize the relation is transactional. Dewey writes: "Try the experiment of communicating, with fullness and accuracy, some experience to another, especially if it be somewhat complicated, and you will find your own attitude toward your experience changing" (1916, MW 9:8). Think of student–teacher transactions.

Those familiar with the later Wittgenstein may easily follow Dewey. The neo-pragmatist philosophers W. V. Quine (1969) and Richard Rorty (1979) have commented on this similarity as has the rhetorician Stephen Toulmin (1984) who studied with

Wittgenstein. Dewey shares Wittgenstein's emphasis on the primacy of practice in co-ordinating human transactions which is why Dewey proclaims, "Education *through* occupations consequently combines within itself more of the factors conducive to learning than any other method" (1916, MW 9:319).[6] The primacy of practice is also important because it puts structured social transactions *before* the emergence of linguistic signs. Derrida follows Saussure in ignoring how linguistic signs (i.e., symbols) emerge. Semiotics does not require quasi-transcendental a priori conditions of possibility.

Before considering essences, let us comment on Dewey semiotic understanding of mental functioning (i.e., intentionality). For Dewey, intentionality is not, contrary to Husserl and Saussure, a psychic substance (*ousia*):

> But a thing which has or exercises the quality of being a surrogate of some absent thing is so distinctive, so unique, that it needs a distinctive name. *As exercising the function we may call it mental.* Neither the thing meant nor the thing signifying is mental. Nor is meaning itself mental in any psychical, dualistic, existential sense . . . . A probable rain storm, as indicated to us by the look of the clouds or the barometer, gets embodied in a word or some other present thing and hence can be treated *for certain purposes* just as an actual rain storm would be treated. We may then term it a mental entity. (1922, MW 13:56–57)

Dewey understands mental functioning as the ability to *take* (or *create*) signs and *use* them to refer to something absent wherein the anticipated absent object can control current conduct whether it ever arrives or not.[7] Human beings function semiotically, hence mentally, in a world without a within; our mind, selves, and signs are not simply located (see Tiles, 1995). Dewey relies on such insights when he declares: "We never educate directly, but indirectly by means of the environment" (1916, MW 9:23). Further, for a cultural-historical being, there is a *continuity* of meaning such that much of our mind and self lies in the past or future while our present personal "identity" is not a transcendental signified. Learning (construction) involves establishing semiotic continuity. Unlearning (deconstruction) involves discontinuity, disruption, otherness, and difference. Growth requires relearning (reconstruction).

Dewey assumes linguistic meaning precedes logical essence. "Essence," he finds, "is but a pronounced instance of meaning; to be partial, and to assign *a* meaning to a thing as *the* meaning is but to evince human subjection to bias" (1925, LW 1:144). He insists, "Essence is never existence, and yet it is the essence, the distilled import, of existence; the significant thing about it, its intellectual voucher, the means of inference" (144). Dewey proclaims, "The name *objects* will be reserved for subject-matter so far as it has been produced and ordered in settled form by means of inquiry; proleptically, objects are the *objectives* of inquiry" (1938, LW 12:122). In Dewey's genetic theory of inquiry, "there will be as many kinds of known objects as there are kinds of effectively conducted operations of inquiry which result in the consequences intended" (1929, LW 4:157). Different *genetic* processes driven by different purposes produce different objects of knowledge as well as linguistic and logical structures.

To convert the contingently constructed falsifiable genetic products of inquiry, including *eidos, arche, entelecheia*, and such, into antecedent metaphysical entities is a terrible mistake. Dewey uses the phrase "*the* philosophic fallacy" to describe "the conversion of eventual functions into antecedent existence" (1925, LW 1:34). This conversion commonly involves hypostatizing the contingent products of inquiry and then reifying them as existing antecedent to inquiry. The a priori transcendent Forms of Plato, transcendental categories of (Kant), or the quasi-transcendental trace of *différance* (Derrida) are examples. The result is to erase the contingent *genetic* trace along with the purposes that guided the construction.

Accounting for change requires some notion of the actual (*energeia*) and potential (*dynamis*), which is why Derrida cannot account for semiotic movement. However, Dewey explicitly rejects "latent" potential;" there is no immanent *entelecheia* to development, human or otherwise (1915, MW 8:13). Dewey reconstructs the actual and potential in terms of transaction. He is a transactional realist for whom "there is no isolated occurrence in nature" (1925, LW 1:207). Existence is comprised of events in actual or potential interaction. The actual event "X" (person, place, object, etc.) actualizes the potential in another event "Y," and conversely. The "identity," subjectivity, and such of all participants in trans-actions are reciprocally trans-formed. Student–teacher transactions provide an example.

Dewey thinks every individual has unique potential (see Cunningham 1994). "Individuality is at first spontaneous and unshaped; it is a potentiality, a capacity of development. Even so, it is a unique manner of acting in and with a world of objects and persons" (1930, LW 5:121). Individuals need otherness and difference to develop their distinctive potentials:

> Individuality itself is originally a potentiality and is realized only in interaction with surrounding conditions. In this process of intercourse, native capacities, which contain an element of uniqueness, are transformed and become a self. Moreover, through resistances encountered, the nature of the self is discovered. The self is both formed and brought to consciousness through interaction with environment
>
> (LW 10:286–287).

Individuality is a potential concretely actualized through transactions with surrounding conditions, especially socio-cultural conditions. Dewey writes, "the environment consists of those conditions that promote or hinder, stimulate or inhibit, the *characteristic* activities of a living being" (1916, MW 9:15). This insight takes us to one of the fundamental ideas of Dewey philosophy of education:

> [T]he only way in which adults consciously control the kind of education which the immature get is by controlling the environment in which they act, and hence think and feel. We never educate directly, but indirectly by means of the environment. Whether we permit chance environments to do the work, or whether we design environments for the purpose makes a great difference. (22–23)

It also tells us something significant about all communication including, of course, communication between teacher and student: "Try the experiment of communicating, with fullness and accuracy, some experience to another, especially if it be somewhat complicated, and you will find your own attitude toward your experience changing; otherwise you resort to expletives and ejaculations" (8). The greater the actual difference, the greater the potential for communicative transformation.

Dewey's pluralistic transactional view of human potentiality places a premium on diversity, otherness, and difference. "Power to grow," he says, "depends upon need for others and plasticity" (57). In "Creative Democracy—The Task Before Us," Dewey declares:

> To cooperate by giving differences a chance to show themselves because of the belief that the expression of difference is not only a right of the other persons but is a means of enriching one's own life-experience, is inherent in the democratic personal way of life. (1939, LW 14:228)

It is also inherent in democratic education.

There is another aspect of Dewey's philosophy that also thematizes diversity and difference. In "Realism Without Monism or Dualism" Dewey declares, "Neither is the disjunction between monistic and dualistic realism exhaustive. There remains pluralistic realism, which is precisely the theory I have advanced" (1922, MW 13:54). According to Dewey, "Dynamic connexions are qualitatively diverse, just as are the centres of action," (1917, MW 10:11). Therefore, he proclaims "pluralism" as "an established empirical fact" and that he is willing to have his position "labeled" as "empirical pluralism" (64). The following depicts Dewey's pluralistic empirical naturalism:

> Nature is characterized by a constant mixture of the precarious and the stable . . . . If existence were either completely necessary or completely contingent, there would be neither comedy nor tragedy in life, nor need of the will to live . . . . Apart from this union, there are no such things as "ends," either as consummations or as those ends-in-view we call purposes. There is only a block universe, either something ended and admitting of no change, or else a predestined march of events.
>
> (1929, LW 4:194–195)

Dewey had referred earlier to the block universe of "William James" (167).

For James (1909/1977), regardless how perfectly unified and complete (*entelecheia*) some essence (*eidos*) appears, there is always something Other, something external, something absent trailing along to alter its signification:

> Pragmatically interpreted, pluralism or the doctrine that it [the universe] is many means only that the sundry parts of reality may be externally related. Everything you can think of, however vast or inclusive, has on the pluralistic view a genuinely "external" environment of some sort or amount. Things are "with" one another in many

ways, but nothing includes everything, or dominates over everything. The word "and" trails along after every sentence . . . . [S]omething else is self-governed and absent and unreduced to unity. (145)

An empirical, naturalistic, and pluralistic universe is eternally incomplete; the meaning of any sign remains forever deferred. It is always possible to anticipate the arrival of something different, something Other after the "and." This is how Dewey and James understand "différance" as difference and deferral.

In a contribution on "pluralism" to a *Dictionary of Philosophy and Psychology*, Dewey remarks that the "needs pluralism serves" are threefold (1902, MW 2:204): (a) "the possibility of real change, or an objectively valid dynamic view;" (b) "the possibility of real variety, particularly in the differences of persons;" and (c) "the possibility of freedom, as a self-initiating and moving power inherent in every real *qua* real" (204). The following is an example of (b):

But when women who are not mere students of other persons' philosophy set out to write it, we cannot conceive that it will be the same in viewpoint or tenor as that composed from the standpoint of the different masculine experience of things . . . . As far as what is loosely called reality figures in philosophies, we may be sure that it signifies those selected aspects of the world which are chosen because they lend themselves to the support of men's judgment of the worth-while life, and hence are most highly prized. In philosophy, "reality" is a term of value or choice. (1919, MW 11:45)

For "women" we may substitute any other perspective.

For Dewey, symbolic expressions, concepts, universals, and such are nonexistential and, therefore, devoid of descriptive empirical content. They perform strictly formal nonexistential functions. The issue turns on "if conceptions are, in any assignable way, *descriptive*;" if so, "then they must be derived by 'abstraction' in the sense in which abstraction means selective discrimination" (1938, LW 12:463). Dewey did not think it possible to directly abstract concepts by selective discrimination. To make his point, he cites most of the following passage where Peirce distinguishes two basic kinds of abstraction:

[W]e shall do well to keep *prescind, presciss, prescission*, and *prescissive* on the one hand, to refer to dissection in hypothesis, while *precide, precise, precision* are used so as to refer exclusively to an expression of determination . . . made free for the interpreter. We shall thus do much to relieve the stem "abstract" from staggering under the double burden of conveying the idea of prescission as well as the unrelated and very important idea of the creation of *ens rationis* . . . this hypostatic abstraction.

(CP 5, 449; see Dewey, 1938, LW 12:463)

Prescission involves empirical selective discrimination; that is, when we are "thinking of a nature *indifferenter*" or "without regard to the differences of its individuals, as when we think of a *white* thing, generally" (CP 2, 428). "White" permits an instance of selective discrimination; it is a linguistically descriptive, existential *general* term. Dewey's example is the empirical description of something as smooth.

Hypostatic abstraction involves thinking form apart from content "as when we think of *whiteness*" (CP 2, 428). Dewey's example is smoothness.

> Smooth*ness*, as an instance of a scientific conception, is not capable of observation and hence not of selective discrimination. For complete absence of resistance and friction nowhere exists in nature. As a scientific conception, smoothness is statable only in a mathematical equation. (1938, LW 12:462–463)

One may describe existential ice as "smooth," but abstract universal "smooth*ness*" is a hypostatic abstraction.

Peirce preferred restricting abstraction to hypostatic abstraction "whereby we regard a thought as a thing, make an interpretant sign the object of a sign" (CP5, 448 footnote). Reified hypostatic abstractions comprise Plato's transcendent realm of forms, Kant's transcendental categories, and Derrida's quasi-transcendental *différance*.

For Peirce, hypostatic abstraction is an "extremely important grade of thinking about thought" (CP 5, 534). Dewey defines abstraction thus: "A term of logic meaning the separation, for *intellectual* purposes only of a quality from the thing to which it belongs, or a relation from the pair of things between which it subsists" (1911, MW 6:359). As understood by Dewey and Peirce, *différance* is a nonconceptual relation between signifier and signified; hence, an instance of hypostatic abstraction, an *ens rationis*, an extremely important grade of thinking about thought.

Dewey championed the genetic method. Remarking on his contributions to *Studies in Experimental Logic*, he expresses this regret: "One of the points which gave much offense in the essays was the reference to genetic method—to a natural history of knowledge . . . . I was to blame for not making the point more explicit" (1916, MW 10:361). In *Democracy and Education*, Dewey mentions:

> Genetic method was perhaps the chief scientific achievement of the latter half of the nineteenth century. Its principle is that the way to get insight into any complex product is to trace the process of its making,— to follow it through the successive stages of its growth. (1916, MW 9:222)

Later, he referred to the "genetic-functional" method wherein data, traits, kinds, descriptive generals, definitional universals, *ousia, arche, teloi, entelecheia, eidos*, and more are all subfunctions of the process of inquiry (see Dewey, 2012, 219, 321, 329, 331, 334). Indeed, "reason" in terms of "identity, contradiction and excluded middle" and the like "are generated in the very process of control of continued inquiry" (1938, LW 12:19). He rejects the view that they are "*a priori* principles fixed antecedently to inquiry and conditioning it *ab extra*" (19). For Dewey putatively a priori principles are merely the reified products of inquiry.

Darwin was most important genealogist of the nineteenth century, although the empirical perspectival naturalism of Friedrich Nietzsche's *Genealogy of Morals* was influential. Dewey and Nietzsche's perspectivalism is not about seeing the same "thing" from different perspectives like the blind men and the elephant. Rather, it involves taking perspectives as participants in natural events influenced by needs, desires, interests, and purposes along with the constraints of various sensory-motor systems.[8] Finite perspectives are exclusionary:

> The favoring of cognitive objects and their characteristics at the expense of traits that excite desire, command action and produce passion, is a special instance of a principle of selective emphasis which introduces partiality and partisanship into philosophy. Selective emphasis, with accompanying omission and rejection, is the heart-beat of mental life. To object to the operation is to discard all thinking. But in ordinary matters and in scientific inquiries, we always retain the sense that the material chosen is selected for a purpose; there is no idea of denying what is left out.
>
> (1925, LW 1:31)

Relevancy shifts with the purposes of finite beings. The excluded Other can be included with an emergent purpose or a shift in ideology. For Dewey, the contingent, perspectival, existential, descriptive *prescission* (not *precision*) from crude anoetic qualitative experience to *ens rationis* as products of inquiry involves exclusions as well as inclusions.

Dewey condemns the "the great vice of philosophy," which is "arbitrary intellectualism" (28). Intellectualism assumes "all experiencing is a mode of knowing, and that all subject-matter, all nature, is, in principle, to be reduced and transformed till it is defined in terms identical with the characteristics presented by refined objects of science as such" (28). He rejects the primarily epistemological thrust of modern philosophy. It is reasonable to ask: If there were a robust theory of learning, would philosophy need epistemology?

The noncognitive provides the context for the cognitive. Signs serve the finite, often unsignified, needs and purposes of those that take (or make) and use them. Dewey's philosophy of education involves a love of wisdom beyond knowledge alone.

Cognition, like signs, mediates among immediate, noncognitive experiences. The immediate presence of anoetic quality is not an instance of a transcendental signified because it is not even a sign:

> *Any* quality as such is final it is at once initial and terminal; just what it is as it exists. It may be referred to other things, it may be treated as an effect or as a sign. But this involves an extraneous extension and use. It takes us beyond quality in its immediate qualitativeness. (82)

Immediate anoetic consciousness of existential quality (e.g., raw pain) is devoid of analytic distinctions, including semiosis or *différance*. Derrida's anti-empiricist quasi-transcendental semiosis is devoid of anoetic quality. For empirical naturalistic perspectival pragmatists this means it cannot comprehend the qualitative experience from whence it arose. Dewey would suspect Derrida of semiotic intellectualism. For those that can follow perspectival difference, it initiates the genetic trace leading to the originary arche-trace of the hypostatic abstraction *différance*.

CONCLUDING POSTSCRIPT

Raphael's frescoe "The School of Athens" portrays Plato pointing heavenwards toward the necessary a priori transcendent Forms and Aristotle downward toward the contingent a posteriori natural world. Empirical naturalism is the excluded Other of Derridean deconstruction while quasi-transcendentalism is the excluded Other of Deweyan reconstruction. In the frescoe, Plato and Aristotle turn toward each other in dialogue. In spite of profound divergence, Derrideans and Deweyans can dialogue in ways edifying for philosophers of education.

ACKNOWLEDGMENTS

The section "Deweyan Pragmatism and Education" draws on Garrison (1999).

NOTES

1. Dewey (2012) argues humankind never was modern.
2. The most serious omission is a discussion of Derrida's "undeconstructables" (Justice, the Gift, Hospitality, and such). Derrida is right that only by accepting the responsibility of deciding the undecidable does one become fully free moral agents. Bernstein (2006) shows how a pragmatist theory of inquiry readily addresses Derrida's aporias of responsibility. Dewey thinks deliberation is only required regarding incommensurable values; otherwise, it is possible to avoid responsibility by using already existing rules of rationality such as utilitarian calculation (see Mousavi and Garrison, 2003). Further, Dewey finds "there are at least three independent variables in moral action" that have different origins and modes of operation and work "at cross purposes and exercise divergent forces in the formation of judgment" (280). The Good, the Right, and Virtue are incommensurable:

   [I]t is characteristic of any situation properly called moral that one is ignorant of the end and of good consequences, of the right and just approach, of the direction of virtuous conduct, and that one must search for them. The essence of the moral situation is an internal and intrinsic conflict; the necessity for judgment and for choice comes from the fact that one has to manage forces with no common denominator. (280)
   Ethical-political conflict is ineliminable. Finally, "The formation of a self new in some respect or some degree is involved in every genuine act of inquiry" (LW 14: 70).
3. Derrida (2004d/1980) reflects on his "aleatory strategy of someone who admits that he does not know where he is going" (128).

4. Michael Peters shows Derrida does not entirely abandon humanism (see Peters and Biesta, 2009, chap. 2, 3, 6).
5. Alexander (2013) extensively explores Dewey's rejection of Parmenides.
6. Dewey objects to education *for* the occupations.
7. It is not necessary to complete the quest for certainty to secure functional presence. Consider using maps.
8. Unlike elephants, humans cannot perceive ultrasound; they may only surmise the experiences of others.

Works Cited

Citations of John Dewey's works are to the thirty-seven-volume critical edition published by Southern Illinois University Press under the editorship of Jo Ann Boydston. In-text citations give the original publication date and series abbreviation, followed by volume number and page number. For example: (1934, LW 10:12) is page 12 of *Art as Experience*, which is published as volume 10 of *The Later Works.*

Series abbreviations for *The Collected Works:*

EW The Early Works (1882–98)

MW The Middle Works (1899–1924)

LW The Later Works (1925–53).

Citations of the critical edition of C. S. Peirce's work are to *Writings of Charles S. Peirce: A Chronological Edition*, "original publication year, Wn,m" where n is the volume and m the page number (e.g., W 1, 299 refers to volume 1, page 299), and to *Collected Papers*, "original publication year, CP n.m" where n is the volume number and m the paragraph number (e.g., CP 1.500 refers to volume 1, paragraph 500).

Alexander, Thomas M. 2013. *The Human Eros: Eco-ontology and the Aesthetics of Existence.* New York: Fordham University Press.

Bernstein, Richard J. 1992. *The New Constellation.* Cambridge, MA: MIT Press.

Bernstein, Richard J. 2006. Derrida: The Aporia of Forgiveness? *Constellations*, vol. 13, no. 3, 394–406.

Cunningham, Craig. 1994. "Unique Potential: A Metaphor for John Dewey's Later Conception of the Self." *Educational Theory*, vol. 44, no. 2, 211–224.

Derrida, Jacques. 1973. *Speech and Phenomena: And Other Essays on Husserl's Theory of Signs.* Translated by David B. Allison. Evanston, IL: Northwestern University Press.

Derrida, Jacques. 1976. *Of Grammatology.* Translated by Gayatri Chakravorty Spivak. Baltimore: Johns Hopkins University Press.

Derrida, Jacques. 1978a. "Structure, Sign, and Play." In *Writing and Difference.* Translated by Alan Bass, 278–293. Chicago: University of Chicago Press.

Derrida, Jacques. 1978b. "Violence and Metaphysics." In *Writing and Difference.* Translated by Alan Bass, 79–153. Chicago: University of Chicago Press.

Derrida, Jacques. 1982. "Différance." In *Margins of Philosophy.* Translated by Alan Bass, 3–27. Chicago: University of Chicago Press.

Derrida, Jacques. 1984. "Deconstruction and the Other." In *Dialogues with Contemporary Continental Thinkers.* Edited by Richard Kearney, 105–126. Manchester, UK: Manchester University Press.

Derrida, Jacques. 1991. "Letter to a Japanese Friend." In *A Derrida Reader*. Edited by Peggy Kamuf, 270–276. New York: Columbia University Press.

Derrida, Jacques. 1995. "Jacques Derrida: Deconstruction and the Other." In *States of Mind: Dialogues with Contemporary Thinkers*. Edited by Richard Kearney, 105–126. New York: New York University Press.

Derrida, Jacques. 2004a [1986]. "The Antinomies of the Philosophical Discipline." In *Eyes of the University: Right to Philosophy 2*. Translated by Jan Plug, 165–174. Stanford, CA: Stanford University Press.

Derrida, Jacques. 2004b [1983]. "The Principle of Reason: The University in the Eyes of its Pupils." In *Eyes of the University: Right to Philosophy 2*. Translated by Catherine Porter and Edward P. Morris, 129–155. Stanford, CA: Stanford University Press.

Derrida, Jacques. 2004c [1982]. "Titles (for the *Collège International de Philosophie*)." In *Eyes of the University: Right to Philosophy 2*. Translated by Jan Plug, 195–215. Stanford, CA: Stanford University Press.

Derrida, Jacques. 2004d [1980]. "The Principle of Reason: The University in the Eyes of its Pupils." In *Eyes Of The University: Right to Philosophy 2*. Translated by Kathleen McLaughlin, 113–128. Stanford: Stanford University Press.

Dewey, John. 1902. "Contribution to Dictionary of Philosophy and Psychology." MW 2: 139–267.

Dewey, John. 1909. "The Influence of Darwinism on Philosophy." MW 4: 3–14.

Dewey, John. 1911. "Contributions to *A Cyclopedia of Education*, Volumes 1 and 2." MW 6: 357–467.

Dewey, John. 1915. "The Subject-Matter of Metaphysical Inquiry." MW 8: 3–13.

Dewey, John. 1916. *Democracy and Education*. MW 9.

Dewey, John. 1916. "Introduction to *Essays in Experimental Logic*." MW 10: 320–365.

Dewey, John. 1917. "The Need for a Recovery of Philosophy." MW 10: 3–48.

Dewey, John. 1919. "Philosophy and Democracy." MW 11: 41–53.

Dewey, John. 1922. "Realism Without Monism or Dualism." MW 13: 40–60.

Dewey, John. 1922. "Education as Politics." MW 13: 329–334.

Dewey, John. 1925. *Experience and Nature*. LW 1.

Dewey, John. 1929. *The Quest for Certainty*. LW 4.

Dewey, John. 1930. *Individualism, Old and New*. LW 5: 41–123.

Dewey, John. 1934. *Art as Experience*. LW 10.

Dewey, John. 1938. *Logic: The Theory of Inquiry*. LW 12.

Dewey, John. 1938. "Does Human Nature Change." LW 13: 286–293.

Dewey, John. 1939. "Experience, Knowledge and Value: A Rejoinder." LW 14: 3–90.

Dewey, John. 1939. "Creative Democracy—The Task Before Us." LW 14: 224–230.

Dewey, John. 2012. *Unmodern Philosophy and Modern Philosophy*. Edited by Phillip Deen, Carbondale: Southern Illinois University Press.

Garrison, Jim. 1999. "John Dewey, Jacques Derrida, and the Metaphysics of Presence." *Transactions of the Charles S. Peirce Society*, vol. XXXV, no. 2, 346–372.

James, William. 1977 [1909]. *A Pluralistic Universe*. Cambridge, MA: Harvard University Press.

Kirk, G. S. and J. E. Raven. 1975 [1957]. *The Presocratic Philosophers*. Cambridge, UK: Cambridge University Press.

Mousavi, Shabnam, and Jim Garrison. 2003. "Toward a Transactional Theory of Decision Making: Creative Rationality as Functional Coordination in Context." *Journal of Economic Methodology*, vol. 10, no. 2, 131–156.

Peters, Michael A., and Gert Biesta. 2009. *Derrida, Deconstruction and the Politics of Pedagogy.* New York: Peter Lang.

Quine, W. V. 1969. Ontological relativity. In *Ontological Relativity and Other Essays.* By W. V. Quine, 26–68. New York: Columbia University Press.

Rorty, R. 1979. *Philosophy and the Mirror of Nature.* Princeton, NJ: Princeton University Press.

Sellars, Wilfrid. 1997. *Empiricism and the Philosophy of Mind.* Cambridge, MA: Harvard University Press.

Spivak, Gayatri. 1976. Introduction to *Of Grammatology.* Translated by Gayatri Chakravorty Spivak, ix–xc. Baltimore: Johns Hopkins University Press.

Tiles, J. E. 1995. "Applying the Term 'Mental' in a World without Withins: Dewey's Realism." *Transactions of the Charles S. Peirce Society,* vol. XXXI, no. 1, 137–166.

Toulmin, Stephen. 1984. "Introduction. The Quest for Certainty." In *John Dewey: The Later Works,* Vol. 4. Edited by Jo Ann Boydston. Carbondale: Southern Illinois University Press.

CHAPTER 18

DEWEY, THE ETHICS OF DEMOCRACY, AND THE CHALLENGE OF SOCIAL INCLUSION IN EDUCATION

MAURA STRIANO

DEWEY'S DEMOCRATIC IDEAL IN AN ERA OF GLOBAL DEMOCRACY AND POSTDEMOCRACY

A current progressive crisis of the democratic narrative in traditionally democratic countries and the failure of the attempts to export democracy in countries struggling for political and social change have been accompanied by the development and dissemination of powerful counter narratives, which continuously challenge the faith in the democratic ideal (Habets 2015).

Moreover globalization, (neo-) liberalization, and privatization together with the development of processes of deregulation, weakening of collective organizations, and loss of collective organizational capacity have progressively eroded democracy from within and defined a postdemocratic scenario, especially for eastern Europe and North American democracies (Rancière 1995, 2002; Crouch 2004).

The risk of degeneration in "bad" forms of populism (Urbinati 2014), the rising power of the media, and the easy manipulation of public opinion (Luckacs 2005) are a constant menace for the maintenance of democracy intended as a pluralist and dialectic form of associated life, warranted by the mediating function of political institutions, individual responsibility, and commitment in the people.

Undoubtedly a decreasing trust in political life (Dalton 2008), negative media reports, disappointed citizens' expectations, and a widespread perception of a weak performance of democratic goverments has caused disaffection toward politics and democratic institutions (Pharr and Putnam 2000). This has required a sound exploration of the role of the public in the promotion and development of democracy (Barber 1998; Diamond 1994), highlighting the features of a democratic social order within which citizens should be educated for political engagement and participation by the civil society as a whole (Bahmuller and Patrick 1999).

Political engagement and participation require, first, the overcoming of all forms of social exclusion, which can be understood as a limitation in the use of different kinds of resources (economic, cultural, social, and structural) causing the deprivation of different forms of capital (financial, human, physical, and social) thereby excluding individuals and groups from access to earnings and wealth, educational opportunities, housing, social interactions, and political power.

This is caused by the presence of cultural and structural barriers to participation—both in the labor market and in society—due to a multidimensional process of progressive social rupture that detaches individuals and groups from institutions and social relations, preventing them from full participation in different types of social activities.

The narrative on democracy is therefore strictly connected to an emerging narrative on social justice and social inclusion, within which we can identify three different dimensions of inclusion defining a new paradigm for social growth, with cultural, practical, and political implications: (a) a socioeconomic dimension based on the categories of capability and participation (Sen 1989, Nussbaum and Sen 1993); (b) an ethical dimension referring to rights, social justice, equity, and equal opportunities based on the categories of difference and recognition (Nussbaum 1997, 2011b; Honneth 1994) and (c) an educational dimension based on the categories of care (Katz, Noddings, and Strike 1999), diversity (Appelbaum 2002), and reciprocity (Kirkness and Barnhardt 2001).

Current debate highlights the necessity to include a variety of perspectives and voices in the democratic discourse, which has generated the development of a dialogic (Giddens 1994, 1998) and inclusive idea of democracy (Young 2002) as well as the acknowledgment of the necessity of listening procedures to support processes of recognition, representation, and reconciliation (Dobson 2014).

While a number of scholars have advocated the need for a "deliberative" version of democracy that should support the construction of a rationally regulated communication and consensus organizing the public sphere (Habermas 1979; Bessette 1980; Bohman and Rehg 1997; Cohen 1997; Guttman and Thompson 2002), this vision has been challenged by others proposing a radical and agonistic version of democracy, taking into account that the process of construction of a democratic social order does not involve consensus but rather conflicts and dissent, which produce a continuous challenging of the oppressive power relations existing in societies (Laclau and Mouffe 1985).

Within this complex scenario, the very idea of democracy must be explored in depth, taking into account its nature and specificity and putting it in relationship with the ideas of social inclusion, social justice, and social development, the latter acknowledged as a process (natural or planned) involving the organization of institutions, resources, and social forces in an increasingly effective way in order to cope with the challenges imposed by the new world scenarios (Cleveland and Jacobs 1999).

Effective conceptual tools for this purpose can be found in Dewey's understandings of democracy as an individual and social task, a moral challenge, an economic and political commitment, and a method of social inquiry. All of them help us in defining a vision of democracy as the main condition to promote and sustain social inclusion according to an emancipatory and participative vision of individual and social development.

THE PREMISES OF A DEMOCRATIC VISION

The roots of Dewey's democratic ideal can be found very early in his career, and are already clearly visible in the 1888 essay "The Ethics of Democracy" (Dewey 1888, EW 1)[1] where he identified the ethical implications of democracy intended as a form of associated life deeply committed to individual growth and to social development, as well as in *Outlines of a Critical Theory of Ethics* (1891, EW 3). At that time Dewey had started to teach philosophy at the University of Michigan, where a contemporary observer, quoted by Westbrook, reported that he and "his mentor and colleague George Sylvester Morris" made the philosophy department "pervaded with a spirit of religious belief, unaffected, pure and independent" (Westbrook 1992, 405).[2]

During his Michigan years Dewey had also the opportunity to meet Jane Addams—a leading figure in the areas of social reform, women's suffrage, and opposition to war—and to visit Hull House, the social and educational life support center for poor and immigrant people that Addams cofounded in Chicago in 1889. As Stengel points out, "Dewey was searching for a way to instantiate his thinking about democracy, about Christianity and about experimentalism" and "it was at Hull House in the company of Jane Addams that Dewey found what he was looking for" (Stengel, in Cunningham et al. 2008, 29). When he moved to Chicago, Dewey's relationship with Jane Addams and Hull House, for which he also became a trustee in 1894, grew deeper and, according to Fesmire, "educated" him in democracy and social life (Fesmire 2015).

As Fesenstein (2014) points out, "an important formative condition" of Dewey's early ethical and political thinking was "the Idealist and New Liberal assault on the misguided individualism of the classical liberal tradition" accused of understanding social life as an "aggregation of inherently conflicting private interests," while it had to be understood "as an organism in which the well-being of each part was tied to the well-being of the whole." But according to Seigfried (1999), Dewey's criticisms of classical liberal individualism "are even more persuasive when seen in the context of the model of the intersubjective constitution of the individual that Addams develops from examining the relation of personal development to social interaction among the women residents of Hull House" (207).

As a consequence, in contrast with the liberal and positivist tradition, Dewey's early political theory in "The Ethics of Democracy" builds up an organicist vision of the relationship between individual and society[3] stating that "democracy approaches most nearly the ideal of all social organization; that in which the individual and society are organic to each other"; therefore, "the organism must have its spiritual organs; having a common will, it must express it" (1888, EW 1:238).[4]

Honneth notes that in this essay Dewey wants to counter "the tendency of the contemporary social philosophy to see in democracy just a mere organizational form of state government" and instead grounds democracy in the process of development of an intersubjective consciousness (Honneth and Farrell 1998). This vision, still rooted in an Hegelian frame of reference, will be slowly dismissed when Dewey comes to realize that this approach "presupposes an untenable teleology of human nature" (767). It is for this reason that he will start, through various studies in psychology, "to work out the social mechanism that could explain, without metaphysical borrowings, the social compatibility of human self-realization" and elaborate a solution that "can be understood in terms of an intersubjectivist theory of human socialization" (Honneth and Farrell 1998, 771).[5]

DEMOCRACY AS AN INDIVIDUAL AND SOCIAL TASK

The encounter and deep friendship with George Herbert Mead was to further contribute to Dewey's understanding of human mind as socially embedded and constructed. As Whipple (2005) notes, "we can elucidate Dewey's democratic ideal through consideration of two of his key social-psychological principles: the experiential act of participation; and, most important for our purposes, his bilevel view of human agency, including habitual and reflective intelligence and the social origin of each" (161).

Accordingly, this approach sustains the development of a powerful notion of human agency intended in relation to individual and personality that Boyte and Finders (2016) see already clearly sketched in "The Ethics of Democracy," where Dewey wrote: "in one word, democracy means that personality is the first and final reality" therefore "the full significance of personality can be learned by the individual only as it is already presented to him in objective form in society" and "the chief stimuli and encouragements to the realization of personality come from society." Nonetheless, he continued, "personality cannot be procured for any one, however degraded and feeble, by any one else, however wise and strong" since "the spirit of personality indwells in every individual and that the choice to develop it must proceed from that individual" (1888, EW 1:244).[6] This vision would be developed in Dewey's psychological writings and later, with stronger ethical and political implications, in the 1922 publication *Human Nature and Conduct: An Introduction to Social Psychology.*

This idea of the "worth" of individual personality indeed is strictly connected with the concept of individual "capability" that Dewey clarified in his first ethical speculations[7], as we can see in the essay "The Metaphysical Method in Ethics" where he wrote that "the ultimate end is the idea of a social universe in which every person's capabilities shall receive their full realization, and in which every person's realization shall contribute to every other person's realization" (1896, EW 5:32).[8]

Dewey's notion of capability as the core of a democratic process of social growth is extremely powerful and can be an important contribution to deeper understanding and development of current trends either in economic or in sociopolitical and ethical studies, which are interconnected in the definition of sustainable perspectives of human and social growth and development. This focus on intersubjectivity makes it essential to understand democracy as a shared enterprise grounded in mutual and reciprocal benefits and responsibilities, defining it as a moral challenge for everyone.

DEMOCRACY AS A MORAL CHALLENGE

Dewey wrote in "The Ethics of Democracy" that "democracy, in a word, is a social, that is to say, an ethical conception, and upon its ethical significance is based its significance as governmental. Democracy is a form of government only because it is a form of moral and spiritual association" (1888, EW 1:240).[9] This means that the choice of democracy as a form of government derives from its being a by-product of morally valuable and spiritually enriching human agency and conduct, as well as the best condition to foster them. Therefore, the development of a theory of democracy requires a theory of ethics, which Dewey believed should be scientifically grounded.

The central idea that interconnects Dewey's theory of democracy with his ethical inquiry is the idea of "growth," which is a consequence of his early organicist vision of the social body and therefore requires the situating of individual and collective conduct within an experiential framework, through a scientific approach that complements a philosophical and practical exploration.[10] A better social order can be achieved through a collective and intersubjective commitment to a shared project of growth for every person.

In the first edition of his *Ethics,* published in 1908, Dewey explains that the main focus and purpose of a theory of ethics should be that of "providing methods for analysing and resolving concrete individual and social situations, rather than of furnishing injunctions and precepts"; in this perspective it should not depend upon fixed values, ideals, standards, and laws but rather be committed to their construction, de-construction and re-construction, and therefore be understood as "a working method for the self-regulation of the individual and of society" focusing on specific social motives (1908, MW 5:57).

Within this framework the main "working social motive" emerging on the basis of the development of a "more generous sense of inherent social relationships" is for Dewey "social justice" considered as "the result of increase of human intercourse, democratic institutions, and biological science" (1908, MW 5:374).

It is interesting to see how Dewey here uses an organismic metaphor derived from biological science applied to human society to explain that the "only ultimate protection against disease is in the general 'resisting power' of the living process." This power "may be temporarily aided by stimulation or surgery, but the ultimate source of its renewal is found in the steady rebuilding of new structures to replace the old stagnation; the retention of broken-down tissues means weakness and danger" (1908, MW 5:540). Social justice is therefore the outcome of a self-renewing and self-healing process of the social organism intended as a growing living creature.

This requires both a scientific analysis of the causes and of the conditions that undermine the full realization of social justice,[11] as well as the reconstruction of intersubjective relationships in terms of "sympathy" and "love," which are human attitudes as well as moral values. Therefore, at the roots of each process of social growth there should be a mechanism of individual and collective moral engagement, resulting from the joint endeavor of a scientific inquiry and of moral reconstruction of social bounds, institutions, and structures.

Accordingly, Anderson (2014) explains that Dewey accomplished a reconstruction of moral theory "by replacing fixed moral rules and ends with an experimental method that treats norms for valuing as hypotheses to be tested in practice, in light of their widest consequences for everyone." This approach is also consistent with Dewey's criticisms of the discontinuity and separation from the world of facts and the realm of values, which, as Putnam highlights, would become a distinctive character of pragmatist thought (Putnam 2002).

Pappas (2008) notes that "the impoverished quality of present moral experience was the underlying concern behind Dewey's democratic vision" and offered to it "plausibility" and "function," but it also offered a broader scope including "habit, character, interaction, communication, and the qualitative dimension of situations" (541).

In the 1932 revised edition of his *Ethics*, Dewey draws a distinction between a "customary morality" and "reflective morality." The first one grounds standards and rules of conduct within an "ancestral habit," while the second "appeals to conscience, reason, or to some principle which includes thought" (1932, LW 7:162). This distinction "shifts the centre of gravity in morality" grounding it on explicit, shared, and validated forms of judgment reflectively constructed (163).

Hickman (1998) notes that Dewey's ethics is "the flower of both his aesthetic theory and his theory of inquiry" (xvi). Accordingly, analyzing the section of Dewey's 1932 *Ethics* titled "The Conception of Virtue in Reflective Morality," Garrison (2004) highlights how Dewey focuses on individual virtues, understanding them within a cultural and social context that offers the possibility to appreciate (in an aesthetical perspective) the different individual contributions to social growth.

Fesmire (1999) highlights the aesthetic and imaginative features of Dewey's moral theory and their implication for his democratic vision: "since our aspirations are not isolated from those of others" we need "a democratized imagination that aesthetically perceives and artistically responds to the entire system of exigencies in a troubled situation" so that we can "skillfully elicit differences and give them a hearing" in order to "reconstruct and harmonize conflicting values so that we can mutually grow" (534).

For Dewey, the exercise of a "reflective morality" requires specific conditions and opportunities as well as a method, "the method of democracy, of a positive toleration which amounts to sympathetic regard for the intelligence and personality of others, even if they hold views opposed to ours, and of scientific inquiry into facts and testing of ideas" (1932, LW 7:329).

The notion of reflective morality is therefore central in his vision of democracy as (a) a form of associated life that must be constructed on the basis of dialogue, shared judgment, co-construction and negotiation of norms and values, and joint exploration of issues and problems and (b) a method of conduct and of inquiry that provides the conditions for reflective morality to be expressed and developed.

INDUSTRIAL DEMOCRACY AND NEW LIBERALISM

Dewey's moral vision is in deep relationship with his early vision of democracy and its impact on economic and social growth. After the Civil War American society was, as Anderson points out, rapidly changing "from a rural to an urban society, from an agricultural to an industrial economy, from a regional to a world power" (Anderson 2014, online). These changes were determining a strong tension between very different and sometimes opposite inner trends. "It emancipated its slaves, but subjected them to white supremacy. It absorbed millions of immigrants from Europe and Asia, but faced wrenching conflicts between capital and labor as they were integrated into the urban industrial economy. It granted women the vote, but resisted their full integration into educational and economic institutions. As the face-to-face communal life of small villages and towns waned, it confronted the need to create new forms of community life capable of sustaining democracy on urban and national scales." These new social conditions called for new forms of social order and new moral and ethical grounds, and Dewey became clearly aware that "neither traditional moral norms nor traditional philosophical ethics were up to the task of coping with the problems raised by these dramatic transformations" (Anderson 2014, online).

Within this framework he developed a vision of democracy strictly connected with equitable economic and social development sustained as Westbrook points out, by a strong commitment to social justice and a profound faith in deliberative citizenship (Westbrook 1991), which he developed and refined both in conversations with Jane Addams as well as through a confrontation with contemporary studies in politics and social sciences (such as those of Westel Woodbury Willoughby, the father of modern political science in the United States, and Leonard Hobshouse, the leading thinker of British "social liberalism").[12]

Indeed Jane Addams' vision of democracy as a "rule of living and a test of faith" (Addams 1907) and her awareness that "uncontrolled industrial capitalism was the primary cause of domestic and international violence" (Addams 1907, 27–28) are consistent with Dewey's understanding of the limits of industrial capitalism, which required reframing according to a democratic ideal.

Dewey's vision was also, as Westbrook (1992) points out, deeply influenced by the cooperativist perspective of the economist Henry Carter Adams, which led Dewey to envision, as a conclusion of "The Ethics of Democracy," the possibility of an "industrial, civil and political" endeavor based on the principle that "all industrial relations are to be regarded as subordinate to human relations" (1888, EW 1:247).

These relations "are to become the material of an ethical realization; the form and substance of a community of good (though not necessarily of goods) wider than any now known" (1888, EW 1:248), as well as a "community of wealth" that Dewey saw as a necessity to accomplish the democratic ideal, overcoming the class divisions of industrial capitalism in favor of a society committed to the full realization of individual and collective growth.[13]

This has also educational implications as Dewey highlighted in the essay "The Need of an Industrial Education in an Industrial Democracy" (1916b, MW 10).

In a letter to Cork (1949), he pointed out that "no existing brand of socialism has worked out an adequate answer to the question of *how* industry and finance can progressively be conducted in the widest possible interest and not for the benefit of one class" and defined himself "a democratic socialist" (450). Accordingly, he did not frame his project of an "industrial democracy" in terms of class struggle since he didn't follow a Marxist approach (as pointed out in "Why I Am Not a Communist" (1934, LW 9) but rather, as explained in Liberalism and Social Action, in terms of a process of advancement in the "liberation from material insecurity and from the coercions and repressions that prevent multitudes from participation in the vast cultural resources that are at hand." Dewey was aware that the process was slow, and required an integration of "old" and "new" models of economic development and social organization as well as beliefs, ideas and values; this integration has to be carried on by "liberalism," to which he assigned a "mediating function," as it places a strong emphasis "upon the role of freed intelligence as the method of directing social action" (1935, LW 11:37).[14]

He strongly advocated for the construction of "a social order" with the chief purpose of establishing the conditions that will move the mass of individuals "to appropriate and use the cultural, the spiritual, resources" that are the product "of the cooperative work of humanity" and therefore affirmed that the most urgent task to be fulfilled was to promote "the socialized extension of intelligence" as well as the socialized use of cultural and spiritual resources that belong to each and every one (1935, LW 11:39).

DEMOCRACY, EDUCATION, AND THE SOCIALIZED EXTENSION OF INTELLIGENCE

For Dewey the reconstruction of social order requires also an educational project aiming at reconstructing human habits and conducts on the basis of a psychological understanding of human growth and agency. This issue was explored in depth in *The School and Society* (1899, MW 1), which addresses two fundamental questions: (a) How can a society be disciplined, organized, ruled in such a manner that all its members can be protected, satisfied, and sustained, while actively and responsibly participating in its development? (b) How can a society develop and grow according to its intrinsic potential?

In a Deweyan perspective, social order is not a matter of general rules imposed on a society from the outside or from above. It is, instead, a matter of individual and collective awareness, reflectivity, and responsibility. For these reasons, an effective social order can be achieved only if and when more and more individuals and groups become able to deal with social problems in a reasonable and reflective manner, using a disciplined method of inquiry into human experiences and relationships. Accordingly, the need for a social order (which is a social need) becomes an educational need as also pointed out in *The Schools of Tomorrow* (1915, MW 8).

In *Democracy and Education* Dewey states that "the extension in space of the number of individuals who participate in an interest so that each has to refer his own action to that of others, and to consider the action of others to give point and direction to his own, is equivalent to the breaking down of those barriers of class, race, and national territory which kept men from perceiving the full import of their activity" (1916a, MW 9:93).[15] The full involvement and participation in the process of construction of societies at all levels and in all dimensions (cultural, economic, political), as well as the effective communication and dissemination of ideas, knowledge, and proposals, requires a "society which is mobile, which is full of channels for the distribution of a change occurring anywhere" and which takes care that all "its members are educated to personal initiative and adaptability." This is because the moral and ideal meaning of democracy "is that a social return be demanded from all and that opportunity for development of distinctive capacities be afforded all" (MW 9:94).

Democracy demands a contribution from each and every person on the basis of the different attitudes, capabilities, and potentialities that each brings into the social arena, through the acknowledgement of equal opportunities of growth, commitment, and participation. According to this approach, social reconstruction requires not only the management and adoption of a method[16] suitable for detecting and exploring social problems, identifying possible solutions following, as Metz points out, a scientific pattern (Metz 1969) but also the construction of collaborative spaces of inquiry and of deliberation within which hypotheses and plans can be criticized, discussed, tested, and evaluated.

As Vanderveen (2011) suggests, "Dewey provides an account of experimental political inquiry," which implies the legitimation and participation of multiple actors to the process of inquiry (160). Inquiry, which represents the intelligent and reflective management of social issues through their critical analysis, problematization, and exploration in order to gain understanding and define hypotheses for possible solutions, emerges through the medium of culture and is developed by involving multiple forms of knowledge and understanding that are inherently social.

In *The Public and its Problems* Dewey explains that "the formation of states must be an experimental process. The trial process may go on with diverse degrees of blindness and accident, and at the cost of unregulated procedures of cut and try, of fumbling and groping, without insight into what men are after or clear knowledge of a good state even when it is achieved. Or it may proceed more intelligently, because guided by knowledge of the conditions which must be fulfilled. But it is still experimental and since conditions of action and of inquiry and knowledge are always changing, the experiment must always be retried; the State must always be rediscovered" (1927, LW 2:257). Inquiry is therefore the condition for the construction, maintenance, and development of the state according to a "pluralistic conception," but it is necessary that "the tools of social inquiry" are forged in places and under conditions close to contemporary events (349) and that "concepts, general principles, theories and dialectical developments which are indispensable to any systematic knowledge be shaped and tested as tools of inquiry." Moreover, "policies and proposals for social action" have to "be treated as working hypotheses" and "be experimental in the sense that they will be entertained subject to constant and well-equipped observation of the consequences they entail when acted upon, and subject to ready and flexible revision in the light of observed consequences" (362).

In this perspective, inquiry comes out of social contexts and contributes to reconstructing and to reorganizing them because a growing number of individuals and groups begin to explore the possibility to overcome and make sense of the conditions they live in. Inquiry may become, therefore, a means to support and sustain social order, since it emerges from the inside of society itself and is controlled by means of dedicated inquiry procedures.

This approach highlights the essential role of public participation in the detection and analysis of social issues and problems, as well as in the selection of the best courses of action to be followed and in the evaluation of their outcomes and results in terms of social growth. Therefore "the essential need, in other words, is the improvement of the methods and conditions of debate, discussion and persuasion" which "depends essentially upon freeing and perfecting the processes of inquiry and of dissemination of their conclusions" (1927, LW 2:366).

Every person is entitled, legitimated, and morally obliged to participate in the processes of inquiry and deliberation that sustain social growth in a democratic society. The "Democratic Ideal" that Dewey sketches out in *Democracy and Education* involves indeed two elements: "greater reliance upon the recognition of mutual interests as a factor in social control" and a deep "change in social habits, a continuous readjustment through meeting the new situations produced by varied intercourse" (1916a, MW 9:92). In a democratic society "voluntary disposition and interest" are the only regulative moral principles of what Dewey calls "associated life."

Democracy, Social Justice, and the Challenge of Social Inclusion

As Stengel (2009, 89) notes, "Dewey speaks in a voice we can still hear today," because in the fabric of his writings we can find embedded ideas that are part of the ongoing discourse. Significant similarities can be found between Dewey's vision and the "capability approach" to economic and social development proposed by Amartya Sen in the early 1980s and its ethical implications in terms of social justice according to the framework defined by Martha Nussbaum in the early 1990s. Indeed, as Zimmerman (2006) points out, "Sen shows—like Dewey—that the concept of freedom and capabilities (in the sense of capability to act and interact) are analytically related" and this is connected to "an understanding of the individual" as "a person who has ideas about what is good for her, who pursues specific aims and performs choices" addressing therefore the person from the point of view of her agency, recognizing "her ability to conceive and fulfil aims, commitments and values, and not only selfish desires" therefore connecting individual interests and social ends (470–471).

In contrast with utilitarianism (an understanding of human agency and rational action that overcomes reduction to personal interest), a vision of the embeddedness of individual agency within complexity and social diversity are elements that ground the capability approach in pragmatism. In particular, they ground Dewey's vision of individual and social development and his idea of individual and collective agency as reflectively oriented. This has not only economic and sociopolitical implications but also educational ones.

In this perspective, Glassman and Patton (2014) see significant relationships between Sen's capabilities approach framework for understanding the human condition and Dewey's democratic vision and educational ideas, acknowledging how together education and democratic values may play important roles in creating contexts that allow individuals and communities to recognize a wide array of human capabilities and to expand them through participatory engagement into processes or economic and social growth, envisaging also a relationship with Freire's pedagogy.

According to the "capability approach" the success or failure of different political systems, as well as the processes of globalization, democratization, development, and economic growth, can be determined taking into account five essential conditions: (a) real freedom in the assessment of a person's advantage, (b) the valorization of individual differences in the transformation of resources into valuable activities, (c) the presence of multivariate activities aimed at producing and maintaining happiness and well-being, (d) a balance of materialistic and nonmaterialistic factors in human welfare, and (e) a shared concern for the distribution of opportunities within society (Sen 1989; Sen in, Nussbaum and Sen 1993).

Nussbaum (2011) puts the capability approach "to work in constructing a theory of basic social justice," adding other notions to the process (such as those of human dignity, the threshold, and political liberalism). She presents a specific list of "central capabilities" that distinguishes between internal and combined capabilities with reference to "two overlapping but distinct tasks of the decent society," which make it possible that, for example, "some societies educate people so that they are capable of free speech on political matters—internally—but then deny them free expression in practice through repression of speech." This distinction is a "useful heuristic in diagnosing the achievements and shortcomings of a society" (Nussbaum 2011a, 21) and in focusing on the basic capabilities that "a minimally just society will endeavour to nurture and support" (28). In this perspective the notion of capability is a useful benchmark to identify democratic societies as those within which the development of basic capabilities is assured and internal capabilities can be fully expressed as combined capabilities.

The capability approach is therefore evaluative and ethical and is very close to Dewey's understanding of democracy, but while Nussbaum focuses on the relationship between individuals and society, Dewey focuses on the relationship among individuals as the context within which the full realization of each individual capability is essential to those of the others. This concept is expressed very clearly in the essay "Philosophy and Democracy" where Dewey explains that equality, in a democratic perspective, does not mean equivalence, which dissolves individual differences and diversities, but, according to a moral and social understanding, it means rather "the inapplicability of considerations of greater and less, superior and inferior"; this implies that "differences of ability, strength, position, wealth" are negligible in comparison with the uniqueness of individual existence, which "must be reckoned with on its own account, not as something capable of equation with and transformation into something else." This vision provides therefore a "metaphysical mathematics of the incommensurable in which each speaks for itself and demands consideration on its own behalf"; accordingly, "democracy is concerned not with freaks or geniuses or heroes or divine leaders but with associated individuals in which each by intercourse with others somehow makes the life of each more distinctive" (1919, MW 11:53).

Dewey's emphasis on the uniqueness of the individual, on differences and diverse "capabilities," and his criticisms of visions of society such as those provided by social Darwinism, which had applied the biological categories of "struggle for existence" and "the survival of the fittest" to the analysis of social and political processes, make his ideas extremely powerful in forming the basis for an inclusive vision of social growth.

This accent on individual uniqueness and diversity is particularly relevant within current cultural, political, and social debates focused on the necessity to assure and acknowledge social equity and social justice not in terms of equivalence of rights, opportunities, and treatment but in terms of balance between individual equality and diversity, which must be developed and sustained mainly through educational processes.

In the essay "Education and Social Direction" Dewey points out that "the unsolved problem of democracy is the construction of an education which will develop that kind of individuality which is intelligently alive to the common life and sensitively loyal to its common maintenance" and calls for "that type of education which will discover and form the kind of individual who is the intelligent carrier of a social democracy" (1918, MW 11:58).

The individual focus of educational processes and practices connects Dewey's vision to current debates on inclusive education intended not as a response to special needs but as an educational approach focused on the valorization of individual differences. Moreover, his insights can provide a fruitful contribution to contemporary debates on social inclusion and education, a contribution that highlights the difference between the perspective of "integration," which is linear, static, and based on processes of assimilation, on the one hand, and the perspective of inclusion, which is bidirectional, dynamic, co-evolutive, and transactional, on the other (Oliver 1990; Booth and Ainscow 2011).

This requires, as Noddings (1999) points out, a deep reframing of the liberalist grounds of educational theories and practices, taking into account the weaknesses of liberalism without losing its great strengths. Dewey's understanding of liberalism as a means for the full achievement of individual and collective freedom—very different from the classic liberal approach grounded on the assumption of the isolated, autonomous individual as the subject of rights—is useful to highlight the strengths and limits of current interpretations of liberalism -either in its "perfectionist" or in its "political" version, according to the framework defined by Nussbaum (2011b). Dewey's approach highlights liberalism's economic, educational, moral, political, and social implications through a reflective and socially shared pattern of inquiry.

Dewey's attention to the value of the community as the dimension within which it is possible to start deconstructing and reconstructing the cultural fabric that is the foundation for public opinion, and his struggle for freedom of individual and collective intelligence (which highlights its critical and creative potential), opens up a dialogue with the approaches of contemporary critical theory (Kadlec 2008; Joas 1992) to social and educational inquiry. Moreover, Dewey's vision of social justice and of social growth highlights the necessity to work out either a sound scientific exploration of the conditions underlying social inequalities or a reconstruction of social bonds and social relationships according to a new frame of shared values. It opens up the possibility to understand "resistance" and power issues by focusing on a transactional vision of human intercourse (Abowitz 2000).

Contemporary issues of social inclusion and social justice, according to Dewey's legacy, have to be approached by using a "dialogue through differences," which involves different perspectives and different kinds of agents at various levels (Stengel 2009; Cunningham et al., 2008; Thrupp and Tomlinson 2005) but also through the reconstruction of individual and collective practices of inquiry and interaction, focusing on the multiple and complex dimensions of individual and collective experience, understood—in a Deweyan perspective—as the "foreground" of human existence.

Dewey's idea of democracy is inclusive and participative (Seigfried 1996; Fischer 2012) and opens up the possibility of a new understanding of his legacy in terms of some contemporary "inclusive" and "deliberative" visions of the democratic task (Young 2002). Moreover, as Bernstein (1985) points out, Dewey's idea of a democratic society is pluralistic, even if according to Talisse (2003) the term "pluralistic," in a Deweyan and pragmatist approach, can be interpreted ambiguously. Nonetheless, it is true that Dewey provides us with a multiperspectival and fallibilist vision of the processes of social inquiry, which should be continuously maintained in order to sustain democracy, intended as a form of communication, inquiry, and deliberation deeply committed to individual and collective social agency and to an inclusive and participative process of social growth.

This vision, based both in "faith in human nature" as well as "faith in the role of consultation, of conference, of persuasion, of discussion, in formation of public opinion, which in the long run is self-corrective" (1939, LW 14:227)—as Dewey states in "Creative Democracy, the Task Before Us"—is extremely powerful and can help us to escape the risk of conceiving Dewey's democratic vision as an external frame of reference, understanding its cultural, economic, political, and social implications within currently complex scenarios. Only on these bases could it be possible to relaunch democracy as a project to be sustained in order to warrant to individuals and communities the best conditions to live and grow thanks to the personal commitment and engagement of everyone.

NOTES

1. As Višňovský and Zolcer (2016) point out, the development of Dewey's democratic theory can be reconstructed by following an articulated genealogy composed of two stages—early and mature—embedding political, ethical, philosophical, and even religious elements, which are interwoven in a complex fabric that incorporates different forms of discourse and different narratives (57).
2. Garrison (1999) reminds us that those were spiritually intense years: "Dewey was active in the Student Christian Association and was a member of the First Congregational Church where he taught Bible classes"; accordingly his "interests in social, political, and economic issues grew increasingly radical as he continued to struggle with issues of unity and religion." Moreover, his marriage, in 1886 to his "self-reliant and politically progressive" student Alice Chipman "seems to have awakened Dewey's deeply ingrained sense of social justice and encouraged his entrance into the world of public affairs" (2).
3. We can see this clearly stated in this passage "the student of society has constantly to be on his guard against the abstract and purely mechanical notions introduced from the physical sciences" since "men cannot be reduced for political purposes, any more than for any other, to bare figure ones" and "a vote is not an impersonal counting of one; it is a manifestation of some tendency of the social organism through a member of that organism" (1888, EW 1:233–234).

4. Therefore "in democracy, at all events, the governors and the governed are not two classes, but two aspects of the same fact—the fact of the possession by society of a unified and articulate will. It means that government is the organ of society, and is as comprehensive as society" (1888, EW 1:239).

5. Indeed, as Good points out, between 1887 to 1891 Dewey did not abandon Hegel but rather abandoned his previous Neo-Hegelianism, and his break with Neo-Hegelianism involved a growing interest in Hegel's *Phenomenology of Spirit*, which clearly influenced his psychological account of human agency and growth (Good 2006). This idea was a powerful factor in producing Dewey's belief "that the not uncommon assumption in both psychology and philosophy of a ready-made mind over against a physical world as an object has no empirical support" and grounded his understanding "that the only possible psychology, as distinct from a biological account of behavior, is a social psychology" (1939, LW 14:17–18).

6. This perspective has deep ethical consequences because from it "result the other notes of democracy, liberty, equality, fraternity—words that are not mere words to catch the mob, but symbols of the highest ethical idea which humanity has yet reached—the idea that personality is the one thing of permanent and abiding worth, and that in every human individual there lies personality" (1888, EW 1: 244).

7. As Rockefeller (1989), notes, "starting with Protestant Christian social values and the Neo Hegelian philosophy of the organic unity of the spiritual and the material, the ideal and the real," Dewey developed "his own philosophy of individual liberation, social transformation, and harmony with the divine"; within this framework "as he reconstructed his early Neo-Hegelian ethical idealism and developed a new brand of humanistic naturalism, which charts a middle way between a tough-minded and tender-minded world view, the idea of democracy remained of central importance" and acquired a strong spiritual connotation (302).

8. As Leys explains in the introduction to the fourth volume of the Early Works, "Dewey was himself seeking a psychological description of the life process that would relate the empirical findings of physiologists and sociologists to man's consciousness of value, but he insisted that a psychological description "cannot involve a different principle." Therefore, "he believed that he had found the 'mediating' standpoint in 'action' or 'activity'" (Leys, in EW 4:xv). This focus on action and activity highlights the fact that Dewey's early account of democracy has strong ethical implications deriving from multiple cultural, experiential, and spiritual "sources."

9. Indeed, "this fulfilling of function in devotion to the interests of the social organism, is not to be put into a man from without. It must begin in the man himself, however much the good and the wise of society contribute. Personal responsibility, individual initiation, these are the notes of democracy" (1888, EW 1:244).

10. Putnam and Putnam (1993) note that "Dewey's picture of human nature is Darwinian and naturalistic, but not reductionist. [. . .] One aspect of Dewey's anti-reductionism is an insistence that the distinction between needs and mere desires, and likewise the distinction between 'values' (which have been intelligently appraised in the course of experience) and mere satisfactions is essential to understanding human action. This does not mean that ethics is a 'special science,' the science that seeks to appraise satisfactions in order to discover what is *valuable*; rather, for Dewey, *every* inquiry tests values as well as facts" (368).

11. An account of this vision, which has significant epistemological and ethical implications, is again clearly visible in *Ethics*, where he acknowledges the "stimulus to foresight, to scientific discovery, and practical invention, which has proceeded from interest in the helpless, the weak, the sick, the disabled, blind, deaf, and insane" and from a "coldly scientific view"

highlights the gains that can be reached "through the growth of social pity, of care for the unfortunate" in terms of social growth (1908, MW 5:335).

12. These scholars shared, according to Miller (1999), "an organic conception of society," which was "viewed as an organism in which the flourishing of each element requires the cooperation of all the others"; accordingly, the aim of social justice is to "specify the institutional arrangements that will allow each person to contribute fully to social well being" (4).

13. According to Rockefeller, in his effort to facilitate the development of industrial democracy, which has been from different perspectives and at different times criticized as impractical and utopian, Dewey tries "to break down the long standing western dualisms between the spiritual and the material, the ideal and the natural, and means and ends" that "have the effect of degrading the material or natural by stripping it of inherent moral and spiritual meaning" with a "dehumanizing and dispiriting effect on the life of the mass of people whose lives are largely bound up with material and industrial concerns." On these bases "industrial democracy means realizing the inherent meaning and value of industrial work and reconstructing the industrial sphere" (Rockefeller 1989, 308).

14. As Kurtz writes in the introduction to the fifth volume of the Later Works, Dewey "sought to work out a new definition of liberalism, emphasizing that liberalism should not be identified with a particular party platform or program but rather with a method of intelligence to be used in a democracy to solve social problems" (Kurtz, in LW 5:xvii).

15. That's why "more numerous and more varied points of contact denote a greater diversity of stimuli to which an individual has to respond; they consequently put a premium on variation in his action. They secure a liberation of powers which remain suppressed as long as the incitations to action are partial, as they must be in a group which in its exclusiveness shuts out many interests" (1916, MW 9:93).

16. As Campbell (1984) points out, in a Deweyan perspective social reconstruction has to be carried on through a "method" that has two levels, each one with a different focus: "the first is largely intellectual and the second is largely practical." "The first level is that in which the problem is formulated and possible solutions are brought forth; the second, that in which the community evaluates these possibilities and enacts the chosen solution" (373).

WORKS CITED

Citations of John Dewey's works are to the thirty-seven-volume critical edition published by Southern Illinois University Press under the editorship of Jo Ann Boydston. In-text citations give the original publication date, series abbreviation, followed by volume number and page number. For example: (1934, LW 10:12) is page 12 of *Art as Experience*, which is published as volume 10 of *The Later Works*.

Series abbreviations for *The Collected Works*:

EW *The Early Works* (1882–1898)

MW *The Middle Works* (1899–1924)

LW *The Later Works* (1925–1953)

Abowitz, K. K. (2000). "A Pragmatist Revisioning of Resistance Theory." *American Educational Research Journal*, vol. 37, no. 4, 877–907.

Addams, J. (1907). *Newer Ideals of Peace*. New York: Macmillan.

Anderson, E. (2014). "Dewey's Moral Philosophy." In *The Stanford Encyclopedia of Philosophy*. Edited by E. N. Zalta. http://plato.stanford.edu/entries/dewey-moral/

Appelbaum, P. (2002). *Multicultural and Diversity Education: A Reference Handbook* Santa Barbara, CA: ABC-CLIO.

Bahmuller, C. F., and Patrick J. (Eds.) (1999). *Principles and Practices of Education for Democratic Citizenship: International Perspectives and Projects*. Bloomington, IN: Eric.

Barber, B. (1998). *A Passion for Democracy: American Essays*. Princeton, NJ: Princeton University Press.

Bessette, J. (1980). "Deliberative Democracy: The Majority Principle in Republican Government." *How Democratic is the Constitution?* Edited by R. Goldwin and W. Shambra. Washington, DC: American Enterprise Institute.

Bernstein, R. J. (1985). "Current Issues in Education." *Varieties of Pluralism*, vol. 5, 1–21.

Bohman, J., and Rehg, W. (1997). *Deliberative Democracy: Essays on Reason and Politics*. Cambridge, MA: MIT Press.

Booth, T., and Ainscow, M. (2011). *Index for Inclusion: Developing Learning and Participation in Schools*. Bristol, UK: Centre for Studies on Inclusive Education.

Boyte, H. C., and Finders, M. J. (2016). "A Liberation of Powers: Agency and Education for Democracy." *Educational Theory*, vol. 66, nos. 1–2, 127–146.

Campbell, J. (1984). "Dewey's Method of Social Reconstruction." *Transactions of the Charles S. Peirce Society*, vol. 20, no. 4, 363–393.

Cleveland. H., and Jacobs, G. (1999). "Human Choice: The Genetic Code for Social Development." *Futures*, vol. 31, nos. 9–10, 959–970.

Cohen, J. (1997). "Deliberation and Democratic Legitimacy." In *Deliberative Democracy: Essays on Reason and Politics*. Edited by J. Bohman and W. Rehg, 67–92. Cambridge, MA: MIT Press.

Cork, J. (1949). "John Dewey, Karl Marx and Democratic Socialism." *The Antioc Review*, vol. 9, no. 4, 435–452.

Crouch, C. (2004). *Post-Democracy*. London: Wiley.

Cunningham, C. A., Granger, D., Fowler Morse, J., Stengel, B., and Wilson, T. (2008). "Dewey, Women, and Weirdoes: or, the Potential Rewards for Scholars Who Dialogue across Difference." *Education and Culture*, vol. 23, no. 2, 27–62.

Dalton, R. J. (2008). *Citizen Politics: Public Opinion and Political Parties in Advanced Industrial Democracies*. London: SAGE.

Dewey, J. (1888). "The Ethics of Democracy." EW 1.

Dewey, J. (1891). *Outlines of a Critical Theory of Ethics*. EW 3.

Dewey, J. (1896). "The Metaphysical Method in Ethics." EW 5.

Dewey, J. (1899). *The Schools and Society*. MW 1.

Dewey, J. (1908). *Ethics*. MW 5.

Dewey, J. (1915). *The Schools of Tomorrow*. MW 8.

Dewey, J. (1916a). *Democracy and Education*. MW 9.

Dewey, J. (1916b). "The Need of an Industrial Education in an Industrial Democracy." MW 10.

Dewey, J. (1918). "Education and Social Direction." MW 11.

Dewey, J. (1919). "Philosophy and Democracy." MW 11.

Dewey, J. (1922). *Human Nature and Conduct*. MW 14.

Dewey, J. (1927). *The Public and Its Problems*. LW 2.

Dewey, J. (1932). *Ethics*, rev ed. LW 7.

Dewey, J. (1934). "Why I Am Not a Communist." LW 9.

Dewey, J. (1935). *Liberalism and Social Action*. LW 11.

Dewey, J. (1939). "Creative Democracy. The Task Before Us." LW 14.

Dewey, Jane M. (1939). "Biography of John Dewey." In *The Philosophy of John Dewey*. Edited by P. A. Schlipp. Evanston, IL: Northwestern University Press.

Diamond, L. (1994). *Nationalism, Ethnic Conflict, and Democracy*. Baltimore: Johns Hopkins University Press.

Dobson, A. (2014). *Listening for Democracy: Recognition, Representation, Reconciliation*. Oxford: Oxford: Oxford University Press.

Fesmire, S. (1999). "Morality as Art: Dewey, Metaphor, and Moral Imagination." *Transactions of the Charles S. Peirce Society*, vol. 35, no. 3, 527–550.

Fesmire, S. (2015). *Dewey*. Abingdon, UK and New York: Routledge.

Festenstein, M. (2014). "Dewey's Political Philosophy." In *The Stanford Encyclopedia of Philosophy*. Edited by E. N. Zalta. http://plato.stanford.edu/archives/spr2014/entries/dewey-political/

Fischer, C. C. (2012). "Pragmatists, Deliberativists, and Democracy: The Quest for Inclusion." *The Journal of Speculative Philosophy*, vol. 26, no. 3, 497–515.

Garrison, J. W. (1999). "John Dewey." In *Encyclopedia of Philosophy of Education*. http://www.ffst.hr/ENCYCLOPAEDIA/11/10/1999

Garrison, J. W. (2004). "The Aesthetics of Ethical Virtues and the Ethical Virtues of Aesthetics." *Interchange*, vol. 35, no. 2, 229–241.

Giddens, A. (1994). *Beyond Left and Right: The Future of Radical Politics*. London: Wiley.

Id. (1998). *The Third Way: The Renewal of Social Democracy*. London: Wiley.

Glassman, M., and Patton, R. (2014). "Capability Through Participatory Democracy: Sen, Freire and Dewey." *Educational Philosophy and Theory*, vol. 46, no. 12, 1353–1365.

Good, J. A. (2006). *A Search for Unity in Diversity: The "Permanent Hegelian Deposit" in the Philosophy of John Dewey*. Lanham, MD: Lexington Books.

Guttman, A., and Thompson, D. (2002). "Deliberative Democracy Beyond Process." *Journal of Political Philosophy*, vol. 10, no. 2, 153–174.

Habermas, J. (1979). "The Crisis of Late Capitalism and the Future of Democracy: An Interview with J. Habermas." *Telos: Critical Theory of the Contemporary*, vol. 39, 163–171.

Habets, I. (2015). "Liberal Democracy: The Threat of Counter-Narratives." *European View*, vol. 14, no. 2, 145–154.

Hickman, L. (Ed.). (1998). *Reading Dewey: Interpretations for a Postmodern Generation*. Bloomington: Indiana University Press.

Honneth, A. (1994). *The Struggle for Recognition: The Moral Grammar of Social Conflicts*. Cambridge, MA: MIT Press.

Honneth, A., and Farrell, J. M. M. (1998). "Democracy as Reflexive Cooperation: John Dewey and the Theory of Democracy Today." *Political Theory*, vol. 26, no. 6, 763–783.

Laclau, E., and Mouffe, C. (1985). *Hegemony and Socialist Strategy: Towards a Radical Democratic Politics*. London: Verso.

Luckacs, J. (2005). *Democracy and Populism. Fear and Hatred*. New Haven, CT: Yale University Press.

Joas, H. (1992). "An Underestimated Alternative: America and the Limits of 'Critical Theory.'" *Symbolic Interaction*, vol. 15, no. 3, 261–275.

Kadlec, A. (2008). "Critical Pragmatism and Deliberative Democracy." *Theoria: A Journal of Social and Political Theory*, vol. 117, 54–80.

Katz, M. S., Noddings, N., and Strike, K. A. (1999). *Justice and Caring: The Search for Common Ground in Education*. New York and London: Teacher College Press.

Kirkness, V. J., and Barnhardt, R. (2001). *First Nations and Higher Education: The Four R's Respect, Relevance, Reciprocity, Responsibility*. https://www.cwu.edu/teaching-learning/sites/cts.cwu.edu.teaching-learning/files/documents/first_nations.pdf.

Metz, J. G. (1969). "Democracy and the Scientific Method in the Philosophy of John Dewey." *The Review of Politics*, vol. 31, no. 2, 242–262.

Miller, D. (1999). *Principles of Social Justice*. Cambridge, MA: Harvard University Press.

Noddings N. (1999). "Renewing Democracy in Schools." *Phi Delta Kappan*, vol. 80, no. 8, 579–583.

Nussbaum, M. (1997). "Capabilities and Human Rights." *Fordham Law Review*, vol. 66, no. 2, 273–300.

Nussbaum, M. (2011a). *Creating Capabilities: The Human Development Approach*. Cambridge, MA: Belknap Press.

Nussbaum, M. (2011b). "Perfectionist Liberalism and Political Liberalism." *Philosophy and Public Affairs*, vol. 39, no. 1, 3–45. http://dx.doi.org/10.1111/j.1088-4963.2011.01200.x

Nussbaum, M., and Sen, A. (Eds.). (1993). *The Quality of Life*. Oxford: Oxford University Press.

Oliver, M. (1990). *The Politics of Disablement*. London: Macmillan.

Pappas, G. (2008). *John Dewey's Ethics: Democracy as Experience*. Bloomington: Indiana University Press.

Pharr, S. J., and Putnam, R. D. (2000). *Disaffected Democracies: What's Troubling the Trilateral Countries?* Princeton, NJ: Princeton University Press.

Putnam, H. (2002). *The Collapse of the Fact/Value Dichotomy and Other Essays*. Cambridge, MA: Harvard University Press.

Putnam, H., and Putnam, R. A. (1993). "Educating for Democracy." *Educational Theory*, vol. 43, no. 4, 361–376.

Rancière, J. (1995). *La mésentente: Politique et Philosophie*. Paris: Editions Galilée.

Rancière, J. (2002). "Éclipse de la politique." *L'Humanité*. http://www.humanite.fr/node/265950

Rockefeller, S. C. (1989). "John Dewey, Spiritual Democracy and the Human Future." *CrossCurrents*, vol. 39, no. 3, 300–321.

Seigfried, C. H. (1996). *Pragmatism and Feminism: Reweaving the Social Fabric*. Chicago: University of Chicago Press.

Seigfried, C. H. (1999). "Socializing Democracy: Jane Addams and John Dewey." *Philosophy of the Social Sciences*, vol. 29, no. 2, 207–230.

Sen, A. (1989). "Development as Capability Expansion." *Journal of Development Planning*, vol. 19, 41–58.

Sen A. (1993). Capability and Well-Being. In: *The Quality of Life*, Edited by M. Nussbaum, A. Sen. Oxford: Clarendon Press.

Stengel, B. S. (2009). "John Dewey at 150: Reflections for a New Century." *Education and Culture*, vol. 25, no. 2, 89–100.

Talisse, R. (2003). "Can Democracy Be a Way of Life?" *Transactions of the C. S. Peirce Society*, vol. 39, no. 1, 1–21.

Thrupp, M., and Tomlinson, S. (2005). "Education Policy, Social Justice and 'Complex Hope.'" *British Educational Research Journal*, vol. 31, no. 5, 549–556.

Urbinati, N. (2014). *Democracy Disfigured: Opinion, Truth and the People*. Cambridge, MA: Harvard University Press.

Venderveen, Z. (2011). "John Dewey's Experimental Politics: Inquiry and Legitimacy." *Transactions of the C. S. Peirce Society*, vol. 47, no. 2, 158–181.

Višňovský, E., and Zolcer, S. (2016). "Dewey's Participatory Educational Democracy." *Educational Theory*, vol. 66, nos. 1–2, 55–71.

Whipple, M. (2005). "The Dewey-Lippmann Debate Today: Communication Distortions, Reflective Agency, and Participatory Democracy." *Sociological Theory*, vol. 23, no. 2, 156–178.

Westbrook, R. B. (1991). *John Dewey and American Democracy*. Ithaca, NY: Cornell University Press.

Westbrook, R. B. (1992). "Schools for Industrial Democrats: The Social Origins of John Dewey's Philosophy of Education." *American Journal of Education*, vol. 100, no. 4, 401–419.

Young, I. M. (2002). *Inclusion and Democracy*. Oxford: Oxford University Press.

Zimmerman, B. (2006). "Pragmatism and the Capability Approach. Challenges in Social Theory and Empirical Research." *European Journal of Social Theory*, vol. 9, no. 4, 467–484.

CHAPTER 19

....

DEWEY AND HIGHER EDUCATION

....

LEONARD J. WAKS

JOHN Dewey wrote relatively little about higher education. Invited to address college education in a 1931 speech, he told the audience that on that topic his mind was blank and they could all go home (Hill 1984). Yet, as I hope to show, Dewey had a well-developed and largely unexplored conception of higher education that remains relevant today.[1]

Dewey's educational ideas have often been extended or applied by other writers to topics in higher education.[2] Unfortunately, many of these either neglect (or even contradict) Dewey's own statements, or overrely on Dewey's ideas for school education, and thus fail explicitly to consider his view of the distinct roles of the university. In this chapter, building on the Dewey corpus, I aim to lay bare Dewey's own conception of higher education.

INQUIRY AS AN INTERMEDIATE STAGE WITHIN LIVED EXPERIENCE

....

We generally think of the university's roles in terms of research, teaching, and community service. Each provides a window into Dewey's view of the university. Teaching and community service, moreover, have served as the basis of two recent book length studies (Benson et al. 2007; Harbour 2014). But first and foremost, the university for Dewey is inquiry's institutional home base. To understand the university—including its teaching and community service roles—as Dewey did, research, or inquiry in its institutional setting, provides the best starting point, and, fortunately, Dewey's ideas about inquiry are well developed.[3]

Inquiry Is a Three-Stage Process

For Dewey inquiry and knowledge formation are always an intermediate (stage 2) part of a three-stage total situation of community experience. Inquiry is stimulated by unsettled, problematic affairs in the community (stage 1). Its results are used in restoring balance and settlement (stage 3). The business of knowledge *production* (stage 2) is functionally distinguishable from the other two stages of life activities.

In *Studies in Logical Theory* (1903), Dewey distinguishes "three distinct forms according to the epochal moment reached in control of experience" (1903, MW 2:318). The first moment, he states, is antecedent to thinking and consists of the situations of living that evoke thought. The second is the moment of thought proper, in which data or immediate materials are presented to thought and acted upon to yield judgment. The third is the moment after thought has considered its data and reached its result; this stage, he says, is the "objective of thought" but lies outside of "thought proper."

In everyday situations, the *antecedent* moment—stage 1—is not an isolated "question" that we seek to answer but "the whole dynamic experience with its qualitative and pervasive continuity" (1903, MW 2:330). The problem in the situation is not merely "subjective" but "objective." It resides in conditions of the situations and only secondarily in our "minds." "It is there; it is there as a whole; the various parts are there; and their active incompatibility with one another is there . . . . it is just this conflict which effects a 'transition in the thought situation" (1903, MW 2:330). The parts as they exist are "actively at war with each other," and the tension motivates some intervention to make a "unified arrangement." But just what form the situation should take "as an organized and harmonious whole is unknown" (1903, MW 2:331).

The second moment, thought proper, has its own "deliberate organization." Some things stand forth as salient "facts," which are not in doubt. But people need to decide just what these facts "mean"—what is their "reference and connection." The facts thus call forth memories and anticipations. Facts and ideas become the "listing of the capital in the way of the undisturbed, the undiscussed, which thought can count upon in this particular problem" because they have been selected with "precisely that end in view" (1903, MW 2:344). Judgment then "makes explicit the assumption of a principle which determines connection." "Inference brings to light the material conditions under which the law ... applies to this case," and thus completes the organization of the subject matter of thought (1903, MW 2:346). The particulars of the situation are now not merely isolated in experience but "interconnected according to a determining principle" (1903, MW 2:352).

At the termination of the second phase, the initial experienced situation is still disturbed but it now has two new elements: (a) an analytic map of its parts and (b) a map displaying many causal connections among them ("C>E"). This map then is available to suggest possible interventions—means to be taken toward a potential new, less disturbed order.

In the third stage, this judgment is carried back into the field of action. The test of thought is not the test of a causal connection (C>E)—the result of thought proper, which completes stage 2. For the intervention C may be made, either bringing about the predicted effects E or failing to do so in the real-world situation. But even if the effects E are brought into existence, they may, instead of ordering the situation, immediately bring new forms of disorder D in their wake. For example, our studies point to additional fertilizer to increase yield per input cost, but as this result is communicated and implemented, the increased demand for fertilizer, not predicted by our model, causes fertilizer prices to rise, with the costs then outweighing the additional yields. Or, to offer another example, our studies show that tear gas would be the most cost-efficient way of dispersing the crowd, but when we disperse the crowd with tear gas as planned, the collective rage leads to a riot a few streets over, followed by unexpected press condemnation, and so on. The causal connections (e.g., fertilizer > yield, or tear gas > dispersion) may be confirmed yet fail as bases for a plan of action. The situations may still be pervaded by unsettlement, demanding further inquiry and suggesting other interventions to restore order. In these cases, while thought at stage 2 has succeeded *internally*, it has failed its ultimate *external* test at stage 3. As Dewey says, "The test of thought is the . . . unity of experience actually affected. *The test of validity of thought is beyond thought*, just as at the other limit thought originates out of a situation which is not dependent upon thought" (1903, MW 2:368; italics added).

This bears repeating: what may be called the first law of experimental logic is that *the context of verification lies outside stage two or the internal context of inquiry proper.*

The Cultural Matrix

Dewey repeats this three-stage pattern thirty-five years later, in *Logic: The Theory of Inquiry* (1938a), but in that work he explicitly distinguishes the underlying biological dimension of thought from its place in culture-shaped human action. In humans, he notes, challenges to habit patterns (stage 1) lead not merely to neural recoding and unconscious habit change but in at least many important cases to conscious recollection of causal connections and their formulation in communicative language. Then "goods or consequences are set up and the intervening process of search becomes more seriated in temporal span and in connecting links" (1938, LW 12:41). The formation of the consequence that, if brought about, would satisfy the need "requires making plans in conjunction with selection and ordering of the consecutive means" (1938, LW 12:41).

Explicitly stated causal relations can be isolated from experienced connections and integrated in logical systems, synthesizing prior results of related scientific inquiries. This increases the power of withdrawing from problematic situations to conceive larger causal patterns and thus means-ends connections. Agents can then construct sign systems of increasing intellectual, goal-directed power "even when nothing referred to is present" (1938, LW 12:58).

All of this takes place during the second stage of thought, or "inquiry proper." Culture, symbols, and the web of accepted knowledge all make cooperative, reflective delay possible, which in turn enables self-conscious recollection and expectation, explicit written documentation, and the institution of new combinations of selected, causally related elements as complex plans. These plans can be further rehearsed in imagination, communicated, investigated, simulated, refined, and improved without irretrievable "real-world" consequences.

RESEARCH AND THE UNIVERSITY

At a certain stage in the development of culture, Dewey notes, human communities institutionalize thinking. The deliberate setting and studying of problems become established features of the cultural landscape. Scholars emerge as a guild of specialists in inquiry, who love problem finding and solving for their own sake. They are members of an "academic class" with their "corporate consciousness" as "members of an organized society of truth-seekers (1903, MW 2:67). University-based scholars are, as he puts it in "Prospects of the Liberal College" (1924a), the community's "specially selected representatives of impartial thinking and communication of knowledge" (1924, MW 15:204). Scientific disciplines emerge as *intermediate institutions*—organizations for systematizing the *second phase* of the process of thought. Scholars express their results openly, including careful descriptions of apparatus and method, which they share in scholarly seminars and conferences and publish in journals. Their results bear on work of distant subcommunities of inquiry and the practical arts.

The development of science thus constitutes a radical refinement of the cultural matrix. It allows symbol systems to develop at a greater remove from ongoing life experience. As he puts this in *Democracy and Education* (1916), this "renders its results remote from ordinary experience" and gives them a "quality of aloofness" (1916, MW 9:189).

Problems of the University

This "aloofness" or institutional separation marks a break in the continuity of living. For once the knowledge-generation process is segregated in a special institution it is no longer situated directly in that "whole dynamic experience with its qualitative and pervasive continuity" (1903, MW 2:330) referred to earlier. The problem situation is no longer "there as a whole." with the conflicts in its "various parts" exercising a pervasive reciprocal influence upon the inquiries of researchers. Instead, members of the specialized technical research profession now can pursue specialized "questions" at one or more institutional removes from the unsettlement of the situations that provoked them. Instead of confronting low crop yields the way a subsistence farmer might, as a life-threatening problem for himself and his family, the professional researcher now experiences and manipulates data and mathematical models. Instead of confronting crowd violence as a police official might, the investigator is removed from the situation of violence. "Verification" no longer lies in the restoration of balance to situations outside of knowledge; for the researchers it becomes internalized within the settling of specialized inquiry in the second phase of thought. This gives rise to two basic problems for the university.

Problem 1:

With the university operating at great remove from the "real life" of the community—of the subsistence farm or the street riot—the research agenda of stage 2 comes to be set by professional scholars based on their own perceptions and interests—which are open to the influence of powerful groups beyond the university. The problems of the larger society (stage 1) no longer shape directly the research agenda. Second, the knowledge created by scholars is evaluated by internal tests at stage 2 (e.g., fitting data to models, making and testing statistical inferences), not against pressing problems in the "real world" beyond the university. Subsequently, research solutions may be "applied" directly to social problems, rather than regarded merely as new and hypothetically useful elements in a total situation. This "application" of knowledge often has disastrous effects.

To outside observers, many university research studies look not merely esoteric and practically useless but self-indulgent and even foolish. Who can forget Senator William Proxmire's famous "Golden Fleece" awards for ludicrous government-funded research projects? One example was the $57,800 study of the physical measurements of airline stewardesses, paying special attention to the "length of the buttocks," a "scientific" study put forth as a contribution to airline safety. Proxmire joked when awarding the fleece award that this study looked like a "big bust" to him.[4]

Many of these inquiries are, however artificial, nonetheless necessary to increase the cumulative power of knowledge and its adequacy to the ever-changing cognitive demands exerted by other institutions of life. Even some of the Golden Fleece winners eventually proved to be valuable, compelling Proxmire to withdraw the awards. Thus, Dewey insists in "The Liberal College and Its Enemies" (1924b), esoteric inquiries must be protected from premature demands for utilitarian application (1924, MW 15:205).

Problem 2:

The university, as a *functionally* distinct institution of knowledge, tends to recruit and develop individual researchers as people who are themselves already relatively removed from the community. Recruits to the academic class are often marked by obsessive attention to mental puzzles isolated from life. "One cannot gaze" upon graduate students preparing themselves for the academic profession, Dewey remarks in "The Modem Trend toward Vocational Education and Its Effect upon the Professional and Non-professional Studies of the University" (1917c), "without being reminded of horses which not only follow a beaten track but which wear blinders to make them unaware of fertile fields and flowery landscapes all about" (1917, MW 10:153).

Meanwhile, challenges to academic freedom are typically if not exclusively directed against those few scholars who turn their research to unsettled social problems. This further encourages academics to become, as Dewey states in "The Case of the Professor and the Public Interest," (1917b), "technical specialists immune from interference because (they) speak in tongues not understood by the public" (1917, MW 10:167). The bad results of this breach include that most citizens outside the university do not care about science, embrace antiscientific ideologies, and reject university-based knowledge even when they have problems where solutions could make direct use of such knowledge.[5]

Repairing the Breach

To make the university a vital force in the community requires that the institution and its specialized inquires (stage 2) remain open at both the agenda setting problem stage (stage 1) and the stage of knowledge utilization (stage 3).

On the front end, the irritations and imbalances experienced in the several areas of everyday life in the community (stage 1) must be gathered and brought to bear upon the problematic of knowledge and the agenda of special inquiries in the university. Universities must be prepared to dedicate some share of their research to "quotidian," everyday problems besetting its surrounding communities.

On the back end, the dissemination and utilization of knowledge must involve collaboration between specialist experts and community representatives. That remains essential regardless of the level of understanding of nonscholars. They must be brought in to contexts of verification as the cumulative knowledge product is put to an appropriate test as an instrument for everyday problem-solving (stage 3). This, Dewey reminds us, is the *ultimate* "context of verification"—because "the test of thought lies outside of thought itself." Only this collaboration can make knowledge formations (provisionally and temporarily) available for "warranted assertability" as knowledge and for use in subsequent social life.

Effectively situating specialized knowledge in society thus requires *concrete communication mechanisms* at two junctures—between stages 1 and 2 (between community members experiencing imbalances and university-based researchers at the research agenda setting juncture) and between stages 2 and 3 (between *internal* knowledge-producing researchers and external community-interest representatives for "verification" at the juncture of phase of "knowledge dissemination and use").

Research in Professional Schools

While Dewey never offers a comprehensive account of research in university-based professional schools, he does offer a monograph length treatment of research in professional schools of education, drawing explicit parallels to schools of engineering and medicine (*Sources of a Science of Education*, 1929, LW 5:4–40). In *Sources*, Dewey reiterates the three-stage model of inquiry and teases out lessons for research programs aimed to inform professional practice. He argues that educational science, like medical science and engineering science, cannot be undertaken independently of professional practice, because the disturbances and anomalies of practice (stage 1) set the problems for inquiry proper (stage 2) (1929, LW 5:24), while the use of research in practice (stage 3) in turn sets the "final test of value of the conclusions of all researches" (1929, LW 5:17).

The problems professional practitioners face are highly complex, arising in situations that are unique and hence cannot be causally mapped. Professional fields all develop simplifying routines and conventions as they respond to day-to-day problems and external pressures. These routines are sustained because they often lead to positive short-term results when viewed in conventional perspective. But there are also negative results and uninvestigated anomalies. For example, practitioners in all fields can get so tied down and habit-bound that they compensate with "impulsive excursions" when "routine has become intolerable" (1929, LW 5:29). And in a jarring departure from his characteristically sober diction that sounds more like A. H. Neill of *Summerhill*, Dewey says that, in education, conventional methods of instruction and discipline are "continuously engaged in manufacturing morbid fixations and dislocations" and that "the increasing number of insane and neurotic is itself evidence of great failure and evil in our educational practices" (1929, LW 5:36). So there are plenty of practical problems and anomalies in educational practice to give rise to research inquiries.

Dewey again points to the yawning gap between professional practitioners and university-based researchers. Practitioners are typically so tied up in immediate problems that they have little time or energy—or background knowledge and training—for research-based reflection. Professors, on the other hand, work at such a remove from school problems that they do not know enough about them to have them control their research agenda, or even know what scientific resources bear on such problems. The problem is not merely one of location in distant organizations but the lack of "intellectual contact of a sympathetic kind" (1929, LW 5:22).

Dewey notes the importance of school reports and records as sources of both qualitative and quantitative data and interpretation for educational research. But he points to a vicious circle that leads to "scientific arrest": the kinds of data researchers seek from practitioners and utilize in their stage 2 inquiries are determined by the existing problematic in research, not in practice. Instead of taking on board the problems as experienced by professional practitioners, professors take up only the data useful for research inquiries they have shaped without practitioner input. As a result, they cannot judge whether the practical solutions stemming from their results are practically useful or merely "accidental and arbitrary" (1929, LW 5:22).

This result again points to the need for effective communication links between professionals and researchers at both the scientific agenda setting stage of inquiry and at the utilization stage. In the case of research for professional use, these links have to be forged between the professional and research communities.

At the agenda-setting stage, problematic practice is the first and best source of research problems, Dewey argues that records and reports generated by teachers and school leaders for their own purposes, as opposed to those generated at the behest of researchers for theirs, are a "neglected" and "almost unworked mine" of data and interpretation for university-based research. And at the stage of utilization, only professional educators can put the results of research to use for learners (1929, LW 5:24). To ease communication between the two communities, educational professionals need to be trained in problem formation and data collection, and researchers have to work more closely with professionals in shaping and testing their inquiries.

What can practitioners expect from research results? Dewey warns against thinking that research can yield universal laws that in turn generate rules for practice. Practice is complex. Every situation is unique in some way. Universal laws based on quantitative research cannot apply directly, because they depend upon repetition and exact uniformity of conditions (1929, LW 5:34). Research results bear on professional practice indirectly, generating deeper understanding and "intellectual instrumentalities," tools to guide attention in observation and interpretation and hence to progressively improve practical intelligence (1929, LW 5:15).

University Teaching

When Dewey died in 1952 only 5 percent of all adults in the United States possessed a bachelor's degree, compared to 25 percent today. Though Dewey saw the university potentially as exercising a pervasive impact on society, he naturally thought of a college education as primarily preparation for professional and leadership roles. Dewey was particularly concerned about the education of those from privileged classes and the indifference it breeds, noting in "Universal Service as Education" (1917d) that "our youth of the more favored class have much done for them, and little is expected in return; there is little to foster public-mindedness" (1917, MW 10:187). He repeated this charge in *Individualism Old and New* (1930), stating that "the distinguishing trait of the American student body" is "an immaturity mainly due to their enforced mental seclusion; there is, in their schooling, little free and disinterested concern with the underlying social problems of our civilization" (1930, LW 5:102).

As a result of this "enforced mental seclusion," Dewey rejected the academic discipline–centered education entrenched in the undergraduate program and instead placed social problems and their amelioration at its core. For Dewey, the overemphasis on disciplinary knowledge, on knowledge already formed and organized in college textbooks, suggested to students that, for the most part, what they need to learn is *already known*. But such pre-existing knowledge is never adequate for complex emergent problems in the community and is frequently quite irrelevant. By failing to make emergent problems central to university teaching, university teachers were indirectly telling students that such problems could be approached by already available "applied" knowledge and were thus not worthy of serious intellectual attention.

The upshot of discipline-based education was thus that the emerging leadership cohort in society would remain indifferent to and largely unaware of society's problems and would be unprepared to work with people within and beyond the university to understand and deal with them. As Dewey put this point in "The Need for Orientation" (1935), discipline based courses with "find the right answer" tests left students with "no clue to the situation in which they are to live" and "at a loss intellectually, morally as well as vocationally" (1935, LW 11:164). While granting that the colleges were a mirror of the existing society, he argued that "the mirror is not passive. It serves to perpetuate the social and economic conditions," indirectly leading students to accept the status quo and thus creating an obstacle to finding or forming new visions that could induce change (1935, LW 11:165).[6]

General Education

How then would Dewey organize college teaching? He accepted the distinction between general education and the specialized major, though he thought that most "foundational" courses in general education could be handled in secondary schools or their junior college divisions, preserving the university's distinct role as the home of research.[7] More significantly, he thoroughly rejected both the "liberal arts" and "the humanities" as organizing principles for general education. In their place he offered an alternative, experimentalist approach that linked general education directly to both social problems and the specialized studies of the major.

The Rejection of the Liberal Arts Framework

Dewey's rejection of "liberal arts" education invites close study. The liberal arts of the ancient world, he notes in *Democracy and Education*, were intended for *liber*, that is, free, citizens with the leisure to study and participate in political life. They aimed "to train intelligence for its proper office, to know" (1916, MW 9:263), where "knowledge" was sharply distinguished from the productive activities from which free men (*liber*) were free. For the ancients, productive doing and making were reduced to a "mere matter of habituation and technical skill" in which knowledge is irrelevant (1916, MW 9:263). The liberal arts philosophy in education, he states in "Challenge to Liberal Thought" (1944), thus

> defines liberal education in terms that are the opposite of what is genuinely liberal. Vocational and practical education was illiberal in Greece because it was the training of a servile class. Liberal education was liberal in Greece because it was the way of life enjoyed by a small group who were free to devote themselves to higher things. They were free to do so because they lived upon the fruits of the labor of an industrially enslaved class. (1944, LW 15:264)

The very concept of liberal arts education thus rests, for Dewey, on social class biases of ancient societies—on the distinction between free and servile people—which are still, at play in modern "liberal arts" education efforts.

> Certain studies and methods are retained on the supposition that they have the sanction of peculiar liberality, the chief content of the term liberal being uselessness for practical ends. This aspect is chiefly visible in what is termed higher education—that of the college and preparation for it. But it has filtered through into elementary education and largely controls its processes and aims. (1916, MW 9:266)

In industrial societies, however, university studies are by contrast bound up with *all* the avenues of productive work: agriculture, engineering, business management, and so on, because *all* productive activity has become infused with theoretical knowledge. For Dewey, therefore, we do not need a new conception of "liberal arts" but rather a new vocabulary of productive and practical arts bound up with advanced scientific knowledge.

The term "vocabulary" should not suggest, however, that the rejection of the term "liberal arts" is just a "mere matter of semantics." For Dewey, the liberal arts contain an ineliminable elitist bias, as well as a pedagogical emphasis on language and literature that provides an obstacle to extending their processes of thought to practical and productive doings. And there is a deeper point about the language of practice. For Dewey, as for Wittgenstein, language is not merely a system of abstract referential symbols. Rather it grows out of and is deeply implicated in human practices. Moves in language—what others might refer to as "language games" or vocabularies—are at the same time also moves in social life and cannot simply be lifted out of social contexts and applied haphazardly in any new ways we wish. Their meaning is (tied up with) their use, and their continued use implies a continuation of forms of social life, at least in attenuated form.

Thus the "liberal arts" enjoy deep internal relations with the values and class roles and privileges of the ancient world. The *trivium* of logic, rhetoric, and grammar are explicitly tied to the arts required by the "liber" in their specific roles (e.g., arguing in law courts or legislative assemblies). The *quadrivium* of mathematical abstractions in turn is tied to the place of contemplation in the ideal life of citizens freed from labor. We cannot simply lift the educational vocabularies of the ancient world and hope to transfer them in our own practices without unwittingly importing primitive survivals of these values and privileges. That implicit importation is precisely why the distinction between the liberal and the vocational in education is for Dewey an *untenable* dualism.

One might ignore this caution and call new educational frameworks for our time "new liberal arts," and so on. A well-known "new liberal arts" initiative was undertaken by the Alfred Sloan foundation in the early 1980s, after an internal position paper by Vice President Stephen White called attention to the growing role of quantification and computer technology applications throughout society. After the expansion and publication of White's (1981) report, the foundation dedicated more than $20 million dollars to new courses in liberal arts colleges to augment education in quantitative reasoning and computer technology literacy. Several of these colleges developed consulting "clinics"; students in new liberal arts courses were required to serve as consultants to client firms, working on quantitative and technological problems and making reports suitable for professional use.

Clearly, the choice of the term "liberal arts" and the dedication of funds to leading liberal arts colleges by the Sloan foundation was intended to endow modern knowledge work with the aura of privilege and prestige from the classical heritage. In the process, the defining sense of "liberal" as free from work, and the antidemocratic implications of the ancient notion, have been thoroughly obscured.

Dewey thought that intellectual and practical clarity demanded a fresh start, with new "arts"—that is, new aggregates of effective means, defined in terms of contemporary human purposes. As he put the point in "Prospects of the Liberal College" (1924a), beyond one or two liberal arts colleges, which "the community might maintain more or less as museums, to adopt the point of view of the liberal arts in the American college … is irrelevant if not cowardly" (1924, MW 15, 200)—a willful refusal to accept their class implications and to face the challenges of building a democratic industrial society.

It is noteworthy that Dewey embraces the term "liberal" in its modern meaning associated—unlike the ancient concept embodied in the liberal arts—with social liberalism, democracy, and social justice. As Dewey argued in "Challenge to Liberal Thought" (1944), "A truly liberal, and liberating, education would refuse today to isolate vocational training on any of its levels from a continuous education in the social, moral, and scientific contexts within which wisely administered callings and professions must function" (1944, LW 15:265).

Despite his rejection of the liberal arts, Dewey's experimentalism offers a compelling vision for contemporary liberal education. But as Frank Wong (2014) has recently observed, "Dewey's American approach has received little attention in the repeated efforts to restore or reform liberal education in the American academy."

The Rejection of the Humanities

Dewey also rejected the ideal of the humanities, which arose in the Renaissance in reaction to the desiccated liberal arts studies of late scholasticism. The humanists' aim, he says, was perfection of the individual learner through emulation of ancient models of virtue, expressed in literary texts. This, he asserts, had two immediate negative effects: (a) the "inner self" replaced contemplation of the Real and the Form of the One as the unifying center of education and (b) the mathematical and scientific subjects of the liberal arts (the *quadrivium*), as a result of the literary bias, lost their central unifying role and were marginalized or eliminated in educating "the humanist." The humanities became an educational program composed almost entirely of literary studies.[8] Thus was born the "two cultures" of humanistic versus scientific-technological-mathematical learning.[9]

Dewey saw this ideal of perfecting the inner self as "rotten." It pulled the individual's energies away from the demands of community life. Further, it displayed a deep metaphysical blunder, resulting from mistaking the individuals we all know—parts of larger social wholes—for free-standing "autonomous" individuals as independent realities. Dewey argues in *Experience and Nature* (1925/1929) that individuality, as individual mental variation, can only be meaningful in a context of social change. When some new variation is introduced it initially represents an inchoate longing, difficult to express, to frame up as belief, to communicate, to place in the social arena so that its meaning and value can be cooperatively assessed. It is private, "too fluid and formless for publication, even to oneself" (1925/1929, LW 1:181). But either the new variant is a "sheer illusion" or else it is social, an "object held in solution, undergoing transformation, to emerge finally as an established and public object" which is "subject to objective requirements and tests" (1925/1929, LW 1:180–181).

For Dewey, in short, inner subjectivity is merely, like the research university it-self, an intermediate position, a preliminary, tentative *stage* in a process of overt and public action. As a result, Dewey argues, the isolated literary education characteristic of the humanities provides merely one more delusory escape from modern problems. However, literary studies—when integrated with the sciences and productive and prac-tical arts—can be a cardinal *resource* for dealing with problematic situations of everyday life. To serve as a useful resource, the subjects groups together as "humanities" must extend beyond literature, narrowly conceived, to include the documentary records of practical fields from science, technology, invention, and architecture to medicine, sur-gery, and law.

Dewey thus rejected both the ontological starting point of the humanities (the inner self to be perfected) and its educational program (literary education isolated from the practical arts).[10] To be clear, Dewey eliminates neither literary texts nor works of art as appropriate subject matters in college education. They both provide both models of ef-fective communication and sources of consummatory experiences that display high forms of human value. Their study in college education, however, would work best not in isolated courses but rather in integrated studies focused on practical transformation of problematic situations.[11]

Dewey's Experimentalist Alternative

Dewey's proposed experimentalist framework for college education stems directly from his view of the university as the institutionalization of the second stage of thinking. Dewey states he states in "Education 1800–1939" (1939) that when he was a student at the University of Vermont in the 1870s there was no college of engineering, or well-equipped science laboratories, and training in the fine arts would have been regarded as out of place. There were no special courses for teachers and no graduate programs to train researchers (1939, LW 14:269). Indeed, so fixed was the course of study that he and his peers went through "a list of courses one after the other, without its even occurring to us that they were prescribed, so much were they a matter of course" (1939, LW 14:270).

But industrialization had by that time *already* called for new specialized practical and productive knowledge, leading to new graduate and professional programs in both the new state universities and the transformed private universities emerging from the elite liberal arts colleges. These new knowledge demands, in turn created a "definite reaction back into the subjects of so-called general and cultural education," which became "more or less pre-professional courses" designed to lay a fairly definite basis for later special-ized training. Meanwhile, the specialized sciences "had reached a stage of development where they played a central role in preparation for intelligent ability to practice success-fully any calling" (1939, LW 14:268–270).[12]

In the new universities developed after 1870, knowledge was reorganized along dis-crete disciplinary lines. To meet the interests of university students—whether intellec-tual, professional, or civic—systematically organized subject matters (i.e., academic disciplines) were, as Dewey recognized, a functional necessity (see 1916, MW 9, esp. ch. 14; 1917a, MW 10:405–408). Only when existing knowledge is systematically ordered within distinct categories, Dewey asserts, can it be made available for efficient use— whether for subsequent inquiries, social applications, or critical public discourses.[13] But as Dewey makes abundantly clear in his three-stage model of thought, disciplined knowledge grows out of social uses—as, for example, developments in the uses of electricity shaped the nineteenth-century discipline of physics. He saw academic disciplines as provisional tools that must be continually shaped and modified for particular subsequent uses.[14] Thus disciplines are constantly evolving with new organizations of subject matter for specific student groups, and thus we find courses like statistics for healthcare, economics for management, and marketing for nonprofit organizations.

The general course of study—in Dewey's day and in ours—has been designed to lead into a specialized major in some disciplinary or professional program and then either advanced research work in a graduate program or advanced professional or technical training. All of these professional end-points presuppose possession of the knowledge stock in those fields bearing upon his work, organized simply and efficiently for use— knowledge to think *with* and *from*. While discipline-based courses and textbooks—and even specialized majors—play a useful subsidiary role, this stock will be most meaningfully and effectively acquired when combined with engagement in the activities of it daily active use.[15]

The problem of general education lies in grasping productively and practically the place and function of disciplinary studies, individually and cumulatively, in the total scene of life. This is both a matter of cognitive understanding, communication, and executive capabilities across various academic, professional, and lay boundaries. Professors could be leaders, not merely in developing (stage 2) knowledge but in establishing effective contact with community members at the stages of agenda setting (stage 1) and dissemination and use (stage 3). But, he says in "Prospects of the Liberal College," (1924b), they have not been "sufficiently the leaders of the community in behalf of their nominal cause" (1924, MW 15:204). Instead of connecting their studies to broad problems, promoting the scientific spirit and method throughout the community, and cooperating with others in testing the cumulative knowledge product for its efficacy in liberating social life, professors have, he adds in "The Liberal College and Its Enemies," *retreated* further and further into specialized studies at ever-farther remove from everyday problems (1924, MW 15:208–209).

The three-stage model of inquiry, however, provides a general template for situating the students' specialized areas of study (located at stage 2) in their larger (stage 1 and 3) social contexts. Major and professional studies must be linked to inquiry-provoking problems (stage 1) and knowledge dissemination and use situations (stage 3). College education can get beyond its present confusion of purpose only by effecting "a more intimate and vital union between theory and practice, science and action, culture and vocation" (1939, LW 14:272).

This, as he states in "Unity of Science as a Social Problem" (1938b), has two broad implications: (a) that science should be taught not merely as bodies of disciplinary subject matter but also as a "method of universal attack and approach" and (b) that specialized, professional, and technical education be directed not merely to narrow ends dictated by special intellectual and professional pursuits but to wide and liberal uses of scientific approaches in all fields of betterment (1938, LW 13:278).[16]

The achievement of this aim would involve directed practical projects, in which students are situated directly into problematic situations, where their growing academic knowledge can be brought to bear directly upon ameliorative efforts. Students could in this way come to grasp the practical upshot of their academic studies and could test university-based knowledge formulations against a practical standard of problem resolution. These projects cannot be organized, however, merely as "add-ons," or situated in periodic cooperative experiences in nonacademic settings. They must be regular components of academic education itself, where students—along with their teachers—combine academic learning directly with problem amelioration.

A Contemporary Example

A contemporary teaching project parallels Dewey's ideas and provides a suggestive example of Dewey's framework for teaching. Professors at Davidson College and Middlebury College have collaborated in creating a "c-MOOC" (essentially a digital seminar) within which students create "communities of inquiry" as they gather and apply scientific knowledge to large unstructured real-world problems, such as: "How might we all maintain well-being and thrive as we age?" Or "how might communities lead the rapid transition to renewable energy?" The MOOC serves as a "collaborative platform where people come together to tackle the world's most pressing issues." One group of students chose to focus their efforts on the question "How might parents in low-income communities in Charlotte, North Carolina, ensure children thrive in their first five years?"

The work of the communities of inquiry proceeds in three stages. In the first or *research* stage (which Dewey would situate as stage 1), "students experienced the value of getting out of the classroom to talk to people, of humanizing these complex issues through face-to-face experiences. They learned to conduct interviews and focus groups with parents, stakeholders, innovators and experts." In the second, or *ideas* stage (which Dewey would situate as the early stage of inquiry proper, the problem clarification of the problem-finding stage), "the students generated specific questions unique to the opportunity areas they discovered in Charlotte, such as 'How might we use community spaces to connect parents to pre-existing resources?'" In the third or *refinement* stage, (which Dewey would consider the later stage of inquiry proper), "the students broke down their big ideas into bite-sized pieces that could be quickly prototyped for feedback. They built physical models and created digital mockups." Then (in what Dewey would consider stage 3), "Students then facilitated sessions with end users for feedback, focusing on testing assumptions and generating insights to inform future iterations of prototypes."[17]

SERVICE TO THE COMMUNITY

Dewey rejected the idea of service to society by university-based scholars as a kind of *noblesse oblige*, where scholars came bearing the gift of their superior knowledge. On the contrary, he held that university-based "knowledge" had no warrant for assertability in subsequent practical situations until it had been employed in complex problematic situations and yielded some measure of control. Community uses afforded university studies the opportunity for practical verification.

As Dewey's views on research and teaching suggest, sound research and university teaching simply cannot be divorced from service to society—they already *are* central elements *of* that service. University research is stage 2 in society's overall three-step process of inquiry, a time-out for reflection between problem awareness and problem resolution. University teaching, on his view, aims at engaging students in the problems of society and in developing *new* knowledge for their resolution precisely through their use of knowledge created in the university. The problem-finding and agenda-setting work for university-based research (stage 1) involves many people, in many occupational roles, working side by side with scholars, as does the utilization of knowledge in ameliorative efforts (stage 3). On Dewey's view the university does not serve society from the outside, as a spectator and external helper, but is an insider; professors and their students are, at least when universities take stock of their social situation, integrally involved in all stages of social activity. This engagement raises the intelligence not merely of academic scholars but of the whole people, and so it advances democracy.

CONCLUSION

The power to create a unity of experience—alleged by the ancients to reside in the liberal arts and especially in the *quadrivium* of contemplative mathematical and scientific studies—is in Dewey's experimentalist higher education framework replaced by the combination of inquiry with the active cooperation in knowledge formation and use among all those seeking to further the human good through the method of intelligence. For Dewey this is the only "unity" worth striving for.

NOTES

1. 'An exception which "proves the rule" is Hogan and Karier (1978), who saw Dewey and his coworkers as ideologists paving the way for the hegemony of the corporate state. More recently, Benson, Harkevy, and Puckett (2007), in *Dewey's Dream*, create what they take to be a "Deweyan" theory of the university, largely by critiquing Dewey's actual views or rejecting them outright, while Clifford Harbour (2015), in *John Dewey and the Fate of the American*

Community College, presents an extensive review of Dewey on college teaching. Because the community colleges are primarily teaching, not research, institutions, however, Harbour explicitly steers away from examining Dewey's views on university-based research.

2. Essays proposing Deweyan approaches to rhetoric, college speech, English composition, logic, the humanities, general education, adult education, and experimental college programs can be found in, for example, Burks (1968); Fishman (1993); Eames (1963); Balkcum (1974); Kaminsky (1962); Harsh et al. (1983); Knode (1940); Benne (1949); and Reynolds (1995).

3. The theory of inquiry is a particularly fortunate vantage point from which to view his ideas on higher education. The theory was formulated early in the century in *Studies in Logical Theory* (1903), developed extensively in *How We Think* (1910), and further clarified in *Logic: The Theory of Inquiry* (1938a). Thus there is a period of thirty-four years when Dewey's views on inquiry—and at least indirectly on research in higher education—matured.

4. "Senator's August Golden Fleece: Stewardesses Shape Surveys Just One Big Bust," *Sarasota Herald Tribune,* August 22, 1975, p. 10-B.

5. The relevance of this concern for the 2016 US presidential election can hardly be overstated.

6. Harbour (2014) is particularly useful in his discussion of Dewey's analysis of the problems of discipline-based teaching. See especially pages 142–145.

7. The first two-year or "junior" colleges were founded in Illinois from 1896 through the early 1900s. The University of Chicago, under William Rainey Harper, founded a junior college division in 1896, during Dewey's tenure. The city of Joliet, Illinois, in partnership with Harper's University, opened a junior college division of its high school in 1902. The purpose of these colleges was to offer college-level general education courses to prepare students for university study. But placing general education for all but the most promising students outside the university permitted the university to protect high academic standards by not accepting students until they had proven themselves to be fully prepared for university study (Harbour 2015, 60–61). Dewey may have formed his views about the proper institutional placement of the "foundational" discipline-based courses while working with Harper at Chicago in the late 1890s.

8. In some medieval universities, the *quadrivium* subjects had already been eliminated; in others they were offered only as nonrequired add-ons to the curriculum. They were seen by Church leaders as vestiges of pagan culture. Arithmetic was at times limited to computing the date of Easter and Music reduced to training for church choirs.

9. Historically, this is accurate. The growth of manufactures, navigation, and trade in the late sixteenth and seventeenth centuries gave rise to demands for useful knowledge. The colleges at Oxford and Cambridge refused to incorporate technical and commercial subjects. The new learning then found its home outside the universities, first at Gresham College, then at the Royal Society—creating an institutional base for the nonliterary culture.

10. Kaminsky (1962) attempts to restate Dewey's position on the humanities. He claims that for Dewey the materials—the recorded data—for the study of complete or reflectively transformed experiences are to be found "primarily in the arts and the humanities" (70–71). Dewey himself sharply rejected that claim.

11. He would warmly embrace Kaminsky's suggestive idea that stories and other artworks become of importance in presenting to us what is involved in the qualitative transformation of experience. Such stories relate the kinds of fused experiences human beings undergo. We are all able to expand ourselves by taking these stories on board in planning for and creating our own individual and collective transformations (see Kaminsky 1962, 70).

12. This distinction between preprofessional and professional studies suggests the familiar distinction between general studies in the first two years of university and the "major" in the past two years. However, as suggested earlier, Dewey appears to favor assigning general studies to preuniversity agencies, preserving the university's identity as the home of inquiry

13. In *Democracy and Education*, chapter 14, Dewey distinguishes between three levels of knowledge. The first is the knowledge acquired incidental to aims-directed everyday action. The second is the knowledge acquired through informal communication with peers, teachers, and community members. The third level is systematic knowledge at the highest degree of abstraction and generality. This kind of disciplined knowledge is the preserve of knowledge specialists. But in a democracy, this third level of knowledge must be widely disseminated, especially through secondary education, at least with regard to understanding how the underlying methods used by specialists make it warranted for use.

14. See *Democracy and Education*, ch. 15. Dewey is worth quoting at length on this point. "Physics developed slowly out of the use of tools and machines; the important branch of physics known as mechanics testifies in its name to its original associations. The lever, wheel, inclined plane, etc., were among the first great intellectual discoveries of mankind, and they are none the less intellectual because they occurred in the course of seeking for means of accomplishing practical ends. The great advance of electrical science in the last generation was closely associated, as effect and as cause, with application of electric agencies to means of communication, transportation, lighting of cities and houses, and more economical production of goods" (1916, MW 9:208–209).

15. Consider this from *How We Think* (1910): "The assumption that information that has been accumulated apart from use in the recognition and solution of a problem may later on be, at will, freely employed by thought is quite false .... the only information which, otherwise than by accident, can be put to logical use is that acquired in the course of thinking" (LW 8:163).

16. Dewey would thus reject the proposal of Harsh et al. (1983) for a general education based on interdisciplinary studies. For Dewey, such studies merely concern relations between disciplines—that is, between several stage 2 processes and results. By contrast, his proposed general education focused upon relations between social problems (stage 1), the disciplines (stage 2), and knowledge utilization (stage 3). He states in "Unity of Science as a Social Problem" that "if a unity could be forged between science and society in that sense, then the problem of unified science—of interdisciplinary integration—would be trivial" (1938, LW 13:278).

17. Allison Dulin Salisbury, "The Inverse MOOC," *Inside Higher Education*, March 12, 2015. https://www.insidehighered.com/blogs/higher-ed-beta/inverse-mooc.

Works Cited

Citations of John Dewey's works are to the thirty-seven-volume critical edition published by Southern Illinois University Press under the editorship of Jo Ann Boydston. In-text citations give the original publication date and series abbreviation, followed by volume number and page number. For example: (1934, LW 10:12) is page 12 of *Art as Experience*, which is published as volume 10 of *The Later Works*.

Series abbreviations for *The Collected Works*:
EW *The Early Works* (1882–1898)
MW *The Middle Works* (1899–1924)
LW *The Later Works* (1925–1953)

Balkcum, Elvin O. 1974. "The Influence of John Dewey's Philosophy on the Founding of the General College." *General College Studies*, vol. 11, 1–29.

Benne, Kenneth. 1949. "John Dewey on Adult Education." *Adult Education Bulletin*, vol. 14, 7–12.

Benson, Lee, Ira Harkevy, and John Puckett. 2007. *Dewey's Dream*, Philadelphia: Temple University Press.

Burks, Don M. 1968. "John Dewey and Rhetorical Theory." *Western Speech*, vol. 32, 118–126.

Dewey, John. 1903. *Studies in Logical Theory*. MW 2:296–376.

Dewey, John. 1910. *How We Think*. MW 8.

Dewey, John. 1916. *Democracy and Education*. MW 9.

Dewey, John. 1917a. "Organization in American Education." MW 10:397–411.

Dewey, John. 1917b. "The Case of the Professor and the Public Interest." MW 10:164–167.

Dewey, John. 1917c. "The Modem Trend Toward Vocational Education and Its Effect upon the Professional and Non-professional Studies of the University." MW 10:151–157.

Dewey, John. 1917d. "Universal Service as Education." MW 10:183–191.

Dewey, John. 1924a. "Prospects of the Liberal College." MW 15:200–204.

Dewey, John. 1924b. "The Liberal College and Its Enemies." MW 15:205–212.

Dewey, John. 1930. *Individualism, Old and New*. LW 5:42–124.

Dewey, John. 1935. "The Need for Orientation." LW 11:162–166.

Dewey, John. 1938a. *Logic: The Theory of Inquiry*. LW 12.

Dewey, John. 1938b. "Unity of Science as a Social Problem." LW 13:271–280.

Dewey, John. 1939. "Education 1800–1939." LW 14:266–272.

Dewey, John. 1944. "Challenge to Liberal Thought." LW 15:261–275.

Eames, S. Morris. 1963. "The First Course in Logic: A Deweyan Approach." *Journal of General Education*, vol. 15, 46–54.

Fishman, Stephen M. 1993. "Explicating Our Tacit Tradition: John Dewey and Composition Studies." *College Composition and Communication*, vol. 44, no. 3, 15–30.

Harbour, Clifford. 2014. *John Dewey and the Future of the American Community College*. London: Bloomsbury.

Hill, Patrick J. 1984. "A Deweyan Perspective on Higher Education." *Liberal Education*, vol. 70, 307–312.

Harsh, Barbara, Paul Haas, and Michael Moore. 1983. "An Interdisciplinary Model to Implement General Education." *Journal of Higher Education*, vol. 54, 42–59.

Hogan, David, and Clarence Karier. 1978. Professionalizing the role of Truth Seekers. *Interchange*, vol. 9, 45–71.

Kaminsky, James S. 1962. "Dewey's Defense of the Humanities." *School Review*, vol. 70, 66–72.

Knode, Jay C. 1940. "The Influence of John Dewey in Higher Education." *New Mexico Quarterly Review*, vol. 10, 17–29.

Reynolds, Katherine C. 1995. "Influence of John Dewey on Experimental Colleges: The Black Mountain Example." Annual Meeting of the American Educational Research Association.

White, Stephen P. 1981 *The New Liberal Arts*. New York: Alfred P. Sloan Foundation.

Wong, Frank. 2014. "The Search for American Liberal Education: Liberal Education and the American Context." *Liberal Education*, vol. 100, no. 4.

CHAPTER 20

....

DEWEY, AESTHETIC EXPERIENCE, AND EDUCATION FOR HUMANITY

....

ANDREA R. ENGLISH AND CHRISTINE DODDINGTON

AESTHETIC experience, Dewey wrote in a 1938 talk to students, is just a way of talking about what experience is in its "best" and "fullest" sense (1938, LW 13:368); it is how we experience the world as fully human. Aesthetic experience describes a process by which we search for meaning and develop dispositions to continue that search. The "possession and appreciation of the meaning of things" is, as Dewey said, "the characteristic human need" (1925, LW 1:272). For Dewey, both society at large, and education systems in particular, had a role to play in providing for this human need. But as Dewey well knew, difficulties arise in every new generation, not only around how best to provide for the needs of the next generation, but also around what constitutes basic human needs in the first place. Dewey found a response to both difficulties through consideration of the question, What is education?, which simultaneously pointed to a deeper, more fundamental question, namely: What does it mean to be human? In Dewey's complex contemplation of these questions, the role of aesthetic experience featured prominently. Here we examine Dewey's thought in relation to aesthetic experience, human nature, and education. In this context, we show how his work sheds light on the crisis in education, not only in his time, but importantly, in the present day as well.

This chapter focuses on examining Dewey's concept of aesthetic experience as it is inextricably tied to his concepts of human nature and education. We begin by exploring the concept of aesthetic experience in the context of Dewey's broader theory of education and growth. We show how, for Dewey, aesthetic experience was experience in its fullest, transformative sense; it involves resistance, exploring in an in-between realm, and coming to completion, and therefore it is educative in that it fosters growth. We then discuss how aesthetic experiences are cultivated in the context of formal learning settings, including classrooms and outdoor environments, paying special attention to the critical and indispensable role of the teacher in creating situations for students' aesthetic experiences. In this context, we discuss Dewey's critique of traditional and progressive education and reveal how his critique is still relevant in today's global education climate. We conclude by discussing the crisis in education as we see it today and suggest that Dewey's views provide three key insights for addressing this crisis: the value of teachers, the role of art as an ethical-political force, and the special place of philosophy of education in the cultivation of shared humanity. Ultimately, we seek to show that Dewey's emphasis on aesthetic experience as the expression of the full potential of human beings is interconnected with his idea of democratic education, such that without the cultivation of aesthetic experiences, there is no possibility for democratic education—and in turn, no possibility for bringing up youths into adults capable of fostering democracy as a way of life.

AESTHETIC EXPERIENCE, LEARNING, GROWTH, AND EDUCATION

Dewey's theory of aesthetic experience is grounded in the idea of human beings as capable of "growth," a term that encapsulates both our capacity for self-growth—the process by which we learn through interactions with our environment—and our fundamental need for others to aid our productive interaction with the environment, a need that serves as the basis for intergenerational educational relationships. Human growth in Dewey's account has two dimensions: "plasticity" and "dependence." These terms taken together describe the underlying basis for the fact that our experience changes and gains shape through the variety of our interactions with objects and with other human beings over time. As we discuss here, for Dewey there was an unbreakable tie among human nature, growth, and experience: growth is both the aim of human experience and the condition for its possibility.

Plasticity, Dependence, and the Human as Social

Dewey's notion of growth aims to account for the fact that human beings do not merely change over time, but rather *learn* from their interactions. The dimension of growth that describes the human ability to learn as a capacity to take in something new and unexpected (a new object or idea) from our environment, consider it, and respond to it in light of our aims and desires is what Dewey refers to as "plasticity."[1] In his use of this term, he was drawing on a long tradition of educational theory connecting to what J.-J. Rousseau called *perfectibilité* ([1762] 1979) and German philosopher J. F. Herbart called *Bildsamkeit* ([1835/1841] 1902, 65, and 1913, 1). To illustrate what plasticity meant for Dewey, we can refer to the example he used in *Democracy and Education*. Dewey described the case of an infant who cannot yet crawl and who is trying to reach an object that is within her visual field, but not within her reach (1916, MW 9:50). With this basic example of learning in the realm of sensory formation, notably one that is also in Rousseau's *Emile* ([1762] 1979, 64) and one that recurs often in Dewey's work, Dewey pointed to something essential about the structure of human learning—namely, that learning entails the experience of limitation: the child experiences what she cannot yet do and does not yet know.

For Dewey, just as for Rousseau, this experience of limitation was not just an aspect of childhood that we "grow out of"; rather, it is fundamental to what it means to be human. But more so than Rousseau, Dewey underscored that this aspect of human nature feeds into our capacity for extended experimentation with our environment. Unlike other animals that mature and become independent quickly, our relatively slow process of physical growth—our extended immaturity, or "prolonged infancy" as Dewey called it in explicitly drawing on bioevolutionary theory—provides us with time to experiment with our surroundings, test out our inclinations, and encounter our limitations to find out what is possible: "The infant has the advantage of the multitude of instinctive tentative reactions and of the experiences that accompany them, even though he is at a temporary disadvantage because they cross one another" (1916, MW 9:50; see also, e.g., 1938, LW 13:291–192). Through this experimental process of testing whether our self-world relations fit together or "cross" one another, the child learns "methods" of interaction that she can use "in other situations"; she learns how to deal with blind spots—that is, with the fact of the negativity of human experience.[2] In this sense, she not only learns something specific, but also learns the structure of learning processes; she "learns how to learn" (1916, MW 9:50).

Another critical point falls out from Dewey's contemplations of the biological fact of prolonged immaturity, and it relates to both our plasticity and our dependence: by nature, human beings are social beings. Human growth is thus a social process. The social comes into play in connection to our plasticity, and the associated capacity for experimentation, in that it relates not only to how we learn to interact with objects, but also to how we learn to be among other human beings. We form relationships with others in part by "testing things out" through trial and error. For example, there is a certain experimental quality in learning to figure out what to say when someone tells us upsetting or joyful news; what to do in certain complex situations of action that could affect others; and also, no less important, what to expect from others in terms of how we are listened to, responded to, and treated.

The social nature of human beings is also underscored in a distinct way in the other dimension of growth, which Dewey termed "dependence." Dewey's aforementioned example of the infant illustrates a need that cannot be met by her established state of capabilities, namely a need for an object, but it also points to her need for other human beings. Dewey used "dependence" to describe this need for others. Like our plasticity, our dependence is a trait of our immaturity, but Dewey pointed out that it is false to assume—as did the popular theories of growth at his time[3]—that growth ends in maturity as a state of "independence."

Independence implies the loss of the need for others. Popular theories of growth in Dewey's time, which viewed human growth as having an end and which greatly impacted how formal education was theorized and practiced, can be seen in part to have their basis in a Kantian idea of enlightenment. Kant defined enlightenment as the release from a self-incurred immaturity (*Unmündigkeit*) to maturity (*Mündigkeit*[4]); this release describes the move from one's inability to use one's mind without direction from authority to becoming an autonomous individual (Kant, [1784] 1990). This idea of independence as autonomy strongly influenced modern concepts of "the educated man" in Dewey's time and after it, for example, in the analytic philosophy of R. S. Peters.[5]

Contrary to the idea of growth ending in adulthood, Dewey argued, dependence is not merely a kind of debilitating helplessness that the child can and should grow out of in becoming "educated." Rather, it remains essential for living throughout a lifetime; it is an aspect of being human that is "constructive" in that it aids further growth (1916, MW 9:50). Although dependence as constructive was to some extent recognized in the then current theories of human nature, the problem, as Dewey saw it, is that human dependence is interpreted as one-sided; there is an assumed dependence of the child on the adult, but not of the adult on the child. As a consequence, this sets up an implicit hierarchical relationship between the dependent child and the independent adult. Dewey highlighted the other, equally significant, side of dependence: the human extended stage of infancy provides time and space for "nurture and affection" from the adult, such that the adult, in developing the feelings of affection and sympathy, is also in that sense "dependent" on his or her relation to the child (1916, MW 9:50). For Dewey, this interdependent intergenerational relationship, an idea that Nel Noddings (2013)[6] has famously furthered in her concept of the reciprocal relationship of caring, provides the basis for valuing others throughout our lives. We start as—and we remain—relational beings. Understood in this way, it logically followed for Dewey that our childhood dependence, combined and viewed together with ongoing human plasticity, does not necessarily lead to individualistic independence or to some kind of prolonged hierarchical dependent relation, but rather can lead to a recognized *inter*dependence (1916, MW 9:49).

Humans as Meaning-Seeking and Meaning-Making Beings

With his notion of growth defined using conceptions of plasticity and dependence, Dewey was not only underscoring the nature of humans as social, as opposed to individualistic; he was also revealing that growth is tied to the human existential need to search for and gain meaning. Our way of being in the world is as a search for meaning; this search is never-ending, not in spite of the fact, but because of the fact, that we *grow* throughout our lives. By tying growth to the search for meaning, Dewey highlighted the connection among growth, human experience, and learning. For Dewey, learning described the process of gaining meaning by way of our experience, where experience here refers to a process of "doing," "undergoing," and making a reflective connection between the two over time (1916, MW 9:146–147).

It is this last aspect, that of "reflection," that is particularly significant for establishing new meaning: new meaning arises, whether for the playful child or the adult scientist, when a connection is made between what one does and what one undergoes in consequence. Dewey illustrated this with an example of a child who touches a flame and feels the pain of a burn. When the child makes the connection between his act of vision and his act of touching the object, he is bringing these acts together to *mean* heat or pain. The child's *acts* in relation to the objects around him now have more meaning, because new connections between the two are perceptible, and these new connections feed into the child's modifications to his self-understanding—that is, how he perceives what he is capable of, what he likes or dislikes—and this in turn influences his choices in future experiences. Equally, the object itself, in this case the flame, "has gained in meaning" for the child, since now the touch means pain, and the light connects to heat. Similarly, for the scientist experimenting with a flame, everything that was already known "about combustion, oxidation, about light, and temperature, may become an intrinsic part of [the flame's] intellectual content" (1916, MW 9:83). Another way to put this is to say that the child's or scientist's self-understanding and understanding of the world have shifted, albeit in different ways; he or she has an expanded sense of what is possible and desirable after hands-on interaction with the world.

However, the idea of "gaining" meaning can be misleading if we fail to consider this terminology in the context of Dewey's theory of growth and learning. When we conceive of learning as a meaning-making process, as illustrated in the example of the child and flame, we can see how learning is grounded in the nature of human experience as involving both encounters with the limitations of our established knowledge and ability—in which we break with our free flow of activity based on an unexpected interaction with the world or others—and reflection upon such encounters—in which we ask ourselves: What happened? What went wrong? The encounters with our own blind spots and the discontinuities in experience and learning that they engender inform meaning, rather than take away from it (English 2013). Accordingly for Dewey, human experience, as a process of growth, should not be understood as reducible to a tacking on of new information; rather, experience is properly described as a transformational process that occurs on the basis of encountering our blind spots—that is, of *undergoing* a world in ways unexpected and unforeseeable. Such encounters are pre-reflective; they are first experienced as an interruption to what we anticipated.[7] To transform them into reflective processes of learning, we have to enter into a process of questioning what we had previously taken for granted as true, real, or justified. This questioning process involves not only questioning the conditions of our interaction with the environment, but also self-questioning: an inquiry into the interruptions in our experiences that helps us determine how our established meanings may prove problematic given the new, unexpected situation.

Reflective thinking is thus our human way of exploring within a realm of ambiguity—an "in-between realm of learning"—wherein we *lose* the sense of the meanings of certain things around us, whether for a split second or for an extended period of time. This in-between is a space between old and new, right and wrong, wherein we have recognized that old values and beliefs no longer guide us, but we have not yet found new ways forward (English 2013, 2016a). Our reflective capacity is an essential part of our human nature. It illuminates how the self and world relate; that is, it seeks to articulate how the "change made [to the world] by [our] action" relates to "a change made in us" (1916, MW 9:147). This is precisely why Dewey made the point that the "value" of a given experience lies in "the perception of relationships" to which it leads; the extent to which the experience is "cumulative," involving increasingly rich reflection on the multiple possible connections between self and world, is the extent to which it "has meaning" (1916, MW 9:147). Enriching established meaning through our experiences was for Dewey the definition of what it means to grow. Dewey spoke of such experiences as "educative": they enhance our perception of the world and thereby give it new meaning via a pathway that includes both loss and gain— that is, a shedding of connections that do not meet the demands of the situation and the building of new connections that are made due to the coming together of established and novel ideas and actions.

Two Senses of the Term "Education"

What is particularly significant in Dewey's discussion of growth and its connection to educative experiences is that he was enhancing a *biological* understanding of human growth with an *educational* understanding of human growth in two ways: first, in his consideration of education as a process of self-formation, and second, in his consideration of education as an intergenerational pedagogical relationship.

Regarding the first point, Dewey's description of the nature of human experience drew on educational thinking during the German Enlightenment going back to Wilhelm von Humboldt's 1792 notion of *Bildung*. According to Humboldt, the human is a being who wants to "sustain" and give "value" and meaning to his existence (Humboldt [1792] 1960, 235).[8] To do this, Humboldt argued, a human being needs to interact with a world that is "not self," that is *other* than self (*NichtMensch*) (Humboldt [1792], 235). This interaction or interplay between self and other is *Bildung*, the German term for education as self-formation and transformation through the interplay between receptivity (*Empfänglichkeit*) and activity (*Selbsttätigkeit*) (Humboldt [1792]1960, 237). The concept of *Bildung* underscores that our encounters with otherness and difference in the world matter; they form us as human beings.

So even though from the biological standpoint the organism's change over a lifetime via interaction with the environment could be called growth, Dewey made clear that from an educational standpoint, not all processes of change are "growth" in a "cumulative," and thus genuinely "educative," sense. Routine, repetitive, and mechanical activities are those with little to no receptivity to difference, and therefore, as Dewey wrote, they hinder growth by limiting new meanings (1916, MW 9:84). It is for this reason that Dewey came to qualify certain experiences as "educative experiences."

Educative experiences are those that involve "interaction" between self and world: a cycle or interplay of actively giving out and receptively taking in.[9] But they also involve "continuity," which refers to making a connection between self and world such that the new associations made in one experience are brought into subsequent experiences (1938, LW 13:25–30). In saying that both *interaction* and *continuity* are constitutive of educative experiences, Dewey sharply distinguished between experiences that are educative and two other modes of being in the world. On the one hand, he was parsing out a mode of being that amounts to *just* interacting without forming continuities. Aside from not being educative, this mode is hardly possible, since living and experiencing as human beings is not simply living in a series of disconnected present interactions—like cattle "fettered to the moment," as Nietzsche put it ([1874] 1983, 60). Rather, we are historical beings with memory, and as such, we form "habits," or what Dewey also called "definite dispositions" (1916, MW 9:51), by "taking" meanings with us from the past and thereby forming continuity from one moment to the next.[10]

On the other hand, Dewey underscored the idea that it is not educative to be in the world with continuity and without interaction. Yet because human beings could exist with the bare minimum of diverse interactions with difference and otherness, Dewey suggested that the possibility of human beings living with continuity and only depleted forms of interaction poses a more serious threat to humankind than does the possibility of existing by interaction without continuity. Dewey's constant reminder throughout his work of the problems of routine and mechanical thinking and being point squarely to this threat and relate to his critical lens on civilization, which we address further later in the chapter.

It is important to note that there is an unresolved tension in Dewey's thinking between his idea of growth along biological lines and his description of growth as an educational phenomenon; his term "educative experiences" proves significant in how he addressed this tension. As Dewey was aware, biologically speaking, growth can occur in many directions for better or for worse. As human beings, we grow just by being alive, in that what we experience in one situation shapes what we can come to experience in future situations. A different way of putting this is to say that our established meanings both make possible and limit the meanings we form in the present situation; they shape how we perceive the features of our environment and ourselves through space and time. These established meanings thus shape what we attend to, or do not attend to; our judgments of the environment; and in turn, our actions. As Dewey explained, in every new experience a "larger system of meanings" we call *mind* "suffuses, interpenetrates, colors what is here and now," and so our vision of what is possible in any given moment is shaped by what we have already experienced (1925, LW 1:231; Alexander 2013, 136).[11] But this fact of human existence also presents a serious problem for human beings in terms of their personal and social growth: Just as our plasticity can flourish and be utilized to experiment and innovate when we encounter something new and unexpected, so too our plasticity can become dense, inflexible, stifled by a lack of richness and an increase in routine in our environment; just as our dependence can flourish such that we grow up to recognize our *inter*dependence and value others, so too our dependence as children can manifest as sustained dependence and reliance on authority, or also as perceived *in*dependence and egoism. And so the need arises to demarcate certain experiences as educative. Dewey qualified an experience as "educative" when it opens up possibilities for further growth, and as "uneducative," or even "mis-educative," when it "distorts the growth of further experience" (1938, LW 13:11).

The problem is that, left to chance, human beings may not have the kind of educative experiences that foster "education" as growth (or *Bildung*), and it is on this basis that Dewey derived the social and ethical need for "education" as a specific kind of intergenerational pedagogical relationship. Dewey wrote of the nature of pedagogical relationships: "It is imperative that every energy should be bent to making the present experience as rich and significant as possible. Then the present merges insensibly into the future, the future is taken care of" (1916, MW 9:61). This second notion of education as a certain pedagogical relationship (like his first notion of education as a self-transformative process or *Bildung*) connects to a long-standing educational philosophical tradition. Dewey was pointing to education as *educare*, to draw forth, or what is referred to in the German tradition as *Erziehung*.[12] Education as *Erziehung* has a moral dimension in that it cultivates the human capacity for *Bildung*, that is, for rich, full, educative experiences. For *Bildung*, a process by which we "strengthen our ideas, abilities and shape our purposes," to be made possible, as Humboldt ([1792]1960) wrote, we need "the whole world [*die Welt*] to interact with, or, at least everything we can imagine the world to be" (237–238).[13] Dewey's concept of "educative experiences" reflects this idea that our human need for meaning dictates our need for diversity—for a whole world of differentiated objects and ideas. His concept of education as a pedagogical relationship makes clear that the educator's moral task is to address this essential human need for meaning; a pedagogical, *educational* relationship is one in which the older generation has the task of spending "every energy" to provide the space for rich, educative experiences for the younger generation.[14]

Aesthetic, Educative Experiences

So what do such rich experiences look like? Such experiences are aesthetic experiences; aesthetic experiences are by definition educative. To an extent, Dewey said, aesthetic experiences are hard to describe—they are ineffable; we know them when we have them (1938, LW 13:364). He came to talk about aesthetic experiences as "*an* experience," which could refer to a range of happenings, including eating a meal, or "the graciousness of a person," wherein the encounter touches our hearts in some way (1934, LW 10:42; 1938, LW 13:359). There are a few key aspects to this kind of experience that are particularly important to Dewey's educational theory. The first is that there is some fulfillment or satisfaction to it, which means it leads us somewhere, as opposed to either just leaving us stuck or being haphazard with no perceivable end. Dewey called the fulfillment that is part of aesthetic experiences "consummation" (1934, LW 10:42).

Although Dewey used the term "satisfaction" to describe the consummatory aspect of aesthetic experience, it would be a misunderstanding to connect this to a highly subjective determination of satisfaction. The consummation of an experience accounts for a world of objects and others that *resist* us—a world that resists our attempts to understand it. Consummatory experiences are those in which we are consciously attending to the moments of resistance, as these are experiences of limitation, which heighten our awareness of the distinct qualities of our environment. As Dewey explained, the first time a child eats an apple "there is no distinction of a me and not-me"; she eats with ease and enjoyment (1892, LW 17: 155). It is not until the world resists the child due to a change in her environment—namely, when she wants an apple a second time and cannot reach it—that her awareness is heightened such that the "seeing and tasting of the apple are no longer bound up together, and accordingly the qualities of color and taste are distinguished in consciousness" (1892, LW 17:155). What the child had once taken for granted as unified now becomes distinct and an object of her reflection, imagination, and inquiry.

As our experiences become more complex, the aspect of resistance from the world becomes even more critical if we are, like Dewey, interested in what makes an experience educative. Dewey is known for the fact that in all of his various discussions of experience as "reflective experience" and as "reflective inquiry," he used very cognitive-sounding terms, such as "uncertainty," "doubt," "perplexity," and "confusion," to describe the moments in which we experience the sort of limitation that sparks our reflection on our interactions with the world.[15] This description of the structure of experience aligns him with the pragmatist focus on doubt as the "birthplace" of thinking.[16] In describing aesthetic experiences, however, Dewey more often used the terminology of "resistance" to connote a *felt* quality.[17] These moments of resistance awaken us to our surroundings, inspiring our imagination, which brings us beyond what Dewey called "the scope of personal, vitally direct experience," which is "very limited" and moves us toward "the full scope" of a situation (1916, MW 9:240).[18] Aesthetic experiences do not ignore resistance, but rather attend to it, and convert "resistance and tensions [. . .] into a movement toward an inclusive and fulfilling close" (1934, LW 10:62).[19] Imagination is essential to aesthetic experiences; it extends our capacity to remain in-between in spaces of ambiguity and take in the resistance, tension, conflict, and struggle that is initiated by our encounters with those things or ideas that are new, different, or difficult to understand; may contradict our beliefs, cause uncertainty, or incite fear; or have the potential to shut us down emotionally and hinder our ability to learn (English 2016b). For this reason, aesthetic experiences are educative; each moment of doing and undergoing within the experience is utilized to inform further perceptions, interactions, and reflective connections between self and world.

An aesthetic experience is experience at its best, because it does what any experience has the potential to do: it breaks apart established meanings that are affecting our interactions with otherness and difference, and in doing so "make[s] us aware of some of the connections which had been imperceptible" (1916, MW 9:83; see also 1925, LW 1:129).[20] By opening our minds to what was taken for granted and revealing our blind spots, Maxine Greene (1995) illustrates, aesthetic experiences contribute to our "wide-awakeness". So while we exist and experience the world as biological beings, we are only fully alive as vitally connected to the *other* by way of aesthetic experiences; they "make living thus contribute to an enrichment of [life's] own perceptible meaning" (1916, MW 9:82). This is why Dewey often described aesthetic experiences using terminology of vitality. Aesthetic experiences are "vital" because through them what we previously took for granted now becomes available to us for the purpose of interpreting new meanings in our environment; in this sense, in simple situations, like that of the child who cannot grab the apple, or in more complex situations, such as moral dilemmas, aesthetic experiences contribute to our development of "a wider reality," "a wider self" (1892, LW 17:156; see also 1938, LW 13:55; Fesmire 2003). As David Granger (2006) notes, for Dewey aesthetic experiences were "revelatory"; in them "a new dimension of the meaning of the human encounter with the world finds expression" (104).

Educative, aesthetic experiences are connected to ongoing growth because they nurture and extend both our plasticity toward increased flexibility in new situations and our dependence toward interdependence as a recognition of the inherent dignity of every human being. So, while it is true that every experience, whether routine and mechanical or aesthetic, contributes to our formation of dispositions toward the world and others—that is, to our character—only aesthetic experiences help us form certain kinds of dispositions that we might call *educative*. Dewey called the two central dispositions formed by aesthetic experiences "sensitivity" and "responsiveness" with the former referring to a deep receptivity to otherness, difference, and newness that contributes to sympathy and willingness to listen and the latter referring to our active engagement with our environment on the basis of our receptivity to distinctions and difference and not in ignorance of them.[21]

On the basis of his conception of experience, or more specifically, as we have argued, his notion of *aesthetic* experience, Dewey found a way to differentiate between an "ordinary definition" of education, which views education as the passing on of "information expressed in symbols" (1916, MW 9:11–12), and a "technical definition" as "the reconstruction of experience." In his technical definition, we find both senses of the term "education." Education as *Bildung* is the "reconstruction of experience" in that it meets two criteria: it must add to meaning—that is, it must contribute to an "increased perception of the connections and continuities" between our doings and undergoings in and with the world—and it must contribute to our understanding of what to expect and anticipate in a new situation, so that we can attempt to direct further experience (1916, MW 9:83; see also Benner 2017). Education as *Erziehung*, that is, as an educational, pedagogical relationship between teacher and learner, is also a type of reconstruction; pedagogical relationships serve to enhance learners' reconstructions of experience by "*reconstructing*" environments to have rich conditions under which such transformative change is made possible (which we examine further in our discussion of the teacher's role). In turn, pedagogical relationships foster learners' desires to form the educative dispositions of sensitivity and responsiveness to perceived differences in their environment.

While on the one hand Dewey wanted to say that having aesthetic experiences is part of how human nature is "built," because such experiences represent the flourishing of our full potentialities within our environment and our exchanges with others, he was also in a sense forced to admit that not all experiences are aesthetic and educative. This is partly due to the fact that Dewey was observant that human beings as social beings are born into groups, communities, and societies that form how they experience the world, and in turn what type of character and associated dispositions they form. As a social critic, Dewey saw that modern society and "civilization," which he at times admired, creates conditions under which human beings have "experiences" that are mechanical and deadening modes of existence; they do not require or support humans to think, reflect on resistance, and make meaningful connections between self and world. Instead, they are a result of the human quest for certainty, reinforced by recurring continuity *without* diverse interactions, which becomes debilitating to individuals and social groups. This quest is what causes "fixed habits," or fixed frames of mind that color our experiences and hinder us from having rich, aesthetic interactions with difference, otherness, and newness.[22] As Dewey pointed out, even the scientist can fall victim to such fixed frames of mind (1938, LW 13: 371). Dewey saw formal education as having a vital role in fostering our ability to avoid such fixation, as we discuss next.

"WIDENING THE MEANING-HORIZON": EDUCATIVE ENVIRONMENTS AND THE TEACHER

In his 1926 essay "Art in Education—Education in Art," Dewey decried the education system precisely because it was perpetuating, rather than mitigating, the loss of genuine, educative, aesthetic experiences (1926, LW 2:112–115). Dewey's notion of aesthetic experience can be seen as a criterion for the evaluation of whether planned systems of educa*ting* others, including the setting up of schools, the selection of subject matter, and the determination of methods of teaching, are actually promoting learners' educative experiences as *Bildung*. His criticism of what he called "old, traditional education" is well known, and to a large extent it reflects what he viewed as the problem in the society of his time. But he also considered the "progressive" or "new" education movement to be failing in several ways. Although in some sense Dewey aligned himself with progressivism, his criticisms of it were severe and cannot be taken lightly if we are trying to understand his positive view of education as a cultivated intergenerational, pedagogical relationship aimed at fostering every individual's growth. Before discussing Dewey's notions of subject matter and teaching, we examine the main features of his criticism of both "old" and "new" education.

The debate between "traditional education" and "progressive education" still goes on today, although it is couched in slightly different terms, such as "transmissive" versus "active" or "dialogic" teaching. In Dewey's time, just as today, critics of transmissive education took issue with how subject matter is treated as final, fixed knowledge that just needs to be passed on from the teacher to the passive mind of the learner, who absorbs this knowledge. In *The School and Society*, Dewey provided us with an image that encapsulated for him what traditional teaching amounts to in practice: the children sit quietly in rows of desks, passively listening (1915, MW 1:21–22). The limitations on the body in such classrooms, as portrayed in the image, are symptomatic of a greater problem for Dewey—namely, that this model of educating assumes a separation of mind and body: the mind is thought "to be purely intellectual and cognitive" and the body "to be an irrelevant and intruding physical factor" (1916, MW 9:147). In practice, this means that educative, aesthetic experiences are not had by learners. There is no doing, but also there is no genuine undergoing and receptivity; rather, there is only "enforced receptivity," as a forced conformity to others' ideas and judgments (1934, LW 9:177).

But Dewey was criticized by philosophers in his time and afterward for a presumed emphasis on "learning by (just) doing"[23] or by simple problem solving, and in turn for a failure to recognize the significant role of subject matter as the heritage of humankind.[24] However, what is less acknowledged is that Dewey was also highly critical of the little attention progressive educators paid to subject matter. While he agreed with progressive education's value on the plasticity of the child and the child's real experiences—something that, as he saw it, is devalued in traditional education—he was distressed by how this often played out in practice in schools.[25] So whereas traditional education lost sight of the child, progressive education went to the opposite extreme: the child's active physical movement and interaction with other children became the fixed focus, such that the teacher, and in turn the subject matter, had little to no place.

At the heart of the matter for Dewey was that neither traditional nor progressive education facilitated the learner's *search for meaning*; neither facilitated educational *growth*. Traditional education's approach failed in that when knowledge is pre-systematized before a child ever encounters it and then merely handed over for the purposes of memorization and regurgitation, the learner cannot make any meaningful connections *from or for* her own life. Thus, there is no educative experience, no recognition of meaningfulness, no expansion of one's "meaning-horizon" (1916, MW 9:84).

On the other hand, the progressive approach valued interaction, including play, bodily movement, and creative making as part of the classroom environment. However, as Dewey viewed it, in practice progressives placed too much emphasis on activity *for its own sake*. Mere activity does not lead to expansion of the learner's meaning-horizon; it leaves to chance the learner's reflection on the *resistance* of undergoing and thus leaves to chance whether the learner will make connections to established knowledge and the broader social values needed for his or her future. The learner's activity, when it is part of an educative, aesthetic experience, must be of a certain kind: it must be doing that "produces observation and reflection, that clarifies and tests ideas, that tempers and expresses emotion" (1934, LW 9:170).

Educative Environments

Dewey's criticisms point to the kind of learning environments he was after. Elements of Dewey's pragmatic thought that have traditionally featured in education include his stress on inquiry and activity, but we can see from Dewey's detailed account of the nature of aesthetic experience that there are other distinctive characteristics that formal learning settings need to offer. Aesthetic experience requires a supportive atmosphere in which openness to embodied and sensate experience is encouraged. Students need opportunities to not only act, but also express and reflect, to discern relationships, all within a context of exchange and association with others and with a sense of immediacy and presence characterizing the learning process (Doddington 2018b, 194). Learning episodes that feature aesthetic experience in the senses we have discussed will often take shape, beginning with a self-initiated engagement with whatever environment, material, or content is present, and with space and opportunity for individuals to draw connections from their previous experiences. An educational commitment to nurturing intellectual growth in this way may see a formal learning episode proceed through a rhythmic dynamic of doing and undergoing to achieve a sense of consummation in which there is "cumulative progression toward the fulfilment of an experience" (1934, LW 10:169). And it is this sense of consummatory fulfillment that gives coherence to the aesthetic experience as a whole. This kind of educative experience should leave individuals transformed, with fresh perspectives and meanings found, as well as an appetite for further growth through similar experiences. Dewey elucidated the value of a sense of transformation in experience:

> The self, whether it succeed or fail, does not merely restore itself to its former state. Blind surge has been changed into a purpose; instinctive tendencies are transformed into contrived undertakings. The attitudes of the self are informed with meaning. (1934, LW 10:65)

A situation in which such organized learning is designed to occur may range in length from the span of an hour to a sequence of sessions. Aesthetic experiences in educational settings then can have the same characteristics of any cultural, situated experience. Steven Fesmire (2014) writes that "acts or events develop over time," and, we might add, as do some learning experiences (51). Fesmire explains further that "as with the act of writing an essay or the event of childbirth, so situations are temporally spread out. From composing a musical score to negotiating a peace treaty, the situational 'spread' includes the immediately felt echo of the prior flow of experience and the dawning sense of the future flow" (51).

In what follows we have chosen to explain how aesthetic experience might be reflected in two different but we hope familiar educational situations that we feel illustrate the significance of the features previously discussed. We summarize from these illustrations some of the "mis-educative" practices that mitigate against or deny aesthetic experience, then our focus shows how the ethos of the classroom and, significantly, the role of the teacher, are crucial.

In our first imagined setting, the learning episode is one in which a poem or image relating to an aspect of humanity is selected as significant by the teacher or by a student for the purpose of sharing with a group of students. Starting points of this kind have been traditionally used for classes in a range of subjects including philosophy, drama, music, and art (Doddington 2012). In this setting, discussion might begin with everyone contributing to collecting and setting out what is provoked by the piece, bringing to consciousness remnants "of the felt echo of the prior flow of experience" (Fesmire 2014, 51). At this point, a quality of openness of response is important. Puzzlement and comments shared go beyond an inquiry for factual information to commentary concerning emotions, recollections, feelings, perceptions, and possible interpretations or limitations. Individually or in groups, students can settle on and then pursue their own line of inquiry, chosen for what they see as most significant to the piece and to them.

In a classroom with sufficient freedom, students could choose in what medium they will then explore the meanings they are finding. This medium might be simply talk, as in dialogue: students might listen to or challenge ideas, discern relationships or resistances, form perspectives and understandings, and try these out alongside others or build on others' ideas. The discussion might fruitfully travel in any direction, since there is no "right" or "true" answer to be discovered, but instead a collective web of possibilities to be shared, which can then emerge or coalesce to give meaning or a feeling of satisfaction to those engaged. The educational value of the situation lies not in the outcome, but in the tonal *quality* of the experience, of the listening and articulation that may have a depth of affect on individuals and alter how they view the original piece or its themes, and how those views in turn might impact their understanding of themselves or aspects of being human. As Dewey commented on the organization of energies, when rhythm pervades the experience of a work of art, there can be "that sudden magic which gives us the sense of an inner revelation brought to us about something we had supposed to have known through and through" (1934, LW 10:175). This is a moment in which meaning is found or understanding dawns, long seen as a mark of richly transformative educational experience.

Alternative expressive media are available for educative experiences of this nature within any standard curriculum. Exploring ideas through drama, using improvisation, role-play, and/or the collective forming of a piece of theater, requires the same features of challenge and openness, attending to others' thoughts and expressions. An individual or group exploration to reveal significance and make sense of the original starting point could occur similarly through writing, painting, collage, or musical composition. The feature of being open to others and what they bring; the "doing" of composing sound, word, or images; and the episodic moments of resistance, reflection, pause, and judgment before continuing to act are tangible characteristics of Dewey's account of significant lived experience. In order to qualify well as aesthetic experience, these engagements need relish and a vital quality of felt intensity and significance. No aspect of this experience could be forcibly induced in a classroom, so the original impulse to engage has to build on what Dewey saw as our natural and significant immaturity and the human quest for meaning.

It is no accident that the arts feature as media for the cultivation and extension of aesthetic experience; they are the ultimate media for symbolic communication. But as we have made clear, aesthetic experience is not exclusive to art. In our second imagined scenario, we turn to the possibilities of outdoor learning. There are many advocates for the value of outdoor experience in education, and many writers in the field acknowledge a debt to Dewey in their justifications of activity in outside environments (Ord and Leather 2011). Beyond the obvious stress on the value for body and activity, teamwork, and so on, justification for outdoor education most recently looks to sustainability and cultural relations (Ross et al. 2014). Although often unacknowledged, these arguments echo many of Dewey's ideas. However, the distinctive nature of aesthetic experience is perhaps under-represented. Yet stepping into an outdoor setting offers immense possibilities for a heightened, felt quality of immediacy and anticipation, with the possibility of new kinds of receptiveness, resistance, and responsiveness (Doddington 2018a, 123). It is not difficult to imagine a group of teacher-led children situated within an urban environment or a forest at the start of an educational "outing" in which "[t]he beginning is initiated by a tensive excitement that compels us to focus on the unfolding experience. Dewey call[ed] this 'seizure' or 'impulsion'" (Alexander 1998, 14).

But reactions alone are not sufficient. Impulsion requires reactions to be "woven as strands into an activity that calls the whole self into play" (1934, LW 10:64). For aesthetic experience and educational value, there needs to be ongoing opportunity for communication, for sharing meaning that helps to reflectively consolidate experience into consciousness and shape. It requires each individual to re-present his felt experience for himself and in relation to others. Where subtle aspects of being situated in the natural world remain ineffable, for example, where "meaning exceeds what can be expressed through language" (Fesmire 2014, 208), articulation can take many forms. A range of expressive and embodied media would again include body, image, and sound as well as language (Doddington 2014, 54, 2015). These reflective pauses to the obvious and significant physical activity provoked by being in an external environment help provide both the intermittent points of undergoing and resistance and the ultimate consummations that mark out aesthetic experience. They ensure that "the field of experience is rendered focused and kept within limits by what Dewey term[ed] 'closure' or 'fusion'[. . .], the sense of bringing the experience to an end" (Alexander 1998, 14).

In both of these illustrations there is an important Deweyan stress on developing the ability to take in the experience of others, for his view was that "the scope of personal, vitally direct experience is very limited" (1916, MW 9:232). This can be achieved in part through the social, collective nature of the learning experience on offer. However, Dewey's emphasis on the need to extend beyond personal, direct experiences indicates the necessity of going beyond social interaction, including in formal learning contexts. His awareness that much of the collected experience of humanity is represented in complex symbolic form meant that access to this was a key feature of the need for formal education. His concern, however, was that in schools this rich resource was often reduced to "bookishness," inert and dry concepts and procedures that students were required to numbingly rehearse or regurgitate for assessment purposes. Since all of humanity's collective understandings and meaning-making originate from experience, Dewey's answer was for students to encounter these "symbolic languages" in ways that enable each student to make vital connections so that she can encounter knowledge with the "urgency, warmth and intimacy of a direct experience in contrast with the remote, pallid, and coldly detached quality of a representative experience" (1916, MW 9:232). This is Dewey's notion of true "appreciation" of what is on offer in subject matter. In both the illustrations given above this is possible.

Subjects such as science, mathematics, the arts, and the humanities, and even technology all offer the opportunity to extend intellectual growth and meaning-making if they are seen by students as relevant to the themes, or the context, that is being studied or explored. Instead of the acquisition of subject matter becoming an end in itself, subjects are to be drawn upon to become the tools with which learners are able to extend their established realm of meanings. Subject matter becomes a tool when it is viewed and presented by teachers as social and human, revealing the human "struggle" that is part of coming to new ideas and knowledge (1909, MW 4). Thus "appreciation," as Dewey termed it, as part of aesthetic experiences enlarges learners' imagined possibilities available for making sense of an encounter with the world beyond their direct, personal experiences (Doddington 2017, 282). Natural science, anatomy, history, literature, art, or indeed any organized subject matter is there as a tool to help extend the sense that learners might find and make in the educational settings previously described.

Experience can also lose its aesthetic nature and worth, which for Dewey amounted to draining experience of its educative capacity. He spoke of two poles that delineate *an* aesthetic experience: "At one pole is the loose succession that does not begin at any particular place and that ends—in the sense of ceasing—at no particular place. At the other pole is arrest, constriction, proceeding from parts having only a mechanical connection with one another" (1934, LW 10:47). In terms of formal education, this would reflect how some children experience episodes within the school day as simply mundane passages of time, or where the fragmented or segmented nature of school activity means that the links and purposes of tasks, although stated by the teacher or even recited by the children themselves, are not necessarily understood or meaningful.

Teacher as Artist

Without pedagogical relationships fostered by teachers, that is, teachers who in Dewey's view could be conceived of as artists, there is no possibility for the next generation to meaningfully engage with their everyday life experiences such that these will extend and expand the body-mind. In the first place, this meant for Dewey that the teacher is neither dictator of the end of learning and growth nor passive bystander to the ways the child would develop without an educator's input; rather, the teacher is one with *vision*. This means the teacher not only sees what is—what the child knows and can do—but has "a long look ahead" at possibilities (1938, LW 13:59 and 21). This vision is based on a careful consideration of the individuality of the child (i.e., the historical, social, and cultural identity that he or she brings to the educational situation)[26] and a knowledge of what is needed for the child to become part of, and contribute to, the growing community of the classroom. The child is thereby coming to realize how she is integrated into the social world. In other words, she is coming to understand and value her *inter*dependence, since the classroom itself is part of the school community and in turn the broader neighborhood community and society.

The teacher's vision, like the artist's, is not a "mold for a cast-iron result," but rather "a starting point to be developed into a plan through contributions from the experiences" of all learners involved (1938, LW 13:47). Dewey called this relationship between teacher and learner a "reciprocal give-and-take," the purpose of which is ever growing and expanding, just as learners' experiences are growing and expanding through their interactions with new objects and others (1938, LW 13:47 and 59). For this relation to be made possible, the teacher must be "responsive," as David Hansen (2005) points out. The teacher's responsiveness is a responsiveness to the child's *response* to the newness of his or her environment, that is, to what the child notices and cares about (Hansen 2005). The teacher is, for Dewey, one who has the disposition of "sensitivity" and "responsiveness." This means she is sensitive and receptive as a listener[27] to the child's established needs and abilities. Like the artist, the teacher is responsive in a way that connects learners' needs to the demands of the situation that is developing.[28] For the teacher this means having flexibility, or what Herbart, drawing on Aristotle's concept of *phronesis*, called "pedagogical tact" (Herbart [1802] 1896; see Aristotle 2000).[29] In Deweyan terms, this can be described as the teacher's skilled, improvisational ability to respond in the moment to what the child demands from the environment for the sake of aiding the child's continued search for meaning.[30]

In teaching, as in making art, material matter will include content, plans, ideas, and attitudes, and it is the teacher-artist's job to form this matter into the live and enlivening experience of the lesson. As in any other creation by an artist, the teacher reconstructs the material of learning so that it becomes a "vehicle of meaning" and works with everything that "emerges serendipitously in the process of creation—the insights, the shifts of attention, the fortuitous associations, the unforeseen opportunities and promises instantly perceived" (Jackson 2000,187–188). On this basis, we can return to Dewey's technical definition of education as the "reconstruction of experience" and show again how it refers not only to education as self-transformation (*Bildung*), but also to education as educating others (*Erziehung*) through *pedagogical* interactions: "Teaching and learning [are] a continuous process of the reconstruction of experience" (1938, LW 13:59; see also 1938, LW 13:59 and 1934, LW 9:198; see also Benner 2017). The teacher's task of reconstruction is indirect; it involves creating situations in which learners' taken for granted modes of thinking and being are productively interrupted, so that they can engage in reconstruction of their own experiences toward an expansion of their meaning-horizons (English 2013).

If an individual's growth is an ongoing process of reconstruction, it may seem that there are no aims to the pedagogical process of educating others. But this would be a false view of Dewey's concept of the teacher as educator-artist. Dewey's notion of growth as *not having* an end, but *being* an end, offers a constraint on the teacher. It recognizes that the teacher cannot know the precise future of the child's development; the child's plasticity remains constant as part of being human. Dewey viewed the systematization of knowledge, and the scientific method's contribution to it, as an important accomplishment of humankind. However, for him, a mind that had acquired systematized and abstracted knowledge was not the end of any given interaction between teacher and learner, nor was it the overall aim of an individual's formal education on the whole. Rather, the aim for the teacher, and for the education system on the whole, is that the learner's ordinary experiences be expanded through planned aesthetic experiences in a way that leads to a sense of never-ending curiosity, "the mark of an actively searching mind on the alert for further knowledge and understanding" (1934, LW 9:181; see also 1938, LW 13:20–21). Curiosity here refers to the desire for continued growth, for continual experiences of difference, newness, and otherness.

Whereas traditional education, as Dewey saw it, leads human beings to *fear* uncertainty and the unknown (1916, MW 9:56), his version of progressive education leads human beings to view uncertainty and the unknown as a space for learning—a space for remaining between old and new to consider possibilities. Aesthetic experiences contribute to our imagination of the possibilities of a situation, and this has moral meaning: they enhance our ability to deliberate what counts as, and what conditions are required for, just responses to others.[31] By extending our "organs of vision," aesthetic experiences contribute to our criticality, because we come to see the possible in the actual, and this is what lies at the heart of positive social change:

> A sense of possibilities that are unrealized and that might be realized are, when they are put in contrast with actual conditions, the most penetrating "criticism" of the latter that can be made. It is by a sense of possibilities *opening* before us that we become aware of constrictions that hem us in and of burdens that oppress. (1934, LW 10:349; emphasis added)

Facing the Crisis in Education: The Value of Teachers, Art, and Philosophy of Education in Democratic Societies

Dewey's notion of a humane and democratizing education that might create a desire for continuous growth stands in stark contrast to an education system organized for discrete and specifiable ends. The current ethos driving educational policies in many countries is resolutely focused on ends that claim, first and foremost, to sustain and promote the economic needs of a nation. It is presumed that educational outcomes can be predetermined and should therefore be measured, and that elements of learning and the curriculum can be prepackaged and "delivered" by the teacher. Dewey's ideas of educational environments, mentioned previously as places for "aesthetic experience," offer us a critical lens on educational policies that measure teachers' efficacy on the basis of meeting fixed curricular or test outcomes: they measure teachers' efficacy on *mis*-educative criteria.

Dewey identified the significance of this problem for education over a hundred years ago in *Democracy and Education*:

> The vice of externally imposed ends has deep roots. Teachers receive them from superior authorities; these authorities accept them from what is current in the community. The teachers impose them upon children. As a first consequence, the intelligence of the teacher is not free; it is confined to receiving the aims laid down from above. Too rarely is the individual so free from the authoritative supervisor, textbook on methods, pre-scribed course of study, etc., that he can let his mind come to close quarters with the pupil's mind and the subject matter. (1916, MW 9:107–108)

With educational policies and practices focused away from understanding how a student can engage with subject matter and focused instead on performance and measurability, we see the growth of what Michael Apple (2007) has described as an *audit culture*. There is a present danger, as Fesmire (2016) warns, of educational institutions "gain[ing] economic efficiency and increas[ing] productivity by frustrating human growth, imagination, and fulfillment (59). The result for the teacher is a loss of scope for professional judgment or the ability to critique what is prescribed. Instead, teachers become viewed as mere technicians (Doddington 2013). Furthermore, in some cases the education of teachers has been shrunk to bare training and even abandoned altogether. For example, in the United Kingdom there has been an increase in unqualified teachers at every level, from nursery to secondary schools.[32]

Recent moves in education globally have widely been attributed to the influence of neoliberalism (Attick 2017). The alignment of education with a business model, resulting in the marketization of education, is one clear strand of this. In the United Kingdom, private education is widespread, and so-called free schools and privately sponsored academies compete for students and against each other, via league tables focused on academic results. Similarly, charter schools in the United States have expanded alongside the closure of public schools, on the basis of offering choice and being accountable in terms of levels of student achievement. In Sweden, for-profit charter schools are encouraged as a competing alternative for state or public education. Unsurprisingly, it is these alternatives to straightforward public or state schools that have seen the greatest increase in unqualified teachers.[33]

Under the guise of promoting "choice," these "alternative" schools, alongside the growth of different kinds of religious faith schools, have been shown to ultimately promote division;[34] according to neoliberalism, this move toward "choice" is a legitimate and desirable response to a society's diversity. But such schools work in striking contrast to the Deweyan concept of the Common School. While some may question whether there was a time when the concept of the Common School was ever fully viable or capable of achieving community (Gerrard 2015), reconsideration of Dewey's original notions has possibly never been more needed or relevant than now. Closely following Dewey, Richard Pring (2007) argues that formal public education is necessary for creating

> a more cohesive and enriching community, shaped by a common culture, from which all benefit, [and that] lies not in the elimination of [. . .] cultural differences, but in the sharing of values and ideals that emphasise our "common humanity" and that see the interaction of cultures as something enriching. (519)

Dewey viewed the creation of aesthetic experiences in school and in life as central to fostering the kind of interaction and communication among diverse groups that is at the heart of democracy as a political system and, as he called it, "a mode of associated living" (1916, MW 9:93). Yet Dewey critically observed that the rise of antidemocratic systems in schools is one with the societal demise of democracy and the rise of fascism, nationalism, racism, and sectarianism, which are all grounded in the denial of the intrinsic dignity of every human being. This "anti-humanist attitude," Dewey warned, is "corrosive"; it engenders "movements that begin by stirring up hostility against a group of people [and] end by denying to them all human qualities" (1939, LW 13:153).

Dewey's response to the crisis of education—at once a crisis of democracy—is one that we believe we can greatly learn from as we move forward in the twenty-first century. We offer here, in conclusion, what we find to be three key insights in his response: the value of the teacher, the role of art as an ethical-political force, and the special place of philosophy of education in the cultivation of humanity.

Rather than turning away from teachers in times of crisis or devaluing them and using them as scapegoats for educational problems, as we see occurring in public discourse today,[35] Dewey's response placed more value on teachers and called for teachers with "social insight" (1934, LW 9:183; see also 1933, LW 9:112–126).[36] Such teachers are in the business of communicating some of the vast resource of human meanings in ways that allow learners to aesthetically experience those meanings and continue to grow and thus, as we previously illustrated, are operating in the role of artists. This role requires teachers' creative vision—a future-oriented look for possibilities to enhance the potential of every human being—which is a far cry from the mechanical delivery and outcome-driven, top-down teaching experience that many contemporary schools demand teachers engage in and that Dewey criticized so vehemently.

Dewey extended his conceptualization of aesthetic experience in *Art as Experience*, and it is here that we also find his understanding of the role of art within humanity. Art is key to how the experiences of humanity can be meaningfully formed or intensified and thus shared in common across culture and time. At the heart of this significance is art's power to communicate: "Every art communicates because it expresses. It enables us to share vividly and deeply in meanings to which we had been dumb" (1938, LW 10:248). Art has this educative force to move us and foster the reshaping of our given meanings precisely because it has the ability to awaken and "let loose" those "elements" that are in the background of our experience and that we thus take for granted (1938, LW 13:367).

While artists may consider their potential audiences, it is not necessary for them to deliberately intend to communicate; the artistic process of expressing material and ordering energies through "a medium which intensifies and clarifies" allows them to create new objects and thus offer "new modes of experience" (1934, LW 10:248). For those engaging with art and finding new modes of experience, Dewey explained that the things produced through art are not themselves the work of art, for "the *work* takes place when a human being cooperates with the product so that the outcome is an experience that is enjoyed because of its liberating and ordered properties" (1934, LW 10:218, emphasis ours). But Dewey was mindful that the idea of art "communicating" is open to assumptions of a simplistic sloganing and messaging using art. He explained that "communication is not announcing things, even if they are said with the emphasis of great sonority" and went on to explain how communication in both the making, and receptive appreciation, of art is of social and personal value:

> Communication is the process of creating participation, of making common what had been isolated and singular; and part of the miracle it achieves is that, in being communicated, the conveyance of meaning gives body and definiteness to the experience of the one who utters as well as to that of those who listen. (1934, LW 10:248–249)

This line of thinking explains some of art's ethical-political power:

> Men associate in many ways. But the only form of association that is truly human, and not a gregarious gathering for warmth and protection, or a mere device for efficiency in outer action, is the participation in meanings and goods that is effected by communication. [. . .] Art breaks through barriers that divide human beings, which are impermeable in ordinary association. (1934, LW 10:249)

Art has the power to bring humanity into communication across diversity in ways beyond mere talk and words, unless these are themselves formed as art. Art's ultimate dependence on meaning places it at the center of aesthetic experience and suggests its extensive educational value for growth.

But Dewey made the salient point that the possibility for experiencing art as *an* experience, one that for him could and should be possible in everyday life and not just in museums and galleries, is dependent on a certain kind of education. Art is not *educative* until "we are educated to enjoy, to realize, [its] educative potentialities" (1926, LW 2:113). So as we look to the future of what formal education can and should consist of, we find ourselves facing the dilemma that Dewey stated early in *Democracy and Education*: "Society determines its own future in determining that of the young" (1916, MW 9:46). As a simple fact, this means that in any society, the older generation is responsible for determining what education looks like for the young, and with that, their established experiences and values unavoidably shape what the next generation experiences. But if we take this shaping of future possibility as a responsibility that is part of cultivating *democratic* societies, it means acknowledging that we, as the adult generation, might not know what is possible, or even desirable, for the next generation; the young too need to have openings for shaping their own experiences. The only way Dewey foresaw resolving this dilemma was through the conversation called *philosophy of education*:

> For all the serious conflicts and struggles that occur in society grow out of different conceptions, expressed or implicit, of what society is and should be. This is true of the conflict of science and religion in its practical aspects, of capital and labor, of the struggle of groups and classes for a more secure position and greater power and freedom with the social order. It is true of the conflict of political parties, through often more so in words than in fact. A philosophy of education, a name that stands for the search for unifying aims and methods in education, is, in reality, a branch of the theory of social ideals and the institutions by which the ideals may be realized. (1936, LW 11:177)

Philosophy of education, for Dewey, was deeply concerned with the question of what education is. But as we have illustrated, answering this question is intimately tied to understanding what human experience looks like at its best and fullest and the conditions under which every human being is given equitable opportunity for a fulfilling experience as a rich search for meaning, a search that inherently has a "social character" (1934, LW 9:195–202; see also 1933, LW 8:80). What makes the need for philosophy of education urgent, in Dewey's time and our own, is the increasing loss of the sense of education as social, wherein individuals realize that "knowledge is a trust for the furthering of the well-being of all" (1934, LW 9:202). Dewey attempted in several writings—arguably throughout his entire corpus—to illuminate our understanding of the full potential of human experience and encapsulated this in the idea of aesthetic experience. But he never claimed to provide a final definition, nor would it be consistent with his thinking to claim that anyone could determine definitively what aesthetic experience amounts to. Instead, Dewey viewed this consideration as the *never-ending* task of philosophers: more precisely, philosophers of education.

In this view, philosophy of education is essential to democratic society's determination of how it might best provide for equitable cultivation and expression of aesthetic experiences for all human beings, which, as Dewey suggested, is the "ultimate problem of free cooperative human living" (1938, LW 13:370). However, one need not think that Dewey sought to return to Plato's philosopher kings. For Dewey, the conversation that is philosophy of education was potentially one that everyone can contribute to, especially teachers. As such, it will involve communication across the diverse groups and communities that are part of democratic societies.

Following Dewey, we could say that the one criterion for joining the conversation of philosophy is one's ability to communicate—which inherently implies, as we have shown, to communicate across difference. Yet in today's global context, in which people constantly become aware of others' experiences that are radically different than their own, it is worth asking whether Dewey's concept of communication is still viable. Genuine communication presupposes that we find some common meanings in our dialogue with one another; yet to do so, there needs to be a search, and that search involves the ability to understand meanings that are *not* common, meanings that are *other* than one's own. Philosopher of education Naoko Saito fruitfully extends Dewey's thinking, showing that in order to begin to understand the meanings others have ascribed to their worlds—to things, events, and ideas—we, as philosophers, need to start by taking a critical eye to our own personal meanings and to those shared by the groups and communities with which we identify. She explains that the philosopher in this way is, and has to be, a "translator," that is, one who examines her own established meanings through the lens of those of others (Saito 2007; Saito this volume).

Taking this extension of Dewey's idea as a criterion for joining the conversation of philosophy of education, we may summarize as follows: one's willingness to listen inwardly, to seek and confront the blind spots and discontinuities in one's experiences, is a condition for contributing to "rebuilding the spirit of common understanding, mutual sympathy and goodwill among all people and races, to exercise the demon of prejudice, isolation and hatred" (1934, LW 9:203–204). The value of any philosophy of education lies in its ability to contribute to this rebuilding process.

NOTES

1. Dewey also uses the term "educability" (e.g., 1916, MW 9:81), which has the same meaning as plasticity.
2. On this concept in relation to Dewey's thinking, see Benner and English (2004), English (2013), and Benner (2017).
3. On the theories of growth that Dewey was responding to, see Oelkers (2017).

4. Though the term *Mündigkeit* is commonly translated as "maturity" and is then easily contrasted with immaturity, a more appropriate translation is "personal sovereignty" (translation AE).

5. See, for example, Peters (1970). See also Martin (1981), in which she presents an early critique of Peters' concept of the educated man on the grounds that it failed to account for women's experiences and perspectives. It sets up an ideal of a person, as she argues, for whom sensitivity to others, imaginative awareness, and emotion are not essential; whom only objectivity and rationality count (Martin 1982, 100–102). For a related discussion of dependence, independence, and interdependence in connection to the Western tradition of philosophy and science, see Griffiths and Smith (1989). In more recent discussions, philosophers of education have presented a nuanced view of Peters, showing him not to be entirely a Kantian philosopher, notably one whom they say may go against Peters' own self-understanding (Cuypers and Martin 2014); see also MacAllister (2016), who indicates how Peters was critical of Kant and draws connections between Peters and Dewey.

6. This is a revised edition of her 1984 work, *Caring: A Feminine Approach to Ethics and Moral Education*, Berkeley: University of California Press.

7. Dewey discusses the precognitive, pre-reflective aspect of experience in connection to his description of the process of inquiry and the meaning of indeterminate situations as existential starting point of inquiry (see, e.g., 1933, LW 8:199–201 and 1938, LW 12:109–111). For an extended discussion of the connections between Dewey's notion of pre-reflective experiences and learning and teaching processes, see English (2013, esp. chs. 3 and 4).

8. In the original German this reads, "Der Mensch" will "seinem Wesen Werth und Dauer verschaffen" (Humboldt [1792] 1960, 235). For a complete English translation of Humboldt's fragment "Theory of Bildung," see Humboldt (2001).

9. See also Doddington (2018b) for a further discussion of experience as transaction between the individual and Dewey's sense of the term "environment."

10. See on this point Alexander (2013), who describes growth as having a "narrative structure" (139–140 and 150).

11. Importantly for Dewey, the mind is connected to our experience in the body and not isolated from it. He writes that a notion of an isolated mind makes us think that aesthetic experience is something that can happen only in the mind, when truly it is an embodied experience of the "live creature" (1934, LW 10:268–269), which he also calls the body-mind. Mark Johnson's work has furthered Dewey's conception of the body-mind; see, for example, Johnson (2007). See also Haskins in this volume.

12. The term *Erziehung* can be translated as "pedagogical interaction" or "moral guidance" in the context of moral education, since the "pedagogue" is not just an observer, but rather is aiming to help the child thoughtfully consider others in his or her thinking, judgments, and actions. Contemporary thinkers have widely agreed that Dewey's ideas of education are connected to the tradition of *Bildung*, but there is disagreement about the extent to which he considers the distinct educator-learner relations identified in the concept *Erziehung*. For example, Gert Biesta (2016), in his recent analysis of Dewey's *Democracy and Education*, argues that Dewey overlooks the idea of education as *Erziehung* and is only talking about education as *Bildung*. However, Dietrich Benner (2017) provides a picture of how Dewey uses both senses of education, as *Bildung* and as *Erziehung*, albeit at different times, in *Democracy and Education*. It seems apparent that across his writings, Dewey is not only concerned with self-transformative processes (*Bildung*), but is specifically concerned with the moral and ethical dimensions of the educator or teacher's role in

supporting the younger generation (as we discuss later in this chapter). See also English (2013) and Stoller (2014).

13. In the original German this reads: "Allein wenn dieser Gegenstand genügen soll, sein ganzes Wesen in seiner vollen Stärke und seiner Einheit zu beschäftigen; so muss er der Gegenstand schlechthin, die Welt seyn, oder doch (den dies ist eigentlich allein richtig) als solcher betrachtet werden" (Humboldt [1792]1960, 237–238).

14. In Dewey's concept of pedagogical relationships, we can see the particular influence of Herbart's theory of pedagogy and instruction; the latter views the entirety of the educator's task in supporting the expansion of the learner's "Circle of Thought" (*Gedankenkreis*) by incorporating differentiated forms of knowledge and participation via the aesthetic representation of the world (Herbart [1804] 1902, [1804] 1887).

15. See for example, his discussion of reflective experience and inquiry in 1916, MW 9, ch. 11; 1933, LW 8; and 1938, LW 12.

16. For a discussion of these connections, see English (2013), who develops the idea of "discontinuity in experience" as part of Dewey's conceptualization of the human experience of limitation and also connects Dewey's thinking to the traditions of pragmatism, phenomenology, hermeneutics, and educational philosophical traditions going back to Plato.

17. See also Granger's (2006) description of this aspect of Dewey's thinking, in which he talks of a "feeling of disharmony" (34–39) arising from pre-reflective immediacy that sparks reflection.

18. On Dewey's concept of imagination and its connection to morality, see Alexander (2013) and Fesmire (2003).

19. On this point in relation to Dewey's aesthetic theory as "embodied aesthetics," see Haskins this volume.

20. See on this point Garrison (1995, esp. 421–423).

21. See Dewey's continual mention of these dispositions in diverse ways throughout his corpus, for example in *Democracy and Education* (1916, MW 9); *Art as Experience* (1934, LW:10); "The Aesthetic Element in Education" (1897, EW 5); and "Foreword to David Lyndsay Watson's *Scientists Are Human*" (1938, LW 13).

22. Nel Noddings (this volume) shows how this quest for certainty, which Dewey so strongly criticizes in *The Quest for Certainty* (1929, LW 4) and elsewhere, finds expression in several ways in the curriculum design of traditional schooling. In a particular connection to our discussion here, she argues that the present-day communication gap between classes is perpetuated by the increase in separation of schools and communities across class lines. We further discuss related issues of current schooling later in this chapter.

23. See Meyer (1997, 2017).

24. Hannah Arendt, as early as 1934 in "The Crisis in Education" (Arendt 2006), criticized the American progressive education movement, and implicitly Dewey, for its emphasis on the newness the child brings to the educational situation and the failure to account for tradition. Her critique certainly applies to much of the movement but overlooks how Dewey himself was critical of these same trends. R. S. Peters (e.g., 1981) is also critical of the child-centered movement and explicitly Dewey. In many ways, Peters's critique of Dewey was an oversimplified interpretation of Dewey's notion of learning (see English 2009). On Dewey and the Hirst-Peters tradition of philosophy of education, see also Martin (2017).

25. See, for example, his discussion of progressive education in "The Activity Movement" (1934, LW 9:169–174) and "The Need for a Philosophy of Education" (1934, LW 9:194–204),

and also "Experience and Education" (1938, LW 13:30–46). On this point see also Kadlec (2007).

26. Notably, in mathematics education research today, this aspect of the teacher's task is now being highlighted as mathematics education reform aims to move away from teacher-centered models of school mathematics instruction, implicitly, when not explicitly, in a Deweyan tradition. Research underscores that an essential aspect of teaching that seeks to rehumanize mathematics is found in acknowledging the valuable diverse ways of mathematizing that children bring from their sociocultural experiences. In this vein, important work is being done with the aim of reconceptualizing school mathematics to include indigenous and other diverse ways of thinking and knowing mathematically (see, e.g., Aikenhead 2017. See also Hintz et al. (2018), who highlight the essential role of the teacher as listener to students' sociocultural resources, ways of knowing, and understandings.

27. There have been significant developments in philosophical and empirical research on the role of the teacher as *listener*, an idea largely underdeveloped until recently (see, e.g., Haroutunian-Gordon 2010; English 2009, 2011, 2016c; Waks 2011, 2015; Haroutunian-Gordon and Laverty 2011; Hintz and Tyson 2015; Hintz et al. 2018). These developments bring to light an aspect of teaching entirely disregarded in traditional teacher-centered teaching, but also often overlooked in today's educational policies that claim to be designed to support educational reform toward student-centered approaches in primary, secondary, and tertiary education.

28. In *Art as Experience*, Dewey explains the connections between the sensitivity or receptiveness of the artist and how it is intimately intertwined with a responsiveness that is based in acute sensitivity to the features of a developing work (see, e.g., 1934, LW 10:58–60). See also Garrison (2009) and Wong (2007) on the Deweyan notion of the teacher as artist.

29. On Herbart's concept of "pedagogical tact" and its connection to notions of teaching in Dewey and other contemporary thinkers, see English (2013, esp. chs. and 7); see also van Manen (1991, 2016). On current educational policy, teacher thinking, and *phronesis*, see Doddington (2013).

30. In connection to this specific meaning of improvisation as a form of expertise, in *Experience and Education* Dewey brings forward another criticism of interpretations of progressive education as implying the teacher should be engaged in "planless improvisation" (1938, LW 13:13).

31. See on this point Fesmire (2003).

32. See the Department for Education School Workforce in England, statistics from November 2016, at https://www.gov.uk/government/uploads/system/uploads/attachment_data/file/620825/SFR25_2017_MainText.pdf, accessed August 1, 2017.

33. See the Department for Education School Workforce in England, statistics from November 2016, at https://www.gov.uk/government/uploads/system/uploads/attachment_data/file/620825/SFR25_2017_MainText.pdf, accessed August 1, 2017.

34. Research today continues to reveal different forms of societal division that has resulted from the Charter/choice movement. For example, research shows that despite the promise to integrate diverse groups into Charter schools, in practice they are leading to resegregation on racial lines (see, e.g., Frankenberg et al. 2012; Orfield et al. 2013). Justice and Macleod (2016) show how school "choice" options can support undemocratic and sectarian interests.

35. See Giroux's (2012) critical analysis of what he shows to be today's "vicious assault" on teachers.
36. This idea of "social insight" here underscores the complexity and moral nature of the teacher's task of having a broad vision of desirable associations to be fostered among the young. Dewey states elsewhere that educating the next generation "cannot be neutral and indifferent to the kind of social organization which exists" since "associations are many and diverse, and some of them are hostile to the realization of full personality [. . . ;] hence for the sake of individual development, [formal] education must promote some forms of associations and community life and must work against others" (1933, LW 8:80).

WORKS CITED

Citations of John Dewey's works are to the thirty-seven-volume critical edition published by Southern Illinois University Press under the editorship of Jo Ann Boydston. In-text citations give the original publication date and series abbreviation, followed by volume number and page number. For example, (1934, LW 10:12) is page 12 of *Art as Experience*, which was published as volume 10 of *The Later Works*.

Series abbreviations for *The Collected Works*:

EW *The Early Works* (1882–1898)

MW *The Middle Works* (1899–1924)

LW *The Later Works* (1925–1953)

Aikenhead, Glen. 2017. School Mathematics for Reconciliation. From a 19th to a 21st Century Curriculum.   https://www.usask.ca/education/documents/profiles/aikenhead/School-Mathematics-for-Reconciliation-vb11.pdf Accessed July 10, 2017

Alexander, Thomas.1998 "The Art of Life: Dewey's Aesthetics." In *Reading Dewey: Interpretations for a Postmodern Generation*, 1–22. Edited by Larry Hickman. Bloomington: Indiana University Press.

Alexander, Thomas. 2013. *The Human Eros: Eco-Ontology and the Aesthetics of Existence*. New York: Oxford University Press.

Apple, Michael W. 2007. "Education, Markets, and an Audit Culture." *International Journal of Educational Policies*, vol. 1, no. 1, 4–19.

Arendt, Hannah. 2006. "The Crisis in Education." In *Between Past and Future*, 170–193. New York: Penguin Books.

Aristotle. 2000. *Nichomachean Ethics*. Edited and translated by Roger Crisp. Cambridge, UK: Cambridge University Press.

Attick, Dennis. 2017. "Homo Economicus at School: Neoliberal Education and Teacher as Economic Being." *Educational Studies*, vol. 53, no. 1,: 37–48.

Benner, Dietrich. 2017. "John Dewey, a Modern Thinker: On Education (as Bildung and Erziehung) and Democracy (as a Political System and a Mode of Associated Living)." In *John Dewey's Democracy and Education: A Centennial Handbook*. Edited by Leonard Waks and Andrea R. English and translated by Andrea R. English and Aline Nardo, 263–279. New York: Cambridge University Press.

Benner, Dietrich, and Andrea English. 2004. "Critique and Negativity: Towards the Pluralisation of Critique in Educational Practice, Theory and Research." *Journal of Philosophy of Education*, vol. 38, no. 3,: 409–428. doi:10.1111/j.0309-8249.2004.00394.x.

Biesta, Gert J. J. 2016. "Democracy and Education Revisited: Dewey's Democratic Deficiency." In *John Dewey's Democracy and Education: A British Tribute*, Edited by Steve Higgins et al., 149–169. London: IoE Press.

Cuypers, Stefaan E., and Christopher Martin. 2014. *R. S. Peters*. New York: Bloomsbury.

Dewey, John. 1892. "Introduction to Philosophy." LW 17:153–160.

Dewey, John. 1897. "The Aesthetic Element in Education." EW 5:202–203.

Dewey, John. 1909. "The Moral Significance of the Common School Studies." MW 4:205–214.

Dewey, John. 1915. "The School and Society." MW 1:1–240.

Dewey, John. 1916. *Democracy and Education*. MW 9.

Dewey, John. 1925. *Experience and Nature*. LW 1.

Dewey, John. 1926. "Art in Education-Education in Art." LW 2:112–115.

Dewey, John. 1929. *The Quest for Certainty*. LW 4.

Dewey, John. 1933. "The Underlying philosophy of Education." LW 8:77–103.

Dewey, John. 1933. "How We Think." LW 8:105–352.

Dewey, John. 1933. "The Crisis in Education." LW 9:112–126.

Dewey, John. 1934. "The Activity Movement." LW 9:169–174.

Dewey, John. 1934. "Education and the Social Order." LW 9:175–185.

Dewey, John. 1934. "The Need for a Philosophy of Education." LW 9:194–204.

Dewey, John. 1934. *Art as Experience*. LW 10.

Dewey, John. 1936. "Anniversary Address." LW 11:171–180.

Dewey, John. 1938. *Logic: The Theory of Inquiry*. LW 12.

Dewey, John. 1938. "Experience and Education." LW 13:1–62.

Dewey, John. 1938. "Does Human Nature Change?" LW 13:286–293.

Dewey, John. 1938. "The Philosophy of the Arts." LW 13:357–367.

Dewey, John. 1938. "Foreword to David Lindsay Watson's Scientists Are Human." LW 13:369–372.

Dewey, John. 1939. "Freedom and Culture." LW 13:63–188.

Doddington, Christine. 2012. "Philosophy, Art or Pedagogy? How Should Children Experience Education?" *Educational Philosophy and Theory*, vol. 46, no. 11, 1258–1269.

Doddington, Christine. 2013. "The Global Search for Better Teaching: How Should Teachers Think for Themselves?" *Education 3-13*, vol. 41, no. 2, 218–232.

Doddington, Christine. 2014. "Education in the Open: The Somaesthetic Value of Being Outside." *Other Education: The Journal of Educational Alternatives*, vol. 3, no. 1, 41–59.

Doddington, Christine. 2015. "Embodied Arts Experience: The Educational Value of Somaesthetics." In *The Routledge International Handbook of the Arts and Education*. Edited by Mike Fleming, Liora Bresler, and John O'Toole, 60–67. Oxon: Routledge.

Doddington, Christine. 2017. "Becoming Experienced: An Alternative Version of Transformative Learning, after Dewey." In *Philosophy as Interplay and Dialogue: Viewing Landscapes within Philosophy of Education*. Edited by Torill Strand, Richard Smith, Anne Pirrie, Zelin Gregoriou, and Marianna Papastephanou, 265–292. Zurich: Lit Verlag.

Doddington, Christine. 2018a. "Education in the Open: Somaesthetic Value of Being Outside." In *Dewey and Education in the 21st Century: Fighting Back*. Edited by Ruth Heilbronn, Christine Doddington, and Rupert Higham, 119–138. London: Emerald Publishing.

Doddington, Christine. 2018b. "Wellbeing and Aesthetic Imagination." In *Wellbeing, Education and Contemporary Schooling*. Edited by Malcolm Thorburn, 188–202. London: Routledge.

English, Andrea. 2009a. "Listening as a Teacher: Educative Listening, Interruptions and Reflective Practice." *Philosophical Inquiry in Education*, vol. 18, no. 1,: 69–79.

English, Andrea. 2009b. "Transformation and Education: The Voice of the Learner in Peters' Concept of Teaching." *Journal of Philosophy of Education*, vol. 43 (October), 75–95. doi:10.1111/j.1467-9752.2009.00716.x.

English, Andrea. 2011. "Critical Listening and the Dialogic Aspect of Moral Education: JF Herbart's Concept of the Teacher as Moral Guide." *Educational Theory*, vol. 61, no. 2, 171–189.

English, Andrea R. 2013. *Discontinuity in Learning: Dewey, Herbart, and Education as Transformation*. New York: Cambridge University Press.

English, Andrea R. 2016a. "Dialogic Teaching and Moral Learning: Self-Critique, Narrativity, Community and 'Blind Spots.'" *Journal of Philosophy of Education*, vol. 50, no. 2, 160–176. doi:10.1111/1467-9752.12198.

English, Andrea R. 2016b. "John Dewey and the Role of the Teacher in a Globalized World: Imagination, Empathy, and 'Third Voice.'" *Educational Philosophy and Theory*, vol. 48, no. 10, 1046–1064. doi:10.1080/00131857.2016.1202806.

English, Andrea R. 2016c. "Humility, Listening and 'Teaching in a Strong Sense.'" *Logos & Episteme*, 7, no. 4, 529–554.

Fesmire, Steven. 2003. *John Dewey and Moral Imagination: Pragmatism in Ethics*. Indiana University Press.

Fesmire, Steven. 2014. *Dewey*. New York: Routledge.

Fesmire, Steven. 2016. "Democracy and the Industrial Imagination in American Education." *Education and Culture*, vol. 1, 53–62.

Frankenberg, Erica, Genevieve Siegel Hawley, Jia Wang, and Gary Orfield. 2012. "Choice Without Equity: Charter School Segregation and the Need for Civil Rights Standards." UCLA: The Civil Rights Project/Proyecto Derechos Civiles, June. http://escholarship.org/uc/item/4r07q8kg.

Garrison, Jim. 1995. "Deweyan Prophetic Pragmatism, Poetry, and the Education of Eros." *American Journal of Education*, vol. 103, no. 4, 406–431.

Garrison, Jim. 2009. "Teacher as Prophetic Trickster." *Educational Theory*, vol. 59, no. 1, 67–83.

Gerrard, Jessica. 2015. "Public Education in Neoliberal Times: Memory and Desire." *Journal of Education Policy*, vol. 30, no. 6, 855–868.

Granger, David. 2006. *John Dewey, Robert Pirsig, and the Art of Living: Revisioning Aesthetic Education*. New York: Palgrave Macmillan.

Greene, Maxine. 1995. *Releasing the Imagination: Essays on Education, the Arts, and Social Change. The Jossey-Bass Education Series*. San Francisco, CA: Jossey-Bass. https://eric.ed.gov/?id=ED418091.

Griffiths, Morwenna, and Richard Smith. 1989. "Standing Alone: Dependence, Independence, and Interdependence in the Practice of Education." Paper presented at the Annual Conference of the American Educational Research Association. https://eric.ed.gov/?id=ED318660.

Hansen, David T. 2005. "Creativity in Teaching and Building a Meaningful Life as a Teacher." *Journal of Aesthetic Education*, vol. 39, no. 2, 57–68.

Haroutunian-Gordon, Sophie. 2010. "Listening to a Challenging Perspective: The Role of Interruption." *Teachers College Record*, vol. 112, no. 11, 2793–2814.

Haroutunian-Gordon, Sophie and Laverty, Megan (eds.) 2011. Philosophical Perspectives on Listening. Special Issue. *Educational Theory*, vol 61. no. 2.

Herbart, Johann Friedrich. (1802) 1896. "Introductory Lecture to Students in Pedagogy." In *Herbart's ABC of Sense Perception and Minor Pedagogical Works*. Edited and translated by William J. Eckoff, 13–28. New York: Appleton.

Herbart, Johann Friedrich (1804) 1887. "Über die ästhetische Darstellung der Welt als das Hauptgeschäft der Erziehung." In *Joh. Friedr. Herbart's Sämtliche Werke in Chronologischer Reihenfolge.* Edited by K. Kehrbach, vol. 1, 259–274 Langensalza: Hermann Beyer and Söhne.

Herbart, Johann Friedrich (1804) 1902. "On the Aesthetic Revelation of the World." In *The Science of Education, Its General Principles Deduced from Its Aim, and the Aesthetic Revelation of the World.* Translated by Henry M. Felkin and Emmie Felkin, 57–77. Boston: D. C. Heath & Co.

Herbart, Johann Friedrich. (1835/1841) 1902. "Umriss Pädagogical Vorlesung." In *Joh. Friedr. Herbart's Sämtliche Werke in Chronologischer Reihenfolge.* Edited by Karl Kehrbach, 10:65–206. Langensalza: Herman Beyer and Söhne.

Herbart, Johann Friedrich. 1913. *Outlines of Educational Doctrine.* Translated by Alexis F. Lange. New York: Macmillan Company.

Hintz, Allison, and Kersti Tyson. 2015. "Complex Listening: Supporting Students to Listen as Mathematical Sense-Makers." *Mathematical Thinking and Learning,* vol. 17, no. 4, 296–326.

Hintz, Allison, Tyson, Kersti, and English, Andrea R. 2018. "Actualizing the Rights of the Learner: The Role of Pedagogical Listening" *Democracy and Education* vol. 26 no. 2 (Article 8), 1–10. https://democracyeducationjournal.org/home/vol26/iss2/8 Accessed: November 1, 2018.

Humboldt, Wilhelm von. (1792) 1960. "Theorie der Bildung des Menschen." In *Wilhelm von Humboldt: Werke in Fünf Bände.* Edited by Andreas Flitner and Klaus Giel, 1:506–518. Darmstadt, West Germany: Wissenschaftliche Buchgesellschaft.

Humboldt, Wilhelm von. 2001. "Theory of Bildung (1792)." In *Teaching as a Reflective Practice: The German Didaktik Tradition.* Edited by Ian Westbury, Stephan Hopmann, and Kurt Riquarts and translated by Gillian Horton-Krüger, 57–61. Mahwah, NJ: Lawrence Erlbaum Associates.

Jackson, Philip W. 2000. *John Dewey and the Lessons of Art.* New Haven, CT: Yale University Press.

Johnson, Mark. 2007. *The Meaning of the Body: Aesthetics of Human Understanding.* Chicago: University of Chicago Press.

Justice, Benjamin, and Colin Macleod. 2016. *Have a Little Faith: Religion, Democracy, and the American Public School.* Chicago: University of Chicago Press.

Kadlec, Alison. 2007. *Dewey's Critical Pragmatism.* New York: Lexington Books.

Kant, Immanuel. (1784) 1990. "On the Question, What Is Enlightenment?" In *Foundations of the Metaphysics of Morals and, What Is Enlightenment.* Translated by Lewis White Beck, 83–89. London: Macmillan.

MacAllister, James. 2016. *Reclaiming Discipline for Education: Knowledge, Relationships and the Birth of Community.* London: Routledge.

Martin, Christopher. 2017. "John Dewey and the Analytic Paradigm in Philosophy of Education: Conceptual Analysis as a Social Aim?" In *John Dewey's Democracy and Education: A Centennial Handbook.* Edited by Leonard J. Waks and Andrea R. English, 304–313. New York: Cambridge University Press.

Martin, Jane Roland. 1981. "The Ideal of the Educated Person." *Educational Theory,* vol. 31, no. 2, 97–109.

Meyer, Meinert. 1997. "John Dewey's Vorstellungen bezüglich der Inhalte des Unterrichts-eine Untersuchung zur historischen Curriculumtheorie." [John Dewey's idea of the content of instruction—An examination of historical curriculum theory.] In *Modernisierung von Rahmenrichtlinien: Beiträge zur Rahmenrichtlinienentwickelung* [Modernisation of curriculum guidelines: contributions to the development of curriculum guidelines]. Edited by Josef Kueffer, 49–80. Weinheim, Germany: Deutscher Studien Verlag.

Meyer, Meinert. 2017. "Subject Matter: Combining 'Learning by Doing' with Past Collective Experience." In *John Dewey's Democracy and Education: A Centennial Handbook*. Edited by Leonard Waks and Andrea R. English, 124–136. New York: Cambridge University Press.

Nietzsche, Friedrich. (1874) 1983. "On the Uses and Disadvantages of History for Life." In *Untimely Meditations*. Translated by R. J. Hollingdale, 57–174. Cambridge: Cambridge University Press.

Noddings, Nel. 2013. *Caring: A Relational Approach to Ethics and Moral Education*. Los Angeles: University of California Press.

Oelkers, Dietrich. 2017. "John Dewey's Refutation of Classical Educational Thinking." In *John Dewey's Democracy and Education: A Centennial Handbook*. Edited by Leonard Waks and Andrea R. English, 279–289. New York: Cambridge University Press.

Ord, Jon, and Mark Leather. 2011. "The Substance beneath the Labels of Experiential Learning: The Importance of John Dewey for Outdoor Educators." *Australian Journal of Outdoor Education*, vol. 15, no. 2, 13.

Orfield, Gary, and Erica Frankenberg. 2013. *Educational Delusions? Why Choice Can Deepen Inequality and How to Make Schools Fair*. University of California Press.

Peters, R. S. 1970. "Education and the Educated Man." *Journal of Philosophy of Education*, vol. 4, no. 1, 5–20. doi:10.1111/j.1467-9752.1970.tb00424.x.

Peters, R. S. 1981. "John Dewey's Philosophy of Education," In *Essays on Educators*. Edited by R. S. Peters, 72–88. London: George Allan and Unwin Ltd.

Pring, Richard. 2007. "The Common School." *Journal of Philosophy of Education*, vol. 41, no. 4, 503–522.

Ross, Hamish, Beth Christie, Robbie Nicol, and Peter Higgins. 2014. "Space, Place and Sustainability and the Role of Outdoor Education." *Journal of Adventure Education and Outdoor Learning*, vol. 14, no. 3, 191–97. doi:10.1080/14729679.2014.960684.

Rousseau, J. J. (1762) 1979. *Emile or On Education*. Translated by Allan Bloom. New York: Basic Books.

Saito, Naoko. 2007. "Philosophy as Translation: Democracy and Education from Dewey to Cavell." *Educational Theory*, vol. 57, no. 3, 261–275.

Stoller, Aaron. 2014. *Knowing and Learning as Creative Action: A Reexamination*. New York: Palgrave Macmillan.

Van Manen, Max. 1991. *The Tact of Teaching: The Meaning of Pedagogical Thoughtfulness*. Albany, New York: State University of New York Press.

Van Manen. Max. 2016. *Pedagogical Tact (Phenomenology of Practice)*. London: Routledge.

Waks, Leonard J. 2011. "John Dewey on Listening and Friendship in School and Society." *Educational Theory*, vol. 61, no. 2, 191–205.

Waks, Leonard J. 2015. *Listening to Teach: Beyond Didactic Pedagogy*. Albany: State University of New York Press.

Wong, David. 2007. "Beyond Control and Rationality: Dewey, Aesthetics, Motivation, and Educative Experiences." *Teachers College Record*, vol. 109, no. 1, 192–220.

VII

AESTHETICS

CHAPTER 21

DEWEY'S *ART AS EXPERIENCE* IN THE LANDSCAPE OF TWENTY-FIRST-CENTURY AESTHETICS

CASEY HASKINS

ON first encounter, *Art as Experience* (1934b, LW 10) can feel like a sprawling novel of ideas that "reads its reader" on more levels than a mind (or body-mind) can process at once. Written in the heyday of twentieth-century cultural modernism, Dewey's book tells a sweeping story, resonant with reconstructed Hegelian, Darwinian, and romantic motifs, about how all human lives are experiential journeys whose destinations are both created and discovered, with no one biographical destination being shared by all. The phenomenologically richest such destinations are *works of art*—experiences of creative agency whose value is at once "instrumental" (they can lead to further valued experiences), "final" (they are prized for their own sakes), and "consummatory" (they are felt fulfillments of purposes internal to the creator's personal life-journey). Works of art, redescribed now as a special subset of consummatory experiences, comprise Dewey's vision of human life at its fullest.

This answer to the proverbial modern question What is Art? represents a radical departure from multiple orthodoxies in the Idealist tradition in aesthetics that dominated American academic conversations about art throughout much of the twentieth century. For example, it redefines a *work of art* not as the finished product of creative activity but as a phase of the creative process itself. "Art," in signifying "a quality of doing and of what is done," is not, Dewey maintains, genuinely a noun but is really adjectival in nature. This anti-reificatory argument carries the further corollary that the most developed instances of experience-as-art are just as likely to occur in such non-fine-art practices as athletics, gardening, blue-collar work, moral deliberation, science, and philosophy as in the visual, literary, and performing arts.[1] In contrast to the high-modernist theories of art history and criticism that emerged out of previous Idealist –influenced aesthetics in the early twentieth century, Dewey's "low" modernist aesthetic characterizes experience-as-art as a culmination of natural processes. Thus redescribed, human creativity takes its mythic meaning not from associations with what lies "above," as in Western theology, or in Kantian-like ideas of pure, supersensible rationality, but from the natural history of an embodied world. One can still speak, phenomenologically, of a kind of aesthetic transcendence in *Art as Experience*, but it is a "horizontal" rather than a "vertical" transcendence.[2]

Framing these thematic moves in turn is Dewey's programmatic rejection of various received dualisms in Western philosophy; these include not only life versus art but also nature versus culture, body versus mind, and practice versus theory. Regarding the first pairing, *Art as Experience* stops short of equating life with art. But it presents modern philosophy's deepest case for the more moderate relationship of *continuity* between these domains, representing an alternative to the high-modernist image of art's vertically transcendent autonomy from everyday life which Dewey disdainfully calls the "compartmental conception of art." He finds that image untenable not only on metaphysical grounds but also because of its role in legitimizing an unholy alliance between the passively consumeristic mindset fostered by the modern museum system and the anti-democratic forces within capitalism.

A rich literature exists on *Art as Experience's* intellectual background and critical reception, as a founding text of pragmatist aesthetics, among twentieth-century thinkers and artists.[3] But what of its influence and reception in the twenty first century? Given how interest in Dewey's book continues to grow within a spectrum of disciplines and subdisciplines that did not exist in 1934—including phenomenological philosophy of mind, neuroaesthetics, feminist aesthetics, black aesthetics, eco-aesthetics, and the aesthetics of everyday life—we sorely need an update that takes stock not only of how *Art as Experience* is shaping aesthetic conversations now but of how the idea of aesthetics as a distinctive field of inquiry has itself evolved in recent decades. Without systematically addressing all of these topics, I will focus here on three subject areas in particular where *Art as Experience* remains a seminal text. One is the literature of "everyday aesthetics," which focuses on the art/life relationship; the second is the literature of "embodied aesthetics," which integrates phenomenological and neuropsychological approaches to art and aesthetic experience; and the third is the ongoing discussion of the relationship between aesthetics and politics, with particular reference to Dewey's philosphical relationship to Theodor Adorno, whose views both challenge and complement Dewey's in instructive ways.

THE AESTHETIC LANDSCAPE SINCE DEWEY

Before we turn to these topics, some further history-of-aesthetics background may be useful. Aesthetics today, unlike in 1934, is understood by many cultural scholars not solely as a subdiscipline of philosophy but as a network of inquiries straddling older boundaries between philosophical aesthetics and the other humanities, between the humanities and the sciences, between analytic and Continental philosophy, and between Western and non-Western cultural perspectives (Haskins 2011). In keeping with Dewey's vision of philosophy as a source of growth in its larger culture, *Art as Experience's* influence now occurs not just in philosophical aesthetics but within this larger network. Two developments after 1934 are particularly relevant to understanding the book's contribution to the larger conversation now.

The first development was the dialectical rise and fall—and then, in more historically self-aware forms, the rise again—of the idea of *aesthetic experience* in academic theorizing about the arts and culture over the past century. A centerpiece of all eighteenth- and nineteenth-century aesthetic theories, this idea increasingly lost academic favor without dying out altogether in the era of twentieth-century modernism. It received a new infusion of life from, among other sources, Dewey's naturalistic reconstruction, which exerted considerable influence among American philosophers, critics, and artists for a number of years after *Art as Experience's* publication in 1934. That influence was then gradually eclipsed, until the later decades of the twentieth century, by the confluence of avant-gardist rejections of traditional notions of beauty as a fundamental norm for criticism in the Cold War era American artworld and the ascendancy of analytic aesthetics as the dominant tradition in American philosophy of art.[4] In addition, the theories and literature of philosophical aesthetics generally became increasingly marginalized within the cultural disciplines. This impulse culminated in the postmodern "anti-aesthetic" movement, epitomized by various amalgams of post-structuralist and neo-Marxist critique.

But by the mid-1990s, beauty and aesthetic experience—newly pluralized and contextualized—were back. Even the most avid anti-aesthetic critics of high modernism, Enlightenment humanism, and the universalizing and essentializing aspirations of academic philosophers still felt, as it turned out—to use a Deweyan phrase that inspired an important book by Michael Kelly (2012)—a "hunger for aesthetics."[5] But "aesthetics" in this late postmodern sense encompasses more than just the phenomenologically unified and unifying situations and objects that mainly concerned Dewey together with the supposedly essential features of art that have preoccupied other philosophers. It also, Kelly notes, involves a complex cross-section of further biological and sociopolitical factors:

> If "hunger" is understood as the complex, evolving, and historical set of human needs, desires, hopes, fears, pleasures, pains and the like, and if "environment" is understood in social-political as well as natural terms, then we can easily see that our relationships with our environment are replete with examples of "temporary absence of adequate adjustment." Dewey believes such absence can be experienced best, if not only, when it is enacted through artistic forms that allow us to separate this type of experience from the general amorphous flow of everyday experience . . . . Art is the enactment in public of our response to an absence of adjustment with our environment after it has left its affective and cognitive imprint on us, which means that art here is as much effect as cause—in Dewey's language, an "undergoing" before a "doing." In

turn, art as enactment provides in nascent form at least the demand for future restoration of an equilibrium with our environment—that is, the imagined elimination of
the absence of adequate adjustment. So art as enactment is also a "doing" in response
to an "undergoing." . . . Art provides the forms of (or for) our affective and cognitive experience of suffering . . . . Just as hunger generates art, art in turn generates a
hunger for aesthetics. (2012, 21–22)

Art that appeals to or satisfies aesthetic hunger, so understood, might deliberately reject
classical ideals of beauty, formal unity, and aesthetic pleasure. Kelly's examples include
paintings by Gerhard Richter, photographs by Sebastiao Salgado, and sculptures by
Doris Salcedo that result from and express a range of politically charged experiences that
include physical and social conflict and trauma. Drawing on Dewey and other recent
thinkers such as Theodor Adorno and Jacques Ranciére, Kelly's *A Hunger for Aesthetics*
is one good benchmark for the eclectic sensibility in aesthetics noted previously.

Consider now a second context for recent interpretations of the art-as-experience
idea. This is the postwar turn in Anglophone philosophical aesthetics away from the
idea that art and aesthetic experience possess "essences" or "natures" that exist in ways
that are ontologically insulated from our evolving practices of interpreting them. Dewey
himself admittedly sometimes uses language in *Art as Experience* that sounds as if he
means to theoretically capture such a classical essence of art. For example, he states in
chapter I that "[T]heories which isolate art and its appreciation by placing them in a
realm of their own, disconnected from other modes of experiencing, are not inherent
in the subject matter but arise because of extraneous conditions" (1934b, LW 10:16).
But if such passages do not imply that there is a universal and timeless "subject matter"
for aesthetics—in the form of experiences whose developmental qualities recur in all
cultures and times—which other aesthetic theories get wrong and Dewey's gets right,
how should we understand them?

Dewey's choice of language here may simply reflect the fact that he delivered *Art as
Experience* originally as lectures to a wide audience. In any case, to get at the deeper
underpinnings of the art-as-experience theme we need to remember another core
tenet of Deweyan pragmatism. This is that all theoretical beliefs about any subject,
however confidently and warrantedly asserted they may be on a given occasion, are internal to the experience of a specific, historically situated inquiring community. Thus
for any normatively charged subject such as the nature of art whose definition comes
under debate, answers to the question "What is art?" can be fully evaluated only in
the further context of an answer to the higher order question, "What makes one answer to 'What is art?' more attuned to the problems and values of this community than
another?" In this and other respects, *Art as Experience*'s entire argument presupposes
Dewey's discussions, in earlier works such as *Experience and Nature* (1925/1929, LW
1) and *The Quest for Certainty* (1929, LW 4) and further developed later in *Logic: The
Theory of Inquiry* (1938, LW 12), of the self-reconstructive and culturally situated nature
of inquiry.

All of these works, moreover, inherit a seminal Peircean theme: Beliefs are habits of action; they are not just things we think but things we *do*. Theoretical inquiry of any kind is, in this sense, a refined and organized form of behavior whose value is always a function of the specific environment to which it responds and contributes. To use a key Deweyan epistemic metaphor, a theorizer is less like a spectator looking at something detachedly through a window than like a kind of agent. Or, to recast the Peircean theme yet again in terms of this essay's framing metaphor, aesthetic theorizing is like journeying over a landscape that sometimes—as with our efforts to understand all cultural subjects, including certainly art—interacts and evolves with those who journey over it.

Having noted these key post-Deweyan developments, we are now in a position to look more closely at the three areas of neo-Deweyan aesthetic discussion mentioned earlier.

Dewey's Everyday Aesthetics

Art as Experience opens with a polemical shot across the bow of traditional Idealist aesthetics. Philosophy of art, Dewey declares, having long placed art on a falsely spiritualized pedestal apart from what ordinary people do, needs to "restore continuity between the refined and intensified forms of experience that are works of art and the everyday events doings, and sufferings that are universally recognize to constitute experience." (1934b, LW 10:9) One face of the art-as-experience thesis emphasizes experience's potential to achieve consummatory status as art in a wide range of settings outside the artworld—that is, in the space of "life." As Dewey puts it in a passage that comes as close as *Art as Experience* gets to a formal definition of art:

> Art is a quality of doing and of what is done. Only outwardly, then, can it be designated by a noun substantive. Since it adheres to the manner and content of doing, it is adjectival in nature. When we say that tennis-playing, singing, acting, and a multitude of other activities are arts, we engage in an elliptical way of saying that there is art *in* the conduct of these activities, and that this art so qualifies what is done and made as to induce activities in those who perceive them in which there is also art. The *product* of art—temple, painting, statue, poem—is not the *work* of art. The work takes place when a human being cooperates with the product to that the outcome is an experience that can be enjoyed because of its liberating and ordered properties. (1934b, LW 10:218)

Two ideas here pose particular challenges to one orthodox approach to conceptualizing art shared by many philosophical aestheticians, art historians, and critics of Dewey's generation. The first is that the *work of art* is not the finished product of an episode of consummatory creative activity; rather, it just *is* that episode itself.[6] An artwork is not something one contemplates but something one *does*, which involves a person's interaction with an environment in ways that transform both person and environment. The other heterodox idea is that works of art, in Dewey's "adjectival" sense, can appear outside the artworld. *Art as Experience* abounds with examples drawn from painting, sculpture, literature, and the performing arts, and many casual readers may find it tempting to interpret it as a "philosophy of the fine arts." But one key implication of the art-as-experience theme is that people lacking artworld affiliations can still be, in a fully dignified sense, artists. This democratic gesture reflects Dewey's rejection of the transcendentalized and universalizing distinction between "fine" and "useful" art, and similarly that between "art" and "craft," which had long been a staple of idealist aesthetic theories. Dewey viewed such theories' dualistic employment of fine art/useful art distinctions as symptomatic of a modalizing style of thought about experience whose origins harked back to ancient dualistic metaphysics and mutated further with the rise of modern capitalism.[7]

In addition to the pushback that Dewey's reconstruction of the art/nonart relationship elicited from idealistically aligned aestheticians of the last century, some new critical discussions of this subject are now emerging. His thesis that art is a special phase of experience that stands out from other phases has here received particular attention. Some commentators find that the logical space Dewey creates for experience-as-art, with its compromise between phenomenological specificity and continuity with other aspects of everday engagement with the world, is just right. Some others find that it pulls too far away from indispensable intuitions about the relative autonomy of fine art practices from everyday life.[8] Yet others, notably Yuriko Saito (2007), have suggested that it does not go far enough. She argues that although the experiences Dewey designates as aesthetic—marked by intense feelings of phenomenological foregroundedness, or unity among qualitative elements, and of cumulativeness within an individual's experiential history—are real and valuable, they only represent part of the larger spectrum of human engagements with the everyday world that deserve the normative cachet of this radically open-textured concept. Deweyan aesthetic experiences have what Saito calls a "stand-out" quality that can be absent from simple activities that nonetheless involve heightened awareness of an object or situation and judgments of attractiveness, unattractiveness, and myriad other value-making qualities. One might in this less stand-out way enjoy the sensuous richness of a cup of tea, or an afternoon working in the garden, or a conversation, none of which need count in Dewey's full developmental sense as "*an* experience." Saito in fact goes further, suggesting that aesthetic "hidden gems" of everyday life can be found, for those who know how to look, even in such initially unarresting phenomena as cracks on floorboards, the growth of mold and mildew, and oil stains on a driveway. Such examples bespeak the influence on Saito's discussion of a Japanese aesthetic tradition that goes unaddressed in *Art as Experience* (as in most works in aesthetics by Western authors).

Saito's quarrel with Dewey is not just terminological. It reflects a deeper question about the ideological implications of any aesthetic theory: In recognizing both that "aesthetics" is a normatively charged term and that its proper usage is a function of our historical practices of using it and reflecting on its usage, do we (however "we" is further defined) want a culture that is maximally restrictive about what receives such honorific attention (as recommended, for example, by high-modernist theories of art and criticism), or maximally inclusive (as implied by Saito's argument), or somewhere in between (as is implied by Dewey's position)? How one answers such a question is likely to reflect the particular cultural purposes one wants aesthetic theorizing to serve. Dewey never clearly poses it in *Art as Experience*, but it has a rightful place within the field's critical conversations at a time when aesthetics has become unprecedentedly multicultural and global in scope.[9]

Another implication of calling art a quality of activities, practices, and products outside of, as well as within, the artworld concerns the aesthetic dimension of moral agency. Dewey's brief but suggestive comments on this subject underscore his rejection of the transcendentalized separation of aesthetics from ethics, which had been a staple of Idealist aesthetic theories since Kant. Here we encounter another strain of Dewey's romantic influence. This is evident, for example, in *Art as Experience's* citation of Shelley's dictum that "the imagination is the chief instrument of the moral good," which is followed by the remark that "art is more moral than moralities" (1934b, LW 10:350). Among recent commentators Steven Fesmire (2003), for example, emphasizes the relevance of Dewey's earlier views on moral imagination to ethical theorizing today, at a time when the explanatory limitations of traditional theories such as Kantian formalism and utilitarianism are widely acknowledged. Drawing upon Dewey's discussions of an effective practical reasoner's engagement in "dramatic rehearsal," Fesmire suggests that a good deliberator is a "moral artist." This is someone who, when obliged to act in a situation where the efficacy of any means to a desired end is uncertain, has a cultivated capacity to imagine different possible scenarios of action in a way that makes more explicit the situation's actual and possible meanings. (More on Dewey's concept of meaning below.) Responsible deliberators must also be responsive, in imaginatively enriched ways, to others, who might conceivably include nonhumans as well as humans. In developing this point, Fesmire hints at a key Deweyan political theme:

> We require a democratized imagination that aesthetically perceives and artistically responds to a situation's "whole system of desires." (LW 7:197)—that is, to the entire system of pressing exigencies in a troubled situation. Because these conflicting tendencies are not localized and isolated from each other, they must be treated comprehensively or, to borrow an increasingly popular term, ecologically. The ecology metaphor highlights that individual parts of a system or situation are intelligible only when understood in their interrelations with other parts of the system . . . . An aesthetically complete moral experience, then, strives for an ecological or democratic ideal.
>
> (Fesmire 1999, 42)

Dewey's moral-artistry theme, so understood, is internally linked to his larger defense of democracy as the premier setting for human moral and aesthetic growth. Fesmire's reference to the moral artist's "ecological" approach to the "whole system of desires" in a situation is suggestive of yet another global-era meaning of Dewey's art-as-experience idea to which we will return at the end.

ART AS EXPERIENCE AND EMBODIED AESTHETICS

As the above discussion suggests, Dewey regarded the question What is an artist? as in some ways more fundamental for aesthetics than What is art? Consider now the first question's further ontological implications. A leitmotif of Dewey's emergent naturalism is that human beings, including all artists and their audiences, are neither Cartesian nor Kantian subjects. We are all fully embodied "live creatures" or "body-minds" who interact with our environments in ways that involve intense phenomenological presence and sometimes also creative practical imagination. Dewey's reinterpretation of the truism that human beings are embodied is for its generation unique in the integration it achieves between Darwinian and romantic themes. This line of thought in turn anticipates later evolutionary-psychological discussions of artistic and aesthetic practices as exaptation-or spandrel-like realizations of genetically based behavioral capacities. At the same time, it also emphasizes an explanatory complexity in the phenomenology of experience that resists traditional forms of physicalistic reductionism.

Dewey's synthesis of biology and phenomenology is evident, for example, in his remark that

> Art is ... prefigured in the very processes of living .... Through consciousness, [man] converts the relations of cause and effect that are found in nature into relations of means and consequence .... What was mere shock becomes an invitation; resistance becomes something to be used in changing existing arrangements of matter; smooth facilities become agencies for executing an idea. In these operations, an organic stimulation becomes the bearer of meanings, and motor responses are changed into instruments of expression and communication. .... Art is the living and concrete proof that man is capable of restoring consciously, and thus on the plane of meaning, the union of sense, need, impulse and action characteristic of the live creature. (1934b, LW 10:30–31)

The references here to how one neurophysiologically registered phenomenon (shock, resistance, etc.) "becomes" another (an invitation, a spur to productive action, etc.) illustrate Dewey's signature theme of the at once biological and ontological emergence of *meaning* out of more general causal processes. Such emergence does not, as in classically "representationalist" philosophies, happen to ontologically distinct minds and bodies in mysterious Cartesian cooperation. Meaningfulness—the core of experience—is itself part of the natural order. It involves the way in which a person's interactions with a physical environment are at once physically felt and manifest to awareness, discursively and prediscursively, as qualities of "situations." Experiences that are aesthetic in Dewey's definition possess qualitative meanings that become objects of interest and attention in their own right, and all of this is also part of the natural order. More traditionally dualistic philosophies of mind would locate the cause of an experience of aesthetic harmony or tension afforded by, say, a work of music or a painting, either on the "mind" side of a mind/nature divide (aesthetic subjectivism) or on the "nature" side (aesthetic objectivism). Dewey, in contrast, understands such causality as emerging out of the interaction between experiencer and environment.

This position's post-Cartesian and post-Kantian naturalistic cast is clear. But further developments within later twentieth-century philosophy of mind and cognitive science were required before *Art as Experience* would come into fresh focus as a pioneering work of what is now variously called "embodied aesthetics" or "the aesthetics of embodied life." One key such development was cognitive science's passage from its classical or first-generation phase into its present second-generation phase. Central to the first phase is an idea inherited from classical empiricism. Cognition is construed as a nonbodily, mental activity governed by purely formal rules that organize symbols; this activity "represents" events and objects in a mind-external world that causes its representations' truth-or -falsity across an otherwise insuperable ontological divide. In the second phase, cognition is itself redescribed as a form of embodied activity. All representational events are now, similarly, understood as forms of interactive behavior at various micro and macro levels of brain/body organization that occur *within* the world they purport to be about.[10] It is in the context of still-evolving second-generation cognitive science, and its transdisciplinary linkage to philosophy of mind, that Dewey has become a key figure for researchers who describe their work under such general rubrics as "embodied cognition" and "enactivism." Dewey is regarded here as a key twentieth-century pioneer of the ideas that mind is "extended" and that consciousness and experience happen not "in our heads" (whether construed in Cartesian representationalist or in first-generation neuroscientific terms) but in the evolving totality of a human being's transactions with a larger world.

Mark Johnson, drawing on this second-generation discussion, finds in *Art as Experience's* account of embodied aesthetic meaning a basis not only for a reconstruction of twenty-first century aesthetic research along Deweyan lines but also for an approach to grounding philosophy *as a whole* in aesthetics. We earlier noted the temporary exile of the idea of aesthetic experience from academic philosophy of art and cultural theory in the late twentieth century. In *The Meaning of the Body: Aesthetics of Human Understanding*, Johnson (2007) suggests that an earlier devaluation of aesthetic experience occurred, ironically, at what is usually considered the birth of modern aesthetics in Kant's *Critique of Judgment*. In characterizing judgments of taste or beauty as disinterested and as grounded not in fully cognitive concepts of experience but in subjective feelings of pleasure, Kant drove a transcendental wedge between aesthetic experience and full-blooded knowledge of the external natural world. This served to further ratify the installation of "epistemology"—defined now as the study of representational activities categorically distinct from empirical events in the brain and body—as the prime organ of philosophy, with aesthetic experience now relegated to being simply, as Johnson puts it, a source of "a certain refined, intellectual kind of feeling" (Johnson 2007, 218).[11]

Dewey's importance for the recent history of aesthetics, Johnson suggests, is due in part to how he naturalistically reconstructs that Kantian move. While retaining the traditional idea that aesthetic experience possesses a discursively noncognitive core, Dewey also maintains that aesthetic experience epitomizes our *meaningful* bodily transactions with our environments. This meaningful dimension of embodied life in turn provides a basis for the possibility of any further knowledge in a way not acknowledged by the representationalism of the Cartesian/empiricist/Kantian tradition. In thus arguing, Dewey points the way to understanding the real "meaning of the body" in one sense of the *double entendre* in Johnson's title. This involves understanding the body not as the mortal, mechanistic vehicle of a separately spiritualized mind but as a fully earthbound locus for the qualitatively rich life of a more organizationally complex body-mind.

Drawing on his earlier work on the bodily basis for the spectrum of human linguistic activity, including especially metaphor, Johnson offers a further account of how the roots of human experience lie in prediscursive, intuitive feelings of unity and disunity as qualities of any situation in which we find ourselves. Following Dewey, he suggests that any experienced feature of an object or event that we consciously or nonconsciously associate with present, past, or possible future experiential transactions with the world are its *meanings*. ("Meanings" in this sense should not be confused with the objects of formal semantic analysis discussed by linguists and mainstream analytic philosophers.) A work of fine art expresses meanings insofar as it embodies qualities undergone in the experience of its creator. The creator then expressively re-integrates that constellation of qualities within a specific configuration of materials according to the conventions of a specific medium (say, literary, visual, or musical). This is done with an intent that those qualities not only reappear, at some level of analysis, in the experiences of audience members, but also lead to those experiences in the sense of being instrumental to bringing them about.

The table on which I am writing possesses various meanings in this sense, corresponding not only to its physical features that support my writing activity but also its affordance of possible future uses. I might eat at the table, converse over it with a friend, and so on. Or consider a more complex artistic example. I am, let's suppose, listening to Billie Holliday's 1943 live recording of "Body and Soul" at the Philharmonic Auditorium. This event had innumerable situation-specific meanings for its original audience. Its meanings now for me include its qualities of harmony, melody, and rhythm, together with lyrics that present further dimensions of meaning. All of these are components of an experience that for me acquires further dimensions of meaning from my recollection of previous encounters with similar harmonic, melodic, and rhythmic elements in jazz, as well as from earlier experiences of mine that I imaginatively link to this song. Since I am a musician, these components possess yet further meanings that are more specific to my own history—say, from my remembered past experiences of performing the song with all of the complex qualitative awarenesses of situations that entailed. Dewey writes that "We lay hold of the full import of a work of art only as we go through in our own vital processes the processes the artist went through in producing the work" (LW 10:328). My experience of this performance of "Body and Soul" (which might be treated either as a token-of-a-type or as a unique work in its own right) reaches its fullest development as a critical response only to the extent that I find a way of imaginatively unifying massive numbers of these dimensions of meaning so that my resultant experience becomes, in the relevant sense, attuned to that of the original artist or artists.[12] Variants on this phenomenological complexity in my experience may be found, in turn, in the art-related experiences of innumerable other human beings in diverse cultural settings.

Another second-generation writer emphasizing the phenomenological impulse of *Art as Experience* is Alva Noë (2015). Drawing on Dewey and other twentieth-century figures including Heidegger and Merleau-Ponty, Noë argues that art's importance for all human beings lies in how its products and experiential processes bring previously unappreciated parts of the world freshly into focus.[13] He takes particular issue with the implication of some recent neuroaesthetic research that aesthetic focusing (like various other intentional states) is straightforwardly analyzable into neurophysiological facts about the brain. This is problematic because doing so obscures, since doing so obscures the explanatory complexity of *experience*.[14] To *focus* on something here is not simply to occupy a certain neurophysiological state, nor is it to "represent" the phenomenon in a sense that ontologically segregates thinking and feeling from acting. It is to consciously *do* something with parts of the world that are already there but that show up and possess new kinds of presence for us because of what we have done to date. We bring something into focus in this way when we freshly experience the form and meaning of a poem, a painting, a musical piece, or other art product. And we do so even more fundamentally when we are creating an artwork ourselves.

Noë emphasizes further that in making or experiencing art, human beings are not simply focusing on various parts of the world. We are continually *organizing and reorganizing* what we do in ways that are driven by our endless curiosity about our situation in the world. This curiosity in turn reflects our ongoing need to create ways of finding our way in a world that is always in different respects concealed from us. Our experience is like a landscape within which such disclosures happen. And artworks—like works of philosophy—are maps that model and hence help us navigate that landscape.

Noë's illustrations of these themes in recent artistic practice provide a welcome update to Dewey's own admittedly truncated and parochial examples.[15] Consider the case of dancing. Here Noë distinguishes between the many kinds of stylized movement that comprise dancing in the term's most broadly descriptive anthropological sense and a higher order companion practice that he variously calls "dance" and "choreography." Danc*ing* is something that, as much as eating or sex or talking, is a lower order, "Level-1 activity." All human beings have impulses to do it, and doing it habitually, like doing anything else habitually, contributes to the organization of our lives. *Dance* or *choreography*, on the other hand, is a "Level 2 practice": it involves a reflective and normative sense of more and less desirable and useful ways of engaging in its lower level counterpart. Dance "reorganizes" dancing; it puts the latter "on display" and "brings it into focus." When, but only when, this happens, dancing becomes genuinely artistic. Dance plays with dancing in ways that not only give the latter form and style but also afford new insight into its further developmental possibilities, which are ultimately, given all the ways dancing is organized into diverse cultures, our own developmental possibilities as human beings. To this extent, dance is also a philosophical practice, in that it provides yet further material for human self-interpretation and self-criticism. Similar observations apply throughout the fine arts. Writing, painting, sculpting, architectural design, music-making, and their emerging hybridizations all exhibit a dynamic of internal self-reorganization and participation in the self-reorganizational life of the larger culture.

In these ways, Noë's argument thus offers an update to Dewey's core theme of the qualitatively special character of fine art as a unique experiential space in a world of bureaucratically driven distractions that, in this century as in the last, can rob experience of its richness. It is worth noting, by the way, that one traditional name for that special character, although neither Noë nor Dewey uses it, is "autonomy." Dewey himself at least may have avoided it because of its past associations with Kantian-style idealism. But Dewey also held that no single school of philosophy has a timeless monopoly on the correct usage of key terminology.[16] It is thus fair to say that the basic intuition of aesthetic specialness or autonomy underwent a significant migration in Dewey, the only major twentieth-century philosopher to systematically transpose the Kantian/Romantic tradition's core aesthetic insights into a naturalistic idiom.

RETHINKING THE DEWEY/ ADORNO CONSTELLATION

The above references to bureaucratic distractions and autonomy may prompt a further question for postmodern era readers: What should we make of *Art as Experience*'s politics? While free of revolutionary rhetoric, it was, for its own time, a subtly political book on various levels. Dewey's naturalistic challenge to Idealist aesthetics invoked the same worldly cultural-political antagonisms as did Darwinism's challenge to traditional theology. In another register, parallels between its critique of Idealist aesthetic theories and those by Marxist-humanist writers have often been noted.[17] Yet *Art as Experience* remains unusual among canonical works of modern aesthetics in its resonance for readers of otherwise polarized sensibilities—idealists and Marxists, modernists and postmodernists, and others. This may be due in part to how its classification as a work of "pragmatist" aesthetics blocked the stereotyping effects of more polarized labels. But more significant here is the interplay Dewey achieved between his key neo-romantic and phenomenological thesis that all experience approximates to an artistic ideal of qualitative unity and intensity and the social-democratic critique of capitalism that was in the foreground or background of all of his mature writings about modern culture.[18]

We see that interplay when Dewey remarks, for example, that

> In an imperfect society—and no society will ever be perfect--fine art will be to some extent an escape from, or an adventitious decoration of, the main activities of living. But in a better-ordered society than that in which we now live, an infinitely greater happiness than is now the case would attend all modes of production. We live in a world in which there is an immense amount of organization, but it is an external organization, not one of the ordering of a growing experience, one that involves, moreover, the whole of the live creature, toward a fulfilling conclusion . . . . To the degree in which art exercises its office, it is also a remaking of the experience of the community in the direction of a greater order and unity. (1934b, LW 10:87)

And, earlier, in *Experience and Nature:*

> We have professionalized amusement as an agency of escape and forgetfulness. But when all is said and done, the fundamentally hazardous character of the world is not seriously modified, much less eliminated. Such an incident as the last war and preparations for a future war remind us that it is easy to overlook the extent to which, after all, our attainments are only devices for blurring the disagreeable recognition of a fact instead of means for altering the fact itself . . . . Comedy is as genuine as tragedy. But it is traditional that comedy strikes a more superficial note than tragedy. (1925/1929, LW 1:45)

Some of these words might have been written by Theodor Adorno, the pre-eminent late twentieth century Marxist theorist of art and culture whose intellectual relationship to Dewey is now receiving fresh attention.[19] Dewey and Adorno are at first sight an odd couple for aesthetic dialogue. In stark contrast to the innocently romantic American optimism of Dewey's prewar writings on art and culture, Adorno's post-Holocaust writings exude a darker European pessimism about the prospects of global justice in an increasingly war-traumatized, bureaucratically managed, and class-dominated modern world. But Adorno's writings on philosophy and culture also provide an essential lens for a new critical assessment of Dewey's aesthetics and pragmatist aesthetics more generally of a kind that can further enrich the multi-traditional dialogue that aesthetics has now become.[20]

Central to such an assessment is that if we take *Art as Experience* and *Aesthetic Theory* (the most important of Adorno's aesthetic works) as representative texts, their relationship is one neither of doctrinal harmony nor of rigid dialectical opposition. A better word is "constellational," in the sense of Adorno's and Benjamin's concept of a relationship between multiple elements within a field that resist reduction to a common denominator. Such elements might include ideas or perspectives within a field of debate that, under the right conditions, challenge those identifying with those perspectives to create new kinds of conversation about a wide array of lower and higher order aesthetic subjects. Such conversations would aim not at classical forms of grand-theoretical unity—which both Adorno and Dewey regarded as unattainable—but at possibilities of belief, action (including coordinated social action), and experience that were not fully implicit in the original elements. A *constellation* in this sense is, to invoke a growing theme within twenty first century social theory, a kind of intellectual network. Here, as in other networks, to fully understand any single node—such as an individual thinker, meme, or set of ideas—one needs to view it in relation to other nodes from which it significantly differs (and with which, to use one of Adorno's favorite Hegelianisms, it is nonidentical).

To put this another way, think of the Dewey-Adorno constellational nonidentity as a complex counterpoint. Its dissonances include their clashing intuitions regarding questions of Idealist or Naturalist methodology, along with further significant—although not total—differences in their cultural politics. Dewey was certainly a radical voice among twentieth-century public intellectuals for his relentless criticisms of various problematic legacies of the Enlightenment.[21] Yet even these criticisms seem mild alongside Adorno's vision of the disenchanting fallout of the Dialectic of Enlightenment. There science appears as hopelessly shackled to bureaucratic-instrumental reason and "identity thinking" and the modern experience of most art, high and low (including the practices of the "culture industry"), is now construed as but so much "false semblance" fueling the forces of political amnesia and domination both before and since Auschwitz.

Dewey (like everyone) lacked the frame of historical reference necessary for a full critical comprehension of such views of art in 1934. In contrast to Adorno's relentless critique of all norms of totality and unity in art and philosophy, *Art as Experience* emphasizes what, in an important early commentary, Stephen C. Pepper called the "organicist" theme of felt and formal unification in aesthetic experience. But it also, Pepper noted, emphasizes "pragmatist" themes of felt conflict and tension in aesthetic consummatory experience.[22] Dewey is clear in the text that he considers a necessary feature of experiences possessing aesthetic quality to be their felt unity. But he was, of course, writing in 1934. Might he have relaxed this requirement had he been privy to more of the pragmatic and experiential contexts of twentieth-century life that fueled Adorno's anti-unificationist critiques?

Speculations about Dewey apart, it is striking that Adorno himself actually became an admirer of Dewey in his later years. In the "Draft Introduction" to his posthumously published *Aesthetic Theory*, Adorno writes:

> That empiricism recoils from art—of which in general it has hardly ever taken notice (with the exception of the unique and truly free John Dewey) other than insofar as it attributes all knowledge that does not agree with its rules of the game to be poetry— can be explained by the fact that art constitutively dismisses these rules of the game, because art is an entity that is not identical with its empiria.
>
> (Adorno 1998, 335)

And later:

> Aesthetics does not proceed with the continuity of scientific thinking. The particular aesthetics of the various philosophies cannot be reduced to a common formulation

as their truth; rather their truth is to be sought in their conflict.... That aesthetics ... wants to find its way out into the open, entirely exposed, imposes on itself the sacrifice of each and every security that it has borrowed from the sciences; no one expressed this necessity with greater candor than the pragmatist John Dewey.[23]

(Adorno 1998, 353)

Adorno does not elaborate on these compliments to Dewey. What possessed twentieth-century philosophy's arch-tragedian about all manner of folk beliefs about the possibility of wholeness and happiness in the various modalized domains of experience—religious, political, moral, aesthetic, and so on—and an arch-critic of American culture to boot, to describe that century's premier pragmatic apologist for the value of everyday appearances, publically accessible art, and democracy as "unique and truly free"? We may surmise at least that, by 1970, Adorno came to appreciate certain pieces of crucial common ground that both thinkers shared. He would have known (whether from direct reading or conversation with colleagues such as Max Horkheimer) that Dewey was, like himself and unlike many other Anglophone philosophers at the time, deeply opposed to the uncritical scientism of Logical Positivism. Indeed, he had his own home-grown version (implicit in passages like that quoted earlier from *Experience and Nature*) of a critique of what Adorno called "identity thinking" in the science-dominated modern world. In a similar spirit, Adorno would have approved of Dewey's portrayal of aesthetic experience as a space for encounters with the world whose qualitative uniqueness allows it to perform the paradoxical service of contributing to social change indirectly, without reducing to crude considerations of utility.[24] Central to Adorno's critique of identity thinking was his rejection of traditional notions of easy translatability between certain works of art and also between certain philosophical texts. This provides a context for his remark that the "truth" emerging from a confrontation between different aesthetic philosophies "is to be sought in their conflict." Reading this alongside the remark's following favorable reference to Dewey, we might wonder whether Adorno saw certain unspecified "truths" about aesthetic subjects emerging from experienced tensions, or relations of irreducible difference, between his and Dewey's approaches to them. (Marxists traditionally call such tensions "dialectics," but Hegel himself came close to calling them simply "experience" [*Erfahrung*].)[25]

As Martin Jay emphasizes in his important book *Songs of Experience: Variations on a Universal Theme in European and American Thought*, Dewey and Adorno were vital contrapuntal voices in the last century's politically charged philosophical debate about the nature of *experience*. This is a concept that had come by the mid-twentieth century to possess no less open-textured and god-term-like a character than "art," "aesthetic," or "culture."[26] We may surmise that Adorno came to appreciate that Dewey, like himself, offered a critical, genealogically framed interpretation of the post-romantic truism that all experience aspires to various kinds of completeness and integration even while it never fully achieves such ideals in particular historical lives or cultures, especially in modern capitalist civilization. The fact that both writers found it important to link questions about the nature and purpose of art to that of the fate of experience (and of "experience") in capitalist civilization underscores the equally seminal significance of both *Art as Experience* and *Aesthetic Theory* for any future discussions of the politics of aesthetics or the aesthetics of politics.

The importance of reading Dewey and Adorno constellationally rather than as simple dialectical opponents is further underscored by a point that both writers, unlike many of their contemporaries, grasped clearly. At a time when the very idea of a single, final, grand unifying aesthetic theory has all but entirely lost its Enlightenment-era credibility, it makes more sense to view specific aesthetic theories—including Dewey's and Adorno's—as time slices in the history of a tradition of inquiry that is in a continual mutually transformative relationship with emerging developments in its culture.[27] (Both thinkers saw all of philosophy this way, as epitomized in Dewey's concept of "philosophical reconstruction" and Adorno's of "negative dialectics.") To this extent both writers provide seminal examples of how theorizing is *itself* a form of experience in the full sense of the rich German word *Erfahrung*. We might indeed say that theorizing—a term whose Greek roots also connote traveling[28]—is a kind of journey (*Fahrt*) from a phenomenologically familiar place in the traveler's history to one whose elements of novelty and risk afford new possibilities of meaning.

AESTHETICS AS "EMBODIED TRAVEL"

What do we gain, philosophically, by metaphorically assimilating aesthetic inquiry, as I have done at different points in this discussion, to travel over a landscape? This is an example of what George Lakoff and Mark Johnson call a "conceptual metaphor," where one conceptual domain is explained via a condensed symbolic linkage with another in a way that then newly shapes both the thought and behavior of language users.[29] Here are some concluding thoughts about why this conceptual metaphor's logic is particularly apt for encouraging fresh thought and action in a Deweyan-pragmatist vein, regarding art and aesthetic experience now.

Dewey himself used a variant of the landscape conceptual metaphor when he remarked in *Experience and Nature* that the experimental method in philosophy "places before others a map of the road that has been travelled; they may accordingly, if they will, re-travel the road to inspect the landscape for themselves" (1925/1929, LW 1:34).[30] As our earlier discussion allows us to appreciate, Dewey's use of landscape and map imagery here condenses his anti-representationalist views about inquiry and experience in a way that implies two key further points. First, maps are not self-standing representations or objects of contemplation but instruments for further action or travel. And second, in a naturalistic world in which change and process occur continually, no map of any territory can be complete. This is because anyone who creates a map or follows it in the course of their travels is ontologically entwined with (rather than a detached contemplator of) their target territory, as is any map they use. And as with actual geographic

maps, so too with their propositional relatives that we call theories, whatever their subject matter. This remains true whether the theory in question pertains to science, or general philosophy, or aesthetic, moral, political, or religious experience.

Speaking of religion, the landscape metaphor takes on yet further meaning in terms
of a romantic theme running throughout the text and margins of *Art as Experience*: the
affinity between aesthetic and religious (or spiritual) experience. Here it is instructive
to read Dewey's book alongside not only his *A Common Faith* (which appeared the
same year[31]) but also Thomas Tweed's more recent groundbreaking study *Crossing and
Dwelling: A Theory of Religion*. Tweed suggests that, given the dynamic character of all
religious traditions, we may think of the higher order practice of theorizing about religion, like the lower order experiences it seeks to describe, as "embodied travel":

> Theory as embodied travel is not a stationary view of static terrain. It is not geography
> or chorography—or even the localized topography of indigenous mapmakers.... [It
> is not] the displacements of voluntary migrants who seek settlement tourists who
> chase pleasure on round-trip journeys, or pilgrims who depart only to return home
> after venerating a sacred site. Theory is purposeful wandering.

(Tweed 2006, 11)

Crossing and Dwelling freshly brings themes from modern anthropological theories
of religious life together with nonrepresentationalist theories of truth, meaning, and interpretation in the pragmatist tradition (with particular reference to James, Dewey, and
Putnam). Echoing Dewey's account of the "religious phase of experience" in *A Common
Faith*, Tweed argues that religions are not institutionally insular compartments of belief and ritual whose internal dynamics stubbornly resist interaction with other such
domains. Rather, they are "confluences of organic-cultural flows that intensify joy and
confront suffering by drawing on human and suprahuman forces to make homes and
cross boundaries" (Tweed 2006, 54). Not only would Dewey, I think, have found this definition congenial; he would have appreciated too how its basic structure generalizes to
the whole spectrum of what *Art as Experience* describes as experience's artistic phase. As
a fan of topographical metaphors himself, he would have affirmed that efforts to theorize
about art too, like efforts to theorize religion, are forms of "embodied travel," in part because the "confluences of organic-cultural flows" they track never sit still long enough for
final mapping. To this we might add that their meaning and value, as forms of travel, is
always connected to their "destinations"—to the possibilities of experience to which they
lead theorists and others who use a theory as a guide for further belief and action.

I have focused on just a few fresh "destinations" to which *Art as Experience* can lead
twenty-first century readers. All can enrich a variety of different conversations that are
gaining new gravity in our self-reorganizing web of aesthetic conversations now. Yet
other destinations deserve more attention than I have been able to give them here. One
obvious example is the continuing suggestiveness of the art-as-experience theme for
interpreting recent work by a rich array of twenty first century professional artists in
all media (see Kelly 2012). But I would be remiss in not mentioning one more major

destination for further conversation that remained off the radar of most mainstream art theory and criticism in the twentieth century. This subject cries out for our attention at the present ecologically imperiled moment for a flood of general and specific reasons. Dewey comes close to explicitly acknowledging some of the general ones when he remarks in "The Live Creature" (this is the passage that inspired Kelly's *A Hunger for Aesthetics*) that

> Every need, say hunger for fresh air or food, is a lack that denotes at least a temporary absence of adequate adjustment with surroundings. But it is also a demand, a reaching out into the environment to make good the lack and to restore adjustment by building at least a temporary equilibrium. (1934b, LW 10:19)

These words certainly apply to the experiential processes of fine artists and their audiences. But their scope is larger, since *Art as Experience's* vision of our biologically based hunger for aesthetics (which serves also as a conceptual metaphor for the sources of human motivation throughout cultural life) presupposes the sweeping metaphysical argument of *Experience and Nature*. Recall here the earlier book's declaration that "[Art]—the mode of activity that is charged with meanings capable of immediately enjoyed possession—is the complete culmination of nature" (1925/1929, LW 1:269). In other words, intelligent human behavior, culminating in art, epitomizes nature's inner development toward self-awareness. This dramatic evocation of art's metaphysical meaning is a key condensation of the book's interwoven Hegelian, Darwinian, and romantic motifs. It takes on more pragmatic meaning when Dewey also remarks that

> Man needs the earth in order to walk, the sea to swim or sail, the air to fly. Of necessity he acts within the world, and in order to be, he must in some measure adapt himself as one part of nature to other parts. In mind, thought, this predicament becomes aware of itself. (1925/29, LW 1:309)

Herein lies a crucial context for *Art as Experience* 's core idea that art is a quality of actions that aim at adjustments between human beings and their "environment" in freshly consummatory ways. Keeping these lines from *Experience and Nature* in mind, we can better appreciate the radical reach of Dewey's aesthetics when he also writes in "The Live Creature":

> Life grows when a temporary falling out is a transition to a more extensive balance of the energies of the organism with those of the conditions under which it lives .... The world is full of things that are indifferent and even hostile to life .... Nevertheless, if life continues and if in continuing it expands, there is an overcoming of factors of opposition and conflict.... Here in germ are balance and harmony attained through rhythm. Equilibrium comes about not mechanically but out of, and because of, tension. Form is arrived at whenever a stable, even though moving, equilibrium is reached ... Order is not imposed from without but is made out of the relations of

harmonious interactions that energies bear to one another. Because it is active . . . order itself develops. (1934b, LW 10:20)

Human experiences of form, balance, order, rhythm, and harmony—all classic marks of the aesthetic—do not issue from a vertically transcendent ideal realm. They arise in bottom-up fashion out of a horizontal environment of tensions, conflicts, and hazards with whose historically shifting features we are continually forging creative (and sometimes, in Fesmire's sense, morally artistic) adjustments. What is finally at stake in these adjustments is not just whether human beings can keep the spirit of art alive in the sense of continuing to enjoy aesthetic experiences afforded by the creations of a special class of producers. Rather, it is the prospect that people of diverse backgrounds within *and* without the fine arts might learn habits and skills for creating new situations exhibiting balance, order, rhythm, and harmony in their everyday transactions with a natural world that keeps prompting us to revise our maps of its surfaces and depths.

Drawing together the above themes of inquiry as travel-on-a-landscape, adjustment between intelligence and environment, and the human hunger for aesthetics, we come finally to what in this century is the most important level at which *Art as Experience,* as I put it at the beginning, reads its embodied readers. Picture the author of the passages just cited (especially the one about how hunger's satisfaction requires "reaching out to the environment") joining us now and surveying the challenges to creative mapping, local and global, facing cultural inquirers in this environmentally imperiled century. Is there any doubt what a time-traveling Dewey would see as the larger landscape of all human travels and an urgent destination for pragmatic aesthetic theorizing today? Far from being limited to the artworld, that landscape is, literally, just the natural world at this point in the history of our planet. The reality of inhabiting the evolving system of natural processes we call Earth itself supplies, as Dewey noted a century ago, the deepest context for our hunger for art and aesthetic experience.

"Environmentalist" may not be the first term that occurs to most people if they are asked to describe Dewey as a philosopher. Neither, for that matter, is "aesthetician." Yet why not read him here as an aesthetic environmental philosopher? For in the end, *Art as Experience* is certainly not only about art in a narrow sense. Rather, it is about creatures who depend for their survival and satisfaction on continually creating better ways of harmonizing means and ends (which is in fact how Dewey defines "art" in *Experience and Nature*)--and, in the process, on inquiring into everything on earth that it means to do so.[32]

NOTES

1. This spectrum of examples underscores how Dewey is interested not only in the classic question *what* is art? but also (anticipating a later discussion by Nelson Goodman) in that of *when* is art? That is: when, or under what conditions, does experience develop into art? This point also provides a crucial context for understanding why Dewey moves, pretty much without comment, back and forth in the text between using "art" in a

traditional fine art-centered sense and in a broader sense that encompasses ordinary-life examples such as those listed previously. This seeming vacillation makes perfect sense when understood as an expression of Dewey's dialectical vision—a carryover from his earlier Hegelian days—of modern democratic civilization as approximating to a future condition where earlier modern distinctions between "fine" and "useful" art fall away and lose their present aura of transcendental permanence within our thinking. In such a condition—whose possibility Dewey only hints at without (sensibly) predicting its arrival—art in his sense finally becomes fully integrated into the daily lives of all citizens. I suggest elsewhere (Haskins 1992) that this amounts in effect to a naturalized reinterpretation *and* inversion of Hegel's "end of art" thesis. In Dewey's version, it is now art—rather than, as in Hegel, philosophy—that gets cast as modern culture's dominant form of modalized intelligence.

2. On the distinction between horizontal and vertical interpretations of transcendence see Johnson (2007), chapter 12. Kestenbaum (2002) argues provocatively that Dewey never fully let go of an unconstructed Idealist longing for transcendence. But this, it seems to me, is at best a gesture of psychoanalytic-like interpretation that refuses to take Dewey at his word when he remarks in *Experience and Nature*, for example, that "Every thought and meaning has its substratum in some organic act of absorption or elimination of seeking, or turning away from, or destroying or caring for ... [O]ur physical names for mental acts like seeing, grasping, searching, affirming, acquiescing, spurning, comprehending, affection, emotion are not just 'metaphors'" (1925/1929, LW 1:221). Especially in light of second-generation cognitive-science discussions like Johnson's, there is no textual basis for supposing that Dewey abandoned this kind of naturalistically "horizontal" thinking even when making such transcendence-suggestive remarks in *Art as Experience* as "We are never wholly free from the sense of something that lies beyond" (1934, LW 10:197). For more discussion, see Haskins (2003).

3. The best book-length discussion of *Art as Experience's* argument and early critical reception remains Thomas Alexander's (1987) *John Dewey's Theory of Art, Experience, and Nature: The Horizons of Feeling*. For an informative further discussion of Dewey's argument and overview of later scholarship see Leddy (2016) and Haskins (2014). Shusterman (1992/2013) broke fresh ground with a Dewey-inspired account of aesthetic experience in the wake of the several-decades-long eclipse of Dewey's once major influence in Anglophone aesthetics by the analytic tradition, epitomized in the work of writers such as Morris Weitz, Arthur Danto, and George Dickie. Shusterman also, following Richard Rorty's renewed appeal to Dewey as a seminal voice in the postmodern era conversation between analytic and Continental philosophy, reframed pragmatist aesthetics as a "promising middle way and mediator between, the analytic and Continental traditions."

4. For more discussion see Haskins (2007). On the recent fortunes of the idea of aesthetic experience in anglophone philosophy, see Shusterman (2000).

5. See Kelly (2012).

6. Dewey's critique of traditional product-centered definitions of art amounts, in effect, to the charge that such definitions commit what in *Experience and Nature* he called the "fallacy of hypostatization," involving a "conversion of eventual functions into antecedent existence" (1925/1929, LW 1:34).

7. Dewey's account of this history inspired later discussions, including Paul Oskar Kristeller's classic 1952 essay "The Modern System of the Arts: A Study in the History of Aesthetics," which in turn inspired Shiner (2001).

8. For example, Monroe C. Beardsley, a commentator who did more than most to champion Dewey's approach to aesthetics during the Cold War era, nonetheless found Dewey's account of fine art to inadequately represent the latter's autonomy. See Beardsley (1982).

9. For a critique of Saito's position, which is part of a larger defense of an "everyday aesthetics" perspective in a Deweyan vein, see Leddy (2014). For a wider-ranging review of all of these writers, see Puolakka (2014).

10. For further discussion of these developments within cognitive science and their relation to Dewey, see Johnson (2007), part II ("Embodied Meaning and the Sciences of Mind").

11. For elaborations on this and other key points in that book, see also Johnson (2015).

12. Dewey is artfully vague about what more exactly such attunement entails. He speaks broadly, without detailed critical examples, of "processes" on the parts of the artist and audience that are gone through in similar ways. And he cautions critics about the methodological pitfalls of the two dialectically opposed positions he calls "judicial criticism" (which imposes artificial formal criteria on the judgment of individual works) and "impressionistic criticism" (a more subjective approach). His approach to circumventing this metacritical dilemma shares some structural features of Hume's classic argument in "Of the Standard of Taste." Criticism, for Dewey, is a kind of *judgment* involving a "search for the properties of the object" (1934, LW 10:312). This search may fall short of its regulative goal but still involves the critic's ability to marshal objective facts about a work's genesis in support of an evaluative conclusion whose value ultimately lies in its instrumentality to further critical experience.

13. See Noë (2015). An important earlier discussion of Dewey's affinities with Continental phenomenologists such as Merleau-Ponty and Husserl is Kestenbaum (1977).

14. Noë's book thus represents—as does Johnson's and as, in an anticipatory way, did *Art as Experience*—an important face of philosophical resistance to efforts to reductively "scientize" subjects of traditionally humanistic study by enthusiasts of first-generation approaches to neuroscience and evolutionary psychology. For an illuminating overview of the surrounding recent debate which accords due weight to the importance of the idea of experience in a way that resonates with many of Dewey's concerns, see Smith (2016).

15. Dewey's examples generally favored the visual arts and literature at the expense of music and dance, for which he apparently had little personal sensitivity. This fact is ironic, given *Art as Experience*'s numerous literal and metaphorical references to "rhythm" as a dimension of artmaking, of experience generally, and of natural processes generally. It seems likely that Dewey was here inspired by reading *The Direction and Rhythm of Motion* by Herbert Spencer, whose views on beauty he discusses elsewhere in *Art as Experience* (I thank Steven Fesmire for this observation).

16. See Dewey's reply to Stephen C. Pepper in "Experience, Knowledge, and Value: A Rejoinder," in Schilpp (1939/1989).

17. As Stefan Morawski notes in a book that reframes the twentieth-century dialogue between Continental and Anglophone aesthetics from a Marxist-humanist perspective: "The aesthetic experience—and here I refer once more to Dewey, expanding on some of his conclusions and slightly modifying others—preserves our familiarity with the world but is at the same time imprinted with strangeness. Although it does not obliterate our psychic habits, it works against their becoming ingrained. It is contemplative and yet opposed to inertia, to that mode of unapprehending rote response which deadens us to the rhythm of life and to persons and things as they authentically are" (Morawski 1978, 311).

18. Another implicitly political dimension in *Art as Experience* emerges from how Dewey defines art broadly enough to accord popular arts generally, along with a wide spectrum

of creative practices in Western and non-Western cultures, a normative status comparable to that of canonical Western white male–created high art. Although Dewey was writing before it became standard to critically interpret aesthetic theories through the lens of identity politics, his implicit politics of identity is certainly inclusive in ways that align with his general political defense of democracy. For this reason, among others, *Art as Experience* is cited as a valuable resource by writers such as Taylor (2016) and Seigfried (1996).

19. See also Hammer (this volume). For an interpretation as well as other more general discussions such as Foster (2007) and Jay (2004). Dewey's published texts provide no evidence of his having known about Adorno (not too surprisingly, given their staggered chronologies), and Adorno's direct knowledge of Dewey's writings was evidently modest. But Adorno had ample opportunities to discuss Deweyan pragmatism with various of their common acquaintances in New York in the 1930s and 1940s. One such acquaintance was Max Horkheimer, who criticized Dewey's views about science but had a more charitable view of *Art as Experience*. See Horkheimer (1975, 2013). Another was art historian Meyer Schapiro, who studied with Dewey at Columbia, who gave Dewey critical feedback on an early draft of *Art as Experience*, and who was friendly with his at-that-time fellow New Yorker Adorno in the late 1930s and early 1940s. See Schapiro (2015).

20. See again Hammer (this volume) for an interpretation of Adorno's philosophy of experience that aligns it sympathetically with Dewey's vis à vis the problem of liberating the idea of experience from insular conceptions of subjectivity, see Foster (2007). On the more general theme of the importance of dialogue between Deweyan pragmatism and other intellectual traditions, see Fesmire (2015, 238ff).

21. His reconstructive targets included, for example, the scientism of Logical Positivism, the Weberian image of modern life organized around plural bureaucratically modalized "spheres of value" (including art and the aesthetic), and the Idealist image of art and aesthetic experience as a disinterested and diversionary "beauty parlor of civilization."

22. Dewey is most explicit about this in his response to Pepper in Schilpp (1939/1989, 552).

23. Theodor Adorno, "Draft Introduction," in *Adorno* (1997, 335 and 353, respectively). In their general tone, these remarks echo Adorno's (1966) earlier reference in *Negative Dialectics* to Dewey's "strikingly humane" version of pragmatism. For further discussion of thematic resonances between Dewey's and Adorno's aesthetic theories, see Posnock (1991, 129–132). Posnock suggests that the differences between Dewey and Adorno are less important than their "shared reorientation of philosophy from metaphysics to critical practice, which historicizes modes of thought by exposing their naturalizing obfuscations."

24. Adorno would in this case be effectively attributing to Dewey a naturalistically horizontalized version of aesthetic autonomy, albeit one certainly more mass-culture friendly than his own. I discuss this last point's implications for a reappraisal not only of the Dewey-Adorno relationship but of how we understand the development of certain tribalized methodological differences in twentieth-century aesthetics in a book in progress, *The Evolution of Autonomy in Aesthetics*.

25. If this was Adorno's thought, it suggests that he would have viewed the intellectual tension between his and Dewey's aesthetics as a basis for what, in *Negative Dialectics*, he called *geistige Erfahrung* ("intellectual experience" or "spiritual experience")—a form of experience that eludes definitive discursive expression and whose recovery is a key challenge for modern philosophy. For further discussion, see Foster (2007).

26. See Jay (2004). For German speakers such as Adorno and Walter Benjamin, the debate about the nature of experience focuses on two words—*Erlebnis* and *Erfahrung*—that

are often indifferently translated with the one English term experience. Although the German terms' connotations sometimes shifted from user to user, *Erlebnis* tended broadly to signify a large spectrum of routinized encounters with the world, whereas *Erfahrung* broadly signified encounters exhibiting elements of phenomenological freshness, awareness of differences between self and object, awareness of the uniqueness of things and situations, and in some contexts also risk and danger. Adorno, like Benjamin and other German critical-theoretic writers, framed many of his deepest criticisms of modern society in terms of how the latter's bureaucratic organization, with its attendant forms of identity-thinking, has a way of extinguishing opportunities for *Erfahrung* in the lives of its inhabitants. I am unaware of any place where Dewey (who read German) commented on these words themselves, but it is, in effect, a variant of the aforementioned distinction that fuels *Art as Experience*'s account of the differences between ordinary experience and "*an* experience." For Dewey, only the latter possesses the consummatory dimension that is a necessary if not sufficient condition for the enlivening and redemptive interactions between people and cultural environments that are aspects of art.

27. Theories that do this would, in effect, be committing yet another higher order version of the reificational error that Dewey called the "fallacy of hypostatization" (see note 7).

28. Actually, the Greek etymology of "theory" encompasses the ideas both of *traveling* (as in the case of a delegation sent by one Greek city to observe and participate in another city's religious festivals) and of *contemplatively observing* (epitomized in post-Pythagorean references to *theoria* as pure intellectual contemplation). Dewey surely knew this history, and we might accordingly interpret his mature vision of intellectual inquiry as a form of guided behavior or practice as a campaign to weaken the second connotation's regulative role within modern conceptions of philosophy while strengthening the first connotation of worldly participation.

29. See Lakoff and Johnson (2003). The authors discuss various conceptual metaphors that are related to the one that concerns us here, as reflected in such familiar locutions as "Life is a journey" or "Love is a journey." Johnson (2007) extends that discussion with an illuminating analysis of "image schemas," which are basically prelinguistic patterns in our multimodal, embodied interactions with the world that then provide material for metaphorical language. One of Johnson's prime examples is the "containment image schema." Here our basic human experiences of literally spatial domains and their boundaries provide myriad possibilities for the linguistic representation of phenomena that are variously associated or dissociated from one another ("His taste is really out there!"; "Count me in!") or that change from one kind of status or context to another ("I'm extending my discussion of Dewey's aesthetics to contemporary theories of cognitive linguistics"). That said, two further aspects of *Art as Experience*'s language invite more discussion than space permits here. First, its central trope of art as something that can be variously conceptualized as a compartment or as something more spatially open is itself also a conceptual metaphor, based on a containment image schema. Second, its argument amounts at this level to a polemic against variations on the image-schematic theme of art or the aesthetic as an autonomous compartment that dominated Idealist aesthetic theorizing from Kant through aesthetic modernism.

30. For a suggestive further discussion of the significance of mapping and journey metaphors for Dewey's larger understanding of the role of inquiry in culture, see Fesmire (2015, 53ff).

31. For further discussion of various parallels between the arguments of *Art as Experience* and *A Common Faith* (especially regarding their respective themes of the "artistic" and "religious" phases of experience), see Haskins (1999).

32. "For all the intelligent activities of men, no matter whether expressed in science, fine arts, or social relationships, have for their task the conversion of causal bonds, relations of succession, into a connection of means-consequence,into meanings. When the task is achieved the result is art: and in art everything is common between means and ends." (1925/29), LW1:277. My description of Dewey as an environmental philosopher echoes another growing genre of "eco-aesthetic" readings of his texts. See in particular Berleant (1997) and Alexander (2013).

Works Cited

Citations of John Dewey's works are to the thirty-seven-volume critical edition published by Southern Illinois University Press under the editorship of Jo Ann Boydston. In-text citations give the original publication date and series abbreviation, followed by volume number and page number. For example: (1934, LW 10:12) is page 12 of *Art as Experience*, which is published as volume 10 of *The Later Works*.

Series abbreviations for *The Collected Works*:

EW *The Early Works* (1882–1898)

MW *The Middle Works* (1899–1924)

LW *The Later Works* (1925–1953)

Adorno, Theodor. *Negative Dialectics*. 1966/1973. Trans. E.B. Ashton. London; Routledge.

Adorno, Theodor. *Aesthetic Theory*. 1970/1998. Trans. Robert Hullot-Kentor. Minneapolis: University of Minnesota Press.

Alexander, Thomas M. 1987. *John Dewey's Theory of Art, Experience and Nature: The Horizons of Feeling*. Albany, NY: SUNY Press.

Alexander, Thomas M. 2013. *The Human Eros: Eco-Ontology and the Aesthetics of Existence*. New York: Fordham University Press.

Berleant, Arnold. 1997. *Living in the Landscape: Toward an Aesthetics of Environment*. Lawrence: University Press of Kansas.

Beardsley, Monroe C. 1982. "Art and Its Cultural Context." In *The Aesthetic Point of View: Selected Essays*, 352–370. Ithaca, NY: Cornell University Press.

Dewey, John. 1925/1929. *Experience and Nature*. LW 1.

Dewey, John. 1929. *The Quest for Certainty*. LW 4.

Dewey, John. 1934a. *A Common Faith*. LW 9.

Dewey, John. 1934b. *Art as Experience*. LW 10.

Dewey, John. 1938. *Logic: The Theory of Inquiry*. LW 12.

Fesmire, Steven. 1999. "The Art of Moral Imagination." In *Dewey Reconfigured: Essays on Deweyan Pragmatism*. Edited by Casey Haskins and David Seiple, 133–150. Albany, NY: SUNY Press.

Fesmire, Steven. 2003. *John Dewey and Moral Imagination: Pragmatism in Ethics*. Bloomington: Indiana University Press.

Fesmire, Steven. 2015. *Dewey*. Abingdon, UK: Routledge.

Foster, Roger. 2007. *Adorno: The Recovery of Experience*. Albany: State University of New York Press.

Haskins, Casey. 1992. "Dewey's Art as Experience: The Tension Between Aesthetics and Aestheticism." *Transactions of the C. S. Peirce Society*, vol. XXVIII, no. 2, 217–259.

Haskins, Casey. 1999. "Dewey's Romanticism." In *Dewey Reconfigured: Essays on Deweyan Pragmatism*. Edited by Casey Haskins and David Seiple, 97–131. Albany, NY: SUNY Press.

Haskins, Casey. 2003. Review of Victor Kestenbaum, *The Grace and Severity of the Ideal: John Dewey and the Transcendent. Transactions of the C. S. Peirce Society*, vol. 29, part 3, 513–519.

Haskins, Casey. 2007. "Beauty." In *American Philosophy: An Encyclopedia*. Edited by John Lachs and Robert Talisse, 70–72. Abingdon-on-Thames, UK: Routledge.

Haskins, Casey. 2011. "Aesthetics as an Intellectual Network." *The Journal of Aesthetics and Art Criticism*, vol. 69, no. 3, 297–308.

Haskins, Casey. 2014. "John Dewey: Survey of Thought." In *Encyclopedia of Aesthetics*, Vol. 2 (2nd ed.). Edited by Michael Kelly, 358–363. Oxford: Oxford University Press.

Horkheimer, Max. 1947/2013. *The Eclipse of Reason*. Eastford, CT: Martino Fine Books.

Horkheimer, Max. 1975. *Critical Theory: Selected Essays*. New York: Continuum.

Jay, Martin. 2004. *Songs of Experience: Variations on a Universal Theme in European and American Philosophy*. Berkeley: University of California Press.

Johnson, Mark. 2007. *The Meaning of the Body: Aesthetics of Human Understanding*. Chicago: University of Chicago Press.

Johnson, Mark. 2015. "The Aesthetics of Embodied Life." In *Aesthetics and the Embodied Mind: Beyond Art Theory and the Cartesian Mind-Body Dichotomy*. Edited by Alfonsina Scarinzi, 23–38. New York: Springer.

Kelly, Michael. 2012. *A Hunger for Aesthetics: Enacting the Demands of Art*. New York: Columbia University Press.

Kestenbaum, Victor. 1977. *The Phenomenological Sense of John Dewey: Habit and Meaning*. London: Humanities Press.

Kestenbaum, Victor. 2002. *The Grace and Severity of the Ideal: John Dewey and the Transcendent*. Chicago: University of Chicago Press.

Kristeller, Paul Oskar. 1952/1980. "The Modern System of the Arts: A Study in the History of Aesthetics." In *Renaissance Thought and the Arts: Collected Essays*, 163–227. Princeton, NJ: Princeton University Press.

Lakoff, George, and Johnson, Mark. 2003. *Metaphors We Live By*. Chicago: University of Chicago Press.

Leddy, Thomas. 2014. *The Extraordinary in the Ordinary: The Aesthetics of Everyday Life*. Peterborough, ON: Broadview Press.

Leddy, Thomas. 2016. "Dewey's Aesthetics." In *Stanford Encyclopedia of Philosophy*. Retrieved from https://plato.stanford.edu/entries/dewey-aesthetics/

Morawski, Stefan. 1978. *Inquiries Into the Fundamentals of Aesthetics*. Cambridge, MA: MIT Press.

Noë, Alva. 2015. *Strange Tools: Art and Human Nature*. New York: Farrar, Straus, and Giroux.

Pepper, Stephen C. 1939/1989. "Some Questions on Dewey's Aesthetics." In *The Philosophy of John Dewey*. Edited by Paul Arthur Schilpp, 369–389. Chicago: Open Court.

Posnock, Ross. 1991. *The Trial of Curiosity: Henry James, William James, and the Challenge of Modernity*. Oxford: Oxford University Press.

Puolakka, Kalle. 2014. "Dewey and Everyday Aesthetics: A New Look." In *Contemporary Aesthetics*. Retrieved from http://contempaesthetics.org/newvolume/pages/article.php?articleID=699

Saito, Yuriko. 2007. *Everyday Experience*. Oxford: Oxford University Press.

Schapiro, Meyer. 2015. Interview. Retrieved from https://thecharnelhouse.org/2015/02/02/the-life-and-works-of-the-marxist-art-historian-meyer-schapiro/

Schilpp, Paul Arthur, ed. 1939/1989. *The Philosophy of John Dewey*. Chicago: Open Court.

Seigfried, Charlene Haddock. 1996. *Pragmatism and Feminism: Reweaving the Social Fabric*. Chicago: University of Chicago Press.

Shiner, Larry. 2001. *The Invention of Art: A Cultural History*. Chicago: University of Chicago Press.

Shusterman, Richard. 1992/2013. *Pragmatist Aesthetics: Living Beauty, Rethinking Art*. Lanham, MD: Rowman & Littlefield.

Shusterman, Richard. 2000. "The End of Aesthetic Experience." In *Performing Live: Aesthetic Alternatives for the Ends of Art*. Ithaca, NY: Cornell University Press.

Smith, Barbara Herrnstein. 2016. "Scientizing the Humanities." *Common Knowledge*, vol. 22, no. 3, 353–372.

Taylor, Paul C. 2016. *Black Is Beautiful: A Philosophy of Black Aesthetics*. Hoboken, NJ: Blackwell.

Tweed, Thomas. 2006. *Crossing and Dwelling: A Theory of Religion*. Cambridge, MA: Harvard University Press.

CHAPTER 22

....

DEWEY, ADORNO, AND THE
PURPOSE OF ART

....

ESPEN HAMMER

UNLIKE much of his other work, John Dewey's aesthetics did not find immediate approval. Soon after the 1934 publication of *Art as Experience* (based on his celebrated 1931 William James Lectures at Harvard University), the influential Italian thinker Benedetto Croce accused Dewey of plagiarism, and for decades it was widely believed to represent a kind of throwback to a bygone, neo-Hegelian mode of thought.[1] Dewey's organicism—his attempt to weave aesthetic experience into the fabric of life (or Spirit, as the Hegelians would say)—struck many commentators as being incapable of acknowledging the apparent consolidation of modern art as an autonomous subdomain of modern culture. As so-called analytic aesthetics started to make an impact in the late 1950s, Dewey's contribution, sometimes formulated in expansive and even speculative terms, was hardly being discussed. However, in the 1970s and 1980s, new interest evolved in Dewey's aesthetics, some of it stimulated by parallel receptions of European thinkers such as Ludwig Wittgenstein, Maurice Merleau-Ponty, and Theodor W. Adorno. Today, Dewey is widely credited for having brought to light a number of issues that recently have been at the forefront of aesthetic debate. Among them are the importance of embodiment for aesthetic experience; a robust challenging of the Kantian idea of disinterested spectatorship; the grounding of aesthetic experience in everyday life; the rediscovery of nature as a source of aesthetic appreciation; the attempt to integrate the faculties of aesthetic experience into a meaningful, self-organizing whole; as well as an emphasis on communication as being essential to art.

One important reason why Dewey's aesthetics has been hard to place and process in the predominantly analytic environment of American aesthetics is its effort to ask not only *what* art is but *why* we have it. While analytic aestheticians have tended to concentrate on the former question, asking for a definition, Dewey focuses decisively on the latter. What are the human interests, he asks, of which works of art, or the experience of them, provide satisfaction?

Dewey, however, is not primarily interested in what it is that *de facto* draws us to art. That would be a psychological or sociological question, answerable in causal or functional terms. Rather, what orients his research is *why we should* (even when we *de facto* take little or no interest, or take an interest for the *wrong* reasons) be interested in art. Like his predecessors Kant, Schiller, and Hegel, he thinks the answer to this question speaks to a fundamental need related to human self-actualization. According to Dewey, art is neither a sensuous stimulus, inviting the ascription of aesthetic predicates, nor a source of insight into how the world happens to be. Nor is it a merely subjective expression, devoid of responsiveness to the world itself.[2] Rather, art offers an emblem of *full, consummatory human experience.* Aesthetic experience provides, or at least anticipates, expressive freedom. As we contemplate aesthetic form, we spontaneously find ourselves in line with the experiential demands posed on us by the world. The subject side and the object side are intertwined, as well as mutually interacting, in such as a way as to allow for experience in its most complete sense.

Although Dewey's idealist precursors have staked out a number of vistas in this terrain, the attempt to relate the aesthetic encounter to the question of experience in general is hardly an easy undertaking. In particular, because it situates aesthetics in the wider dimensions of the everyday and the nonaesthetic, in which he thinks the conditions of experience are less than ideal, the challenges are considerable. In this chapter I discuss how Dewey characterizes and motivates such an undertaking. In particular, I consider Dewey's account in the light of aesthetic modernism, represented by the work of Adorno. While in certain key respects (in particular the dialectical and normative emphasis on the concept of experience) similar to that of Dewey, Adorno's aesthetics opposes that of Dewey in ways that I claim pose serious problems for the latter's view. For Dewey, a successful work of art is supposed to unify all the things that modern life, as he sees it, disastrously tears apart: reason and sensibility, reason and emotion, fact and value, mind and body, freedom and necessity, subject and object, ego and alter, and so on. A work of this kind registers the tragic dimension of modern life while bringing comic resolution and solace. For Adorno, by contrast, a successful work of art insists on the presence of tragic division, diremption, and dissatisfaction in order to open the door to some future and utopian reconciliation. On Adorno's view, the kind of work that would satisfy Dewey's constraints can at best bring false reconciliation and false affirmation. While, according to Adorno, all artistic form is illusory in the sense that it intimates some sort of integral wholeness or unity that cannot be attained under modern conditions, the advanced Adornian work of art (exemplified by Berg, Webern, Beckett, and Kafka) rebels against illusion (and harmonious beauty) for the sake of holding open the possibility of a transcendent state of full integrity.

ART AND EXPERIENCE

The key to Dewey's aesthetics consists in his effort to ground the understanding of art in an account of human experience.

For esthetic experience is experience in its integrity. Had not the term "pure" been so often abused in philosophic literature, had it not been so often employed to suggest that there is something alloyed, impure, in the very nature of experience and to denote something beyond experience, we might say that esthetic experience is pure experience. For it is experience freed from the forces that impede and confuse its development as experience; freed, that is, from factors that subordinate an experience as it is directly had to something beyond itself. To esthetic experience, then, the philosopher must go to understand what experience is.

(1934, LW 10:278)

Aesthetic experience is pure experience. In order to understand what experience is, the philosopher must turn to aesthetic experience. These are strong and at first sight somewhat counterintuitive claims. Would it not be more plausible to think of aesthetic experience as a particular kind of experience, a subset of what human experience is about, rather than a key to experience as such?

A quick glance at what many philosophers, especially in the empiricist tradition, have taken aesthetic experience to involve may seem to suggest that it cannot coherently be presented as a stand-in for experience in general. The available accounts have often been of a psychological or broadly naturalistic nature, such that what it is to experience a work of art, and indeed what art and its purpose might be, becomes a function of the psychological traits that motivate or dispose us to take an interest in art. These traits may include various types of emotion, sentiments, empathy, discernment, or imagination, and to engage with a work of art is to exercise one or more of them such that a causal or functional account can be offered of how the work impacts on the mind. Typically, such views consider art as capable of triggering a particular type of response. We become, say, emotionally engaged, and our experience of the work of art is analyzed in terms of the felt quality of the emotion itself.[3] While some aestheticians take emotions to have a cognitive import, there is in this tradition no disagreement about the fundamentally subjective nature of the relevant experience itself. Whatever cognitive import an emotional state might have, it can at best provide knowledge indirectly, by appealing to inferences drawn by reason. It is *our* psychological makeup that aesthetics interrogates, and to experience art is to entertain the kind of state that causally or functionally corresponds to a particular kind of input (in this case the work of art itself as presented to one's senses). For precisely this reason it seems that any attempt at investigating the nature of experience more broadly with reference to aesthetic experience must fail: In order for mental activity to qualify as an act of experience, it must aim at objectivity. It must be intentional. Aesthetic experience seems too subjective to fit the bill.

While a self-avowed naturalistic empiricist, Dewey was not an empiricist in the traditional sense of seeking to identify inert sensory states to be used as foundational building blocks in an account of experience. He does not offer the kind of causal or functional account I just mentioned. Nor does he analyze aesthetic experience in terms of "the inner" as opposed to "the outer." In *Experience and Nature* (1925, LW 1:25) and elsewhere, he criticizes empiricism for *reducing*, as he puts it, the experienced object to "traits connected with the *act of experiencing*." Thus, in the opening chapter of this work, he ridicules how the empiricist would claim to experience a chair:

> Logically, the chair disappears and is replaced by certain qualities of sense attending the act of vision. There is no longer any object, much less the chair which was bought, that is placed in a room and that is used to sit in, etc. If we ever get back to this total chair, it will not be the chair of direct experience, of use and enjoyment, a thing with its own independent origin, history, and career; it will be only a complex of directly "given" sense qualities as a core, plus a surrounding cluster of other qualities revived imaginatively as "ideas."
>
> (1925, LW 1:25)

Empiricism, at least in its classical guise, is in other words not true to its own project of grounding knowledge in direct experience. Instead it reduces the sensed world to its supposed sensory correlates (the sense qualities together with the "ideas" or inferential structures holding the qualities together so as to make up a meaningful unity), which themselves are analyzed atomistically. The "chair itself" is left out of the picture. The result is that nature becomes "an indifferent, dead mechanism" (1925, LW 1:28). This is not the world we take ourselves to be relating to as agents; thus, for the "veil of ideas" empiricist "the cord that binds experience and nature is cut" (1925, LW 1:29).

> The isolation of traits characteristic of objects known, and then defined as the sole ultimate realities, accounts for the denial to nature of the characters which make things lovable and contemptible, beautiful and ugly, adorable and awful. It accounts for the belief that nature is an indifferent, dead mechanism; it explains why characteristics that are the valuable and valued traits of objects in actual experience are thought to create a fundamentally troublesome philosophical problem.
>
> (1925 LW 1:28)

According to Dewey, empiricism's failure to bring the world properly into view is not just a philosophical failure but a way of thinking that is intimately bound up with our lives as modern agents. While inadequate as a philosophical doctrine, empiricism offers a pretty good picture of how agents in modernity tend to interpret themselves. We are, Dewey thinks, alienated from the world (of experience), locked inside, as it were, a vision of ourselves as agents merely of representation, contemplation, and calculation. Central to the emergence of this self-interpretation is scientism, the interpretation of science as an authoritative guide not only to nature but to experience itself. At stake is an intellectualist vision that is closely aligned not only with empiricism but with a certain kind of Cartesian self-interpretation. Dewey sees such intellectualism as the "great vice of philosophy" (1925 LW 1:28). It is a position in which "all experience is a mode of knowing, and [. . .] all subject-matter, all nature, is, in principle, to be reduced and transformed till it is defined in terms identical with the characteristics presented by re-fined objects of science as such" (1925 LW 1:28). For the intellectualist approach, experi-ential content must satisfy formal constraints associated with scientific method in order to count as evidence.

Unlike leading thinkers in the European tradition such as Husserl, Heidegger, and Adorno, Dewey never works out a detailed genealogy or account of this state of alien-ation. It is clear, though, that he believes it is related to the modern emergence of a sci-entific and intellectualist worldview. The intellectualist asks for the world to be viewed in terms of value-neutral, calculable properties. His or her attention is predominantly directed toward primary rather than secondary or tertiary sense-qualities (indeed the scientific mind precisely distinguishes between these various qualities, assigning merely subjective reality to secondary and tertiary ones), and he or she rigorously seeks to dis-tinguish between reason on the one hand and desire, imagination, and emotion on the other, excluding the latter from any methodological commitments. For the intellectu-alist/scientist mindset, nature—in the way Kant also defined it—is the sum total of eve-rything that exists under causal law.

The human capacity for spontaneity, by contrast, the ability to act and think on the basis of self-chosen principles, becomes questionable; and to the extent that the exist-ence of the creative mind is acknowledged, it is viewed in psychological, empirical, and minimalist terms, involving a disembodied approach to the world.

In his admittedly quite cursory effort to chart the emergence of experiential aliena-tion, Dewey also points to the dominance of procedure over attention to the particular. In modern bureaucracies, for example, agents treat particulars as having a certain value and as qualifying for the ascription of predicates and the attribution of descriptions, insofar as they can be taken to satisfy certain general criteria or fall into particular classes or categories. Under capitalism, Dewey adds, the tendency toward abstraction is exacerbated as exchange value, to use a Marxian terminology, is assigned a priority over use value. What something is as a singular individual, or what its use value as such may be, may be of less importance to the entrepreneur and the investor than its functional (instrumental) or monetary value.[4]

What, then, according to Dewey, would full, consummatory experience look like? We may infer from his criticism of classical empiricism that he seeks to *save the phenomena* as they present themselves in experience. However, in order to do so, it is not enough simply to be in possession of justified beliefs. A belief such as "The cat is on the mat" might be both entertained, true, and justified, yet without anything like completely de-veloped experience correlating to it. While experience, on the other hand, is meant to issue in belief and ultimately be able to settle it, it is in no way reducible to justified be-lief, or belief supported by evidence. We therefore need to search elsewhere for Dewey's outline of normative satisfaction conditions of full, consummatory experience—the conditions, in short, that must be satisfied in order for a given act of experience to count as disclosive of the phenomena as they really, and in the fullest possible sense, present themselves. If any of these conditions are not satisfied, the phenomenon has not been disclosed adequately.

Central to Dewey's pragmatism is that things are discovered primarily *as we act upon them*—treat them, use them, enjoy, and endure them. The world is disclosed to us, and reconfigured, as we do things, rather than in acts of passive experiential intake or contemplation. The chair that was mentioned earlier is not primarily an inert object with properties but a use-object, something we encounter in the act, say, of sitting down. From the engaged point of view, which involves a first-person perspective, the world, moreover, is revealed as laden with *value*. Indeed, to engaged agents values become apparent as being properties of the world and not mere subjective projections. Qua such properties they make demands on us, prompting our engagement with the world in various ways. A person is kind, the sky is sublime, a chair is pleasant to sit on, a building is ugly, the act of forgiving someone is generous, and so forth.

However, value cannot be discerned independently of the *emotions*. Thus, Dewey maintains that the disinterested spectatorship of scientific inquiry should be viewed as an exception to the otherwise emotionally charged responses with which human subjects interact with the environment: "An emotion is implicated in a situation, the issue of which is in suspense and in which the self that is moved in the emotion is vitally concerned. Situations are depressing, threatening, intolerable, triumphant" (1934, LW 10:72). Dewey further motivates this view by claiming that emotions have an intentional structure; the notion of the self-sufficient emotion or affect, complete and felt independently of that to which it relates, makes no phenomenological sense: "an emotion is *to* or *from* or *about* something objective, whether in fact or in idea" (1934, LW 10:72).

In what is clearly an attempt to correct Max Weber's famous picture of the modern world as disenchanted, the notion of consummatory experience reveals for Dewey a world of significance in relation to which creative agents not only have reasons to care based on various types of inference but do immediately care. Prior to reasoning about its significance, a particular situation or event matters in that it has prompted us to view it in a certain light, as calling for a particular type of response.

For such acknowledgment of significance to be possible, however, the agent must also display a capacity for *imagination*. Like Kant and later Husserl, Dewey sees the imagination as fundamentally involved in the kind of attentive engagement with the world that marks full experience. Rather than being a mere capacity for entertaining thoughts and representations without reference, the imagination enlivens, as it were, the perceived object, situating it in a larger context while providing both temporal, spatial, and evaluative depth. Thus, the imagination provides a horizon of possibilities, a background, against which a particular object, event or situation may emerge as a subject of interpretation and reconstruction. In ever-widening interpretive circles of recollection, anticipation, and confirmation, consciousness understands its relation to the world in terms, ultimately, of a sense of unity: the object of experience necessarily belongs to an indefinitely extended totality of meaning. Within this totality, we experience events not discreetly and, as it were, along a linear axis of temporal progression (as though time and space could be held rigorously apart); rather, events reveal rhythms of partly a natural and partly a social nature.

Dewey syncopates his account of experience with a vision of human subjectivity as an active, world-responsive (or intentional) organic unity of body and consciousness, with the latter being an integrated unity of intellect, emotion, desire, impulse, and will. The term "organic," while perhaps connoting a more romantic view than that on offer in Dewey, is meant to indicate the dependence of each of the subject's parts on the functioning of all the other, as well as the unity of all the mutually interacting parts. The behavior of a part can only be made fully intelligible in purposive terms (in relation to its role and function within the organic unity as a whole)—and any mere causal analysis, except in specific cases, is bound to fail. To be a subject is to be a self-organizing system, open to the world yet also absorbed in its presence to one.

Far from being a separate substance, consciousness is thus wholly *embodied*—neither identical with the body (which would entail functionalism or eliminativism) nor distinguishable from it in the sense of not being located and intentionally structured (thereby comporting itself toward the world). Indeed, Dewey's view anticipates positions in current debates over "extended minds" and perhaps even the very recent resurgence of panpsychism. There is no spatiotemporal location for the mind to properly inhabit. To have a mind is to be able to entertain a first-person point of view on the world, one that is active, engaged, and discerning. As Sartre would later argue, consciousness discovers itself in action, in being involved with the world of its various concerns.[5] It is fundamentally a form of activity with no substantive structure or ego-pole.

The final point to be mentioned concerning fully developed experience is that it is *cumulative*. It is not cumulative in a straightforward, linear fashion of the kind entertained in pre-Kuhnian accounts of scientific progress, moving from one falsified hypothesis to the next. Rather, there is a cumulative continuity such that the habits we form in intercourse with the world allow us to retain the meaning of things and events as an integral part of the self. As the agent confronts the new and the strange, he or she inevitably seeks to integrate the experience in a larger, familiar totality of already adopted beliefs, values, and practices. The account of cumulative continuity is central to Dewey's understanding of expressiveness: to be expressive, to carry significance, things and events must be encountered within the framework of an already established mode of inhabiting the world, one that is based on a long-standing interaction between self and its environment. Thus, experience is open to alterity while being prepared to take it up as an element of a larger whole, comprising the self in its ongoing encounters with the world. Ultimately, since it draws on existing concepts, meanings, and practices, the possession and mastery of which require education, such a process refers the individual to his or her community, the intersubjective space in which shared senses of significance and propriety are embodied in traditions, practices, and norms.

In hermeneutic thinking, this idea might be formulated in terms of the hermeneutic circle of moving back and forth between anticipatory horizon (mediated by the past) and actual discovery: those who are already *experienced* (in the everyday sense of the term) will also be better at *experiencing*.[6] If consciousness, as in classical empiricism, were some kind of complex registering and responding device, devoid of the organically structured and expanding horizon of meaning that Dewey associates with cumulative experience, it would not be capable of any genuine acts of individual experience.

I mentioned that Dewey's goal as an aesthetician is to consider art in the light of his account of experience—hence *Art as Experience*, his 1934 study. However, from Dewey's actual formulations of this relation it is not always easy to extract a clear and determinate meaning. Some passages very strongly stress the *continuity* between art and experience.[7] What he calls normal processes of living are recovered or rediscovered in aesthetic experience. At other times—and here I take it that he refers to the human intellect, the capacity for conceptual thinking—he claims that art operates at a level of more *immediate* experience than does everyday life. In yet another set of passages he emphasizes how art *intensifies* everyday experience. He also refers to how, through art, "meanings of objects that are otherwise dumb, inchoate, restricted, and resisted are clarified and concentrated, and not by thought working laboriously upon them, nor by escape into a world of mere sense, but by creation of a new experience" (1934, LW 10:138). "Clarification" and "concentration" may perhaps be helpful notions by which to account for the specificity of aesthetic experience. Yet could it not be argued that scientists must be committed to those principles as well? The right response seems to be that, in the precise sense outlined by Dewey, they could not. Scientists distinguish rigorously between conceptual thinking, which is supposed to be abstract and quantitative, and sense perception, which is supposed to be as noninterpreted and neutral as possible. The idea of the "new experience" seems to indicate, as in Schiller, a different kind of interplay between reason and sense, or perhaps some alternative to the traditional understanding of this interplay.

The notion of there being a qualitative continuity between art and the everyday is surely central to Dewey's project.[8] It is, however, very much at odds with Kantian ideas of art's autonomy.[9] Indeed, Dewey seems to risk having to identify every act of experience as harboring an aesthetic component. Yet if that is the case, then every object is potentially an art-object, and Dewey will be unable to draw a line between art and non-art. Some commentators welcome such a view. Richard Shusterman (2000), for example, thinks that one of the great achievements of Dewey's pragmatist aesthetics is to have decisively broken with the traditional barriers between art and the everyday. Just as scientific rationality may be viewed as founded upon everyday learning processes involving habit, responsiveness to the environment, and openness to incremental revision, so what counts as aesthetic experience depends on the configurations of everyday experience. Note, though, that from premises such as "being dependent upon" or "continuous with," no statement about identity follows. While systematically relating aesthetic experience to the everyday, Dewey does not seek to eviscerate the distinction between the two domains. Rather, his aim, ultimately, is to highlight *both* continuity and difference. Only with the dialectic of continuity and difference in mind can Dewey's attempt to provide an aesthetically oriented critique of experience become intelligible.

Art, according to Dewey, is uniquely valuable precisely in that it provides insight—from the first-person point of view—into what full, consummatory experience involves: "Art is the living and concrete proof that man is capable of restoring consciously, and thus on the plane of meaning, the union of sense, need, impulse and action characteristic of the live creature" (1934, LW 10:31). It is, one might say, a form of second-order experience—an experience of experience. Dewey is not claiming that every encounter with objects to which we are prepared to assign aesthetic value satisfies this ideal. Some works of art may simply leave us indifferent and unengaged. Rather, his fundamental thesis is that aesthetic experience, when at its most intense, discerning, and fulfilling, is all that human experience can possibly be. It is a model of authentic experience.

Normative conceptions of experience have been defended with some frequency throughout the history of philosophy. For the Kant of the *Critique of Pure Reason*, experience is fully developed when culminating in objective judgment (judgment having objective truth-value). However, such objectivity is itself made possible by objectivizing conditions, including space and time considered as a priori forms of intuition and categories considered as a priori normative constraints on thought. Ideas of art as providing a privileged space for modeling the nature of full, consummatory experience can be traced back to Kant's *Critique of the Power of Judgment* and has had a long trajectory from Schelling and the German romantics via Schopenhauer and Nietzsche to Adorno, Heidegger, and Merleau-Ponty. For Dewey the aesthetic realm is supposed to be a sanctuary from the alienating effects of everyday life. However, considered as a sanctuary, and being related to the everyday, it is also meant to provide a critical check on experience, helping us to cultivate practices capable of yielding more fulfilling ways of being in the world. Thus, in addition to being aesthetically pleasing, art serves a pedagogical purpose: it is a means for the development of a more satisfying, authentic form of selfhood. In objects of art, the recipient encounters an expressive language, meaningful yet not reducible to conceptual paraphrase, that invites and encourages more concrete and more integrated interaction with the environment. In the formed matter of which the object of art is composed, the meanings at stake are available only insofar as the imagination and the body are actively engaged. Art thus brings about "a union of necessity and freedom, a harmony of the many and the one, a reconciliation of sensuous and ideal" (1925, LW 1:269–270).

It is not entirely clear *how* art encourages and permits such a reconciliation. Does all art do this? And, if it does, are modern agents generally able to experience art at its most satisfying level? In the next section, turning to the challenge of aesthetic modernism, I explore these critical issues.

ADORNO AND AESTHETIC NEGATIVITY

Dewey may seem to saddle art with a task for which it is not prepared. Is it true that art performs the task of providing a model for a more fulfilling way of being in the world? The question immediately bifurcates into two, equally important, issues. First, is not the experience of genuine art precisely *unreal*, or perhaps even illusory, divorced from the goings on of "real life" (the life, that is, of more formal transactions and objectivizing experience, in short the everyday life of essentially modern agents)? The motivating consideration here is not just that certain of the arts—the novel, for example, or film—call for a distinctive ontological account due to their "fictional," "non-real" nature but that the experience art offers seems indifferent to the demands of everyday life, the life we normally think of as "real." Second, is it true that art in general displays the kind of harmony that Dewey attributes to it? Is it not rather that much art seems to resist the vision of successful integration of the sensuous and ideal, and with that a union, as Dewey puts it, of necessity and freedom, and a harmony of the many and the one?

The first question points to a dilemma for Dewey. The more he stresses the continuity of art and everyday life, the harder it becomes to portray art as taking up a critical stance toward everything existing outside it. On the other hand, the more he stresses the critical dimension of art, the more he needs to view art as autonomous, hence divorced from everyday life, and therefore also potentially "unreal" or "illusory." In general it can be said that Dewey had a remarkably undeveloped sense of art's autonomy, especially in the period he mainly seems to be dealing with, namely modernity. However, for his view of art to make sense, it seems that he needs some sort of account of how art is able to determine itself, direct itself, and make "claims" (in the "language of art") independently of nonartistic spaces of sense-making, action, and interaction.

The second question harbors an empirical dimension. What kind of art is Dewey actually referring to? To be sure, his aesthetics purports to be universally valid. Dewey sets no limits to its purported valid application. Yet quite a lot of art does not fall in line with Dewey's reconciliatory prescriptions and language. This is perhaps most evidently true of modernist art. Indeed, most of the art that Dewey refers to in *Art as Experience* is from the eighteenth and nineteenth centuries. With the exception of Cézanne, Renoir, and Matisse (who, by the way, were favorites of his friend and art collector Alfred C. Barnes), the references cluster around such household classics as Milton, Goethe, Schiller, Tolstoy, Titian, Rembrandt, and Delacroix. Kafka, Joyce, Eliot, Schönberg, and Picasso, artists who radically challenged artistic conventions, and who did so when Dewey was developing his aesthetic ideas, are conspicuously missing.

Adorno, who published on aesthetics from around 1930 until his death in 1969 (his main work in aesthetics, *Aesthetic Theory*, emerged posthumously), agrees with Dewey that the highest task of art, at least in modernity, is to provide a space for the most concrete and fullest form of human experience. Like Dewey, he invokes art in an effort to counter the kind of experience he believes is pervasive in rationalized modernity, including a narrowly instrumental view of things, a reduction of "mattering" to calculable properties (under capitalism, most obviously exchange value), a radical subjectivization of value, a rampant individualism that isolates the individual from wider contexts of meaning, as well as a disengaged, unimaginative, and unemotional attitude toward the world and other human beings. More than Dewey ever did, Adorno places much of the blame for these distortions of experience with how capitalism supposedly transforms the particular into universality, driving out any sense of the significantly concrete individual:

The marrow of experience has been sucked out; there is none, not even that apparently set at a remove from commerce, that has not been gnawed away. At the heart of the economy is a process of concentration and centralization that has the power to absorb what is scattered. It leaves traces of independent existences only for professional statistics and permeates the most subtle spiritual innervations often without its being possible to perceive the mediations.

(Adorno 1997, 31)

Adorno, however, is a lot less sanguine than Dewey about the prospects for a genuine rejuvenation and revitalization of human experience *within* the framework of rationalized modernity.[10] Since, as he claims in this passage from *Aesthetic Theory*, the effects of rationalization, objectivization, and instrumentalization have "repercussions for the most recondite intellectual processes," there can be no "sanctuary," continuous with everyday experience yet able to crystallize or intensify its key, constitutive features, to which agents may turn in order to lead more integrated, full lives. Indeed, Adorno argues that appeals to immediacy, intensity, and meaningfulness (of the kind that one finds in Dewey) stand in danger of misrepresenting the object of experience, which in most cases cannot be isolated from the abstractive tendencies of society as a whole. As long as Dewey is unwilling to grant aesthetic experience some kind of formal autonomy, instead aiming to break down the barrier between fine art and reified experience, his account of aesthetic experience risks being ideological, affirming status quo, rather than critical. Only with regard to art that aspires to formal autonomy (a genuine and total separation from standard contexts of meaning-making), which for Adorno is found in advanced, high modernism—the music of Schönberg, novels by Beckett, and so on—is it possible to conceive of a kind of reconfiguration or normative rethinking of human experience that does not fall into the trap of simply elevating a false particular. (Adorno's criticism is often scathing when it comes to what he sees as pseudo-experience and pseudo-concreteness—types of experience, often promoted by mass media or advertising, originating in manufacturing, manipulating contexts of meaning-making.)

Adorno's account of aesthetic autonomy is complex and fraught with dialectical tensions. He does not believe that art can ever escape society and its integrative logic completely. While a yearning that came to define the development of nineteenth-century bourgeois art (reflecting the more general project of attaining full personal autonomy in a liberal society), any attribution of complete autonomy to cultural artifacts in a commercially driven society would be an illusion. Also, if aesthetic autonomy entails some sort of vision of art as capable of creating a counterrealm of meaning, opposed to the empirical world, then for Adorno this would make art deeply affirmative: it would create the impression of art as a place to go to find solace but not being able to assume a critical stance toward everyday social reality. Adorno does, however, believe that advanced works of art can be understood as *aspiring* to autonomy. Echoing Kant's account of the autonomy of aesthetic judgment, the particular kind of experience they offer cannot be reduced to, or be derived from, other types of experience, including those of knowing, desiring, or rationally determining something. Advanced works of art aspire to autonomy at the level of form. However, form for Adorno is not just, as it is for Dewey, a principle accounting for the mode of art's presentation, the configuration of matter, but it is also, and more importantly, the element of art responsible for creating tension and potential disunity in the work itself. Art needs to aspire to autonomy; if not, it would be absorbed in society and unable to take up a free, critical stance toward it. However, aesthetic autonomy itself is generative of illusion: the illusion, in short, of the work being divorced from the world, to be admired purely for the way it impresses us aesthetically. In modernist art, Adorno sees a progressive unease being displayed with the very achievement of autonomy that the modernist movement had demanded. In the attempt to articulate truth—the truth not of empirically given states of affairs as such, but about the nature of experience itself, the socially determined and sanctioned conditions at stake when agents take a stance toward the world—the formal dimension of art starts to dominate to such an extent that any harmony of the Deweyean kind becomes impossible. In truly sophisticated works of modernist art such as Alban Berg's operas or Picasso's mature paintings, Adorno detects images of what human experience has come to be like. These are works that, in their hyperorganization, make plain to their audiences the pain and dissatisfaction (Adorno often uses the term "dissonance") involved in our everyday, instrumental orientation toward the world: "What the enemies of modern art, with a better instinct than its anxious apologists, call its negativity is the epitome of what established culture has repressed and that toward which art is drawn. In its pleasure in the repressed, art at the same time takes into itself the disaster, the principle of repression, rather than merely protesting hopelessly against it" (Adorno 1997, 19).

Adorno's semiautonomous works of art are not true to reality by depicting or imitating its mode of appearance to us. Insofar as they have what Adorno calls "truth-content," it is because they set up an intuitive tension for us between the universal and the particular, between the rational subject and its other, such that the deformations of experience can become manifest. However, by making those deformations manifest, Adorno thinks they anticipate their overcoming. We can at this point see a stark contrast with Dewey. In Dewey's view, art is a reservoir of meaning. Adorno, by contrast, looks to art that actively rejects meaning—intimating, that is, that there is no meaning—in order better to anticipate true, authentic meaning. For Adorno, the experience of truth content is far from edifying or enjoyable. Rather, it tends more toward a kind of unease or even pain as the reality of untrue or false social practices, including our very ability to experience the world properly and interact with it, becomes apparent.

For Dewey, the aesthetic dimension primarily offers *joy* and *delight*. The voluptuous qualities of his favorite painter Renoir's nudes, he writes, "give delight with no pornographic suggestion" (1934, LW 10:101). "What is expressed is the experience Renoir himself had of the joy of perceiving the world" (1934, LW 10:134). As it did for Schiller, the beauty entertained in the recipient's enjoyable encounters with works of art is supposed to reconcile the ideal and the sensuous, form and matter, allowing the recipient to take pleasure in her own experience of an object:

[Beauty – E. H.] is properly an emotional term, though one denoting a characteristic emotion. In the presence of a landscape, a poem or a picture that lays hold of us with immediate poignancy, we are moved to murmur or to exclaim "How beautiful." The ejaculation is a just tribute to the capacity of the object to arouse admiration that approaches worship. [. . .] In case the term is used in theory to designate the total esthetic quality of an experience, it is surely better to deal with the experience itself and show whence and how the quality proceeds. In that case, beauty is the response to that which to reflection is the consummated movement of matter integrated through its inner relations into a single qualitative whole.

(1934, LW 10:135)

Adorno, on the other hand, thinks of at least modernist art as being more at home in the register of the *sublime*.[11] For him, the experience of sublimity amounts to an intuitive insight into the natural basis of man's existence, that which resists ideality and form. Via the sublime, and hence via the experience of advanced works of modernist art, an act of remembrance is supposed to take place: while unpleasant, we are meant to discover nature as the normally repressed other of reason.

It is to be suspected that the differences between Dewey's and Adorno's aesthetic views come down to more than a disagreement about the purpose of art. Dewey writes about art in the spirit of the reformer, seeking incrementally to correct social ills yet without any desire for radical social change. Adorno locates his thinking about art in an ambitious yet highly pessimistic critique of Western civilization itself. While, for Dewey, modern agents tend be unaware of the true potentials of human experience, Adorno and Horkheimer (1979, 43–80), in their reading of the Homeric epics, consider our understanding of reason's demands to have been distorted and misinterpreted from the very onset of civilization. In "The Influence of Darwin on Philosophy," for example, Dewey (1909 MW 4:3–14) understands reason to have a particular genealogy, intimately tied up with a Darwinian, naturalistic account of the interacting, self-preserving, and self-organizing organism. In agreement with Dewey's naturalistic emphasis yet in sharp disagreement with his Hegelian orientation toward life as a dynamic interplay of interrelated and interdependent elements, Adorno theorizes the formation of subjectivity as wholly predicated on the ability to create distance, opposition, and objectivity via the exercise of formal-instrumental reason. Ultimately, whereas Dewey thinks of social critique as amounting to a reconstitution of the organic relation between people and their environment based on an appeal to intelligent self-reflection, Adorno increasingly loses faith in the progressive potential of much social criticism, believing that reason, in the form of philosophical self-reflection he refers to as negative dialectics, must itself critique the self-distortion that supposedly generates so many social ills. Moreover, Adorno, as we have seen, also assigns to art the task of conducting a critique of reason.

It is often claimed that Dewey's organicism can be traced back to his early interest in Hegel. However, his aesthetics also harbors a Romantic side—a side that becomes particularly evident when compared to Schiller.[12] Like Dewey, Schiller strongly emphasized the need to overcome the Kantian distinction between reason and sensibility, which he argued does not do justice to any of them. Introducing the notion of the play-drive (*Spieltrieb*), Schiller put forward an account of beauty as the unity of reason and sensibility (or form and matter).[13] It is worth highlighting the fact that Herbert Marcuse, a thinker who in many ways was close to Adorno, drew direct inspiration from Schiller in his own thinking about art. Like Dewey he treated art as a model or even sanctuary of full experience, dismissing the concerns about aesthetic autonomy, and therefore also the commitment to high modernism, that informs Adorno's aesthetics. Unlike Schiller, Dewey, and Marcuse, Adorno accepts Kant's differentiation not only of reason and sensuousness but of science, morality, and art as well. His acceptance, however, does not follow from a belief in the essential or necessary (or a priori) difference between them. Adorno's view is that the differentiations are socially and historically real: with the emergence of rationalized modernity, art lost its erstwhile connection to other spheres of human meaning-making (such as science, religion, and morality) and achieved autonomy. Art, Adorno claims, accepted, as it were, that, rather than being continuous with conceptually determinate, instrumentally structured domains of validity such as science or even morality, it operates under a different set of laws, adhering to conditions of adequacy and success that emerge as incommensurable with both ordinary life and other, differentiated expert cultures. The language of art is thus enigmatic and in need of deciphering; rather than aiming at validity in the senses familiar to us from science and morality (acceptability to all rational agents), it aspires to a form of immediate expression that, while addressing the emotions, amounts to a form of distinctive *aesthetic* truth. Dewey thinks that aesthetic insight can directly inform everyday practice. Adorno, however, while asking us to consult advanced works of art for their capacity to interrupt and challenge other forms of experience, sees art as essentially heterogeneous and indefinable, impossible to interpret satisfactorily in conceptual terms.

CONCLUSION

Since the great upheavals of the 1960s art world when, in particular, the high modernism espoused by Clement Greenberg and later Michael Fried gave way to conceptual and postconceptual art practices, conceptions of aesthetic autonomy have not found much favor among critics and theorists of art. On some views, commodification is to blame. There is no space for art outside the imperatives and pressures of the art-market. On other views, the high-low distinction often espoused by autonomy theorists is elitist and incompatible with any critical role for art. Finally, many theorists view the modernist tradition, in its steadfast demand for decisive articulation of medium specificity and cult of aesthetic value for its own sake, as having exhausted itself and become sterile. For serious art to continue after the demise of modernism, it would have to incorporate the vernacular and the everyday and view itself as in the business not of expressing opaque truths via the constellation of aesthetic properties but of communicating meanings and messages with a view to enriching and reflecting upon human experience at large. Ultimately, as Alva Noë puts it in his recent reflection on Dewey, art should be viewed as the consummation of life qua meaning-making, experiential activity:

> Every experience, insofar as it is *an* experience, is integral. It has form and meaning. And it is made. It is achieved. In other words, for Dewey, it is *aesthetic*. Life itself is a meaning-making activity. All experience, insofar as it *is* experience, happens in an aesthetic space. For to be integral, to be integrated, to be organized, is to *be* aesthetic.
>
> Perceiving itself, thinking, wondering, no less than dancing and singing, are aesthetic. For Dewey, to fail to be aesthetic is not to fail to be art; it is to fail to be experience at all.
>
> So in a way it is Dewey's view that we are all artists. For we are all engaged in the making of experiences, in comprehending the form and meaning in the cycles of doing and feeling, of acting and undergoing the consequences of our actions, that organize our lives at the most basic biological life. Life itself is an activity of making experience.
>
> And that is exactly what art is. Art is experience, for Dewey. Artists don't make things. They make experiences.
>
> (Noë 2015, 204–205)

In this chapter I have explored Dewey's reasons for holding such a view of the purpose of art. However, via my references to Adorno, I have also suggested reasons to be skeptical of Dewey's continuity thesis regarding the life/art relation. If art is to inform and, in conformity with both Dewey's and Adorno's perfectionism, critique (everyday) experience, then it needs to do so from a vantage-point other than the typically available ways of meaning-making presented to us as agents in a modern society. I have not been ascribing to Dewey an "end of art" thesis. Yet it is worth pondering that his essentially democratic vision of art may turn out to be at odds with the sense of importance and authority that previous cultures have assigned to art. That said, it may of course also be that the oppositional stance associated with Adorno's conception of aesthetic autonomy is so deliberately "other-worldly" that its capacity to spurn changes in social life necessarily must falter. If that is the case, then perhaps Noë is right after all in identifying Dewey as the aesthetician best capable of articulating the needs of a democratic age.

NOTES

1. See Croce (1948, 203–207, esp. 203), where Croce wonders whether Dewey has "availed himself of some Italian authors" in writing the book. See also the more blatant claim in Croce (1952, 1–6), where Dewey is accused of having "arrived on almost every point at the same conclusions regarding art which had been reached in Italian aesthetics during the past thirty years."

2. For an overview of the general approaches to art available to twentieth-century American aesthetics, see Eldridge (2014).

3. For a particularly elaborate defense of such a view, see Robinson (2005).

4. See Bernstein (2010, 148): "Like the early Marx (and Hegel), Dewey was distressed by the fragmentation and alienation characteristic of so much of modern life. Dewey's vision of the good society is aesthetic insofar as he calls for the type of education and social reform that can enrich experience. See also Westbrook (1991, 401–402), where he claims that *Art and Experience* "was not incidental to the radical politics that absorbed Dewey in the 1930s. Indeed, it was one of the most powerful statements of that politics, for it clearly indicated that his was not a radicalism directed solely to the material well-being of the American people but directed as well to the provision of consummatory experience that could be found only outside the circulation of commodities."

5. See Sartre (1986, 39): "Thus in what we shall call the world of the immediate, which delivers itself to our unreflective consciousness, we do not first appear to ourselves, to be thrown subsequently into enterprises. Our being is immediately 'in situation;' that is, it arises in enterprises and knows itself first in so far as it is reflected in those enterprises."

6. For the standard version of the hermeneutic circle in contemporary debate, see Gadamer (1989, 265–271).

7. Dewey (1934, LW 10:9): "When artistic objects are separated from both conditions of origin and operation in experience, a wall is built around them that renders almost opaque their general significance, with which esthetic theory deals. Art is remitted to a separate realm, where it is cut off from that association with the materials and aims of every other human effort, undergoing, and achievement. A primary task is thus imposed upon one who undertakes to write upon the philosophy of the fine arts. This task is to restore continuity between the refined and intensified forms of experience that are works of art and the everyday events, doings, and sufferings that are universally recognized to constitute experience. Mountain peaks do not float unsupported; they do not even just rest upon the earth. They *are* the earth in one of its manifest operations."

8. For a particularly insightful account of Dewey's continuity-thesis, see Johnson (2007, 209–234).

9. For a later, Greenbergian critique of Dewey on this score, see Kuspit (1968, 96): "For Dewey the formal object of art disappears; its reality is diffused in the process of its natural development. Dewey discusses not the form of the work of art but the form of experience. The formal work of art is no more than a fulfillment of experience; presupposing this, Dewey has no need to account for the art-object, because the end of art is fulfillment in experience, not the production of ad hoc objects."

10. For an illuminating reflection on Dewey from precisely this point of view, see Eldridge (2010, 242–264).

11. See Adorno (1997, 196–197): "The sublime, which Kant reserved exclusively for nature, later became the historical constituent of art itself. The sublime draws the demarcation line between art and what was later called arts and crafts."

12. For a useful discussion of Dewey's relation to Romanticism, see Alexander (1987, ch. 5). I disagree, though, with Alexander's interpretation of romantic expression theory. According to Alexander (who mainly refers to Coleridge and Wordsworth), romantic expression theory operates with a sharp divide between the inner and outer, arguing that a work of art should be viewed as an externalization of inner and subjective emotion. He

rightly understands Dewey to be rejecting such a theory. For him, the emotion cannot be divorced from its vehicle or expression. His reading of Romanticism, however, seems in this regard to be deeply misleading. Neither Coleridge nor Wordsworth (or Novalis or Schelling, for that matter) espouse such an inner/outer division. They persistently claimed that expression unites inner and outer, mind (or freedom) and world.

13. See Schiller (1965, letter 25).

WORKS CITED

Citations of John Dewey's works are to the thirty-seven-volume critical edition published by Southern Illinois University Press under the editorship of Jo Ann Boydston. In-text citations give the original publication date and series abbreviation, followed by volume number and page number. For example: (1934, LW 10:12) is page 12 of *Art as Experience*, which is published as volume 10 of *The Later Works*.

Series abbreviations for *The Collected Works*:

EW *The Early Works* (1882–98)

MW *The Middle Works* (1899–1924)

LW *The Later Works* (1925–53)

Adorno, Theodor W. 1997. *Aesthetic Theory*. Translated by Robert Hullot-Kentor. Minneapolis: University of Minnesota Press.

Adorno, Theodor W., and Max Horkheimer. 1979. *Dialectic of Enlightenment*. Translated by John Cumming. London and New York: Verso.

Alexander, Thomas M. 1987. *John Dewey's Theory of Art, Experience, and Nature: The Horizons of Feeling*. Albany: State University of New York Press.

Bernstein, Richard J. 2010. *The Pragmatic Turn*. Oxford: Polity Press.

Croce, Benedetto. 1948. "On the Aesthetics of Dewey." *Journal of Aesthetics and Art Criticism*, vol. 6, 203–207.

Croce, Benedetto. 1952. "Dewey's Aesthetics and Theory of Knowledge." *Journal of Aesthetics and Art Criticism*, vol. 11, 1–6.

Dewey, John. 1907/1909. *Journal Articles and Book Reviews in the 1907-1909 Period, and The Pragmatic Movement of Contemporary Thought and Moral Principles in Education*. MW 4.

Dewey, John. 1925/1929. *Experience and Nature*. LW 1.

Dewey, John. 1934. *Art as Experience*. LW 10.

Eldridge, Richard. 2010. "Dewey's Aesthetics." In *The Cambridge Companion to Dewey*. Edited by Molly Cochran, 242–264. Cambridge, UK, and New York: Cambridge University Press.

Eldridge, Richard. 2014. *An Introduction to the Philosophy of Art*, 2nd ed. Cambridge, UK, and New York: Cambridge University Press.

Gadamer, Hans-Georg. 1989. *Truth and Method*. Translated by Joel Weinsheimer and Donald G. Marshall. London: Shed & Ward.

Johnson, Mark. 2007. *The Meaning of the Body: Aesthetics of Human Understanding*. Chicago: University of Chicago Press.

Kuspit, Donald B. 1968. "Dewey's Critique of Art for Art's Sake." *Journal of Aesthetics and Art Criticism*, vol. 27, 93–98.

Noë, Alva. 2015. *Strange Tools: Art and Human Nature*. New York: Hill and Wang.

Robinson, Jenefer. 2005. *Deeper than Reason: Emotion and its Role in Literature, Music, and Art*. New York: Oxford University Press.

Sartre, Jean-Paul. 1986. *Being and Nothingness: An Essay on Phenomenological Ontology*. Translated by Hazel E Barnes. London: Methuen.

Schiller, Friedrich. 1965. *On the Aesthetic Education of Man in a Series of Letters*. Translated by Reginald Snell. New York: Frederick Ungar.

Shusterman, Richard. 2000. *Pragmatist Aesthetics: Living Beauty, Rethinking Art*. Lanham, MD, and Oxford: Rowman & Littlefield.

Westbrook, Robert. 1991. *John Dewey and American Democracy*. Ithaca, NY: Cornell University Press.

VIII

INSTRUMENTAL LOGIC, PHILOSOPHY OF TECHNOLOGY, AND THE UNFINISHED PROJECT OF MODERNITY

CHAPTER 23

DEWEY, PRAGMATISM, TECHNOLOGY

LARRY A. HICKMAN

INTRODUCTION

DEWEY identified a central component of his philosophical method as instrumentalism. His vast published work is replete with discussions of tools and machines: technical and technological metaphors are among his favorite narrative devices. Nevertheless, among the twentieth century's philosophical debates about the nature and direction of technology he often appeared an outlier, less interested than was Martin Heidegger or the critical theorists of the Frankfurt School, for example, in advancing a coherent philosophical treatment of technology. He was, and continues to be, better known for his efforts to reform education, philosophy, ethics, democratic institutions, logic, and even religion than for his account of technology.

This situation invites several questions. First, since Dewey's treatment of technology is not concentrated in any one of his publications, is it possible to distill his ideas into a coherent account that is more accessible than the one he left us? Second, in what sense was his project pragmatic? Third, how does his project differ from other twentieth-century approaches?[1] Fourth, how does his project relate to some of the main twenty-first century vectors and debates within the philosophy of technology? Finally, how radical was Dewey's pragmatic account of technology?

DISTILLING DEWEY'S ACCOUNT OF TECHNOLOGY

Dewey understood technology in one of its senses as inquiry into tools and techniques in the same sense in which geology is inquiry into the earth's materials, processes, and structures, and biology is the study of life and living organisms. Although his treatment of technology is widely dispersed and has many facets, the following distillation arguably captures his view in its generality: technology is systematic inquiry into the invention, development, and production of tools and other artifacts (conceptual as well as material) as they are cognitively deployed to raw materials and intermediate stock parts (conceptual as well as material) with a view to the resolution of indeterminate or problematic situations. In its narrow, more abstract form, technology may be said to be inquiry into the tools and methods of such inquiry itself. It may be said to be the *logos* of *technē* (in the general sense of making and doing) (Parry 2014).[2] In its broader form it may be said to be inquiry into the tools, methods, and materials of specific disciplines and practices.

Dewey distinguished these narrow and broad systematic senses of technology from technique as craft in the same sense that he distinguished the experimental science of the seventeenth and following centuries from the empirical or classificatory protoscience of Aristotle, for example. Further, even though Dewey does not use the term "technoscience," which was coined much later to refer to the interdependence between allegedly "pure" science and the instrumentation that has been an essential component of its development, it is clear that he would have been comfortable with the concept. Dewey was clear: in his view, the scientific revolution(s) of the seventeenth century should be identified as revolution in the way that tools and techniques were conceptualized and employed as a result of systematic inquiry.

It may be helpful to think of technology in its more abstract form—inquiry into the tools and techniques of inquiry—as the warp on which the weft of disciplinary inquiries into tools and techniques are woven. Dewey thought that specific disciplinary inquiries into tools and techniques are active in law, historiography, the arts, and religion, for example, as well as in disciplines that are more commonly known as technological. As these practices are woven across the warp of the more technical form of technology as inquiry into inquiry, they contribute their unique colors and textures to the rich textile of cultural life.

Dewey's Account of Technology as Pragmatic

Dewey's view of technology is grounded in his pragmatism. But what form does his pragmatism take? This matter is of particular importance given that several varieties of pragmatism have appeared as a result of its revival of interest during the last decades of the twentieth century and the first decades of the twenty-first.

In one of its senses "pragmatism" refers to a movement within American philosophy that was at its peak during the last decades of the nineteenth century and the first decades of the twentieth century. Speaking generally, the pragmatism of Charles

S. Peirce, William James, and John Dewey was based on the idea that the meaning of a conception lies in its conceivable practical effects. Pragmatism was thus a reaction against essentialism and foundationalism, as well as the idea that the developing norms of knowledge and value are grounded in sources that lie outside of human experience. For Dewey more specifically, this meant that meanings are not representational but fluid and contextual: they emerge within processes of inquiry as a result of the interplay between means and ends that allows them to "breed" new meanings.

His characterization of meaning is implicitly technological: "Meaning, fixed as essence in a term of discourse, may be imaginatively administered and manipulated, experimented with. Just as we overtly manipulate things, making new separations and combinations, thereby introducing things into new contexts and environments, so we bring together logical universals in discourse, where they copulate and breed new meanings" (1925/1929, LW 1:152). Further, knowledge is what has been warranted by prior experimental inquiry and is therefore assertible under relevantly similar future conditions.

In a 1905 letter to A. W. Moore, Dewey complained that the term "pragmatism" had been abused. He objected to its use to refer to his own work except in a very limited sense.

> I have never known a myth grow so rapidly as that of "pragmatism." To read its critics one would think it was a positive system set forth for centuries in hundreds of volumes, & that its critics were the ones engaged in a tentative development of new & undogmatic ideas. But I object root and branch to the term "pragmatism" (except in its origin limited sense)
>
> [...]
>
> Any name can only be one[-]sided, and so it seems a pity to have any. Radical empiricism begs as few as any, tho I should prefer the term experimentalism to empiricism. Philosophy is Functionalism in the sense that it treats only of functions of experience (not of facts, nor of states, ideas, &); it is Geneticism [a]s a mode of analyzing & identifying these functions; it is Instrumentalism as a theory of the significance of the Knowledge-function; it is Experimentalism as a theory of the test of worth of all functions. If I were a German I could stick all these words together and announce a new system. Doubtless. Meanwhile I think there is nothing to do but to peg away at the analyses of particular problems. 1905.01.02 (01827): John Dewey to A. W. Moore

Even though Dewey was willing to apply the term "pragmatism" to his own work solely in its "origin[al] limited sense," his functionalism, geneticism, instrumentalism, and experimentalism are methods that have played a significant role in pragmatism as a school of thought. In what follows, "pragmatism" is used to refer to Dewey's version of those basic ideas.

More specifically, a nonexhaustive characterization of what could arguably be called Dewey's pragmatic method would include a Darwinian, naturalistic *experimentalism* that rejects fixed essences, foundations, and external or a priori impositions from outside of processes of inquiry. Dewey distinguished what is experimental from what is empirical in terms of the intervention of tools: he characterized experiment as "the art of conducting a sequence of observations in which natural conditions are intentionally altered and controlled in ways which will disclose, discover, natural subject-matters which would not otherwise have been noted" (1925/1929, LW 1:339). He viewed experimentation as breaking down "the wall that had been erected between theory and practice" (1925/1929, LW 1:339).

Dewey's *functionalism* is perhaps best understood in terms of the way that the term "functional" relates to the terms "process" and "structure." He notes that "[b]y process is meant the manifestation of energy in a change; by structure the arrangement of energies in a relatively static or enduring form; by function, the consequences that give meaning or significance to processes and structures . . . . Processes refer to the (relatively) dynamic factor; structure to the (relatively) static, and function to the 'ends' maintained and subserved–the phase of use and purpose" (1923, MW 15:247).

It is in this sense that Dewey functionalizes the difference between material and conceptual tools, since it is their function in practice and not their structural features that determine them as instruments.[3] His functionalism also reveals his view of the traditional "problem" of the status of logical objects. In a 1916 lecture at Columbia University, for example, he specifically rejected the idea that logical objects such as numbers and classes are either physical, psychological, or metaphysical. His alternative was that they are among the tools of inference in the same sense in which plows are among the tools of agriculture. He even suggested that his proposal might be applicable to the field of metaphysics, that is, that "those lost souls of philosophical theory which go by the name of essences and subsistences may be just such tools" (1916, MW 10:91–93).

Dewey's pragmatism is *instrumental* in the sense that means are treated as both instruments and as intermediate ends of inquiry. Aims, or what he calls "ends-in-view," are treated both as ends of inquiry and as instrumental for further inquiry. The "laws" of science and nature are treated neither as universal nor particular but as universaliz*able* in the sense of instruments that can be used in appropriately relevant contexts to secure desired ends. It is important to note that even though Dewey's himself referred to his variety of pragmatism as instrumentalism, his instrumentalism was but one of the tools in his philosophical kit and it is quite different from the interpretation that some of his critics have attributed to it.

DEWEY'S MILIEU: MAIN TWENTIETH-CENTURY ACCOUNTS OF TECHNOLOGY

In order to understand how radical Dewey's philosophy of technology was, especially for its time, it may be helpful to contrast it with more or less contemporaneous debates about the nature and function of technology. The late nineteenth and early twentieth century in Dewey's America was what Cicilia Tichi has termed a "gear and girder" age. The professional engineer was presented as an American hero of can-do optimism in more than "one hundred silent movies and in best-selling novels approaching five million copies in sales between 1897 and 1920" (Tichi 1987, 98). In 1928 Americans elected Herbert Hoover, an engineer, as their president. It was the age of Thomas Alva Edison, Alexander Graham Bell, and the Wright brothers—an age of invention and rapid technological change. Dewey was not immune to the excitement and optimism of technological progress; his early work includes references to the telegraph, the telephone, the locomotive, the self-binding reaper, and other modern tools and machines.

Among Dewey's contemporaries there were positivists who argued that the only legitimate approaches to human problems were scientific or technological. On the side of science, they tended to argue that the methods of the sciences are paradigmatic for other areas of experience and that they are value free. On the technological side there were technocrats who promoted the doctrine of the "technological fix." They were positive about the future of technology in two senses. In one sense they bubbled with optimism about technological progress, and in the other they tended to adopt the reductive methods of positivism that often lacked adequate consideration of contexts and consequences. They exuded confidence that the historical momentum of progress was so sure-footed that bold technological projects could be advanced without adequate consideration of environing factors, since whatever problems "technology" created, "it" could also fix.

This was arguably the view of technology adopted by those who planned and implemented the American military engagement in Southeast Asia in the 1960s and 1970s and the invasion of Iraq in 2003. They appeared to believe that if the right tools were employed, even vague ends would take care of themselves. In other words, *their means became their ends*. We shall see that Dewey also held the view that when tools and techniques fail then more, not less, technology is called for. But what he meant by that is far more subtle and complex than what the "technological fix" technocrats had in mind. It is also clear that Dewey rejected the core doctrines of scientism: that the methods of the natural sciences are paradigmatic for all areas of experience, that such methods are value free, and that the conclusions of the natural sciences are universally applicable to all areas of experience. Dewey's characterization of technology is not imperious: he thought that there are vast areas of experience in which technology has no business.

A related twentieth-century approach relied on what the critical theorists rejected as "instrumental rationality" and what Langdon Winner termed "straight line" instrumentalism (Winner 1977, 228). On this view, tools and techniques merely serve as means to independently formulated ends, and their use is justified once a decision is made to secure those ends. In other words, *ends justify means*. This idea also lacks attention to context and consequences. As a method it has led to embarrassing problems such as the radioactive waste at Hanford, Washington, and the melting of the ice packs at the earth's poles. This was also the doctrine of the "scientific" Marxists of the Soviet era, whose continuing legacy includes the radiological and chemical waste dumps in central and eastern Europe and the melt-down at the Chernobyl nuclear reactor.

On the other end of the spectrum there were philosophers—they were primarily European—who responded to technology (or, perhaps better, technological change) with despair or defiance. Neither positive nor positivist, Martin Heidegger's 1927 *Being and Time* built on the phenomenology of Edmund Husserl by making helpful distinctions such as the difference between tools as objects and tools as instrumental (that is, in use), but he went too far for some of his critics during the 1930s when he adopted the "blood and soil" metaphors of the National Socialists. For post–World War II Heidegger, as well as for neo-Heideggerians such as Albert Borgmann, technology has often been portrayed as a source of alienation, failure of authenticity, and forgetting of Being (Heidegger 1976, 1996; Borgmann 1999). Critics of this school, including Peter-Paul Verbeek, have charged Heidegger's project with (a) dogmatic exclusion of alternative approaches; (b) simplistic romanticizing of earlier technological epochs, tools, and techniques, and (c) obscurantist abstractions. Perhaps the most trenchant criticism of the work of the later Heidegger has been that it is backward-looking: that it moves backward from the existence of tools and artifacts to considerations of the conditions for their possibility (Verbeek 2005, 47–95).

Whereas Heidegger offered a dystopian scenario from the political right, the neo-Marxist critical theorists offered a more moderate version of dystopianism. Members of the first generation attempted to construct a social science that would foster emancipation from instrumental rationality, which they identified as the methods of the technosciences. The second generation focused on tools to promote communication and avoid colonization of the lifeworld by technoscientific rationality. Jürgen Habermas, for example, posited a gulf between the technosciences and the enterprises of communicative and emancipatory action, whose job it is to keep instrumental rationality at bay (Hickman 2000). Fellow critical theorist Herbert Marcuse pushed back on this position somewhat by arguing that there might be a postrevolutionary scientific technology (Hickman 2001, 165).

This dystopian umbrella also sheltered Jacques Ellul, whose idiosyncratic blend of Calvin, Heidegger, and Marx advanced the idea that technology has become autonomous in ways that leave little or no room for human agency. Ellul was particularly critical of what he regarded as the effects of "technique" on the mysteries of religion, which he thought essential to human life (Ellul 1964).

Until the last decades of the twentieth century most philosophers of technology failed to see that Dewey had a coherent account of technology because his work did not fit into any of the available categories. Those who did read his work tended to identify his instrumentalism with instrumental rationality as characterized by the critical theorists, or worse, as providing support for the worst practices of American business. But during the last decades of the twentieth century, as we shall see, some important accounts of technology began to move in the direction of the position he had taken since the early days of the twentieth century.

KNOWING AS A MODE OF TECHNOLOGY

In a book-length typescript that Dewey thought lost but was recovered, edited, and published by Phllip Deen in 2012, Dewey characterized knowing as a mode of technology which has two phases.

> The view that, philosophically speaking, knowledge is one form, a central form, of technology does not mean that its subject matter and products are specifically similar to technologies exhibited in production of commonalities and services in the electrical industry or in transportation or application of bio-chemistry in agriculture. It means that knowledge is, first, a form of technology in the methods it employs in producing more knowledge and improving its own methods, and, furthermore, is *capable* of being a technology in human social guidance of technologies now called such but whose human and social consequences are left a matter of pulling and hauling of conflicting customs and institutions which are hardly touched by effective use of the method of intelligence at work. What I called the first affair constitutes the philosophical problem of knowledge in its narrower sense. The second matter defines the philosophical problem of knowledge in its wider human and moral sense.
>
> (Dewey 2012, 244)

In Dewey's characterization, one of the phases of knowing as a form of technology involves knowledge producing more knowledge in ways that are systematic and self-corrective. This form of technology, although inspired by the family of technoscientific methods that have developed since the seventeenth century, is not identical with the methods of the sciences and engineering since it both involves inquiry into the tools of inquiry itself and is informed by inquiry in nonscientific fields, such as law. Moreover, it *can be* at work in any field, including the plastic and visual arts, or even religion, in which there is systematic inquiry into the materials, tools, and techniques of a particular discipline. In the second phase, knowledge is technology as an art in its "wider human and moral sense" of tools of inquiry used and developed. Dewey's implicit argument is that when tools and techniques are inadequate or fail, then more technology—more systematic knowledge-getting—is called for. As such, his analysis rejects the dystopian views previously discussed (Hickman 1990).

Technology is thus in Dewey's view neither a thing, nor an organization, nor a system. In contrast to Heidegger and some neo-Heideggerians, technology is not a source of alienation, failure of authenticity, or forgetting of Being. A fruitful account of technology does not move backward from the existence of tools and artifacts to considerations of the conditions for their possibility but forward in ways that engage human concerns.

In contrast to the critical theorists, technology does not rely on instrumental rationality as a method. Technology is instead instrumental in the sense, already described, that means are treated as both instruments and as intermediate ends of inquiry. Aims, or what he calls "ends-in-view," are treated both as ends of inquiry and as instrumental for further inquiry. More specifically, in contrast to Habermas, Dewey recognizes no chasm between technology and efforts to improve communication within and across boundaries, nor is technology an impediment to emancipation from bad decisions with respect to tools, methods, and artifacts. Technology in Dewey's sense provides the tools for enhanced communication and for emancipation from the dead weight of custom and tradition. In contrast to Jacques Ellul, technology is not a system, and it is certainly not autonomous.

Put somewhat differently, technology is in one of its senses an evolving set of methods for getting new knowledge, which is in turn a way of managing the tools of means/ends relationships. This is the sense in which Dewey could say that science is a type of art, or technology, thus reversing that relationship as it is generally characterized. Since this point has often been misunderstood, it should be emphasized that Dewey drew an important distinction between the various arts (as opposed to art in its more general sense) and the sciences. He finds that the various arts *express* meanings, whereas the sciences *state* meanings. The arts express materials, whereas the sciences pursue a maximal substitutivity of variables (1934, LW 10:90). It was never Dewey's aim to "rub out" the distinction between the arts and the sciences, as at least one of his interpreters has suggested (Rorty 1982, 51).

The second aspect of technology referred to in the preceding quotation refers to inquiry within fields that we more commonly refer to as "technologies" but also include the humanities and the various arts, among other disciplines. Because technology in its narrow, more technical sense involves inquiry into the tools and methods of inquiry itself, in the best of circumstances it can serve as a guide to the more specific inquiries within these technological fields at the same time that it is also informed by the tools and techniques proper to their various projects.

But if technology in the technical sense is said to involve inquiry into the tools and methods of inquiry that are used to pursue aims, or ends-in-view, does that not commit Dewey to the idea that technology is by definition good? It does indeed, but not in the sense that the positivists had in mind. Because of his identification of technology in its narrow, technical sense with inquiry into tools and techniques of inquiry, Dewey thought that the cure for technical failure was more technology. He was positive about the development of new tools and artifacts, but he embraced neither the ill-considered "technological fix" projects of the technocrats nor their unsustainable ideas about means/ends relations. He took into account the contextual features of inquiry into tools and techniques by means of careful attention to the details of means/ends relationships.

Dewey's characterization of technology in *What I Believe* reflects this commitment as well as providing an example of his pragmatic method at work. He wrote that "'[t]echnology' signifies all the intelligent techniques by which the energies of nature and man are directed and used in satisfaction of human needs; it cannot be limited to a few outer and comparatively mechanical forms. In the face of its possibilities, the traditional conception of experience is obsolete" (1930, LW 5:270).

By "intelligent techniques" Dewey means those techniques that have been experimentally vetted (and thus that have functioned as ends-in-view) and that are therefore warranted in future inquiries in their role as means or instruments with respect to the production of new ends-in- view. How are such techniques vetted? They are regarded as functional aspects of problematic situations. As functions they are analyzed in genetic terms, identifying them, supplementing them, and locating them in a wider context. And as instruments they are examined in terms of their potential for generating wider significance. As already indicated, technology in Dewey's sense is not a thing, or an organization, or a system. Technology is thus a way of producing new knowledge—both in terms of inquiry into methods of such production and in terms of the production of new knowledge within specific disciplines in ways that expand the "wider human and moral sense."

To put this somewhat differently, Dewey thus stakes out his position between the extremes of undisciplined optimism on one side and dogmatic pessimism on the other. His view is *genetic*: he accepts the use of tools and techniques as a key feature of the historic development of human beings as within and a part of nature. His view is *critical*: technology is intelligent because it involves inquiry into methods for making tools and techniques more intelligent. Because technology is inquiry involving tools and techniques, that process can no more be bad or evil than biology as inquiry into forms of life is bad or evil.

Tools and techniques can of course be employed in ways that are unintelligent, just as theories of biological development (such as social Darwinism) can be unintelligent because diverted to narrow interests. Perhaps most important, Dewey rejects the idea that "technology is indifferent to the uses to which it is put." He argues that "[a]s long as that statement remains as true as it is at present time, it signifies that something else is sure to decide the uses to which it is put—traditions and customs, rules of business and of law—which exist now because they came into existence in the past, superficially sugared over by moralistic condemnations and exhortations" (Dewey 2012, 244).

Dewey thus argues that the tools and techniques that properly serve human beings will emerge not from traditions, rules, ideologies, or party loyalty but from the very processes by which those traditions, rules, and ideologies are subjected to inquiry in the service of continual reconstruction with a view to social good. That argument is articulated and enlarged in his 1939 identification of democracy and education as experimental, that is, as a technological project. A careful reading of his remarks reveals why, on his view, neither technology nor democracy can be exported. Tools and techniques may be exported, but systematic inquiry into their use cannot. Inquiry is always grounded in context.

[D]emocracy is belief in the ability of human experience to generate the aims and methods by which further experience will grow in ordered richness. Every other form of moral and social faith rests upon the idea that experience must be subjected at some point or other to some form of external control; to some "authority" alleged to exist outside the processes of experience. Democracy is the faith that the process of experience is more important than any special result attained, so that special results achieved are of ultimate value only as they are used to enrich and order the ongoing process. Since the process of experience is capable of being educative, faith in democracy is all one with faith in experience and education. All ends and values that are cut off from the ongoing process become arrests, fixations. They strive to fixate what has been gained instead of using it to open the road and point the way to new and better experiences.

(1939, LW 14:229)

Dewey's Pragmatic Technology in the Context of Recent and Continuing Vectors in the Philosophy of Technology

After 1990, Don Ihde incorporated elements of Dewey's pragmatic treatment philosophy of technology into his own position, which he named "postphenomenology" (Ihde 1993). Ihde articulated a descriptive type of phenomenology that turns away from foundationalism of phenomenology's earlier versions in order to focus on the complex issues of human/world mediation. His work has been especially rich and productive in the area of imaging technology. Like Dewey, he holds that mediation is richly perspectival. Like Dewey, he rejects the idea that tools are neutral, arguing instead that they are multivalent. Like Dewey, he stresses embodiment relations (although Ihde's treatment is much better developed) (Ihde 2002). Like Dewey, he functionalizes subject and object as aspects of a relational context. Like Dewey, he emphasizes and explores the interplay between means and ends. From the standpoint of Dewey's pragmatism, however, as Paul Durbin and Carl Mitcham have pointed out, there remains the challenge "to consider in what ways Ihde's phenomenology might be a basis for societal, political, and technological reform" (Mitcham 2006, 31).

Mitcham is correct that Dewey's project of identifying technology with inquiry into tools and techniques has broader social, political, and educational application than can be found in Ihde's project, even given its many important insights. What this means is that, for Dewey, wherever there are tools and techniques, whether they are material or conceptual, whether they are used in engineering, in journalism, or in jurisprudence, for example, there are general patterns of inquiry that are both applicable to those fields and in turn informed by them. In contrast to what Heidegger's critics have characterized as his retrograde project, Dewey's project looks forward. He called for experimental inquiry into what things do now and how they can be improved so that undesirable or problematic situations can be ameliorated, especially in their social and environmental implications.

Dutch philosopher Peter-Paul Verbeek, who has been influenced by Ihde, has argued that it is now time to "bracket" Heidegger's work on technology (Verbeek 2005). He notes that there has been an "empirical" turn in the philosophy of technology that has pivoted away from concern with *Dasein* toward consideration of what things do. This move attracted a new generation of analytic philosophers who "bracketed" the efforts of earlier analytic efforts to map out what they regarded as the distinctions between science and technology. This new generation was interested in what engineers do, for example, as well as other problems touching on the relations between technology and society.

The empirical turn encouraged the more muscular phenomenological account of the relations between humans and their tools and artifacts that we find in Ihde's postphenomenology. Like Durbin and Mitcham, however, Verbeek is concerned that what may have been lost in this approach was the larger picture. Focus on the details of actual technological practices tended to obscure the larger normative context.

This led to another turn—an "ethical" turn that fostered specific enterprises such as environmental ethics, the ethics of food biotechnology, engineering and architectural design ethics, animal ethics, and so on.[4] But there was a tendency in some of these fields to ignore or neglect what Verbeek called "the interwoven character of technology and morality." He therefore called for a third "turn"—an "ethics of accompanying technology" that would combine the best of both empirical and ethical turns. His list of areas of theory and practice that could be impacted by such a turn included ethics, philosophical anthropology, political philosophy, and even metaphysics (Verbeek 2010).

This is more or less what Dewey had been calling for from the early decades of the twentieth century. He claimed that all inquiry is ethical at the very least in the sense that it is concerned with choices about what should be done. It is social in the sense that decisions about tools and techniques have consequences for the manner in which socialization occurs. Such decisions are therefore closely connected with educational technology. The production of successful outcomes involves inquiry into the often competing claims of goods, rights, and virtues; if they are to be intelligent, there is no a priori way of knowing in advance what tools will be required for such deliberations. They are always open ended. This is no less true in the arts than in the technosciences. Given Dewey's naturalism, together with his rejection of the traditional body/mind and material/conceptual splits, he was able to argue that intelligence in ethics is of the same type that invents the telephone (1891, EW 3:95). He thus rejected the idea of "nonnatural" moral concepts that have been advanced by philosophers such as Derek Parfit (Parfit 2011). The norms of ethics are constructed and reconstructed just as are other technical tools and artifacts.

Andrew Feenberg, who was trained in the methods and outlooks of critical theory, has proposed a similar turn—a turn away from some of that school's earlier tenets and toward positions that are similar to those that Dewey articulated in the early and mid-decades of the twentieth century. Feenberg has rejected the notion of technology as ideology and has replaced an essentialist understanding of technology with one that is functional. He has emphasized the role of networks and compromise as a part of technical decision-making. He has moved toward a version of social constructivism. All of these positions were components of Dewey's pragmatic treatment of technology (Feenberg 1999, 2010; Hickman 2007, 79–91).

There are also components of Dewey-type pragmatism in the work of Bruno Latour's sociological approach to technology. First, Latour's functionalist notion that the meanings of objects lie in their traces is similar to Dewey's functionalist view that objects are objectives. Second, in both views the meanings of objects are contextual. Third, whereas Dewey argued that a tool can function as an object in one context and an instrument in another, Latour describes situations in which objects as "completely silent intermediaries become full-blown mediators" (Latour 1993, 81). Fourth, both Latour and Dewey object to reifying organizations: they are treated instead as functions. They are the ways in which the actors that constitute them are organized and reorganized around a shifting set of common ideas and they are the ways in which they affect other organizations, or what Dewey called "publics."

There is, however, an interesting divergence in their interpretations of modernity. For Latour, "we have never been modern" means that the nature/culture split that was a part of the project of modernity was never fully accepted in practice and that, furthermore, that it has lost favor as the technosciences have advanced. Although Dewey does not use the phrase, he comes very close, arguing that we have never been modern in a different sense. As he put the matter to Christine Chisholm Frost in a 1941 letter, "many of the fundamental ideas of the old [Medieval] synthesis were not discarded but were carried over into the systems that attempt new philosophical formulations, and thereby has prevented the development of a synthesis which actually corresponds to the vital conditions and forces of the present" (1941.01.23 [13074]: John Dewey to Christine Chisholm Frost).

In other words, the reason we have never been modern is not that we never really accepted the nature/culture split of modernity, as Latour suggests but that the modernist project was hamstrung from the outset because it failed to engage and reconstruct the Medieval synthesis. It was content with its substance/accident metaphysics, its mind/body split, and its quest for certainty. Worse, the premodern synthesis continues to block progress in areas of social interaction such as education, democracy, and even the technosciences.

Although a detailed discussion Dewey's pragmatism as it relates to trends in the sociology of science and technology is outside the scope of this essay, it is worth noting that Andrew Pickering's work embraces a nonrepresentational agenda similar to Dewey's. Moreover, his "mangle" is reminiscent of Dewey's experimental, or denotative, method, and he views machines as multivalent (Pickering 1995).

A brief mention of Weib Bijker also seems relevant. His work was a part of the project known as social construction of technology (SCOT). His response to the "technological determinism" debates of the late twentieth century was to argue that human action shapes technology. He initially left aside the question of the extent to which technology shapes society. As a result of later research, however, he suggested that even such factors as "technological obduracy" are also socially constructed, and his emphasis shifted from "social" to "construction." Just as Dewey did, SCOT took up ethical and even political issues associated with technology (Bijker 2009, 88–94).

Dewey's approach to ends/means relations and his broad characterization of technology emphasized social construction of technology, to be sure, but the ways in which tools shape social choices was also important to him. His treatment of ends/means relations, which has already been discussed, is relevant in this connection. Also relevant is the argument in his 1896 essay "The Reflex Arc in Psychology," which might be paraphrased as follows: human beings live in a dynamic relation with their environment, including their tools, which both shapes them and is shaped by them. In problematic situations interest and context aid selection of aspects of the environment, such as tools, whose use then produces new meanings that condition further behavior, including new interests and potentially novel types of tools use (1896, EW 5:96–109).

Recent work by a quasi-critic of Dewey's account of technology suggests a rich vein of new scholarship. Drawing on the work of Roland Barth, for example, Andrew Wells Garnar has argued that a Deweyan "philosophy of technology can be brought together with postmodern philosophy in order to make sense of what is distinctive about contemporary 'postmodern' technology" (Garnar 2012, 232).

Finally, it should be noted that not everyone is convinced of movements within the philosophy of technology that have been described here as reflecting some of the central components of Dewey's project. Zwier, Blok, and Lemmens (2016), for example, have questioned the very basis of the empirical turn (specifically, Ihde's postphenomenological project). They argue that it conceals a theoretical approach to technology that Heidegger termed "Enframing." They call for a turn against what has been described here as the functional component of Dewey's project in order to reconsider what Verbeek dismissed as the: classical period of the philosophy of technology. They call for a "rehabilitation of the ontological dimension in the philosophy of technology."

CONCLUSION

Some of the recent accounts of technology presented here have moved in the direction that Dewey occupied already in the early decades of the twentieth century. But it is arguable that Dewey's pragmatic treatment of technology remains more radical in some respects than those alternative accounts that have been presented in this essay. This situation suggests new vectors in Dewey scholarship. First, Dewey's concept of technology transcends and provides a context not only for those disciplines normally called "technologies" but for other disciplines as well, such as the arts and religion. Beyond that, his concept of technology probes deeply into the methods of philosophy, treating logical objects such as classes as tools and providing a place for a critique of the tools and methods of inquiry in its technical sense.

His view suggests a path to overcoming the constraints of premodern concepts that continue to create a drag on human progress. Dewey argues that there is a cultural lag even within philosophy because of failures to appropriate the tools and methods that have been developed as a part of technological progress. By this he does not mean only advances in computing technology or medical technology, for example, but also advances across a broad spectrum of cultural disciplines and practices, including logic and religion. Nevertheless, he does not arrogate to philosophy the solution of the problems that have been the result of failure to analyze and reconstruct failed concepts and practices, since that is the work of "all elements of society working together" (Dewey 2012, 284). But he does think that philosophy can have a positive result insofar as it is able to clean up some of the mess it has created. Among other things, this would mean rejecting the idea that theory is the highest form of knowledge. He argues that theory should be regarded as a type of practice.

Dewey's pragmatic concept of technology is radical in a literal sense: it goes to the root of the problem that he is addressing. It involves a call to reconstruct received ways of thinking about our cultural practices. It is a call for experimentalism to supplant received dogma, for a recognition of the fact that structural constructs are aspects of processes and can often be expressed in terms of functions, for an organic holism to replace mind/body and material/conceptual splits, and for greater attention to the demands of both continuity and context and means/ends relationships. It was in this vein that Dewey called for religious institutions to become more relevant to the needs of their adherents by periodically reconstructing their tools and techniques and for the reform of logic in the sense that propositions should no longer be understood as truth-bearing units of meaning but as rather as proposals, valid or invalid, relevant or irrelevant with respect to particular sequences of inquiry.

Finally, Dewey's pragmatic concept of technology is radical in the sense that doubt is baked into his project. Far from being a barrier to technological progress, doubt is featured as a key element in its successes. Without uncertainty there is no motivation for reconstruction and innovation either of technology in its narrow technical sense, or in the sense in which technology is at work in disciplinary methods, or in the sense in which it is the *sine qua non* of the reconstruction of cultural practices more broadly.

NOTES

1. In what follows the terms "twentieth century" and "twenty-first century" will be employed somewhat loosely. Heidegger and Ellul, for example, provide accounts of technology that are associated with the twentieth century. In terms of his remarks on technology, Habermas is also treated as a part of the twentieth century. On the other hand, although Ihde's appropriation of some of the key elements of pragmatism dates from about 1990, he is here associated with the twenty-first century because of his continuing influence in the field.
2. This is an excellent article on the various Greek senses of *technē* from Xenophon to Plotinus.

3. Dewey illustrates his analysis with a helpful metaphor. "Process may be compared to the energy of a stream (itself constituted of an immense number of unit-processes), and structure to the banks, the bed, etc. Function may be compared with the consequences or uses to which the stream is put, irrigation, milling, etc." (MW 15:247).

4. There is a great deal of important work being done in these fields by individuals who have been influenced by Dewey's pragmatism. Although there are too many to mention in this brief note, a partial list includes the work of Erin McKenna on animal ethics, Paul Thompson on food biotechnology, Andrew Light and Bryan Norton on environmental ethics, Steven A. Moore on architectural design, Tibor Solymosi and Mark Johnson on cognitive science, and David Hansen, Leonard Waks, and Jim Garrison on education. This list is far from exhaustive.

WORKS CITED

Citations of John Dewey's works are to the thirty-seven-volume critical edition published by Southern Illinois University Press under the editorship of Jo Ann Boydston. In-text citations give the original publication date and series abbreviation, followed by volume number and page number. For example: (1934, LW 10:12 is page 12 of *Art as Experience*, which is published as volume 10 of *The Later Works*.

Series abbreviations for *The Collected Works*:

EW The Early Works (1882–98)

MW The Middle Works (1899–1924)

LW The Later Works (1925–53)

Citations of Dewey's correspondence are to *The Correspondence of John Dewey, 1871–2007*, published by the InteLex Corporation under the editorship of Larry A. Hickman. Citations give the date, reference number for the letter, and author followed by recipient. For example: 1973.02.13 (22053): Herbert W. Schneider to H. S. Thayer.

Bijker, Weibe E. 2009. "Social Construction of Technology." In *A Companion to the Philosophy of Technology*. Edited by Jan Kyrre Berg Olsen, Stig Andur Pedersen, and Vincent F. Hendricks, 88–94. Malden, MA: Wiley-Blackwell.

Borgmann, Albert. 1999. *Holding on to Reality*. Chicago: University of Chicago Press.

Dewey, John. 1891. "Moral Theory and Practice" (EW 3:93–109). Carbondale and Edwardsville: Southern Illinois University Press.

Dewey, John. 1896. "The Reflex Arc Concept in Psychology" (EW 5: 96–109). Carbondale and Edwardsville: Southern Illinois University Press.

Dewey, John. 1916. "Logical Objects" (MW 10:89–97). Carbondale and Edwardsville: Southern Illinois University Press.

Dewey, John. 1923. *Syllabus: Social Institutions and the Study of Morals* (MW 15: 229–272). Carbondale and Edwardsville: Southern Illinois University Press.

Dewey, John. 1925/1929. *Experience and Nature* (LW 1). Carbondale and Edwardsville: Southern Illinois University Press.

Dewey, John. 1930. "What I Believe" (LW 5:268–278). Carbondale and Edwardsville: Southern Illinois University Press.

Dewey, John. 1934. *Art as Experience* (LW 10). Carbondale and Edwardsville: Southern Illinois University Press.

Dewey, John. 1939. "Creative Democracy—The Task Before Us" (LW 14:224–240). Carbondale and Edwardsville: Southern Illinois University Press.

Dewey, John. 2012. *Unmodern Philosophy and Modern Philosophy*. Edited by Phillip Deen. Carbondale and Edwardsville: Southern Illinois University Press, 2012.

Ellul, Jacques. 1964. *The Technological Society*. New York: Vintage Books.

Feenberg, Andrew. 1999. *Questioning Technology*. London and New York: Routledge.

Feenberg, Andrew. 2010. *Between Reason and Experience*. Cambridge, MA, MIT Press.

Garnar, Andrew Wells. 2012. "Hickman, Technology, and the Postmodern Condition." *Techné*, vol. 16, no. 3, 231–251.

Heidegger, Martin. 1976. "Only a God Can Save Us: *Der Spiegel's* Interview with Martin Heidegger." *Philosophy Today*, vol. 20, no. 4, 267–284.

Heidegger, Martin. 1996. *Being and Time*. Translated by Joan Stambaugh. Albany, NY: SUNY Press.

Hickman, Larry. 1990. *John Dewey's Pragmatic Technology*. Bloomington: Indiana University Press.

Hickman, Larry. 2000. "Habermas's Unresolved Dualism: *Zweckrationalität as Idée Fixe.*" In *Perspectives on Habermas*. Edited by Lewis Edwin Hahn, 501–513. Chicago and La Salle, IL: Open Court.

Hickman, Larry. 2001. *Philosophical Tools for Technological Culture*. Bloomington: Indiana University Press.

Hickman, Larry. 2007. *Pragmatism as Post-Postmodernism*. New York: Fordham University Press.

Ihde, Don. 1993. *Postphenomenology: Essays in the Postmodern Context*. Evanston, IL: Northwestern University Press.

Ihde, Don. 2002. *Bodies in Technology*. Minneapolis: Minnesota University Press.

Latour, Bruno. 1993. *We Have Never Been Modern*. Cambridge, MA: Harvard University Press.

Mitcham, Carl. 2006. "From Phenomenology to Pragmatism: Using Technology as an Instrument." In *Postphenomenology: A Critical Companion to Ihde*. Edited by Evan Selinger. Albany, NY: SUNY Press.

Parfit, Derek. 2011. *On What Matters*. Oxford: Oxford University Press.

Parry, Richard. 2014. "Episteme and Techne." In *The Stanford Encyclopedia of Philosophy*. Edited by Edward N. Zalta. http://plato.stanford.edu/archives/fall2014/entries/episteme-techne/

Pickering, Andrew. 1995. *The Mangle of Practice: Time, Agency, and Science*. Chicago: University of Chicago Press.

Rorty, Richard. 1982. *The Consequences of Pragmatism*. Minneapolis: University of Minnesota Press.

Tichi, Cecelia. 1987. *Shifting Gears: Technology, Literature, Culture in Modernist America*. Chapel Hill: University of North Carolina Press.

Verbeek, Peter-Paul. 2005. *What Things Do*. University Park: Pennsylvania State University Press.

Peter-Paul Verbeek. 2010. "Accompanying Technology: Philosophy of Technology after the Ethical Turn." *Techné*, vol. 14, no. 1, 49–54.

Winner, Langdon. 1977. *Autonomous Technology*. Cambridge, MA: MIT Press.

Zwier, Jochem, Vincent Blok, and Peiter Lemmens. 2016. "Phenomenology and the Empirical Turn: A Phenomenological Analysis of Postphenomenology." *Philosophy and Technology*, vol. 29, 313–333.

CHAPTER 24

....

DEWEY'S CHICAGO-
FUNCTIONALIST
CONCEPTION OF LOGIC

....

F. THOMAS BURKE

INTRODUCTION

....

LITTLE will seem familiar to most contemporary logicians who might browse through
the pages of Dewey's 1938 *Logic*. Dewey's ideas will seem outdated and naïve (Nagel 1986;
Suppes 1969a; Russell 1939). Yet, such assessments will be laden with presuppositions
regarding what *normal* mathematical logic is—presuppositions that are now practically universal, reflecting confidence in many cumulative achievements throughout the
twentieth century. These presuppositions prevent a fair assessment of Dewey's views on
what logic is. We will elucidate Dewey's approach to logic here by relating its origins and
development to various milestones in the history of contemporary mathematical logic.
We may get a better sense of what Dewey was doing by mapping it onto what we already
understand.

Dewey's approach to logic is to contemporary approaches to logic what a functionalist approach to psychology was to a structuralist approach to psychology circa 1895.
Dewey's functionalist approach to logic renders deductive inference in terms of its
functional role in inquiry. Contemporary logic has yet to outgrow structuralist biases
as originated in Frege's and Russell's logicism. But these two approaches are not irrecon-
cilable. The real story here is not one of "Dewey versus the logicians" but rather one of
functionalist logic versus structuralist logic.

Dewey developed his conception of logic at the same time that Russell and others
were establishing the mathematical and philosophical credentials of contemporary
symbolic logic. Dewey's take on the subject was shaped well before formal first-order
deduction systems became a designated landmark in the philosophical landscape.
From the 1890s onward, Dewey cut a trail into the frontier of logic that more commonly

came to be approached by other routes that more quickly led to fertile ground. Looking back, it seems that those taking more travelled roads have nicely mapped and settled that frontier even if there may be patches of wilderness that still warrant exploration. Where in this domain might Dewey's lightly traveled trail have led? It may have led to interesting places, but it may also have entered the domain of logic in only shallow and glancing ways.

Yet, what if the frontier of logic were more extensive than what is now familiar territory? This is what Dewey was advocating (Nagel 1986) though he did not put it that way given that what is familiar territory today was still largely an unfamiliar frontier that did not yet provide reliable reference points in Dewey's day. What is now familiar to contemporary logicians is in fact only part of what Dewey regarded as the domain of logic.

Dewey's conception of logic did not originate entirely with Dewey. Peirce had outlined a similar view in 1877–78, presenting the logic of science as a normative study that includes a survey of three different kinds of inference—abductive, deductive, inductive—along with a discussion of how they complement one another in scientific inquiry. Dewey's trail in fact coincides with portions of Peirce's trail (acknowledged in the preface of Dewey's 1938 *Logic*) even if Dewey's trajectory was ultimately different. Nagel (1986, xi–xii) points out that, besides Peirce, others preceded Dewey in characterizing logic as a theory of inquiry, citing Aristotle, Descartes, Arnauld, Mill, Bosanquet, Lotze, and Sigwart. Contrasts with these earlier thinkers are not where we should begin to best understand Dewey's approach to logic. We begin instead by contrasting it with Bertrand Russell's approach.

Dewey's and Russell's approaches to the study of logic are similar in that their respective mature conceptions of logic emerged as reactions to nineteenth-century idealism. Dewey's turn away from Hegel had begun by 1893. Russell's embrace of British idealism was just beginning in 1893, though his revolt against it was done by 1898. Their respective anti-idealist efforts had achieved escape velocity by 1903—exhibited in Russell's *Principles of Mathematics* and in Dewey's *Studies in Logical Theory*—though their anti-Hegelian trajectories were different.

RUSSELL'S ANTI-HEGELIAN TURN

In 1893 Russell was awarded a first-class BA in mathematics at Trinity College, Cambridge. Under the influence of contemporaries at Cambridge and elsewhere (Bradley, Bosanquet, McTaggart, Ward, Stout, and others), Russell's dalliance with British neo-Hegelianism spanned roughly the years from 1893 to 1898. Russell's 1897 dissertation was a neo-Hegelian treatment of the foundations of post-Kantian geometry. But his attempts from 1896 to 1898 to apply the same approach to foundations of post-Kantian physics went nowhere as he began to comprehend that physics cannot be an a priori science in the way that geometry was alleged to be (Garciadiego 1991, 51–61). Russell came to realize that the doctrine of internal relations, while indispensable to neo-Hegelian idealism, stood in the way of synthesizing the foundations of physics from the antinomies of geometry. In effect, the antinomies began to outpace efforts at synthesis (Garciadiego 1991, 60). Apparently, one could only try in vain to extend neo-Hegelian methods beyond what might have been made of geometry in the first place (Griffin 1988, 34).

Such efforts were among Russell's earliest attempts to carry out his so-called Tiergarten Programme—a plan to produce "a comprehensively Hegelian dialectic of the sciences, complete with dialectical supersessions and culminating in a metaphysical science of the Absolute Spirit" (Griffin 1988, 19). A dialectical account of a priori foundations of physics was supposed to succeed that of geometry, while a dialectical account of arithmetic was supposed to precede it. But in 1896 Russell studied Cantor's 1883 work in set theory while reviewing two books that had cited Cantor. Though Russell rejected the notion of transfinite numbers, he was exposed to non-idealist work in the foundations of arithmetic. In 1897 Whitehead suggested to Russell that he read not just neo-Hegelians but Hegel's own works on logic. Russell concluded that Hegel's views of arithmetic were "ignorant and stupid," as Whitehead probably expected (Garciadiego 1991, 62–64). Meanwhile, Russell's growing discomfort with neo-Kantian psychologistic aspects of his own investigations of arithmetic together with the impasse presented by physics and the doctrine of internal relations led to a blanket rejection of idealism. By 1898 he was able to turn his attention to the foundations of arithmetic without idealist spectacles. If there were still "deposits" of idealism in Russell's thinking in 1898, they were dismissed by the end of the year (Carey 2016; Griffin 1984).

Russell instead came to favor a modernesque empiricist epistemology sporting a commonsense realist metaphysics, buttressing an increasing interest in mathematical logic as a general-purpose analytical tool in philosophy. His discussion in 1903 of what is now known as "Russell's paradox" generated considerable interest in set theory and symbolic logic. The publication of *Principia Mathematica* with Whitehead (1910–1913) provided footing for subsequent developments in the mathematical study of deduction. This propelled the use of related methods of formal-linguistic analysis in philosophy. If we can define the word 'the' in terms of the words 'all' and 'some', then maybe the sky is the limit? Russell's (1905) "On Denoting" and Moore's (1919) "Internal and External Relations" are prototypical examples of how to do philosophy in this formal-analytic vein—using first-order formalisms (though vaguely formulated) to reveal ambiguities in what various philosophical theses say.

DEWEY'S ANTI-HEGELIAN TURN

We review more of Russell's story later. Meanwhile, how did Dewey's story begin, and where did his anti-idealism take him as far as logic is concerned? Dewey viewed logic as more than a mathematical study of deduction. It was a normative study that subsumed and integrated all three kinds of inference that Peirce had identified.

Why was Dewey disposed to see it this way? It was due more to Hegel's influence than to Peirce's. Dewey backed away from Hegel more carefully than did Russell. Hegel did not leave less of a deposit on Russell's thinking than on Dewey's, but Dewey (1930) held onto what he thought valuable in Hegel's views while avoiding old pre-Kantian philosophical battlegrounds which by then had become wastelands. For example, debates in which the doctrine of internal relations makes sense (affirmed or denied) are artificial so far as Dewey was concerned. To ricochet from absolute holism to absolute atomism would achieve nothing, as if those two poles exhausted all options. Dewey saw this. Russell qua logical atomist had to learn it the hard way.

Dewey's Hegelianism was initially fostered during his two years of graduate study at Johns Hopkins under the influence of George S. Morris. Dewey (1930) later noted that Morris's Hegelianism was tinged by "his early Scotch philosophical training in a commonsense belief in the existence of the external world." Morris apparently "had no difficulty in uniting Aristotelianism with Hegelianism." Morris's Hegelianism was not British neo-Hegelianism. A confluence of events in the 1890s moved Dewey not to reject this influence but to naturalize it "into functional, organic, evolutionary, and bio-psycho-social equivalents of thought and action, intellect and practice" (Johnston 2014, 71).

Menand (2001, 299–330) asserts that Dewey's turn away from Hegel was affected by several factors including at least (a) his reading and teaching of James's *Principles of Psychology* (1890), (b) pivotal conversations with Jane Addams (Menand 2001, 312–315), and (c) some empirical psychological work of two colleagues at Chicago (Angell and Moore 1896). Other influences on Dewey's thought at this time include the advance of evolutionary theory in the nineteenth century, an increasing emphasis on the relevance of scientific methodology in philosophy, Dewey's long-term collaborations with George Herbert Mead and James Tufts, and his growing appreciation of Peirce's conception of inquiry. But the three crucial influences that Menand highlights deserve attention.

When eighty years old, Dewey stated that James's two-volume *Principles of Psychology* was the one greatest influence in the development of his thought—the greatest but not the only influence; not that he did not disagree with some of it but that it greatly influenced him. It awakened Dewey from a dogmatic slumber, so to speak, and continued (along with James's later radical empiricism) to shape his thinking (Schilpp 1939). "The impact of James's *Principles* was revolutionary in showing that the idealist's proffered solution of a 'synthetic power' as a unifying condition of experience was simply not needed because experience didn't require 'synthesis' to begin with" (Alexander 2008, 565). Dewey's correspondence in 1893 (CJD, vol. 1) shows his coming around to the view that "the self as *activity*" is a dynamic integration of social, psychological, biological, and ecological transactions and, while just as *real*, is not reducible to any one such party to the process. We can also sense his dismissive attitude toward unfettered metaphysics, pre-Kantian or otherwise. Still, this alone does not indicate how an inversion of Hegel's dialectic fits into Dewey's emerging conception of human experience.

Jane Addams's influence on Dewey here was pivotal. In a letter to his wife Alice (CJD vol. 1: 1894, 00206) after contemplating "an argument" with Addams concerning strikers' use of force during the 1894 Pullman strike in Chicago, Dewey wrote: "I can sense that I have always been interpreting the dialectic wrong end up—the unity as the reconciliation of opposites, instead of the opposites as the unity in its growth" (Hickman 2008, 574). Addams (Nobel laureate, 1931) had insisted that such conflict was never justified, whether or not it aligned with Hegel's dynamic of conflict and resolution in human history. Dewey was slow to admit missteps, but his Hegelian footing in this case proved to be unsure.

The cumulative result by 1894 was that Dewey turned Hegel's dialectic upside down and inside out, and revised it in ways that became unrecognizable as "Hegelian." An inversion of Hegel's pattern of human history became Dewey's pattern of individual growth and development. It became for Dewey the pattern of inquiry, of habit formation, of learning—even of particular experiences. It became the generic pattern of any dynamic episode of achievement in regard to which we may meaningfully speak of something as having a "functional role."

Chicago Functionalism

Tangible evidence of this shift can be seen in Dewey's founding of the "Laboratory School" in 1896 as a way to test, develop, elaborate, and apply his new view of experience, the emphasis being on learning not as an effort to *achieve unity* but as an effort to cultivate growth of the *innate unity* of the student qua experiencer. The goal of schooling in this view was not just acquisition of knowledge but more so the cultivation of intelligence—that is, the cultivation of capacities to grow in knowledge in efficient, effective, and fruitful ways. This notion of intelligence ultimately became Dewey's generalized version of Peirce's conception of science as presented in "Illustrations." Dewey's view of the best methods of intelligence coincide with Peirce's view of the best ways of fixing belief, namely, scientific methods broadly conceived. A propensity to use those "best methods" was for Dewey what schooling should aim to impart to students such that the growth of knowledge would more likely take care of itself over the course of a lifetime. The Laboratory School was designed to elaborate and test this claim.

The experimental and interpretive work of James Angell and Addison Moore at Chicago in 1895 pushed such ideas in psychological and epistemological directions. Angell and Moore proceeded in 1895 to replicate reaction-time experiments conducted by Ludwig Lange in Wilhelm Wundt's laboratory a few years earlier (Lange 1888; Carleton 1982; Backe 2001). In Lange's experiments, subjects in one group were to focus on an anticipated sensory stimulus (sensing a flash of light and then pressing a button) while subjects in another group were to focus on a designated mode of muscular response (pressing a button when prompted by a flash of light). Reaction times were thus of two types: S times for subjects anticipating a stimulus and R times for subjects anticipating a response. After many initial trials to familiarize subjects with the experimental setup, reaction times were then recorded. Only later times were regarded as meaningful. It was found that R times were typically shorter (with less variance) than S times. Citing Wundt's (1874) five-stage account of the "reflex arc," Lange conjectured that anticipation of stimuli affects the causal linkage between stimulus and response in different ways than does anticipation of responses. Basically, the data was explained by the hypothesis that R reactions "pass through much less grey matter" than do S reactions where the latter would more likely add drag (and variability) to causal stages involving perception ("entry into the *field* of consciousness") and apperception ("entry into the *focus* of consciousness").

Meanwhile similar experiments elsewhere were yielding different results, either with faster S reactions or with no significant difference between S times and R times (Breitwieser 1911). This undermined Lange's reliance on Wundt's particular depiction of a reflex arc. Dewey had no sympathy for Wundtian interpretations of the data, and the opportunity to explain Lange's results in alternative ways presented an opportunity to clarify Dewey's emerging post-Hegelian conception of experience. On this view, Lange's experiments were exhibiting a process of habit formation (growth and development, the pattern of learning—the pattern of human history writ small, characterizing even the most mundane human experiences).

Angell's and Moore's experiments were similar to Lange's, though they recorded both early and late reaction times. Lange recorded reaction times as useful data only after the subject was amply practiced and sufficiently trained so as to be familiar with the experimental setup. Angell and Moore tracked reaction times in such sequences of trials from start to finish insofar as *the training process* was the object of interest. They aimed to test the idea that differences in S and R reaction times depended on whether or not the coordination between motor-responses and sensory-stimuli were habitual. It was expected that early reaction times would reflect a relative absence of coordination and thus be longer than later more coordinated reaction times. With enough training, either type of reaction time, S or R, might be shorter than the other. Angell and Moore found this to be the case.

In effect, Lange's retrospective interpretation of his data in terms of a generic five-stage Wundtian reflex arc scheme (sensation → perception → apperception → volition → action) was suspect. Angell and Moore replaced it with a view emphasizing a process of training and coordination—a process that was evidenced throughout the course of the trials and that was invisible when looking only at later trials. The experimental trials from start to finish traced out a pattern of coordination (learning, habit formation, growth, development) but in different ways geared respectively to the subject's initial focus.

The upshot was that experiments performed by Wundt and others were based on a misconception of animal experience. Dewey's reflections on this were published in his 1896 "Reflex Arc" paper, arguing that the "New Psychology" of Wundt and his students had not yet shed various debilitating presuppositions of eighteenth-century epistemology. This paper also exhibited Dewey's measured move away from Hegel insofar as Dewey's depiction of the general pattern of a "unit of behavior" reflected a scaled-down inverted version of Hegel's pattern of human history. It was, again, the pattern of learning, of habit formation, of growth—a pattern of particular dynamic processes with respect to which a notion of "functional role" makes sense.

The explanation proposed by Dewey and the "Chicago School" entailed that the distinction between sensory inputs and motor outputs should not be identified with the distinction between *stimuli* and *responses*. This required a fundamental terminological shift. Positively, an animal's *living* is a dynamic whole—a unified manifold of "doings and undergoings"—which may be dissected, analyzed, and resolved into various constituent units (within units, parts within parts) which share a common pattern. This basic "unit of behavior" is to be identified with a process of habituation (learning, coordination) in which, first, relatively discordant sensory inputs and motor outputs constitute a *stimulus* (as presented in Lange's early experimental trials) and where, second, a *response* is a learned (evolved, educated, habituated) coordination of such inputs and outputs—a formation of routine modes of behavior in which respective inputs and outputs are reliably coordinated (as achieved in Lange's later experimental trials). Each of Lange's experimental trials initiated a particular input/output "arc" that could be timed, but these times were officially recorded only for later trials. The actual *stimulus* for the experimental subject was the presentation of an unfamiliar experimental setup as a whole—an unfamiliar setting calling for certain input/output interactions. The respective *response* was the subject's learned (routinized, habituated, coordinated) ability to function well (or as well as it's worth) in those circumstances. The respective unit of behavior here is thus not just a sensory input nor a motor output nor even a linear mechanistic arc-like causal linkage from the former to the latter. It is rather an *episode* of nondeterministic resolution (of habituation, of learning, of fixation) in which discordant manners of input/output interactions are eventually coordinated. This pattern traces not a one-dimensional causal *arc* but rather the unfolding of an episode of growth of an uncoordinated manifold of such arc-like sense/act interactions into one that is coordinated. With various qualifications, this schematic pattern was cast by Dewey as the pattern of inquiry (1938), the pattern of particular experiences (Dewey 1934), the pattern of individual growth and learning (Dewey 1933; Dalton and Bergenn 1996), the episodic pattern of evolution (Dewey 1910, 1922)—all of which are recognizable versions of Hegel's pattern of human history scaled down to commonsense proportions.

STRUCTURALIST VERSUS FUNCTIONALIST LOGIC

When Russell's Hegelian spectacles fell away, he was already in the midst of investigating the foundations of arithmetic and questioning his earlier studies of geometry. He proceeded to manipulate and utilize compound spectacles with interchangeable lenses already introduced by Frege, Dedekind, Cantor, and others (in support of his mathematical logicism), by Platonist realism (positing the reality of universals independent of mind and language), by British empiricism (to shore up logical atomism), by rationalism (such that knowledge independent of experience is possible), and by other kinds of off-the-shelf eyewear.

When Dewey's Hegelian spectacles fell away, he instead began to see things through spectacles of a post-Hegelian pro-Darwinian design. These spectacles disclosed Hegel's pattern of human history in even the most mundane episodes of ordinary life and experience. Hegel's absolute (dialectical) idealism was a brand of metaphysics—positing a dynamic cosmological actualization of the identity of mind and reality, thought and being. Dewey's inversion of this view was not a brand of metaphysics. It was a kind of phenomenology—a normative phenomenology of inquiry, so to speak—based on scientific studies of human nature. It was aimed not at salvaging details of pre-Kantian epistemology but at answering to the revolutionary impact of Darwinism and a growing emphasis on the use of science-like methods in philosophy. Structuralist psychology was one of his earliest targets (1896), and educational methodology was one of the earliest domains in which he made positive attempts to explore, apply, and test the new spectacles (EW 5, MW 1).

Russell's anti-Hegelian fallback maneuvers reflected a structuralist approach to logic. Dewey's anti-Hegelian flanking maneuvers reflected a functionalist approach. At issue here is the meaning of the word 'logic'. Dewey's functionalist conception of logic is different from contemporary conceptions precisely because it is functionalist—not that functionalism and structuralism are mutually exclusive, though Dewey's conception of logic is and was broader than usual.

Current views of mathematical and philosophical logic are built around a study of deductive inference. It is no coincidence that deductive inference is the one kind of inference that is amenable to structuralist methods. Logicians today assume that logical inference is nothing other than deductive inference (Woods et al. 2002). To study logic is to study deductive inference. To teach an academic logic course today is to teach propositional and first-order grammars and respective deduction systems. Libraries of logic texts from around the world show this to be a fact. This reflects why it is argued that there is no "logic" of induction (Popper 1959; Putnam 1963). The latter would reduce induction to deduction, which is absurd. Inductive (statistical) inference is not deductive inference. It is a principled kind of inference with correctness standards that nevertheless do not guarantee the truth of conclusions drawn from true premises. It does not pass muster as deductive inference, so there is no "logic" of induction.

In contrast, logic for Dewey is built around a study of three kinds of inference—deductive, inductive, abductive—structurally in themselves but also functionally in regard to how they work independently and together in the course of inquiry. We thus find Dewey referring to logic as a study of inquiry, not just a study of deduction. Just as there is a logic of deduction, there is a logic of induction and a logic of abduction, though these are three different logics, or three aspects of logic as such.

A BRIEF HISTORY
OF STRUCTURALIST DEDUCTIONISM

A review of some historical twists and turns will help to clarify this contrast. To understand the trajectory of mainstream twentieth-century philosophical logic, we need to understand Russell's post-Hegelian trajectory. This requires that we understand the trajectory of mathematics from the nineteenth century into the twentieth century—a trajectory that Russell did not originate but which he translated into a jargon and method that became influential in twentieth-century philosophy. Philosophers are not typically good mathematicians, and vice versa. Nevertheless, due to Russell's mediation, logic and philosophy in the twentieth century were impacted by mathematical developments in the nineteenth century. The linguistic turn that took place in philosophy was driven largely by such a turn that took place in mathematics almost a century earlier.

Mathematics in the nineteenth century advanced on several fronts (geometry, analysis, algebra) in reaction to discoveries of non-Euclidean geometries, of discrepancies in the notions of continuity versus differentiability, of nonnumerical and noncommutative algebras. Increasing emphasis on argumentative rigor emerged in light of the confluence of these advances. Rightly or wrongly, mathematical rigor was understood to be deductive rigor—attainable by cleaning up the language of mathematics, eliminating ambiguities and insisting on clear and thorough statements of all assumptions (definitions of primitive concepts, formulations of axioms, enunciation of permissible deduction rules). These aims were presented in Pasch's *Lectures on Modern* (projective) *Geometry* (Pasch 1882) and later in Hilbert's *Foundations of* (Euclidean) *Geometry* (Hilbert 1899). By the end of the nineteenth century, mathematical language and its style of argumentation aspired to be entirely *verbal*. Diagrams and motions were cast as nonessential heuristic aids lying outside of the language and logic of mathematical analysis and geometry. Verbal rigor in turn required some kind of verbal regimentation.

By 1899 Russell was immersed in these developments, and he was clearly up to speed by 1903. Russell's impact on philosophy at large came by way of his efforts to press on with Frege's attempt to ground arithmetic in "logic"—even after finding the same "antinomy" in Frege's (1884) *Grundgesetze der Arithmetik* that Zermelo had uncovered in Cantor's "naïve set theory" a year earlier. Russell was drawn to this project because in many respects it mirrored the Tiergarten Programme sans dialectical negativism. "Logic" was to serve as the foundation for mathematics by way of arithmetic; and these in turn were foundational for physics and science at large insofar as the language of science called for precision and clarity. Presumably, this project should extend in a fairly straightforward way to philosophy, assuming that analytical clarity and argumentative rigor were of prime importance in philosophy. The upshot was that quantificational predicate grammars yielded standards of expressive clarity and deductive rigor against which the language and conduct of science and philosophy were to be measured.

Subsequent developments of this approach to philosophy did not pan out. Russell mounted a formidable effort throughout the first decade of the twentieth century, yielding his first-order quantificational treatment of definite descriptions (Russell 1905) and the three-volume *Principia Mathematica* (Russell and Whitehead 1910–1913). Progress thereafter did not stop so much as it roared ahead in ways that Russell had not envisaged. In particular, the early Wittgenstein (1921) was inadvertently spoiling things from within, leading in his *Tractatus* to the notion that legitimate philosophical discourse should be contained wholly within the purview of (infinitary) propositional deductive logic while at the same time establishing that such pure deduction from scratch could offer nothing beyond trivialities so far as deducible truths go. That is, pure deductive inference could not reach outside of itself to ground anything so substantive as arithmetic. So much for logicism.

This knocked Russell off his horse. Yet members of the Vienna Circle (along with sympathizers from the Berlin Society, the Lvov-Warsaw School, and others) were surging ahead at this point, pondering the substance and methodological potentials of the *Tractatus*. The resulting swath of thought was something like the following. Logic and mathematics are purely formal, consisting only of referentially empty tautologies. The latter are not meaningless, but they do not exhaust the domain of meaningful statements. A "verifiability criterion of meaningfulness" is also allowed. Namely, a statement is meaningful just in case it or its negation is tautological *or else* its truth or falsity is (perhaps indirectly if not inconclusively) verifiable in principle. There are thus just two kinds of meaningful statements: those that are analytically (necessarily) true or false (a priori) and those that are synthetic (contingent) and whose truth or falsity is purportedly verifiable (a posteriori). This composite criterion threatened entire disciplines built around contingent statements whose truth or falsity is not subject even in principle to empirical verification ("murder is wrong," "there is no first cause," "Elvis is handsome," "God is love"). So far as legitimate philosophy goes, ethics, metaphysics, aesthetics, and theology should be ostracized because, by this criterion, they rest on grounds that are ultimately meaningless. The alleged problem is that we trick ourselves into talking nonsense in these latter enterprises because of sloppy background grammars and semantics. The obvious solution is to clean up our language (to better avoid playing grammatical tricks on ourselves) and to be resolutely disciplined empiricists when it comes to putting semantic meat on the formal bones of grammar.

This program was dubbed "logical positivism" by Feigl and Blumberg in 1931 and later, more moderately, as "logical empiricism" (Feigl 1943). In contrast with Hegelian "dialectical negativism," it pictured science as a single unified edifice of contingent facts and natural laws (encompassing physical, psychological, and social subject matters) that were to be progressively discovered and systemized by way of proper use of something like the hypothetico-deductive method—namely, (a) welcoming hypotheses whatever their sources may be but then (b) subjecting them to thorough analysis at least so far as to deduce consequences that could be empirically tested and then (c) performing such empirical tests. Deductive "logic" was in fact the linchpin of this program, whether labeled as positivist or empiricist.

Notably, logical empiricism assumed this shape only retrospectively in the 1940s and 1950s. Logical empiricism was otherwise a marginal and inchoate moving target throughout the same period in which Dewey was working out a different conception of logic and science. Before we return to explicating Dewey's conception of logic, we review several currents in the development of twentieth-century analytic philosophy insofar as these supply standards against which Dewey's or anyone else's conception of logic are now measured.

Formal-linguistic efforts to realize logicist and logical empiricist ideals quickly stalled in the face of significant headwinds. In the 1930s, Wittgenstein's rejection of his own *Tractatus* was a major influence in this regard. So-called ordinary language philosophy emerged in the late 1940s and 1950s at Oxford (initiated by Austin, Ryle, Strawson, and others) in reaction against the notion that formal-linguistic methods provide overriding standards of clarity in philosophical analysis. Russell's first-order account of definite descriptions was in fact *not* being successfully extended, while Strawson and others argued that that account was misleading from the start. It was claimed that the study of philosophical concepts might be better served by careful examination of the use of respective terminology in ordinary discourse. A paradigmatic example is Anscombe's 1957 book *Intention*. This work bucked both formal-linguistic and logical-empiricist trends, first, by its style of conceptual analysis via studies of how the term 'intention' and its cognates are used in ordinary discourse and, second, by pioneering an analytic approach to *ethics* by means of this conceptual analysis and because of its relevance to the philosophy of action.

At the same time, a sober and measured study of mathematical deduction persisted throughout the 1930s and 1940s on several fronts with key results achieved by a number of mathematicians and logicians. For instance, the Löwenheim-Skolem theorem and the respective Skolem paradox had been established by Skolem (1920) by way of generalizing an earlier result by Löwenheim (1915). Hilbert (1928) and Hilbert and Ackerman (1928) introduced an explicit theory of deduction for first-order languages, essentially baptizing *metalogic* (and proof theory in particular) as an area of mathematical study by highlighting the central importance of notions like deductive consistency, provability, completeness, decidability. On such grounds, Gödel's (1930, 1931) famous (in)completeness theorems undermined Hilbert's formalist program by driving a wedge between deductive logic and arithmetic, establishing in effect that there can be no complete axiomatic ground for mathematics. Church (1936, 1941) and Turing (1937, 1938) independently explicated notions of computability (λ-computability, Turing computability), which allowed them to prove the undecidability of Hilbert's "decision problem," serving to elucidate the limited scope of deductive logic per se versus mathematics proper. Meanwhile, Tarski (1933, 1936a, 1936b, 1944) essentially created model theory (versus proof theory) by showing how to do for formal first-order languages what early Wittgenstein had done for formal propositional languages, namely, providing recursive semantic definitions of "truth" and "consequence" for all but atomic sentences in such a language. First-order models provided for Tarski what truth tables provided for early Wittgenstein.

This far-from-exhaustive list of key developments in the mathematics of deduction in the first half of the twentieth century is not random but fails by itself to reflect the size of the army of mathematicians (also including Post, Fränkel, Schönfinkel, von Neumann, Bernays, Herbrand, Weyl, Gentzen, Kleene, and many others) who helped to discover and explore such results throughout the 1930s and 1940s. Ordinary language philosophy may have been blunting the force of formal-linguistic trends in some philosophical circles, but the study of formal deduction continued to flourish among mathematicians.

The impact of ordinary language philosophy thus should not be ignored nor should it be overemphasized. In the late 1940s and early 1950s, Quine (1947, 1953, 1956) voiced misgivings about the coherence of (pre-Kripkean) "modal logic." He accentuated Church's 1936 anti-formalist undecidability result "that there can be no generally applicable test of contradictoriness" (Quine 1948), and he convincingly argued that logical-positivist versions of the analytic/synthetic distinction are unworkable (Quine 1951). The latter essentially eviscerated logical positivism. Yet all such critiques by Quine were aimed not at undermining the use of formal-linguistic and/or empiricist methods in philosophy and science but, rather, at reconceptualizing those methods in more meaningful ways. Namely, the study of first-order deductive inference requires no prior metaphysical commitments, but first-order languages provide formal templates for clarifying ontological commitments inherent in various ways of speaking. In short, the study of first-order deductive inference constitutes a kind of meta-metaphysics. Quine promoted a formal-methodological first-order nominalism such that asserting the existence of certain entities (photons, leprechauns, Napoleons, Dr. Watsons) requires ways of speaking in which such entities are regarded as "particulars"—ways of speaking such that to *be* is to be the possible value of a first-order variable, no more and no less. In one sense, numbers may be regarded as universals but not as existent entities (e.g., at the farmers' market where so many bunches of beets or pounds of snow peas cost so many dollars) while, in another sense, numbers may be regarded as particulars and thus as existent entities (as in Peano arithmetic, or in elementary school where one is memorizing the single-digit times table). Where Russell tried to ground first-order analysis once and for all in atomistic terms, Quine (following Carnap and Duhem) cast it more flexibly in holistic terms. On Quine's (1951) view, "our statements about the external world face the tribunal of sense experience not individually but only as a corporate body." First-order deductive analysis might isolate and explicate any aspect of the fabric of science at whatever level of analysis may seem appropriate, so long as it measures up to the prescriptions of first-order deductive analysis.

In this light, by 1960 or so, factions within Anglo-American philosophy were proceeding in comparatively sober terms to promote methods of mathematical logic insofar as such methods might improve practices of philosophical analysis.

For example, Kripke (1959, 1963) did for "modal logic" what Tarski had done for "first-order logic" by providing basic outlines for a possible-worlds semantics for formal modal grammars. The latter work was pursued largely in light of Carnap's (1950, 1956) work on modal logic, not to mention that of C. I. Lewis (1918). These efforts spurred interest in "intensional logic," promising to make better sense of words that express "propositional attitudes" that are better regarded as "operators" (i.e., like quantifiers or modalities) rather than as "properties" or "relations." We do not pursue the details here, but this work effectively disposed of Quinean conundrums regarding modal logic.

Contrary both to Russell's logical atomism and to logical positivist conceptions of a singular "unified science," Suppes (1960, 1962, 1965) pioneered a so-called semantic view of scientific theories—emphasizing mathematical modeling where a scientific theory was characterized as a collection of models (even allowing pairwise inconsistent models) rather than as a single syntactic structure with carefully chosen axioms. This added more nails to logical positivism's coffin.

Meanwhile, at Oxford, Grice (1957, 1968) inadvertently managed to threaten if not undermine ordinary-language methodology from within, focusing on conversational norms and developing a notion of conversational implicature (versus literal meaning) that undermined Strawson's critique of Russell's treatment of definite descriptions.

At MIT, Chomsky (1957, 1963, 1965) developed a fruitful approach to the study of syntax for artificial and natural languages, introducing a new array of formal techniques into the "scientific" study of language. Formal linguistics was here to stay.

Davidson (1967, 1974) promoted the idea that natural language is *like* a formal language with a Tarski-like semantics even if it might not be formalized quite so cleanly. At minimum, formal linguistics seemed to provide a fruitful attitude if not a quasi-formal methodology for philosophical analysis. This had been illustrated in Moore's (1919) use of vaguely devised first-order formal techniques to reveal ambiguities in various troublesome philosophical theses.

Kaplan (1968, 1978, 1989) took such methods to new heights, employing various higher-order predicates (belief predicates, a denotation predicate, a representation predicate, even a rigid-designation predicate) in his treatments of demonstratives and quantification into opaque contexts. No rigorous formalism for such analyses were presented, but a kind of intuitive facility for translating natural-language sentences into a symbolic jargon analogous to Russell's first-order treatment of definite descriptions seemed to legitimate the use of such methods.

Montague (1970, 1973), on the other hand, began in the 1950s to apply mathematically rigorous formal techniques in his studies of natural language. This produced precise formal treatments of nontrivial fragments of ordinary English, which were early contributions to a surge of similar work in subsequent decades.

DEWEY VERSUS THE DEDUCTIONISTS

The preceding limited survey of some important post-Russellian developments in mathematical linguistics illustrates the fecundity of Russell's "analytic logic." Russell aided the emergence of twentieth-century mathematical deductive logic and formal linguistics, though only in its earlier stages. His logicism was just the Tiergarten Programme in a new post-Hegelian guise—the product of *Hegelian* deposits in his own thinking that were not fully eradicated, his rejection of British idealism notwithstanding. Within a decade after the appearance of *Principia Mathematica*, it was clear that Russell's atomistic logicism would not work. We have briefly traced a history of how that failure was exposed while the growth of mathematical deductive logic and formal linguistics continued to flourish. So where might Dewey's conception of logic be located with respect to any of these accomplishments?

Today, Russell (1909, 1919, 1939, 1940, 1945) remains the most vocal critic of Dewey's conception of logic. His criticisms suggest that Dewey's conception of logic was developed in blissful irrelevance to any of the formidable developments outlined above. Quine, Nagel, Suppes, and others appeared to be more sympathetic in their respective dismissals of Dewey's philosophy of logic, but the sentiments were similar. In polite but dismissive ways, Church (1945) and Smullyan (1947) reviewed some papers attributed jointly to Dewey and Bentley (Bentley 1945a, 1945b; Dewey and Bentley 1945a, 1945b, 1945c). Such reviews were like the kiss of death.

Such reviews may be discounted for two reasons. First, the several materials that were reviewed when read in isolation are not representative of the full-bodied functionalist conception of logic that Dewey had developed over the preceding fifty years. These reviews presupposed a structuralist tradition that was foreign to Dewey's functionalist conception of logic: like apple trees being assessed in regard to their fitness as apples. Second, the reviewed materials were the product of a collaboration that reflected Bentley's sensibilities as much as Dewey's. This complicates efforts to assess Dewey's conception of logic by looking only at these particular articles. The Dewey/Bentley collaboration was an extended happenstance that, by 1945, was still not well developed. This collaboration coincided with many pivotal and accelerating developments in mathematical deductive logic. Bentley and Dewey were at pains to accommodate such results that on their terms were difficult to pinpoint both terminologically and conceptually.

One of Dewey's admitted weak points was mathematics, specifically regarding how to characterize mathematics as a full-bodied inquiry into abstract subject-matters. The collaboration with Bentley after 1940 did Dewey favors in this regard but otherwise do not reflect his functionalist conception of logic in relation to contemporary mathematical deductive logic. Dewey paid attention to the development of mathematical logic after 1903. In "Logical Objects" (Dewey 1916) he summarized his functionalist conception of inference (as "the use of things as evidence of other things") and of logic as the study of inference. He then critically assessed several aspects of Russell's "analytic logic" as presented in 1914 (when Russell was still in his logical-atomist heyday). This was years before the full force of mathematical methods were brought to bear in the study of deduction by Wittgenstein, Carnap, and others. Yet Dewey clearly pinpointed discrepancies between his own functionalist view of logic versus Russell's logical atomism and a respective kind of metaphysics designed to accommodate first-order extensionalism.

Dewey's correspondence with Bentley and others is certainly one place to look for evidence of Dewey's unfiltered take on such developments as they were emerging at the time. Dewey was not untroubled by these developments even as his own distinctive conception of logic progressed independently well into the 1940s. Basically, these mainstream developments offered no frontal challenge to Dewey's conception of logic but were nevertheless unacceptable primarily because they portrayed logic as much less than what Dewey would want to allow and, as such, involved essential terminological and conceptual differences that worked against their being incorporated unaltered into Dewey's conceptual framework.

DEWEY ON OBJECTS AND SATISFACTION

We thus finish here by surveying a number of issues that Dewey raised against mainstream developments in mathematical logic in his day. We may still wonder whether Dewey has anything positive to add to these ongoing developments, but that goes beyond what we can comfortably address here. We look at some questions and problems that Dewey himself posed and try to explain what he was getting at in light of his functionalist approach to logic versus the structuralist approach initiated by Russell, Wittgenstein, and the logical positivists.

With Bentley's prodding in 1948, Dewey took Tarski's work seriously enough to question his notion of "satisfaction" of (first-order) formulas by (sequences of) "objects" and, in particular, the assertion that "a sentence is true if it is satisfied by all objects." The latter may be puzzling when encountered point-blank, that is, until one understands Tarski's use of set theory in a generic extensionalist theory of truth for first-order languages. But Dewey was puzzled by more subtle aspects of Tarski's terminology that clashed with his own. In particular, Dewey balked at Tarski's treatment of "sentences" and "objects":

> [Tarski] certainly falls back on "objects," without telling how he gets to them. If he had taken 'sentence' or 'assertion' as one constituent of an extensive transactional system, 'object' might have been understood as that designated by the system in a way that "satisfies" and is "adequate" to each member of the transaction as spatially and temporally extending, proceeding. . . . While 'thing' may be a semantic term, can 'object' and 'satisfied by' be semantic in the semanticist sense? Looks to me like an attempt to "keep" the extra-semantic after having not eaten it but put it in the garbage can. But I don't know Tarski firsthand.
>
> (CJD 1948.02.22 (15115): John Dewey to Arthur Bentley)

What Dewey is grasping at here can be understood if what he meant by the word 'object' is likened to what Tarski might have meant by phrases like 'fully worked out model' or, better, 'fully worked out classes of multiscale models' in a dynamic framework in which models might be progressively (transactionally) developed and tested (as if in a process of inquiry). On this score, in contemporary parlance, Dewey was basically trying to get his head around the idea of "an object *satisfying* a sentence" but thinking in terms of "a sentence being *true* in a class of models." It did not make sense.

In his 1938 *Logic* (LW 12:122), Dewey had already highlighted relationships among "objects" (as settled results of inquiry), "objectives" (as possible ends-in-view of respective inquiries) and "objectivity" (of inquiries, of outcomes of inquiry). In 1944, in reply to Bentley's queries, he voiced concerns regarding Tarskian extensionalism similar to those that he later voiced in 1948:

> Whatever the proper use of (the words) 'object, objects', it is not in connection with the theory of knowledge. We may speak of the "objective" of the latter as that which inquiry, or know*ing*, is concerned with in particular cases. But it is not engaged in collecting "objects" as a child collects pretty pebbles, or a connoisseur pictures, or a buyer samples of wares. (These cases are intended to suggest the context in which the word 'objects' has pertinence). There are "subjects" of inquiry—topics, themes, and some aspects of these subjects of study may be properly called *objectives* or ends-held-in-view, as directives of behavior. But the substitution of the word 'objects' for the word 'subject' which latter word was alone in use in connection with the theory of knowledge until the seventeenth century is wholly a product of the epistemological mentalistic mind-world metaphysical dualism in which mind as knower retained the *super*natural attributes of soul or spirit while being set over against the *natural* world of science—which was then exclusively "physical" and "material" in its traditional disparaging metaphysical sense.
>
> (CJD 1944.08.29 (15366): John Dewey to Arthur Bentley)

If anyone did, Dewey knew how to put traditional metaphysics in its place. In this passage, we have Dewey, the philosopher, lecturing Tarski, the mathematician, about the care that must be taken to avoid muddy philosophical ditches. Such lectures fell on deaf ears because of terminological conflicts. Who, for instance, was substituting the word 'objects' for the word 'subject'? In the course of ignoring the progressive character of modeling, Tarski and cohorts were doing just that. They were essentially, in practice, treating "subjects" (as in subject-matters, subjects of study) simply as classes of what they called "objects," whether in the form of "domains of discourse" or as "ranges of quantification." For Dewey, subject-matters generally cannot be reduced to classes of individuals, though squaring away such subject-matters determines the objectives of inquiry. Set theory, extensional semantics, and methodological nominalism all have a place in a normative account of inquiry, but that cannot be all there is to semantics.

Dewey was not ready in either 1944 or 1948 to voice such concerns publicly, but he was clearly perplexed. It was not until the 1940s and 1950s that Tarski's "semantic conception of truth" was becoming visible and taking hold in Anglo-American philosophy (Tarski 1944; Tarski and Vaught 1956; Henkin 1961). The significance and content of Tarski's work in the 1930s and 1940s was then and still is up for debate in the arena of mathematical deductive logic itself (Schlick 1934; Neurath 1934, 1936; Carnap 1942; Black 1948; Etchemendy 1990; Mancosu 2010).

It is no surprise that Dewey in the 1940s would also question Tarski's conception of truth even if from a distant vantage point. In retrospect, debates about correspondence versus coherence conceptions of truth in light of Tarski's Convention T—about whether or not Tarski presupposed a fixed universe of discourse, about the distinction if any between a universe of discourse and a range of quantification—were results of not being sufficiently clear about the functional role of deduction in inquiry (scientific or otherwise). Neurath's references to the current state of some kind of progressive encyclopedia of acknowledged "truths" or Carnap's insights about the time-dependency of confirmation (but not of truth) are but faint inklings of what Dewey had already seen as the need to cast logic in terms of an overarching framework of progressive inquiry with reference to which notions of modeling, representation, correspondence, coherence, truth, confirmation, discourse, language, object, and so on might be *functionally* characterized.

DEWEY ON LOGICAL VALIDITY

Another terminological conflict concerns the words 'valid' and 'validity', 'invalid' and 'invalidity', 'validate' and 'invalidate'. Dewey had been using these terms in mutually consistent ways since the 1880s in his logical writings and elsewhere—not that their meanings did not evolve for Dewey, but that he used them in accordance with ordinary usage (as in 'a valid reason', 'a valid contract', 'a valid question', 'a valid point'). Their meaning in his logical writings reflected the normative sense that we would want to distinguish valid (properly validated) versus invalid (properly invalidated) conclusions of inquiry. In a letter commenting on a draft of Dewey's 1939 *Theory of Valuation*, Charles W. Morris made the following suggestion:

> 4. Is 'valid' the best term to apply to statements in technological discourse when these are controlled in terms of statements in scientific discourse? (See pp. 34, 50, 70, 74.) It may be confused with the use of 'valid' in the sense of Carnap etc. Perhaps 'grounded' is possible? In any case, it might be noted that the present use must not be confused with 'valid' as a term in syntax.
>
> (CJD 1939.03.23 (08029): Charles W. Morris to John Dewey)

Dewey graciously responded as follows:

> 1. Personally, as appears in some passage of my Logic, I do not accept the view that validity is formal or syntactical correctness. But since the point is not particularly relevant to the word as used in the mss., I have struck 'valid' out and substituted another word, usually 'warranted'. If there are any passages where I have failed to do so, it will be all right if you make the change.
>
> (CJD 1939.03.24 (08030): John Dewey to Charles W. Morris)

Both Morris and Dewey were talking about a syntactic rather than a semantic conception of validity. As of 1939, Morris's take on Carnap's thinking will have been informed as much or more by the latter's 1934/1937 *Logical Syntax of Language* and his

1935 *Philosophy and Logical Syntax* as by the 1939 *Foundations of Logic and Mathematics* (to which Morris had editorial access). Dewey probably will have been acquainted only with some of Carnap's pre-1939 work that emphasized formal syntax (such that truth and validity were indeed regarded as "terms in syntax"). Dewey's own pre-1939 conception of validity was functional, neither syntactic nor semantic in the sense of Carnap or Tarski. (Note, for what it is worth, that Peirce (1869, 1877–78) also used the word 'valid' in more than just Carnap's deductionist sense.)

What is validity in Dewey's pre-1939 sense? Logic for Dewey is a study of inquiry— a normative study aimed at distinguishing better and worse methods of inquiry, presupposing (a) that this study can be pursued in a principled way and (b) that inquiry in general is subject to normative principles. A normative study of inquiry in general is broader than Peirce's normative study of scientific inquiry (1877–78). Peirce had sketched a single basic pattern of inquiry (as a pattern of stabilizing belief in response to the presence of destabilizing doubt) which Dewey recognized as an example of his own inversion of Hegel's pattern of human history—a single basic pattern of growth (chunked into units or episodes of experience, learning, forming and reforming habits). In 1896, this was the structure of a "unit of behavior." As such, a given inquiry should typically come to some (tentative) conclusion—a belief, a judgment, a response to a problem, an answer to a question—which will have been formulated and validated using properly executed methods of inquiry. Such a conclusion to an inquiry will be *valid* just to the extent that the inquiry will have been properly executed. Logic is a study of what it is for inquiries to be properly executed.

This perspective on inquiry is not unrelated to Kuhn's (1977) more limited discussions of scientific change and theory choice, namely, where normal science may hope to proceed on the basis of ongoing changes and choices (theoretical, experimental, instrumentational; sometimes profound and sometimes not) that have been made in some principled way (i.e., properly validated). What are the principles by which such choices are made? Under what circumstances are such choices said to be properly validated? All of this is well within range of what Dewey had been talking about all along, since 1890 or so, as a primary concern of logic as a normative theory of inquiry.

DEWEY ON LOGIC AS SUCH

None of the latter makes sense if logic is a normative theory of inquiry which in turn is a normative syntactic/semantic study of deductive inference. What is meant by the word 'logic' may be the most fundamental terminological conflict at issue here. Ownership of as much word choice as possible may be given to contemporary versions of mathematical deductive logic at Dewey's expense. Dewey was willing to replace talk of "valid" judgments with talk of "warranted" judgments. Many such terminological conflicts may be so easily resolved. Such acquiescence does not extend to the word 'logic'.

For Dewey, logic is a normative (prescriptive) theory of inquiry (a) because it is a study of inference and (b) because inference must be understood functionally as well as structurally to be understood at all. But it must be understood functionally in what sense?

There are three kinds of inference—abductive, deductive, inductive. Each kind of inference has been studied to various extents over the last century and a half. Mostly, each has been studied separately from the others, and each is studied structurally if at all. This structural balkanization has yielded interesting results such that (a) "mathematical logic" has come to be defined as a study of deductive inference, (b) statistical (inductive) inference has become a highly refined discipline that is not generally regarded as an integral part of the subject matter of "mathematical logic," and (c) abductive inference remains an enigma that is not part of the subject matter of "mathematical logic" at all. In such a view, to ask whether there could be a "logic" of induction or a "logic" of abduction would be like asking if induction or abduction were reducible to deduction.

Two Types of Functionality in Inquiry

On the other hand, Dewey's conception of logic involves different presuppositions and asks different questions. The issue at hand concerns what it means to understand abduction, deduction, and induction functionally, not just structurally. It thus means two things. It means (A) that to understand what abduction, deduction, and induction are, we must understand how they mutually support, rely on, and otherwise relate to one another—not just what each is in isolation from the other two. In this first sense, the three-way relation among abduction, deduction, and induction involves a feedback circuit: we hypothesize, we analyze, and we actualize, which impels us further to hypothesize, analyze, actualize. Hypotheses are abduced to explain (as sufficient conditions for) targeted data, other implications of these hypotheses are deduced while seeking empirically testable predictions, the latter are subjected to observational and experimental tests to induce how well they comport with those predictions, which will result in new data in light of which tested hypotheses are modified (rejected, elucidated) or new hypotheses are abduced. This is a progressive three-way functional relation.

Understanding abduction, deduction, and induction functionally also means (B) that we must understand how (when, why) implementations of this three-way dynamic are initiated and utilized (well or badly) for what ends. A study of functional relations among abduction, deduction, and induction in the first sense is inherently normative in that there will be rules and standards of correctness for each kind of inference, each by itself as well as in terms of its interdependencies with the other two kinds of inference. Nowhere in this normative study will one find reasons explaining why the functioning of inference should proceed in this or that direction beyond the presumption that it should proceed correctly. But there are other kinds of good and bad reasons—involving purposes, preferences, interests, commitments, allegiances, investments, aims, goals, ends-in-view—that affect where our inferences take us, motivating them and rendering them more or less worthwhile, for better or worse.

Why think that "logic" could explain this broader kind of rationality in principled ways without devolving into mere psychology or political theory? Dewey's answer is that it can do this if we think of logic not just as a study of inference but as a study of inquiry in a broadly generic sense. When we consider inference and inferences as procedures (processes, activities) occurring within respective inquiries and thus materially affecting the course of these inquiries, we assume the second perspective on how to functionally characterize the workings of inference. Besides having to measure up to norms of internal correctness, inferences must also measure up to standards regarding their usefulness in promoting progress in and completion of given inquiries. It falls to logic to articulate norms in both the latter and former senses.

In this light consider the fact that each kind of inference may be and often is studied more or less in isolation from the other two; yet any set of A-type principles that determine norms for what serves as better and worse instances of any one kind of inference will inevitably make reference to the other two kinds of inference. For instance, the now-standard distinction between valid and invalid deductive arguments is distinctly owned by the logic of deduction. On the other hand, the now-standard distinction between sound and unsound deductive arguments is not distinctly owned by the logic of deduction insofar as the notion of soundness also requires but does not provide principled and generally applicable ways to determine whether given premises are indeed true or false (in this or that model so that deductive arguments are respectively sound or not only in this or that model). Such principles and methods instead fall within the purview of the logic of induction.

For example, the U.S. Office of the Surgeon General cannot legitimately tell from scratch whether a perfectly valid deductive argument concluding that tobacco-smoking causes cancer is sound. It will be necessary to consider observational and experimental procedures and results that are claimed to have yielded convincing support for inducing that the premises of that argument are true. In such contexts, the argument may be assessed as to its soundness though usually without perfect confidence—so that a yes/no answer as to whether and which warning statements are to appear on cigarette packages will be based implicitly on statistics and probabilities.

In short, deductive soundness can be assessed only if truth of deductive premises can be assessed. Doing so in a reliable way falls largely to the logic of induction precisely because only inductive inference proactively faces the question of truth head on. It begins with deductively-clarified hypotheses and, by submitting them to tribunals of methodologically-proper experimentation and observation, ends if at all with yes/no decisions regarding those hypotheses. These decisions are based on material (methodological, statistical, probabilistic) norms, but they are yes/no decisions. Yes, smoking cigarettes causes cancer. No, immunizations do not cause autism.

If such results are unexpected, they will raise further questions despite whatever inductive precautions will have been taken to support them. Such questions invite further abductive inferences. Persistent questioning calls for abducing new or modified ("but what if . . . ") hypotheses that would account for new data (re-examining and refining original hypotheses). This requires further deductive analysis and thus new observational studies and experimental tests. Such cyclical workings of three kinds of inference may proceed indefinitely so long as their mutual coherence remains elusive, yet they may converge on conclusive results where hypotheses are consistently confirmed. Thoroughly confirmed hypotheses may later raise questions. Inductive surprises may come out of the blue, or they may reflect well-known annoyances that have so far been ignored. Either way, the logic of abduction (typically) takes the results of inductive inference as its premises, its givens, rather than as final conclusions.

On this score, a distinction that professional deductionist logicians tend to ignore works directly against common appreciation of the logic of deduction. Namely, formally valid deductive arguments may be materially empty or meaningless. How is it that deductive arguments involving meaningless Ps and Qs may be valid yet irrelevant to anything in one's experience? Why is it logically true that P implies that Q implies P, even if Q and P are mutually unrelated in any relevant way? If so, then the true statement that $2 + 2 = 4$ is implied by any true or false statement, for example, that Mickey Mouse is green. Deductive validity is blind to norms of material relevance requiring that Ps and Qs pertain to a common subject matter.

Likewise, deductive arguments involving meaningful Ps and Qs may be invalid and yet express analytic entailments. Namely, deductive consequences of given premises may not be validly deducible from those premises (see the treatment of "analytic consequence" in Barker-Plummer et al. 2011). The fact that Bart is a bachelor analytically entails that he is unmarried, yet we have to reach outside of formal deductive logic to justify this argument. Deductive validity is blind to norms of intensional relevance acknowledging that the contents of predicate symbols, names, descriptions, and such have deductive force that is not covered by norms of first-order extensional deductionist logic.

Deductive inference (valid or not) gains practical traction when premises are not just true or false but are materially and intensionally relevant to each other and to things that matter. One of the primary A-type functions of abductive inference is to produce, endorse, or modify plausible premises on the basis of inductive (induced) results of activities designed to test "prior" premises presumed to matter enough to justify investigatory effort. Deductive inferences gain relevance from the deliverances of abductive inference, to put it simply, which may then be secured by results of inductive inference—presumably for some purpose or in pursuit of some goal.

This brings us to B-type functionalism—what Dewey labeled as "instrumentalism." The preceding discussion of A-type functionalism draws on an image of a circle (circuit, cycle) of functionality—namely, where deductions rely on deliverances of abduction, abductions rely on deliverances of induction, inductions rely on deliverances of deduction, and around it goes. According to B-type "Chicago functionalism" circa 1895, this circuit may or may not come back on itself. B-type functionality pertains to how actions, events, things, states, hypotheses, data, and so on function (James will have said "work") in the movement from a situation where inferential processes are irregular (discordant, do not quite come back on themselves) to one where they are regular (concordant, reliably and stably do come back on themselves). We hypothesize further only if prior hypotheses do not rationally and/or experimentally measure up. We settle, if we can afford to, only when things can indeed be settled.

Anyone who is technically skilled in some real-world art (chemistry, mathematics, guitar, parenting) might sum this up as a kind of perfection principle—something like "practice makes perfect"—in regard to mastering various skills required for doing their art in the way they do it. The present point regarding B-type functionalism is only that this summary principle presupposes a fundamental common pattern characterizing episodes of learning, episodes of accomplishment, in which unsettled and irregular activities become settled and regular activities—a common pattern characterizing what Dewey referred to in 1896 as "units of behavior." It is within and with respect to such episodes of resolution that different forms of inference function together in service to achieving (securing, establishing, becoming attuned to) various kinds of unforced regularity in response to sufficiently prominent irregularities. Such conclusions typically are fallible but are warranted ("valid") or not to the extent that procedures used to achieve those results comport with logical norms.

Logical norms thus cannot be limited to deductive norms. (a) Deductive norms address things like formal validity (truth preservation from premises to conclusions). (b) Norms for inductive (statistical) inference rely on probability theory (essentially a formal mathematical discipline) but also, therefore, on factors like avoidance of biased observation and experimental methods, assuring sufficiently large sample sizes, implementation of proper controls against hidden causal influences, and so forth. (c) Norms for abductive (ampliative) inference are not well understood. They are clearly exemplified, nevertheless, by differences between a medical doctor who can quickly and reasonably surmise (hypothetically) that a given patient exhibiting given symptoms is suffering from this or that malady, versus the intern who pauses to consult medical texts to explore possible diagnoses for the apparent symptoms. Abductive inference is a kind of inference that connects empirical dots (for better or worse) when the dots are not enough by themselves to determine a connection. Innocence provides innovative freedom that respectively may be devoid of trajectory, while experience provides trajectory but perhaps at the expense of innovative flexibility. A general account—a logic—that distinguishes better and worse kinds of abductive inference ultimately is charged with elaborating normative principles that clearly distinguish legitimate versus illegitimate ways of balancing such options. As illustrated by concrete examples, medical or otherwise, this involves not formal or methodological factors essential to deductive and inductive logic, respectively, but what are essentially psychological factors like training, learning, conditioning, expertise, even sanity.

Dewey's conception of units of behavior as resolutions of discordant situations into concordant situations reveals a distinctive feature of B-type functionalism. The latter plays a crucial role in a theory of inquiry (experience, learning) that would avoid the Scylla of Russell's atomism and the Charybdis of Quine's holism. Dewey's theory of inquiry presupposes that discordant situations are foisted on us in a perilous world. What does this have to do with logic? Well, such situations objectively determine how detailed one must be in transforming them, which kinds of actions count as primitive, which kinds of actions require dissection and modification, what counts as data or evidence versus what is speculative or hypothetical, and so forth. These are *functional* designations, matters to be determined neither once and for all as Russell's atomism requires nor arbitrarily as Quine's holism would allow. It is *the situation* that determines what counts as an atomic proposition, for instance; and the content of an atomic proposition in one situation may be a complex subject matter in another. Compare the content of "My shoes are tied" in a situation where one is late for an important early morning business appointment versus a situation where one is yet to master the whole shoe-tying process. "Situations" in Dewey's theory of inquiry are meant to anchor logic in the real world as we experience it, providing concrete contextual constraints that put things into perspective in light of which appropriate levels of discernment may be exercised.

DEWEY VERSUS THE LOGICIANS?

So where do we stand regarding Dewey's logical theory? One lesson here is that almost anything resulting from the development of twentieth-century deductionist logic might be incorporated into a Deweyan theory of inquiry. Having to choose between Frege, Russell, and Carnap versus Dewey is a false dilemma, not requiring an exclusive choice. It is not a zero-sum decision. Dewey was not always on the mark, just as Frege, Russell, and Carnap were not. Dewey's conception of logic as a normative theory of inquiry nevertheless introduces a perspective that would render it just as mathematical and abstract as it is practical and concrete.

WORKS CITED

Citations of John Dewey's works are to the thirty-seven-volume critical edition published by Southern Illinois University Press under the editorship of Jo Ann Boydston. In-text citations give the original publication date and series abbreviation, followed by volume number and page number. For example: (1934, LW 10:12) is page 12 of *Art as Experience*, which is published as volume 10 of *The Later Works*.

Series abbreviations for *The Collected Works*:

EW *The Early Works* (1882–98)

MW *The Middle Works* (1899–1924)

LW *The Later Works* (1925–53)

Citations of Dewey's correspondence are to *The Correspondence of John Dewey*, 1871–2007, published by the InteLex Corporation under the editorship of Larry Hickman. In most cases, citations give the date, reference number for the letter, and author followed by recipient. For example: 1973.02.13 (22053): Herbert W. Schneider to H. S. Thayer.

Alexander, Thomas M. 2008. "Comments on James Good: *A Search for Unity in Diversity.*" *Transactions of the Charles S. Peirce Society*, vol. 44, no. 4, 563–568.

Angell, James Rowland, and Addison W. Moore. 1896. "Studies from the Psychological Laboratory of the University of Chicago. I. Reaction-Time: A Study in Attention and Habit." *Psychological Review*, vol. 3, 245–258.

Anscombe, Elizabeth. 1957. *Intention.* Oxford: Blackwell.

Backe, Andrew. 2001. "John Dewey and Early Chicago Functionalism." *History of Psychology*, vol. 4, no. 4, 323–340.

Barker-Plummer, Dave, Jon Barwise, and John Etchemendy. 2011. *Language, Proof, and Logic*, 2nd ed. Stanford, CA: CSLI Publications.

Bentley, Arthur Fisher. 1945a. "On a Certain Vagueness in Logic, I." *Journal of Philosophy*, vol. 42, no. 1, 6–27. Appeared as sections I–III of "Vagueness in Logic" in Dewey and Bentley 1949, chapter I (LW 16:8–32).

Bentley, Arthur Fisher. 1945b. "On a Certain Vagueness in Logic, II." *Journal of Philosophy*, vol. 42, no. 2, 39–51. Appeared as sections IV–X of "Vagueness in Logic" in Dewey and Bentley 1949, chapter I (LW 16:32–45).

Black, Max. 1948. "The Semantic Definition of Truth." *Analysis*, vol. 8, no. 4, 49–63.

Breitwieser, J. V. 1911. *Attention and Movement in Reaction Time.* New York and Oxford: Science Press.

Cantor, Georg. 1883. "Ueber unendliche, lineare Punktmannichfaltigkeiten (5)." *Mathematische Annalen*, vol. 21, no. 4, 545–591. Published separately as a monograph: *Grundlagen einer allgemeinen Mannigfaltigkeitslehre (Foundations of a General Theory of Aggregates)*.

Carey, Rosalind. 2016. "Russell's Metaphysics." In *The Internet Encyclopedia of Philosophy.* http://www.iep.utm.edu/

Carleton, Lawrence Richard. 1982. "The Rise of Chicago Functionalism." *Erkenntnis*, vol. 18, no. 1, 3–23.

Carnap, Rudolf. 1934. *Logische Syntax der Sprache [The Logical Syntax of Language].* Vienna: Springer-Verlag. English translation, London: Routledge and Kegan Paul, 1937.

Carnap, Rudolf. 1935. *Philosophy and Logical Syntax.* London: Kegan Paul, Trench, Trubner and Company.

Carnap, Rudolf. 1939. "Foundations of Logic and Mathematics." In *International Encyclopedia of Unified Science*, vol. 1, no. (3). Chicago: University of Chicago Press.

Carnap, Rudolf. 1942. *Introduction to Semantics.* Cambridge, MA: Harvard University Press.

Carnap, Rudolf. 1950. "Empiricism, Semantics, and Ontology." *Revue Internationale de Philosophie*, vol. 4, 20–40. Included in Carnap 1956.

Carnap, Rudolf. 1956. *Meaning and Necessity: A Study in Semantics and Modal Logic*, 2nd enlarged ed. Chicago: University of Chicago Press.

Chomsky, Noam. 1957. *Syntactic Structures.* The Hague: Mouton.

Chomsky, Noam. 1963. "Formal Properties of Grammars." In R. D. Luce, R. R. Bush, and E. Galanter, eds., *Handbook of Mathematical Psychology.* New York: Wiley.

Chomsky, Noam. 1965. *Aspects of the Theory of Syntax.* Cambridge, MA: MIT Press.

Church, Alonzo. 1936a. "A Note on the *Entscheidungsproblem.*" *Journal of Symbolic Logic*, vol. 1, 40–41.

Church, Alonzo. 1936b. "An Unsolvable Problem of Elementary Number Theory." *American Journal of Mathematics*, vol. 58, 345–363.

Church, Alonzo. 1941. *The Calculi of Lambda-Conversion.* Annals of Mathematics Studies, vol. 6. Princeton, NJ: Princeton University Press.

Church, Alonzo. 1945. "Review of the First Three Chapters of Dewey and Bentley 1949." *Journal of Symbolic Logic*, vol. 10, no. 4, 132–133.

Dalton, Timothy C., and Victor W. Bergenn. 1996. "John Dewey, Myrtle McGraw, and *Logic*: An Unusual Collaboration in the 1930s." *Studies in History and Philosophy of Science*, vol. 27, no. 1, 69–107.

Davidson, Donald. 1967. "Truth and Meaning." *Synthese*, vol. 17, 304–323.

Davidson, Donald. 1974. "On the Very Idea of a Conceptual Scheme." *Proceedings of the APA*, vol. 47, 5–20.

Dewey, John. 1910. *The Influence of Darwin on Philosophy, and Other Essays in Contemporary Thought*. New York: Henry Holt. Essays reprinted separately in EW and MW. Critical edition reissued in 2007 (Carbondale: Southern Illinois University Press).

Dewey, John. 1922. *Human Nature and Conduct: An Introduction to Social Psychology*. New York: Henry Holt. Reprinted in MW 14.

Dewey, John. 1930. "From Absolutism to Experimentalism." In George P. Adams and William P. Montague, eds., *Contemporary American Philosophy*, vol. II, 13–27. New York: Macmillan. Reprinted in LW 5:147–160.

Dewey, John. 1933. *How We Think*. Chicago: Henry Regnery. Reprinted in LW 8:105–354. Revised and expanded version of 1911 edition (Boston: D. C. Heath), reprinted in MW 6:177–356.

Dewey, John. 1934. *Art as Experience*. New York: Henry Holt. Reprinted in LW 10.

Dewey, John. 1938. *Logic: The Theory of Inquiry*. New York: Henry Holt. Reprinted in LW 12.

Dewey, John. 1939. *Theory of Valuation*. Chicago: University of Chicago Press. Originally appeared in the *International Encyclopedia of Unified Science: Foundations of the Unity of Science* series, vol. 2, no. 4 (ed. Otto Neurath). Reprinted in LW 13:189–254.

Dewey, John, and Arthur Fisher Bentley. 1945a. "A Search for Firm Names." *Journal of Philosophy*, vol. 42, no. 1, 5–6. Appeared as "Introduction: A Search for Firm Names" in Dewey and Bentley 1949, xi–xiii (LW 16: 6–7).

Dewey, John, and Arthur Fisher Bentley. 1945b. "A Terminology for Knowings and the Known." *Journal of Philosophy*, vol. 42, no. 9, 225–247. Appeared as "The Terminological Problem" in Dewey and Bentley 1949, chapter 2 (LW 16:64–73).

Dewey, John, and Arthur Fisher Bentley. 1945c. "Postulations." *Journal of Philosophy*, vol. 42, no. 24, 645–662. Appeared as "Postulations" in Dewey and Bentley 1949, chapter 3 (LW 16:74–95).

Etchemendy, John. 1990. *The Concept of Logical Consequence*. Cambridge, MA: Harvard University Press.

Feigl, Herbert. 1943. "Logical Empiricism." In Dagobert D. Runes, ed., *Twentieth Century Philosophy*, 371–416. New York: Philosophical Library.

Feigl, Herbert, and Albert E. Blumberg. 1931. "Logical Positivism: A New Movement in European Philosophy." *Journal of Philosophy*, vol. 17, 281–296.

Frege, Gottlob. 1884. *Grundgesetze der Arithmetik*. Breslau: Verlage Wilhelm Koebner. Translated as *The Foundations of Arithmetic: A Logico-Mathematical Enquiry into the Concept of Number*, by John L. Austin (Oxford: Blackwell, 1950; 2nd rev. ed., 1974).

Garciadiego, Alejandro Ricardo. 1991. *Bertrand Russell and the Origins of the Set-Theoretic "Paradoxes."* Basel: Birkhäuser.

Gödel, Kurt. 1930. Die Vollständigkeit der Axiome des logischen Funktionenkalküls. *Monatschefte für Mathematik und Physik*, vol. 37, 349–360. Translated as "The Completeness of the Axioms of the Functional Calculus of Logic" in Heijenoort 1967, 582–591.

Gödel, Kurt. 1931. "Über formal unentscheidbare Sätze der *Principia mathematica* und verwandter Systeme I." *Monatschefte für Mathematik und Physik*, vol. 38, 173–198. Translated as "On Formally Undecidable Propositions of *Principia Mathematica* and Related Systems, I" in Heijenoort 1967, 596–616.

Grice, H. P. 1957. "Meaning." *Philosophical Review*, vol. 66, no. 3, 377–388.

Grice, H. P. 1968. "Utterer's Meaning, Sentence Meaning, and Word Meaning." *Foundations of Language*, vol. 4, 225–242.

Griffin, Nicholas. 1984. "Bertrand Russell's Crisis of Faith." *Russell: The Journal of Bertrand Russell Studies*, vol. 4, no. 1, 101–122.

Griffin, Nicholas. 1988. "The Tiergarten Programme." *Russell: The Journal of Bertrand Russell Studies*, vol. 8, no. 1, 19–34.

Henkin, Leon. 1961. "Some Remarks on Infinitely Long Formulas." In *Infinitistic Methods: Proceedings of the Symposium on Foundations of Mathematics*, 167–183. Oxford: Pergamon Press.

Hickman, Larry A. 2008. "Dewey's Hegel: A Search for Unity in Diversity, or Diversity as the Growth of Unity?" *Transactions of the Charles S. Peirce Society*, vol. 44, no. 4, 569–576.

Hilbert, David. 1928. "Die Grundlagen der Mathematik." *Abhandlungen aus dem Seminar der Hamburgischen Universität*, vol. 6, 65–85.

Hilbert, David. 1971 (1899). *Foundations of Geometry*. La Salle, IL: Open Court. Translation from the 10th German edition by Leo Unger, revised by Paul Bernays. First edition originally published as *Grundlagen der Geometrie* (Stuttgart: B. G. Trueder, 1899).

Hilbert, David, and Wilhelm Ackermann. 1928. *Grundzüge der theoretischen Logik (Principles of Theoretical Logic)*. Berlin, Heidelberg: Springer-Verlag.

James, William. 1890. *The Principles of Psychology* (2 vols.). New York: Henry Holt. Reprinted in the *Works of William James series* (Cambridge, MA: Harvard University Press, 1981).

Johnston, James Scott. 2014. *John Dewey's Earlier Logical Theory*. Albany: State University of New York Press.

Kaplan, David. 1968. "Quantifying." *Synthese*, vol. 19, 178–214.

Kaplan, David. 1978. "Dthat." In Peter Cole, ed., *Syntax and Semantics*, vol. 9. New York: Academic Press.

Kaplan, David. 1989. "Demonstratives: An Essay on the Semantics, Logic, Metaphysics, and Epistemology of Demonstratives and Other Indexicals." In Joseph Almog, John Perry, and Howard Wettstein, eds., *Themes from Kaplan*, 481–563. New York: Oxford University Press.

Kripke, Saul A. 1959. "A Completeness Theorem in Modal Logic." *The Journal of Symbolic Logic*, vol. 24, no. 1, 1–14.

Kripke, Saul A. 1963. "Semantic Considerations in Modal Logic." *Acta Philosophica Fennica*, vol. 16, 83–94.

Kuhn, Thomas S. 1977. "Objectivity, Value Judgment, and Theory Choice." In *The Essential Tension: Selected Studies in Scientific Tradition and Change*, 320–339. Chicago: Chicago University Press.

Lange, Ludwig. 1888. "Neue Experimente über den Vorgang der einfachen Reaction auf Sinneseindrücke." *Philosophische Studien*, vol. 4, 479–510. Translated as "New Experiments on the Process of the Simple Reaction to Sensory Impressions" by David D. Lee, 2009 (http://psychclassics.yorku.ca/LangeL/NewExperiments.pdf).

Lewis, Clarence Irving. 1918. *A Survey of Symbolic Logic*. Berkeley: University of California Press. Reprinted 1960 (New York: Dover) with the omission of chapters 5–6.

Löwenheim, Leopold. 1915. "Über Möglichkeiten im Relativkalkül." *Mathematische Annalen*, vol. 76, no. 4, 447–470. Translated as "On Possibilities in the Calculus of Relatives" in Heijenoort 1967, 228–251.

Mancosu, Paolo. 2010. *The Adventure of Reason: Interplay Between Philosophy of Mathematics and Mathematical Logic, 1900–1940*. Oxford: Oxford University Press.

Menand, Louis. 2001. *The Metaphysical Club: A Story of Ideas in America*. New York: Farrar Straus Giroux.

Montague, Richard. 1970. "English as a Formal Language." In B. Visentini et al., ed., *Linguaggi nella Società e nella Tecnica*. Milan: Edizioni di Communità. Reprinted in Montague 1974.

Montague, Richard. 1973. "The Proper Treatment of Quantification in Ordinary English." In J. Hintikka, J. Moravcsik, and P. Suppes, eds., *Approaches to Natural Language: Proceedings of the 1970 Stanford Workshop on Grammar and Semantics*. Dordrecht: D. Reidel. Reprinted in Montague 1974, chap. 8.

Moore, George Edward. 1919. "Internal and External Relations." *Proceedings of the Aristotelean Society*, vol. 20, 40–62.

Nagel, Ernest. 1986. "Introduction to Dewey's *Logic: The Theory of Inquiry*." LW 12:ix–xxvii. Carbondale: Southern Illinois University Press.

Neurath, Otto. 1934. "Radikaler Physikalismus und 'wirkliche Welt'" [Radical Physicalism and the "Real" World]. *Erkenntnis*, vol. 4, 346–362.

Neurath, Otto. 1936. "Erster Internationaler Kongress für Einheit der Wissenschaft in Paris 1935." *Erkenntnis*, vol. 5, 377–406.

Pasch, Moritz. 1882. *Vorlesungen über Neuere Geometrie*. Leipzig: B. G. Teubner.

Peirce, Charles Sanders. 1877–78. "Illustrations of the Logic of Science." *Popular Science Monthly*, 12–13. In six parts. Reprinted together in EP1, chaps. 7–12. Reissued with supplementary material in 2014, ed. Cornelis de Waal (Chicago: Open Court).

Popper, Karl. 1959. *The Logic of Scientific Discovery*. New York: Harper & Row. Translation of *Logik der Forschung*, 1934.

Putnam, Hilary. 1963. "The 'Corroboration' of Theories." In Paul Arthur Schilpp, ed., *The Philosophy of Rudolf Carnap*, 121–137. La Salle: Open Court.

Quine, Willard van Orman. 1947. "The Problem of Interpreting Modal Logic." *Journal of Symbolic Logic*, vol. 12, 42–48.

Quine, Willard van Orman. 1948. "On What There Is." *Review of Metaphysics*, vol. 2, 21–38. Reprinted in Quine 1953, 1–19.

Quine, Willard van Orman. 1951. "Two Dogmas of Empiricism." *Philosophical Review*, vol. 60, 20–43. Reprinted in Quine 1953, 20–46.

Quine, Willard van Orman. 1953. *From a Logical Point of View*. Cambridge, MA: Harvard University Press.

Quine, Willard van Orman. 1956. "Quantifiers and Propositional Attitudes." *Journal of Philosophy*, vol. 53, 177–187.

Russell, Bertrand. 1897. *An Essay on the Foundations of Geometry*. Cambridge: Cambridge University Press.

Russell, Bertrand. 1905. "On Denoting." *Mind*, vol. 14, 479–493.

Russell, Bertrand. 1909. "Pragmatism." *Edinburgh Review*, vol. 209, no. 428, 363–388. Includes remarks on Dewey's *Studies in Logical Theory* (1903).

Russell, Bertrand. 1919. "Professor Dewey's *Essays in Experimental Logic*." *Journal of Philosophy*, vol. 16, no. 1, 5–26.

Russell, Bertrand. 1939. "Dewey's New *Logic*." In Paul Arthur Schilpp, ed., *The Philosophy of John Dewey*, 135–156. New York: Tudor.

Russell, Bertrand. 1940. "Warranted Assertibility." In *An Inquiry into Meaning and Truth*, 400–410. New York: George Allen & Unwin.

Russell, Bertrand. 1945. "John Dewey." In *A History of Western Philosophy*, 819–828. New York: Simon & Schuster.

Russell, Bertrand, and Alfred North Whitehead. 1910–1913. *Principia Mathematica*. 3 vols. Cambridge: Cambridge University Press.

Schilpp, Paul Arthur (Ed.). 1939. *The Philosophy of John Dewey*. The Library of Living Philosophers, vol. 1. New York: Tudor Press.

Schlick, Moritz. 1934. "Über das Fundament der Erkenntnis" [On the Foundation of Knowledge]. *Erkenntnis*, vol. 4, 79–99.

Skolem, Thoralf. 1920. "Logisch-kombinatorische Untersuchungen über die Erfüllbarkeit oder Beweisbarkeit mathematischer Sätze nebst einem Theoreme über dichte Mengen." *Videnskapsselskapet Skrifter, I. Matematisk-naturvidenskabelig Klasse*, vol. 6, 1–36. Translated as "Logico-Combinatorial Investigations on the Satisfiability or Provability of Mathematical Propositions: A Simplified Proof of a Theorem by L. Löwenheim and Generalizations of the Theorem" in Heijenoort 1967, 252–263.

Smullyan, Arthur Francis. 1947. "Review of Dewey and Bentley 1947." *Journal of Symbolic Logic*, vol. 12, no. 3, 99.

Suppes, Patrick. 1960. "A Comparison of the Meaning and Use of Models in the Mathematical and Empirical Sciences." *Synthese*, vol. 12, nos. 2–3, 287–301. Reprinted in Suppes 1969, 10–23.

Suppes, Patrick. 1962. "Models of Data." In E. Nagel, P. Suppes, and A. Tarski, eds., *Logic, Methodology, and the Philosophy of Science: Proceedings of the 1960 International Congress*, 252–261. Stanford, CA: Stanford University Press. Reprinted in Suppes 1969, 24–35.

Suppes, Patrick. 1965. "Logics Appropriate to Empirical Theories." In J. W. Addison, Leon Henkin, and Alfred Tarski, eds., *Symposium on the Theory of Models*, 364–375. Amsterdam: North-Holland.

Suppes, Patrick. 1969a. "Nagel's Lectures on Dewey's *Logic*." In S. Morgenbesser, P. Suppes, and M. White, eds., *Philosophy, Science, and Method: Essays in Honor of Ernest Nagel*. New York: St. Martin's Press.

Suppes, Patrick. 1969b. *Studies in the Methodology and Foundations of Science: Selected Papers from 1951 to 1969*. Dordrecht: D. Reidel.

Tarski, Alfred. 1933. "The Concept of Truth in Formalized Languages" (in Polish). *Prace Towarzystwa Naukowego Warszawskiego, Wydzial III Nauk Matematyczno-Fizycznych*, vol. 34. Warsaw. First presented to the Warsaw Scientific Society in 1931. Revised and modified as Tarski 1936.

Tarski, Alfred. 1936a. "Der Wahrheitsbegriff in den formalisierten Sprachen" [The Concept of Truth in Formalized Languages]. *Studia Philosophica*, vol. 1, 261–405. English translation in *Logic, Semantics, Metamathematics*, 152–278 (Oxford: Clarendon Press, 1956).

Tarski, Alfred. 1936b. "On the Concept of Logical Consequence." English translation in *Logic, Semantics, Metamathematics*, 409–420 (Oxford: Clarendon Press, 1956). New translation as "On the Concept of Following Logically" by Magda Stroińska and David Hitchcock, in *History and Philosophy of Logic*, vol. 23(2002), 155–196.

Tarski, Alfred. 1944. "The Semantic Conception of Truth and the Foundations of Semantics." *Philosophy and Phenomenological Research*, vol. 4, 341–375.

Tarski, Alfred, and Robert Vaught. 1956. "Arithmetical Extensions of Relational Systems." *Compositio Mathematica*, vol. 13, 81–102.

Turing, Alan. 1937a. "Computability and λ-Definability." *Journal of Symbolic Logic*, vol. 2, 153–163.

Turing, Alan. 1937b. "On Computable Numbers, with an Application to the *Entscheidungsproblem*." *Proceedings of the London Mathematical Society*, Series 2, no. 42, 230–265.

Turing, Alan. 1938. "On Computable Numbers, with an Application to the *Entscheidungsproblem*. A Correction." *Proceedings of the London Mathematical Society*, Series 2, no. 43, 544–546.

Wittgenstein, Ludwig. 1961 (1921). *Tractatus Logico-Philosophicus*, trans. D. F. Pears and B. F. McGuinness. London: Routledge and Kegan Paul.

Woods, John, Ralph H. Johnson, Dov M. Gabbay, and Hans Jürgen Olbach. 2002. "Logic and the Practical Turn." In Dov M. Gabbay, Ralph H. Johnson, Hans Jürgen Olbach, and John Woods, eds., *Handbook of the Logic of Argument and Inference: The Turn Towards the Practical*, 1–39. Studies in Logic and Practical Reasoning. Amsterdam: North-Holland.

Wundt, Wilhelm Maximilian. 1874. *Grundzüge der physiologischen Psychologie*. Leipzig: Engelmann. Translation of volume 1 of the fifth German edition by E. B. Titchener as *Principles of Physiological Psychology* (New York: Macmillan, 1904).

DEWEY, HABERMAS, AND THE UNFINISHED PROJECT OF MODERNITY IN *UNMODERN PHILOSOPHY AND MODERN PHILOSOPHY*

PHILLIP DEEN

INTRODUCTION

THE central contention of *Unmodern Philosophy and Modern Philosophy* is provided by the title itself. John Dewey argued that what we know as "modern" philosophy has never been truly that and not because it began centuries before our own. Rather, what has been called modern philosophy still carries with it the stultifying philosophical baggage that arose during a premodern period. The technoscientific revolution has overturned virtually every aspect of human association with the natural world and with each other and has provided new vistas of scientific knowledge. Meanwhile, the modern philosophical enterprise, with its focus on epistemology, continues to ask whether knowledge is even possible and refuses to incorporate the technoscientific method into moral life encompassing the full range of aesthetic, moral, political values.

The text itself is composed of roughly 750 loose manuscript pages Dewey wrote largely between 1941 and 1942. *Unmodern Philosophy and Modern Philosophy* (*UM&MP*) evolved from a work on the origins of science in relation to common sense into the final project on the present era's unmodernity. The manuscript was famously reported by the *New York Times* and speculated on by Dewey scholars to have been left in a cab outside the Deweys' New York City home, but the true story of how the pages disappeared and, even more mysteriously, how they were eventually entered into the Dewey Papers at Southern Illinois University to lay unexamined for decades, remains unknown. Though the published work is edited from the remaining pages of an evolving and incomplete manuscript, the final result contains a surprisingly coherent and powerful argument.[1]

However, the focus of the *Oxford Handbook of Dewey* is not on the past, either of the manuscript or of the pragmatist philosophical tradition. Echoing Dewey's own call in "The Need for a Recovery of Philosophy," this handbook explicitly calls for scholars to do more than simply to chew philosophical cud, to bring up well digested pragmatist material (1917, MW 10: 47). The present task, rather, is to think about the next stage of Dewey scholarship, which is consistent with his ongoing demand that philosophy address not only its own problems but the problems of humanity. My focus in this chapter, then, will not be to provide a historical account of *UP&MP* or simply to summarize its contents. Instead, it is to provide one compelling path for future work in the wake of this "new" book.

The sad fact is that Dewey did not come close to completing the manuscript. The plan for the text was for it to have three parts—historical, theoretical, and practical. After a critical genealogy of our unmodern present, he followed with an analysis of the outworn theoretical dichotomies that reflect our unmodernity—those between mind and body, things and persons, practical and theoretical, and material and ideal. After that, Dewey planned to write on the practical upshot of a truly modern philosophy that had overcome these antiquated dichotomies but did not. Scholars who wish to work out the implications of this unfinished book have been given a few promising avenues. It contains a sparkling section on his philosophy of technology, an ontology of events, and threads to critique philosophy's ongoing and unfortunate epistemological project. All of these are worth pursuing.

However, in this chapter, I make the case that we need to elaborate a Deweyan account of modernity and modernization. Perhaps this is for idiosyncratic reasons. When I first heard of the missing manuscript, I wanted to find it first and foremost to find Dewey's theory of modernity. As my original, motivating interest in the mysterious missing manuscript would have answered in his unwritten third part, this is frustrating. Since finding the pages, I have wondered what Dewey would have or should have written.[2] Reflecting the influence of Hegel's thought, Dewey believed that to think is to articulate the meaning of the present, however messy or self-contrary that present may be. In this chapter I try to provide some initial understanding of what Dewey meant by modernity, to sketch a few ideas about what the present crisis of modernity is, and to outline future research.

To sharpen our understanding of Dewey's theory of modernity, I engage another thinker who thought that modernity was unfinished but well worth completing rather than turning to antimodernism, premodernism, or postmodernism—Jürgen Habermas.[3] In 1980, Habermas was awarded the Adorno Prize, named after his teacher and founding member of the Frankfurt School of Western Marxism. He took the occasion to speak on modernity and those who have turned against it in the name of either premodern tradition or an antimodern rejection of reason in the name of aesthetic nihilism. He sought to diagnose the pathologies of modernity and to propose a cure. That piece was published under the title "Modernity: An Unfinished Project," and Habermas went on to further develop its argument in *The Philosophical Discourse of Modernity* and other texts (Habermas 1980/1997, 1985/1987, 1992, 1996/2001). Because Habermas' central project here bears an elective affinity with Dewey's, and because it offers a way of framing our discussion of Dewey's work in a very different way from those typically found in the pragmatist literature, I attack the problem of modernity in Dewey by whetting it against three of Habermas' points: (a) the meaning of modernity, (b) diagnosis of the pathologies of modernity through discussion of social and cultural modernization and their relationship to the lifeworld of everyday human practice, and (c) proposed cures for the pathologies of "unmodernity" shifting from a philosophy of subjective consciousness to one of communicative action.

Three opening provisos: First, this is not an attempt to explore Habermas' social theory thoroughly, which is vast and dense, but only to use it as a jumping off point to elaborate Dewey's analysis of modernity in a new and, hopefully, productive way. Second, I am not taking up Habermas' critique of postmodernism, premodernism, and antimodernism, though Dewey had some interesting and compatible things to say, particularly regarding the problem of skepticism. Third, I do not want to slight those who have fruitfully explored the intersection of Dewey and Habermas' work, but I do narrow focus to the primary texts alone.[4] With those prophylactic comments out of the way, we can proceed.

MODERNITY AND HOMEWORLD

Dewey famously acknowledged that Hegel had left a "permanent deposit" in his thought (1930a, LW 5: 154). Habermas shares with Dewey the Hegelian aspiration to reconcile the contradictions of modernity. In particular, they both desired to find a new, modern homeworld lost in the wake of the failure of the Medieval synthesis. Human reason had come to replace the unity provided by the Church as traditional ideologies and institutions were torn apart by the rise of capitalism, industry, technology, and science. But they also shared Hegel's optimism that building a reconciled world was possible but now would embody universal freedom. Dewey and Habermas do not want us to wearily resign to the world ushered in by the technoscientific revolution, nor are they nostalgic thinkers. They are hopeful, since the overcoming of tradition makes it possible for individuals to find a new home based in the free exercise of reason.

The question of the meaning of the modern has been raised many times. In many ways, modernity is defined by the asking of that question, as modernity is an awareness of the new, of the present moment as a beginning and a breaking with the past. To be modern is to ask what it means to be modern. Therefore, the question of modernity has come up every time an era becomes aware of itself *as* an era (Habermas 1980/1997, 39–42; 1996/2001, 131–132). For both Habermas and Dewey, this question needs to be asked today because a truly modern social existence has become possible but has gone unrealized. They do not possess the optimism that we have escaped our self-imposed immaturity and taken responsibility as free and rational beings for our future history, as marked Kant's earlier awareness of his own modernity in "What Is Enlightenment?" (Kant 1784/1991). Instead, we have missed critical opportunities. For Habermas, we had (and have) the opportunity to escape subject-centered reason and take up communicative action. For Dewey, the technoscientific revolution has prepared us to apply the methods of experimental inquiry to human values. Unfortunately, neither opportunity has been seized. The result is a culture in conflict with itself.

As Dewey discusses in detail in the first half of *UM&MP*, conceptual tools and categories developed during premodern times continue to shape how we approach both our value-rich everyday lives and abstract reflection on them. The cultural contradictions of today are the result of a blend of the modern and the unmodern. We refuse to apply the advances in method in the area of natural science to the realm of human affairs. We are left with philosophical dualisms of thought / practice, thing / person, mind / body, material / ideal, and nature / humanity—the analysis of which comprise the second half of the book. "The dualisms which are the staple of modern philosophy are, in the first place, reflections, mirrorings, of clashes, cleavages in the cultural life of the West" (1952, LW 16:407) and "are, fundamentally, expressions of the split within our culture between the 'scientific' and the 'moral'" (Dewey 2012, 94). The result is something posing as modern philosophy reflecting a not-yet-modern culture. "[W]hat is called 'modern' is as yet unformed, inchoate. Its confused strife and its unstable uncertainties reflect the mixture of an old and a new that are incompatible. The genuinely modern has still to be brought into existence" (1948, MW 12:273).

The question of modernity is then born of confusion, not confidence. Perhaps this is because, for both thinkers, our modernity is not anchored in a return to the ancients presumed to have intuited eternal Truths. Our modernity is a not a re-naissance or recovery of what had been lost in the so-called Dark Ages. Instead, it is an unanchored time that is left to develop its own operative norms out of the stuff of the lived experience itself. The scientific method is self-correcting and portable, but it lacks an infallible foundation in the Absolute, and this can be unsettling to those who think the Absolute is necessary to feel safe in the world. While writing *UM&MP*, Dewey repeatedly transcribed a quotation from Matthew Arnold that opens chapter 6, "Wandering between Two Worlds": "Modern times find themselves with an immense body of institutions, established facts, accredited dogmas, customs and rules, which have come to us from times not modern. In this system their life has to be carried forward; yet they have a sense that their system is not of their own creation, and that it by no means corresponds exactly with the wants of their actual life; that, for them, it is customary, not rational. *The awakening of this sense is the awakening of the modern spirit*" (Dewey 2012, 92). Modernity is then liberating but terrifying. To recall a phrase from a book that significantly influenced *Unmodern Philosophy*, Gilbert Murray's *The Four Stages of Greek Religion*, the retreat into epistemology and fundamentalism with their quests for epistemic and moral certainties, is the result of a "failure of nerve." While the experimental search for knowledge has made peace with the loss of a fixed anchor, the realm of value has not and retreats into a traditional desire for certainty. This realm is then "unmodern" because it does not recognize, using Steven Fesmire's (very Deweyan) technological metaphor, "Wherever we drop anchor, our anchorage inevitably moves" (Fesmire 2015, 44).

To discuss modernity is then not to conceptualize a reconciled homeworld that already exists in fact—as we might imagine the ancients to have had—but to conceptualize our present contradictions, as in modern art typified by Picasso's *Guernica*. This is true for Habermas as well, as I argue through the rest of this chapter. Drawing from strands of Left Hegelianism, both Dewey and Habermas are trying to rationalize the world by showing the contradictions of modernity and, in so doing, opening the possibility of reconciliation in fact rather than merely represented in thought or art. And this will require overcoming a pseudoscientific philosophy that is on a quest for certainty or reliant on certain subjective intuitions (as we find even among "modern" philosophers like John Locke).

Pathologies of Societal and Cultural Modernization

To be modern in our unmodern era is then to feel not at home in one's awareness of the new. The question follows of why we feel this way. As Dewey and Habermas frame it, the modern era demands a resolution: modernization. Habermas' Weberian analysis of modernization opens an interesting angle for reading Dewey's. Drawing from German sociologist Max Weber's work, Habermas identifies two forms of modernization—cultural and societal. Through these lenses, he diagnoses the pathologies of modernity. Though Dewey's diagnosis certainly differs from Habermas' in important ways, the parallels are illuminating.

Cultural modernization is the process by which cultural spheres are differentiated. The scientific, moral-legal, and aesthetic spheres develop as fields of social life each according to their own internal logic, resulting in universal judgments grounded in unique validity claims of truth, rightness, and authenticity. This is exemplified in the rise of aesthetic modernism and art for art's sake. In this understanding, artworks are not to be evaluated by their capacity to represent reality or by their capacity to promote moral goodness in their audience; rather, they are judged by their internal standards of beauty or aesthetic experience. Recall Oscar Wilde's introduction to *The Portrait of Dorian Gray* in which he argued that art uses truth and lies or pieties and immoralities for its own purposes and serves no ends other than its own. As Wilde argued for aesthetic modernism, so too did Habermas argue for the other cultural spheres. Science is oriented toward judgments of objective knowledge while the moral-legal sphere seeks universally valid judgments of rightness. This cultural differentiation was fully articulated, according to Habermas, in Kant's three *Critiques* in which, for example, the norm of disinterested pleasure allowed for universally valid aesthetic judgments while isolating them from scientific or moral purposes (Habermas 1980/1997, 42–48).

In itself, such cultural modernization is not a threat. It allows each sphere to develop rapidly and attain universally valid judgments appropriate to each. We stop trying to judge art or truth by moral standards, scientific findings by aesthetic and moral standards, and so on. However, this development, taking place within the lifeworld of everyday social experience, is threatened on two fronts. First, as each sphere differentiates, it becomes more the domain of experts—scientists, moral and legal theorists, and artists and art critics. The various communicative practices of the lifeworld are left behind and the advantages of differentiation are lost. Public life is being impoverished as experts go into relative self-exile. This point was made also by Dewey in his critique of Walter Lippmann's democratic elitism in *The Public and Its Problems* and throughout *Art as Experience*. Second, cultural modernization rooted in the everyday practices of the lifeworld is threatened by societal modernization.

Societal modernization, distinguished from cultural modernization, is an extension of Weber's analysis of the expansion of instrumental-purposive rationality as manifested in economic and administrative-bureaucratic reason. According to Weber, modernity is being increasingly encased in an "iron cage" of such thinking. This type of rationality attends only to the efficiency of means and not the substantive ends being pursued. It asks only how well we can do something, not what should be done in the first place. It is the reason of the bureaucrat who follows orders as crisply as possible, or the product engineer who follows the higher-ups' demand to maximize profits and eliminate waste. As efficiency becomes an end in itself, other substantive epistemic, moral-legal, and aesthetic interests are pressed into service of the market or the state. Extending the Frankfurt School's critique of instrumental reason, Habermas charges that everything is becoming either a commodity or an object to be administered. All of social life is taken to be a system to be rationalized. Art becomes a commodity or propaganda. Science becomes a means to sell widgets or to maximize the state's military and administrative power. The lifeworld is "colonized."

Habermas' diagnosis on the pathologies of modernization then calls for a reversal of the colonization of the lifeworld and a reconnection of differentiated cultural spheres not with each other but with the undifferentiated lifeworld practices from which they sprang. However, before turning to how this is to be done, let us compare Habermas' diagnosis with Dewey's rejection of this sort of narrow technological reason.

In my reading, Dewey would agree with Habermas' critique of societal modernization but disagree with that regarding cultural. Though the Frankfurt School and many other critics reduced pragmatism to a crude instrumentalism that cares only about efficiency of means and collapses into the cultural logic of late capitalism, this charge has always been far afield from the truth. Dewey was a fierce critic of such instrumentalism, despite its sharing a favored name for his own theory of inquiry. He sharply rejected this sort of technological reason, nor did he cheer on technological mastery of nature for its own sake. Addressing such tools, he wrote, "They are not now controlled in any fundamental sense. Rather do they control us. They are indeed physically controlled. Every factory, power-house and railway system testifies to the fact that we have attained this measure of control. But control of power through the machine is not control of the machine itself . . . . We are not even approaching a climax of control; we are hardly at its feeble beginnings" (1930b, LW 5:86; see also 1944, LW 17:451–453).

The best, if brief, statement of Dewey's theory of technology is found in *UM&MP*, in which he explicitly describes knowing as a "mode of technology." This is not meant in a reductive sense in which thought is valuable only as a means of obtaining certain ends or control of the environment. Rather, this distorted understanding of knowing and of technology both result from our premodern baggage, the genealogy of which is provided in the first half of the book (Dewey 2012, 242–251). Knowing is an activity involving creative use and development of conceptual tools. As its etymology would indicate, the *logos* of *technê* is not mere tools but rational reflection on craft itself. Further, any theory of inquiry that did not understand ends-in-view as themselves part of the situation to be reconstructed, and therefore as open to revision as any means to achieve them, was truncated and dangerous. Experimental inquiry must inquire into ends in light of their means, as well as the reverse.

Further, Dewey was a democratic socialist radicalized by the failures of state capitalism during the Great Depression. He argued that one of the central failings of capitalism was that it submitted to crude instrumentalism. Drawing explicitly on Thorstein Veblen's engineer-businessman distinction, Dewey argued that the former is interested in solving problems while the latter would direct social productive potential into private profit by exploiting breakdowns of the market. Business-as-usual turns the public potential of human practice to narrow ends external to the needs of the situation.

Lastly, Dewey argued that this rapacious search for profit and efficiency was rendering everyday experience an-aesthetic, numbing and cheapening the lifeworld of value-rich social practice. So, in that, Dewey would agree that we must reverse societal modernization, while conceding with Habermas that instrumentality is not an evil in itself so long as it remains within its proper domain.

However, like Bruno Latour, the contemporary social theorist who famously declared that "we have never been modern," Dewey argues that cultural differentiation must be understood only functionally. It is not intrinsic. In *UP&MP*, and particularly in the final extant chapter "Experience as Life-Function," Dewey again voiced his regret, found originally in his re-introduction to *Experience and Nature*, that rather than the word "experience" he should have used "culture" to best express what he meant. It is the rich network of socially meaningful human practice akin to Habermas' lifeworld. The epistemological *aporia* of Subject-Object inherited from the so-called moderns from Locke to Kant is better understood as culture-in-nature. A virtue of this approach is its holism. There is no sharp separation between the knower and the known or between valuing truth, goods, or aesthetic richness. Spheres of life are not isolated but only functionally distinguished by how they work in our already value rich experience, and it is the job of philosophical inquiry to act as a liaison officer between various cultural inquiries, articulating and sharing the best techniques for problem-solving (1925, LW 1:306).

Dewey articulates the merely functional separation of the aesthetic and the instrumental in his *Art as Experience* (discussed further in a moment). While aesthetic experience is that phase of activity in which appreciation dominates, in which we focus on the consummated meaning at hand, that does not mean that it can be appreciated sharply cut off from the process that has been consummated. Further, in appreciation, we must take up a position akin to that of the producer of the artwork, just as the artist must take up the position of the appreciator while producing it. In this, Dewey does not think that it is truly possible to isolate art for art's sake from a process of production. It is itself the outcome of a productive process, induces a similar one in the audience, and may provide the experiential material for further production. And all along, it uses the material of scientific inquiry and moral ends as raw aesthetic material. But we may also say that the artwork as appreciated need not further any purposes external to itself; then again, we may say that of any consummating experience. The engineer or legislator may also aesthetically appreciate the outcome of his or her hard work. The case of the aesthetic then illustrates a larger point—that a cultural sphere may be functionally distinguished from others but that we may not isolate them essentially as distinct realms of life with intrinsically separate norms.

For Dewey, any differentiation between cultural spheres is functional, local, and against the backdrop of everyday culture / experience. It is dangerous to divide everyday social experience into isolated epistemic, moral or aesthetic domains, as it results in scientific inquiry without regard for moral or aesthetic values and moral inquiry without the use of the best methods of inquiry. As noted earlier, for Dewey, sharp differentiation of spheres like that between science and morals contributes to the pathologies of the lifeworld. The ongoing power of antiquated philosophical dualisms rooted in cultural contradictions prevents the development of the moral and aesthetic spheres. The problem is not that those areas have been unable to develop independently from technoscientific methods of solving problems and acquiring knowledge but precisely that we have failed to extend those methods into the realm of human values. Even Habermas, taking a cue from Abrecht Wellmer, implies that the sharp separations of the three cultural spheres does not exist with the communicative practices of everyday life (Wellmer, 1997). Rather, they interpenetrate.

Dewey agreed that we should not impose scientific-technical problems, tools, and solutions on to all aspects of culture—just as we would not impose aesthetic or moral problems, tools, and solutions on to all of culture—but that is not because they have an intrinsically different kind of universal validity but because reconstructions are local. He would, however, agree that expert culture must be reintegrated into the everyday if it is to be resistant to the encroachment of vulgar instrumentalism driven by the market.

EXPERIMENTAL AND
INTERSUBJECTIVE REASON

With that, let us turn to the final part of my attempt at an analysis of modernity—what needs to be done. Despite their grim analyses of the failure of modernization, Dewey and Habermas both held out hope. Dewey was a perpetual optimist, at least in the sense that it was always possible to ameliorate present problems—not that utopia would ever be at hand or that it was inevitable, only that there is always hope to improve present circumstances. Even Habermas once sunnily defined modernity as "the epoch that lives for the future, that opens itself to the novelty of the new" (1985/1987, 5).

Habermas seeks to overcome the philosophical centrality of epistemology—using Dewey's critical definition of epistemology as the search for certain knowledge through the connection of supposedly isolated Subject and Object—though that is not how he presents his project. Rather, it is the overcoming of the philosophy of consciousness / subjective reason. In his own diagnosis of the history of philosophy, Habermas regrets a missed opportunity. Modernity made a great leap forward when it overcame the limits imposed on reason by political and ecclesiastical authority. Humanity could think for itself without first swearing loyalty to some authority outside of itself. Instead, moral and legal commands must bring themselves before the tribunal of reason. However, this reason was understood as that of the isolated subject who, at the same time, was universal because of the universality of reason. Reason was understood through the lens of the self-aware thinking subject. From this foundational subjectivity, humanity was finally free to follow its own, universally valid moral law. Normativity was derived from within (Habermas 1996/2001, 133; Kant 1784/1991). This project is still alive, if stunted, and guides those who would fulfill the prospect of the Enlightenment. Modernity still "has to create its normativity out of itself" (Habermas 1985/1987, 7).

However, this subjective formulation of reason was torn by a series of internal divisions within the mind and between the mind and world. In the thought of the young Hegel was an opportunity to skirt these *aporia* of reason identified by Kant. Kant had unwittingly identified the dead end of thinking that reduces to the experiences of the subject and attempts to judge validity claims by reference to that subjectivity. The triremption of reason into science, morality, and aesthetics articulated by Kant was, for Hegel, to be reconciled in ethical life, but that was ultimately understood through the lens of subjectivity. Hegel opened the door to an alternative conception of reason in his early Jena writings but backslid by absolutizing subjectivity as Spirit understood as unconditional self-relation and self-realization. Historical reason came into its own as God reached self-knowledge (funnily enough) in Hegel's *Bildungsroman, The Phenomenology of Spirit*. But to Habermas, this can reconcile thought to itself, perhaps, but not thought to reality and vice versa. Hegel came up short because of his inability to break with subjective reason. Unknowingly agreeing with Dewey, Habermas saw that this unmodern reason could not replace the Medieval synthesis (Habermas 1996/2001, 135). Subject was cut off from Object and, for both Habermas and Dewey, philosophy reduced to epistemology (or its reactionary negation through Romanticism) and social thought to crudely instrumental reason.

Hegel's missed route for an ethical totality was through communicative action, which appeals to the norms operative internal to the linguistic practices of the intersubjectively constituted lifeworld—those practices that differentiate their own internal epistemic, moral-legal, and aesthetic validity. Internal to those practices are universally valid communicative norms—truth, rightness, authenticity—that could resist the invasion of the lifeworld by economic / bureaucratic / instrumental rationality. The norms of communicative action are still present immanently whenever we communicate, so the path is still there to be taken. Habermas' solution is to free communicative action, and thereby the lifeworld of everyday cultural practice, from instrumental reason. This reversal of societal modernization is to be paired with the return of experts to the lifeworld, to blunt the downside of cultural modernization and to reconcile them in the everyday practice—"expert culture is appropriated from the perspective of the lifeworld" (Habermas 1980/1997, 52).

For Habermas, the reason we have never truly been modern is that we have allowed purposive-instrumental rationality to predominate where it does not belong. This has long been the Frankfurt School's explanation for the failure of Marx's critique of political economy to account for the rise of late capitalism and totalitarianism rather than socialism: Marx himself did not see the dangers of instrumental or technological reason. As noted previously, this critique was also targeted at the classical pragmatists, particularly at William James and Dewey's Chicago School of instrumentalism, so it is particularly ironic that the resources for Habermas' critique of societal modernization and the colonization of the lifeworld, and for the elaboration of his concept of communicative action, arose from his engagement with the pragmatists Charles Peirce and George Herbert Mead (1992, 149–204; 1981/1985, 1–112; 1983/1995, 116–194). Their social pragmatist account of meaning and self-realization revitalized the Hegelian path not taken.

However, it seems to me that his theory of communicative action is still lacking. It centers on the norms of practice generally that arise out of the norms of communicative practice specifically. Universally valid norms governing each are said to arise out of the general requirements of each type of communication in the differentiated cultural spheres (though each is universally valid within its domain). For example, when we talk about morality, we implicitly appeal to the norm of mutual understanding even when saying vile and exclusionary words. The ethical totality comes not from the supposed unity of a subject / consciousness but from an ideal, unforced consensus of undistorted communication implicit in communication itself. Therefore, we may charge the fascist with a performative contradiction when their communication violates its implicit communicative norms.

But, ultimately, this strikes me as overly discursive. Rather, I would make the Deweyan point that the norms of practice arise from the needs of concrete practice in its many aspects. Further, I worry that Habermas' communicative solution sounds too close to Peirce's third method of fixing belief—that a belief "appeals to reason"—only this time reason is understood as intersubjective (which is, admittedly, an improvement). The problem is that the fact that we are able to reach consensus does not mean that we have engaged a recalcitrant external reality that pushes back. Discursive reason, however intersubjective, would seem to be weaker than an experimental reason that treats those immanent discursive norms as hypotheses to be tested in social practice. Their validity would seem to require that they "work" in the broadest possible sense, taking into account the many values and agents in play, rather than just securing agreement between people. Experimental action is no less intersubjective or communicative than communicative action, but it takes place in the context of experimentation to determine whether what can obtain consensus also gets the world to agree.[5]

Put more simply, Habermas hopes to fight the twin dangers of social and cultural modernization by appealing to the norms internal to communicative action. This will protect independent spheres dedicated respectively to scientific truths, moral rightness, and aesthetic value or emancipation from being reduced to mere instruments of bureaucratic capitalism. The norms are ever-present in uncoerced communication. But it is not clear that these norms are distinct, or only functionally distinguished according to the needs of the lived situation. Further, to assert that a scientific, moral, or aesthetic conclusion is true because it arose from uncoerced communication is sufficient to establish truth seems to overlook the critical role of extra-discursive reality. External reality's role in determining truth can be found only through experimentation. Dewey's understanding of intersubjectivity as that of the experimental community then seems to better address the risks of societal and cultural differentiation. Conceptually, his idiosyncratic model of technological reason seems to be a more promising route for understanding where reason went off the rails into unmodernity. It is more contextual, concrete, and experimental.

As noted, the problem for Dewey is not technoscientific reason as such; rather, it is one that has been coopted by the profit motive and reduced to crude instrumentalism. In his model, the problem is that knowing, understood as a mode of technology in a broad sense, has been "colonized" by technology in the narrow sense of mere means or "technological reason." Dewey explicitly asserts that if we would only incorporate this insight, "the entire epistemological, subject-object, mind-reality industry drops away. And this line is the only one that can be taken if the theory of knowledge is based upon knowing, as knowing is exhibited and made evident in scientific inquiry" (Dewey 2012, 242). As the critique of the rise of the epistemology industry is the core theme of the work, this places the notion of technology at the center.

According to Dewey, and long predicted by Larry Hickman's analysis of Dewey's philosophy of technology, the problem is that "technology" is insufficiently technological (Hickman 1990, 2001, 2007). We have developed astounding means / instruments / tools, but we have not brought ends into the inquiry. Technology would properly be a rational accounting of productive practice broadly understood to include technical, moral, and aesthetic production. Both ends and means are adjusted, abandoned, or improved in the course of testing our hypotheses against the world. That is, "technological" and "experimental" are the same. The problem is not that we have colonized instrumental reason into the lifeworld but that technological reason has itself been warped by economic and bureaucratic forces external to itself. A fundamental point of conflict between the Frankfurt School and philosophical pragmatists is that the former have denied that technoscientific inquiry may be reflective while the latter have disagreed. Both have been critical of a crude instrumentalism bound up with money and power, but they have differed over whether technoscience necessary serves the dominant cultural logic or if it may be a means of democratic emancipation.[6]

CONCLUSION

Let me try to put these initial thoughts on modernity, as structured by an engagement with Habermas' "Modernity: An Unfinished Project," into order. To specialists in American pragmatism, the idea that Dewey would argue that we are not truly modern because we carry an antiquated philosophical legacy comes as no surprise. *UP&MP* has some compelling new insights and provides depth to some familiar arguments, but it is not a radical turn from Dewey's other works. However, one does profit from reading it with and against Habermas' own critique of our failure to be modern.

Both hope to realize the still inchoate Enlightenment dream that reason and emancipation might still be linked, and both place the blame on the corrupting and totalizing effects of crude instrumentalism serving capital. Where they differ is over the need to develop differentiated norms with distinct cultural practices and whether technoscientific reason offers the means to realize modernity. This project is well worth our time. The fears that motivated them both—that culture has failed to unleash the potential of modernity's turn toward discourse and experimentation, away from absolutes available to introspective reason, and that philosophy has abdicated its critical role to uncritical markets and governments—certainly should motivate us today. The free exercise of public reason continues to suffer in an age of 140-character political debate, epistemic bubbles, and media consolidation. Unless that is corrected, data mining political operatives and conglomerates, media or otherwise, will have sway. While Dewey's and Habermas' analyses of modernization may be dense and technical, they are certainly not "academic." In this attempt to articulate the concept of modernity underlying *UP&MP* by whetting it against Habermas' own, I hope that paths forward both for research on *UP&MP* and for social reconstruction have been made clearer.

NOTES

1. For a far more detailed account of the manuscript's history and content, and of the editorial process and principles I used when preparing it, see the "Introduction" and "Editor's Introduction" (Dewey 2012, xiii–xlvi).

2. In this vein, and as a companion to the present chapter, I sketched some thoughts on a Deweyan cultural critique in the third part of my introduction to *UP&MP* (Dewey 2012, xxvi–xxxviii). For more on how *UP&MP* is related to Dewey's theory of historical inquiry, see also Deen (2013).

3. Hence, my not-terribly-subtle reference to the anthology on Habermas titled *Habermas and the Unfinished Project of Modernity* (D'Entrèves and Benhabib, 1997).

4. Because of Habermas' own focus on Peirce and Mead over Dewey, others have tended to do the same. Notable worthwhile examples of those discussing Dewey and Habermas / third generation Critical Theory include Antonio and Kellner (1992), Shalin (1998), Honneth (1998), Aboulafia et al. (2002), Whipple (2005), and Kadlec (2007).

5. In this, I find myself siding with experiential accounts of pragmatism against the linguistic, particularly those epistemic-pragmatist justifications of democracy that understand pragmatism to be saying that truth is uncoerced discursive agreement rather than agreement mediated by experimentation and the ensuing resistance of the world.

6. I am open to the possibility that I have projected too much of the classical Frankfurt School into Habermas. Scientific inquiry is one sphere of culture oriented toward objective knowledge, which may indicate that it is distinct from purposive rationality as such.

WORKS CITED

Aboulafia, Mitch, Myra Bookman, and Cathy Kemp, eds. 2002. *Habermas and Pragmatism*. New York: Routledge.

Antonio, R. J., and D. Kellner. 1992. "Communication, Democratization, and Modernity: Critical Reflections on Habermas and Dewey." *Symbolic Interaction*, vol. 15, no. 3, 277–298.

Deen, Phillip. 2013. "Pragmatist Historiography in Unmodern Philosophy and Modern Philosophy." *European Journal of Pragmatism and American Philosophy*, vol. 5, no. 1, 131–139.

d'Entrèves, Maurizio Passerin, and Seyla Benhabib. 1997. *Habermas and the Unfinished Project of Modernity: Critical Essays on the Unfinished Project of Modernity*. Cambridge, MA: MIT Press.

Dewey, John. 1917. "The Need for a Recovery of Philosophy." MW 10:3–63.

Dewey, John. 1925. *Experience and Nature* LW 1.

Dewey, John. 1930a. "From Absolutism to Experimentalism." LW 5:147–160.

Dewey, John. 1930b. *Individualism, Old and New*. LW 5:41–123.

Dewey, John. 1944. "Between Two Worlds." LW 17:451–465.

Dewey, John. 1948. "Reconstruction as Seen Twenty-Five Years Later." MW 12:256–277.

Dewey, John. 1952. "Modern Philosophy." LW 16:407–419.

Dewey, John. 2012. *Unmodern Philosophy and Modern Philosophy*. Edited by Phillip Deen. Carbondale: Southern Illinois University Press.

Fesmire, Steven. 2015. *Dewey*. New York: Routledge.

Habermas, Jürgen. 1980/1997. "Modernity: An Unfinished Project." In *Habermas and the Unfinished Project of Modernity: Critical Essays on the Unfinished Project of Modernity*. Edited by Maurizio Passerin d'Entrèves and Seyla Benhabib, 38–55. Cambridge, MA: MIT Press.

Habermas, Jürgen. 1981/1985. *The Theory of Communicative Action*. Vol. 2. Boston: Beacon Press.

Habermas, Jürgen. 1983/1995. *Moral Consciousness and Communicative Action*. Cambridge, MA: MIT Press.

Habermas, Jürgen. 1985/1987. *The Philosophical Discourse of Modernity*. Cambridge, MA: MIT Press.

Habermas, Jürgen. 1992. *Postmetaphysical Thinking*. Cambridge, MA: MIT Press.

Habermas, Jürgen. 1996/2001. "Conceptions of Modernity: A Look Back at Two Traditions." In *The Postnational Constellation*, 130–156. Cambridge, MA: MIT Press.

Hickman, Larry. 1990. *John Dewey's Pragmatic Technology*. Bloomington: Indiana University Press.

Hickman, Larry. 2001. *Philosophical Tools for Technological Culture: Putting Pragmatism to Work*. Bloomington: Indiana University Press.

Hickman, Larry. 2007. *Pragmatism as Post-Modernism: Lessons from John Dewey*. New York: Fordham University Press.

Honneth, Axel. 1998. "Democracy as Reflexive Cooperation: John Dewey and the Theory of Democracy Today." *Political Theory*, vol. 26, no. 6, 763–783.

Kadlec, Alison. 2007. *Dewey's Critical Pragmatism*. Lanham, MD: Lexington Books.

Kant, Immanuel. 1784/1991. "An Answer to the Question: What Is Enlightenment?" In *Kant: Political Writings*. Edited by H. S. Reiss, 54–60. Cambridge, UK: Cambridge University Press.

Shalin, Dmitri. 1998. "Critical Theory and the Pragmatist Challenge." *American Journal of Sociology*, vol. 98, no. 2, 237–279.

Wellmer, Albrecht. 1997. "Adorno, Modernity, and the Sublime." In *The Actuality of Adorno: Critical Essays on Adorno and the Postmodern*. Edited by Max Pensky. Albany, NY: SUNY Press.

Whipple, Mark. 2005. "The Dewey-Lippmann Debate Today: Communication Distortions, Reflective Agency, and Participatory Democracy." *Sociological Theory*, vol. 23, no. 2, 156–178.

IX

DEWEY IN CROSS-CULTURAL DIALOGUE

CHAPTER 26

DEWEY AND CONFUCIAN PHILOSOPHY

A Dialogue on Becoming Persons

ROGER T. AMES

GROUNDS FOR A DIALOGUE

As a promising beginning for dialogue, we might be encouraged by the fact that immigrant A.N. Whitehead, a self-confessed "American" philosopher, said in reference to his half-brother John Dewey: "If you want to understand Confucius, read John Dewey. And if you want to understand John Dewey, read Confucius" (Whitehead 1954, 176). In *Process and Reality*, Whitehead further allows that his own "philosophy of organism seems to approximate more to some strains of . . . Chinese thought" (Whitehead 1985, 7). The same Whitehead elsewhere announces (quite shamelessly for some) that when philosophizing, "it is more important that a proposition be interesting than that it be true" (Whitehead 1985, 259). Taking these several comments in sum, we might be buoyed by concluding that a philosopher of Whitehead's stature would recommend a tandem reading of Dewey and Confucius, if not as a source of truth then, even better, as a very interesting exercise. But nothing could be farther from the truth. Whitehead seems quite oblivious to the process sensibilities he shares with both Confucius and Dewey and in fact dismisses both of these philosophers explicitly as "pragmatists" whose commitment to what he considers to be a naïve empiricism precludes any but the most uninteresting of philosophical adventures[1] (Whitehead 1954, 176–177). Indeed, we are on the shakiest of grounds if we try to appeal to the authority of Whitehead as a warrant for our Confucian-Deweyan dialogue.

Even so, Whitehead's dismissive comments can be helpful if only to stimulate us to defend Dewy and Confucius against his philosophical condescension. In what follows, I explore resonances between these two traditions to argue that both Dewey and Confucius are indeed interested in what Whitehead calls "silly" and "superfluous" questions to the extent that such questions are of consequence in enhancing if not indeed enchanting the human experience.

We might remember that any suggestion of a fruitful comparison between Dewey and Confucius in Whitehead's own historical moment would have seemed as baffling to his philosophical colleagues as it was to him. And yet, I argue that from our present vantage point we can identify a set of seemingly disparate yet interrelated historical circumstances that years hence might be interpreted as having anticipated just such a conversation. Over one generation, precipitated largely by the rise of China, the economic and political order of the world has undergone a dramatic sea change and we have witnessed the rise of China as a world power. At the macro international level, it can be fairly argued that the United States and China share the most important economic and political relationship in the world today. Question: Will a changing world cultural order follow in the wake of this geopolitical transformation, and to what extent will distinctively American Deweyan pragmatism and distinctively Chinese Confucian philosophy be drawn upon as resources for this global revolution?

This increasingly complex relationship between the United States and China, although driven by opportunities for obvious mutual benefit, remains not only fragile and unstable but also, because of a profound lack of cultural understanding, largely underdeveloped. Said another way, were the United States and China able to realize a relationship of mutual trust and accommodation, the twenty-first century could be secured and its problems could be addressed with some real confidence. In the search for shared values and a common vocabulary needed to give them expression, there are clear reasons not only for the United States and China but for the world community broadly to promote a Confucian-Deweyan dialogue.

One obstacle to this dialogue is that, for most of the last century in our seats of higher learning, Western philosophy—that is, almost exclusively European philosophy—has constituted the mainstream curriculum worldwide. This exclusionary fact has been as true in Beijing, Tokyo, Seoul, and Delhi as it has been in Boston, Oxford, Frankfurt, and Paris. And if indigenous Asian and American philosophies have been largely ignored abroad, they have also been significantly marginalized within their home cultures.[2] A seemingly reticent William James had it almost right when he prefaced his 1901-2 Gifford lectures by admitting that "it seems the natural thing for us [Americans] to listen whilst the Europeans talk," except that he might have included the Asian philosophers along with the Americans as the natural audience for European philosophy (James 1985, 11).

The good news is that this Eurocentric self-understanding of professional philosophy, while still persistent, is gradually giving way in our own time in which the call for pluralism and diversity has become a mantra in higher education. It is clearly the case that there has been a powerful resurgence of interest in the American pragmatists over the past several decades and that non-Western traditions of philosophy too are now being taught more and more in tertiary institutions. While these indigenous, non-European traditions are still a long way from the mainstream, both American pragmatism and

Confucian philosophy at least have the shared responsibility of continuing to exert pressure on the discipline of philosophy to be more open and inclusive.

PHILOSOPHY IN CHINA AND "CHINESE" PHILOSOPHY

Turning to the Chinese academy, it would be fair to say that while contemporary Western philosophy has, until very recently, largely ignored the Chinese tradition, Confucian philosophy within China has been true to its own narrative in being porous and resolutely "comparative." That is, going as far back as the first wave of Western learning when Buddhist philosophy entered China in the second century CE, Confucianism has, over the centuries and down to the present day, evidenced a syncretic and hybridic pattern of absorbing into itself whatever would offer it its best competition.

Important for our anticipated dialogue is that in first encounter between Dewey and Confucianism in 1919, Confucianism had been under a sustained attack by the intellectuals identified with the New Culture Movement (1915–21). These reformers reviled Confucian philosophy as plaque clotting the intellectual arteries of China, retarding the vital circulation of the new Western ideas of "Mr. Democracy" and "Mr. Science" that would be necessary for a beleaguered China to emerge into the modern world. Indeed, in this historical context, Dewey, especially with his advocacy of progressive education, was prescribed by some as an antidote to the ills of Confucianism.[3] This initial encounter between Dewey's pragmatism and Confucianism was short-lived. An increasingly sinozized variation of Marxist-Leninism was contending with Yan Fu's (1854–1921) appropriation of Western liberalism in the late Qing dynasty (1644–1911) to serve China as the new political and cultural orthodoxy. And this Chinese version of a Marxist socialism was bent on smothering this still inchoate Deweyan pragmatism, and at the same time, on burying the last vestiges of Confucianism. In response to the rise and ultimate victory of Chinese communism, several of the most distinguished representatives of the New Confucianism movement fled the Chinese revolution to man the academic battlements abroad and defend the integrity of the Confucian tradition. Philosophers such as Tang Junyi, Mou Zongsan, and Fang Dongmei from their perches in Hong Kong and Taiwan looked to Europe, largely Germany, for philosophical ideas that could be drawn upon to fortify their Chinese philosophical resources. What these philosophers shared was the mission of, individually and together, formulating their own disparate versions of a hybridic New Confucianism to apply as a tourniquet to stop the hemorrhaging of a cultural tradition under full assault.

Today the keen interest in what had become Marxist-Maoism has, in marked degree, subsided among academic Chinese philosophers themselves. We can now look back over the past century and trace a steady progression in the Chinese academy among those Western philosophers who were being marshalled and absorbed into contemporary Chinese philosophy. There is a clear path from Kant and Hegel in the earlier days, to Whitehead, Wittgenstein, and, in particular, to phenomenology and Heidegger today. And it is germane to our Confucian-Deweyan dialogue that the shift of interest from Kant to Heidegger among Chinese philosophers has been motivated, in important degree, by the perceived resonances between Heidegger and their own indigenous ways of thinking.[4] In fact, the reestablishment of Chinese sovereignty in the mid-twentieth century and the exponential emergence of China as a world power over the last generation are fueling within China a renewed awareness of its own cultural tradition as a resource for self-understanding and as a platform for engaging its delayed but now ineluctable process of globalization. Today Confucianism in particular is being promoted vigorously by both government agencies and within the academy itself as the spiritual root of this living tradition.

This series of complementary and interpenetrating conditions has set the stage for a conversation between a revitalized Deweyan pragmatism and a Confucianism in ascent that are placeholders for the rich and varied resources that define in some important degree the predominant and persistent cultural sensibilities of their native soils (Thompson and Hilde 2000; Fei 1992).[5]

CONFUCIANISM AND DEWEYAN PRAGMATISM AS RADICAL EMPIRICISMS

In our own historical moment, a default ideology of liberal individualism prevails both within Western cultures and among Asian urban elites. This individualism is an ideology to the extent that, in our post-Marxist, postcollectivist era, liberal assumptions about what it means to be a person have come to have a monopoly on human consciousness that does not brook any influential alternatives. Our current discourse in ethics and social and political philosophy has become dominated by an understanding of the human being that takes a foundational individualism as its starting point and, as such, appeals to the familiar vocabulary cluster of agents, acts, generic virtues, human rights, entitlements, character traits, autonomy, motivation, reasons, choice, freedom, principles, consequences, and so on. Confucianism and Deweyan pragmatism would both reject any suggestion that persons are autonomous individuals that, on the basis of their autonomy, can be accurately described, analyzed, and evaluated independently of their contextualizing environments. They would both contend that persons can only be measured first and foremost by their dealings with other human beings and the quality of the bonds they are able to grow in these interpersonal relationships. Indeed, I would argue that perhaps the most important contribution these two traditions have to make to our contemporary philosophical discourse is their robust alternatives to individualism—that is, Confucianism's conception of the relationally constituted "consummate person" (*ren* 仁), and the neologism Dewey develops and deploys to challenge what he denounces as a "new individualism," that is, his notion of "individuality."

Both the Confucian and Deweyan notions of person begin from the fact of association. Everything we do as human beings—physically, psychologically, socially, environmentally—is transactional and collaborative. Nothing and nobody does anything by itself. Persons are radically embedded as narratives nested within narratives and are "events" rather than individual "things"—they are intertwined histories rather than marbles in a jar. A corollary to this fact of association is the primacy of vital relationality. Relationships—our roles in family and community and as participants in the natural world as well—are first order, while our putative discreteness is a second-order abstraction. This shared doctrine of internal relations means that persons are particular configurations of relations and are thus themselves constituted by these roles and relationships. As irreducibly social, we humans are in the business of quite literally "making" friends, where the friendship is first order and the persons as discrete "individuals" are second-order abstractions from these relations. Such a conception of intrinsic relationality stands in stark contrast to external relations—that is, the idea that we begin as discrete, autonomous individuals who then establish relations between ourselves and other separate and independent individuals and that, when the dissolution of such relationships happens to occur, we still retain our initial identity and integrity as individuals.

Another Confucian and Deweyan corollary to associated living and the primacy of vital relationality is their radical empiricism. Confucian philosophizing begins from and seeks its warrant in the ordinary affairs of the day. This commitment to empiricism is captured in the "aspectual" language that serves as the key philosophical vocabulary for this tradition. By aspectual language, I mean that the terms of art, rather than providing analytic distinctions that allow for the diremption into separate parts of the manifold of elements in experience, speak to different perspectives on the same phenomenon. The often-evoked Confucian philosophical terminology such as "the inseparability of knowing and doing" (*zhixing heyi* 知行合一) and "the inseparability of forming and functioning" (*tiyong heyi* 體用合一) expresses a holistic worldview in which theoretical philosophizing is derived from and must be authenticated in our practices. Further, knowing and doing are just two different ways of looking at the same experience. Again, given the focus and field nature of our experience, the cosmic totality is adumbrated in each impulse of experience. As Mencius famously states, "The myriads of things all find their fruition here in me" (*Mencius* 7A4). The ultimate Confucian project is to transform what is ordinary into the extraordinary through a regimen of personal, communal, and cosmic cultivation—that is, to elevate and enchant the everyday. In the first and most fundamental of the canonical *Four Books*, the *Expansive Learning* (*Daxue* 大學), this project is stated explicitly in the following terms: "cultivate your person" (*xiushen* 修身), "set you family right" (*qijia* 齊家), "bring proper order to the nation" (*zhiguo* 治國), and "promote peace in the world" (*pingtianxia* 平天下). These several radial dimensions of personal cultivation are coterminous and mutually entailing, where the ultimate source of meaning is cultivated personal relations and where a world at peace provides the ideal context for personal growth and our consummation within family and polity. As we transform ourselves, we transform our environing context.

Dewey captures this same commitment to empiricism in his early 1896 publication on the reflex arc in psychology. This article challenges the traditional, fragmenting, and decontextualizing stimulus-response understanding of interactions derived from the "old" Cartesian psychology with a new, transactional, and holographic paradigm. The argument is that a person's entire complex narrative is entailed in how one is drawn into particular activities and in how one responds to such stimulation. In this interpretation of experience, a young Dewey sets his career trajectory of eschewing the familiar dualisms that have become fundamental to our commonsense—mind-body, agent-action, subjective-objective, self-other, and so on—and of reinstating context as a necessary condition for understanding any and all of experience. For Dewey, the relationship between organism and environment is invariably one of doing and undergoing, of shaping and being shaped.

Another key clarification that the young Dewey offers for experience as it is to be understood in this new pragmatism is his 1905 statement of the postulate of immediate empiricism in which he rejects the nonempirical assumptions about "things-in-themselves," whether they be atoms or a priori concepts. His starting point is that experience is always "experience of *thats*." And given the inseparability of the subjective and the objective in everything we see and do, an understanding of the content of our experience requires that we ask: "What is *that* experienced *as*?" Such a question applies not only to the furniture of our experience but also to our philosophical terms of art such as "subjective, objective, physical, mental, cosmic, psychic, cause, substance, purpose, activity, evil, being, quantity—any philosophic term, in short." In this seminal article, Dewey is rejecting the epistemic fallacy that equates reality with knowledge, arguing that all experience is equally real. And if we want to know what something "really" is, he says "go to experience and see what it is experienced as."

CONFUCIANISM AND THE AESTHETICIZATION OF THE HUMAN EXPERIENCE

Having established this radical empiricism as a shared interpretive context for Confucianism and Deweyan pragmatism, we can now turn specifically to the notions of person that emerge from their shared assumptions about the primacy of relationality, the eventful nature of experience, and the role that context has in the understanding and explanation of any particular event.[6] For both conceptions of person, we might begin by challenging the familiar, essentializing expression "human being" with the neologism, "human becomings" to underscore the processional and thus gerundive nature of these shared cosmological assumptions.

There are several organically related terms that we will need to include in our exploration of the Confucian notion of *ren*仁 that in different contexts can be translated as either "consummate persons" or "consummate conduct." *Ren* is necessarily plural as "persons" here because, as suggested by the graph itself which combines "person/s" (*ren* 人) and the number "two" (*er* 二), in this tradition, we need each other to become persons. As Herbert Fingarette famously opines, "For Confucius, unless there are at least two human beings, there can be no human beings" (Fingarette 1983, 217). Another way of making this same point with the translation of *ren* as "consummate conduct" is to register the irreducibly transactional nature of "conduct" itself (L. *condūcō*: "a bringing together").

The first term we need in understanding how personal identity is realized for consummate "human becomings" is *li* 禮: "aspiring to propriety in one's roles and relations." Going back to the high culture of the Shang dynasty, formally prescribed rites and rituals were performed at stipulated times to reinforce the political and religious status of the participants within the extended family lineages and to punctuate the seasons of the life at court. Originally such ritual performances were narrowly defined, formal, religious procedures enacted by the ruling class and its entourage to fortify their relationship with nature and with the inhabitants of the other penumbral world. These rituals were often constituted in imitation of perceptible cosmic rhythms as a means of strengthening the coordination of the human, natural, and spiritual environments. They were used to reinforce a sense of human participation within the regular operations of the cosmos. Gradually over the ensuing centuries these ritual activities were extended outwards radially from rulers themselves to the community more broadly, thereby investing in these life forms an increasingly social significance. In these extended ritual observances, participants would have their proper status and place, and to the extent that persons were not fully cognizant of what the details and spirit of the ritual procedures required of them, they would quite literally not know where to stand and what to do.

In Confucius's account of his own personal growth found, he states that "by fifteen I had set my purposes on learning, and by thirty I had taken my stance," (*Analects* 2.4) referring thereby to the assiduous effort he was making in his continuing project of personal cultivation. In the unfolding of one's narrative, education in its broadest sense was learning where to stand and what to say. Importantly, throughout the *Analects*, such terminologies are closely linked to the governing metaphor of "advancing resolutely on one's way" (*dao* 道). It is repeatedly stated throughout the Confucian canons that it is "ritual propriety" (*li*)—also frequently translated as "rites," "ceremony," "etiquette," "decorum," "manners"—that enables persons to determine, consolidate, and display virtuosity in the relational transactions in the course of their daily lives. What recommends the translation of *li* as "propriety" is that it along with other words such as "appropriate," "proper," and "property," is derived etymologically from the Latin, *proprius* with its core meaning of "making something one's own." The substance of *li*, unlike formal rules and regulations, is dependent upon a process of assiduous personalization—that is, it is the aspiration to make the unique role of this particular daughter in her relationship with this father, something moving and magical.

But not everyone can "live" *li* in an equally felicitous way. It is the cultivated quality of the persons involved in the ritualized life forms that determine the virtuosity expressed through *li*. And only those who are consummate in their conduct are able to truly express the meaning and the musicality of the ritually aestheticized life:

> The Master said: "What have persons who are not consummate in their conduct to do with achieving ritual propriety in their roles and relations? What have persons who are not consummate in their conduct to do with the playing of music?"

> (*Analects* 3.3)

Although these *li* life forms clearly have their formal and redundant structures, still the preponderant significance of such activities in defining family and communal life lies in those informal, personal, and particular aspects that conduce to and are necessary for the real religious experience of binding tightly within our families and communities. The *li* have an important affective aspect wherein feelings suffuse and fortify all of our relational activities, providing the communal fabric a tensile strength that resists the inevitable tensions and rupture that attend associated living. *Li* also have a profoundly somatic dimension where body is often as effective as language in communicating the deference necessary to strengthen the bonds among those participating in the various life forms. Pursuing refinement through the performance of *li* must be understood in light of the uniqueness of each participant engaged in the profoundly aesthetic project of becoming this exceptional and always inimitable person. *Li* is a process of personal articulation—the growth and disclosure of an elegant disposition, an attitude, a posture, a signature style, and, ultimately, a persistent and singular identity.

When we turn to Confucian role ethics, one way to distinguish the inclusive and holistic Confucian vision of the moral life from more formalized and hence reductionistic principled-based ethical theories is to give an account of how the particular, the informal, and the contextualizing aspects of experience, far from being discounted and marginalized, in fact take on a central importance as those resources that can be drawn upon to maximize the productive outcome of always particular human activities. This aesthetic dimension—the need for moral artistry in ethics—is integral to this holistic understanding of human conduct in which all aspects of experience have more or less relevance and thus have some value for determining a worthwhile outcome. It is because the moral vision of Confucian role ethics is concerned with coordinating the contribution of each aspect of experience in achieving the totality of the effect that the normative language it appeals to are, in the Whiteheadian sense, fundamentally aesthetic terms (Whitehead 1938, 53–60). The moral quality of conduct itself is most often characterized in the texts in the qualitative language of authenticity and genuineness or duplicity and pretense rather than by appeal to the rationalizing language of right or wrong, good or evil. There is a perceived, inseparable relationship between elegance and morality and, conversely, between baseness and immorality.

Since morality itself in this Confucian tradition is nothing more than those modalities of acting that conduce to the enhancement of relations, any kind of conduct that has a disintegrative effect on the fabric of family or community is perceived as fundamentally immoral. Lifestyle takes on crucial import when we consider the corrosive consequences on the community of those who live lives without style. Carelessness becomes of major concern when we have to worry about those who could care less. And ignorance in the sense of ignoring the needs of others far from being detached or neutral, is in fact to inflict a violence upon their persons (Dalmiya, 1998). Graciousness, on the other hand, has gravity when we reflect on the relevance that charm and deportment have for an overall sense of fittingness and propriety. Morality is much more than formal correctness, emerging as it does importantly from poise and deportment in our transactions with others.

In addition to the term *li* 禮 as "achieving propriety in one's roles and relations," the second, hugely significant factor we must consider in the process of realizing and focusing a persisting, personal identity and its coherent horizons of relevance—that is, in becoming "consummate persons" (*ren*)—comes with the cognate term, the "lived body" (*ti* 體). The structure of our understanding and our habitude is rooted in and shaped by the fact of our embodied experience in its visceral connection to the world. At the most primordial level, the body via three mutually entailing modalities—our discursive, our vital, and our carnal bodies—serves as the bond that coordinates our subjectivity with our environments and that mediates the processes of thinking and feeling within our emerging patterns of conduct. Human procreativity expressed in our physicality provides the birthing of distinctive and unique persons from those who are genealogically prior. At the same time, within this ongoing, ceaseless, and overlapping process of embodiment, the many prior progenitors persist in this continuing process of transforming into someone else. That is, while persons emerge to become specifically who they are as unique creatures, the parents and grandparents of such persons continue to live on in them, most obviously in their physicality but, more importantly, in how they think and feel. The eventful process continues as the progeny too in their turn are alive in their own descendants. And this "living on" is not meant merely rhetorically Even more obvious and significant than the transmission of physical likenesses are the substantial continuities of the cultural tradition itself—its language, institutions, and values that are embodied and transmitted by each succeeding generation.[7]

In this Confucian tradition, "body" (*ti* 體) and its cognate character "aspiring to propriety in one's roles and relations" (*li* 禮) are correlative and aspectual in the sense that they express two ways of looking at the same phenomenon. That is, these two graphs reference "a living body" and "embodied living," respectively. The notion of *li* 禮 denotes a continuing, complex, and always novel pattern of invested institutions and significant behaviors that is embodied, authored, and reauthorized by successive generations. *Li* is the persistent cultural authority that serves to unify the family lineages (*shizu* 氏族) and clans (*jiazu* 家族) and that, in the fullness of time, comes to constitute the genealogical identity of a living people (*minzu* 民族).

It should be clear that what we are referencing here is not simply the transmission of a physical lineage. The living body and our embodied living is the conveyance of the cultural corpus of knowledge—linguistic facility and proficiency, religious doctrines and mythologies, the aesthetics of refined living, the modeling of mores and values, instruction and apprenticeship in cognitive technologies, and so on—through which a living civilization itself is preserved and extended. Our bodies are certainly our physicality, but they are much more. They are also conduits through which the entire body of culture is inherited, interpreted, elaborated upon, and reauthorized across the ages. For this holistic Confucian philosophy, our unique persons in their physical and narrative entirety penetrate so deeply into human experience that it would be a nonsense to try to separate out some reality that stands independent of them. Said another way, our reality is our lived, embodied experience, and nothing else.

Dewey's Neologism: "Individuality"

We now turn from the Confucian conception of "consummate persons" (*ren*) as their identities are achieved through "embodied living" (*li*) and the "living body" (*ti*), to Dewey's somewhat resonant notion of "individuality." Dewey in *Individualism Old and New* worries over the growth of an aberrant form of individualism that had broken with Emerson's promise to conjure forth for us a nonconformist and self-reliant American soul. Dewey rues the fact that real "individuality," the end of the Emersonian project in which each one of us aspires after the highest quality of our own personal uniqueness, had degenerated into the then prevailing ideology of a self-interested and contentious "individualism." Such a "new" individualism gives us little other than a zero-sum mercantile culture of winners and losers:

> The spiritual factor of our tradition, equal opportunity and free association and intercommunication, is obscured and crowded out. Instead of the development of individualities which it prophetically set forth, there is a perversion of the whole ideal of individualism to conform to the practices of a pecuniary culture. It has become the source and justification of inequalities and oppressions.
>
> (1930, LW 5:49)

The first point Dewey would make is that we need to abandon our commonsense assumption that we live our lives inside our skins and recognize the extent to which life is "out there" in a way that is organic, interactive, and fully collaborative with the changing world:

> The thing essential to bear in mind is that living as an empirical affair is not something which goes on below the skin-surface of an organism: it is always an inclusive affair involving connection, interaction of what is within the organic body and what lies outside in space and time, and with higher organisms, far outside.
>
> (1925/1929, LW 1:215)

For Dewey, "individuality" is not initially quantitative: it is neither a pre-social potential nor a kind of isolating discreteness. Rather, "individuality" is first and foremost qualitative, arising through distinctive service to one's community. Individuality is "the realization of what we specifically are as distinct from others (1891, EW 3:326)," a realization that can only take place within the context of a flourishing communal life. "Individuality cannot be opposed to association." says Dewey. "It is through association that man has acquired his individuality, and it is through association that he exercises it."[8] An individual so construed is not a "thing" but a "patterned event" describable in the language of uniqueness, integrity, social activity, relationality, and qualitative achievement. Dewey's conception of what I have called a "human becoming" provides us with a gerundive notion of unique and interdependent persons for whom relationality, particularity, and sociality are the source and expression of their individuation and for whom such individuation—their distinctiveness—far from excluding relationships with others, is to be measured by the virtuosity they are able to achieve within the patterns of the relations that come to constitute them. Our "individuality" is neither an initial condition nor exclusive of others; on the contrary, we become distinctive and even distinguished as the immediate product of the quality of the relations we have been able to effect with others. And it is in the achievement of this distinctiveness that "individuality" becomes quantitative, allowing us to stand out as unique and inimitable persons.

To further explore Dewey's understanding of individuality then, we will need several additional terms, the first of which is his idiosyncratic use of "habits." Dewey is keenly aware that he is using "habits" in an unfamiliar way. That is, he develops a distinctive language of habits to describe the various modalities of association that enable human beings to add value to their activities and to transform their mere associative relations into a fully communicating community. He justifies this choice of terms by claiming that:

> we need a word to express that kind of human activity which is influenced by prior activity and in that sense acquired; which contains within itself a certain ordering or systematization of minor elements of action; which is projective, dynamic in quality, ready for overt manifestation; and which is operative in some subdued subordinate form even when not obviously dominating activity.
>
> (1922, MW 14:31)[9]

We might appeal to some Deweyan observations on habits of personal growth as an alternative vocabulary that might provide us with an associative analogy for this Confucian relational, situational, and transactional notion of personal conduct. First, Dewey is critical of the hypostatization of conduct as a concept of discrete agency that locates instincts within isolated individuals:

> A combination of traditional individualism with the recent interest in progress explains why the discovery of the scope and force of instincts has led many psychologists to think of them as the fountain head of all conduct, as occupying a

place before instead of after that of habits. The orthodox tradition in psychology is built upon isolation of individuals from their surroundings. The soul or mind or consciousness was thought of as self-contained and self-enclosed.

(1922, MW 14:93–94)

Dewey in rejecting the priority of an ostensive autonomous "self" over that of a habitude—an organic configuration of relations—appeals to the actual situated human experience as we live it. He makes the argument that shared cultural life forms or "habits" must have priority over instincts by observing that any infant isolated from its dependent relations would quickly become a dead infant; that is, infants left to their own devices without access to, or intervention by culturally informed relations could not survive for a single day. Even the meaning of the actions and gestures of infants is derived from the mature communal context within which they reside:

> The inchoate and scattered impulses of an infant do not coordinate into service-able powers except through social dependencies and companionships. His impulses are merely starting points for assimilation of the knowledge and skill of the more matured beings upon whom he depends. They are tentacles sent out to gather that nutrition from customs which will in time render the infant capable of independent action. They are agencies for transfer of existing social power into personal ability; they are means of reconstructive growth.
>
> (1922, MW 14:94)

Dewey is, in his own tradition, a flat-out revolutionary in insisting upon the primacy of the relationally constituted, concrete situation as the garden in which to cultivate social intelligence and as the locus for the pursuit of the consummate life. The optimally appropriate response to our ever-present uncertainties, and to any confident resolution of these uncertainties, can only be negotiated within the actual circumstances themselves, with individual agency itself being an abstraction from them. Using Dewey's own language, this unique relational individuality stands in contrast to what he refers to as an "old psychology" that is based upon the assumed presence of some superordinate "soul" or "mind" or "self" as its principle of individuation:

> The traditional psychology of the original separate soul, mind or consciousness is in truth a reflex of conditions which cut human nature off from its natural objective relations. It implies first the severance of man from nature and then of each man from his fellows.
>
> (1922, MW 14:60)

As his radical alternative to what has become our commonsense understanding of the discrete person, Dewey argues that only the hold of a traditional conception of the singleness and simplicity of soul and self blinds us to perceiving what they mean: the relative fluidity and diversity of the constituents of selfhood. There is no one ready-made self behind activities. There are complex, unstable, opposing attitudes, habits, impulses, which gradually come to terms with one another, and assume a certain consistency of configuration.

(1922, MW 14:96)

In a thinly veiled criticism directed at his mentor and philosophical inspiration, William James, and at the internal inconsistencies that remained in James's groundbreaking *Principles of Psychology* with the stream of consciousness it endorses, Dewey insists that

the doctrine of a single, simple and indissoluble soul was the cause and the effect of a failure to recognize that concrete habits are the means of knowledge and thought. Many who think themselves scientifically emancipated and who freely advertise the soul for a superstition, perpetuate a false notion of what knows, that is of a separate knower. Nowadays they usually fix upon consciousness in general, as a stream or process or entity. . . . Now it is dogmatically stated that no such conceptions of the seat, agent or vehicle will go psychologically at the present time. Concrete habits do all the perceiving, recognizing, imagining, recalling, judging, conceiving and reasoning that is done.

(1922, MW 14:123–124)

How extreme is Dewey in this social construction of the person? As we have seen, he certainly rejects the idea that human beings are in any way complete outside of the associations they have with other people. But does Dewey go too far in the other direction when he claims that for the human being, "apart from the ties which bind him to others, he is nothing (1932, LW 7:323)?" For Dewey, the familiar contrast between an erstwhile discrete individual and society is a fiction, with the error lying in assuming that persons *are* individuals as opposed to understanding that their individuality and uniqueness is a social achievement won through the quality of their associated lives together. To seek a greater degree of individual freedom is in fact to attempt to change one's current configuration of social relations for a different, better configuration of relations that allows for a greater degree of participation in the activities that constitute the community.

Dewey follows his notion of individuality as a dynamic habitude to its logical conclusion, arriving at a holographic, focus-field conception of person in which the entire cosmos is entrained in each moment of experience:

We find also in all these higher organisms that what is done is conditioned by consequences of prior activities; we find the fact of learning or habit-formation. . . Thus an environment both extensive and enduring is immediately implicated in present behavior. Operatively speaking, the remote and the past are "in" behavior making it what it is. The action called 'organic' is not just that of internal structures; it is an integration of organic-environmental connections. It may be a mystery that there should be thinking but it is no mystery that if there is thinking it should contain in a 'present' phase, affairs remote in space and in time, even to geologic ages, future eclipses and far away stellar systems. It is only a question of how far what is "in" its actual experience is extricated and becomes focal.

(1925/1929, LW 1:213)

Dewey and the Social, Political, and Religious "Idea" of "Democracy"

Dewey, as with his terms "individuality" and "habits," demands much from his ideosyncratic use of the term "democracy," putting it to work as the method for achieving our "individuality" as unique persons through optimizing the possibilities provided by our associations:

> In one word, democracy means that *personality* is the first and final reality. It admits that the full significance of personality can be learned by the individual only as it is already presented to him in objective form in society; it admits that the chief stimuli and encouragements to the realization of personality come from society; but it holds, none the less, to the fact that personality cannot be procured for anyone else, however degraded and feeble, by any one else, however wise and strong.

(1882-1898, EW 1:244)

Dewey in clarifying the social production of persons, introduces an important distinction between the "idea" (and sometimes "ideal") of democracy, and democracy as a political form. In *The Public and Its Problems*, Dewey is holistic in looking for the real substance of democracy in the informal, the concrete, and the everyday—the lives and relationships of particular people in their own particular communities. He defines "the democratic idea in its generic social sense" in the following terms:

> From the standpoint of the individual, it consists in having a responsible share according to capacity in forming and directing the activities of the groups to which one belongs and in participating according to need in the values which the groups sustain. From the standpoint of the groups, it demands liberation of the potentialities of members of a group in harmony with the interests and goods which are common.

(1929, LW 2:327-28)

Dewey's insight is simple. We do not come into relationships but begin from being radically situated in and constituted by our relations. For Dewey, the "idea" of democracy then, is a social, a political, and, for him, ultimately a religious ideal that seeks to take full advantage of the opportunity that the human life provides us. The "idea" of democracy is the cosmological answer to the question: How do we grow initially inchoate, constitutive relations of persons-in-community to make them optimally productive? And in thus growing such relations, how can we optimize the possibilities of the human experience? The idea of democracy is thus both aesthetic and moral. It is the aesthetic of optimizing the creative possibilities of the communicating community and thus getting the most value and meaning out of the human experience. And it is moral in providing a concrete strategy for cultivating our interpersonal relations and maximizing their growth. For Dewey, the "doings and undergoings" of each and every person in this "Great Community" is the source and substance of real democracy—the optimal and virtuosic relationality of focal, holographic "individuals" as each of us uniquely and cooperatively shapes and is shaped by the emerging and shared communities to which we belong.

There is for Dewey a logic here. It begins from the observation that if we are constituted by our relations, it follows that when our neighbors do better, we do better. Positively stated, the idea of democracy is a strategy for getting the most out of the relations that constitute a community, and, negatively stated, it is a clear acknowledgment that any coercion in these roles and relationships is a diminution in the creative possibilities of the community. To be clear, Dewey's "idea" of democracy is not one possible option for associated living that exists among other alternatives; it is not one political system among many. Democracy is rather the never-to-be-realized, completed, or perfected ideal of consummate relatedness. As Dewey insists, the "idea" of democracy is nothing less than "the idea of community life itself" (1929, LW 2:328).

Confucian "Family Reverence" (*xiao*) and the Optimizing of Experience

Returning to the Confucian conception of "consummate persons" (*ren*) as "human becomings," there is its analog to Dewey's notion of "democracy" and its consequent Great Community as a strategy for optimizing of the human possibilities. Importantly, in the Confucian context, it is family rather than community that serves as the primary social nexus. Indeed, the term "family reverence" (*xiao* 孝) is the governing moral imperative in classical Confucianism and the tradition that follows from it. In the *Chinese Classic of Family Reverence*, Confucius declares that this "way of family reverence" is the very substance of morality and education. He declares specifically, "It is family reverence (*xiao*) that is the root of moral virtuosity, and whence education (*jiao*) itself is born" (Rosemont and Ames 2009, 105).

Like the notion of "consummate persons" (*ren* 仁) that requires us to access and to build upon our own existential sense of what it would mean to become consummate as "persons" in our relations with specific others, *xiao* too has immediate reference to our lived experience in a narrative of succeeding generations as we remember our own parents and grandparents, and attend to our own children and grandchildren. *Xiao* quite literally means the roles and relationships that conjoin the elders and the youth of successive generations, and the relations between the present generation and those generations that have gone before. *Xiao* references the quality achieved in the roles of grandparents, daughters, and grandsons, and in the roles of progenitors and their progeny.

It is because the entry point for developing moral competence in the Confucian vision of the moral life is family relations in the broadest sense that *xiao* as "family reverence" has a singularly important place in the Confucian canons. But in exploring the notion of *xiao*, we must make an effort to clarify the particular nature and significance of the institution of family within this Confucian context. The distinguished sociologist Fei Xiaotong draws a contrast between the nuclear "family" that for anthropologists takes on its major significance as the site of reproduction, and the dominant historical pattern of premodern Chinese families. Such families are lineages of persons with the same surname and, by extension, are clans made up of several lineages who the share the same surname. While lineages also have the function of reproduction, Fei insists that within the Chinese experience they have served as "a medium through which all activities are organized" (Fei 1992, 84). That is, in addition to the perpetuation of the family, lineages have complex political, economic, and religious functions that are expressed along the vertical and hierarchical axis of the father-son and mother-daughter-in-law relationships. Lineage relations are again reinforced socially and religiously through the institutions of ancestor reverence, a continuing practice that archaeology tells us dates back at least to the Neolithic Age.

Of course, given the fact that the structure of Chinese family lineages has changed dramatically over time, such generalizations must be qualified by time and place—by regional and temporal variations. Having said this, historian Yiqun Zhou marshals scholarly consensus behind her claim that premodern Chinese society was "for several thousand years largely a polity organized by kinship principles" (Zhou 2010, 19). In weighing the extent to which social order was derived from and dependent upon family relations, Zhou insists that, in contrast with the Greeks, "the Chinese state was never conceived as a political community that equaled the sum of its citizens" and that "the relationship between the rulers and the ruled was considered analogous to the relationship between parents and children" (Zhou 2010, 17–18n51). She cites the late Qing scholar Yan Fu who claims that imperial China from its beginnings was "seventy percent a lineage organization and thirty percent an empire" (Zhou 2010, 19n55). It is this persistent, family-based sociopolitical organization of Chinese society that has within this antique culture, late and soon, elevated the specific family values and obligations circumscribed by the term *xiao* to serve as the governing moral imperative.

Given the primacy of vital relationality, if the Latin root of "religious" as *religare* does in fact mean "binding tightly" (as in "ligament," "obligation," "league," and "ally")—then "family reverence" (*xiao*) has a profoundly religious import as well, referencing those familial and communal bonds that together constitute a resilient and enduring social fabric (Hoyt 1912, 126–129).[10] And it is in this profoundly religious sense of "binding tightly"—that is, the strengthening of the family and communal bonds—that we interpret the Master's autobiographical response when asked by his disciple Zilu what he would most like to do:

> I would like to bring peace and contentment to the aged, share relationships of trust and confidence with friends, and to love and protect the young.
>
> *(Analects* 5.26)

In reflecting on Confucian religiousness, we might begin from the distinguished French sinologist Marcel Granet who observes rather starkly that "Chinese wisdom has no need of the idea of God" (Granet 1934:478). Granet in this succinct assertion is rejecting the relevance of the Abrahamic One-behind-the-many model of religiousness that follows from the doctrine of strict transcendence. We find that Confucianism does not appeal to an independent, retrospective, and substantive Divine Agency as the reality behind appearance and as the source of all cosmic significance. The world is an autogenerative, "self-so-ing" process—*ziran er ran* 自然而然—that has the energy of its ongoing self-transformation resident within it. It is an inside without an outside. And human religious feelings themselves are a motor of religious meaning, understood prospectively as an unfolding and inclusive spirituality achieved within the qualitatively inspired activities of the family, the community, and the natural world. Human beings are both a source of, and contributors to the numinosity that inspires the world in which we live.

DEWEY'S RELIGIOUSNESS

Dewey, like Confucianism, has a human-centered rather than a God-centered conception of religiousness. He rejects conventional "religion" as institutionalized dogmatism competing with equally misguided modern science in their claims about "Truth." Yet Dewey in his writings still insists on retaining not only the term "religious," but even the term "God," to connote "the sense of the connection of man, in the way of both dependence and support, with the enveloping world that the imagination feels is a universe" (1933-34, LW 9:36). Dewey not only rejects supernaturalism but sees the organized religion built around it as a very real obstacle to the possibility of realizing a religiousness that is not a separate kind of experience but a quality that can be achieved in all aspects of the human experience. The institutions and rituals of conventional religions that entail a kind of assimilation of their practitioners are not only unproductive of such a quality of experience but are indeed anathema to the distinctive individuality that Dewey believes to be the ground of such inspired living.

In Dewey's use of the term "religious," as with "democracy" and "individuality," he again inverts popular wisdom. He does not begin from the familiar conception of Deity that infuses social forms with religious meaning—a Godhead that stands as the ultimate arbiter and guarantor of truth, beauty, and goodness. Rather, Dewey starts from ordinary social practices that, when they achieve a certain breadth and depth of meaning, reveal a religious sensibility that emerges out of one's full commitment of oneself to one's own cultured human community and the sense of felt-worth and belonging that comes with this investment. The religious quality of experience emerges out of one's solidarity with a continuing humanity, and, importantly, out of one's reverence for the natural world.

What Dewey does want to preserve of traditional religiousness is its natural piety: a sense of awe and wonder and humility that precludes any temptation to seek control and, in its stead, encourages an attitude of cooperation and coordination with the natural complexity that surrounds us in the broadest sense. His adjustment to the "religious" lies in replacing institutionalized worship with the creative role that deliberate human activity has in the appreciation and enchantment of experience for the flourishing community. Indeed, it is nothing less than inspired human living that is the source of spirituality.

Some Differences

In the concept of relationally constituted persons, in morality as growth in these relations, and in inspired, even religious living that follows such an understanding of the human experience, we find much resonance between Deweyan pragmatism and Confucian philosophy. But the differences abound as well. Just to take one example, in spite of Dewey's radical departure from an entrenched foundational individualism, in spite of his sustained commitment to the ultimacy and the complexity of the concrete situation in his rejection of an abstract moral idealism and, most importantly, in spite of his awareness of the vital role of early childhood education and his own intense personal experience as a much-engaged parent, he still does not develop the seemingly obvious implication that the generalizable site of associated growth for most people is going to be their families. Indeed, the uniquely Confucian perception of how we become persons departs fundamentally from the Deweyan conception of personal cultivation in its stress upon our immediate family roles and relations as the entry point and the ground for acquiring moral competence.

Positively speaking the underlying wisdom in this Confucian tradition is simple. Family is that single human institution to which persons are most likely to give themselves utterly and without remainder. But of course, this Confucian appeal to family as the organizing metaphor for the human experience is not altogether benign. Traditionally it has been the imbalance between partiality and impartiality that has been the source of corruption in the Confucian world, an imbalance that is not there in Dewey's communal model. Inappropriate intimacy in relations is China's primary obstacle on its own road to democratization. It has been slow to produce the formal, more "objective" and "transparent" institutions necessary to sustain the kind of democracy that would truly allow for the optimization of the human experience for everyone.

If we are persuaded that there is a basis for dialogue and that such a dialogue would be mutually advantageous, the question we are left with is how do we, inspired by the models of social activism provided by both Dewey and Confucius, move from an academic conversation among what some less kind than us might characterize as freeloading intellectuals, to thick social practices?

NOTES

1. Whitehead, having criticized Christian theology roundly for banishing novelty by trying to formularize truth, then turns to a criticism of both Confucius and Dewey for abjuring questions about the "ultimacies" that underlie the simple facts of experience. Here Whitehead is criticizing both thinkers explicitly for being pragmatists who, in limiting their interest to the bald facts, preclude the fruitful consequences that emerge when we ask "silly" and "surperfluous" questions—that is, metaphysical questions—and in so doing, give rise to novelty. He is particularly harsh on Confucius who occasioned "a time when things ceased to change" and whom he blames for "the static civilization of China." For commonalities and differences between Whitehead and Dewey's metaphysical assumptions, see "Dewey, Whitehead, and Process Metaphysics" by William T. Myers in this volume.
2. It is true as Raymond Boisvert (1998) reports that in the first part of the twentieth century, American philosophers were honored in both Europe and Asia. But beyond a passing gesture of courtesy, whatever influence there might have been had certainly disappeared before the Second World War. In the United States itself, Harvey Townsend (1934, 1) reports on the status of American philosophy during his generation:

   American philosophy is a neglected study in America. This is due, at least in part, to an apologetic deference to things European. The call of Emerson and Whitman to Americans to think their own thoughts and sing their own songs is still too often unheeded. It has not entirely convinced Americans that they have a soul of their own.

   More than two generations later, this bias was still in evidence. In the preface to *The Oxford History of Western Philosophy*, the general editor Anthony Kenny (1994), in referring to the authors of the various sections of the text, reports that "all the authors belong to the Anglo-American style of philosophy in the sense that they have been trained in or have taught in, that tradition." In the body of the work itself, however, there is no mention of American thought— no Edwards, Emerson, Peirce, James, or Dewey. The only references to things American indexed are the "American Revolution," "Thomas Paine," and "Thomas Jefferson"—with the latter being mentioned in the text as "a friend of Paine." The ostensive conclusion is that, up until the last few decades, American philosophy, even as assessed by Anglo-American thinkers, has not had much effect in shaping the character of contemporary Western philosophy.
3. Dewey arrived in China in 1919 three days before the beginning of the May Fourth movement. During the twenty-six months of his China sojourn, he was hosted by his Columbia students such as Hu Shi and Jiang Menglin who had, since their return to China, risen to prominence both professionally and as reformers in the New Culture Movement. During

his visit, Dewey lectured all over China and was much reported upon in the new vernacular press. Robert Clopton and Tsuin-chen Ou (1973, 13) report that "Dewey did not gain followers among the professional philosophers on the faculties of Chinese universities, most of whom continued to follow the German and French schools of philosophy in which they had been trained in Europe." Given the difficult times, Dewey's ideas were ostensibly "misread" by an activist audience in such a way as to have more influence on the current social and political needs than they did on professional philosophy, a "misreading" that one can only assume Dewey would have condoned if not encouraged. See Gu Hongliang's *Shiyong zhuyi de wudu* (A Misreading of Pragmatism) and also Zhang Baogui's *Duwei yu Zhongguo* (Dewey and China). In defense of Hu Shi, the usual target of this "misreading," Dewey's American students during this period did not do much better in understanding the profundity of the disjunction Dewey's contribution was introducing into the Western philosophical narrative.

4. Witness Zhang Xianglong's *Cong xianxiangxue dao Kongfuzi* (From Phenomenology to Confucius). It should be noted that, for an academic book, this title on publication met with inordinate popularity.

5. This assertion is taken quite literally in the arguments offered in Thompson and Hilde, *The Agrarian Roots of Pragmatism* and in Fei Xiaotong's *Xiangtu Zhongguo* (From the Soil).

6. In this discussion of the Confucian conception of person, I am excerpting some text from a manuscript I am presently writing tentatively titled "Theorizing 'Persons' for Confucian Role Ethics: A Good Place to Start."

7. The sense of immortality implied by the expression "living on" is difficult to see if the body is taken as "belonging" only to an individual. The opening chapter of the *Chinese Classic of Family Reverence* makes clear that, for Confucius, the body is an inheritance and on loan from one's family lineage and that the first obligation we have to this lineage is to maintain its integrity by avoiding any kind of desecration. See Rosemont and Ames (2009, 105).

8. *The Class Lectures of John Dewey*, Volume 1, p. 122.

9. See Steven Fesmire (2003, 10) wherein he sheds some light on the deliberately imprecise habits by describing them as "pre-established social circuits."

10. Hoyt (1912) provides some interesting textual evidence for this very old and often disputed etymology.

WORKS CITED

Citations of John Dewey's works are to the thirty-seven-volume critical edition published by Southern Illinois University Press under the editorship of Jo Ann Boydston. In-text citations give the original publication date and series abbreviation, followed by volume number and page number. For example: (1934, LW 10:12) is page 12 of *Art as Experience*, which is published as volume 10 of *The Later Works*.

Series abbreviations for *The Collected Works*:

EW *The Early Works* (1882–98)

MW *The Middle Works* (1899–1924)

LW *The Later Works* (1925–53)

Boisvert, Raymond. 1998. *John Dewey: Rethinking Our Time*. Albany: State University of New York Press.

Clopton, Robert, and Tsuin-chen Ou. 1973. *John Dewey: Lectures in China 1919-1920*. Honolulu: University Press of Hawaii.

Dalmiya, Vrinda (1998). "Linguistic Erasures." *Peace Review*, vol. 10, no. 4.

Dewey, John. (1882). *Early Essays*. EW 1.

Dewey, John. (1922). *Human Nature and Conduct*. MW 14.

Dewey, John. (1925/1929). *Experience and Nature*. LW 1.

Dewey, John. (1929). *The Public and Its Problems*. LW 2.

Dewey, John. (1930). *Individualism Old and New*. LW 5.

Dewey, John. (1933/1934). *A Common Faith*. LW 9.

Dewey, John, and James H. Tufts. (1932). *Ethics*. LW 7.

Fei Xiaotong [Fei Hsiao-t'ung]. 1992. *Xiangtu Zhongguo* (From the Soil: The Foundations of Chinese Society). Translated by Gary G. Hamiliton and Wang Zheng. Berkeley: University of California Press.

Fesmire, Steven. 2003. *John Dewey and Moral Imagination: Pragmatism in Ethics*. Bloomington: Indiana University Press.

Fingarette, Herbert. 1983. "The Music of Humanity in the *Conversations of Confucius*." *Journal of Chinese Philosophy*, vol. 10.

Granet, Marcel. 1934. *La pensée Chinoise*. Paris: Editions Albin Michel.

Gu, Hongliang. 2000. *Shiyong zhuyi de wudu: Duwei zhexue dui Zhongguo xiandaizhexue de yingxiang* (A Misreading of Pragmatism: The Influence of Dewey's Philosophy on Modern Chinese Philosophy). Shanghai: Huadong Normal University Press.

Hoyt, Sarah R. 1912. "The Etymology of Religion." *Journal of the American Oriental Society*, vol. 32, no. 2.

James, William. 1985. *The Varieties of Religious Experience*. Cambridge, MA: Harvard University Press.

Kenny, Anthony (Ed.). 1994. *The Oxford History of Western Philosophy*. Oxford: Oxford University Press.

Rosemont, Henry Jr., and Roger T. Ames. 2009. *The Chinese Classic of Family Reverence: A Philosophical Translation of the* Xiaojing. Honolulu: University of Hawai'i Press.

Thompson, Paul, and Thomas Hilde (Eds.). 2000. *The Agrarian Roots of Pragmatism*. Nashville, TN: Vanderbilt University Press.

Townsend, Harvey. 1934. *Philosophical Ideas in the United States*, New York: American Book Company.

Whitehead, A. N. 1938. *Modes of Thought*. New York: Macmillan.

Whitehead, A. N. 1954. *Dialogues of Alfred North Whitehead*, as recorded by Lucien Price. Boston: Little, Brown.

Whitehead, A. N. 1985. *Process and Reality*. Donald Sherbourne corrected edition. New York: Free Press.

Zhang, Baogui. 2001. *Duwei yu Zhongguo* (Dewey and China), Shijiazhuang: Hebei Peoples Press.

Zhang, Xianglong. 2001. *Cong xianxiangxue dao Kongfuzi* (From Phenomenology to Confucius). Peking: Shangwu yinshuguan.

Zhou, Yiqun. 2010. *Festivals, Feasts, and Gender Relations in Ancient China and Greece*. Cambridge: Cambridge University Press.

CHAPTER 27

TWO-WAY INTERNATIONALIZATION

Education, Translation, and Transformation in Dewey and Cavell

NAOKO SAITO

INTRODUCTION

OUR global age is characterized by diverse political emotions, sometimes manifest, sometimes hidden, involving religious and ethnic tensions, homelessness and immigrancy, and divisions of identity. The anxieties of the "risk society" (Beck 1986/ 1992) couple with both cynicism and docility in various forms and a sense of futility in relation to seemingly overwhelming threats constituted by environmental despoliation, the proliferation of weaponry, and most imminently terrorism. Democracy calls for the cultivation of a new political sensibility that particularly acknowledges such negative political emotions as fear, doubt, and anger. Such anxieties are felt by those outside seeking to enter a society, those inside concerned about immigration, and those inside but at the margins and resistant to the pressures of inclusion. Social science research tends to be blind to such emotions as it focuses on conditions of consent, equality, and social inclusion. It does not give sufficient attention to the existential and emotional aspects of individual political lives. Scant space is given to the more subtle, darker manifestation of emotions, whether expressed by overt dissent or by the silent majority.

Against this background, one of the most urgent tasks of political education is the cultivation of political emotions—in response to the hidden sense of the deviant and the peripheral, to the dimension of human being that cannot be fully captured by the framework of agreement, mutual recognition, and respect for diversity. Such political education would involve some transformational aspect of our political life, allowing us to reconsider the way we are engaged with different cultures as *other* cultures—the other that is beyond our comprehension. The challenge for education is to turn the tragic sense of guilt, anxiety, isolation, and loss toward a hope for living together with others again.

In response to this challenging task of democracy and education, this chapter explores the possibility of John Dewey's pragmatism, in particular its perfectionist antifoundationalism and idea of democracy as a way of life (1939, LW 14). I argue that the transformational experiencing of linguistic incommensurabity epitomized in translation is essential to enhancing the potential of Dewey's idea of democracy on a global scale, especially in response to the pressing need for the understanding of other cultures. In order to go beyond certain limits of Dewey's antifoundationalist perfectionism and democracy as a way of life—one that is tied up with the idea of recognition—it is proposed that Dewey's pragmatism can be further translated through Stanley Cavell's idea of *philosophy as translation*. In conclusion an alternative route to political education is to be explored for internationalization through the art of translation in a manner that is genuinely two-way, where translation is a matter of transformation.

DEMOCRACY AND EDUCATION IN JAPAN

When Dewey paid a visit to China and Japan in the late 1910s and the early 1920s, he called for mutual understanding between the East and the West for the cause of democracy. In Japan, however, almost a century ago, from February 9 until April 28, 1919, he faced the real difficulty of putting into practice his democratic principle of mutual learning from difference. Dewey's visit to Japan was a test case in which he was caught out by a real gap in cross-cultural communication—a foreign place where the English word "democracy" was untranslatable. He was confronted with a severe challenge to his hope of attaining mutual understanding and universal democracy beyond national and cultural boundaries—the real difficulty of crossing borders (Saito 2003). He left Japan with a remark: "It takes more force, more moral courage to be an outspoken critic of the politics and social condition of one's nation, to be a dissenter, in Japan, than in any other country in the world" (1921, MW 13:257). Yet by confronting and surmounting difference in ways of thinking, value systems, and habits of mind in other countries, Dewey still proposed the importance of an understanding that reached "the inner spirit and real life of a people" (267) and that such contact with another nation become "a real means of education, a means of insight and understanding" (263).

Today, almost a century after his visit to Japan, the political life of Japanese society has been undergoing a massive change with regard to democracy. Against the current government's direction toward the revision of Article 9 of the Japanese constitution in a militaristic direction, young students and mothers, joining hands with nonaligned citizens, have started a nationwide antiwar demonstration. Political emotions have been stirred in the voicing of political slogans on the street. Furthermore, the minimum age for the right to vote has been reduced from twenty to eighteen years. Some high school students voted for the first time in 2016. Japanese high schools are facing an immediate need to improve political education for democratic participation and citizens.

Beneath the apparent advancement of democracy and education, however, the facile discourse of political slogans—in particular, the ideological, partisan "anti-" slogans that differentiate too easily between the good and the bad, the we and the they—effects a kind of inclusion: the inclusion of the inarticulate into the visible, in clear-cut categorization. The political language toward inclusion manifests a foundationalist drive that muffles or even oppresses the marginalized. This occurs through a sensationalization of political emotions—whether it is for the love of children or for the love of humanity. Such inclusive and foundationalist modes of thinking are akin to the problem-solving assumptions of educational policy documents—those that constantly lure us to apparently secure ground. Epitomizing the dichotomy of reason and emotion in our political life, this presents the danger of a pupulist sensationalization of political emotion—what might be called pupulist emotivism. This is the kind of emotion that is concomitant with conformist thinking, with the suppression of critical thinking.

Meanwhile, behind the outward and direct manifestation of the political sentiments of ordinary people, there exists some inward turn in democracy around the world— whether it secretly manifests itself in the exclusion of the foreign, the immigrant, what is beyond our grasp, or in the inward turn of young people who are reluctant to study abroad, concealed though this may be by the call for internationalization in higher education. The political discourse of the ideological partisanship covers over deeper sentiments involving anxieties of human existence.

In response to the hope and challenges posed by democracy in Japan today, Dewey's antifoundationalist conception of democracy can be appreciated anew.

DEWEY AND DEMOCRACY AS A WAY OF LIFE

> Regarded as an idea, democracy is not an alternative to other principles of associated life. It is the idea of community life itself. It is an ideal in the only intelligible sense of an ideal: namely, the tendency and movement of some thing which exists carried to its final limit, viewed as completed, perfected. . . . The idea of ideal of a community presents, however, actual phases of associated life as they are freed from restrictive and disturbing elements, and are contemplated as having attained their limit of development. (1927, LW 2:328)

Creative Democracy, Perfectionist Antifoundationalism

John Dewey and his pragmatism can give a powerful theoretical backbone to challenges illustrated by democracy and education in Japan. In the passage quoted above , Dewey expresses his perfectionist idea of democracy—democracy as an ideal that is always to be achieved in the daily events of life. Dewey's creative democracy exemplifies a third way "beyond relativism and objectivism" (Bernstein 1983), in an alternative horizon of *perfectionism*—the ateleological idea of perfection without final perfectibility (Saito 2005).

Dewey's cross-cultural experience illustrates such an antifoundationalist-perfectionist idea of creative democracy, and this is based on his pluralistic vision of a global community. He claims a need for global understanding that is supported by the notion of unity in diversity, a solidarity among human beings that is made possible only through interaction between different perspectives. Dewey emphasizes that the heart and final guarantee of democracy is its capacity to cultivate the "habit of amicable co-operation" among friends (1939, LW 14:228).[1] In his idea of creative democracy, a drive toward crossing the national and cultural borders of America is entailed. As Bernstein says, "[Dewey] was deeply involved in encouraging democratic practices throughout the world" (Bernstein 2010, 88): and as Hickman says, Dewey is a global citizen (Hickman 2003). Indeed with his perfectionist aspiration Dewey believes that global boundaries should be and can be transcended:

> Territorial states and political boundaries will persist; but they will not be barriers which impoverish experience by cutting man off from his fellows; they will not be hard and fast divisions whereby external separation is converted into inner jealously, fear, suspicion and hostility. Competition will continue, but it will be less rivalry for acquisition of material goods, and more an emulation of local groups to enrich direct experience with appreciatively enjoyed intellectual and artistic wealth. (1927, LW 2:370)

Dewey's quest for democracy on a global scale does not rely on the universalist foundation of humanism: neither is it assimilated into the global tide of economy. If there is any *global* dimension in his pragmatism, it is the global that is to be achieved from within: "Democracy must begin at home" (368).[2]

It is here the cultivation of what might be called the global mentality is called for in his vision of democracy and education. The key here is how to cultivate the mind that can cross borders beyond one's limit. In *Democracy and Education*, Dewey emphasizes in particular the cultivation of "open-mindedness."

> Openness of mind means accessibility of mind to any and every consideration that will throw light upon the situation that needs to be cleared up, and that will help determine the consequences of acting this way or that . . . . [I]ntellectual growth means constant expansion of horizons and consequent formation of new purposes and new responses. These are impossible without an active disposition to welcome points of view hitherto alien; an active desire to entertain considerations which modify existing purposes. (1916, MW 9:182)

> Open-mindedness is not the same as empty-mindedness. To hang out a sign saying "Come right in; there is no one at home" is not the equivalent of hospitality. But

there is a kind of passivity, willingness to let experiences accumulate and sink in and ripen, which is an essential of development. (183)

In the first passage, Dewey calls for the expansion of horizon, as it were to presage Charles Taylor's reference to Gadamer's idea of "fusion of horizons," and his own call for learning "to move in a broader horizon" (Taylor 1992, 67). In the second passage, Dewey suggests that such a turning point in expanding one's horizon requires a particular attitude of passivity, lending an ear to others. We might say that he anticipated the necessity of two-way internationalization—the active will of going out and the passive mode of receiving the other. Dewey indicates a way of achieving such bidirectional internationalization as follows:

> Travel is known to have a broadening effect, at least if the traveller is willing to keep his mind open. The amount of enlightenment which is gained from travel usually depends upon the amount of difference there is between the civilization from which the traveller starts his journey and that of the country at which he arrives. The more unlike the two are, the more opportunity there is for learning. (1921, MW 13:262)

Here, by using the metaphor of travel and journey, Dewey expresses his antifoundationalist idea of democracy on the way—democracy as a way of life that is always being created and still to be created through mutual learning from difference.

Nearly one hundred years after his disheartening visit to Japan, what would Dewey have said if he saw the contemporary situation of Japan—where young people and mothers demonstrate on the street, raising their voices against war? Or, vice versa, how would Dewey's words ring true to those ordinary people on the street?

Limits of Pragmatism, Limits of Recognition

As Richard Bernstein says, we should think about "what we may still learn from Dewey in our own attempts to understand and foster democratic practices" (Bernstein 2010, 71). This means that in response to the needs of our times Dewey's pragmatism and his idea of democracy and education must be exposed to what he himself calls "reconstruction in philosophy" (1920, MW 12). There are some philosophical-practical challenges to his pragmatism. First and foremost, to what extent can his antifoundationalist perfectionism sustain itself in the face of the dualistic foundationalist drive inherent in the political ideology exchanged in the discourse of "anti-"?

Second, how can his anti-dualism of reason and emotion, in his idea of "creative intelligence" (1934, LW 10:351), resist the tide of what might be called the emotivist democracy—a kind of democracy driven by the popular sentiment? The more emotions are expressed in an easy-to-access vocabulary, the more the space for critical thinking seems to narrow down. Dewey's idea of the "criticism of criticisms" (1925/1929, LW 1:298) is, on Hilary Putnam's account, a matter of "higher-level criticism," involving "'standing back' and criticizing even the ways in which we are accustomed to criticize ideas, the criticism of our ways of criticism" (Putnam 2004, 96). Critical thinking is risk-taking by nature, involving an awakening to what has not been thought before, an adventure into the realm of the unknown. In the emotional burst of political scenes around the world, such space for criticism is obliterated. An appeal to humanitarian discourse (oftentimes on the foundationalist, universalist assumption of human being) is not an exception. What would be an alternative route to the cultivation of political emotion, one that could resist more fully the tide of emotivist democracy? Where can we find an alternative language and way of thinking for responding to people's despair and aspiration for democracy?

Third, while Dewey is sensitive enough to pay attention to the different voices of others and other cultures, to what an extent can we rely on his discourse of mutual learning from difference? While Dewey acknowledged that "Japan *is* a unique country, one whose aims and methods are baffling to any foreigner" (1919, MW 11:171), his pragmatist response to the experience of the unknown is to sustain a hope for democracy, to retain the pragmatist "antiscepticism" (Putnam 1995, 20) or "antiskeptical nonfoundational fallibilism" (Bernstein 2016). Pragmatism deals with skepticism in its "*healthy* awareness of human fallibility" (Putnam 1995, 68, italics added). Bernstein says that the wisdom of pragmatism is to "exorcise" Cartesian anxieties (Bernstein 1983). In view of what is beneath the series of terrorist attacks around world, and of what does not surface and is covered over by the vocal political slogans, there does seem to exist a kind of human sentiment that awaits an alternative route for expression, perhaps beyond the healthy attitude of pragmatism. Would pragmatist *anti*-skepticism be powerful enough to expel the anxious voice of the peripheral, the unexpressed, and the unknown?

Fourth is the metaphor of *the expansion of horizons* in the idea of mutual learning. As much as pragmatist wisdom of crossing borders is all the more significant today, such a move accompanies the destabilizing experience of one's familiar standpoint. The metaphor of expansion, however, can embody and exercise an assimilating force when an encounter with the very difference does not necessarily lead to the experience of expansion. We can easily expand *our* horizons without radically changing our own framework. Is an active will to open one's mind sufficient for the *understanding* of others in two directions? The cultivation of political emotions requires subtler attention to the way we cross (or cannot cross) borders and what happens in the very precarious moment when we *are crossing* borders, being affected by what is beyond our grasp.

This leads us to the fifth related challenge to Dewey's pragmatism. How can it retain a "rooted cosmopolitan" position, as Bernstein puts it, (Bernstein 2010, 88)—one that retains Americanness (if there is such a thing), while crossing its boundaries to become cosmopolitan? To what extent can pragmatism exercise the power of transcending "American rootedness" by exercising the power of "transcend[ing] the limitation of [its own] context" (Bernstein 1992, 834)? It would require a thorough way of standing on the border so that it will be brought back to neither identity politics with national sentiment nor to cosmopolitan sentiment for universalized humanity.

Bernstein points out the common ground of Dewey's idea of democracy with that of Axel Honneth who has contributed much in the development of the theory of recognition and who appreciates Dewey's ideas of "expanded democracy" and "social cooperation"(Bernstein 2010, 86). Bernstein says with Dewey that "one must do more than protect the rights of minorities and dissenters; one must work toward developing a culture in which plurality and difference of opinion are encouraged" (85). This is the politics of recognition, and there is indeed such element (or at least an inclination that triggers such politics) in Dewey's pragmatism. These five limits of Dewey's pragmatism, however, indicate that there is a need to take a turn from the discourse of recognition so that the possibilities of his antifoundationalist-perfectionist vision of creative democracy can be viable today: American philosophy is still to be translated. This means then that pragmatism has exposed itself to criticism.

In his talk, "Global Resurgence of Pragmatism," Bernstein says that pragmatism is part of "a global philosophic movement" involving European and Anglophone thinkers (Bernstein 2016, 11). It is not a "marginal provincial movement" but has been crossing boundaries between different contexts and streams of thought. Truly pragmatism has a global power, one that carries itself beyond the borders of America. This simultaneously means, however, that it exposes itself to the effects of other cultures; the effects cannot be one way. It is in such *bidirectional* movement that the genuine power of the global reach of pragmatism is tested in response to these challenges. Internal criticism of *American* pragmatism is called for to release its cosmopolitan proclivity.

American Philosophy in Translation

Within such a two-way critique, I turn *from comparison to translation* (Standish 2011). Translation represents the whole way of thinking—antifoundationalist thinking on the way, with its focus on the very moment of crossing a border. Dewey's antifoundationalist-perfectionist idea of creative democracy can be further enhanced from the perspective of translation—as democracy in translation. Some characteristic features of his pragmatism discussed above endorse the transitory and transformative nature of democracy. As philosophy in service to life, pragmatism challenges dualisms typical of modern Western philosophy—of reason and emotion, of facts and values, and of right and wrong. To go beyond these divides, and to live the antifoundationalist way of life, we must learn to live in crossing borders. Translation is a metonym of such transformative experience. With Emerson's idea of "transla[ing] the world," the recently published edited collection *Translate the World* (Alfonso and LaRocca 2015a) justifies the attempt to read American philosophy from the scope of translation and in terms of the mediation of American transcendentalism. Translation in the Emersonian sense is the experience of encountering "the difficulty of knowing that we do not know" (Alfonso and LaRocca 2015b, 15), of encountering the other—to be surprised by what is beyond our grasp (Saito 2015). The book invites us to reread the texts of Emerson, as the American Scholar, through a cross-cultural lens: it re-presents what is called transcultural studies as a matter of translation and transformation.

PHILOSOPHY
AS TRANSLATION: TRANSLATING DEWEY'S
LANGUAGE THROUGH CAVELL'S

Philosophy as Translation and Understanding Other Cultures

It is in part in response to the challenges of democracy and education that Kyoto University's SPIRITS project, "Philosophy as translation and understanding other cultures: Interdisciplinary research in philosophy and education for bidirectional internationalization," was established.[3] (See figures 27.1 and 27.2.)

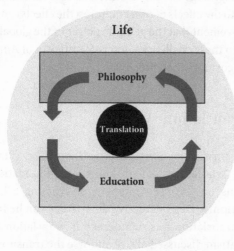

- Thinking from and in life
- Thinking through education, not through pedagogy as a discipline
- Transcending the application model of theory and practice
- Broadening the concept of translation to involve the rebirth of human beings

FIGURE 27.1 Intersections of philosophy and education, mediated by translation.

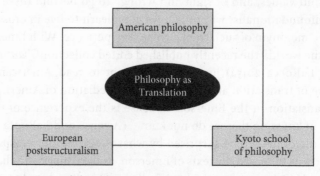

FIGURE 27.2 American philosophy, Kyoto School of Philosophy and European poststructualism.

Our aim was to conduct interdisciplinary research in philosophy and education in order to convert ways of thinking about and understanding other cultures and to realize cultural identities in authentic, liberating, and bidirectional ways.

Beyond the literal sense of translation between two "different" language systems, translation in the SPIRITS project developed in relation to the following four orientations:

1. Translation is a mode of bridging different streams of thought (of Europe, America, and Asia), beyond fixed terms of comparison, and acknowledging gaps and incomprehensibility as the potential for mutual transformation.
2. Identities of culture, thought, and person are always to be translated.
3. Translation is internal to the nature of language.
4. Translation highlights the fact that the translation of our words is accompanied by the transforming of our own selves, destabilizing the ground on which our practices of telling and describing stand.

While these points suggest *bidirectional* internationalization in higher education, this does not imply a humanist universalism. Neither is bidirectionality equivalent to exchangeability in a global economy. If there is anything *global*, it is to be achieved from within one's culture, with acknowledgement of asymmetries and gaps. (See figure 27.3.)

One of the ongoing discoveries was the need for the overturning the overturning of the center-periphery structure through the perspective of translation so that we can reencounter different cultures as other from the *peripheral* standpoint of border-crossing. (See figures 27.4 and 27.5).

The apparently peripheral voice of the female is appreciated anew for its power of overturning the dominantly masculine discourse in philosophy (Saito 2016). The appropriation, and worse, the theft of the feminine voice, shows the necessity for sensitivity to what cannot be said, to the obscure (Saito 2017), and to the peripheral. We then came to thematize *the cultivation of political emotions* as a crucial component of philosophy as translation. It is from this perspective that Stanley Cavell's American philosophy can usefully be brought into the picture.

Cavell, Perfectionism, and Political Emotions

> Happiness ... Cheerfulness, in a democracy, is what I call a political emotion. Your democracy requires that morale be kept up. It's difficult.
>
> —Stanley Cavell (Cavell and Standish 2012, 272)

It is Cavell who enables us to take a shift beyond the plane of recognition toward the sentiment of the peripheral, the dissenting and the immigrant in our understanding of other cultures. Cavell's Emersonian moral perfectionism elucidates a *political* strain in his ordinary language philosophy and reiterates its *American* democratic accent on

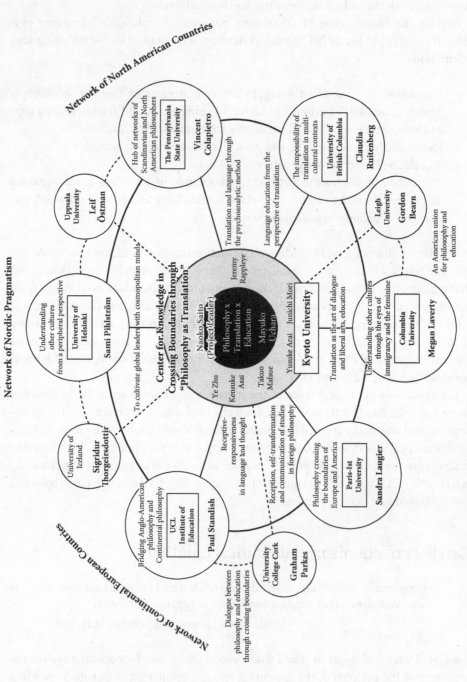

FIGURE 27.3 Development of the international network of the SPIRITS project.

Network of North American Countries

Network of Nordic Pragmatism

Network of Continental European Countries

Hub of networks of Scandinavian and North American philosophers

The Pennsylvania State University

Vincent Colapietro

The impossibility of translation in multi-cultural contexts

University of British Columbia

Claudia Ruitenberg

Translation and language through the psychoanalytic method

Language education from the perspective of translation

Uppsala University

Leif Östman

Leigh University

Gordon Bearn

An American union for philosophy and education

Understanding other cultures from a peripheral perspective

University of Helsinki

Sami Pihlström

Translation as the art of dialogue and liberal arts, education

Understanding other cultures through the eyes of immigrancy and the feminine

Columbia University

Megan Laverty

Center for Knowledge in Crossing Boundaries through "Philosophy as Translation"

Jeremy Rappleye

Naoko Saito (Project Leader)

Philosophy × Translation × Education

Mayuko Uchara

Ye Zhu   Kensuke Asai   Takao Matsue

Yusuke Arai   Junichi Mori

Kyoto University

To cultivate global leaders with cosmopolitan minds

University of Iceland

Sigridur Thorgeirsdottir

Receptive-responsiveness in language and thought

Reception, self-transformation and communication of studies in foreign philosophy

Philosophy crossing the boundaries of Europe and America

Paris-1st University

Sandra Laugier

Bridging Anglo-American philosophy and Continental philosophy

UCL Institute of Education

Paul Standish

University College Cork

Graham Parkes

Dialogue between philosophy and education through crossing boundaries

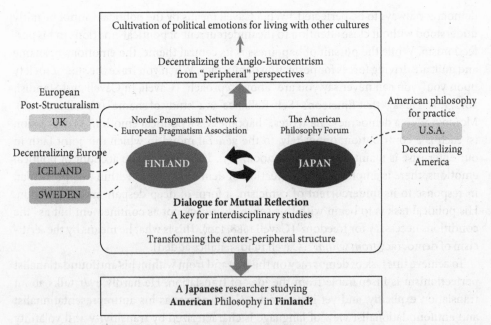

FIGURE 27.4 Dialogue among peripheral voices, crossing borders.

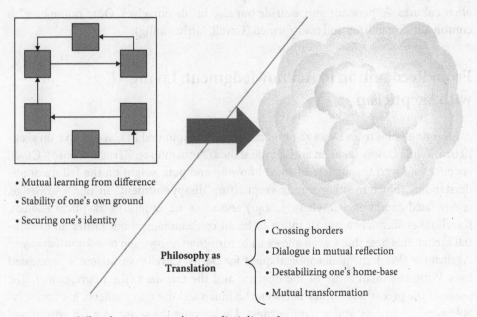

FIGURE 27.5 What does it mean to be interdisciplinary?

democracy always to be perfected.[4] What Cavell means by the political cannot be fairly understood without close attention to the undercurrent of political emotions in his perfectionism. While the pursuit of happiness is its central theme, the emotions of shame and guilt are driving forces for perfecting democracy. When you "take the sins of society upon you," you can never say you are "above reproach" (Cavell, in Cavell and Standish 2012, 162). He says that Emerson's "Self-Reliance" is a "study of shame" (Cavell 1990, 47). Moreover, "In a democracy," he writes, "happiness is a political emotion, as depression is; each is a contribution, oppositely, to the general mood in which our joint faith in our enterprise is maintained" (Cavell 2004, 183). Here also, in the account of political emotions, there is emphasis on the creation of democracy from within—in particular, in response to its undercurrent of cynicism, a form of deep despair and resignation. His political task is to begin with this sense of privacy not as confinement but as "the conditions necessary for freedom" (Cavell 1988, 120). This is what he means by the "criticism of democracy *from within*" (Cavell 1990, 3, italics added).

To achieve this task of democracy on the way and from within, his antifoundationalist perfectionism is inseparable from the idea of translation. He hardly ever talks about translation explicitly, and yet it permeates Cavell's texts as his antirepresentationalist and antifoundationalist view of language is characterized by transitivity and volatility (Cavell 1992, 27). Thoreau expresses this with the phrasing: Truth refuses to be finally fixed: it is "instantly *translated*" (Thoreau 1992, 217). Engagement with the process of translation inevitably brings us into the dimension of the obscure, the unknown. It is in the light of this that Cavell presents his position with regard to the understanding of *other* cultures—others not only outside but also inside ourselves. Our "home base" is continually destabilized and transformed (Cavell, forthcoming).

From Recognition to Acknowledgment: Living with Skepticism

A diverging point from Dewey's pragmatism is foregrounded in Cavell's take on skepticism. While Dewey takes an antiskeptic stance (Putnam 1995; Bernstein 2010), Cavell is concerned with the anxiety of (not) knowing and puts weight on the failure of understanding. Since in other minds skepticism, "disappointment" in our knowledge, is our fated condition (Cavell 1979, 440) and since we cannot be skeptical enough, Cavell takes skepticism not so much to be an epistemological but rather an existential matter. It is here that Cavell allows us to turn *from recognition to acknowledgment*.[5] Against the (Western) philosophical quest for clarity, Cavell's worldview is permeated by a Wittgensteinian sense of the obscure and the transient (the ungraspable). The sense of the precarious border between the inner and the outer reflects his unresolvable sense of anxiety and groundlessness. Undergoing the sense of a rift within and without the self is at the heart of the experience of translation. In translation we must be "on some boundary or threshold, as between the impossible and the possible" (Cavell, forthcoming).

This requires us to pass through "crossroads" (Cavell 1979, 19)—the moment of crisis in one's life when one moves from "darkness to light" (102). Here is expressed a sense of taking a risk, being on the edge, in "onward thinking" (Cavell 1992, 135). In living with the anxieties of our existence, Cavell's point of acknowledgment is to recover the pathos of our lives, a hope for living with others with eternal gaps. "Human beings do not naturally desire isolation and incomprehension, but union or reunion, call it community. It is in faithfulness to that desire that one declares oneself unknown" (463).

Acknowledgment involves us in the *anxieties of inclusion*. These are emotions we experience when we have to live with dissent, exposing ourselves not simply to different but also to discordant and dissonant voices—to the disturbing, the irritating, and the unsettling. Such emotional destabilizing goes beyond the political language of mutual recognition and of respect for different values, insofar as such differences are construed in quest of secure ground. Such destabilization is the precondition of the self: it is necessary for cultural criticism from within, which is a powerful means of affecting the world. This, however, can be subverted by what Cavell calls the "problem of the humanitarian" tendency towards inclusion as assimilation (Cavell 1979, 437). He warns us against an instinct inherent in humanitarian discourse, "a wish to convert the outcast into a social role," "a wish to view outcasts as beings different from oneself, about whose good they themselves did not require consulting" (436–437). He calls this inclination "emotional imperialism" (437). Duties to other human beings are "dischargeable," whereas an acknowledgment is not (435).[6]

To live with the anxieties of inclusion means to learn to stand on the border, by taking up the obscure and thinking in "the twilight zone of inquiry" (1916, MW 9:155). This opens up an alternative horizon in our political life—before and beyond our ideological partisanship of "anti-."

To think and live without fixed ground does not mean that anything goes. This is best illustrated by Emerson's idea of *finding as founding* (Cavell 1989, 109). This is an idea of perfection without final perfectibility, without abrogating the quest for a better life (Cavell 1990; Saito 2005). Emersonian perfectionism has a strong focus on its process of perfecting here and now, with no final state of perfectibility (Cavell 1990, 3; Saito 2005). Dewey also says, "Perfection means perfect*ing*, fulfillment, fulfill*ing*, and the good is now or never" (1922, MW 14:200, italics added). Cavell presents us with what might be called an Emersonian perfectionist antifoundationalism—which retains the perfectionist and Emersonian (and hence Nietzschean affirmative) thrust of *American* philosophy (one that does not itself acquiesce in relativism but that does fully acknowledge and live with negative doubt), while at the same time refusing to settle down on fixed ground.

This is in tune with what Bernstein describes as pragmatism's way of attending to the "tragic dimension of human life without submitting to Schopenhaurian pessimism" (Bernstein 2016, 15). And yet Cavell's Emersonian and Thoreauvian mode of thinking and use of language sustain the *betweenness* of a radical nature—in a way more thoroughly antifoundationalist than pragmatism's, always on the way. Dewey takes chance to be the crucial element. Taking a chance, the moment of the leap, is at the heart of his experimentalism and philosophy for action. Cavell's Emersonian perfectionist antifoundationalism definitely shares this scheme of thinking, and yet it elaborates and dives into the vague territory of our lives.

To recover, in the face of anxiety and from within despair and disappointment, the desire to say "I think" is at the heart of the Cavellian cultivation of political emotions. It is in full resistance to the foundationalist inclination of emotivist democracy. And certainly Dewey's pragmatism and his idea of democracy as a way of life can be translated in such terms.

POLITICAL EDUCATION AND TWO-WAY INTERNATIONALIZATION: TRANSLATION AS TRANSFORMATION

> Creative activity is our great need; but criticism, self-criticism, is the road to its release.
> —Dewey, "Construction and Criticism" (1930, LW 5:143)

In the case of Japanese education, despite the lowering of the voting age to eighteen years, when it comes to political education and citizenship education, high schools and teachers have been trapped in the dichotomous thinking between the political inculcation of ideology or the neutrality.[7] Political education tends to teach students how to vote, the mechanism of democratic processes, and the structure of the political system. In the study of politics, the dimension of internal transformation as it is related to the experience of translation has hardly ever been discussed—as it is considered to be an untouchable realm.

In the interconnected concepts of translation, acknowledgment, and the anxieties of inclusion, Cavell's "extended sense" of the political reminds us that our political life is inseparable from our relation to language (Cavell 2010, 431).[8] It connects the psychological and the existential with the political—involving our unlimited answerability to others and the sense of shame that goes with this. The two paths cannot be achieved within a horizon of the politics of recognition, nor understood primarily in terms of the adjustment of conflicting interests and the resolving of disagreement. Dewey's idea of democracy as a way of life does certainly imply such alternative sense of the political. This political is therapeutic and transformational by nature—being inseparable from translation. The provision of this, in Cavell's view, is the task of philosophy, and this is to be distinguished from the polemical discourse of politics-as-usual. Involving philosophy in *praxis*, Cavell's philosophy as translation converts the relationship between active and passive. This corresponds to Emerson's conversion of Kant's idea—active power of thinking in passion, passive demonstration of action. It broadens the concept of action and praxis that is at the heart of Dewey's pragmatism.

The focus on the anxieties of inclusion does not exempt us from thinking but asks us to rethink what it means to think (in Dewey's spirit of the "criticism of criticisms"), to think more rigorously, driven by a passion for democracy. Such passionate though passive criticism discloses the violence hidden behind the apparently secure, benevolent, humanist language of politics and behind the aggressive political language of partisanship.

The cultivation of political emotions requires the integration of reason and emotion, and this is a key to realizing democracy as a way of life in a thoroughly antifoundationalist way as Dewey wished it to be, without our yielding to populism or to idealizations of rational autonomy. And yet, perhaps, more radically than Dewey challenging us to cross borders, inside and outside, and challenging Dewey to translate his language, a Cavellian political education would encourage teachers and students to think in "extra-vagance" in Thoreau's words (Thoreau 1992, 216), in the manner of "Man Thinking," in Emerson's (Emerson 2000, 52)—to think beyond existing limits: to resist our fated tendency toward inclusion, assimilation, and settlement. Challenging inclusion, it asks us to think critically about ourselves, about what excludes us from ourselves, our ignorance, our failures of understanding.

American philosophy indicates a perfectionist way toward the understanding of other cultures. With the experience of untranslatability, of the rift between ways of thinking, and of the abyss that lies beneath what we say and do with words, translation is the experience of a mutual unsteadying of standpoints. Putting into question one's standpoint is the process of self-criticism that is at the heart of understanding other cultures. Such experience opens us to anxiety, making us vulnerable to the response of the other. Translation in this sense uproots ethnocentric ways of comparison or communication based upon one's secure ground. Translation as a form of cultural criticism begins within the culture, before and while we are engaged in intercultural understanding.

The anxieties of inclusion are what we experience when we confront the real difficulty of *including* what is separate from us, without assimilating it to our own illusionary secure ground. Our own standpoint might be shattered involving an "anxiety that our expressions might at anytime signify nothing" and the "fear" of "inexpressiveness," in which "I am not merely unknown, but in which I am powerless to make myself known" (Cavell 1979, 351). And we might say it is this realm of the unsaid toward which Dewey's language needs further to be translated. His line of thinking can then lay the way for a method of cultural criticism from within, disturbing the "rootedness" of American philosophy and exposing it to the effects of *other* cultures. This is the very implication of any cosmopolitan tendency in American philosophy, if such there be.

Such destabilization from within—cultural criticism from within—is an alternative way to affect the world. This requires "genuine intellectual humility and humane practical wisdom," as Bernstein says about William James (Bernstein 2016). Translation is a mode of conversation to effect such mutual transformation. In this sense philosophy as translation is inseparable from what Dewey calls "philosophy as the general theory of education" (1916, MW 9:338) and from what Cavell calls "philosophy as the education of grownups" (Cavell 1979, 125; Saito and Standish 2012). This may be one of the most important and practical lessons today in the global resurgence of pragmatism.

Hence there is a need for cultivating *the art of translation*—translation broader than linguistic exchange. Dewey says that communication is at the heart of creative democracy and communication is the art of mutual learning. To further develop this idea, and to resist more thoroughly a symmetrical and exchangeable form of communication, translation accompanies the experience of anxiety and hope, exposing us to what is dissonant, inside and outside ourselves: it is a metonym of our asymmetrical life. This involves a constant struggle with *self*-knowledge, which is the precondition of understanding *other* cultures. *Bi*directionality involves the experience of mutually destabilizing of standpoints. The art of translation requires standing "on tiptoe" (Thoreau 1992, p. 11), on precarious borders, so that we shall be brought back neither to an identity politics, with its inclination to nationalism or ethnocentrism, nor to a bland cosmopolitan orientation that lacks the sense of the difficulty of crossing borders. It converts the relationship between the established and the dissenting, the center and the periphery. Translation then is a precondition for achieving two-way internationalization.

Political education for two-way internationalization is a sole way in which democracy begins at home, while at the same time disturbing one's "rootedness" in the native culture. In this sense this is a kind of cosmopolitanism still to be achieved, on the way, and always from within. Political education in this sense is linguistic education. Translation requires a higher form of *foreign* language education, one that already begins with native language education—where the foreign in the familiar is encountered by allowing ourselves to be affected by *other* cultures and by redefining, transcending, and crossing borders. The point of understanding other cultures in acknowledgment and through translation is to find the moment of the "flying Perfect" (Emerson 2000, 252) when "mutual attunement" (Cavell 1979, 115) takes place across unending divisions. This is the mode of "neighboring" others in "perpetual nextness" (Cavell 1992, 108).

This requires a broader sense of education, involving the translation of our own ways of living and thinking, and of the society as a whole.

ACKNOWLEDGMENT

This research has been supported by Grant-in-Aid for Scientific Research (Japan Society for the Promotion of Science).

NOTES

1. "To cooperate by giving differences a chance to show themselves because of the belief that the expression of difference is not only a right of the other persons but is a means of enriching one's life experience, is inherent in the democratic personal way of life" (1939, LW 14:228).

2. "It is said, and said truly, that for the world's peace it is necessary that we understand the peoples of foreign lands. How well do we understand, I wonder, our next door neighbors? It has also been said that if a man love not his fellow man whom he has seen, he cannot love the God whom he has not seen. . .. A man who has not been seen in the daily relations of life may inspire admiration, emulation, servile subjection, fanatical partisanship, hero worship; but not love and understanding, save as they radiate from the attachments of a near-by union. Democracy must begin at home, and its home is the neighborly community" (1927, LW 2:368).

3. SPIRITS stands for "Supporting Program for Interaction-based Initiative Team Studies," a project funded and promoted by Kyoto University. Our research theme is "Philosophy as Translation and Understanding Other Cultures: Interdisciplinary Research in Philosophy and Education for Bidirectional Internationalization" (2013–2017, Principal Investigator: Naoko Saito). URL: http://www.educ.kyoto-u.ac.jp/nsaito/

4. Emersonian perfectionism has a strong focus on its process of perfecting here and now, with no final state of perfectibility (Cavell 1990, 3; Saito 2005).

5. Acknowledgment is an alternative mode of knowing: "to fall in love with the world," while living with doubt (Cavell 1979, 431).

6. "I have found that the hedging of my acknowledgment of humanity in others hedges my own humanity, shows me the limits of human nature in me" (Cavell 1992, 434); The "call upon me, my answerability, is unrestricted" (436).

7. *Yomiuri Newspaper,* July 6, 2016

8. "From the root of speech, in each utterance of revelation and confrontation, two paths spring: that of the responsibilities of implication; and that of the rights of desire. It will seem to some that the former is the path of philosophy, the latter that of something or other else, perhaps psychoanalysis. In an imperfect world the paths will not reliably coincide, but to show them both open is something I want of philosophy" (Cavell 2005, 185); and "Speaking for myself, I went on to testify that my life too has been transfigured by the experience [in Mississippi] in unpredictable ways, both in psychological ways, as well as, in some extended sense, in political" (Cavell 2010, 430–431).

WORKS CITED

Citations of John Dewey's works are to the thirty-seven-volume critical edition published by Southern Illinois University Press under the editorship of Jo Ann Boydston. In-text citations give the original publication date and series abbreviation, followed by volume number and page number. For example: (1934, LW 10:12) is page 12 of *Art as Experience*, which is published as volume 10 of *The Later Works*.

Series abbreviations for *The Collected Works*:

EW *The Early Works* (1882–1898)

MW *The Middle Works* (1899–1924)

LW *The Later Works* (1925–1953)

Alfonso, Ricardo Miguel and LaRocca, David (eds). 2015a. *A Power to Translate the World: New Essays on Emerson and International Culture.* Leanon, New Hampshire: The University Press of New England on Behalf of Dartmouth College Press.

Alfonso, Ricardo Miguel and LaRocca, David (eds). 2015b. "Introduction: Thinking Through International Influence." In *A Power to Translate the World: New Essays on Emerson and International Culture.* Leanon, New Hampshire: The University Press of New England on Behalf of Dartmouth College Press, 1–28.

Beck, Ulrich. 1986/1992. *Risk Society: Towards a New Modernity*. Trans. Mark Ritter London: SAGE.

Bernstein, Richard J. 1983. *Beyond Objectivism and Relativism: Science, Hermeneutics, and Praxis*. Philadelphia: University of Pennsylvania Press.

Bernstein, Richard. 1992. "The Resurgence of Pragmatism." *Social Research*, vol. 59, no. 4, 813–840.

Bernstein, Richard. 2010. *The Pragmatic Turn*. Cambridge, MA: Polity Press.

Bernstein, Richard J. 2016. "Global Resurgence of Pragmatism." Keynote speech at the special session organized by SPIRITS project at Kyoto University co-organized with the American Philosophy Forum of Japan, June 11, Kyoto University.

Cavell, Stanley. 1979. *The Claim of Reason: Wittgenstein, Skepticism, Morality, and Tragedy*. Oxford: Oxford University Press.

Cavell, Stanley. 1988. *In Quest of the Ordinary: Lines of Skepticism and Romanticism*. Chicago: The University of Chicago Press.

Cavell, Stanley. 1989. *This New Yet Unapproachable America: Lectures after Emerson after Wittgenstein*. Albuquerque, NM: Living Batch Press.

Cavell, Stanley. 1990. *Conditions Handsome and Unhandsome: The Constitution of Emersonian Perfectionism*. Chicago: University of Chicago Press.

Cavell, Stanley. 1992. *The Senses of Walden*. Chicago: University of Chicago Press.

Cavell, Stanley. 2004. *Cities of Words: Pedagogical Letters of a Register of the Moral Life*. Cambridge, MA: The Belknap Press of Harvard University Press.

Cavell, Stanley. 2010. *Little Did I Know: Excerpts from Memory*. Cambridge, MA: Belknap Press of Harvard University Press.

Cavell, Stanley. Forthcoming. "Walden in Tokyo." In *Stanley Cavell and the Thoughts of Other Cultures*. Eds. Paul Standish and Naoko Saito. (Manuscripts under review)

Cavell, Stanley, and Standish, Paul. 2012. "Stanley Cavell in Conversation with Paul Standish." *Journal of Philosophy of Education*, vol. 46, no. 2, 155–176.

Dewey, John. 1916. *Democracy and Education*. MW 9.

Dewey, John. 1919. "Liberalism in Japan." MW 11:156–173.

Dewey, John. 1920. *Reconstruction in Philosophy*. MW 12.

Dewey, John. 1921. "Some Factors in Mutual National Understanding." MW 13:262–271.

Dewey, John. 1922. *Human Nature and Conduct*. MW 14.

Dewey, John. 1925/1929. *Experience and Nature*. LW 1.

Dewey, John. 1927. *The Public and Its Problems*. LW 2.

Dewey, John. 1930. "Construction and Criticism." LW 5:127–143.

Dewey, John. 1934. *Art as Experience*. LW 10.

Dewey, John. 1939. "Creative Democracy—The Task Before Us." LW 14:224–230.

Emerson, Ralph Waldo. 2000. *The Essential Writings of Ralph Waldo Emerson*. Ed. Brooks Atkinson. New York: Modern Library.

Hickman, Larry. 2003. "John Dewey's Pragmatic Technology." Paper presented at the International Symposium: "Pragmatism and the Philosophy of Technology in the 21st Century," Center for Philosophy, University of Tokyo, December 12.

Putnam, Hilary. 1995. *Pragmatism*. Cambridge, MA: Blackwell.

Putnam, Hilary. 2004. *Ethics without Ontology*. Cambridge, MA: Harvard University Press.

Saito, Naoko. 2003. "Education for Global Understanding: Learning from Dewey's Visit to Japan." *Teachers College Record*, vol. 105, no. 9 (December 2003), 1758–1773.

Saito, Naoko. 2005. *The Gleam of Light: Moral Perfectionism and Education in Dewey and Emerson*. New York: Fordham University Press.

Saito, Naoko. 2015. "Emerson and Japan: Finding a Way of Cultural Criticism." In *A Power to Translate the World: New Essays on Emerson and International Culture*. Leanon, New Hampshire: The University Press of New England on Behalf of Dartmouth College Press, 217–235.

Saito, Naoko. 2016. "The Feminine Voice in Philosophy: Cavell and Perfect Pitch" (SPIRITS International Project, "Philosophy as Translation and Understanding Other Cultures: The Cultivation of the Aesthetic Imagination," Clock Tower Centennial Hall, Kyoto University, March 12.

Saito, Naoko. 2017. "Realism of the Obscure and Philosophy as Translation." In *Stanley Cavell and Philosophy as Translation: "The Truth is Translated."* Eds. Paul Standish and Naoko Saito. London: Rowman & Littlefield, 11–23

Saito, Naoko, and Standish, Paul, eds. 2012. *Stanley Cavell and the Education of Grownups*. New York: Fordham University Press.

Standish, Paul. 2011. "Social Justice in Translation: Subjectivity: Identity, and Occidentalism." *Educational Studies in Japan: International Yearbook*, no. 6, 69–79.

Taylor, Charles. 1992. *Multiculturalism and "The Politics of Recognition": An Essay with Commentary*. Princeton, NJ: Princeton University Press.

Thoreau, Henry, D. 1992. *Walden and Resistance to Civil Government*. Ed. William Rossi. New York: W. W. Norton.

CHAPTER 28

....

EXPERIMENTAL DEMOCRACY
FOR CHINA
Dewey's Method

....

SOR-HOON TAN

DEMOCRACY is in peril as never before. Its supposed universal appeal is being eroded by the increasingly dismal political, economic, and social performances of countries wearing that label. Some countries which embarked on democratization in recent years are drifting toward a new authoritarianism. Nondemocratic countries with stellar economic growth in the era of global capitalism offer alternative models of development and government, while enemies of democracy rub their hands with glee and pronounce the death of democracy, all too eager to bury it for good. Could John Dewey's philosophy of democracy guide us through these dangerous waters? Is Dewey's understanding of democracy still relevant for those who continue to harbor hopes for democratization in the People's Republic of China?

Dewey visited China in 1919, during a time that seems diametrically different from the present. Troubled by political reversals in the efforts to establish a republican government after the fall of the Qing dynasty, following a century of weak imperial government that could not defend China's sovereignty against foreign encroachments, many Chinese intellectuals believed that nothing less than a new culture was needed to save China. Dewey was welcomed and feted during his visit as the "philosopher of democracy," bringing to China "the best that America has to offer," ideas of progressive education that would support China's modernization understood in terms of the adoption of science and democracy. Historian Barry Keenan's study of Dewey's visit to China concludes that his Chinese followers' "Dewey experiment" to transform China culturally through education reforms failed because of the inapplicability of Dewey's ideas (Keenan 1977, 156–57, see also Ching 1985). Alan Ryan and Robert Westbrook both consider Dewey to have limited influence on China (Westbrook 1992, 249–52; Ryan 1995, 206).

However, nearly three decades after his visit, a 1947 Chinese monograph evaluating "prominent works in contemporary philosophy" comments, "pragmatism has become the conscious or unconscious tenet of social thought and action of contemporary

Chinese society" (Yang and Wang 2014, 95). After the Chinese Communist Party (CCP) orchestrated virulent attacks on Dewey and his student Hu Shih during the 1950s and 1960s as purveying the most pernicious form of "subjective idealism" supporting imperialist-capitalist class interests, Chinese scholars in the post-Mao era have reassessed Dewey's influence on China more positively, including his influence on Mao Tse-tung (Sun 1999). While it might be "unrealistic to ask for a single total assessment of Dewey's visit to China" (Smith 1985, 255–56), most Chinese commentators acknowledge his significant influence on the modernization of Chinese education (Su 1995; Zhou and Xiang 2001; Wu and Li 2016). Others suggest that his Chinese followers might have misinterpreted him (Gu 2000; Zhang 2003). However, one must remember that getting Dewey "right" is not the same as thinking and acting well as a Deweyan pragmatist in real situations. Dewey offers no absolute dogma, and Chinese pragmatists such as Hu appropriately treated his ideas as tools to solve China's problems (Tan 2004a). Whether or not one agrees with the outcome of their inquiry, Dewey's fallible instrumentalism permits and even requires that such a process would transform his ideas, hopefully in ways that advance rather than distort pragmatism.

At a talk I gave on Dewey's pragmatist method in 2017 in Beijing, a retired Chinese academic observed that, despite the excitement of Dewey's visit, those who flocked to his public lectures were disappointed that he offered no solution to China's problems. If his Chinese audience expected direct solutions to China's problems from Dewey, then they did not understand his philosophy. Dewey was more aware than most people of the complexity of China's situation and never pretended that he had any ready-made solutions or blueprint for "saving China."

> But the task of reorganization, of transformation, of union of old and new, is so vast, so appalling in its complexity, that neither any wholesale forecast of the future nor any simple remedy is worth the paper it is written on. The things that are certain are few. Either failure or success will entail tremendous consequences for the rest of the world, so that no one can afford to be indifferent. A great number of specific enterprises and experiments, converging to a common end, will have to be undertaken. There is no situation in the world more calculated to justify distrust of panaceas and wholesale remedies. (1921, MW 13:95)

These words of Dewey, writing nearly a century ago about "Old and New China," could very well also describe the situation now when it comes to China's democratization.

DEMOCRATIZING CHINESE (CONFUCIAN) CULTURE

Democracy is not merely a method of selecting government officials through universal suffrage, competitive elections, and regulating government and citizens' actions through specific political institutions. According to Dewey, "Democracy is a form of government only because it is a form of moral and spiritual association" (1888, EW 1:240). James Tiles suggested that "what Dewey took to be a more inspiring sense of 'democracy' was a form of culture—a set of practices, attitudes, and expectations, which in an ideal society would pervade every aspect of human interaction" (Tiles 1997, 121). Democracy is valued as a way of life that enables all to pursue the moral end of human growth in every sense. It does not differ from other ethical conceptions of government (e.g., the Aristocratic ideal) in its goal of the best form of association which harmonizes the varied needs, capacities, desires of human beings, it differs in how that goal is to be achieved: not by a select few through specialized institutions or organizations within society, but by the participation of every person (1888, EW 1:243).

Ethical governments must serve the governed. From the democratic perspective, this purpose cannot be achieved unless each member of the community shares in selecting its governors and determining their policies (1927, LW 2:327), so political institutions are not unimportant. However, the democratic ideal does not and cannot only work through political participation, certainly not if it is limited to voting every few years for government representatives. "Regarded as an idea, democracy is not an alternative to other principles of associated life. It is the very idea of community life itself." (1927, LW 2:328). Democratic politics for Dewey consists of publics engaging in social inquiries to find solutions to shared problems arising from the indirect consequences of transactions meriting regulation. The democratic way of life, that is, participation in cooperative inquiries, must also prevail in the family, the neighborhood, places of religious worship, schools, and at the workplace (1927, LW 2:325). This is an ideal that has not been realized even in Western democracies: "democracy in this sense is not a fact and never will be" (1927, LW 2:328). Its significance lies in the normative standards it provides to guide democratic practice and measure democratic achievements.

Dewey considered an ideal to be "the tendency and movement of some thing which exists carried to its final limit, viewed as completed, perfected" (1927, LW 2:328). Democracy, as the ideal of community, therefore presents "actual phases of associated life as they are freed from restrictive and disturbing elements, and are contemplated as having attained their limit of development" (1927, LW 2:328). In other words, his conception of democracy is rooted in the imperfect ways of life of American communities—communities which have developed what we identify as democratic political institutions to remedy certain unsatisfactory social experience, in particular individuals' experience of oppression and injustice. As such, is the conception culturally specific and therefore irrelevant to cultures which are radically different?

The cultural differences between China and America was the very reason his Chinese followers believed Dewey's visit could help China achieve the cultural transformation needed in order to democratize, which they equate with modernization. Times have changed, and modernization theory which presumes a universal path of human development for all societies has been replaced by discourses of cultural pluralism and multiple modernities (Tu 2000). While the May Fourth iconoclasts were more than willing to take America as its model in the pursuit of science and democracy, today those sympathetic to Dewey emphasize that it is reductionist "to equate American liberal democracy with democracy itself" (Sun 2008, 58). China's spectacular rise in the changing global political economy and geopolitics since the 1990s have seen a surge in Chinese nationalisms—including a form of cultural nationalism closely associated with the revival of Confucianism-centered traditional Chinese culture (Kang 2008) and a state nationalism that appropriates China's Confucian legacy as the CCP's new ideological prop (He and Guo 2000, 28–30).

Part of current nationalist discourses in China is the rejection of Western models, especially liberal democracy, as unsuited to China, from the perspective of both its current unique circumstances and its traditional culture. Indeed, given the shift of economic power to Asia, and China in particular, and the political crises plaguing North America and Europe, Chinese nationalists have progressed from championing everything with "Chinese characteristics" as a defense of China's uniqueness and sovereignty to asserting the superiority of "China models" in various domains. Even when not the intent of their authors, very often academic works that legitimately challenge the hegemony of Western ideas have unfortunately fed the fires of Chinese nationalism. Given the perception that American imperialism involves the "export" of liberal democracy to other parts of the world, it is not surprising that Chinese nationalisms tend to be antidemocratic, and when they are not, they tend to assume that China already has a democracy "with Chinese characteristics" that is more democratic than other countries. Even academic forms of Chinese nationalism are often linked to neo-conservative and neo-authoritarian thought highly critical if not outright opposed to democratization. Moreover, the promotion of "national studies" since the 1990s has marked a "retreat from the public" by intellectuals (Xu 1999, 80) and the apparent "depoliticization" of traditional culture evident in popular appropriation also could work against democracy by encouraging political apathy and refusing to question the undemocratic political status quo.

While traditional Chinese culture should not be reduced to Confucianism, the latter has been very much at the center of contemporary discourses that challenge Western models of democracy, just as it had been the chief target of May Fourth iconoclasts who adopted the slogan to "demolish the Confucian shop" in the pursuit of democracy. There is a rich and growing literature on the relationship between Confucianism and democracy, ranging from agreement with Samuel Huntington that a Confucian democracy is an oxymoron, proposals of Confucian meritocracy or Confucian Constitutionalism as alternatives to liberal democracy, attempts to discover democratic elements or at least the seeds of democracy in ancient Confucian texts or in ancient China, to arguments that Confucian philosophy could be justifiably interpreted or reconstructed to be compatible with some kind of democracy. The struggle over the "lost soul of Confucianism" goes beyond academic debates, for Confucianism has become a convenient tool in "the politics of civilization," in which it is deployed in resistance to democratization (Zheng 2004, chapter 3).

Andrew Nathan pointed out that the failures of China's democratic experiments— "efforts to establish legislatures that were chosen in relatively open, competitive elections, and which tried to exercise their constitutional powers; and efforts to establish freedoms of speech and organization" (Nathan 1993, 4)—are overdetermined, with possible causes ranging from ideology, national security problems, militarism, political culture, underdevelopment, peasant mass, constitutional and institutional flaws, moral failures of supporters of democracy, interactions and behavior of the political elites. Culturalist arguments that China *cannot* democratize because of its traditional culture, or that China *should not* democratize because democracy is incompatible with its cultural traditions, adopt reductionist, static, essentialist, totalizing, and consequently hegemonic views of culture (Dirlik 1985, 94–95; Boudon and Bourricaud 1989). This contrasts strongly with the Deweyan understanding of cultures as dynamic, changing ways of life, consisting of ideas, practices, and artifacts shared and transmitted in processes which at their best (though not always) develop the imagination, refine tastes, and deepen intellectual insights. A country's culture(s) neither determines whether it can become democratic, nor does it justify particular norms for a people. Treating culture as the answer to explanatory or justificatory problems invariably oversimplifies and essentializes a way of life, and ignores its complexity as a process comprising of multiple interlocking problems which require dynamic solutions over time.

Dewey reconstructed the concept of culture so that his conception of democracy as culture could be adopted without falling victim to American ethnocentrism (Tan 2008). According to Dewey, "philosophy deals with cultural problems, using culture in the broad sense which the anthropologists have made clear to us—dealing with the patterns of human relationships" (1947, LW 17:466). He defines culture as "the complex of conditions which taxes the terms upon which human beings associate and live together" (1939, LW 13:67). In his philosophy, democratization does not involve imposing a particular culture of a specific society on all others; it requires that each democratizing society works with its own particular set of cultural problems to find better alternatives for human association in its specific circumstances to enable moral growth for all members and groups. All cultures can and should democratize and the democratizing project is an on-going one even for the oldest "democracies" of the world, none of which can claim a culture that is fully democratic by Dewey's standard. Chinese culture can democratize without losing its distinctiveness or becoming just like other democratic cultures.

Within the contemporary discourse on the relationship between Confucianism and democracy, some scholars have attempted to reconstruct conceptions of Confucian democracy that explore the possibilities of democratizing Confucian societies by elucidating certain similarities inter alia between Dewey's philosophy of education and Confucian teachings on personal cultivation, and their conceptions of persons and ethical relations (Hall and Ames 1999; Tan 2004b). They begin with the incompatibility of Confucianism with the conventional understanding of liberal democracy as premised on possessive individualism, treating social relations as valuable only when voluntary, competitive and conflicting relationships as inevitable and even desirable, cooperation as justified only on the basis of calculative self-interests, and government as legitimate only with checks and balances and focused on the protection of individual civil and political rights. They then highlight the differences between this (mis)understanding of democracy and Dewey's conception of democracy, which they argue provides a way of democratizing that would be compatible with Confucian values and ideal practices.

Their conceptions of Confucian democracy are ways of life, that is, cultures which would be both Confucian and democratic. They have been labeled "Deweyan Confucian Communitarians" as their versions of Confucian democracy are based on a fundamentally social view of individuals and emphasize the value of community on par, perhaps even above the values of freedom and equality.

PHILOSOPHICAL RECONSTRUCTIONS AS TOOLS

Part of Dewey's appeal for Confucian democracy projects lies in his critique of political institutions of American democracy during his time, even as he defended the ethical ideal. This is important in two ways: the current problems of de facto American democracy therefore cannot count against Deweyan Confucian democracy philosophically or practically, and it opens up new possibilities for the institutional forms democratization in China can take, instead of a procrustean attempt to impose already malfunctioning democratic institutions on China. Political theorist Sungmoon Kim recently criticizes "Confucian Deweyan Communitarians" for emphasizing the intrinsic value of democracy as a way of life to the exclusion of democracy's instrumental value which emphasizes political institutions (Kim 2016, 243–44). Although he absolves Dewey from this, implying that the Deweyan Confucians misunderstand Dewey, Kim's criticism is reminiscent of criticisms of Dewey for overlooking the political, or at least not adequately grasping certain aspects of political life (e.g., Wilkinson 2012). Neither Dewey's own nor the Deweyan Confucians' emphases on the nonpolitical ignore the need for democratic political institutions or their importance, but they all reject the assumption that prevailing institutions of countries purporting to be democratic are the only or best alternative for all who aspire to democracy.

Contrary to Kim's reading, Dewey's major work in political philosophy, *The Public and Its Problems*, does not offer "primarily an overarching scaffolding of political institutions" (Kim 2016, 240).

> There is no sanctity in universal suffrage, frequent elections, majority rule, congressional and cabinet government. These things are devices evolved in the direction in which the current was moving, each wave of which involved at the time of its impulsion a minimum of departure from antecedent custom and law. (1927, LW 2:326)

Rather, the work is an exercise in philosophical reconstruction of the ideas of the democratic state, of democracy and its intrinsic values of freedom, equality, and community. In tracing how the political institutions of existing democracies were the products of contingent historical changes, Dewey was emphasizing that they are changeable, and it is preferable that changes come about through intelligent direction than happenstance. In the case of not yet democratic countries, democratization must proceed through intelligent direction of conditions already present for change, rather than "import" others' institutions just because they seem more desirable. And when such import of institutions occur, as has happened with democratization in many second- and third-wave democracies, they invariably need to be modified and adapted to local conditions in order to function at all. In suggesting that ideas such as freedom supporting or justifying Western democratic institutions were not their cause but intellectual terms that express the democratic movement (1927, LW 2:289), Dewey was not derogating "the important and even superior claims of democracy as an ethical and social ideal" (1927, LW 2:287). Nor was he relegating the intrinsic value of democracy to dependency, contrary to Kim's claim that intrinsic value is conditional upon instrumental value; Kim argues that it is only after democratic political institutions have been adopted for instrumental reasons, as better ways of "coordinating complex social interactions under the circumstances of modern politics," that citizens could live "the democratic way of life, which make democracy intrinsically valuable." (Kim 2016, 244–245). Dewey's pragmatism does not impose a rigid sequential order placing institutional democratization before realization of democratic ways of life or the fostering of democratic cultures. Quite the contrary, he inquired "whether political freedom can be maintained without that freedom of culture ... If it is true that the political and legal react to shape other things, it is even more true that political institutions are an effect, not a cause" (1939, LW 13:67).

Kim's study of South Korea as a Confucian democracy, wherein democratic political institutions adopted for its instrumental value are consolidated as a way of life attaining the intrinsic value of democracy through mediation and negotiation with the Confucian public culture (Kim 2016, 246), is pragmatic in starting with actual problems of democratization. It provides a case study of intelligently directed social change, showing how a Confucian culture could democratize even as it Confucianizes democracy in Korea in a theoretical model of "mutual accommodation" between democracy and Confucianism in public life instead of the replacement of the latter in the "liberal congruence thesis" he attributes to other theorists attempting to reconcile Confucianism and democracy (Kim 2016, 247). However, his dismissal of competing conceptions of Confucian democracy based on philosophical reconstructions of Confucian and democratic ideas to produce Confucian democratic ideals are not warranted by Dewey's pragmatism, in which philosophical reconstructions have an important role. Indeed, the process of democratic consolidation in Confucian societies described by Kim could meet Dewey's standard of intelligently directed change only if there are appropriate criteria for determining whether the result of any mediation and negotiation between Confucian public culture and democratic political institutions is Confucian and democratic enough. The inherited ideas of both Confucianism and democracy cannot serve as such criteria for they are products of different times and express different forms of Confucianism and democracy that are no longer relevant in the new Confucian democracy. Such old ideas need to be reconstructed philosophically to produce the criteria for guiding the mediation and negotiation between Confucianism and democracy in Kim's Confucian democracy.

Rather than meaning that intrinsic value is always conditional upon instrumental value, their inseparability in Dewey's philosophy precludes rendering the intrinsic value of democracy or democratic culture a passive effect in a linear causal process. An intrinsic value is always also an instrument, and an instrumental value is always also an end. Dewey rejected "intrinsic values" in the sense of "ends-in-themselves" which are not also means (1939, LW 13:226). Means and ends are not merely causally, externally, related; they are internally related in that the meaning of each cannot be fully understood without the other, and they can mutually transform each other in reality. An intrinsic value as an end is not an absolute end-in-itself independent of all relations. Instead, "anything taken *as end* is in its own content or constituents a correlation of the energies, personal and extra-personal, which operate as means" (1939, LW 13:216). Dewey understands intrinsic values as ends-in-view, "constituted in terms of the conditions of its actualization" (1939, LW 13:218). The human activity of valuation involves generalizing about means-ends. Value propositions imply "an aversion to an existing situation and attraction toward a prospective possible situation" and are pragmatic to the extent that they include explicitly or implicitly "a *specifiable and testable relation between the latter as an end and certain activities as means for accomplishing it*" (1939, LW 13:202, original italics).

Democracy has intrinsic value only when it serves as an "end-in-view," which is itself a means of transforming the unsatisfactory undemocratic situation, and therefore has instrumental value. In the discourse of Confucian democracy, philosophical reconstructions provide new democratic Confucian ideals that encompass the intrinsic values of democracy (such as freedom, equality, community). Their reconstructions are premised on past unsatisfactory experiences of Confucian and democratic institutions and practices, and as Deweyan reconstructions, intended not as absolute ends-in-themselves but as ends-in-view, which are means to critique and improve the status quo in practice. The reconstructed philosophical ideals of Deweyan Confucian democracy, while encompassing the intrinsic values of democracy and Confucianism, must have instrumental value in diagnosing current problems, critiquing or assessing current political institutions and social practices, as well as setting out more concrete steps toward a democratic way of life. Rather than always being "conditional on" and resulting from living under democratic political institutions, an understanding of the Confucian-democratic ideals as intrinsic values are also needed to specify actions that need to be taken, what kind of political and other institutions need to be established, or which existing ones need to be reformed and how such reforms might be accomplished, in order to move in the direction of Deweyan Confucian democracy.

Intrinsic values do not become relevant and motivating only after they have been realized by means of political institutions as Kim claims. Functioning as ends-in-view, intrinsic values are also instrumental values, and, even if abstract, they can still have motivational force while serving as guides for intelligent direction of social change. Philosophical reconstructions emphasizing the intrinsic value of democracy as a way of life are important in China's democratization because they can serve as tools to question ideological claims such as the CCP's claim that China has built a "socialist political democracy with Chinese characteristics," and to criticize existing political as well as nonpolitical institutions and practices by specifying where and how they have failed to live up to the ethical ideal of democracy, stunting citizens' moral growth and communities' flourishing. Justified philosophical reconstructions of Confucian ideals based on interpretations of Confucianism grounded in the ancient texts can serve as tools to challenge appropriations of Confucianism in aid of authoritarianism, which serve elite interests much more than they benefit the rest of the population. The battle for democracy in China is as much ideological as it is practical, and intellectual tools are needed for both.

Experimenting for Democracy

Dewey insists that "democratic ends demand democratic methods for their realization" (1939, LW 13:187). However, democratic methods are not limited to the political institutions of countries calling themselves democracies. Dewey himself never made the mistake of simply prescribing American political institutions, or any ideal institutional forms he himself might have invented, as the panacea for all countries aspiring to democracy (Clopton and Ou 1973, 88). For Dewey, democratic methods are "methods of consultation, persuasion, negotiation, communication, cooperative intelligence, in the task of making our own politics, industry, education, our culture generally, a servant and an evolving manifestation of democratic ideas" (1939, LW 13:157). Instead of some specific political machinery, such as representative government elected via universal suffrage, independent judiciary, and so on, democratic methods can be found in all social interactions. While some political theorists might frown upon the diminished emphasis on the political, this is likely to be more fruitful in China's context, given the CCP's control over the political machinery, but fortunately not quite total control over every aspect of Chinese citizens' lives, and widespread skepticism among the Chinese population and others about the wisdom of a wholesale adoption of known democratic political institutions.

The expansion of democratization to the non-political aspects of people's daily life should not be mistaken for escapist de-politicization which turns a blind eye to political institutions that obstruct democratization. During his visit to China, Dewey was asked, "Where should we start in reforming our society?" He answered, "We must start by reforming the component institutions of the society. Families, schools, local governments, the central government—all these must be reformed" (Clopton and Ou 1973, 62). Just as there is no total reconstruction of a society, there cannot be one single starting point. As Dewey said of the problems of an earlier time, "a great number of specific enterprises and experiments, converging to a common end, will have to be undertaken" (1921, MW 13:1935). Democratic methods promote democratic habits and create the conditions for democratic participation beyond the social relations in which they were first applied. If it is unrealistic or unwise to attempt a top-down wholesale democratization of political institutions, or a populist uprising which in any case is not guaranteed to bring about a Deweyan democracy—in fact it is unlikely to do so since its methods would be undemocratic—then one must apply the democratic methods in nonpolitical areas of social life where each person could begin the process of democratization by reforming whatever social relations he or she engages in, with the hope that this will nurture capacities for self-governance and desire for political democracy. The path to genuine government by the people and the institutional forms this will take in China must be sought in the activities of the Chinese people themselves, in which organized intelligence will be employed to solve shared problems, including the problems of governance. Such activities are most likely to be found in the many social experiments being carried out in the country.

The last three decades have seen many experiments in China, from agricultural responsibility system, contract labor, industrial parks co-developed with foreign partners, special economic zones and technology zones, and many other policy and institutional innovations in market reforms, to experiments with privatization of housing, healthcare financing reform, household registration reform, rural cooperatives, legalizing nongovernment organizations' activities that address social problems, cross-sector collaboration between the party-state and civil society organizations, community-based urban management, integrating international immigrants into local community, methods of managing conflicts and maintaining social stability, electoral democracy at the village and county levels, elections within the CCP, and other experiments of representation and consultation. Experimental programs and experimental zones are explicitly incorporated into the state's development plans since the nineties (Heilmann and Melton 2013). A national level awards program for best practices in local governance innovation was established in 2000. Policy innovation and experimentation are included in the measures for evaluating party cadres. This experimental and adaptive approach is considered a major contributor to China's economic success and a key characteristic of the "China model" (Chen and Naughton 2017, 22; see also Mukand and Rodrik 2005; Florini, Lai, and Tan 2012). Decentralized experimentation is a regular feature of Chinese policy making process in which the CCP top leaders set the main directions while encouraging local officials to experiment with various ways of achieving the goals of central policies, and the results of such experiments are then fed back into national policy making. Very often the results of experiments have been used to overcome opposition to change in the struggle among policy makers over the direction of the country. The process also encourages bottom-up initiative, inclusion of local knowledge, and adaptive policy learning while allowing top decision-makers to retain ultimate control over which experiments are confirmed, revised, terminated, or spread and at the same time reduce the political risk of reforms and avoid nationwide mistakes that could prove disastrous for a large and complex country like China.

National replications of local experiments, as well as assessment of their successes on other independent criteria, vary from case to case. Not all successful experiments are due to national orchestration. The privatization of township and village enterprises and state-owned enterprises, for example, were "more a result of central authorities responding positively to local innovations that the former had had no role in fostering, rather than part of a larger economic design" (Florini, Lai, and Tan 2012, 5). Despite the hierarchical nature of Chinese Communist rule and the inflexibility of most Communist Party-states elsewhere, some experiments seem to have been motivated more by the desire to solve local problems, individual preferences for innovative solutions, opportunity, and the effect of imitating peers' innovations than they have been responses to the incentives to innovate provided by the central authorities; and some experiments are even contrary to central command (Teets, Hasmath, and Lewis 2017, 514). In most cases, it is difficult to distinguish between bottom-up and top-down initiatives, as there is an interplay between local initiative and central sponsorship in the initial stages of major experimental efforts (Heilmann 2008, 10).

Just as there are a variety of views about the likely future for China—collapse (Gorrie 2013), authoritarian resilience (Nathan 2003), trapped transition (Pei 2008), or democratic evolution (Ogden 2002; Gilley 2004), among others—studies of Chinese reform experiments vary in their assessment of where these are leading the country. While Florini and her co-authors argue that, despite the absence of "any immediate prospects for democratic rule in China, in the sense of freely contested multiparty elections backed by fully realized freedoms of press, assembly, and voice," the multitude of experiments reveal information flows, participation and accountability mechanisms, and other practices and institutions that might yet contribute to democratization as they re-shape the habits, norms, and expectations of Chinese citizens and their political leaders (Florini, Lai, and Tan 2012, 6, 164). Others see China's experimentalism as a key factor in its authoritarian resilience or "adaptive authoritarianism," as the approach enhances the CCP's ability to meet major economic, political, social, and environmental challenges, thereby enhancing its performance legitimacy and entrenching its regime (Heilmann 2008, 2; see also He and Thøgersen 2010; Yan and Ge 2017, 421). At times, policy experimentation could even be manipulated as a political symbol to delay reform (Zeng 2015).

Chinese policymakers employ a methodology of "proceeding from point to surface (*youdian daomian* 由点到面)," in which experimental points are established to try out some solutions to specific problems, each limited to a particular locale and policy area or economic sector (Heilmann 2008, 7), driven by local initiative with formal or informal support of higher level policymakers, whose endorsement of the results of particular experiments allow "model experiences" to be extracted from them and spread through extensive media coverage, high-profile conferences, study visits, and calls for emulation in more and more regions (Heilmann 2011, 63). Instead of policymaking and legislation always preceding implementation, this distinctive process innovates through implementation before adoption or finalization of policies and drafting of regulations and laws (Heilmann 2008, 4). During the process, generalizable policies are formulated and refined progressively with reiterations of the initial experiments according to local circumstances. The concrete pattern of decentralized experimentation in the Chinese policymaking process has its historical and ideological roots in the revolutionary experience of the CCP before the founding of the People's Republic of China, which provides the mechanism that legitimizes local initiative while leaving hierarchical control intact within the party-state (Heilmann 2011, 63). The distinctive vocabulary and methods of "point to surface" policy experimentation were established as a method of the CCP political leadership by the mid-1950s. During the Great Leap Forward and the Cultural Revolution, policy experimentation was reduced to "preconceived, centrally imposed model propagation and emulation" (Heilmann 2011, 75). It was left to the reformers of the 1980s to recover "point-to-surface" policy experimentation as the "concretization" of the CCP's best tradition of "seeking truth from facts," although even party members are often oblivious to its prereform history (Heilmann 2011, 64, 72).

Deng Xiaoping's reform policies based on "seeking truth from facts" and "crossing the river by feeling for stepping stones" have sometimes been described as "pragmatism" (Fewsmith 2001, 55), although many Chinese publications have protested that Deng's emphasis on practice and using concrete experience to guide policy is Marxist rather than pragmatist and generally distinguish Marxism from pragmatism (Yang and Wang 2014, 259). The acknowledged authority of Deng's "let practice be the sole criterion for testing truth" is Mao's essay, "On Practice" (Mao 1965, 296). While neither Deng nor Mao would endorse Deweyan pragmatism or pragmatist democracy, recent Chinese research on Republican China tends to question a strict divide between Dewey, Mao, and Marx and "argue for a Marxian influence on Dewey and a Deweyan influence on Mao" (Schulte 2012, 106). Heilmann's study shows that, contrary to official CCP historiography, "Communist experimentation is a part of a much bigger story about widespread efforts at experimentation in extremely uncertain times during China's Republican era," and he presents convincing evidence for "the Deweyan imprint on Mao's experimental approach" (Heilmann 2011, 77–79). Part of that story is Dewey's influence on that period and his followers' emphasis on the experiment-based approach to social reforms, most evident in Hu's translation of "pragmatism" as "experimentalism (*shiyan zhuyi* 实验主义)," in order to highlight "what this philosophy pays the most attention to, the method of experiment" (Hu 1996, 212). Besides the Chinese studies of Dewey's influence on Mao, Herbert Marcuse reportedly saw "more of Dewey than Marx" in Mao's "On Practice" (Schram 1984, 106).

Among the variety of experiments being conducted in China, some could already be relatively closer than others to Deweyan paradigms. Kyoung Shin identifies the emergence of a "post-hierarchical" architecture of what he calls "community-driven experimentalist governance . . . enacted through a set of community-driven practices between the protagonists, such as joint framework making or platform making, collective learning about local conditions, joint problem solving, and peer review and social sanctioning" (Shin 2017, 607–8). He explicitly uses "experimentalist governance" in the sense it is employed in the works of Charles Sabel and his collaborators and cites Sabel and Zeitlin's works on experimentalist governance in the European Union for comparison in his analysis (Shin 2017, 611, 626). This concept of experimentalist governance, "a recursive process of provisional goal setting and revision based on learning from the comparison of alternative approaches to advancing them in different contexts," is "experimentalist in the philosophical sense of American pragmatists like John Dewey (1927) because they systematically provoke doubt about their own assumptions and practices, treat all solutions as incomplete and corrigible, and produce an ongoing, re-ciprocal readjustment of ends and means through comparison of different approaches to advancing common general aims" (Sabel and Zeitlin 2012, 169–170). Besides being a response to challenges of governance under conditions of complex uncertainty, experi-mentalist governance also offers an answer to the question of what Dewey's pragmatism requires of democratic institutions beyond vague ideals, although it is not without its critics from both pragmatist and other perspectives (Sabel 2012; cf. Allen 2012; Ralston 2012; Pappas 2012, 68–72).

Another area which could prove productive for Dewey inspired research into China's potential for democracy and obstacles to democratization is the "deliberative democ-racy" experiments such as the deliberative polling conducted in Zeguo, Zhejiang prov-ince (He 2008; Fishkin et al. 2010), and other experiments aimed at increasing the people's participation in decision-making processes the outcomes of which have im-pact on their lives. While different theories of deliberative democracy show a variety of philosophical inspiration and influences, Dewey's conception of democratic politics in terms of social inquiries conducted by publics formed in the process externalities of transactions requiring regulation has often been cited as a source of deliberative approaches to democracy. However, Gregory Pappas criticizes political theories of deliberative democracy for failing to use Dewey in the most productive way. Despite affinities and similarities, such theories differ significantly in their understanding of de-liberation from what Dewey requires of democratic social inquiries (Pappas 2012, 57–67). Beyond these theoretical concerns, the consultative and deliberative experiments in China are more authoritarian than democratic, even though they are important in propagating and promulgating the idea that people should have a decisive voice when major decisions are made that affect their lives (He and Thøgersen 2010), and therefore still marks an important step toward "government by the people."

While none of them point unequivocally in the direction of a Deweyan democ-racy, the Chinese reform experiments provide a rich field for Deweyans to explore the relevance and validity of Dewey's theory of democracy to China, if we take seriously Dewey's insistence that democratization must begin from the specific circumstances and prevailing conditions of a country. The CCP's "experimentation under hierarchy" differs from Dewey's experimental method in significant ways. In what ways does the CCP's experimentation methodology fail to be a "method of organized intelligence" which Dewey identifies with the democratic method? To what extent and how do the undemocratic aspects of the former impede its effectiveness in solving problems, or achieving the individual moral growth and community flourishing of a Deweyan de-mocracy? Or was Dewey mistaken that the two are synonymous? Do currently undem-ocratic policy experiments have the potential to become or to include Deweyan social inquiry, and would actualizing that potential increase their effectiveness and contribute to democratization? How might one go about actualizing that Deweyan potential, if it exists? While we may see no clear path in today's China to a democratic regime fa-miliar to us and taken as a norm by most democratic theories—in which top political leaders are appointed through competitive elections and universal suffrage and basic freedoms are protected by rights—this should not be criterion to measure the success of our inquiry, if we take seriously Dewey's fallibilism about the political institutions of democracy. Following his method, we should work from ground up, by inquiring into the conditions in various domains, locales, and activities that might offer opportunities for Deweyan social inquiries, thinking through how obstacles to successful social inquiries could be removed, and reflecting on the possible directions such social inquiries might take in China, without being prejudiced by what we already know about previous democratic transitions. The exact forms of China's democratic institutions if they are realized with Dewey's method must be the collaborative results of the Chinese people's social inquiries into the varied problems of their experience.

WORKS CITED

Citations of John Dewey's works refer to the thirty-seven-volume critical edition published by Southern Illinois University Press under the editorship of Jo Ann Boydston. In-text citations give the original publication date and series abbreviation, followed by volume number and page number. For example: (1934, LW 10:12) is page 12 of *Art as Experience*, which is published as volume 10 of *The Later Works*.

Series abbreviations for *The Collected Works*:

EW *The Early Works* (1882–98)

MW *The Middle Works* (1899–1924)

LW *The Later Works* (1925–53)Allen, Barry. 2012. "Experiments in Democracy." *Contemporary Pragmatism* 9(2):75–92.

Boudon, Raymond, and François Bourricaud. 1989. *A Critical Dictionary of Sociology*. Chicago: University of Chicago Press.

Chen, Ling, and Barry Naughton. 2017. "A Dynamic China Model: The Co-Evolution of Economics and Politics in China." *Journal of Contemporary China* 26(103):18–34.

Ching, Julia. 1985. "China's Responses to Dewey." *Journal of Chinese Philosophy* 12:261–281.

Clopton, Robert W., and Tsuin-chen Ou, eds. 1973. *John Dewey: Lectures in China, 1919–1920*. Honolulu: University of Hawaii Press.

Dirlik, Arif. 1985. *Culture, Society and Revolution: A Critical Discussion of American Studies of Modern Chinese Thought*. Vol. 85-01. Durham, NC: Asian/Pacific Studies Institute, Duke University.

Fewsmith, Joseph 2001. *China since Tiananmen: The Politics of Transition*. Cambridge: Cambridge University Press.

Fishkin, James S., Baogang He, Rpbert C. Luskin, and Alice Siu. 2010. "Deliberative Democracy in an Unlikely Place: Deliberative Polling in China." *British Journal of Political Science* 40(2):435–448.

Florini, Ann, Hairong Lai, and Yeling Tan. 2012. *China Experiments: From Local Innovations to National Reform*. Washington DC: Brookings Institution Press.

Gilley, Bruce. 2004. *China's Democratic Future: How It Will Happen and Where It Will Lead*. New York: Columbia University Press.

Gorrie, James R. 2013. *The China Crisis: How China's Economic Collapse Will Lead to a Global Depression*. Hoboken, NJ: Wiley.

Gu, Hongliang 顾红亮. 2000. *The Misreading of Pragmatism* 实用主义的误读. Shanghai: East China Normal University Press.

Hall, David L., and Roger T. Ames. 1999. *Democracy of the Dead: Dewey, Confucius, and the Hope for Democracy in China*. La Salle: Open Court.

He, Baogang 何包钢. 2008. *Deliberative Democracy: Theory, Method and Practice*（协商民主：理论，方法和实践）. Beijing: Chinese Academy of Social Sciences Press.

He, Baogang, and Stig Thøgersen. 2010. "Giving the People a Voice? Experiments with Consultative Authoritarian Institutions in China." *Journal of Contemporary China* 19(66):675–692.

He, Baogang, and Yingjie Guo. 2000. *Nationalism, National Identity and Democratization in China*. Brookfield, VT: Ashgate.

Heilmann, Sebastian. 2008. "Policy Experimentation in China's Economic Rise." *Studies in Comparative International Development* 43(1):1–26.

Heilmann, Sebastian. 2011. "Policy-Making through Experimentation: The Formation of a Distinctive Policy Process." In *Mao's Invisible Hand: The Political Foundations of Adaptive Governance in China*, edited by Sebastian Heilmann and Elizabeth J. Perry, 62–101. Cambridge, MA: Harvard University Asia Center.

Heilmann, Sebastian, and Oliver Melton. 2013. "The Reinvention of Development Planning in China, 1993–2012." *Modern China* 36(6):580–628.

Hu, Shih. 1996. *Collected Essays of Hu Shih* (胡适文存). Hefei: Huangshan Press.

Kang, Xiaoguang 康晓光. 2008. *Come Back China: Contemporary Mainland Chinese Cultural Nationalism Movement (Zhongguo guilai: dangdai zhongguo dalu wenhua minzu zhuyi yundong yanjiu)* (中国归来：当代中国大陆文化民族主义运动研究). Singapore: Bafang Wenhua.

Keenan, Barry. 1977. *The Dewey Experiment in China*. Cambridge, MA: Harvard University Press.

Kim, Sungmoon. 2016. "Pragmatic Confucian Democracy: Rethinking the Value of Democracy in East Asia." *The Journal of Politics* 79(1):237–249. doi: http://dx.doi.org/10.1086/687762

Mao, Tse-tung. 1965. "On Practice." In *Selected Works of Mao Tse-tung*, 295–309. Beijing: Foreign Language Press.

Mukand, harun W., and Dani Rodrik. 2005. "In Search of the Holy Grail: Policy Convergence, Experimentation and Economic Performance." *American Economic Review* 95(1):374–383.

Nathan, Andrew. 2003. "Authoritarian Resilience." *Journal of Democracy* 14(1):6–17.

Nathan, Andrew J. 1993. "Chinese Democracy: The Lessons of Failure." *Journal of Contemporary China* 2(4):3–13.

Ogden, Suzanne. 2002. *Inklings of Democracy in China*. Cambridge, MA: Harvard University Press.

Pappas, Gregory Fernando. 2012. "What Would John Dewey Say about Deliberative Democracy and Democratic Experimentalism?" *Contemporary Pragmatism* 9(2):57–74.

Pei, Minxin. 2008. *China's Trapped Transition: The Limits of Developmental Autocracy*. Cambridge, MA: Harvard University Press.

Ralston, Shane J. 2012. "Dewey and Hayek on Democratic Experimentalism." *Contemporary Pragmatism* 9(2):93–116.

Ryan, Alan. 1995. *John Dewey and the High Tide of American Liberalism*. New York: Norton.

Sabel, Charles F. 2012. "Dewey, Democracy, and Democratic Experimentalism." *Contemporary Pragmatism* 9(2):35–55.

Sabel, Charles F., and Jonathan Zeitlin. 2012. "Experimentalist Governance." In *Oxford Handbook of Governance*, edited by David Levi-Faur, 169–184. Oxford: Oxford University Press.

Schram, Stuart R. 1984. "Mao Studies: Retrospect and Prospect." *The China Quarterly* 97:95–125.

Schulte, Barbara. 2012. "The Chinese Dewey: Friend, Fiend, and Flagship." In *The Global Reception of John Dewey's Thought*, edited by Rosa Bruno-Jofré and Jürgen Schriewer, 83–115. New York: Routledge.

Shin, Kyoung. 2017. "Neither Center nor Local: Community-Driven Experimentalist Governance in China." *The China Quarterly* 231:607–633.

Smith, John E. 1985. "Pragmatism at Work: Dewey's Lecture in China." *Journal of Chinese Philosophy* 12:231–259.

Su, Zhixin. 1995. "A Critical Evaluation of John Dewey's Influence on Chinese Education." *American Journal of Education* 103(3):302–325.

Sun, Youzhong. 1999. "John Dewey in China: Yesterday and Today." *Transactions of the Charles S. Peirce Society* 35(1):69–88.

Sun, Youzhong. 2008. "Globalizing Democracy: A Deweyan Critique of Bush's Second-Term National Security Strategy." In *Democracy as Culture*, edited by Sor-hoon Tan and John Whalen-bridge, 53–62. Albany: State University of New York Press.

Tan, Sor-hoon. 2004a. "China's Pragmatist Experiment in Democracy: Hu Shih's Pragmatism and Dewey's Influence in China." *Metaphilosophy* 35:44–64.

Tan, Sor-hoon. 2004b. *Confucian Democracy: A Deweyan Reconstruction*. Albany: State University of New York Press.

Tan, Sor-hoon. 2008. "Reconstructing 'Culture': A Deweyan Response to Antidemocratic Culturalism." In *Democracy as Culture*, edited by Sor-hoon Tan and John Whalen-Bridge, 31–49. Albany: State University of New York Press.

Teets, Jessica, Reza Hasmath, and Orion Lewis. 2017. "The Incentive to Innovate? Behavior of Local Policymakers in China." *Journal of Chinese Political Science* 22:505–517.

Tiles, James E. 1997. "Democracy as Culture." In *Justice and Democracy*, edited by Ron Bontekoe and Marietta Stepaniants, 119–131. Honolulu: University of Hawaii Press.

Tu, Wei-ming. 2000. "Multiple Modernities: A Preliminary Inquiry into the Implications of East Asian Modernity." In *Culture Matters: How Values Shape Human Progress*, edited by Samuel P. Huntington and Lawrence E. Harrison, 256–267. New York: Basic Books.

Westbrook, Robert. 1992. *John Dewey and American Democracy*. Ithaca: Cornell University Press.

Wilkinson, Michael A. 2012. "Dewey's 'Democracy without Politics': On the Failures of Liberalism and the Frustrations of Experimentalism." *Contemporary Pragmatism* 9(2):117–142.

Wu, Hongcheng 吴洪成, and Chen Li 李晨. 2016. "Dewey's Populist Education Thought and Its Influence on China 杜威的平民主义教育思想及其对中国的影响." *Journal of Guangzhou University (Social Science Edition)* 15(4).

Xu, Ben 1999. *Disenchanted Democracy: Chinese Cultural Criticism after 1989*. Ann Arbor: University of Michigan Press.

Yan, Xiaojun, and Xin Ge. 2017. "Reforming Governance under Authoritarianism: Motivations and Pathways of Local Participatory Reform in the People's Republic of China." *Democratization* 24(3):405–424.

Yang, Shoukan, and Chengbing Wang. 2014. *Pragmatism's Chinese Travels (*实用主义的中国之旅*)*. Beijing: Chinese Academy of Social Sciences Press.

Zeng, Jinghan. 2015. "Did Policy Experimentation in China Always Seek Efficiency?" *Journal of Contemporary China* 24(92):338–356.

Zhang, Rulun 张汝伦. 2003. "Dewey's Fate in China (杜威在中国的命运)." *Reading (*读书*)* 7:126–132.

Zheng, Yongnian. 2004. *Will China Become Democratic? Elite Class and Regime Transition.* Singapore: Marshall Cavendish.

Zhou, Hongyu 周洪宇, and Zongping Xiang 向宗平. 2001. "The Spread of Dewey's Educational Thought in China and Its Influence 杜威教育思想在中国的传播及其影响." *Journal of Hebei Normal University (Education Sciences)* 3:59–65.

X

THE AMERICAN PHILOSOPHICAL TRADITION, THE SOCIAL SCIENCES, AND RELIGION

CHAPTER 29

....

JOHN DEWEY'S DEBT TO
WILLIAM JAMES

....

JAMES CAMPBELL

THE NOTION OF DEBT

....

DEBT is the natural condition of every human.[1] All of us have benefitted and suffered from the contributions of others, most of whom will remain ever unknown to us. In a cumulative discipline like philosophy, we all have debts to those who have gone before us. Philosophers especially bear these debts because of the complexity of their concerns and their rich inheritance from earlier thinkers who have addressed these concerns. The work of philosophy as the pursuit of wisdom would be a much sadder endeavor if it had to begin anew with each individual inquirer. At times, the complexity of this debt is brushed aside, as when Alfred North Whitehead suggests that "[t]he safest general characterization of the European philosophical tradition is that it consists of a series of footnotes to Plato" (1929/1969, 53). It is far better to consider our philosophical debts as multiple, so that we can recognize the diversity of the many interacting philosophical streams and recognize philosophy as a pluralistic inquiry.

As we consider the thought of John Dewey, we recognize that there are many non-Jamesian—not necessarily anti-Jamesian—influences on him, from his studies of Plato, Hegel, and Thomas Hill Green, to his interactions with Charles Sanders Peirce, George Herbert Mead, James Hayden Tufts, and Jane Addams. Finally, of course, there is the inspiration that both James and Dewey drew from Ralph Waldo Emerson.[2] In this chapter, however, I focus only on Dewey's debt to James and make as explicit as possible how I see Dewey to have been shaped by James's thought.

Perhaps the best introduction to any consideration of Dewey's debt to James is through an examination of their interactions over a series of Decennial Publications of the University of Chicago.[3] Of special importance is volume 11 of the second series of these Publications, the 1903 *Studies in Logical Theory*, that Dewey and his fellow contributors dedicated to James "[f]or both inspiration and the forging of the tools with which the writers have worked."[4] Dewey writes directly to James in March of that year that "so far as I am concerned your Psychology is the spiritual progenitor" of the volume (1903d/2002, 215) and in December that "I wonder sometimes if you fully appreciate how much of all of this is in your two volumes of Psychology" (1903e/2002, 346). In early 1904, James published a brief essay titled "The Chicago School" in which he announces that "Chicago has a School of Thought!—a school of thought which, it is safe to predict, will figure in literature as the School of Chicago for twenty-five years to come."

Unlike some universities that "have plenty of thought to show, but no school," and other universities that have "plenty of school, but no thought," in these Publications the philosophy department at Chicago "shows real thought and a real school." In particular, James praises Dewey and "his disciples" for having "collectively put into the world a statement, homogeneous in spite of so many cooperating minds, of a view of the world, both theoretical and practical, which is so simple, massive, and positive that, in spite of the fact that many parts of it yet need to be worked out, it deserves the title of a new system of philosophy" (1904a/1978, 102).[5]

In his 1925 essay, "The Development of American Pragmatism," Dewey returns to this time, and, writing in the third person, he notes that in the *Studies in Logical Theory* "the instrumentalists recognized how much they owed to William James for having forged the instruments which they used." He also indicates that "in the course of the studies, the authors constantly declared their belief in a close union of the 'normative' principles of logic and the real processes of thought, in so far as these are determined by an objective or biological psychology and not by an introspective psychology of states of consciousness." Dewey continues that "the 'instruments' to which allusion is made" appeared before James's *Pragmatism* and that "it is among some of the pages of his *Principles of Psychology* that one must look for them." He further emphasizes that *The Principles* developed "two distinct themes." The first of these he describes as "a re-interpretation of introspective psychology, in which James denies that sensations, images and ideas are discrete and in which he replaces them by a continuous stream which he calls 'the stream of consciousness.'" The second theme that James develops in *The Principles* is a more biological theme that "shows itself in its full force in the criterion which James established for discovering the existence of mind." Here Dewey quotes the following passage from *The Principles*: "'The pursuance of future ends and the choice of means for their attainment are thus the mark and criterion of the presence of mentality* in a phenomenon' [1890, 1:21]," and then notes that James "develops this idea in the chapter on reasoning where he says that 'the only meaning of essence is teleological, and that classification and conception are purely teleological weapons of [the] mind' [1890, 2:961]" (1925b, LW 2:15–16). Thus vital to the work of the Chicago pragmatists were James's central ideas that consciousness must be understood as a stream rather than atomistically and that the purpose of thinking is to help solve the problems of living.

While it is clear that Dewey followed a generally Jamesian trajectory in his work, it is perhaps a good idea to note initially a few places where he rejects James's position. One explicit instance is Dewey's bristling at James's connection in *Pragmatism* of his position on truth with personal satisfaction. There James writes: "Dewey says truth is what gives 'satisfaction.' He is treated as one who believes in calling everything true which, if it were true, would be pleasant" (1907/1975, 112). Dewey replies, in "What Pragmatism Means by Practical," to James's misstatement of his position that "I do not think I ever said that truth is what *gives* satisfaction" and that "I have never identified any satisfaction with the truth of an idea, save *that* satisfaction which arises when the idea as working hypothesis or tentative method is applied to prior existences in such a way as to fulfill what it intends" (1908a, MW 4:109). Another place of disagreement is Dewey's 1939 introduction to a reprint of James's *Talks to Teachers* that rejects James's belief that "school-keeping" requires that "much if not most of the work will of necessity be dull and at first repulsive" and that "[t]o get this repellant work done he [James] considered that the teacher must use 'external methods.'" Opposing this view, Dewey, the educator who most strongly emphasizes the integration of ends and means, writes that James "was wrong in thinking the school has to be essentially the kind that he had known, that study and learning have to be repellant" (1939, LW 14:339).[6] Behind both of these points is the general individual versus social stance that represents James's and Dewey's fundamental difference and that will reappear later in this chapter.

DEWEY'S EXPRESSED DEBT

We can consider initially a number of places where Dewey makes his debt to James explicit by indicating values in James's thought that he aspired to or tried to champion. In a memorial after James's death in 1910, for example, Dewey emphasizes that James was trained as a scientist and was "far and away the greatest of American psychologists." At the same time, Dewey notes that James's "sense of reality" was his "foremost trait." He continues that "the business of philosophy is to generalize and to systematize," and, as a result, too often philosophers find themselves "under a greater temptation than others to follow the bent of their own leading principles, to fill in missing considerations and to overlook contrary indications." For his part, however, James was "extraordinarily free from this defect" (Dewey 1910b, MW 6:98–99). Dewey also points to James's "power of literary expression" that "strikes both the layman and the professional philosopher, and strikes them at first glance." Dewey, himself often criticized for his lack of literary grace, writes that in James's work we find "[t]he picturesqueness of reference, the brilliant accuracy of characterization, by which he has enriched philosophic literature." We also find in James, Dewey continues, a vital appreciation "for the concrete, and for the varied aspects of the world." James was thus "not a philosopher who by taking pains acquired a literary gift; he was an artist who gave philosophic expression to the artist's sense of the unique, to his love of the individual" (Dewey 1910b, MW 6:100).

Further, James had a "religious belief in the possibilities of philosophy," in "the human significance of philosophy." Most professional philosophers, Dewey laments, write in an obscure style for a narrow professional audience. Under these circumstances, it is hardly possible to appreciate or carry forward James's "genuine faith in its simplicity." As these academicians advance within the discipline of philosophy, any chance to preserve plain speech too often "gets lost in the mazes of scholarship; wrapped in the napkin of specialization and buried in the ground of professionalism; or it dissipates along with the disillusionizing of early ardent hopes" (Dewey 1910b, MW 6:101–102). James was, however, "everywhere and always the moralist" (Dewey 1910a, MW 6:92), one who offered us an "honest acceptance of the facts of science joined to a hopeful outlook upon the future," and a "courageous faith in our ability to shape the unknown future" (Dewey 1910a, MW 6:96). Dewey also expresses the hope that "[w]hen our country comes to itself in consciousness, when it transmutes into articulate ideas what are still obscure and blind strivings," it will be realized that the two individuals who will "stand out as the prophetic forerunners of the attained creed of values" (1910a, MW 6:96–97) will be Emerson and James.

In a later essay, his 1930 autobiographical statement "From Absolutism to Experimentalism," Dewey points to four factors that operated on his own development: his direct involvement with the practice and theory of education, his ongoing reaction against the dualism of science and morals, his growing recognition of the importance of social categories like communication and participation, and "the influence of William James." It was this last factor that he identified as the "one specifiable philosophic factor which entered into my thinking so as to give it a new direction and quality" (Dewey 1930a, LW 5:157). Elsewhere, when he discusses the specific content of James's impact on him, Dewey again indicates that it was not the themes from *The Will to Believe*, *Pragmatism*, or *A Pluralistic Universe*, which are often thought to be James's greatest philosophic contributions. Rather, what Dewey emphasizes is the importance of *The Principles of Psychology* to advancing "the fundamental idea of an open universe in which uncertainty, choice, hypotheses, novelties and possibilities are naturalized." Further, Dewey notes that the more that we study James "in his historic setting the more original and daring will the idea appear" (1927b, LW 3:149). Dewey even writes on James's centenary in 1942 that "the *Principles of Psychology* is the greatest among the great works of James." Dewey offers this evaluation because he believes that in *The Principles* James has shown that "experience is intimately connected with nature instead of existing in a separate world" (1942, LW 15:11).

Returning to "From Absolutism to Experimentalism," we see that Dewey there takes note of what he sees as "two unreconcilable strains in the *Psychology*" (1930a, LW 5:157). James, of course, had admitted that *The Principles* was dualistic, in part a representation of the new physiological psychology that aspired to become a natural science and in part a continuation of a more traditional psychology whose "waters of metaphysical criticism leak" into the presumed science "at every joint" (1892/1984, 400; cf. 1890/1981 3:1183–1184; 1895/1978, 88). Dewey phrases this dualism in his own way. He points initially to James's "adoption of the subjective tenor of prior psychological tradition," such that even when past work was "radically criticized," the inherited vocabulary lived on. So, for example, even the tremendous advance of what James calls "the stream of thought" or "the stream of consciousness" over "discrete elementary states" still implied "a realm of consciousness set off by itself." In addition to this subjective strain in *The*

Principles, there is also an objective strain that had "its roots in a return to the earlier biological conception of the *psyche*, but a return possessed of a new force and value due to the immense progress made by biology since the time of Aristotle" (Dewey 1930a, LW 5:157).

Dewey indicates his doubt that "we have as yet begun to realize all that is due to William James for the introduction and use of this idea" of biology; and he is thus not greatly disappointed that even James had not "fully and consistently realized it himself." In any case, Dewey continues, this rethinking of biology "worked its way more and more into all my ideas and acted as a ferment to transform old beliefs." This rethinking is especially prominent, Dewey notes, in James's recognition of the living and experiential over the mechanical. As he writes, James "had a profound sense, in origin artistic and moral, perhaps, rather than 'scientific,' of the difference between the categories of the living and of the mechanical." While Dewey further notes that "[m]any philosophers have had much to say about the idea of organism," he emphasizes that in general "they have taken it structurally and hence statically." James, on the other hand, showed us how "to think of life in terms of life in action." It was even possible to "show how the most distinctive factors in his general philosophic view, pluralism, novelty, freedom, individuality, are all connected with his feeling for the qualities and traits of that which lives." Thus, Dewey concludes, when we fully recognize "the revolution introduced by James," we will be better able to work to eliminate the bad psychology that was embedded in philosophy and to reconstruct philosophy "to the significant issues of actual experience" (1930a, LW 5:157–158).

In a 1940 essay, "The Vanishing Subject in the Psychology of James," Dewey returns to *The Principles* and explores again the "two incompatible strains in the Jamesian psychology" (1940, LW 14:166). The first of these strains is James's "official acceptance of epistemological dualism," however tentative and hypothetical James intended this acceptance to be. "According to this view, the science of psychology centres about a *subject* which is 'mental' just as physics centres about an *object* which is material." The other strain in James's psychology is the decreasing presence of the subject in the course of *The Principles*. As Dewey writes, "James's analysis of special topics tends ... to reduction of the subject to a vanishing point, save as 'subject' is identified with the organism, the latter, moreover, having no existence save in interaction with environing conditions." This latter strain is thus not dualistic, and "subject and object do not stand for separate orders or kinds of existence but at most for certain distinctions made for a definite purpose *within* experience" (1940, LW 14:155). Dewey continues that in James's 1904 article "Does 'Consciousness' Exist?" he writes that the consciousness that was an essential part of this dualism in *The Principles* is better understood as " '[a] mere echo, the faint rumor left behind by the disappearing "soul" upon the air of philosophy' [James 1912, 3–4]." Dewey further notes "the tendency of the separate subject as knower to disappear even in the *Psychology*," and he quotes James's admission that " 'for twenty years past I have mistrusted "consciousness" as an entity; for seven or eight years past I have suggested its nonexistence to my students' [James 1912, 4]" (1940, LW 14:156). Dewey indicates that this twenty-year period would take James's mistrust of consciousness to a time before *The Principles* was published.

In spite of James's admission that dualism was mistaken, however, Dewey notes that James "never reworked his *Psychology* so that all phases and aspects of psychological phenomena were observed and reported from this point of view." And, rather than actively opposing the quest for psychology as a natural science, he shifted his focus to philosophy. Partly as a result of James's shift, psychological theory still remained in 1940 "the bulwark for all doctrines that assume independent and separate 'mind' and 'world' set over against each other" (Dewey 1940, LW 14:166–167). Dewey's point, of course, is that philosophy must finally do away with this dualism. In this task, he believes that James's alternate emphasis upon the organism in the environment points the way. He quotes, for example, such pragmatic passages from *The Principles* as: " 'My thinking is first and last and always for the sake of doing, and I can only do one thing at a time' [1890, 2:960]," and " 'There are no "truer ways of conceiving" [understanding or interpreting] things than any others; there are "only more important ways; more frequently serviceable ways" ' [1890, 2:962]" (Dewey 1940, LW 14:160). Still, Dewey continues, "[t]he influence of the dualism is so strong that James does not follow out the implication of his hypothesis that the brain—and nervous system generally—functions as an organ in the behavior constituted by interaction of organism and environment" (1940, LW 14:161).

On James's death in 1910, Dewey points to his importance in the public realm of ideas. James was "almost the only philosopher of the day whose death marks an event in the world of letters and of public affairs, as well as in the realm of university teaching and scholarship" (Dewey 1910a, MW 6:92). Over twenty-five years later, Dewey continues in his praise of James that "in respect to many-sidedness he is the most significant intellectual figure the United States has produced" (1937, LW 11:464). Rather than cultivating a professional career, James "constitutes a memorable turning point in the story of American philosophic thought precisely because the human man always took precedence of the professional philosopher" (Dewey 1937, LW 11:469). Dewey continues that he knows of no "other modern thinker whose philosophy owes so little to dialectics and to tradition, to the second hand generally, and so much to predicaments that were vitally experienced; and in the large and proper sense of the word were moral in quality" (1937, LW 11:473). Dewey notes further that, because of his practicalist orientation, James showed little interest in philosophy's usual rearward focus. In James, Dewey writes, "[t]here are no signs of concern with the spectacle of history." Dewey takes this orientation as a positive one, "an indication not of an insufficient but of an abundant sense of life, of life irrespective of chronology." James's world was thus "intensely contemporary," with an interest that was in what "*is* rather than *was*." In "his contemporaneousness," James's concerns were with "the problems and predicaments in which mankind finds itself implicated under all skies at all times" (Dewey 1937, LW 11:464).

At one point, Dewey even notes that "James's contribution" (1920b, MW 12:250) to philosophy was his powerful sense of meliorism, the belief that, in Dewey's words, "the specific conditions which exist at one moment, be they comparatively bad or comparatively good, in any event may be bettered" (1920a, MW 12:181–182), or as James himself puts it, "improvement is at least possible" (1907/1975, 61). Dewey writes that "James develops the concept of a dependable future which is active and flexible, and which can be freely created by those who live in it; his radical liberalism is a philosophy which invites each man to create his own future world" (1920b, MW 12:250). In this open future world, the common person can help create something better. Dewey further points to James's admission that "the greater part of philosophic problems and especially those which touch on religious fields are of such a nature that they are not susceptible of decisive evidence one way or the other." As a result, individuals have a democratic right in some situations to adopt "beliefs not only in the presence of proofs or conclusive facts, but also in the absence of all such proof" (Dewey 1925b, LW 2:10). Dewey writes that "if democracy be a serious, important choice and predilection it must in time justify itself by generating its own child of wisdom, to be justified in turn by its children, better institutions of life." Further, he notes that "[i]t is not so much a question as to whether there will be a philosophy of this kind as it is of just who will be the philosophers associated with it"; and at the head of this list Dewey wants to place James "through whom this vision of a new mode of life has already spoken with beauty and power" (1919, MW 11:53).

DEWEY'S UNEXPRESSED DEBT

There are also a number of places where Dewey builds upon James's ideas without acknowledging that he is doing so. Perhaps his borrowing in these cases was without his recognition; more likely Dewey thought that what he was doing would be so obvious to his audience that any mention of his debt to James was unnecessary. Here we consider just six such instances.

We can begin with a consideration of Dewey's unspoken debt to James through an examination of their accounts of the reflex arc in psychology. James's account of the reflex arc in *The Principles* is a straightforward discussion of the stages of the physiological process by means of which, for example, a child becomes interested in, burned by, and then wary of a candle flame. As he presents this process, the stimulus of the candle flame "arouses the grasping reflex" on the part of the child as well as the eventual idea of "the consequent pain." Having once been burned, the child learns to act "in *anticipation* of future things," and, as a consequence of this learning, "[t]he grasping will be arrested in mid-career, the hand drawn back, and the child's fingers saved" (1890/1981, 1:37–38). Dewey begins his article "The Reflex Arc in Psychology" by referencing James's "familiar" account in *The Principles*, but he quickly suggests that explanations like James's remain dualistic in their separation of stimulus and response. For Dewey, we should not begin "with a sensory stimulus" like a candle flame "but with a sensori-motor co-ordination, the optical-ocular," such that "in a certain sense it is the movement which is primary, and the sensation which is secondary." For him, "the real beginning is with the act of seeing; it is looking, and not a sensation of light" (1896, EW 5:97). Dewey continues that "the reflex arc idea, as commonly employed, is defective in that it assumes sensory stimulus and motor response as distinct psychical existences, while in reality they are always inside a co-ordination and have their significance purely from the part played in maintaining or reconstituting the co-ordination" (1896, EW 5:99). Beginning as early as 1903, however, Dewey focuses on James's emphasis on continuity rather than his discussion of stages. As Dewey writes in the Jamesian volume *Studies in Logical Theory*: "The significance of the evolutionary method in biology and social history is that every distinct organ, structure, or formation, every grouping of cells or elements, is to be treated as an instrument of adjustment or adaptation to a particular environing situation" (1903b, MW 2:310). Sounding very much like James in 1930, Dewey writes that "[b]ehavior is serial, not mere succession." While for heuristic purposes—as James had done in his discussion of the reflex arc—action is often separated "into discrete acts," Dewey emphasizes that "no action can be understood apart from the series to which it belongs" (1930b, LW 5:221).

Another place where Dewey builds upon James's ideas is in his discussion of habit in *Human Nature and Conduct* (1922, MW 14:15–62) that fails to mention James's discussion of habit in *The Principles* (1890/1981, 1:109–131) or in *Talks to Teachers* (1899/1983, 47–54).[7] With regard to this large topic of habit, we can consider here only one important theme: the connection between habit and morality. James characteristically emphasized individual aspects. He writes, for example, that while people tend to speak "of good habits and of bad habits," their emphasis "in the majority of instances" is on the latter. "They talk of the smoking-habit and the swearing-habit and the drinking-habit," he writes, "but not of the abstention-habit or the moderation-habit or the courage-habit." For his part, however, James wants to emphasize that "our virtues are habits as much as our vices." The individual's life, to the extent that it has what he calls "definite form," is simply "a mass of habits—practical, emotional, and intellectual" that are "systematically organized for our weal or woe, and bearing us irresistibly towards our destiny, whatever the latter may be" (1899/1983, 47).

Dewey's emphasis is different. His interest in bad habits is less in personal failings than in customs that are "out of date" or "unintelligent." As he writes in *Ethics*, "[w]hen social life is in a state of flux, moral issues cease to gather exclusively about personal conformity and deviation." In times of social conflict, moral issue center around "the value of social arrangements, of laws, of inherited traditions that have crystalized into institutions, in changes that are desirable. Institutions lose their quasi-sacredness and are the objects of moral questioning" (1932, LW 7:314–315). In *Human Nature and Conduct*, he writes that "in a changing world, old habits must perforce need modification, no matter how good they have been." These traditions tend to persist, however, "because individuals form their personal habits under conditions set by prior customs." We are habitual beings whose imagination of what might be is constrained by what is familiar. Moreover, too often our educational procedures function as "the art of taking advantage of the helplessness of the young" so that "the forming of habits becomes a guarantee for the maintenance of hedges of custom." Still, Dewey is hopeful for the future. As he sees the situation, "because of present mobility and interminglings of customs," individuals are "now offered an enormous range of custom-patterns, and can exercise personal in-genuity in selecting and rearranging their elements." Thus, if we can "intelligently adapt customs to conditions, and thereby remake them," we can create a better future. In doing so, we will not be choosing "between a moral authority outside custom and one within it." Our choice is rather "between adopting more or less intelligent and significant cus-toms" (Dewey 1922, MW 14:41, 43, 47, 54, 58). This choice remains difficult, he writes in *The Public and Its Problems*, because our habitual ways "generate ease, skill and in-terest in things to which we have grown used" and preclude any desire to test them, and also because habits "instigate fear to walk in different ways" (1927a, LW 2:335). James, of course, had made just this point when he writes of the onset of "[o]ld-fogyism" (1890/ 1981, 2:754), and of the end of curiosity when the "mental grooves and channels" become set and "the power of assimilation" is diminished (1890/1981, 2:1021).

Dewey also makes use of James's ideas when he discusses what he calls the "problem of good" as opposed to the "problem of evil." The former goes unrecognized, he notes, while the latter "is a well-recognized problem." We take goods "for granted; they are as they should be; they are natural and proper." As a result, he continues, "it is difficult for the goods of existence to furnish as convincing evidence of the uncertain character of nature as do evils. It is the latter we term accidents, not the former, even when their adventitious character is as certain" (1925a, LW 1:45–46; cf. 1931, LW 6:19). Although Dewey does not acknowledge it, James had earlier written in a similar fashion about our attempts "to overcome the 'problem of evil,' the 'mystery of pain,'" while at the same time failing to recognize any "'problem of good'" (1897/1979, 70). James continues in this vein that while "[t]he existence of evil forms a 'mystery'—a 'problem' ... there is no 'problem of happiness'" (1879/1978, 34).

A fourth use of James's insights can be found in Dewey's "test of the value of any phi-losophy which is offered us" that he elaborates in the following pair of questions. Does a philosophy "end in conclusions which, when they are referred back to ordinary life-experiences and their predicaments, render them more significant, more luminous to us, and make our dealings with them more fruitful?" Or does that philosophy "termi-nate in rendering the things of ordinary experience more opaque than they were before, and in depriving them of having in 'reality' even the significance they had previously seemed to have?" While philosophies of the former sort integrate our values and our experiences, philosophies of the latter sort lead their adherents "to measure the sub-limity of their 'realities' as philosophically defined by remoteness from the concerns of daily life," and cause what he calls "cultivated common sense to look askance of philos-ophy" (1925a, LW 1:18). We can compare this test with what James had written earlier—in a more general way but in the same mood—that "[o]n pragmatic principles we can not reject any hypothesis if consequences useful to life flow from it" (1907/1975, 131). Thus for James both universal conceptions and particular sensations have meaning and reality only if they play a useful role in the context of life's larger meanings, and the choice of a life path, whether a marriage or a career or a spiritual stance, can be justified in the absence of any present proof by evidence of its potential success. While Dewey was in general leery of James's will to believe, his recognition of the role of faith in his own social and political commitments must have shown him how close he came at times to James's position that belief can create its own verification (see 1897/1979, 80).

Another place where James's ideas form the background of Dewey's position would be Dewey's presentation of the social nature of the self. James explores this topic primarily in the chapter "The Consciousness of Self" in *The Principles*. While this theme is not central to James's overall thought, it was part of the general psychological milieu that he was surveying in 1890. He writes that "*a man has as many social selves as there are individuals who recognize him* and carry an image of him in their mind." As an example of this multiplicity, he considers the case of a boy whose saintly persona, familiar to his parents and teachers, is replaced by another that "swears and swaggers like a pirate among his 'tough' young friends." James continues more broadly that "[w]e do not show ourselves to our children as to our club-companions, to our customers as to the laborers we employ, to our own masters and employers as to our intimate friends" (1890/1981, 1:281–282). In addition, through our interactions in community, we try on the lives and personalities of others and learn more of the fullness of what it is to be human. As we move through life and respond to new situations, we also find ourselves modifying our ideas and choosing new reference groups. He writes that "when, as a protestant, I turn catholic; as a catholic, freethinker; as a 'regular practitioner,' homeopath, or what not, I am always inwardly strengthened in my course and steeled against the loss of my actual social self by the thought of other and better *possible* social judges than those whose verdict goes against me now" (1890/1981, 1:300).

Without discussing James explicitly, Dewey offers a largely parallel account of the social nature of the self that appears in a number of his volumes.[8] In *Reconstruction in Philosophy*, he writes that a series of fundamental questions of a social and moral nature "become the starting-points of inquiries about every institution of the community when it is recognized that individuality is not originally given but is created under the influences of associated life" (1920a, MW 12:193). In *Human Nature and Conduct*, he notes that, as enculturated beings, "[i]t is of grace not of ourselves that we lead civilized lives" (1922, MW 14:19). A few years later, in *The Public and Its Problems*, Dewey writes that "[e]verything which is distinctively human is learned, not native, even though it could not be learned without native structures which mark man off from other animals." He continues in this vein with the remarkable claim that we *learn* to be human. We are not just acquiring particular skills that fill out our original potentials, like learning to speak this language rather than that, or to play the violin rather than the piano. For Dewey there is more: "To learn to be human is to develop through the give-and-take of communication an effective sense of being an individually distinctive member of a community; one who understands and appreciates its beliefs, desires and methods, and who contributes to a further conversion of organic powers into human resources and values" (1927a, LW 2:331–332). It is in this sense of becoming a unique self that "all distinctively human action has to be learned" (Dewey 1927a, LW 2:335). In *Ethics*, Dewey discusses another aspect of the social self: our interdependence. "No one is born except in dependence on others," he writes. "Without aid and nurture from others, he would miserably perish" (1932, LW 7:227). Dewey continues in this vein at times further than James ever went. For example, he writes that "[a]part from the ties which bind him to others, he is nothing" (1932, LW 7:323).

Finally, we can consider their shared experiential understanding of religion. In both James's volume *The Varieties of Religious Experience* and Dewey's *A Common Faith*, we find an approach that avoids the doctrinal and dogmatic, bypasses liturgies and ceremonies, and short-circuits theological traditions. The focus of both of their inquiries into the meaning and importance of religion is upon experience. They differ, of course, on the focus of this experience as individual or communal. For James, religious experience involves a "living sense of commerce with a God" (1904b/1920, 211). While he made no claims to having had such "commerce," he still believed that personal religion was "the primordial thing." Religious organizations, he writes, "live at second-hand upon tradition"; but their founders claimed a "direct personal communion with the divine" (1902/1985, 33). For James, it is this personal communion with the divine that makes religion an eternal part of human life. For Dewey, the religious aspect of experience is communal, concerned not with any of the sorts of commerce with a God that tend to manifest themselves in bouts of crushing guilt or infusions of redemptive grace. Rather, his interest is with expanding our attempts to advance ideals of cooperation and community. He writes that "religions now prevent, because of their weight of historic encumbrances, the religious quality of experience from coming to consciousness and finding the expression that is appropriate to present conditions, intellectual and moral" (1934, LW 9:8). To attain these values, Dewey continues, it is necessary that "their identification with the creeds and cults of religions must be dissolved" (1934, LW 9:20) and that the values inherent in communal striving be recognized. For Dewey, attitudes are religious when they "lend deep and enduring support to the processes of living" (1934, LW 9:12).

The Complexity of Debt

There are, of course, many other Jamesian themes in Dewey that might be considered; but I hope that what I have mentioned will spur further discussion. In closing, I briefly note a parallel theme. In this consideration of Dewey's debt to James, I have only hinted at Dewey's debt to Peirce—a debt that, while not as deep as his debt to James, is still worthy of our serious consideration. It is a familiar idea that Dewey drew strongly from both Peirce and James, combining their insights, and others', in his new situations. H. S. Thayer, for example, writes that in Dewey "we witness the coalescence of the critical and scientific motives of Peirce's pragmatism with the moral implications and ideals of James." Of course, as Thayer continues, those two perspectives are not just combined in Dewey's work. They are, he notes, "intensified through a long lifetime devoted to exploration and analysis of their respective consequences in a variety of philosophic contexts, and to their continuous expansion under inquiry responsive to new currents of thought" (Thayer 1981, 165). In a similar fashion, Darnell Rucker writes: "The pragmatism that John Dewey and his colleagues and their students collaborated on there [at the University of Chicago] had its roots in James and Peirce, but what emerged from their efforts was distinctly their own and reflected more truly the soil from which it sprang than did either James's or Peirce's thought." Their situation was the emerging problematic urban world of the twentieth century. Rucker emphasizes that Dewey and his colleagues "shared James's practical orientation, in contrast to Peirce's emphasis on theory," while at the same time accepting "Peirce's broad view of the method of science and its application, as opposed to James's fear that science, too narrowly interpreted, was a threat to human values." Given the importance of action to Dewey and the others, Rucker continues, "they proceeded to derive an entire philosophy from the analysis of action" that became "a pragmatism different from both Peirce's logic-centered thought and James's psychology-based work" (1969, vi).

Philosophers, like all humans, live in debt to those who have gone before. Dewey, the focus of this essay, was no exception. As I have tried to show, he owed a special debt to James. Since our debts, philosophical and otherwise, are complex, however, no presentation of a Jamesian Dewey will encompass his thought completely. Still, no consideration of Dewey's thought can be adequate if it overlooks his debt to James.

NOTES

1. Justus Buchler writes: "Man is born in a state of natural debt, being antecedently committed to the execution or the furtherance of acts that will largely determine his individual existence. He moves into a contingent mold by which he is qualitied and located, and related to endless things beyond his awareness. From first to last he discharges obligations. He is obligated to sustain or alter, master or tolerate, what he becomes and what he encounters" (1955, 3).
2. See especially James (1903/1982) and Dewey (1903c).
3. The University of Chicago was founded in 1892, and it celebrated its first decade with a series of Decennial Publications.
4. This dedication appears at the end of the preface to *Studies*. In full it reads: "For both inspiration and the forging of the tools with which the writers have worked there is a preeminent obligation on the part of all of us to William James, of Harvard University, who, we hope, will accept this acknowledgment and this book as unworthy tokens of a regard and an admiration that are coequal" (Dewey 1903a, MW 2:296–297; James, 1904, 217).
5. The *Studies* contain four essays by Dewey as well as further essays by Helen Bradford Thompson, Simon Frasier McLennan, Myron Lucius Ashley, Willard Clark Gore, William Arthur Heidel, Henry Waldgrave Stuart, and Addison Webster Moore.
6. This essay lists William Heard Kilpatrick as co-author (Dewey 1939, LW 14:337n); but, even if the final text was by Heard, the sentiments were clearly Dewey's as well.
7. Dewey does explicitly consider James and habit in the 1932 *Ethics* that he wrote with James Hayden Tufts, where he quotes a bit from *The Principles* (1932, LW 7:205–207). Dewey's discussion of habit in the 1908 edition of *Ethics*, also written with Tufts, does not mention James (1908b, MW 5:309–311).
8. Tufts explicitly discusses James's position on the social self in his portion of both editions of the *Ethics* (Dewey, 1908b, MW 5:85–86; Dewey, 1932, LW 7:77–79).

Works Cited

Citations of John Dewey's works are to the thirty-seven-volume critical edition published by Southern Illinois University Press under the editorship of Jo Ann Boydston. In-text citations give the original publication date and series abbreviation, followed by volume number and page number. For example: (1934, LW 10:12) is page 12 of *Art as Experience*, which is published as volume 10 of *The Later Works*.

Series abbreviations for *The Collected Works*:

EW *The Early Works* (1882–1898)

MW *The Middle Works* (1899–1924)

LW *The Later Works* (1925–1953).

Buchler, Justus. 1955. *Nature and Judgment*. New York: Columbia University Press.

Dewey, John. 1896. "The Reflex Arc Concept in Psychology." EW 5:96–109.

Dewey, John. 1903a. "Preface." *Studies in Logical Theory*. MW 2:295–297.

Dewey, John. 1903b. "The Relationship of Thought and Its Subject-Matter." MW 2:298–315.

Dewey, John. 1903c. "Emerson—the Philosopher of Democracy." MW 3:184–192.

Dewey, John. 1903d/2002. Letter to William James, 20 March 1903. In *Correspondence of William James*. 12 vols. Edited by Ignas K. Skrupskelis and Elizabeth M. Berkeley, 10:214–216. Charlottesville: University Press of Virginia.

Dewey, John. 1903e/2002. Letter to William James, 19 December 1903. *Correspondence of William James*. 12 vols. Edited by Ignas K. Skrupskelis and Elizabeth M. Berkeley, 10:346–348. Charlottesville: University Press of Virginia.

Dewey, John. 1908a. "What Pragmatism Means by Practical." MW 4:98–115.

Dewey, John. 1908b. *Ethics*, with James Hayden Tufts. MW 5.

Dewey, John. 1910a. "William James." MW 6:91–97.

Dewey, John. 1910b. "William James." MW 6:98–102.

Dewey, John. 1919. "Philosophy and Democracy." MW 11:41–53.

Dewey, John. 1920a. *Reconstruction in Philosophy*. MW 12:77–201.

Dewey, John. 1920b. "Three Contemporary Philosophers." MW 12:205–250.

Dewey, John. 1922. *Human Nature and Conduct: An Introduction to Social Psychology*. MW 14.

Dewey, John. 1925a. *Experience and Nature*. LW 1.

Dewey, John. 1925b. "The Development of American Pragmatism." LW 2:3–21.

Dewey, John. 1927a. *The Public and Its Problems*. LW 2:235–372.

Dewey, John. 1927b. "The Pragmatic Acquiescence." LW 3:145–151.

Dewey, John. 1930a. "From Absolutism to Experimentalism." LW 5:147–160.

Dewey, John. 1930b. "Conduct and Experience." LW 5:218–235.

Dewey, John. 1931. "Context and Thought." LW 6:3–21.

Dewey, John. 1932. *Ethics*, with James Hayden Tufts. LW 7.

Dewey, John. 1934. *A Common Faith*. LW 9:3–58.

Dewey, John. 1937. "The Philosophy of William James." LW 11:464–478.

Dewey, John. 1939. Introduction. In *James's Talks to Teachers*. LW 14:337–340.

Dewey, John. 1940. "The Vanishing Self in the Psychology of William James." LW 14:154–167.

Dewey, John. 1942. "William James as Empiricist." LW 15:9–17.

James, William. 1879/1978. "The Sentiment of Rationality." In *Essays in Philosophy*, 32–64. Cambridge, MA: Harvard University Press.

James, William. 1890/1981. *The Principles of Psychology*. 3 vols. Cambridge, MA: Harvard University Press.

James, William. 1892/1984. *Psychology: Briefer Course*. Cambridge, MA: Harvard University Press.

James, William. 1895/1978. "The Knowing of Things Together." In *Essays in Philosophy*, 71–89. Cambridge, MA: Harvard University Press.

James, William. 1897/1979. *The Will to Believe, and Other Essays in Popular Philosophy*. Cambridge, MA: Harvard University Press.

James, William. 1899/1983. *Talks to Teachers on to Psychology, and to Students on Some of Life's Ideals*. Cambridge, MA: Harvard University Press.

James, William. 1902/1985. *The Varieties of Religious Experience: A Study in Human Nature*. Cambridge, MA: Harvard University Press.

James, William. 1903/1982. "Emerson." In *Essays in Religion and Morality*, 109–115. Cambridge, MA: Harvard University Press.

James, William. 1904a/1978. "The Chicago School." In *Essays in Philosophy*, 102–106, 217–218. Cambridge, MA: Harvard University Press.

James, William. 1904b/1920. Letter to James Henry Leuba, 17 April 1904. In *The Letters of William James*. 2 vols. Edited by Henry James, 2:211–212. Boston: Atlantic Monthly Press.

James, William. 1907/1975. *Pragmatism: A New Name for Some Old Ways of Thinking*. Cambridge, MA: Harvard University Press.

James, William. 1912/1976. *Essays in Radical Empiricism*. Cambridge, MA: Harvard University Press.

Rucker, Darnell. 1969. *The Chicago Pragmatists*. Minneapolis: University of Minnesota Press.

Thayer, H. S. 1968. *Meaning and Action: A Critical History of Pragmatism* (2nd ed. 1981). Indianapolis: Hackett.

Whitehead, Alfred North. 1929/1969. *Process and Reality: An Essay in Cosmology*. New York: Free Press.

CHAPTER 30

MEAD, DEWEY, AND THEIR INFLUENCE IN THE SOCIAL SCIENCES

DANIEL R. HUEBNER

JOHN Dewey's influence in the social sciences is inextricable from his relationship with George Mead, both in the sense that Dewey's ideas relevant to the social sciences have been developed in substantial collaboration with Mead and in the sense that Dewey has been interpreted by later social scientists primarily through Mead's work and the work of Mead's students. Thus, this chapter seeks to accomplish two interrelated tasks: to trace novel aspects of the relationship between Mead and Dewey, especially as it is relevant to the social sciences, and to identify major aspects of Dewey's reception in and engagement with the social sciences in relation to the reception of Mead in those disciplines.

This endeavor draws substantially from a renewed body of literature in the sociology of knowledge that takes as its focus the "knowledge-making practices" of scholars and that draws theoretically from the philosophy of American pragmatism in this endeavor (Camic et al. 2011; Huebner 2014). This perspective emphasizes the actual practices of knowledge production, both in terms of the collaborative social projects in which they are embedded and motivated and in terms of modes of working on real problems of investigation instead of the speculative movement of ideas. In particular, this means taking seriously the role of collaborators and teacher–student relationships in understanding the work of scholars, recognizing the ways in which professional lives are not fully separable from personal lives, and placing the development of scholars' work in the context of actual attempts to make knowledge over time in such endeavors as laboratory experiments, acts of writing, travels and inspections, and the like. However, it also suggests that the connections between people are not simply direct lines of conveyance for information but must be understood as dynamic and selective relationships in response to changing situational contexts. The specificity of this approach offers the possibility of empirical investigations whose findings may go beyond obvious claims about the dependence of ideas on sociohistorical context. In the case of Dewey, this means taking seriously the role of George Mead—and the role of the Mead family in relation to the Deweys—in Dewey's work as it changed over time, as they worked together in laboratories, taught and learned from students, advocated on one another's behalf, and reflected on one another's ideas. It means also tracing identifiable connections by which particular people claim to take certain ideas from Dewey and the situations in which such claims are made.

One route for assessing the relation between Dewey and Mead (or any other published scholars) is, of course, to collate the references to one another in their respective published works. This is problematic for a number of reasons, most notably because citations are not a clear reflection of intellectual influence and because conventions about citing others' work change over time. While published references are part of the story, the attempt to reconstruct social relationships must also rely on a variety of historical documents and in this sense must be more a research endeavor than a literature review. In the text that follows, I attempt to indicate some of the underutilized archival documents by which such research could be carried further. One of the key untapped resources, along with personal correspondence, is the body of extant student notes and papers from Mead's and Dewey's classes. As Dewey himself once noted, "It would be a serious reproach to me if my associates [i.e., students at Columbia University] had not attained a juster understanding of what I had said in my written work than is likely to exist in the case of those who have only the latter to consult" (1939, LW 14:4).

The following sections are organized so that they trace chronological aspects of the relationship between Dewey and Mead and indicate some of the ways in which their encounters in each of these periods influenced the social sciences of the time and later. The chapter then examines some of Dewey's more independent influences on the social sciences and the recent renaissance of pragmatist orientations in the social sciences. Throughout, the chapter points out some of the major unanswered questions and unexplored sources of documentation on these topics in the hopes of suggesting productive avenues for further research.

UNIVERSITY OF MICHIGAN, 1891–1894

The basic outlines of Dewey's early relationship with Mead are well known, having been recounted in a number of major biographical and historical works on Dewey or Mead (Dykhuizen 1973; Coughlan 1975; Aboulafia 1991; Rosenthal and Bourgeois 1991; Cook 1993; Westbrook 1993; Martin 2003). The discussion that follows focuses on reassessing the work of their period together at the University of Michigan by highlighting efforts by Dewey and Mead that have been overlooked in previous accounts and by seeking evidence from their correspondence and publications of the work they thought of as most important. In 1891, Dewey needed someone to teach the courses normally taught by his junior University of Michigan colleague, James H. Tufts, who had decided to pursue advanced study in Germany. William James may have drawn George Mead to Dewey's attention, although Tufts may also have directly suggested Mead when they briefly overlapped in Germany. At that time, Mead was studying philosophy and psychology at the University of Berlin and treated James as something of a mentor and advisor (Huebner 2014, 43). Mead was hired for a position teaching courses in physiological psychology, including developing laboratory experiments, and the history of philosophy, while another former Harvard student, Alfred H. Lloyd, was hired for a position focusing on logic and psychology.

From 1891 to 1894, Dewey, Mead, and Lloyd began to develop innovative new lines in a number of aspects of philosophy. The most important outcomes of this work as far as Mead was concerned were Dewey's foundational works in functional psychology, the "The Theory of Emotions" series of articles and "The Reflex Arc Concept in Psychology" (1894–95, EW 4:152–188; 1896, EW 5:96–109), to both of which Mead referred extensively in subsequent published and unpublished writings. These works sought to explain mental phenomena such as sensation and attention as phases within the normal behavioral processes of biological organisms and drew upon the work of William James (cf. Campbell, this volume).

During this period Mead was much more thoroughly engaged in the development of psychological experiments than has previously been acknowledged (Huebner 2014, ch. 2). The nascent development of functional psychology was, in Dewey's view, finally giving direction to the design of experiments and an explanatory framework for their results, instead of haphazard experimenting without purpose. Mead worked with Dewey and Lloyd to develop psychophysiological experiments that were not merely unprincipled tests but could target issues of how perception, mental imagery, attention, and sensation were related to organic conduct. This fact is most easily traced in Dewey's correspondence with James R. Angell for this period (especially 1892.04.25 [00466]: John Dewey to J. R. Angell; 1893.05.10 [00478]: John Dewey to J. R. Angell). Mead also made histological and anatomical studies of neural tissue, studied the behavior of microscopic organisms, dissected animal specimens, observed problem-solving behavior among live animals, wrote a criticism of psychophysical measurements, and studied and spoke about hypnotic suggestion as a possible medical practice. Evidence from correspondence suggests that Dewey was heavily involved in the theory and design of these efforts as a practical component of the functional psychology he was developing.

These ideas came together in a seminar Mead gave in 1893–1894 titled "Special Topics in Psychology," documentation of which is preserved in the notes of student R. Clair Campbell (Campbell Family Papers: box 2, folder 2). This course included critical discussions of the reflex arc, the physiological theory of emotion, the social interrelation of action projects, the functional nature of mental images, the coconstitution of organism and environment, and the differences between human and other animal consciousness—all before those ideas were put into print by either Mead or Dewey. Mead apparently used William James's *Principles of Psychology* and George Trumbull Ladd's *Elements of Physiological Psychology* as his texts. He also discussed a number of specific physiological and behavioral observations that are not otherwise recorded in the work of Dewey and Mead on the macro- and microscopic structure of the nervous system and sense organs, the relation of first-order and second-order sensations, brain localization of mental functions, and the comparative evolution of the organs of sense and motility.

When Mead's laboratory work is brought into the picture of the University of Michigan philosophy department in the early 1890s, it is possible to begin reconstructing the development of functional psychology on a more practical basis. Dewey and his junior colleagues did not invent their approach by some revelation or unfolding of ideas alone. Their claims were developed in relation to their own actual experimental tests made primarily by Mead with input from Dewey. Later commentaries on this early functional psychology (as well as Mead's later philosophical developments) often miss the extent to which these ideas can be understood to be grounded in experimental studies of biological processes. In this regard, Dewey later gave much credit in correspondence to Mead's work at the University of Michigan for "biologizing" his approach (1945.05.21,22 [15449]: John Dewey to A. F. Bentley; 1945.09.14 [13694]: John Dewey to E. O. Sisson; 1946.07.09 [07139]: John Dewey to Joseph Ratner).

Dewey and Mead also began to connect around issues of the social and political sciences. For example, in 1892 Dewey and Mead worked together with Alfred H. Lloyd and Fred Newton Scott on a project that failed to materialize but nevertheless seems to have had an influence on their thinking: a proposed edited volume of contributions to the psychology of Ancient Greek philosophy from a social standpoint. Dewey wrote to James Angell that he sought to "interpret the history of thought more from the anthropological and political standpoint—as a social phenomenon" and that this idea had particular urgency for him because he was engaged in "an attempt to interpret Plato less as a philosopher at large and more as an expression of and reflection back upon Athenian social life" (1893.05.10 [00478]: John Dewey to J. R. Angell). Mead's contribution was to have been a reinterpretation of Pythagoras and the development of the "idea of space" out of the practical distinction between "space and place" (quoted in Huebner 2016, 57). What Lloyd's or Scott's contributions were to have been, I have been unable to discover. Mead had been hired to teach not only in physiological psychology but also the history of philosophy, and Dewey was likewise conversant with the discipline's history. But what makes this project novel in studies of the history of philosophy is its focus on interpreting the history of thought as a "social phenomenon," as Dewey termed it.

Grounding the history of thought in historical social processes is an underexplored aspect of the work of Dewey and Mead, but we find such an emphasis very early on in their work—long before Dewey and Mead came to the attention of social scientists. Mead developed a thoroughly social approach to explaining the history of thought in a number of talks, manuscripts, and classes throughout his career, and his thoughts on Ancient Greek philosophy are the earliest evidence of these efforts (Huebner 2016). Indeed, later in his career, Dewey acknowledged Mead to have an unsurpassed insight into the history of thought (1932a, LW 6:308; 1916.02.29 [03234]: John Dewey to H. M. Kallen; 1917.05.10 [03260]: John Dewey to M. C. Otto), as evidenced in works such as his "Scientific Method and Individual Thinker" (Mead 1917) for the collaborative pragmatist volume *Creative Intelligence*. Although it is difficult to work out the details of this failed project on Ancient Greek thought (much in the same way other potentially related failed projects of this period, including "Thought News," are difficult to reconstruct; see Coughlan 1975, 93–108; Dykhuizen 1973, 71–72; Feffer 1993, 82–86; Rockefeller 1991, 172–198; Westbrook 1993, 51–58), it is clear that the contributors sought to consider how the social sciences might reframe philosophical insights. Of course, Dewey was already teaching classes in political philosophy in this period (including to foundational sociologist Charles H. Cooley, whose notes from Dewey's course are extant [Charles Horton Cooley Papers:box 4]), and much has been made of how Dewey's writings on ethics shifted away in the early 1890s from Hegelian idealism toward practical social action. These efforts may well have influenced Mead's own shift toward social philosophy.

Although it would only become apparent later, the most direct influences that Dewey had on individual social scientists during this period at the University of Michigan were upon Charles Cooley, who taught at the University of Michigan his entire subsequent career and became an important early American sociologist, and Robert E. Park, who was a newspaper writer in Michigan at the time but later became a collaborator of Booker T. Washington at Tuskegee Institute and the central figure of the "Chicago School" of sociology after World War I (a topic discussed further later). For his part, Cooley's view of Dewey's influence in his work changed over time: in his diary from the period he wrote that he was "much influenced also by Dewey's lectures on Political Philosophy heard in the fall of [18]93," but in a 1928 autobiographical statement he acknowledged only the "lasting mark" of Dewey's "personality" rather than his "lectures," and he claimed that he "had already arrived at a somewhat similar view" to Dewey by the time of taking his class (quoted in Ross 1992, 241). Cooley was an influential early author and teacher in sociology, and some of his prominent students, including Read Bain and Robert C. Angell, engaged with Dewey's work in their own scholarship. The relationship of Mead and Cooley is perhaps even more contentious. Mead referred substantially to Cooley in many of his courses (as documented in extant students' notes),[1] but he also wrote a critical evaluation of Cooley's work after he died that has been cited as an important source of Cooley's relative decline in importance in the sociological canon (Jacobs 2009). Cooley seems never to have substantially discussed Mead's ideas in a major publication or credited him with an important influence.

In any case, some later commentators have indicated that the key innovation made by pragmatism as developed by Dewey and Mead to sociological thought is precisely a double grounding of human action in both biological and social processes. Hans Joas (1985, 1996) has argued that the core of Mead's philosophy is "practical intersubjectivity": practical in the sense that action is the function of the corporeal biological organism in relation to situations encountered in the course of living and intersubjective in the sense that this practical action is fundamentally social from its very genesis and is oriented toward living with other humans. Both of these features first appear in fragmentary but compelling form in the relatively short period at the University of Michigan in the work of both Dewey and Mead and precisely in projects that they engaged in together. In a letter to Arthur F. Bentley, Dewey recalled that he owed much to Mead in "getting me over to a biological-sociological approach" and in one to E. O. Sisson that

Mead was "a student of biology and also of social relations," indicating that Dewey was aware both of the intrinsic connection between biology and sociology in his philosophical approach and of the importance of his relationship with Mead in developing that insight (1945.05.21,22 [15449]: John Dewey to A. F. Bentley; 1945.09.14 [13694]: John Dewey to E. O. Sisson).

Interpersonally, the Dewey family and the Mead family socialized regularly, and their relationship with one another seems also to have pushed their thinking on child psychology and international politics. The families both had children during their short period in Michigan together: Morris Dewey, the Deweys' third child born in 1893, and Henry C. A. Mead, the Meads' first and only child born in 1892. Their correspondence from this period indicates that the families helped one another raise their children and that Alice Chipman Dewey's modern parenting style influenced the Meads. They frequently looked after one another's children and spent substantial time together. Indeed, some of their correspondence seems to indicate that they were interested in the interpretation of infant language and behavior, a topic documented professionally by Dewey's publication of "The Psychology of Infant Language" (1894, EW 4:66–69) and by the later work of Dewey and Mead on early education and the development of language and self in children. Additionally, George Mead's wife, Helen Kingsbury (née Castle) Mead, was the child of one of the wealthiest families from the Hawaiian Islands that made their fortune on sugarcane plantations and merchandise shipping. Indeed, Alice Dewey and Helen Mead traveled together to Hawaii in the spring of 1892 when Helen was pregnant; and Helen's brother, George Mead's best friend from his days at Oberlin College, Henry Northrup Castle, came to stay with the Meads for a period in 1893 and participated in courses and private discussions of the Deweys and Meads (1892.06.01 [00079]: H. C. Coleman to A. C. Dewey; 1893.06.10 [14129]: H. N. Castle to S. N. and M. T. Castle; 1894.03.26 [00097]: H. C. Coleman to John and A. C. Dewey). The Hawaiian Revolution in which the American settlers to the islands led a revolt that overthrew the native monarchy in favor of republican government and annexation to the United States occurred while the Meads and Deweys were together at the University of Michigan, and the close ties of the Meads-Castles to the situation must have influenced their discussions. Dewey's later involvement in progressive education in Hawaii was largely the result of his relationship with the Meads, a topic further discussed later.

UNIVERSITY OF CHICAGO, 1894–1904

Much has been written also about the development of the relationship between Mead and Dewey at the University of Chicago after they moved there (Dewey, 1939; Rucker, 1969; Cook, 1993; Feffer, 1993; Martin, 2003). In the spring of 1894 Dewey was engaged in negotiations with the president of that new institution, William Rainey Harper, and his correspondence reveals that he worked seriously to secure a place for Mead, whom he thought of as an important collaborator and original philosopher (1894.03.26

[11895]: John Dewey to J. H. Tufts; 1894.03.27 [00502]: John Dewey to W. R. Harper; 1894.04.10 [00503]: John Dewey to W. R. Harper). Dewey took up the chairmanship of the philosophy department at the University of Chicago. The philosophy department also taught the psychology courses and developed courses in education and pedagogy over the next decade. Mead arrived as an assistant professor in the same department with the understanding that he would shift away from experimental physiological psychology into comparative psychology and general philosophy. Throughout the subsequent decade together in Chicago, the Meads and Deweys became even closer interpersonally. They stayed with one another on occasion, they corresponded frequently when out of town, they held joint get-togethers, they cared for one another's children and parents, they attended events and performances together, and they clearly talked frequently about a whole host of topics.

At the University of Chicago from 1894 onward, many of the ideas first introduced at the University of Michigan were further developed in terms of functional psychology, social and behavioral psychology, education and pedagogy, and social reform. Functional psychology and its relation to philosophical logic and epistemology came to fruition in a series of major publications, which drew the attention of William James (1904), who dubbed Dewey and his students the "Chicago School" of philosophy. Their central work, in James's view, was the *Studies in Logical Theory* (1903, MW 2:295–375), which Dewey edited as a collaborative volume with essays from students who had taken his advanced seminar in logic. Most notably included were James R. Angell and Addison W. Moore, who would become long-term contributors to functional psychology and pragmatist philosophy at the University of Chicago, and most notably absent were George Mead and Alfred H. Lloyd, who of course were not among Dewey's new students but worked with him previously to develop this functional perspective. Mead's most important contribution to this literature came in the form of his "The Definition of the Psychical" (Mead 1903), which Dewey acknowledged as an influence on his thinking about how to overcome the need for a separate "psychical" or mental substance in thinking about human behavior and how to restate judgment as a practical act but which he nevertheless acknowledged was difficult to understand because of Mead's writing style (1903.03.11 [00798]: William James to John Dewey; 1903.08.25 [01831]: John Dewey to H. H. Bawden; 1945.09.14 [13694]: John Dewey to E. O. Sisson). Dewey also acknowledged Mead's influence on his thinking about the nature of emotional attitudes (1894–95, EW 4:152–188), and Mead in turn acknowledged the influence of Dewey's publications on emotions for his own work in that domain (Mead 1895) and of Dewey's critique of the "reflex arc" concept for his work to reformulate the nature of the "psychical" (Mead 1903) and the relation of philosophical disciplines to one another (Mead 1900) in terms of the act. Throughout this period and later, Dewey took on the role of defending and supporting Mead against critics in private and in relation to promotion at the university.

After Mead turned over the experimental psychology laboratory to James Angell and with the neurobiological aspects of psychology primarily the concern by H. H. Donaldson, Jacques Loeb, and others at the new university, Mead developed the first courses in "comparative psychology" at any major American college (Huebner 2014, 56). Mead's major topic in these courses was animal intelligence: if animals are acknowledged to respond functionally to their environments and consequently to have different ways of being "intelligent" than humans, the topic of psychology is dramatically reframed away from human subjective consciousness toward the adaptive or functional conduct of organisms. The clearest published articulation of this work is in Mead's (1907) "Concerning Animal Perception," in which Mead again credits Dewey's critique of the reflex arc concept for providing the analysis by which animal perception may be redefined objectively as a process of mediation within action.

Mead observed behavioral experiments on animals conducted by John B. Watson and others in the comparative psychology laboratory at the University of Chicago, and his comparative psychology courses were taken by Watson, sociologists W. I. Thomas and Charles A. Ellwood, economist Wesley Clair Mitchell, and others (Huebner 2014, 56). The orientation Mead developed in his comparative psychology courses was key to providing the path to Mead's objective and social understanding of mind and self through the observable behavior of organisms in the context of simultaneously practical and social-cooperative problems of adaptation.

According to Dewey, Thomas was particularly impressed by the approach that Mead took in his comparative psychology courses and viewed it as a new method that could be applied to sociology and anthropology. Dewey considered Thomas a "valuable ally" and the "first outpost" of the philosophy that he and Mead had introduced to Chicago (1894.12.12,14,15 [00246]: John Dewey to A. C. Dewey). Thomas would later recall that Mead had been a significant influence on his thought (along with Cooley) but that he had probably influenced Dewey as much as Dewey influenced him, through Thomas's work in ethnology and the interpretation of cultures (Baker 1973, 245). Dewey's own important early contribution to this literature was his "Interpretation of Savage Mind," in which he notes that he was "indebted to Dr. Thomas (through personal communication as well as from his articles) for not only specific suggestions, but for the point of view here presented to such an extent that this article is virtually a joint contribution" (1902, MW 2:43). Thomas reprinted Dewey's article in his influential *Source Book for Social Origins* (Thomas 1909). This article and Dewey's "Psychology and Social Practice" (1900, MW 1:131–150) also caught the attention of Albion W. Small (1900, 1901, 1902), the inaugural chairman of the sociology department at the University of Chicago, who referred repeatedly to these works by Dewey in this period as providing a perspective that may make it possible to synthesize the sociological and psychological sciences.

The direct contact of Dewey and Mead with the social sciences undoubtedly expanded during this period, perhaps especially with sociology, economics, and political science. In economics, Thorstein Veblen is often seen as an important faculty interlocutor and Wesley Clair Mitchell an influential early student, and in political science, Charles E. Merriam is often seen as a faculty interlocutor and Arthur F. Bentley as an early student (and later collaborator). Other institutional economists, including Clarence E. Ayres and John R. Commons, evince clear influences from Dewey's writings. Commons (1934, 150–156) was particularly clear in arguing that the theory of institutions developed by this school of economists drew heavily from the "social prag-matism" of Dewey. Here, the key insight appears to be Dewey's notion of custom and habit, providing a way of conceptualizing how the conventions of economic transactions change. Institutional economics fell out of favor in the United States for many years, and its "new institutionalist" rebirth has apparently not drawn as heavily on the older Deweyan conceptualization of institutions as have new institutionalist authors in soci-ology.[2] Merriam's (and Mead's) later group of political science students, perhaps espe-cially Harold Lasswell, may also be mentioned in this connection as evincing Dewey's influence. In these cases, the influence of Dewey is difficult to disentangle from that of Mead and of others in the social sciences of the University of Chicago, but it is clear that the "institutional" approach to economics and the "behavioral" approach to political science pioneered at the University of Chicago have a family resemblance with Deweyan pragmatism.[3]

Although this period of Mead's work does not feature much in discussions of his mature philosophy, it is key to the development of his analysis of the functions of speech and manual manipulation (both forms of "gesture" in Mead's adaptation of Wilhelm Wundt's terms) in the formation of human reflective intelligence. Extending this claim even further, the work of Mead in comparative psychology is completely absent from the literature on Dewey, despite the fact that the ideas Mead developed first in this context also appear in some of Dewey's later works. For example—at the hazard of prematurely indicating some of Dewey's developments after leaving the University of Chicago—Dewey developed an analysis of language symbols in "Knowledge and Speech Reaction" (1922a, MW 13) and in chapter 5 of *Experience and Nature* (1925, LW 1:132–160) that he later acknowledged was strongly indebted to Mead (quoted in Morris, 1932, 322n1). In this later period Mead adopted "behaviorism," the coinage of his former student John Watson, to describe his own (and Dewey's) perspective on the study of the nature of language and consciousness (Mead 1922), with the caveat that their work was more satisfactory than Watson's because it examined the broader social processes in which behavior was formed and did not seek to exclude subjective phenomena in the manner that Watson did. Dewey, in turn, also identified his own collection of earlier essays as having been written from "the standpoint of what is now termed a behavioristic psychology" (1916, MW 10:319), but only shortly thereafter he criticized the behaviorists (with the "marked exception" of Mead) for dangerously "oversimplifying" and ignoring the "obvious facts" of subjective experience (1922a, MW 13:7). While Dewey's philosophical developments at the University of Chicago arguably centered on logic and ethics, Mead broadened the perspective into comparative psychology and into the social nature of the mind (a topic also discussed in subsequent sections).

In addition to the work on psychology, Dewey and Mead also both made contributions to pedagogy and education. Other contributions to the present handbook discuss these in further detail, so I only highlight one additional aspect of Dewey's educational work. As already mentioned, Helen Mead's family became very interested in the progressive education work being done under Dewey's leadership in Chicago. The Castles provided funds to help set up and furnish the University Elementary School in the late 1890s, they arranged to have both Francis W. Parker and Dewey come to Hawaii for summer teacher training programs and educational revivals during that period, they recruited teachers trained under Dewey to come to Hawaii to teach, and some of the Castles (notably Harriet Castle Coleman and Mabel Wing Castle) came personally to Chicago to study with Dewey (Castle 1989, 2004, 2012; Huebner 2014, ch. 3). The influence of Dewey and Mead on the educational system of Hawaii has been well documented in the literature on the history of education in that state (Castle 1989; Potter and Logan 1995; McEwan 2015), but it has had little impact on the study of Dewey (*pace* Martin 2003) despite the specificity it might give to discussions of Dewey's early progressive education efforts, as well as Dewey's later world travels and his views on Americanization, imperialism, and democracy.

The other major projects in which Mead and Dewey worked together were issues of social reform, and again other contributions to the present handbook address these topics. It is worth pointing out, however, that Jane Addams and a few of the other major social reformers of the era have been increasingly reclaimed as foundational authors in American sociology (e.g., Deegan 1990, 2013; Lengermann and Niebrugge-Brantley 1998) and that the relationships of Dewey and Mead to Addams centered intellectually on shared interests in the reconstruction of social responsibilities and the democratization of social and economic institutions (Dewey 1939; Seigfried 1996).

Mead's major works along these lines at the turn of the twentieth century are his "The Working Hypothesis in Social Reform" (Mead 1899) and a bit later "The Philosophical Basis of Ethics" (Mead 1908), and Dewey's are undoubtedly his influential *Ethics* (coauthored with James H. Tufts and published in 1908 but no doubt begun informally before 1904 [Dewey and Tufts 1908, MW 5]) and perhaps his essays on ethics and morality including "The Logical Conditions of a Scientific Treatment of Morality" (1903b, MW 3:3–39), which Mead (1908, 315) thought provided the underlying logic that makes it possible to locate the "moral interpretation of our experience" within "experience itself." Dewey and Tufts's *Ethics* was used as the standard textbook for the ethics courses at the University of Chicago long after Dewey left, including those by Mead, and Mead clearly drew from this work in his own publications and lectures. Much has also been made of the importance of practical social reform activities on the development of the work for which Mead is primarily known, his theory of the social nature and genesis of the self and his work on democratic theory (Joas 1985; Shalin 1988; Cook 1993; Deegan 2008; Carreira da Silva 2010).

The Chicago School and Symbolic Interactionism

After John Dewey left Chicago in 1904, he and George Mead worked at two different institutions for the remainder of their lives, although they maintained frequent contact and they continued to work along complementary philosophical lines. Dewey's departure also left behind all the other members of the Chicago School of philosophy—the core faculty consisted of Mead, James H. Tufts, Addison W. Moore, and Edward S. Ames—who continued to develop many of the lines of thought. Dewey's departure also precipitated the split between the philosophy and psychology departments, the latter initially headed by James Angell. Both Dewey and Mead developed arguably their most important and thoroughgoing insights into social phenomena after they were no longer colleagues, including, for example, Dewey's work on habit and institutions and Mead's work on the social nature of the self. I do not propose to review those accomplishments in detail here but rather to highlight a few of the most important professional issues that help to identify key moments in the reception of Dewey in the social sciences.

Mead wrote substantially about Dewey throughout his later career (Mead 1935, 1930, 1929a, 1929b, 1926), and discussions of Dewey were a constant refrain in Mead's social psychology and other courses at the University of Chicago, including references to Dewey's early work in psychology, logic, and ethics, and his later *How We Think* (1910, MW 6) and *Democracy and Education* (1915, MW 9). But Mead was evidently disappointed by Dewey's own "Introduction to Social Psychology," *Human Nature and Conduct* (1922b, MW 14). He wrote, but did not publish, a critical review (later published by Cook 1994), in which he criticized Dewey for relying on outdated theories of imitation, failing to conceptualize the development of the self as taking-the-role-of-the-other, and largely rehashing ideas from *How We Think*—in effect, for ignoring Mead's own advances in social psychology and the advances of the field more generally since they had parted company. On Dewey's part, the article "Knowledge and Speech Reaction" (1922a, MW 13) is the only major exception to this neglect of Mead's later social psychological writings published prior to Mead's death. In contrast to his reaction to *Human Nature and Conduct*, Mead apparently considered the publication of Dewey's *Experience and Nature* (1925, LW 1), which connected this social psychology with issues of the constitution of nature itself, to be a major intellectual event. He put together a special advanced seminar for the winter 1926 quarter wholly concerned with the discussion of the book and its relation to Dewey's other work and to contemporary relativistic theories of nature. Documentation from this course still exists in the form of notes archived in the George Herbert Mead Papers (box 9, folder 2) taken by student George Dykhuizen, who would later write a major biography of Dewey. Late in his career, Mead referred extensively to *Experience and Nature* in lectures and writings; most of these references appear in the posthumously published volumes compiled by Mead's former students and colleagues (Mead 2015, 79; 1938, 517; 1936, 334; 1932, 18) and in a few of his late essays (Mead 1926, 383; 1929b, 84; 1930, 229). It is probably not overestimating its importance to say that Mead viewed *Experience and Nature* as Dewey's most encompassing work to that date and one that gave a major new reference point in philosophy. Dewey later acknowledged privately the substantial influence of Mead on the development of the ideas in *Experience and Nature* (1931.06.16 [08009]: John Dewey to C. W. Morris; 1945.09.14 [13694]: John Dewey to E. O. Sisson).

It is worth highlighting Mead's teaching and writing about Dewey's social psychology, precisely because the latter's most important inroads into the social sciences came primarily through the mediation of Mead and his students at the University of Chicago. Indeed, Dewey's most obvious influence on the social sciences, or at least the body of literature with the most substantial explicit reference to him and his ideas, is the so-called Chicago School of sociology of the 1920s and 1930s, a topic examined in several major studies (Carey 1975; Lewis and Smith 1980; Bulmer 1986; Ross 1992; Abbott 1999; Gross 2007).

Typically the leader of this Chicago School is seen as Robert E. Park, an early student of Dewey's at Michigan when Park was a newspaper reporter. Park avowed that Dewey "inspired and encouraged" him in "an intellectual curiosity in regard to the world" (Baker 1973, 253). Dewey taught Park that "thought and knowledge were to be regarded as incidents of and instruments of action" (Baker 1973, 254), and throughout his subsequent career Park frequently referred to the key insight that society exists only in communication as one he took from Dewey's *Democracy and Education* (Park 1921, 14–15; 1938, 192–193; 1943, 728). This insight provided the basis for an interactional approach by which Park and others sought to overcome the problems of earlier collective psychologies and social-organismic metaphors in describing the dynamics of society. Park was also a long-time colleague of Mead at the University of Chicago, and he once indicated that Mead "has made a more penetrating analysis of the relations we describe as social than anyone else I happen to know" (Park 1942, 218). The work of Park and his students have been particularly influential in the study of race and ethnic relations, urban ecology, and collective behavior.

Still, Park was not the most important member of the Chicago School of sociology to influence Dewey's reception, an appellation that should instead go to the relatively forgotten Ellsworth Faris, a student of Mead's after Dewey left Chicago, who ultimately replaced W. I. Thomas as a faculty member. A lapsed Christian missionary, Faris's work (collected in Faris 1937) developed a social psychological approach critical of explanations of human behavior that relied upon fixed psychological "elements" (such as instincts, faculties, or reflexes), because they were treated in such explanations as if they were merely activated in behavior rather than themselves being formed in the course of human social actions. At least part of his motivation appears to have been to counter the implicit racism and ethnocentricity often found in attempts to apply such psychological accounts to other cultures. In crafting this social psychology, he was the most influential and earliest author to argue that Dewey, Mead, William James, W. I. Thomas, Charles H. Cooley, Robert E. Park, and a few others constituted a coherent alternative school of thought to existing psychological accounts of human behavior (Huebner 2014, 187–189). This grouping consists primarily of those authors about whom Mead taught in his social psychology courses (Dewey, James, Cooley) alongside Mead's and Faris's colleagues (Thomas, Park). It is largely the institutional and rhetorical success of these efforts that yoked Dewey and Mead together as supposed predecessors to what came to be called "symbolic interactionism" in the work of Faris's most famous student, Herbert Blumer (1969) and from there into the general sociological literature (Huebner 2014, ch. 7).

This is despite the fact that there is no evidence suggesting these supposed predecessors saw themselves as constituting such a coherent school. These selected authors were not without substantive disagreements, and from different perspectives other groupings of authors (such as Charles S. Peirce, James, Dewey, and Mead) would seem at least as coherent.

For symbolic interactionists, the key insights that these predecessors gave to sociological theory were a social account of the development of personality and identity, including the concepts that could be developed into an attendant theory of social roles, reference groups, and socialization and an apparent emphasis on the formation of meanings and symbols through social interaction, providing the seeds of a novel approach to communication, knowledge, and agency. With such a consistent emphasis on social interaction and the social self, this perspective has not been without critics who charge that it ignores broader social dynamics and structures or that its authors tend to read their supposed predecessors' works primarily through a restrictive lens, potentially missing other connections or insights. Symbolic interactionism was originally conceived as an alternative to mainstream sociology but no longer maintains this outsider status. In this literature, Mead is almost always the key foundational author and Dewey is often read in relation to Mead (e.g., Blumer 1969, 1). An added irony is that the aspects of Mead's work most often discussed come primarily from volumes published after his death compiled by Mead's former students and colleagues, especially *Mind, Self, and Society* (Mead 2015), in which Dewey was at least marginally involved and, more importantly, for the interpretation of which Dewey published key reference points.

Dewey's renewed attention to and discussion of Mead in the late 1920s and early 1930s came in the context of the decline of the Chicago School of philosophy and Mead's subsequent death. The University of Chicago hired the young Robert M. Hutchins as president in 1929, and he immediately began to remake the university divisions. The so-called Hutchins Controversy (Cook 1993) saw him attempt to appoint his acquaintances to philosophy positions over the objections of long-time faculty, who perceived in his actions a serious disdain for their accomplishments and professional status. James H. Tufts resigned as chairman in 1929 leaving Mead as acting chair, and the following year Mead and several junior faculty members likewise resigned in protest. Dewey responded to this by negotiating an invitation for Mead to take up a position at Columbia University in the 1931–1932 school year, and he began corresponding with Chicago philosophers T. V. Smith, Charles Morris, and Edward S. Ames in an effort to honor Tufts and Mead with some *festschrift* or other memorial. An unintended consequence of Hutchins's efforts to disassemble the pragmatist orientation of the University of Chicago philosophy department was to help push many like-minded scholars into the reformulated social science departments and university college, where Dewey, Mead, and other pragmatists were prominent fixtures of the curriculum throughout the middle of the twentieth century (Huebner 2014, 314–315).

Mead fell fatally ill in early 1931 and died in April of that year. Dewey was present at Mead's funeral and gave a eulogy that was published as "George Herbert Mead as I Knew

Him" (1931, LW 6:22–28). Dewey was kept informed as definite plans for posthumous publications were made, and he subsequently wrote "Prefatory Remarks" for Mead's Carus lectures (1932a, LW 6:307–310), an "Introduction" to the essay of Mead's student Theodore T. Lafferty that primarily discussed Mead, not Lafferty (1932b, LW 6:311–312), and a review in the *New Republic* of two other posthumously published works compiled under Mead's name by his students and colleagues (1936, LW 11:450–453), all within the first few years after Mead's death. These pieces together constitute Dewey's most sustained written engagement with Mead's ideas and influence, and they include substantial insights into the intimate personal and scholarly relationship of these two men. Dewey's accounts of the manner in which Mead developed his philosophy have had a significant impact on the biographical literature on Mead.

Throughout the remainder of his professional life, Dewey became an important interpreter and apologist for Mead and a mentor to younger scholars who sought to work in the tradition of American pragmatism. In his published correspondence may be found substantial discussions of Mead with a wide variety of philosophers, pedagogues, social scientists, novelists, and professionals, including Arthur F. Bentley, Justus Buchler, Lyle Eddy, James T. Farrell, John D. Graves, W. G. Houston, Grace de Laguna, C. Wright Mills, Charles Morris, Joseph Ratner, John H. Randall, Edward O. Sisson, and Paul D. Wienpahl. In these exchanges, Dewey repeatedly sought to insist upon Mead's influence on the development of his own thought and to excuse many problems of interpretation as stemming not from bad ideas but from somewhat antiquated or stilted language.

DEWEY'S INFLUENCE

The standard line in contemporary interactionist sociology about the relationship between Dewey and Mead is well expressed by Norbert Wiley (2016, 113), that "Dewey helped Mead institutionally, but Mead helped Dewey theoretically." And while it is certainly true that Mead is important to the understanding of Dewey's relation to the social sciences, there are a number of avenues of influence that are at least semi-independent from the interpretation of Mead and ideas for which Dewey, not Mead, is primarily credited. One starting point is to trace personal and institutional relationships, especially student–teacher relationships and schools of thought in which Dewey figures.

Perhaps the most obvious route for this influence is Dewey's presence for much of the early twentieth century at Columbia University. Here Dewey's influence is seen in the work of sociologist Robert S. Lynd, especially his *Knowledge for What* (Lynd 1940), which argues for a socially responsive form of social science and makes reference to insights from *How We Think* (1910, MW 6) and *Human Nature and Conduct* (1922b, MW 14). C. Wright Mills was, for a period, also a high-profile faculty member in sociology at Columbia who was influenced by Dewey's (and especially Mead's) pragmatism.

Mills wrote his dissertation on "A Sociological Account of Pragmatism" (posthumously published as Mills 1966) and corresponded with and cited Dewey in the development of his work in the "sociology of knowledge." Dewey was also cited in work by sociologists Robert K. Merton and Robert S. MacIver at Columbia, although it is not clear what influence, if any, he actually had on their thought. The specialist in sociology of education and the family, Willard W. Waller, was also influenced by Dewey and apparently taught some of Dewey's ideas in classes, but he was somewhat isolated from the regular Columbia sociologists as a faculty member at Barnard College. Overall, the Columbia sociology department was at least somewhat receptive to Dewey's ideas, and several of the major left-leaning social scientists who were graduate students there evince engagement with Dewey's social and political writings, including Daniel Bell, Nathan Glazer, Alvin Gouldner, Seymour M. Lipset, and Philip Selznick (although their engagement with Dewey comes at least as much from his essays in the magazine *Commentary*—which critically engaged with some of these authors [esp. 1947, LW 15:224–238; 1949, LW 16:369–382]—as from his philosophical monographs).

Also at Columbia University, Dewey had a long-term intellectual exchange with foundational anthropologist Franz Boas, and they even apparently co-taught a seminar on "comparative ethics" in 1914–1915. Torres Colón and Hobbs (2015) argue that Dewey's conceptualization of experience as simultaneously natural and cultural—found in his works including *Human Nature and Conduct* (1922b, MW 14), *Experience and Nature* (1925, LW 1), and the recently rediscovered and published *Unmodern Philosophy and Modern Philosophy* (Dewey 2012)—was influenced by Boas's (1911) notion of "culture," although in those works Dewey also contributes fundamental insights not found in Boas regarding the nature of communication in experience. They likewise trace evidence of Dewey's influence on other anthropologists who studied with or critically responded to Boas, including Ruth Benedict, Gene Weltfish, Alexander Lesser, and Leslie White.[4]

Other influential individual figures in sociology, such as methodological innovator George A. Lundberg and early Dewey student Charles A. Ellwood (Turner 2007), also evince a clear influence from Dewey's sociologically oriented work on psychology, logic, and epistemology. As with Jane Addams, W. E. B. Du Bois has increasingly been reclaimed as an important foundational sociologist (Morris 2015), and he likewise held an ongoing dialogue with Dewey. While a number of authors have compared and contrasted the views of Du Bois and Dewey (see Sullivan, this volume), I am unaware of any major study that claims to show one as a major influence over the other. Indeed, no sustained body of literature of which I am aware has taken the same care to trace Dewey's influence in the social sciences at Columbia or other institutions as has been done for Dewey's and Mead's influence at Chicago. And in cases such as those of Addams, Du Bois, and Boas where the relationships are not hierarchical, the task for scholars is even more challenging. Perhaps the body of literature that examines the mutual influence of Dewey and Mead can be a reference point for conceptualizing such relationships.

In the broader international literature in social theory, Dewey's influence has historically been only somewhat independent of Mead, although his incorporation in this literature has been fragmentary, and Mead and Dewey have increasingly come to be combined in discussions of American pragmatism. For example, foundational French sociologist Émile Durkheim gave critical lectures in 1913–1914 on *Pragmatism and Sociology* (Durkheim 1983) that refer specifically to Dewey's *Studies in Logical Theory* (1903, MW 2:295–375) and *How We Think* (1910, MW 6)—and not any work by Mead, but Durkheim was apparently unable to find in them a satisfactory sociological account of knowledge and truth (a problem that later authors would consider Durkheim's failure to read Dewey fairly and independently from William James rather than Dewey's own failing [Joas 1993; Deladalle 2002]). Dewey's influence on early French social sciences seems to go no further than this, and much the same can be said for other international audiences in the social sciences prior to the end of World War II (see Joas [1993] for discussion), although this is certainly a topic upon which further research may be warranted. In the later twentieth century, there was a resurgence of interest in pragmatism among German social theorists, notably in the work of Karl-Otto Apel and Jürgen Habermas on Peirce and Hans Joas and Axel Honneth on Mead. To a certain extent the subsequent European reception of pragmatism is in dialogue with later American philosophical interpretations of Dewey, especially the work of Richard Rorty. Among these scholars, Dewey is often seen as important for his work on the nature of the democratic public sphere and communication rather than his writings on logic, metaphysics, and other aspects of traditional philosophy.

More recently, there has been considerable discussion of a "revival of pragmatism," as the title of a volume edited by Morris Dickstein (1998) phrases it, and this revival has had a notable influence on the reception of Dewey and Mead in the social sciences. Indicators of this trend in recent years include new editions and translations of work by Mead and several international conferences on Dewey, Mead, and pragmatism in the social sciences.[5] This literature has also included attempts to indicate the relevance of classical American pragmatism to burgeoning contemporary fields including cognitive science, environmental studies, democratic and social epistemology, and pragmatist historiography (e.g., Joas and Huebner 2016).

Although a large number of publications have appeared in the social sciences recently that are explicitly oriented toward the pragmatism of Dewey and Mead, very little has been published attempting to examine and synthesize this trend more generally. Such work will certainly need to be undertaken not only to bring our understanding of the influence of these pragmatists on the social sciences up to date but also to reflect more substantially on whether there are coherent fundamental principles that have motivated the reception of Dewey and Mead, whether the nature of that reception has changed over time, and what other aspects of their work have not been (but could be) more substantially built upon in these disciplines. As a starting point for such work to systematically trace paths of influence and to use that work to rethink possible new approaches, the present chapter has sought to indicate the major distinctive ways in which twentieth-century social scientists have drawn explicitly upon the work of Dewey and Mead and to highlight some of the features of the practical relationship of Dewey and Mead that have not been sufficiently explored.

Acknowledgments

I wish to acknowledge the helpful comments I received on drafts of this chapter from Steven Fesmire and Hans Joas.

Notes

1. According to the most recent research, there are at least seventy-nine sets of student notes of varying length and quality still extant from Mead's courses (Huebner 2014, appendix 2), and the analysis in the present paper draws upon this corpus to make claims about the content of Mead's courses. These sets of notes have not figured in the literature on Dewey's relationship to Mead or to the social sciences in any significant way.
2. John Dewey's brother, Davis R. Dewey, was an economist and statistician at MIT whose descriptive and historical studies put him conceptually close to the institutional economists. I am unaware of any literature that seriously traces the connection of economics to John Dewey through his brother's work.
3. The history of the humanities and social sciences is riddled with "Chicago Schools" of philosophy, sociology, economics, political science, and others—all of which have problematic internal and external boundaries (see, for example, discussion in Abbott, 1999). In economics, in particular, the ideas of the earlier pragmatically-inclined institutional economics are rather antithetical to those of the more well known post–World War II Chicago School of neoclassical economists led by Milton Friedman and others.
4. Some archival resources have recently become available to study the influence of Mead and Dewey on American anthropologists at the University of Chicago: the Milton Singer Papers, 1925–1999, and the Clifford Geertz Papers, 1930s–2007. Singer wrote his 1936 master's thesis on "George Herbert Mead's Social-Behavioristic Theory of Mind," and Geertz wrote a 1950 undergraduate comprehensive exam paper on "G. H. Mead: Social Positivist"; both were taught substantially about Dewey and American pragmatism as students: Singer from David M. Miller at the University of Texas and Charles Morris at the University of Chicago and Geertz from George R. Geiger at Antioch College.
5. New editions of Mead's *Mind, Self, and Society*, in particular, have appeared in both English and French in recent years and the publication of Dewey's (2012) lost *Unmodern Philosophy and Modern Philosophy* might also be mentioned. Examples of conferences include a 2009 conference in Opole, Poland, resulting in *The Continuing Relevance of John Dewey* (Hickman et al. 2011), a 2011 conference in Opole resulting in *George Herbert Mead in the Twenty-first Century* (Burke and Skowronski 2013), a 2013 conference in Chicago resulting in *The Timeliness of George Herbert Mead* (Joas and Huebner 2016), a 2013 conference in Cagliari, Italy, resulting in *La filosofia sociale di George H. Mead* (Nieddu 2016), and an August 2015 conference at the University of Chicago on "Pragmatism and Sociology" and a 2017 follow-up at Radcliffe Institute.

Works Cited

Citations of John Dewey's works are to the thirty-seven-volume critical edition published by Southern Illinois University Press under the editorship of Jo Ann Boydston. In-text citations give the original publication date and series abbreviation, followed by volume number and page number. For example: (1934, LW 10:12) is page 12 of *Art as Experience*, which is published as volume 10 of *The Later Works*.

Series abbreviations for *The Collected Works*:

EW *The Early Works* (1882–98)

MW *The Middle Works* (1899–1924)

LW *The Later Works* (1925–53)

Citations of Dewey's correspondence are to *The Correspondence of John Dewey*, 1871–2007, published by the InteLex Corporation under the editorship of Larry Hickman. Citations give the date, reference number for the letter, and author followed by recipient. For example: 1973.02.13 (22053): Herbert W. Schneider to H. S. Thayer.

Abbott, Andrew. 1999. *Department and Discipline: Chicago Sociology at One Hundred.* Chicago: University of Chicago Press.

Aboulafia, Mitchell. 1991. *Philosophy, Social Theory, and the Thought of George Herbert Mead.* Albany: State University of New York Press.

Baker, Paul J. 1973. "The Life Histories of W. I. Thomas and Robert E. Park." *American Journal of Sociology*, vol. 79, no. 2, 243–260.

Blumer, Herbert. 1969. *Symbolic Interactionism: Perspective and Method.* Englewood Cliffs, NJ: Prentice-Hall.

Boas, Franz. 1911. *The Mind of Primitive Man.* New York: Macmillan.

Bulmer, Martin. 1986. *The Chicago School of Sociology: Institutionalization, Diversity, and the Rise of Sociological Research.* Chicago: University of Chicago Press.

Burke, F. Thomas, and Krzysztof Piotr Skowronski, eds. 2013. *George Herbert Mead in the Twenty-First Century.* Lanham, MD: Lexington Books.

Camic, Charles, Neil Gross, and Michèle Lamont. 2011. "Introduction: The Study of Social Knowledge Making." In *Social Knowledge in the Making.* Edited by Charles Camic, Neil Gross, and Michèle Lamont, 1–40. Chicago: University of Chicago Press.

Campbell Family Papers, 1860–1865, 1879–1949. Bentley Historical Library, University of Michigan–Ann Arbor.

Carey, James T. 1975. *Sociology and Public Affairs: The Chicago School.* Beverly Hills, CA: SAGE.

Carreira da Silva, Filipe. 2010. *Mead and Modernity: Science, Selfhood, and Democratic Politics.* Lanham, MD: Lexington Books.

Castle, Alfred L. 1989. "Harriet Castle and the Beginnings of Progressive Kindergarten Education in Hawai'i 1894-1900." *Hawaiian Journal of History*, vol. 23, 119–136.

Castle, Alfred L. 2004. *A Century of Philanthropy: A History of the Samuel N. and Mary Castle Foundation*, revised edition. Honolulu: Hawaiian History Society.

Castle, Alfred L. 2012. "Introduction." In *The Collected Letters of Henry Northrup Castle.* Edited by George Herbert Mead and Helen Castle Mead, ix–xxiv. Athens: Ohio University Press.

Charles Horton Cooley Papers, 1872–1930. Bentley Historical Library, University of Michigan–Ann Arbor.

Commons, John R. 1934. *Institutional Economics: Its Place in Political Economy*, Vol. I. New York: Macmillan.

Cook, Gary A. 1993. *George Herbert Mead: The Making of a Social Pragmatist.* Urbana: University of Illinois Press.

Cook, Gary A. 1994. "George Herbert Mead: An Unpublished Review of John Dewey's *Human Nature and Conduct.*" *Journal of the History of the Behavioral Sciences*, vol. 30, 374–379.

Coughlan, Neil. 1975. *Young John Dewey: An Essay in American Intellectual History.* Chicago: University of Chicago Press.

Deegan, Mary Jo. 2008. *Self, War, and Society: George Herbert Mead's Macrosociology.* New Brunswick, NJ: Transaction.

Deegan, Mary Jo. 1990. *Jane Addams and the Men of the Chicago School, 1892–1918.* New Brunswick, NJ: Transaction.

Deegan, Mary Jo. 2013. "Jane Addams, The Hull-House School of Sociology, and Social Justice, 1892–1935." *Humanity & Society*, vol. 37, no. 3, 248–258.

Deladalle, Gérard. 2002. "French Sociology and American Pragmatism: The Sociology of Durkheim and the Pragmatism of John Dewey." *Transactions of the Charles S. Peirce Society*, vol. 38, nos. 1–2, 7–11.

Dewey, Jane. 1939. "Biography of John Dewey" In *The Philosophy of John Dewey.* Edited by Paul Schilpp, 3–45. New York: Tudor.

Dewey, John. 1971a [1894]. "The Psychology of Infant Language." Vol. 4 of *The Early Works*, 1882–1898. Edited by Jo Ann Boydston. Carbondale: Southern Illinois University Press.

Dewey, John. 1971b [1894–1895]. "The Theory of Emotions." Vol. 4 of *The Early Works*, 1882–1898. Edited by Jo Ann Boydston. Carbondale: Southern Illinois University Press.

Dewey, John. 1972 [1896]. "The Reflex Arc Concept in Psychology." Vol. 5 of *The Early Works*, 1882–1898. Edited by Jo Ann Boydston. Carbondale: Southern Illinois University Press.

Dewey, John. 1976a [1902]. "Interpretation of Savage Mind." Vol. 2 of *The Middle Works*, 1899–1924. Edited by Jo Ann Boydston. Carbondale: Southern Illinois University Press.

Dewey, John. 1976b [1900]. "Psychology and Social Practice." Vol. 1 of *The Middle Works*, 1899–1924. Edited by Jo Ann Boydston. Carbondale: Southern Illinois University Press.

Dewey, John. 1976c [1903]. *Studies in Logical Theory.* Vol. 2 of *The Middle Works*, 1899–1924. Edited by Jo Ann Boydston. Carbondale: Southern Illinois University Press.

Dewey, John. 1977 [1903]. "The Logical Conditions of a Scientific Treatment of Morality." Vol. 3 of *The Middle Works*, 1899–1924. Edited by Jo Ann Boydston. Carbondale: Southern Illinois University Press.

Dewey, John. 1978 [1910]. *How We Think.* Vol. 6 of *The Middle Works*, 1899–1924. Edited by Jo Ann Boydston. Carbondale: Southern Illinois University Press.

Dewey, John. 1980a [1915]. *Democracy and Education.* Vol. 9 of *The Middle Works*, 1899–1924. Edited by Jo Ann Boydston. Carbondale: Southern Illinois University Press.

Dewey, John. 1980b [1916]. "Prefatory Note to *Essays in Experimental Logic*." Vol. 10 of *The Middle Works*, 1899–1924. Edited by Jo Ann Boydston. Carbondale: Southern Illinois University Press.

Dewey, John. 1981 [1925]. *Experience and Nature.* Vol. 1 of *The Later Works*, 1925–1953. Edited by Jo Ann Boydston. Carbondale: Southern Illinois University Press.

Dewey, John. 1983a [1922]. *Human Nature and Conduct.* Vol. 14 of *The Middle Works*, 1899–1924. Edited by Jo Ann Boydston. Carbondale: Southern Illinois University Press.

Dewey, John. 1983b [1922]. "Knowledge and Speech Reaction." Vol. 13 of *The Middle Works*, 1899–1924. Edited by Jo Ann Boydston. Carbondale: Southern Illinois University Press.

Dewey, John. 1985a [1931]. "George Herbert Mead as I Knew Him." Vol. 6 of *The Later Works*, 1925–1953. Edited by Jo Ann Boydston. Carbondale: Southern Illinois University Press.

Dewey, John. 1985b [1932]. "Introduction to *Studies in Philosophy*." Vol. 6 of *The Later Works*, 1925–1953. Edited by Jo Ann Boydston. Carbondale: Southern Illinois University Press.

Dewey, John. 1985c [1932]. "Prefatory Remarks in *The Philosophy of the Present*." Vol. 6 of *The Later Works*, 1925–1953. Edited by Jo Ann Boydston. Carbondale: Southern Illinois University Press.

Dewey, John. 1987 [1936]. "The Work of George Mead." Vol. 11 of *The Later Works, 1925–1953*. Edited by Jo Ann Boydston. Carbondale: Southern Illinois University Press.

Dewey, John. 1988 [1939]. "Experience, Knowledge and Value: A Rejoinder." Vol. 14 of *The Later Works, 1925–1953*. Edited by Jo Ann Boydston. Carbondale: Southern Illinois University Press.

Dewey, John. 1989a [1947]. "Liberating the Social Scientist: A Plea to Unshackle the Study of Man." Vol. 15 of *The Later Works, 1925–1953*. Edited by Jo Ann Boydston. Carbondale: Southern Illinois University Press.

Dewey, John. 1989b [1949]. "Philosophy's Future in Our Scientific Age: Never Was Its Role More Crucial." Vol. 16 of *The Later Works, 1925–1953*. Edited by Jo Ann Boydston. Carbondale: Southern Illinois University Press.

Dewey, John. 2012. *Unmodern Philosophy and Modern Philosophy*. Edited by Phillip Deen. Carbondale: Southern Illinois University Press.

Dewey, John, and James H. Tufts. 1978 [1908]. *Ethics*. Vol. 5 of *The Middle Works, 1899–1924*. Edited by Jo Ann Boydston. Carbondale: Southern Illinois University Press.

Dickstein, Morris, ed. 1998. *The Revival of Pragmatism: New Essays on Social Thought, Law, and Culture*. Durham, NC: Duke University Press.

Durkheim, Émile. 1983. *Pragmatism and Sociology*. Edited by J. B. Allcock. Translated by J. C. Whitehouse. Cambridge, UK: Cambridge University Press.

Dykhuizen, George. 1973. *The Life and Mind of John Dewey*. Carbondale: Southern Illinois University Press.

Faris, Ellsworth. 1937. *The Nature of Human Nature: And Other Essays in Social Psychology*. New York: McGraw-Hill.

Feffer, Andrew. 1993. *The Chicago Pragmatists and American Progressivism*. Ithaca, NY: Cornell University Press.

George Herbert Mead Papers, 1855–1968. Special Collections Research Center, Joseph P. Regenstein Library, University of Chicago.

Gross, Neil. 2007. "Pragmatism, Phenomenology, and Twentieth-Century American Sociology." In *Sociology in America: A History*. Edited by Craig Calhoun, 183–224. Chicago: University of Chicago Press.

Hickman, Larry A., Matthew C. Flamm, Krzysztof P. Skowronski, and Jennifer A. Rea, eds. 2011. *The Continuing Relevance of John Dewey: Reflections on Aesthetics, Morality, Science, and Society*. New York: Rodopi.

Huebner, Daniel R. 2014. *Becoming Mead: The Social Process of Academic Knowledge*. Chicago: University of Chicago Press.

Huebner, Daniel R. 2016. "On Mead's Long Lost History of Science." In *The Timeliness of George Herbert Mead*. Edited by Hans Joas and Daniel Huebner, 40–61. Chicago: University of Chicago Press.

Jacobs, Glenn. 2009. "Influence and Canonical Superiority: An Analysis of How George Herbert Mead Demoted Charles Horton Cooley in the Sociological Canon." *Journal of the History of the Behavioral Sciences*, vol. 45, no. 2, 117–144.

James, William. 1904. "The Chicago School." *Psychological Bulletin*, vol. 1, 1–5.

Joas, Hans. 1993. *Pragmatism and Social Theory*. Chicago: University of Chicago Press.

Joas, Hans. 1996. *The Creativity of Action*. Chicago: University of Chicago Press.

Joas, Hans. 1997 [1985]. *G. H. Mead: A Contemporary Re-Examination of His Thought*. 2nd re-vised edition. Translated by Raymond Meyer. Cambridge, MA: MIT Press.

Joas, Hans, and Daniel R. Huebner, eds. 2016. *The Timeliness of George Herbert Mead*. Chicago: University of Chicago Press.

Lengermann, Patricia, and Jill Niebrugge-Brantley. 1998. *The Women Founders: Sociology and Social Theory*. New York: McGraw Hill.

Lewis, J. David, and Richard L. Smith. 1980. *American Sociology and Pragmatism: Mead, Chicago Sociology, and Symbolic Interaction*. Chicago: University of Chicago Press.

Lynd, Robert S. 1940. *Knowledge for What? The Place of Social Science in American Culture*. Princeton, NJ: Princeton University Press.

Martin, Jay. 2003. *The Education of John Dewey*. New York: Columbia University Press.

Mead, George H. 1895. "A Theory of Emotions from the Physiological Standpoint." *Psychological Review*, vol. 2, 162–164.

Mead, George H. 1899. "The Working Hypothesis in Social Reform." *American Journal of Sociology*, vol. 5, 367–371.

Mead, George H. 1900. "Suggestions Towards a Theory of the Philosophical Disciplines." *Philosophical Review*, vol. 9, 1–17.

Mead, George H. 1903. "The Definition of the Psychical." *Decennial Publications of the University of Chicago*, 1st Series, vol. 3, 77–112.

Mead, George H. 1907. "Concerning Animal Perception." *Psychological Review*, vol. 14, 383–390.

Mead, George H. 1908. "The Philosophical Basis of Ethics." *International Journal of Ethics*, vol. 18, 311–323.

Mead, George H. 1917. "Scientific Method and Individual Thinker." In *Creative Intelligence: Essays in the Pragmatic Attitude*. Edited by John Dewey et al. New York: Henry Holt.

Mead, George H. 1922. "A Behavioristic Account of the Significant Symbol." *Journal of Philosophy*, vol. 19, 157–163.

Mead, George H. 1926. "The Nature of Aesthetic Experience." *International Journal of Ethics*, vol. 36, 382–392.

Mead, George H. 1929a. "The Nature of the Past." In *Essays in Honor of John Dewey*. Edited by John Coss, 235–242. New York: Henry Holt and Co.

Mead, George H. 1929b. "A Pragmatic Theory of Truth." *Studies in the Nature of Truth*. University of California Publications in Philosophy, vol. 11, 65–88.

Mead, George H. 1930. "The Philosophies of Royce, James, and Dewey in Their American Setting." *International Journal of Ethics*, vol. 40, 211–231.

Mead, George H. 1932. *The Philosophy of the Present*. Edited by Arthur E. Murphy. Chicago: Open Court.

Mead, George H. 1935. "The Philosophy of John Dewey." *International Journal of Ethics*, vol. 46, 64–81.

Mead, George H. 1936. *Movements of Thought in the Nineteenth Century*. Edited by Merritt H. Moore. Chicago: University of Chicago Press.

Mead, George H. 1938. *The Philosophy of the Act*. Edited by Charles W. Morris, John M. Brewster, Albert M. Dunham, and David L. Miller. Chicago: University of Chicago Press.

Mead, George H. 2015 [1934]. *Mind, Self, and Society: The Definitive Edition*. Originally edited by Charles W. Morris, annotated edition by Daniel R. Huebner and Hans Joas. Chicago: University of Chicago Press.

Mills, C. Wright. 1966. *Sociology and Pragmatism: The Higher Learning in America*. New York: Oxford University Press.

Morris, Aldon. 2015. *The Scholar Denied: W. E. B. Du Bois and the Birth of Modern Sociology*. Berkeley: University of California Press.

Morris, Charles. 1932. *Six Theories of Mind*. Chicago: University of Chicago Press.

McEwan, Hunter, ed. 2015. Special Issue: John Dewey in Hawai'i. *Educational Perspectives: Journal of the College of Education/University of Hawai'i at Manoa*, vol. 47. nos. 1–2.

Nieddu, Anna Maria, ed. 2016. *La filosofia di George H. Mead: Analisi, interpretazioni, prospettive*. Milano: Mimesis.

Park, Robert E. 1921. "Sociology and the Social Sciences: The Social Organism and the Collective Mind." *American Journal of Sociology*, vol. 27, no. 1, 1–21.

Park, Robert E. 1938. "Reflections on Communication and Culture." *American Journal of Sociology*, vol. 44, no. 2, 187–205.

Park, Robert E. 1942. "Modern Society." In *Biological Symposia*, Vol. 8: *Levels of Integration in Biological and Social Systems*. Edited by Robert Redfield, 217–240. Lancaster, PA: Jaques Cattell Press.

Park, Robert E. 1943. "Education and the Cultural Crisis." *American Journal of Sociology*, vol. 48, no. 6, 728–736.

Potter, Robert E., and Linda L. Logan. 1995. *A History of Teacher Education in Hawai'i*. Honolulu: Hawaii Education Association.

Rockefeller, Steven C. 1991. *John Dewey: Religious Faith and Democratic Humanism*. New York: Columbia University Press.

Rosenthal, Sandra, and Patrick Bourgeois. 1991. *Mead and Merleau-Ponty: Toward a Common Vision*. Albany: State University of New York Press.

Ross, Dorothy. 1992. *The Origins of American Social Science*. Cambridge, UK: Cambridge University Press.

Rucker, Darnell. 1969. *The Chicago Pragmatists*. Minneapolis: University of Minnesota Press.

Seigfried, Charlene Haddock. 1996. *Pragmatism and Feminism: Reweaving the Social Fabric*. Chicago: University of Chicago Press.

Shalin, Dmitri. 1988. "G. H. Mead, Socialism, and the Progressive Agenda." *American Journal of Sociology*, vol. 93, no, 4, 913–951.

Small, Albion W. 1900. "The Scope of Sociology III. The Problems of Sociology." *American Journal of Sociology*, vol. 5, no. 6, 778–813.

Small, Albion W. 1901. Review of *The Problem of Conduct* by A. E. Taylor. *American Journal of Sociology*, vol. 7, no. 1, 122–125.

Small, Albion W. 1902. "The Scope of Sociology VIII. The Primary Concepts of Sociology." *American Journal of Sociology*, vol. 8, no. 2, 197–250.

Thomas, William I. 1909. *Source Book for Social Origins: Ethnological Materials, Psychological Standpoint, Classified and Annotated Bibliographies for the Interpretation of Savage Society*. Chicago: University of Chicago Press.

Torres Colón, Gabriel A., and Charles A. Hobbs. 2015. "The Intertwining of Culture and Nature: Franz Boas, John Dewey, and Deweyan Strands of American Anthropology." *Journal of the History of Ideas*, vol. 76, no. 1, 139–164.

Turner, Stephen. 2007. "A Life in the First Half-Century of Sociology: Charles Ellwood and the Division of Sociology." In *Sociology in America: A History*. Edited by Craig Calhoun, 115–154. Chicago: University of Chicago Press.

Westbrook, Robert B. 1993. *John Dewey and American Democracy*. Ithaca, NY: Cornell University Press.

Wiley, Norbert. 2016. *Inner Speech and the Dialogical Self*. Philadelphia: Temple University Press.

CHAPTER 31

IDEALISM AND RELIGION IN DEWEY'S PHILOSOPHY

RANDALL E. AUXIER AND JOHN R. SHOOK

JOHN Dewey's relationship with philosophical idealism, like his philosophy's approach to religion, is a difficult interpretive challenge. Identifying what counted as "idealism" as understood by Dewey, and by his idealist contemporaries, must be sensitive to its many variations and associations. Idealism was changing significantly during the period of 1870 to 1940, no less so than Dewey's philosophy over that time. Dewey's relationships with idealism and naturalism were bound up with his view of experience, including religious experience. Questions of interpretation are inevitable. Is experience ultimately more ideal or more natural for Dewey, or should experience be de-emphasized to avoid metaphysics? Does religious experience have an independent role, or is it just a type of aesthetic experience? Such issues revolve around decisions, faced by Dewey himself, about what metaphysics can and cannot accomplish in a pragmatic, radically empirical philosophy.

The stance taken on Dewey's metaphysics is usually predictive of a scholar's viewpoint on the role of idealistic themes and religious experiences in Dewey's philosophy. Hostility toward all metaphysics including idealism characterizes some commentators, while some others appreciate metaphysics so long as it is not idealistic. There are also scholars wary of metaphysics who only offer epistemological interpretations of Dewey. As for scholars who are not antithetical to idealism, there are those who acknowledge Dewey's association with idealistic views,[1] and there are also those who argue that Dewey is best understood through the lens of idealism.[2] Not surprisingly, commentators taking idealism quite seriously, as we do, are more open to the significant role that religious experience plays throughout Dewey's thought from his early to late periods. This chapter examines the major encounters between Dewey and idealism and the roles that religion played in those episodes.[3]

CHRISTIAN IDEALISM

The Congregationalism that dominated much of New England, including the Vermont of Dewey's birth, proved amenable to a pious theistic idealism for those seeking a philosophical worldview. God, for this idealism, is the supreme personal spirit guiding an ideal world appearing as material. Dewey accepted this God during his college years. His later memories of an "inward laceration" from a strict religious upbringing were not about resentment or hostility toward religion but only a painful recollection of strict moral demands placed on a young cerebral boy. Dewey was well aware how his selection of an idealistic philosophy from alternatives available during the 1870s and 1880s was a thoughtful response on both ethical and intellectual levels.

At Dewey's seventieth birthday party, his Columbia colleagues presented Dewey with a copy of Coleridge's *Aids to Reflection*. They recorded him saying that this book "was our spiritual emancipation in Vermont," and "Coleridge's idea of the spirit came to us as a real relief, because we could be both liberal and pious; and this *Aids to Reflection* book, especially Marsh's edition, was my first Bible."[4] Dewey's rare autobiographical reflections must not be treated as gospel, especially his accounts of intellectual debts, but this one was sincere. His Calvinist upbringing was no false memory either, nor was his laborious escape from it, after embracing idealism at the University of Vermont during 1875–79.

During Dewey's teenage years, the liberality and universalism of his church's minister, Lewis O. Brastow, encouraged the welcome view that reason and religion can and must cohere. Dewey studied this standpoint under his philosophy professor at the University of Vermont, H.A.P. Torrey, who taught from James Marsh's edition of Samuel Taylor Coleridge's *Aids to Reflection* and *The Remains of the Rev. James Marsh* (Shook 2004, 304–309; Dykhuizen 1973, 9–18). Coleridge and Marsh happened to be two of the earliest philosophical thinkers in England and America, respectively, to study Kant, Hegel, Schelling, and other idealists in their German editions.

The liberating creed heard from Coleridge declared that neither speculative reason nor scientific theory, with their didactic and static principles, can take precedence over the living processes and practicalities of human life: "[I]t must be the Practical Reason of Man, comprehending the Will, the Conscience, the Moral Being with its inseparable Interests and Affections—that Reason, namely, which is the Organ of Wisdom, and (as far as man is concerned) the Source of living and actual Truths. . . . Christianity is not a Theory, or a Speculation: but a Life;—not a Philosophy of Life, but a life and a living Process" (Coleridge 1829, 115, 131; see Dalton 2002, 23–40).

As for Marsh, Dewey cites him in one of his earliest articles, "Soul and Body" (1886), while proposing that "soul" and "body" are related as "function and organ, as activity and instrument" (EW 1:112). Marsh had stated: [W]e recognize the body, each as his own body, and the life of the body, as *his own life*. It belongs to him, as a part of his being, as the *outward form* and *condition* of his *existence in space*. . . . It is not merely an *organ*, or material *mechanism*, to be conceived as distinct from our personal self, but *it is our proper self as existent in space*, in the order and under the laws of *nature*" (Marsh 1843, 256–257, italics in original)

After graduation, Dewey taught at a high school in Oil City, Pennsylvania. An interview with Dewey by Max Eastman for *The Atlantic* in 1941 recounts his "mystic experience" in Oil City while reading Wordsworth. The experience was, in Eastman's summary, "an answer to that question which still worried him: whether he really meant business when he prayed." The feeling of oneness, which Dewey likened to Whitman's "oneness with the universe," assured him he need not worry about existence or his place in the universe. It "was not a very dramatic mystic experience," but, as Eastman reported, there was "just a supremely blissful feeling that his worries were over." In Dewey's own prosaic words, "What the hell are you worrying about anyway? Everything that's here is here and you can just lie back on it." Dewey then told Eastman, "I've never had any doubts since then, nor any beliefs. To me faith means not worrying." He further opined that mystical experiences are "purely emotional and cannot be conveyed in words." Dewey concluded, "I claim I've got religion, and that I got it that night in Oil City" (Eastman 1941, 672–673).

Dewey was no longer someone at war with his religious well-being, and idealism was already more vexing to him than his own religiosity. He had learned enough about Kant and idealism to pursue some of transcendental idealism's puzzles. Dewey was willing to identify God with "the Absolute" in the sense of a perfectly personal being that encompasses and guarantees the organic wholeness to this vision of personal selves residing within dynamic nature. Knowledge remained the vital issue for Dewey: how was this vision to be knowable by humanity, so that knowledge stays unified with what is known? Cartesian dualism situated all knowing on one side of an ontological chasm, apart from matters to be known. Materialism leaves other minds unknowable at best and all minds unreal at worst. Classical empiricism kept the factual units of experience unrelated to each other and hence unintelligible for real knowledge. And Kantianism kept Reason's role for knowledge too dependent on unknowable things-in-themselves. Dewey sought a philosophical system able to explain how selves relate to each other and the whole without rendering essential factors unknowable.

ABSOLUTE IDEALISM

Dewey's neo-Hegelian tutelage was conducted during the 1880s under Johns Hopkins University professor George S. Morris, and (by eagerly reading) Oxford's T. H. Green and Glasgow's Edward Caird. These idealists were formulating critiques of rival philosophies, especially empiricism and materialism, in order to expound the culminating thesis that the perfectly unified mind of the Absolute is both the epistemic ideal and ontological ground for each human intelligence. Dewey also heard Charles S. Peirce's lectures on logic and scientific methods at Johns Hopkins, but little influence from Peirce is visible during this early period.

Morris was more fitting to Dewey's temperament and need. Morris's absolute idealism was tempered by an engagement with the Greeks as taught by his own professors in Germany, F. A. Trendelenburg and Hermann Ulrici. Dewey adopted its organic idealism, regarding every real thing as functionally contributing to the ongoing vitality of the whole of reality, joining a philosophical heritage tracing back to F. W. J. Schelling and J. G. Herder (Shook 2000, 2017). Morris made a deep personal impression as well. After Morris died in 1889, Dewey's eulogistic remembrance noted that "Professor Morris never held his philosophy by a merely intellectual grasp, since it was fused with his personal character, and gained its color and tone from his own deeper interests" (EW 3:7). A religious affinity was also shared between them. One of Morris's lectures, incorporated into his book *British Thought and Thinkers* (Morris 1880), describes his own religious experience. Dewey later recalled that account, explaining why it "is worth quoting, both because of its rarity and because it reveals how early his mind sought the philosophic channel" (EW 3:5; see Wenley 1917, 308–321). Dewey viewed this sort of unusual experience as characteristic of a "philosophic" channel at the core of one's character, indicating how he respected mystical states for exploring philosophical questions.

Dewey acquired from absolute idealism the imperative that human experience and knowledge cannot be left unaccountable or unconnected to environing reality. The successive editions of his *Psychology* from 1886 to 1891 display a drift away from rationalism as he sought to reasonably fulfill this imperative. He formulated version after version of his own "experimental idealism," as he labeled it in *The Study of Ethics: A Syllabus* (1894; EW 4:264). He was distancing himself from neo-Hegelian absolutism because the perfections of divine Mind seemed too aloof from the actionable knowledge achievable by human intelligence. The resolution of Dewey's boyhood doubts was maturing: not only can we lie back on what *is*, but we also do not *know* what we *do not know*. It is more intellectually honest to accept intelligence's limitations than to place trust in abstract reason's perfections. Unbidden experiences about the bare necessity of things may not be capturable by conceptual formulations, but exaggerating our capacity for knowing all of reality is just the adult version of avowing to get right with our savior. Relax—what is here, really is here.

The first (1887) edition of *Psychology* had agreed with T. H. Green that "Psychology is the science of the reproduction of some universal content or existence, whether of knowledge or action, in the form of individual, unsharable consciousness." (EW 2:11) Specifically, "The knowledge of the finite individual is the process by which the individual reproduces the universal mind, and hence makes real for himself the universe, which is eternally real for the complete, absolutely universal intelligence, since involved in its self-objectifying activity of knowledge." (EW 2:lxxix). This second statement was deleted for the 1889 revised edition. Dewey had judged that philosophy cannot justify the assertion of an Absolute Mind, and the term "God" could no longer properly refer to that Absolute. With this move away from Absolute idealism, he was also letting go of the personal God as a spiritual absolute.

By the late 1880s, Dewey was seeking a third alternative between the Absolute as a projector of knowledge to humanity and God as a projection of human knowledge. In an 1889 exposition of Green's philosophy, Dewey offered an interpretation that had more to do with his own evolving view of God:

> The statement that God is the ideal, or even the true self of man, is liable to interpretation from the wrong side, and, indeed, has often been so interpreted. It is taken to mean that God is only a projection of man; that he is an ideal that man forms of what man would be were he perfect, and that, therefore, God has no reality excepting as a conception of man's ideal, and that God becomes real in the degree in which man realizes his ideal. But this is a complete inversion of Green's thought. The reality of God in himself is a condition of our having the notion of Him as our own ideal self, of our attempts, our striving to make this ideal real, and of our measure of success. Human nature is rather the projection of God, that is, the reproduction of Him, through physical conditions, than God the projection of man's ideal.
>
> (EW 3:26)

Dewey never accepted the first interpretation of God as mere projection, in his early or late philosophy, and hence anthropomorphism was never acceptable to him. Nor was Dewey quite comfortable with the "reproduction" of God in us. What is being reproduced, exactly? If God is participating in our material strivings toward our ideals, none of God's eternal perfections would be relevant or helpful, for all we can know is our own ideals and the environing world enabling our progress, and neither of those things can be known by us as perfect. God understood as a *paraclete* or helper, another idea which endowed God with personality, was becoming a problem.

The relationship that Dewey sought between knowing selves and the knowable whole was proving to be too unstable: either absolute reality is a rational Self constituting reality's completed unity while finite selves within that whole create nothing or individual selves must constitute a known world without universal reason (in the Coleridgean or Hegelian sense). The former view forbids people from doing anything morally real, while the latter forbids people from knowing anything objectively real. Dewey well understood the import of both alternatives. His 1888 book on Leibniz had accused monodology of implicating two very different Gods: (1) a supreme monad eliciting the development of all other monads so thoroughly that the whole amounts to spiritual pantheism and (b) a perfected monad needing so little interaction with lesser monads that the aggregate amounts to subjective idealism. Yet Dewey discerned a third conception of God hinted at in Leibniz's writings that can satisfy Leibnizian principles:

> God is the harmony of the monads,—neither one among them nor one made up of them, but their organic unity ... God *is* the pre-established harmony. This conception, like that of harmony, may have either a mechanical interpretation (according to which God is the artificial, external point of contact of intelligence and reality, in themselves opposed) or an organic meaning, according to which God *is* the unity of intelligence and reality. ... According to this view, the opposition between ideal

inclusion and real exclusion vanishes. God *is* the harmony of the real and ideal, not a mere arrangement for bringing them to an understanding with one another.

(EW 1:421–422)

A similar view was defended by some American personal idealists, such as George Holmes Howison, during the 1890s. William Ernest Hocking later developed this view into his own type of organic idealism. The conception of the Self (whether divine or human) as the dynamic harmonization of the real and ideal became Dewey's overriding concern, and he was among the first philosophers to work out this idea. Could the ultimate reality of individual selves fulfill that conception? Personal idealism also erupted in Britain with Andrew Seth's (1887) *Hegelianism and Personality*.

Dewey refused to join these personalists and their paramount mission to uphold individual moral responsibility against absolute idealism.[5] He was already making his own determinations about the nature of the individual self. His 1890 article "On Some Current Conceptions of the Term 'Self,'" while nominally directed at confusions among definitions for the "self" in Seth's book, concludes by stating that the self can neither be the synthetic unity of sense and thought nor a transcendent activity behind all experience. Dewey ends this article by exonerating Green from hypostatizing an abstraction of the Self, without endorsing Green's supreme absolute. (EW 3:74).

Experimental Idealism

Dewey was revealing his new theory of the self to allies, such as William James. In 1891 he wrote to James (1890) about closely reading his *The Principles of Psychology*, urging an even more radical interpretation of consciousness. Its chapter on "The Consciousness of Self" proposes a fundamental field of "sciousness"—the stream of interrelated phenomena prior to the self/not-self distinction. Dewey tells James,

> that is a much better statement of the real core of Hegel than what you criticize later on as Hegelianism. Take out your "postulated" "matter" & "thinker," let "matter" (i.e. the physical world) be the organization of the content of sciousness up to a certain point, & the thinker be a still further unified organization [not a unify-ing organ as per Green] and that is good enough Hegel for me. And if this point of view had been worked out, would you have needed any "special" activity of attention, or any "special" act of will? The fundamental fact would then be the tendency towards a maximum content of sciousness, and within this growing organization of sciousness effort &c could find their place. ... the unity of Hegel's self (& what Caird is driving it [sic]) is not a unity in the stream as such, but of the function of this stream—the unity of the world (content) which it bears or reports. ... But Hegel's agent (or Self) is simply the universe doing business on its own account.

(1891.05.06, 00458: Dewey to James)

The primal field of "sciousness" would be labeled as "experience" by James and Dewey in later writings to formulate the "postulate of immediate empiricism" (Dewey) or "radical empiricism" (James).

Experience is wider than consciousness; consciousness is a broader realm than a self's thinking; and thinking has a wider range than known objects. Experience per se is not known, and experience does not merely exist for this or that conscious self, although everything that a thinking self is and produces occurs within experience and its known products are also within experience. Subjective idealism is too narrow because objective reality is vastly larger than anything happening for self-consciousness, so experience extends beyond any personal self, for Dewey. Although James is agnostic about that final point, they did agree that Absolute idealism is ill-founded. In spite of Royce's (1885) ingenious arguments in *The Religious Aspect of Philosophy*, James eventually judged, along with Dewey, that the vast extent of experience is not already known by any self—not even a divine or transcendent self—so far as we know or *can* know.[6] Royce's "proof" from the reality of error showed at most that a concept of the Absolute is intellectually inevitable, but it failed to establish that such a being *exists* or *must* exist in accord with that concept.

Dewey and James, along with Royce, firmly agreed that materialism is mistaken because anything postulated as material must be conceived only in dynamic relationships with thoughtful knowers. Dualism only multiplies the errors of subjective idealism and materialism. Since personal idealism and absolute idealism also seemed inadequate to Dewey and James, they were driven toward radical empiricism by the first decade of the twentieth century. Metaphysics remained contentious. James chose a synoptic neutral monism, while Dewey formulated a pluralistic and naturalistic version of organicism (on categorizing naturalisms see Shook 2011). James remained more of a personalist. As for Dewey, by 1900 it was becoming difficult to ascertain the degree of affiliation he retained with idealism.

Readers of Dewey's article "Moral Theory and Practice" and his *Outlines of a Critical Theory of Ethics*, composed during 1890 and published in 1891, were the first to encounter his reconstruction of the individual self. First, an individual self is always active and only real in that activity: there is no unmoved spiritual mover behind personal agency. Second, ideals have no reality nor efficacy outside of that ongoing activity of conduct. The only remaining role that moral ideas could play is this: the degree to which an action is thoughtful, heeding conditions and consequences essential to this acting, constitutes its ideal aspect and eligibility for moral evaluation. A moral end, on Dewey's definition, enhances overall coordination, unifies one's character, and permits worthier achievements. Although individuality captures the "personal" side of committed participation in social progress, and the growth of that *individuality* (which includes personality) is a manifestation of that moral priority (e.g., in genuine education), there is no separate ontological status for the individual. The moral individual exemplifies that dynamic harmonization of the real and ideal carried out in social conduct. Dewey elaborated this theory of social ethics in later works such as *Ethics* (1908).

In 1892 Dewey openly rejected Green, declaring that a perfect and static Absolute/ God can play no role in human intelligence or morality (EW 3:159–161). If the growth of human mind is not a poor reduplication of God's perfect mind, what happens to our view of intelligence, once that God is abandoned as unreal? Dewey thus eliminated the middle term of God, so that the idealized community (as intelligence unified) is the spiritual ideal for each individual member of that community (as intelligence growing). Furthermore, around 1894 his church attendance ceased, never to be renewed.

With the departure of the Absolute, there was an important adjustment in Dewey's conception of reality: it cannot be an intelligibly unified whole in itself. If nature is not already perfectly ordered, then no perfect God is responsible for that, and the growth of human intelligence is not about representing for ourselves some perfect order that God had laid down. All the same, human ideals remain powerful here and now, even if they are not immanent in the Whole. Human intelligence is capable of appreciating whatever order happens locally to as prevailing in nature, because intelligence is participating that order's alteration and development. Dewey no longer needed a metaphysical God to explain human knowledge, but he did need a potentially intelligible world for human knowing. Fortunately, his philosophy did not have to start from an unprovable postulate, since much intelligibility is already evident, and no sensible objection can disprove that. James would continue to struggle with the immediacy of pure experience, but Dewey's worries had faded years before. What is here *exists*, as he said in 1941 of his 1881 experience.

Christianity, after theism, must be thoroughly reconstructed. Dewey's 1893 essay "Christianity and Democracy," identifies Christianity's prioritization of the full realization of each individual with the devotion to the endless advancement of genuine community. How could a single religion turn out to be the ultimate moral end of all humanity for all time? First, what Christianity stands for must be liberated from historical accident to reveal its universal significance. (Dewey anticipates Royce's *The Problem of Christianity* by twenty years.) Second, what religiosity stands for must be connected to that *same* universal significance. That is why Dewey denies that Christianity is just a religion (EW 4:4). What is a religion? "Every religion is an expression of the social relations of the community; its rites, its cult, are a recognition of the sacred and divine significance of those relationships." (EW 4:3) Going further, if "the community" should consist of all intelligent agents, then a potentially universal religion is no longer a religion but just the ongoing revelation of Truth itself. That revelation is not *from* God—that revelation *is* God. "God is essentially and only the self-revealing, and the revelation is complete only as men come to realize Him. ... The revelation is, and can be, only in intelligence. ... Beyond all other means of appropriating truth, beyond all other organs of apprehension, is man's own action" (EW 4:6–7). For Dewey, "Christianity, if universal, if revelation, must be the continual unfolding, never ceasing discovery of the meaning of life." (EW 4:4).

What is socially universal, for Dewey, can therefore only be democracy itself:

> It is in democracy, the community of ideas and interest through community of action, that the incarnation of God in man (man, that is to say, as an organ of universal

truth) becomes a living present thing, having its ordinary and natural sense. This truth is brought down to life; its segregation removed; it is made a common truth enacted in all departments of action, not in one isolated sphere called religious.

(EW 4:9)

Like nature, God has no meaning or reality outside of an integration with us, through our transformation of the cooperative world.

Dewey had arrived at an empiricist and functionalist version of Leibniz's third conception of God as a growing unity of intelligence and reality, grown through progressive social experience. Other idealists, such as Howison and Seth, were plodding toward the same idea but not boldly enough to situate God firmly within human energy and achievement. Heaven was not a democracy for the personal idealists, not even for Royce. For Dewey, to self-consciously and devoutly participate in the democratic and scientific growth of intelligence (the inclusive moral end urged by Dewey) is not to seek God or to become "like" God—it is to be unified *in* God, wherever social intelligence is growing. To be religious is to be ethical, which is to be devoted to the advancement of intelligent culture, which is nothing less than the democratic pursuit of free intelligence itself (Shook and Good, 2010). Royce could agree up until the last clause; he wanted the authentic *agapic* community now, not democracy's tumultuous hopes for public community. Dewey took up controversies over God with Royce, discussed in the next section, but he published nothing about James's (1902) *The Varieties of Religious Experience*, although its influence on Dewey's *A Common Faith* is discussed in the last section.[7]

Democracy would be religious enough for Dewey's philosophy, as he proceeded with confidence to expound his ethical, pedagogical, and social theories from 1896 to 1924, culminating with *Democracy and Education* (1916) and *Human Nature and Conduct* (1922). Most other idealists during that era defended democracy sincerely enough. However, philosophers offering idealism as a substitute for revelation had less tolerance for social disorder and political deliberation, needing a metaphysically guaranteed order in reality before they can believe that more good than evil is achievable in society.

THE CRITIC OF ABSOLUTE IDEALISM

Dewey's sharp criticisms of idealism during the first two decades of the twentieth century allowed many of his readers to think that he had fully abandoned idealism. However, his autobiographical reflection in 1930, "From Absolutism to Experimentalism," emphasizes how adopting experimentalism was his decisive transition, which flowed from "experimental idealism," as he called his view after 1891. Dewey was still labelling his philosophy as experimental idealism in 1929 in *The Quest for Certainty* (LW 4:134). His assembly of this philosophy from organicist and idealistic theses without needing an Absolute provided him with argumentative grounds for criticizing metaphysical idealisms.

In 1900 Dewey reviewed Royce's *The World and the Individual, First Series*, examining its conception of the Absolute. Why is an Absolute of infinitely perfect experience implicated by our limited and incomplete experiences? Having denied that reality could be utterly unlike experience, Royce infers that all reality consists of experience only, but that leaves his absolutism exposed to Dewey's dilemma: how can one and the same purposive experience be known as poorly fulfilled and also as completely fulfilled? If a purpose is only partially fulfilled, then it cannot be simultaneously known as completely fulfilled within the Absolute (otherwise, we would rest content with that experience). On the other hand, if we know an experience as perfectly fulfilled (as it really is within the Absolute), then we would not regard it as merely human experience.

Royce cannot dodge this dilemma since flawed human experiences are the only evidence, and he cannot prove the Absolute's reality by logic alone, Dewey argues. An unproven Absolute cannot condemn all human experience as irredeemably unsatisfactory, even if, as Dewey admits, only a greater fund of wider experience can reveal where our purposes can become more successful, or exposed as fruitless. For Dewey's experimental idealism, Royce's "identification" (as Dewey interprets the argument) of Absolute experience with human experience is not philosophically justifiable. A weaker conclusion is proffered by Dewey: our purposes attain or lose their relative validity in the course of further guided experiences intended by those plans. There is no need to presume any perfected achievements but only postulated outcomes attainable through effort in actual human experiences.

Dewey's criticism of Royce echoes his previous repudiation of T. H. Green, and it was at work in Dewey's even earlier critique of Leibniz (EW 1:415–418). Rationalism's preference for complete metaphysical identity (as Dewey takes Royce to be asserting), while leaving empirical difference inexplicable, was too static and formal for Dewey. He preferred a dynamic "organic unity"—a dynamic identity despite differences that attains unity through those differences. For Dewey, only changing and interrelating processes are real, while the real for Royce includes logical relations that compel our thinking and provide norms for our reflective acts. Was Dewey more of a process philosopher than Royce?

No phase of Dewey's career demarcates when "process" philosophizing first infused his thought. Going back to his earliest publications, Dewey used the word "process" in most of his writings with high frequency, describing practically every significant matter under discussion as a process, and often as an activity as well. Among early process thinkers in America, calling attention to one's philosophy as basically about "process" came much later. However, that delay does not mean that Dewey was unaware or unaffected by his fundamental allegiance to process. In 1903 he wrote revealing letters to William James, explicitly pointing out the importance of process. One letter mentions how George H. Mead (the student of both James and Royce) calls reality a "Life-Process" (1903.03.15?, 00797: Dewey to James), and a follow-up letter to James expressed his own commitment to process.

It may be the continued working of the Hegelian bacillus of reconciliation of contradictories in me that makes me feel as if the conception of process gives a basis for uniting the truths of pluralism and monism, and also of necessity and spontaneity. . . . I cannot help feeling that an adequate analysis of activity would exhibit the world of fact and the world of ideas as two correspondent objective statements of the active process itself—correspondent because each has a work to do, in the doing of which it needs to be helped out by the other. The active process itself transcends any possible objective statement (whether in terms of facts or of ideas) simply for the reason that these objective statements are ultimately incidental to its own ongoing— are for the sake of it.

(1903.03.27, 00800: Dewey to James)

Although this "active process itself" was metaphysically sufficient for Dewey, functioning as absolute enough for his experimentalism, he refused to credit Royce (and related idealists such as Bowne, Howison, and Hocking) with this process view. Subsequent debates allowed each to talk past Dewey, and vice versa, on crucial topics from truth and reality to experience and the absolute (Oppenheim 2005, 291–300). This argumentative futility widened the growing divisions among the next generation of philosophical witnesses. The pragmatists around Dewey and James, along with the new realists, felt justified in dismissing idealism, and that distrust was sustained during the rest of the twentieth century. Ironically, that ill-repute attached to idealism also left Dewey's idealistic debts in obscurity, especially for later pragmatists anxious to stay safely naturalistic.

Dewey did praise Royce's work in logic (MW 2:360–361) while developing his own logical theory. He sent a copy of *Studies in Logical Theory* (1903) to Peirce, who responded with a book review and two stern letters in reply. Peirce accused Dewey of psychologism by reducing logical relations to psychological processes and objected to Dewey's turn away from transcendence and whatever realities it may harbor with a mere logical interdiction. There is no logical or empirical basis to foreclosing an extension of inquiry into what is only possible, for Peirce. Concomitantly, Dewey was too comfortable with metaphysical and religious agnosticism, and Royce agreed with that assessment. These disagreements could not be easily reconciled. Peirce's "idealistic" pragmatism occupied a middle ground between Royce's insistence upon the hypothetico-logical knowability of the Absolute and Dewey's limitation of logic's reach to generalizations from actual experience. For Peirce, one cannot say in advance what inquiry into the structure of possibility in mathematics and abduction in logic might confirm in the future. Post-Kantian problems haunted all three philosophers. Something transcends the ongoing work of intelligence. How should it be treated as a recognizable aspect of experience?

EMPIRICAL NATURALISM

In 1904 Dewey left the University of Chicago for Columbia University and its unique philosophical atmosphere. Naturalism, as it was developing there, was far from just materialism or monistic realism. Dewey adapted this open and pluralistic naturalism to fit with his experimentalism. He began publishing articles in *The Journal of Philosophy*, continuing to expound his criteria for philosophical adequacy and his view of dynamic reality, and contrasting his views with both idealisms and realisms. Put concisely, two requirements play a paramount role. First, a metaphysical requirement: all of human experience is within the same reality as everything else that is also real. Nothing about experience segregates it apart from the rest of what is real. Second was an epistemological requirement: an account of experience's continuity with the rest of reality is compatible with understanding that continuity. Nothing about experience prevents our knowing how experiences are within reality.

Dewey asserted the identity of experience and reality in such articles as "The Realism of Pragmatism" (1905b), "The Postulate of Immediate Empiricism" (1905a), and "Reality as Experience" (1906). The first article seemed to assert materialism, with a decidedly Darwinian flavor: "Psychical things are thus themselves realistically conceived; they can be described and identified in biological and physiological terms, in terms (with adequate science) of chemicophysical correspondents. . . . Their origin as existences can be stated *and must be stated* in terms of adjustments and maladjustments among habits, biological functions" (MW 3:154–155, our emphasis). The second article sounded like subjective idealism: "things are what they are experienced to be" (MW 3:159). The third article affirmed a tenet associated with absolute idealism: "the assimilation to each other of the ideas of experience and reality" (MW 3:101). Dewey expected such pronouncements to be mutually coherent and supportive; most of his readers were left confused, despite another ten years of clarifications.

These three views can be reconciled, starting with the way that mental events are within experience, but noting how experience is a vastly broader realm for Dewey than whatever reaches self-awareness or thoughtful attention. Dewey agreed with James's empiricist claim that consciousness does not have its own kind of existence, so "experience" is not consciousness and certainly not just the content of mental matters. He also agreed with Frederick Woodbridge's naturalistic statement of this same view, taking the objects of experience to be real entities rather than simulacra of objects composed of some "stuff" called experience (MW 3:156; Woodbridge 1905). Since natural objects around us are in lived experience, mental events in experience are attempted adjustments of biological functions and biological activities are interactions with environing matters. Therefore, experiencing encompasses both the purposeful organism and the environing matters with which that organism is engaged.

Dewey's abiding appeal to experience for adjudicating the real and the unreal is understandably reminiscent of idealism's prioritization of mind over matter. His repudiation of mechanism and materialism as metaphysically inadequate, coupled with his emphasis on the efficacious power of ideas and ideals, also sound like idealistic views. He was not rejecting his experimental idealism that dated back to 1891, but it was undergoing adaptation for the context of evolution, naturalism, and the scientific attitude. Idealism's antipathy toward science's account of nature arouses his complaint that scientific method must not be subordinated to rationalist dialectic. Yet Dewey withholds from science the right to dictate what is more or less real. Reality does not consist *only* of known matters; anything experienced yet not knowable deserves ontological parity with everything confirmed by science. Everything really is what it is experienced to be, by his postulate of immediate empiricism. Identity, then, is not about reducing external things down to experiential status but instead about situating experiences within the natural realm.

> If biological development be accepted, the subject of experience is at least an animal, continuous with other organic forms in a process of more complex organization. . . . And experience is not identical with brain action; it is the entire organic agent-patient in all its interaction with the environment, natural and social.
>
> (MW 10:26)

Science can determine where and how experienced events actually persist, by ascertaining how much of nature, which includes the organism, is involved with an experiential episode. (If the subject is peremptorily taken out of nature, the question is begged against Dewey's ontology, and dualisms proliferate.) Visual illusions are engagements with a very local region of nature—what happens to be focally in the line of sight and its perceptual processing in the brain (MW 8:53–54). Colors have vastly greater import, as they are reliably where broad fields of electromagnetic radiation are activating duly sensitive nervous systems, so colors are neither only external or internal (LW 1:25, 254). Meaningful import therefore correlates with natural extent—that is what Dewey means by the capacity of inference to stretch into nature.

Dewey always insisted that experiential episodes cannot be entirely reduced to, or completely identified with, brain events. Although what the brain is doing cannot be omitted from a full scientific explanation for how the organism is experiencing, no knowledge of brain activity is possible without wider reference to the behavioral guidance the brain is providing, as well as that behavior's purpose within an environing context. In his essay "How Is Mind to Be Known?" (1942) Dewey again explains that

> behavior . . . even on the biological level (without reference to behavior as it is culturally constituted), includes a great deal more than "brain events." Indeed, I have difficulty in seeing how any one can give an intelligible account of cerebral behavior unless that limited mode of behavior is itself descriptively determined in connection with the whole scheme of what is known about behavior in its widest biological sense—a sense in which interaction with environmental conditions is included.
>
> (LW 15:33)

Even if cortex, conduct, and circumstance are so coordinated, what really is experience, that philosophy must be so mindful of it? If Dewey's mature philosophy truly left idealism behind in order to frame a pragmatic naturalism adequately, why should the term "experience" survive to denote anything ontologically important? Yet Dewey refused to surrender the term, at the high cost of perpetuating metaphysical misunderstandings. His final despair at evading modern philosophy's view of experience as psychological and subjective allowed him to suggest "culture" as a substitute (LW 1:361–362). However, while human experience is thoroughly cultural, "culture" is not a full substitute for the ontological and epistemic roles that Dewey required from "experience." For Dewey, animals such as fish, frogs, and finches are experiencing the world without culture; and new knowledge is learned by specialized inquirers far in advance of their culture. Furthermore, the variety of naturalism advocated by Dewey must challenge subjectivist categorizations for experience with arguments more ontological and metaphysical than anthropological. Such arguments are at the heart of his major books, such as *Experience and Nature* (1925), *The Quest for Certainty* (1929b), and *Logic: The Theory of Inquiry* (1938).

Experience and Nature announces what and where experience is:

> [E]xperience is of as well as in nature. It is not experience which is experienced, but nature—stones, plants, animals, diseases, health, temperature, electricity, and so on. Things interacting in certain ways are experience; they are what is experienced. Linked in certain other ways with another natural object—the human organism— they are how things are experienced as well. Experience thus reaches down into nature; it has depth. It also has breadth and to an indefinitely elastic extent. It stretches. That stretch constitutes inference.
>
> (LW 1:12–13)

To ensure than inference, as a mental process, is entirely experiential *and* natural (not subjective or transcendental), Dewey denied that mind and body could be ontologically separated, even if they should be functionally and logically distinguished. *Experience and Nature* proposes "body-mind" to characterize complex organisms.

> Unless vital organizations were organizations *of* antecedent natural events, the living creature would have no natural connections; it would not be pertinent to its environment nor its environment relevant to it; the latter would not be usable, material of nutrition and defence. In similar fashion, unless "mind" was, in its existential occurrence, an organization *of* physiological or vital affairs and unless its functions developed out of the patterns of organic behavior, it would have no pertinency to nature, and nature would not be the appropriate scene of its inventions and plans, nor the subject-matter of its knowledge.
>
> (LW 1:217–218)

Dewey's view that experiencing is entirely natural contravenes abiding presumptions in philosophy. Critics either insisted that he must be a materialist willing to discard what is so experiential for what is just physical or that he must be an idealist eager to absorb into the subjective what is truly objective. Yet his philosophy transcends those dichotomies. Scientific materialism mistakenly holds that nature is only what nature may do when human thinking is absent; intellectualist idealism mistakenly holds that nature is only what nature must do when human thinking is present. Dewey's empirical naturalism instead credits nature with an indefinite multiplicity of interacting activities, with organic perceiving and exploring among them. Knowing is a rigorous mode of thoughtful exploratory engagement *with* and *within* nature, and there is nothing about observation or knowledge rendering it unnatural.

In *Experience and Nature* (1925), Dewey refers to his philosophy as "empirical naturalism" (LW 1:4). In response to George Santayana's accusation that Dewey unduly privileges experience's perspective on nature, he replied that nature is nothing but perspectival: everything is both particularly somewhere and inherently related to other matters.

> Since experience is both individualized and associational and since experience is continuous with nature as background, as a naturalist I find nature is also both. In citing Mr. Santayana's denial that nature has here, now, and perspective, I found myself in stating my own view compelled to use the plural form:—heres, nows, perspectives. ... It is absurd to confer upon nature a single here, now, and perspective, and if that were the only alternative, I should agree with Mr. Santayana in his denial. But there are an indefinite multitude of heres, nows, and perspectives. As many as there are existences.
>
> (LW 3:80)

That multiplicity to existence/experience allows for a perspectival and pluralistic naturalism.

This admitted multiplicity elicits idealism's offer to explain experience's organization into the meaningful consistencies and necessities for knowledge. Dewey declines that offer without making empiricism's typical retort, that perception undistorted by idealized inference conveys abundant information for knowing. *The Quest for Certainty* (1929b) points out their common premise, which is also shared by self-proclaimed realists, that knowledge's test is some pre-established reality to which human thinking should conform. Irrespective of whether that reality is pre-set by reason, perception, or nature, those philosophies agree that the contribution of thinking must not stray into originality if it aims at knowledge of truth (LW 4:87). Dewey took the contrary view: ideas selectively track the evident associations among things to discover interconnections useful for reliably transforming those things. That intellectual function for ideas is exemplified in science. "It was logically inevitable that as science proceeded on its experimental path it would sooner or later become clear that all conceptions, all intellectual descriptions, must be formulated in terms of operations, actual or imaginatively possible" (LW 4:95). Ideas must make a real difference to the surrounding world, not because thought pre-sets what the world must be but because thinking transforms what the world can be. "A genuine idealism and one compatible with science will emerge as soon as philosophy accepts the teaching of science that ideas are statements not of what is or has been but of acts to be performed ... ideas are worthless except as they pass into actions which rearrange and reconstruct in some way, be it little or large, the world in which we live" (LW 4:111).

For Dewey to encourage an idealism compatible with science, rather than a scientific realism aligned with science, makes one wonder how naturalistic his philosophy could be. *Logic: The Theory of Inquiry* (1938) emphasizes how logic and philosophy of science must adapt to modern science's interest in relations, not essences or substances. The function of theoretical descriptions of postulated entities is primarily to render natural changes more predictable, not to represent inherent features of those entities accurately. What is most realistic about well-confirmed conceptions of theoretical entities is their detectably dynamic characters—their propensities for altering while affected by other changing entities. Accordingly, experienced qualities of our environs are in no way threatened by science (LW 12:119–120). To worry that objects known by science lack familiar qualities, and then rescue those qualities by situating them in a subjective realm apart from nature, opens up pointless metaphysical puzzles and leaves scientific method mysterious.

At the conclusion of the *Logic*, Dewey sorts out major theories of knowledge by their treatment (well, maltreatment) of reflective inquiry. Subjective empiricisms and idealisms, and every type of positivism, place their confidence in "verifiable" evident matters while distrusting scientific inferences that alter the import of those matters (LW 12:511–512, 518–521). Rationalist idealisms (Kant is the primary target) ignore the experimental inquiries into transformable situations where reasonings acquire their limited power, instead erecting reason into a universally normative power to guarantee uniform necessities (LW 12:521–524). As for absolute idealism, it admits the incompleteness of human judgment but faults judgment for falling so short of knowledge's final unity that such inadequacy is only redeemable by the prior ultimate reality of that unity (LW 12:524–526). The rivals to Dewey's empirical naturalism each exaggerate the importance of one chosen phase of inquiry, and those philosophies only maintain a dialectical advantage by faulting another isolated phase of inquiry for inadequacy.

IDEAL-REALISM

Dewey's mature philosophy of instrumentalism, or experimental idealism, can be equally viewed as a perspectival naturalism that combines idealism with realism. Insights and improvements between 1925 and 1938, influenced by C. S. Peirce and A. N. Whitehead, include his recasting of knowing as an intrinsically temporal process, so that transformation and transaction are the operational basis of inquiry. Inquiry also became, for Dewey, a deeply human form of engagement with nature not only as it can be known but also as it can be appreciated, revered, and valued for our moral and political prospects. The metaphysical chasm between knowing and the known was closed, but the greater project remained: the functional unification of fact and value and the demonstration that ideals are real. In *Individualism, Old and New* (1929a), Dewey described his philosophy: "a naturalism which perceives that man with his habits, institutions, desires, thoughts, aspirations, ideals and struggles, is within nature, an integral part of it, has the philosophical foundation and the practical inspiration for effort to employ nature as an ally of human ideals and goods such as no dualism can possibly provide" (LW 5:114).

Two central works by Dewey offer the philosophical fulfillment of this naturalism: *Art as Experience* (1934) and *A Common Faith* (1934). Dewey's aesthetics falls outside the purview of this chapter; here we examine the organicism inherent to his approach to ethical ideals. The 1932 edition of *Ethics* by Dewey and James Tufts presents a pragmatist moral psychology and moral philosophy, without determining the ontology of values and ideals. *A Common Faith*, Dewey's Terry Lectures, accounts for the real potency of ideals by invoking religious experience, piety, and God.

The topic had been re-opened for Dewey when he accepted the invitation five years earlier (1929) to present the Gifford Lectures to explore natural theology by addressing "the religious phases of experience" (LW 9:4). His thinking came to maturity in the Terry Lectures. He expected that subtracting supernaturalism from religiosity would dismay traditional theists, while situating God within nature would disappoint atheists. Overtly, the three chapters of *A Common Faith* explain what it means to be religious, how religiously-held ideals function, and where ethico-religious communities can flourish. The first chapter effectively supplies Dewey's response to James, the second chapter responds to Santayana,[8] and the third chapter constitutes his response to Royce. These three philosophies surround his own empirical naturalism with partially agreeable yet divergent worldviews. James is the sensitive experimentalist who was held back by underdeveloped categories (unlike Royce); Santayana is the metaphysical materialist who stunted the individual self (unlike James); Royce is the righteous communitarian who forestalled tragedy with unnatural hopes (unlike Santayana). Dewey sought a combination of experimental, natural, and communal perspectives in order to occupy the middle ground, as neither toughminded nor tenderminded, twice-born in James's sense, with assurances that intelligence is our best hope for worthy societies as the common fruit of religious experience.

Dewey begins on common ground with James's second lecture of the *Varieties of Religious Experience* on the course of historical religions and the significance of personal faith for religions. However, he rejects certain categories upon which James relied, especially what James called "religion in general" and its supposed link with "unseen powers" (LW 9:6–8). Dewey focuses only on what James described as "the essence of religious experiences, the thing by which we finally must judge them," which for both pragmatists "must be that element or quality in them which we can meet nowhere else" (James 1929, 45). Dewey goes further than James by clarifying why "the religious" is no separate matter destined only for cultivation within religion. Religious exclusivity is instilled through institutionalized doctrine to perpetuate supernaturalist religions. Regrettably, that insularity distorts the natural function of religiosity and renders mysterious the role played by devout faith within social affairs.

According to Dewey, people do not have religious experiences because there are religions, nor do religions deserve credence because people have religious experiences.

James more than flirted with the first view, but he did not sufficiently appreciate the implications of the second view. If "the religious" should only denote "attitudes that may be taken toward every object and every proposed end or ideal" and "lend deep and enduring support to the processes of living" (LW 9:8, 12) then that distinctive quality may be present in anyone's ongoing devotion to worldly affairs. Religiosity enlivens every individual's committed participation in communal improvement. Dewey denies any monopoly claimed by religions over arousing such commitment—religious fidelity is already immanent within the ethical life, or it is nowhere. Religiosity must morally unify the self (as James had claimed), and Dewey adds that a person's ideal ends must unify one with the world where moral action makes its difference (LW 9:16–17). If devotion to a religion instead sets an individual's duties against each other and ensures conflicts among the endeavors that one pursues, this disunity is more unethical and fanatical than religious.

Dewey concludes the first chapter by presaging his dispute with Santayana, who had notably praised the naturality and justness of piety in *Reason in Religion* (1905). In Dewey's own view,

> Natural piety is not of necessity either a fatalistic acquiescence in natural happenings or a romantic idealization of the world. It may rest upon a just sense of nature as the whole of which we are parts, while it also recognizes that we are parts that are marked by intelligence and purpose, having the capacity to strive by their aid to bring conditions into greater consonance with what is humanly desirable. Such piety is an inherent constituent of a just perspective in life.
>
> (LW 9:18)

Dewey agreed that a sense of reverent dependency on the world's ways is essential to mature religiosity. The second chapter develops his alternative to Santayana's materialistic fatalism and purely aesthetic religiosity.

Dewey was hostile toward the supremely unseen and unknowable, in either its spiritualist manifestations (inflating "liberal" religion) or its materialist versions (echoing Herbert Spencer), calling it "a shadow cast by the eclipse of the supernatural" (LW 9:57). Dewey had already complained that Santayana's version of naturalism is inhumanly "inarticulate, a kneeling, before the unknowable" (LW 3:74), in reaction to Santayana's 1923 lecture "The Unknowable" where he allied with the Unknowable of Spencer (Santayana 1936, 162). Santayana judges, as does Dewey (and Royce), that philosophy should not postulate the intrinsically unknowable, although human knowledge is evidently limited and fallible. But Dewey parts ways with Santayana when skepticism, even when grounded on what is known of nature, dictates too much about life. Santayana asserts: "How far knowledge is possible, therefore, can never be determined without first knowing the circumstances; and the very notion of knowledge ... is a notion that never could be framed without confident experience of sundry objects known and of persons able to know them" (Santayana 1936, 170–171). The single word "first" in this passage divides Dewey from Santayana. We do not have to know the circumstances (the what and the who) before framing our conception of the object of faith. Does any survey of what is now known, even the knowledge from the physical sciences, really have the right to dictate how intelligence operates and what it may operate upon? For Dewey, Santayana's fatalistic materialism is just as culpable for isolating religious experience from the rest of life as any revelatory religion.

Dewey warns against "the general tendency to mark off two distinct realms in one of which science has jurisdiction, while in the other, special modes of immediate knowledge of religious objects have authority. This dualism as it operates in contemporary interpretation of mystic experience in order to validate certain beliefs is but a reinstatement of the old dualism between the natural and the supernatural" (LW 9:26–27). This warning is delivered to science just as sternly as religion: scientific experience, even generously construed (as in Spencer and Santayana), has no more privileged access to truth and existence than religious experience has. The way that Santayana denies to the objects of religious contemplation any efficacy in the world does not exempt his synoptic naturalism from Dewey's critique. Imagination is surely essential to our appreciation of ideals, but our anticipation of what could become real through effort is the point of imagining, not a mystical adoration of the impossible. Dewey scolds Santayana in the first chapter for letting imagination play only a ancillary role instead of a harmonizing role in the ongoing life of the self (LW 9:13–14). The second chapter closes the trap on Santayana. Isolating faith's object in its own realm of being, as Santayana does, because our capacities seem so feeble in contrast to nature's powers, corrupts the true nature of ideals:

> It is admitted that the objects of religion are ideal in contrast with our present state. . . . The assumption that these objects of religion exist already in some realm of Being seems to add nothing to their force, while it weakens their claim over us as ideals, in so far as it bases that claim upon matters that are intellectually dubious. The question narrows itself to this: Are the ideals that move us genuinely ideal or are they ideal only in contrast with our present estate?
>
> (LW 9:29)

In the next paragraph, in defiance of both supernaturalism and materialism, Dewey sketches a realistic conception of a potently ideal God amenable to intelligence and effective action.

Is Dewey's God naturally real or merely ideal as a subjective idea or transcendental postulate? Unless "ideal" is summarily relegated to "fantasy," ideals are naturally real precisely where, like anything real, they make a dynamic difference: "the reality of ideal ends as ideals is vouched for by their undeniable power in action" (LW 9:30). Where is this dynamic activity? God is transactionally real where environing forces work in concert with ethical achievements (LW 9:34–35; see Shook 2018). But this natural God in itself is not destined to be the object of religious faith. Person and world, in a unified whole, are the objectives of religious faith. They are neither merely felt nor merely known, and they are not felt or known in their fullness. The fullness comes by way of imagination; the proper philosophical response is audacious speculation, albeit with due humility. Yet these are the ideal ends whereby the "self" is unified through religious experience. Our faith is that we can together become what we ardently desire to be as flourishing persons.

In the third chapter, Dewey argues that the natural home of religiosity must be larger than any church, or an entire religion. Dewey adapts from Royce the language of community in a most democratic and pluralistic vein. In its totality, the "community of causes and consequences" in which all persons actual and future are entwined has to exceed intellectual knowing but not imaginative valuation (LW 9:56). Dewey's final task in *A Common Faith* is to adjust Royce's idealistic philosophy of religion to his own imaginative vision. Royce's ideal ends were *not* imagined, although they did call out to the loyalty of whoever served a cause. Here Dewey and Royce agree: devoted service and human desire is the requisite power of response to religious experience. For Royce (1913), as *The Problem of Christianity* and other writings argue, proper objects of faith can be logically inferred from fragmentary and tragic experience. Dewey did not accept this kind of logical method, yet the ideal of community defended by Royce resonated with Dewey's view of the ideal unification of person and world. Within this encompassing growing whole, Dewey finds reason to seek grace in the doings and sufferings of the human community (LW 9:57).

Dewey's ideal-realism, exemplified in *A Common Faith*, represents the culmination of his reconstruction of absolutism into the experimentalism needed for an empirical naturalism. The fundamental unity of experience and existence in his philosophy is the key to interpreting Dewey's relationship with idealism, religion, and metaphysics.

Notes

1. They include John J. McDermott, Richard Bernstein, H. S. Thayer, Raymond Boisvert, Douglas Anderson, Richard Hart, Cornel West, and Dwayne Tunstall.
2. These names come to our mind: Henry Nelson Wieman, Victor Kestenbaum, Jennifer Welchman, Frank Oppenheim, James A. Good, and Stephen Rockefeller. We wish to particularly draw attention to Oppenheim (2005).
3. With regret we cannot do justice to most of the idealist-minded philosophers in dialogue with Dewey. Charles S. Peirce was a keen critic from 1894 until 1904, while Josiah Royce was prominent during 1910 until 1916. Edgar Sheffield Brightman was perhaps the most talented idealistic critic from the late 1920s onward. A.O. Lovejoy, C.I. Lewis, John Elof Boodin, William Ernest Hocking, and Charles Hartshorne were also important voices in the "idealistic" critique of Dewey.
4. Quoted by Herbert W. Schneider in Lamont (1959, 15). Dewey was referring to Coleridge (1829).
5. Dewey makes one more mention of personalism as a rival to totalitarianism, which he still perceived as an excessive individualism (LW 15:220–221). Dewey is probably referring to Emanuel Mounier's (1938) *A Personalist Manifesto* (chap. 2), but he oversimplifies its view. Dewey also mentioned personalism in a letter to Sidney Hook (1946.03.08, 13145), citing

Jacques Maritain by name. What Dewey thought about the label of personalism does not deter our exposition. Personalism is the convenient label for a metaphysical stance held by James, Royce, arguably Peirce, and many more idealists during Dewey's times such as B. P. Bowne, G. H. Howison, and E. S. Brightman. See Bengtsson (2006).

6. A close comparison of Royce's *Religious Aspect of Philosophy* with James's *The Principles of Psychology* shows how James preserves the empirical and phenomenological insights of Royce but denudes them of their dialectical and explicitly idealist context, especially with regard to theories of attention, the stream of consciousness, and the role of doubt in relation to postulation (Auxier 2013, chap. 7). Royce and James should both be credited with the primary insights; they were in more or less constant conversation from 1882 onward, but Royce published his book first. As for Dewey, he perceived Royce's position but kept a greater distance. Dewey does cite *The Religious Aspect of Philosophy* three times in his *Outlines of a Critical Theory of Ethics* (1891), which Royce promptly reviewed.

7. James's *Varieties of Religious Experience* kept Dewey cognizant of religious experience as a subfield in psychology and social thought. Dewey told a friend that "a chapter in his Varieties of Religious Experience are I think the best statements of 'pragmatism'" (1906.05.26, 02507: Dewey to Frank Manny).

8. Santayana's widely read essay "Ultimate Religion" (1933) made a response to his views especially important at that moment.

Works Cited

Citations of John Dewey's works are to the thirty-seven-volume critical edition published by Southern Illinois University Press under the editorship of Jo Ann Boydston. In-text citations give the original publication date and series abbreviation, followed by volume number and page number. For example: (1934, LW 10:12) is page 12 of *Art as Experience*, which is published as volume 10 of *The Later Works*.

Series abbreviations for *The Collected Works*:

EW *The Early Works* (1882–98)

MW *The Middle Works* (1899–1924)

LW *The Later Works* (1925–53)

Citations of Dewey's correspondence are to *The Correspondence of John Dewey*, 1871–2007, published by the InteLex Corporation under the editorship of Larry Hickman. In most cases, citations give the date, reference number for the letter, and author followed by recipient. For example: 1973.02.13 (22053): Herbert W. Schneider to H. S. Thayer.

Auxier, Randall E. 2013. *Time, Will, and Purpose: Living Ideas from the Philosophy of Josiah Royce*. Chicago: Open Court.

Bengtsson, Jan. 2006. *The Worldview of Personalism*. Oxford: Oxford University Press.

Coleridge, Samuel Taylor. 1829. *Aids to Reflection*, with a preliminary essay by James Marsh. Burlington, VT: Chauncey Goodrich.

Dalton, Thomas C. 2002. *Becoming John Dewey: Dilemmas of a Philosopher and Naturalist*. Bloomington: Indiana University Press.

Dewey, John. 1886. "Soul and Body." EW 1:93–115.

Dewey, John. 1889. "The Late Professor Morris." EW 3:3–13.

Dewey, John. 1894. *The Study of Ethics: A Syllabus*. EW 4:219–362.

Dewey, John. 1886. *Psychology*. EW 2.

Dewey, John. 1888. *Leibniz's New Essays Concerning the Human Understanding: A Critical Exposition*. EW 1:251–435.

Dewey, John. 1889. "The Philosophy of Thomas Hill Green." EW 3:14–35.

Dewey, John. 1890. "On Some Current Conceptions of the Term 'Self.'" EW 3:56–74.

Dewey, John. 1891a. "Moral Theory and Practice." EW 3:93–109.

Dewey, John. 1891b. *Outlines of a Critical Theory of Ethics*. EW 3:237–388.

Dewey, John. 1892. "Green's Theory of the Moral Motive." EW 3:155–173.

Dewey, John. 1893. "Christianity and Democracy." EW 4:3–10.

Dewey, John. 1900. "Review of Josiah Royce's *The World and the Individual, First Series*." MW 1:241–256.

Dewey, John. 1902. "Review of Josiah Royce's *The World and the Individual, Second Series*." MW 2:120–138.

Dewey, John. 1903. *Studies in Logical Theory*. MW 2:293–388.

Dewey, John. 1905a. "The Postulate of Immediate Empiricism." MW 3:158–167.

Dewey, John. 1905b. "The Realism of Pragmatism." MW 3:153–157.

Dewey, John. 1906. "Reality as Experience." MW 3:101–106.

Dewey, John. 1908. *Ethics*. MW 5.

Dewey, John. 1916. *Democracy and Education*. MW 9.

Dewey, John. 1922. *Human Nature and Conduct*. MW 14.

Dewey, John. 1925. *Experience and Nature*. LW 1.

Dewey, John. 1929a. *Individualism, Old and New*. LW 5:41–124.

Dewey, John. 1929b. *The Quest for Certainty*. LW 4.

Dewey, John. 1930. "From Absolutism to Experimentalism." LW 5:147–160.

Dewey, John. 1934. *A Common Faith*. LW 9.

Dewey, John. 1938. *Logic: The Theory of Inquiry*. LW 12.

Dewey, John. 1942. "How Is Mind to Be Known?" LW 15:27–33.

Dykhuizen, George. 1973. *The Life and Mind of John Dewey*. Carbondale: Southern Illinois University Press.

Eastman, Max. 1941. "John Dewey." *The Atlantic* 168: 671–685.

Hickman, Larry A. 1986. "Why Peirce Didn't Like Dewey's Logic." *Southwest Philosophy Review* 3: 178–189.

James, William. 1890. *The Principles of Psychology*. New York: Henry Holt.

James, William. 1929. *The Varieties of Religious Experience*. New York: Modern Library.

Lamont, Corliss, ed. 1959. *Dialogue on John Dewey*. New York: Horizon Press.

Marsh, James. 1843. *The Remains of the Rev. James Marsh*. Boston: Crocker and Brewster.

Morris, George S. 1880. *British Thought and Thinkers*. Chicago: Griggs.

Mounier, Emmanuel. 1938. *A Personalist Manifesto*. London: Longmans, Green.

Oppenheim, Frank. 2005. *Reverence for the Relations of Life: Re-imagining Pragmatism via Royce's Interactions with Peirce, James, and Dewey*. Notre Dame, IN: University of Notre Dame Press.

Royce, Josiah. 1885. *The Religious Aspect of Philosophy*. Boston, Houghton, Mifflin.

Royce, Josiah. 1900. *The World and the Individual, First Series*. New York: Macmillan.

Royce, Josiah. 1913. *The Problem of Christianity*. New York: Macmillan.

Santayana, George. 1933. "Ultimate Religion." In *Septimana Spinozana: Acta Conventus Oecumenici in Memoriam Benedicti de Spinoza Diei Natalis Trecent*. The Hague: Martinus Nijhoff, 105–115.

Santayana, George. 1936. "The Unknowable." In *Obiter Scripta: Lectures, Essays, and Reviews*, ed. J. Buchler and B. Schwartz. New York: Charles Scribner's, 162–188.

Seth, Andrew. 1887. *Hegelianism and Personality*. Edinburgh: W. Blackwood.

Shook, John R. 2000. *Dewey's Empirical Theory of Knowledge and Reality*. Nashville, TN: Vanderbilt University Press.

Shook, John R. 2004. "Jonathan Edwards's Contribution to John Dewey's Theory of Moral Responsibility." *History of Philosophy Quarterly* 21: 299–312.

Shook, John R. 2011. "Varieties of Twentieth Century American Naturalism." *The Pluralist* 6: 1–17.

Shook, John R. 2017. "The Nature Philosophy of John Dewey." *Dewey Studies* 1: 13–43.

Shook, John R. 2018. "A Unity with the Universe: Herder, Schelling, and Dewey on Natural Piety." In *The Routledge Handbook of Religious Naturalism*, ed. Donald Crosby and Jerome A. Stone. London and New York: Routledge, 55–67.

Shook, John R., and James A. Good. 2010. *John Dewey's Philosophy of Spirit, with Dewey's 1897 Lectures on Hegel*. New York: Fordham University Press.

Wenley, Robert M. 1917. *The Life and Work of George Sylvester Morris*. New York: Macmillan.

Woodbridge, Frederick J. E. 1905. "The Nature of Consciousness." *Journal of Philosophy* 2: 119–125.

CHAPTER 32

·····

PHILOSOPHY AND THE MIRROR OF CULTURE

On the Future and Function of Dewey Scholarship

·····

ERIN MCKENNA AND SCOTT L. PRATT

DEWEY scholarship is often framed against a background of Dewey's philosophical periods (early, middle, and late) or the received categories of academic philosophy (ethics, epistemology, metaphysics, and so on). Richard Rorty's "recovery" of Dewey in the 1980s established a different frame: scholarship of the "old" or nineteenth-century Dewey of *Experience and Nature* and that related to the "postmodern" Dewey of *The Quest for Certainty*. For some of Rorty's readers, this distinction marked the difference between careful, text-based considerations and scholarship driven by the reader's own agenda with a desire to enter into mainstream philosophical conversations. For others, Rorty's reconception of Dewey provided a new philosophical resource with which to engage the "linguistic turn" that had come to dominate American academic philosophy. While "traditional" Dewey scholarship continued to be marginalized in the discipline, a new generation of philosophers following Rorty and his students established a new division of work tracing its roots to Dewey. One side read Dewey in the context of twentieth-century Continental philosophy (in relation to Maurice Merleau-Ponty and Martin Heidegger, for example), and the other side read him as part of Anglo-American language philosophy (in relation to Wilfred Sellars, W. V. O. Quine, Hilary Putnam, and Donald Davidson), with the latter strongly supported by the work of Robert Brandom, Cheryl Misak, Colin Koopman, and others.

Rather than framing Deweyan philosophy against a background defined by the categories and debates of the past seventy years of American academic philosophy, we think that the more promising future for Deweyan philosophy is in the context he proposed in his 1931 paper, "Philosophy and Civilization." Dewey wrote:

> Philosophy ... sustains the closest connection with the history of culture, with the
> succession of changes in civilization. It is fed by the streams of tradition, traced at

critical moments to their sources in order that the current may receive a new direction . . . . But philosophy is not just a passive reflex of civilization that persists
through changes . . . [P]hilosophy marks a change of culture. In forming patterns to
be conformed to in future thought and action, it is additive and transforming in its
role in the history of civilization.

(1927, LW 3:7)

Philosophy on this account can be understood against a background framed by two
dispositions, one "a passive reflex" and the other "additive and transformational." The
resulting frame is both critical and constructive. On one hand, it provides a means
of assessing a philosophical work in terms of its relation to the culture from which it
emerges. It provides a means of examining the consequences of such a view—both its
ability to reflect the culture and time and its implications for the life of the culture. On
the other hand, as a constructive frame, it also supports the development of philosophical work that challenges the status quo, resists its commitments, and offers something
in its place. The two sides are not sharply separated since the constructive side turns on
an informed critique of the dominant ways of thinking that result from a careful examination of philosophy that starts as a passive reflex.

Dewey carried out this sort of analysis through most of his career. Perhaps the most
often ignored example was published in 1915 as *German Philosophy and Politics*.[1] The
book began as three lectures given at University of North Carolina, Chapel Hill in
February 1915. World War I had begun just six months earlier. Dewey's thesis in the
lectures was that German philosophy (mostly identified with Immanuel Kant) had
made war likely. His claim was not that philosophy by itself caused the war but that it
served at least as a mirror reflecting "contemporary social struggles" and, as a mirror,
provided a "definitely practical aid" in realizing the ends it reflected (1915, MW 8:199).
Twenty-seven years later and three years into World War II, Dewey published a second
edition of *German Philosophy and Politics* where he concluded in his new introduction
that Hitler's rise depended on these same philosophical commitments.

In this discussion, we consider contemporary Deweyan philosophy in the context
of Dewey's contrast between "reigning philosophies" (1915, MW 8:199) that mirror the
commitments of the culture and philosophies of resistance that seek to change those
commitments. As a mirror of culture, philosophy re-presents and formalizes widely
held commitments to problem-solving practices and beliefs that are how individuals
in a culture understand themselves and the world. Philosophy in this form is an engine
of conservation feeding back into the culture through its institutions a rationale for its
main commitments, guarding it against disruption, and promoting the smooth progress of its people and ideas along a shared path. Philosophies of resistance, by contrast,
begin as responses to experienced problems that emerge when established institutions
and the habits of daily life fail. Philosophy of this sort emerges when widely held beliefs
and practices of inquiry do not address the problems at hand. Criticism gives way to a
search for alternative ways of thinking and acting. Philosophies of resistance are not,
for Dewey, simply the negation of existing ideas. Such either/or philosophy reflects a

reigning philosophy and serves as a means of conserving present culture by affirming or negating it whole. Either way, the status quo is preserved as the ever-present structure that determines the central commitments of the culture (1938, LW 13:7–8).

First, we consider Dewey's analysis of the reigning philosophy focusing on the two aspects that he held were responsible for its support of war and later the rise of Nazism in Germany: the commitment to absolute moral norms and the separation of reason and experience. We then argue that linguistic pragmatism likewise mirrors present American culture and consider in particular the work of Robert Brandom.[2] What the mirror reveals is that while American culture has set aside a commitment to absolute moral principles, it has retained a commitment to the separation of reason and experience, now manifested as a separation between language and experience. We argue that in this case the reigning philosophy has not yet brought world war but aid for the political movement that elected Donald Trump in 2016. Following Dewey, the passive reflex of a reigning philosophy also provides the resources necessary for resistance. By reading linguistic pragmatism through this lens, we can find means to respond to the experience of living in "Trump's America." Dewey's analysis in 1915 directs his twenty-first century readers, who face the prospect of new wars and violence, to use philosophy as a critical tool. We conclude with a survey of some of those resources—philosophies of resistance and some of the basic concepts that can serve as new resources in the American philosophical tradition.

THE LOGIC OF FANATICISM

When Dewey gave his lectures in 1915, he declared that German philosophers had evaded "the logic of experience, only to become, in the phrase of a recent writer, the spoil of a 'logic of fanaticism.' Weapons forged in the smithy of the Absolute become brutal and cruel when confronted by merely human resistance" (1915, MW 8:159). By separating experience from reason, Dewey argued, Kant had laid the groundwork for the rise of political absolutism and its attendant violence. The phrase "the logic of fanaticism" was from George Santayana. In November 1914, just three months after war was declared across Europe, Santayana wrote a piece for *The New Republic* in which he argued that Germany was simultaneously seen as the height of "Culture" and the epitome of barbarous behavior. Germans were the height of "Culture" because they had surpassed individualism and "subdued their souls for the better service of the State[.]" But their barbarian side, according to Santayana, was seen in being "ruthless, appealing deliberately and even from a sense of duty to any and every means which is expected to further their national purposes; and again on the deeper ground that they are singly determined to carry out an a priori impulse or Absolute Will, which their philosophers have found to be agitating the whole universe and more particularly their own bosoms" (1914, 18). This sense of being ordained to lead the world to some "absolute and supreme end" is what compelled them to take ruthless action on behalf of the good of the world.

But the discounting of individuals in the pursuit of some absolute end is also what made them barbarians. Santayana continued, "The pursuit of any single end, ravishing and incomparable as it may seem to the enthusiast, strains and impoverishes human nature, and sometimes, by detaching it too much from common and humble feelings, actually debauches it. Indeed, the inhumanity of fanaticism does not lie chiefly in the conscientious crimes which it dictates here and there; It lies rather in the miserable Imaginary end Itself, for the sake of which those crimes are committed" (1914, 19). In other words, the logic of fanaticism allows the end to justify the means, but the end pursued is necessarily disconnected since individual thought and imagination have not been part of forming the end pursued and the end is artificially fixed and static.

This article was clearly on Dewey's mind when he prepared his 1915 lectures.[3] Santayana emphasized the willingness of Germans to subordinate themselves to the State as the source of the logic of fanaticism. Dewey sought to explain that willingness in philosophical terms. While standard accounts of the conflict, now and at the time, focused on political or economic causes, Dewey argued for the centrality of a philosophical view as a necessary condition of the war. Alone, perhaps, among the commentators, Dewey attributed the origins of the conflict to the philosopher of *Perpetual Peace*, Immanuel Kant.

Throughout this text Dewey pointed to the impact ideas have on practical and political action—that is, he was focused on the centrality of philosophy for people's lives. While he acknowledged that politics also serve to control the development of philosophical ideas, he stressed philosophy's formative role in the unfolding conflict of the time. He said that even if he did no more than convince the reader that philosophical ideas *reflect* a society's view of itself he would still have made the case for the impact of philosophy on politics in *this* case because the views reflected perpetuated the idea that Germany and the German people took themselves to be the ultimate development of Truth and Reason. "When what a people sees in its intellectual looking glass is its own organization and its own historic evolution as an organic instrument of the accomplishment of an Absolute Will and Law, the articulating and consolidating efficacy of the reflection is immensely intensified" (1915, MW 8:199). The logic of German thinking, Dewey held, was the conclusion that a German victory was a victory for all of humanity. "First, the German Luther who saved for mankind the principle of spiritual freedom against Latin externalism; then Kant and Fichte, who wrought out the principle into a final philosophy of science, morals and the State; as conclusion, the German nation organized in order to win the world to recognition of the principle, and thereby to establish the rule of freedom and science in humanity as a whole" (1915, MW 8:181).

This division of freedom and science is the key for Dewey's analysis of Kant. Kant's main contribution, according to Dewey, was that reason rules in the sensible world and results in science, but reason also rules in the supersensible (noumenal) world and results in moral duty and freedom. The rule of reason in science resulted in the "unsurpassed technical efficiency and organization in the varied fields of action" (1915, MW: 151)—foreshadowing the technological efficiency of the Third Reich's Final Solution. However, while science can free humans from superstition and sentimentalism, it cannot achieve true freedom. That is only found in the supersensible world and the idea of moral obligation. "The fact of duty, the existence of a categorical command to act thus and so, no matter what the pressure of physical surroundings or the incitation of animal inclinations, is as much a fact as the existence of knowledge of the physical world . . . . The very existence of a command in man to act for the sake of what ought to be—no matter what actually is—is thus of itself final proof of the operation of supersensible reason within human experience . . . within moral experience" (1915, MW 8:149–150). Being rational, regardless of experience, is what puts humans above the rest of nature for Kant; there is no freedom in the sensible world, only in the supersensible, moral world. So, Dewey affirms Santayana's analysis that Germany represents a dualism of commitment, but for Dewey this dualism is captured by Kant's division between the sensible and supersensible so that Germany can lead the world in science and technical efficiency *and* be committed to an abstract ideal independent of experience. That is, Kant brings "an imaginative synthesis" that helps to "formulate a sense of national mission and destiny" (1915, MW 8:152). But for Dewey this sense of national mission and destiny is more dangerous than helpful.

"A physical catastrophe, an earthquake or conflagration, acts only where it happens," Dewey said. "While its effects endure, it passes away." Philosophical ideas for Dewey can be more dangerous than an earthquake since they are abstract, "that is to say, severed from the circumstances of their origin, and through embodiment in language capable of operating in remote climes and alien situations. Time heals physical ravages, but it may only accentuate the evils of an intellectual catastrophe—for by no lesser name can we call a systematic intellectual error" (1915, MW 8:143). The "intellectual catastrophe" in this case is the separation of the sensible and supersensible and the accompanying belief that the freedom of agents is independent of experience. These ideas are made still more dangerous because philosophers claim "to be concerned not with contemporary problems of living, but the essential Truth and Reality viewed under the form of eternity" (1915, MW 8:143–144). This means philosophical ideas are meant to be separable from experience; they are meant to be objective, eternal, and universal.[4]

Freedom for Dewey is found in the ability to apply creative intelligence to problems as they arise in one's life so that one opens up future possibilities for action. Freedom is not simply had but achieved by constant transactive adjustment to one's environment and other people in that environment. Part of the problem for Dewey is that, on the German model, freedom becomes a fixed concept found only in the rational mind or will. "Freedom is *consciousness* of freedom. Liberty of action has little to do with it" (1915, MW 8:195). Further, the only way to achieve this inner freedom is to subordinate oneself physically and politically to the State. "In contrast with this realm of inner freedom stands that of civil and political action, the principle of which is obedience or subordination to constituted authority" (1915, MW 8:157). On this model, an individual's first duty is to the State (1915, MW 8:193) of which the individual only exists as a member. The law of reason leads people to the State, not natural sociability (1915, MW 8:171). This is, in part, why Kant embraced duty and rejected the give and take of utilitarianism and rights. Dewey says, "[T]he conception of duty is one-sided, expressing command on one side and obedience on the other, while rights are at least reciprocal." He attributes to French philosophy the focus on social and political rights that are formed and achieved through discussion, compromise, and mutual adjustment. Similarly, he finds English philosophy's focus on the intelligent self-interest of utilitarianism to be a philosophy rooted in the social nature of human beings and the developing and adaptive nature of moral philosophy. "[T]he characteristic moral contribution of English thought— intelligent self-interest . . . at least evokes a picture of merchants bargaining, while the categorical imperative," he concluded, "calls up the drill sergeant" (1915, MW 8:166).

That Kant dismisses sociability and happiness concerned Dewey. "[P]ersons who profess no regard for happiness as a test of action have an unfortunate way of living up to their principle by making others unhappy. I should entertain some suspicion of the complete sincerity of those who profess disregard for their own happiness, but I should be quite certain of their sincerity when it comes to a question of my happiness" (1915, MW 8:166–167). While many take discounting happiness as a sign of moral maturity, Dewey saw it as a dangerous sign of callousness and inhumanity. Not only is duty a threat to happiness, but it is also a threat to intelligent experimentation and adjustment. "A gospel of duty separated from empirical purposes and results tends to gag intelligence. It substitutes for the work of reason displayed in a wide and distributed survey of consequences in order to determine where duty lies an inner consciousness, empty of content, which clothes with the form of rationality the demand of existing social authorities" (1915, MW 8:164). *Duty is separated from experience.* Claiming that justice must be the revelation of spirit rather than the "mere means" of securing human welfare is a kind of emotional rhetoric. Dewey says that "During an ordinary course of things, it passes for but an emotional indulgence; in a time of stress and strain, it exhibits itself as surrender of intelligence to passion" (1915, MW 8:165).

Duty separated from experience results in a reliance on a priori absolutes and rules out experimentalism in the realm of morals. "The situation puts in relief what finally is at issue between a theory which is pinned to a belief in an Absolute beyond history and behind experience, and one which is frankly experimental. For any philosophy which is not consistently experimental will always traffic in absolutes no matter in how disguised a form. In German political philosophy, the traffic is without mask" (1915, MW 8:182). The commitment to absolutism is clear and is clearly an error—an "intellectual catastrophe." Once experience and experimentalism are set aside, moral self-righteousness can reign. When this is combined with a sense of national destiny, unrestrained patriotism can lead to dreams of world domination in which everyone is "free." "Philosophical justification of war follows inevitably from a philosophy of history composed in nationalistic terms. History is the movement, the march of God on earth through time. Only one nation at a time can be the latest and hence the fullest realization of God . . . . The idea that friendly intercourse among all the peoples of the earth is a legitimate aim of human effort is in basic contradiction of such a philosophy" (1915, MW 8:197).

On Dewey's account, these philosophical commitments resulted in a German state that believed it had the duty to conquer and control others in the name of progress. In contrast, he suggests that this kind of philosophy had not gained a grip in the United States, outside of a few intellectual circles, because "Our social organization commits us to this philosophy of life. Our working principle is to try: to find out by trying, and to measure the worth of the ideas and theories tried by the success with which they meet the test of application in practice. Concrete consequences rather than *a priori* rules supply our guiding principles" (1915, MW 8:200). Dewey argued that German philosophy sees social constitutions as something to be developed in the abstract in order to guide social development. In contrast, American philosophy sees them as the "cumulative result of a multitude of daily and ever-renewed choices" (1915, MW 8:200).

Dewey clarified that this American philosophy is an experimental rather than an empiricist philosophy. Empiricism catalogues occurrences but they have no directing power. By contrast, "In an experimental philosophy of life, the question of the past, of precedents, of origins, is quite subordinate to prevision, to guidance and control amid future possibilities. Consequence rather than antecedents measure the worth of theories. Any scheme or project may have a fair hearing provided it promise amelioration in the future; and no theory or standard is so sacred that it may be accepted simply on the basis of past performance" (1915, MW 8:201).

The problem with German philosophy, for Dewey, was not its conscious method and organization. In fact, much can be learned from their "methodic and organized intelligence" (1915, MW:202). The problem was that this intelligence was put in the service of ends that were predetermined by the State rather than using such intelligence to arrive at the ends themselves. On the German model, the ends are absolute and not revisable, and everything is subordinated to those ends. On Dewey's American model, ends are hypothetical, tentative and to be improved upon (1915, MW 8:202).

Dewey says that for America "our history is too obviously future" so we rely on "inventive imagination" checked by "results achieved." "I can but think that the present European situation forces home upon us the need for constructive planning. I can but think that while it gives no reason for supposing that creative power attaches *ex officio* to general ideas, it does encourage us to believe that a philosophy which should articulate and consolidate the ideas to which our social practice commits us would clarify and guide our future endeavor" (1915, MW 8: 202–203). This experimental philosophy turns ideas into experiences, which then shape future ideas and experiences. In order to most effectively carry out this experimental philosophy, peace and increased social intercourse should guide our endeavors.

Peace is a goal, for Dewey, not because it equals a lack of disturbance but because peace allows for fruitful cooperation and experimentation among peoples. But he wonders if even America is yet up to the task of living by its own philosophy.

> Promoting the efficacy of human intercourse irrespective of class, racial, geographical and national limits. Any philosophy which should penetrate and particulate our present social practice would find at work the forces which unify human intercourse. An intelligent and courageous philosophy of practice would devise means by which the operation of these forces would be extended and assured in the future.

> An American philosophy of history must perforce be a philosophy for the future, a future in which freedom and fullness of human companionship is the aim, and intelligent cooperative experimentation the method.
>
> (1915, MW 8:204)

One might object that this is itself an idealism. But in Dewey's terms this is an end-in-view that guides intelligent thought and action even if it is never fully achieved.

That this aim was not fulfilled in the wake of World War I was made evident when Germany, this time under the leadership of Hitler, began a second world war. Hitler was not a disciple of Kant and Hegel, but his rise depended on the philosophical dispositions and doctrines developed by Kant and inculcated in German education (and philosophical education worldwide) and in German notions of the state. On this German account, one cannot encounter "experience" except through the mediation of reason. The philosophical disposition that makes duty the primary means of life and reason the realm of freedom uniquely (or at least distinctively) connected German philosophy and politics and prepared the German people to follow an autocratic leader into a war that disrupted the lives, economies, and culture of Germany and the rest of Europe. When Dewey returned to the topic in 1943, he argued that the rise of Hitler was made possible by the very same philosophical disposition. This latter argument was framed more especially around the apparent German willingness to accept authoritarian leadership without question. Here the failure or inability to question could be attributed, again, to the separation of experience and reason explicit in Kant's philosophy and implicit in the philosophical disposition of German culture. We claim that the phenomenon of the 2016 presidential campaign and election also trades on the presence of a philosophical view that parallels the German philosophy Dewey describes.

THE GAGGING OF INTELLIGENCE BY THE LINGUISTIC TURN

Kant was imperial Germany's philosophical mirror and provided direction for its politics. As Dewey claimed, "Even if we went so far as to say that reigning philosophies simply reflect as in a mirror contemporary social struggles, we should have to add that seeing one's self in a mirror is a definite practical aid" (1915 MW 8:199). We claim that philosophy after the "linguistic turn" is the mirror of Trump's America and provides direction for its politics. For most linguistic turn philosophers, it seemed clear that experience, whatever it involved, could only be approached through language. Such philosophy had two virtues. It recognized that absolutes—whether claims about duty or truths of God—were relative to the language that expressed them and that language and experience are separate. Eliminating Kant's commitment to absolute duty answered one of Dewey's worries, but the separation of language and experience ignored his second.

As Richard Rorty observed, in the resulting "linguistic philosophy," "philosophical problems are problems which may be solved (or dissolved) either by reforming language or by understanding more about the language we presently use" (1967, 3). The philosophical mirror of American culture indicates that solving or dissolving problems is a matter of changing language not experience. From the end of World War II to the present day, linguistic philosophy, in various forms, has come to dominate the philosophic world, clearing the way for Trump's America.

By severing the connection between experience and reason, language becomes the one way of motivating and framing action. Freedom is no longer something that is achieved and tracked in experience but something that is talked about in certain ways. Policies and politicians become judged by how their language squares with the language that is affirmed as stating values ("Support the troops!" "Cut taxes!" "Preserve the Second Amendment!"). Our claim is not that such politicians are fascists but that their views have elements of an oppressive philosophy that is parallel (or shares a logical or ordering structure) with the strand of German philosophy that Dewey identified. Hitler was a product of Kantian thought as surely as Trump was a product of the linguistic turn.

What is primarily at work here is the notion that separation of reason and experience is the problem. Language philosophers who reduce pragmatism to a method are as fanatical in this separation as German philosophy was in separating the sensible from the supersensible. To believe that one can separate reason and experience is to follow the German model and "gag intelligence."

> A gospel of duty separated from empirical purposes and results tends to gag intelligence. It substitutes for the work of reason displayed in a wide and distributed survey of consequences in order to determine where duty lies an inner consciousness, empty of content, which clothes with the form of rationality the demands of existing social authorities. A consciousness which is not based upon and checked by consideration of actual results upon human welfare is none the less socially irresponsible because labeled Reason.
>
> (1915, MW 8:164–165)

For Dewey, "Kant detected and formulated the direction in which the German genius was moving, so that his philosophy is of immense prophetic significance" (1915, MW 8:152). Kant serves as a diagnostic tool for understanding the rise of authoritarianism in Germany. We think that twentieth and twenty-first century language philosophy is similarly prophetic.

Dewey's response to German philosophy was to propose a counterveiling American philosophy. On one hand, America was too new to have a single philosophy and so was able to engage in the process of inquiry within experience and, on the other, America is (presumably) able to avoid absolutism. The resistance Dewey recommends is twofold. One sort challenges absolutism, the singular devotion to duty where duty is dictated by the state. The other challenges the separation of experience and reason. One could easily argue that the United States adopted the first form of resistance and for much of the twentieth century challenged state absolutism in its various forms. One could even argue that, for many, especially in the academy, the challenge to absolutism needed to be as aggressively pursued at home as it was abroad in opposing authoritarian regimes. At home, the challenge, led by the pragmatists in the early century and then by a wide range of thinkers later in the century, took on the idea that there are "absolute" truths—in religion, in science, in ethics, and in politics. In fine Deweyan form, intellectuals challenged the unquestioned truths of religion and politics, arguing that present circumstances showed the limits of "truths" adopted for different times in light of different inquiries and problems.

Dewey, in his assessment of the American philosophical attitude, was, of course, too optimistic. In Jim Crow America where Blacks were forced into separate schools and backseats, women were prohibited from voting in national elections, indigenous people were held on reservations, and the poor had little or no support, freedom was something at best limited to a certain group and at worst was accessible to almost no one thanks to the conditions required to maintain the social hierarchy. Still, the outlook recommended had the potential to respond to even these pervasive American problems because it demanded attention for experienced problems and rejected the idea that answers would be framed by absolutism. One can argue that only one side of Dewey's response to German politics became central to philosophy in America and its politics.

By mid-century in the wake of World War II the rejection of absolutism became the primary philosophical goal. The logical positivism that came to dominate American academic philosophy in the 1940s and 1950s was predicated on the idea that philosophy needed to separate itself from all forms of philosophical absolutism, replacing its concern with a focus on understanding how claims about the world could be verified. The unverified and unverifiable claims of absolutism were, in the view of philosophers like Otto Neurath and Rudolph Carnap, responsible for the rise of totalitarianism in Europe and the fall of philosophy. If philosophy was to make any contribution to the postwar world, it would be as a steadfast critique of absolutism and adherence to claims that were empirically meaningless. The shift of philosophical focus to the verification of claims led to a shift in the central questions of philosophy, what Gustav Bergmann called the "linguistic turn." By the 1950s, however, the positivists' quest for verification came to be seen as a new dogma that itself needed to be set aside if philosophy was to remain committed to its opposition to absolutism in all its forms. The linguistic turn became a discipline-wide focus on language as the fundamental subject matter for philosophical investigation.[5]

From a Deweyan perspective, the language philosophers, like Kant, were not involved in independent speculation but rather were in conversation with their culture. In this case, the effective rejection of absolutism implies the sharp separation of language from experience even as language also was understood as the sole source of meaning. If Dewey is right about philosophy as a culture-work in dialogue with dominant habits of thought and problem-solving, then it is not a surprise that language philosophy emerged alongside an increasing skepticism of principles and institutions that claimed universal truth and application. The dominant philosophical disposition of American culture was in conversation with its philosophers and often set aside absolutes in favor of concern about the saying of things. Language finally achieved the role that reason held in a Kantian universe. Like reason, language became the sole resource for making experience meaningful and for the verification of claims. The vision of Deweyan democracy where inquiry is of experience, and absolutes do not exist, is overridden by a focus on the language one chooses to account for the experience. Just as Dewey uses Kant as a means of understanding German politics, so language philosophy can be used as a means of understanding American politics. While there are many points of entry to understanding the relation of language philosophy and American politics, we choose linguistic pragmatism because it inherits parts of Dewey's project but rejects its overall mission.

Robert Brandom is, for us, a case in point. As a pragmatist of the linguistic turn, Brandom puts "language at the center of philosophical concerns and [understands] philosophical problems to begin with in terms of the language one uses in formulating them" (2011, 22). Such a pragmatist, Brandom observes, "take[s] it that the most important feature of the natural history of creatures like us is that we have *come into language*" which requires, theoretically anyway, addressing three questions concerning the issues of demarcation, emergence, and leverage (2011, 26). Demarcation is definitional; marking the difference between "sentience" and "sapience" distinguished by the "core practices" of sapient beings: giving and asking for reasons. Emergence explains how such discursive creatures can emerge from a world of "non- or pre-linguistic creatures" or, as he puts it elsewhere, what "distinguishes us from the beasts of the forest and field" (2009, 154). And leverage characterizes "the massive qualitative difference in capacity between linguistic … creatures" and those same beasts (2011, 27).

The demarcation question turns out to be central for Brandom and for our Deweyan analysis of the relationship between language philosophy and American politics. For Brandom the demarcation of rational human agents from other creatures is a basic Kantian idea, "the axis around which all [Kant's] thought turns, … that what distinguishes exercises of judgment and intentional agency from the performances of merely natural creatures is that judgments and actions are subject to distinctive kinds of *normative* assessment" (2011, 1–2). The normative assessment, from the linguistic pragmatist perspective, is the ability to give and ask for reasons for judgments and actions. The necessary demarcation here serves the same function as the separation Dewey identified in Kant as the separation between the external realm of science and causation and the internal moral realm in which agents are responsible for their judgments.

For Kant, the internal realm is where individuals can be free. Brandom says "Kantian positive freedom is the *rational* capacity to adopt *normative statuses*: the ability to *commit* oneself, the *authority* to make oneself *responsible*" (2009, 59). For Brandom as a linguistic pragmatist, this capacity is linguistic and involves our ability to commit to a "vocabulary" in terms of which we can give reasons. The choice of vocabulary we use marks who we are as agents and how we relate to each other and our own sense of meaning. "For what we really, essentially are, *in* ourselves, depends on what we are *for* ourselves. It depends on which vocabulary for self-description we adopt, endorse, interpret ourselves in terms of, and so identify with" (2009, 155). Freedom is our ability to commit to, to choose, a vocabulary that makes us who we are and establishes our grounds for judgment: this is the language in which we ask for and give reasons. The separation between the realms of the beast and the realms of rational human beings leaves behind *merely* sentient responses to the environment, experience in some direct sense. Here, the beasts are wordless, and their experience, whatever it may be, remains inaccessible.

Unlike Kant, however, Brandom's external world of beasts is not a world of science and causation. Where Kant's external world is a world of order, Brandom's is a jungle, inaccessible to reasons and outside concern. For Kant, the separation of the internal from the external means that the processes of reason are separated from actual experience and so the principles established by reason are not subject to empirical test or reform. For Brandom, vocabularies are likewise protected from experience in that experience can enter into the space of reasons for purposes of inquiry only if it enters that space as language, as part of the vocabulary that makes reasoning possible. The separation of reason from experience in Kant is mirrored by the separation of language and experience in Brandom.

Dewey argued that German philosophy was committed to absolutism and that American politics—or at least American culture—could not abide absolutism of this sort. Brandom's language philosophy is consistent with this cultural character. That there is no antecedent determination of which is the best vocabulary for us to choose allows his view to escape with Dewey from the absolutism of the Kaiser and Hitler. If American politics mirrors language philosophy, it is not an absolutist affair. But does it support the democratic community that Dewey sought?

The world of American politics, if we analyze it as a manifestation of language philosophy, is rather a politics framed by the battle of vocabularies that provide us with the self-descriptions to which we can commit and which make us who we are. The choice of vocabularies is not a matter of inquiry, or of truth and falsity as these emerge in the process of inquiry, since the selection of a vocabulary is itself a process of choosing the language with which truth and falsity will be determined. For Kant, the key to German politics is the ability of the people to be at once free and ordered by the state. For American politics, the key is to be at once free and not ordered by the state because the nonlinguistic world is empty of meaning, and order (such as it is) is a matter of the language we choose.[6]

And now it should be clear how Dewey's assessment of German philosophy and politics is relevant to American philosophy and politics in the mainstream. For many, one of the most confusing aspects of the 2016 presidential election was the apparent ability of the candidate Donald Trump to make claims that were patently false and yet were endorsed with enthusiasm by millions of Americans. At the same time, candidate Hillary Clinton, who was also fact-checked constantly, was routinely found to be more truthful than her rival. The observation led many in the press to accuse Trump supporters of being ill-informed, gullible, or just plain stupid. A Deweyan analysis of American politics in light of our discussion of language philosophy should lead us to give this aspect of the election a second look. If the philosophical commitments of these many supporters of Trump (and perhaps of Clinton as well) were animated by a philosophical disposition of the sort captured by Brandom's linguistic pragmatism, then the really important feature of Trump's and Clinton's speeches was not their veracity as some product of inquiry but rather their ability to be endorsed as formative vocabularies for large groups of people seeking meaning. From this perspective, that Trump spoke in contradictions or repeated conspiracy theories or attacked women and racial minorities did not affect his supporters because they shared the idea that language and experience are separable. What was important for his supporters was the way his claims about the world provided a sense of meaning and self-description, how the claims helped formulate who they are as agents. What Dewey said of German philosophy's gospel of duty could also be said about the rhetoric of Trump. "During an ordinary course of things, it passes for but an emotional indulgence; in a time of stress and strain, it exhibits itself as surrender of intelligence to passion" (1915, MW 8:165).

In the wake of the election, many supporters reported that they did not think that the winning candidate would actually do the things he said. The specific calls to action, or claims about the world, were not what led to a positive vote. Instead, they reported that what Trump said marked a new direction, or expressed frustration that they shared, or gave voice to things that the opposing candidate's language failed to express. Brandom can account for such an approach as part of what he called the "most sophisticated conception of sapience." In this conception, we are "creatures of our positive expressive freedom—beings structured and driven by the description of ourselves that we endorse at each stage in our development—hence self-creating beings, who can change what we are in ourselves by changing what we are for ourselves, by identifying with new descriptions of ourselves, by adopting new vocabularies" (Brandom 2009, 154–155). For Brandom, Trump gave many the vocabulary necessary to change who they were—from agents who felt excluded from opportunity they imagined their parents had and who felt afraid of the ways in which "their people" were no longer the dominant people to agents confident of their future and place in the world. This is the intellectual error that worried Dewey—it leaves the vulnerable more vulnerable in actual experience.

Returning to Dewey's worry about German philosophy, the philosophical dispositions of Germany, however justified they may be for those who adopted them, led to war. By separating reason and experience, the German mainstream could follow a path to war without the ability to question it, to see its potential consequences and change course. The same separation emerging in the American mainstream runs comparable risks. Separating vocabularies of self-creation from the experiences and consequences of such self-creation runs the clear risk of leading to, in fact already has led to, violence and exclusion and the inability to hear alternative views and to formulate shared concerns and social action. From a Deweyan point of view, language philosophy provides us with valuable resources to understand present politics but also highlights that language philosophy must be examined for its inherit dangers as a philosophical view that has catastrophic consequences. Recall Dewey's words: "Time heals physical ravages, but it may only accentuate the evils of an intellectual catastrophe—for by no lesser name can we call a systematic intellectual error" (1915, MW 8:143). The catastrophe here is that when linguistic pragmatism gags intelligence, through appeals to reason or language separated from experience, "the logic of fanaticism" is unleashed again.

RECONSTRUCTED MIRRORS OF CULTURE

We have argued that philosophy matters for the world. But it matters in different ways, and these differences are important to understand in order to make some suggestions about future Dewey scholarship. A common way for Dewey scholars to understand the idea that philosophy matters for the world is the idea that philosophy should take up practical social and political concerns of the day—that philosophy should be engaged with real-world problems. Many who study the work of Dewey take this seriously and put his (and other) views to work in the world by taking up specific problems related to gender, race, power, war, the environment, and animals. We conclude with a few examples of scholarship that takes seriously both the mirror of culture and the need to transform culture. We also point to work that seeks to reconstruct mirrors that open up new and different possibilities.

If Dewey is right, philosophers can and should help reconstruct American culture in light of the experience of a pluralistic world at increasing environmental and economic risk. Resources for reconstruction are already available in American philosophies of resistance, including the work of the classical pragmatists Peirce, James, and Dewey— read outside the mirror of linguistic philosophy—and the broader tradition of activist philosophers including W. E. B. Du Bois, Jane Addams, Mary Follett, Horace Kallen, Alain Locke, Rachel Carson, Angela Davis, Vine Deloria Jr., and many others. For these thinkers, philosophy worth the name began in response to experienced problems— situations marked by confusion, doubt, indeterminacy—and then returned to these problems, aiming to change and reconstruct them in ways that allowed the inquirer to go forward, to encounter still more experience. Philosophy as a mirror became a means of resistance and a tool of transformation.

Some of this work is done by starting with careful analysis of the texts and showing how the real-world problems arise in Dewey's work itself. Gregory Fernando Pappas's (2008) *John Dewey's: Ethics: Democracy as Experience* and Steven Fesmire's (2015) *Dewey* are examples of this kind of work. *The Pluralist, The Transactions of the Charles S. Peirce Society, The Journal of Speculative Philosophy, Educational Theory, Dewey Studies*, and the *Inter-American Journal of Philosophy* are journals that often include work on Dewey's thought and writings. Scholarship in this vein is important for several reasons. First, while it builds on previous Dewey scholarship (such as work by Thomas Alexander and Larry Hickman), it often corrects earlier incomplete or incorrect readings of Dewey's work. Second, it introduces Dewey's work to an audience who may have had no exposure to his thinking. Third, it shows how Dewey's writing has been, and can continue to be, a resource for addressing pressing problems. This then supports those who are more engaged in scholarship directly applying Dewey's thinking to such problems.

Some examples of this "applied" scholarship include *The Human Eros: Eco-ontology and the Aesthetics of Existence* by Thomas M. Alexander (2013), which uses Dewey to provide a pragmatic ecological philosophy; *Living as Learning: John Dewey in the 21st Century* by Jim Garrison, Larry Hickman, and Daisaku Ikeda (2014) uses Dewey and Buddhism to provide resources for navigating an increasingly globalized world; *John Dewey, a Peace-Minded Educator* by Charles F. Howlett and Audrey Cohan (2016) documents Dewey's complex views of, and commitment to, pacifism and show how his views on this are an important resource for the world today. Charlene Haddock Seigfried's (2001) *Feminist Interpretations of John Dewey* both gathered emerging work using Dewey in a feminist context and inspired work that continues today some of which can be found in *Contemporary Feminist Pragmatism* (Bardwell Jones and Hamington 2012). Contemporary Dewey scholarship also includes numerous journal articles that use Dewey to address pressing present problems. A few examples will have to suffice to make this point: Steven Fesmire's "Useful for What? Dewey's Call to Humanize Techno-Industrial Civilization," Erin McKenna's "Eating Apes, Eating Cows," and Shane Ralston's "A Deweyan Defense of Guerilla Gardening." In addition to the journals mentioned already, *Pragmatism Today* and *Contemporary Pragmatism* are some of the journals that regularly feature work using Dewey to discuss contemporary issues, and this is work that needs to continue.

This kind of scholarship is important for several reasons. First, as with the more "historical" work, it introduces Dewey to people interested in working on contemporary problems who may never have encountered Dewey or who have read accounts that argue that Dewey is irrelevant to such concerns. Second, it lives out the Deweyan spirit of philosophy by putting philosophy in the service of real-world problems more than in the service of the profession of philosophy itself. Third, it pushes Dewey's thinking in new directions, provides corrections to limitations in Dewey's thought, and encourages philosophy as a discipline to understand itself as engaged thinking that makes a difference in people's lives.

Both of these kinds of scholarship need to continue, but we think there also needs to be special attention paid to a set of key ideas: power, resistance, boundary, place, pluralism, agency, fallibilism, and hope. Power is often understood as the ability to act, but it can also be understood as the ability to dominate or the ability to cooperate ("power over" and "power with" as Mary Parker Follett described it). Resistance involves responding to power as domination, but it also involves reconstructing the situations at hand and building new opportunities. Using collaborative power focuses on the importance of understanding agency not just of individuals but of communities and others with whom we share the environment. Differences among agents are essential to fostering collaboration, and the conservation of differences provides a means of sustaining pluralism across boundaries.

To understand the power of people and nature, for example, it is important to understand how the place of the specific people and nature has helped shape who they are, the experiences they have had, and the sense of agency with which they live. This kind of situated knowledge includes some awareness of boundaries that help delineate specific peoples and natures and allows for the possibility of understanding within and across borders. Encountering difference (pluralism) is also part of what shapes peoples and nature—sometimes in ways found to be positive, sometimes in ways found to be negative, and sometimes in ways that remain uncertain in value. Learning to make pluralism more often an asset than a threat or harm is an important topic for Dewey scholarship in an increasingly diverse but connected world as it is an important source of hope for humans living with each other and the earth in a positive and sustainable way.

Hope requires, at least in part, an approach to difference that entails humility and openness in the face of others rather than fear or the desire to dominate. The Peircean idea of fallibilism is taken up by Dewey (and others) to argue for an attitude of open questioning and flexible revision in the face of evolving experiences. While one can find elements of all of these key ideas in Dewey, they are not all fully developed, and most require some updating based on new understandings and experiences that have emerged in the time since Dewey's death (see Sullivan in this volume for examples of this). While this list is not exhaustive, we hope it gives the reader (and future Dewey scholars) some ways to focus future historical and applied work connected to Dewey.

There are examples of writing that, while not always explicitly focused on Dewey, use a genuine Deweyan approach and take up topics related to the themes mentioned here. Such work seeks to create alternative mirrors of American culture. They are efforts to respond to real problems and to preserve difference as they seek alternative goods. For example, work by Eddie S. Glaude Jr. (2016: *Democracy in Black: How Slavery Still Enslaves the American Soul*), Melvin Rogers (2012: *The Undiscovered Dewey: Religion, Morality, and the Ethos of Democracy*), and Patricia Hill Collins (2006: *Black Sexual Politics: African Americans, Gender, and the New Racism*) all attempt to reimagine black politics and provide a philosophical mirror for a different part of American culture than does linguistic pragmatism. Though not specifically Deweyan, many indigenous philosophies are reflective of part of the philosophical character of America and its problems. Thomas Norton Smith reconstructs the work of Nelson Goodman in ways that recall the classical pragmatism of William James in order to frame an alternative conception of American Indian philosophy at its intersection with Western culture. The result is the *Dance of Person and Place* (Goodman 2010). Leanne Simpson (2011) argues for political resurgence in North America through the recovery of indigenous languages, stories, governance, and land in *Dancing on Our Turtle's Back*. These and other Native thinkers recall the long tradition of indigenous resistance to settler colonialism manifested along the border between Native and European America including the work of nineteenth-century Native prophets, turn-of-the century writers such as Charles Eastman, and late twentieth-century thinkers such as Vine Deloria Jr. and Gerald Vizenor.

Chris Tirres's (2014) *The Aesthetics and Ethics of Faith: A Dialogue between Liberationist and Pragmatic Thought* and Gregory Pappas's (2011) *Pragmatism in the Americas* both expand and challenge notions of pragmatism and the philosophies of the Americas. Just in this volume there are a number of chapters that challenge more conservative takes on education (something at the heart of Dewey's work)—Leonard

Waks, Maura Striano, and Jim Garrison are specific examples. Jerry Rosiek and Kathy Kinslow's (2016) *Resegregation as Curriculum: The Meaning of the New Racial Segregation in U.S. Public Schools* is an example of Deweyan work that is not "about" Dewey but rather puts Dewey's ideas to work on important issues in the world today. Similarly, Erin McKenna's (2014) *Pets, People and Pragmatism* and *Livestock: Food, Fiber, and Friends* (McKenna 2018) examine human relationships with other animal beings through a version of Deweyan inquiry and ethics. Lisa Heldke's piece in this volume, "John Dewey and Pragmatist Feminist Philosophy," both takes up and challenges Dewey's work as she seeks to push both feminist thought and pragmatist scholarship to consider new ways of understanding gender, self, and community.

Dewey saw philosophy as a mirror of culture that provides an opportunity for reflection on how we think and insight into how to realize our philosophic vision. But such mirrors do not exhaust a vision of a culture or community. Even as Kant and the Western tradition reflected the dominant culture in Germany and the Anglo-American world at the beginning of the twentieth century, Dewey recognized the possibility of resistance. Brandom's philosophy is likewise a mirror of the dominant American culture that elected a president and a supportive Congress for whom language was a tool of self-creation separable from the facts. Just as Dewey called for a philosophy of resistance at the outset of World War I, he would, we think, call for new resistance today. Dewey scholarship is not just about solving problems but also about taking the perspectives of people who are not part of the mainstream in order to build new mirrors. Our history *American Philosophy: From Wounded Knee to the Present* (McKenna and Pratt 2015) reconstructs the history of American philosophy to represent a broader story—more people, more perspectives, and more problems. Our goal was to set the stage for the possibility of seeing other mirrors long present in American culture that we called the philosophy of resistance. This philosophy "is one that challenges dogma and settled belief from a perspective that recognizes the pluralism of experience and the value of growth and change. It is resistance in an expected way because it takes on systems of domination as a necessary step in a process of liberation. At the same time, American philosophies of resistance do not rest with criticism but actively work to establish alternative ways of thinking and living" (McKenna and Pratt 2015, 6). Mirrors to reflect people and problems in order to see the way to a better world require other voices, different angles on experience, and ends-in-view that respond to the diversity of peoples, their hopes, and their futures—that is the constructive future of Dewey scholarship.

NOTES

1. Shannon Sullivan (this volume) briefly includes *German Philosophy and Politics* in her discussion of Dewey's assessment of World War I.
2. A similar analysis could be make of other authors such as Richard Rorty, but given the pressures of space we look at only one example.

3. Dewey references Santayana's piece in *German Philosophy and Politics*, page 159.
4. It is important to note that Dewey's interpretation of Kant in *German Philosophy and Politics* is based on the scholarship of the day and may or may not represent the meaning of Kant's claims in present scholarship.
5. For further discussion of this account of mid-twentieth century, see McKenna and Pratt (2015).
6. Joe Margolis, in his discussion of linguistic pragmatism (this volume) argues that Brandom and the so-called "Pittsburgh School" divide experience and language in a way similar to what we describe. Margolis does not develop the implications of the split, namely, that language becomes an instrument of self-construction unbound by the "facts," by the commonsense use of language to express experienced states of affairs encountered in the everyday and which political action sets out to ameliorate. Instead, politics is about what we say and not what we do or what is done. Margolis is on the right track, but he misses just why Brandom and his colleagues are central to American thought in the era of Trump and not simply a philosophical view that is inadequate. Linguistic pragmatism is a philosophical mirror of early twenty-first century American culture. David Hildebrand also challenges Brandom's view by citing the division between experience and language.

WORKS CITED

Citations of John Dewey's works are to the thirty-seven-volume critical edition published by Southern Illinois University Press under the editorship of Jo Ann Boydston. In-text citations give the original publication date, series abbreviation, followed by volume number and page number. For example: (1934, LW 10:12) is page 12 of *Art as Experience*, which is published as volume 10 of *The Later Works*.

Series abbreviations for *The Collected Works*:

EW *The Early Works* (1882–98)

MW *The Middle Works* (1899–1924)

LW *The Later Works* (1925–53)

Alexander, Thomas M. 2013. *The Human Eros: Eco-ontology and the Aesthetics of Existence*. New York: Fordham University Press.

Bardwell Jones, Celia, and Maurice Hamington, eds. 2012. *Contemporary Feminist Pragmatism*. New York: Routledge.

Brandom, Robert. 2009. *Reason and Philosophy: Animating Ideas*. Cambridge, MA: Belknap Press.

Brandom, Robert. 2011. *Perspectives on Pragmatism: Classical, Recent, and Contemporary*. Cambridge, MA: Harvard University Press.

Collins, Patricia Hill. 2006. *Black Sexual Politics: African Americans, Gender, and the New Racism*. New York: Routledge.

Dewey, John. 1915. *German Philosophy and Politics*, in MW 8. Carbondale: Southern Illinois University Press.

Dewey, John. 1927. "Philosophy and Civilization," in LW 3. Carbondale: Southern Illinois University Press.

Dewey, John. 1938. "Experience and Education," in LW 13. Carbondale: Southern Illinois University Press.

Fesmire, Steven. 2015. *Dewey*. New York: Routledge.

Fesmire, Steven. 2016. "Useful for What? Dewey's Call to Humanize Techno-Industrial Civilization." *Pragmatism Today*, vol. 7, no. 1, 11–19.

Garrison, Jim, and Larry Hickman, Daisaku Ikeda. 2014. *Living as Learning: John Dewey in the 21st Century*. Cambridge MA: Ikeda Center.

Glaude, Eddie S. Jr. 2016. *Democracy in Black: How Slavery Still Enslaves the American Soul*. Portland OR: Broadway Books.

Howlett, Charles F., and Audrey Cohan. 2016. *John Dewey, a Peace-Minded Educator*. Carbondale: Southern Illinois University Press.

McKenna, Erin. 2014. *Pets, People, and Pragmatism*. New York: Fordham University Press.

McKenna, Erin. 2015. "Eating Apes, Eating Cows." *The Pluralist*, vol. 10, no. 2, 133–149.

McKenna, Erin. 2018. *Livestock: Food, Fiber, and Friends*. Athens: University of Georgia Press.

McKenna, Erin, and Scott L. Pratt. 2015. *American Philosophy: From Wounded Knee to the Present*. New York: Bloomsbury.

Pappas, Gregory Fernando. 2008. *John Dewey's: Ethics: Democracy as Experience*. Bloomington: Indiana University Press.

Pappas, Gregory Fernando, ed. 2011. *Pragmatism in the Americas*. New York: Fordham University Press.

Ralston, Shane. 2012. "A Deweyan Defense of Guerilla Gardening." *The Pluralist*, vol. 7, no. 3, 57–70.

Rogers, Melvin. 2012. *The Undiscovered Dewey: Religion, Morality, and the Ethos of Democracy*. New York: Columbia University Press.

Rosiek, Jerry, and Kathy Kinslow. 2016. *Resegregation as Curriculum: The Meaning of the New Racial Segregation in U.S. Public Schools*. New York: Routledge.

Rorty, Richard. 1967. *The Linguistic Turn*. Chicago: University of Chicago Press.

Santayana, George. 1914. "The Logic of Fanaticism." *The New Republic*, November 28, 18–19.

Seigfried, Charlene Haddock. 2001. *Feminist Interpretations of John Dewey*. State College: Pennsylvania State University Press.

Simpson, Leanne. 2011. *Dancing on Our Turtle's Back*. Winnipeg, Manitoba: Arbeiter Ring.

Smith, Thomas Norton. 2010. *Dance of Person and Place*. Albany, NY: SUNY Press.

Tirres, Chris. 2014. *The Aesthetics and Ethics of Faith: A Dialogue between Liberationist and Pragmatic Thought*. Oxford: Oxford University Press.

XI

PUBLIC PHILOSOPHY AND PRACTICAL ETHICS

CHAPTER 33

DEWEY AND PUBLIC PHILOSOPHY

NOËLLE MCAFEE

Philosophy recovers itself when it ceases to be a device for dealing with the problems of philosophers and becomes a method, cultivated by philosophers, for dealing with the problems of men.

—John Dewey (1917, MW 10:46)

INTRODUCTION

A chapter on John Dewey and public philosophy should begin with an explanation of the term "public philosophy" itself. But this, as we shall see, is exactly the problem that this chapter sets out to answer. Is it philosophy done for a public audience or a public purpose? Does it aim to educate the public or learn with the public? Does its practice keep philosophy itself intact or does the practice transform philosophy itself? So in lieu of an initial definition, let me trace two uses of the term: one as a public theory and another as a practice.

First there is the notion of public philosophy as a widely-shared view about politics. Walter Lippmann titled his book of 1955 "The Public Philosophy" and in it he (a) lamented the weakening of a shared vision of what American democracy ought to be and (b) developed the outlines of what a strong public philosophy would be: namely one that was based on natural law theory and civility. Here "public philosophy" is a kind of political doctrine, a coherent philosophy that could be widely shared. In another vernacular, it is the same thing as an ideology, though that term came to be shunned because of its Marxist overtones (Statham 2002, 4). Lippmann and his followers in political science are looking for a political philosophy that can be widely shared, or again in another vernacular, hegemonic. The ideal public philosophy would seem as natural as the air we breathe, just the way things really are.

This use of the term "public philosophy," especially in political science, continues to the present, most notably in the title of Michael Sandel's book *Democracy's Discontent: America in Search of a Public Philosophy*. "By public philosophy," Sandel writes, "I mean the political theory implicit in our practice, the assumptions about citizenship and freedom that inform our public life" (Sandel 1996, 4). Though he uses Lippmann's term, Sandel argues in that book for a fundamentally different kind of public philosophy: republican, not liberal, participatory, not minimal. Lippmann's view rested on a notion that citizens need not do much for representative government to work, but they at least need to subscribe to the basic structure of society. Sandel is arguing for a more participatory role for citizens, and this too requires a shared orientation. Still, this notion of public philosophy as some kind of shared political doctrine is not, at least not directly, the subject of this chapter.

Instead, the focus here is on a second notion of public philosophy, which emerged from the public scholarship movement beginning around 1990 to ameliorate the seeming disconnect between higher education and public life (Brown and Witte 2015; Sandmann 2016). As Ernest Boyer, then executive director of the Carnegie Foundation for the Advancement of Teaching, wrote, "The campus is seen as a place for faculty to get tenured and students to get credentialed, but what goes on there is not seen as relevant to many of our social problems" (Boyer 1990). Or, as David Brown put it,

> Even those professors who see "politics" and "power" in every text and institution nonetheless pursue their critiques in very orthodox academic fashion. They deconstruct, but they do not communicate with the larger public. They labor for the approval of their peers, but not for the sake of that public. There are clearly rewards for their academic performance, but very little of it benefits the real-world constituencies that inspire their scholarship.
>
> (Brown and Witte 2015, 7)

To address this problem, Boyer asked whether it was possible "for the work of the academy to relate more effectively to our most pressing social, economic, and civic problems." The historian Thomas Bender called for "the opening up of the disciplines . . . that have become too self-referential" (Bender 1993, 143). In the 1990s many state humanities councils made a concerted effort to get the humanities more engaged in public life (Veninga and McAfee 1997). In the late 1990s, a group of scholars and national leaders founded Imagining America (IA) to take a lead in this effort. As IA's website recounts,

> By the late 1990s, the national conversation about higher education's civic purpose was well established, reinvigorated during the previous decade. Newly created centers for service-learning and community partnerships were advancing higher education's commitment to engagement. However, values of reciprocity and mutual benefit sometimes went unrealized, and humanities, arts, and design were underrepresented.
>
> Imagining America was launched at a 1999 White House Conference initiated by the White House Millennium Council, the University of Michigan, and the Woodrow

Wilson National Fellowship Foundation. The name Imagining America reflected the theme of the White House Millennium Council that focused on renewing participation in all walks of U.S. life: "Honor the Past—Imagine the Future."

(http://imaginingamerica.org/about/)

Today colleges and universities throughout the country have offices of public engagement, initiatives in public scholarship and now digital humanities, and campaigns to bridge the divide through civic work between town and gown. Many academic disciplines have efforts for public engagement, including organizations such as the National Council on Public History, bibliographies of public sociologists, literature reviews of civic humanities, and more recently conference and organizations for public philosophy.

While philosophy was a little late in taking up public work, in the early 2000s the American Philosophical Association (largely thanks to John Lachs' advocacy and fundraising) set up an ad hoc standing committee on public philosophy. (I was one of its first members.) The now standing Committee on Public Philosophy has its own website (http://www.apaonline.org/group/public) and is quite active, holding sessions at the various divisional meetings of the American Philosophical Association (APA) and running an annual op-ed contest. Its understanding of public philosophy is capacious: "On the belief that the broader presence of philosophy in public life is important both to our society and to our profession, the basic charge of the committee will be to find and create opportunities to demonstrate the personal value and social usefulness of philosophy." Out of the committee's work, many other ventures have spun off, including the Public Philosophy Network (https://www.publicphilosophynetwork.net) and its four (to date) large conferences bringing together philosophers who do a wide range of work from teaching philosophy in prisons to working internationally on climate change.

VARIETIES OF PUBLIC PHILOSOPHY AS PRACTICE

Those who say they practice public philosophy engage in a variety of activities, including teaching in public settings, writing for a popular audience, and more, including the following activities listed on the APA's committee on public philosophy page:

1. Organize and support programs that demonstrate the personal value and social usefulness of philosophy, such as suitable lecture series, and radio and television appearances by philosophers.
2. Organize and support programs that bring public attention to philosophy and philosophers, such as book signings.

3. Establish ties to national and local media.

4. Prepare appropriate news releases for the divisional meetings of the APA and for other events of philosophical significance.

5. Serve as a conduit so that media and other inquiries can be channeled to appropriate individuals in the profession.

6. Create or support the creation of audio tapes and videotapes useful for calling attention to philosophy and for garnering support for philosophy.

7. Encourage APA members to engage in public debate about significant issues by such means as sponsoring op-ed essay contests.

8. Establish contact with politicians, civil servants, and opinion makers to impress upon them the full scope of the contributions philosophers can make.

9. Make common cause with ethics institutes and other organizations in promoting the engagement of philosophy with broader publics.

But ask philosophers what the term "public philosophy" actually means, and one will hear starkly different views, from being something to help edify or even just entertain the public to something that should help strengthen and transform both public life and philosophy itself. More than a variety of views, they are competing. For example, recently I responded to a philosophy blogosphere query about the meaning of public philosophy with this:

> If we took a non-elitist view of philosophy and a non-condescending and more Deweyan view of the public, we'd get this kind of answer: public philosophy is a collective (philosophers with the help of publics) inquiry into what is at the root of our troubles and what might be done to ameliorate them. I worry that notions of public philosophy as aiming to educate the masses completely miss this point. Public philosophy ought to change what WE do not just what the public knows. Our own work should change — should become more engaged with the world — if we're doing our work from a public point of view. Then some supposed problems become pointless to pursue and others that we might have otherwise ignored loom large. This still leaves plenty room for other philosophers to work on things that might seem pointless today. Tomorrow they could serve a huge point. Think Whitehead's process philosophy or Spinoza's passions.

To this, another philosopher replied anonymously,

> Noelle, I think that the definition of "public philosophy" should be kept as politically unloaded as possible. A "public toilet" is a toilet for use by the public. A "public park" is a park for use by the public. A "public orchestra performance" is an orchestra performance to be accessed and enjoyed by the public. This is so, whether they are toilets, parks and performances that serve the public well, or do their job badly. Likewise, "public philosophy" should mean philosophy to be accessed and used by the public. If we label only a subset of philosophy accessed and used by the public as "public philosophy," that will cause much confusion I think.

Rather than tarry with confusion, he suggests, we should stick with the simple adjectival notion of public. But readers of this handbook on Dewey can easily imagine that reducing "the public" to the users of parks or toilets would make Dewey apoplectic. Additionally, for Dewey, as I discuss shortly, what anyone does with philosophy is itself a vitally important matter.

This anonymous philosopher's view is common, but here with Dewey I want to argue against it for a number of reasons. A thin conception of the public is not only elitist and condescending, it undermines democracy and misses out on reflexive transformations of philosophy. It is thin in the sense that it is merely a descriptor that points to those who are the recipients of whatever goods are being made public, whether bathrooms, highways, or concerts. The public has no role, qua public, in the production of the good. It is elitist and condescending in the sense that the choice and the production of the good is left to experts who may easily look down on what the public could contribute to the good's production. So, as I discuss later, a thin notion of the public lends itself to a top-down expert model of specialized knowledge production as opposed to horizontal relationships that are characteristic of democracy. And finally, this thin notion denies the public any role in transforming the discipline that is at work.

But historically, the elitist notion has prevailed. Consider Plato's public philosophy. With his allegory of the cave, Plato offered what may be the most powerful—and problematic—image of philosophy's role for the public. After the philosopher has seen the light, literally, of truth and the ultimate reality of things, he then ventures back into the cave of everyday human experience and error to enlighten those entranced by shadows and images. But as Plato noted then and many philosophers note now, the public was not terribly grateful for this enlightenment. They prefer spectacles and illusions to truth, which is a paramount reason that the people cannot govern themselves well. Better to have enlightened philosophers govern them than leave the people to their own devices. In Plato's view, philosophers serve as correctives to the public's proclivities.

So how would Dewey answer? That is the subject of this chapter. It calls for speculation, for as I noted in Dewey's day the term was used to denote a shared ideology, not a way of doing philosophy. But I believe we can piece together very clearly what Dewey would think by interrogating what he thought about the two constitutive parts of the phrase—public and philosophy—and then putting those together.

DEWEY'S RECOVERY OF PHILOSOPHY

"A philosophy which abandoned its guardianship of fixed realities, values and ideals, would find a new career for itself"

(Dewey 1929, LW 4:248).

In much of his work, especially the texts *Reconstruction in Philosophy* (1920) and *The Quest for Certainty* (1929), Dewey develops an antifoundationalist and contextualist account of philosophical knowledge (Kadlec 2007). It is antifoundationalist in that it values experience and is wary of claims to transcendent knowledge or truth, and it is contextualist in that it sees philosophical inquiry as always connected with lived human experience and history.

Dewey's recovery of philosophy is largely a rebuke to the view of philosophy held by Plato and most of the tradition that followed. Where Plato thought of philosophy as the search for absolute and unchanging truths above and beyond the phenomenal world in which people live, Dewey argued that "the distinctive office, problems and subject matter of philosophy grow out of stresses and strains in the community life in which a given form of philosophy arises, and that, accordingly, its specific problems vary with the changes in human life that are always going on and that at times constitute a crisis and a turning point in human history" (1920 MW, 12:256).

Moreover, Dewey points out that, despite the philosophical tradition's pretense to be objective and independent from actual human affairs, it is instead a product of them and for the most part in the end beholden to them. While philosophy gave itself the mission to "extract the essential moral kernel out of the threatened traditional beliefs of the past" it could never quite shake off authority of those social institutions. So "it became the work of philosophy to justify on rational grounds the spirit, though not the form, of accepted beliefs and traditional customs" (1920 MW, 12:90).

And where Plato, Kant, and others saw philosophy as the queen of the sciences, as the arbiter of what was really real and true, Dewey wanted to make room for science, seeing philosophy as a liaison officer between the discoveries of science and social life. Instead of looking for ultimate Truths and Reality, philosophy ought to inquire about "human affairs and hence into morals" (1920 MW, 12:266).

Thinking of philosophy in this way, something new is gained:

> What is lost from the standpoint of would-be science is regained from the standpoint of humanity. Instead of the disputes of rivals about the nature of reality, we have the scene of human clash of social purpose and aspirations. Instead of impossible attempts to transcend experience, we have the significant record of the efforts of men to formulate the things of experience to which they are most deeply and passionately attached. Instead of impersonal and purely speculative endeavors to contemplate as remote beholders the nature of absolute things-in-themselves, we have a living picture of the choice of thoughtful men about what they would have life to be, and to what ends they would have men shape their intelligent activities.

So Dewey views philosophy as a practice that is embedded in human social life and history yet at the same time deeply involved in inquiry about how life should be lived, about what we ought to do, about what kind of action would be intelligent and productive, and what would not be so. Philosophers are not distant onlookers but participants in public life.

Having uncovered the paradox that philosophy that sought to be above it all has been instead deeply enmeshed in social conditions, Dewey writes that what philosophy has been doing all along, under cover, it should henceforth do openly and intentionally. This could be the "new career" that Dewey later suggests.

> When it is acknowledged that under disguise of dealing with ultimate reality, philosophy has been occupied with the precious values embedded in social traditions, that it has sprung from a clash of social ends and from a conflict of inherited traditions ... it will be seen that the task of future philosophy is to clarify men's ideas as to the social and moral strifes of their own day. Its aim is to become so far as is humanly possible an organ for dealing with these conflicts.
>
> (1920 LW, 12:94)

On the Public

Lippmann's Phantom Public

Plato's public philosophy arose in reaction and opposition to the Athenian experiments in democracy, and it called for correcting the public's seeming inability to rule itself wisely. By Dewey's day, more than two millennia after Plato, after popular revolutions of the eighteenth century that gave rise to democratic governance, Plato's public philosophy was still at work through Madison's safeguards against factions, through representative structures, and through the rise of a new professional and expert class trusted with managing the complexities of modern societies. So even democratic governance retained a modicum of Plato's legacy, remaining in large part, to use Whitehead's phrase, a footnote to Plato's political philosophy. In liberal democracies, representative government keeps democracy from being too direct; a culture of expertise and professionalism keeps citizenship an amateur activity; a trip to the voting booth only every two years or so is the general extent of citizens' political involvement. And that is as it should be, noted Walter Lippmann, one of the realists of the early twentieth century, channeling Plato's political philosophy best, arguing that the "omnicompetent" citizen that democracy claims there is hardly exists. Because the public does not have the wherewithal to know what was best, modern societies need an elite class of guardians to run things, experts not lay people, which would include experts in the humanities, philosophers included.

Lippmann laid out his critique in two widely read books, *Public Opinion* (1922) and *The Phantom Public* (1925), and on the pages of the *New Republic* magazine. He argued that the people themselves were too diffuse and preoccupied to attend to public problems. What we call a public, Lippmann famously observed, is merely a phantom. We invoke the phantom public to make ourselves feel that we have a real democracy.

But look around, he noted: people seem to be unable to fathom the complexities of the problems that beset them; much less are they able to engineer solutions. They barely know what is going on. They are like the theater-goer who shows up in the middle of the second act and leaves before the curtain closes, having stayed just long enough to figure out who the villains and the heroes are.

Also at this time, as Theda Skocpol has noted, where before many nongovernmental activities, such as philanthropy, were carried out by volunteers, soon these activities became the province of professionally run organizations, effectively relieving citizens of any duty beyond staying informed enough to cast a modicum of an intelligent vote.

Lippmann's solution, outlined in his books of the 1920s, was for an elite group of decision-makers and social scientists to do the work of governing. As Alison Kadlec points out, Lippmann was not entirely hostile to democracy, certainly not like Plato was. He did see a role for the public: to call out the expert leaders whenever they acted in self-interest rather than the public interest and to vote them out of office as needed. Kadlec stresses that "Lippmann's decidedly myopic equation of democracy with voting for 'the Ins when things are going well and the Outs when things are going badly' is not exactly based on an elitist contempt for the masses" (2007, 91). He did want a role, however limited, for the public. But that role had to stop short of trying to manage the vast complexities of modern society, otherwise "to ask an average citizen to exercise anything in the vicinity of self-rule is like [asking someone] to 'navigate a ship from dry land'" (Kadlec 2007, 92).

Dewey's Theory of the Public

John Dewey took seriously Lippmann's reservations about the public but offered a robust counter-story in his 1927 book *The Public and Its Problems*. Where Lippmann and other progressive realists called for developing a class of guardians to solve public problems, Dewey focused on understanding and reconstituting the public. He defined the public simply as all "those indirectly and seriously affected for good or evil" by the "human collective action" of some particular group of people (Dewey 1954, 27, 34–35). Whenever any group's actions have consequences for a community as a whole, this community is a political public. There's no doubt that some people's actions have consequences for the whole of society; but a problem arises when this public cannot find itself, when it is bombarded but inchoate. Writing in the early twentieth century Dewey noted how complex and difficult to fathom were the kinds of issues facing this public. When problems become immense and their consequences difficult to perceive, the problems begin to eclipse the public. In Dewey's day, as in ours, observers lamented the public's indifference to social problems, its apathy. But apathy, Dewey noted, is best understood as "testimony to the fact that the public is so bewildered that it cannot find itself" (Dewey 1954, 123).

> At present, many consequences are felt rather than perceived; they are suffered, but they cannot be said to be known, for they are not, by those who experience them, referred to their origins . . . . Hence the publics are amorphous and unarticulated.
>
> (Dewey 1954, 131).

The public can find itself, or to put it more aptly, *make* itself by coming together to talk about the pressing problems of the day, to identify the sources of problems, to see how these problems differentially affect others, to try to decide together what should be done. Out of these processes, processes that all amount to what we call public deliberation, might emanate informed public opinion about what should be done. This information has a special status. Dewey put it this way, "The man who wears the shoe knows best that it pinches and where it pinches, even if the expert shoemaker is the best judge of how the trouble is to be remedied" (Dewey 1954, 207). Public problems are best fathomed by the public itself. It may enlist experts or governments to fix the problems, but it alone is the best judge of what needs to be addressed and whether the remedy is successful (McAfee 2004).

Here is what John Dewey proposed:

- To find itself, the public needs to be able to fully fathom the consequences of human actions and the origins of actions.
- The public needs to able to know "what to make of" the relationships they come to understand. They need to know what they can do, and what the implications of their own actions will be.
- People need to have more and better opportunities to find each other, in actual places where they can meet face to face. If the knowledge stays locked up inside themselves, it cannot help feed the public as a public.

Dewey's solution is three-pronged and interconnected: First, to find itself, the public needs to be able to fully fathom the consequences of human actions and the origins of actions. An example today might be accepting (a) that there is in fact global warming that is upsetting the climate, ecosystems, and habitats and (b) that this change is the result of our unprecedented use of fossil fuels, of policies and geopolitics that promote this dependence, and of the practices of industries that profit from it. As Dewey sees it, one does not discover such consequences of human action alone. Consequences are discovered by engaging others, inquiring how they are affected by events.

Dewey argues that, to be able to make such connections, and make good political judgments thereafter, the public needs increased intelligence—not on the minutiae of geology and meteorology but the kind of intelligence needed to "judge of the bearing of knowledge" that geologists and meteorologists produce (Dewey 1954, 208–209). In my view, to the extent that public deliberation is about ends, about deciding what kind of political communities the deliberators want to produce, deliberators decide "what to make of" particular facts in light of their broader purposes and aims. At the end of the day, they need knowledge of where they want and are willing to move as a political community given all the constraints, consequences, trade-offs, competing values, aims, and necessary sacrifices they discover in their deliberations. Such intelligence is not an attribute of experts nor of individual citizens but something possessed by a community. It is what I call *public knowledge*.

This last point brings me to the third prong of Dewey's solution. To create this kind of intelligence or public knowledge, Dewey calls for a "practical re-formation of social conditions," namely people's reconnection to their local communities, where face-to-face intercourse can occur (Dewey 1954, 211). Dewey's impetus here is not a nostalgic longing for an Aristotelian *polis* or for communitarian virtue but a pragmatic observation that any individual's ideas are "broken and imperfect" unless they are "communicated, shared, and reborn in expression" (Dewey 1954, 218).

> Signs and symbols, language, are the means of communication by which a fraternally shared experience is ushered in and sustained. But the wingèd words of conversation in immediate intercourse have a vital import lacking in the fixed and frozen words of written speech. Systematic and continuous inquiry into all the conditions which affect association and their dissemination in print is a precondition of the creation of a true public. But it and its results are but tools after all. Their final actuality is accomplished in face-to-face relationships by means of direct give and take. Logic in its fulfillment recurs to the primitive sense of the word: dialogue.
>
> (Dewey 1954, 218)

In this passage, Dewey points to the importance of verbal communication, which political theorists might refer to today as public deliberation. Such public talk makes possible a "fraternally shared experience" or understanding of political phenomena *as* phenomena that are perceived and felt by a public. Dewey observes that when people inquire together about political matters, they create more knowledge of these matters and of themselves as a public. This is not merely the result of aggregating their bits of knowledge. Rather, it is the result of being able to weave together the interconnections, dispersed consequences, and multiple and sometimes clashing aims that the public can conceive only when it talks together. As the people talk together and begin to fathom the roots and effects of public problems, they begin to form and identify themselves as a public, as actors who might be able to channel and direct public action.

Dewey's Public Philosophy

While I have treated them separately, Dewey's recovery of philosophy and his account of the public are thoroughly intertwined. The public career for philosophy should ultimately be to improve social conditions, including thinking critically about what obstacles are in the way and what paths should be pursued.

Lest the philosopher think most of the public work is on its side, note the need for the intelligence that, according to Dewey, only a public can provide. The public does so by identifying problems that affect people jointly, tracing the origins of these problems, communicating and deliberating together about what ought to be done, and enlisting the structures of governance to follow the agendas that the public sets.

Philosophy and the public come together for Dewey not just conceptually for the philosopher but for the public as well. In a speech on democracy being a way of life, Dewey pointed out how the public can serve an epistemic function, pulling together the knowledge needed for public problems to be addressed. "The foundation of democracy is faith in the capacities of human nature; faith in human intelligence, and in the power of pooled and cooperative experience. It is not belief that these things are complete but that if given a show they will grow and be able to generate progressively the knowledge and wisdom needed to guide collective action" (Dewey 1986, vol. 11). Because the people know where the shoe pinches, they can point to what problems need to be addressed.

Because there are so many social and material obstacles to the public forming, the people need allies in their public work. And here the philosopher can help by standing with the public, collaboratively, to help identify those obstacles and work with the public to overcome them. By seeing the public philosopher's work as parterning with the public, we can which kinds of practices of public philosophy are really democratic and socially useful and which are not, including what kinds of practices might be well-meaning but pernicious. In a 2013 report to the Kettering Foundation on public philosophy, Sharon Meagher sums up some common conceptions of the roles of philosophers in public life, including:

- As expert
- As gadfly/critic (Socrates)
- As public liaison officer (Dewey)
- As offering useful skills such as deliberation
- As citizen
- As tour guide to unfamiliar places and perspectives

To assess these, she offers five theses on public philosophy, which I find to be very compatible with Dewey's pragmatism:

1. Public philosophy should be transformative, that is, it should not just aim to bring the public good of philosophy to the public but be ready to transform itself. Meagher quotes Linda Alcoff: "the public arena is a space where intellectual work is done, where problems emerge to be addressed, and where knowledge and experience are gained that can address a variety of issues. . . . Furthermore, one can receive vital feedback concerning one's positions, which can suggest needed modifications." So too the self-styled role of gadfly or critic can distance the philosopher from the public.

2. Public philosophers should not be understood as "experts." Meagher cautions that in a technocratic age it is tempting to take up the role of expert with unassailable knowledge but that public philosophers aim to provide an antidote to technocratic thinking. Moreover, philosophers should "reflect critically on their roles within various publics" and also be critical of any claim to neutrality and objectivity (Meagher 2013, 10). Also, philosophy is not about having the right answers but asking good questions. So too, as I discussed earlier, Dewey's recovery of philosophy aims to topple claims to absolute truth and search instead for publicly situated intelligence. The role of philosopher as expert entirely undermines that Deweyan understanding of social inquiry.

Moreover, Dewey makes room for the expert only once the public has gathered and begins to carry on its inquiries. The expert is at the service of the public, providing information needed for the public to make wise decisions. Acknowledging that contemporary social problems involve complexities that the average person may not know, Dewey sees a need for expert knowledge. To the extent that contemporary problems involve technical matters, "they are to be settled by inquiry into facts; and as the inquiry can be carried on only by those especially equipped, so the results of inquiry can be utilized only by trained technicians" (Dewey 1954, 125). But solving problems is not just a matter of fact but a matter of interest, value, and purpose, and "a class of experts is inevitably so removed from common interests as to become a class with private interests and private knowledge, which in social matters is not knowledge at all" (Dewey 1954, 207). Social or public matters call for what I am calling *public knowledge*, which includes an understanding of how policies affect what people need and care about. "No government by experts in which the masses do not have the chance to inform the experts as to their needs can be anything but an oligarchy managed by the interests of the few" (Dewey 1954, 208).

3. Public philosophy demands collaborative and interdisciplinary work. Meagher offers a number of reasons for this:

> first, if we are working on problems in which members of one or more publics has a stake, then our work cannot be the exclusive domain of philosophers. Particularly in cases where philosophers are working on issues concerning democracy, civil society, and participation, it is critically important that the philosophical practices incorporate participatory and democratic ideals . . . . Relatedly, if we agree with the thesis that public philosophy should be transformational, then the public philosopher must be open to dialogue with, and learning from, others. Secondly, if we agree that many problems in the civic domain are "wicked problems," that is problems that are large and ill-defined, involved or affect large numbers of people, and are interdependent on other problems ("Poverty is linked with education, nutrition with poverty, the economy with nutrition, and so on") . . . , the work requires collaboration with others and interdisciplinary work. Certain kinds of problems can't be managed unless the public acts—and keeps on acting. A public that can

act effectively is needed most when communities face . . . "wicked" problems . . Because of the interdependence of people and of social problems, those who practice public philosophy require strategies that entail a collaborative approach that facilitates discussion on deliberation on both how to define the problem in a way that makes sense to all stakeholders and then how to work together to find meaningful solutions.

4. Public philosophers must be committed to assessing their work and being accountable to their public partners. While not all philosophical work requires any collaboration, "if we understand publicly engaged philosophy as the practice of philosophy with the intent of some public or civic good, then publicly engaged philosophers should take responsibility for their work and take public criticisms and evaluation seriously" (Meagher 2013, 12). And again, with Dewey, philosophical knowing is a social enterprise. It involves continuous learning, reflection, education, and self-correction.

5. Public philosophy demands that we work to make philosophy more inclusive and representative of various publics. This may not have been a concern at the forefront of Dewey's thinking, but it does seem to follow from his ideas about how all members of a community can find themselves to be a public. I think it also follows from a question that any effort to address public problems should ask: to solve this problem, who else needs to be at this table? And if they are not at this table, why not? How can we get everyone together?

So of the possible roles listed here, clearly the roles of expert and critic/gadfly are not in keeping with a Deweyan notion of public philosophy. But these roles do work:

- As public liaison officer (Dewey)
- As offering useful skills such as deliberation
- As citizen
- As tour guide to unfamiliar places and perspectives

I think we could add two more roles, one that Gramsci offered: organic intellectual, someone who sees his or her intellectual work as rooted in a community and aimed at addressing that community's concerns. But this organic intellectual would need to submit his or her ideas to public scrutiny and debate and never act as a stand in for the public. Second, there is the need for a critical pragmatist practice, which Dewey engaged in during the Depression, of identifying and finding alternatives (perhaps framed for public deliberation) to systems of communicative distortion, obstacles to public politics and social order (Kadlec 2007).

So, given this Deweyan account of public politics, we can clarify which kinds of practices of public philosophy are democratic and which are not. To put the difference starkly, Table 33.1 differentiates the Platonic idea of public philosophy from a more democratic one.

During this new century, many philosophers have taken up the mantle of public philosophy, but sadly many think that the goal is to simply perform philosophy in public, or to broadcast widely their own brilliant arguments, and maybe to become lauded as a public intellectual. Many well-meaning philosophers are trying to help improve the public, to help them think more rationally, argue more deliberatively (e.g., like a philosopher), think more critically, spot logical fallacies, vote against bad politicians and policies, support good policies and good arguments, and perhaps see the light about the existence or nonexistence of God or creationism, truth or bullshit, science or myth. Unfortunately, none of this is public work in a robustly democratic way, for all of it usurps the role of a public to identify problems, their causes and possible solutions, and skips over any need for public deliberation and choice.

Philosophers can do public work by helping the public find itself. If Dewey is right that publics form when people begin to see how problems jointly affect them, then public philosophers can work with the public to help people make these connections, that is, between what people are experiencing and what trouble is brewing. And they can lay out possible courses of action. The key is for philosophers to stop short of making the connections themselves or advocating for a certain courses of action. Rather, they can help lay out what the implications and costs of each option are. The public itself needs to make the difficult choices and trade-offs. Otherwise there will be neither the public knowledge nor the public will for sustainable change.

Table 33.1 provides a general framework for philosophical public work. The public philosopher will be more of a pragmatist and less of a realist, in the Platonic sense, about what the right choices are. Rather than convening spaces for education they will help convene spaces for inquiry. They will engage the public in public work rather than dazzle them with philosophical brilliance. They will see the public as agents, not audiences. Their relationship with the public will change from a vertical one of professional to amateur to a horizontal one of citizen to citizen.

It is not possible to say that any particular activity is public or not. Content and context matter. One philosopher can write an op-ed to exhort the public to agree to a particular position, and another can write an op-ed to show a new perspective on an old problem. The first op-ed is probably not very helpful for democracy, but the second one is. One philosopher might hold a reading at a bookstore to sell more books, another to invite a conversation. Likewise, the second one is likely to be more democratic. Public philosophy includes framing issues for public deliberation (e.g., some work on climate change); working with communities addressing problems (e.g., prison work); revising how philosophy understands a problem (e.g., on issues of race, gender, and disability); and critical philosophies that try to identify those who have been sidelined and need to be at the table. There is much good work to do.

Had Walter Lippmann appreciated Dewey's solution to the phantomness of the public, he might not have directed so much attention to the need for "the public philosophy" that could bind the public together in a civic patriotism to a very thin kind

Table 33.1. Varieties of Public Philosophy in Very Broad Strokes

	Realist	Pragmatist
Inspirations	Plato (also Russell, Lippmann)	Dewey (also Arendt)
Character	Elitist	Democratic
Aims	Education	Inquiry
"	Small-scale intellectual growth	To help a public find itself
"	Entertainment	Engagement
"	Better argumentation	Increasing democracy
Direction	Top-down/vertical	Colllaborative/horizontal
"	Professional –> Amateur	Citizen <–> Citizen
Who Learns	The Interested Masses	Both the public and the philosophical community
Conceptions of the Public	Thin	Thick
	Audience	Agent
	Amateurs	Agents
Attitudes toward the public	Condescending	Respectful
Philosophers' Role	Kings	Citizens
Ways of Working	Popularizing Philosophical Issues	Framing Public Problems for public choice and action
"	Explaining how philosophers view an issue	Learning what publics know about an issue that philosophers could use to think about it better
"	Doing what we philosophers already do	Rethinking what we are doing
According to Dewey	Defending the status quo	Aiming for change

of democratic society. The public philosophy that Lippmann longed for would provide order and stability; it would ensure that everyone would do their role and that the expert leaders and professionals would guide the ship of state well. He wanted a public that could spot when fools and cads took the helm and then vote the frauds out of office. But he could not see much role for them beyond that. Dewey did not need any kind of hegemonic ideology to bind the people to the state. He wanted a state that was robustly authored by a public through the squalls and changes that history throws. Instead of expertise, he looked for way to cultivate public intelligence. Philosophers would do well to help with this project of public cultivation.

Some of the best current work in pubic philosophy is being curated at the *Public Philosophy Journal,* an online venue for engaged and public scholarship: http://

publicphilosophyjournal.org/. Also, the Philosophy and the City group holds conferences all over the world, bringing together a global community of scholars focusing on urban issues: http://philosophyofthecity.org/. Additionally, the Public Philosophy Network holds conferences every two years.

WORKS CITED

Citations of John Dewey's works are to the thirty-seven-volume critical edition published by Southern Illinois University Press under the editorship of Jo Ann Boydston. In-text citations give the original publication date and series abbreviation, followed by volume number and page number. For example: (1934, LW 10:12) is page 12 of *Art as Experience*, which is published as volume 10 of *The Later Works*.

Series abbreviations for *The Collected Works:*

EW *The Early Works* (1882–1898)

MW *The Middle Works* (1899–1924)

LW *The Later Works* (1925–1953)

Bender, Thomas. 1993. *Intellect and Public Life: Essays on the Social History of Academic Intellectualism in the U.S.* Baltimore: Johns Hopkins University Press.

Boyer, Ernest L. 1990. Scholarship Reconsidered: Priorities of the Professoriate. New York: The Carnegies Foundation for the Advancement of Teaching.

Brown, David W., and Deborah Witte, eds. 2015. *Higher Education Exchange.* Dayton: Kettering Foundation.

Dewey, John. 1986. *The Collected Works of John Dewey, Later Works.* Carbondale: Southern Illinois University Press.

Dewey, John. 1954. The Public and Its Problems. Athens, OH: Swallow Press.

Kadlec, Alison. 2007. *Dewey's Critical Pragmatism.* Lanham, MD: Lexington Books.

Lippmann, Walter. 1922. *Public Opinion.* New York: Harcourt, Brace and Company.

Lippmann, Walter. 1925. *The Phantom Public.* New York: Macmillan.

Lippmann, Walter. 1955. *The Public Philosophy.* Boston: Little, Brown.

McAfee, Noëlle. 2000. *Habermas, Kristeva, and Citizenship.* Ithaca, NY: Cornell University Press.

McAfee, Noëlle. 2004. "Public Knowledge." *Philosophy and Social Criticism*, vol. 30, no. 2, 139–157.

Meagher, Sharon. 2013. "Public Philosophy: Revitalizing Philosophy as a Civic Discipline." Report to the Kettering Foundation. January 13, 2013. http://api.ning.com/files/C*75Xw4bA4cU7vHOHS-zlLRmkdBskXa9IzuVBCJKtjhmSgMrQy8tWT u1s9vqumPuG2gyJfaPzwWJ1Tu4*NoJIUVYUXtPpC37/KetteringreportfinalcorrectedFeb2 013.pdf

Sandel, Michael. 1996. *Democracy's Discontent: America in Search of a Public Philosophy.* Cambridge, MA: Belknap Press of Harvard University Press.

Sandmann, Lorilee R., ed. 2016. *Journal of Higher Education Outreach & Engagement: 20th Anniversary Issue.* Vol. 20:1. Athens: University of Georgia.

Statham, E. Robert Jr. 2002. *Public Philosophy and Political Science: Crisis and Reflection.* Lanham, MD: Lexington Books.

Veninga, James F., and Noëlle McAfee, eds. 1997. *Standing with the Public: The Humanities and Public Life.* Dayton, OH: Kettering Foundation Press.

CHAPTER 34

....

DEWEY AND ENVIRONMENTAL PHILOSOPHY

....

PAUL B. THOMPSON AND ZACHARY PISO

THE Burlington of John Dewey's boyhood was quite unlike the environmentally conscious community where his earthly remains now reside outside the chapel at the University of Vermont. The city was a bustling center for manufacturing and a hub for shipping. The surrounding countryside was a denuded cutover with little of the beauty we now associate with the second growth forest of deciduous hardwoods. Vermont has become a hotbed for environmental consciousness in the twenty-first century, but there was really no such thing as environmental consciousness (much less hotbeds of it) when Dewey lived there. This essay on Dewey's connection to environmental philosophy begins with some observations that situate awareness of environmental issues historically and moves on to review Dewey's role in the dawn of that awareness. Given the fact that Dewey's direct contributions to environmental philosophy were negligible, the fact that Dewey's thought now *is* quite influential among many philosophers and political theorists writing on environmental issues is remarkable. Indeed, the list of authors who have argued that Dewey can be helpful in thinking through environmental issues is so long that we will not even try to summarize this literature. Instead, we take a more forward-looking approach, tracing this influence to Dewey's elaboration of the *concept* of environment. This is a feature that runs throughout much of his thought. We close the essay with some suggestions on how future scholarship on Dewey's philosophy and future work in environmental philosophy might each benefit from closer collaboration.

Environmental Philosophy from 1900 to the Present Day

Environmental philosophy begins with recognition of an environmental crisis (or at least undergoes a decisive turn in its development). This genesis is located historically in the early decades of the twentieth century, and the North American continent was an important locus for its early expansion. Inquiry into the questions that now comprise environmental philosophy coincides with the dawning awareness of nature's vulnerability to human encroachment and devastation. In the United States, this dawning took form in the closing of the frontier noted by Frederick Jackson Turner in 1893 and through social movements to preserve (or conserve) tracts of "untrammeled" land. Institutions such as the US National Parks and state or federal forests, prairies, and wetlands were the instruments of early-phase environmentalism. The writings of John Muir and the leadership of Gifford Pinchot (who established the US Forest Service during the Theodore Roosevelt administration) are cited as key sources (Norton 1991). Human alterations of the North American landscape began to be perceived as "threats" demanding a response, and environmental philosophy took shape in the creation and dissemination of arguments, rationales, and policies that could serve to justify as well as critique the institutions that emerged *as* a response (Nash 1967). The sense of crisis broadened especially in connection with Rachel Carson's *Silent Spring* in 1962, which demonstrated a new class of threats taking shape within domesticated environments such as farms, urban parklands, and even suburban lawns. The threats of environmental pollution from industrial activities were extending right into our homes and bodies, and efforts to "clean up" air and water were the proposed response (Dunlap 1981). Although these efforts met with significant success, the sense of impending crisis continued to expand in forms ranging from unrestrained human population growth, exhaustion of key resources, and finally the pervasive and practically irreversible mechanisms of climate change. Throughout these expansions and shifts in the meaning of environmental crisis, environmental ethics underwent corresponding shifts in the rationales and argument forms that were seen as important for conceptualizing observed and predicted environmental change as a problem.

Of course, to cite this genesis for environmental philosophy is not to imply that it was universally recognized. Environmental philosophy encompasses both the rationales for interpreting such changes in the world around as threats or crises on the one hand as well as for *denying* that there is anything to get excited about on the other. Furthermore, the historical and geographical locus for the genesis narrative is open to contestation. For some commentators, the environmental crisis is an apocalyptic threat that is visible on the near horizon, but for most Native American tribes, the apocalypse has already occurred. For at least a century they have been coping with a despoiled environment that is long past the tipping point where "response" could hope to restore the balance or integrity envisioned by many white environmental philosophers (Whyte 2015). One may view resource depletion, loss of biodiversity, and climate change as an impending threat or as the continuation of an unjust and unjustifiable process. Or, as some climate-change deniers do, one can insist that everything is just fine. Each perspective reflects a philosophical standpoint on "the environment" that was shaped by events of the late nineteenth through mid-twentieth centuries.

Once the expanding aura of crisis that spawned the environmental activism of the twentieth century began to be supported with philosophical reflection and the development of new themes in ethics and policy, philosophers began to notice and draw upon a much older and more continuous literature. In North America, this included neglected traditions of Native American thought and culture and also in the nineteenth-century transcendentalists, especially Emerson and Thoreau. With this turn, the themes of environmental philosophy expanded once again, this time less inspired by crisis than by the recognition that appreciation of natural areas could be grounded in aesthetics and by exploring the sense in which a natural or built environment comes to characterize the human condition. At the same time, humanism itself was undergoing a unique set of challenges, less from its traditional opponents who saw it as a threat to religious authority than from those who wanted to stress the continuity between humankind and other animal species. Unlike the crises discussed earlier, this turn of thought was more obviously philosophical in its orientation. It challenged implicit assumptions about the interface between ethics and the philosophy of mind, for example. Like the crisis literature in environmental philosophy, calls for better treatment or even rights for nonhumans has highly significant practical implications, ranging from reform in biomedical research and diet (e.g., Thompson 2015) to protection and preservation of natural habitats. In short, environmental philosophy *begins* with a sense of urgent crisis tied to human incursions against what had previously been thought to be unaffected areas of the natural world, but this beginning rapidly expands to include a large set of additional themes.

One important expansion to environmental philosophy since the 1980s is the recognition of environmental injustice, which stresses the peculiar forms of vulnerability to environmental threats experienced by poor or politically marginalized groups. The 1987 report of the World Commission on Environment and Development, chaired by Gro Haarlem Brundtland, is one signal of this decisive turn. The Brundtland Commission had been convened through the United Nations, and its report brought the notion of "sustainable development" to prominence. This concept has a philosophical history of its own, but we argue that whatever else it did or did not accomplish, the Brundtland report did reshape "the environmental problem" by setting it within a global context. However threats to environments, such as national parks or wildlife sanctuaries, are *valued*, they are seen in the post-Brundtland context as embroiled in the complexities and politics of global development. Accordingly, industrialized nations are heavy *users* of natural resources and *emitters* of pollution, including greenhouse gases. They also score much higher on quality of life indices than nations in the less industrialized regions of Africa, Latin America, and Asia. In the three decades since the Brundtland report, China and India have seen marked improvement in quality of life indicators and have also joined the ranks of industrial polluters. In an era of climate change, we contend that one can no longer see the preservation of natural beauty or endangered species as a problem that is distinct from distributive justice at a global scale (see Thompson 2010).

Hence the question: What is the connection between the thought and legacy of John Dewey, on the one hand, and this burgeoning field on the other? The rapid growth of interest in environmental ethics occurs in the 1970s, two decades after Dewey's death. The history just recounted shows that it has points of origin well within the years when Dewey was at his intellectual peak. We begin, thus, with the question of whether Dewey himself can be said to have participated in the dialogs and debates that mark the birth of environmental philosophy between 1859—the year of his birth in Burlington, Vermont—and 1952, the year that he died in New York City. Succinctly, the answer to this question is "no." The main reason to think that John Dewey *might* have some relevance to environmental philosophy is that a school of contemporary scholars writing on present-day environmental issues have created what is known as "environmental pragmatism." Initiated by Anthony Weston and given significant impetus by the 1996 anthology of that name compiled by Andrew Light and Eric Katz, environmental pragmatism emerged in the 1990s as an attempt to steer philosophical scholarship on environmental issues away from what were perceived to be very arcane theoretical debates over the value of nonhumans including ecosystems and threatened populations. For some self-described environmental pragmatists, pragmatism just meant a resolute focus on topics having practical implications. For others, the attraction lay in an approach to valuation that relied neither on psychological states of human beings (such as pleasure, pain, or satisfaction of preferences) nor on bald assertions of intrinsic value that seemed without further warrant (Light and Katz 1996). This latter approach has been advocated by Bryan Norton (1991, 2005) in a series of books and articles that make frequent reference to Peirce, Dewey, and Quine and also to Carnap and Habermas as representative pragmatists. Norton's use of pragmatist source material has also been significantly expanded by Ben Minteer (2011). Hugh McDonald (2004) produced an extended response to environmental philosophers who stressed intrinsic values through detailed accounts of Dewey's naturalism, his instrumental epistemology, and his moral holism. Although critics have responded to the emergence of environmental pragmatism within environmental philosophy, they mainly attend to the work of Light and Norton, rather than Dewey, and we do not engage that literature here.

THE MISSING EMPHASIS ON ENVIRONMENTAL ISSUES IN DEWEY'S WORK

Although Dewey engaged in many of the important public issues of his time, one cannot go to Dewey's texts expecting to find much that could be used to cast him as friend *or* foe of the environment. One cannot undertake the analysis of Dewey's significance for environmental issues without first admitting that he was notably insensitive and unresponsive to the environmental discourse of his own time. Dewey's written work is replete with references to the environment, but so far as we have been able to determine, all of them focus on environing conditions that frame responsive activity, a theme we discuss at greater length later. Dewey's conception of an environment is fundamental to his thought and serves as a crucial link to Darwinian themes that are of considerable importance in mainstream environmental philosophy today. Environments serve as the field, domain, or order in which organisms, reproducing populations, social groups, and even structured activities such as education, science, or art are situated. With respect to the latter, culture itself can be understood as "an environment" in which both individuals and institutions function. While we argue later that this broad understanding of what environments are can be a source of insight for understanding why environments matter, it is important to recognize that Dewey's usage of the word "environment" encompasses many senses that have nothing whatsoever to do with that sense in which there is thought to be an environmental crisis. More tellingly, however, we have been unable to locate discussions in Dewey's published work that reference the literature, debates, or figures—such as Muir or Leopold—that present-day environmentalists cite as precursors to their own interests.

Dewey's writings betray what most American environmentalists would regard as a shocking lack of interest in burgeoning projects such as the campaigns to expand national parks and national forests that were led by John Muir and Gifford Pinchot and given impetus by Theodore Roosevelt. He offers no endorsement to Benton Mackeye's efforts to establish the Appalachian Trail and shows virtually no awareness of impending environmental crisis. To be fair, Dewey is quite like many of his philosophical contemporaries in this respect. One would also search in vain through the writings of G. E. Moore (1873–1958), Ludwig Wittgenstein (1889–1951) or Edmund Husserl (1859–1938) for signs of environmental consciousness. Yet other contemporaries—Henri Bergson (1859–1941), Martin Heidegger (1889–1976), and Alfred North Whitehead (1861–1947)—did notice the rise of environmental issues, even if their treatment of them was nascent and not fully formed. Dewey's failure to engage environmental issues might be seen as especially egregious in light of his proximity to fellow Vermonter George Perkins Marsh (1801–1882), whose 1862 book *Man and Nature* was one of the earliest treatises on environmental decline.

More seriously, Dewey's occasional and not infrequent references to the progress of industrialization during the first half of the twentieth century show no cognizance of environmental costs and risks that we have been able to detect. Dewey was a keen social critic of the industrial revolution, noting how employment within the factory system had created jobs that were as boring and unfulfilling as they were hazardous to workers. He understood how unfettered markets for wage labor drove workers' compensation down to levels that were incapable of sustaining basic needs, not to mention unjust in the levels of wealth that were accruing to industrialists. He did not, however, suspect that the fossil fuels that were powering factories were finite, that obtaining resources through mining and drilling was having irreversible impact on landscapes and ecosystems, or that the emissions from combustion were sources of pollution, threats to public health, and causes of environmental changes that would last for millennia. Nor did he notice (as did Marx) that the emerging industrial agriculture made possible by mechanization and the Haber-Bosch process was depleting soils and threatening renewable sources of potable water.[1] As historian Stephen Stoll has shown, soil conservation was closely linked to rural community health in traditions of American agricultural writings that date back to the mid-eighteenth century (Stoll 2003). Thomas Jefferson's writings on agriculture and democracy were situated within this tradition. Although Dewey noticed Jefferson's interest in democracy, he did not see how it was connected to questions of environmental sustainability. The debate over sustainability, soil conservation, and community health was being vigorously pursued in Dewey's lifetime under the auspices of the Country Life Commission, initiated by President Theodore Roosevelt and led by Liberty Hyde Bailey, yet we have found no evidence that Dewey was engaged in this debate.[2]

Finally, it is worth noting another series of events occurring during Dewey's lifetime that, while less patently environmental in their focus, are important elements in the narrative of present-day environmentalism. These are debates over the safety and efficacy of "patent medicines" popular in the last quarter of the nineteenth century and concerns over the adulteration of foods that accompanied the growth of rail transport, canning, and other forms of preparation that concealed key aspects of the supply chain from end consumers. They were a target of Harvey Wiley in the Bureau of Chemistry at the US Department of Agriculture, who was developing new toxicological and epidemiological methods to evaluate foods and medicines. Wiley became the first administrator of the Food and Drug Administration (FDA) after it was established in 1906. Significantly, Upton Sinclair's novel of social reform *The Jungle* was a key driver for the creation of the FDA. Intending to create sympathy for the plight of immigrant workers in Chicago's packing plants, Sinclair had described an episode where a worker slips and falls into a rendering vat, only to be ground into the sausage being made. Noting how public alarm over the incident led to passage of the Pure Food and Drug Act, rather than social reform, Sinclair remarked that he had aimed to affect America in its heart but had instead hit its stomach. Social controversies over the toxic effects of additives and industrial processing continued unabated throughout the twentieth century. The book *100,000,000 Guinea Pigs* documented abuses in the 1930s and spurred the creation of the Consumers Union, now the publisher of *Consumers Reports*. These concerns over the toxicity of industrial products and processes are now pillars of contemporary environmental consciousness, and the value-laden nature of epidemiology and toxicology continue to be contested issues (Katikireddi and Valles 2015; Elliott and Resnik 2014). It seems impossible that Dewey could have been unaware of these debates, yet his published writings neither discuss the underlying philosophical issues nor do environmental health impacts appear as examples in his writings on the scientific method. In short, anyone hoping to portray Dewey as a source for contemporary environmental philosophy must face up to the fact that his published writings provide virtually no direct support for such a claim. Perhaps Dewey considered these issues relatively unimportant or saw little role for philosophers in addressing them. Alternatively, he was just preoccupied with other things. In any case, there were many opportunities for engagement with momentous environmental issues that remained unrealized.

DEWEY'S INTERPRETATION OF "THE ENVIRONMENT"

Ironically, Dewey's arch nemesis Bertrand Russell makes one of his own rare references to the "nonhuman environment" while offering a cautionary warning against Dewey's "power philosophy," which Russell calls a "cosmic impiety." Russell writes,

> The concept of "truth" as something dependent on facts largely outside human control has been one of the ways in which philosophy has hitherto inculcated the necessary element of humility. When this check on pride is removed, a further step is taken on the road to a certain kind of madness—the intoxication of power which invaded philosophy with Fichte, and to which modern man, philosophers or not, are prone.
>
> (Russell 1961, 214)

He describes the nonhuman environment as largely outside of human control. Russell's use of the words "environment" and "control", while consistent with common usage, is very much at odds with Dewey's. Indeed, a failure to suspend vernacular conceptualizations of environment and control can lead to a serious misreading of Dewey's significance for environmental philosophy. Piers H. G. Stephens points out that notable environmental philosophers Eric Katz, Holmes Rolston, and Eugene Hargrove have all issued critiques of pragmatism on the basis that the philosophy begets "excessive anthropocentrism, subjectivism and instrumentalism" (2012, 26).

For example, George Sessions, a founding voice in "deep ecology," endorses Russell's critique of Dewey, stating that Dewey was promoting a humanistic, technological ethos that has led to environmental decline in "China, Japan and Mexico, as well as the United States" (Sessions 1974, 73). In a more subtle critique, C. A. Bowers argues that Dewey's emphasis on "the method of intelligence" marks an implicit and generally unreflective commitment to Western scientific rationality. Bowers interprets this in much the same way as Sessions, implying a Baconian vision in which science domesticates nature, bending natural forces to the human will (Bowers 2003). Focusing more on Norton and Minteer than Dewey himself, Jacoby Adeshi Carter argues that environmental pragmatism is committed to the idea that an economizing rationality can be deployed to manage environmental disruptions (Carter 2012). Given the omission of environmental issues within Dewey's work, these critical comments are not entirely unwarranted. These authors, however, do seem to be understanding control as control *over* the environment, a view that Larry Hickman has critiqued as "straight-line instrumentalism" (Hickman 2007).

A more thorough explication of Dewey's account of environment and control is helpful, and it is useful to begin by focusing more narrowly on reflex actions, a class of behaviors that were of interest to the psychologists of his day. As is so often the case, Dewey's 1896 "The Reflex-Arc Concept in Psychology" is seminal (1896, EW 5:96–109). The reflex arc was proposed to explain sensory-motor behavior through the association of stimulus and behavioral response. Reflexive responses were taken to be mechanisms that could be conditioned to occur through repetitive associations with arbitrary events detected by an organism's sensory apparatus. Ivan Pavlov (1849–1936) and his salivating dogs are the celebrated example. Dewey's paper argues that this model understates the semiotic quality of such responses, even for a dog. The dog (or any organism) is situated or disposed toward sensory stimuli in an anticipatory manner: it is poised. "Control" indicates the repertory of possible responses that the dog might make when changes occur. The dog's environment is as much the depot of past and anticipated occurrences that characterize the situation and fix its dispositions as it is a world of external stimuli. Control in this sense does not imply that an organism has or desires the capacity to manipulate its situation in every particular. It simply means that organisms will respond to change in their environment by continuously adjusting their dispositional posture. Once a dog has incorporated the ringing bell into the posture with which it anticipates the arrival of food, salivation is itself a form of control. In Dewey's view, a mechanistic stimulus-response model is not only incapable of explaining control; strictly construed it suggests that it is impossible.

Importantly, being environmentally situated is distinct from being spatio-temporally located for Dewey. Neither the time-space continuum nor the four-dimensional Cartesian grid are proper environments, given Dewey's usage: they are instead spatial constructs that encompass or surround entities in much the same way that a circle drawn around a dot on a page encompasses the dot. In *Logic: The Theory of Inquiry*, this contrast is noted in Dewey's clarification that "an organism does not live *in* an environment; it lives by means of an environment" (1938, LW 12:32). The clarification echoes Dewey's remarks from *Experience and Nature*, where he charges that "to see the organism *in* nature, the nervous system in the organism, the brain in the nervous system, the cortex in the brain is the answer to the problems which haunt philosophy. And when thus seen they will be seen to be *in*, not as marbles are in a box but as events are in history, in a moving, growing never finished process" (1925/1929, LW 1:224). These characterizations of organism-environment interaction can be found throughout Dewey's writings—one especially lucid elaboration can be found in the opening four chapters of *Democracy and Education*—and are often offered as foundational discussions that set the context for readers. For all organisms, environments are habitats; they are the sphere within which the organism lives and exerts influence. In this sense, the environments of organisms are bounded (though imprecisely) by the degree to which events can impinge upon the organism. A well-disposed organism might be said to have incorporated all those elements that *might* impinge within its nexus of control. Nevertheless, Dewey's concept is not limited so that only sentient beings have environments.

The general sense in which pragmatism itself is inherently oriented toward environment was well articulated by Sandra B. Rosenthal and Rogene A. Buchholz (1996):

> From the backdrop of the non-spectator understanding of human experience, humans and their environment—organic and inorganic—take on an inherently relational aspect. To speak of organism and environment in isolation from each other is never true to the situation, for no organism can exist in isolation from an environment, and an environment is what it is in relation to an organism. The properties attributed to the environment belong to it in the context of that interaction. What we have is interaction of an indivisible whole, and it is only within such an interactional context that experience and its qualities function. (40)

In this very general sense, pragmatism might well have been *called* environmentalism. It would not imply that one was interested in the political project of preserving ecosystems or endangered species. Rather it frames meaning, valuation, and judgment as processes that reflect the emergence of centeredness or orientation in relationship to a set of environing conditions.

Dewey specifies this general pragmatist kind of environmentalism in both biological and sociocultural terms. Sticking with biology for the moment, responsiveness to environing conditions is a defining characteristic of organisms. Organisms as such exhibit a capability for directed or controlling response to their environment. This capability might be described as active, purposeful, or even intentional in many instances, but what is crucial would be an aptitude that can only be characterized in terms of the interactive totality of organism-in-an-environment. No environment, no organism; no organism, no environment, properly said. The response-ability indicative of the organism-environment system is reflected in the language that we apply to it. A flower responds to its environment through metabolic processes that draw upon water to dissolve soil minerals, producing materials that will be incorporated into its own tissues. A stone that is worn away by the constant flow of water is not responding to its environment, even if it is affected by processes in the environment. The difference between response or aptitude on the one hand and mere causal effect on the other is an ontological difference. Of course, observers of the difference may be wrong about any particular case; Dewey *is* a fallibilist, after all. But the propensity for responsiveness marks the categorical separation of organism-environmental relations from those propensities for change that bear no sense of order or teleology whatsoever.

Environmental Values

The organism-environment relation licenses intentional, interested, or purposeful descriptions of the organism *as* situated within this relational totality. The communicative utility of such descriptions in turn authorizes our vernacular tendency to speak as if the organism and its environment are distinct entities. What one might call (with some trepidation) the *form* of the organism/environment relation is exhibited widely. Staying within biology, a species or breeding population is situated within an environment, for example. Moving to social behavior, the reproducibility of group identity hangs upon being environed in a manner that generates situatedness and its attendant mechanisms of control. Perhaps even within the brain we might speak of habits themselves as being environed by a neurological situation comprising memory systems, sensory-motor response capabilities, and a legacy of "learned" (e.g., retained) responses archived within neural networks. "Being disposed" in one way rather than another can thus be analyzed both in terms of the way that a person is situated within that environment we commonly refer to as "the world" *or* in terms of the way that neural networks have been configured as a function of learning within the basic architecture of the human brain. Discussing the behavior/brain relationship in such a manner takes the conceptual point well beyond anything one might find in Dewey, but the example is illustrative of the way that he might have intended to generalize his conceptual point.

The organismal pole of the organism-environment relationship is in some instances amenable to description as a "point of view." It is worth noting that not all of the entities having this relational status merit classification as intentional, but for those that do, the possibility of control (in Dewey's sense) may indicate (or generate) a version of the organism-environment totality that we associate with "perspective."[3] Nevertheless, the orientation or point of view that is ascribed to any given organism avails the descriptive orientation that is peculiar to many characteristically human activities. The phenomenology that was being developed in Dewey's lifetime by Husserl, Heidegger, Marcel, and others provided an approach to philosophizing that, when combined with the *Umwelt* of biologist Jakob von Uexküll (1864–1944), yields something quite like Dewey's organism-environment totality as approached from the perspective of the organism. Von Uexküll had argued that the subjectivity of an organism (his paradigm was the lowly tick) was constitutively fixed by its capacities for interaction with its *Umwelt*—a word that might be translated alternately as "environment" or "surrounding world." Heidegger drew upon von Uexküll to discuss the difference between Dasein (the characteristic being of human subjectivity) and the subjectivity of animals, which he characterized as "poor in world" (Heidegger 1995, 192–195). In noticing "the worldhood of the world" Heidegger is pointing out the way in which Dasein exhibits an environed centeredness characteristic of human beings. Dasein is always already cast into an Umwelt, though for humans (as distinct from ticks) the environing world is a richly cultural artifact.

Dewey would not have disagreed with the "richly cultural" observation. Yet Dewey and other pragmatists also maintain a vocabulary for describing behavior from a position *outside* the center of orientation (the subjectivity) that marks the organismal pole of an organism-environment totality. This is to describe the organism, as it were, from the perspective of the environment—a deeply ironic formulation, of course, for the environment cannot have a perspective save, perhaps, the self-nullifying "view from nowhere" identified by Thomas Nagel. To speak this way is to speak "as if," as Dewey was keenly aware. Yet he was also aware (and equally keenly) that describing the organism-environment relation in just these imaginative terms was instrumental for many of the projects in which scientists were and are engaged. Thus while Dewey was able to philosophize about "being environed" in a sense commensurate with phenomenology, he was not committed to a view that denied the possibility or coherence of an observer's perspective on organism-environment relations.

Nevertheless, scientists who observe an organism responding to environmental change do express aspects of their own situatedness. We are situated as scientists within institutions (e.g., habitualized practices) that reinforce particular dispositions for control (again, in Dewey's sense). That means that qua scientist, our observation is a particular form of socially reinforced control that attunes our perceptual and communicative capacities toward a specific class of possible responses. An aesthete on a nature walk or a hunter might observe the organism in an entirely different way, but here, too, a particular situatedness is crucial. What matters for scientists is that we are seeing how the organism is itself situated; this is a feature of what it means to *observe* an organism in a scientific way. Although our own situatedness as scientific observers informs this seeing, it also recedes into the background, becoming a component of the pragmata—the depot of past experiences—that makes scientific activity meaningful.

It is tempting to say that we project our own situatedness, our own possession of a perspective, onto the organism that we are observing, but it would be equally valid to hypothesize causal relationships running in the opposite direction: We are able to grasp the sense in which we ourselves *have* something we might call a perspective, a standpoint or a view because we have projected a relationship that we have seen in the behavior of other organisms back onto our own experience. Dewey's frequent praise of science as availing more developed reflective abilities may well be grounded in the latter possibility. What is more, this possibility distinguishes Dewey's view from that of phenomenologists who presume (perhaps following Descartes) that the subjectivist perspective has ontological priority. For Dewey, an ability to contemplate alternative perspectives on perspective taking (to see that others might take competing views) is a form of developmental growth for the person (the organism). It is an achievement, and not an ability that we can presume all people will share. Dewey goes on to turn this reflection into a prescription: we should create environments (our schools) where this kind of growth (the ability to take a perspective on perspective taking) is adaptive. These seemingly tangential observations are material to our later discussion of how Dewey can help us respond to the issues that we characterize as "environmental" in a more prosaic sense.[4]

As Dewey scholars know, Dewey applies the situated nature of inquiry well beyond epistemology. His aesthetics draw upon the situatedness of an experiencing subject to characterize art. Art is not the artifact (the painting or performance), and Dewey's aesthetics is not predicated on features of paintings, musical compositions, or literary texts. The work of art is the creative experience, an experience that must be had by the viewer, reader, or listener in order for a genuinely aesthetic moment to occur. As observation and collection of data are for scientific research, this experience is exposited as an instance of the organism-environment relationship, this time in terms of the way that the viewer of a painting or sculpture brings a prior orientation to seeing it, undergoing a series of transformative changes in response and finally culminating in a consummation that makes the experience of viewing a work of art into a unified whole. Dewey's account of aesthetic experience is of singular importance for his discussion of the organism-environment relation because it is in these consummatory encounters that the participatory dimensions of the relation are most fully realized. Here, dropping back to a spectator's perspective would actually block the participatory engagement that is essential to aesthetic consummation.

Dewey's aesthetics also provide a point of entry for his discussion of valuation as a form of engagement, an expression of the organism-environment response-ability that is most meaningfully described from the perspective of a socially committed participant. Valuations are responses to problematic situations. They emerge through a process of inquiry in which one probes a number of hypotheses to ascertain which will address the problem. In a sense, the orientation that will lend normative force to an evaluation is implicit within the elements of one's environing conditions that made the situation problematic at the outset. In other words, the better or worse ways of valuing a situation are "objective characteristics of the situation" when it is interpreted as structured by relationships between organism and environment. This objectivity hardly means that situations are valuable independent of our (an organism's) valuation of them. For human communities, it is quite likely that the cultural dimensions of one's environment will contain prior commitments that require resolution through the process of valuation. Much of what makes a situation ethically significant will derive from those commitments and will hence be reflected in the felt need, the call to response, that is implied by the urgency of moving through the various phases of inquiry toward some action that resolves (or at least ameliorates) the tensions that provoke moral inquiry in the first place.

In sum, Dewey's theory of value is inherently environmental (as are other pragmatisms) in the sense that they accord both ontological and conceptual significance to environments. Dewey extends the power to shape those situations that propound response *to* the environing world of the organism and sees life itself as emerging from the ability to be responsive to environments. Crucially, values are products of the environment, of the history that organisms accrue in their various adventures of parry, control, and response. This does not necessarily mean that any organism—including a human one—will problematize a given situation in terms of the need for preservation and conservation of ecosystems or in terms of duties to or the value of nonhumans, including other nonhuman organisms. It is thus a fair criticism to say that there is nothing inherent in Dewey's philosophy as we have construed it that would make him an environmentalist in the contemporary sense of the word. As we have already noted, Dewey was regretfully inattentive to those elements in his own experience that might have sensitized him to the growing suite of environmental problems that were accruing as a result of industrialization and the spread of capitalism. Nevertheless, as several authors have argued, Dewey's basic philosophical orientation—his metaphysical environmentalism—does provide both a strong basis for recognizing environmental problems today and for formulating responses to them for tomorrow.

WHAT DOES DEWEY OFFER
TO ENVIRONMENTAL PHILOSOPHIES
OF THE FUTURE?

Dewey's conception of the environment provides resources for ameliorating contemporary public problems that confront environmental science, management, and policy. Here we focus on three frontiers for engaged philosophy—interdisciplinarity, transdisciplinarity, and environmental justice.

After the globalization of the environment with the Brundtland report of 1987 and the subsequent studies of the Intergovernmental Panel on Climate Change, it has become increasingly important to conceptualize environmental issues in ways that are amenable to multidisciplinary and transdisciplinary inquiry. The notion of "wicked problems"— a concept formulated with the aid of C. West Churchman, a pragmatist philosopher working at Berkeley in the 1960s and 1970s who remains unappreciated by fellow philosophers—has been influential (cf. Norton 2015). As described by Horst Rittel and Melvin Webber in 1973, wicked problems are value laden and characterized by uncertainty, high stakes, irreversible consequences, multiple constituencies, lack of clarity in problem definition or what would count as a solution, and the presence of important factors that are beyond the control of any analyst or decision-maker. Churchman had emphasized the importance of approaching wicked problems with a profound sense of one's potential culpability and moral responsibility—an attitude that was in deep conflict with the ideal of "value-free science." While the division of scientific inquiry into disciplinary specializations had proven useful for the solution of "tame" problems, environmental crises are all wicked.

The trouble is that scholars and practitioners of multi-, inter-, and transdisciplinary research have taken the usefulness of tamed, disciplined scientific practices as testament to science carving nature at its joints. On this view, biology is reliable and predictive because biological theories represent the one way that the world actually is, but so is physics, and ecology, and perhaps economics. Scientists forget the ways that their methods and theories developed in order to navigate problematic situations— sometimes these situations were artfully constructed in the laboratory, but sometimes these situations were wicked problems demanding new knowledge and technology. By wresting scientific culture from the environment in which it is wedged tightly, it is too easy to think of the signs and symbols of that culture as value free (cf. Knorr Cetina 1999). This presents a seemingly insurmountable challenge for interdisciplinary inquiry, since the *integration* of these supposedly value-free disciplines appears to lack any objective standard for bringing disciplinary perspectives together (Klein 2014; Boix Mansilla 2010).

Dewey anticipated the challenge of interdisciplinary integration as early as *Experience and Nature*, warning:

> Over-specialization and division of interests, occupations and goods create the need for a generalized medium of intercommunication, of mutual criticism through all-around translation from one separated region of experience into another. Thus philosophy as a critical organ becomes in effect a messenger, a liaison officer, making reciprocally intelligible voices speaking provincial tongues, and thereby enlarging as well as rectifying the meanings with which they are charged.
>
> (1925/1929, LW 1:306)

Theorists of interdisciplinarity are pursuing all-around translation, but their tack is to motivate ontological and epistemological theories that themselves purport a value-free substrate or methodology to which we hold diverse disciplines accountable (Piso 2015). Dewey is not after that sort of translation. Instead of grand philosophical theories that let us off the hook for the choices that we make, liaison officers excavate the ways that specialized cultures create meaning in the pursuit of diverse goods (Hickman 2007). Disciplinary cultures provide tools that help us to bring about these goods, and in particular disciplinary descriptions and theories must also be taken as tools, since language is "the tool of tools" (1925/1929, LW 1:134). At stake in interdisciplinary collaboration is not the discovery of the environment as it really exists apart from organism-environment interaction; as Dewey demonstrates, that sense of environment is incoherent, but even if we could make sense of it, it would provide little guidance for how we, as organisms, ought to act. Rather, what is at stake in interdisciplinary collaboration is how we ought to navigate the environment, an environment that admits of plural goals and goods, but plural goals and goods that are often in tension with one another (Piso 2016).

Philosophers as liaison officers are tasked then with showing how provincial tongues are situated within particular problem-solving endeavors. This is a far cry from thinking of science as value-free; indeed, a main task of liaison officers is to make explicit the values that specializations hold dear and to submit these values to deliberation and criticism. In Dewey's call for enlarging the meaning of provincial tongues, though, he is calling for more than analysis of the ways in which science is value-laden. We enlarge meaning in these collaborations by locating the ways that particular practices bear on the pursuit of goals outside of the purview of their originating discipline. After all, our attempts to ameliorate the ecological dimensions of wicked problems can bear on the agricultural dimensions, or the anthropological dimensions, or the artistic. Here philosophy must partake in inquiry, must serve as a plain member within interdisciplinary collaboration, in hypothesizing ways in which reconstruction in one corner of life bears on the reconstruction of another (Lake, Sisson, and Jaskiewicz 2015).

By thinking of disciplinary descriptions as tools, Deweyan environmental philosophers appreciate the distinctively pragmatic challenge of interdisciplinary inquiry. Wicked problems require reflection and deliberation on the values that are at stake when we orient ourselves to an indeterminate situation. Crucially, however, this turn to the valuational aspects of inquiry is not, for Deweyans, a turn away from objectivity (Putnam 2002). Values exist as part of a situation, in the relation between an organism and its environment, rather than as detached perspectives of a disembodied subject. Here it is important to remember that inquiry is initiated by the indeterminacy of the situation in which we find ourselves and that there is work to be done in transforming an indeterminate situation into a problematic situation (Brown 2012). When we orient ourselves, we are taking certain values to be of higher priority than others, and we are sparing some of our practices from reconstruction (in Dewey's *Logic*, propositions serve this role of scaffolding our inquiry, and it is only judgment arising out of doubt that can properly be said to be true or false). Ultimately, interdisciplinary integration is a matter of wielding the right tools for navigating a properly problematized but initially indeterminate situation.

Transdisciplinary inquiry differs from interdisciplinary inquiry in that the former enrolls publics (who, if specialists, are not specialists in the traditional academic disciplines). Transdisciplinarity can be understood as an embrace of the pragmatics of inquiry and a recognition that the way that we problematize an indeterminate situation admits of norms—that there are more or less right ways of taking the situation to be problematic. Theorists of various forms of transdisciplinarity often warrant such inquiry on both epistemic and ethical grounds. Epistemically, transdisciplinarity often brings to bear local knowledge, ecological and otherwise, to propose novel solutions to wicked problems (Folke 2004). Ethically, transdisciplinarity legitimates science and science-based policymaking by providing a forum in which stakeholders endorse the ways that academic specialists orient themselves to the situation (Thompson and Whyte 2012; Swanson et al. 2012; Popa, Guillermin, and Dedeurwaerdere 2015). Yet once inquiry is understood as reconstruction of the totality of the situation—including both organisms and the environment—then these two justifications become difficult to disambiguate (Anderson 2004; Welchman 2002). Values are not external to the situation and brought to bear in legitimating explanations of and interventions within the external world. Values, as part of the situation, are themselves subject to reconstruction. In transdisciplinary inquiry, we mobilize reasons for problematizing the situation one way rather than another, and our reasons abide by shared norms regarding when the pursuit of one value ought to yield to another.

What a Deweyan theory of inquiry maintains is that this rivalry of goods does not give way to relativism. A community deliberating over the appropriate way to problematize a situation is inquiring into the correct use of a shared moral vocabulary (Clough 2008; Anderson 2004). When navigating wicked problems, there is sometimes the suspicion that there is no sense in which various problematizations are more true than others, that disagreements regarding value judgments are incommensurable (Clough 2015). On the Deweyan theory of inquiry, however, transdisciplinary inquiry aims at warranting assertions about the causal and valuational features of indeterminate situations. While community leaders may register an inchoate sense that the situation is a problem, they call on diverse publics to speak to underappreciated goods and overlooked exigencies in the pursuit thereof (Brister 2012).

Finally, we endorse a theme that has been central to Norton and Minteer's appropriation of Dewey's thought: the commitment to valuational inquiry provides important resources for environmental policy in general, and emerging problems of environmental justice are especially relevant. Dewey's account of democratic deliberation is rich, attending to the ways that science as well as narrative, drama, and the arts all contribute to widening our imagination and warranting collective action. These deliberative practices find parallels in current social science, where environmental scientists and managers draw on tools from participatory mapping, modeling, and visioning to convene with stakeholders and rehearse potential futures (Olabisi et al. 2016; Dunn 2007). As Norton has stressed in his proposals for adaptive management, Dewey offers us both a dynamic procedure through which community goals and commitments are expressed and a theory of inquiry that preserves objectivity in flux. Dewey's call for a science of values is grounded in the recognition that values can, and often must, change and that communities must experiment in order to find harmonious ways of configuring their values (Norton 2015). Above all else, environmental justice calls for recognition of the ways that land use and the burdens of environmentally pollution have been systematically and disproportionately borne by people who are marginalized in virtue of race, gender, and social class. Ironically, advocacy on behalf of the environment can be co-opted in ways that further marginalize the traditional victims of environmental injustice. While in one sense the work of Jane Addams may be more directly relevant to the restorative aspect of environmental justice, Dewey provides a complementary metaethics wherein value judgments are accountable to shared social norms and the concrete situations in which we find ourselves. He counters the pervasive view that values are simply a subjective statement of one's preferences. But, more importantly, Dewey's elaborate account of deliberation offers resources for cultivating common ground in the face of radical differences. This aspect of Dewey's thought *is* the element that has heretofore been the primary focus of environmental pragmatists (Chaloupka 1987; Minteer 2011; McDonald 2004).

Interdisciplinarity, transdisciplinarity, and environmental justice offer three frontiers for environmental philosophy, especially for engaged philosophers working with scientists and stakeholders. That said, the ways that environmental philosophy weaves together philosophy of science, ethics, social and political philosophy, and so on cuts across "divisions of interests, occupations, and goods" in academic philosophy. While Deweyans have long appreciated the permeable boundaries between these specializations, there is a need for further philosophical reflection on these liminal spaces. Sorting out the ways in which Dewey's theory of inquiry is accountable to his conception of democracy, and vice versa, provides guidance for thinking about public problems today. Dewey's characterization of philosophy as the "liaison officer" that brings the strands of inquiry into coherence is pertinent, and even within Dewey scholarship tracing the threads between *Democracy and Education* and *The Quest for Certainty* might help us liaise that environment that constitutes us as a social organism.

NOTES

1. Editor Steven Fesmire brought to our attention an especially telling oversight in Dewey's remarks on agriculture: "When chemical fertilizers can be used in place of animal manures, when improved grain and cattle can be purposefully bred from inferior animals and grasses, when mechanical energy can be converted into heat and electricity into mechanical energy, man gains power to manipulate nature" (1920, MW 12:120). Dewey's naivety with respect to ecological dynamics here leads him to praise the manipulation of nature, but this naive praise is actually in tension with, rather than the logical extension of, his attention to organism-environment interaction.

2. Bailey himself was a well-regarded educational reformer as well as the leading agricultural scientist of his day. In his writings on education, Bailey stressed experiential methods. He was the leading advocate of outdoor nature experiences that would draw upon students' involvement in gardening, camping, hiking, or hunting and scavenging to pique their interest in biology. In his role as dean of the nation's first agricultural college at Cornell University, Bailey promoted educational opportunities for women and appointed the first woman faculty member at Cornell (see Thompson, 2010). Dewey was, of course, undertaking similar experiments in education at the University of Chicago, and one might have expected there to be some relationship or interchange of ideas that would have given him an opportunity to at least reflect on Bailey's methods. Doing so might well have brought him into engagement with the environmental issues being raised by the Country Life Commission and with Bailey's interest in farming's impact on the natural resource base, yet we have found no evidence of any direct connection between Dewey and Bailey.

3. Perspective in our metaphorical sense does not imply anything that would properly be characterized as a view in the ocular sense. The metabolic processes within a microorganism reflect an orientation toward an environing world, yet it would be metaphorical to describe a bacterium's relation to its environment as a "point of view." Perspective and point-of-view *do* yield or license intentional descriptions. Views (as distinct from mere orientations) are characteristic of most humans, and presumably many other vertebrates, but they reflect the orientation of only a minority of the organisms that respond to their respective environments.

4. In fact, much of Dewey's epistemology starts from a spectator's perspective on the work of scientists in order to mobilize a rich vocabulary for describing the process of inquiry and categorizing its elements. This philosophical practice does not contradict the claim that Dewey's epistemology could only have been developed from the perspective of an active organism (Dewey himself) reconstructing its environment. When Dewey refers to "the situation," he is generally describing the organism-environment totality of an inquiring scientist—an organism responding to a thoroughly socialized environment through practices (control mechanisms) of observation and inference. The situatedness of situations is simply the way in which inquiring scientists are oriented to their environing world in much the same way cockroaches are oriented to their environments by hunger, fear, or the need for sleep. In each case, orientation reflects a prior state of the organism-environment totality, along with whatever features are calling for response at the moment—the features that make the situation "problematic." Although situations can be attributed to a problem-solving scientist in much the way that the environment of a wetland can be characterized as the environment of a frog, Dewey's use of the word "situation" within epistemology carries with it the sense or feeling of being situated as an organism working to maintain continuous

life functions in a precarious world. Situations are in this sense much less than "everything in the universe" (a wholly pointless if logically consistent way to understand "the environment"), at the same time that they are more. They are less in that the scientist (the organism) has selected a subset of possible stimuli for attention. They are more in that situations are *meaningful*; they connote how an organism is always oriented within an environment. This orientation reflects the habits of accumulated organism-environment interactions as well as ongoing projects and current needs. Orientation becomes acute when some feature in the surrounding environment intrudes upon the situation to demand proximate (if not immediate) attention and response.

WORKS CITED

Citations of John Dewey's works are to the thirty-seven-volume critical edition published by Southern Illinois University Press under the editorship of Jo Ann Boydston. In-text citations give the original publication date and series abbreviation, followed by volume number and page number. For example: (1934, LW 10:12) is page 12 of *Art as Experience*, which is published as volume 10 of *The Later Works*.

Series abbreviations for *The Collected Works*:

EW *The Early Works* (1882–98)

MW *The Middle Works* (1899–1924)

LW *The Later Works* (1925–53)

Anderson, Elizabeth. 2004. "Uses of Value Judgments in Science: A General Argument, with Lessons from a Case Study of Feminist Research on Divorce." *Hypatia*, vol. 19, no. 1, 1–24.

Boix Mansilla, Veronica. 2010. "Learning to Synthesize: The Development of Interdisciplinary Understanding." In *The Oxford Handbook of Interdisciplinarity*. Edited by Robert Frodeman, Julie Thompson Klein, and Carl Mitcham, 288–306. Oxford: Oxford University Press.

Bowers, C. A. 2003. "The Case Against John Dewey as an Environmental and Eco-Justice Philosopher." *Environmental Ethics*, vol. 25, 25–42.

Brister, Evelyn. 2012. "Distributing Epistemic Authority: Refining Norton's Pragmatist Approach to Environmental Decision-Making." *Contemporary Pragmatism*, vol. 9, no. 1, 185–203.

Brown, Matthew J. 2012. "John Dewey's Logic of Science." *HOPOS: The Journal of the International Society for the History of Philosophy of Science*, vol. 2, no. 2, 258–306.

Carson, Rachel. 1962. *Silent Spring*. Boston: Houghton Mifflin.

Carter, Jacoby Adeshi. 2012. "Environmental Pragmatism, Global Warming and Climate Change," *Contemporary Pragmatism*, vol. 9, 133–150.

Chaloupka, William. 1987. "John Dewey's Social Aesthetics as a Precedent for Environmental Thought." *Environmental Ethics*, vol. 9, 243–260.

Clough, Sharyn. 2008. "Solomon's Empirical/Non-Empirical Distinction and the Proper Place of Values in Science." *Perspectives on Science*, vol. 16, no. 3, 265–279.

Clough, Sharyn. 2015. "Fact/Value Holism, Feminist Philosophy, and Nazi Cancer Research." *Feminist Philosophy Quarterly*, vol. 1, no. 1, 7.

Dewey, John. 1896. "The Reflex Arc Concept in Philosophy." EW 5.

Dewey, John. 1920. *Reconstruction in Philosophy*. MW 12.

Dewey, John. 1925/1929. *Experience and Nature*. LW 1.

Dewey, John. 1938. *Logic: The Theory of Inquiry*. LW 12.

Dunlap, Thomas. 1981. *DDT: Scientists, Citizens and Public Policy*. Princeton, NJ: Princeton University Press.

Dunn, Christine E. 2007. "Participatory GIS—A People's GIS?" *Progress in Human Geography*, vol. 31, no. 5, 616–637.

Elliott, Kevin C., and David B. Resnik. 2014. "Science, Policy, and the Transparency of Values." *Environmental Health Perspectives*, vol. 122, 647–650.

Folke, Carl. 2004. "Traditional Knowledge in Social-Ecological Systems." *Ecology and Society*, vol. 9, no. 3, 7.

Heidegger, Martin. 1995. *The Fundamental Concepts of Metaphysics: World, Finitude, Solitude*. Translated by W. McNeill and N. Walker. Bloomington: University of Indiana Press.

Hickman, Larry A. 2007. *Pragmatism as Post-Postmodernism: Lessons from John Dewey*. New York: Fordham University Press.

Katikireddi, S. V., and Sean A. Valles. 2015. "Coupled Ethical-Epistemic Analysis of Public Health Research and Practice: Categorizing Variables to Improve Population Health and Equity." *American Journal of Public Health*, vol. 105, no. 1, 36–42.

Klein, Julie Thompson. 2014. "Discourses of Transdisciplinarity: Looking Back to the Future." *Futures*, vol. 63, 68–74.

Knorr Cetina, Karen. 1999. *Epistemic Cultures: How the Sciences Make Knowledge*. Cambridge, MA: Harvard University Press.

Lake, Danielle, Lisa Sisson, and Lara Jaskiewicz. 2015. "Local Food Innovation in a World of Wicked Problems: The Pitfalls and the Potential." *Journal of Agriculture, Food Systems, and Community Development*, vol. 5, no. 3, 13–26.

Light, Andrew, and Eric Katz, eds. 1996. *Environmental Pragmatism*. New York: Routledge.

McDonald, Hugh. 2004. *John Dewey and Environmental Philosophy*. Albany, NY: SUNY Press.

Minteer, Ben. 2011. *Refounding Environmental Ethics: Pragmatism, Principle, and Practice*. Philadelphia: Temple University Press.

Nash, Roderick. 1967. *Wilderness and the American Mind*. New Haven, CT: Yale University Press.

Norton, Bryan G. 1991. *Toward Unity Among Environmentalists*. Oxford: Oxford University Press.

Norton, Bryan G. 2005. *Sustainability: A Philosophy of Adaptive Ecosystem Management*. Chicago: University of Chicago Press.

Norton, Bryan G. 2015. *Sustainable Values, Sustainable Change: A Guide to Environmental Decision Making*. Chicago: University of Chicago Press.

Piso, Zachary. 2015. "Integration, Language, and Practice: Wittgenstein and Interdisciplinary Communication." *Issues in Interdisciplinary Studies*, vol. 33, 14–38.

Piso, Zachary. 2016. "Integration, Values, and Well-Ordered Interdisciplinary Science." *The Pluralist*, vol. 11, no. 1, 49–57.

Popa, Florin, Mathieu Guillermin, and Tom Dedeurwaerdere. 2015. "A Pragmatist Approach to Transdisciplinarity in Sustainability Research: From Complex Systems Theory to Reflexive Science." *Futures*, vol. 65, 45–56.

Putnam, Hilary. 2002. *The Collapse of the Fact/Value Dichotomy and Other Essays*. Cambridge, MA: Harvard University Press.

Rosenthal, Sandra B., and Rogene A. Buchholz. 1996. "How Pragmatism Is an Environmental Ethic." In *Environmental Pragmatism*. Edited by Andrew Light and Eric Katz, 38–49. New York: Routledge.

Russell, B. 1961 *The Basic Writings of Bertrand Russell: 1903–1959*. Edited by R. E. Egner and L. E. Dennon. London: Routledge.

Schmitt Olabisi, Laura, Jelili Adebiyi, Pierre Sibiry Traoré, and Mayamiko Nathaniel Kakwera. 2016. "Do Participatory Scenario Exercises Promote Systems Thinking and Build Consensus?" *Elementa: Science of the Anthropocene*, vol. 4, 000113. doi: 10.12952/journal.elementa.000113.

Sessions, George. 1974. "Anthropocentrism and the Environmental Crisis." *Humboldt Journal of Social Relations*, vol. 2, no. 1, 71–81.

Stoll, Stephen. 2003. *Larding the Lean Earth: Soil and Society in Nineteenth-Century America*. New York: Hill and Wang.

Swanson, J. C., Y. Lee, P. B. Thompson, R. Bawden, and J. A. Mench, 2012. "Integration: Valuing Stakeholder Input in Setting Priorities for Socially Sustainable Egg Production," *Poultry Science*, vol. 90, 2110–2121.

Thompson, Paul B. 2010. *The Agrarian Vision: Sustainability and Environmental Ethics*. Lexington: University Press of Kentucky.

Thompson, Paul B. 2015. *From Field to Fork: Food Ethics for Everyone*. Oxford: Oxford University Press.

Thompson Paul, and Kyle Powys Whyte 2012. "What Happens to Environmental Philosophy in a Wicked World?" *Journal of Agricultural and Environmental Ethics*, vol. 25, 485–498.

Welchman, Jennifer. 2002. "Logic and Judgments of Practice." In *Dewey's Logic Theory: New Studies and Interpretations*. Edited by F. Thomas Burke, D. Micah Hester, and Robert B. Talisse, 27–42. Nashville, TN: Vanderbilt University Press.

Whyte, Kyle Powys. 2015. "Indigenous Food Systems, Environmental Justice and Settler Industrial-States. In *Global Food, Global Justice: Essays on Eating under Globablization*. Edited by Mary C. Rawlinson and Caleb Ward, 143–156. Newcastle, United Kingdom: Cambridge Scholars Publishing.

....

CHAPTER 35

DEWEY AND BIOETHICS

....

D. MICAH HESTER

> Within the circle of professional philosophers and in the teaching of phi-
> losophy in institutions of learning, differences in the conclusions that
> constitute systems and isms have their place. But for the public, they are
> of slight importance compared with the question of what philosophers are
> trying to do and might do if they tried. The interest of the public centers in
> such questions as . . . . How is [philosophy] related to those concerns and
> issues which today stand out as the problems of men?
>
> (Dewey, 1946, LW 15:155)

JOHN Dewey (1859–1952) challenged the field of philosophy to focus less on logic and
conceptual puzzles and more on affecting lived experience. And while Dewey himself
was known for his public engagements, from the development of progressive education to the development of the American Association of University Professors, from
supporting Hull House to supporting the political inquiries, Dewey was not without his
own blinders. For example, Dewey said and did little about race relations during the
post–Civil War/Jim Crow era in which he was working. Further, it is worth noting that
in his major work, *Ethics* (1908/1932, MW 5; LW 7), his coauthor, James Tufts (1862–
1942), wrote the "applied" chapters while Dewey focused on the theoretical debates
among virtue ethics, consequentialism, and deontology. Even in the 1946 volume, *The
Problems of Men*, Dewey's concern is with broad public issues like education, human nature, and value, not poverty, war, or the environment (1946, LW 15).

But maybe it is not necessary for Dewey to be all things to all people and just enough
for him to provide a theoretical basis that can "engage in the act of midwifery that was
assigned to [philosophy] by Socrates twenty-five hundred years ago" (1946, LW 15:169).

In fact, one place he may have indirectly succeeded is in the field of bioethics.
Bioethics is a contemporary professional endeavor that looks to the moral issues raised

by bio-eco-medico-practices. The term "*Bio-Ethik*" was coined by Fritz Jahr (1895-1953) in the first part of the 20th century as a broad principle of moral conduct in relation to all living beings. In the early 1970s, scientist Van Rensselaer Potter (1911–2001) picked up the term "bioethics" and applied it to moral concerns raised by the fracturing of the natural sciences. At almost the same time as Potter, but seemingly independently, Sargent Shriver (1915–2011) coined the term "bioethics" as a concatenation of biology and ethics in relation to the development of a new ethics of science institute at Georgetown. Since that time, the term has been focused as narrowly as clinical ethics—the ethics of patients and providers—and as broadly as eco-ethics—the ethics of "bios" and ecology. And yet, however broadly or narrowly we construe the field of bioethics, it is an endeavor with both conceptual and practical considerations woven into the very heart of that endeavor.

That bioethics arose out of the late 1960s is one thing; *how* it came to arise is another. During the first half of the 20th century, philosophical discussions of practical matters were sparse. Even if we take Dewey/Tuft's *Ethics* as an exception, metaethics trumped practical ethics for much of the century—with debate about the epistemology and psychology of moral claims taking center stage. It is out of this environment that bioethicist Albert Jonsen (1931–) notes

> Many of us have wondered how the desiccated moral philosophy of the 1960s turned into the vigorous ethics of bioethics . . . . My fantasy is that the ghosts of our two great American philosophers, William James and John Dewey, silently presided over the transformation . . . . It is my impression that philosophers who have become bioethicists have followed, unknowingly, the lead of these preeminent American philosophers.
>
> (Jonsen 1997, 19)

This chapter explores what Jonsen's "fantasy" means, particularly in relation to the work of John Dewey. To do so, the discussion begins with a brief explanation of the subject matter of bioethics and then turns to a discussion of key features of pragmatism that are infused throughout current bioethical theory and practice. Last it turns to an exploration of Dewey's own words about physicians and health to show how his work grounds the pragmatic approach of bioethics.

THE SUBJECT MATTER OF BIOETHICS

Before looking more closely at Jonsen's fantasy, it will help to sketch briefly the subject matter of bioethics itself. For the purposes of this chapter, bioethics shall be construed as medical, clinical ethics, and this field looks at the moral space in which healthcare is provided by clinicians for the sake of patients. Bioethics concerns human well-being in the face of medical circumstances and situations that call forth a response by healthcare providers. As such bioethics is about conditions and relationships—specifically, about the conditions of health and illness that are the basis of the relationship between patient and provider.

Edmund Pellegrino (1920–2013) rightly noted over 35 years ago that medicine is about making "a decision 'good' for *this* patient" (Pellegrino 1979, 173). To meet this demand is to be particular, not generic; individual, not global. The provider's actions in a patient's storyline can be promoting, protective, or acquiescent; they can generate new ends, avoid particular outcomes, or go with the existing flow. But if they meet with *this* patient's life story as he or she (or his or her parents) has been developing it, any of those actions empower the patient—in the face of whatever vulnerabilities befall him or her.

Bioethics speaks to conditions of wellness and affliction, and these conditions occur within human experience and differ for each human being. Within the context of health and illness, a certain kind of relationship arises between humans as they seek health and well-being and the healthcare providers who offer knowledge, skills, and experience with the purpose of promoting health through preventing and eradicating, illness, diseases, and injuries. However, this relationship begins with a substantive and unavoidable imbalance of power (where "power" is defined simply as "an ability to do"). Physicians have long held a position of authority in the society at large and in medical encounters in particular. Obviously, there are important reasons for this. Physicians have a kind of knowledge not possessed by most of their patients (which is why patients seek them out), and this fact leads to an imbalance of status and power in medical encounters. In the words of Richard Zaner (1933–), "[Patients] realize that to be sick is to be disadvantaged and compromised both by the illness and by the relationship to the doctor, who has the edge over the patient in knowledge, skills, resources, and social legitimation and authority" (Zaner 1993, 10). There is a fundamental "asymmetry" in patient–provider relationships.

> [This] asymmetry of power in the helping relationship is marked by the '*peculiarly vulnerable* existential state' of the patient and the power of the professed healer(s) . . . .
> From the perspective of the patient, illness or injury forces breaks with the usual flow of daily life.
>
> (Zaner 1988, 55; emphasis added)

This "break" disables the patient in ways that force him/her to place trust in the physician, "and obliges the patient to rely on the care of other persons" (Zaner 1988, 55). Meanwhile, the physician, by way of his or her technical ability and scientific knowledge, is empowered within and by the relationship, and though most likely a stranger to the patient, he or she is implicitly entrusted with a responsibility to help the patient.

It is this fundamental imbalance in the relationship between the professional's empowered abilities and knowledge and the patient's "peculiar vulnerability" that leads to an important moral response—namely, that the moral responsibilities of healthcare providers simply differ from those of patients and their families. Now this may seem obvious on its face, but it is important to see *why* the responsibilities differ in order to see *how* they differ. The power imbalance requires mitigation (if not elimination), and the responsibility for doing so weighs more heavily on the side of those in power, not on those who are vulnerable. Vulnerability is a state of concrete risk of harm, but often that which endangers the vulnerable subject is unknown to the subject him- or herself. The "power" spoken of by Zaner is precisely the power of both knowledge and skill that can enlighten and empower the otherwise vulnerable patient. While patients and their families do have their own responsibilities and obligations in light of the vulnerabilities they have and face, there is a particular moral challenge of responsibilities born by those in power in patient–provider encounters (viz., healthcare professionals).

Bioethics, then, is a field of inquiry concerned with the ethics of particular relationships and conditions—medical, healthcare relationships and the well-being and/or afflictions of humans as they live their lives. It is a field that morally requires providers to focus, not simply on disease or illness, not on health and well-being, but on the conditions and outcomes of specific patients in their lived experiences.

JONSEN'S "FANTASY": PRAGMATIC BIOETHICS

Of course, humans have experienced health and illness since the dawn of the species, but bioethics as a field of inquiry is a relatively new phenomenon. There are a number of historical factors—both in society at large and in medicine—that contributed to the development of bioethics as a "demi-discipline" (Jonsen 1997) in the second half of the 20th century. But Jonsen's fantasy is philosophical in nature, not sociohistorical. It speaks to a possible theoretical stimulant for the development of bioethics (viz., pragmatism). In his book, *The Birth of Bioethics* (2003), Jonsen further argues, rather than fantasizes, that "American bioethics" is what it is because the "spirit of American philosophy" (articulated by John Smith) permeates bioethical theory and activity. It is worth noting that Jonsen's fantasy is not held by him alone. Susan Wolf (1959–) claims that bioethics' more recent emphases in empirical data and taking the experiences of women and minorities seriously is a mark of a deep pragmatic strain in the discipline. She states, "Bioethics and health law have always been 'applied' or practical. But in shifting their respective approaches increasingly away from something principle- or rule-driven to something more inductivist and empirical, their approach to the practical becomes pragmatic" (1994, 399). John Arras (1945–2015) has even gone so far as to say that "There is a sense in which we [bioethicists] are all (or at least most of us are) pragmatists now" (Arras 2003, 70). So what does this mean?

While there is, of course, no one philosophical system that is "pragmatism," the "spirit" it captures can be found in a group of philosophical positions and theories that emphasize the practical outcomes of philosophical inquiry for human purposes. These outcomes and purposes arise from the intelligent and contextual nature of inquiry, take seriously the centrality and continuity of experience, and stress the evolution and habitual underpinnings of character. And though some may object to the fact that pragmatism is not clearly defined in one system, "The resistance of pragmatism to a precise definition is a mark of its vitality, an indication that it is a living philosophy rather than an historic relic" (Talisse and Aikin 2008, 3).

It is fair to say, then, that what stands as "pragmatism" is reasonably debatable. However, it may be possible to map some of the features that are shared by most pragmatist philosophical positions. Such features include *aiming* at practical consequences, *grounding* in naturalism, *recognizing* fallibility, and *integrating* human thought and action. Of course, it is not difficult to find professed pragmatists who may differ or deviate from these features. Furthermore, it is the case that other philosophical movements—existentialism, phenomenology, empiricism—share some or all of these features to some degree. However, pragmatism does so in light of themes that arise from a primarily practical and consequentialist take on epistemology and ethics. Also, many versions of pragmatic philosophy develop a substantive theory emphasizing some form of meliorism, while eschewing foundationalism. For our purposes here, there are three key features of pragmatism:

Pragmatic Consequentialism

Pragmatism lays heavy emphasis on identifying the purposes behind our conceptual and practical determinations, but although purpose drives us, outcomes give meaning to our purposes. The practical outcomes of our conceptions are directly relevant to their meaning. What we mean is less a matter of our intentions than how others interpret and are affected by our words and actions. In other words, consequences give significance to our concepts and actions. Pragmatism argues that those consequences are best derived through careful inquiry, which, like scientific inquiry, is typically inductive and, thereby, always fallible.

Pragmatic Meliorism

Taking Charles Darwin (1809–1882) seriously, pragmatism treats agents as continuous with the world they inhabit. As such, truths are not "out" in the world, merely to be discovered. Instead, both in questions of truth and in concerns for the good, pragmatism argues that human action is necessary for either to come to full fruition. "The heart of pragmatism was," Hilary Putnam (1926–2016) tells us, "the insistence on the agent point of view" (1988, 70). Agency, then, is human interaction with its environment, an environment not passively received but humanly developed. Ethically, then, the *responsibility* for the moral condition of the world is placed upon each of us.

Pragmatic Anti-Foundationalism

Pragmatism avoids epistemological absolutes, and along with its emphasis on consequences and meliorism, pragmatism is led to an antifoundationalist position on justification. In Dewey's language, truth is but "warranted assertibility," where method, inquiry, and consensus ground knowledge (scientific and moral), not correspondence of ideas with objective, external reality.

Jonsen's fantasy should be seen in the context of pragmatism writ-large. But, then, where is Dewey's ethical theory in all this? While others in this volume speak more fully to Dewey's moral theory, it is important to sketch briefly a particular feature of his moral thought to see pragmatic elements therein.

In both the 1932 version of the Dewey/Tuft volume *Ethics* and his essay, "Three Independent Factors in Morals" (1930), Dewey argues that the history of Western moral philosophy has been one attempt after another of trying to find a single principle of ethical determination and action, but in fact, "ethics" is a concept that arises from in-dependent sources. Colloquially, ethics concerns how each individual deals with "right" and "wrong," "good" and "bad." But, more reflectively, we speak about our *personal* ethics, and frankly most, if not all, of us believe we are good people who have "ethics." We judge our actions and the actions of others with "praise and blame [that] are so spontaneous, so natural, and as we say 'instinctive'" so as to "operate as reflex imputations of virtue and vice" (1930, LW 5:286). This sense of ethics is tied closely to *values* and *character*.

In addition, though, we also recognize that we have roles as members of communities and professions that are governed by "ethics" in a different sense. This governing authority is manifest in rules and regulations, codified in laws and codes of ethics, but it also resides in our sense of what inhabiting that role—be it spouse, friend, citizen, or professional—is all about and what the responsibilities and obligations are that come along with the actions we perform in our roles. "Right, law, duty, arise from the relations which human beings intimately sustain to one an-other ... from the very nature of the relation that binds people together" (Dewey 1932, LW 7:219). This sense of ethics is often associated with judgments of actions or behaviors as *right* and *wrong*.

Finally, we carry with us our values, interests, and desires, and we begin to recog-nize that others, too, have their own as well. Further, the roles we play each carry corresponding obligations. Often, between personal interests, cultural values, and professional and relational obligations, it is not uncommon to find ourselves in con-flict with others, with institutions, even with the many aspects of ourselves. Here con-flicting concerns often lead to questions regarding ends we really should pursue and what means are appropriate in those pursuits. "There can ... be no such thing as a reflective morality except when men seriously ask by what purposes they should direct their conduct, and why they should do so" (Dewey 1932, LW 7:184). This sense of ethics can be characterized as weighing *good* and *bad*, *better* and *worse*.

Dewey's argument is that none of these three senses of "ethics" can be reduced to the others, and that to ignore any one of them is to cut off deliberation prematurely. Each of us is a "values carrier" and appraiser of action, whether as a product of biology, nurturing, education, or some other means. Further, we do, in fact, find ourselves in re-lation to others—familial, professional, and so forth—and those relationships commit us to others and to expectations for which we are held accountable. At the same time, in a finite universe of limited abilities and resources, with a plurality of individual and communal interests, we are confronted often by concerns for what we should do and why.

For Dewey, ethics concerns each of these aspects of moral living—values (character), duties (roles), and goods (ends). We might say, then, the "field" of ethics—that is, the territory of values and interests covered by moral considerations—comprises those *evaluations* of human (and some other animal) conduct, both arising from and affecting character, which result in appraisals of "good" and "bad," "right" and "wrong." So, in Dewey's development of pragmatic ethics, moral considerations must take ends seriously, but those ends are inextricably tied to motivations and means, character and action. Thus both what constitutes a "good" and what constitutes appropriate ways to achieve our goods are open for debate, because "it is the characteristic of any situation properly called moral that one is ignorant of the end and of good consequences, of the right and just approach, of the direction of virtuous conduct, and that one must search for them" (Dewey 1930, LW 5:280).

Given this openness, the very development of moral goodness and rightness remain in our hands. That is, ethics is a form of meliorism—since the "truth" of ethics is developed through our interests, choices, and agreements. To navigate these complex interactions of independent factors of morality, Dewey suggests a reflective process that moves from the merely "desired" end to a judgment that it is, in fact, "desirable." This reflective process weighs the independent factors marrying means to ends, moving from what Dewey calls merely "de facto" interests to "de jure" goods (cf. 1929, LW 4:ch. 10). But then this implies that goods are not determined in advance. They are grounded first in experience, and using experience, culture, knowledge, along with precepts, norms, and reason leads us to determine actions worthy of pursuit. All this, then, entails a "soft" *particularist*[1] approach to moral thought, since the context of our actions and the specifics of the interests, goods, and purposes must be attended to in order to fashion a morally acceptable vision of what to do and whom to become.

DEWEY THE BIOETHICIST

Jonsen (1997; 2003) has suggested that pragmatic moral thought undergirds bioethics (particularly, bioethics construed as inquiry in to the clinical practice of medicine), and I have explained briefly some of the insightful and important components of pragmatic moral thought and how they are instantiated in Dewey's own work because Jonsens's fantasy does not simply imply the importance of pragmatism to bioethics but the impact of Dewey's work specifically. As noted already, the field of bioethics did not exist in Dewey's time, and while he may have been at the forefront of many public issues, bioethics was never explicitly one of them. What I hope to show is that Dewey's work applies the salient features of his moral philosophy, specifically a meliorism that entails a soft particularist focus on outcomes, to the concept of health and the practices of healthcare providers in order to ground a clear moral approach to the subject-matter of bioethics.

As discussed earlier, the subject matter of bioethics are the conditions that patients find themselves in and the relationships that those conditions stimulate with healthcare providers. Health, as we noted, is particular, and the relationships that follow from our striving to be healthy are particular as well. In fact, I have argued elsewhere that we must begin by recognizing that patients, far from being mere accidental tourists in health care, are, in fact, *members* of the healthcare community (Hester 2001). Community, here, then, is no mere descriptive term but a normative concept. One explanation of normative community comes from John Dewey when he says, "The parts of a machine work with a maximum of coöperativeness for a common result, but they do not form a community. If, however, they were all cognizant of the common end and all interested in it so that they regulate their specific activity in view of it, then they would form a community." (1916, MW 9:8) The contrast highlighted by Dewey's illustration is between a mere gathering of individuals and a community, and it is also a contrast between passive activity and meliorist influence. The individual members of a gathering work toward their own ends which, by either chance or external construction of the situation, may or may not fit well with the ends of others in the group. The coworkers (nurses, specialists, and subspecialists) in a hospital, for instance, can easily find themselves members of a "mere" social gathering in their daily activities to the extent that their activities are routinized and their pursuit of ends is limited to their individual tasks. No clear connections are sought, and no purpose is truly sought. These bonds are strengthened to form a community, however, when individuals become aware of the ends of others, take others' ends as common and shared, and recognize that satisfying the interests of others in the community is of value to themselves. Members of a community while attempting to fulfill their own interests take note of others' desires and adjust and regulate their activities and employ means appropriate to the mutual fulfillment of common ends. This awareness of mutually fulfilling interests manifests itself through a sharing of activities—through truly shared experiences where a common perspective is forged—and responsibilities in order to consummate the desires of all members of the community. The actions of all purposefully affect the outcomes, and the outcomes are sought together as common and connected.

In health care, taking on an attitude in which patients are members of this normative community empowers them—members of communities have status and access that non-members do not. Patients, then, become subjects who deserve care, not objects who need fixing. Dewey's insightful words resonate here, "Not man in general but a *particular* man suffering from some *particular* disability aims to live healthily, and consequently health cannot mean for him exactly what it means for any other mortal" (1920, MW 12:176).

Community, then, must make room for individual experiences and interests; it is found in a "society which makes provision for *participation in its good of all its members on equal terms* and which secures flexible readjustments of its institutions through interaction of the different forms of associated life" (1916, MW 9:105 [emphasis added]). And members of such a community will find that their own "[s]ocial perceptions and interests can be developed only in a genuinely social medium—one where there is give and take in the building up of a common experience" (1916, MW 9:368). By fostering a sense of community of which patients are a part, we set conditions that warrant robust patient participation, not merely consent and dissent. And finally, by opening ourselves to patients as fellow members of health care, we start them on the road to healing, to healthy living even while infirmed—paradoxical, maybe, but possible and worthy of our pursuits.

Community itself becomes a concept central to health and healing. It establishes the moral ground for the patient–provider relationship. But how can healthcare providers go about the task of addressing patients as members of the community? First, we must recognize that what is being requested of providers is a significant ethical approach to their efforts. They must, as Dewey argues, be artists in their craft.

> Just in the degree in which a physician is an artist in his work he uses his science, no matter how extensive and accurate, to furnish him with tools of inquiry into the individual case, and with methods of forecasting a method of dealing with it. Just in the degree in which, no matter how great his learning, he subordinates the individual case to some classification of diseases and some generic rule of treatment, he sinks to the level of the routine mechanic. His intelligence and his action become rigid, dogmatic, instead of free and flexible.
>
> (1920, MW 12:176)

Such an artistic turn implies an ethical requirement of moral epistemology. Ethical determinations are a form of practical judgment, a particular form of intellectual pursuit. Practical judgment involves the establishment of "facts" in order to decide what must be done. As Dewey tells us, "The survey and inventory of present conditions (or facts) are not something complete in themselves; they exist for the sake of an intelligent determination of what is to be done, of what is required to complete the given" (1915, MW 8:18).

This, then, is a deeply morally reflective moment where Dewey's ethical insights come into stark relief. In order to make this move from what is given to what must be done—from *de facto* to *de jure*—moral deliberation is necessary. Moral deliberation embraces all three independent factors of morality—character, consequences, and intentions (virtues, goods, and duties)—by weighing these factors. It requires intimate contextual understanding of the people involved, the institutions in which acts and decisions are occurring, and the principles to be considered. But all of this is for the sake of moving ahead, of finding a path forward. This can all seem quite distant and impersonal.

> As a part of a practical judgment, the discovery that a man is suffering from an illness is not a discovery that he must suffer, or that the subsequent course of events is determined by his illness; it is the indication of a needed and a possible course by which to restore health. Even the discovery that the illness is hopeless falls within this principle. It is an indication not to waste time and money on certain fruitless endeavors, to prepare affairs with respect to death, etc. It is also an indication to

search for conditions which will render in the future similar cases remediable, not hopeless. The whole case for the genuineness of practical judgment stands or falls with this principle [of practical judgment—namely, that facts are contextual and call for an intelligently determined response].

(1915, MW 8:18–19)

Practical judgment seeks out principles of actions and thought.

At the same time, though, we must be reminded, "How to live healthily . . . is a matter which differs with every person" (Dewey 1920, MW 12:175). That is, it is the experience of each human being that dictates what health means. Again, Dewey says,

> [Health] varies with [each person's] past experience, his opportunities, his temperamental and acquired weaknesses and abilities. Not man in general but a *particular* man suffering from some *particular* disability aims to live healthily, and consequently health cannot mean for him exactly what it means for any other mortal. Healthy living is not something to be attained by itself apart from other ways of living. A man needs to be healthy in his life, not apart from it, and what does life mean except the aggregate of his pursuits and activities? . . . Surely, once more, what a man needs is to live healthily, and this result so affects all the activities of his life that it cannot be set up as a separate and independent good.".

(1920, MW 12:175–176, emphasis added)

As such, these principles of action must remain "free and flexible" in order to meet with the individual conditions of particular human lives. It is the personal and professional meaning of the conditions and principles that make up the ethical landscape of the situation. The interests at play are personal. They are individual to adult patients and mature minors. They are particular to parents. They are peculiar to children. They are the values and beliefs that are unique to the stories in which they have arisen. No "distant" ethic can speak to the ethical conditions of a case without venturing "inside."

The implications, then, are that moral epistemology only succeeds when it applies its tools to the particularities of situations at hand. It is this kind of ethical approach that makes Dewey's work important to bioethics, conceived of as a kind of clinical endeavor. Again, the subject matter of bioethics is the health and well-being of human beings when those conditions are brought into relationship with healthcare providers. Dewey's work locates the conditions of health and illness within the individual human experience, which implies the need for healthcare providers to incorporate the subtleties of patient lives within the community of healthcare. It does not simply implore physicians and others to act but shows them why and how actions in healthcare occur in normative communities where individuality must be recognized and fostered. It lays groundwork for careful attention to judgment, not for the sake of theory but for the sake of concrete, practical conditions at hand.

LOOKING AHEAD

Bioethics as a field is moving to greater levels of specialization, with scholars focusing on specific areas of medicine. Pragmatism, generally, and the work of Dewey, specifically, is finding its way into these more specialized discussions. To list just a few instances:

- Clinical ethics (Joseph Fins, Frank Miller, Matthew Bacchetta; D. Micah Hester)
- End-of-life issues (Fins; Hester)
- Genetics (Mary Mahowald; Glenn McGee)
- Neuroethics (Fins; Eric Racine)
- Nursing ethics (Ekaterini Halarie; Karen Rich)
- Patient-provider relationships (Hester; Griffin Trotter)
- Pediatric ethics (Hester; Mahowald; Jonathan Moreno)
- Psychiatric ethics (David Brendel)
- Research ethics (Brendel; Miller)
- Reproductive issues (Hester; Mahowald; McGee)

The point here is that Dewey and pragmatism are not only influencing the contemporary conversation of bioethics writ-large but a great many specific subtopics that fall within the larger field.

To expound on just one of the previous examples, in their 1997 article, "Clinical Pragmatism: A Method of Moral Problem Solving," Fins, Bacchetta, and Miller herald an approach to clinical ethics carefully and overtly tied to a Deweyan approach to moral inquiry. The article argues for consensus as central to moral deliberation, emphasizing the methodological character of pragmatism. Using a case of an elderly Parkinson's patient, the analysis identifies the importance of communication with all parties concerned—getting clear about the medico-clinical details, helping the patient's family understand those details and what follows from them, understanding the patient's (and patient's family's) socio-situation. This inductive approach leads to the fashioning of moral ends through a partnership among all parties. Rather than trying to fit this unique situation into predefined, morally acceptable categories—whether these be characterized by rules, principles, or theories—Fins et al. employ "a disciplined process of inquiry" (141) that starts *within* situations in order to develop contextually sensitive moral judgments and actions that rely on reflectively developed warrant. Clinical pragmatism is democratic, experimental, and fallible, attempting to make decisions in full recognition of the need to act in the face of uncertainty. Further, it recognizes, as well, meliorism—that is, the power of human conviction and action to create (not simply recognize or accept) moral outcomes.

Here again we see those features of an approach to ethics, bioethics, and clinical ethics considerations that is distinctively Deweyan and pragmatic. Features such as contextual, narrative sensitivity, and falliblist experimentalism can be found readily in the work of those who are looking at ethical issues that arise from such practices as deep brain stimulation to considerations of parental authority in pediatric decision-making. It is precisely because John Dewey's approach to ethics, to community, to health, and to professional activity speaks to the subject matter of bioethics and the need for special attention to the individuals and institutions that affect and are affected by issues of health and healthcare. His meliorism and concern for outcomes, his practical focus grounded in theoretical considerations, are part and parcel of a pragmatist ethical account that undergirds Jonsen's bioethical "fantasy" that thinkers like Dewey, while not themselves concerned with what has become the field of bioethics, make the field not only possible but rich and rewarding.

Notes

1. Epistemological particularism is the belief that one can identify specific experiences without first having identified conceptual categories that would frame our identification of those experiences (see Chisholm 1973). Moral/ethical particularism is the belief that moral deliberation is not a principled-based activity (see Dancy 1993). What I am calling "soft" particularism trades on Dewey's belief in grounding morality in specifics of experience/ situations and his conception of principles, not as absolutes but as experientially determined rules of thumb. Principles, as Dewey has said, "represent conditions which have been ascertained during the conduct of continued inquiry to be involved in its own successful pursuit.... [P]rinciples are generated in the very process of control of continued inquiry" (Dewey 1938, LW 12:19). Like Charles Peirce before him, Dewey calls these kinds of principles "guiding" or "leading" principles. "According to this view, every inferential conclusion that is drawn [i.e., every result of inquiry] involves a habit (either by way of expressing it or initiating it) in the *organic* [i.e., living and evolving] sense of habit, since life is impossible without ways of action sufficiently general to properly be called *habits*" (Dewey 1938, LW 12:19). These habits as they are investigated, formulated, and developed become the leading principles of future inquiry. Experience determines the character of principles, and continually brings those principles into question, reshaping them as needed, given the contexts in which they arise and are to be applied. In this way, Dewey holds no unqualified moral principles but does acknowledge usefulness of habits in the process of reasoning. For some particularists, this might disqualify Dewey as a particularist, but these are not *pro tanto* principles (cf. Gaut 2001); they are contingent, even heuristic, principles (cf. Väyrynen 2011), and as such I characterize Dewey's position as a modified particularism, where we do begin in experience without the benefit of universals or absolutes or a prioris, but experience and inquiry also provide us insights that can be used to help make determinations beyond immediate situations—even if those same insights must be adjusted or abandoned as inquiry continues.

Works Cited

Citations of John Dewey's works are to the thirty-seven-volume critical edition published by Southern Illinois University Press under the editorship of Jo Ann Boydston. In-text citations give the original publication date and series abbreviation, followed by volume number and page number. For example: (1934, LW 10:12) is page 12 of *Art as Experience*, which is published as volume 10 of *The Later Works*.

Series abbreviations for *The Collected Works:*

EW *The Early Works* (1882–1898)

MW *The Middle Works* (1899–1924)

LW *The Later Works* (1925–1953)

Arras, John. 2003. "Freestanding Pragmatism in Law and Bioethics" In *Pragmatic Bioethics*, 2nd edition. Edited by Glenn McGee, 61–76. Cambridge, MA: MIT Press.

Chisholm, Rodrick. 1973. *The Problem of Criterion*. Milwaukee, WI: Marquette University Press.

Dancy, Jonathan. 1993. *Moral Reasons*. New York: Wiley-Blackwell.

Dewey, John. 1916. Democracy and Education. MW 9.

Dewey, John. 1915. "The Logic of Judgments in Practice." MW 8.

Dewey, John. 1920. Reconstruction in Philosophy. MW 12.

Dewey, John. 1929. The Quest for Certainty. LW 4.

Dewey, John. 1930. "Three Independent Factors in Morals." LW 5.

Dewey, John. 1938. Logic: The Theory of Inquiry. LW 12.

Dewey, John. 1946. "Introduction." In *Problems of Men: The Problems of Men and the Present State of Philosophy*. LW 15.

Dewey, John, and James H. Tufts. 1908. Ethics. MW 5.

Dewey, John, and James H. Tufts. 1932. Ethics, rev. ed. LW 7.

Gaut, B. 2001. "Art and Ethics." In *The Routledge Companion to Aesthetics*. Edited by B. N. Gaut and D. M. Lopes, 341–352. New York: Routledge.

Hester, D. Micah. 2001. *Community as Healing: Pragmatist Ethics in Medical Encounters*. Lanham, MD: Rowman & Littlefield.

Jonsen, Albert. 1997. "The Birth of Bioethics: The Origins and Evolution of a Demi-Discipline." *Medical Humanities Review*, vol. 11, no. 1, 9–21.

Jonsen, Albert. 2003. *The Birth of Bioethics*. New York: Oxford University Press.

Pellegrino, Edmund. 1979. "The Anatomy of Clinical Judgment" in Clinical Judgment: A Critical Appraisal, Edited by H. T. Engelhardt, S. F. Spicker, and B. Towers. Dordrecht, Holland: D. Reidel Publishing, 169–194.

Putnam, Hilary. 1988. *The Many Faces of Realism*. Bloomington, IN: Open Court Press.

Talisse, Robert B., and Scott F. Aikin. 2008. *Pragmatism: A Guide for the Perplexed*. London: Continuum.

Vayrynen. 2011. "Moral Particularism." In *Continuum Companion to Ethics*. Edited by C. B. Miller, 247–260. New York: Continuum Press.

Wolf, S. M. 1994. "Shifting Paradigms in Bioethics and Health Law." *American Journal of Law and Medicine*, vol. 20, 395–415.

Zaner, Richard. 1988. *Ethics and the Clinical Encounter*. New York: Prentice Hall.

Zaner, Richard. 1993. *Troubled Voices*. New York: Pilgrim Press.

Index

Figures, notes, and tables are indicated by f, n, and t following the page number.